Encyclopedia of
Health Care
Management

Encyclopedia of
Health Care
Management

EDITOR
Michael J. Stahl
University of Tennessee, Knoxville

A SAGE Reference Publication

SAGE Publications
International Educational and Professional Publisher
Thousand Oaks ▪ London ▪ New Delhi

For information:

 Sage Publications, Inc.
2455 Teller Road
Thousand Oaks, California 91320
E-mail: order@sagepub.com

Sage Publications Ltd.
6 Bonhill Street
London EC2A 4PU
United Kingdom

Sage Publications India Pvt. Ltd.
B-42, Panchsheel Enclave
Post Box 4109
New Delhi 110 017 India

Printed in the United States of America

REF. RA 971 .E52 2004

Encyclopedia of health care
management

Library of Congress Cataloging-in-Publication Data

Encyclopedia of health care management / edited by Michael J. Stahl.
    p. cm.
Includes bibliographical references and index.
ISBN 0-7619-2674-7 (cloth)
    1. Health services administration—Encyclopedias. 2. Public health administration—Encyclopedias.
I. Stahl, Michael J.
RA971.E52 2004
362.1´068—dc222

                                    2003015576

03   04   05   06   07   10   9   8   7   6   5   4   3   2   1

Acquiring Editor:	Rolf Janke
Developmental Editor:	Vince Burns
Editorial Assistant:	Sara Tauber
Production Editor:	Sanford Robinson
Typesetter:	C&M Digitals (P) Ltd.
Copy Editor:	Linda Purrington
Indexer:	Molly Hall
Cover Designer:	Michelle Lee

Contents

List of Entries

Reader's Guide

HUMAN RESOURCES

INTERNATIONAL HEALTH CARE ISSUES

LEGAL AND REGULATORY ISSUES

Professional Standards Review Organizations
Qui Tam Actions
Referral
Rehabilitation Act of 1973
Scope of Practice
Self-Referral
Sentinel Event
Settlement
Standard of Care
Stark Law
Statute of Limitations
Structured Settlement
Summons
Tail Coverage
Title VII of the Civil Rights Act of 1964
Unanticipated Outcome Disclosure
Vicarious Liability
Women, Infants, and Children (WIC) Program

MANAGED CARE

Ambulatory Care
Carve-Out
Compensating Differentials
Enrollee
Enrollment
Evidence-Based Medicine
Fee-for-Service
Health Care Reform
Health Maintenance Organizations (HMOs)
Length of Stay
Managed Care
Managed Care Plans
Mandated Coverage
Medical Care
Out-Of-Network Services
Patterns of Care
Per Diem Payments
Per Member Per Month (PMPM)
Prospective Payment System (PPS)

MARKETING AND CUSTOMER VALUE

Adopter Categories
Advertising
Ambulatory Care
Comparative Advertising
Complementary Products
Customer
Customer Relationship Management (CRM)
Customer Satisfaction Research
Customer Value

Database Marketing
Direct Marketing
Environmental Scanning/Analysis
Exclusive Distribution
Expansion Strategies
First-Mover Advantage
Franchising
Goods–Services Continuum
Hypercompetition
Integrated Marketing Communications
Intensive Distribution
Licensing
Loyalty in Health Care Consumer
Maintenance of Scope
Market Entry Strategies
Market Opportunity Analysis
Market Segmentation
Marketing Concept
Marketing Mix
Marketing Plan
Marketing Research
Marketing Value
Mass Customization
Mystery Shoppers
Non Price Competition in Hospitals
One-to-One Marketing
Patient Expectations
Perceptual Gaps in Services Quality
Physician-Patient Relationship
Press Releases
Product
Product Classes
Product Line Extensions
Product Life Cycle (PLC) Analysis
Product Mix
Public Relations
Sales Forecasting
Selective Distribution
Service Area Competitor Analysis
Service Quality
Services
Social Marketing
Substitute Product
Wellness
Women as Major Health Care Consumers

OPERATIONS AND DECISION MAKING

Capacity and Capacity Utilization
Clinical Decision Making
Decentralization of Decision Making

Decision
Decision Support Systems
Economic Order Quantity (EOQ)
Empowerment (Delegation of Authority)
Enterprise Resource Planning
Excess Capacity
Facilities Management
Future Search
Geographic Information System
Health Care Service Operation
Health Production Functions
Just In Time and Health Care Management
Mass Customization
Nominal Group Technique (NGT)
Operations Management
Outsourcing
Production Possibilities Curve
Queuing
Root Cause Analysis
Sales Forecasting
Service Operation
Statement of Operations
Supply Chain Management
Technology Assessment
Technology Change
Theory of Constraints
Utilization Review
Value Chain for Health Care
Waiting Time

PHARMACEUTICALS AND CLINICAL TRIALS

Adverse Drug Reaction (ADR)
Adverse Event (AE)
Adverse Selection and Impact
Alternative Medicine (Complementary Medicine,
    Integrative Medicine, Unconventional Medicine)
Assurance
Belmont Report
Biotechnology
Blinding
Case Report Form (CRF)
Clinical Research
Clinical Trials
Contract Research Organization (CRO)
Control Group
Critical Paths
Data Management
Declaration of Helsinki Laws
Demographics
Drug Coverage

Effective Dose
Efficacy
Exclusion Criteria
Food and Drug Administration (FDA)
Formularies
Generic Drug
Good Clinical Practices (GCPs)
In Vitro Testing
In Vivo Testing
Inclusion Criteria
Informed Consent
Investigational New Drug Application (IND)
Investigator (Principal Investigator)
Kefauver-Harris Amendments
Longitudinal Study
Medical Genetics
MedWatch Program
National Institutes of Health (NIH)
New Drug Application (NDA)
Off Label
Open-Ended Study
Open-Label Study
Orphan Drug
Out-of-Network Services
Over-the-Counter (OTC)
Phase I Study (Phase I Clinical Trial)
Phase II Study
Phase III Study
Phase IV Study
Pivotal Studies
Placebo
Preclinical Testing
Premedicate (Premedication)
Prescription
Price Control in the Pharmaceutical Industry
Protocol (Involving Human Subjects)
Quality Assurance
Randomization
Recruitment
Standard Operating Procedures (SOPs)
Standard Treatment
Study Arms
Subinvestigator
Subject, Human Research
Vital Signs
Vulnerable Research Subject Population

QUALITY

Academic Degrees
Care Management

Case Management
Clinical Practice Guidelines/Pathways
Common Cause Variation
Continuous Quality Improvement (CQI)
Control Chart
Disease Management
Electrocardigram (EKG or ECG)
Flowchart
Global Blood Safety Projects
Health Status Indicators
Hippocratic Oath
Length of Stay
Maternal and Child Health
Medical Care
Medical Errors
Morbidity
Mortality
National Committee on Quality Assurance (NCQA)
Outcomes Research
Pareto Chart
Patterns of Care
Plan-Do-Study-Act Cycle
Quality Assurance
Quality Improvement Cycle
Quality Management
Root Cause Analysis
Run Chart
Service Quality
Six-Sigma Program
Special Cause Variation
Statistical Process Control (SPC)
Statistical Thinking
Supply Chain Management (SCM)
Utilization Review
Wellness
Zero Defects

STATISTICS AND DATA MINING

Adverse Selection
Common Cause Variation
Control Chart
Epidemiology
Database
Database Marketing
Data Management
Pareto Chart
Randomization
Run Chart
Six-Sigma Program

Special Cause Variation
Statistical Process Control
Statistical Thinking
Zero Defects

STRATEGY

Alliances
Authority
Balanced Scorecard
BCG Portfolio Analysis
Boards of Directors
Breakeven Analysis
Business Plan
Coalitions
Collaborative Partnership
Competitive Advantage
Competitive Strategy and Groups
Contraction Strategy
Cooperation Strategies
Co-opetition
Critical Success Factors
Culture and Culture Change
Culture and Strategy
Diversification Strategies
Divestiture Strategies
Emergent Strategy
Environmental Analysis
Expansion Strategies
Generic Strategies
Harvesting Strategies
Horizontal Integration
Industry Analysis
Internal Environmental Analysis
Long-Range Planning
Managed Competition
Managing Organizational Change
Market Entry Strategies
Merger and Acquisition
Mission
Networks
Niche Strategies
Nonprice Competition in Hospitals
Objectives
Organizational Change
Organizational Design and Discontinuous Change
Product Life Cycle Analysis
Service Area Competitor Analysis
Strategic Alternatives
Strategic Assumptions

Contributors

Alexander, Greg R., PhD
University of Alabama at Birmingham

Allen, Tammy D., PhD
University of South Florida

Alvarez, Benito A., MD, MBA
Cleveland, OH

Anderson, Frederick A., MD
University of Massachusetts Medical School

Askew, Jerry W., PhD
St. Mary's Health System, Knoxville, TN

Atchley, E. Kate, PhD
University of Tennessee

Austin, Charles J., JD
Hilton Head Island, SC

Behn, Bruce, PhD
University of Tennessee

Biancaniello, Thomas M., MD
University Hospital, State University of New York at
    Stony Brook

Blake, Gregory H., MD
UT Medical Center & Graduate School of Medicine,
    Knoxville, TN

Burgess, Jennifer R.D., PhD
Bradley University

Burgess, Jerry, MBA
HealthCare 21 Business Coalition,
    Knoxville, TN

Burgiss, Samuel G., PhD
University of Tennessee
Burns, Lawton Robert

Burke, Ronald, PhD
York University

Burkhardt, Jeffrey H., PhD
University of Alabama at Birmingham

Burns, Lawton R., PhD
University of Pennsylvania

Capper, Stuart A., PhD
Tulane University

Chesney, Alan P., PhD
University of Tennessee

Christoph, Richard T., PhD
Dakota State University

Cimino, Linda M., MS, RN
State University of New York at Stony Brook

Clark, Don P., PhD
University of Tennessee

Clarke, Richard, CPA
Westchester, IL

Clemens, Bruce W., PhD
James Madison University

Cole, Michael S., PhD
Auburn University

Colovos, Nick, MD
Allegheny General Hospital

Culbertson, Richard A., MD
Tulane University Medical Center

Daley, Brian J., MD
University of Tennessee Medical Center
    at Knoxville

Daves, Phillip R., PhD
University of Tennessee

Day, Doreen T., MS, RN
State University of New York at Stony Brook

Dean, Peter J., PhD
University of Pennsylvania

DiMartino, Theresa, JD
New York, NY

Duncan, W. Jack, PhD
University of Alabama at Birmingham

Elenkov, Detelin, PhD
University of Tennessee

Ellis, Randall P., PhD
Boston University

Falaschetti, Dino, PhD
Montana State University

Feild, Hubert S., PhD
Auburn University College of Business

Fell, Daniel, MBA
DDN Group, Chattanooga, TN

Ferrara, Kathleen, MS, RN
Stony Brook University Hospital,
   Stony Brook, NY

Fisher, Bruce D., JD
University of Tennessee

Flynn, Barbara, PhD
Wake Forest University

Ford, Eric W., PhD
Pennsylvania State University

Gandhi, Ramesh K., MD, MBA
Digestive Specialists, Dayton, OH

Gardial, Sarah, PhD
University of Tennessee

Garrison, Christopher J., MD, MBA
Baylor University

Getzen, Thomas E., PhD
Temple University

Ginter, Peter M., PhD
University of Alabama at Birmingham

Glascoff, David W., PhD
Western State College of Colorado

Gniatczyk, Laura, PhD
ArvinMeritor- Human Resources

Gossage, David L., MD, MBA
The Allergy, Asthma & Sinus Center,
   Knoxville, TN

Grabowski, David C., PhD
University of Alabama at Birmingham

Griffin, Patti Elaine, PhD
Lipscomb University

Grigsby, David W., PhD
Clemson University

Grossman, Michael, PhD
National Bureau of Economic Research

Gutman, Arthur, PhD
Florida Institute of Technology

Haley, George T., PhD
University of New Haven

Haley, Usha C. V., PhD
University of New Haven

Hankins, Charles T., MD, MBA
Baylor University

Helland, Katherine R., PhD student
University of Tennessee at Knoxville

Henderson, Barry, MD, MBA
Atlanta, GA

Ho, Vivian, PhD
University of Alabama at Birmingham

Hochron, Stuart, MD, JD
Family Medical Center, Woodbridge, NJ

Houser, Frank, MD, HCA
Nashville, TN

Hughes, Harry N., CPA
University of Tennessee

Hughes, Julia A., PhD
Tulane University

Ippolito, Anthony J., MD
State University of NY at Stony Brook

Jirak, George V., MD, MBA
Wheeling, WV

Judge, William Q., PhD
University of Tennessee

Kaluzny, Arnold D., PhD
University of North Carolina at Chapel Hill

Kaplan, Robert S., PhD
Harvard University

Karakaya, Fahri, PhD
University of Massachusetts—Dartmouth

Erica L. Katz

Katz, Robert I., MD
State University of New York at Stony Brook

Kaufman, Darren S., PhD
State University of NY at Stony Brook

Khouqeer, Fareed A., MD, MBA
King Faisal Specialist Hospital and Research Centre—
   Jeddah, Saudi Arabia

Kotler, Philip, PhD
Northwestern University

Kucera, Edna Lee, MS, RN
State University of New York at Stony
   Brook Hospital

Kurz, Richard S., PhD
St. Louis University

Ladd, Robert T., PhD
University of Tennessee

LaForge, R. Lawrence, PhD
Clemson University

LaFrance, Kevin G., MD
Baylor University

Leap, Terry, PhD
Clemson University

Lee, Nancy R., PhD
Social Marketing Service, Inc., Mercer Island, WA

Lee, Shoou-Yih Daniel, PhD
University of North Carolina—Chapel Hill

Leigh, James H., Jr., MD, MBA
Atlanta, GA

León, Ramón V., PhD
University of Tennessee

Levick, Donald, MD, MBA
Allentown, PA

Liao, Jack S.L., MD, MBA
Atlanta, GA

Lighter, Donald E., MD, MBA
University of Tennessee

Lyle, Linda, PhD
University of Tennessee

MacStravic, Scott R., PhD
University of Colorado

Malvey, Donna M., PhD
University of Central Florida—Brevard
   Campus

Mariotti, John L., MB
The Enterprise Group, Knoxville, TN

Marks, Michael R., MD, MBA
Norwalk, CT

Massingale, Cheryl S., JD
Knoxville, TN

Matuk, Judy, MS
State University of New York at Stony Brook

McDermott, Michael E., PhD
Hofstra University

McKinney, Anne M., JD
Knoxville, TN

McLaughlin, Curtis P., DBA
University of North Carolina at Chapel Hill

Menachemi, Nir, PhD
University of Alabama at Birmingham

Mennemeyer, Stephen T., PhD
University of Alabama at Birmingham

Mentzer, John T., PhD
University of Tennessee

Meyers, James F., MD
US Army—Baylor University Program in Health
  Administration

Michael, Max III, PhD
University of Alabama at Birmingham

Mirvis, David M., MD
University of Tennessee Medical Center, Memphis

Mock, Curtis Alec, MD, MBA
Memorial Hospital of Rhode Island

Moller, Daryn H., MD
State University of New York at Stony Brook

Montalvo, Raúl F., MD, MBA
Ponce, Puerto Rico

Moon, Mark A., PhD
University of Tennessee

Moore, Terry, MBA
The Xtend Group Inc., Knoxville, TN

Morrisey, Michael A., PhD
University of Alabama at Birmingham

Mulkey, Shonna L., MD
US Army—Baylor University

Nabrit-Stephens, Barbara A., MD, MBA
Blue Cross-Blue Shield, Philadelphia, PA

Nader, Francois, MD, MBA
Aventis, Morristown, NJ

Nelson, Leonard J. III, PhD
Samford University

Ann Nevius
Balanced Scorecard Collaborative, Lincoln, MA

Ng, Bernard T., MD, MBA
State University of New York at Albany

Nicola, Ray M., MD
Centers for Disease Control, Seattle, WA

Noon, Charles E., PhD
University of Tennessee

Nuñez, Jr., Miguel A., MD, MBA
Green Cross Health Systems Inc., Miami, FL

Oetjen, Dawn M., PhD
University of Central Florida

Okolo, Ken Oranefo, MD
Tennessee Department of Finance and Administration,
  Nashville

Payne, Terry L., PhD
Oak Ridge National Laboratory, Oak Ridge, TN

Parsons, Steve
Washington University

Peat, Jillian A., PhD student
University of Tennessee

Pedigo, Thurman L. Sr., MD, MBA
Vanderbilt University

Pershing, Edward, CPA
Pershing, Yoakley & Associates, Knoxville, TN

Petersen, Donna J., PhD
University of Alabama at Birmingham

Pirkle, Kipling M., PhD
Washington and Lee University

Porterfield, Rebecca Irene, PhD
University of North Carolina—Wilmington

Poteet, Mark L., PhD
Organizational Research & Solutions, Inc., Tampa, FL

Preston, Gregory, MD, MBA
Keystone Mercy Health Plan, Philadelphia

Quay, Steven C., MD, PhD
Nastech Pharmaceutical Company, Hauppauge, NY

Raju, Ramanathan, MD, MBA
Coney Island Hospital, New York, NY

Ray, Amy W., PhD
Bentley College

Reizenstein, Richard C., PhD
University of Tennessee

Richardson, Woodrow D., PhD
Ball State University

Richter, Jennifer L., JD
University of Tennessee

Robertson, Kenneth R., MD, MBA
Memphis Children's Clinic, Memphis, TN

Robin, Richard A., DO, MBA, MPH
East Greenwich, RI

Rossiter, Louis F., PhD
Virginia Commonwealth University

Rotarius, Timothy, PhD
University of Central Florida

Samuelson, Carole W., PhD
University of Alabama at Birmingham

Schmidhammer, James L., PhD
University of Tennessee

Schumann, David W., PhD
University of Tennessee

Seat, Elaine, PhD
University of Tennessee

Senlet, Pinar, MD, MBA, MPH
US Agency for International Development, Ankara,
  Turkey

Sileno, Anthony, PhD
Nastech Pharmaceutical Company Inc., Hauppauge, NY

Slovensky, Donna J., PhD
University of Alabama at Birmingham

Smith, Elizabeth M., PhD student
University of Tennessee at Knoxville

Spencer, Barbara, PhD
Mississippi State University

Srinivasan, M. M., PhD
University of Tennessee

Srivastava, Alok, PhD
Georgia State University

St. John, Caron H., PhD
Clemson University

Stahl, Michael J., PhD
University of Tennessee

Steiner, Kenneth D., MD, MBA
Family Medical Center, P.C., Woodbridge, NJ

Stover, Thomas L., MD, MBA,
Akron General Medical Center, Akron, OH

Stretton, Jean, MD, MBA,
Philadelphia, PA

Stuart, C. Bevan, MD, MBA
Riverside Community Hospital, Riverside, CA

Sundstrom, Eric D., PhD
University of Tennessee

Swayne, Linda E., PhD
University of North Carolina, Charlotte

Sym, Donna, PharmD
State University of New York at Stonybook

Totten, Jeffrey W., PhD
Southeastern Louisiana University

Trekell, Melissa, MD, MBA
Tennessee Breast Center, Maryville, TN

Van Matre, Joseph G., PhD
University of Alabama at Birmingham

Vitkun, Stephen A., MD, PhD, MBA,
State University of New York at Stony Brook

Weiner, Bryan J., PhD
University of North Carolina at Chapel Hill

Williams, David R., PhD
University of Alabama at Birmingham

Young, Carlton C., PhD
University of Alabama at Birmingham

Younggren, Bradley N., MD
Ft Lewis, WA

Zink, Donald L., JD
Evergreen, CO

Preface

What is the relevance of an *Encyclopedia of Health Care Management?* Why do patients, physicians, other providers, employees of health care providers, students of health care, and consumers of health care insurance need to understand the business and management issues in the health care industry?

When the health care industry was stable in the 1980s, there was little need for such knowledge. Now that health care has become one of the largest and most dramatically changing industries in the United States, the need to understand the changes has grown exponentially. As the baby boom generation ages; as new, expensive health care technology emerges; as new pharmaceutical products become available, there are huge increases in the demand for health care services. Indeed, there are forecasts from the Centers for Medicare and Medicaid Services in Washington that total expenditures on health care services will surpass $2 Trillion in 2007 and account for 17% of Gross Domestic Product. This is a strong growth from $1 Trillion and 14% of GDP in 1996. We are spending more on health care in total dollars and more as a percentage of the total economy.

Along with the growth in health care expenditures, the government is assuming a greater role. Compliments of growth in Medicare and Medicaid to deliver health care services to elderly and poor patients, respectively, almost 50% of the above health care expenditures were controlled by federal and state governments as of this writing in 2003. Then, the U.S. Congress was debating prescription drug coverage in Medicare with estimates of the various plans adding between $400 million and $1 Trillion to the preceding share of health care expenditures passing through government hands.

Compliments of the growth of the Internet, patients and consumers were able to research health care topics during the process of choosing health care insurance coverage and receiving care. This empowerment helped consumers and patients to be more demanding about the value received for health care purchases.

As of this writing, new advances were being made to increase the quality of delivered health care services. The power of information systems was being implemented among health care providers, including hospitals, to reduce errors and control costs.

These changes were occurring so rapidly in 2003 that patients, physicians, other providers, employees of health care providers, students of health care, and consumers of health insurance could no longer sit back and assume stability. This *Encyclopedia of Health Care Management* is intended to help them understand the business and management issues in the health care industry.

Given such a large industry with so many different issues, there are about 600 keywords defined in this volume. The keywords are classified into 16 general categories. Please see the Reader's Guide for the categories and the keywords. Additionally, there are tables on medical degrees, medical specialties, medical organizations, medical legislation, and health care acronyms to facilitate understanding of the business and management issues in the health care industry.

Please feel free to e-mail me at mstahl@utk.edu with your comments on this *Encyclopedia of Health Care Management.*

—Michael J. Stahl

Acknowledgments

As editor of the *Encyclopedia of Health Care Management,* I fully acknowledge that the work of many, many others made this book possible. Without their work, this book would not exist.

First, I must recognize the Editorial Advisory Board consisting of Drs. Kate Atchley, Peter Ginter, Linda Swayne, and Steve Vitkun. These professionals helped to design the list of keywords for the book, helped to recruit some of the authors, and wrote some of the keywords themselves. Given the breadth and depth of their experience, they added great insight to the topic. Kate Atchley added great insight into the development of the leadership and management keywords; she leads the Leadership Development Program in the Physician Executive MBA at The University of Tennessee. Peter Ginter, University of Alabama at Birmingham, added expertise to the development of the strategy and management keywords; he teaches Health Care Strategy and is coauthor of a widely cited text in that area. Linda Swayne, who led the development of the marketing keywords, teaches Health Care Marketing at the University of North Carolina in Charlotte and is a textbook coauthor with Peter Ginter. As an M.D. and a Ph.D. on the faculty of the Medical and Pharmacology Schools at the State University of New York in Stony Brook, Steve Vitkun added great insight to the medical practice and pharmacological keywords in the book.

Second, I must recognize the authors. More than 160 professionals wrote the book's innovative material. I am proud to call them partners in this educational venture.

Please see the Contributing Author List. Note the high level of education and the educational diversity of the author team as represented by the number of PhDs, MDs, MBAs, CPAs and JDs. Please also note the diversity of institutional affiliations with universities, hospitals, medical schools, pharmaceutical companies, clinics, accounting firms, and law firms. These diverse educational and institutional backgrounds provide unique perspectives into the business of medicine.

I need to recognize the efforts of Mr. Thomas Brown, Program Coordinator, Physician Executive MBA, University of Tennessee. Tom developed the Excel spreadsheets and the listings in the Web pages to manage the keywords and work status. Dr. Lee Wortham verified all the Internet addresses in the Further Readings.

Certainly, I need to acknowledge the work of Mr. Rolf Janke, Vice President at Sage Publications. Rolf developed the original idea of the *Encyclopedia of Health Care Management* and has been a product champion of the concept throughout its life. Sara Tauber, assistant to Rolf Janke; Vince Burns, developmental editor; Sanford Robinson, senior production editor; and Linda Purrington, copy editor, were all instrumental in implementing the idea.

All of the above experts made this book possible. I recognize them individually and collectively for their contributions.

—Michael J. Stahl

About the Editor

Michael J. Stahl, Ph.D., is Director of the Physician Executive MBA Program and Distinguished Professor of Management in the College of Business at the University of Tennessee, Knoxville. He received his B.S. in Electrical Engineering from the State University of New York at Buffalo and his Ph.D. in Management from Rensselaer Polytechnic Institute. In the early 1970s, he was a program manager on the design of a communications satellite at the Space and Missile Systems Organization in Los Angeles. From 1982 to 1989, he was Head of the Management Department at Clemson University. He was Associate Dean in the College of Business at the University of Tennessee from 1989 to 1997, and a member of the Leadership Steering Committee for the Total Quality Forums from 1992 to 1998. He was Principal Investigator with a team of nine researchers on a three-year, $400,000 research grant concerning Customer Value from the National Science Foundation, involving Eastman Chemical Company.

Dr. Stahl has published more than 50 journal articles in a variety of areas including Strategic Management, TQ, and health care, as well as twelve books including *Strategic Management, Perspectives in TQ,* and *The Physician's Essential MBA.* He teaches strategy and business planning in the Physician EMBA, Taiwan EMBA, and MBA programs. From 1997 to 2000 he served on the Board of Directors and chaired the Board's Development Committee for the Florence Crittenton Agency. He currently serves on the Board of Catholic Charities—Knoxville, and on the Board's Development Committee.

ACADEMIC DEGREES

Academic Degree Abbreviation	Degree Title
Associate Degrees	
A.A.	Associate of Arts
A.A.S.	Associate of Applied Science
A.S.	Associate of Science
A.B.A.	Associate of Business Administration
Bachelor Degrees	
A.B.	Bachelor of Arts
B.A.	Bachelor of Arts
B.B.A.	Bachelor of Business Administration
B.E.	Bachelor of Engineering
B.E.E.	Bachelor of Electrical Engineering
B.S.	Bachelor of Science
B.Sc.	Bachelor of Science
B.S.E.	Bachelor of Science in Engineering
B.S.N.	Bachelor of Science in Nursing
B.N.	Bachelor of Nursing
B.Pharm.	Bachelor of Pharmacy
Master Degrees	
M.A.	Master of Arts
M.S.N.	Master of Science in Nursing
M.S.	Master of Science
M.Ed.	Master of Education
A.M.	Master of Arts
M.B.A.	Master of Business Administration
M.S.E.E.	Master of Science in Electrical Engineering
M.S.E.	Master of Science in Engineering
M.M.M.	Master of Medical Management
M.S.H.S.	Master of Science in Health Science

M.L.S.	Master of Library Science
M.P.S.	Master of Professional Studies
M.P.H.	Master of Public Health
L.L.M.	Master of Legal Letters
M.P.P.	Master of Public Policy
M.P.A.	Master of Public Administration
M.H.A.	Master of Hospital Administration
M.S.Ed.	Master of Science in Education
Th.M.	Master of Theology
M.Phil.	Master of Philosophy
M.Div.	Master of Divinity
M.S.W.	Master of Social Work
Doctoral Degrees	
M.D.	Doctor of Medicine
D.O.	Doctor of Osteopathic Medicine
O.D.	Doctor of Optometry
D.C.	Doctor of Chiropractic
D.Ch.	Doctor of Chiropractic
D.P.H.	Doctor of Public Health
Dr.P.H.	Doctor of Public Health
D.B.A.	Doctor of Business Administration
J.D.	Juris Doctor (Law)
N.D.	Doctor of Nursing
D.N.Sc.	Doctor of Nursing Science
Sc.D.	Doctor of Science
D.Sc.	Doctor of Science
Ph.D.	Doctor of Philosophy
Ed.D.	Doctor of Education
D.P.M.	Doctor of Podiatric Medicine
D.S.W.	Doctor of Social Work
M.B., Ch.B.	Bachelor of Medicine and Surgery
M.D., C.M.	Doctor of Medicine/Master of Surgery
M.B.B.S.	Bachelor of Medicine and Surgery
D.A.	Doctor of Arts
D.Arts	Doctor of Arts
Psy.D.	Doctor of Clinical Psychology

D.D.S.	Doctor of Dental Surgery
D.M.D.	Doctor of Medical Dentistry
Au.D.	Doctor of Audiology
Th.D.	Doctor of Theology
D.Phil.	Doctor of Philosophy
D.D.	Doctor of Divinity
Pharm.D.	Doctor of Pharmacy
D.V.M.	Doctor of Veterinary Medicine

—Steven A. Vitkun

ACADEMIC MEDICAL CENTER (AMC)

Academic medical centers (AMCs) were established after World War II, with federal funding for university-based science programs. Federal funding has continued to be their primary funding source; Medicare and Medicaid legislation provides explicit support for medical education and delivery of medical services to specific populations such as the poor and the elderly. However, recent drastic cuts in governmental funding have threatened the future of AMCs and prompted doubts about their ability to survive in highly competitive markets.

An AMC consists of an allopathic or osteopathic school of medicine, at least one other health professional school or program, and one or more owned or affiliated teaching hospitals. Beyond that, they are less easily defined, because the organization and structure of an AMC vary. It has been said that if you have seen one AMC, you have seen one AMC. For example, an AMC can be a component of private or public universities or statewide systems as in California or New York, or it can be a freestanding institution. AMCs vary widely in size, with some consisting of a few small hospitals with just over a hundred beds, whereas others have dozens of affiliated hospitals and over a thousand beds. Larger AMCs have revenues exceeding $500 million annually, whereas smaller ones have more modest budgets. Thus generic strategies can probably not be applied to AMCs. To develop and implement successful strategy, AMCs must integrate assumptions about the environment, their missions, and core competencies into the planning process.

However, the 120 AMCs located throughout the United States have in common their multiple missions. AMCs are the nation's primary source of health professions education, cutting-edge research, and provision of highly critical tertiary care to those in need, including the poor. It is estimated that AMCs provide approximately 40% of indigent care in the United States.

PROBLEMS FACED BY AMCS

Whether through market forces or governmental reforms, AMCs face a marketplace in which competitive pressures demand more cost-effective, high-quality care.

Drastic government funding reductions have underscored the need for a stable source of private funding to support their multiple missions, because these activities typically do not pay for themselves. Furthermore, they have slight chance of profitability and reduce the AMC's ability to compete with local community providers. Advised to behave in a more businesslike manner, AMCs have adapted business strategies such as merging and integrating that have met with questionable results. For example, the evidence from mergers has reported more high-profile failures, such as the mergers between the University of California at San Francisco and Stanford Health or between New York University and Mount Sinai medical centers, than successes. AMCs have also been criticized for copying strategies that have failed when community hospitals implemented them. For example, strategies aimed at transforming the AMC into an extensive community-based health care system by developing physician networks have been, for the most part, financial disasters for both community hospitals and AMCs. The lesson learned was that a network agreement did not guarantee physician referrals.

—Donna M. Malvey

See also Integrated Delivery System

FURTHER READING

Blumenthal, D., Weissman, J. S., & Griner, P. F. (1999). Academic health centers on the front lines: Survival strategies in highly competitive markets. *Academic Medicine, 74,* 1038–1049.

Krauss, K., & Smith, J. (1997). Rejecting conventional wisdom: How academic health centers can regain their leadership positions. *Academic Medicine, 72*(7), 571–575.

Managing academic health centers: Meeting the challenges of the new health care world. (2000). A Report of the Commonwealth Fund Task Force on Academic Health Centers. Washington, DC: Commonwealth Fund.

Van Etten, P. (1999). Camelot or common sense? The logic behind the UCSF/Stanford merger. *Health Affairs, 18*(2), 143–148.

ACCESS

Access to health care is the ability of the patient to gain entry to the system for care that is available, timely, appropriate, and affordable. Public policy debate has focused on access as the 10th goal of the U.S. surgeon general in the *Healthy People 2010.* In this report, the surgeon general advances the goal to "improve access to comprehensive, high-quality health care services" as a public health goal for the nation. Recent public attention to access has focused on economic barriers to care and resultant health disparities among population groups, but the surgeon general acknowledges broader and more complex roots involving "the patient, provider, and system of care."

Specific policy objectives to measure and evaluate access have been proposed as national access objectives. Notable among these objectives are "the reduction to 0% of the proportion of children and adults younger than 65 without health care coverage; increasing to 95% the proportion of people with a specific source of primary care; and increasing to at least 90% the proportion of individuals who have access to rapidly responding prehospital emergency medical services" (U.S. Department of Health and Human Services, "Access to Quality Health Services," *Healthy People 2010*, pp. 1–13. As these disparate objectives demonstrate, the concept of access is complex and has far-reaching policy implications for the health system.

The study of access to health care has an extensive history and several critical dimensions that make the problem of access of key interest to policymakers.

These dimensions of access can be understood as variations on a set of critical "A" terms: availability, affordability, appropriateness (quality), and acceptability. Solving any one of these problems does not assure solution to the overall political problem of access, which has plagued health policy makers with a ferocity nearly equal to that of societal concern for health care expenditures.

AVAILABILITY

Health policy makers initially concentrated on availability of health care services during the "golden era" of American medicine when fee-for-service physician payment and charge-based hospital reimbursement were the norm. The 1946 passage of the landmark Hospital Construction Act (P.L. 79-725), better known as the Hill-Burton Act after its congressional sponsors, provided direct support through grants and loans for the construction and refurbishment of the nation's hospitals. A national standard of access, defined as four hospital beds for each 1000 people, was established, presumably to benefit largely rural locations without hospital facilities. During the early years of the program established by Hill-Burton, the policy emphasis was clearly on expanding the nation's supply of beds. Unrecognized at this time was a key provision of the act, to be enforced 30 years later, that mandated facilities receiving these funds to furnish a "reasonable volume of services to those unable to pay" and to make their services "available to all persons residing in their service areas" (P.L. 79-725). These provisions are clearly obligations to facilities to assure access to care in return for receipt of federal funds. The act was later amended in 1954 to include nursing homes, rehabilitation facilities, chronic disease centers, and diagnostic or treatment facilities.

Similar concerns existed with regard to the availability of physicians and other health professionals. Policymakers concurred that a health provider shortage existed across professions and that an increase in supply of professionals was the proper response. As early as 1963 the Health Professions Education Assistance Act (P.L. 88-129) provided construction money to health professions schools, with the stipulation that enrollments be increased. Direct federal support was provided to medical schools for the first time, and loans and scholarships were provided for students. In 1971 further legislation (P.L. 92-157) known as the Pell Act, provided for a wide range of health professions schools to receive funds in exchange for specified increases in enrollment. For the first time the federal government directly entered the effort to increase the supply of primary care providers, a key access strategy that continues today.

Policy direction to address availability shifted dramatically from an attempt to increase absolute numbers of providers and facilities, to a strategy of proper distribution of these resources through planning. A perception emerged that both providers and facilities were becoming too plentiful and that the nation had moved from shortage to oversupply. This refocus of priorities coincided with increasing concerns for the cost of health care and the notion that increasing supply of providers and facilities led to increased and often inappropriate utilization as expressed in Roemer's law that "a built bed is a filled bed."

Availability of service has evolved to a point that providers are generally regarded as free to make decisions concerning location and offering of services in response to market forces. The role of government, once quite directive, has been reduced to providing incentives to serve underserved populations through Disproportionate Share payments under the Medicare program and to provide primary care services through preferential payment policies of federal reimbursement. These preferential sources of payment are quite important to the fiscal well-being of "safety net" providers such as public hospitals and clinics that provide substantial services to disadvantaged populations through "open door" policies for access to care. The federal government has refrained, however, from major policy initiatives to affect availability at a time when concerns are once again being expressed regarding a shortage of hospital beds and a critical shortage of physicians and nursing, pharmacy, and other health professionals.

AFFORDABILITY

As concerns over the cost of health care have increased in recent decades, so has the concern over affordability of health care and the relationship of unaffordable care to lack of access. This concern has primarily been expressed for the uninsured, who have no way to pay for increasingly expensive services other than through personal means. The negative consequences of uninsured status are potentially financially ruinous: Medical expenses are the leading cause of current personal bankruptcy filings.

Another dimension of the affordability issue, however, is that of the underinsured. Although the individual may possess adequate means for some services, other vital services, such as prescription drugs for the elderly, may be beyond financial reach.

THE UNINSURED

The Kaiser Family Foundation reported 38.4 million uninsured Americans in 2000, and various recent estimates place this number as high as 44 million. These figures approximate one in every seven Americans. Almost two thirds of the uninsured, or 64%, are defined as poor or near poor. According to the Kaiser Family Foundation, the uninsured report the greatest problems of access to care, across all racial segments. Of the uninsured, 34% have no usual source of care, a strong indicator of actual access, as opposed to 13% in the general population. Although non-workers are twice as likely to be uninsured as are employees, 61% of the uninsured are members of households headed by a full-time, full-year worker.

Medicare has lifted the threat of uninsured status from the vast majority of those over 65, and Medicaid provides comparable assurance to those eligible for assistance. The needs of the working poor and families remain a significant issue, however.

To assure access to care, children in these households have received special attention. Adjustments to the Medicaid program have created more liberal eligibility guidelines to allow extension of public insurance to children. This policy has support from research that finds uninsured children are less likely to receive preventive checkups and care for chronic conditions such as asthma. Nevertheless, 15% of children under age 18 remain uninsured.

The uninsured problem increases for young adults, 30% of whom lack coverage. This age group is at high risk for trauma and accidents. Access of a limited sort has been assured through the stipulation in the Emergency Medical Treatment and Active Labor Act of 1986 that anyone seeking treatment at a hospital emergency department must be examined and receive appropriate stabilization.

THE UNDERINSURED

A more recent development impacting access is the increase in underinsured individuals. This includes health care needs that are not covered at all in a given plan, such as outpatient drug coverage, or that are covered but with high copayments that result in the patient sacrificing care. As health insurance premiums have risen since 2000, an increasing percentage of cost is borne by employees rather than by employers, as was traditional. Limitation of access to care may result from increasing the employee share of coverage, switching carriers and products, reduction of covered services, tightening eligibility requirements, and/or reducing the employer's role in insurance.

Underinsurance is of special concern as a factor reducing use of preventive services. Stable relationships between providers and patients are a predictor of effective use of primary care, a prime *Healthy People 2010* objective. This relationship is threatened as individuals are called on to pay directly for these services even though such health care may prevent more costly care later.

APPROPRIATENESS

A service that is inappropriate to the need of the consumer or that is delivered with inferior quality is of little benefit, no matter how attainable access to the service may be. Great attention has been devoted by health policy makers to balancing the system of care to assure access to appropriate services.

A prominent example is the recognition of the magnitude of chronic illness in the population and the need for access to services that are routinely available to monitor and adjust ongoing care. This philosophy is a departure from earlier system responses that emphasized curative services delivered to inpatients through specialty-trained personnel.

Primary care professional services are another established access strategy. Policymakers have advocated primary care services as less costly but also of greater quality, because the level of service is more likely to be matched to the health needs of the vast majority of the population.

Managed care has posed a particular problem for consideration of access. The popular idea is that managed care plans are committed to denying access to care through medical review, case management, and other management strategies. Philosophically, however, managed care is based on a foundation of appropriate care in keeping with patient needs and on a recognition that unlimited access may result in overutilization of and inappropriate services.

The effort to achieve balance in determining appropriateness of care has been a major financial and public relations challenge for the managed care industry, because the public has focused on the negative message that access to care is sometimes denied.

ACCEPTABILITY

Access to care may be readily available but still rejected by patients as unacceptable. The *Healthy People 2010* priority of eliminating racial and ethnic disparities in health care has paid great attention to cultural gaps between providers of care and those disadvantaged populations with less than optimal access to care. Specific programs have been initiated to address these concerns by increasing the supply of minority health professionals. An example is the Association of American Colleges' "3000 by 2000" program to increase the number of entering minority medical students to 3,000 per year.

Services may not be accessed because patients are uninformed regarding their availability. An example is screening services to detect diabetes in the adult population. In the absence of routine primary care, these services are often available at little or no cost, but the target population may be unaware of their existence. In addition, patients may also be uninspired to access such services because the patients lack basic health information on the consequences of untreated diabetes and the readily available means by which most diabetes may be controlled.

Patients may not trust the system, as in preventive dental services. Finally, the discomfort associated, in the mind of the patient, with care may result in failure to access the system.

CONCLUSION

Access is a multidimensional issue that includes not only provider availability but also fundamental economic considerations and issues of patient acceptance. It remains a significant policy issue complicated by inequality of access and systemic barriers to care.

—Richard A. Culbertson

See also Medicaid, Public Hospital

FURTHER READING

Aday, L. (2001). *At risk in America: The health and health care needs of vulnerable populations in the United States.* San Francisco: Jossey-Bass.

Institute of Medicine. (2000). *America's health care safety net: Intact but endangered.* M. Lewin & S. Altman (Eds.). Washington, DC: National Academy Press.

Kaiser Family Foundation. (2002). *Trends and indicators in the changing health care marketplace.* Menlo Park, CA: Kaiser Family Foundation.

Litman, T., & Robins, L. (1997). *Health politics and policy* (3rd ed.). Albany, NY: Delmar.

U.S. Department of Health and Human Services (DHHS). *Healthy people 2010* (Vol. 1). Washington, DC: U.S. Government Printing Office.

ACCREDITATION OF HOSPITALS

See Joint Commission on Accreditation of Healthcare Organizations (JCAHO)

ACCRUAL-BASED ACCOUNTING

Accrual-based accounting is a procedure intended to match revenues reported in financial statements with the expenses associated with generating those revenues. Financial statements pertain to specific time periods (that is, the month, quarter, year, and so on).

In the accrual system, revenues and expenses are not solely identified with the actual collection of cash from the client or the payment of cash to a supplier or creditor. Revenue is recognized or recorded in the income statement when the rendering of the services is deemed completed; likewise, expenses are recognized or recorded when incurred or when we acknowledge responsibility for them.

Cash may have been received from a client before the services are rendered, as a prepayment, or after the services are rendered, such as the collection of a client copayment and/or collection from the client's insurer. Under the accrual system, when the services are performed the revenue is considered earned, regardless of whether or not cash has been received.

Cash payments for liability insurance premiums are paid in advance of the coverage period, whereas payment for utility services is made after the services have been provided. With respect to the insurance premiums, the expense is considered to have been incurred with the passage of the policy coverage period. Regarding the utilities, the expense is considered to have been incurred as the utility services were received. In both preceding cases, under the accrual system expenses are considered to have been incurred with the passage of time, not when the actual payment of cash is made.

—Harry N. Hughes

FURTHER READING

Harrison, W. T., Jr., & Horngren, C. T. (2001). *Financial accounting* (4th ed.). Upper Saddle River, NJ: Prentice Hall.

Keiso, D. E., Weygandt, J. J., & Warfield, T. D. (2001). *Intermediate accounting* (10th ed.). New York: Wiley.

Warren, C. S., Reeve, J. M., & Fess, P. E. (2002). *Financial and managerial accounting* (7th ed.). Mason, OH: South-Western.

ACCUMULATED DEPRECIATION

Unlike supplies, which are physically consumed during the course of practice, fixed assets, such as computers, office furniture, X-ray equipment, and laser equipment are used or reused for several periods. The total verifiable costs associated with various fixed assets are normally reported on the balance sheet in a fixed assets section. As the cost of a fixed asset is consumed, the periodic amount is shown as depreciation expense in the income statement and is aggregated in the accumulated depreciation account on the balance sheet.

The cost of the particular depreciable asset should be maintained on the balance sheet. By using the accumulated depreciation account, the total estimate as to the amount of the asset's cost that has expired with the passage of time or usage is also reflected on the balance sheet.

For example, suppose a computer is purchased at a total cost of $8,500. If it is estimated the computer will have a total useful life of 5 years with no residual or salvage value, its cost can be spread over the 5 years of its use on an equal basis by using straight-line depreciation. The annual depreciation expense reported on the income statement would be $1,700, and the accumulated depreciation on the balance sheet would show the aggregate of the annual depreciation expense amounts. Using the preceding data, the computer would be reported on the first and second year's balance sheets as follows:

For the first year's balance sheet:		
Computer	$8,500	
Less accumulated depreciation—computer	*1,700*	6,800*
For the second year's balance sheet:		
Computer	$8,500	
Less accumulated depreciation—computer	*3,400*	5,100*

*The 6,800 and 5,100 amounts are referred to as the book value of the asset. Note that as the asset's cost is consumed, the book value approaches zero, which is the expected salvage value in this illustration.

—Harry N. Hughes

FURTHER READING

Harrison, W. T., Jr., & Horngren, C. T. (2001). *Financial accounting* (4th ed.). Upper Saddle River, NJ: Prentice Hall.

Warren, C. S., Reeve, J. M., & Fess, P. E. (2002). *Financial and managerial accounting* (7th ed.). Mason, OH: South-Western.

ACQUISITIONS

See Merger and Acquisition

ACTIVITIES OF DAILY LIVING

See Long-Term Care

ACTIVITY-BASED COSTING

Activity-based costing (ABC) can provide health care professionals with the necessary information to address the critical questions required to manage any organization. ABC is based on the very simple, yet very powerful, principles that activities consume resources and services use the output of these activities. ABC focuses on the management and cost of activities, whereas traditional costing systems focus on departmental or service costs. ABC improves the costing of products and services by more accurately assigning overhead or indirect costs on a cause-and-effect basis.

Activity-based costing is a tool organizations can use to develop more accurate cost information to enhance managerial decision making. Health care costs are going up again. Government officials, corporations, and individuals are all calling for health care organizations to lower costs. Why does everyone appear to be concentrating on reducing costs rather than finding ways to bring in more revenue? In simple terms, if costs are greater than 50% of revenues (as in the current health care environment), organizations receive a greater return on their investment dollar from decreasing costs than from increasing revenues.

Not only is reducing overall costs important, but improving the accuracy of costing information is also becoming much more critical to enhancing organizational performance. Remember: no margin, no mission. As indirect costs (such as overhead) become a larger portion of organizations' overall costs, it becomes crucial that these costs be allocated accurately. In most cases the information received from the organization's costing systems is of very little value to its managers in making strategic decisions. Organizations have information to satisfy auditors and receive reimbursements (and sometimes even this doesn't work very well), but do they have the requisite information to accurately accumulate what a particular managed care contract is costing? Or how much it is really costing for a particular procedure? In other words, do organizations have the information available to accurately calculate profitability by patient group, procedure, doctor, and insurance carrier? The answer is usually no. ABC can assist in this endeavor.

In addition, traditional costing procedures allocate indirect costs based on some sort of volume measure (encounters, dollar value of reimbursements). When this occurs, the highest-volume (usually lowest-complexity) departments or procedures get allocated the largest percentage of costs, even though this department or procedure may not be actually using (or absorbing) that amount of indirect costs. Therefore, a cross-subsidy of costs occurs, where one department or procedure, although very complex by nature (but low volume), absorbs very little of the indirect costs.

These cross-subsidies of service costs can cause all sorts of disrupting behavior in organizations. ABC is a tool to help uncover and correct these cross-subsidies.

How does activity-based costing work? Resources (such as general ledger costs) are first allocated to organization activities (such as locating charts and patient preparation), and these activity costs are allocated to cost objects (such as procedures and insurance carriers). For a simple example, let's assume $1,000 of salary costs. Using time spent, this $1,000 is allocated to the activities actually performed. If 50% of the time was spent performing procedures, 30% of time was spent doing paperwork, and 20% of the time was spent searching for charts, the $1,000 of salary costs would be allocated as follows: $500 to the procedure activity, $300 to the paperwork activity, and then $200 to the searching for charts activity.

Next these costs would be allocated, in some fashion, to the cost objects the manager is trying to analyze. For example, if the manager wanted profitability by insurance carrier these activity pools would have to be allocated to the various insurance carriers in a cause-and-effect way so that the carriers who used more of the resources would be charged with more of the costs. So let's assume seven insurance carriers require different levels of paperwork to be processed. Carrier A requires 30% of the effort, and carrier B requires 20% of the effort; the remaining five carriers each use 10% of the effort. Using ABC, you would then allocate 30% of the $300 paperwork activity pool to carrier A ($90) and 20% of the $300 paperwork pool to carrier B ($60). In this manner the insurance carriers that are using more of the resources of the organization are assigned more of the costs.

—Bruce Behn

FURTHER READING

Baker, J. J. (1998). *Activity-based costing and activity-based management for health care.* Gaithersburg, MD: Aspen.

ACTIVITY RATIOS

See Ratio Analysis

ACUTE CARE

See Hospitals

ADMINISTRATIVE SERVICES ORGANIZATION (ASO)

An ASO is an organization that provides a wide variety of administrative services to managed care organizations that outsource these services. This allows the managed care organization to concentrate on its primary mission of providing quality, cost-effective medical care.

The ASO oversees the administrative aspects of the company's payroll, workers' compensation insurance, health insurance, retirement plans, disability, state and federal unemployment insurance management, and government compliance issues.

Services specific to health care offered by ASOs include the following:

Eligibility and enrollment processing

Benefit plan setup

Member services

Claim adjudication

Claim repricing

Capitation processing

Coordination of benefits

Physician profiling

HEDIS (Health Plan & Employer Data & Info Set) reporting

Management reporting

—Donald Levick

FURTHER READING

checkpointhr.com/about_overview.asp
Med On Web Introduces the First Electronic Administrative Service Organization (EASO). (2000, April 17). *PR Newswire* (New York).
www.netpeo.com
www.peoinfo.com/html/ASO.htm
www.stratummed.com/ASO.htm

ADOPTER CATEGORIES

The term *adopter categories (AC)* classifies what might be more generally described as market segments, buyer or customer groups, and related similar terms. Groups of customers adopt (make purchase decisions) different choices based on differing reasons and criteria. Sorting these prospective clients or customers into groupings is a common practice, and *adopter categories* is just one of many names given to these groups. Much of this definition is devoted to the nature of adopter categories and the criteria and decisions associated with them.

All markets can be segmented into prospective purchasers based on specific needs and wants. These adopter categories or market segments may be based on geography, age, demographics, social status, economic status, racial or gender segmentation, risk classification, and many other parameters.

Understanding the adopter categories being served is a critical step in the establishment of marketing plans, service definition, pricing, and delivery methods. Market research is a common tool used to define market segments and thus understand adopter categories. The more distinctive the characteristics of adopter categories, the more specifically targeted the marketing attention to it can be. Products and services are frequently developed or adapted to adopter categories with the expectation that tailoring them to specific decision criteria of prospects and customers will enhance the likelihood of competitive success.

Pricing is a major issue for most adopter categories. Although there are many sacrifices a purchaser must make to acquire something he or she wants or needs, price is usually near the top of the decision list. Positioning the price of the goods or services depends heavily on competitive conditions in the market segment (AC) chosen as the target. At times, an error in pricing can completely eliminate a competitor from consideration, which is why pricing is so important in those cases. In other cases, such as health care services or accident insurance where a third party is paying, price may be far down the list in users' decision criteria, but it will still be high on the payer's priority list.

Location and geography are important criteria for adopter categories, because many other factors usually depend on it. To save time, some adopter categories choose locations that are convenient. Other adopter categories exclude locations that are too remote or inconvenient.

An old saying in retailing is "There are three very important decisions a retailer must make: location, location, and location." Location is often a key decision criterion for adopter categories. This is why facilities serving like adopter categories cluster. Doctors' offices often cluster in locations near hospitals, as do specialty pharmacies. Many retail stores seek neighborhoods that benefit from traffic of adopter categories shopping in the same area; large supermarkets attract smaller specialty stores such as dry cleaners, fast food restaurants, and so forth in strip malls. These are all cases of sellers attempting to take advantage of the shopping patterns of adopter categories to make their offering more attractive than those of competitors.

Once the adopter categories and their needs, wants, and preferences are clearly defined and understood, many other decisions can be built on that knowledge. Age and gender are frequent criteria for defining adopter categories. Certain marketing approaches and advertising media choices are much more successful with some age-groups than with others. Certain age-groups are largely unresponsive to appeals that would be hugely successful with other age-groups. For example, skateboards are unlikely to have much appeal to people over age 70, whereas canes and walkers are equally unlikely to be a major purchase interest for those under age 20!

Although that is an extreme example, in many cases, marketers spend good money on promotion or communications where large parts of the target market have absolutely no interest in the product or service! Such waste just emphasizes the importance of clearly understanding and accurately defining the target adopter categories.

Finally, it is important to reiterate that marketing communications, promotion, advertising, and so on are important tools in pursuing specific adopter categories. Targeting of adopters with specific products, services, pricing, locations, hours of operation, affinity marketing, and so forth can result in a much more effective use of facilities, personnel, and resources.

When relative parity on one or more of the decision factors occurs, then adopter categories search to the next criteria on their priority list for a decision basis. If products and services, price, and location are equal, perhaps the speed of service, facility attractiveness, or conveniences such as parking and covered walkways becomes a decision factor.

Key factors such as quality (conformance to specification) are usually gatekeepers for adopter categories and thus merit only a passing discussion. Without a minimum level of acceptable quality, prospective suppliers will be excluded from consideration in the decision process.

In some instances different levels of "specification quality" may be offered, but these are essentially product differences and adopter categories consider them on that basis. (For example, both Timex and Rolex watches keep time accurately enough to satisfy nearly all adopter categories, but their prestige differs widely, and these two similar products appeal to quite different adopter categories).

The familiar "doc in a box" urgent care medical facilities are highly desirable to some adopter categories for their convenience and long hours, but are abhorrent to others, who insist on more conventional medical care based on a longer-term relationship. Whether the choice is one of an urgent care clinic or a hospital outpatient clinic or emergency room, understanding the adopter categories preferences is absolutely critical in positioning both facilities as service providers to customers (in this case, patients).

Understanding these kinds of psychological segmentation and purchaser motivation is critical in understanding adopter categories and making decisions on services to be provided, location, pricing, and advertising and promotional efforts. Understand your adopter categories' preferences and characteristics, wishes, likes, dislikes, needs and wants, and behavior patterns. The job of meeting those preferences and capitalizing on those characteristics will be much easier, and the outcome will also be much more successful.

—John L. Mariotti

See also Market Opportunity Analysis, Marketing Research, Market Segmentation

FURTHER READING

Engel, J. F., Blackwell, R. D., & Miniard, P. W. (1995). *Consumer behavior.* Fort Worth, TX: Dryden Press.

ADVANCED HEALTH CARE DIRECTIVES

Advanced health care directives are written documents in which people provide guidance on their health care decisions in the event they become unable either to communicate their own personal medical care choices or to decide appropriately what those choices should be. Directives let people state prospectively their wishes and instructions about treatments they want or do not want if they become unable in the future to understand or communicate with health care providers.

These directives are made in the form of instructions as to medical treatment such as living wills and DNR (do not resuscitate) orders; these instructional directives are a person's statements about what treatment or care should or should not be performed in the event of certain medical conditions. Directives also delegate legal authority to another person(s) to make treatment decisions; examples are durable powers of attorney for health care and declarations of preferences for mental health treatments. These directives give another person (an attorney-in-fact, agent, proxy, or surrogate) the power to decide on treatment and care for the individual granting the power (the principal) if that person is unable to do so.

The most widely used advanced health care directives (as mentioned earlier) include living wills, which provide a person's instructions concerning death-delaying procedures when that individual is in a terminal condition; DNR orders, also concerning death-delaying procedures; durable powers of attorney for health care, which are delegations of authority to another concerning a wide range of health care decisions; and declarations of preferences for mental health treatment, which represent the delegation of authority dealing only with mental illness.

Advanced health care directives may be effective immediately on the individual's signature, meaning that they may be invoked immediately on an individual's inability to make decisions, weigh treatment alternatives, or give informed consent, or directives may only become effective on the individual's incompetence as declared by physician(s) or as otherwise determined under the terms of the directive. Directives becoming effective only on the declaration of incompetence usually require a certified statement of incompetence by a physician who has treated the person within a stated period of time or by the person's attending physician. Except for the somewhat rare declaration of preferences for mental health care directives, advanced health care directives are revocable until an individual becomes incapable of communicating revocation. In many states revocation may be made orally as well as in writing.

The form and effectiveness of advanced health care directives are usually guided by state law. Directives drafted in compliance with the laws of an individual's state of residence are normally honored by health care professionals, because of their familiarity with the directives as well as their awareness of the authority behind the enforcement of the directives. Health care professionals acting in reliance on such directives are generally protected by state law from liability for such actions.

Through advanced health care directives, people can preserve their privacy and autonomy. If drafted correctly, directives can avoid the need for judicial involvement in individuals' health care decisions by eliminating the need to appoint guardians or conservators.

—Anne M. McKinney

See also Durable Powers of Attorney for Health Care (DPAHC), Living Wills

FURTHER READING

Krohm, C., & Summers, S. (2002). *Advance health care directives: A handbook for professionals.* Chicago: ABA Publishing.

ADVERSE DRUG REACTION (ADR)

An adverse drug reaction (ADR) is an unintended reaction to a drug. For an approved drug, it is an unintended reaction to the drug at normally used doses for prophylaxis, diagnosis, or treatment of a disease, or for the modification of physiological function. In clinical trials, an ADR includes an injury related to overdosing, an abuse or dependence, as well as unintended interactions with other medications or products. In clinical trials, the term *adverse drug reaction* may be incorporated into the more general term *adverse event* (AE), which includes any negative experience encountered by the participant during the course of a clinical trial. An ADR is associated specifically with the drug being tested. In clinical trials, ADRs or AEs are graded on a severity scale and must be reported to the FDA.

Any adverse drug reaction, no matter how minor, has the potential to do harm. When we consider that in clinical trials testing, a drug may be given to 1,000 participants under controlled conditions, adverse events that occur with a frequency of less than 1/1,000 may go undetected prior to marketing. Some adverse reactions may be predicted by the drug's pharmacology or mechanism of action. However, some idiosyncratic reactions may be related to other causes, such as interactions with other medications, or genetic or environmental factors.

Several strategies can be used to detect adverse reactions after marketing of a drug. These include cohort studies, case control studies, and meta-analysis of pre- and postmarketing studies. Because these techniques have limitations, individual reports may be very helpful to identify adverse drug reactions. The U.S. Food and Drug Administration has an Internet-based Adverse Event Reporting System. This computerized database supports the FDA's postmarketing safety surveillance program for all approved drug and therapeutic biologic products. Reports are reviewed by clinical reviewers at the Center for Drug Evaluation and Research and at the Center for Biologics Evaluation and Research. Based on this information, manufacturers may update package inserts, or physicians and other health care providers may receive warning letters from the drug manufacturer if a significant problem is found with a drug or other biological compound. Ultimately, the reporting system seeks to identify potential problems and improve patient safety.

—Stephen A. Vitkun

FURTHER READING

Bohaychuk, W., & Ball, G. (1999). *Conducting GCP-compliant clinical research.* Chichester, UK: Wiley.

Ginsberg, D. (1999). *The investigator's guide to clinical research* (2nd ed.). Boston: Centerwatch.

Hardman, J. G., & Limbird, L. E. (2001). *Goodman & Gilman's The pharmacological basis of therapeutics* (10th ed.). New York: McGraw-Hill.

www.FDA.gov/cder/aers/default.htm

ADVERSE EVENT (AE)

An adverse event is any undesirable, unexpected medical symptom or finding that a study subject experiences while taking a study medication or using a study device.

Causality, or the relationship between cause and effect (study medication or device and medical occurrence), is generally not implied. For example, adverse events include such diverse circumstances as headaches, colds, vomiting, or motor vehicle accidents. The term *adverse drug reaction* (ADR) more accurately implies that a particular drug caused an untoward event. The database of adverse reactions to marketed products is known as AERS (Adverse Event Reporting System).

Adverse events can be categorized as either serious or nonserious. A serious adverse event is one that is fatal or life threatening, results in hospitalization or prolongs hospitalization, is significantly disabling or incapacitating, or is a congenital anomaly or birth defect. The FDA GCP guidelines include overdose as a serious adverse event.

All adverse events, serious and nonserious, must be recorded in source documents and case report forms. The investigator must immediately report all serious adverse events to the sponsor. The sponsor is then obligated to expedite the dissemination of this information to all concerned investigators, institutions, institutional review boards or institutional ethics committees (IRBs or IECs), and regulatory authorities. The term *unexpected adverse event* is used when the nature or severity of the event is inconsistent with product labeling (as detailed in the investigator brochure for an approved experimental drug or device) or the data sheet (package insert for a marketed product).

A grading system should be applied to the relationship of an adverse event to the study medication or device. Although regulatory documents do not specify this grading system, the following suggested system illustrates the intent of such a system:

None: AE is definitely not associated with study drug or device.

Remote: AE is not likely associated with study drug or device.

Possible: There is a reasonable causal relationship between event and study drug or device, but AE could have been caused by participant's clinical state or other therapies participant has received.

Probable: There is a reasonable causal relationship between event and study drug or device, event subsides when study item is discontinued, and event cannot be explained by study subject's usual clinical state.

Highly Probable: There is a reasonable causal relationship between event and study drug or device, event subsides when study item is discontinued, and event reappears with repeat exposure to study drug or device.

The intensity and severity of the adverse event should also be graded on a scaled system. As with the grading of the causal relationship between a study drug or device and adverse event, there is no standard as to how to grade severity. The following suggested system illustrates the intent of such a system:

Mild: AE is transient, does not require medical treatment, and does not interfere with subject's daily routine.

Moderate: AE produces minor discomforts and concerns that may slightly interfere with subject's daily routine but are relieved with simple therapeutic measures.

Severe: AE interrupts the subject's daily routine and requires systematic medical treatment. .

—Linda M. Cimino

See also Case Report Form (CRF), Good Clinical Practices (GCPs)

FURTHER READING

Bohaychuk, W., & Ball, G. (1999). *Conducting GCP-compliant clinical research.* Chichester, UK: Wiley.

Chow, S.-C., & Liu, J.-P. (1998). *Design and analysis of clinical trials: Concepts and methodologies.* New York: Wiley.

Day, S. (1999). *Dictionary for clinical trials.* Chichester, UK: Wiley.

Kolman, J., Meng, P., & Scott, G. (1998). *Good clinical practice* (pp. 2–3). Chichester, UK: Wiley.

ADVERSE SELECTION

Adverse selection occurs when individuals or groups with higher expected health care utilization join a risk pool designed for those with a lower expected utilization. A necessary condition for adverse selection is that the individual or group knows more about his (or her) future claims experience than does the insurer. In contrast, favorable selection occurs when those with lower future expected utilization join a plan designed for those with higher expected use.

Adverse selection poses a major challenge to health insurers. Consider an insurer that assigns all insureds to a single insurance pool. This is simple community rating. In such a plan, all those with coverage pay the same premium based on the average expected claims experience plus loading costs. If an individual knows he is likely to use a lot of medical care, he has an incentive to join this plan because his premiums will likely be less than the expected claims. Someone who knows she is a low user has an incentive not to join because the premium is well above the likely use of covered services. After people have joined the plan, the insurer discovers that claims experience was greater than anticipated and premiums are likely to be insufficient to cover costs. Adverse selection is the reason for this. High-cost individuals joined and low-cost individuals avoided an insurance plan designed for average-cost individuals.

Because of adverse selection, insurers engage in underwriting. This is an effort to put individuals or groups into insurance pools or classes that reflect their likely future claims experience. Underwriting is based on relatively easily measured characteristics that are related to future claims experience. Thus individuals may be in different risk classes based on their age, gender, and prior health conditions. Group contracts can also entail adverse selection. Insurers deal with adverse selection in this case by underwriting based on the credibility of the group's prior claims experience relative to the insurer's overall book of business or by retrospective experience rating. In the latter case, the group's premium is based exclusively on the actual claims experience of the group in the current year. Such experience-rated premiums often include a stop-loss clause designed to limit the group's exposure to particularly high individual claims or to an unusually high overall claims experience.

Most empirical evidence on adverse selection comes from employer data on worker choices among the plans offered. Additional evidence comes from the Medicare program. The studies are nearly unanimous in finding biased selection (see Cutler & Zeckhauser, 2000, in the Further Reading section for this entry). Much of the research has examined enrollment into health maintenance organizations (HMOs) in contrast to conventional health insurance; the literature concludes that HMOs tend to attract people who use less health care. Many of these studies are designed to examine the utilization of workers before they have a choice of health plans. For example, let's say all workers for a firm are in a conventional employer-sponsored health insurance plan in year 1. In year 2 the firm offers a choice of a conventional plan and an HMO. Workers choose one or the other plan. Examining the claims experience of each set of workers in year 1 typically shows that those who ultimately chose the HMO had lower prior claims experience.

Evidence of adverse selection in the Medicare program has led Congress to change the way Medicare HMOs are paid. Payments for Medicare beneficiaries selecting an HMO are now "risk adjusted" to reflect prior utilization as well as age, gender, institutional and welfare status, and location.

Risk adjustment methodologies are also used to meaningfully compare premiums across insurers or groups by adjusting for factors associated with the cost of expected future utilization. Methods rely on demographic characteristics, measures of health status, and prior utilization. Prior utilization tends to be among the best predictors (see Van de Ven & Ellis, 2000).

—Michael A. Morrisey

FURTHER READING

Cutler, D. M., & Zeckhauser, R. J. (2000). The anatomy of health insurance. In A. J. Culyer & J. P. Newhouse (Eds.), *Handbook of health economics* (Vol. 1, pp. 564–643). Amsterdam: Elsevier Science.

Van de Ven, W., & Ellis, R. P. (2000). Risk adjustment in competitive health plan markets. In A. J. Culyer & J. P. Newhouse (Eds.), *Handbook of health economics* (Vol. 1, pp. 755–845). Amsterdam: Elsevier Science.

ADVERTISING

Advertising is the promotion of goods or services in exchange for compensation, usually monetary. Advertising is an important but single component of an overall strategic health care marketing plan. Effective advertising requires thoughtful attention to what to say, how to say it, through what means to say it, and to whom the message is intended, that is, its target audience.

In thinking about advertising one useful concept is the AIDA model, which proposes that consumers go through four stages in making a buying decision: awareness, interest, desire, and action. Ad campaigns can be geared to the particular stage(s) a business seeks to affect. Another tenet of effective advertising is to promote benefits, not features, in offering products and services: Consumers value how they will be helped far more than the mechanisms involved.

An often-forgotten useful advantage of ad campaigns is the retention of customers. Keeping such components as brand awareness and the business's unique advantages in the minds of customers who can "vote with their feet" further justifies inclusion of considerable advertising dollars in a firm's annual budget.

Late-19th-century retailer John Wanamaker famously remarked that half of his advertising was wasted, but he did not know which half. Today, the availability of detailed localized quantitative information, such as demographic data, allows for more rational advertising and other marketing decisions. Nonetheless, the art of advertising undoubtedly contributes to marketing effectiveness. The choice of individuals and agencies knowledgeable and experienced in health care is of strategic importance to the success of health care professionals and organizations.

Public relations (PR) is the promotion of a product or service for which one does not have to pay, such as in holding a health fair, being active in community service, or being quoted as an expert in the media. PR has been used effectively in marketing physician and health care services.

Health care advertising has seen geometric growth since a 1980 landmark ruling by the Federal Trade Commission against the American Medical Association's broad prohibitions on the solicitation of patients and its proscription of almost all forms of advertising and promotion by its members. The FTC reasoned that advertising forms an indispensable function in society in allowing for more competition and thus better pricing. However, that assertion may find challenge in the history of health care costs subsequent to the decision.

The Code of Medical Ethics of the American Medical Association serves as a key source for detailed opinions regarding health care advertising, publicity, telecommunications services, and standards of professional responsibility in media communications. The key issue is whether advertising or publicity, regardless of form or content, is true and not materially misleading.

Direct-to-consumer (DTC) pharmaceutical advertising has increased greatly since 1997, when the Food and Drug Administration (FDA) eased certain requirements, such as listing voluminous information about potential side effects. Advertisements must still list major health risks and include a means for consumers to obtain information about side effects. DTC advertising proponents point to improvements in patient education, involvement, and compliance. Opponents cite cost considerations and studies purporting that physicians are swayed from good medical judgment by demands for drugs advertised directly to consumers.

—Barry Henderson

See also Customer Relationship Management (CRM), Electronic Commerce, Marketing Concept, Press Release, Public Relations

FURTHER READING

Meade, P. S. (1998). *Healthcare advertising and marketing.* New York: McGraw-Hill.

Ogilvy, D. (1985). *Ogilvy on advertising.* New York: Random House.

www.ama-assn.org/ama/pub/category/8600.html

AFFIRMATIVE ACTION IN EMPLOYMENT

The general term *affirmative action* is used to describe any number of proactive steps that organizations take to reduce discrimination on the basis of race, color, religion, sex, or national origin. An affirmative action plan or affirmative action program (AAP) states the specific types of actions planned within a particular organization.

AFFIRMATIVE ACTION IN ORGANIZATIONS

There are three circumstances under which an organization would adopt an affirmative action program. By Executive Orders 11246 issued in 1965 and 11375 issued in 1967 by President Lyndon Johnson, the federal government mandates that government contractors and subcontractors have an affirmative action plan. The Office of Federal Contract Compliance Programs (OFCCP) enforces the executive order in much the same way that the Equal Employment Opportunity Commission (EEOC) enforces claims of discrimination. Yet there are clear distinctions between the jurisdictions of the two government offices. One notable difference is that the OFCCP refers cases involving discrimination against one person (that is, adverse selection) to the EEOC; the OFCCP typically takes cases charging patterns of discrimination against groups of people. Also unlike the EEOC, the OFCCP has both enforcement and administrative authority. In other words, the office may impose sanctions against companies not abiding by the executive orders. These sanctions may include the withdrawal of current agreements and deeming contractors ineligible for future contract awards.

The second circumstance under which an organization would adopt an affirmative action program is a court ruling or consent decree. Private organizations may be ordered by a court of law to formulate and abide by an affirmative action program as redress for the court's findings of past discrimination. Court mandates for affirmative action are typically handed down only in the most egregious of discrimination cases; therefore, companies have fewer degrees of freedom in this circumstance, as further discussed later.

In the third case, private organizations may adopt affirmative action plans voluntarily; however, these plans are not monitored by any federal agency. Individuals or groups of individuals taking exception to these voluntary affirmative action plans must litigate through Title VII of the Civil Rights Act. Court decisions have established that voluntary programs must be temporary, free from adverse impact against white male employees, and designed specifically to reduce imbalance between minority and majority groups in order to comply with Title VII.

COMPONENTS OF AN AFFIRMATIVE ACTION PLAN

In its most basic form, the term *affirmative action* refers to a continual, four-step process that involves both analysis and action steps:

1. A *utilization analysis,* in which the organization compiles the percentage of workers in each protected class that are currently employed.

2. An *availability analysis* in which the availability of qualified men, women, and nonwhites present in the relevant labor market is ascertained.

3. *Identification of problem areas,* in which comparisons are made between the percentages used and the percentages available; if marked differences exist with regard to any protected class, corrective action must be planned.

4. *Corrective action* is carried out to increase the parity of protected class percentages between the organization and the labor market. Goals and timetables are included so that progress toward parity can be monitored.

Corrective actions may include a variety of steps deemed necessary to move toward an employee composition that more closely mirrors the composition of the relevant labor market. For instance, corrective actions may include more focused recruitment of applicants from underrepresented groups. Organizations may participate in specialized job fairs or advertise for positions in publications that may appeal more strongly to a particular protected class. Corrective action may also include training and educational programs designed to break down stereotypes among employees and otherwise make the organization a more welcoming place for currently underrepresented groups. Finally, corrective action may entail monitoring selection techniques to ensure they are not adversely impacting members of a protected class. If adverse impact is found, the selection practice may be modified or augmented. For example, some law enforcement agencies offer training courses before administering physical abilities tests, to optimally prepare women candidates, who often do not fare as well as men in endurance and strength testing.

Note that nothing in the basic affirmative action plan requires an organization to hire unqualified individuals. Furthermore, the intentional hiring of an individual because of his or her protected class status is illegal. By extension, quota systems in which a certain number of applicants in a protected class must be hired, regardless of qualifications, are also illegal. Often affirmative action plans are assumed to encompass these circumstances even though they are not intended. Rather, goals and timetables are flexible, and they are a means of measuring progress, rather than ends in and of themselves. Of course, in the implementation stages organizations may in fact give preferential treatment on the basis of race or gender. This is strongly discouraged and is not in keeping with the spirit of affirmative action guidelines. The only exception to the preceding is in the case of court-mandated programs, which may include requirements to hire a certain number of workers from a protected class in a specific timeframe.

THE DEBATE SURROUNDING AFFIRMATIVE ACTION

Thirty-five years after its inception, debate continues over the worthiness of affirmative action to correct past instances of discrimination. Proponents of affirmative action, on the one hand, cite the increases in women and minorities in the workplace and the accompanying opportunities for training and education as evidence of its success. Opponents, on the other hand, argue that affirmative action leads to preferential treatment in hiring and that it usurps attention from competence and ability as the most important worker characteristics. Also, opponents argue, affirmative action has unintended, negative social consequences. Although underrepresented worker opportunities are seemingly increased, research has shown that perceptions of individuals hired under affirmative action programs are negative; they are perceived to be less competent and qualified than other employees.

Currently, both the court system and state lawmakers are shaping the future of affirmative action. The U.S. Supreme Court hears affirmative action cases each year, and policymakers in California have been very active in formulating affirmative action at the state level.

—Jennifer R. D. Burgess

See also Adverse Selection, Civil Rights Acts of 1964 and 1991, Labor Markets, Title VII of the Civil Rights Act of 1964

FURTHER READING

Fisher, C. D., Schoenfeldt, L. F., & Shaw, J. B. (1999). *Human resource management* (4th ed.). Boston: Houghton Mifflin.

Gatewood, R. D., & Feild, H. S. (2001). *Human resource selection.* Fort Worth, TX: Harcourt Brace.

Grossman, R. J. (2001, March). Behavior at work. *HR Magazine, 46,* 50–54, 56, 58.

Heilman, M. E., Rivero, J. C., & Brett, J. F. (1991). Skirting the competence issue: Effects of sex-based preferential selection on task choices of women and men. *Journal of Applied Psychology, 76,* 99–105.

Locke, E. A. (1997). Individualism: The only cure for organizational racism. *Industrial Organizational Psychologist, 34*(4), 128–129.

United Steelworkers v. Weber, 433 U.S. 193 (1979).

www.dol.gov

AGE DISCRIMINATION IN EMPLOYMENT

The Age Discrimination in Employment Act (ADEA) was passed in 1967 and was amended in 1978 and 1986 to prohibit employment discrimination against employees 40 years of age and older. Discriminatory practices include recruiting younger applicants or forcing people to retire early for the purpose of maintaining a younger workforce. The legislation was created to resolve practices following stereotypical perceptions of older workers being unsuitable for the workforce. As such, the rules do not apply to workers under 40 years old. Under the ADEA, employers must have a valid reason for all employment decisions regarding employees over the age of 40, which includes hiring, pay, benefits, training, and promotion. The legislation is applicable to private firms that employ at least 20 individuals, governments, unions, and employment agencies. Exceptions to the law include individuals in key management positions (such as vice presidents and CEOs), those whose pensions would be more than $44,000 annually, and pilots who have a mandatory retirement at age 55. Despite these laws, American businesses paid approximately $200 million for age discrimination lawsuits between 1996 and 1998, and the U.S. Equal Employment Opportunity Commission (EEOC) reported a 9% increase in age-related discrimination charges filed in 2001. In the health care system, these types of charges are likely to occur in the nursing population, because the average age for RNs (registered nurses) has increased rapidly from 37.4 years in 1983 to 44.5 years in 2000. Remedies to age discrimination include paying the offended individual or mitigating damages (such as replacing the lost job with a similar job). In age discrimination, a complaint should first be filed with the EEOC. If a satisfactory outcome cannot be reached, the worker can pursue the discrimination complaint with a lawsuit.

—Jillian A. Peat

See also Aging Society, Employment Discrimination, Equal Employment Opportunity Commission (EEOC), Title VII of the Civil Rights Act of 1964

FURTHER READING

Guttman, A. (2000). *EEO law and personnel practices.* Thousand Oaks, CA: Sage.

Letvak, S. (2002). Myths and realities of ageism and nursing. *Association of Operating Room Nurses, 75*(6), 1101–1107.

www.aarp.com

www.eeoc.gov/laws/adea.html

www.eeoc.org

AGING SOCIETY

The share of the population that is elderly is rising rapidly in developing countries because the baby boom generation is aging. The 2000 census reported that 12.4%

of the U.S. population was age 65 or older. This figure is projected to rise to 18.5% in 2025. Most elderly people live on a limited budget while facing declining health and rising health care expenditures. The working-age population must save in advance for retirement while raising children and perhaps serving as caregivers for aged parents. There is also concern that the increasing needs of the elderly may reduce resources for the nonelderly, particularly children. The aging society will be influenced by public policies that provide for the health care and economic well-being of the elderly. Evolving factors in the private sector will also influence future cohorts of elderly people.

The Medicare program represents the largest source of public funding for the purchase of medical care for the U.S. elderly. People age 65 and over are entitled to receive most inpatient and outpatient care, subject to a set of annually declared deductibles and copayments, along with modest monthly premium rates for ambulatory services. In 2000, Medicare expenditures reached $224 billion, just over 2% of gross domestic product (GDP). These expenditures are projected to reach 4.5% of GDP in 2030, and the trust fund that covers Medicare payments for hospital care is projected to go into deficit in 2031.

Medicare expenditures have grown rapidly, in part because of the development and diffusion of increasingly sophisticated medical technologies. Policymakers hoped the introduction of Medicare HMOs would restrain cost growth. Although Medicare managed care enrollment has increased substantially, total program costs continue to escalate. If Medicare expenditures continue to rise rapidly, policymakers will be forced to limit access to certain costly health care interventions for Medicare beneficiaries, increase payroll taxes used to finance the system, or increase deductibles, copayments, or premiums for Medicare recipients.

The Medicaid program provides the largest source of public funding for long-term care (LTC) in the United States. Each state administers its own Medicaid program with partial funding from the federal government. Although only 10% of Medicaid recipients are age 65 and over, this group accounted for 29% of Medicaid expenditures in 1998. Elderly individuals qualify for nursing home care under the Medicaid program if their income and asset levels fall below certain thresholds, which vary across states. Limited Medicaid resources have led to low reimbursement to nursing homes for Medicaid patients in some states and to concerns regarding the quality of care that Medicaid nursing home patients receive. Less than 10% of Americans ages 55 to 64 have purchased private LTC insurance. Most aging Americans appear to view the Medicaid program as their source of LTC insurance. Subsidizing the purchase of LTC may save costs for governments in the long run, if such policies reduce future Medicaid expenditures. However, this possibility has not been proven.

Rising expenditures on outpatient drugs among the elderly have led to calls for government intervention in this health care sector. Policymakers are considering expansion of the Medicare program to include coverage for outpatient prescription drug costs. Other policy options include price controls in the brand-name drug sector, reimportation of drugs from other countries which have lower prices, and policies that encourage price competition from producers of cheaper generic drugs.

Individuals age 65 and over in the United States support themselves financially through a combination of Social Security benefits, private pension benefits, asset income, and earnings. The latter three sources of income are sizeable, although not all elderly receive income from each of these three sources. In contrast, almost all are eligible at age 65 for full Social Security benefits, because of their previous work history or because they are beneficiaries as spouses of qualified workers. The full eligibility age for Social Security rises to age 67 for people born in 1960 or after.

Because the elderly are expected to support their retirement using a variety of income sources, Social Security payments have been maintained at relatively low levels since the initiation of the program. Thus the program serves as a social safety net and has been demonstrated to alleviate poverty among the elderly. The Social Security program is a pay-as-you-go system, with payroll taxes of current workers going toward the benefit payments of current elderly individuals. Because the ratio of the elderly to current workers will increase in the future, the Social Security Trust Fund is predicted to go into deficit in 2041. The real rate of return at retirement on taxes paid into the Social Security program by current workers is also predicted to be extremely low. These concerns have led some policymakers to recommend partial privatization of the Social Security system, allowing some Social Security payroll taxes to be invested in private markets.

To compound retirement concerns in the aging society, employers have been providing less support to workers for retirement savings. In previous decades, most large employers offered workers defined benefit pension plans, which provided a guaranteed stream of income in retirement. Now most large firms provide contribution plans, which require workers to assume more risk in saving and investing for retirement. Empirical evidence suggests that many working-age individuals are poorly educated regarding the need to save for retirement and often begin saving too late in life. Thus in old age many people must sharply curtail their expenditures.

Although public funding for senior citizens improves their health status and economic well-being, these expenditures come at a cost to other members of society. Each 1% increase in the elderly population has been estimated to crowd out public spending directed toward the nonelderly at a rate of −0.33%. The elderly will represent an increasing financial burden for society in the future. Overall increases in productivity and economic growth will be necessary to support an aging population, while maintaining the economic status of both young and old people in society.

—Vivian Ho

FURTHER READING

Gruber, J., & Wise, D. (2002). An international perspective on policies for an aging society. In S. Altman & D. Schactman (Eds.), *Policies for an aging society: Confronting the economic and political challenges* (pp. 34–62). Baltimore: Johns Hopkins University Press.

Schulz, J. H. (2002). *The economics of aging* (7th ed.). Westport, CT: Auburn House.

AID TO FAMILIES WITH DEPENDENT CHILDREN (AFDC)

The Aid to Families with Dependent Children (AFDC) program was a federal entitlement program that provided financial and work support, as well as child care assistance, to financially distressed families with children. After the passage of the Welfare Reform Law of 1996, AFDC was repealed and supplanted by the Temporary Assistance for Needy Families (TANF) program.

ADFC was a component of the national welfare program that also included the Job Opportunities and Basic Skills Training program as well as the Emergency Assistance Program. As originally formulated, AFDC was funded by both the federal and state governments. The federal government specified the overall program requirements and overall guidelines, leaving the states to promulgate the rules governing determination of benefits and program administration. Each state determined eligibility for benefits based on that particular state's standard of need and on the income and other resources and support available to the applicant.

Under a given state's AFDC program, an eligible family was required to have a dependent child who met the following criteria:

1. Less than 18 years of age

2. Lack of parental support

3. Living at home with the parent or close relative

4. Resident of the state

5. U.S. citizen or resident alien

As noted, eligibility for benefits was, in part, based on the particular state's standard of need, that is, the income and resources a family needed to live in that state. Determination of eligibility involved a two-step process. First, the gross income of the "assistance unit" was determined. Some family income and other resources available to the family were excluded, such as some income earned by students and the earned income tax credit. Second, the gross income, net of allowable disregards, was compared with the need standard for that state. Once eligibility was confirmed, a calculation of the exact benefits to be provided to the assistance unit was made based on the total income available as applied to the need standard, net of all applicable disregards.

As noted, the AFDC program was replaced by TANF in 1996 (AFDC was eliminated and replaced with the CalWORKs program in 1997). Oversight for the TANF program is provided by the Office of Family Assistance, which itself operates under the auspices of the U.S. Department of Health and Human Services (DHHS), Administration for Children and Families. TANF provides federal funds (in the form of block grants) to states, which in turn design and administer their own individual welfare programs. The specifics of the TANF regulations were designed to foster the return of beneficiaries to the workforce and provide a transitional program for the cultivation of self-sufficiency, to transform welfare into a temporary assistance program.

—Darren S. Kaufman

FURTHER READING

www.acf.dhhs.gov/programs/afdc/afdc/.txt
www.acf.dhhs.gov/programs/ofa/exsumcl.htm

ALLIANCES

The term *alliance* refers to the combination of two or more organizations for the promotion of common interests or the joint exercise of functions. Alliances differ from mergers, acquisitions, and other combinations in that the united organizations remain legally independent corporations after the alliance. The motivation to form alliances stems from mutual needs and willingness to cooperate to reach common objectives that no single organization can accomplish alone. Several motivations prompt alliance formation: to gain competitive advantage, to leverage critical capabilities, to gain economies of scale or scope, to increase the flow of innovation, and to improve flexibility in responding to market and technology changes.

Alliances are not monolithic. Differentiations can be made regarding whether the alliance is considered strategic or not. A *strategic alliance* meets two conditions. First, the partners share the rewards and risks of the alliance and exercise mutual control over joint tasks. Second, partners make repeated contributions or exchanges in one or more strategic areas (such as manufacturing, distribution, or marketing) in the involved organizations' core businesses.

Strategic alliances can be further divided into three groups, each formed on the basis of its own value-creating logic. In *co-optation alliances,* organizations entice potential rivals or producers of complementary goods or services (for example, suppliers or distributors) to combine forces by joining the alliance. Co-optation alliances create value by neutralizing competitive threats, building critical mass, and capturing "nodal positions" in the market. The value created can be substantial if strong first-mover advantages exist (such as allying with the only multispecialty physician practice in a market). In cospecialization alliances, organizations meld their distinctive assets, competencies, positions, and relationships to create new forms of value. A distinct motivation of *cospecialization alliances* is to develop and exploit new market opportunities (such as fully capitated Medicaid managed care). Finally, in *learning alliances* participating organizations seek to internalize the embedded capabilities of other organizations. The exchange of distinct know-how among participants may lead to the creation of new competencies and novel opportunities across multiple product markets (such as alliances between health care systems and physician practice organizations).

Some alliances are considered nonstrategic. An example is *service alliances,* also known as *pooled* or *lateral alliances.* They involve similar types of organizations (such as hospitals) with similar needs that unite to achieve scale economies, enhance access to scarce resources, and increase political clout. The domain of such alliances can encompass a wide array of technical, financial, human resource, and management services. Although service alliances can evolve into strategic alliances, they typically do not touch the core of member organizations' business. As such, they do not figure centrally in the organization's efforts to position itself in the market.

Alliances can also assume various legal and organizational forms. They can be structured on the basis of equity or contracts. *Equity-based alliances* sometimes involve the creation of a new entity as when, for example, a hospital and a physician group form a closed physician–hospital organization for managed care contracting, utilization management, and quality improvement. There are also equity-based alliances without creating a new entity. For example, a hospital may form an alliance with a physician group by purchasing minority ownership shares, to encourage joint marketing, service production, and managed care contracting. *Contract-based alliances* are mainly for the purpose of service provision. They tend to entail longer-term mutual dependence than do traditional arms-length contracts.

Health care examples of contract-based service alliances include group purchasing alliances, industry research consortia, and cooperatives that provide members with information and programs to improve operational efficiency and clinical effectiveness. Contract-based strategic alliances differ even more sharply from traditional contractual exchanges, because the former involve not only long-term interdependence but also shared managerial control and continuous transfers of technology, services, or know-how between partners. Health care examples of contract-based strategic alliances include "virtually" integrated delivery systems, community care networks, and interindustry alliances such as between health care systems and pharmaceutical companies.

GROWTH OF ALLIANCES IN HEALTH CARE

Health care organizations face unrelenting demands for cost containment, service quality, access to care, technology advancement, and public accountability. Several adaptive responses, including alliance formation, have emerged to deal with these pressures. The federal health reform effort and the subsequent market-based interventions in the mid to late 1990s also stimulated the formation of alliances in health care. Many hospitals and physician groups, for example, formed co-optation alliances to gain market power vis-à-vis managed care organizations and to prevent market encroachment by other emerging health care systems. Generally, such alliances served defensive purposes such as neutralizing potential competitors, protecting existing market share, assuring continued access to referrals, and blocking "divide and conquer" strategies by health plans.

The 1990s also witnessed the growth of cospecialization alliances as health care organizations sought to provide a coordinated continuum of health services to a defined population and to accept clinical and fiscal accountability for the outcomes and health status of the population served. As a mechanism for building "virtually" integrated delivery systems, cospecialization alliances may offer many of the potential benefits of vertical integration without the disadvantages associated with asset ownership. The significant capital outlays and high fixed costs tend to reduce vertically integrated systems' flexibility to adjust to changes in technology, financing arrangements, government regulation, and consumer preferences. In turbulent, unpredictable environments, such disadvantages become particularly salient, critical, and difficult to manage.

Health care organizations have also formed cospecialization alliances with health and human service organizations and other community groups to address community-level risk factors that lead to overuse of health services, increased costs, and other adverse outcomes. Such alliances— known as *community care networks* or *community health partnerships*—are prompted by a recognition that providing a broad range of health services to an enrolled population may have little impact if the larger context in which the population lives and works is not conducive to good health. Activities common to this type of alliance include measuring and tracking community health status, providing multifaceted services to defined populations, developing community problem-solving capacity, and restructuring local health and human service delivery systems.

Finally, interest has also grown in learning alliances as health care organizations seek to enhance quality, assure state-of-the-art care, and exploit emerging market opportunities. For example, the National Cancer Institute's Community Clinical Oncology Program has created a learning alliance between academic centers and community hospitals to increase participation in the National Cancer Institute's approved clinical trials, thereby providing access to state-of-the-art care in local communities. A similar arrangement is under way involving the National Institute of Drug Abuse and the Center for Substance Abuse Treatment and Community-Based Treatment Program. Some health care systems have also formed learning alliances with local mental health and social service agencies to gain access to skills in case management. Such skills enhance health care systems' ability to offer Medicaid managed care services and disease management programs.

Environmental conditions play a critical role in shaping the formation and sustainability of alliances. Many of the pressures, such as cost containment, quality improvement, and technology transfer, that stimulated alliance formation in the 1990s remain strong. Other factors—such as capitation and other risk-sharing financial arrangements and policy concerns about the plight of the uninsured and underinsured—have waned in strength. Although health care organizations continue to use alliances to create value and improve their market positions, the nature, composition, and dynamics of alliances in the coming decade are likely to differ and will reflect the emerging trends in the health care industry.

OPERATING AN ALLIANCE

To realize the potential benefits of an alliance, health care managers must carefully design and manage the alliance. Six challenges arise. First, managers must seek agreement among partners on the scope of the alliance, including the areas of mutual interest, the expected value of the alliance, the apportionment of that value, and the activities to be performed jointly. Second, managers must design governance arrangements, management processes, and operational interfaces that fit the external and internal demands of the alliance. Third, managers must rigorously assess each partner's contribution to the alliance, including their own, to assure that contributions are indeed synergistic

or complementary. Fourth, managers must define how alliance performance will be measured and continuously monitor progress against specific benchmarks. Fifth, managers must recognize that the strategic purposes and operating context of alliances may shift over time, requiring adjustments in the scope, membership, operation, and performance assessment of the alliance. Finally, managers must anticipate and manage the challenges that commonly arise when organizations with historical, cultural, and operational differences attempt collaboration (as in, for example, building trust, facilitating information exchange, and maintaining commitment).

ASSESSING ALLIANCE PERFORMANCE

A critical concern among alliance participants is "How do alliances perform?" Research on alliance performance is currently lacking, and findings of the few studies are largely inconsistent. Recent studies conducted by researchers at the Virginia Commonwealth University showed that members of local hospital alliances had higher net revenues but were ineffective at cost control. As a result, the net revenues generated did not translate into higher cash flow. Furthermore, the performance of local hospital alliances varied significantly according to such market conditions as managed care penetration and competition from other local alliances. An analysis by the federal General Accounting Office (GAO) has found that purchasing alliances among hospitals do not necessarily yield scale economies and efficiency. Prices negotiated by purchasing groups often are higher than are paid by hospitals negotiating directly with a vendor.

Although current evidence may not offer much comfort and guidance, several principles may assist health care managers in defining and assessing the effectiveness or performance of their alliance. For example, Rosabeth Kanter, a renowned Harvard Business School professor, suggests that effective alliances share the attributes of "six I's":

1. The alliance is seen as Important, with strategic significance and getting adequate resources and management attention.

2. The alliance is seen as a long-term Investment, from which members will be rewarded relatively equally over time.

3. Alliance partners are Interdependent, maintaining an appropriate balance of power.

4. The alliance is Integrated to manage communication and appropriate points of contact.

5. Each alliance member is Informed about plans for the alliance and for each other.

6. The alliance is Institutionalized, with supporting mechanisms that permeate interorganizational activities and facilitate trust relationships among members.

On the basis of these six I's, alliance partners and managers can devise relevant indicators and procedures for assessing alliance performance. Such assessment may take both the variance and process approaches. The variance approach focuses on outcomes, seeking to identify organizational and market conditions that explain variation in performance. For example, are identifiable changes in market share or financial performance among participating organizations attributable to alliance membership? Does the creation of a separate corporate entity or formal governing board reduce the redundancy of services provided by member organizations and increase the number of managed care contracts? This approach is appropriate for analyzing the effect of alliance formation on various indicators of performance and factors that account for specific features of organizational arrangements or innovation adoptions. The process approach emphasizes particular conditions, events, and stages in the overall development or specific organizational change processes. Example questions include the following: Are problems faced in the early stages of alliance development different from those experienced in later stages? Is there any change in the decision-making processes of the alliance and the pattern of communication among members after the formation of a governance board with representatives from member organizations? This process approach is appropriate in considering the interaction among various factors as alliances and participating organizations adapt over time.

Performance assessment can be applied to the alliance as a whole and to organizations that make up the alliance. It is important to consider the achievement of goals shared by all member organizations. Yet attention should also be paid to the individual needs of member organizations and whether alliance membership increases each member's ability to achieve its stated objectives, satisfy its key stakeholders, and gain access to needed resources. Another important yet often neglected dimension is the performance of alliances as seen by key external stakeholders (such as state regulatory agencies, health care plans, and community advocacy groups), who may be affected by or otherwise interested in the alliance and its impact. Incorporating those stakeholders' perspectives in the performance assessment of alliances may increase the legitimacy of and earn unexpected support for the alliance, particularly during financial downturns.

—Bryan J. Weiner, Shoou-Yih Daniel
Lee, and Arnold D. Kaluzny

See also Merger and Acquisition

FURTHER READING

Doz, Y. L., & Hamel, G. (1996). *Alliance advantage: The art of creating value through partnering.* Boston: Harvard Business School Press.

General Accounting Office. (2002, April 30). *Group purchasing organizations: Pilot study suggest large buying groups do not always offer hospitals lower prices.* GAO-02-690T. Washington, DC: U.S. Government Printing Office.

Kaluzny, A. D., Warnecke, R. B., & Associates. (1996). *Managing a health care alliance.* San Francisco: Jossey-Bass. Reprinted 2000 by Beard Books, Washington, DC.

Kaluzny, A. D., Zuckerman, H. S., & Ricketts, T. C. (1995). *Partners for the dance: Forming strategic alliances in health care.* Ann Arbor, MI: Health Administration Press. Reprinted 2002 by Beard Books, Washington, DC.

Kanter, R. M. (1989). When giants learn to dance. New York: Touchstone.

Lamb, S., Greenlick, M. R., & McCarty, D. (Eds.). (1998). *Bridging the gap between practice and research: Forging partnerships with community-based drug and alcohol treatment.* Washington, DC: National Academy Press.

Weiner, B. J., & Alexander, J. A. (1998). The challenges of governing public–private community health partnerships: Lessons from the Community Care Network[SM] Demonstration Program. *Health Care Management Review, 23*(2), 39–55.

Weiner, B. J., Alexander, J. A., & Zuckerman, H. S. (2000). Strategies for effective management participation in community health partnerships. *Health Care Management Review, 25*(3), 48–66.

Yoshino, M. Y., & Rangan, U. S. (1995). *Strategic alliances: An entrepreneurial approach to globalization.* Boston: Harvard Business School Press.

ALLIED HEALTH PROFESSIONAL

See table in Specialty

ALTERNATIVE EVALUATION

See Buyer Behavior

ALTERNATIVE MEDICINE (COMPLEMENTARY MEDICINE, INTEGRATIVE MEDICINE, UNCONVENTIONAL MEDICINE)

In 1993 Dr. David Eisenberg and his associates published a landmark study titled "Unconventional Medicine in the United States—Prevalence Costs and Patterns of Use," in which they showed that the frequency of use of unconventional therapies in the United States was much higher than expected and that most people don't report their use of these therapies to their medical doctors. This study propelled the established medical community to pay closer attention to alternative treatments and to study them using more rigorous scientific processes. The report showed an estimated 60 million Americans in 1990 used alternative medical treatments and spent nearly $14 billion. The study also showed that the number of visits for alternative medicine exceeded the number of visits to all U.S. primary care physicians. In 1990 visits to alternative medicine providers numbered 425 million, whereas visits to primary care physicians numbered 388 million. Of respondents who sought unconventional therapies, 72% never mentioned that fact to their medical doctor.

A follow-up survey was conducted in 1997. In both the 1990 and the 1997 surveys, alternative therapies were used mainly for chronic conditions such as back pain, allergies, anxiety, depression, and headaches. The authors of the survey found that extrapolating their results to the entire U.S. population suggested a 47.3% total increase in visits to alternative practitioners, from 427 million to 629 million (more than the number of visits to all U.S. primary care physicians). Out-of-pocket expenditure on alternative therapies was estimated at $27.0 billion in 1997.

Why complementary and alternative medicine (CAM) have become so popular remains unclear. Some have suggested it may be a fad related to a cultural change with a renewed interest in the paranormal, which remains popular no matter how much evidence refutes it. Perhaps an increased anxiety about health across society, even though people are living longer and healthier with greater emphasis on healthy lifestyles, has also contributed to the growing interest. Some have suggested that much of CAM's popularity lies with the "worried well."

Since the advent of modern refined pharmaceuticals, such as aspirin in 1899, Western medicine has trended toward the application of the scientific method to treatment protocols. Other scientific advances in molecular and biological chemistry have refined our understanding of many body processes, leading to a rigorous science-based approach in Western conventional medicine. Before this the practice of health care varied greatly, with little to distinguish what was "conventional" and what was "alternative."

What has perhaps suffered with the evolution of socialized systems of health care and of managed care is the time that in centuries past health care providers took in understanding, listening to, and visiting their patients and thereby providing "tender, loving care." With the evolution of study into the mind–body interactions and the effectiveness of placebos, it is possible that what people have missed with the lack of tender, loving care (TLC) in the modern medical

practice is in some way filled by complementary or alternative medicine. At the same time as conventional medicine places greater emphasis on preventive care and lifestyle, some of these issues have been more aggressively marketed and the needs filled with CAM practices. Many rigorous scientific studies are now under way to test the efficacy and discover underlying mechanisms of action for CAM.

Currently, several prestigious academic medical institutions in the United States have opened up programs in complementary and alternative medicine or integrative medicine. Duke University started its Duke Center for Integrative Medicine in December 2000. Harvard Medical School (HMS) in July 2000 established the Division for Research and Education in Complementary and Integrative Medical Therapies, headed by Dr. David Eisenberg. Their mission statements include the following directives: (a) Structure scientific research involving complementary and integrative medicine therapies according to traditional investigative and evaluative techniques, including controlled clinical trials; (b) share evidence-based resources across HMS and its teaching affiliates; (c) coordinate educational programs and policy development in such areas as credentialing, referrals, and comanagement of patient care; and (d) develop criteria to responsibly recommend the use or avoidance of herb/supplements and other complementary therapies. The University of Arizona has long been a leader in integrative medicine under the leadership of the popular Dr. Andrew Weil as director of the program in integrative medicine. M. D. Anderson in Texas has also started up a program in complementary and alternative medicine education and research. It is not clear for how long these practices will continue to be called "alternative" when they are quickly becoming part of the mainstream.

The U.S. government started the National Center for Complementary and Alternative Medicine (NCCAM) as a part of the National Institutes of Health (NIH) in 1998. The center has the following areas of focus:

- *Research.* Support clinical and basic science research projects in CAM by awarding grants across the country and around the world; we also design, study, and analyze clinical and laboratory-based studies on the NIH campus in Bethesda, Maryland.
- *Research training and career development.* Award grants that provide training and career development opportunities for predoctoral, postdoctoral, and career researchers.
- *Outreach.* Sponsor conferences, educational programs, and exhibits; operate an information clearinghouse to answer inquiries and requests for information; provide a Web site and printed publications; and hold town meetings at selected locations in the United States.

- *Integration.* To integrate scientifically proven CAM practices into conventional medicine, we announce published research results; study ways to integrate evidence-based CAM practices into conventional medical practice; and support programs to develop models for incorporating CAM into the curriculum of medical, dental, and nursing schools.

In addressing the concepts of what today is being called *complementary and alternative medicine* (CAM), it is important to first define some of the terms associated with these practices. The term *conventional medicine* refers to medicine as practiced by holders of M.D. (medical doctor) or D.O. (doctor of osteopathy) degrees, some of whom may also practice complementary and alternative medicine. Other terms for conventional medicine are *allopathy, biomedicine,* and *Western, regular,* and *mainstream medicine.*

ALTERNATIVE MEDICINE

Therapeutic approaches taken in place of traditional medicine and used to treat or ameliorate disease are called *alternative medicine.*

COMPLEMENTARY MEDICINE

Therapies that complement traditional Western (or allopathic) medicine are called *complementary medicine.* Professor Edward Ernst, who holds a chair in CAM at Exeter University in the UK, provided the following definition: "Complementary medicine is diagnosis, treatment and/or prevention which complements mainstream medicine by contributing to a common whole, by satisfying a demand not met by orthodoxy or by diversifying the conceptual frameworks of medicine" (Ernst, 2000, p. 34).

COMPLEMENTARY/ALTERNATIVE MEDICINE (CAM)

The terms "complementary" and "alternative" are often used interchangeably, when in fact they are two different therapeutic approaches. The British have approached this from a slightly different angle. A more encompassing definition of CAM is provided on the Cochrane Collaboration Web site (see Further Reading): "A broad domain of healing resources that encompasses all health systems, modalities, and practices and their accompanying theories and beliefs, other than those intrinsic to the politically dominant health systems of a particular society or culture in a given historical period."

COMPLEMENTARY/INTEGRATIVE MEDICINE

Complementary/integrative medicine combines traditional Western (or allopathic) and complementary approaches and supplements but does not replace conventional therapy. It is used for

- Managing symptoms
- Increasing wellness (quality of life, reported sense of well-being)
- Improving treatment efficacy

Basic Principles of Integrative Medicine

The basic principles of integrative medicine, as stated by the University of Arizona program in integrative medicine (see Further Reading), are as follows:

- A partnership between patient and practitioner in the healing process
- Appropriate use of conventional and alternative methods to facilitate the body's innate healing response
- Consideration of all factors that influence health, wellness, and disease, including mind, spirit, and community as well as body
- A philosophy that neither rejects conventional medicine nor accepts alternative medicine uncritically
- Recognition that good medicine should be based in good science, inquiry driven, and open to new paradigms
- Use of natural, less invasive interventions whenever possible
- The broader concepts of promotion of health and the prevention of illness as well as the treatment of disease
- Practitioners as models of health and healing, committed to the process of self-exploration and self-development

Complementary and Integrative Medicine (CIM)

The term *complementary and integrative medicine,* or *CIM,* is used when describing the study or use of traditional Western (or allopathic) and complementary medicine approaches when studied or used together.

NCCAM'S MAJOR DOMAINS OF COMPLEMENTARY AND ALTERNATIVE MEDICINE (FOR CONSUMERS AND PRACTITIONERS)

Complementary and alternative medicine (CAM) and health care are those health care and medical practices that are not currently an integral part of conventional medicine. The list of practices that are considered CAM changes continually as CAM practices and therapies that are proven safe and effective become accepted as "mainstream" health care practices. Today, CAM practices may be grouped within five major domains: (a) alternative medical systems, (b) mind–body interventions, (c) biology-based treatments, (d) manipulative and body-based methods, and (e) energy therapies. The individual systems and treatments in these categories are too numerous to list in this book. Thus, only limited examples are provided within each.

Alternative Medical Systems

Alternative medical systems involve complete systems of theory and practice that have evolved independent of and often prior to the conventional biomedical approach. Many are traditional systems of medicine that are practiced by individual cultures throughout the world, including a number of venerable Asian approaches.

Traditional Asian medicine emphasizes the proper balance or disturbances of *qi* (pronounced chi), or vital energy, in health and disease, respectively. Traditional Asian medicine consists of a group of techniques and methods, including acupuncture, herbal medicine, oriental massage, and *qi gong* (a form of energy therapy described more fully later). Acupuncture involves stimulating specific anatomic points in the body for therapeutic purposes, usually by puncturing the skin with a needle.

Ayurveda (eye-yer-VAY-duh) is India's traditional system of medicine. Ayurvedic medicine (meaning "science of life") is a comprehensive system of medicine that places equal emphasis on body, mind, and spirit, and strives to restore the innate harmony of the individual. Some of the primary Ayurvedic treatments include diet, exercise, meditation, herbs, massage, controlled breathing, and exposure to sunlight.

Other traditional medical systems have been developed by Native American, Aboriginal, African, Middle Eastern, Tibetan, and Central and South American cultures.

Homeopathy and naturopathy are also examples of complete alternative medical systems. Homeopathy is an unconventional Western system based on the principle that "like cures like," that is, the same substance that in large doses produces the symptoms of an illness, in very minute doses cures it. Homeopathic physicians believe that the more dilute the remedy, the greater its potency. Therefore, homeopaths use small doses of specially prepared plant extracts and minerals to stimulate the body's defense mechanisms and healing processes to treat illness.

Naturopathy views disease as a manifestation of alterations in the processes by which the body naturally heals itself and emphasizes health restoration rather than disease treatment. Naturopathic physicians employ an array of healing practices, including diet and clinical nutrition; homeopathy; acupuncture; herbal medicine; hydrotherapy (the use of water in a range of temperatures and methods of applications); spinal and soft-tissue manipulation; physical therapies involving electric currents, ultrasound, and light therapy; therapeutic counseling; and pharmacology.

Mind–Body Interventions

Mind–body interventions employ a variety of techniques designed to facilitate the mind's capacity to affect bodily function and symptoms. Only a subset of mind–body interventions are considered CAM. Many that have a well-documented allopathic theoretical basis, such as patient education and cognitive-behavioral approaches, are now considered "mainstream." In contrast, meditation; certain uses of hypnosis; dance, music, and art therapy; and prayer and mental healing are categorized as complementary and alternative.

Biology-Based Therapies

The biology-based therapies category of CAM includes natural and biology-based practices, interventions, and products, many of which overlap with conventional medicine's use of dietary supplements. Included are herbal, special dietary, orthomolecular, and individual biological therapies.

Herbal therapies employ an herb or a mixture of herbs for therapeutic value. An herb is a plant or plant part that produces and contains chemical substances that act on the body. Special diet therapies, such as those proposed by Drs. Atkins, Ornish, Pritikin, and Weil, are believed to prevent or control illness as well as promote health. Orthomolecular therapies aim to treat disease with varying concentrations of chemicals, such as magnesium, melatonin, and megadoses of vitamins. Biological therapies include, for example, the use of laetrile and shark cartilage to treat cancer and bee pollen to treat autoimmune and inflammatory diseases. These can be further subdivided into the following categories:

Herbal/Plant Therapies. A specific dictionary definition of an herb is any seed-producing plant that does not have persistent woody tissue but rather dies down at the end of a season. A general definition is a plant valued for its medicinal, savory, or aromatic properties.

Nutrition and Special Diets. In Webster's dictionary, the term *nutrition* is defined generally as the act or process of nourishing; specifically, it is the sum of the process by which an animal or plant takes in and uses food substances. Diets commonly used by patients with cancer may be described as restrictive, supplemental, or simply as requiring changes in food habits.

Biologic/Organic/Pharmacologic. Nonplant biologic (related to life—again, as in the dictionary), organic (derived from living organisms), pharmacologic (drugs or substances used as medications) substances make up the remaining category of biological therapies that are usually swallowed, injected, or applied to the skin.

Manipulative and Body-Based Methods

The category of manipulative and body-based methods includes methods that are based on manipulation or movement of the body. For example, chiropractors focus on the relationship between structure (primarily the spine) and function, and how that relationship affects the preservation and restoration of health, using manipulative therapy as an integral treatment tool. Some osteopaths, who place particular emphasis on the musculoskeletal system, believing that all the body's systems work together and that disturbances in one system may affect function elsewhere in the body, practice osteopathic manipulation. Massage therapists manipulate the soft tissues of the body to normalize those tissues.

Energy Therapies

Energy therapies focus either on energy fields originating within the body (biofields) or those from other sources (electromagnetic fields).

Biofield therapies are intended to affect the energy fields, whose existence is not yet experimentally proven, that surround and penetrate the human body. Some forms of energy therapy manipulate biofields by applying pressure or manipulating the body by placing the hands in, or through, these fields. Examples include qi gong, Reiki, and Therapeutic Touch therapies. *Qi gong* is a component of traditional Asian medicine that combines movement, meditation, and regulation of breathing to enhance the flow of vital energy (*qi*) in the body, to improve blood circulation, and to enhance immune function. *Reiki,* the Japanese word representing universal life energy, is based on the belief that spiritual energy channeled through the practitioner heals the spirit, which in turn heals the physical body. Therapeutic Touch is derived from the ancient technique of "laying on of hands" and is based on the premise that the healing force of the therapist promotes the patient's recovery and that the body heals when its energies are in balance. By passing their hands over the patient, these healers identify energy imbalances.

Bioelectromagnetism-based therapies involve the unconventional use of electromagnetic fields, such as pulsed fields, magnetic fields, or alternating current or direct current fields, to treat, for example, asthma or cancer, or manage pain and migraine headaches.

BRITISH CATEGORIES OF ALTERNATIVE THERAPIES

The British have opted for a somewhat different grouping of alternative therapies, as seen in their recent reports to the House of Lords Select Committee on Science and Technology. The grouping is based on a judgment as to how much evidence is available to support each therapy:

Group 1. Professionally organized disciplines, with their own diagnostic approach. They have some scientific evidence of effectiveness and recognized systems of training for practitioners: acupuncture, chiropractic, herbal medicine, homeopathy, osteopathy.

Group 2. Complementary therapies that lack a firm scientific basis and are not regulated to protect the public but that give help and comfort to many people: Alexander technique, aromatherapy, Bach flower remedies, bodywork therapies, including massage, counseling stress therapy, healing, hypnotherapy, Maharishi ayurvedic medicine, meditation, nutritional medicine, reflexology, shiatsu, yoga.

Group 3. Alternative disciplines that have no established evidence base to support their claims for safety and efficacy.
> 3a: long-established and traditional disciplines with very specific philosophies: anthroposophical medicine, Ayurvedic medicine, Chinese herbal medicine, Eastern medicine (Tibb), naturopathy, traditional Chinese medicine.
> 3b: Other alternative disciplines: crystal therapy, dowsing, iridology, kinesiology, radionics.

—Miguel A. Nuñez, Jr.

FURTHER READING

Astin, J. A. (1998). Why patients use alternative medicine: Results of a national survey. *JAMA (Journal of the American Medical Association), 279,* 1548–1553.

British Medical Association. (1993). *Complementary medicine: New approaches to good practice.* Oxford, UK: Oxford University Press.

Budd, S., & Mills, S. (2000). *Professional organisation of complementary and alternative medicine in the United Kingdom 2000: A second report to the Department of Health.* Exeter, UK: University of Exeter.

Eisenberg, D. M. (1997). Advising patients who seek alternative medical therapies. *Annals of Internal Medicine, 127,* 61–69.

Eisenberg, D. M., Davis, R. B., Ettner, S. L., et al. (1998). Trends in alternative medicine use in the United States, 1990–1997: Results of a follow-up national survey. *JAMA (Journal of the American Medical Association), 280,* 1569–1575.

Eisenberg, D. M., Kessler, R. C., Foster, C., et al. (1993). Unconventional medicine in the United States. *New England Journal of Medicine, 328,* 246–252.

Ernst, E., & White, A. (2000). The BBC survey of complementary medicine use in the UK. *Complementary Therapies in Medicine, 8,* 32–36.

Ernst, E., et al. (1995). Complementary medicine—a definition [letter]. *British Journal of General Practice, 5,* 506.

Fisher, P., & Ward, A. (1994). Complementary medicine in Europe. *British Medical Journal, 309,* 107–111.

Goldbeck-Wood, S., Dorozynski, A., Lie, L. G., et al. (1996). Complementary medicine is booming worldwide. *British Medical Journal, 313,* 131–133.

http://integrativemedicine.arizona.edu/publications/index.html

http://nccam.nih.gov

Landmark Healthcare. (1998). *The Landmark Report on public perceptions of alternative care.* Sacramento, CA: Landmark Healthcare.

Mills, S., & Peacock, W. (1997). *Professional organisation of complementary and alternative medicine in the UK: A Report to the Department of Health.* Exeter, UK: University of Exeter.

Pelletier, K. R., Marie, A., Krasner, M., et al. (1997). Current trends in the integration and reimbursement of complementary and alternative medicine by managed care, insurance carriers, and hospital providers. *American Journal of Health Promotion, 12,* 112–122.

www.chiro.org/alt_med_abstracts/DISCONTINUED/House_of_Lords/CHAPTER_I.html#a2)

www.dukehealth.org/health_services/integrative_medicine.asp

www.mdanderson.org/departments/cimer/

www.publications.parliament.uk/pa/ld/ldsctech.htm

AMBULATORY CARE

Ambulatory care is medical care provided on an outpatient basis or care delivered to people who are not confined to a hospital. The care provided in an ambulatory setting includes diagnostic services, observation, surgical services, and rehabilitation. The 1990s in health care was marked by a fundamental shift from most care taking place in an inpatient environment to taking place in the outpatient or ambulatory setting. In some areas, more than 80% of surgeries are done in an outpatient setting. The primary driver has been cost. Payers don't want patients in the hospital when the care can be and is being delivered in lower-cost outpatient facilities. Many procedures once performed only at the inpatient hospital are now done at freestanding outpatient surgery and diagnostic centers. As would be predicted, the cost of the procedures at these centers is much lower than it is at a large inpatient facility. Acceptance by patients is excellent, and quality does not suffer.

Sophisticated diagnostic tools, such as MRIs, CT scans, low-risk cardiac catheterization, chemotherapy for malignancies, and endoscopic surgical procedures such as arthroscopy and laparoscopy are routinely performed in an ambulatory setting.

The patient is more involved with his or her care when surgery is done on an outpatient basis and when there is a payment differential between a procedure or diagnostic test performed in an inpatient versus an outpatient setting. As an inpatient, the patient is basically passive; when the patient must go to one of these centers, he or she is taking some responsibility for the care delivered. Consumer market research studies have demonstrated that patients prefer to receive health care services on an ambulatory basis.

As this outpatient segment of health care continues to grow, for-profit companies have emerged to deliver this care. The best known and one of the largest is Health South, a $4 billion company (annual total sales/revenues) that started as a rehabilitation facility but now has diagnostic and surgery centers all over the United States.

Because of a more favorable payer mix at better reimbursement rates, many procedures previously done in an inpatient setting are now much more profitable when done as an outpatient procedure. A recent example is cardiac testing. At one time, many of these tests were considered too risky to be done anyplace except the hospital but are now being performed in the physician's office. Cardiologists, like most other physicians, have watched their reimbursement drop on many inpatient procedures. Performing some of the low-risk testing, such as echocardiography, in the office has helped maintain income. Physician-owned "heart hospitals," which are outpatient specialty centers for a single disease, can be found all over the United States. The main issue is that physicians now feel safe in providing this care in an outpatient setting and the reimbursement can enhance falling revenues.

In some areas, this trend toward specialty facilities has been at the expense of not-for-profit hospitals. Providing care for the indigent is not included in many for-profit ambulatory centers. Many integrated health care delivery systems have developed innovative joint ventures with their medical staff to compete with the pure for-profits such as Health South.

The doctor's office has been the mainstay of health care in the United States and represents ambulatory care in its purest form. Patients still consider the doctor's office as the entry point to the health care delivery system. However, in most markets the days of the individual solo practitioner seem over. Costs are diluted when spread over a larger group of providers, and therefore many physicians have joined into large single-specialty groups called independent practice associations (IPAs) or into multispecialty groups. The Mayo Clinic practice model is the benchmark for the multispecialty group practice.

The scope for ambulatory services continues to broaden every day, and many health care systems have responded by taking the initiative of providing easy access to outpatient centers. One such system is Akron General Health System in Akron, Ohio. Its leadership recognized very early in the evolution of the outpatient market that taking health care to its constituents, rather than asking the patient to come to the large tertiary medical center, made sense. The system built a series of seven outpatient centers in a spoke-and-wheel model around the Akron area. Akron General is now known as the leader of outpatient delivery in the area despite major competition. Having the reputation as the leader in outpatient care has enhanced the inpatient side, because the patient is familiar with the quality delivered in the outpatient centers. When illness or accident occurs, many choose Akron General as their preferred inpatient provider based on the quality of care delivered in the outpatient settings. Akron General has also entered into a joint venture with its surgical staff to own and manage an existing freestanding outpatient surgery center.

In conclusion, a major shift in where health care is delivered has been and continues to be toward the outpatient setting. Patient acceptance and favorable outcomes along with lower cost have emerged as the major drivers of this change. As technology advances, and as more information is made available via the Internet, more testing and procedures will be done outside the hospital walls.

The hospitals will remain, but the acuity (severity of illness) of the patient mix will be higher because of the aging population. The patients will be sicker. The care of chronic illnesses will become the mainstay of the hospital; length of inpatient stays will increase, and the resources used for this population will cost more. These factors will all drive up the cost of an inpatient stay; therefore, to remain viable and competitive, health care systems must have the ability to deliver low-risk testing and procedures in the outpatient setting.

—Thomas L. Stover

FURTHER READING

Sennett, C. (2000). *Ambulatory care in the new millennium: The role of consumer information.* Gaithersburg, MD: Aspen.

Shortell, S. M., Gillies, R. R., Anderson, D. A., Erickson, K. M., & Mitchell, J. B. (2000). *Remaking health care in America.* San Francisco: Jossey-Bass.

Zuckerman, A. (1998). *Ambulatory care in integrated delivery systems.* San Francisco: Jossey-Bass.

AMERICAN BOARD OF MEDICAL SPECIALTIES (ABMS)

The American Board of Medical Specialties (ABMS) membership consists of 24 approved medical specialty boards in the United States. The ABMS, formed in 1933, functions to provide information to the public, the government, the profession, and its members concerning certification in medicine. Its mission is "to maintain and improve the quality of medical care by assisting the member boards in their efforts to develop and utilize professional and educational standards for the evaluation and certification of physician specialists" (see the ABMS Web site at www.abms.org). The certification process for physicians provides assurance to the public that the physician specialist certified by a member board has completed the required training and evaluation in an approved program and successfully completed an examination by that member board. Physicians who gain certification by this process become diplomates of the member boards. The process is designed to create educational standards to assess the knowledge, skills, and experience believed to be required to assure that the physician is capable of proving quality care to patients in that specialty.

Each member board designates voting representatives to the ABMS based on the number of certificates issued during the previous 5 years and three members from the public.

The ABMS maintains a list of all board-certified diplomates. The member boards include Allergy & Immunology, Anesthesiology, Colon & Rectal Surgery, Dermatology, Emergency Medicine, Family Practice, Internal Medicine, Medical Genetics, Neurological Surgery, Nuclear Medicine, Obstetrics & Gynecology, Ophthalmology, Orthopedic Surgery, Otolaryngology, Pathology, Preventive Medicine, Psychiatry & Neurology, Radiology, Surgery, Thoracic Surgery, and Urology.

—Thomas M. Biancaniello

FURTHER READING

www.abms.org

AMERICAN BOARD OF PREVENTIVE MEDICINE (ABPM)

The American Board of Preventive Medicine (ABPM) is a member board of the American Board of Medical Specialties (ABMS). The board was originally known as the American Board of Preventive Medicine and Public Health, incorporated in 1948. Its name was changed in 1952. ABPM was formed to promote preventive medicine by encouraging the study of the specialty, to improve standards of care, and to promote the cause of preventive medicine. The board, which consists of preventive medicine practitioners, is a nonprofit entity.

In 1953 the ABMS and the Council on Medical Education and Hospitals of the American Medical Association authorized certification of specialists by the ABPM. The ABPM grants certification to licensed physicians who have completed appropriate educational programs in specialty areas and who have passed certifying exams. Physicians who gain certification by this process become diplomates of the member boards. The ABPM grants certification in three primary specialties: Aerospace since 1953, Occupational Medicine since 1955, and General Preventive Medicine since 1960 and combined into Public Health and General Preventive Medicine in 1983. And in 1989 the ABPM granted a subspecialty certification in Undersea Medicine and in 1992, Medical Toxicology.

—Thomas M. Biancaniello

FURTHER READING

www.abprevmed.org

AMERICAN COLLEGE OF HEALTHCARE EXECUTIVES (ACHE)

The American College of Healthcare Executives (ACHE) is a professional organization of health care executives whose goal is to improve the health of U.S. society by working to advance health care leadership and management excellence. The membership consists of 14,195 active participants and 5,762 diplomates who have successfully completed the requirements for certification. The mission, as noted on the ACHE Web site, is to provide educational opportunities, offer leadership development programs, and promote high ethical standards and conduct. It provides knowledge, skills, and values to enable its members to advance health. The focus of the ACHE is to help its members meet the daily challenges that face health care executives and to enhance career development. Programs available, through education, to members of ACHE include credentialing, new health initiatives, and advanced learning tools. ACHE also publishes material used in college curriculums.

ACHE offers its members advice on business decisions affected by both global and societal issues. Professional executives meet yearly to reinforce and explore health care issues. The ACHE networks with other organizations to provide additional resources to meet members' needs.

In addition, ACHE publishes *Journal of Healthcare Management* and the *Healthcare Executive* magazine. Its publishing division, Health Administration Press, is a leading publisher in management of health care publishing books, textbooks, and journals.

—Thomas M. Biancaniello

FURTHER READING

www.ache.org

AMERICAN DENTAL ASSOCIATION (ADA)

The American Dental Society (ADA) was formed in August 1859, by 26 dentists. The ADA is a professional society committed to improving oral health by advancing the profession and science, promoting ethical practice, and developing standards for care, education, and research.

Today the ADA has 141,000 members and includes 53 state territorial and 529 local dental societies advocating for its members and oral health. The administrative body of the ADA is a board of trustees. The House of Delegates is the legislative body of the ADA and consists of delegates from the constituent societies, federal dental services, and the American Student Dental Association (ASDA).

The 11 ADA councils study issues related to their specialties and make policy recommendations to the board of trustees and the House of Delegates. Each council has members in its specific specialty. The nine recognized specialty areas are dental public health, endodontics, oral and maxillofacial pathology, oral and maxillofacial surgery, orthodontics and dentofacial orthopedics, pediatric dentistry, periodontics, prosthodontics, and radiology.

The ADA publishes the *Journal of the American Dental Association, ADA News,* and the *ADA Guide to Dental Therapeutics.* The U.S. Department of Education officially recognizes the Commission on Dental Accreditation for its education programs.

—Thomas M. Biancaniello

FURTHER READING

www.ada.org

AMERICAN HOSPITAL ASSOCIATION (AHA)

The American Hospital Association (AHA) is a national trade organization that serves and represents hospitals and health care networks, and their patients and communities. Founded in September 1899 by eight hospital superintendents, it was originally known as the Association of Hospital Superintendents. The name was changed in 1906 to the AHA, and in 1918 organizational membership structure was instituted. In addition to representing its membership, it also advocates in the public interest. Membership in the AHA now includes single members and diversified groups.

The mission is to advance the health of individuals and communities. It represents and advocates for its members and is committed to health care improvement. It sponsors research and demonstration projects in the delivery of health care services, conducts educational programs, gathers and analyzes data, and communicates through publications to keep members informed of trends and national developments.

Contributions by the AHA include establishing the Hospital Service Plan Commission, which became Blue Cross, and establishing of the Hill-Burton program, which provided free care for patients. The AHA was also instrumental in establishing the Commission on Financing of Hospital Services, which ultimately led to the creation of the Medicare program.

—Thomas M. Biancaniello

FURTHER READING

www.hospitalconnect.com

AMERICAN MEDICAL ASSOCIATION (AMA)

The American Medical Association (AMA) is a professional organization of physicians, founded by Dr. Nathan Davis in 1847. The purposes of the AMA are to promote the science and art of medicine and the betterment of public health.

Early in its history, the AMA established standards for medical education and a code of medical ethics was written and published. The AMA has been an advocate for public health throughout its history, promoting sanitary standards, developing quarantine regulations, establishing a board to examine remedies, promoting automobile safety belts and infant and child car seats, reporting on the hazards of cigarette smoking, and forming a council to promote public health education. In 1922 the AMA published *Hygeia* (subsequently *Today's Health*), the first family health magazine.

In 1869 the AMA began publishing medical journals and currently publishes 13 in the United States. The AMA began supporting research in 1898, establishing a Committee on Scientific Research to provide grants for medical research.

The AMA continues to promote standards for medical education, pharmaceutical manufacturing and advertising, and graduate medical education. It established standards for the approval of teaching hospitals and medical specialty training. It has set standards for terminology, disease classification, and procedural codes. In 1972, it opened its membership to medical students.

The AMA has been active politically, establishing the American Medical Political Action Committee in 1961. Patients' rights, confidentiality, reimbursement for health care services, and environmental safety have been areas of concern for the AMA. The AMA views itself as the main voice for physicians and patients.

—Thomas M. Biancaniello

FURTHER READING

www.ama-assn.org

AMERICAN NURSES ASSOCIATION (ANA)

Headquartered in Washington, D.C., the American Nurses Association (ANA) has the distinction of being the only professional organization representing the entire population of registered nurses in the United States. Providing the strongest voice for the nursing profession and workplace advocacy, the ANA's reach encompasses Congress, federal agencies, boardrooms, hospitals, and other health care facilities.

Through its 54 constituent state and territorial associations and over 180,000 members, the interests of the nation's 2.6 million registered nurses are represented by the ANA. The ANA is the strongest labor union for the nursing profession, because more than 25 of its constituent associations act as collective bargaining agents for nursing.

Committed to meeting the needs of nurses as well as health care consumers, the ANA is committed to ensure that an adequate supply of highly skilled and well-trained nurses is available. The ANA advances the nursing profession through several mechanisms, namely projecting a positive and realistic view of nursing, fostering high standards of nursing practice, promoting the economic and general welfare of nurses in the workplace, and lobbying Congress and regulatory agencies on health care issues affecting nurses and the general public.

Through the ANA's political and legislative program, the association holds firm positions on such diverse issues as Medicare reform, patients' rights, whistleblower protection, adequate reimbursement, and access to health care. The ANA is dedicated to expand the scientific and research base for nursing practice, to gain better compensation and better working conditions for nurses, and to implement new ways in which nursing services can be delivered to respond to current and future demands for cost-effective, quality health care.

—Linda M. Cimino

FURTHER READING

www.ana.org

AMERICAN PUBLIC HEALTH ASSOCIATION (APHA)

The American Public Health Association (APHA) is composed of a large, broad-based membership that includes health care professionals, administrators, scientists, and educators working in the field of public health. This membership currently exceeds 50,000 individuals from diverse sectors of the public health arena.

Public health, per se, is a diverse field, and can be thought of as both the processes and activities as well as the individuals and organizations that seek to promote health and well-being and to prevent illness and disease, injury, and premature death. In addition, the process of developing public health seeks to create an environment in which the health and safety of the public can be maintained and improved.

Given the broad scope of interests, activities, and responsibilities of the APHA membership, the mission of this large, diverse organization is implemented via subgroups within the APHA. These subgroups are formally organized into 25 specialty-based sections and 7 special primary-interest groups. The specific discipline-based sections include Alcohol, Tobacco, and Other Drugs; Chiropractic Care; Community Health Planning and Policy Development; Environment; Epidemiology; Food and Nutrition; Gerontological Health; Health Administration; HIV AIDS; Injury Control and Emergency Health Services; International Health; Laboratory; Maternal and Child Health; Medical Care; Occupational Health and Safety; Oral Health; Podiatric Health; Population; Family Planning and Reproductive Health; Public Health Education and

Health Promotion; Public Health Nursing; School Health Education and Services; Social Work; Statistics; and Vision Care. The special interest groups represented within APHA include Alternative and Complementary Health Practices, Community Health Workers, Disability Forum, Ethics Forum, Health Law Forum, Radiological Health, and Veterinary Public Health.

The APHA communicates and documents its stance regarding key public health issues via APHA Policy Statements, which are made available to interested individuals and the public through a searchable database on the Web at www.apha.org/legislative/policy/policysearch/index.cfm. In addition, APHA members can access online proposed policy statements awaiting vote by the APHA governing council.

—Darren S. Kaufman

FURTHER READING

www.apha.org

AMERICAN RED CROSS (ARC)

The American Red Cross is a humanitarian organization made up of volunteers whose mission is to provide relief to victims of disasters and help people prevent, prepare for, and respond to emergencies. Being made up of volunteers, the American Red Cross is not funded by the government. Thus it depends on the generosity of its donors to provide funds for its budget. Of the 1.2 million members, 60% are adults and 40% are young adults and youth. The American Red Cross is the largest humanitarian organization in the United States. Its volunteers serve in various roles. This would include management positions such as leaders of youth councils, supervisors on disaster relief operations, and chapter managers. These volunteers provide services such as training in CPR, first aid, and HIV/AIDS education. In addition, volunteers are involved in support activities such as volunteer recruitment, marketing and public relations, fundraising, serving on advisory groups, and delivering services to youth. Each year this organization mobilizes relief to victims of more than 63,000 disasters nationwide and has been the major supplier of blood and blood products in the United States for over 50 years. It also trains many people in vital life-saving skills, provides relevant community services, and assists international disaster and conflict victims in more than 50 countries. The American Red Cross is able to accomplish its goals through the charitable dedication of its volunteers, who provide services without pay for personal, humanitarian reasons.

—Anthony J. Ippolito

FURTHER READING

www.RedCross.org

AMERICANS WITH DISABILITIES ACT (ADA) OF 1990

· The Americans with Disabilities Act (ADA)[1] was enacted by Congress in 1990 with the major intent to extend the privileges and duties of the Rehabilitation Act of 1973[2] to most private employers, all local and state governmental entities, and to most establishments in the private sector serving the public. Among its findings supporting passage of the act, Congress asserted that "some 43,000,000[3] Americans have one or more physical or mental disabilities" that had caused society to isolate and segregate them, and to discriminate against individuals with disabilities in areas such as employment, public accommodations, education, and other areas of intentional exclusion.

The ADA has four substantive titles (sections).[4] Title I addresses the employment relationship, and has accounted for the larger part of the litigation activity concerning interpretation and application of the ADA. Title II covers public entities, that is, state and local governments. Title III relates to public accommodations and commercial facilities offered by private entities. Title IV provides for telecommunications relay service for speech- and hearing-impaired individuals, and closed captioning of public service announcements.[5]

Under Title I, employers[6,7] having 15 or more employees are prohibited from discriminating against "otherwise qualified" employees or job applicants because of a disability. All aspects of the employment relationship are addressed, including recruitment, hiring, training, promotion, wages, etc. There are three key concepts in Title I. "*Disability*" means "a physical or mental impairment that substantially limits one or more of the major life activities . . . ; a record of such an impairment . . . ; or being regarded as having such an impairment." A "*qualified person with a disability*" is defined as "an individual with a disability who, with or without reasonable accommodation, can perform the essential functions of the employment position that such individual holds or desires." *Reasonable accommodation*s may include modifying existing facilities to make them more readily accessible to disabled persons, or modifying the job itself, through restructuring, modifying work schedules, reassignment to a different job, modifying equipment, or providing interpreters or readers. Generally, employers are not required to provide an accommodation if to do so would impose "undue hardship," meaning significant expense[8] or difficulty, nor is the disabled person entitled to the accommodation of his or her choice. Ideally, the employer will engage in a meaningful dialogue with the disabled person to seek a reasonable accommodation, if possible.

Interpretation and application of the ADA in the workplace is fact intensive. EEOC regulations define "substantially limits" as "unable to perform a major life activity[9] that the average person in the general population can perform; or . . . significantly restricted as to the condition, manner or duration under which an individual can perform a major life activity." Three decisions by the U.S. Supreme Court in 1999 set some boundaries. The decisions, although differing in their details, all stood for the proposition that the severity of an impairment, and therefore whether the impairment constituted a disability, needed to be evaluated by looking at the degree of severity after it had been mitigated, that is, subjected to correction or treatment.[10] In the first case, twin visually impaired female airline pilots were found not to be disabled, because their vision was correctable to better than 20/200 with corrective lenses.[11] An amblyopic truck driver was found not to be disabled because he used monocular visual cues to compensate for his impairment.[12] A mechanic with high blood pressure was not disabled because he was able to maintain his blood pressure at normal levels with medication.[13]

The Supreme Court issued three other decisions of significance in 2002. In the first case,[14] the Court further addressed "major life activities," focusing on manual tasks and working. The plaintiff in that case had severe carpal tunnel syndrome that prevented her from performing all the manual tasks required of all members on her work team, and she was ultimately fired for poor performance. The Court stated, "When addressing the major life activity of performing manual tasks, the central inquiry must be whether the claimant is unable to perform a variety of tasks *central to most people's daily lives,* not [just] the tasks associated with her particular job" (emphasis added).[15] In another case,[16] the Court addressed the issue of when a direct threat to health or safety of others was sufficient not to require an employer to hire an individual with a disability. The Court upheld the employer's refusal to hire a job applicant because of abnormalities in his liver, caused by Hepatitis C, that would be exacerbated by toxic solvents and chemicals present in the refinery where he sought employment.[17] In its third case,[18] the Court ruled that a job reassignment requested as a reasonable accommodation need not be granted if it would conflict with a seniority system, whether collectively bargained for, or unilaterally imposed.

Title II covers state and local governments, whether or not they are recipients of federal financial assistance. Qualified individuals with a disability are not to be excluded from participation in, nor denied the benefits of "services, programs, or activities" offered by the public entity. A "qualified individual with a disability" is one who "with or without reasonable modifications to rules, . . .

practices, [or removal of barriers], meets the essential eligibility requirements for the receipt of services or participation in [the] programs or activities provided." Examples include building curb ramps on public streets, improving access to public buildings, and using appropriate formats to provide public information to people with hearing, vision, or other impairments. Licensing or certification programs may not impose discriminatory requirements or eligibility criteria, and may be required to accommodate testing conditions. For example, the New York Board of Law Examiners agreed to provide a visually impaired applicant with a large-print copy of the examination, a separate room with enhanced lighting, and other modifications.[19] In contrast, requiring a motorist with cerebral palsy to take a road test when he sought to renew his license was found not to be discriminatory, because he would operate his vehicle with hand controls.[20] The Court found the requirement to be a proper balance of the need to ensure safety on streets and highways with the rights of the disabled applicant. Title II also addresses public transportation, and requires, for example, that fixed-route bus service be supplemented with paratransit service and that rail and bus transportation be accessible to disabled passengers.

Title III requires commercial facilities and places of public accommodation, owned or operated by private entities, to be accessible to the disabled. Commercial facilities include office buildings and factories. The broader classification is public accommodations, generally any establishment or business open to the public, such as restaurants, hotels, theaters, shopping centers, stadiums, hospitals, doctors' offices, and day care centers. Such places must ensure there are no barriers to access, including policies and practices as well as physical barriers, and must provide accommodations or alternative services if the barriers cannot be removed. For example, a brewery was required to modify its "no animals" policy, where a blind visitor sought to be accompanied by his guide dog while taking a public tour.[21] More familiar and common examples include accessible parking spaces and wheelchair seating spaces in theaters, auditoriums, and so on.

Finally, note that at this writing courts have not settled the extent to which states are subject to the requirements of Titles II and III. Lower courts have disagreed whether states' Eleventh Amendment immunity was properly abrogated when the ADA was enacted, and the U.S. Supreme Court has yet to decide the issue.

—Donald L. Zink

NOTES

1. Pub. L. No. 101-336, 104 Stat. 327 (1990) (codified at 42 U.S.C. 12101 *et seq.* and 47 U.S.C. 225, 771).

2. The Rehabilitation Act (see entry) only covers programs or activities that receive federal financial assistance. Most of the basic concepts, including disability, reasonable accommodation, program and facility accessibility, and discrimination are defined identically under the two statutes. The legislative history of the ADA indicates that it should be interpreted in conformity with precedents from the Rehabilitation Act. An amendment of the ADA in 1992 sought to "harmonize" the two statutes.

3. The magnitude of this estimate has not been universally accepted.

4. Title V has various miscellaneous provisions, such as enforcement, attorneys' fees, and insurance issues. Title V also specifically excludes certain conditions as qualifying as a disability, such as homosexuality, compulsive gambling, kleptomania, and substance abuse disorders because of current illegal use of drugs.

5. Because of the complexity of the statute, the given examples are only suggestive of the full range of issues brought under the ADA.

6. Excluded as an employer are "the United States, a corporation wholly owned by the government of the United States, or an Indian tribe; or . . . a bona fide private membership club (other than a labor organization)."

7. In *Board of Trustees of the University of Alabama v. Garrett* (1998), 531 U.S. 356, in a ruling carefully limited to application of Title I of the ADA, the U.S. Supreme Court held that Congress had not validly abrogated the Eleventh Amendment immunity of state governments when it passed the ADA. States, therefore, are immune from suit by their employees under Title I of the ADA. However, municipalities, counties, or subordinate governmental units still are covered.

8. Several studies have suggested that the actual costs of most accommodations are minimal.

9. The ADA itself also does not define "major life activities." Title I regulations and guidance memoranda give the examples of "caring for oneself, performing manual tasks, walking, seeing, hearing, speaking, breathing, learning, and working" as well as other examples.

10. EEOC guidance memoranda directed that the impairment should be looked at "without regard to the availability of mitigating measures." The U.S. Supreme Court did not defer to the position held by EEOC.

11. *Sutton v. United Airlines* (1999), 527 U.S. 471.

12. *Albertsons, Inc. v. Kirkingburg* (1999), 527 U.S. 555.

13. *Murphy v. United Parcel Service* (1999), 527 U.S. 516.

14. *Toyota Motor Mfg., Ky., Inc. v. Williams* (2002), 534 U.S. 184.

15. Tasks central to daily life included household chores, bathing, and brushing teeth. Because Williams could perform those tasks, she was not disabled. The Court left open whether working per se was a "major life activity." Justice O'Connor had stated earlier in *Sutton* that "there may be some conceptual difficulty in defining 'major life activities' to include work." It is arguable that a substantial limitation in working, without more, is not enough to constitute a disability.

16. *Chevron U.S.A., Inc. v. Echazabal* (2002), 536 U.S.

17. Title I defines "direct threat" as a "significant risk to the health or safety *of others* that cannot be eliminated by reasonable accommodation" (emphasis added). EEOC regulations expand the definition by adding the phrase "*of the individual or*" (emphasis added). In this instance, the Supreme Court did defer to the EEOC regulations.

18. *US Airways, Inc. v. Barnett* (2002), 535 U.S.

19. *D'Amico v. New York State Bd. of Law Examiners* (1993), 813 F. Supp. 217 (W.D.N.Y.).

20. *Theriault v. Flynn* (1998), 162 F.3d 46 (1st Cir.).

21. *Johnson v. Gambrinus Co.* (1997), 116 F.3d 1052 (5th Cir.).

ANNUAL PERCENTAGE RATE (APR)

The annual percentage rate (APR) associated with a loan is the effective rate that you pay on an annual basis. If i is the annual rate, and m is the number of times a year you make payments, then the APR is

$$APR = (1 + i/m)^m - 1$$

Various other terms for i are the *quoted rate, stated rate, nominal rate,* or *annual rate.* The APR is different from the stated rate and must be calculated and disclosed, because otherwise banks would only reveal the lower, stated rate. This difference is best illustrated thus: Suppose you have a mortgage at a stated annual rate of 9% per year, and you make monthly payments. Then you pay an interest rate of $9\% \div 12 = 0.75\%$ per month. The quoted rate is 9%, but because you are making monthly payments you are actually paying a higher effective rate. This is because you are making your interest payments throughout the year instead of only at the very end. The annual percentage rate for this loan is

$$APR = 1.0075^{12} - 1 = 9.38\%$$

Your effective rate is 9.38%, and your stated rate is 9%. Whenever you make more than one interest payment per year, your annual percentage rate will be more than the stated rate.

—Phillip R. Daves

See also Compound Growth Rate, Time Value of Money

FURTHER READING

Brigham, E. F., & Ehrhardt, M. C. (2001). *Financial management* (10th ed.). Mason, OH: South-Western.

ASSETS

Assets can broadly be described as resources owned by a company used to produce future benefits. Ownership of an asset can generally be obtained through the use of internal equity in the company or through external financing. Assets are generally categorized as either short term or long term. Short-term assets represent resources that will be converted into cash within one year from the balance sheet date. The balance sheet date represents a snapshot of the financial position of a company at a certain point in time. Long-term assets represent resources intended to be used for the benefit of the company at a point in time beyond 12 months from the balance sheet date.

Within each of the two categories, short-term assets and long-term assets, various classes of assets are commonly found on a company's balance sheet. Several types of short-term assets are typically found in most health care organizations: cash and cash equivalents, marketable securities, accounts receivable, inventory, and prepaid expenses.

Cash and Cash Equivalent—Cash provides the basis for measuring all financial statement accounts. Cash can be maintained on site at the company, for example in a petty cash fund (small amounts of cash to cover day-to-day needs). In addition, cash can be maintained by an external financial institution. Even though the cash is not physically located at the company, authorized company personnel can initiate transactions with the external financial institution to use the cash resources. Cash equivalents are highly liquid instruments or instruments that can easily be converted into cash.

Marketable Securities—Marketable securities are investments that can include stocks and bonds in other publicly traded companies. Not all investments in stocks and bonds qualify as short-term marketable securities. To qualify as a marketable security, the company must intend to convert the investment into cash within one year from the balance sheet date. Company management generally bases this intent on the company's day-to-day cash needs.

Accounts Receivable—Accounts receivable arise from a company selling its products or services to customers who do not immediately pay cash. For most health care organizations, accounts receivable arise from the treatment of a patient and the related billing of the patient or the patient's third-party insurer. Health care providers such as hospitals must establish the gross value of the accounts receivable at the prevailing charge for each service rendered. However, given the nature of third-party payer contracts, the expected collections for those services are usually significantly less than established charges. As a result, management must estimate the allowance for uncollectible amounts because of contractual arrangements. Accounts receivable appear on the balance sheet during the time period between the recognition of revenue and the receipt of the related cash payment. In addition, the likelihood is inevitable of some accounts receivable not being collected as a result of bad debt. Companies account for these expected bad debts by using an "allowance for bad debts" account.

Inventory—Inventory most often represents items held for sale or use in producing goods and service in the ordinary course of business. Inventory is most common in manufacturing and retail companies, whose operations involve selling inventory as part of their operations. Inventory in most health care organizations includes medical supplies and pharmaceuticals used in treating patients.

Prepaid Expenses—Prepaid expenses represent amounts paid by a company for benefits that have not yet been received. For example, a company may pay an insurance premium for coverage over the next year. The company should record the amount paid as a prepaid asset and amortize the asset as the benefits of that insurance are received. Another example is a maintenance contract on equipment. The company may prepay a three-year maintenance contract and record the amount paid as a prepaid asset. Subsequently, the company should amortize the prepaid asset over the life of the maintenance agreement.

Long-term assets provide benefits that extend beyond the current operating period. The most common type of long-term assets are fixed assets, such as land, buildings, furnishings, and equipment owned by the company. These fixed assets are normally recorded at their cost and then depreciated over their useful lives. A subjective estimation is normally involved in determining the useful life of a particular fixed asset. The matching principle states that expenses should be matched against revenues in the period when the benefits are recognized. The cost of acquiring a long-term asset, which is expected to generate revenues in the future periods, is therefore capitalized in the period of acquisition. As the revenues associated with the long-term asset are recognized, these costs are depreciated.

Intangible assets are another type of long-term assets. Intangible assets represent the rights, privileges, and benefits of possession, rather than physical existence. By their nature, intangible assets can have a higher degree of uncertainty than tangible assets. Examples of intangible assets include the costs of acquiring copyrights, patents, trademarks, trade names, licenses, and goodwill. Much like fixed assets, intangible assets generally have a useful life. Likewise, determining the estimated useful life for an intangible asset can be a subjective task. Intangible assets are amortized over their useful lives in accordance with the matching principle just discussed.

—Edward Pershing

ASSET TURNOVER RATIOS

See Ratio Analysis

ASSURANCE OF COMPLIANCE (FEDERAL WIDE ASSURANCE, FWA)

The filing of an assurance of compliance (referred to as a *federal wide assurance*, or FWA) is required under U.S. Department of Health and Human Services (DHHS) regulations for all institutions conducting federally funded research involving human subjects. The assurance is a formal declaration to DHHS that the institution will conduct such research in accordance with the federal policy that addresses the protection of human participants (Subpart A of the Code of Federal Regulations at Title 45: Public Welfare, Part 46: Protection of Human Subjects [45 CFR 46]), generally referred to as the Common Rule (because of its acceptance by several federal agencies in addition to DHHS). Without such an assurance on file with the Office for Human Research Protections (OHRP), an institution cannot receive federal funds supporting such research. Any collaborating institution, or institution to which the main awardee subcontracts, is also mandated to comply with the filing requirement (even if located outside of the United States).

The terms of the FWA require that detailed written procedures (such as informed consent requirements, institutional review board review procedures) and necessary resources and staff are in place by the institution to ensure the protection of human subjects. The issue of appropriate training of personnel involved in such research activities is addressed as well.

The FWA itself requires certain specific declarations, including the disclosure of the ethical principles by which the institution will be guided in the review and conduct of human subject research.

The principles outlined in the *Belmont Report* are those most commonly adopted by institutions within the United States, whereas international sites can rely on primary ethical guidance from the Declaration of Helsinki. To express their commitment to protecting human subjects, many institutions extend their assurance of compliance not only to include compliance with all subparts of 45 CFR 46

(A, B, C, and D) but also to include coverage of all human participant research, regardless of funding status or source.

Monitoring of compliance with the assurance requirement is under the jurisdiction of the DHHS office specifically responsible for human subject research, the Office for Human Research Protections (OHRP).

—Judy Matuk

See also Belmont Report, Office for Human Research Protections (OHRP)

FURTHER READING

http://ohrp.osophs.dhhs.gov/irbasur.htm
www.access.gpo.gov/nara/cfr/waisidx_99/45cfr46_99.html

ATMOSPHERICS

See Facilities Management

AUTHORITY

Historically in management, *authority* is defined as the right to require or prohibit actions of others. This definition has led to the formal theory of authority that states that all authority (rights) flow from the top to the bottom of an organization. The CEO gets her authority from the board of directors, vice presidents get their authority from the CEO, and so on.

The formal theory of authority was challenged in 1938 by Chester Barnard, who proposed the acceptance theory and viewed authority in an entirely different way. According to Barnard, managers get their right to influence employees because employees accept the legitimacy of management. Authority is most likely to be accepted when it is considered legitimate, legal, and necessary. In this view, ironically, authority flows from the bottom to the top of organizations.

The arguments regarding the formal and acceptance theories are primarily of academic rather than practical interest. From a management perspective, the important issue is how managers exercise the authority they possess, regardless of the source. It is generally recognized that successful managers are good at delegating their authority. The effective delegation of authority allows managers to expand their abilities, manage their time, and provide employees with valuable decision-making experiences.

The universal agreement that the ability to delegate authority is an important skill for successful managers raises an interesting question. If delegation is so important to managerial success, why do managers often hesitate to delegate? The answer has to do with accountability. Because authority is a right, the manager is free to temporarily give up the right to someone else. The manager, however, can never be relieved of the accountability for the exercise of the authority. Delegation is risky. If a manager delegates authority to a person who does not act responsibly, the manager who delegated the authority remains accountable for any lack of performance. Hence the maxim one hears so often, "If you want to be sure something is done right, do it yourself."

Delegation of authority, as stated, is risky business; there is no denying this reality of organizational life. However, successful management entails a number of risks. It is risky to try new ideas and to delegate authority, but these risks are inherent in the practice of management.

Organizations are effective when different units coordinate their efforts toward a common goal. This coordination is a primary responsibility of management, and authority is one of the tools—along with leadership, persuasion, and inspiration—that managers use to ensure coordination. Authority, in fact, has been called the supreme coordinating force in any organization.

—W. Jack Duncan

FURTHER READING

Barnard, C. I. (1938). *Functions of the executive.* Cambridge, MA: Harvard University Press.

Mooney, J. D., & Reiley, A. C. (1932). *Principles of organization.* New York: Harper & Row.

Simon, H. A. (1976). *Administrative behavior* (3rd ed.). New York: Free Press.

Urwick, L. F. (1944). *Elements of administration.* London: Harper.

Weber, M. (1947). *The theory of social and economic organization.* A. M. Henderson & T. Parsons (Eds. and Trans.). New York: Free Press.

AUTONOMOUS HEALTH CARE PLAN/STRUCTURE

An autonomous health care plan, broadly defined, is an organization that acts as a financial intermediary, typically for an employer, to which the assumption of financial risk, attendant to the obligation to pay for the delivery of health care services needed by the firm's employees, can be outsourced. Traditional health plans subserve only basic insurance functions, that is, actuarial services and risk pooling. Managed care plans create value by taking on marketing and utilization review functions as well.

Four types of autonomous health care plans currently exist:

- Traditional indemnity
- Preferred provider organization (PPO)
- Point-of-service plan (POS)
- Health maintenance organization (HMO)

The latter three health care plans constitute the various types of managed care plans.

PREFERRED PROVIDER ORGANIZATION (PPO)/POINT OF SERVICE (POS)

The preferred provider organization (PPO) represents an early foray of health care plans beyond the usual and customary (UC) payment system. Under the UC payment system, providers charged the health care plan what was felt to be a "usual, customary, and reasonable" fee. As provider fees escalated, the health care plan (at that time the plans were indemnity insurers) simply raised premiums. The PPO represents a discounted fee-for-service plan in which care rendered by physicians belonging to the PPO network is covered. However, enrollees can go outside of the network as long as they are willing to pay a greater proportion of the provider's, albeit discounted, fee. A point-of-service (POS) plan is similar to a PPO in that the enrollee is afforded choice but is required to pay a greater percentage of the provider's fee.

HEALTH MAINTENANCE ORGANIZATIONS (HMOS)

Health maintenance organizations (HMOs) represent the full implementation of managed care. These health care plans subserve the basic insurance functions, noted earlier, as well as formalized utilization review, to control costs and aggressive marketing to foster growth of enrollment in the plan. Because many enrollees are willing to pay a premium for a choice option, many plans offered by HMOs also allow for point-of-service options.

—Darren S. Kaufman

FURTHER READING

Enzmann, D. (1997). *Surviving in health care.* St. Louis, MO: Mosby.

AUTONOMOUS WORK GROUPS

See Team-Based Organizations

AVERAGE COLLECTION PERIOD (ACP)

The average collection period (ACP) is the average amount of time that it takes a business to collect its accounts receivable. It is easily calculated from the balance sheet (rather than the more tedious approach of making a list of the amount of time that each individual customer takes to pay and then averaging). If *AR* is the level of accounts receivable and *S* is the annual sales or revenues, then *ACP* is

$$ACP = (AR \times 365)/S$$

For example, if Internal Specialists LLC has annual revenues of $20 million and at year-end has $5 million in accounts receivable, then its average collection period is $(5 \times 365) \div 20 = 91.25$ days. This means that Internal Specialists takes, on average, 91 days to collect payment on an account.

A long average collection period means the firm has more money tied up in its accounts receivable. Decreasing the ACP, either through improved collection procedures or through factoring, frees up money that can be used elsewhere in the business. For example, if Internal Specialists could reduce its ACP from 91.25 days to 60 days, then the accounts receivable balance would decrease from $5 million to $(60 \times \$20 \text{ million}) \div 365 = \$3.29$ million. This would free up $5 million – $3.29 million = $1.71 million in funds that could be used to purchase new equipment, or paid out in salary or bonus. Note, though, that this $1.71 million would be a one-time cash flow—it would not occur year after year.

—Phillip R. Daves

See also Factoring of Accounts Receivable

FURTHER READING

Brigham, E. F., & Daves, P. R. (2002). *Intermediate financial management* (7th ed.). Mason, OH: South-Western.

B

BACKWARD VERTICAL INTEGRATION

See Vertical Integration

BAD DEBT LOSS

A bad debt loss arises when a health care provider is unable to fully, or partially, collect amounts rightfully due it, as a result of the failure of a patient or third party to fulfill payment obligation. Generally, bad debt losses are associated with accounts receivables generated in the normal course of business. A common example is the failure of an individual to pay for services provided and billed. In the health care environment, a bad debt loss is different from a contractual adjustment or charity care. A contractual adjustment is the difference between normal or standard charges and amounts that are contractually due the health care provider under various contracts (such as with commercial insurance carriers, Medicare, or Medicaid). Charity care represents amounts that are not collected but for which there was never an expectation of payment, because of the patient's financial resource limitations.

Bad debt losses, in contrast, are amounts the organization has a right to collect and for which it fully expects payment at the time services are rendered. If the patient or third party (such as an HMO or a commercial insurance company) does not make the payment, these amounts are recorded as bad debt losses. Bad debt losses are shown as an operating expense in the health care provider's income statement, similar to other types of expenses, and may be the actual write-offs during a period or an estimate based on historical expense. Any future recoveries of amounts

written off as bad debt losses may be recognized as income when received.

—Edward Pershing

BALANCE SHEET

The balance sheet (BS) is one component of the financial statements. A standard set of financial statements includes the balance sheet, income statement, statement of cash flows, and associated footnotes. These statements can be issued on a daily, monthly, quarterly, or annual basis. If accounting is the basic language of business, then financial statements are the fundamental scorecards that report organizational performance, and the balance sheet is the operational snapshot of an organization's financial situation at a particular point in time (for example, organization X's balance sheet as of December 31, 2008). The income statement and statement of cash flows depict the activities of the organization over a period of time (such as organization X's income statement for the year ending December 31, 2008).

A typical balance sheet has three sections: assets, liabilities, and owners' equity. Assets are resources the organization owns that will provide the organization with future benefits (that is, that have a quantifiable monetary value), such as cash, equipment, and buildings. Liabilities are organizational obligations that will require future cash outlays, such as accounts payables, pension liabilities, and long-term debt. Owners' equity has several components. Owners' equity includes the cumulative effect of common and preferred stock transactions and retained earnings. Retained earnings represent, since the organization's inception, the total net income earned less any dividends that have been paid to owners.

The balance sheet also has an order (structure) to how individual elements are classified. For example, all asset entries are listed on the balance sheet in order, from current to long-term assets. Current assets are those assets that are the most liquid (can most easily be turned into cash). So on a typical balance sheet, items such as cash and accounts receivable are listed under current assets, whereas items such as property, plant, and equipment are listed under long-term assets. Liabilities are also classified from current to long term on the balance sheet.

Another way to look at the balance sheet is in equation form: Assets = liabilities + owners' equity. Under the dual-entry system of accounting, assets must always equal liabilities plus owners' equity. So if assets equal $100,000, liabilities equal $30,000, and owners' equity must equal $70,000. In other words, this equation says that all company assets, accumulated throughout the years, are owned (or claimed) by some entity. A portion of the assets is claimed by creditors (these are liabilities), and some of the assets are claimed by the owners (owners' equity).

Although financial statements, including the balance sheet, are based on a number of different assumptions, it is important that health care professionals understand that accounting financial statements provide valuable data that are reliable, comparable, and consistent. In addition, financial statements provide us with timely data that enhance our ability to assess future cash flows, assist in decision making (an information role), and monitor debt covenants and bonus arrangements (a stewardship role).

—Bruce Behn

FURTHER READING

Cleverley, W. O., & Cameron, A. E. (2002). *Essentials of health care finance* (5th ed., pp. 124–129). Gaithersburg, MD: Aspen.

BALANCED BUDGET ACT (BBA) OF 1997

The Balanced Budget Act (BBA) of 1997 contains important and significant changes to welfare, Medicare, and Medicaid programs. Other provisions of the BBA, such as concern Food Stamps and housing, are not discussed here.

MEDICARE

The BBA expands the list of choices for Medicare beneficiaries that is referred to as Medicare + Choice. The following options are provided for coverage of health care services in the BBA:

Traditional fee-for-service Medicare: Seniors can continue to receive traditional coverage of a fee-for-service nature and can also opt to return to the fee-for-service plan if they try another type of plan such as an HMO (see later).

Provider-sponsored organizations (PSOs): A PSO is operationally equivalent to an HMO. However, the entity is run by medical providers as opposed to by an insurance company.

Medical savings accounts (MSAs): A Medicare MSA allows the Medicare beneficiary to make tax-free contributions into the Medicare MSA. This account is controlled by the beneficiary and is used to cover expenses incurred for qualified health care services.

Private fee-for-service plans: These plans provide the Medicare beneficiary with the option of obtaining unrestricted fee-for-service health care insurance.

Private plans and health maintenance organizations (HMOs): These plans provide access to care for Medicare beneficiaries via a panel of preselected providers. In general, such plans afford beneficiaries an expanded spectrum of benefits, as compared with traditional Medicare, and at a reduced cost. However, choice of provider is more restricted.

Preferred provider organizations (PPOs): These plans allow Medicare beneficiaries to receive care from providers who do not participate in the HMO's provider panel. Hence, while maintaining the cost benefits of participation in an HMO, PPOs allow the beneficiary to choose a provider.

The BBA spells out how payments are made to Medicare + Choice plans, including stipulation of the minimum monthly payments to the plans, a payment formula that blends average national and local costs (so as to attract more plans to low-cost areas while maintaining plan availability in higher-cost areas), and guaranteed minimum percentage increases for payments. In addition, the "50:50" rule is eliminated (this rule required Medicare + Choice plans to enroll a minimum of half of enrollees in non-Medicare plans). Importantly, the BBA carves out medical education costs from Medicare + Choice payments and diverts these funds directly to teaching hospitals.

The BBA addresses the issue of consumer protection by mandating the continuous availability of medical care to enrollees, and prohibition of so-called gag rules that prevent providers from discussing all treatment options, including noncovered services. The BBA provides for grievance and appeal procedures, the availability of emergence care, and the confidentiality of health information. In addition, the BBA delineates how payments will be made to providers. Home health care spending not incurred subsequent to confinement in a skilled nursing facility or hospital, under the terms of the BBA, is reallocated to Medicare Part B (previously covered by Part A). The BBA formalizes a number of antifraud measures that go beyond those spelled out in the Health Insurance Portability and Accountability Act of 1996.

The Future of Medicare

The BBA mandates the creation of a commission to investigate the impact of the projected increase in the number of Medicare enrollees expected with the retirement of the "baby boom" generation. This commission is charged with making recommendations to Congress with regard to how the Medicare program can maintain long-term solvency.

MEDICAID

The BBA seeks to reduce Medicaid costs while improving the cost-effectiveness and quality of care to low-income persons. The states are afforded greater flexibility with regard to setting provider payment rates. In addition, states are permitted, under the terms of the BBA, to provide Medicaid services through managed care without the need to first obtain a waiver. Other measures to alleviate the financial burden imposed on the states of providing Medicaid services are also created, such as elimination of the states' obligation to pay for Federally Qualified Health Centers and Rural Health Centers, and changes in federal Medicaid matching rates for some locales.

CHILDREN'S HEALTH

The BBA provides increased health care coverage for uninsured children and for increased spending on children's health care. States are provided increased access to grants that provide for expanded access of eligible children to health care insurance coverage. In addition, states are afforded increased flexibility with regard to how mandated matching funds, paid by the state, can be used, for example, to expand Medicaid coverage, to provide health services such as immunizations, well-child care, and so forth. Importantly, children who became ineligible for Medicaid as a result of the more rigorous eligibility requirements for Supplemental Security Income (SSI) as defined in the welfare reform act, are restored to Medicaid eligibility.

—Darren S. Kaufman

FURTHER READING

www.cmwf.org/programs/taskforc/Reute249.asp
www.house.gov/budget/papers/mainsumm.htm

BALANCED SCORECARD AND HEALTH CARE

The balanced scorecard (BSC) is an organizational measurement and management system that links strategy to financial and nonfinancial objectives. The BSC measures organizational performance across four perspectives: financial, customer, internal process, and learning and growth (see Exhibit 1). Executives translate the organization's vision and strategy into linked objectives and measures in the four balanced scorecard perspectives.

Exhibit 2 shows a general health care strategy map, based on the balanced scorecard. The map's causal linkages provide a framework to articulate strategy and a road map for executing and evaluating the strategy.

1. The high-level financial objective "financial viability" is supported through two basic approaches, revenue growth and productivity. Revenue growth comes from (a) deepening relationships with existing customers, such as by offering multiple services and delivering complete solutions; and (b) selling new services to new customers and in new markets. A productivity strategy also has two components: (a) lowering direct and indirect expenses and (b) reducing the working and fixed capital needed to support a given volume of activity. Every strategy requires a balancing act between growing revenues and managing costs.

2. A health care organization must deliver attractive value propositions to its key constituencies (customers). The value proposition is the unique mix of product, price, service, relationship, and image that an organization offers its customers to differentiate itself in the market. Typical value propositions can be lowest total cost, product leadership, and complete (one-stop) customer solutions. Constituencies could include patients and their families, referring physicians, payers, academics, government and advocacy groups, and communities.

The customer perspective typically includes several generic measures—customer satisfaction, customer retention, new customer acquisition, and market and account share in targeted segments—of the successful outcomes from a well-formulated and implemented strategy. It should also include value proposition measures. Typical customer perspective measures include patient satisfaction surveys, referrals by physicians, number of patient complaints, and presence on preferred provider lists.

3. To support its financial and customer objectives, the organization must excel in key internal processes, both clinical and administrative. It must articulate and measure for the effectiveness and efficiency of both clinical processes and important nonclinical and administrative

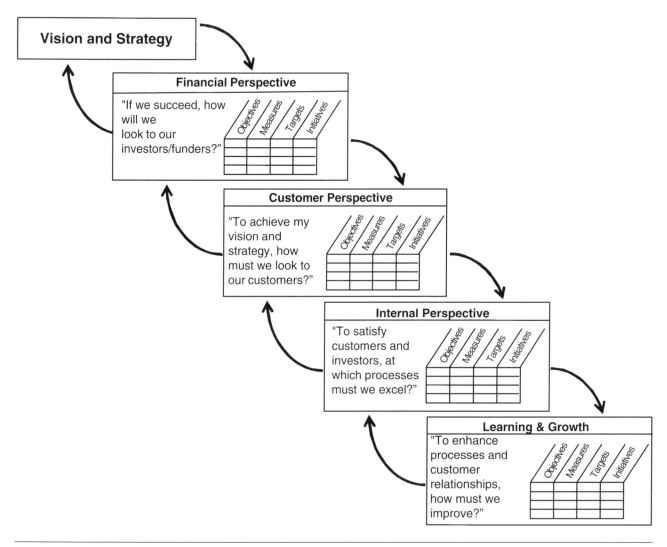

Exhibit 1   The Balanced Scorecard

processes. The key processes include admission and discharge, planning, innovation, relationship management with constituencies, clinical outcomes, and operations.

4. The learning and growth perspective establishes objectives for the health care staff to be recruited, trained, and provided with the tools and environment necessary to do their job effectively and efficiently. Objectives in the learning and growth perspective define the employee capabilities and skills, technology, and corporate climate needed to support the strategy. It shows where businesses must invest and improve in reskilling their employees, enhancing information technology and systems, and aligning organizational procedures and routines.

IMPLEMENTATION AND IMPACT

The process of building a balanced scorecard and strategy map brings together an organization's health care

professionals from diverse backgrounds, training, and experiences to develop an integrated and shared view of the organization's strategy for success. One professional stated that the balanced scorecard gave him a framework for treating management from a systems approach, much like physicians think of human health as a system. Just as a physician would not diagnose a condition without considering multiple symptoms and running various tests, a health care organization should not articulate, measure against, and diagnose its strategy without a systems approach—the causally linked four BSC perspectives.

A project starts with a senior project team, drawn from among physicians, nurses, and managers, meeting to define the strategy. The team wrestles with the tradeoffs required to meet the multiple missions and constituency goals of health care organizations. For example, one hospital defined its mission in terms of customers—"our patients, their families, and referring physicians"—and its value proposition as to "provide the best, most compassionate

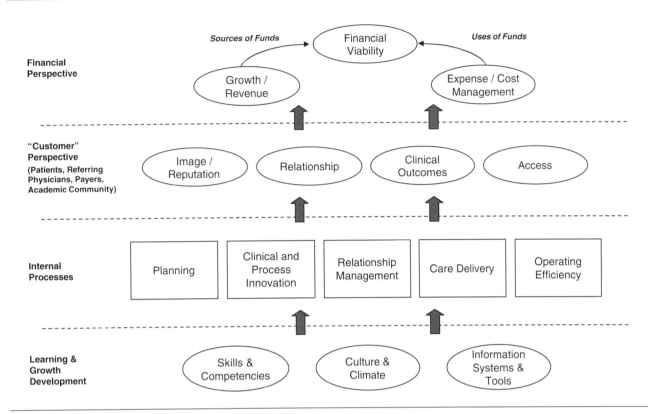

Exhibit 2   A General Health Care Strategy Map

care, and excel in communications." The mission was expressed in its balanced scorecard with measures for patients, families, and primary care physicians. But the scorecard also recognized the importance of financial solvency, with objectives for cost reduction and revenue growth. The scorecard led to the re-engineering of existing processes and to the development of entirely new processes that delivered on both the mission and substantial financial improvements.

At Montefiore Medical Center, New York City, the chief operating officer of the acute care center led her senior team through a process culminating in two high-level and easy-to-understand strategies:

- Be "all things to some people": Develop a population-based approach focused on providing a full spectrum of health care services to specific populations (children, women, and seniors) in MMC's immediate area.
- Be "some things to all people": Develop specialty centers, such as cancer, cardiology, and maternal/child services, to attract patients from neighboring communities.

MMC's new business strategy endeavored to strike the difficult balance between providing population-based health care, which emphasized providing full and

cost-effective service for the general population, and developing centers of excellence (cardiovascular, cancer, children's health, women's health, and HIV) that could attract a large base of new customers.

Early adopters in health care have received the following benefits from their new management system based on the BSC:

- A structure and framework to align their organizations around a more market-oriented customer-focused strategy. The strategy helped them do the right things, not just do things right.
- A focus not just on areas to cut costs but on specific customer segments for revenue growth, along with the necessary infrastructure and processes to broaden consumer and physician relationships.
- A powerful communication and collaboration mechanism for all employees, along with team-based accountability for achieving strategic objectives.
- A management process for resource allocation to achieve targeted outcomes.
- A continual feedback, review, and learning process to monitor, learn, and improve the strategy.
- A framework for adapting the strategy to changes in the regulatory, competitive, technological, and consumer environment.

—Robert S. Kaplan and Ann Nevius

FURTHER READING

Inamdar, S. N., & Kaplan, R. S. (2002, May–June). Applying the balanced scorecard in healthcare provider organizations. *Journal of Healthcare Management, 47,* 179–196.

Kaplan, R. S., & Norton, D. P. (1996). *The balanced scorecard: Translating strategy into action.* Boston: HBS Press.

Kaplan, R. S., & Norton, D. P. (2001). *The strategy-focused organization: How balanced scorecard companies thrive in the new business environment.* Boston: HBS Press.

Meliones, J. (2000, November–December). Saving money, saving lives. *Harvard Business Review, 78,* 57–67.

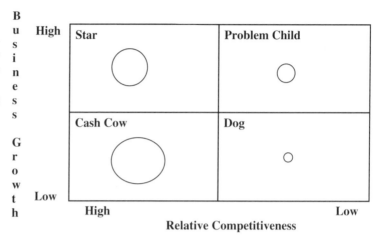

Figure 1   Generic BCG matrix

BCG PORTFOLIO ANALYSIS

BCG Portfolio Analysis takes its name from its corporate developer, the Boston Consulting Group. The BCG is a two-dimensional portfolio-matrix model with business growth rate on the vertical axis and relative competitiveness (the company's market share divided by its largest competitor's market share) on the horizontal axis. The BCG assumes that a high-growth business is superior to a low-growth one, and that a high relative market share is superior to a low one. Each axis represents an index scale measurement of its respective characteristic, and is split into high and low levels, thereby resulting in a matrix with four intersecting boxes (see Figure 1): *High Growth/High Competitiveness* (Star box); *High Growth/Low Competitiveness* (Problem Child box); *Low Growth/High Competitiveness* (Cash Cow box); and *Low Growth/Low Competitiveness* (Dog box).

RELATIVE COMPETITIVENESS

In using the BCG, a company locates each of its business units, major products, or product groups (referred to collectively as a *business*) in the matrix's four boxes with a circle. The size of the circle will vary in direct proportion to the relative importance of each business to the company—greater importance equals greater size. The proportion of the company's revenues or profits that a business generates generally determines its relative importance to the company.

When a business is rated as belonging to one of the four categories, Star, Cash Cow, Problem Child, or Dog, the model implies certain generic strategies as appropriate to consider. *Note that the model's implied strategies are appropriate for consideration, not definite strategies to follow.* Competing companies in similar strategic situations have been equally successful using diametrically opposed strategies. The strategic suggestions for each of the categories are as follow:

Star. Continue to invest in and to build the business and its profits.

Cash Cow. Minimize investment in building the business but seek to maximize short- and medium-term profits. Harvest those profits to invest in Stars and those Problem Children considered worthy of trying to build into Star businesses.

Problem Child. Determine which Problem Children have substantial potential to become Stars and which do not. Invest in those with the best potential to become Stars and divest the rest.

Dog. Divest the Dogs.

Business definitions can have substantial effects on analysis. For instance, one may define the analgesic market in many ways: the total analgesic market, legend analgesics (controlled substances), OTC analgesics, nonaspirin OTC analgesics, nonaspirin/nonacetaminophen analgesics, and so on. Business definitions affect projections of relative competitiveness and business growth rates, perceptions of largest competitors, and a host of other factors. A related important factor in services is the market's geographic extent. For medical clinics or hospitals, the geographic limit that administrators place on their markets, whether it is the clinic's neighborhood, city, county, or region (such as East Tennessee, northeastern United States), state, national, or international (for example, Mayo Clinic), will have a dramatic effect on market size, market growth rates, market share/relative competitiveness, and so on.

The company's situation can also have a serious effect on how a business is viewed. What may be a Problem Child for a large multinational company may be a Star for a smaller company, and what may be considered a Star by any company may pose a colossal problem for a small or medium-sized company if it does not have the resources to exploit the business's potential. This was what happened in the case of Dolby Labs in the UK (the inventors of Dolby Sound technology), which eventually had to sell itself to Sony to take full advantage of the Dolby technology's potential.

The emphasis on market share in determining relative competitiveness is based on the assumption that the greater a company's market share, the greater will be its profitability. This assumption can be valid but remains a weakness, because substantial exceptions can be created by such variables as market preference for a particular product or supplier, patent protection for a specific technology, efficiencies not related to market share, and various other factors.

Although growth is an important factor in determining the attractiveness of a particular business, other factors are also important. For example, the company's ability to take full advantage of the business may be a factor. Or perhaps the business's growth is due to a fad; for example, growth in demand for traditional Chinese medicines may be related to a fad for Asian culture. Or perhaps demand for a product or business has been distorted by a crisis situation such as the anthrax scare or by a strike causing short- to medium-term scarcity of alternative medications and treatments.

The relative competitiveness measure does not take the industry structure into consideration. Does the company operate in a highly fragmented industry (one in which no single competitor has a significant market share, such as a private medical practice in a large city) or a highly consolidated industry dominated by a few large competitors (such as pharmaceuticals). In the former situation, there is little true difference between being the largest competitor with a 1.2 competitiveness rating on a semilog scale or a medium-sized competitor with a 0.67 competitiveness rating. In the latter situation, the implications for the two competitors could be huge.

—George T. Haley

See also Market Opportunity Analysis, Positioning Strategies

FURTHER READING

Hamermesh, R. G. (1986). *Making strategy work*. New York: Wiley.

Hedley, B. (1977, February). Strategy and the business portfolio. *Long Range Planning, 32,* 41-57

Wheelen, T. L., & Hunger, J. D. (1998). *Strategic management and business policy* (6th ed.). Reading, MA: Addison-Wesley.

BED OCCUPANCY

Bed occupancy is expressed as the total number of occupied beds by the total number of available beds. Usually the calculation is expressed in the percentage (%) of occupancy. These numbers are used for a great many financial calculations and projections.

Reimbursement for the prospective payment system (Medicare) is predicated on the projected occupancy rate for each hospital. The following graph can help explain the calculations.

Bed Types	Available Beds	Occupied Beds	Percentage of Occupancy
Acute medical	250	240	96%
Acute surgical	200	150	75%
Acute oncology	50	40	80%
Acute NICU	30	30	100%
Acute pediatric	150	100	66.6%
Maternity	100	78	78%
Total	780	638	81.8%

In acute care institutions, the census at midnight is usually the point that is used to identify the occupancy rate. Although a cutoff point is needed, this census does not necessarily express the total volume of patients for the day. An excellent example is a surgical unit. At midnight you may have a patient in the bed who is ready to go home. Once discharged, the bed is available and very likely will be filled by another patient coming from the operating room. The census will show one patient in the bed, but two occupied the same bed in one 24-hour period. The total number of patients admitted and then discharged provides a better picture of the total census each day. Staffing patterns need to reflect these calculations as well.

Prospective payment under Medicare is an advanced payment to the health care provider (the hospital) according to predefined rates. The diagnosis-related groups (DRG) system drives the payment structure for these patients. The DRG payment system was started in 1983 for most states and in 1986 for all states in the United States. These groups included risk-adjusted, severity-of-care, and expected-length-of-stay projections.

The DRG system groups like diagnoses together to simplify the payment for prospective payments. The assumption is that the care rendered will be of an acute nature and a covered service.

If, however, the care rendered is not of an acute nature or not a covered service under Medicare the reimbursement for that time frame will be deducted when determination is made. One of the downsides to this payment system is that the payment is made based on the payment schedule from a rate determined by costs of one or more years ago. That means, for example, that the funds received in 2004 (prospective payment) are calculated on the costs for 2002. As costs continue to escalate, it can be understandably difficult to manage with the level of funds based on prior years' costs.

Bed occupancy drives other financial decisions. Staffing patterns, equipment and supplies, food supplies, and other major needs are determined by the anticipated bed occupancy levels. These are measured by census figures and the projected growth based on these numbers. The bed occupancy figures help the administrative staff forecast what is required to maintain the organization and what state and federal regulatory requirements may be anticipated.

—Edna Lee Kucera

FURTHER READING

www.cms.org

www.ipro.org

BELMONT REPORT

The *Belmont Report* was conceived in 1979 by the National Commission for the Protection of Human Subjects of Biomedical and Behavioral Research. Both the report and the commission were mandated by the National Research Law (Public Law 93-348), promulgated on July 12, 1974. The report identifies and provides relevant applications for the three ethical principles that must be followed by investigators who must conceive and conduct, and for institutional review boards (IRBs) who must review and assess, research involving human participants. The *Belmont Report* provides the basis for the federal regulations governing the protection of human participants (Code of Federal Regulations at Title 45, Public Welfare, Part 46, Protection of Human Subjects; 45 CFR 46).

The ethical principle of "beneficence" requires that the investigator "Do no harm." Although this end is ultimately desired, it is not necessarily guaranteed in a research setting. It may, in fact, be the variable being tested, as when an investigator is assessing adverse effects of an experimental drug that is being administered to a human participant for the first time. The *Belmont Report* allows for this and extends the "Do no harm" principle to research by expanding the concept to one of "Minimize risk and maximize benefit."

The ethical principle of "justice" requires that the decision of who should be included and who should be excluded from a particular research activity should not be done arbitrarily and should make ethical sense, given the aims of the research activity. The report speaks of social justice, that is, there should be some order of preference for inclusion, based on the vulnerability of a subject population. For example, adults should be included in the research before children, as should nonpregnant women before pregnant women.

The ethical principle of "respect for persons" speaks to consideration of the subject as an individual, not as a means to collect data. One of the most basic ways to respect the subject as an individual is to provide that person with all the information needed to make the decision regarding whether or not to be in the research study, that is, to allow for self-determination. An ethical and noncoercive informed consent process is one of the critical tenets of principles governing human subjects research. Another aspect of this principle is the requirement to protect subjects who cannot by themselves make the decision to participate. An example of this type of "vulnerable" subject is a minor, who is considered too immature to make such a decision. IRBs must ensure that additional protections are in place to protect such a population, for example by ensuring parental permission and minor assent where applicable.

—Judy Matuk

See also Institutional Review Board (IRB), Vulnerable Research Subject Populations

FURTHER READING

National Commission for the Protection of Human Subjects of Biomedical and Behavioral Research. (1979). *The Belmont report: Ethical principles and guidelines for the protection of human subjects of research.* Available on the Web at ohrp. osophs.dhhs.gov/humansubjects/guidance/belmont.htm

BENEFIT AND COST ANALYSIS

See Cost–Benefit Analysis (CBA)

BENEFIT PACKAGE

A benefit package is the array of benefits and covered services available in a particular health care insurance plan. This array differs in scope according to the negotiated contracts with the company benefit contractor. The costs of services often dictate what is included and what is not.

The package iterates the covered and noncovered services as well as details and defines the rights for expedited review and other covered challenges. It has become increasingly important to the insured to know and exercise their appeal rights. With rapid advances in treating disease and life-saving therapies, treatments are often not "covered" under the benefit package and require vigorous challenge to provide payment. These "experimental" clauses often deny life-saving care. The expedited appeal process is the avenue for the patient and family to pursue.

Medicare and Medicaid services require a basic minimum of service that a managed care company must provide to receive federal funds for these populations. For example, acute and subacute rehabilitation services for posthospital care must be included in the package. Dental coverage need not be included. Dental services are not included for the Medicare beneficiary and therefore need not be included in the benefit package offered to its clients by a managed care company. Acute and subacute rehabilitation services are included under Medicare and thus must be included. These "risks" are included in the total cost the insurance companies will charge for the Medicare and Medicaid contracts.

—Edna Lee Kucera

FURTHER READING

www.thehealthpages.com

BENEFIT SEGMENTATION

See Segmentation

BILLING

Billing is the process of submitting a request for payment for services rendered or goods provided to a client. In the health care system, this may take several forms. A bill may be submitted directly to the patient or to a third party (such as an insurance company, an intermediary as in Medicare, or an administrative agent for a self-insured employer) who is responsible for paying for the services. If the bill is submitted to the patient, the patient may in turn submit it to a third party for reimbursement. Or bills may be submitted to both the third party and to the patient, with the patient responsible for paying the difference between the charge and the amount paid by the third party, a process known as *balance billing*. The health care provider may,

however, agree to accept the amount paid by the third party as payment in full; in this case, the provider is said to accept *assignment*.

Bills may be generated based on charges for different units of service. A charge may be generated for each individual service that is performed, or may be *bundled* to include charges for all services provided during an episode of illness (for example, surgeon's fees that include preoperative and postoperative care as well as the operation itself, or all hospital costs incurred during a hospitalization) or for all services delivered on a particular day (*per diem* billing). Bills for individual services may be based on usual and customary charges in the community (such as for conventional fee-for-service systems), a fee schedule based on bids or negotiation as in managed care models, or on a legislated or administratively determined fee schedule as in Medicare and many Medicaid plans. Administratively set schedules may, in turn, be based on actuarial studies, estimated resource use (as in the resource-based relative value scale), or other determinations.

Bills may be subject to various forms of deductions before payment is made. These include *deductibles* and *copayments* that the patient must pay and discounts negotiated between the payer and provider. In addition, bills may not be paid if the claim is denied because, for example, the service is not covered by the payer or because the patient cannot or does not pay. Bills that are expected not to be paid represent charity care, and those that are expected to be paid but are not paid represent bad debt. The sum of bad debt and charity care represents uncompensated care.

Bills may be submitted for payment in two basic forms: manual or electronic. Manual billing involves the completion of paper forms that are sent from the provider or patient to the payer. Electronic bills are generated from data input to a computer at the site of care and transmitted electronically to the payer; automated systems then determine the patient's eligibility and payment rates, and generate an electronic payment back to the provider.

The Health Insurance Portability and Accountability Act (HIPAA) of 1996 has mandated electronic billing using standard formats for most billing transactions. This law requires the health care industry to develop and implement data and transaction standards, including the use of a single electronic format, for providers to use to bill for their services. Health plans must be able to accept transactions in this format, and providers may either directly bill in electronic form or submit manual bills to a clearinghouse that will convert these bills into the standard electronic form.

—David M. Mirvis

See also Bad Debt Loss, Deductibles, Electronic Claims, Health Insurance Portability and Accountability Act (HIPAA), Prospective Payment System

FURTHER READING

www.ahcpr.gov/data/hipaa1.htm

BILLING FRAUD

See Billing

BIOTECHNOLOGY

The term *biotechnology* is best defined by defining each of its parts. "Bio" refers to the use of biological processes; "technology" refers to how to solve problems or make useful products. Biological processes have been manipulated for millennia for multiple uses. The growing of crops and the raising of animals for the purposes of providing food and clothing are basic examples. Through research and education conducted over the last 30 years, our manipulation of biological processes has expanded to direct manipulation at the molecular and cellular levels. Thus biotechnology engineering of cellular and molecular processes can be used to solve problems and make products.

The attributes of cells and biological molecules on which biotechnology capitalizes are DNA and proteins. DNA (deoxyribonucleic acid) is the genetic material of almost all living things. DNA provides instructions for the development and maturation of cells as well as for the tasks a particular cell is to undertake. The role of proteins is to provide the building materials and perform all the functions of cells. A cell has many different kinds of proteins, assigned to specific tasks. DNA determines the production of proteins and coordination of their activities. DNA contains the information for making these proteins. From this perspective, DNA serves as the command center of the cell.

The presence of DNA at the level of cells and molecules unifies life. DNA represents the same genetic language between cells. DNA can be transferred from one cell to another and can be used by the recipient cell. These interactions between cells are quite specific. To accomplish this transfer of DNA information, biotechnologists must use focused, precise instruments and processes. These processes can be used to solve specific challenges. This manipulation of cellular matter forms the basis of modern biotechnology.

—Anthony J. Ippolito

FURTHER READING

Day, S. (1999). *Dictionary for clinical trials.* Chichester, UK: Wiley.
www.bio.org

BIOTERRORISM

The term *bioterrorism* (BI-oh-TER-e-riz-em) is derived from the words *biological* and *terrorism.* By definition, it is the intentional threat or actual use of a biological agent(s), which includes both micro-organisms (bacteria, parasites, viruses, and fungi) and toxins (chemicals) produced by micro-organisms, plants, or animals.[1] Each has the ability to produce disease, illness, or intoxication in a susceptible population.[2] The explicit intent of such threat or use in the pursuit of political, religious, or ideological goals is to create fear and panic to coerce and intimidate governments or societies. Such agents may be dispersed in either an overt or covert fashion, with a malevolent intent.[3] Although the disease pathogens are assumed to target human populations, they may also be directed toward animal or plant species. Regardless of the end target, the explicit purpose of such agents is to cause disease or death in human, animal, or plant populations.

Under Title 18 of the United States Code, section 2332(a), the Weapons of Mass Destruction Act, it is illegal to use, threaten, attempt, or conspire to use a weapon of mass destruction, including any biological agent, toxin, or vector. U.S. law continues to evolve to address the specific issues of criminal prosecution as it relates to bioterrorism. Hence, the development of the Biological Weapons Anti-Terrorism Statute of 1989 (BWAT). Under this statue Title 18 of the United States Code, section 175, identifies the use of biological agents or toxins as a criminal violation in the United States. In general, whoever develops, produces, stockpiles, transfers, acquires, retains, or possesses, a biological agent, toxin, or delivery system for use as a weapon is in violation. Current U.S. statutes identify fines or imprisonment for whoever possesses, uses, or exercises control over a select agent in a manner constituting reckless disregard for the public health and safety. People whose acts result in bodily harm or death face fines and life imprisonment.[4]

—Nick Colovos

NOTES

1. "Biological Terrorism." (2001). Center for the Study of Bioterrorism & Emerging Infections, Saint Louis University School of Public Health.
2. LAPublichealth.org
3. www.dtic.mil/doctrine/jel/new pubs/jpl 02.pdf
4. www.fas.org/sgp/congress/2001/hr3160.html

BIRTHING CENTER

A birthing center[1] is a facility, alternative to the traditional hospital setting, for healthy pregnant women to give birth in. Birthing centers provide women with a comfortable health care environment that maintains patient safety, and skilled medical attention, at a reduced cost to the patient, in a more homelike, family-centered environment than is available in a hospital. The birthing center is geared to appeal to women who have had uneventful past deliveries. They are designed about a wellness model for pregnancy and delivery.

In a article in the *New England Journal of Medicine*,[2] study outcomes for 11,814 women at 84 freestanding birthing centers were reported. The women had lower-than-average risk of a poor outcome. In addition, cesarean section delivery was less common at birthing centers than for similar low-risk pregnancies at hospitals. The study concluded "that birth centers offer a safe and acceptable alternative to hospital confinement for selected pregnant women, particularly those who have previously had children, and that such care leads to relatively few cesarean sections." Nearly 100% of the women who used the center said they would recommend this alternative to friends and would be happy to return to the center again themselves.

Quality is monitored in states that have licensed, accredited birthing centers, and birthing centers demonstrate outcome data similar to hospital facilities. To maintain quality, surveys are required. National standards were established in 1985, and 37 states currently license birthing centers to ensure patient safety and quality.

The creation of birthing centers provides women with a place to deliver at a reduced cost while maintaining patient safety. In rural areas, these centers offer women care that otherwise would necessitate excessive travel. At a birthing center, families can experience childbirth in a more relaxed environment. Programs are even extended to include grandparents. Hospitals are also responding to the need to create a more family-friendly atmosphere by creating birthing rooms and recognizing the role of the nurse midwife for selected women.

Cost-effective operation is achieved by eliminating hospital overhead, reduced requirements for expensive equipment and technology ("high touch" rather than "high tech"), and lower personnel requirements, including staffing only when women are in labor. Improved patient and family satisfaction is achieved through the more personal, family-centered atmosphere. In addition to the delivered babies, these centers may also provide laboratory services, education, home visits, and initial newborn evaluations.

Staffing of birthing centers is only available when an actual admission occurs. Technologically advanced equipment is not available at the birthing center. By initiating a self-help method of treatment, the center also saves on staffing.

—Thomas M. Biancaniello

NOTES

1. www.birthcenters.org.

2. Rooks, J. P., Weatherby, N. L., Ernst, E. K., Stapleton, S., Rosen, D., & Rosenfeld, A. (1989). Outcomes of care in birth centers. The National Birth Center Study. *New England Journal of Medicine, 321*(26), 1804–1811.

BLINDING

Blinding is a technique used to minimize bias in a study by preventing the participants from knowing which treatment option they are allocated to receive. Blinding can take three main forms: single, double, and triple blinding.

Single blinding involves the subjects being unaware of their treatment regimen. In a study comparing a new drug to a drug already in use, a subject may have a preconceived notion that one drug is more effective than the other. This can cause a potentially exaggerated effect (see placebo effect) for either the standard or the investigational treatment.

Double blinding involves keeping both the investigator and the subject unaware of the treatment assignment. This eliminates potential investigator bias for measuring efficacy or detecting potential adverse events associated with a treatment.

Triple blinding involves keeping the treatment assignments unknown to the subject, to the investigator, and to the person performing the data analysis.

Various study designs can be blinded to varying degrees. To be considered scientifically sound, most study designs require double blinding. The use of quantification and universal statistical criteria (p value $< .05$, and so forth) often eliminates any potential bias that could be introduced at the data analysis level. If a study involves a subject or investigator being "blinded," this information should appear in the consent form. For studies involving a placebo, this placebo blinding, as well as under what conditions the "blind" may be broken, must also be explained in simple language in the consent form. Washington, DC., or ohsr.od.nih.gov/mpa/

—Daryn H. Moller

FURTHER READING

National Institutes of Health, Human Subject Research Advisory Committee. (1998). Washington, D.C., or ohsr.od.nih.gov/mpa/

BLUE CROSS AND BLUE SHIELD (BCBS)

Blue Cross and Blue Shield are independent, locally operated insurance plans. They have existed for over

70 years. One in four Americans carry this insurance. The Blue Cross Blue Shield Association is the trade association for 43 local member companies.

In the beginning, Blue Cross and Blue Shield Plans marked the birth of prepaid health care coverage in America. Blue Cross was for hospital care coverage, and Blue Shield included physician services. Most plans have now combined to offer both services under one umbrella.

Blue Cross began in 1929 to guarantee hospital coverage for schoolteachers in Dallas. Soon other groups joined, and national attention was drawn to the plan. Around the early 1900s, Blue Shield was born in the mining and lumber camps in the Pacific Northwest. Physicians were paid monthly fees to provide medical care for the laborers. The Blue Cross and Blue Shield Association is the result of a merger between the Blue Cross Association and the National Association of Blue Shield Plans.

In the 1920s, the Blue Cross and Blue Shield companies were the first to forge partnerships with physicians and subscribers. Instead of just paying for health benefits, they created partnerships with hospitals, physicians, and other health care providers.

Although they were traditionally not-for-profit companies, some plans, such as the Empire Plan of New York, have applied for and been granted for-profit status. Blue Choice Senior Plan is a division of Blue Cross Blue Shield that deals with the Medicare population.

—Doreen T. Day

FURTHER READING

www.bluecares.com
www.bsbsvt.com

BOARDS OF DIRECTORS

Within the health care organization, the board of directors is the ultimate authority with legal responsibility for total financial and organizational stewardship. The board has legal control of the organization and is responsible for ensuring the continued existence of the organization. It possesses legal authority to take those actions essential to the governed entity's financial well-being as well as to the quality of service delivered by the organization and through its agents. It is, to paraphrase Harry S. Truman, where the buck stops.

The board is given wide-ranging authority to oversee the affairs of the organization within the laws of the state and federal governments and within the restrictions set by the organization's charter and bylaws. The board is the direct representative of the owners of the organization and is obligated to act in the best interest of the owners as a class. A range of ownership possibilities exist, and these have significant ramifications for the process of board selection. In addition, the board of a health care organization must also be cognizant of the interests of physicians and other professionals, employees, consumers of service, and the broader public.

TYPES OF BOARDS

Not-for-profit ownership. The traditional hospital organization has been organized as a not-for-profit entity established by a philanthropic individual or association; or alternatively by a religious body. In the first instance, board members are typically nominated and elected from the membership ranks of the establishing organization, or from the broader community served. In recent years a movement toward the election of independent directors on a corporate model has gained in popularity, although it is still unusual. In the case of religious boards, the members are often appointed from the ranks of the vocationally religious or from members of the sponsoring denomination.

For-profit boards. Although investor-owned facilities compose a minority of hospitals in the United States, they constitute the majority of organizations engaged in long-term care, home health services, managed care financial services, and medical group practice. Boards of directors in these settings act as representatives of shareholders or partners as a group. They are empowered to make decisions according to their best judgment while being mindful of trusteeship obligations to the shareholders' interests. Directors are typically elected by the shareholders or by members of the group.

Public boards. Public organizations provide substantial health services in hospital, public health, and educational sectors throughout the nation. Public boards, often labeled *boards of trustees* or *boards of governors,* may be found in organizations directly operated by government. In such instances, members are usually appointed by political bodies, or directly elected in a minority of cases. A growing trend is the conversion for operating purposes of governmental entities to public benefit agencies, with board selection and authority more closely resembling the not-for-profit model.

BOARD MEMBER ATTRIBUTES

Board members are typically selected for one or more of three *W*'s: wisdom, work, and wealth. Each of these dimensions mirrors a vital board function.

Wisdom reflects the traditional expectation that members will bring to the board expertise in dealing with complex business and professional problems, especially those that can benefit from community involvement. Board members have been drawn from occupations such as law, accounting, banking, and the health professions. It is customary to consult the board members from a given area of expertise on problems in that realm provided no conflicts of interest between personal interests and fiduciary duty exist.

Work signals the obligation of the board member to conscientiously discharge duties by preparing for, and allocating appropriate hours of service to, board activities. This effort includes service on board committees and specific projects such as special committees or search efforts.

Wealth implies various dimensions, given the type of organization. In the not-for-profit sector, board members are often expected to make donations to the organization or at a minimum participate in philanthropic endeavors. In the for-profit arena, board members are usually presumed to hold some equity stake in the organization through stock ownership or other form of investment in the enterprise. Wealth is not a usual criterion in governmental boards, although campaign contributors are sometimes rewarded with such appointments.

CURRENT CONSIDERATIONS IN BOARD MEMBERSHIP

Diversity of board members is an increasing concern of health care organizations. As the workforce has diversified as a matter of policy direction, so too has the profile of ideal board composition. Public and private boards are increasingly recruiting women and members of minorities to serve as members, to fulfill a stated policy objective.

Physicians as members of boards represent a special case for consideration. In hospital organizations, thinking has shifted in the last two decades away from a policy of minimal involvement of physicians at the board level to one that encourages or even mandates physician membership. Historic concerns about potential conflicts of interest on the part of physicians, expected to be reflected in an inability to separate professional interests from organizational duties of stewardship, have diminished. Instead, the wisdom of physicians is actively sought on issues affecting the medical aspects of the institution as well as other board issues. This in part reflects the boards' growing concern for patient safety and quality of care within the organization. Conversely, physician organizations are often required by state law or Internal Revenue Service code to include nonphysician representatives on their governing boards, to assure consideration of alternate perspectives.

BOARD ORGANIZATION

Boards are led by an elected or appointed chairperson and other officers as necessary to carry out work. The chair usually oversees all board activities, including appointment of committees and establishment of agendas. The chair also directs planning for leadership succession, evaluating the CEO, self-evaluating the board itself, and assuring its own regeneration and renewal through education and new appointments.

Board size has become more controversial, with a move toward smaller corporate model boards of 15 or fewer members. This trend is in contrast to earlier large representative boards of as many as 75 members that characterized not-for-profit governance. These large boards were often managed by smaller executive committees, effectively thwarting the wide participation a larger board would imply. The model of the smaller working board conforms to contemporary notions prevalent in for-profit corporate governance that seek to align governance and management activities as fully as possible, to increase effectiveness.

To permit broader participation, the work of boards is often carried out by committees. Usual examples include but are not limited to finance, quality of care, strategic planning, and community relations. These committees may include members drawn from the community and the staff of the organization but gain their authority by reporting to the full board. In addition, boards often have a nominating committee for selection of new members and officers and a compensation committee specifically charged with reviewing payment of the top management.

A special case in the contemporary environment is the audit committee. This committee reports directly to the board and consists exclusively of outside directors, to assure objectivity in dealing with any controversial findings.

DUTIES OF THE BOARD

The board is charged with the critical duty of appointing and evaluating the CEO. The board delegates the conduct of the internal operations to this key individual and should refrain from direct involvement in operations. The board is responsible for monitoring CEO performance in meeting agreed-on key objectives and for collaboratively overseeing critical areas of performance in partnership with the CEO, such as finance and quality of care. Although the board is cautioned to refrain from involvement in managing the organization, establishment of policies in key operating areas such as quality and finance has obvious implications for management and must be carefully considered.

MISSION DEVELOPMENT

The board is charged with adopting the mission statement of the organization. Once the mission statement is adopted, the board is obligated to evaluate and monitor the accomplishment of the mission through the activities of the CEO and the organization. Analysts have observed that missions in the for-profit arena are often quite focused on the fiscal performance of the organization and on its obligations to its shareholders, whereas not-for-profit missions are general and amorphous. This lack of focus leads to ambiguity in the next critical area of responsibility to be discussed, strategic planning.

Strategic planning is generally regarded as a key aspect of the CEO role in developing the plan itself. The board is responsible for developing the framework within which the strategic plan is developed, in the form of the mission and goals of the organization. Within this framework, the CEO develops the objectives for performance. The board assesses and approves the strategic plan, either as a committee of the whole or through its strategic planning committee, and uses the assessment of the plan's attainment in fulfilling its key responsibility to evaluate the CEO's performance.

RELATIONS WITH MEDICAL STAFF

A special issue for the board is its relationship with the medical staff. Historically, the medical staff has enjoyed a quasi-autonomous relationship with the board, mediated through the CEO and the joint conference committee. Yet as early as 1965 the famous *Darling v. Charleston Community Memorial Hospital* (1966) decision established the accountability of boards for the quality of care in their facilities. The recent move to include physicians as governing board members is in part prompted by recognition of the complex yet critical process of evaluating quality of care and by the desire of boards to include the wisdom of experts in this quest.

Credentialing of physicians and other health professionals through staff membership and privileges is a clear board accountability and a key component of the quality process. This role includes establishing policies for granting credentials on the recommendation of the medical staff. The Joint Commission on Accreditation of Healthcare Organizations (JCAHO) insists on the active involvement of boards in this process with documented evidence supporting this involvement.

KEY POLICIES

Boards are charged to fulfill a fiduciary role on behalf of the organization, in which the board member is to place the best interest of the organization ahead of self-interest. As a result, many boards have adopted policies defining and regulating conflicts of interest on the part of members to avoid self-serving behavior in board decision making. Confidentiality policies are another standard element of board policy in which members are obliged to observe confidentiality of the organization's deliberations.

Boards are increasingly called on to review and approve ethics policies and codes of conduct for behavior throughout the organization. In some instances ethics committees

of the board have been created, whereas in a few instances ethics officers report directly to the board.

SYSTEM VERSUS FACILITY BOARDS

In larger organizations, a division of labor between corporate or system boards and facility boards is necessary. Strategic and capital financing issues are often reserved to the system board, with operating finance and quality responsibilities delegated to facility boards under general oversight of the system board. Wide variations exist in these patterns, depending in part on style of ownership.

THE FUTURE OF GOVERNANCE

Perhaps at no time has it been more difficult for a director to be a "prudent person," as the minimal test of the law demands. Business scandals in the corporate and health care sectors have eroded public confidence in the efficacy of board stewardship in protecting the public interest. Patient safety itself is increasingly called into question, and the smug self-assurance that a health care organization is doing good simply by fulfilling its mission is likewise called into question. Exciting yet threatening technological advances promise to remake the face of health care. Director recruitment and retention and the provision of minimal protection to directors (who are often volunteers) through liability insurance and indemnification assure challenges to effective health care governance in the future.

—Richard A. Culbertson

See also Ethical Code, Strategic Planning

FURTHER READING

Darling v. Charleston Community Memorial Hospital (1966), 33 Illinois 2d 326, 211 N.E. 253 (1965), cert. denied 383 U.S. 946.

Pointer, D., & Ewell, C. (1994). *Really governing: How health system and hospital boards can make more of a difference.* Albany, NY: Delmar.

Pointer, D., & Orlikoff, J. (1999). *Board work: Governing health care organizations.* San Francisco: Jossey-Bass.

Taylor, B., Chait, R., & Holland, T. (1996, September–October). The new work of the nonprofit board. *Harvard Business Review, 74*(5), 29–40.

Tyler, J. L., & Biggs, E. (2001). *Practical governance.* Chicago: Health Administration Press.

BOARDS OF HEALTH

Boards of health provide governance and/or recommendations (advisory) to state and local public health agencies to promote the health of their respective communities. State law or policy determines the establishment of a board of health, its role, and its composition, which therefore vary significantly from state to state.

In states where the board of health governs the public health agency, it is responsible for enforcing federal, state, and local health laws and regulations and for establishing policies to protect and promote the health of the state's residents. The board appoints a health official who oversees the operation of the agency. There are usually local boards as well as a state-level board.

In states where state and/or local boards are advisory, the health official is usually appointed by and reports to an elected official, with the board advising the elected official. In some states, there are no boards of health, and health officials report directly to an elected official such as the governor, mayor, or county commission.

The composition and appointment of board members also varies greatly. Members may be appointed by an elected official, be elected or appointed by various health associations, or even be elected directly by citizens of a political jurisdiction. In most cases, state law establishes specific criteria that must be met by board members to ensure a knowledgeable and community-based board. A membership association, the National Association of Local Boards of Health (NALBOH), is available to provide assistance. Some states also have state associations for local boards.

—Carole W. Samuelson

See also Health Officer and Health Commissioner, Public Health

FURTHER READING

www.naccho.org
www.nalboh.org

BOOK VALUE

The book value of a fixed asset is the historic acquisition cost of the asset minus accumulated depreciation and write-offs. It may also be referred to as the *carrying value,* because it is the value carried on the books of an organization at any point in time. Depreciation is based on allocating the cost of the asset over a period of time, usually considered the asset's useful life. This depreciation is accumulated over the asset's life and then deducted from the original asset cost to produce the book value. Book value does not represent the earning capacity of the asset, nor does it associate any potential risks surrounding the asset. There is no true relationship between the book value and the market value of a fixed asset. Market value is the price as determined dynamically by buyers and sellers in an open market.

For example, let's assume that ABC Medical Center purchased a magnetic resonance imaging (MRI) machine in 2000 for $1,000,000. The MRI machine is assumed to have a useful life of 10 years. In addition, the machine is assumed to have a salvage value of approximately $100,000. The salvage value is the expected value of the asset at the end of its useful life. The depreciable basis of the machine is the original cost ($1,000,000) less the salvage value ($100,000), or $900,000. The annual depreciation on the MRI machine is calculated by dividing the depreciable basis of $900,000 by the estimated useful life of 10 years. Thus ABC would record $90,000 per year as depreciation on the machine.

Based on this information, the book value of the MRI machine after three full years of service is

Original cost	$1,000,000	
Less accumulated depreciation	(270,000)	3 years × $90,000 annual depreciation charge
Book value	$730,000	

Book value is important in determining the gain or loss associated with the disposal of an asset. On the sale of an asset, the book value is compared with the sales price. If the sales price is equal to the book value, then no gain or loss is experienced for financial statement purposes. If the sales price is greater than the book value, the difference in the two values is considered as a gain. If the sales price is less than the book value, the difference in the two values is considered a loss. The book value for income tax purposes may differ from that for financial statement purposes, because of different depreciation methods. In that case, gains or losses for tax purposes also differ.

—Edward Pershing

BREAKEVEN ANALYSIS

Breakeven (BE) analysis is a management decision-making tool, useful particularly when fixed costs are a significant portion of an organization's cost structure. Sometimes referred to as *cost–volume–profit analysis,* BE analysis calculates the level of sales (in units or in dollars) such that an organization earns zero profit on a specific product or project. If the level of sales exceeds the breakeven level, the organization makes a profit; sales lower than breakeven generate a loss.

When referring to units in the BE calculation, the unit must first be clearly defined, because it can be stated with a variety of terms. In a general sense, organizations are

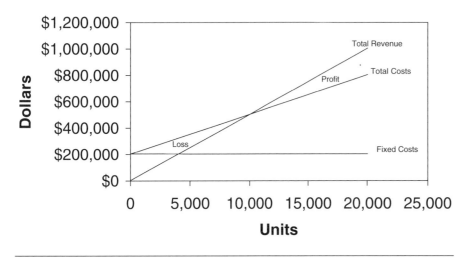

Figure 1

interested in measuring the number of physical units produced, or the productivity of human or machine, which would encompass service applications. On a macro level, health organizations may be interested in measuring number of cases, or patient days, or unique visits to a facility. Measuring activity on the micro level may refer to the number of procedures or lab tests. Regardless of the measure, the units being measured must be consistent; the analysis is applied to only one measure of output at a time (for example, a lab makes one breakeven calculation for a blood test and another completely different calculation for a skin fungus test, because the costs involved with each test are likely very different).

BE requires an understanding of fixed costs and variable costs within an organization. Total cost represents the sum of fixed and variable costs. BE is the amount of sales, stated in units or in dollars, that equals total cost; at this level of sales, earnings before interest and taxes (EBIT) equal zero. (See Figure 1.)

The breakeven point is defined as follows:

BE in quantity terms: Fixed costs / contribution margin in dollars

Breakeven in dollar terms: Fixed costs / contribution margin ratio

Contribution margin: Unit selling price – unit variable cost

Contribution margin ratio: Contribution margin / unit selling price

Original Example Data: The Physical Therapy Clinic (PTC) has fixed costs of $200,000 per year. The average variable cost per patient for providing service is $30 per appointment. The average charge to a patient for each appointment is $50, generating a contribution margin per appointment of $20. The contribution margin ration is $20 / $50 = 0.40. To reach a breakeven point and exactly cover fixed costs, the clinic must generate 10,000 patient appointments for the year:

BE in units: $200,000 / $20 = 10,000 patients

BE in dollars: $200,000 / .40 = $500,000

To reconcile using totals,

Total revenue: 10,000 patients × $50 = $500,000

Total costs:

Fixed costs: $200,000

Variable costs: 10,000 patients × $30 = $300,000

_____

EBIT $0

Appointments beyond 10,000 will generate a positive EBIT:

Assume 15,000 patients, which is 5,000 patients above BE:

5,000 × $20 = $100,000 EBIT

To reconcile using totals:

Total revenue: 15,000 patients × $50 = $750,000

Total costs:

Fixed costs: $200,000

Variable costs: 15,000 patients × $30 = $450,000

_____

EBIT $100,000

OPERATING LEVERAGE

Assuming fixed costs remain at $200,000 in the preceding example, a 33% increase in patients from 15,000 to 20,000 would generate an EBIT of $200,000, a 100% increase. Similarly, a 20% decrease in patients from 15,000 to 12,000 would decrease EBIT to $40,000, a drop of 60%. Higher fixed costs create the potential for greater variability in EBIT, in both positive and negative directions. A number of industries, including health care, auto, airline, and manufacturing in general are highly susceptible to the volatility resulting from operating leverage. Any organization that purchases expensive equipment or that owns significant assets such as buildings, or that has a high fixed payroll, increases the potential effects of operating leverage. Off-balance-sheet strategies such as equipment leasing or the use of temporary employees can reduce an organization's exposure to operating leverage.

SENSITIVITY ANALYSIS

To be useful in a health care setting, relevant questions pertaining to BE are cast from a more practical operations perspective. For instance, managers want to have an intuitive feel for the sensitivity of EBIT to changes in the patient load. As budgets are set in place for the coming year, management and staff have estimated the patient load they will be facing, and have hired staff and made purchase commitments accordingly. By using the contribution margin, managers can conduct a sensitivity analysis on their projected data to determine the effects of possible swings in services demanded by patients. Suppose in the original PTC data that management has projected 15,000 patient appointments for the coming fiscal year, which generates a projected EBIT of $100,000. But if patient demand falls off, what are the consequences to the organization? The president of the company has established a working minimum target EBIT of $60,000 for the coming year, to keep stakeholders happy. What change in patient demand can PTC experience and still achieve the minimum goal of $60,000 EBIT? Based on a contribution margin of $20, the clinic can experience a drop in patient demand of 2,000 visits and still achieve the desired minimum EBIT:

Change in EBIT / contribution margin = unit change in demand

($100,000 – $60,000) / $20 = 2,000 fewer patients

Stated from another perspective, what is the required sales level, in number of patients, necessary to achieve an EBIT of $60,000?

Required revenue in dollars = fixed costs + variable costs + target EBIT

$50Q = $200,000 + $30Q + $60,000

Q = 13,000 (a decrease of 2,000 patients)

Where

Q = number of patients

$50 = charge to patient per visit

$30 = variable cost per visit

$200,000 = total fixed costs

$60,000 = target EBIT

EXTENSION: OUTSOURCING

Using the original PTC data, the PTC management is debating whether to outsource some of the physical therapy work to a firm that employs a pool of therapists that is hired out on a case-by-case basis. The outsourcing firm will provide supplies and charge an hourly rate for the therapist. The net effect will be an increase in the variable cost per patient visit to $35 (reducing the contribution margin from $20 to $15), and the reduction of fixed costs by $60,000 (based on employing one less full-time physical therapist). Given competitive pressures, management would like to hold the patient charge to $50. What is the new breakeven point in patient visits required to generate a target EBIT of $60,000?

Required visits = (fixed costs + target EBIT) / contribution margin

Required visits = ($140,000 + $60,000) / 15 = 13,333 visits

EXTENSION: PRICE CHANGES

PTC's newest competitor has just opened, offering basic visits for $40. Should PTC match the offer? What is the effect on the BE point over the next year? Using the original PTC data, the variable cost remains at $30 per visit and fixed costs are $200,000. The contribution margin is now $40 – $30 = $10 and the contribution margin ratio is $10/$40 = 0.25. The new BE point is calculated as follows:

BE in units: $200,000 / $10 = 20,000 patients

BE in dollars: $200,000 / 0.25 = $800,000

PTC now has an estimate of the amount of business necessary to break even at the lower pricing point. This information will help, along with other considerations, in making an informed decision.

CAPITAL BUDGETING AND INCREMENTAL BUSINESS EXPANSION

Breakeven analysis can also be used to help make decisions concerning equipment purchases or incremental business expansion decisions.

Here's an example: Community Hospital (CH) is debating whether to purchase a new MRI machine, which costs $1.0 million. The fixed costs per year to operate the machine total $300,000 including $200,000 in depreciation and $100,000 in hospital overhead. The variable cost to operate the machine for each patient is $600, including $200 in materials and $400 in personnel time. The charge to a patient is $1,000 for each MRI; therefore the contribution margin is $400 per patient and the contribution margin ratio is $400 / $1,000 = 0.40. To reach the breakeven point on the MRI machine, CH must schedule 750 patients each year:

BE in units: $300,000 / ($1,000 − $600) = 750 patients

BE in dollars: $300,000 / 0.40 = $750,000

EXTENSION: LEASE OPTION

Suppose CH is able to lease the MRI machine for $100,000 per year, so that fixed costs equal $200,000, including the $100,000 in overhead. The patient charge is still $1,000, and the variable cost per patient is $600. The BE point is now 500 patients:

BE in units: $200,000 / 400 = 500 patients

BE in dollars: $200,000 / 0.40 = $500,000

This option represents lower risk in terms of breaking even but also diminishes the potential for a larger EBIT on the upside. CH must also trade off other issues that affect the decision, such as the potential to build equity in the MRI machine by purchasing versus the risk of technological obsolescence.

For example, let's say Home Health Care Inc. (HHC) has recently opened a new office, and revenues are growing quickly. In anticipation of further demand growth, the president of the company is considering hiring an additional registered nurse (RN). The incremental fixed cost will total $60,000 per year, including benefits and payroll taxes. The average charge to the patient for a home visit by an RN is $70. The average variable cost for each home visit by an RN is $20, for a contribution margin of $50 and a contribution margin ratio of 0.714 ($50/$70). To reach a breakeven point on the hire, the nurse must make 1,200 visits, or 100 per month:

BE in units: $60,000 / ($70 − $20) = 1,200 visits

BE in dollars: $60,000 / 0.714 = $84,000 (rounded)

CAPITATION RATES

Health care organizations that accept capitation rates also use breakeven analysis in structuring their delivery

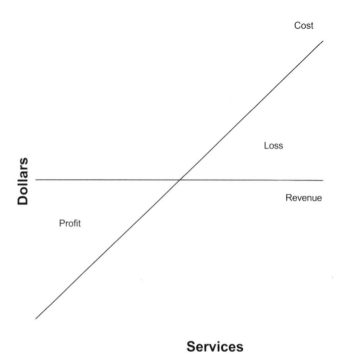

Figure 2

systems. A capitation environment is a payment system in which health care providers receive payment in advance for the defined health care needs of a specific population for a set period of time. The provider must budget in advance how much it is willing to spend on fixed costs, such as equipment and salaries. Going forward, revenue is fixed, and of course total variable costs and therefore total costs will change with the number of patients that access the system. In this case, the provider is typically interested in minimizing the amount of service or visits for a fixed number of people. In contracting to accept a capitation rate, the provider must carefully estimate its cost structure and then determine the maximum amount of service to provide. As seen from Figure 2 the picture is reversed relative to traditional breakeven analysis. The organization makes a profit if it holds patient visits below the breakeven point. Beyond the breakeven point, the organization loses more money (equivalent to the variable cost expended) on each additional patient.

—Kipling M. Pirkle

See also Activity-Based Costing, Capitation/Capitated Health Plans, Contribution Margin, Earnings Before Interest and Taxes (EBIT), Outsourcing

FURTHER READING

Brealey, R. A., & Myers, S. C. (2002). *Principles of corporate finance.* New York: McGraw-Hill.

Brigham, E. F., & Houston, J. F. (2001). *Fundamentals of financial management.* New York: Harcourt College.

Cleverly, W. O., & Cameron, A. E. (2002). *Essentials of health care finance.* Gaithersburg, MD: Aspen.

Collin, P. H. (2001). *Dictionary of business.* London: Peter Collin.

Horngren, C. T., Harrison, W. T., & Robinson, M. A. (1996). *Accounting.* Upper Saddle River, NJ: Prentice Hall.

Weygandt, J. J., Kieso, D. E., & Kimmek, P. D. (2002). *Managerial accounting: Tools for business decision making.* New York: Wiley.

www.toolkit.cch.com

BUREAU OF LABOR STATISTICS (BLS)

The Bureau of Labor Statistics (BLS) is the principal agency of the federal government charged with tracking labor and economic indicators. Although the BLS is an independent agency, it also serves as a statistical resource for the U.S. Department of Labor. The BLS collects and analyzes various data pertaining to employment, prices and living conditions, import and export price indexes, productivity, and compensation. For example, the national unemployment rate and current conditions regarding employee hours and wages are among the most well-known and most-requested statistics provided by the BLS. In many instances, data can also be provided according to region or to industry. Moreover, data are updated on a regular basis, the frequency of which depends on the statistic in question. For example, monthly changes in the national unemployment rate are available. The BLS also regularly conducts national surveys, the results of which are of great interest to organizations. For instance, the Employee Benefit Survey details the percentage of organizations offering various forms of health and medical benefits. Data are conveniently available from the BLS via the agency's internet home page.

—Elizabeth M. Smith

See also U.S. Department of Labor

FURTHER READING

www.bls.gov

BUSINESS PLAN

A business plan (BP) may be defined as a comprehensive selling document that communicates the promise of a business to potential backers. Thus a BP needs to fit the audience and convey excitement and promise.

Typically, the purpose is to raise funds in support of a new business, product, or service. Given the many changes in the health care industry, there are an increasing number of examples of BPs to gain funds. Indeed, there may be three broadly different situations requiring a BP. These include startup ventures seeking funding, existing firms seeking additional financing, or new activities within existing companies. In the first category, a group of physicians may develop a BP to seek debt financing from a bank to develop an ambulatory surgery center. An existing pharmaceutical company might seek equity funding from investment bankers to acquire a biotechnology company in the second situation. In the third situation, an existing acute care hospital may develop a BP to gain support to launch home health care services.

Because a health care BP may seek millions of dollars in funding, the document should include a substantial, comprehensive description of the business, in about 25 pages. BPs of fewer than 10 pages often do not do justice to the business, whereas 100-page BPs may not be read because of their imposing size. In those 25 pages, the major parts of a BP include the executive summary; a company overview, often with statements of mission, vision, values, and goals; the strengths and weaknesses inside the business, as well as the opportunities and threats in the external environment; strategies for delivering value to customers and for beating competitors; processes for conducting stable operations; a time-phased financial plan; and an implementation action plan. The implementation is especially important to persuade the investor that the plan is more than a dream. Thus, good business plans are full of specifics such as milestone dates, budgets, and specific responsibilities by person so that investors can measure and track results.

To develop a comprehensive understanding of the business, investors often use the following questions to evaluate a BP: Are investor expectations realistically addressed? Is the financial justification realistic? How marketable is the product or service? Are the operational processes to deliver the service or product realistic? How experienced is the management team charged with integrating the business?

Given that a BP is a selling document, intended to persuade backers to finance the business, there are at least four ways to attract potential investors. The most important is evidence of customer acceptance, because if sales and revenue cannot be realized in an income statement, losses will be substantial. A hospital with a high occupancy rate and an increasing length of stay among patients can readily document customer acceptance. Demonstration of a proprietary position can be exciting to investors, because it increases the odds that the revenues will continue. Backers welcome evidence of focus by the business and appreciation of investor needs.

Similarly, there are at least four ways to repel investors. Unrealistic growth projections and unrealistic financial projections can damage the credibility of the entire BP. A hospital that assumes companies will always accept escalating prices for in-hospital care may be rudely surprised to see such financial projections unmet. Custom engineering can be dysfunctional, because it will preclude expansion of scale and limit sales revenue. Infatuation with a product can be a warning signal that the management team may miss important customer requirements.

Even if all the preceding parts are included, backers still ask some strategic questions of the entire BP: Is it internally consistent? Does it fit the external environment? Does it deliver value to customers while beating competitors? Is it specific? Is it feasible? An answer of no to any of these questions may kill outsider investment in the BP.

An often used description of the business planning process is given in Rich and Gumpert's paperback book *Business Plans That Win $$$* (see Further Reading section). Business Plan Pro is a user-friendly software program that contains short tutorials to help the user understand the characteristics of the specific parts of the BP and the contribution to the whole BP.

—Michael J. Stahl

See also Debt Financing, Equity, Income Statement (IS), Mission, Objectives, Revenues, SWOT (Strength–Weakness–Opportunity-Threat) Analysis, Values (Gulding Principles), Vision

FURTHER READING

Berry, T. (1998). *Business Plan Pro Version 3.0.* Palo Alto, CA: Palo Alto Software.

Rich, S. R., & Gumpert, D. E. (1985). *Business plans that win $$$: Lessons from the MIT Enterprise Forum.* New York: Harper & Row.

Tiffany, P., & Peterson, S. D. (1997). *Business plans for dummies.* Foster City, CA: IDG Books Worldwide.

BUSINESS VALUATION

A business valuation is a process by which analysts determine the amount a business is worth. Such a valuation might be conducted for several reasons, discussed in the following sections.

ESTABLISH BID PRICE

Buyers conduct a valuation of their potential acquisitions to determine the maximum amount they should pay. In doing this they might ask, How will this acquisition generate enough cash flow to justify its cost? How will this acquisition complement my existing business? Are there duplicate services or expenses that can be eliminated? Do I have special experience or expertise that can be used to improve the acquisition's performance?

A clever buyer also performs a valuation from the seller's perspective, to see the minimum amount the seller would be willing to accept. This knowledge can be very helpful in negotiations.

ESTABLISH ASKING PRICE

Similarly, the seller conducts a valuation to determine the minimum acceptable selling price and sets the asking price higher than this price. However, in a sense the seller is at an informational disadvantage relative to the buyer. The buyer knows his or her maximum price, and often has enough information to value the business from the seller's perspective and so has a good idea of the seller's minimum selling price. Typically the seller does not have enough information about the buyer to determine the maximum amount he or she would be willing to pay. Thus if the buyer makes good use of business valuation techniques, he or she will have an advantage in negotiating a transaction price.

ESTABLISH VALUE FOR TAX PURPOSES

When a business owner gives or leaves a business to family members, there are often estate tax implications. A business valuation may be necessary to establish a value of the business so that estate taxes can be levied.

TO DETERMINE THE COST OF BUYING IN

The value of the business must be established when a new partner is allowed to buy into it. If the buy-in price is set too low, the existing partners are selling a portion of the business for too little; if the price is set too high, the new partner will overpay. Although the buy-in price is subject to negotiation, just as with any other sale, an impartial business valuation provides a common starting point for negotiations.

TO HELP MAKE MANAGERIAL DECISIONS

An often-overlooked use of business valuation techniques is to help managers make better decisions. If a sophisticated valuation model has been developed, it is relatively straightforward to see how potential operating changes translate into changes in the value of the business.

For example, a valuation model might be used to determine how much extra value is generated when a business tightens up its inventory or accounts receivable policy. If the additional value generated is greater than the cost of the changes, then the owners will be better off making the change. Using a valuation model to help make managerial decisions is called *value-based management*.

VALUATION TECHNIQUES

Valuation techniques fall roughly into two categories: (a) the multiples approach and (b) the cash flow approach.

Multiples Approach to Valuation

The oldest and simplest valuation technique is the multiples approach. In it, to reach a value of the firm the analyst multiplies a representative measure of the firm's performance, such as earnings per share, number of customers, sales, or covered lives, by a multiplier. A common multiplier is the P/E ratio. Earnings per share multiplied by a price divided by earnings gives, algebraically, price. In practice an analyst might observe that the average P/E ratio for firms in the drug industry is 25. Then if a new drug company has earnings of $2 per share, its per share price would be $50 if it had the same P/E ratio as the average firm in its industry.

For some firms, earnings are a poor indicator of value. For example, during the Internet stock craze many firms had consistent negative earnings but had positive stock prices. An alternate commonly used multiplier is the price-to-sales ratio. For example, the industry average ratio of per share price to per share sales is about 4.4 for the pharmaceuticals industry. If a new pharmaceuticals company had $40 million in sales and 10 million shares outstanding, then it would have per share sales of $4 per share. Using the industry sales per share multiple of 4.4 gives a per share price of $4 × 4.4 = $17.60.

The advantage of the multiplier technique is that it is very easy to implement. If you know the appropriate multiple to use, then finding the accounting data to multiply it by is usually simple. The disadvantage is that finding the appropriate multiple is more art than science. Multiples vary from firm to firm because of differences in growth opportunities, financing choices, profitability, technology, and a host of other firm-specific and market factors. Using an industry average multiple, as in the preceding example, is guaranteed to give an answer, but not necessarily the correct answer.

Cash Flow Approaches to Valuation

A more sophisticated valuation technique is to project future cash flows and find their present value (see the entry for *Time Value of Money* for a discussion of how to find present values). Many variations, modifications, and proprietary models are available; we discuss two generic techniques: the cash-flow-to-equity method and the corporate value method.

CASH-FLOW-TO-EQUITY METHOD

As the name implies, the cash-flow-to-equity method identifies the cash flows available to stockholders and finds their present value. This present value is the total equity value, which when divided by the number of shares outstanding yields the projected price per share. In what follows, assume that r_S is the required rate of return for equity holders (see entries for *Capital Asset Pricing Model* and *Cost of Capital* for a discussion of the required rate of return).

Cash flow to equity is defined in various ways. The simplest is to define cash flow to equity as the dividends the company pays out. Under this definition, the value of the stock is given by the discounted dividend model:

$$\text{Price} = \sum_{t=1}^{\infty} \frac{D_t}{(1+r_s)^t}$$

where the D_t equals the expected dividends each year forever. A simplification of this model is to assume that dividends will grow at a rate $g < rS$. We don't show the modification here, but if you assume that dividends grow at a constant rate, g, then the preceding expression simplifies considerably:

$$\text{Price} = \frac{D_1}{r_s - g} = \frac{D_0(1+g)}{r_s - g}$$

where D_0 is the most recent annual dividend. This is called the "constant growth rate dividend model" or just the "constant growth model."

Although dividends are certainly the cash flows the corporation pays out to its shareholders, many companies don't pay dividends, and even for those that do, their individual divisions don't pay separate dividends, so the formulas just given have only limited use. And even for companies that do pay dividends, the payments may be larger or smaller than what the company can sustain in the long run, so the price obtained using the dividend growth formula is a good estimate of the value of a business only under some very limited circumstances.

A more robust measure of the cash flow to equity takes into account that to replace equipment or grow, firms must reinvest some of their earnings, and that the amount that must be reinvested is not really available to be paid out to shareholders. It also takes into account that not all firms pay dividends. Cash flow to equity, or CFE, is computed as follows:

$$CFE = \text{net income} - \text{required net investment in assets} - \text{required dividends on preferred stock}$$

Required net investment in assets is the investment in assets required to support sales growth but doesn't include investment in such things as marketable securities or accumulation of cash. This investment is net of depreciation and can also be calculated as required gross investment in assets minus depreciation that was charged during the year.

Of course, this greater precision comes at a cost; the analyst must actually make projections of required net investment in assets (the dividends on preferred stock are set contractually, so they are easy to calculate). However, an analyst who is serious about evaluating a business will almost certainly learn enough about that business to make such projections—at least over a five-year period. Given these projections, the equity value can be calculated as

$$\text{Price} = \sum_{t=1}^{\infty} \frac{CFE_t}{(1 + r_s)^t}$$

And just as with the dividend growth model, if we assume that CFE grows at a constant rate this can be simplified to

$$\text{Price} = \frac{CFE_1}{r_s - g}$$

In practice, analysts make specific projections for as many years as they feel they have good information, and then assume constant growth after the period of explicit projections. So if there are N years worth of specific projections the combination of the two valuation formulas becomes

$$\text{Price} = \sum_{t=1}^{N} \frac{CFE_t}{(1 + r_s)^t} + \left(\frac{1}{(1 + r_s)^N} \right) \left(\frac{CFE_{N+1}}{r_s - g} \right)$$

THE CORPORATE VALUATION MODEL

Another commonly used valuation technique is the corporate valuation model. In this model the total cash flows generated from the firm's operations are discounted at the company's aggregate cost of capital (see entry for *Cost of Capital*). The difference between this method and the cash-flow-to-equity method is that (a) the total after-tax cash flows, including interest payments, rather than the cash flows to equity, are used, (b) the aggregate cost of capital, rather than the cost of equity, is used as the discount rate,

and (c) the values of debt, any preferred stock, and nonoperating assets are accounted for.

The best way to understand how the corporate valuation model works is to think of the firm as consisting of two separate pieces: operations and nonoperating assets. Operations are what the firm does on a day-to-day basis, such as producing and selling its products. Nonoperating assets are things the firm owns but doesn't use in operations, marketable securities and equity investments in other firms. The sum of the value of operations and the values of the nonoperating assets is the total value of the firm. Several constituencies own this total value. Of course, the firm has stockholders, but the firm may also have bondholders or bankers who have a claim on the assets, as well as preferred stockholders. This gives us two different ways of partitioning the total value of the firm:

Total Value of Firm	Total Value of Firm
Value of operations	Value of equity
+ Value of nonoperating assets	+ Value of debt
	+ Value of other financing securities

If we are interested in valuing the equity in the firm, then we calculate

Value of operations

+ value of nonoperating assets

− value of debt

− value of other financing securities

= value of equity

Many times the value of the nonoperating assets is easy to determine—if they are marketable securities, then it is just the market value of those securities. At other times, such as in the case of equity interest in nontraded companies, the determination is more difficult, and a separate valuation must be done. And the same goes for other financing securities: If preferred stock is outstanding, then its value is the market value. The value of debt is usually easy to approximate; unless the firm's riskiness has changed, or interest rates have moved a great deal since the debt was issued, then the value of debt is close to its book value. That leaves only the value of operations to estimate.

The value of operations is the present value of all the free cash flows (FCFs), where the free cash flow in a given year is the sum of all the after-tax cash flows available to all the various investors after taking into account any required reinvestment in the company. For an uncomplicated company, FCF can be approximated by this equation:

EBIT $(1 - T)$

– required net investment in operating assets

= *FCF*

where *EBIT* is earnings before interest and taxes and *T* is the company's tax rate.

Once an analyst has projected free cash flows for *N* years, the value of operations is determined like the cash-flow-to-equity method:

$$\text{Value of operations} = \sum_{t=1}^{N} \frac{FCF_t}{(1 + r_{\text{corporate}})^t} + \left(\frac{1}{(1 + r_{\text{corporate}})^N} \right) \left(\frac{FCF_{N+1}}{r_{\text{corporate}} - g} \right)$$

See the *Cost of Capital* entry for a discussion of how to calculate the aggregate cost of capital, $r_{\text{corporate}}$, which is also known as the weighted average cost of capital. The value of the equity is then calculated as shown here.

—Phillip R. Daves

See also Cost of Capital

FURTHER READING

Brigham, E. F., & Daves, P. R. (2002). *Intermediate financial management* (7th ed.). Mason, OH: South-Western.

BUYER BEHAVIOR

See Customers' Desired Purposes or Goals

CANADIAN HEALTH CARE SYSTEM

The Canadian health care system is run by the government and provides all citizens of Canada with universal health care coverage and hence access to all available health care services. By definition, no one is medically uninsured in Canada. As opposed to all other industrialized nations, Canadians are not permitted to purchase private health care insurance. In contrast, health care services in the United States are paid for by either employer-based health care plans, or, in the case of the elderly and financially distressed, by Medicare and Medicaid. Hence, in the United States, many people are uninsured who are unemployed and not elderly, disabled, or poor. This is a growing and unresolved problem in the United States.

THE DEVELOPMENT AND EVOLUTION OF THE CANADIAN HEALTH CARE SYSTEM

In 1957 the House of Commons created legislation that provided funding to any province that administered and helped to finance universal hospital insurance. In 1968, medical insurance was added to this. By 1971, all 10 Canadian provinces were participating in the federally funded program in which the federal government paid half of the province's costs of health care. By 1984, via the Canada Health Act, physicians were forbidden to charge a fee that exceeded the provincial benefit schedule. The Canada Health Act, however, does not provide for universal drug coverage or nursing home care. Drug coverage is provided to the elderly and poor. Some home health services are covered.

Over the last two decades, the proportion of health care costs underwritten by the Canadian federal government has declined, with a greater percentage of the burden of these costs being shouldered by the provincial governments. By 1997, only 23% of health care expenditures were covered by the federal government. These budget cuts, on the part of the federal government, were undertaken to reduce medical costs and to mitigate the growth of Canada's rather sizable deficit spending.

Through the Canada Health and Social Transfer, federal subsidies for provincial health care, education, and social programs were bundled, to allow the provinces to set their own priorities. This further reduced funds available for health care services.

DETERIORATION OF THE CANADIAN SYSTEM

As a result of the decrement in available funds to support Canadian health care services, there has been a dramatic decrease in the ability of the Canadian health care system to meet the demand for services. This has led to long waiting times for access to diagnostic tests, surgery, and other tests and treatments. Moreover, enrollment in Canadian medical schools declined and hospitals merged or closed, further decreasing the number of available hospital beds. Purchases of expensive capital equipment such as lithotriptors and magnetic resonance imaging (MRI) machines were curtailed.

FUTURE DIRECTIONS

The Canadian public as well as Canadian health care providers are quite concerned about the lack of access to care and to the latest health care technology. Nevertheless, continuing the current, publicly funded system is preferred to implementing either private insurance for low-risk patients, or a multitiered system.

—Darren S. Kaufman

FURTHER READING

Inglehart, J. (2000). Revisiting the Canadian health care system. *New England Journal of Medicine, 342,* 2007–2012.

CAPACITY AND CAPACITY UTILIZATION

Capacity is the maximum amount that can be produced in a given period under normal conditions.

Capacity may be stated in terms of output units or input units. For example, the capacity of a clinic may be expressed as the maximum number of patients that can be seen per day, whereas the capacity of a hospital may be stated as the total number of beds. Most often, capacity is expressed as a rate per time period.

Although the term *capacity* implies a constraint on the amount that can be produced, the notion of capacity is quite flexible and is affected by a number of factors in both the long term and short term. Obviously, capacity can be increased in the long term through capital improvements and increased staffing. These investments may result in expanded physical facilities that provide more hospital beds, improved technology that allows patients to be treated faster, an expanded workforce to better handle patient loads, and better information that reduces patient waiting times. Major investments of this type must be carefully coordinated, because expanded physical facilities without appropriate increases in staffing levels, or vice versa, may not be effective in increasing capacity.

It may not be as obvious that capacity can also be altered in the short term. Temporary staffing, overtime, and subcontracting are ways to increase capacity in the short term. Temporary additions to the staff or overtime may be used to increase capacity in unusual situations involving, for example, large-scale vaccination programs. Subcontracting may involve sending lab specimens to an external laboratory for testing rather than using hospital facilities. In this manner, capacity is increased in the short term to provide the needed customer service, although extra cost may be involved.

Efficiency of the workforce also plays a role in determining the capacity of a system. With a fixed level of equipment/facilities and personnel, training and education may play an important role in increasing capacity through more efficient operations.

Capacity utilization is an important measure that tells us what percentage of the available capacity is actually being used. Capacity utilization should reflect conscious decisions made by management to forecast demand and provide the necessary resources.

The target or planned level of capacity utilization is a strategic decision. A hospital administrator would probably like to see a high level of capacity utilization with respect to the number of beds in the hospital. A high projected use level may be necessary to justify the purchase of a major piece of diagnostic equipment. A doctor's office may call patients a day in advance to remind them of their appointment, so that a high level of capacity utilization can be maintained. In many cases, however, the planned level of capacity utilization should allow for a buffer to handle surges in demand. A prime example is the hospital emergency room, where the need to maintain a state of readiness necessarily results in low average capacity utilization. In planning for the target level of capacity utilization, the cost of not being able to provide service (which could be catastrophic in the emergency room) must be weighed against the cost of idle capacity.

—R. Lawrence LaForge

FURTHER READING

Blackstone, J. H., Jr. (1989). *Capacity management.* Cincinnati, OH: South-Western.

Haksever, C., Render, B., Russell, R. S., & Murdick, R. G. (2000). *Service management and operations* (2nd ed.). Upper Saddle River, NJ: Prentice Hall.

CAPITAL ASSET PRICING MODEL

The capital asset pricing model, developed by William F. Sharpe and John Lintner in the middle 1960s, is the theoretical relationship between the required rate of return on an investment and the investment's risk.

The required rate of return on an investment is the rate of return that investors require to compensate them for the risk of undertaking the investment. For example, investing in one-year Treasury Bills is a very safe investment. In modern times the U.S. Treasury has never defaulted on an interest or principal payment, and investment in U.S. Treasury instruments is for all intents and purposes risk free. But because there is very little risk, the rate of return is also very low: Currently, one-year Treasury Bill rates are on the order of 1.5% to 2.0%. In contrast, investing in common stock is very risky, and investors expect rates of return in excess of 10% per year to compensate them for bearing this risk.

The capital asset pricing model specifies that the expected (or required) rate of return, ER_S, on an investment in security S is equal to

$$ER_S = R_f + \beta_S (ER_M - R_f)$$

where R_f is the risk-free rate, ER_M is the expected rate of return on the market portfolio, and β_S is the security's beta.

Of the three variables on the right-hand side of the equation, only the risk-free rate is easy to estimate. Practitioners use the yield on a long-term (20 to 30 years) Treasury bond as the risk-free rate. This rate can be found in the *Wall Street Journal* and in a variety of online sources.

The expected return on the market portfolio is the most difficult to estimate. First, in theory the market portfolio should consist of all investment assets. In practice we use the S&P 500 (Standard & Poor 500), which is just an approximation. Second, ER_M is supposed to be what investors expect, at the current time, they will earn in the future on an investment in the market portfolio. Behavioral economists have found this expectation changes over time, with inflation, with the state of the economy, and for other reasons. In particular, it is *not* generally equal to the rate of return that happened to occur on the market portfolio over some past time period. Instead, financial economists try to estimate the quantity in parentheses, $ER_M - R_f$, also called the *market risk premium*, which is thought to be more stable and is usually in the 4% to 6% range.

The firm's beta, β_S, is supposed to be a measure of how the stock's performance is expected to correlate with the market's performance. In practice, financial practitioners assume that β is stable and estimate it from historical stock returns and market returns as

$$\beta = \frac{\sigma_S \rho_{S,M}}{\sigma_M}$$

where σ_S is the standard deviation of the stock's returns, σ_M is the standard deviation of the market's returns, and $\rho_{S,M}$ is the correlation coefficient between the stock's returns and the market's returns.

So, for example, consider the following information for a company:

$$\sigma_S = 0.60$$

$$\sigma_M = 0.35$$

$$R_f = 0.06 = 6\%$$

$$\rho_{S,M} = 0.80$$

$$ER_M - R_f = 5.5\%$$

Then $\beta = [(0.60)(0.80)] \div (0.35) = 1.37$ and the stock's required rate of return is $r_S = 6\% + (1.37)(5.5\%) = 13.535\%$. Investors should expect to receive an annual return of 13.5% on this stock.

—Phillip R. Daves

FURTHER READING

Brigham, E. F., & Daves, P. R. (2002). *Intermediate financial management* (7th ed.). Mason, OH: South-Western.

CAPITAL FINANCING

See Capital Structure

CAPITAL INVESTMENT

See Long-Term Investments

CAPITAL STRUCTURE

See Balance Sheet

CAPITALIZATION RATIOS

See Ratio Analysis

CAPITATION/CAPITATED HEALTH PLANS

See Health Insurance, Health Maintenance Organizations (HMOs)

CARE MANAGEMENT

Care management is "a comprehensive systems approach to medical care that combines the latest medical knowledge on the best clinical methods, population-based outcomes measurement and evaluation, and advanced practice tools" (Juhn, Solomon, & Pettay, 1998). From this definition, several elements of effective care management can be inferred:

- *Comprehensiveness.* The disease or preventive care options for a clinical condition are well characterized and supported by scientific evidence or, at least, consensus among experts in the disease entity. This level of understanding requires literature reviews and meetings of health care practitioners to identify best practices in diagnosis and treatment, idealized pathways of care and outcomes, and objective performance measures and indicators.

- *Risk stratification.* Target populations with the disease or risk factor can be identified using available data sources, including demographic information, diagnosis categories, resource utilization, costs, and epidemiological markers. The database must be sufficiently robust to provide methods of stratifying the population by some criteria, for example age, laboratory parameters, diagnosis codes, or procedure codes.

- *Focus on improvement or cure.* Interventions should not just focus on caring for expensive aspects of patient care; they also must concentrate resources on preventive and palliative modalities that reduce the disease burden of the population. Individuals in the population in the early stages of the disease process or who are at risk for developing the clinical condition should receive appropriate interventions, such as education or early disease detection testing kits, to help prevent or detect the disease. Patients in the intermediate or advanced stages of a clinical condition should be managed using protocols and pathways that allow customization of the care within guidelines determined by experts and literature evidence.

- *Resource allocation to preventive services.* Education and empowerment of individuals with a clinical problem leads to better outcomes, in general (Morgan, 1998). In addition to the improved clinical outcomes, patients often are able to reduce the cost of care through better preventive management, reducing the net cost of investments in preventive modalities.

- *Continuity of care.* People with chronic medical illnesses, such as AIDS or behavioral disorders, need the support of practitioners, case managers, and other health professionals to ensure that the treatment regimens are followed precisely. Frequently, a care manager assumes responsibility for these coordination and compliance processes, establishing close relationships with patients so that the rapport can translate into better clinical care and support services. Treatment and diagnostic modalities can often be uncomfortable to endure or difficult to implement in daily life, and the relationship established with a care manager can provide the impetus for an individual to comply, despite the inconvenience or discomfort. In addition, as a care manager becomes more familiar with a patient, subtle indications of changes in the patient's condition may be detected early enough to reduce complications and prevent death.

- *Robust data management.* Insurance data management systems and office billing systems do not usually contain enough data for care management, although they may be used for analyzing populations and identifying the target population. Clinical records from the hospital and physician's office also do not supply enough information to perform care management, because of inconsistent data recording and legibility issues. To manage care effectively and particularly to reduce the disease burden in populations at risk, a more robust source of clinical information is required. Systems such as electronic medical records, telemedicine (see entry), and Internet communications strategies make care management programs substantially more effective.

Care management companies that specialize in a specific disease entity, such as AIDS, or in behavioral health problems have advanced data management systems that record, store, and analyze clinical data in the same manner as a computerized patient record. Tracking and monitoring the appropriate parameters of an individual's health to help an individual maintain or improve his health status requires current and accurate data, and population health management requires detecting trends in health and disease burden before they become costly.

Care management programs have been implemented in a number of settings. Managed care organizations adopted this approach when the traditional utilization management method of controlling costs met with increasing resistance from providers and the public. Traditional managed care methods required physicians and other health professionals to request permission to perform particular high-cost diagnostic and therapeutic procedures, usually with appeals to insurance company nurses using protocols developed by companies that create guidelines by consensus. When this process became onerous to practitioners and patients in the late 1990s, managed care organizations began adopting a care management approach and attempted to collaborate with physicians to better care for patients. Using this approach, the managed care nursing staff may use the same guidelines, but the nurse becomes a partner with the physician, suggesting alternative approaches and facilitating care for the patient through reminder systems and management of referrals. The effect of this change in approach is still being evaluated.

Other organizations have adopted the care management approach. Hospitals and providers, such as physician groups, use the care management model to segment the population into groups for interventions. Thus a population might be stratified into four categories:

- Patients with the disease in late stages of clinical manifestations

- Patients with the disease in middle stages of clinical manifestations
- Patients with the disease with mild clinical manifestations
- People at risk for the clinical condition

Each of these categories is managed differently. People with the most severe manifestations may require intensive case management to ensure they receive medications, complete referral appointments, have necessary procedures performed, and carry out important monitoring tests (such as blood sugar checks for diabetics) that will slow or stop further deterioration. On the other end of the spectrum, people at risk for the clinical condition may be targeted for education and monitoring to reduce the possibility of developing the symptoms or complications of the condition. By using tools specific for each of the categories of care, patients can receive better quality care, and the cost of care may be reduced by diminishing the disease burden of the population.

Care management can improve the quality of care by ensuring access to needed services and a focus on prevention. Automating the clinical health record helps make this approach even more effective, by improving the ability to identify patients at risk, evaluating care received by patients, anticipating medical needs and communicating effectively with patients, performing population-based studies on patterns of care to identify best practices, and maintaining a collaborative approach to care among patient, physician, and payer. The methods used in care management are appropriate for providers and payers, and as an approach to supervising and providing health care, care management holds great promise.

—Donald E. Lighter

FURTHER READING

Forman, S., & Kelliher, M. (1999). *Status One: Breakthroughs in high risk population health management.* San Francisco: Jossey-Bass.

Institute of Medicine. (Ed.). (2001). *Crossing the quality chasm: A new health system for the 21st century.* Washington, DC: National Academy Press.

Juhn, P., Solomon, N., & Pettay, H. www.kpnw.org/permjournal/pring98pj/cmi.html

Lighter, D., & Fair, D. (2000). *Principles and methods of quality management in health care.* Gaithersburg, MD: Aspen.

Morgan, A. I. (1998, September–October). Evaluating the economic impact of member attitudes on managed care disease management programs. *Disease Management, 1*(5), 247–254.

Todd, W., & Nash, D. (Eds.). (2001). *Disease management: A systems approach to improving patient outcomes.* San Francisco: Jossey-Bass.

Weed, R. (1998). *Life care planning and case management handbook.* Boca Raton, FL: CRC Press.

www.ahrq.gov/clinic/cpgsix.htm

CARE MAPS

See Clinical Pathways (Care Maps ™ or Critical Paths)

CARVE-OUTS

A "carve-out" refers to health care benefits that are paid for or delivered differently from the remainder of services covered under an insurance policy or managed care contract. This may occur in two general ways. First, certain services covered under a policy may be delivered or financed using managed care methods, whereas the remainder of services are delivered and financed under conventional indemnity model systems. For example, an indemnity policy may carve out behavioral health benefits to be managed by a behavioral health organization using capitated payments to providers and strict use management controls, whereas all other services are provided under a conventional fee-for-service model.

Second, all services may be delivered using a managed care model. However, certain services may be carved out from the basket of services that a provider is obligated to deliver under its contract. Those carved-out services are then provided under a separate financial agreement and, commonly, by a different delivery system. Payment for these carved-out services is provided above and beyond the capitation rate that covers all other services that are included in the managed care contract. For example, prescription drug services may be carved out from a comprehensive managed care contract. A provider group may receive a capitation-based contract to provide all services except prescription drugs to members. Prescription drugs may then be provided though a separate organization under a separate financial arrangement, such as direct reimbursement for costs. The most common services that are carved out include behavioral health services, prescription drugs, catastrophic care, and transplantation.

Thus carve-outs serve to separate the health insurance function into categories by disease or service groups, with each group provided under a separate service or contractual arrangement. Carve-outs have several potential advantages. They permit employers, for example, to introduce managed care in a limited way without incurring the backlash against more comprehensive managed care plans. Carve-outs to highly specialized groups may enhance quality of care by promoting care by providers and delivery systems specifically oriented to certain conditions or services. In addition, carve-outs may protect against underutilization of specialized services by separating funds for these services from the general pool available for all care, and they may reduce the incentive for managed care plans to avoid enrollment of patients with certain conditions that, in the absence of a carve-out, would result in above-average expenditures.

The major objective is, however, to reduce costs of care. In the case of predominantly indemnity coverage, carving out selected services for a managed care approach may reduce costs through utilization review, discount contracting, and so on. This approach is particularly valuable for services such as behavioral health that are less well defined than other services and for pharmaceutical drugs in which use controls are highly specialized. In comprehensive managed care models, carving out selected services allows rigorous use control and, possibly, quality management, by highly specialized service delivery and finance systems. Carve-outs have been shown to reduce the intensity of both outpatient and, particularly, inpatient behavioral health services.

Substantial disadvantages also exist. Carving out particular services from the remaining services leads to fragmentation of care and may, paradoxically, increase overall costs. For example, carving out behavioral health services from physical health care inhibits or precludes the management of mild and common behavioral health conditions such as depression by primary care providers and interrupts continuity and integration of care services. This may lead to reduced or duplication of services. Finally, by establishing administrative boundaries between the responsibilities of different groups, carve-outs create conditions conducive to cost shifting. For example, if pharmaceuticals are carved out, a capitated provider is more likely to opt for drug therapy for a condition that may also be treated by nonpharmacologic means. Carve-outs may also increase expenses by adding substantial administrative costs.

—David M. Mirvis

See also Managed Care

FURTHER READING

Ma, C. A., & McGuire, T. G. (1998). Costs and incentives in a behavioral health carve-out. *Health Affairs, 17*(2), 53–69.

CASE MANAGEMENT

As health care has become more complex, the need for an organized approach to providing care has become mandatory. Individuals with chronic health disorders must often access a variety of health services, diagnostic procedures, and therapies that require coordination to ensure that appropriate services are provided at appropriate times. This need for coordination becomes even more important in the current era of health care, because services that are traditionally defined as "health care," that is, are provided by a physician or in the hospital, now interface with numerous social services, such as counseling, exercise programs, and transportation services. The goal of case management involves creating a support structure to ensure that patients receive appropriate services at the appropriate time with an expected outcome.

As defined by the Case Management Society of America, "Case management is a collaborative process which assesses, plans, implements, coordinates, monitors and evaluates options and services to meet an individual's health needs through communication and available resources to promote quality cost-effective outcomes" (www.casemanagement.com/, July 2002). Case management is an integral part of care management, an approach to health care that takes into account the various stages of a disease process or clinical condition and musters the health care system to provide appropriate resources throughout the continuum of the condition. Case management usually is applied to the most seriously ill people first, because those are the most likely to need health care services and coordination of care to ensure the best outcomes. For these types of patients, a case manager performs a number of functions:

- Thoroughly understanding the patient, the diagnosis, stage of illness, and the environment in which the patient lives, including local medical and social services, as well as family resources
- Gathering appropriate background and resource information regarding the best methods of treating the patient's illness at each stage
- Understanding the treatment regimen prescribed by attending and consulting physicians in the context of availability of resources in the patient's environment
- Working with the patient, family members, and health care providers to formulate an acceptable and appropriate plan for the patient's care
- Implementing processes to assure that the patient receives the required care, performs the necessary monitoring procedures, and undergoes diagnostic testing and therapeutic procedures at the scheduled times
- Monitor care and communicate with providers, family members, and the patient in an effective and timely manner
- Monitor the financial and insurance issues in the patient's care to ensure adequate financial resources for services and procedures

The attention to detail required for this process generally requires a health care professional dedicated to managing the process of care, and in most cases, nursing professionals serve as case managers. Depending on the clinical condition, the nursing professional can be a registered nurse, but sometimes an advanced practice nurse's expertise is required. The case manager must have a good grasp of the clinical condition or disease entity, as well as of the many variations that may occur in the clinical course. Case managers become intimately familiar with health conditions in ways that are unique to their position in the health care management team.

Case management relies heavily on teamwork concepts, because coordinating care among many health care providers requires collaboration with providers at many levels in the system. Effective case management can necessitate educating patients, families, and providers on the exigencies of the health care system. For example, patients and families need to understand the nature of the disease process, as well as what to expect at each stage of the illness and what their responsibilities are for following the diagnostic and treatment plans outlined by providers. Health care providers, in contrast, often need to increase their understanding of the financial constraints imposed by the patient's health insurance and financial situation, so that the treatment program can be modified to fit the patient's circumstances. The case manager often acts as the resource person for this information, particularly if the patient's care is divided among a number of different providers. The advent of the World Wide Web and electronic modes of communication, such as e-mail and telemedicine, has revolutionized the methods by which case managers carry out their work.

The complexity of many chronic clinical conditions, such as diabetes, asthma, and congestive heart failure, has led to the formation of companies that specialize in case management for specific diseases. These companies create a system of dealing with a particular disease and become familiar with resources available in a number of locales so they can effectively manage patients in disparate communities, with different health care providers and resource environments. Case managers in these companies are often nursing professionals who become familiar with a few communities so they can effectively work with providers, families, and patients. An effective computerized medical record and tracking system forms the cornerstone of these organizations to evaluate treatment regimens, compare diagnostic and therapeutic outcomes to benchmark data, trigger reminders for case managers and patients regarding needed care, and manage the patient's care within budgetary limits and available financial resources.

In addition to these specialized companies, many health insurance plans create their own case management programs to address those clinical conditions of significance to the health plan, either in terms of cost, frequency, or risk. The health plan usually structures the case management program much like the case management companies, with a physician manager to direct the medical operations, a business-oriented professional to assess financial implications, and staff members (typically registered nurses) with interest and expertise in the management of the disease entity. Both specialty companies and health insurance plans require similar resources:

- Computerized patient record system
- Tracking system for patient appointments for diagnosis and therapy
- Analysis systems for evaluating patterns of care
- Benchmarking system for evaluating and recommending care options (often expressed as clinical pathways)
- Effective communications tools to acquire patient data, interact with patients and providers, and educate everyone involved in the process of care
- Financial assessment systems to evaluate the cost of care in monetary and resource use terms
- Relationships with health care providers to ensure seamless care for the patient
- Financial resources and processes to maintain the systems in the highest state of performance

Case management services are offered in a number of other settings as well. In addition to specialty organizations and insurance companies, other organizations that implement case management services include health departments, hospitals, medical groups, specialty physician groups, and home health agencies. Each of these organizations may have a slightly different approach to performing case management, because each has specific skills and services to offer. However, to be successful every case management program must address all the patient's needs.

A number of organizations have arisen to promote the profession of case management, including the following:

- *American Academy of Case Management* (www. aihcp.org). Provides educational programs and certification testing.
- *American Board of Quality Assurance and Utilization Review Physicians* (www.abqaurp.org). Originally started to certify physicians in medical management reviews, this organization has added a case management educational and certification program.
- *Case Management Society of America* (www. cmsa.org). This group offers educational programs and a membership program for case managers and also has a division that promotes case management education internationally.

In addition, a few university nurse education programs offer specialized training curricula leading to certificates in case management for graduates.

The evidence for the efficacy of case management is somewhat mixed. Rosen and Teesson found that evidence-based case management for psychiatric clients in the United Kingdom and Australia was an effective method of management, but also discovered that programs could be subject to bias that may influence the quality of the program. Holloway and Carson reviewed the literature with regard to case management in psychiatry and found little evidence validating the approach, but a few instances of the approach seemed promising. Rasmussen and associates evaluated the approaches used for managing pediatric respiratory illnesses in developing countries and found that case management was one of the most effective tools for ensuring adherence to medication regimens and follow-up visits. However, when applied to public health nursing support of adolescent mothers, the case management approach adopted by a public health department led to equivocal improvement in parenting competence, social support, and self-esteem in teen mothers case managed by public health nurses. The authors of the study were guarded in their analysis, however, because the failure to achieve significant gains in the outcome measures could be attributed to the intervention approach, rather than to the use of case managers. As with many other types of health care services, the caseload of a case manager can influence performance.

The other aspect of efficacy, namely cost efficiency, has not been well studied or reported in the literature. Assessing the cost effectiveness of any intervention such as case management requires an evaluation of the benefits and costs of the program. Benefits can be defined in several ways: for example, by cost savings realized by avoiding unnecessary or duplicative tests, by decreases in hospitalization rates caused by the work of a case worker, or by economies of scale caused by more effective pharmaceutical management in groups of people with the same clinical condition. Costs usually entail the actual costs of care, cost of staff and overhead associated with providing case management, and capital expenditures such as computer systems and software. Additional benefits are measured by improved patient function and a greater number of quality-adjusted life years for patients with chronic conditions. Because case management is applied in so many different clinical situations, these studies may demonstrate varying value, but the information would be highly beneficial.

In summary, case management is an approach to organizing, monitoring, and directing the care of an individual or population with a specific clinical condition. Because of the nature of the services provided by case managers, these professionals generally have clinical experience, particularly in the specific disease entity under management. Case management has the potential for reducing cost of services through greater application of preventive care to reduce or delay onset of complications caused by progression of the clinical condition. In addition, individuals with a clinical problem can benefit from a case management program through improved adherence to treatment regimens, follow-up with physicians and other health providers, and closer monitoring of health parameters that indicate a need for revision of a care plan. Case managers depend heavily on information, and specialized computer programs with the ability to store clinical data, track laboratory and imaging studies, and monitor drug regimens provide case managers with the infrastructure necessary to effectively supervise health care services. As care management is adopted more extensively throughout the health care delivery system, case management can be expected to grow as well.

REFERENCES

Holloway, F., & Carson, J. (2001, Autumn). Case management: An update. *International Journal of Social Psychiatry, 47*(3), 21–31.

Rasmussen, Z., Pio, A., & Enarson, P. (2000, September). Case management of childhood pneumonia in developing countries: Recent relevant research and current initiatives. *International Journal of Tuberculosis and Lung Disease, 4*(9), 807–826.

Rosen, A., & Teesson, M. (2002, December). Does case management work? The evidence and the abuse of evidence-based medicine. *Australian and New Zealand Journal of Psychiatry, 35*(6), 731–746.

Young, A. S., Grusky, O., Sullivan, G., Webster, C. M., & Podus, D. (1998, September). The effect of provider characteristics on case management activities. *Administrative Policy in Mental Health, 26*(1), 21–32.

—Donald E. Lighter

FURTHER READING

www.aihcp.org

www.abqaurp.org

www.cmsa.org

Powell, S. (Ed.), & Ignatavicius, D. (2001). *CMSA core curriculum for case management.* Philadelphia: Lippincott, Williams, & Wilkins.

Siefker, J., Garrett, M., & Van Genderen, A. (1998). *Fundamentals of case management: Guidelines for practicing case managers.* St. Louis, MO: Mosby-Year Book.

Weed, R. (1998). *Life care planning and case management handbook.* Boca Raton, FL: CRC Press.

CASE MIX

According to Center for Medicare and Medicaid Services (CMS), a hospital's case mix index represents the average diagnosis-related group (DRG) relative weight for that hospital. It is calculated by summing the DRG weights and dividing by the number of discharges. The CMS assigns relative weights to each DRG and reviews them every year. States that have their own DRG scheme (such as New York) use different weights from those assigned by CMS. When there is a mix of Medicare and non-Medicare discharges, the case mix is a weighted average of the respective weights.

Basically, the case mix is an attempt to express the acuity of the patient population against costs for the services. The prospective payment rates, based on DRGs, have been established as a basis of the Medicare hospital reimbursement system. This patient classification system (DRG) better identifies the types of patients treated and the costs associated by the hospital. Since 1983 when DRGs and the prospective payment system were introduced, there have been many revisions. Initially, DRGs were meant to include only the elderly but today they include newborn and pediatric populations. Hospitals use this classification system (case mix index) to measure the effectiveness of the care management of care with costs and measurement from year to year, against the hospitals themselves.

—Edna Lee Kucera

FURTHER READING

http://cms.hhs.govwww.ipro.org
www.cms.gov

CASE RATE REIMBURSEMENT

Case rate reimbursement is a payment to the provider based on a preagreed fee that includes all aspects of care regardless of additional various costs incurred for the care. These global fees are commonly used in surgical cases. For example, a case rate may include preoperative care and one or two postsurgical visits. Although this is not an actual financial "risk" to the provider, the costs for the entire spectrum of care for some cases may be higher than what the provider gets paid. Efficiency and coordination of care are essential to make these payments beneficial for both the payer and the provider.

The advent of extensive cardiac surgical advances may illustrate the issue.

The managed care company contracts with a provider for coronary artery bypass graft (CABG) at $25,000 per case. The lives covered in the managed care contract would be included as potential cases. The health range in this population would vary greatly from very frail with many health care problems, to hearty with few or no health care problems. Two individuals come to the hospital, both for the CABG surgical procedure. One is a 40-year-old man with no prior medical history except high cholesterol. The other is a 70-year-old man with a history of diabetes, hypertension, and two myocardial infarcts (MIs). It is not too hard to imagine that the younger patient may consume fewer resources than the older patient with the more extensive medical history. The provider is paid the same for both patients, but one uses more resources and time for the same surgery.

The managed care companies and the providers (physicians and hospitals) contract the rates for this reimbursement scheme to benefit all parties. The costs of care have been lowered by hospitals by assuring that the presurgical testing is completed with a standard set of laboratory tests, EKGs, and radiologic services. Standard sets of orders and services are extremely important in this environment to establish an efficient and timely care pattern. Clinical pathways may be used to establish medically sound and cost-conserving services.

Clinical pathways are created by the health care teams, including the physicians and nursing staff as well as other health care providers involved in the care of the specific procedure or disease in question. The team looks at present practice at the hospital and does a literature search to identify the best practices in other institutions. They then generate the pathway, delineating what the care will be for each step or day of care. Order sets with all the appropriate treatments in the correct sequences are completed. After training and "buy-in" from the remaining team members, the clinical pathway is ready for use. It is important to recognize that a physician champion must verbalize to the physicians the need for using the pathway. In addition, the chairs of each of the medical departments must endorse the clinical pathway for the selected population. Data from experience with the pathway constitute important feedback to the physicians and teams, to measure positive outcomes and assess for any changes that may be needed. Good information support systems and administrative commitment to the clinical pathways assure decreased costs and standardized, predictable quality, making case rate reimbursement a viable and reasonable payment method.

—Edna Lee Kucera

FURTHER READING

www.cms.orgwww.UHC.com

CASE REPORT FORM (CRF)

Case report forms (CRFs) are the official documentation of a clinical trial. The primary purpose of CRFs is to collect research data, whereas the primary purpose of source documents is to care for study subjects from a clinical perspective. The study researchers design these documents to collect only the data necessary to support the research hypothesis. The information in the CRFs provides the basis for the final clinical study report. These data are used in any study-related publications. This information is also necessary for regulatory approval of a new drug.

CRFs must reflect the study protocol exactly. All the information requested in the study protocol must be reflected in these documents. Only information requested in the study protocol is necessary. Unrequested information is not included in the analysis or in the final report. The clinical study protocol specifies what information is to be recorded on the CRF. A clinical research site's standard operating procedures outline the proper methods for completing these forms, review of these forms for accurate transcription from source documents, and the time frame for retaining these forms.

CRFs are the official documentation of the clinical trial for the regulatory authorities, and together with the source documents are closely examined during an audit or inspection.

—Linda M. Cimino

See also Protocol (Involving Human Subjects), Standard Operating Procedures (SOPs)

FURTHER READING

Bohaychuk, W., & Ball, G. (1999). *Conducting GCP-compliant clinical research.* Chichester, UK: Wiley.

Day, S. (1999). *Dictionary for clinical trials.* Chichester, UK: Wiley.

Kolman, J., Meng, P., & Scott, G. (1998). *Good clinical practice—standard operating procedures for clinical researchers.* Chichester, UK: Wiley.

CASH AND CASH EQUIVALENTS

Cash, in its most basic form, is the legal tender amount of currency (and/or coins) valued by a monetary unit, such as the U.S. dollar, is held by an organization (or individual), and can be used to purchase goods and services. Cash consists of all monies immediately available for disbursement without restriction and includes the amount of currency and coins currently on hand, the amounts held by a bank or other financial institution, as well as any undeposited checks or deposits currently in transit to, but not yet posted by, the bank or financial institution.

Within a financial statement, such as a balance sheet or statement of financial position, which is presented in

accordance with generally accepted accounting principles (GAAPs), cash is recorded at its face value and is listed as the very first current asset, because it is considered the most liquid of all assets (the reported value of the asset can be most easily converted into cash on hand and used for the purchase of goods and services). Not all monies held by an organization can be included within the cash line item of a financial statement. For example, amounts held that have had internal or external restrictions placed on them that limit their use would not be presented in a financial statement as cash, because the amounts would not meet the liquidity criteria and might not be used to satisfy current liabilities of the organization. Restrictions that limit the use of cash could come from a designation by the board of directors stating that the monies are to be used strictly for making an upcoming bond payment or even from an outside donor stating that his or her contribution must be used to purchase capital improvements.

In most cases, cash is not reported on its own within a set of GAAP financial statements but is instead combined with other certain highly liquid assets known as *cash equivalents.* These assets are normally various investments and are cash equivalents because of the ease with which they can be converted into physical cash on hand. Financial Accounting Standard No. 95 (www.fasb.org), "Statement of Cash Flows," defines a cash equivalent as a "short-term, highly liquid investment" that will mature within three months or less after being acquired by the organization. Examples of common cash equivalents include monies held in money market accounts, U.S. Treasury obligations, commercial paper, and certificates of deposits that have a maturity date less than three months from the time of their purchase. It is expected that, if needed, these types of investments could be withdrawn, retired, or sold in a timely manner in order to make additional cash available to the organization, which could then be used to meet current operational needs. As with cash, to be included in the cash and cash equivalents line item within a set of financial statements, the potential cash equivalents cannot be restricted in any form that would prevent them from being easily converted to cash on hand and used to purchase goods and services.

The amount presented as cash and cash equivalents can provide the reader of the financial statements with useful information about the organization. Not only does this line item provide a snapshot of the current cash position of the organization at a given point in time, but it can also be used to measure the entity's ability to meet its current obligations and operational needs. The amount of cash and cash equivalents can be used in a number of financial ratios that provide a reader of the financial statements with a benchmark for the organization, measured not only against itself at another point in time but also against other organizations within the same industry or region. The most common ratio using cash and cash equivalents is the "days cash on hand" ratio. This ratio is calculated by dividing the total amount of cash and cash equivalents by the product of the total expenses for the period minus depreciation divided by 365. Once calculated, this ratio tells the user how many days the entity can cover its expenditures given the current amount of cash and cash equivalents.

—Edward Pershing

CASH BASIS OF ACCOUNTING

The cash basis of accounting is one in which revenues are not recognized until cash is received and expenses are not recognized until cash is disbursed. The cash basis of accounting is considered an "other comprehensive basis of accounting" (OCBOA), as that term is used in accounting literature. These bases of accounting are often used when they have a substantial basis of support and may serve as an alternative to the more comprehensive and complex basis of accounting known as *generally accepted accounting principles* (GAAPs). However, use of an alternative basis of accounting, such as the cash basis, must be appropriate in the circumstances.

Under the cash basis of accounting, no effort is made to use the matching accounting principle, which seeks to match revenue in the same accounting period in which the related expense occurs. This matching is typical of the accrual basis of accounting. The accrual basis of accounting recognizes revenue when goods are sold or a service is performed and not when the money is received. Costs are incurred and expenses are recognized in the period in which the revenues they helped produce are recognized. As a result, the accrual basis of accounting more accurately depicts how the entity is performing.

Under the cash basis of accounting, revenue recognition is delayed until cash is collected. Expense is recognized when cash is disbursed. As a result, income or loss for any period is simply the difference between cash disbursed and cash received. Therefore, net income for an entity using the cash basis of accounting can be very deceiving. For example, if an entity receives a large sum of money in the current year to finance a construction project to be completed in the following year, revenue will be overstated in the current year and expenses will be overstated in the succeeding year. Therefore, the cash basis of accounting often does not allow management or outsiders to obtain a realistic view of how the company is performing.

The cash basis of accounting is often used by physicians, as well as by other professionals. Professionals choose to use this type of accounting because professionals provide services, bill their clients, and generally receive their fees in a timely manner. They usually have limited or no inventories. Professionals also usually have limited investments in period assets such as buildings and equipment. Those who do have significant holdings in long-term fixed assets often choose to use the modified cash basis, which differs from the pure cash basis in that long-term assets are accounted for using the accrual basis of accounting. The cash basis of accounting is also used by many smaller business entities, including other small health care providers.

For larger entities where inventories are an important aspect of how revenue is generated, such as merchandisers and manufacturers, the Internal Revenue Service (IRS) does not allow use of the cash basis of accounting for tax purposes. The accrual basis of accounting may be required for those types of entities.

—Edward Pershing

CASH FLOW

See Discounted Cash Flows

CASH MANAGEMENT

See Cash and Cash Equivalents, Cash Basis of Accounting

CENTERS FOR MEDICARE AND MEDICAID SERVICES

The Centers for Medicare and Medicaid Services (CMS), formerly the Health Care Financing Administration (HCFA), is the federal agency responsible for administering Medicare and Medicaid. These programs provide medical and medically related services to 75 million of the nation's low-income children and their families, as well as to the aged, blind, disabled, and medically needy. Another 10 million Medicaid-ineligible and uninsured children receive services through the State Children's Health Insurance Program (SCHIP). CMS spends over $360 billion per year to purchase health care services for these program recipients.

Thomas A. Scully, current Administrator of CMS, oversees program administration conducted in three agency centers that are supported by several offices: the Center for Medicare Management, the Center for Beneficiary Choices, and the Center for Medicaid and State Operations.

Created in 1965, Medicare consists of a hospital insurance program that covers most people 65 years or older, a voluntary supplemental health insurance, and a program to help less poor elderly individuals with out-of-pocket expenses. Medicaid is a joint federal/state entitlement program that pays for medical assistance for certain individuals and families with low incomes and resources; it expanded the existing federal/state income assistance programs.

Management of Medicare and Medicaid was assigned to the U.S. Department of Health, Education, and Welfare, later reorganized into the U.S. Department of Health and Human Services (DHHS). The Social Security Administration (SSA) had responsibility for administering Medicare. The Social and Rehabilitation Service (SRS) had responsibility for Medicaid. HCFA was created in 1977 to consolidate the administration of Medicare and Medicaid under the Department of Health and Welfare, now DHHS.

—Barbara A. Nabrit-Stephens

See also Aid to Families with Dependent Children (AFDC), Medicaid

FURTHER READING

http://cms.hhs.gov/about/history
http://cms.hhs.gov/about/history/Califano2.asp
http://cms.hhs.gov/about/history/pre35.asp
Inglehart, J. K. (2001). The Centers for Medicare and Medicaid Services. *New England Journal of Medicine, 345,* 1920–1924.
www.ssa.gov/regs/ssasect.htm

CHANGING CORPORATE CULTURE

See Culture and Culture Change

CHARISMATIC LEADERSHIP

See Leadership

CHARITY CARE

See Indigent Health Care

CHIEF MEDICAL OFFICER/ MEDICAL DIRECTOR

Chief medical officers or medical directors are physicians who are employed, either full-time or part-time, by an organization involved in delivery of health care services. These doctors' administrative responsibilities usually include oversight to ensure that health care provided by the employing institution is of optimal quality. Other responsibilities can vary based on the employing institution's needs, product, and perspective on the role. The terms *chief medical officer* and *medical director* tend to be used interchangeably.

The idiom *medical director* has been used in the United States at least since the Civil War. Dr. LaFayette Guild in 1862 referred to himself as "Medical Director Army of Northern Virginia" in his reports to the surgeon general of the Confederate Army.

Hospitals and hospital organizations may employ a number of medical directors, each with varying responsibilities and time commitments needed to meet various institutional needs. Large individual hospitals frequently include a medical director, who may also be called *chief medical officer* (CMO) or *vice president for medical affairs* (VPMA), on the facility's senior administrative team. This individual may or may not have formal training in administration. Typically, this is a full-time role filled by someone who has been a member of the hospital's active medical staff in the past and who is employed by the facility to provide the primary interface between the voluntary medical staff and the administration of the institution.

Hospitals, especially larger facilities, may employ part-time medical directors or may appoint medical staff members as medical directors to oversee the care delivery provided in specific service areas. For example, if the hospital includes a psychiatric unit, emergency services, a rehab unit, or a cancer center, a part-time medical director may be employed or appointed for each unit. Medicare conditions of participation require certain units to have medical directors. Typically, these physicians are on the active medical staff and have specialty training and certification in their respective area.

Organizations of physicians that provide direct medical care may function under the direction of a medical director or chief medical officer. In large physician groups, be they multispecialty or single-specialty, the medical director may function more in a CEO-type role and may be responsible for the financial performance of the group as well as for the quality of care provided. Most medical schools include physician faculty members who provide direct patient care. These clinicians are usually organized in a physician faculty organization, which has a medical director as head of the group.

Health insurance companies frequently employ a chief medical officer or medical director to oversee the care of insured individuals. This role is always present in federally qualified HMOs. Physicians in these insurance roles typically oversee the plan's utilization review function in addition to its quality assurance efforts.

A number of governmental and quasi-governmental agencies employ chief medical officers/medical directors. Again, these positions typically are responsible for overseeing the quality of care. For example, regional Emergency Medical Services (EMS) have a physician responsible for assuring the quality of emergency services. Most public health agencies in the United States are led by a physician responsible for the quality of care at public health clinics and for disease surveillance and disease prevention in the geographic region of responsibility. Directors of state public health agencies are designated "state public health directors" rather than as chief medical officers.

Large private employers may also employ medical directors. These individuals frequently are responsible for overseeing the health benefits provided by the employer.

—Frank Houser

FURTHER READING

Stahl, M. J., & Dean, M. J. (Eds.). (1999). *The physician's essential MBA.* Gaithersburg, MD: Aspen.

www.acpe.org

www.amda.com

CHRONIC DISEASE

Disease states or conditions are either acute or chronic. This discussion is about chronic diseases. To be classified as a chronic disease, the condition must have some of the following characteristics: It is nonreversible, leaving the individual with a residual disability, and generally requires specialized treatment for a long period of time. Patient education is important to help the patient cope with the chronic condition. These conditions/diseases do not resolve spontaneously and are rarely cured completely.

The focus on treating chronic diseases, when possible, should be to work on prevention rather than treatment. Treatment is directed at keeping the condition under control rather than at a cure.

Understanding chronic disease and possible treatments is vital to developing a national policy to address the significant financial impact these conditions have on the amount of total health care dollars spent. In 1994, the medical costs of people with chronic diseases accounted for more than 60% ($400 billion annually) of all medical costs. These same conditions accounted for 70% of all deaths in the United States. The dramatic widespread impact of chronic diseases on society is felt because almost 75% of adults older than 65 have more than one chronic illness.

The Centers for Disease Control and Prevention (CDC) has pointed out that chronic diseases affect more than just

health care dollars. These illnesses have financial, personal, and occupational costs that go beyond only health care expenditures. Unfortunately, the societal impact of these long-term conditions is rarely considered.

Examples of chronic diseases are Alzheimer's disease, arthritis, cancer, cardiovascular disease, chronic obstructive pulmonary disease (COPD), diabetes, epilepsy, and osteoporosis. Because of their impact both socially and financially, these conditions have been the major beneficiaries of government financing, in the hope of finding cures for these "incurable" diseases.

Statistics are important in understanding the impact these conditions have on society. Researchers estimate that more than 1.5 million osteoporotic fractures occur each year. The direct health care expenditure for treating these fractures is $14 billion. About 2.3 million Americans require treatment for epilepsy. Diabetes affects 16 million Americans, and the condition also leads to blindness, renal failure, amputations, and heart disease. Diabetes costs society more than $98 billion yearly. Smoking leads to COPD, which causes more than 100,000 deaths yearly. Cardiovascular disease affects 58 million Americans. In 1999, the cost for treating these diseases was $287 billion. The American Cancer Society estimates that 8.4 million Americans have a history of cancer, with 1.2 million cases being diagnosed in 2000. Cancer is the second leading cause of death in the United States, with approximately 550,000 deaths per year. Arthritis affects 43 million Americans, with a cost of $65 billion annually in medical care and lost productivity. Alzheimer's disease affects more than 4 million people, with a cost of $152 billion.

The societal impact of chronic disease on society is monumental.

—Michael R. Marks

See also Disease Management, Epidemiology, Episodes of Care, National Institutes of Health (NIH), Wellness

FURTHER READING

www.cdc.gov

www.nih.gov

CIVIL RIGHTS ACTS OF 1964 AND 1991

The Civil Rights Act of 1964 was enacted by Congress in order to create and clarify additional rights and privileges under federal law for individuals and classes of individuals. Congress enacted the Civil Rights Act of 1991 in response to several Supreme Court decisions that Congress found to have weakened the scope and effectiveness of federal civil rights laws. In addition to clarifying congressional intent with regard to the proper interpretation of the Civil Rights Act of 1964, with the Civil Rights Act of 1991 Congress further established additional remedies available to prevent and deter unlawful discrimination.

In an effort to expand the reach of antidiscrimination laws to the actions of individuals, with the 1964 act Congress used its authority under the U.S. Constitution to regulate interstate commerce. Before the Civil Rights Act of 1964, it was not always clear whether the actions of private business owners and public establishments were covered by constitutional provisions or other civil rights laws. By using its right to regulate interstate commerce, Congress made clear that any establishment involved in providing goods, services, lodging, or any places of entertainment, restaurants, gasoline stations, theaters, or any other service open to customers (and thus involved in commerce or the business of the nation), must provide full and equal enjoyment of such goods and services, regardless of race, color, religion, or national origin. The provision of medical services is included in this expansive view of commerce.

Congress did not apply the Civil Rights Act of 1964 to private clubs, such as country clubs, or establishments that are not open to the public, unless such clubs or establishments make their facilities available to customers and patrons outside of the organization. If a club opens such facilities to the public, then those areas that have been opened must be offered in a nondiscriminatory manner.

A key section of the Civil Rights Act of 1964, known as Title VII, covers employment discrimination. This section of the act is perhaps the greatest support for employment law litigation. Title VII makes it unlawful for an employer to discriminate (on the basis of race, color, religion, sex, or national origin) against applicants or employees in the hiring, firing, or promotion process, or in any terms, conditions, or benefits afforded to employees. Prohibition of sex discrimination makes it illegal to treat employees differently because of pregnancy, childbirth, or related medical conditions. The act also encompasses sexual harassment, making it illegal for employers to engage in or allow sexual harassment at the workplace.

Title VII generally applies to all employers who have 15 or more employees. In addition, Title VII applies to labor unions and employment agencies but does not apply to bona fide private membership clubs.

The Civil Rights Act of 1991 expanded the remedies available to a complaining party to include compensatory and punitive damages in cases of intentional discrimination in employment and the right to a jury trial. The act also includes some statutory limitations on the amounts of such awards, depending on the size of the employer.

—Jennifer L. Richter

See also Employee Rights, Equal Employment Opportunity Commission (EEOC)

FURTHER READING

www.dol.gov
www.eeoc.gov

CLAIM

A formal written notification for monetary damages being sought from the health care provider or entity for an alleged injury. A claim may be made by a patient or by the patient's family, legal guardian, or attorney. Copies of all correspondence and any other available information related to receipt of a claim should be forwarded to the risk manager, medical malpractice insurer, or other designated party as soon as possible. The professional liability malpractice insurance policy generally defines what constitutes a claim that requires reporting. If resolution is not achieved and formal legal action is pursued in the judicial system, the claim then becomes a lawsuit.

—Kathleen Ferrara

FURTHER READING

Youngberg, B. (1990). Claims and litigation management. In L. M. Harpster & M. S. Veach (Eds.), *Risk management handbook for healthcare facilities* (Chapter 26). Chicago: American Society for Healthcare Risk Management.

CLAIMS MADE COVERAGE

See Claim, Claims Management

CLAIMS MANAGEMENT

Claims management is a process of early identification, investigation, and resolution of potentially compensable events. Potentially compensable events are poor patient outcomes that are usually associated with a patient's request for monetary damages. A claims management process involves a programmatic approach that outlines the institutional philosophy of how adverse events are communicated and handled in anticipation of litigation. The development of policies should guide staff regarding

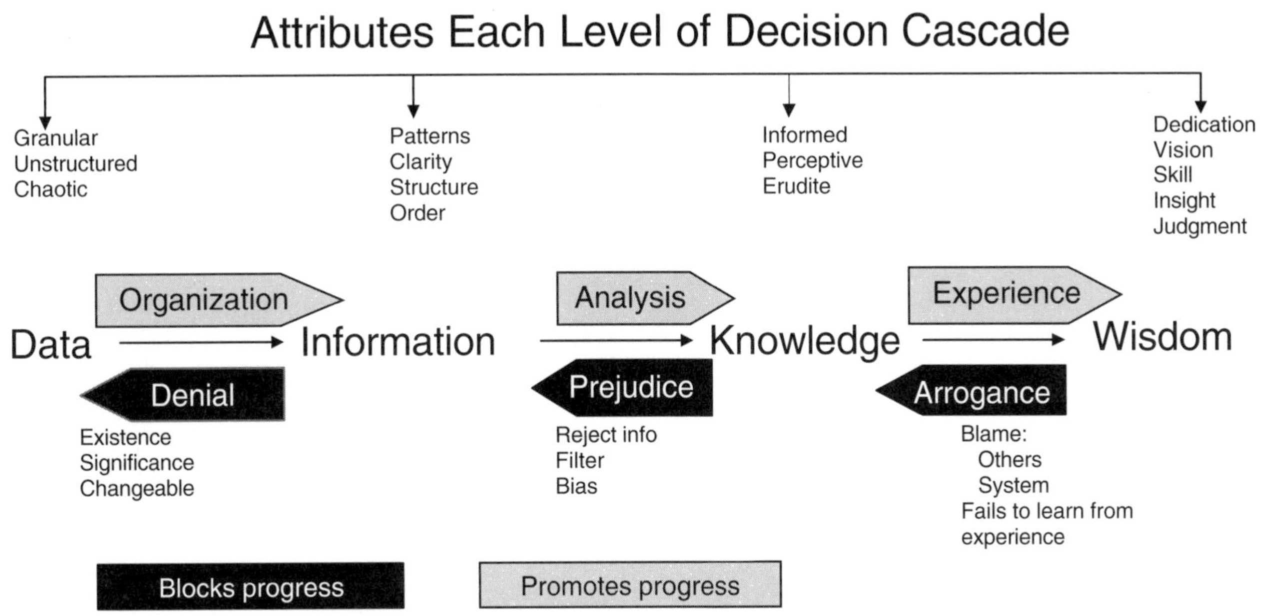

Attributes Each Level of Decision Cascade

Granular
Unstructured
Chaotic

Patterns
Clarity
Structure
Order

Informed
Perceptive
Erudite

Dedication
Vision
Skill
Insight
Judgment

Organization

Data ———→ Information ———→ Knowledge ———→ Wisdom

Analysis

Experience

Denial

Prejudice

Arrogance

Existence
Significance
Changeable

Reject info
Filter
Bias

Blame:
    Others
    System
Fails to learn from
experience

Blocks progress   Promotes progress

Figure 1

notification, classification, and disposition of information that has been identified as entailing potential or actual liability. This handling of information is a risk management function. The risk manager receives reports of professional and general liability claims against the institution, its employees, and agents and manages them to conclusion.

—Kathleen Ferrara

FURTHER READING

Youngberg, B. (1998). *The risk manager's desk reference* (2nd ed., pp. 256–265). Gaithersburg, MD: Aspen.

CLINICAL DECISION MAKING

The reader leaving this discussion with a healthy appreciation of "just in time" versus "just in case" knowledge will have been well served. The objective is to shed light on the concepts, characteristics, tools, and process of clinical decisions. The cascade of the decision process is graphically depicted in Figure 1.

The change in the clinical decision process, even its mention in publications, has undergone meteoric growth in recent times, largely as a result of information technology and the creation of the Internet. From an obscure beginning envisioned as an indestructible defense communication system, the Internet has grown to the World Wide Web (WWW) with undefined borders. This revolutionary

change may be rivaled only by the invention of descriptive language and Gutenberg's printing press. Like the press, the Internet has become the property of the people and, absent some catastrophic natural event, will not be turned back. A recent AMA survey found that almost half of physicians report the World Wide Web (WWW) has had a major impact on their practice of medicine. The Internet in medicine functions as a powerful resource, much as medical reference texts did 50 years ago. It is impossible to discuss clinical decision making today without considering the WWW impact.

Briefly, and for purposes of this article, a decision is "a position, an opinion, or a judgment reached after consideration" (American Heritage Dictionary). To a degree, by implication, decision signals closure and reduces uncertainty. Decisions are often driven by an individual's latest, or most disastrous, experience. Frailties sometimes overpower strengths, and errors usually decline as the knowledge base expands. Faulty or incomplete data carry a serious risk of failure, and until recently, a structured approach was uncommon. A search of Medline, which dates from 1960, using the phrase "medical decision" found only three references in the early 1960's: Two discussed court decisions, and a third reviewed contraceptives. Diabetes articles increased from 960 in 1965 to 10,416 in 2001; during the same time, articles on decision making increased to 21,847 or nearly 60 times the rate of increase in diabetes articles.

Anyone practicing for a few years can likely recall an experience with a patient in which the physician noted subtle changes unsupported by objective data and in which, nevertheless, additional testing confirmed a dangerous illness in an early stage. Justifiable pride can be taken in this metaphor of the indispensable human factor, because it will be a long time before a computer performs this diagnostic function. Yet computers do aid diagnostic decisions.

By the late 1980s several medicine-oriented programs entered the market, created for the personal digital assistant (PDA). Today, increased use of mobile devices foretells the replacement of pocket reference books. Reliable Web resources abound and Web sites formerly restricted to the academic medical centers, such as Medline, are now open to the world. Although a long way from *Star Wars,* this new system has the potential of ushering in the dawn of a new era in medical quality.

—Thurman L. Pedigo, Sr.

CLINICAL INVESTIGATION

See Clinical Trials

CLINICAL PATHWAYS (CARE MAPS™ OR CRITICAL PATHS)

Clinical pathways (treatment plans, also referred to as Care Maps™ or critical paths) are important tools for all participants in the health care system. This includes the patient, clinicians, nurses, other health care workers, managed care organizations, and other payers. Clinical Pathways allow an institution to achieve high-quality and cost-effective care. Clinical pathways are useful in planning, coordinating, communicating, and evaluating patient care.

Clinical pathways allow for the development of collaborative care teams that set the plan or goals for a specific case type or diagnosis. Teams are made up of physicians, nurses, therapists, administrators, and others who are part of the team caring for a patient with a specific diagnosis. The outcomes that have been reviewed and agreed on by an entire team are more likely to be achieved. The changes or variations in outcome are more easily explored and addressed.

The use of clinical pathways also allows for a "data driven" process related to outcomes. This helps both payers and health care providers agree on resources for care provision. The data (benchmarking) are then incorporated into future pathways for a specific diagnosis allowing for improvement of care (best practices) as well as input into the payer's guidelines for determining reasonable care.

Clinical pathways, which define a map or plan of care for a specific diagnosis, imply coordination of all clinical activities or "time limited" paths, clarifying that the goal of resource coordination is to minimize the duration of care. It is important to recognize that we strive for an appropriate length of stay while maximizing efficiency of care and minimizing variances in quality of care. Pathways may include preprinted order sheets, daily goals of treatment, tools for documenting care, and patient/staff education materials. Evaluation of variances (variations in care) are used to help improve the quality of care.

The pathway or map, then, provides an overview of the entire process from start to finish. Any individual piece in the process can be evaluated, updated, or eliminated as dictated by the collaborative care team and best medical practices. The algorithms of a clinical pathway can help guide clinicians through an "if–then" decision process for a particular treatment or condition. As an educational tool, clinical pathways are data driven and apply evidence-based medicine.

In various settings, clinical pathways have been used to guide inpatient care, complete episodes of care, specialized applications or procedures, and life and health management. The use of clinical pathways can help an institution, physician, or other health care worker to

- Clarify the "big picture."
- Plan and coordinate care.
- Establish expectations.
- Reduce variation of care.
- Educate staff, students, and residents.
- Benchmark.
- Improve communication among clinicians, patients, families, payers, and others.
- Improve the work environment.
- Design menu-driven physician order entry systems (electronic medical records).

Working with the hospital administration and finance departments, it is possible to estimate the cost of a specific care program. The collaborative care team working on a clinical pathway or clinical practice guideline can obtain information on the current cost of care of a specific diagnosis, as well as on the cost of care on a clinical pathway being developed. This allows all members of the hospital team (clinical, administrative, and financial) to see the current costs, as well as the potential opportunities for savings using a clinical pathway (clinical practice guideline, care map, or critical pathway).

An approach to clinical pathways development is through developing collaborative care teams that work in conjunction with a clinical pathways oversight committee. This committee is responsible for making sure the clinical pathways comply with other hospital policies regarding chart forms as well as other regulatory requirements. The oversight committee is also charged to form a clinical collaborative team to develop a pathway for a specific diagnosis (a high-cost or high-volume diagnosis). It also reviews compliance with the pathways and reviews reports of variances to help the collaborative teams evaluate system processes that may be responsible for the variances.

In the near future, clinical pathways may well serve as a menu-driven interface for physician computer order entry systems as part of an electronic medical record. When a clinical pathway is updated in an electronic system, any changes made to the clinical pathway (to represent a change in best practice, and so forth) on the computer system server are immediately available so that the very next patient is treated with the updated clinical pathway. Even prior to implementing a physician computer order entry system, the Internet (or intranet) may prove useful as a repository for storing an institution's clinical pathways. Even if a clinical pathway is printed out from the computer, hand annotated, and placed on the patient's chart, this ensures that the most current clinical pathway is immediately available for patient care.

—Stephen A. Vitkun

See also Care Maps, Clinical Practice Guidelines/Pathways

FURTHER READING

Kongstvedt, P. R. (1996). *The managed health care handbook* (3rd ed.). Gaithersburg, MD: Aspen.

Lighter, D. E., & Fair, D. C. (2000). *Principles and methods of quality management in health care.* Gaithersburg, MD: Aspen.

CLINICAL PRACTICE GUIDELINES/PATHWAYS

Well-designed clinical practice guidelines should recognize and filter strong and weak evidence, expert opinion, and conflicting information from many sources in a way that makes the information useful to a specific audience. Good guidelines should acknowledge that their uses may differ from user to user, but no matter how the guideline is applied, the use should not conflict with valid scientific evidence. Wise choice and use of authoritative guidelines eliminate for clinicians the improbable task of sorting through the information maelstrom in which we now exist.

Practice guidelines are developed by experts acting on behalf of professional societies, guideline companies, health plans, medical organizations, pharmaceutical manufacturers, disease management vendors, government agencies at all levels from CMS to local health departments,

research organizations, purchasers of health care services, advocates, and consumer groups. These policies contribute to decisions about every aspect of the delivery of health care from timeliness of the delivery of preventive health services to legislation regarding malpractice. It is important to identify the validity of the recommendation, the end user, the target population, and the desired result of proper application of the guideline.

The selection process for choosing one set of guidelines over another may lead a physician in a group practice to choose asthma management guidelines developed by colleagues who practice in the specialty of allergy and immunology. Pediatricians in the same group may choose the same guideline produced by the Academy of Pediatrics (2002). Many guideline developers have selected physicians as the audience for their materials.

Clinicians may have been the principal target for the use of guidelines in the treatment of their patients. However, clinical guidelines have a number of useful applications outside of the direct care of a patient. David Eddy (1990–1991) described the uses of practice policies in terms of flexibility of their application. The most flexible application of clinical guidelines is to advise practitioners about the choices available to them during an episode of direct patient care. Clinicians may consider this cookbook medicine unless they realize that the choice and consequence remain theirs. No matter how specific a guideline may be, no matter how brief the episode of care to which it applies, the choices offered only apply to a segment of the target population. It is the practitioner's skill that determines to whom, and at what time, a clinical recommendation makes sense. Thinking in these terms makes physician clinical guidelines the most flexible use to which these decision support tools may be applied. Although compliance with guidelines is expected to affect outcomes, level of compliance is difficult to measure. Most measures of compliance are related to intermediate outcomes. For example, pediatric immunization rates, mammography screening rates, and other measures of steps in the care process are used to estimate compliance. Measured thus, physician performance varies substantially.

Clinical pathways, which are more structured than clinical guidelines, are used principally by nonphysician practitioners to deliver timely care over a set period of time and require higher levels of compliance than clinical guidelines. They rely on the same evidence but generally require a deliberate justification for variation, often in writing in the medical record. A pathway should be considered a management tool for applying a clinical guideline (see Kelly & Bernard, 1997).

For years health plans have used a type of clinical pathway known as *utilization management guidelines* to support the decision-making process of nurse and physician reviewers in their use management departments. In this application a registered nurse is trained to acquire medical information and organize it so that it fits a diagnostic category, to determine whether a service requested by a clinician is medically necessary for the patient, timely in its delivery, not in conflict with some other service or condition, and delivered in a setting that is both safe and effective for the individual who is receiving care. Managed care organizations measure inter-rater reliability to determine whether the guidelines are followed. Typical compliance expected among nurse reviewers is 90%. In this setting, a nurse can only approve services. If the nurse states any uncertainty regarding necessity or safety, a physician reviewer is asked to evaluate the request. As with clinical pathways in the hospital, physicians can record reasons for varying from the guideline or for interpreting the clinical condition differently from the nurse. Given the same set of circumstances, health plans expect to achieve 80% inter-rater reproducibility for physician reviewers.

Finally, guidelines can be written into public policies as laws or into contracts as health care benefits. In such cases, policy, and not necessarily medical necessity, dictates the decision process. Guidelines at this level are so restrictive that they can actually define a situation where care should not be delivered. An extreme example of such a practice policy concerns medicinal marijuana. Whether prescription or use are supported by evidence and indicated or not, a policy can make it not legal to prescribe or to use. A less dramatic policy may govern whether or not an individual has health insurance that pays for certain types of service or technology. In many cases the absence of the benefit reduces or eliminates the likelihood that a person will seek those services and guides the person to seek other effective services from the physician.

An attempt to coordinate all the elements of health care delivery guided by clinical policies from least to most restrictive has evolved over the past 15 to 20 years. The concept of disease management represents a strategy to incorporate clinical guidelines, clinical pathways, insurance benefits including formulary selections, provider reimbursement, and information management into a patient's health care. Disease management is a patient- and family-centered strategy to improve quality of life for people with chronic conditions. This application engages the affected individual, his or her health care providers, the health plan, and sometimes the community to reduce the frequency and severity of exacerbations in the illness.

Guidelines are only useful to support informed decisions. Their validity must be evaluated on a regular basis. New information needs to be screened for effectiveness, incorporated into existing guidelines, and disseminated to the selected audience. Even with wide availability of valid guidelines, measurement of compliance in practice remains elusive. Until routine reporting methods are introduced, the effect of clinical guidelines on the health of large populations is difficult to assess. As information tools, however, clinical guidelines should be considered effective.

—Gregory Preston

FURTHER READING

American Academy of Pediatrics. (2002). Practical guide for the diagnosis and management of asthma. In *Pediatric clinical practice guidelines & policies: A compendium of evidence-based research for pediatric practice* (2nd ed., pp. 5–56). Elk Grove, IL: Author.

Eddy, D. (1990–1991). Background and definitions. In American College of Physicians (Ed.), *Assessing health practices & designing practice policies: The explicit approach* (pp. 5–15). Philadelphia: Author.

Kelly, J. T., & Bernard, D. B. (1997). Clinical practice guidelines: Foundation for effective disease management. In W. E. Todd & D. Nash (Eds.), *Disease management: A systems approach to improving patient outcomes* (pp. 157–177). Chicago: American Hospital Publishing.

CLINICAL RESEARCH

Clinical research is the process by which a new drug or therapeutic modality is introduced into common clinical practice. A clinical trial has three distinct phases or subtypes. Using a new drug as an example, a Phase I trial is the first exposure of a drug or intervention in a human. Frequently researchers have experimented on animals to determine an approximate dose range and potential adverse effects. However, because of differences between humans and other animals, dose range, absorption, excretion, side effects, metabolism, and efficacy must be investigated. Phase I trials are frequently of small size and involve a large amount of data collection, because researchers may find unexpected or unexplained responses or effects in humans. Most drugs that reach a Phase I trial move to a Phase II trial, which is frequently larger in scope, enrolls more participants and further investigates the dose range and efficacy of the drug compared with existing treatments. Potential side effects discovered in the Phase I trial are further investigated and potentially managed. If the results of a Phase II trial show a new drug is effective, then investigations proceed to a Phase III trial. The purpose of this series of investigations is to determine how the new treatment compares with existing modalities. Occasionally, two experimental treatments are directly compared with one another. Phase III trials often require a large number of participants to detect subtle differences that may exist between the new and existing treatments. Frequently these studies involve more than one medical center, to obtain a sufficient sample size in a timely fashion. During both Phase II and Phase III trials, participants are often randomized to either the new treatment or an existing treatment without the knowledge of the clinicians directly treating the patients. This is done to minimize potential participant and investigator biases. (See entry for *Blinding*.) The individuals receiving the new treatment are the experimental group and the individuals receiving the standard modality are the control group. A Phase III trial may also be used to compare different dosing schedules or regiments of pre-existing modalities, to determine which is most efficacious. An additional Phase IV may be added as a postapproval and marketing study to further investigate the side effects and efficacy of a drug.

Whenever human research is conducted, all experimental protocols must be reviewed by a committee known commonly as an institutional review board (IRB). The IRB is frequently composed of physicians and other health care professionals, lawyers, researchers, and members of the community. The responsibilities of the IRB are to ensure that the researcher is qualified to conduct the study, to determine if the trial is well planned, and to ensure that patient recruitment, enrollment, confidentiality, and compensation are appropriate. As any human study requires informed consent, the IRB is also responsible for ensuring that the information given to patients is complete and in an easily understandable format. Throughout the duration of the study, the investigator and IRB must remain in communication with regard to unexpected side effects and adverse events. The IRB also has the ability to postpone or terminate a study if it is felt the potential risks to the participants involved outweigh the potential benefits. The study may also be closed prematurely based on the data collected. As the study is ongoing, the preliminary data may show that the new drug or treatment modality is not as efficacious as initially proposed, or even potentially harmful, showing side effects not seen during Phase I and II trials. It is therefore unethical to continue to expose participants to increased risk. Likewise, if the new treatment is shown to be significantly better than the standard treatment, the ongoing trial can be halted and all patients could then receive the newer, more efficacious treatment.

—Daryn H. Moller

See also Clinical Trials, Food and Drug Administration (FDA), Good Clinical Practices (GCPs), National Institutes of Health (NIH), Phase 1 Study (Phase 1 Clinical Trial), Phase 2 Study, Phase 3 Study, Phase 4 Study,

FURTHER READING

Chow, S.-C., & Liu, J.-P. (1998). *Design and analysis of clinical trials: Concepts and methodologies.* New York: Wiley.

Friedman, L. M., Furberg, C. D., & DeMets, D. L. (1998). *Fundamentals of clinical trials* (3rd ed.). New York: Springer.

CLINICAL TRIALS

Clinical trials are investigations with human participants to discover or verify the clinical, pharmacologic, or other pharmacodynamic effects of an investigational drug product. A clinical trial also characterizes absorption, distribution, metabolism, and excretion of a drug product with the object of determining its safety and efficacy.

Approval of a preclinical submission by a regulatory agency, usually the submission of an investigational new drug (IND) application, determines the start of clinical trials. The design of clinical trials is related to the particular type drug under investigation.

A clinical program starts with three main strategic phases and a postmarketing phase, each with its own specific set of objectives.

The phases are as follows:

Phase I. This phase is intended for the initial testing in healthy normal volunteers. These studies usually consist of shorter studies in a small number of participants (20 to 80), to determine the levels of toxicity, absorption, pharmacologic effects, drug interaction, metabolic effects, dose ranges, and the preliminary evidence of effectiveness.

Phase II. These studies are usually larger than Phase I trials and are required to determine effectiveness and relative safety of the drug product. They are the first controlled studies, and they are intended to discover whether a new drug is effective for one or more clinical indications, at a specified dose and frequency of administration. The studies are usually employed as double-blind, placebo-controlled trials and include anywhere from 100 to 200 patients on the drug. These trials are intended to establish primary efficacy end points, to help design the Phase III trials. After completing phase II trials, the drug company usually arranges a meeting with the regulatory agencies to get the agencies' "buy-in" (agreement to proceed) on the Phase III program.

Phase III. These studies are expanded controlled and uncontrolled trials after preliminary evidence of effectiveness and safety has been established in the previous phases. This phase establishes the clinical requirements of regulatory agencies and provides the company's marketing department with information on which to base marketing themes.

Phase III studies are usually double-blind, placebo-controlled trials that include an increase in patient number, exposure, and length of drug administration. It is important during Phase III studies to arrange several meetings with the regulatory agencies to discuss the format of the registration application, any new indications, and the core of the clinical submission.

Phase IV. The fourth phase is intended for postmarketing trials to elucidate the incidence of adverse reactions, and explore specific pharmacologic effects. Phase IV studies can also supplement premarketing data, study new patient populations, and explore other indications.

The sponsor should acquire qualified individuals (biostatisticians, clinical pharmacologists, physicians) throughout all phases of the clinical trials, to determine the design of the protocols, case report forms, and establish the appropriate clinical end points. It is also recommended that sponsors submit the appropriate chemistry, manufacturing, and controls documentation during Phase II and Phase III studies.

—Anthony Sileno

See also Longitudinal Study, Pivotal Studies, Placebo, Study Arms

FURTHER READING

Cato, E. C. (Ed.). (1988). *Clinical trials and tribulations.* New York: Marcel Dekker.

Food and Drug Administration (FDA). FDA guidance for the industry. (1997). *General considerations for the clinical evaluation of drugs.* Washington, DC: U.S. Government Printing Office.

Food and Drug Administration (FDA). FDA guidance for the industry. (1999). *INDs for Phase 2 and 3 studies of drugs, including specified therapeutic biotechnology-derived products; chemistry, manufacturing and controls content and format.* Washington, DC: U.S. Government Printing Office.

Guarino, R. A. (Ed.). (1987). *New drug approval process.* New York: Marcel Dekker.

U.S. Department of Health and Human Services, Food and Drug Administration, Center for Drug Evaluation and Research, Center for Biologics Evaluation and Research. (1996, April). *Good clinical practice: Consolidated guidance.* Rockville, MD: International Conference on Harmonization of Technical Requirements for Registration of Pharmaceuticals for Human Use.

CLOSED SYSTEMS

See Culture and Culture Change

COALITIONS (BUSINESS)

Aggregations of businesses often act in concert to attain specific goals. Some mutual benefit societies in the area of life and health insurance are over 200 years old in this country. Members-only insurance has a long tradition in many fields, where common interest is the basis of common action. As employers began to sponsor group insurance policies for employees, they also formed alliances to improve costs and the efficiency of their purchasing. Contemporary business coalitions also seek influence in the health arena at local and national levels, channeling diverse business entities into consistent activities.

Membership composition, requirements, and activities vary among coalitions. Some include employers of all sizes, and some have size restrictions. Some limit membership only to employers who purchase health plans, and others include both insurers and health providers. Many are primarily purchasing coalitions, which take advantage of economies of scale. Often organizations belong to more than one coalition, in their home state plus wherever large concentrations of employees are found.

Characteristically, coalitions serve their members through dissemination of information, efforts to influence health policy, plus quality and cost control initiatives. Quality initiatives are a core activity for business coalitions, because comparative information about health care quality and cost is necessary for value-based health care purchasing. The National Business Coalition on Health (NBCH, at www.nbch.org), a coalition of coalitions, reports 90% of their members collect and analyze data such as Health Plan & Employer Data & Info Set, or HEDIS®, hospital and physician health claims, and leapfrog quality indicators. Founded in 1989, NBCH has a membership of about 90 employer-led coalitions representing over 7,000 employers and 34 million covered lives. Nearly 60% of their member coalitions offer a pharmacy benefit carve-out. HMO plans, PPOs, mental health benefits, vision, and dental plans are examples of other group discounts available.

Other examples of business coalitions focused on health plans and public policy include the following:

Washington Business Group on Health (at www.wbgh.org), founded in 1974, which is the only national not-for-profit organization exclusively devoted to representing the perspective of large employers. The membership consists of 160 large employers, with 39 million covered lives.

The Midwest Business Group on Health (at www.mbgh.org), formed in 1980, has over 70 members in eleven states.

The Pacific Business Group on Health (at www.pbgh.org), a California-based organization founded in 1989, has 47 purchasers of health plans as members, representing about 3 million covered lives and $4 billion in annual health care expenditures.

The National Coalition on Health Care (at www.nchc.org), founded in 1990 and perhaps the most broadly representative alliance, has 96 employers and other groups as members and represents about 100 million individuals.

Leapfrog (at www.leapfroggroup.org), founded by the Business Roundtable (at www.brt.org), has 100 public and private member organizations representing 32 million individuals in 50 states.

The National Association of Manufacturers (at www.nam.org) has 14,000 member companies and represents 18 million individuals, and also devotes considerable efforts to health care issues, both purchasing and public policy.

—Jerry Burgess

CODE OF ETHICS

ETHICAL ISSUES FACED BY MANAGERS

Ethical issues are present even in routine daily decisions of a manager. Managing involves ethics at every level from small personal decisions to large public policies. It may be appropriate to regard most managerial decisions as being permeated by ethics, rather than to regard ethical considerations as tangential issues. Because managers have power that affects people's lives, there is a potential for them to act in a good or evil manner. Managers who make incorrect decisions to promote their own interests are unethical. In addition, any situation that is less favorable than it could have been is ethically compromised. Managers should attempt to distribute resources in a fair manner; however, a fair distribution is not always an equal distribution. Managers design and enforce organizational rules. Their ethical responsibility is to produce a system of shared values and expectations that is realistic and fair. Managerial decisions may be ethical because they may test the manager's personal values. These types of conflicts involve discrepancies between personal and organizational values. Managers act as the link between organizational success and the lives of the individuals whom they manage.

Ethical behavior may be encouraged by designing organizations with optimal distribution of power and minimizing pressures that might otherwise encourage unethical behavior. Managers should seek to create a corporate culture of openness and cooperation. Efforts should be made to understand the factors in organizations that enhance or distort human values and behavior.

Four examples of ethical issues for managers follow:

- External effects of
  - Unsafe consumer products or services
  - Arrogance in dealing with "foreign" people—people who are different from "ourselves"
- Internal conflicts
  - Negligence in guaranteeing the health and safety of employees
  - Foot-dragging among members with regard to affirmative action
  - Foot-dragging among members regarding equitable promotions
- Conflicts of
  - Decisions to shut down a profitable unit, leaving local individuals and managers to handle the fallout
  - Rushed schedules that jeopardize health and safety regulations
- Stakeholder value conflicts on (for example)
  - Issues related to placement of an MRI machine
  - Possible safety hazards, costs, resource depletion
  - Return on investment and long-term health of the company

HEALTH CARE ORGANIZATIONAL ISSUES

Obvious organizational issues that present opportunities for physician leaders to lead with ethics include the following:

- Employee rights: due process, privacy
- Sexual harassment
- Whistle-blowing
- Misuse of power
- Discouraging intrinsic motivation
- Selection and placement
- Corporate culture
- Corporate social responsibility
- Agreed-on incentive system versus actual system
- Terminations
- Organizational structure, design, and politics
- Performance appraisals
- Drug testing, physical exams
- Diversity/discrimination
- Planning, policy, control
- Government relations
- Safety/health issues
- Technical development
- Foreign payments
- Environment protection
- Product safety, reliability
- Quality management
- Purchasing (gifts, bribes)
- Automation, robotics
- Confidentiality

- Inappropriate requests
- Intellectual property
- Truth in claims
- Organizational versus individual needs
- Customer and user participation
- Conflicts of interest
- Personal biases
- Individual and population differences
- Appropriate interventions
- Intervention consequences
- Fair pricing

STANDARDS ETHICS THAT OFFICERS UPHOLD

The standards for ethical practice to be upheld by professionals include the following:

Integrity. Professionals are honest, play fair, and act in good faith with others in all dealings for the company. They seek to know their own preferred belief systems, values, needs, and limitations, to understand how they may differ from others, and to be conscious of the potential effect of these differences on their work. They refrain from making false, misleading, or deceptive statements and provide accurate information. They avoid conflict-of-interest relationships as well as expensive gift giving, bribery, nepotism, and abuse of government relationships. Professionals clarify to all parties the exact nature of their performance and function. They act with an expectation that each exchange in business is in effect one of many more to come. They act with the intent of a long-term business relationship.

Productivity. Professionals are expected to be knowledgeable about all aspects of their profession and to perform their work in an exemplary fashion. They exercise careful judgment to protect those for whom they are responsible. Professionals use appropriate information, resources, incentives, research, and applications to secure the best service for each stakeholder. They are aware of cultural, individual, and role differences involving age, gender, race, ethnicity, national origin, religion, sexual orientation, disability, language, and socioeconomic status. Professionals work continuously to eliminate the effect on work in the company of biases based on the listed differences. They do not condone or participate in unfair discriminatory practices of any kind. They strive to advance individual and organizational learning, performance, and development while mitigating the causes preventing stakeholder welfare. They comply with laws and social policies that serve the interests of stakeholders, the public, society, and the environment. Moreover, professionals should possess skills such as the following:

- Establishing and managing client relationships
- Conducting analyses

- Identifying root causes of conflicts
- Building partnership within firm
- Negotiating skills
- Conflict resolution skills
- Technical skills
- Consensus and commitment-building skills
- Project management skills
- Speaking skills
- Facilitating the leadership, implementation, and management of change

Responsibility. Professionals uphold the law and these ethical standards and prevent harm to any stakeholder. They consult with colleagues and clients regarding ethical compliance in their professional duties. They engage in proper business conduct to prevent unethical dilemmas. They share credit for work accomplishments when appropriate and to be worthy of trust as professionals. They serve the company by honoring all contracts, promises, and any agreed-on commitments. Moreover, they are aware of their professional responsibility to the community in which they work and live, to the society in which they belong, and to a livable planet. They understand that there is a necessary confluence of a healthy ecosystem, stable governments, a healthy economy, and healthy organizations. Professionals have an obvious responsibility not to bring harm to another individual, department, division, company, community, or any other element in society.

Respectfulness in Relationships. Professionals recognize, respect, and are concerned about the intrinsic worth of individuals, their interactions with each other, as well as their rights to privacy, confidentiality, and self-directedness within the context of fundamental dignity, financial information, and worth of all people. They advocate that restrictions on the rights of individuals by managers at work should be limited and used only with clear business justifications. They are alert to the fact that legal obligations manifested as compliance policies and procedures may lead to inconsistency and conflict with the exercise of the rights of individuals. When conflict does occur among stakeholders' obligations, concerns, and rights, they seek to resolve these conflicts in a responsible and ethical manner, avoiding or minimizing harm to others. They are sensitive to power differences among all stakeholders and do not mislead or exploit other people before, during, or after professional work exchanges. Respectfulness in relationships creates confidence among stakeholders.

Physician leaders are uniquely positioned to influence ethical awareness in the workplace. Understanding the basic underpinnings of ethical theory and empirical research in ethics gives physician leaders a grounding in the ethical implications of their decisions.

Here are some things a physician leader should *not* do:

- Violate professional, academic, or business ethics by being less than honest in billing or submitting low proposal bids and higher final bills
- Promise solutions will work when the opposite may be true
- Make false return-on-investment (ROI) claims
- Use client information for personal gain
- Falsify data
- Compromise the technology for any personal or political gain by providing interventions that are acceptable to the client but incorrect for the context
- Take credit for the work of another
- Make false claims about any professional's behaviors or potential accomplishments

PRACTICAL ETHICAL CODE FOR DECISIONS

A survey of organizations indicated the materials and formats most commonly used in ethics training:

- Codes of ethics (79%)
- Lectures (63%)
- Workshops and seminars (53%)
- Case studies (46%)
- Films and discussion (41%)

(Perry, Bennet, & Edwards, 1990, p. 8)

Case studies and discussions have been found most effective. "They give participants a sense of how to analyze and resolve ethical problems in a way that is consistent with the company's code or standards of corporate conduct" (Perry, Bennet, & Edwards, 1990, p. 8).

The actual process of making ethical decisions is seldom as easy as simply selecting the correct alternative. Although physician leaders sometimes face clear choices between obvious right and wrong, extenuating circumstances usually exist, so they face tough choices between one right and another right. With such choices, it is helpful to apply a step-by-step decision-making process. When confronted with choosing between two "right" alternatives, ethical decisions depend on both the decision-making process and the experience, intelligence, and integrity of the decision maker. Sometimes training and coaching can both enhance the decision-making process and enrich the experience of the decision maker (Dean, 1993). Most, however, contain the same basic processes represented in Werhane's (1992) model for ethical decision making.

Werhane's model has seven steps in the process (Dean, 1993):

1. *Identify the relevant facts.* Key factors that shape the situation and influence ethical issues must be identified.

2. *Define the ethical issues.* All issues related to the situation must be identified and the ethical issues separated from the nonethical issues. Issues may be identified at all levels of the organization.

3. *Identify the primary stakeholders.* Those individuals and groups involved in the situation that will be affected by a decision are the primary stakeholders. The impact of a decision on them must be considered.

4. *Determine the possible alternatives.* All alternative interventions need to be identified.

5. *List the ethical implications of each of the alternatives.* Each alternative needs to be evaluated according to the impact on the stakeholders and the three ethical theories.

6. *List the practical constraints.* Any factors that might limit the implementation of alternatives or render it too difficult or risky must be identified.

7. *Determine which actions should be taken.* After weighing the information provided in steps 1 through 6, an alternative needs to be selected and an implementation strategy identified.

THE NEED FOR AN ORGANIZATIONAL CREDO

The reason for an organizational credo is to place the leadership values of particular ethical importance front and center. Physician leaders can be the stewards for the following values:

- Open communication
- Well-being of the whole organization
- Care of the well-being of the individual
- Model of integrity and respect

And they can empower employees to do the same in modeling these values.

Ethics can be seen in an organizational credo. Also, the credo helps to demonstrate a responsibility to more than the patient.

- Management is a profession. As with any other profession—physicians, accountants, lawyers—the organization needs a code or credo to establish its culture.
- Medical ethics and business ethics are the same but different when interacting within an organization. All stakeholders need to be aware of both sets of responsibility: to the patient and to the organization.
- Without an organizational credo, staff and patients will be unaware of the nature, rules, regulations, and varieties of managed care and the financial parameters of their health benefits.

An organizational credo draws attention to and creates a standard acceptance of common policies for concerns such as

- Use of patient information other than for patient use
- Lack of confidentiality safeguards for electronic records (e-records)
- Information availability to nonclinicians
- Medical laws and standards that may not apply, because managed care organizations are businesses
- The usual lack of standards for the handling, storage, or destruction of medical records obtained by managed care organizations

—Peter J. Dean

FURTHER READING

Dean, P. J. (1992). Making codes of ethics "real." *Journal of Business Ethics, 11*(4), 285–291.

Dean, P. J. (1993). A selected review of the underpinnings of ethics for human performance technology professionals. Parts 1 and 2. *Performance Improvement Quarterly, 6*(4), 3–49.

Dean, P. J. (1994, Nov/Dec). Some basics about ethics. *Performance and Instruction, 33,* 42–45.

Perry, D., Bennet, K., & Edwards, G. (1990). *Ethics policies and programs.* Washington, DC: Ethics Resource Center.

Werhane, P. H. (1992, July). *Corporate moral and social responsibility.* Paper presented at Ethics Practice and Teaching Workshop, Colorado Springs, CO.

COLLABORATIVE PARTNERSHIP

A collaborative partnership is one in which two or more separate organizations depend on each other to be successful in the marketplace. Sometimes this interdependence is informal and short-lived; usually it is a contractual relationship that has a longer time span. Either way, collaborative partnerships are an important vehicle for health care providers to work together within their fragmented industry.

In the 1990s, the health care industry was forced to become more integrated. It did this through outright acquisitions and collaborative partnerships. Collaborative partnerships are most appropriate when an organization is faced with a situation where the outcome desired is strategically important and the initiator needs to preserve an independent relationship with the collaborator(s). Although many organizations have or are currently experimenting with this new approach to delivering value, the leadership skills required to be successful are often quite different from those required to be successful in isolated organizations.

Collaborative partnerships have fueled much innovation in the health care industry. For example, Drugstore.com partnered with Amazon.com to expand use of the Internet for pharmaceutical purchases. Similarly, HealthSouth Corporation partnered outside of the health care industry with Oracle Corporation to create a wireless information network and centralized medical records database. Within the health care consumer network, the U.S. Department of Defense and the Veterans Administration are forming numerous collaborative partnerships, and health care business coalitions are gaining in strength and reach. Perhaps the greatest exploration of the power of collaborative partnerships comes from the many community health improvement partnerships between hospitals and physicians.

—William Q. Judge

See also Alliances, Co-opetition, Cooperation Strategies, Negotiations, Networks

FURTHER READING

Blair, J., Savage, G., & Whitehead, C. (1989). A strategic approach for negotiating with hospital stakeholders. *Health Care Management Review, 14*(1), 15–22.

Judge, W., & Ryman, J. (2001). The shared leadership challenge in strategic alliances: Lessons from the U.S. healthcare industry. *Academy of Management Executive, 15*(2), 71–79.

Pellet, J. (2001). HealthSouth's digital dream. *Chief Executive, 173,* 32–36.

Zukoski, A., & Shortell, S. (2001). Keys to building effective community partnerships. *Health Forum Journal, 44*(5), 22–25.

COLLECTION FLOAT

See Float Management

COLLECTIVE BARGAINING

Collective bargaining is a process by which individual workers combine to negotiate with an opposing party (usually an employer or employer group). The object of collective bargaining is for the workers to gain strength through numbers. The National Labor Relations Act (NLRA or "Wagner Act") sets out mandatory subjects of collective bargaining, which must be discussed between the workers' representative (the union, if the employer's workers are unionized) and the employer. The mandatory subjects of bargaining are wages, hours, and working conditions.

—Bruce D. Fisher

FURTHER READING

Fisher, B. D., & Phillips, M. J. (2004). *The legal, ethical, and regulatory environment of business* (8th ed., chapter 17). Mason, OH: Thomson-South-Western.

COMMON CAUSE VARIATION

Common cause variation is variation that is inherent to a process, caused by unknown factors, resulting in a random but well-defined distribution of process measurements. It describes the natural noise in a process and is a direct result of how the process is designed, constructed, and managed.

A process that is subject only to common cause variation can be regarded as stable and predictable, in the sense that the process average and process variation can computed and used to predict the future behavior of the process. However, even though the process variation can be regarded as stable, it may still be too large to be acceptable. For example, a stable process, subject only to common cause variation, may be consistently producing output that is too large or too small. If the magnitude of the process variation allows the output to meet requirements, the process is said to be *capable*. If the magnitude of the process variation is so large that requirements are consistently not met, the process is said to be *not capable*. A reduction in common cause variation requires a change to the process itself and is generally the responsibility of management.

A control chart displaying measurements from a process that is subject only to common cause variation displays a random pattern, almost always with all points within the control limits, and with no runs, shifts, or trends. Points that occur outside the control limits, or which display shifts or trends, are regarded as due to special cause variation.

For patients seeking care in a walk-in clinic, the amount of time it takes for a patient to be seen by a physician is variable. It could depend on a number of unpredictable factors, including the number of other individuals seeking care, the nature of care required, the staffing, and so on. Taken as a whole, these different sources of variation constitute the common cause variation in this process. If something extraordinary happens, say all the physicians run out of the clinic to take care of the victims of a traffic accident, then the wait times become extremely long, and this is called special cause variation.

COMMON STOCK

See Equity

COMMUNITY-BASED HOSPITAL

Hospitals have been the cornerstone of the American health care delivery system. Community-based hospitals (CBHs), providing care to the local community, are categorized as being nonfederal, short term (less than 30 days), general and special hospitals. University-based and federal (Veterans Administration, for example) hospitals are also extremely important, but the U.S. system wouldn't work if the health care delivery system didn't have a local emphasis. The basic mission of all these institutions is to improve the health and quality of life of individuals and the communities in which they serve.

These CBHs must be able to provide the basic, routine services needed in the local community. But these institutions realize they cannot provide the full spectrum of specialized services offered by university-based hospitals. Such services include heart and lung transplants, separation of twins connected at birth, and experimental cancer surgical and medical treatments, to name a few. However, many CBHs are involved in clinical trials and research, either in conjunction with university hospitals or on their own.

Traditionally, graduate educational programs for physicians have been university based, with CBHs providing additional educational opportunities through affiliations with university hospitals. However, CBHs have been able to expand their educational offerings beyond physicians by focusing on ancillary health care providers that university-based hospitals have traditionally ignored. Such providers include nurses, physician assistants, nurse practitioners, physical therapists, and occupational therapists, to name a few.

Most CBHs have found their surgical patient population has undergone a transition from mostly inpatient to outpatient. It is now common for more than 70% of surgeries in CBHs to be done on an ambulatory basis. Many of these hospitals have therefore lowered their bed count, because patients have shorter stays for medical conditions and inpatient surgeries, and more surgery is done on an outpatient basis. Therefore the physical makeup of these institutions has changed. Many have developed freestanding ambulatory surgery centers (ASCs) to improve the efficiencies (both financial and time) of delivering surgical care.

The length of stay for patients has shortened significantly over the past decade. This change has prompted these hospitals to re-engineer. They have used now-empty floors in hospitals to develop nursing home–type units and rehabilitation units and created new services such as sleep labs and wound care centers. Many hospitals have opened emergency care walk-in centers in neighboring towns, to reach out further into the local community and to make getting care even easier.

More and more CBHs are putting on health fairs and speakers programs to convey disease management and preventive health care measures to the members of their community. These programs are designed to help create loyalty to these CBHs.

During the past decade, the number of hospitals in the United States has decreased as managed care has put financial pressures on hospitals. Some have been merged into larger institutions, whereas others have closed their doors. As health care continues to change, to remain vital and viable institutions, CBHs will continue to evolve to meet the demands of their community.

—Michael R. Marks

See also Ambulatory Care, American Hospital Association (AHA), Case Management, Community Health, Hospitals

FURTHER READING

www.aha.com

COMMUNITY HEALTH

"Community health" is the health status of a defined population organized by common identity and/or an identified geographic location. Elemental to community health is the definition of the community and its culturally influenced understanding of health. Health administrators are often challenged in providing health care when the culture of a community significantly influences its understanding of health. Culturally framed definitions of health are developed over generations and across the fabric of cultural activities. Health care is a central component of a community, and its management has developed well beyond simply coordinating the provision of health services. Health care leaders are now key players in the support and improvement of community health. The three central areas of action in community health are health promotion, health protection, and the provision of health services.

DEFINING COMMUNITY

The first building block for sustained community health is a clear understanding of the membership or boundaries associated with the community. Although communities are most commonly thought of as a population defined by some geographic boundary, communities can also be bound by a mutual identity outside a specific physical boundary. Often a community achieves a high sense of cohesion by organizing around common themes, cultural identities, and shared interests or goals.

For assessing community health, it is important to use a common baseline understanding of the definition of the specific community. Community health status indicators, epidemiologic studies, and strategies for activities in health promotion, health protection, and the provision of health services use this baseline as a platform for assessment, planning, and action.

DEFINING HEALTH

The World Health Organization (WHO) generally defines health as a harmonious state of complete physical, mental, and social well-being—not merely the absence of disease or illness. This harmonious state is achieved within the context of cultural norms and values. Whereas physical and mental well-being are often understood within the context of a culture's medical or science model, social well-being draws on broader elements of the cultural life of the community. To get a complete picture of the health of a community, an assessment of social well-being includes areas such as ecosystems and social support systems. Social support systems include public health, school health, and other tax-supported sectors such as public safety and justice systems.

Health, as a state of physical, mental, and social well-being, is built on a complex web of underlying determinants. These determinants are best understood through four main categories: lifestyle, social and physical environment, human biology/genetics, and access to health care. Historically, health administration has focused on access to and delivery of health services. Research on the determinants of health indicates that of the four categories listed, access to health care services represents only about 10% of the causal pathway to health. As health administrators assume a larger role in community health, focus will shift more to the impact of human biology (20%) and environment/lifestyle (70%) on health.

Health administrators play a key role in helping communities define health broadly and build strategies to promote and protect health within the multiple causal pathways found in their unique cultural settings. Leaders in not-for-profit health service organizations are increasingly legitimizing tax-exempt status by addressing their role in community health as part of a successful business plan. The central focus of successful social partnerships between the hospital and the community it serves is the establishment of culturally informed and framed definitions of health. Community health councils or coalitions are examples of partnerships of key community stakeholders, including members from health service organizations, who define the health priorities of their communities and work to build community capacity to resource and support efforts to improve community well-being. Healthy community partnerships best serve their community when they combine grassroots coalitions with tax-supported health promotion, health protection, and health service delivery activities.

HEALTH PROMOTION

"Health promotion" is educational and social support processes aimed at enabling people's ability to increase control over and improve their health, and reinforcing that behavior over time. Rooted in the social and behavioral sciences, health promotion activities focus on changing unhealthy behaviors, sustaining/promoting healthier behaviors, and influencing healthy public policy. At the individual level, this includes activities aimed at promoting healthy behaviors and moving people with unhealthy behaviors through stages of change from awareness to healthy action. At the community level, this includes activities that bring greater community capacity to improve health. Central to this effort is building social capital through educational, organizational, political, and cohesion-building activities. These activities often include public health practices, school health education, worksite health programs, personal health practices, recreational services, health professions practices, and legal/legislative practices.

HEALTH PROTECTION

"Health protection" is community intervention aimed at environmental health risk factors. Rooted in the scientific foundation of community health, health protection draws from human ecology, environmental sciences, demography, and epidemiology. The major categories of health protection are injury control (intentional and unintentional), water safety, food safety, vector/zoonoses control, waste control, atmospheric pollution control, and environmental issues of the residence and workplace.

PROVISION OF HEALTH SERVICES

The final category of community health is the provision of health services. Provision of health services includes strategic planning, service provision, and health services evaluation provided to a community. Health administration is often introduced to broader participation in community health through this area of involvement. Although coordinating health service provision is a primary responsibility

of the health administration profession, health planning and evaluation are most effective when they include community participation. Local community health services and personal health services are an integral part of the overall provision of care in a community. Community health is best served when continuously improving community capacity includes the full continuum of health services from community care settings to traditional tertiary care institutions. To ensure the broadest possible access to and accurate development of resources and services, community health services planning should include full collaboration between health administrators and the key culturally rich stakeholders of the communities they serve.

—James F. Meyers

See also Community Health Status Indicators

FURTHER READING

Bowen, G. L., Martin, J. A., Mancini, J. A., & Nelson, J. P. (2000). Community capacity: Antecedents and consequences. *Journal of Community Practice, 8*(2), 1–21.

Green, L. W., & Ottoson, J. M. (1999). *Community and population health.* Boston: WCB McGraw-Hill.

Johnson, K., Grossman, W., & Cassidy, A. (1996). *Collaborating to improve community health.* San Francisco: Jossey-Bass.

Weil, P. A., Bogue, R. J., & Morton, R. L. (2001). *Achieving success through community leadership.* Chicago: Health Administration Press.

www.ache.org/policy/Respon.cfm

COMMUNITY HEALTH STATUS INDICATORS

Community health status indicators are specific measures of distinct aspects of the overall health of a population residing in a defined geographic area. They provide easily usable information important to health planners, policymakers, and health care providers. By definition, these measures should be community based and should encompass dimensions of health status attainment relevant to the entire population. Because health status is a function of both public health and health care, community health status indicators include direct measures of health, such as mortality and disease incidence rates, and related measures of the major determinants of health, including sociodemographic characteristics, health services availability, health care use, environmental conditions, social connectedness, and general well-being. Community health status indicators often complement data from within health care organizations derived from medical records or from clinical or administrative databases, by describing factors relevant to health that exist or occur outside the health care organization. Although typically generated and used by public health professionals, health care management organizations may find community health status indicators useful in monitoring the external environment for strategic planning and management.

SOURCES AND USES OF COMMUNITY HEALTH STATUS INDICATORS

Community health status indicators are typically derived from population-based data systems such as vital records, federal health databases, national or state health surveys, surveillance systems, and data compiled by national, professional, and research organizations. The systematic collection of community health status indicators over time allows for the ongoing assessment of needs, the identification of emerging or waning trends, and the introduction of accountability into health systems. The community and population focus of these indicators is important in monitoring health status trends and in evaluating the effectiveness of health promotion and disease prevention strategies across a population, regardless of health insurance status, health plan affiliation, or health care use history.

Because health status is not only a function of health care, health management organizations attend to these measures of trends in emerging diseases or population characteristics, because they can suggest needed modifications to the portfolio of health care services offered by the organization. Political leaders also monitor community health status indicators, which often serve as important windows on the overall state of a community. Adverse changes in community health status indicators may predict issues that will be of concern to members of the public and that may motivate them to community action.

Unlike the findings from a single research study, community health status indicators provide routine, stable measures of the quality of life and health in a given community. Classic examples are the rates for infant mortality, adolescent pregnancy, motor vehicle fatalities, and the incidence of HIV. Broader measures can include the percentage of the population uninsured, emergency room use rates, high school graduation rates, and the air quality index.

PERFORMANCE MONITORING

Since the performance measurement movement gained momentum in the 1990s, public health agencies and health care organizations have been experimenting with the use of community health status indicators as measures of health system performance. Traditional indicators of community health status such as the rates of completed immunizations at 2 years of age or the rates of early initiation of prenatal care are being applied to specific populations such as the patient population of a health plan or Medicaid enrollees. As in the past, community health status indicators are useful for monitoring the overall well-being of a defined population and in combination with system-level indicators, can suggest areas in need of improvement. Such indicators, if based on consistent measurement strategies, can be used to compare performance across health plans or to compare an individual health organization's performance against that of the larger community.

THE MINNESOTA CHILD HEALTH MONITORING SYSTEM

As one example of an extensive monitoring system based on a set of community health status indicators, the Minnesota Department of Health developed a set of measures for the purpose of monitoring the health of children across the state. The table on the opposite page illustrates this child health monitoring model, which depends on the focused collection and examination of indicators in four specific areas: general child health status, child health services utilization, the health system, and the larger societal context within which children and families live. In this model, indicators specific to one sector of the overall health care system can be used in concert with indicators of the broader community to paint a portrait of the overall health of children and to point to areas perhaps amenable to intervention. Note also that this model incorporates the notion of community assets in addition to community health concerns.

CRITERIA FOR COMMUNITY HEALTH STATUS INDICATORS

The process of developing and selecting community health status indicators can be an arduous one, involving various experts as well as representatives of the community. In any case, certain criteria should be met before a community health status indicator is adopted (from Petersen & Alexander, 2001, pp. 75–77):

Simplicity: The indicators should be conceptually straight-forward, well defined, reliable, and valid.

Stability: The indicators should represent events with sufficient occurrence to provide stable estimates, that is, estimates without dramatic fluctuation due to small numbers.

Table 1   Minnesota Child Health Monitoring Model

Health Status	Health Utilization	Health Systems	Population Context
• Mortality rates • Incidence of communicable diseases • Mental health • Youth risk behavior • Adolescent pregnancy • Low birth weight • Confirmed cases of child abuse and neglect • Incidence of injuries • Nutritional deficiency	• Immunizations • Barriers to use • Emergency room visits • School screening • Well-child visits • EPSDT • School clinic use • Mental health service use • Specialty services used by children with special health care needs • Community resources used by children with special health care needs	• Health insurance coverage • Type and number of pediatric providers available • Type and number of specialty providers available • Type and number of support services available • Perceived availability of care • Denials of service • Uncompensated care • Out-of-pocket expenditures	• Children in poverty • Children in special ed • School dropout rate • Adolescent arrest rate • Community violence • Pre-1970 housing units • Housing as percentage of income • Urgent care facilities • Public libraries, books • Law enforcement level • Adult CE programs • Youth vocational ed • Open/green spaces • Bike and walking paths • Voting in elections • Alcohol outlets • Food shelf use

Source: D. J. Petersen (1997), *Monitoring the health of Minnesota's children and families in an era of reform: The Minnesota MCH Indicators Project* (Minneapolis: Minnesota Department of Health).

Note: EPSDT, Early and Periodic Screening, Diagnostic, and Treatment.

Timeliness: The data needed to calculate the indicators should be readily available at the level at which they will be used, the state, county, or health management organization.

Logical: The indicators must be meaningful to those for whom they are intended to be useful and must reflect the goals and objectives of the program and/or the health status conditions they are intended to measure.

Equity: The indicators selected should reflect the potential health status concerns of the majority of any subdivisions that exist within the larger entity using the indicators (counties, communities, clinics, and so forth). This is particularly important if the indicators may be used in resource allocation decisions.

—Donna J. Petersen

FURTHER READING

Durch, J. S., Bailey, L. M., & Stoto, M. A. (Eds.). (1997). *Improving health in the community: A role for performance monitoring.* Washington, DC: National Academy Press.

Petersen, D. J., & Alexander, G. R. (2001). *Needs assessment in public health: A practical guide for students and professionals.* New York: Kluwer Academic Press.

www.aspe.hhs.gov

www.hrsa.gov

COMMUNITY RATING

See Community Health

COMPARATIVE ADVERTISING

In comparative advertising, a company publicly compares its product or service with other competing products or services. Firms usually compare their products with a single product, but in some situations a product has been compared with multiple competitive products. For example, manufacturers of Tylenol and other over-the-counter (OTC) pain relievers describe their products as better and faster pain relievers than specific, named competing brands or sometimes just use the leading brand words as points of comparison. Although it is not illegal in the United States to name competing brands, it is not wise, because doing so can start self-defeating competitive price wars.

The variety of comparative advertisements includes television, radio, print media, and the Internet. In recent years, various Internet sites have compared product prices and specifications to aid potential buyers make informed decisions. Similarly, buyers also visit different company Web sites to compare prices.

Today it is uncommon for hospitals, other medical facilities, and medical professionals to employ comparative advertising. However, we do not know how competitive the medical field will be in the future. When the medical field is saturated by health care providers, health care providers may resort to comparative advertising. It was once uncommon for attorneys to advertise, but we have seen numerous law firms using advertisements strongly appealing to fear on television and other media during the last decade.

—Fahri Karakaya

See also Advertising, Competitor Analysis

FURTHER READING

Perrault, W., & McCarty, J. (2002). *Basic marketing* (14th ed.). Boston: Irwin McGraw-Hill.

COMPARATIVE STATICS

Comparative statics is a field of study that examines how changes in market conditions influence the positions of the demand and supply curves and therefore the equilibrium levels of price and output (see Santerre, 2000).

Comparative statics involves comparing the initial and new equilibrium points after an external change alters the market. This tool can therefore be used to explain the effects of market changes in the past or to forecast future market outcomes. For example, suppose the market for physician services in Chicago is initially in equilibrium. Then a local economic boom increases average consumer income by $1,000 per year. The quantity of physician services demanded at every given price rises, shifting the demand curve for physician services to the right. At the original equilibrium price, the quantity demanded of physician services exceeds the number of visits physicians are willing to supply. Patients bid up the price of physician visits, which gives physicians an incentive to increase the number of visits provided. This process continues until the market price and quantity of visits reach the intersection of the original supply curve and the new demand curve. Thus, comparative statics predicts that a higher price and number of physician visits are associated with an increase in consumer income.

—Vivian Ho

FURTHER READING

Santerre, R. E., & Neun, S. P. (2000). *Health economics: Theories, insights, and industry studies.* Orlando, FL: Dryden Press.

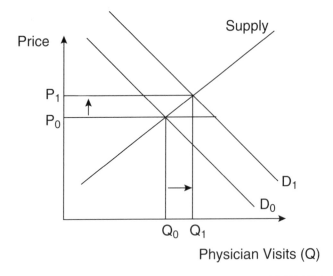

Figure 1 Comparative Statics

COMPENSATING DIFFERENTIALS

"Compensating differentials are the observed wage differentials required to equalize the total monetary and nonmonetary advantages or disadvantages among work activities and among workers themselves," says Sherwin Rosen, a modern labor economist, in "The Theory of Equalizing Differences," *The Handbook of Labor Economics* (Rosen, 1986).

The principle of compensating differentials, as noted, is based on an economics paradigm holding that this formulation is based on market clearing, in which the problem of wage differentials involves heterogeneous workers and jobs. "This is in contrast to the standard market paradigm, where the identities of the traders is immaterial to final outcomes and indeed is the ultimate source of efficiency of a decentralized competitive market system, with whom and for whom one works is generally of considerable importance for achieving efficient labor allocations" (Rosen, 1986).

Medical economics differs from the policies of a competitive market system. The medical system is not a free-market system and is not based on a free-market economy. There is no remaining method in the U.S. health care economy that is based on supply and demand.

In the past, fees and choice of location of care were determined by the interaction between the patient and the physician. Today, compensating differentials in the economics of the current medical system are skewed by the dominant third-party payer system in the United States. From the Medicare program, with its establishment in

1965; to the Medicaid or Welfare system, in the mid-1960s; to the fee-for-service model, which most closely represented a free-market system (prior to third-party coverage); to "usual and customary" reimbursement; to capitation models; to prospective payment; to DRGs (diagnosis-related groups) and APGs (ambulatory patient groups), the health care economic picture has moved totally away from any system that is recognized as free market, whereby workers receive payment from employers based on economic principles of efficiency in a decentralized competitive market system.

All the reimbursement forms just listed interfere with the compensating differentials as discussed in economic models. Regardless of whether provided by individuals or by organizations, health care reimbursement has moved away from the transactions that mirror supply and demand. The concept of a competitive market system where price fluctuates freely, adjusted spontaneously and in consideration of other factors (such as quality of service, timeliness of service, type of services, and location, in addition to cost) is no longer present in health care management. Health care has lost a driver. Attempts to relocate one have fallen short even after limiting services, attempting gatekeeper models, measuring, and valuing "quality issues" or outcomes.

Health care reimbursement companies, as third-party payers, do not employ physicians to provide health care, unless in the staff model scenario, which is dying across the country. The agreement between the physician providers and the third-party payer relates to accepted reimbursement as a set amount (usually set unilaterally by the payer). This amount is lower than charges and is expected to compensate for services provided to members. However, the negotiated amount may still be denied by the third-party payer. Consistent with economics, if there is an oligopoly in the third-party payer arena, the compensation for the health care entity or the provider is limited by the lack of competition between payers. In the current health care environment, this fact allows the payer to dictate reimbursement without effective recourse. There is no avenue for the end organ, as the recipient of care, to seek other alternatives. The recipient in the health care marketplace is forced to accept the care as dictated by the insurance plan, contracted to control provider (hospital and physician) costs. The "choice" claims that can be heard in the setting of an insurance oligopoly remain under the umbrella of unilaterally controlled, nonnegotiable compensation; the choice is in the level of copayment for which the member or patient will be responsible.

For these reasons, compensating differential is a misnomer in the health care industry when considered according to the classic economic paradigm.

Compensating differentials for physicians include geographic location and desirability of location. Concentration of certain specialties in one area and concentration of different health care reimbursement companies seem to have the greatest effect. The differentials for physicians providing health care services are also affected by specialty. Using a component of the compensating differential paradigm (that is, comparing wage differentials across the spectrum, holding worker ability constant), physicians of the same specialty and training command higher salaries in less desirable areas of the country. Geographic location shows that the Southeast United States is the least desirable and the highest reimbursed area of the country to practice medicine, and New England and the North Central regions are the least reimbursed and the most desirable areas of the country to live. The variance for single specialty follows the geographic distributions. Another differential is population density. Single-specialty primary care receives lower salaries in more densely populated areas. In subspecialty nonprimary care, the salaries are higher in areas of more dense populations. For example, a specialist in internal medicine/pediatrics commands a much higher salary to practice in the rural Midwest than would be provided in urban Boston. Confounding this trend, the same specialty may be reimbursed at a lower rate in an undesirable area of an inner-city setting, such as in a federally qualified community health center in an impoverished, crime-riddled urban area. Serving in this undesirable area should command higher reimbursement, but this does not hold true; probably because of lack of funding, both from the private paying patient and governmental funding.

Physicians may see differing compensating differentials in employment, even within similar locations. RVUs (relative value units) were instituted following a Harvard University review commission recommendation during the Clinton administration. This form of payment differential attempts to supply compensation based on level and intensity of service as constants, with other geographic expenses as variants. Providers vie for a base level of RVUs to achieve adequate productivity to cover expenses for their position in a particular site of practice.

Other forms of compensating differentials for payment to physicians include total gross productivity, which drives visits and charges without crediting other factors. Net reimbursement (gross charges minus third-party payer discounts) proved a more accurate record of financial performance but has been found to cause physicians to preferentially select their patients by the kind of coverage the patients possess.

Capitation is another form of reimbursement that has been used to differentiate compensation. A physician provider receives financial credit for the size of a "panel" of patients. The larger the panel, the greater continuity of care and the higher the number of visits provided to a population with a set amount of reimbursement. Capitation had many admirable aspects in its original mission: cutting costs by sharing risk with providers, employers, and third-party payers; focusing attention on regular evaluation for wellness, not only illness; and providing comprehensive care to avoid referrals to more costly subspecialists. The capitation bubble has burst, and this form of reimbursement is seldom used these days.

Another common form of compensation, although commonly accompanied by a financial loss, is a salaried position. This allows a physician to expect a certain amount of reimbursement and frequently does not account for productivity level or other nonreimbursable forms of benefit to a medical practice. Therefore, physicians are frequently content to provide a minimal level of work under this system of compensation.

Creative compensation plans have been developed using a combination of many different aspects of the component parts of a successful medical practice. A physician may receive a base salary with added financial incentives for differing aspects of practice involvement, including community involvement, administrative functions in the practice, chairing meetings, developing initiatives within the practice, leading hospital and organizational change, developing the practice by increasing his or her own practice membership, contracting or negotiating on behalf of the practice, accepting responsibility for clinical support of associate clinicians (nurse practitioners or physician assistants), marketing, and leading fellow members of the practice through dispute resolution.

These plans usually are difficult to institute as compensating differentials in established practices, because there is always disagreement about the financial value of differing aspects of contributions by different members of the practice. Once established, however, these plans have been found mutually beneficial to physicians as well as to the organization that employs them. A critical component of most such plans is the financial backing needed to supply the "seed money" that provides the initial bonus pool for the providers in the first cycle of the new compensation plan. When the bonus pool is secured, these plans frequently generate adequate revenue to exceed expenses, sustaining the plan.

—Curtis Alec Mock

FURTHER READING

http://econpapers.hhs.se/paper/fipfedfap/96-07.html

Rosen, S. (1986). The theory of equalizing differences. In O. Ashenfelter & R. Layard (Eds.), *The handbook of labor economics* (Vol. 1). Amsterdam: North Holland.

www.ssa.gov/history/briefhistory3.html

COMPENSATION SYSTEMS

No issue generates more emotion, controversy, and frustration within an organization than pay. Therefore, the compensation system and an organization's members' understanding of that system is a key ingredient in the success of the organization. The compensation system is the set of rules and logic an organization uses to determine the pay of individuals within the organization. It consists of direct compensation (base pay, differential pay, bonuses, and cash recognition awards) and indirect compensation (benefits, income replacement programs, and employee services). The compensation system is developed with the following considerations: legal requirements, internal equity, external competitiveness, reward strategies, and compensation administration. Each of these components of a compensation system is discussed here.

Both state and federal government have enacted laws that define aspects of the employment relationship between an employer and an employee. Laws such as the Fair Labor Standards Act of 1938, the prevailing wage laws (such as the Davis-Bacon Act of 1931), and equal rights legislation, which also govern employee benefits, are all examples of how government affects compensation systems. The maze of federal and state laws present both challenges and opportunities for compensation systems in health care organizations. Many hospitals have significantly changed their present packages to meet federal regulations and reduce costs. Managers and compensation specialists must be aware of the laws and how they may directly or indirectly affect the compensation system.

Within an organization, internal equity establishes equal pay for work of equal value and pay differences for work of unequal value. This principle focuses attention on a pay structure that reflects the relative worth of jobs within the organization. The pay structure, then, is a system of differing pay rates for different work or skills within a single organization. The pay structure is divided into various pay grades. Individual pay differences within pay grades may be supported by three criteria: work performed, competencies (such as certification), or work outcomes. In addition, the pay structure may group jobs into families. Job families are jobs of the same nature but requiring different skills and responsibility levels. For example, a nursing job family might consist of nurse assistant, licensed practical nurse, registered nurse, and nurse practitioner. Compensation experts may develop pay structures that are appropriate to particular job families within an organization.

A fundamental tool in determining a job's value to an organization is the job evaluation method. The job evaluation method should have two characteristics. First, it should provide a quantifiable method of ranking or rating jobs within an organization, and second, it should involve a process designed to gain acceptance of the pay structure by those within the organization. The job evaluation process, then, involves systematic data collection on jobs, analysis of those jobs according to a predetermined criterion, and a method of placing jobs into a pay structure that is perceived as fair. Because the pay structure is constantly revised, this task is never fully completed.

Five job evaluation methods are currently used by organizations. The method varies from qualitative to quantitative and according to whether it involves job-to-job comparisons or job-to-standard comparisons. The least quantitative job evaluation is a *job-ranking approach* in which all jobs are ranked from lowest to highest on overall job importance. This method is easy to administer but is inappropriate for large organizations because it lacks reliability, and it does not measure the relative value of one job compared with another. The *job classification method* involves grouping jobs into a predetermined number of classifications or grades. The job classification method is easily understood by employees, is used by the U.S. government, and is easily administered. However, this method focuses on the whole job and may be ambiguous and subjective. The *point factor method,* the most frequently used method, involves using specific factors (such as know-how, problem solving, and accountability) to evaluate relative job worth. This method produces reasonably objective and defensible results, good documentation, and a systematic process. It is, however time-consuming and difficult to explain to employees. The factor comparison method is rarely used, because it does not respond to market conditions and it is labor intensive. The factor comparison method involves ranking jobs on comparable factors, identifying weights to those factors, and then assigning a dollar amount to those factors. The market-based evaluation is not a job evaluation at all but involves using market salary data to determine the relative worth of jobs in an organization. This method is less legally defensible than the traditional job evaluation methods.

Once a job has been described and has been rated relative to other jobs in the organization, it is necessary to set up a pay structure. Pay structure is the array of pay rates for different jobs within a single organization; pay rates focus attention on differential compensation paid for work of unequal worth. Typically, large organizations have a pay structure that consists of approximately 30 or so pay grades. A pay grade is a group of jobs with the same or similar values for compensation purposes. All jobs in a pay grade have the same pay range (maximum, minimum, and midpoint). Currently, many organizations are moving to a pay structure that involves 5 or fewer pay grades. Broad-banding, as this structure is known, has the advantage of simplifying the compensation system and providing more autonomy to managers. It has the disadvantage of lacking career ladders. Organizations that are "de-layered" find broad-banding useful.

External pay competitiveness is the comparison of an organization's compensation to relevant external organizations that compete in the same product or labor market. An organization may decide to be a market leader, to pay the market average, or to lag behind the market. Whatever the decision, it is essential that an organization be aware of how its pay structure compares with the market. This knowledge requires two pieces of information: a definition of market, and a market survey.

Defining the market is a process of identifying which other employers an organization competes with for employees. Choices may be made on the basis of geography, occupational grouping, organizational product, or competition for labor. Wage or salary surveys are part of the information organizations use to determine a strategy to recruit and retain workers. Surveys must be structured so that similar jobs are being compared between organizations and so that total compensation is accounted in the analysis. Total compensation includes salary plus indirect compensation, which is reflected in the costs of additional benefits, such as time off, health insurance, retirement accounts, and other insurance (life, disability, worker's compensation, unemployment, and long-term care).

The relationships between pay and both internal and external equity are very complex. An employee's perception of pay equity is related to both expectations of pay levels and perceptions about how others are paid. However, the situation is further complicated because satisfaction with pay is only one determinant of retention and productivity. Research demonstrates that the nature of the job itself, relationships with coworkers and supervisors, commitment to the organization, and opportunities for advancement are equally important variables in explaining productivity and retention. A competitive advantage rewards health care organizations that have a clear market strategy for all job families within the organization and that have a clear understanding of how pay affects productivity and retention.

The third component of a pay structure is the reward system to determine individual salaries within an organization. Here the organization must decide and articulate which individual qualities to reward. Possibilities are merit, length of service, skills, and economic need. Merit-based pay is pay for performance and is designed to reward employee behavior that supports the achievements of the organization's goals and objectives. Merit pay is defined as "a reward that recognizes outstanding past performance." It can be given in the form of lump sum payments or as increments to the base pay. Merit programs are commonly designed to pay different amounts (often at different times) depending on the level of performance. Merit increases may or may not take into account a person's position in the salary range. The major obstacle to merit pay is defining and then measuring merit. When merit is defined in quantitative terms, then quality may suffer. Merit pay, which depends on performance appraisal, is seen as unfair if the performance appraisal is seen as unfair. Remember that many employees think they are above-average performers being paid a below-average salary.

Length of service, or longevity, has been used frequently as a merit criterion because it rewards loyalty to the organization and is easy to measure. Employees frequently assume a person who has worked for a particular organization for a longer period of time should be paid more than someone "just hired off the street." So longevity pay has the added advantage of being popular among the current workforce. Organizations may find competitive advantage in offering longevity pay or bonuses to certain groups of professional employees. Hospitals may be able to demonstrate that registered nurses who stay 5 or 10 years are more productive and therefore should be paid a longevity bonus to retain their services.

Skill is another basis for rewarding individual employees. Skill-based pay links pay to the depth and breadth of the work-related skills, abilities, and knowledge that a person acquires or demonstrates. The criterion chosen can influence employee behaviors by describing what is required to get higher pay. Rewards for certifications or degrees are examples of skill-based pay. One advantage of skill-based pay is that measurement of skills is viewed as objective and is frequently done by an external agent. Carefully placed rewards for demonstrated skills can improve employee retention and productivity.

Individual rewards may also be based on economic need. An example of need-based rewards is the across-the-board increase. Such increases are frequently tied to a cost-of-living calculation. Need-based increases are viewed by employees as entitlements: They feel their salary or wage should at least keep pace with inflation. The idea that a wage should be tied to economic need is the basis for establishing a minimum wage law and the living wage movement. As organizations continue to move away from the concept of rewards based on economic need, a result may be increased employee support for across-the-board increases and improving the pay of the lowest-paid employee. Health care organizations where there are large disparities between higher-level employees and lower-paid employees seem particularly vulnerable to the argument that pay should be sufficient to take care of basic economic needs.

Whatever compensation system is adopted by an organization, it must be fairly administered and clearly communicated to employees at all levels. A fair compensation system provides for both distributive justice (the amount of reward distributed to employees) and procedural justice (the process used to determine the amount of reward employees receive). There are at least three reasons why

it is essential to clearly communicate an organization's compensation strategy and methodology. First, for the system to influence employee behavior, employees must understand it. If an organization attempts to reward employees for giving good customer service, but the employees do not understand that intent, then they will not give good service. Second, employees tend to think the system is more compressed (no room for raises) than it in fact is. This perception will diminish motivation. An employee who feels there is no chance for a salary increase will give up trying to earn one. Third, being open about how salaries are established engenders trust in the organization. Employees who trust their managers and organization are most likely to stay and be productive. Ultimately, the compensation system is a part of the organization's culture and its overall human resources strategy.

—Alan P. Chesney

FURTHER READING

Dressler, G. (1999). *Human resource management* (8th ed.). Upper Saddle River, NJ: Prentice Hall.

Fower, E. (1990). *Strategic pay: Aligning organizational strategies and pay systems.* San Francisco: Jossey-Bass.

Milkovice, G., & Newman, J. (1996). *Compensation* (5th ed.). Chicago: Irwin.

Society for Human Resource Management. (2000). *The SHRM learning system: Module Five, Compensation and benefits.* Alexandria, VA: Society for Human Resource Management.

COMPETITIVE ADVANTAGE

Competitive advantage is the factor or series of factors that allows one organization to outperform competitors relative to the primary measure of success in its market (profit, patient satisfaction, market share, and so on). For this reason, competitive advantage is, in a sense, the Holy Grail of strategy: It is the thing organizations seek but rarely find. When found, most often competitive advantage cannot be sustained, so the quest begins again.

Executives and researchers have searched for competitive advantage in many places. For years, perhaps generations, "location, location, location" was considered the key to organizational success in virtually any market. The Internet, jet airplanes, and telecommunications put an end to that prescription. Other business leaders have tried to configure their organizations in ways that provided an advantage over competitors. Some have argued that speed is the key. In rapidly changing environments, if you respond faster to critical stakeholder needs, competitive spoils are yours for the taking. The promise of speed encouraged many organizations to focus on flexibility rather than on efficiency. In some industries, the price of a product or service was less important than speed of delivery.

MORE RECENT VIEWS

More recently, the quest for competitive advantage has centered on resources. The resource-based view (RBV) of competitive advantage proposed that organizations that control critical resources such as land, labor, and capital have an advantage over those that do not control critical resources. It seemed somewhat obvious that organizations with more financial resources should have an advantage over those with less. However, when Wal-Mart overwhelmed Sears at a time when the latter had much deeper pockets, the resource-based view became suspect. Upstarts in an industry so dominated by firms such as IBM deepened the suspicion of the resource-based view.

The importance of knowledge-based industries today has caused some to suggest that knowledge and the ability of an organization to learn and change are the real keys to competitive advantage. Much is written about the competitive value of knowledge and its proper management as a strategic resource.

COMPREHENSIVE FRAMEWORK

In fact, competitive advantage can be achieved by capitalizing on resources, competencies, or capabilities. Resources, tangible and intangible, can provide competitive advantage. The reputation (intangible resource) of the Mayo Clinic provides a tremendous competitive advantage over other less well-known medical facilities. Distinct competencies (skills that no other competitors possess) can also provide a competitive advantage. The competencies of physicians in leading-edge stem cell transplant centers provide a competitive advantage that not even the Mayo Clinic can overcome with regard to these specialized procedures. Finally, organizations can obtain a competitive advantage by their integrative or management abilities. Some—relatively few—organizations seem unusually good at bringing together resources and competencies, leveraging them, and thereby obtaining exceptional synergies.

KEY QUESTIONS FOR COMPETITIVE ADVANTAGE

Regardless of whether one is talking about resources, competencies, or capabilities, the things an organization is counting on to provide a competitive advantage must meet some rather specific criteria. These criteria are value, rareness, ease of imitation, and sustainability. For any resource, competence, or capability that might provide a competitive advantage, strategic leaders must ask the following questions and obtain definite responses. First, "Is the resource, competence, or capability of value to our patients, doctors, and other stakeholders?" The answer must be yes. If stakeholders do not value it, it cannot be the source of competitive advantage. Second, "Are we essentially the only competitor who possesses the resource, competence, or capability?" The answer must be yes. If all the competitors possess it, it cannot be the source of competitive advantage. Third, "Is our resource, competence, or capability difficult for our competitors to imitate?" The answer must be yes. If it is not difficult to imitate, competitors will imitate it as soon as they recognize that you have an advantage. Finally, "Can we sustain the resource, competence, or capability?" The answer must be yes. If you cannot sustain it, it cannot be the source of competitive advantage.

—W. Jack Duncan

FURTHER READING

Barney, J. B. (1995). Looking inside for competitive advantage. *Academy of Management Executive, 9*(4), 49–61.

Bartlett, C. A., & Ghoshal, S. (2002). Building competitive advantage through people. *Sloan Management Review, 43*(2), 34–41.

Berman, S. L., Down, J., Davis, J., & Hill, C. W. L. (2002). Tacit knowledge as a source of competitive advantage in the National Basketball Association. *Academy of Management Journal, 45*(1), 13–31.

Duncan, W. J., Ginter, P. M., & Swayne, L. E. (1998). Competitive advantage and internal organizational assessment. *Academy of Management Executive, 12*(3), 6–16.

Greve, H. R. (2001). From Silicon Valley to Singapore: Location and competitive advantage in the hard disk drive industry. *Administrative Science Quarterly, 46*(3), 794–796. Review of book by J. McKendrick, R. F. Doner, & S. Haggard.

Lubit, R. (2001). Tacit knowledge and knowledge management: The keys to sustainable competitive advantage. *Organizational Dynamics, 29*(3), 164–178.

McEvily, S. K., & Chakravarthy, B. (2002). The persistence of knowledge-based advantage: An empirical test for product performance and technological knowledge. *Strategic Management Journal, 23*(4), 285–305.

Ofeh, E., & Sarvary, M. (2001). Leveraging the customer base: Creating competitive advantage through knowledge management. *Management Science, 47*(11), 1441–1456.

Rindova, V. P., & Kotha, S. (2001). Continuous "morphing": Competing through dynamic capabilities, form, and function. *Academy of Management Journal, 44*(6), 1263–1280.

Wiggins, R. R., & Ruefli, T. W. (2002). Sustained competitive advantage: Temporal dynamics and the incidence and persistence of superior economic performance. *Organizational Science, 13*(1), 82–105.

COMPETITIVE BIDDING

Competitive bidding is a method for determining, by comparing rival offers, the price at which a good is sold. The need to win business against rivals forces participants to disclose their lowest acceptable price.

Competitive bidding can take many formats and can be used either to sell an item to many potential buyers or to buy an item from many potential sellers. A familiar example is an oral auction where the auctioneer asks if anyone will pay a certain amount to buy an item. If more than one person agrees to that price, the auctioneer suggests a higher price until only the winner is left. Another example is a sealed bid process, in which sellers are asked to submit their prices in writing so that their rivals will not see them. The seller offering the lowest price wins the sale if all other conditions, such as time of delivery and technical specifications, are met.

In "English" auctions, the auctioneer starts with a low price and progressively raises it until a winner is determined, whereas in a "Dutch" auction the price starts high and is lowered until someone agrees to that price. Both approaches are called "first price" auctions because the price named is the one at which the sale occurs. In a "second price" auction, the winner pays (or is paid) the price of the runner-up, that is, the next-to-highest (or next-to-lowest) bid. Which auction format yields the lowest price to a buyer, or highest price to a seller, is a matter of intense theoretical research.

Which format is used depends on the time available, the need to document the process, and whether bidders wish to keep some information private. A hospital seeking to buy a CT scanner may use a sealed bid auction, because it must weigh the technical merits of different machines against price. By agreeing not to publicly disclose the conditions offered by the sellers, the hospital hopes to secure a more favorable price.

Competitive bidding is frequently used by private health maintenance organizations to procure the services of clinical laboratories and other suppliers. It is not used routinely by the federal government to determine payment for services under Medicare. Studies by the federal General Accounting Office and the inspector general of the U.S. Department of Health and Human Services have found that Medicare payment rates are higher than those of many private insurers and are sometimes higher than prices offered to the public in retail stores. Under a demonstration project of competitive bidding for durable medical equipment in Polk County, Florida, in 2001, Medicare reports that it saved an average of 20% compared with its standard rates after selecting winners based on considerations of price, quality, and accessibility. The long-term use of competitive bidding in the Medicare program is a matter of intense controversy, because it has the potential to lower payment rates and possibly limit the number of suppliers who can participate in the program.

—Stephen T. Mennemeyer

See also Centers for Medicare and Medicaid Services (CMS), Health Maintenance Organizations (HMOs), Medicaid, Medicare

FURTHER READING

http://cms.gov/media/press/release.asp?Counter=399

McAfee, R. P., & McMillan, J. (1987). Auctions and bidding. *Journal of Economic Literature*, 25(2), 699–783.

Milgrom, P. R. (1987). Auction theory. In T. F. Bewley (Ed.), *Advances in economic theory—Fifth World Congress*. Cambridge, UK: Cambridge University Press.

www.healthaffairs.org

COMPETITIVE EQUILIBRIUM

A competitive equilibrium occurs in a competitive market when there is no tendency for the market price or quantity exchanged of a good or service to change further. This equilibrium is located at the intersection of the market demand curve and the market supply curve in a graph of price against quantity (see Figure 1, opposite). If the market price for aspirin exceeded the equilibrium price, the quantity of aspirin supplied would exceed the quantity demanded; sellers would want to sell more aspirin than consumers wished to buy. Sellers would gradually lower their price, and consumers would gradually increase their quantity demanded, until the market returned to equilibrium. If the market price for aspirin were lower than the equilibrium price, then the quantity of aspirin demanded would exceed the quantity supplied by sellers. In this case consumers would gradually increase the price they offer to sellers, and sellers would gradually increase their quantity supplied, until the quantity of aspirin demanded equaled the quantity supplied at the market clearing price. A competitive market describes a market for a particular good or service that has many buyers and sellers, so individual buyers and sellers have little or no ability to affect prices. Therefore, a competitive equilibrium is reached through the actions of many buyers and sellers; no one buyer or seller can single-handedly influence the equilibrium price and quantity exchanged for the overall market.

—Vivian Ho

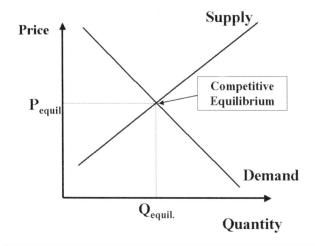

Figure 1

FURTHER READING

Santerre, R. E., & Neun S. P. (2000). *Health economics: Theories, insights, and industry studies.* Orlando, FL: Dryden Press.

COMPETITIVE STRATEGY AND GROUPS

The competitive strategy of a health care organization is a formal plan for dealing with the market movements made by competing health care firms. A competitive strategy facilitates the positioning of your firm in the right place at the right time with the right product, thus establishing a competitive advantage for your firm. Your competitive strategy creates value when it allows your firm to create new competitive advantages faster than competitors can mimic your existing competitive advantages.

A health care firm with a relatively small set of products (for example, a two-physician pediatric medical group) may be able to operate effectively with a single competitive strategy (because the geographic market is well defined and the competing physicians are likely to be stable within the market). However, a large, integrated health care system, such as one that has a 650-bed hospital that also serves as a Level I trauma center, owns three rural feeder hospitals, offers expanded home health services, and is a teaching hospital for the nearby medical school, would likely use multiple competitive strategies. Given the wide variation on products and services offered, this complex health care organization competes in several markets, each defined very differently.

Organizations tend to be labeled according to their competitive strategy perspective. Miles and Snow suggest there are four organization types, based on competitive strategy: defenders, prospectors, analyzers, and reactors. Defenders search for stability in the market and work to maintain the status quo of their competitive position. They do not actively search out new product opportunities and seldom seek new avenues for existing products.

Prospectors specialize in research and development. They are in a continuous state of advance and seldom focus on any one idea for very long. Prospectors rarely receive all the possible benefits of a new product, because they move on to the next new idea before exhausting all the efficiencies from the "older" product.

Analyzers typically remain true to their core business, while actively seeking out diversified opportunities. They attempt to maximize both the value in being an efficient defender with the possible value of being a first-mover prospector.

Reactors are seen as not really having a defined competitive strategy. Instead of developing a deliberate competitive posturing plan, reactors are unable to respond or are inconsistent in their response to their competitors' market movements. Although reactors seem to do little conscious strategic planning, this "strategy" may actually be feasible in highly regulated environments where innovation is not readily rewarded.

Porter provides another competitive strategy categorization scheme. He overlaps the two factors of strategic target (for example, the product appeals to either a broad or narrow audience) and strategic advantage (for example, the value of the service is derived by either its "customization and high cost" or its "standardization and low cost"). For example, a county hospital would likely be seen as offering standardized, low-cost health care services to a broad population base. In contrast, an ophthalmology practice focusing on customized, high-cost laser eye surgery would likely be seen as having a narrow target audience.

—Dawn M. Oetjen and Timothy Rotarius

See also Strategic Groups, Strategic Management

FURTHER READING

Miles, R. E., Snow, C. C., Meyer, A. D., & Coleman, H. J., Jr. (1978). Organizational strategy, structure, and process. *Academy of Management Review, 3*(3), 546–562.

Montgomery, C. A., & Porter, M. E. (Eds.). (1991). *Strategy: Seeking and securing competitive advantage.* Boston: Harvard Business School Press.

Porter, M. E. (1980). *Competitive strategy.* New York: Free Press.

Porter, M. E. (1985). *Competitive advantage.* New York: Free Press.

COMPETITOR ANALYSIS

See Service Area Competitor Analysis

COMPLEMENTARY MEDICINE

See Alternative Medicine

COMPLEMENTARY PRODUCT

A complementary product is a product that has a particular value to the customer because of its use with another product. An example of complementary products are the compact disk (CD) and the CD player. Neither can perform its appropriate function without the other, and thus neither has any particular value without the other. The sales of the two products are intimately related. People do not buy CDs unless they have CD players, and initially people were not anxious to buy CD players until they were convinced that their desired music, including previously released recordings, would be available in that format.

Another aspect of complementary products involves pricing strategies. At a fast food restaurant, a "value meal" includes the drink, potato or other starchy food, and entrée. Each item is also available for separate purchase. However, because the restaurant believes that the items will be regularly purchased together as complementary products, it practices the "value meal" pricing strategy or *bundling,* in which it is more economical for the purchaser to buy all the items as a unit. Other examples of *bundling* of complementary products include pricing by hotels in which the room rate also includes a "free" breakfast that cannot be unbundled from the room rate, and computers in which the operating system comes preloaded on the machine.

The pricing of complementary products may also include estimations of the demand relationship such that the manufacturer may, for example, be willing to lose money on a razor in order to make up for it on the blades or the grocer to lose money on the shortcake but make up for it on the strawberries and cream.

Because of the intimate usage relationship between the two complementary products, marketers need to be attentive not only to the prices they charge but also to the product development and distribution actions by the manufacturers of the related product. For years many comedians drew knowing laughs from customers about the fact that hot dogs and buns were packaged in mismatched counts: eight or twelve buns, but ten hot dogs, in a package.

—David W. Glascoff

COMPLIANCE

In health care, compliance refers to efforts by providers, contractors, and suppliers to ensure that the company or group and their physicians and employees adhere to the laws and regulations governing the workplace and the health care field. Voluntary compliance programs are strongly encouraged by the government. A well-crafted compliance program demonstrates the company's commitment to the ethical and proper way to do business, communicates company values and procedures to employees, requires adherence to the laws and rules governing health care practices, discovers and addresses problems, and constantly monitors to ensure the efficacy of the program.

There are many reasons for a company to implement a compliance program. The chief reason is to ensure that the company's values and safeguards are known and observed throughout the company. An effective compliance program must include a commitment to inform and educate employees and to define the legal and ethical obligations of each individual within the company. Key to the success of any compliance program is a clear, accessible means of reporting problems or concerns. The reporting procedures should provide for anonymity, but if the communicator is known, there must be assurances that the communicator's privacy will be protected and that the person will not be subject to any form of retaliation. Follow-up is equally important. Also essential is a well-defined system for investigating and addressing problems once they are made known. A successful program must demonstrate its ongoing commitment to compliance by performing regular audits and evaluations to ensure that the numerous aspects of the program are working properly and being followed. The compliance program should also include policies and procedures for redressing problems discovered and, where appropriate, should include mechanisms for reporting errors and overpayments to the proper authorities.

The Office of Inspector General (OIG) of the U.S. Department of Health and Human Services is charged with oversight of protecting the integrity of federal health care payment programs. OIG has issued health care guidelines for establishing and overseeing a compliance program in several areas of the health care field. The program elements are similar for differing segments of the health care market, but for this discussion the focus will be on the "Guidance for Individual and Small Practice Physicians."

This OIG guide gives a clear road map for any health care provider or practice seeking to institute a compliance plan. Compliance programs for physicians should be viewed as a form of "preventive medicine." Physicians have a duty to ensure that claims submitted to Medicare, Medicaid, and other federal health care programs are true and accurate. An effective compliance program is the best mechanism to ensure that billing rules are followed and that problems are discovered and corrected.

The OIG guide for implementing a compliance plan identifies the following steps:

1. Audit and monitor.

2. Establish practice standards and procedures.

3. Designate compliance officer or contacts.

4. Conduct appropriate training and education.

5. Develop a plan to respond to detected offenses and conduct corrective action interviews.

6. Develop open lines of communication.

7. Develop disciplinary standards through well-publicized guidelines.

Compliance programs can be narrow or broad. A basic program for physicians would focus primarily on billing issues. A more comprehensive program would include billing compliance, employment, safety, privacy, and other fraud and abuse laws. A comprehensive program should be the long-term goal. This is especially important in the current health care environment given recent efforts by federal enforcement agencies and *qui tam* relators to claim that many kinds of health care violations create a false claim or statement when billing for Medicare or Medicaid reimbursement.

Important organizational steps must be taken before establishing a compliance program. The group or practice must first gain the support and commitment of the board, management, providers, and staff. Financial support must be committed to the program. Such support is required for development and startup costs, hiring a compliance officer and staff, funding for education, and sufficient resources for ongoing operations.

Actual implementation of the program should begin with step 1 of the OIG guide—auditing and monitoring. This step requires an internal assessment to determine current practices and problems, identify risk areas, and establish areas of responsibility and patterns of information flow. Policies and procedures should be clear written statements concerning all aspects of the compliance program. These must be communicated to all members and employees of the practice and should include clear endorsements by top management and, where relevant, the board. Oversight responsibilities should be assigned and a compliance officer appointed. Education and training programs should be conducted to ensure that every person in the organization is made aware of the specifics of the program and knows the identity of the compliance officer and how to report concerns.

Perhaps the most essential and important aspect of the program is the institution of a hotline or other means of reporting problems. Great care should be taken that reported concerns are investigated and addressed in a timely manner and that "messengers" do not suffer any negative consequences. Where appropriate, it may even be advantageous to reward individuals for their efforts to report and correct problems. Systematic auditing and monitoring measure the effectiveness of the program. Finally, the program must establish protocols for correcting problems, sanctions for noncompliant behavior, and policies for reporting mistakes and returning overpayments to government or private payers.

The goals of an effective compliance program include prevention, discovery, and correction. When problems are found and promptly reported, the threat of severe sanctions imposed by the government may be significantly reduced. Although the existence of a compliance program does not insulate a group from the imposition of penalties, it can influence the severity of any penalties and may help avoid criminal prosecution. Under the Federal Sentencing Guidelines, the existence of an effective compliance program is a mitigating factor to be taken into consideration when applying mandatory sanctions.

A compliance program may also help avoid a corporate integrity agreement (CIA). A CIA is a government-imposed "compliance program" that can be quite onerous. A typical CIA is imposed for a five-year period, and compliance with a CIA can be quite expensive in terms of time, effort, and money.

The benefits of a voluntary compliance program are numerous and tangible. Such programs raise awareness, reduce the risk of whistleblower actions, serve as a mitigating factor in fraud investigations and assessment penalties, and demonstrate commitment to responsible and ethical practices in the health care system.

—Cheryl S. Massingale

See also Qui Tam Actions

FURTHER READING

Office of Inspector General. Compliance program for individual and small group physician practices. (2000, October 5). *Federal Register, 65,* 194.

Withrow, S. (2000, October). Compliance guidance for physicians: Blustering about clustering. *Health Care Fraud & Abuse Newsletter, 3*(9), 5–6.

COMPONENT CARE

See Episodes of Care

COMPOUND GROWTH RATE

The compound growth rate for a pair of values, V_1 and V_2, and a number of time periods, n, is the constant growth rate, g, that will cause V_1 to grow to V_2 over n time periods. In equation form, g must satisfy

$$V_2 = V_1(1 + g)^n$$

If you know V_1, V_2, and n, then you can solve for g:

$$g = n\sqrt{\frac{V_2}{V_1}} - 1$$

The following examples can help explain the uses of the compound growth rate formulas.

Suppose sales increased from $100 million in 1999 to $180 million in 2003. What is the average annual sales compound growth rate? We know sales increased by a total of 80% over these four years. However, this does not represent an annual sales growth rate of $80 \div 4 = 20\%$. Rather, the annual sales growth rate is

$$g = 4\sqrt{\frac{180}{100}} - 1 = 0.1583 = 15.83\%$$

The growth rate is less than 20% because of compounding. At a growth rate of 15.86%, sales will grow as follows:

Year	Sales	
1999	$100	
2000	$100 × (1.1583)	= $115.83
2001	$115.83 × (1.1583)	= $134.17
2002	$134.17 × (1.1583)	= $155.41
2003	$155.41 × (1.1583)	= $180.00

In 2000, sales increased by 15.83% of $100, or $15.83. In 2001, sales increased by another $15.83 plus 15.83% of the additional $15.83 sales in 2000. Thus not only does the initial $100 in sales grow by 15.83% each year, but the additional sales in each year will also grow by 15.83%.

The same calculations apply to interest earnings. If you invest $100 in a savings account at 6%, then in one year you will have $106. In two years you will have $106 × (1.06) = $112.36. In three years you will have $112.36 × (1.06) = $119.10. In the second and third year you earned interest on the $100, plus interest on the interest you had earned earlier. This is called *compound interest*. See the entry for *Time Value of Money* for a discussion about compound interest.

COMPOUNDING INTERVALS

The compound growth rate depends on the beginning and ending values and on the number of compounding intervals. For example, if you started with $100 in a stock account and five years later you had $146.93, then the annual compound growth rate, which is also equal to the annual compound rate of return, would be

$$g = r = 5\sqrt{\frac{146.93}{100.00}} - 1 = 0.080 = 8\%$$

However, if you wanted to know the monthly compound rate you earned, the calculation would be

$$g = r = 60\sqrt{\frac{146.93}{100.00}} - 1 = 0.006433 = 0.643\% \text{ per month}$$

This is not equal to $8\% \div 12 = 0.667\%$.

—Phillip R. Daves

See also Annual Percentage Rate (APR), Time Value of Money

FURTHER READING

Brigham, E. F., & Ehrhardt, M. C. (2001.) *Financial management* (10th ed.). Mason, OH: South-Western.

COMPOUND INTEREST METHOD

See Compound Growth Rate

COMPRESSED WORKWEEKS

The term *compressed workweek* refers to an alternative work schedule that can be used by employers who are trying to implement creative work scheduling to meet either work demands, customer needs, or the personal commitments of employees. This type of work schedule typically involves employees regularly working longer hours on some workdays, so that they can have all or part of another workday off. Compressed workweeks specifically involve work schedules wherein the employee continues to work a full-time schedule (such as 40 hours per week), but according to a work schedule that entails fewer workdays in a workweek than the typical five 8-hour workdays.

Typical examples for compressed workweek schedules are four 10-hour workdays, followed by a three-day weekend or working 80 hours during nine workdays. Within the health care profession, nurses frequently work on a compressed schedule to maximize both work and personal time. Frequently, nurses may be assigned to three successive 12-hour shifts, resulting in a three-days-on, four-days-off weekly work rotation. This type of work arrangement could be considered a compressed workweek.

This type of work schedule offers employees flexibility to obtain an additional weekday or part of a weekday to address personal matters (such as family obligations, child/elder care, or travel). Moreover, it may allow the employer to better meet customer demands, because the regular hours of operation may be extended beyond the typical 8-hour workday. Compressed workweeks are one of several work-scheduling alternatives an employer may want to consider offering. Other options include flextime and telecommuting.

—Laura Gniatczyk

See also Flextime, Telecommuting

FURTHER READING

Bureau of National Affairs. (2001). *Alternative schedules.* Washington, DC: Author.

CONCENTRIC DIVERSIFICATION

See Diversification Strategies

CONFLICT MANAGEMENT

Conflict in any organization is inescapable, and managers spend a sizable amount of their workweek managing conflict. An organization's bottom line can be significantly affected by unresolved conflict in terms of lost productivity, employee turnover, reduced employee morale, and increased litigation. People who effectively manage conflict are perceived as more competent managers than those who cannot. In addition, effective conflict management increases employee perceptions of fairness and job satisfaction, reduces worker stress and health-related problems, and results in fewer employee lawsuits (Jameson, 1999).

The cost of conflict to an organization can be enormous. Possible variables to factor into a cost analysis include amount of wasted employee time (calculated as a fraction of total monthly compensation, including benefits), employee turnover costs (150% of total annual compensation to account for recruitment, hiring, training, and so on), sabotage/theft costs, reduced job motivation (usually estimated by a percentage of annual salary), and days lost because of stress-related health issues and absenteeism. For example, consider an ongoing conflict between two staff nurses (each earning $6,000 per month in total compensation) and a hospital pathologist ($18,000 per month total compensation). This conflict results in all three workers wasting 8 hours per month for three months, and ultimately causes one nurse to find other employment. Using conservative estimates, the unresolved conflict results in a $112,500 loss to the hospital:

- Cost of nurses' wasted time: $6,000/160 work hours per month × 24 hours over 3 months × 2 nurses = $1,800
- Cost of pathologist's wasted time: $18,000/160 work hours per month × 24 hours over 3 months = $2,700
- Replacement of departing nurse: $72,000 total compensation × 150% = $108,000

A conventional definition of conflict is any situation where there are discordant goals or ideas between individuals or groups. Conflict arises for a multitude of reasons, including differences in values, attitudes, and perceptions; incompatible goals and objectives; miscommunication; unclear job boundaries; misattributions of others' motives; and competition over limited resources. Many people perceive all conflict as destructive and something to be avoided. In fact, conflict may be either positive or negative, depending on its outcomes. Negative or dysfunctional conflict occurs when an individual's or group's productivity is impeded, morale is undermined, and people become more polarized on issues. Positive or constructive conflict clarifies important issues, generates better-quality decisions, and creates new ideas (Thomas, 1990).

When seeking to manage conflict, the goal is to minimize dysfunctional conflict and maximize constructive conflict. Conflicts can be made more constructive by discovering the root cause of the issue, to correct misperceptions and miscommunications. In addition, an atmosphere of collaboration can be built by emphasizing common goals and objectives held by the involved parties. Increasing the amount of information shared, in terms of both quality and quantity, is also key to managing conflict. Organizations can help manage conflict and its impact on performance by sponsoring team-building activities, mandating negotiation or conflict management training, encouraging regular staff meetings, and formalizing a dispute resolution process.

—E. Kate Atchley

See also Group Norms, Group Performance, Groupthink, Merger and Acquisition, Negotiations

FURTHER READING

Dana, D. (1997). *How to build better relationships at work and home* (2nd ed.). Prairie Village, KS: MTI Publications.

Gebelein, S. H., Stevens, L. A., Skube, C. J., Lee, D. G., Davis, B. L., & Hellervik, L. W. (2001). Manage conflict. In *Successful manager's handbook: Development suggestions for today's managers* (pp. 466–480). Minneapolis: Personnel Decisions International.

Jameson, J. K. (1999). Toward a comprehensive model for the assessment and management of intraorganizational conflict: Developing the framework. *International Journal of Conflict Management, 10*(3), 268–295.

Thomas, K. W. (1990). Conflict and negotiation processes in organizations. In M. D. Dunnette & L. M. Hough (Eds.), *The handbook of industrial and organizational psychology* (2nd ed., Vol. 3, pp. 651–717). Palo Alto, CA: Consulting Psychologists Press.

CONGLOMERATE DIVERSIFICATION

See Diversification Strategies

CONSENT

See Informed Consent

CONSOLIDATION

See Merger and Acquisition

CONSUMER

See Customer Perceptions

CONSUMER ADOPTION PROCESS

See Diffusion of Innovation

CONSUMER CHOICE AND DEMAND

See Customers' Consequences, Customers' Desired Purpose or Goals, Customer Value

CONSUMER-CHOICE HEALTH PURCHASING GROUP

See Coalitions, Health Plan Employer Data and Information Set (HEDIS)

CONSUMER PERCEPTION OF SERVICE

See Customers' Consequences, Customers' Desired Purpose or Goals, Customer Value

CONSUMER PRICE INDEX (CPI)

The consumer price index (CPI) is a price index whose movement reflects changes in the prices of goods and services purchased by the average consumer. It is the ratio of the cost of a basket of goods and services at current prices to the value of the identical items at constant prices of a base year. The percentage change in the CPI from one year to the next is taken as a measure of the nation's inflation rate, or the rate a household's income would have had to increase to keep up with the cost of goods and services the household buys. Recent changes in the medical component of the CPI reveal that medical prices have increased much more rapidly than prices of other goods and services.

Thousands of goods and services enter the market basket for the CPI. The U.S. Department of Commerce's Bureau of Labor Statistics (BLS) determines the composition of this basket. Major categories of items in the CPI include housing, food and beverages, apparel, transportation, medical care, entertainment, and "other" goods and services. The BLS determines what it would cost to purchase a fixed basket of goods and services in a base period and in the current period. Each period's CPI is the ratio of the current cost of the basket divided by its base period cost. Published price indexes multiply this ratio by 100, presumably to make it easier to interpret. For example, if the consumer price index for the current period is 154.3, this means the cost of purchasing a fixed basket of goods and services rose 54.3% between the current year and the base period.

The CPI is computed with a fixed market basket that presumably reflects what households buy. Individual prices are weighted by base year quantities obtained from consumer expenditure surveys. The composition of this basket remains constant for relatively long periods. It is revised about once each decade to account for consumption pattern changes and the introduction of new goods and services. Critics of the CPI argue the basket composition should be revised more frequently. Price indexes that use a fixed market basket tend to overstate the importance of items that rise in price and understate the importance of items that fall in price, because consumers tend to switch spending from the former to the latter. Despite problems associated with calculating the CPI, it is the most widely used price index in the United States.

CPI indexes, along with price indexes for various categories of medical services, are available on the Web at www.hcfa.gov/stats. Price indexes are available for such medical spending items as medical services, physician services, dental services, hospital services, and prescription drugs.

—Don P. Clark

FURTHER READING

Feldstein, P. J. (1999). *Health care economics* (5th ed.). Albany, NY: Delmar.

Folland, S., Goodman, A. C., & Santo, M. (2001). *The economics of health and health care* (3rd ed.). Upper Saddle River, NJ: Prentice Hall.

Ford, I. K., & Sturm, P. (1988). CPI revision provides more accuracy in the medical care services component. *Monthly Labor Review, 111,* 17–26.

Norwood, J. L. (1981). Indexing federal programs: The CPI and other indexes. *Monthly Labor Review, 104,* 60–65.

CONSUMER SATISFACTION SURVEYS

See Customer Satisfaction Research

CONTINGENCY PLANNING

See Environmental Analysis, Strategic Management

CONTINUITY OF CARE

Although no references earlier than 1965 appear in a Medline search, in the last 20 years continuity of medical care has been increasingly acknowledged and advocated. Studies have sought to define the term and evaluate the benefits of continuity. Such studies have evaluated continuity, using a model based on the style of practice. Some of the earliest studies were reported in nursing and public health journals. Later efforts have sought to evaluate hospitalization emphasizing the patients' perception of care and outcomes. The multidimensional nature of these studies leaves most issues surrounding continuity unresolved, although remarkable progress has been achieved.

This entry reviews the past, considers the present, and explores the future for answers to the value of continuity. Humans have been described as pack or herd animals, showing a degree of cultural constancy and reliability, as opposed to loners. This craving isn't restricted to medicine or personal physicians. It pervades all aspects and facets of life: People like to use the same hairdresser or grocer, eat at the same restaurants, attend the same church, vote for the same political party, hire the same lawyer; many buy their automobile from the same dealer for years. This continuity represents brand loyalty, with its appreciation of a predictable product, dependable availability, and less effort expended in decisions. Thus humans may instinctively also seek continuity when selecting someone for advice on health issues, one of the most important aspects of life. This decision to choose continuity, like others, frequently occurs after experiencing an urgent need of such services.

Many reminisce about the "good old days" of medical practice, the romanticized Norman Rockwell model. That model still lives, in this era, with young, dedicated physicians caring and devoted to both patients and science. The tools for continuity have changed with the advent of new technology. The age of specialization, sometimes leading to fragmentation, created a drastic upheaval of our notions of continuity of medical care. Such concerns led Donald Berwick, M.D., referring to his wife's recent hospitalization, to comment, "Before, I was concerned; now, I have been radicalized." In this chain of incidents, Berwick, a tireless health care reformer, witnessed firsthand the frailties of the system. Continuity, by definition, must include follow-through, monitoring, appropriate course adjustments, and outcome management—attributes Berwick found lacking in this health care crisis.

A face-to-face encounter, though valuable, is not required for continuity, but an in-depth, organized, longitudinal, integrated record is essential. In the United States, records are usually stored as bits and pieces of fragmented data. A laboratory bit or two here, a vital sign there, and historical information buried somewhere else, however, hardly constitute a continuum. The fragmented pieces of text today are often so voluminous that important facts may escape notice, buried deeply in a forest of data. Here competing needs collide, the needs for both information continuity and for privacy. Reconciling these concerns presents a challenge.

The team delivery system (TDS), a complementary restructure of our health care, has the potential to advance our continuity. Whereas teams gained early favor in Japanese manufacturing, the TDS had a slow start in medicine, and few outcome studies exist. In the manufacturing and service sectors, self-directed work teams are small groups of workers, with complementary skills, who share a common approach to basic purpose, performance goals, and mutual accountability. Such teams typically feature empowered members who learn and thrive in open, encouraging environments. Research in other industries has shown that self-directed work teams work effectively to improve results in quality and outcome.

During training, physicians usually work in teams with faculty members and students. Typically, after training they move into private practice. TDS restores medical providers to the more efficient, integrative, and supportive team model. The highly trained specialists, the relatively isolated rural physicians, mid-level practitioners, and other health care providers combine their assets in ways that would be improbable without the technology-supported TDS. This process can provide unrivaled high-quality health care services to the participating systems. Likewise, ancillary members of the team, such as spiritual and social support staff, emergency medical technicians (EMTs), paramedics, and patient educators, when trained to work together, are much better prepared to provide higher-quality patient care than if they were each operating in isolation.

Some consider the old model of health care delivery inefficient and sometimes deficient. Physicians are challenged by rapid advancements in medical knowledge, while faced with limited time to absorb continually expanding amounts of new literature, with resulting wide variations in medical practice and patient care. The explosion of information created by expanding research and discovery soon outdates hard-won knowledge.

TDS, in contrast, creates an environment of continuous learning and a culture of professional excellence and communication. The team incorporates training into its daily life, featuring the use of frequent electronic communications and monthly technology-supported meetings in which

specialists both gain knowledge of local experience and provide on-the-job mentoring for less experienced team members. In this model, the team members are encouraged to participate fully and to constantly review data on treatments and outcomes to develop and update clinical practice guidelines.

Specific goals such as expected outcomes are established, and progress toward those goals is measured, establishing trust and confidence. This trust and confidence allows the team to design appropriate prereferral protocols, so that patients referred to specialists can maximize the effectiveness of their first visit. For instance, an orthopedic referral for herniated disc includes the appropriate images for the specialist to make the diagnosis and begin the treatment plan on the first visit. In some cases, after early appropriate workup and treatment, a referral may not be required. For TDS to work, a team needs structure and definition. Team members must understand their roles and limits.

The goal of the "coherent whole" of health care delivery is today closer to realization. The attention focused on quality, and the lack thereof, is more encouraging than material advances. Typically, such advances come in waves, and it is foolhardy to predict when they will crest and trough. However, medical providers of tomorrow, just as Newton, standing on the shoulders of today's advances, must reach for the excellence achievable through a vibrant and coherent health care system.

—Thurman L. Pedigo, Sr.

CONTINUOUS QUALITY IMPROVEMENT (CQI)

The term *continuous quality improvement (CQI)* is frequently used in the literature on health care quality and patient safety. Its has two different but related interpretations. The first, more encompassing, use of *CQI* is as a synonym for *total quality management (TQM)* or *quality management (QM)*. Here, it represents the entire set of principles, methods, and tools that constitute a quality management organizational initiative. Such principles typically include top management leadership, customer/patient focus, the development of customer–supplier relationships, and more, but perhaps the most important of these is the continuous improvement of processes. It is this latter sense of CQI, as the core of the "CQI movement," that is more fully discussed here.

Quality management holds that every product, service, and patient outcome is the output of a process. Thus, if the quality of the process output is deficient on some dimension (such as time, cost, clinical outcome, or patient satisfaction), then the process must be improved. Further, in a dynamic world of emerging technologies, shifting patient and employer expectations, regulatory change, and competitive developments, processes must be *continuously* improved. W. Edwards Deming's famous chain reaction illustrated that process improvements (reductions in rework, scrap, and errors) lead to improved efficiency and decreased costs. The initial emphasis of industrial quality control was largely directed toward these ends. The quality gurus offered rather uniform prescriptions to enhance process improvement. These included an emphasis on teamwork so that complex and cross-functional processes could be addressed; the injunction to "drive out fear/blame" so that the problem of false data could be minimized; and the study of variation because of the information it furnishes on the state of the process.

An organization's processes are especially improved when the organization uses a systematic effort rather than haphazard change directed by hunches and intuition. To promote effective process change, organizations need to use a structured approach or template to guide each improvement project. This guide is the scientific method or some variant thereof such as the PDSA/PDCA (Plan-Do-Study-Act/Plan-Do-Check-Act) cycle (championed by Walter Shewhart and Deming), the diagnostic and remedial journeys of Joseph Juran, or the Seven-Step Method (Hitoshi Kume, Brian Joiner, and others).

In a wonderfully succinct description, George Box defined quality management as the democratization of the scientific method. Unfortunately, many workers would have difficulty in defining the scientific method, much less in operationalizing the definition (translating it into operations), so the models of process improvement just described were created. The models serve as practical guides for an inexperienced person or team and emphasize the use of data and the analytical tools of process improvement such as flowcharts, Pareto charts, and cause-and-effect diagrams. Intermountain Health Care, under the leadership of Brent James, has been a pioneer in applying CQI principles to clinical processes. Success stories there include a 50% reduction in adverse drug reactions, 80% reduction in the decubitus-ulcer rate, and an improvement in complete breast cancer pathology reports from 84% to 99%. CQI case studies can be found regularly in the *Joint Commission Journal on Quality Improvement*, the Institute for Healthcare Improvement's Web site (at www.ihi.org/resources/successstories), and the National Association for Healthcare Quality's Web site (go to www.nahq.org/journal, then click on "On-Line Articles").

—Joseph G. Van Matre

See also Discontinuous Change, Pareto Chart, Plan-Do-Study-Act Cycle, Quality Improvement Cycle, Run Chart, Statistical Process Control (SPC)

FURTHER READING

Berwick, D. M., Godfrey, A. B., & Roessner, J. (1990). *Curing health care: New strategies for quality improvement.* San Francisco: Jossey-Bass.

Gordon, D. B., et al. (2000). A quality improvement approach to reducing use of meperidine. *Joint Commission Journal on Quality Improvement, 26,* 686–699.

McLaughlin, C. P., & Kaluzny, A. (1999). *Continuous quality improvement in health care: Theory, implementation, and applications* (2nd ed.). Gaithersburg, MD: Aspen.

CONTRACT RESEARCH ORGANIZATION (CRO)

A contract research organization (CRO) is an organization contracted by the sponsor to conduct preclinical, clinical, and other trial-related functions. CROs can be classified into four basic categories: brokers; Phase I organizations; Phase II, III, and IV monitoring groups; and full-service CROs.

Brokers or site management organizations (SMOs) provide names of potential clinical investigators needed for the development of products. The conduct of the whole clinical trial then depends on the sponsor.

Phase I CROs conduct studies and support for drug interaction, drug metabolism, bioavailability and bioequivalence, pharmacokinetic, and special patient population studies.

Phase II, III, and IV CROs conduct studies for pivotal trials in support of regulatory registration. Their services include identifying suitable investigators, conducting contract negotiations, holding investigator meetings, initiating the study, and monitoring. They can supply everything, from the protocol and case report forms, to obtaining institutional review board (IRB) approval.

Full-service CROs perform all the functions from all regulatory aspects and operations, to preclinical to clinical trials and marketing approval.

A sponsor may transfer some or all of the responsibilities of the trial to the CRO, such as

Preclinical management, which includes consulting on the design of studies, conducting the preclinical trials, identifying laboratories and methods for testing, conducting liaisons with the FDA, and preparing pharmacology and toxicology regulatory submissions

Phase I development, which includes consulting on the design of studies, conducting the Phase I trials, pharmacokinetic program development, pharmacokinetic and pharmacodynamic modeling, FDA liaison, representation at FDA meetings, and drug interaction study design and support

Phases II to IV, which include consulting and design of studies, conducting the Phase II to IV studies, efficacy and safety end point analysis, FDA liaison and representation at FDA meetings, and statistical analysis and plan

Medical and technical writing, which includes preclinical and scientific reports, investigational new drug summary sections and annual reports, investigators' brochures, protocols and patient informed consent, clinical statistical reports, medical device applications, and new drug application compilation and writing

Chemistry, manufacturing, and controls (CMC) sections, which include auditing and identifying contract manufacturers and laboratories, good manufacturing training, standard operating procedure writing, preparing drug master files and validation protocols, conducting stability studies, analytical support, and liaison with FDA chemists

Regulatory submissions, which includes investigational new drug application submissions, registration activities, new drug application submissions, liaison with the FDA, and setting up FDA meetings

Postmarketing, which includes consulting on new indications, liaison with regulatory authorities on safety issues, supplements to new drug applications, publication writing support, market support studies, and FDA annual reports

It is appropriate to choose the most ideal CRO to handle your trial needs. Basically, this role should be perceived as an extension of the sponsor's own in-house expertise, with the goal of helping the sponsor meet clinical research and development objectives in a timely manner.

The CRO should have an adequate staff of experienced personnel skilled in each facet of drug development. It should have a good network of clinical study sites and be in full compliance with FDA, state, and foreign regulations.

CROs can specialize in certain therapeutic areas such as cardiovascular disease, central nervous system disorders, urology, oncology, and infectious disease trials. Choose the CRO that offers the most expertise.

In addition, review the curriculum vitae (résumés) of the CRO staff and investigators who are involved in your project. This will help you identify the experience the clinical CRO staff members have in your area.

A global CRO may also be important if you want your drug approved in other countries besides the United States. CROs can offer a global presence in regulatory and scientific staff.

Finally, get a study budget from your CRO. It is important to get price quotes from different CROs. Then negotiate the price that fits your budget.

—Anthony Sileno

FURTHER READING

Cato, E. C. (Ed.). (1988). *Clinical trials and tribulations.* New York: Marcel Dekker.

CONTRACTION STRATEGY

Contraction strategies decrease the size or scope of operations for an organization either at the corporate level or business level. Contraction strategies include divestiture, liquidation, harvesting, and retrenchment.

With divestiture, an operating unit is sold off as a result of a decision to permanently and completely leave the market despite the market's current viability. Generally, the service or business to be divested has value and will continue to be operated by the purchasing organization. An organization may divest a service because it needs cash to fund more important operations for long-term growth, the service may not be achieving management's goal, or the service is too far from the organization's core business or management's area of expertise. For example, many multihospital systems have divested their insurance operations (HMOs) to concentrate on care delivery.

Liquidation involves selling the assets of an organization. The assumption underlying a liquidation strategy is that the unit or service cannot be sold as a viable and ongoing operation. However, the assets (facilities, equipment, and so on) still have value and may be sold for other uses. Common reasons for pursuing a liquidation strategy include bankruptcy, the emergence of a new technology that results in a rapid decline in the use of the old technology, and the desire to dispose of nonproductive assets. For example, an aging hospital building may be sold for its property value or an alternative use.

A harvesting strategy is selected when the market has entered long-term decline. Although the organization may have a relatively strong market position, industrywide revenues are expected to decrease. The organization "rides the decline," allowing the business to generate as much cash as possible but at the same time investing no new resources. In a harvesting strategy, the organization attempts to reap maximum short-term benefits before the product or service is eliminated. Such a strategy allows the organization to make an orderly exit from a declining segment of the market by planned downsizing. In the pharmaceutical industry, harvesting strategies are common for drugs that are being replaced by more potent or effective drugs.

A retrenchment strategy is a response to declining profitability often brought about by increasing costs. The market is still viewed as viable, and the organization's products or services continue to have wide acceptance. Retrenchment typically involves a redefinition of the target market, selective cost elimination, and asset reduction. Retrenchment may be directed toward reduction in personnel, the range of product or services, or the geographic market served. It represents an effort to reduce the scope of operations. In some cases, a health care organization expands to new markets but may find that costs are more than anticipated, that the organization is "spread too thin" to adequately serve the market, and that local competitors are better positioned to provide quality services at lower cost. Therefore, the organization retrenches to its original or a more focused market.

Peter M. Ginter

See also Divestiture Strategies, Harvesting Strategies, Liquidation, Retrenchment Strategies

FURTHER READING

Duncan, W. J., Ginter, P. M., & Swayne, L. E. (1998). *Handbook of health care management.* Malden, MA: Blackwell.

Ginter, P. M., Swayne, L. E., & Duncan, W. J. (2002). *Strategic management of health care organizations* (4th ed.). Oxford, UK: Blackwell.

Harrigan, K. R. (1980). *Strategies for declining businesses.* Lexington, MA: D. C. Heath.

CONTRACTUAL ADJUSTMENTS

Most health care providers participate in contracts with third-party payers that reimburse the provider less than the amount charged for services. The difference between established rates charged by a health care provider for services rendered to a patient and the amount actually paid for those services by a third party under a negotiated payment contract is recognized in the financial statements as a contractual adjustment. The third-party payer contract may be negotiated with an insurance company, health maintenance organization, preferred provider organization, employer, or state and federal governments.

Contractual adjustments may result from many different types of payment methods, such as contracts that pay a fixed percent of charges, prospective payment contracts that pay a set amount based on diagnosis, contracts with prospective per diem rates, or cost-based contracts that are subject to retrospective adjustments to estimated interim payments. To report patient revenue in the period in which services are provided, which is in accordance with generally accepted accounting principles, health care entities must determine the amount ultimately realizable under terms of a payment contract. Contractual adjustments are estimated, then recorded on current charges, the terms of the contract, and historical payment data for different payment contracts. Gross patient service charges as such are

not meaningful in a health care provider's financial statements. Revenue net of the appropriate contractual adjustment is the expected measure for operations.

—Edward Pershing

CONTRIBUTION MARGIN

See Margins

CONTROL CHART

A control chart is a graphical tool that provides the ability to monitor a process for changes that occur, and can be used to identify and characterize different sources of variation that act on a process. Most commonly, control charts plot the values of some characteristic of a process over time. In addition to the individual points, a control chart also displays three other (vertical) lines: a center line at the process average, an upper control limit (UCL) located three standard deviations above the center line, and a lower control limit (LCL) located three standard deviations below the center line. This chart provides the ability to distinguish random variation that is inherent to the process (called *common cause variation*) from sporadic variation that is not part of the normal process and produces a localized change to the process (called *special cause variation*). Special cause variation can be identified by applying rules that seek to distinguish it from common cause variation. Most commonly, any point that occurs more than three standard deviations away from the mean is identified as stemming from a special cause. Other rules seek to identify process shifts (such as a series of seven or more points all on the same side of the center line), or process trends (a series of seven or more points where each point is greater or less than the immediately preceding point).

Various kinds of control charts have been developed to handle different types of data and different methods of data collection. Attributes data describe data that are based on counts. The p chart is a type of control chart that plots the proportion, *p,* of items that possess a certain attribute (for example, the proportion of patients in a hospital that contract a particular kind of infection each month). The c chart and the u chart display either the count or the rate of occurrence of attributes that occur in a fixed period of time (or space), such as the number of inspection violations per week (or room).

Variables data describe quantitative measurements (such as length of time, dollars spent, or physical measurements). If data are collected in small subgroups over time, the X-bar chart displays the averages of the values in each subgroup, and the R chart displays the ranges of the values in each subgroup. Thus, the process can be monitored for both changes in average, and changes in variation. As an example, the emergency room at a hospital could select (at random) five individuals who present themselves for treatment and measure the amount of time until they have been seen by a physician. This could be done daily for a month, with the averages plotted in the X-bar chart, and the ranges plotted in the R Chart.

If the data cannot be aggregated in subgroups, but rather individual measurements occur over time, then these can be plotted using an X chart (also called an *individuals chart*). An example might be the number of prescriptions filled in a pharmacy each day.

Control charts have proven themselves to be extremely useful tools for better understanding the dynamics of processes.

—James L. Schmidhammer

CONTROL GROUP

A control group is a population, within a study, that is compared with an experimental group. An attempt is made to make the control group as like as possible to the experimental group in all factors except in the factor of interest. A historical control group involves using individuals or data that were collected earlier in time than the experimental group. As risks, prognosis, and management can vary over time, using a historical control group introduces a potential bias into the experiment. To eliminate these potential variables, a case–control study can be used where both the experimental and control groups are chosen at the same time and matched as closely as possible except for the experimental variable. In a case–control study, a person with a disease (a case) is compared with the control population, consisting of people with the same risk factor but without the disease of interest. Bias is introduced, because individual recall of exposure to risks factors plays a significant role. However, this study design is frequently used as a preliminary investigation because data are relatively quick and inexpensive to obtain. In a randomized controlled trial (a type of prospective study), the participants are randomly allocated to either the experimental or the control group. The experimental design introduces the study variable and the data must be analyzed to determine if the two groups differ statistically with regard to nonexperimental variables. In a crossover study, each individual receives each specific treatment and functions as his or her own individual control.

—Daryn H. Moller

See also Clinical Investigation, Clinical Trials

FURTHER READING

Portney, L. G., & Watkins, M. P. (2000). *Foundations of clinical research* (2nd ed.). Upper Saddle River, NJ: Prentice Hall.

COOPERATION STRATEGIES

Cooperation strategies are formal or informal agreements between multiple entities that are designed to create advantages for all the participating entities. Cooperation strategies, intended to gain access to external resources, are frequently employed to maintain or increase the size or scope of operations for an organization. Cooperation strategies may be used at either the corporate or business level to increase the organization's ability to compete against other organizations. Cooperation strategies are typically considered when planning or implementing strategies such as new markets or services development, market or services diversification, and horizontal and/or vertical integration. Cooperation strategies are a means of obtaining or maintaining desirable resources through cooperation with other entities. This cooperation combines resources and capabilities to obtain common goals through efficient use of resources by economies of scale and scope.

Cooperation strategies include formalized cooperation such as mergers, acquisitions, and joint ventures, as well as less formal cooperation arrangements such as working agreements or strategic alliances. The principal functional distinctions between these arrangements are the degree of ownership, control, and permanency. The degree of formality in cooperation strategies can be described as a linear relationship between the extremes of merger at one end of the continuum, and simple informal cooperation at the opposite end of the continuum. Formal cooperation strategies are frequently typified by various types of written legal agreement that delineates the rights, obligations, and responsibilities of the parties involved. Formal agreements governing cooperation are used when it is desirable to limit the risk of opportunistic behavior on the part of external cooperating entities, and when well-defined lines of authority and responsibility are desired. Informal agreements are most often based on goodwill and trust between the entities and are desirable when the initial costs of establishing cooperation agreements do not warrant the greater resource expenditures or loss of flexibility inherent in formal agreements.

Cooperation strategies are occasionally referred to as "quasi-firms," which, like cooperation strategies, are a means of obtaining or maintaining desirable resources by cooperating with other entities by combining resources and capabilities to achieve a common goal via efficient use of resources in economies of scale and scope.

Knowledgeable legal counsel should be consulted before effecting any cooperation strategies involving health care organizations, because of extensive federal and state antitrust regulations and laws, including laws proscribing direct payments to reduce or limit services, as well as self-referral and antikickback regulations governing many agreements between health care providers and organizations.

MERGERS

In a merger, two or more independent entities are combined into one new entity that retains the resources of the two previous entities, and the independent existence of both merging entities ceases. The newly created entity possesses the resources of the prior entities and has complete ownership and control over these resources. Mergers tend to occur when a long-term relationship is advantageous and reduces the exposure of organizational resources to the risk of opportunistic behaviors from cooperating entities. Mergers are complex arrangements that require the dedication of significant organizational resources, are difficult and complex to accomplish effectively, and are difficult and complex to disintegrate once accomplished. Two of the chief difficulties resulting from mergers are the potential for cultural conflict resulting from remnants of the pre-merger cultures of the independent organizations and from the organizational stresses of restructuring duplicative resources.

ACQUISITIONS

In an acquisition, two or more independent entities are combined through the acquisition of one entity by another, with the surviving entity obtaining ownership and control of the resources of the acquired entity. The resulting entity retains the identity of the acquirer, the independent existence of the acquired entity ceases, and the acquiring entity's existence continues.

JOINT VENTURES

In a joint venture, two or more entities combine their resources for a common purpose and share in the gain or loss as the case may be. Joint ventures differ from other types of cooperation strategies mainly in that joint ventures are typically meant to pursue a single venture or goal, even though this effort may take years to accomplish. Given the limited scope of joint ventures, the operational structure may be designed to insulate the parent organizations from adverse consequences resulting from the activities of the joint venture; to limit the risk exposure of the parent organizations, for example, a new corporate entity may be formed. In contrast to joint ventures, other forms of cooperation strategies typically are formed and sustained to accomplish more than one specific goal or endeavor. The term *joint venture* describes the strategic relationship between the entities and does not reflect the legal or operational structure of the entities themselves.

STRATEGIC ALLIANCES

In a strategic alliance, two or more entities cooperate in pursuit of common goals or objectives. Strategic alliances tend to be formed in pursuit of more general organizational goals, as opposed to joint ventures, which are typically formed to pursue a specific goal or endeavor. Strategic alliances do not have the structural or operational permanency or integration implicit in mergers or acquisitions. In health care, a strategic alliance often takes the form of profession or trade organizations, such as a state hospital association or physicians' association. Strategic alliances are of indeterminate longevity and may be short term or long term in nature as the common goals dictate.

—Carlton C. Young

See also Expansion Strategies, Merger and Acquisition

FURTHER READING

Duncan, W. J., Ginter, P. M., & Swayne, L. E. (1998). *Handbook of health care management.* Malden, MA: Blackwell.

Ginter, P. M., Swayne, L. E., & Duncan, W. J. (2002). *Strategic management of health care organizations* (4th ed.). Oxford, UK: Blackwell.

Miller, W. J. (Ed.). (1991). *Health care law sourcebook: A compendium of federal laws, regulations and documents relating to health care.* New York: Matthew Bender.

CO-OPETITION

The term *co-opetition,* which has emerged from game theory, encourages rivals to consider collaborating with each other in productive ways for end consumers and for each competitor's mutual benefit. Although most observers agree that collaborative partnerships are frequently the way forward within the vertical supply chain, there is considerable debate about cooperation between horizontal competitors. Both sides agree benefits accrue to cooperation between competitors, but some argue this cooperation can be done in a way that promotes healthy competition, whereas others argue such cooperation is simply "market rigging by another name."

In the past, most management thinking has focused on getting larger and larger portions of an existing "pie." Given the growing interdependencies between businesses and the opportunities created by new information technology, management thinking has expanded to consider not only "cutting the pie, but also expanding the pie." The new term *co-opetition* describes competitors collaboratively expanding the market in creative win/win arrangements.

One prominent way co-opetition is being explored in the health care industry is through competing hospitals' collaborative efforts on community-based health promotion and wellness programs while simultaneously competing with each other for provision of acute and chronic disease treatment procedures. To make these collaborative partnerships between competing entities work, health care executives clearly need a new mind-set.

—William Q. Judge

See also Alliances, Collaborative Partnership, Cooperation Strategies, Negotiations, Networks

FURTHER READING

Brandenburger, A., & Nalebuff, B. (1996). *Co-opetition.* New York: Doubleday.

Dixit, A., & Nalebuff, B. (1992). *Thinking strategically: The competitive edge in business, politics, and everyday life.* New York: Norton.

Market rigging by another name. (1996, July). *Management Today,* p. 3.

Quint, B. (1997). Co-opetition: Sleeping with the enemy. *Information Today, 14(1),* 7, 47.

CORPORATE COST OF CAPITAL

See Cost of Capital

CORPORATE CULTURE

See Culture

CORPORATE GOVERNING BOARD

See Boards of Directors, Governing Boards

COST-BASED REIMBURSEMENT

Cost-based reimbursement is a retrospective payment system in which the payer agrees to reimburse the provider for allowable costs incurred while providing health care services to the covered population. Allowable costs are generally defined as all costs related to the health care services provided. Cost-based reimbursement is based on how much a medical service costs rather than on how much the provider charges for the service.

This system of payments resulted in increasing medical expenditures, because a cost-based reimbursement system encouraged health care spending rather than limited it. The payer assumed all the financial risk for providing health services, because the provider was assured of reimbursement for all costs incurred in providing care. Consequently, this system of reimbursement contributed to excessive use of medical services and overinvestment in capital assets.

Medicare payments to hospitals were under this form of payment beginning in 1965 when the Medicare program was signed into law. Cost-based reimbursement for most hospitals ended in 1983 and ended for the physician/provider population in 1992 as prospective payment systems were implemented. In the Medicare program, cost-based reimbursement was replaced by a prospective payment system implementing diagnosis-related groups (DRGs) for payment of hospital inpatient services, and ambulatory payment classifications (APCs) for hospital outpatient services.

—Jeffrey H. Burkhardt

See also Prospective Payment System

FURTHER READING

Gapenski, L. C. (2001). *Understanding healthcare financial management* (3rd ed., pp. 73, 77–78). Chicago: Health Administration Press.

Zelman, W. N., McCue, M. J., & Millikan, A. R. (2000). *Financial management of health care organizations: An introduction to fundamental tools, concepts, and applications* (pp. 343, 347–349). Malden, MA: Blackwell.

COST–BENEFIT ANALYSIS (CBA)

Cost–benefit analysis (CBA) provides a framework for evaluating the social desirability of a proposed public program and for evaluating alternatives. It is intended to promote the efficient use of society's scarce resources by comparing the monetary value of all benefits of a social program with all costs associated with the program. A program improves society's welfare if the benefits associated with it exceed the costs. The socially optimal level of the program is attained when the change in social benefit associated with the last increment of the program equals the change in social cost. In other words, the social optimum is achieved when the marginal social benefit and marginal social cost coincide. Interest in health care CBA stems from concerns about the rising costs of providing health services. Policymakers and health care providers conduct formal analyses of benefits and costs to help them promote greater efficiency in providing health care services. CBA can be applied to evaluate the social desirability of health initiatives such as disease screening programs, alternative treatment procedures, new health care technologies, and medical research. Managed care providers can use CBA to determine which care programs are worth the cost.

Conceptually, CBA is a simple application of marginal analysis. Information is gathered on the value of social benefits and social costs associated with a proposed program. Net benefits of the program are expressed in terms of the sum of a future stream of discounted benefits relative to costs. When the present value of social benefits exceeds the present value of social costs, a program will hold positive net benefits for society. Such a program becomes a candidate for adoption. The CBA is often used to evaluate alternative programs. All else equal, a program with a lower CBA will be preferable to an alternative with a higher CBA.

COSTS AND BENEFITS

Decision makers confront many practical and conceptual difficulties when applying CBA principles. These include challenges associated with identifying costs and benefits, measuring costs and benefits, and accounting for the long-term nature of health projects.

Costs and benefits must be identified. All resources used in the activity must be taken into account when measuring costs. Relevant resources to consider are those that could have been used elsewhere if the activity had not been undertaken. Some costs are obvious, including costs of labor, buildings, machinery and equipment, and supplies. These are direct costs, or the costs of resources purchased directly to run an activity. Other costs are less obvious. Included here are such indirect costs as the value of a patient's time, lost earnings, the value of a volunteer's time, and other social costs. Benefits of a program include the net benefits accruing to the patient and organizations as well as indirect benefits such as productivity improvements or gains accruing to family members and other third parties.

Monetary values must be attached to all costs and benefits. This poses a challenge for most health care projects, because competitive markets often do not exist for evaluating costs and benefits of public projects. Even where markets exist, resulting market prices and factor costs do not reflect true marginal social cost and marginal social benefit when they are distorted by monopoly pricing. Hospital cost accounting is not set up to facilitate CBA. It is an extremely difficult task to attach monetary values to nonmedical costs, such as time away from work and the cost of family disruptions.

Difficulties associated with imputing monetary costs in health care project evaluations have led analysts to embrace the economic concept of opportunity costs. When resources are devoted to one project, they are unavailable for other projects. The opportunity cost of a given resource is the value of the resource when used in the next best alternative. Opportunity costs form the basis for all costs. What society gives up to provide the project is the true cost of the project. When competitive market prices are unavailable, cost measurement begins with the assessment of opportunity costs.

CBA measures benefits in dollar terms. Benefits are typically defined in terms of the maximum amounts that informed individuals are willing to pay for a program. Willingness to pay represents the amount of other goods and services, measured in monetary terms, that an individual is willing to forgo to enjoy program benefits. Total program benefits can be obtained by summing willingness to pay of all people whose welfare is affected by the program. Equity issues often enter benefit calculations. If willingness-to-pay calculations place undue emphasis on well-being of wealthier people, decision makers adjust the weights to reflect preferences of low-income people.

When program evaluators find it difficult to express benefits in monetary terms, they often turn to cost-effectiveness analysis (CEA). Here, costs are measured in monetary terms, but benefits are expressed in terms of some standard of clinical outcome, such as mortality rates or quality-adjusted life years. Cost–utility analysis (CUA) is a subset of CEA in which the objective is measured in quality-adjusted life years or some other measure that takes into account an individual's preference for health. When decisions are being made about resource allocation in health care programs, CBA is preferred to CEA, because CBA measures both resource costs and health benefits in monetary terms. CEA and CUA are appropriate when program evaluators want to value specific health outcomes relative to each other.

DISCOUNT RATE

Health care decisions often involve a substantial investment component. Evaluating, for example, the decision to construct a public hospital would involve calculating costs and benefits spread over many years. When effects of a decision are generated over a long period of time, it is necessary to reduce the time stream of costs and benefits to a single number. This is accomplished by calculating the net present value of a project. Future net benefits are converted into present dollars by discounting them at some rate of interest, or discount rate. Cost–benefit calculations are sensitive to the choice of discount rate. High discount rates penalize projects with long payoff periods, whereas low discount rates make projects with benefits accruing far in the future look more attractive. A discount rate should reflect the rate at which society as a whole is willing to trade off present costs and benefits for future ones. This is known as the *social discount rate*. The appropriate social discount rate value for health projects is a matter of considerable debate.

—Don P. Clark

See also Public Goods

FURTHER READING

Folland, S., Goodman, A. C., & Santo, M. (2001). *The economics of health and health care* (3rd ed.). Upper Saddle River, NJ: Prentice Hall.

Garber, A. M., & Phelps, C. E. (1997). Economic foundations of cost-effectiveness analysis. *Journal of Health Economics, 16,* 1–31.

Sloan, F. A. (1995). *Valuing health care: Costs, benefits, and effectiveness of pharmaceuticals and other medical technologies.* Cambridge, UK: Cambridge University Press.

Warner, K. E., & Luce, B. R. (1982). *Cost–benefit and cost-effectiveness analysis in health care.* Ann Arbor, MI: Health Administration Press.

COST EFFECTIVENESS

See Cost–Benefit Analysis (CBA)

COST LEADERSHIP STRATEGIES

See Generic Strategies

COST OF CAPITAL

A company's cost of capital is the rate of return it requires to undertake a new project that is of the same riskiness as the existing business. It is calculated as an average of the costs of the various sources of financing it uses.

As sources of financing, companies use equity (stock), debt (bonds or bank loans), and sometimes preferred stock.

Each of these sources has a different cost, or required rate of return, which is based on its relative level of riskiness. From the investor's perspective, debt is the safest. If the company misses an interest payment or in some other way defaults, the various debt holders can take over the company to be repaid. Because of this power, debt holders are said to have a primary claim on a company's cash flows.

Preferred stock, if a company has any outstanding, is the next most risky financing tool. It is riskier than debt, because a company is not obligated to make preferred stock dividend payments; if the company is doing badly, it can omit the preferred stock dividend without risking bankruptcy. It is less risky than stock, from the investor's perspective, because typically if a company omits its preferred dividend payment then it cannot pay any common stock dividends until the preferred dividends are paid.

Common stock is the most risky investment because the debt holders and the preferred stockholders must all be paid before the common stockholders can receive anything. Because of this the cost of debt, r_d, is usually less than the cost of preferred stock, r_{Pf}, which is less than the cost of common stock, r_S.

The cost of debt, r_d, is just the yield on the outstanding bonds, or the interest rate on the debt owed to a bank. However, because the company gets to deduct interest payments from income when calculating taxes, the actual cost to the company is $r_d(1 - T)$, where T is the company's tax rate. The cost of preferred stock with constant per share dividend, D, and current market price P, is $r_{Pf} = D/P$. The cost of equity is usually calculated using the capital asset pricing model. See the *Capital Asset Pricing Model* entry for this calculation. The overall cost of capital is just a weighted average of these costs:

$$\text{Cost of capital} = w_d r_d (1 - T) + w_{Pf} r_{Pf} + w_S r_S$$

where w_d = market value of debt divided by the total value of the firm (the market values of the debt plus preferred stock plus common stock), w_{Pf} = market value of preferred stock divided by the total value of the firm, and w_S = market value of common stock divided by the total value of the firm. The firm's cost of capital is also called its *weighted average cost of capital,* or *WACC.*

For example, consider a publicly traded managed care company with the following financing information:

Stock: $100 million with a required return of 13% (see entry for *Capital Asset Pricing Model*)

Bonds: $50 million with a yield of 9%

Preferred stock: $10 million with a market price per share of $100 and dividend per share of $6

Tax rate: 40%

The proportion of debt, w_d, is $50 \div (100 + 50 + 10) = 0.3125 = 31.25\%$. The proportion of preferred stock is $10/160 = 0.0625 = 6.25\%$, and the proportion of equity is $100/160 = 0.625 = 62.5\%$. The required rate of return on the preferred stock is its annual dividend divided by the current price, $6/100 = 0.06 = 6\%$. Given this information, the cost of capital is

$$\begin{aligned}
\text{Cost of capital} &= 0.3125[(0.09)(1 - 0.40)] \\
&\quad + 0.0625(0.06) + 0.625(0.13) \\
&= 0.102 \\
&= 10.2\%
\end{aligned}$$

—Phillip R. Daves

FURTHER READING

Brigham, E. F., & Daves, P. R. (2002). *Intermediate financial management* (7th ed.). Mason, OH: South-Western.

COST SHIFTING

Cost shifting exists when a hospital, physician group, or other provider raises prices to one set of buyers *because* it has lowered prices to some other group. The term has also been applied to managed care firms that are similarly said to have raised premiums to one set of purchasers because it had to lower premiums to some other set.

The term has been commonly used in debates over health care reform. Some have argued, for example, that efforts to reduce Medicare expenditures by lowering payments to hospitals under the Medicare prospective payment system, or through the encouragement of Medicare managed care plans, may save money for Medicare but will increase costs to younger folks. This is said to occur because to make up the difference, hospitals will simply raise their prices to private insurers. Insurers, facing higher hospital prices, will then tell employers they have to raise health insurance premiums because they are "being cost-shifted against" by hospitals.

Simply charging one group a higher price than another group does not constitute cost shifting. Firms in many industries do this: Airlines routinely charge different prices to people on the same plane. Movie theaters routinely charge different prices to adults and children. Restaurants and banks give senior citizen discounts. Hotels offer convention rates.

Cost shifting is different. Not only must the provider charge different prices to different payers, but also it must raise prices to one payer in response to lower prices from another. To be able to do this, two things are necessary.

First, the provider must have market power, that is, it must have the ability to set prices above costs. Second, and critically important, the provider must not have *already* fully exercised its market power.

The first condition is straightforward. Suppose a hospital had no market power. When it attempted to raise its prices to, say, private insurers, the insurers would drop them from their network of participating hospitals and the insurers' subscribers would get their care from other hospitals in town. If there is substantial competition in the relevant provider market, cost shifting cannot occur.

The second condition is more subtle. A profit-maximizing firm with market power takes advantage of its power. Suppose it has two groups of buyers: Medicare and private insurers. It charges Medicare the most the government will allow. It sets the private price based on the marginal revenue and marginal cost of privately insured patients. (Note that the relevant cost of a private patient may be the Medicare revenue given up.)

If Medicare decided to lower its payment rate, a profit-maximizing hospital can't make it up by charging private insurers more. It is already charging the profit-maximizing price. The economics imply that the hospital will reduce the number of beds it is willing to fill with Medicare patients and shift that capacity to privately insured patients, who are now relatively more profitable. However, to get more privately insured patients it must lower (not raise) its price to private insurers. Thus, a profit-maximizing provider that has market power still will not shift costs. Instead, it will *lower* its prices. Similarly, if Medicare raises its payment rates, providers will raise their private prices.

Cost shifting can occur if a hospital with market power "likes" privately insured patients in the special sense that it is charging them less than it profitably could. Under this circumstance, when Medicare lowers its payment rate the hospital can raise its price to the privately insured. Notice that this ability to shift cost is limited. Once the hospital has reached the profit-maximizing price, any effort to raise private prices further reduces profits and is self-defeating.

Finally, notice that the foregoing discussion does not imply all nonprofit hospitals with market power will shift costs. Their ability to do so depends on their mission. Suppose a hospital has a mission to provide care to the poor. It does so by maximizing profits from paying patients and then using the profits to provide care for the poor. Even with market power, this hospital is unable to shift costs. In fulfilling its mission, it has charged the profit-maximizing price to private insurers. There is no more profit to be extracted from them when Medicare cuts its payment rates.

A number of studies have sought to empirically examine the existence and magnitude of cost shifting. See Morrisey (1994, 1996) for detailed reviews of much of the literature. Two of the best studies are by Hadley, Zuckerman, and Iezzoni (1996) and by Dranove and White (1998). Hadley et al. used a national sample of hospitals over the 1987–1989 period to examine the effects of financial pressure and competition on the change in hospital revenues, costs, and profitability, among other things. They found that hospitals with lower base year profits increased costs less and increased their efficiency. With respect to cost shifting, "We found no evidence to suggest that cost shifting strategies that might protect hospital revenues in the face of financial pressure were undertaken successfully" (Hadley et al., 1996, p. 217).

Dranove and White (1998) used 1983 and 1992 California hospital data to compare changes in net prices paid by Medicaid, Medicare, and privately insured patients. They conclude, "We find no evidence that Medicaid-dependent hospitals raised prices to private patients in response to Medicaid (or Medicare) cutbacks; if anything, they lowered them" (Dranove & White, 1998, p. 163).

—Michael A. Morrisey

FURTHER READING

Dranove, D., & White, W. D. (1998). Medicaid-dependent hospitals and their patients: How have they fared? *Health Services Research, 33*(2), 163–186.

Hadley, J., Zuckerman, S., & Iezzoni, L. I. (1996). Financial pressure and competition: Changes in hospital efficiency and cost-shifting behavior. *Medical Care, 34*(3), 205–219.

Morrisey, M. A. (1994). *Cost shifting: Separating evidence from rhetoric.* Washington, DC: AEI Press.

Morrisey, M. A. (1996, December). Hospital cost shifting, a continuing debate. *EBRI Issue Brief,* No. 180. Washington, DC: Employee Benefit Research Institute.

COST–UTILITY ANALYSIS

See Cost–Benefit Analysis (CBA)

CREDENTIALING

Credentialing is the process by which a health care practitioner becomes entitled to practice medicine, to practice a subspecialty, or to perform certain procedures and functions. In determining whether an individual should be credentialed in a particular area of medicine or to do certain procedures, the credentialing process takes into consideration the individual's education, training, past and current experiences, and board certification.

Board certification is one form of credentialing. The American Board of Medical Specialties recognizes 24 boards, with some having sub-boards in special areas. Candidates must have completed the appropriate training, pass a written exam, and, for some, pass an oral exam. Successful candidates are certified in the specialty or subspecialty and are designated as diplomates of that board. Periodic recertification is often required.

Hospitals, other health care facilities, insurance carriers, and managed care companies all credential health care practitioners. In hospitals and health care facilities, health care practitioner education, training, board certification status, current competency, and experience are reviewed by a credentials committee consisting of peers and sometimes other health care professionals. They then make recommendations to the person's department as to whether or not he or she meets criteria for credentialing. That recommendation is then reviewed by the medical staff organization and then is sent to the governing body of the institution for approval. The person may then practice in the areas for which he or she is credentialed.

Insurance companies and managed care organizations may either delegate the credentialing to the medical staff or perform their own evaluation of the practitioner through a similar process.

—Thomas M. Biancaniello

CREDIT RATING

A credit rating is a measure of a health care organization's overall creditworthiness and financial stability. An organization's credit rating provides the public and other interested third parties with an independent evaluation of the organization's financial ability to primarily secure indebtedness for the short and long term and also provides solid evidence of the organization's perceived ability to service debt or lease payments. A credit rating is typically provided by an independent third party that specializes in providing these ratings to the public and private investor communities. Some of the most recognized providers of credit ratings include *Standard & Poor's, Moody's Investor Services,* and *Fitch.* These firms are known rating agencies, whose primary business is providing these ratings to public and private companies. These rankings are noted by a three-letter format and range from AAA to BBB for companies considered investment grade, with companies rated below this range being termed speculative or "junk" investment grade. The credit rating is a key determinant of the organization's borrowing cost and is closely correlated with the interest rate it obtains from the public or private debt markets. A more highly rated organization receives a lower interest rate and a resulting lower annual or semiannual payment on its indebtedness. The converse relationship is true as well. An organization that receives a lower credit rating has a higher interest rate and overall cost of borrowing. As such, an organization with a higher credit rating has a higher debt capacity.

As the following chart indicates, each rating agency has its own format for a credit rating and provides the basis for comparing companies on the merits of their creditworthiness.

Credit Risk	Moody's	Standard & Poor's	Fitch
Prime	Aaa	AAA	AAA
Excellent	Aa	AA	AA
Upper Medium	A	A	A
Lower Medium	Baa	BBB	BBB
Speculative	Ba	BB	BB
Very Speculative	B, Caa	B, CCC, CC	B, CCC, CC, C
Default	Ca, C	D	DDD, DD, D

A rating agency also provides "outlooks" for an entity that offers guidance on what the next rating for the organization may be in the next ratings cycle. An outlook can be characterized by the rating agency as *stable, negative, positive,* or *uncertain.*[1] Although ratings may be changed at any time, the change or addition of an outlook is an early indication to provide guidance to investors prior to a new review cycle. The credit-rating process is typically undertaken by an organization when they are considering issuing debt or maintaining an ongoing rating. Whereas a credit rating is provided by a third party, the cost for obtaining the rating is paid for by the organization.

A credit rating is determined on both quantitative and qualitative measures. From a quantitative perspective, an organization's credit rating is determined by a myriad of financial ratios and performance criteria. The financial ratios are measurements that capture a firm's liquidity, leverage, and operating performance and allow it to be compared with its industry peers. These ratios are typically calculated in a predetermined manner, and the building blocks of the credit rating are determined by how the organization falls within certain ranges that are developed for the credit ratings from AAA to unrated or speculative investments. The ratios are typically compared with the medians of the various rating bands. For example, according to Moody's, the median operating margin for hospitals or health care systems rated Aa in 2000 was 3.1%, with a minimum operating margin of 3.1%, a maximum of 7.4%, and an average of 2.5%.[2]

The financial ratios that are measured for an organization are divided into three categories and are referred to as *liquidity, leverage,* and *operating ratios.* A liquidity ratio would include ratios such as the current ratio, days cash on hand, and days in accounts receivable. Leverage ratios include such ratios as debt-to-equity and debt-to-cash flow. Operating ratios include the organization's operating margin and excess or net margin and return on assets and equity. Other crucial metrics for a health care organization are their performance metrics, which include use ratios such as average length of stay, Medicare case mix, and maintained bed capacity. These metrics, coupled with an organization's payer mix (which provides the percentage of revenue derived from sources such as commercial insurance, Medicare, and Medicaid), begin to provide an overall picture of how the health care organization compares with its peers. Further, other important metrics include the nature of admissions and the power or concentration that a few admitters (physicians or physician groups) may have on the organization. If a large number of admissions or volume is concentrated in only a few physicians, that organization is perceived as riskier, and significant changes or problems with one group or physician can adversely affect the organization. A selection of ratios that are considered by the rating agencies are noted in Table 1 (p. 114) along with their general definition.[3]

The overall size (as measured by total revenue or assets) of the organization is also considered by the rating agencies. An organization that has larger amounts of assets and revenue is perceived to have the ability to weather financial and operational downturns and gets a higher credit rating than its peers in a given category.

Qualitative issues are also an important part of a credit rating and are considered by the rating company's analyst. The qualitative issues considered by a rating agency include business or market position for the organization's service area; competitiveness of the service area; quality and effectiveness of senior management and the board of directors; local and demographic and economic trends; risks associated with medical staff size and third-party payers; and local and national regulatory environments.[4] One qualitative measure that receives much scrutiny is senior management's role in the organization. It is critical for management to demonstrate a strong history of developing and implementing a successful business plan for the organization. A rating agency conducts a round of interviews with both senior management and the board of directors, to understand the role of the board of directors and its interaction with senior management. It is expected that senior management is accountable to the board of directors and that the board is not simply a "rubber stamp" for management. In addition, a rating agency expects senior management to provide financial projections coupled with the short- and long-range plans and goals for the health care organization. These financial projections provide a basis for the health care system to support a particular rating on a prospective basis. If the credit rating is being obtained for the new project that requires a significant amount of new debt, it is important for the rating agency to be able to understand the ability of the organization to carry the additional debt load and to generate the associated revenues.

Table 1   Selected Ratios Considered by Rating Agencies

Ratio	Computation
Accounts receivable (days)	(Net patient accounts receivable × 365) / net patient revenue
Annual debt service coverage (x)	Net revenue available for debt service / (principal payments + interest expense)
Average age of plant (years)	Accumulated depreciation / depreciation expense
Average payment period (days)	(Total current liabilities × 365) / (total operating expenses − depreciation and amortization expenses)
Cash on hand (days)	(Unrestricted cash and investments × 365) / (total operating expenses − depreciation and amortization expenses)
Cash-to-debt (%)	Unrestricted cash and investments / long-term debt + short-term debt)
Current ratio (x)	Total current assets / total current liabilities
Cushion ratio (x)	Unrestricted cash and investments / estimated future peak debt service
Debt-to-capitalization (%)	(Long-term debt + short-term debt) / (long-term debt + short-term debt + unrestricted fund balance)
Debt-to-cash flow (x)	(Long-term debt + short-term debt) / (excess of revenues over expenses + depreciation and amortization expenses)
Excess margin (%)	(Total operating revenue − total operating expenses + nonoperating income) / (total operating revenue + nonoperating income)
Maximum annual debt service coverage (x)	Net revenue available for debt service / estimated future peak principal payments and interest expense
Medicare case mix index	Measurements comparing acuity of Medicare patients among hospitals
Net debt ($000)	Total debt outstanding − trustee-held bond funds
Operating cash flow margin (%)	(Total operating revenue − total operating expenses + interest expense + depreciation and amortization expenses) / total operating revenue
Operating margin (%)	(Total operating revenue − total operating expenses) / total operating revenue
Return on assets (%)	Excess of revenues over expenses / total assets
Unrestricted cash and investments ($000)	Unrestricted cash + short-term investments + board-designed cash and investments

Another crucial qualitative measure is the organization's relationships with the physician community. A rating agency considers the number and types of physicians that admit patients to the health care system. The rating agency may interview physicians and physician groups to understand how the organization interacts and works with physician groups in the community. An organization's managed care relationships are also critical to its performance and creditworthiness. An organization that participates in the larger managed care plans and contracts in its markets provides for a stronger credit rating given its access to the patients in the region in relation to the managed care community.

In sum, a credit rating is the judgment by an independent third party of a company's ability to meet current and future debt obligations. It is determined by financial and operational measures and ratios and nonfinancial indicators such as market share, demographics, and management effectiveness.

—Edward Pershing

NOTES

1. Moody's Investors Services, Municipal Credit Research (2001, September), *Not-for-Profit Healthcare 2001 Outlook and Medians*; and Standard & Poor's Public Finance (2001, May), *Health-System Ratios: Then and Now*. New York: Author.

2. Moody's Investors Services, Municipal Credit Research (2001, September), *Not-for-Profit Healthcare 2001 Outlook and Medians*. New York: Author.

3. Moody's Investors Services, Municipal Credit Research (2001, September), *Not-for-Profit Healthcare 2001 Outlook and Medians*. New York: Author.

4. Standard & Poor's Research Ratings Direct (2001, September), *2001 Nonprofit Median Health Care Ratios.* New York: Author.

CRITICAL SUCCESS FACTORS

Critical success factors are those relatively few things that must be accomplished for the individual or the organization to be considered successful by important stakeholders. Critical success factors are important to identify and understand because they focus attention on the things that matter most rather than on the trivial things that consume most of the manager's time.

Henry Mintzberg argues, based on his observations of real managers, that the manager's job is not characterized by careful planning, organizing, and controlling. Instead, managers jump from emergency to emergency and rarely spend 10 consecutive minutes on any task. The manager's job, according to Mintzberg, is characterized by fragmentation and brevity. A primary cause of this fragmentation is lack of attention to critical success factors.

The concept of critical success factors was developed more than 20 years ago to help managers focus on the things that make the difference between success and failure. Critical success factors are unique for each industry and in some cases differ by industry segment. The critical success factors, for example, in long-term care will be different than those in emergency medicine. The leadership team of a local public health department identified the following seven factors as critical to the department's success:

1. Accurate assessment of community health needs

2. Delivery of high-quality services

3. Appropriately qualified staff

4. Adequate financial resources

5. Clear legal authority for health policy leadership

6. High credibility with favorable public image

7. State-of-the-art technology

Regardless of industry or service category differences, if managers are to manage using critical success factors, a series of actions must be accomplished. First, those factors that are absolutely crucial to the success of the organization must be identified. Once identified, the critical success factors must be stated as clearly and concisely as possible, to assist in communicating them to others. It is not enough for executives to understand the critical success factors; everyone in the organization must understand them and agree these are the things that really make the difference. Third, the factors must be ranked in terms of their importance.

Finally, to monitor progress, performance measures must be developed for each factor.

Critical success factors require constant attention and are, therefore, an important aspect of management control. More important, however, is the potential role of critical success factors in goal setting. One of the best ways to ensure that critical success factors receive constant and careful attention is to use them as the basis for setting strategic goals. Setting strategic goals anchored directly in critical success factors focuses individual attention on the things that absolutely must be done right if the organization is to be successful.

—W. Jack Duncan

FURTHER READING

Duncan, W. J. (1999). *Management: Ideas and actions.* New York: Oxford University Press.

Friesen, M. E., & Johnson, J. A. (1995). *The success paradigm: Creating organizational effectiveness through quality and strategy.* Westport, CT: Quorum Books.

Mintzberg, H. (1973). *The nature of managerial work.* New York: Harper & Row.

Rockart, John F. (1982). The changing role of information systems executives: A critical success factors perspective. *Sloan Management Review, 23,* 3–13.

CULTURE AND CULTURE CHANGE

The concept of organization culture has become increasingly important in recent years, as health care managers have struggled to compete in more competitive and unpredictable environments. The study of culture emphasizes the significance of understanding the sociological and psychological underpinnings of the organization as a guide to managing its human resources more effectively. Culture has proven an instrumental concept in developing the "self-directed" and "self-managing" work groups that are vital to the complex systems common in today's health care delivery organizations.

Organizational culture is defined as the shared understanding of an organization's members about the organization itself, as reflected in its members' patterns of values, beliefs, and ways of thinking. In a strong organizational culture, these patterns are widely held, deeply felt, and taught to new organizational members as correct. The culture provides members with a sense of organizational identity, common purpose, and commitment to the organization's mission. Culture may also be seen as the "collective wisdom" of the organization, which is accumulated over time and guides the actions of members in the absence of more direct instructions or guidelines. In his best-selling book on national cultures, Geert Hofstede described culture as the "software of the mind." According to Richard L. Daft, culture serves two critical functions in organizations. First, it serves as an internal integration mechanism, providing members a means of knowing how to relate to each other and work together by developing a collective identity. The culture also provides a mechanism for external adaptation by guiding members' actions with outside organizations, clients, and customers.

An example of the latter is provided by the "Credo" of Johnson & Johnson Inc. The essence of the company's culture is embodied in this 308-word statement. Adopted in 1948, the "Credo" continues to guide the actions of the company today. It simply states that, at Johnson & Johnson, responsibility to customers (doctors, nurses, patients) comes first, responsibility to employees second, responsibility to the community and the world third, and responsibility to the company's stockholders comes last. The "Credo" is credited with providing management with critical guidance during the Tylenol-tainting incidents of 1982 and 1986, in which capsules of the company's product were adulterated with cyanide and used as murder weapons. Management moved quickly to recall the entire inventory on store shelves and in warehouses despite enormous short-term financial losses. The result was that the company's reputation was quickly restored, enabling it to survive, prosper, and continue to serve its customers with an assurance of safety.

OBSERVING THE CULTURE

As powerful as the concept of culture is, it is important to keep in mind that because the essence of culture exists only as a shared understanding among members, one cannot observe the culture directly but only make inferences about the various aspects of an organization's culture from its observable expressions. It is therefore incumbent on the manager to become adept at observing the outward signs of culture and skilled at interpreting their meaning in the context of the organization and its environment. Some of the typical signs of culture are the stories, symbols, ceremonies, and slogans related to the organizational values.

Stories, often based on true events, are shared by an organization's members and told to new members to relate a cultural ideal. They typically involve an example of exemplary behavior, such as extraordinary service to a client or customer. In a large regional hospital in the Midwest, new organization members are often told stories about the hospital staff's dedication to patients during a five-day winter storm in the 1980s. A majority of the hospital's staff stayed on the job continuously throughout the storm, making sacrifices to ensure that patients had the very best care possible under the circumstances. Culture-based stories often

feature the founder or namesake of an organization. At the Salk Institute for Biological Research in La Jolla, California, the ideals of the founder, Jonas Salk, are exemplified in stories related to Dr. Salk's dedication and hard work in developing the first effective vaccine for polio.

Ceremonies and rites serve an important function in communicating aspects of the culture to members. Awards ceremonies, for example, tell members what is valued. Rites of passage, such as the celebration of promotions, serve to reinforce feelings of inclusion. Events can also carry more than one meaning. At the Medical University of South Carolina, an annual picnic for past patients of the hospital's pediatric coronary unit serves not only as a reunion for staff and patients but also as a strong reminder to the staff of the organization's basic purpose.

Physical symbols, often seen as abstract forms, may be used by organizations to express an aspect of the organization's culture. The Nordstrom company symbolizes the importance of its lower-level employees by depicting the organization chart upside down, with a set of hands supporting each level from the level below. Removing fixed interior walls in a typical modern office is often symbolic of the organization's commitment to openness, teamwork, and enhanced communication.

Language is also used to communicate culture, often through the use of slogans. At Children's Memorial Hospital of Chicago, the slogan "Where Kids Come First" embodies the organization's widely held belief that no child in need of care should be turned away. When insurance and financial arrangements threaten a child's access to expensive care, the hospital staff works together to find innovative ways to deliver the needed care. The slogan serves as an ever-present reminder of this value.

As seen by these illustrations, the study of culture directs attention to almost every aspect of organizational life. The insight that organization members often find meaning in small things has been expressed by author Karl Weick and others as a part of the concept of the "social construction of reality."

ORIGINS OF CULTURE

The origins of organizational culture are as varied as its many manifestations and include both systematic, intentional aspects as well as unintended ones. In health care organizations, culture has its roots in the overall culture of the health professions. The shared understandings of an organization's members are based, to a large extent, on the values imparted through extensive education and clinical training. The Hippocratic oath serves as a foundation to guide actions and decisions regarding patient care.

The organization's environment and its strategic emphasis also contribute to the formation of the organization's culture. In *Corporate Culture and Organizational*

Effectiveness (1997), Daniel Denison proposed that there is an inevitable fit among strategy, environment, and culture. In the case of health care organizations, the organization's strategic emphasis is most likely to be external, that is, emphasizing the needs of clients and the community rather than the owners and employees.

According to Denison, an external strategic emphasis can give rise to two prototypical culture types. When the environment emphasizes the need for stability and direction, the organization is most likely to adopt a mission culture, in which cultural ideals adhere to notions of service to the client above all other goals. Exemplary employee behavior is described in terms of adherence to this ideal, as in the case of the snow-bound hospital cited above. In contrast, when the environment emphasizes the need for change and flexibility, organizations are more likely to adopt the norms of an adaptability culture, which emphasizes the value of providing a response to changing conditions. The cultures of emergency medical response teams, for example, often relate stories of their members' skill at improvising solutions in response to unexpected conditions. At the U.S. Centers for Disease Control (CDC), an adaptability culture overlays the essential mission-driven focus and allows for the flexibility to respond to unexpected outbreaks all over the world.

CULTURE CHANGE

Given the benefits of a strong and positive culture, the question inevitably arises of whether an organization's culture can be managed over time to better align itself with the organization's strategic direction. Perhaps the most common approach to managing the culture is the attempt to instrumentally use the observable expressions of culture. For example, managers who want to instill a greater sense of inclusiveness and "buy-in" among employees might initiate new ceremonies and events. Although such manipulation of the symbols of culture may produce some results, these attempts carry some potential negative consequences. Research indicates they are at best short-term tools. An even greater problem pointed out by the research is that they often lead to resentment, because many employees see them as superficial fixes or unwanted forms of ideological control. The best evidence regarding the possibility of affecting deeply based and long-lasting culture change, however, comes from the literature on the learning organization.

The concept of the learning organization was popularized in Peter M. Senge's best-selling book *The Fifth Discipline* (1990). Senge described the benefits that accrue to firms that not only learn, but "learn to learn." In other words, firms that build cultures that value the search for continuous improvement. According to Senge, this can best be achieved by having the organization's management adopt a new view of leadership embracing the concept that leaders should strive to become inspirers, teachers,

and stewards rather than disciplinarians, judges, and accountants.

In a widely cited *Harvard Business Review* article, David A. Garvin (1993) laid out a more practical approach to achieving the goal of becoming a learning organization. According to Garvin, a firm needs to engage in five main activities:

1. *Systematic problem finding and problem solving.* The learning organization builds a culture that constantly questions whether it is engaged in the right pursuits and adopts systematic ways of finding solutions to them.

2. *Experimentation.* They also build cultures that constantly experiment with ongoing programs and demonstration projects and that are committed to change.

3. *Learning from past experiences.* By encouraging a mind set that treats success and failure the same, the culture of the learning organization creates additional opportunities to discover what works and what does not.

4. *Learning from others.* The culture of the learning organization values benchmarking the best practices of other organizations and values listening to and observing its clients.

5. *Transferring knowledge.* The learning organization values the sharing of ideas and adopts mechanisms to ensure the widest possible dissemination of them throughout the organization by using the best combination of written, visual, and on-site learning mechanisms.

Garvin's suggestions point to a highly engaged but lengthy process, and one that consumes a large percentage of the organization's energy and resources, especially during an initial adoption period. The benefits are tremendous, however. By internalizing the culture of continuous improvement, members of the learning organization require little direction from management, become more committed to serving the needs of clients, and become more cooperative with others in the organization. They also adopt increasingly higher aspirations in their own performance, which translates into higher performance for the organization as a whole.

—David W. Grigsby

FURTHER READING

Daft, R. L. (2001). *Organization theory and design* (7th ed., pp. 314–325). Mason, OH: South-Western.

Dennison, D. R. (1997). *Corporate culture and organizational effectiveness*. Denison Consulting. New York: Wiley.

Garvin, D. A. (1993, July–August). Building a learning organization. *Harvard Business Review, 78*, 78–91.

Hofstede, G. (1980). *Culture's consequences*. London: Sage.

Hofstede, G. (1991). *Culture and organizations: Software of the mind*. London: McGraw-Hill.

Kotter, J. P., & Heskett, J. L. (1992). *Corporate culture and performance*. New York: Free Press.

Morgan, G. (1997). *Images of organization* (2nd ed.). Thousand Oaks, CA: Sage.

Peters, T. J., & Waterman, R. H. (1982). *In search of excellence*. New York: Harper & Row.

Senge, P. M. (1990). *The fifth discipline*. New York: Doubleday.

Smircich, L. (1983). Concepts of culture and organizational analysis. *Administrative Science Quarterly, 28*, 339–358.

Smircich, L., & Calas, M. (1987). Organizational culture: A critical assessment. In F. M. Jablin, L. Putnam, K. Roberts, & L. Porter (Eds.), *Handbook of organizational communication* (pp. 228–263). Newbury Park, CA: Sage.

Trice, H., & Beyer, J. (1993). *The cultures of work organizations*. Englewood Cliffs, NJ: Prentice Hall.

Weick, K. E. (1995). *Sensemaking in organizations*. Thousand Oaks, CA: Sage.

www.childrensmemorial.org/whatsnew/pbs.asp

www.jnj.com/our_company/our_credo/index.htm

CULTURE AND STRATEGY

Health care organizations find themselves in turbulent environments. Managers of successful organizations have to choose strategies that enable them to adapt and to exploit environmental opportunities. The strategic choices that managers make inevitably display subjective factors. This section analyzes culture as one subjective factor that affects strategy in organizations.

Harrison Trice and Janice Beyer emphasized that organizational cultures have six major characteristics: They are (a) *collective*—cultures emerge from individuals interacting with one another; (b) *emotionally charged*—emotion and meaning infuse the structures and forms of cultures; (c) *historically based*—particular cultures draw on the unique histories of particular groups of people coping with unique sets of ideas and cultural practices; (d) *inherently symbolic*—symbolism and expressiveness dominate cultures rather than technicalities and practicalities; (e) *dynamic*—cultures change and adapt; and (f) *inherently fuzzy*—fuzziness marks the peripheries of cultures, while core values generate enough consensus to induce cooperation among members.

The substance of cultures includes ideologies. Janice Beyer defined *ideologies* as shared, coherently inter-related sets of emotionally charged beliefs, values, and norms that bind some people together and help them explain their worlds in term of cause-and-effect relationships. Beliefs, values, and norms form distinct concepts. Beliefs express cause-and-effect relationships, for example, that certain behaviors will lead to certain outcomes. Values express preferences for certain behaviors or certain outcomes. Norms express which behaviors others expect and offer culturally acceptable ways to attain outcomes. Organizations' strategies reflect their major stakeholders' ideologies. Usha Haley identified how U.S. multinational corporations operating in South Africa found themselves exposed to competing ideologies from American consumers, governments, and stockholders, as well as from South African governmental agencies with which they interacted, increasing the range and diversity of their symbolic responses.

Environmental jolts and organizational strategies acquire meanings from ideologies that determine whether managers perceive the jolts as dilemmas, opportunities, or aberrations. Alan Meyer observed that two San Francisco hospitals had different ideologies with different effects on their successful strategies in response to an environmental jolt. The first, Memorial Hospital, had a "lean and hungry" ideology that saw meetings, conferences, and memos as frivolous. The administrators believed that setting up and maintaining a formal, bureaucratic structure incurred too many costs, and therefore they avoided it. The hospital relied on tradition and efficiency to control costs. Consistent with this ideology, Memorial Hospital had a low ratio of employees to patients, the controller prepared and typed his own financial reports, the administrators answered their own phones, and the culture discouraged meetings and outside relationships. The hospital ran as a tight ship. The second, Community Hospital, had an ideology of entrepreneurial pluralism, which valued a loose federation within the hospital, each unit focused on a distinct program or type of patient. Other beliefs encouraged innovation and links with the outside environment. The administrators spent about 70% of their time managing relationships with community organizations and planning agencies. Internally, the hospital appeared chaotic.

The environmental jolt occurred when the community's hospital-based anesthesiologists went on strike for one month to protest an enormous increase in the cost of malpractice insurance. Most surgeons and referral physicians joined the strike, causing abrupt declines in hospital admissions, bed occupancy, and cash flows.

Because it did not customarily watch its environment, Memorial Hospital did not foresee the strike and did little to change because of it. Its normally lean ways gave it a favorable cash position, and it could continue as before to weather the strike. The strike enabled Memorial to reaffirm the value of its self-reliance and lean ways and also to dramatize its commitment to employees, none of whom it laid off. In contrast, Community Hospital anticipated and predicted the strike and changed because of it. It used the strike to experiment and to learn new tactics in external relations. The strike enabled Community Hospital to reaffirm the value of its adaptive dexterity and also to dramatize its delegative style. The strike led to permanent changes in Community Hospital that built new coalitions and new community-based programs.

—Usha C. V. Haley

See also Decision, Strategy

FURTHER READING

Beyer, J. M. (1981). Ideologies, values and decision-making in organizations. In P. C. Nystrom & W. H. Starbuck (Eds.), *Handbook of organizational design: Vol. 2. Remodeling organizations and their environments* (pp. 166–202). New York: Oxford University Press.

Haley, U. C. V. (2001). *Multinational corporations in political environments: Ethics, values and strategies.* River Edge, NJ: World Scientific.

Meyer, A. (1982). How ideologies supplant formal structures and shape responses to environments. *Journal of Management Studies, 19*(1), 45–61.

Trice, H. M., & Beyer, J. M. (1993). *The cultures of work organizations.* Upper Saddle River, NJ: Prentice Hall.

CURRENT ASSETS

See Assets

CURRENT ASSETS/LIABILITIES

See Ratio Analysis

CUSTOMER

A customer is an individual or entity that is the recipient of a good or service made available by a supplier or provider, usually in exchange for something of value that is generally but not always monetary in nature. A customer may or may not be the end user of the good or service; for example, a customer may be an intermediary such as a wholesaler or a retailer, which purchases and then resells an item to another individual or entity. In the case of health care, the customer/end user may be a patient, who is the recipient of the services of a physician in exchange for a monetary payment, or a physician, who is the recipient of medical supplies such as hypodermic syringes or gauze for the clinic, also in exchange for financial compensation. Similarly, in the services arena a customer of an HMO or other third-party payer could be a company that participates in its plan. An example of a customer/intermediary might be a pharmaceutical benefits management firm that purchases pharmaceutical drugs from a manufacturer and then resells them to an end user member of a health care plan for which that pharmaceutical benefits management firm has been contracted to provide pharmaceutical drugs by a health insurance organization.

A customer orientation is becoming increasingly critical for success in health care, as in other industries. It costs significantly more to gain a new customer than to retain an existing, loyal, profitable customer. Thus a primary emphasis in both products and services associated with health care firms of all types is being placed on developing long-term relationships with loyal, profitable customers for goods as diverse as medical equipment and supplies, services provided by physician practices to referring physicians, and services provided to individual end users by hospitals, clinics, or private practices.

CONSUMER AS A TYPE OF CUSTOMER

The term *consumer* is often incorrectly used as being synonymous with *customer.* A consumer is a particular type of customer who is the end user of a packaged good purchased in a retail establishment. (The term *consumer* is rarely used in connection with a service.) A consumer is always an end user whereas a customer is not. A consumer, being an end user, cannot be an intermediary. This type of customer/consumer differentiation is used for product types such as (but not limited to) over-the-counter (OTC) drugs, pharmaceutical drugs sold at retail pharmacies, and other consumer packaged goods (CPGs) such as adhesive strips, antiseptics, and other items sold to individual end users by retail establishments. This classification would also hold for products such as medical supplies or pharmaceutical products sold or given to hospitals, clinics, and physicians' offices, then provided to consumer end users as samples. The manufacturer of such merchandise provides its goods to an intermediary such as a retailer or a wholesaler (a customer). Those products then proceed through the distribution channel to the point where they are ultimately sold (or given as samples to promote future sale) to the consumer end user.

—Richard C. Reizenstein

See also Customer Relationship Management (CRM)

FURTHER READING

Armstrong, G., & Kotler, P. (2003). *Marketing: An introduction.* Upper Saddle River, NJ: Prentice Hall.

Herzlinger, R. E. (1997). *Market-driven health care: Who wins, who loses in the transformation of America's largest service industry.* Reading, MA: Addison-Wesley.

Woodruff, R. B., & Gardial, S. F. (1996). *Know your customer.* Cambridge, MA: Blackwell.

CUSTOMER PERCEPTIONS

See Customers' Consequences, Customers' Desired Purpose or Goals, Customer Value

CUSTOMER RELATIONSHIP MANAGEMENT (CRM)

WHAT IS CUSTOMER RELATIONSHIP MANAGEMENT (CRM)?

Customer relationship management (or CRM) is an emerging managerial philosophy closely aligned with the intersection of marketing and information technology. CRM suggests that the goal of a business organization should be to develop, enhance, and maintain relationships with its "best customers." (The term *customer* is used here to include both end-user consumers and business-to-business customers.) Terms such as "strengthening the bond between customer and company," "customer-focused strategy that drives profitability," and "customer retention" are often associated with CRM. In this view, not all customers are created equal, and it is in the organization's interest to create long-term relationships with a strategically targeted segment of the customer population that will best contribute to the organization's success. Often success is defined in terms of profitability (for example, "the 20% of the customer base that is responsible for 80% of the revenues"), although customers may also contribute to organizational success through enhancing the organization's image, word of mouth, or other types of influence. However success is defined, the intention is to identify, target, and nurture those customer relationships that are most critical to that goal.

TRENDS CONTRIBUTING TO CRM

CRM is the outgrowth of two recent trends across industries. First, customers in all markets have more choices and more power than ever before. In industry after industry, managers agree that customers are "setting the bar higher" and what used to be considered satisfactory customer response (in terms of products and services) is no longer adequate. Several factors are driving this trend:

1. *Increased competition.* The more alternative providers are in the marketplace, the more customers can and will demand from those providers, because they can "vote with their feet" (or dollars) and switch providers with relative ease.

2. *Splintered markets.* As markets become more competitive, more "specialists" or "niche" players begin to emerge. Competitors aggressively go after subsegments of the total marketplace, fracturing the market into smaller, more tightly focused customer groups, each demanding and receiving specialized attention from willing providers.

3. *Product information proliferation.* Aggressive promotion by providers, as well as increasing access to free and plentiful "public information," such as the Internet, means customers are better educated about their own needs as well as options for fulfilling them.

Second, new technology (computing power, databases, and data analysis techniques) has created an explosion of customer information, often at the level of a single transaction. This has exponentially increased an organization's ability to track, understand, target, and form more lasting relationships with customers, down to the level of an individual customer. The CRM philosophy embraces the concepts of "mass customization," literally a one-to-one approach to the marketplace. The combination of these two trends (more demanding customers and superior ability to track them at a micro level) has created a fertile environment where being "customer focused" can be accomplished with a precision never before attempted. CRM as a philosophy is a strategic response to these two trends.

THE RELATIONSHIP BETWEEN CRM AND MARKETING

CRM builds on many of the traditional concepts associated with marketing, including segmenting the marketplace, targeting a specific group of customers, positioning the product or service in the customer's mind, understanding the customer through research, and using marketing tactics (such as pricing, promotion, distribution, and product) to create an offering of unique value to customers. However, one might think of CRM as marketing seen through a specific lens. This "view" of the marketplace reorients traditional marketing thinking in the following ways:

Traditional Thinking	CRM Thinking
New customer acquisition	Customer retention
Share of market	Share of the customer's wallet
Transaction based (one exchange)	Loyal relationships (lifetime exchanges)
Mass customer markets	One-to-one responses
Focus on provider's offering	Focus on customer's needs

What is also new about CRM is the emergence of several business-level tactics in their importance to planning and delivering customer value. These include database analysis and data mining, lost customer analysis, customer information systems management, brand equity management, customer service programs, and particular attention to all points of contact between an organization and its customers.

—Sarah Gardial

FURTHER READING

Barnes, J. G. (2001). *Secrets of customer relationship management.* New York: McGraw-Hill.

Lee, D. (2000). *The customer relationship management survival guide.* St. Paul, MN: HYM Press.

Newell, F. (2000). *Loyalty.com: Customer relationship management in the new era of Internet marketing.* New York: McGraw-Hill.

Peppers, D., & Rogers, M. (1993). *The one to one future.* New York: Doubleday.

CUSTOMER SATISFACTION RATING

See Customer Satisfaction Research

CUSTOMER SATISFACTION RESEARCH

Customer satisfaction research is conducted to determine the customer's reaction to or feeling about the value received from products or services purchased or provided (usually, but not always, for some type of compensation). Such research usually evaluates a specific product or service offering during or after use, usually through the vehicle of a customer satisfaction survey. Such surveys, using customer satisfaction rating and other evaluative techniques, yield a "report card" of the provider's strengths and weaknesses that the provider can then use to improve the product or service being offered. Customer satisfaction research is used across the spectrum of industries, including a wide array involved in various aspects of health care, from pharmaceutical companies to hospitals, clinics, and private practice, to medical equipment suppliers.

Most customer satisfaction research focuses on product or service attributes or features in terms of their importance or how well the organization performs in delivering them. These attributes or features are measured against what is referred to as a *comparison standard,* in essence a benchmark for that particular area of the product or service performance. For example, patients of a physician practice, clinic, or emergency room, all have mental benchmarks from past experience and personality characteristics of the individual as to how long is acceptable to be in a waiting room. That time frame is usually a range of acceptability, the comparison standard.

If that range of acceptability is exceeded, the customer experiences what is characterized as negative disconfirmation, or dissatisfaction with that aspect of the service being offered by that particular provider. This dissatisfaction or negative disconfirmation grows greater in direct proportion to the amount by which the comparison standard is exceeded. Conversely, if the range of acceptability is less than the comparison standard, the customer experiences what is referred to as positive disconfirmation, or satisfaction with that aspect of the service offered by that provider. This positive disconfirmation or satisfaction grows greater as that aspect of the product or service improves as contrasted to the comparison standard. If the improvement is truly notable, the customer may experience a phenomenon known as customer delight, in which the product or service, such as waiting room time, is so positively noteworthy that it is truly memorable.

There are several different types of comparison standards that can be used in customer value research. These include expectations (how the user believes the product/service will perform), ideals (how the user wishes the product/service would perform), experience with other competitors in the same product/service category (such as a specific competitive clinic or practice with which a patient has had experience), industry norms (the average or typical performance of competitors in the same product/service category), other competitors in a different product/service category (such as a private practice in contrast to a 24-hour clinic), and marketing promises (whether what is promised in marketing campaigns in areas such as promotion of a clinic is fulfilled by the actual service delivered to the patient).

CUSTOMER SATISFACTION AND CUSTOMER VALUE

As noted, customer satisfaction as commonly viewed revolves around attributes or features. Any entity needs to understand how well it performs at the attribute level in relation to its direct and indirect competition to function well in the marketplace, but that is not sufficient. There must also be evaluation beyond the attribute level. To be optimized, customer satisfaction research and surveys should incorporate all three levels in the value hierarchy: attributes, consequences, and end states. Attributes describe the product or service, consequences describe the user–product interaction, and end states describe the goals of the person or organization. (For further information, see the entry for *Customer Value*.)

CUSTOMER SATISFACTION SURVEYS

The purpose of developing a customer satisfaction survey is to measure the performance of a service or entity in providing the value dimensions (attributes, consequences, and end states) outlined in the value hierarchy. Questions in such surveys are generally designed to address overall performance as well as the individual value dimensions outlined in the value hierarchy. In addressing the value dimensions, the questions should address all three of these levels rather than focusing primarily or exclusively on attributes or features as has generally been the case in such survey work. These value dimensions should be generated by interviews of customers representative of the segment of users to whom the satisfaction survey is targeted, rather than internally by the administering organization. Thus the value dimensions to be assessed in a customer satisfaction survey by a hospital emergency room should be generated through in-depth interviews of emergency room patients rather than by an internal brainstorming process by administrators of the hospital or of the emergency room, or internally by emergency room physicians or other personnel. The customer should provide the value dimensions for customer satisfaction survey work and research.

Customer satisfaction surveys can assess performance of the entity under consideration, importance of certain value dimensions from attributes through end states, or both. This is normally done through a combination of customer satisfaction rating questions, open-ended questions, and demographic information. Customer satisfaction rating questions normally occur first in such survey work and can range from rank-order preference questions to questions based on rating scales, the most commonly used being importance scales and Likert scales (*Strongly Agree* to *Strongly Disagree*). Care must be taken that questions are asked about areas that are actionable (about which something can be realistically accomplished), that are important to the customer, that are not overly redundant with other questions, and that do not ask about multiple dimensions within the same question.

Such customer satisfaction rating questions are usually followed by demographic information so that rating scale responses can be cross-classified by demographic

descriptors such as age, education, gender, race, and type of health insurance. Open-ended questions are recommended for inclusion at the end of satisfaction surveys, to provide in-depth insights into key areas of strength and weakness of the provider regarding the product or service in question. Satisfaction surveys of key market segments should be done at least quarterly to be of maximum usefulness to the entity seeking customer satisfaction information.

—Richard C. Reizenstein

See also Customer Satisfaction Research, Customer Value

FURTHER READING

DiPaula, A., Long, R., & Wiener, D. E. (2002, Fall). Are your patients satisfied? *Marketing Health Services, 22,* 28–32.

Gale, B. T. (1994). *Managing customer value: Creating quality and service that customers can see.* New York: Free Press.

Gardner, B. (2001, November). What do customers value? *Quality Progress, 34,* 41–48.

Garver, M. S. (2002, September 16). Try new data-mining techniques. *Marketing News, 36,* 31–33.

Naumann, E., Jackson, D. W., Jr., & Rosenbaum, M. S. (2001, January–February). How to implement a customer satisfaction program. *Business Horizons, 44,* 37–46.

Slywotzky, A. J. (1996). *Value migration: How to think several moves ahead of the competition.* Cambridge, MA: Harvard Business School Press.

Woodruff, R. B., & Gardial, S. F. (1996). *Know your customer.* Cambridge, MA: Blackwell.

CUSTOMERS' CONSEQUENCES

See Customer Value

CUSTOMERS' DESIRED PURPOSE OR GOALS

See Customer Value

CUSTOMER VALUE

Customer value represents the difference between the benefits the customer (whether an intermediary or an end user) realizes from the use of a product or service and the costs (monetary, psychological, or other) that the customer incurs through that use. A patient, for example, could receive positive customer value through the benefit of having a bacterial infection controlled by an antibiotic with a high level of efficacy. The price paid for the drug is one potential cost; convenient availability of the drug in terms of where it can be purchased, another. The net customer value to that patient/customer would likely be positive if the bacterial infection were controlled promptly, unless the cost was exorbitant. Negative customer value could accrue if the side effects of such a drug were so severe that they produced a condition more medically threatening than the original infection. Similarly, a referring physician likely would be perceived as deriving positive customer value if the specialist to whom the patient was referred saw the patient promptly and diagnosed and treated the patient's condition effectively. Negative customer value might well be the result if the referral specialist saw the patient after so long a delay that the patient's condition had deteriorated significantly.

Customer value must be determined by finding out what the customer of a firm, a hospital, an individual, an intermediary, or another entity wants. Those "wants" are referred to as *value dimensions*. Costs to obtain those value dimensions must also be understood, to be able to assess what customer value represents in a particular situation, and whether it is positive or negative.

CUSTOMER VALUE AND THE VALUE HIERARCHY

The value hierarchy is a multilevel representation of how customers deal with products and services in more depth and at greater levels of abstraction. Three levels of the hierarchy exist: attributes, consequences, and values or desired end states. These are interconnected such that the lower levels are the means by which the ends or the higher levels are achieved. At the base of the hierarchy are those *attributes* or features that the customer immediately perceives on thinking of a product or service. These are the elements that are most objectively defined, what is at the "top of the mind." In an outpatient clinic, for example, patients who are customers of the clinic might indicate that they are seeking friendly staff, short waiting room time, efficient appointment scheduling, and knowledgeable physicians and support personnel—all concrete features, components, or characteristics that are being sought. No matter what the customer constituency, the first value dimension that occurs to a customer is usually at the attribute level.

Beyond attributes, however, are higher levels of value dimension, which give a more in-depth perspective on how products or services relate to customers but which also tend to be more abstract in nature. Above the basic attributes in the value hierarchy is the consequence level, which characterizes the product or service interaction with the customer. Consequences are, in fact, logical extensions of attributes and are thus higher-order value dimensions. They represent the customer's subjective opinion of what the product or service does for them in terms of both benefits and costs. Patients who indicate that a knowledgeable physician is an attribute/feature that they want in an outpatient clinic might have as higher-level value dimensions the consequences that they want to have confidence that the treatment recommended will be beneficial, that it will ameliorate their medical conditions, and that it will be covered by their medical insurance.

The last and highest level of value dimension in the hierarchy is the desired end state or value. These tend to be long term in nature, the most abstract and subjective of the value dimensions. These tend to focus on users and their core values, purposes, or long-term goals. The customer tends to focus on these goals through multiple means or life experiences (such as lower-level value dimensions, both attributes and consequences). The levels in the value hierarchy are thus interconnected in that the lower levels are the means by which the higher levels are obtained. Thus, long life or good health might be desired end states. These might be achieved by the means of knowledgeable physicians (attribute) in an outpatient clinic who recommend treatment that will improve the patient/customer's medical condition (consequence), leading to long life or good health (desired end state or value).

The stability of the highest-order value dimensions is greatest even as they are the most abstract, with those at the lower levels being progressively less stable as well as more concrete. The hierarchy itself tends to have a pyramid shape, with many attributes, fewer consequences, and a small number of desired end states. In addition, the desired end states, being most stable, are the most oriented to the formation of long-term strategy regarding groups of homogeneous customers (in marketing, known as *market segments*) where the lower levels of the hierarchy are less compatible with a long-term orientation because of their greater instability, and are thus more compatible with short-term solutions and implementation approaches.

Value hierarchies are a very useful way to visualize what homogeneous groups of customers want in a product or service. They must, however, be developed with great care to be sure that the group under study is indeed homogeneous in nature and that the relationships among attributes, consequences, and desired end states are understood for the product or service under study. Personal interviewing of at least 8 to 10 people in each segment is usually needed to glean the full array of value dimensions at each level of the hierarchy and to comprehend the relationships among them that ultimately lead to the desired end state level. This interviewing permits both strategies and appropriate implementation mechanisms to be developed to deal with each segment and the hierarchy that represents the benefits and costs important to each customer group.

The terms *customer value* and *customer satisfaction* are frequently used incorrectly as synonymous. In fact, *customer value* should refer to the use of the *full* value hierarchy. Customer satisfaction, in contrast, is frequently used to implicitly reference the measurement of the effectiveness of an organization in satisfying the attribute level only of the hierarchy, although in more sophisticated research customer satisfaction measures can incorporate all three levels of the value hierarchy. (See the entry for *Customer Satisfaction Research.*)

—Richard C. Reizenstein

See also Customer Perceptions, Customers Consequences, Customer Satisfaction Research, Market Segmentation

FURTHER READINGS

Judge, W. Q., & Ryman, J. A. (2001, May). The shared leadership challenge in strategic alliances: Lessons from the U.S. healthcare industry. *Academy of Management Executive, 15,* 71–79.

Naumann, E., Jackson, D. W., Jr., & Rosenbaum, M. S. (2001, January–February). How to implement a customer satisfaction program. *Business Horizons, 44,* 37–46.

Vandenbosch, M., & Dawar, N. (2002, Summer). Beyond better products: Capturing value in customer interactions. *MIT Sloan Management Review, 43,* 35–42.

Woodruff, R. B. (1997). Customer value: The next source for competitive advantage. *Journal of the Academy of Marketing Science, 25,* 139–153.

Woodruff, R. B., & Gardial, S. F. (1996). *Know your customer.* Cambridge, MA: Blackwell.

Woodruff, R. B.. & Gardial, S. F. (1999). Building advantage through customer value. In M. J. Stahl (Ed.), *Perspectives in total quality.* Cambridge, MA: Blackwell.

DATABASE

A database is an organized collection of data that can be manipulated to produce information specific to a user's needs. Conceptually, a database is an electronic filing system with an indexing structure linking to specific data elements. Some databases also may be referred to as *data repositories.*

DATABASE ORGANIZATION

The basic element of a database is a *field,* or variable. Each field in a database is specified as a fixed (maximum) number of characters, each equivalent to a byte of data. The data elements may be text, such as a patient name, or numeric, such as a birth date. Text data also can be coded, or converted to numeric values. For example, in a diagnostic database the value 250.0 represents a diagnosis of diabetes mellitus, using the International Classification of Diseases coding system. Specifications for the number of characters, the type of data, code definitions for all fields, data relationships, and other data structure characteristics are stored in a centralized repository called the *data dictionary.* The data dictionary is a vital part of the database management system.

A group of related fields is called a *record.* Typically a record contains data related to a person, location, or time-based event, such as an episode of care. Fields including patient demographics, diagnostic and procedure codes, and charge data might constitute that patient's financial record. The financial records of all patients would comprise the billing *file,* a collection of related records. A spreadsheet program such as Microsoft Excel can be used to construct a simplistic row-by-column "flat" file. In this structure, each cell on the worksheet is a field, and the columns show all observed values for a given variable. Rows are equivalent to records. Billing files, cost accounting files, insurance benefits files, and other related files could constitute a financial database, a pool of related and integrated data.

DATA MODELS

Data stored in the database are organized in logical and physical configurations. The physical design, which determines where individual data elements are recorded on the storage medium, is the purview of computer technicians. The logical structure is conceptual, specifying data relationships used to group related variables. For example, all data elements needed to process a patient bill would be grouped. This design element determines the ultimate utility of the database. Thus involving end users of the database in the logical design process is critical.

The individual data elements and their relationships may be visually specified in a data model, a diagram similar to a flowchart, that shows the relationships and levels of data. A hierarchical model is a branching tree structure, where each level represents all possible elements of the level above it. For example, the personnel database might begin with all job classifications, one of which is nursing. The nursing classification might branch to nurse practitioners (NPs), registered nurses (RNs), and licensed practical nurses (LPNs). The RNs might branch to employment status (full-time regulars, part-time floaters, and temporary contract employees) and clinical assignments (medical, special care, postsurgical, psychiatric). This branching would continue to the individual employee level. Only one path exists from the starting point to the final element.

A network model may have shared relationships, and an element may be connected to two or more elements in the level above it. Extending the hierarchical example, individual floater nurses may be assigned to more than one clinical specialty depending on staffing needs.

Hierarchical and network models don't allow for re-specification of data relationships once the database has been designed and data entry has begun. Therefore, it is difficult to expand the database without redesigning it.

Relational, or logical, databases are the most frequently used model. Data are stored in row-by-column tables. Data can be manipulated by selecting rows/records, by eliminating columns not required for the query, and by joining tables using unique identifiers to link records from the various tables. A unique identifier or common data element is the key attribute for connectivity in a relational database. An identifier is even more important in linking records from disparate databases. Consider the challenge of compiling a patient's health information that has been generated in several organizations. The quest continues for a unique personal identification number (UPIN) that is universally employed.

DATA ACCESS

Users access combinations of the data elements or fields in a database or repository through various application programs, which typically are specific to a function such as personnel benefits management or patient accounts. Application programs are connected to the database through a database management system (DBMS), a program that serves as an interface to access the data elements required by the various programs and to enable users to enter, select, manipulate, and retrieve data. Users may access the data and acquire information through reports or queries. Reports are prespecified collections or aggregations of individual records in an ordered format, generally including information that is used routinely and compared across reporting periods.

Data also may be retrieved and manipulated by using structured query language (SQL), a set of commands that allows the user to create, modify, or delete variables, tables, and files. Through these manipulations, the user can extract unique combinations of data to meet specific information needs.

HEALTH INFORMATION DATABASES

Databases used in health care range from spreadsheet-type files generated for a single purpose by a single user to extremely large, national-level databases such as the Medicare claims databases maintained by the Centers for Medicare and Medicaid Services (CMS). Databases such as this are aggregates of millions of individual patient records, storing personal and demographic data, financial records, clinical findings, and administrative information. Information derived from this database is used to pay providers for health care services, to conduct clinical and health services research, and to plan for the future of Medicare.

Provider Medicare claims are reported to CMS using the Uniform Bill–92; thus, these data elements are standardized despite the hundreds of points of capture. Unfortunately, standardization of data and information across the health care industry is not the norm. Until a standard clinical vocabulary is adopted industrywide, the ability to link data across entities is seriously compromised.

—Donna J. Slovensky

See also Electronic Medical Record, Health Information Systems Management

FURTHER READING

Baron, J. A., & Weiderpass, E. (2002). An introduction to epidemiological research and medical databases. *Annals of Epidemiology, 10*(4), 200–204.

DATABASE MARKETING

Database marketing is an approach to communicating with customers and prospective customers that relies on the use of sophisticated customer databases. A customer database is a comprehensive collection of information about customers and prospective customers that includes geographic, demographic, and behavioral information. A customer database is much more than a mailing list, which normally contains only contact information. A true customer database is an interactive tool that is constantly updated with new information about individual customer purchase behaviors, inquiries, or other contacts with the company. Thus it allows a company to engage in dialog with customers, rather than simply to carry on one-way conversations.

Customer databases are used both in business-to-business (B2B) and in business-to-consumer (B2C) situations. An example of a B2B customer database might be one maintained by a supplier of disposable hospital supplies. A typical customer entry in this database would include products the hospital has bought previously, the timing of those purchases, key contacts, information about what competitors are providing to the hospital, any current or pending contracts between the hospital and the supplier, and customer service information including "complaint and resolution" history. This database would be particularly useful for sales representatives from the disposable hospital supply company, who would access this information to develop strategic sales plans, and who would constantly update this database to keep it current. An effective salesperson would access this database both before a call on the customer, to keep abreast of any recent purchase information or customer service issues, and after the call, to update the database with new competitor intelligence or changing customer needs. With current information such as this, market analysts can examine buying patterns at different types of hospitals, as well as positions of strength and weakness of key competitors. Such information is also crucial to help this company forecast future sales, which is critical to effective supply chain management.

An example of effective B2C database marketing would be a physician who maintains a comprehensive database of patients and who can use that database to proactively communicate with those patients. Something as simple as a phone call to a patient reminding him or her that it's time to schedule an annual physical exam is an example of B2C database marketing at work. Such a database would also allow physicians to identify all patients who have been prescribed a particular medication and, should a superior medication become available, to inform those patients of the change.

Companies can use database marketing in a number of ways to build customer loyalty and to enhance sales. A very popular use of customer databases is to "profile" customers based on previous purchases and to decide which customers should receive particular offers. A well-known example of a company that uses this approach very effectively is Amazon.com. Amazon uses sophisticated statistical techniques to "cluster" customers into different categories based on previous purchases. Then, when a new product becomes available that would potentially appeal to this cluster of customers, an email message is sent out, informing those customers of the new product. Such database marketing can significantly enhance a company's ability to build loyalty in its customer base. A database can also help companies identify customers who may need upgrades or replacements for previously purchased products. For example, General Electric (GE) Medical Imaging Systems maintains a comprehensive customer database that includes the installation date of each of its imaging systems. This allows GE to identify customers who may need replacements or upgrades to their current equipment and to proactively propose such new solutions.

Although the benefits from database marketing can be profound, effective use of database marketing requires significant investment. Such investment takes two broad forms: systems and culture. The investment in systems includes computer hardware, database software, communication links, and skilled technical personnel. In addition to these foundation investments, further system investment in software specifically designed to analyze customer databases is required, and the purchase and installation of such systems can potentially run into the millions of dollars. Also, significant investment is often required to link various systems together to maximize the effectiveness of the customer database. For example, customer information from customer service is often maintained in one system, whereas customer information from salespeople may be in

a different system. These systems must be designed to share information if they are to work as a truly integrated database marketing system.

Perhaps the most important investment is in culture. To effectively implement a database marketing approach, companies must often change their cultures from intuition-based decision making to data-driven decision making. In addition, the usefulness of the customer database is highly dependent on its accuracy and timeliness. Especially in B2B marketing situations, the accuracy and timeliness of the customer database requires that customer-facing personnel (specifically, sales and customer service people) use and properly maintain the customer records.

A critical issue involving database marketing involves protecting the privacy of customers. Although companies are able to collect extensive information about customers and use that information to "microtarget" their selling efforts, consumer advocates are becoming increasingly troubled that detailed information about customers will go on the open market, available to the highest bidder, raising serious personal privacy concerns. In an effort to police itself, industry groups such as the Direct Marketing Association (DMA) have launched initiatives that require member companies to abide by specific guidelines designed to protect consumers from potential privacy violations.

—Mark A. Moon

FURTHER READING

Lee, D. (2000). *The customer relationship management survival guide.* St. Paul, MN: HYM Press.

Newell, F. (2000). *Loyalty.Com: Customer relationship management in the new era of Internet marketing.* New York: McGraw-Hill.

Peppers, D., & Rogers, M. (1993). *The one-to-one future: Building relationships one customer at a time.* New York: Currency Doubleday.

DATABASE SERVER

See Database

DATA MANAGEMENT

Data management is the process of collecting the raw data, entering them in computers for analysis, analyzing them, writing reports, formatting them for submission to regulatory agencies, and proper long-term storage.

Most research teams use standardized and newly created tools to collect, process, analyze, and audit data. Tools vary in format from visual analog scales to open-ended questionnaires. Examples of tools for participants to use to self-report data include diaries, calendars, logs, and surveys. The case report form is the basic tool of data abstraction. Many reports use a Web-based format; others are paper based. The National Cancer Institute (NCI) is constructing an informatics system that will reduce the extensive paperwork often associated with clinical trials. For example, the Common Toxicity Criteria (CTC), a Web-based, interactive application, uses standardized language to identify and grade adverse events in cancer clinical trials. Forms are also available for rapid reporting of adverse events, electronically or by telephone, to alert researchers to potential safety issues. The Adverse Event Expedited Reporting System (AdEERS) is a Web-based program that enables researchers using NCI-sponsored investigational agents to expedite the reporting of serious and unexpected adverse events directly to the NCI and the FDA.

A written data management plan (DMP) is a critical element in conducting a successful clinical study or trial. The DMP is usually very general during the protocol development stage, but immediately before study initiation it should become very detailed. A typical DMP provides detailed descriptions of how the following areas will be addressed during the clinical trial:

- *CRF processing:* How will completed CRFs be tracked, filed, and handled in the data entry area?
- *Data entry:* How will staff be trained? Will data be double-entered? How will differences in the data be resolved?
- *Validation and query generation:* Who decides how data will be verified? What documentation is needed? How will programming be tested?
- *Query management:* How will queries be tracked? How will queries be resolved? How will the main database be updated?
- *Coding:* Which questions have open-ended text that needs to be grouped for table presentations? Which questions need to be coded with standard medical terminology, and what standard medical terminology should be used?
- *Filing:* Where will CRFs be filed? Who should have access to the files, and how will access to them be controlled? How many copies of each CRF should be made? How should updated data be recorded on the original forms and on copies of them?
- *Audits:* What types of audits are useful? How much of the data should be audited? How should auditing results be interpreted? What changes should be made to processes based on the results of an audit?

—Steven C. Quay

DAYS CASH ON HAND

Days cash on hand is a hypothetical indicator of an entity's ability to pay its daily operating expenses without the benefit of future cash inflows. Days cash on hand is one of the most important indicators of an organization's liquidity. In the course of daily operations, an organization must continue to meet its payroll demands, accounts payable payments, interest payments, and many other cash outflows necessary to operate the entity. Days cash on hand provides management, shareholders, and creditors a worst-case scenario glimpse at the organization's abilities to meet those demands.

The formula for calculating days cash on hand is as follows:

$$\text{Days cash on hand} = \text{cash and investments}$$
$$\div \text{periodic operating expense per day}$$

where periodic operating expense per day equals operating expenses excluding depreciation and amortization/days in period.

Days cash on hand is computed by dividing cash and investments by the entity's operating expense per day. Operating expense per day is determined by dividing periodic operating expenses (excluding depreciation and amortization expenses) by the number of days in the period. Days cash on hand is computed by dividing liquid assets by the quotient of operating expenses (less depreciation expense) to the number of days in the period. Usually the ratio is used to review a company's annual position. Therefore, 365 is used in the calculation. The denominator in the calculation indicates an average day's cash outflow. Depreciation and amortization are removed from the calculation because they are noncash operating expenses. Operating expenses are costs incurred through the daily operations of the entity.

Cash and cash equivalents include short-term cash deposits as well as marketable securities. Marketable securities are short-term investments that can be sold quickly and converted to cash in the open market. Some organizations include investments categorized as long-term assets, assets whose use is limited, or board-designated funds. The inclusion of such assets is generally determined by the restrictions, if any, placed on those assets. For example, if an organization has investment assets whose use has been stipulated by the donor of those assets to be used only for capital equipment, those investments are excluded from the calculation of days cash on hand. They are excluded because they are assets not available for use in meeting the daily cash expense requirements of the organization. Typically, the definitions of which assets to include in the numerator of the calculation of days cash on hand are

Balance Sheet as of December 31, 200x

Assets		Liabilities and Fund Balance	
Cash and investments	$6,263	Accounts payable and accrued expenses	$10,357
Accounts receivable	21,840	Notes payable	825
Inventories	3,177	Current portion of LTD	2,150
Net plant and equipment	119,998	LTD and capital leases	30,582
TOTAL ASSETS	**$151,278**	**TOTAL LIABILITIES**	**43,914**
		Fund balance	107,364
		TOTAL LIABILITIES AND EQUITY	**$151,278**

Income Statement for the 12 Months Ended December 31, 200x

Total operating revenue	**$114,805**
Expenses	
Salaries and wages	82,910
Benefits	10,250
Provision for uncollectibles	3,328
Provision for malpractice	1,320
Depreciation	4,130
Interest	1,542
Amortization	5,424
TOTAL OPERATING EXPENSES	**$108,904**
TOTAL OPERATING INCOME	**$5,901**

explicitly detailed in an organization's bond indenture agreement, corporate investment policy, or other authoritative document.

For example, assume the following for XYZ Medical Center ("XYZ"):

The numerator is simply the $6,263 in cash and investments. The denominator is computed by taking total operating expenses of $108,904 and removing noncash expenses, including depreciation and amortization expenses of $4,130 and $5,424 respectively. This produces total cash operating expenses of $99,350. If we are looking at XYZ from an annual days-cash-on-hand perspective, we would then take total cash operating expenses of $99,350 and divide by 365 days. XYZ has approximately 23 days of cash on hand.

$$\$6,263$$

$$(\$108,904 - \$4,130 - \$5,424) / 365 \text{ days} = \$272.19 \text{ day}$$

$$\$6,263/\$272.19 \text{ day} = 23 \text{ days}$$

In recent years, health care entities have seen operating cash balances decline because payers have created more complex and restrictive reimbursement structures. Payer denials have also increased, therefore decreasing the amount of cash an entity receives.

—Edward Pershing

FURTHER READING

Gapenski, L. C. (1991). *Understanding health care financial management* (6th ed.). Ann Arbor, MI: Health Administration Press.

Moyer, R. C., McGuigan, J. R., & Kretlow, W. J. (1998). *Contemporary financial management* (7th ed.). Cincinnati: South-Western.

Pavlock, E. J. (1994). *Financial management for medical groups.* Englewood, CO: Center for Research in Ambulatory Health Care Administration.

Zelman, W. N., McCue, M. J., & Millikan, A. R. (1998). *Financial management of health care organizations: An introduction to fundamental tools, concepts, and applications.* Malden, MA: Blackwell.

DAYS IN ACCOUNTS RECEIVABLE

See Average Collection Period (ACP)

DEBT

See Liabilities

DEBT FINANCING

See Liabilities

DEBT SERVICE COVERAGE

Debt service coverage is a common financial metric used to measure an organization's ability to service or repay its long-term indebtedness. Repayments for debt include both interest and principal payments that are amortized over a scheduled period. This metric is typically used to measure the ability an organization has to pay for its principal and interest payments in a given time period. The debt service coverage (DSC) ratio is computed as follows:

$$DSC = EBITDA \div \text{annual debt service}$$

Earnings before interest, taxes, depreciation, and amortization (EBITDA) is sometimes referred to as "net revenue available for debt service" and is often defined in loan documents and bond covenants. Annual debt service includes interest payments, principal reductions, and certain lease payments if they are classified as capital leases. The amount of interest paid on debt is correlated to the current principal balance, the time length and frequency of repayments, and the opportunity cost of lending money over the given period (also known as the *yield curve*).

In short, this calculation provides several important indicators to lenders, creditors, and investors in that it provides insight into the organization's timely repayment of its indebtedness. For example, if the DSC ratio is 2.5, the organization can pay for its indebtedness 2.5 times and the lender or creditor has a margin of safety of 1.5 times above and beyond the repayment of debt.

EBITDA		*Annual Debt Service*		*Debt Service Coverage*
$51,584,601	÷	$20,633,840	=	2.5

Fundamentally, this ratio is driven by the ability of a company to generate enough revenue from operations to cover operating costs and the cost to borrow money. All other things kept constant, an increase in revenue will positively affect the debt service coverage ratio. In contrast, fluctuations in operating expenses will inversely affect this ratio. In situations where a company has agreed to variable rates of interest on debt, fluctuations in the interest rate may significantly affect the amount of annual debt service, leaving the ratio at risk from general economic conditions.

If this ratio approaches a level of 1.0, there is an indication that the organization can only meet its debt payments for its current obligations and cannot make other capital expenditures or investments nor could it provide any dividends or distributions to its owners or investors. As such, all stakeholders in an organization typically analyze this critical financial ratio to determine not only the current financial performance of the organization but also its long-term viability and financial performance.

The DSC ratio is most often used in the context of general financial analysis or loan or bond covenants for the organization. Loan and bond covenants are found in the bond legal documents such as a trust indenture or loan agreement, which states the requirements the organization must meet to be in compliance with the loan or bond documents. Often an officer of the organization or its auditor must provide a certificate or letter to the lender or bond trustee as to the accuracy of this ratio.

—Edward Pershing

DECENTRALIZATION OF DECISION MAKING

Decentralization of decision making is the act of moving the responsibility for decisions and actions away from central management authority and outward to those people closest to the situation. A central tenet of good management is that decisions should be made by the people with the most knowledge of the circumstances, principles, and objectives of the decision. Moreover, those closest to the customer are usually best qualified to create and deliver what the specific customer values.

The effect of decentralizing decision making, done properly, is to use local knowledge of the process, product, customer, supplier, department, plant, or division to arrive at the best possible decision. Decentralization also places the responsibility for results in the hands of people with unique local knowledge.

For-profit corporations frequently decentralize to more accurately assign costs where they are incurred and to determine the relative profitability and asset use of the business units that make up the corporation. The same principle works equally well in not-for-profit organizations, with minor adaptations for differences such as fund accounting.

Although decentralization remains popular for the reasons just listed, it has been declining in popularity for several reasons. One of the first reasons for the recent trend back to centralization is that it gives the impression of, and can actually result in, tighter control by the parent organization or its top management. During difficult economic times, this control, especially in the priority ranking of resources, is both necessary and desirable.

A major challenge of decentralization is achieving synergy among related business units, functions, or divisions. When each unit can make independent decisions, standardization and coordination usually suffer. Each unit tends to optimize decisions based on its own needs, which are not the same across many units. The more widely the units are spread about markets or geography, the more challenging it becomes to achieve synergistic leverage in a decentralized environment.

A final drawback of decentralization is the trapping of resources in local units, making it either difficult or impossible for the larger enterprise to use them. People, facilities, know-how, equipment, and even capital may be hoarded for the benefit of the decentralized unit, although it denies the larger enterprise access to them. When resources and talent are scarce, this suboptimal resource use may be the most dangerous drawback of decentralization.

In summary, decentralized decision making has many benefits: It puts local knowledge close to customers, markets, and decisions and thus should yield the best decisions and courses of action; it also clearly assigns costs, revenues, and profits where they are most directly created or incurred.

Along with these benefits, decentralization has some notable drawbacks: Multiple decentralized units, each with its own overheads, practices, and cultures, create complexity and difficulty in creating synergy or leverage. The most difficult problem of decentralization is that of trapped resources—usually human resources but also equipment, technology, facilities, and market access—with the result that some decentralized decision-making units may perform superbly, but others, and the overall enterprise, may suffer.

Choosing how far to decentralize decision making is a key strategic decision for any enterprise.

—John L. Mariotti

See also Vertical Integration

DECISION

A decision involves coming to a conclusion about a course of action or an issue. The complex process of decision making involves many factors. A decision situation most often involves alternative courses of action and possible future events. The field of decision theory provides a rational framework for many decision situations.

Most decision making occurs under conditions of uncertainty. This means that the possible future events, referred to in decision theory as *states of nature,* are not known. In this case, the decision maker may be able to identify the possible states of nature and estimate the likelihood that each will occur.

A decision matrix can then be constructed, with the decision alternatives represented by rows and the possible states of nature, and their associated probabilities, represented by columns. Each cell in the matrix represents a decision–outcome combination, and the "payoff" of each combination can be recorded in the matrix. The payoff may represent dollars in profit or savings, or some other performance measure associated with the decision.

The decision matrix just described provides a framework to analyze the decision alternatives, but the final decision is often influenced by the propensity of the decision maker for risk taking.

When a series of decisions must be made in sequential fashion, a decision tree can be constructed to show the series of decision options and resulting states of nature. Each branch along the tree represents a combination of decisions and outcomes. Analysis of each branch results in the expected payoff of each sequence of decisions.

—R. Lawrence LaForge

FURTHER READING

Russell, R., & Taylor, B. W., III. (1998). *Operations management: Focusing on quality and competitiveness* (2nd ed.). Upper Saddle River, NJ: Prentice Hall.

DECISION SUPPORT SYSTEMS

Decision support systems (DSSs) are computer-based applications that use data, models, and knowledge for enhancing effective decision making. The premise is that a decision maker is likely to select the best alternative when all pertinent information regarding each choice and its potential outcome is available. A decision maker can thus evaluate the implications of each decision alternative and choose the one most likely to accomplish the goal. DSS applications are proactive and become the basis for effective planning.

DSS applications use factual historical information ("what was" and "what is") to provide the ability to forecast ("what can be") scenarios. By using appropriate representations (models) of a phenomenon, a DSS lets the user evaluate the potential outcome of various assumptions and alternatives. Such applications of information technology are proactive in nature, with the ability to perform various analyses to optimize the process of alternative selection in uncertain (lack of appropriate information) and complex (too many attributes) situations.

Data-based DSS applications are designed for the retrieval of relevant information. Such applications may integrate information from several databases or a data warehouse. Retrieval of patient information and treatment histories is an example. By combining such records with similar profiles, a doctor may become better able to diagnose or predict medical disorders. Model-based DSSs use various mathematical representations to combine several attributes of a phenomenon. Appropriate models can be used to maximize revenues, improve scheduling and staffing, and manage inventories of various supplies. Knowledge-based DSS applications use qualitative expertise and rules (expert systems) to make the expertise of several specialists available to the health care professional.

Health care applications of DSS technologies can be categorized into clinical, financial, and administrative applications. Clinical applications combine the use of medical/clinical knowledge with a patient's characteristics to accurately diagnose a patient's condition, determine proper drug dosage, administer preventive services to given patients at specific times, and carry out diagnostic or therapeutic procedures (Wong, 2000). Many such applications combine the expertise of several specialists. Through such an application, Vanderbilt Hospital has demonstrated huge savings by eliminating unnecessary orders, unnecessarily high drug costs, and delays in patient recovery caused by insufficient information (Morrissey, 2002).

Susquehanna Health System, a multihospital system, is realizing benefits of implementing a comprehensive decision support system that uses data-warehousing technology to provide pertinent patient, administrative, and procedural information (Orefic, 2001). Such systems allow users to determine the optimum service by integrating all relevant facts about the patient, provider network, hospital, and health plan resulting in various efficiencies (Troy, 1999).

Financial applications allow users to analyze the performance of various procedures and processes to best use available resources. Examples include monitoring the financial performance of each activity, determining cost savings, improving collections, and forecasting future financial needs. Administrative applications may include scheduling personnel, managing inventories of supplies, determining staffing requirements, and managing relationships with business partners.

—Alok Srivastava

See also Decision, Health Information Systems Management, Information Technology

FURTHER READING

Morrissey, J. (2002). Doctor's orders. *Modern Healthcare, 32,* 16, 32–34.

Orefic, J. J. (2001). Moving to the next level. *Health Management Technology, 7,* 46–47.

Troy, T. N. (1999). The strength and success of unity. *Managed Healthcare, 8,* 30–32.

Wong, H. J. (2000). The diffusion of decision support systems in healthcare: Are we there yet? *Journal of Healthcare Management, 4,* 240–253.

DECLARATION OF HELSINKI LAWS

The Declaration of Helsinki is the formal code of ethics adopted by physicians in 1964 at the 18th World Medical Assembly meeting in Helsinki, Finland. This declaration is a worldwide standard for medical personnel who conduct human research trials. It has been revised by the World Medical Assembly in Tokyo, Japan, in 1975, in Venice, Italy, in 1983, in Hong Kong in 1989, and in South Africa in 1996. Physicians are not exempt from criminal, civil, and ethical responsibilities and penalties under the laws of their own countries, because the standards outlined in the code are considered only a guide to physicians worldwide.

The assembly recognized several basic principles regarding biomedical research involving human subjects. These principles are as follows. The purpose of such research must be to improve diagnostic, therapeutic, and prophylactic procedures and the understanding of the etiology and pathogenesis of disease. The research must conform to generally accepted scientific principles and be based on adequately performed laboratory and animal experimentation as well as on a thorough review and knowledge of the scientific literature. An experimental protocol detailing the design and performance of each experimental procedure is to be submitted for consideration, comment, guidance, and ultimately approval to a specially appointed independent committee that is in compliance with the laws and regulations of the country where the research will be performed. The research will only be conducted by scientifically qualified persons and under the supervision of clinically competent medical personnel. Responsibility for the human participant always rests with a medically qualified person and never on the participant regardless of the fact that he or she has given consent. Careful assessment of predictable risks compared to foreseeable benefits must precede every study involving human participants. Physicians should stop any investigation if hazards are found to outweigh potential benefits. The interests of the participant must always prevail over the interests of science and society. Physicians must protect a research participant's rights to privacy and minimize the study's impact on the integrity of his or her physical, mental, and/or personality status. When publishing research results, physicians are obligated to preserve the accuracy of these results. Results from experimentation not in accordance with this declaration's principles should not be accepted for publication. Potential participants must be adequately informed of the aims, methods, anticipated benefits, and potential hazards and discomforts associated with participation in the study. They can decline participation and withdraw consent at any time. Physicians must obtain participants' freely given, written informed consent. Physicians should not obtain informed consent from a potential participant with whom the physician has a dependent relationship. In cases of legal incompetence, the legal guardian can provide informed consent. For minor participants or those with physical or mental incapacity, permission for participation can be given by a responsible relative. Minor participants can give consent in conjunction with that of their legal guardian. The research protocol must contain a statement of the ethical considerations associated with the conduct of the research.

In addition to these basic principles, the declaration also provides for guidelines for the proper conduct of medical research combined with professional care (clinical research) and nontherapeutic biomedical research involving human subjects (nonclinical biomedical research).

The following definition of the standard concerning human research trials is the most current, as detailed in the declaration's revised Section 29, dated October 2000: "The benefits, risks, burdens and effectiveness of a new method should be tested against those of the best current prophylactic, diagnostic, and therapeutic methods. This does not preclude the use of placebo, or no treatment in studies where no proven prophylactic, diagnostic or therapeutic method exists."

—Linda M. Cimino

See also Informed Consent; Subject, Human Research

FURTHER READING

Chow, S.-C., & Liu, J.-P. (1998). *Design and analysis of clinical trials: Concepts and methodologies.* New York: Wiley.

Glossary: Clinical research terminology. (2001, December). *Applied Clinical Trials,* 36–48.

Kolman, J., Meng, P., & Scott, G. (1998). *Good clinical practice.* Chichester, UK: Wiley.

Wittemore, R., & Grey, M. (2002, Second Quarter). The systematic development of nursing interventions. *Journal of Nursing Scholarship,* 115–120.

DECLINE STAGE OF PRODUCT LIFE CYCLE

See Product Life Cycle (PLC) Analysis

DEDUCTIBLES

The use of deductibles by third-party payers, including insurance companies, health maintenance organizations (HMOs), and other managed care organizations, is a method of minimizing financial risk to the payer and sharing responsibility of payment with the patient. Deductibles require the patient to pay a predefined amount before insurance coverage begins. For instance, if the total cost of an inpatient stay at a health care institution is $500 and the patient is required to pay a $200 deductible per year, the insurance covers the remaining $300. The specified amount of the deductible and coverage terms varies, depending on the type of health insurance contract. In most catastrophic or major medical insurance contracts, deductibles are used as a standard to eliminate routine medical care costs.

Insurers benefit by placing a portion of the financial burden on the patient, reducing expenses to the insurer. Another reason insurers use deductibles is to reduce use of medical care. By being required to pay a portion of the costs each time medical care is sought out, patients are less inclined to overuse medical care. Deductibles are typically established at reasonable rates, affordable to the average person, but are designed to encourage people to consider whether the care is necessary. Insurers benefit by requiring patients to pay deductibles, but if the patient does not seek care until the illness becomes severe, higher costs may result in the long run.

—Edward Pershing

FURTHER READING

Griffith, J. R. (1999). *The well-managed healthcare organization* (4th ed., p. 16). Chicago: Health Administration Press.

Zelman, W. N., McCue, M. J., & Millikan, A. R. (1998). *Financial management of health care organization: An introduction to fundamental tools, concepts, and applications* (p. 351). Malden, MA: Blackwell.

DEFAULT

See Liabilities

DEMAND

Each good and service has its own characteristics that determine the quantity consumers are willing and able to buy. The most important influence over how much of a good or service consumers will buy is its price. Other important determinants include prices of related goods and services, income, consumer preferences, and demographic characteristics. The demand for physician visits, for example, depends on the price of visits, prices of related goods and services such as hospital outpatient services or home care services, income, age, health status, and insurance coverage. Demand analysis seeks to determine which factors are most influential in determining how much health care people are willing and able to purchase. Measures of the responsiveness of consumer demand to changes in prices and incomes represent important policy parameters. Understanding these factors help us formulate health care policies, explain variations in the use of medical services, determine effects of health insurance practices, provide more accurate forecasts of use, and assist in pricing medical services.

Consumers demand good health. It makes them feel happier and provides a return, just like an investment good, in the form of increased earnings or a decrease in sick days. Consumers produce health by purchasing medical inputs in the market as well as by devoting time to preventive measures. The demand for health care is derived from the more basic demand for health. It is a medical input used to produce health. Health care economists focus attention on the demand for health care. Analyzing the demand for health care as a derived demand provides a better understanding of factors that determine how much health care consumers will buy. This, in turn, helps in formulating health care policies.

Consider the demand for physician visits, a type of health care. A demand schedule (curve) for physician visits shows the relationship between price and quantity demanded during a particular period, all other things being unchanged. Consumers tend to purchase more physician visits at lower prices than at higher prices. This inverse relationship between the price of visits and quantity demanded is known as the *law of demand.* Changes in quantity of physician visits demanded in response to the change in price are reflected in movements along the demand curve.

When assessing the relationship between price and quantity of physician visits demanded, it is important to understand the true price of this service. Consumption of a health care service often requires a considerable amount of waiting and travel time. When the value of time a consumer gives up represents a significant portion of the money price of a health care service, the value of time should be taken into account when calculating the true or full price of that service.

Health care demand studies focus on the price elasticity, or the percentage change in the quantity demanded resulting from a given percentage change in price. Price elasticity values are negative because prices and quantities demanded move in opposite directions. Health care economists are interested in the magnitude of the response and often refer to these elasticity values in absolute value terms. Price elasticities are affected by the nature of the good or service, the availability of substitutes, and whether the good or service is used alone or in combination with other items. Consumers perceive few substitutes for health care, so their purchases are not very price responsive. Price elasticity values for medical care tend to be in the inelastic range, indicating, for example, that a given percentage increase in price will lead to a smaller percentage decrease in quantity demanded. Information on the responsiveness of consumers to changes in price is used to determine the effects of health insurance practices and government policies.

Many other factors influence the amount of physician visits that people will buy. A change in any one of the variables held constant in constructing the demand curve would change the quantities demanded at each and every price. Changes in buying patterns are represented by shifts in the demand curve rather than movements along the curve. When consumers decide to buy more physician visits at a given price than they did before, their demand is said to have increased. Demand has decreased when buyers take less than they formerly did at a given price. When factors other than the price of a physician visit change, the result is a shift in demand. These factors are known as demand shifters. Examples of demand shifters include changes in income, prices of related goods and services, demographics, and health insurance coverage.

One of the most important causes of a shift in demand is changing income. Rising incomes increase the demand for office visits. The responsiveness of consumer demand to changes in income is called the *income elasticity of demand,* which measures the percentage change in demand resulting from a given percentage change in income. Normal goods have positive income elasticities, and inferior goods have negative income elasticities. As families earn more, the composition of their expenditure changes. Demand for luxury goods rise more rapidly than demand for necessities. Necessities are items with income elasticities that range from 0 to +1. Luxuries have income elasticities that exceed 1. Empirical evidence shows income elasticities for medical services are positive and less than 1. This means consumers perceive health care to be a necessity.

Demand is also influenced by prices of related goods. The demand for physician visits rises when the prices of its substitutes (hospital outpatient services, visits to other providers) rise, and falls when their prices fall. A reduction in the price of a complement (diagnostic services) will increase the demand for physician visits, and an increase will reduce demand. The extent of the demand shift is given by the cross-elasticity of demand, which measures the percentage change in demand resulting from a given percentage change in price of the related item. If consumers buy more of one item when the price of a related good rises, the cross-price elasticity of demand is positive. When they buy less, the cross-elasticity is negative. Substitutes have positive cross-elasticities and complements have negative cross-elasticities.

Demographics also influence the demand for health care. The number of buyers affects the quantity of a service bought. Population growth can be expected to increase demand for physician visits. Health status tends to vary by age. As the proportion of the population over age 65 increases, the demand for physician visits will also increase.

Coinsurance influences the demand for physician visits. Most patients do not pay the full price of their office visit. An insurance company pays a portion of the bill. The part paid by the consumer is called the *coinsurance rate.* More insurance coverage will lower the coinsurance rate. By lowering the effective price of health care, more insurance coverage also makes consumers less responsive to price changes. Reducing the coinsurance rate increases the demand for physician visits and also makes the demand curve less price elastic. Increasing coinsurance rates have the opposite effect.

—Don P. Clark

See also Consumer Choice and Demand, Elasticity of Demand, Spending on Health Care

FURTHER READING

Acton, J. P. (1975). Nonmonetary factors in demand for medical services: Some empirical evidence. *Journal of Political Economy, 83,* 596–614.

Feldstein, P. J. (1999). *Health care economics* (5th ed.). Albany, NY: Delmar.

Folland, S., Goodman, A. C., & Santo, M. (2001). *The economics of health and health care* (3rd ed.). Upper Saddle River, NJ: Prentice Hall.

DEMOGRAPHICS

Demographics are a set of characteristics used to describe or define the members of a population. Common demographic factors include age, gender, ethnicity, genetic background, and sexual orientation. Other common social factors used to describe a population include religion, income level, geographic location, education, medical conditions, behavior patterns and preferences, and so forth. Demographic information regarding the entire population of the United States or specific regions can be provided by organizations such as the U.S. Bureau of the Census, local governmental agencies, or private organizations (through survey data). The trending of demographic data can be used to allocate resources or to determine prospective markets. By looking at the size of a particular segment of the population (for example, age over 70), forecasts can be made regarding health care utilization or potential markets for medications or services that are commonly used by people in that group.

When used for research purposes, demographic data can be used to select a particular study population. This way, the prevalence of the question addressed in the hypothesis will be higher, and the required sample size will be smaller without decreasing the power of the study. Demographic data can be used to analyze a population subset from which the sample for study will be drawn. Statistics can be applied to determine if the sample selected for study matches the greater population to be examined and to determine how this is reflective of the entire population. For example, does the percentage of Asian female participants in the study match the percentage of Asian females in the population of interest, and how does this reflect the percentage of Asian females in the United States as a whole? By comparing the actual sample enrolled in the study to the population of interest, the potential unseen effects of confounding variables can be minimized and the results of the study will reflect what is expected to occur in the entire population.

In other studies, such as an epidemiologic study of a toxic exposure, the demographic data become descriptive. The age, gender, ethnicity, and so on of the exposed group can be compared with the general population as well as the incidence of a specific disease in the study group versus the general population. If the demographics of the exposed group do not match the demographics of the general population, a control group may be selected that did not have that exposure but would match the demographics of the study group. This is again done to have the two populations mimic each other, thereby minimizing the effects of other variables.

—Daryn H. Moller

FURTHER READING

Day, S. (1999). *Dictionary for clinical trials.* Chichester, UK: Wiley.

DEMOGRAPHIC SEGMENTATION

See Segmentation

DEPRECIATION

Depreciation is a concept most commonly associated with long-lived assets, such as property and equipment, and represents a process whereby the cost of the assets, less any residual or salvage value, is charged to income in a rational and systematic manner over the estimated useful life of that asset. Depreciation is a process of allocation, not valuation.

The key elements in the process of depreciation accounting are the estimate of the useful life of the asset and the method used. The useful life must contemplate obsolescence caused by technological or other changes, and the pattern of wear and tear caused by physical usage. The depreciation method used is typically based on a function of time or actual physical usage.

Useful lives of medical equipment and facilities are typically based on prior experience with similar assets or on commonly accepted guidelines in the industry. The American Hospital Association's *Estimated Useful Lives of Depreciable Hospital Assets* is an example of such a source. The estimate of a useful life for a particular asset in the health care industry should consider the rapid changes in technology in this industry and the likelihood of equipment made obsolete or inadequate by technological advances.

A variety of depreciation methods are used in the depreciation accounting process to allocate the cost of the asset over its estimated useful life. Again, the method must be systematic and rational and, in theory, match the cost of the asset with the revenue that asset produces over a period of time.

One of the most common methods of depreciation is a straight-line method. This method is simple and is easily applied. The straight-line method is theoretically acceptable when the decline in the economic utility of the asset is a function of time rather than usage. This method also assumes a consistent use in each period over the life of the asset and a consistent level of maintenance.

Other depreciation allocation methods based on time reduce depreciation charges over the life of the asset. In other words, under these methods depreciation expense is higher in the early years of the asset's life and lower in later years. These accelerated methods are theoretically acceptable when the contribution of the asset to the organization's operations is greater in the early years and declines over time. Another underlying premise in these methods is

increasing maintenance costs over time, so that the total cost related to the asset is held somewhat level.

The accelerated methods of depreciation are varied as to the mechanics used in the calculations to allocate depreciation over the estimated useful life of the asset. The most common are declining balance and a "sum-of-the-years-digits" method. They both accelerate depreciation.

The declining balance method simply applies an assumed constant depreciation rate to the net cost of the asset each period. Therefore, as the net cost declines the depreciation rate in the subsequent period also declines. The rate used takes into account the asset's cost, salvage or residual value, and estimated life.

The "sum-of-the-years = digits" method simply applies a fraction, the constant denominator of which is the sum of the years of estimated economic life and the numerator of which for each year is the remaining years of life, to the depreciable cost of the asset. For example, the fraction in year 1 of an asset with a five-year life would be $5/(5 + 4 + 3 + 2 + 1)$, or 5/15, or 332%. The method is simple and produces the desired accelerated deprecation result.

The most common methods of depreciation based on usage rather than on the passage of time are based on some units of service or service hours. These methods often produce a better match of the allocated cost with the revenue produced by the asset. Such methods lend themselves well to medical equipment, for which the life of an asset directly correlates with its use. Care must be taken in estimating the hours or units, and again, the impact of advancing technology must be considered.

Depreciation also has meaning with respect to other assets, such as investments. Here, depreciation is a valuation concept and is most commonly applied to a decline in value of an asset such as an investment. Often the decline in value is not realized until the investment is sold. However, the unrealized depreciation is a financial consideration, particularly if the investments are recorded at fair value in the financial statements of an organization.

—Edward Pershing

FURTHER READING

www.hospitalconnect.com

DERIVED DEMAND

See Demand

DIFFERENTIATION STRATEGIES

See Generic Strategies

DIFFUSION OF INNOVATION

Medical advances ranging from heart catheterization to cancer-fighting drugs hold benefits for society but raise costs associated with providing health care. New health care technologies are adopted gradually. Some providers adopt quickly, some slowly, and some not at all. Because an innovation does not exert its full economic impact until the adoption process is well under way, it is important to understand factors that determine the rate at which firms in the industry adopt an innovation. The spread of health care technologies can be viewed as a diffusion process by which the proportion of potential users adopting an innovation grows over time. Research conducted by Edwin Mansfield identifies several factors that determine the rate at which firms adopt an innovation. The probability that a firm will adopt a new technique is an increasing function both of the proportion of firms already using it and of the profitability in doing so, and a decreasing function of the size of investment required to adopt it.

DETERMINANTS OF THE DIFFUSION RATE

It takes time for health care providers to widely adopt a new innovation. Increases in the proportion of firms that already use an innovation can be expected to raise the adoption rate. Implementing a new health technology involves risk. Perceived risk seldom disappears after only a few providers adopt the technology. Profitability of using a new technology is viewed at first with considerable uncertainty. As more information becomes available and experiences accumulate, risk associated with using a new technology declines. Innovations differ in the time required to cut risk of use to an acceptable level. When a large proportion of health care providers adopt the technology, this signals to others that the innovation will benefit both the patient and practice. Competitive pressures force risk adverse providers to consider the innovation more favorably. The adoption process tends to build on itself, at an increasing rate, until most potential adopters have acted. Resource availability and risk tolerance dictate an upper limit on the proportion of providers that will accept a new innovation. As this upper limit is approached, adoption rate tends to slow.

Health care providers are more likely to adopt an innovation if it is expected to boost profits by raising revenue relative to costs. The more profitable an investment in technology is relative to others that are available, the greater is the chance that profitability estimates will be high enough to compensate for risks associated with use of the new technology. Firms adopt a new technology when the present value of future profits associated with the innovation is positive. As the relative profitability of this technology grows, others respond more quickly. Waiting too long may result in a loss of market share that may be difficult to regain.

Adoption rates tend to be smaller for innovations that require relatively large investments. Providers are more cautious before committing themselves to products entailing large financial commitments. Financing becomes a challenge, and payoff periods increase with the size of initial outlays. This leads to the expectation that larger providers will introduce new techniques and smaller ones will follow as both risk and investment requirements associated with the technology decline over time.

The economic theory of innovation suggests additional factors that may influence adoption rates. Regulation may exert a negative effect on the rate of innovation. For example, payment ceilings lower the profitability of new technologies, particularly those requiring high operating costs and initial investment outlays. Sales and promotion efforts may speed the adoption process by stimulating demand for the product or service using the new technology. When a market is growing at a rapid rate, the innovation is introduced quickly to accommodate growth in the market. If there is little or no market growth, introduction must wait until existing equipment is replaced.

MEASURING THE DIFFUSION RATE

Innovations in health care are adopted gradually. Adoption occurs slowly at first, then at an increasing rate, and later at a decreasing rate as an upper limit is approached. Growth over time in the proportion of providers that have adopted a new technology can be approximated by a logistic function, or an S-shaped curve. The logistic growth function provides a convenient way to describe the growth path over time for any variable for which an upper limit exists, and the observed change in this variable in each period depends both on the cumulative value attained in the preceding period and on the remaining distance to the upper-limit value. Both these characteristics are likely to be exhibited by the dependent variable, the proportion of users adopting a new technology i. This share is denoted by P_i at time t. The maximum proportion of potential adopters is K_i. Growth in the proportion of users adopting the new technology is positively influenced by both prior adoption rates and by the remaining distance to the upper-limit value in the preceding period. In other words, the proportion of users adopting the new technology should slow as the ceiling value is approached. These two opposing effects together lead to the S-shaped growth path exhibited by the logistic function.

The logistic specification is given by $\ln[P_{it}/(K_i - P_{it})] = \alpha_i + \beta_{it} + \mu_i$, where α_i is a constant of integration that positions the logistic curve on the time axis, β_{it} is the slope coefficient that reflects the growth rate of the proportion of potential users adopting the new technology (diffusion rate), and μ_i is a random disturbance term. Estimates of the diffusion rate of an innovation (β_i) can be obtained using a variety of econometric techniques.

—Don P. Clark

See also Product Life Cycle (PLC) Analysis, Technology Change

FURTHER READING

Escarce, J. J. (1996). Externalities in hospitals and physicians adoption of a new surgical technology: An exploratory analysis. *Journal of Health Economics, 15,* 715–734.

Folland, S., Goodman, A. C., & Santo, M. (2001). *The economics of health and health care* (3rd ed.). Upper Saddle River, NJ: Prentice Hall.

Griliches, Z. (1957). Hybrid corn: An exploration in the economics of technological change. *Econometrica, 25,* 501–522.

Mansfield, E. (1961). Technical change and the rate of imitation. *Econometrica, 29,* 741–766.

Mansfield, E., & Hensley, C. (1960). The logistic process: Tables of the stochastic epidemic curve and applications. *Journal of the Royal Statistical Society, Sec. B, 22,* 332–336.

DIRECT MARKETING

Direct marketing is an approach to communicating with customers that consists of direct contact with carefully targeted individuals both to obtain an immediate response and to cultivate a long-term relationship. Direct marketing can be thought of in contrast to mass marketing, in which broad customer segments are reached with standardized messages, typically delivered through such tools as print and media advertising, sales promotion, and public relations. In a direct marketing approach, very narrow segments are targeted, and customized communications are directed at these narrow segments, based on common needs or response objectives from each segment.

Direct marketing can take many forms. Personal selling is an example of direct marketing, where companies use a direct sales force to individually understand customer needs and propose solutions. For example, pharmaceutical companies have traditionally relied heavily on personal selling as a way to communicate directly with physicians about advantages and benefits of new drug formulations. Direct mail is another direct marketing tool, which involves sending an offer, announcement, reminder, or other form of communication, directly to a consumer or business customer at a particular address. Companies that use direct mail are able to select very narrow target markets, to personalize the communication to the specific needs of that narrow target, and to easily measure the responses generated by the communication. Traditionally, direct mail was paper based and delivered through the U.S. Postal Service, but technology has made possible lower-cost alternatives, such as fax mail, e-mail, and voice mail. Of course, with reduced cost has come an explosive growth in direct mail, and consumer annoyance has also increased. Telephone marketing is also a direct marketing tool, and companies use both outbound telephone marketing to proactively sell to consumers or business customers, and inbound telephone marketing to reactively receive orders from customers. Outbound telephone marketing has many of the advantages of personal selling, such as the ability to tailor the message to needs of the individual consumer and ability to respond to objections directly. This tool delivers these advantages at a fraction of the cost of face-to-face personal selling. Again, however, with cost advantages come the ability of marketers to over-use the tool, and consumer privacy and annoyance concerns have grown as the tool has become more popular.

Many companies are shifting resources away from mass marketing and toward a direct marketing model. In some companies, traditional mass marketing tools are being supplemented with direct marketing tools, whereas in other companies a direct marketing approach has become the primary tool for communicating with customers. An excellent example of this transformation is Amazon.com, which has almost exclusively used a direct marketing approach, primarily with e-mail, and has successfully built a strong brand name and a large following of very loyal customers. For sellers, direct marketing is a powerful tool for building relationships with individual customers. Effective use of customer databases allows companies to conduct an ongoing dialog with customers, rather than the one-way communication that is the hallmark of mass marketing.

—Mark A. Moon

FURTHER READING

Peppers, D., & Rogers, M. (1993). *The one-to-one future: Building relationships one customer at a time.* New York: Currency Doubleday.

DIRECTOR'S AND OFFICERS' LIABILITY

See Boards of Directors

DISCONTINUOUS CHANGE

See Organizational Change

DISCOUNTED CASH FLOWS

Cash flows are the amount of money that is expected to be generated from an investment. Sometimes these are all positive, and sometimes they are of mixed sign. Discounted cash flows are the cash flows after they have been reduced to account for the time value of money. This reduction is accomplished by dividing each cash flow by $(1 + r)^n$ where r is the discount rate and n is the number of periods that the cash flow is discounted. For example, a $100 cash flow to be received from an insurance company in 1 year with a discount rate of 8% is worth $100/(1 + 0.08)^1 = 100/1.08 = \$92.59$. A $100 cash flow to be received in 2 years is worth $100/(1.08)^2 = \$87.73$. Of course, $100 to be received now is worth $100.

We say that "the present value of $100 to be received in one year at a discount rate of 8% is $92.59" or "the discounted present value of $100 is $92.59."

Discounted cash flows are used in net present value calculations.

—Phillip R. Daves

See also Net Present Value (NPV), Time Value of Money

FURTHER READING

Brigham, E. F., & Ehrhardt, M. C. (2001). *Financial management* (10th ed.). Mason, OH: South-Western.

DISEASE MANAGEMENT

Disease management can be considered a major component of care management, which is "a comprehensive systems approach to medical care that combines the latest medical knowledge on the best clinical methods, population-based outcomes measurement and evaluation, and advanced practice tools" (Juhn, Solomon, & Pettay, 1998). Disease management is a specific application of the care management approach to a disease entity, and organizations that perform disease management must have the infrastructure to manage the disease from before the onset of symptoms in high-risk populations, through the end stages of the illness. The process involves the following elements:

- Stratifying populations at risk for the illness
- Creating interventions for each degree of the illness
- Implementing the interventions for the appropriate stratum
- Monitoring the effects of the interventions as well as clinical, economic, and social outcomes

The backbone of an effective disease management program is a comprehensive data management system, preferably automated. Collecting, managing, and trending large volumes of data require a degree of sophistication that cannot be achieved in a manual data processing system. Systems used for disease management are among the more sophisticated electronic patient records available.

The concept of disease management was developed in the 1980s by the Boston Consulting Group, and the term was coined in the early 1990s (Boston Consulting Group, *HealthCare Practice,* www.bcg.com/practice/health_care.asp). The approach has been applied in many different types of organizations since that time, including

- Health maintenance organizations (HMOs)
- Hospitals
- Medical groups
- Pharmacy benefit management organizations
- Disease management organizations
- Home health agencies
- Governmental health-related agencies
- Public health programs
- Health-related charitable organizations

Each of these organizations has a different purpose for applying disease management. For example, health maintenance organizations use disease management techniques to better manage the care of high-cost patients to avoid duplication of services and inappropriate, high-cost procedures (Agovino, 2001). Charitable organizations may use disease management for clinical conditions such as acquired immune deficiency syndrome (AIDS) to improve access to services for clients with the disease. Medical groups may offer disease management services to their patients to decrease the workload of the physician by appropriately tracking and monitoring patients using clinical practice guidelines that provide instructions for care by allied health professionals. Pharmacy benefit management organizations (PBMOs), in fact, evolved as an outgrowth of the concept of disease management. PBMOs provide a number of services to health care payers, from processing pharmacy claims to contracting with participating pharmacies for medication delivery and evaluation of patterns of drug use based on claims evaluations. Regardless of the reason for applying the principles of disease management, the approach is essentially the same.

The process of disease management is based on the premise that specific interventions are effective at various phases of an individual's progression along the continuum of a clinical condition. Most disease management programs stratify populations according to their level of severity of the disease state. For example, a population at risk for diabetes could be divided into five groups, as in Table 1.

The stratification process is conducted on administrative or clinical data, depending on the organization's focus. The clinical data may be obtained from a review of medical charts or from risk-screening surveys that may be administered by staff members of the organization via telephone, by mailed surveys, or over the Internet.

Most organizations form teams to implement the disease management program, consisting of representatives from the many service areas involved in delivering care to patients. The key people on a disease management team include the following:

- Physician expert in the disease
- Nurse leader
- Administrator
- Health education specialist
- Information specialist
- Special services providers, such as home health, durable medical equipment, and so on
- Specialized health professionals, such as physical therapists
- Representatives from other industries that must interface with the patient, such as the educational system or political representatives

Once the team has stratified the population, the interventions for each group may be implemented. Modes of intervention depend heavily on the nature of the population. For example, a relatively poorly educated population requires more media-based interventions, such as public service announcements or videotapes, whereas printed materials may be more appropriate for highly educated individuals. Educational specialists can usually design effective programs based on population demographics.

Case management services for the most severely affected and moderately affected individuals include relatively aggressive educational programs to provide a knowledge base that enhances the person's ability to manage the illness, detect early signs of deterioration, and adhere to treatment regimens in partnership with a provider. The case management program depends heavily on interactions with both organizational providers and practitioners in the community who will be treating the patient. These collaborations are key to maintaining a patient's health over the long period of time during which case managers deal with the individual. Most case managers are health professionals, usually nurses, and their work is directed by clinical

Table 1　Stratification of Population for Diabetes Mellitus

Group	Identifying Factors	Approach
I	No clinical abnormalities; family history of diabetes OR obesity	Lifestyle counseling, weight loss, periodic checkups; educational program on identification of diabetes
II	Prediabetic; mildly abnormal glucose tolerance test; slightly elevated HbA1c	Aggressive lifestyle counseling for weight loss, exercise, reduction in fat consumption
III	Diabetic, minimal manifestations	Aggressive lifestyle counseling, quarterly checkups, glucose monitoring, medication management
IV	Diabetic, no more than one episode of ketoacidosis or hypoglycemia per year	Aggressive lifestyle counseling, monthly checkups, glucose monitoring, medication management, limited case management
V	Diabetic, more than one episode of ketoacidosis or hypoglycemia per year	Case management services

protocols (clinical practice guidelines) that detail expected steps in the process of the patient's care. The protocols may be developed by the organization, purchased from a vendor that has created them from literature evidence and consensus panels, or designed by specialty societies by physicians who are expert in the clinical condition. Automating the protocols makes them even more effective.

Disease management provides an organized approach to deal with a population of individuals with varying levels of risk for a clinical condition and with varying levels of severity of the illness in the population. A number of approaches have been developed, mostly relating to the type of provider implementing the program.

—Donald E. Lighter

FURTHER READING

Agovino, T. (2001, August 9). Disease management popular among HMOs: Control of chronic illness may save millions in long-run. *Detroit News.* www.detnews.com/2001/business/0108/09/b03-264515.htm.

Juhn, P., Solomon, N., & Pettay, H. (1998, Spring). Care management: The next level of innovation for Kaiser Permanente. *Permanente Journal.*

Lighter, D., & Fair, D. (2000). *Principles and methods of quality improvement in health care.* Gaithersburg, MD: Aspen.

Mallarkey, G. (2000). *Opinion and evidence: Disease management. Parsippany, NJ.* Adis International Ltd.

Todd, W., & Nash, D. (2001). *Disease management: A systems approach to improving patient outcomes.* San Francisco: Jossey-Bass.

www.ahrq.gov/clinic/cpgsix.htm

DISENROLLMENT

The term *disenrollment* is used for an insured member dropping his or her insurance coverage. This may occur when the individual leaves a job and goes to another or when the premiums are too costly to maintain. Medicare and Medicaid beneficiaries may "trade" their traditional Medicare/Medicaid benefits and sign them over to a managed care company. They thus disenroll from Medicare to go to another insurance plan.

Typically, the Medicaid beneficiary may disenroll up to three times in a given period without penalty.

The ability to make changes or the need to make changes in insurance coverage has caused some concerns in the federal government.

Getting information about health care status, the sharing of this information, and "pre-existing condition" exclusions have caused serious difficulties for many people. As a result, the federal government has passed the Health Information Portability and Accountability Act (HIPAA), which provides legal guardianship for protected health information, and limits how that information is shared and with whom. There are three areas of focus: privacy, security, and administrative simplification. In each of these focus areas, there are very specific responsibilities that all health care providers, associates, vendors, and others who have real or potential access to protected health care information are obliged to address and carry out.

As HIPAA touches on every aspect of health care, compliance with the changes is expected to cost millions of dollars.

—Edna Lee Kucera

FURTHER READING

http://cms.hhs.gov
www.healthprivacy.org
www.hipaalawyer.com

DISPROPORTIONATE SHARE HOSPITAL (DSH)

Disproportionate share hospital (DSH) programs provide additional payments to hospitals with a large number of low-income inpatients. Established in the early 1980s, Medicaid and Medicare DSH payments reached almost $20 billion in 1992, primarily through the growth of Medicaid DSH.

Medicare DSH payments are uniformly applied across the nation. Large urban teaching hospitals (5% of hospitals) receive one third of Medicare DSH payments. In 1997, after the program reached 6% of total hospital payments, Congress reduced payments by 1% per year through 2002. Payments remain concentrated to large urban facilities; 250 hospitals receive half of all DSH payments.

After 1985 states began to finance their share of the Medicaid DSH program through provider taxes and voluntary donations, usually from hospitals. Total Medicaid DSH payments grew to 15% of total Medicaid spending by 1992. DSH payments became huge parts of some states' Medicaid programs, for example, 51% in New Hampshire and 36% in Louisiana.

After Congress severely limited provider taxes and voluntary contributions in 1991, states began to transfer funds from government-owned hospitals to the Medicaid agency through intergovernmental transfers (IGTs) as a means to continue funding DSH. In 1993 IGTs were restricted to again limit the growth of the Medicaid DSH program.

Although the history of the DSH program, especially in Medicaid, is a complex dance between federal legislative intent and creative state budgeting, the program serves to maintain the safety net of public hospitals that provide the bulk of care to low-income people.

—Max Michael

See also Balanced Budget Act (BBA) of 1997, Medicaid, Public Hospital

FURTHER READING

Fagnani, L., & Tolbert, J. (1999). *The dependence of safety net hospitals and health systems on Medicare and Medicaid disproportionate share hospital payment programs.* Washington, DC: Commonwealth Fund.

Ku, L., & Coughlin, T. A. (1995). Medicaid disproportionate share and other special financing programs. *Health Care Financing Review, 16*(3), 27–54.

DIVERSIFICATION STRATEGIES

The term *diversification* is used to describe a business strategy based on variety. Diversification strategies are the plans that involve choosing one or more options to improve the likelihood of success in diversification. There are many forms of diversification, and describing a few of them will illustrate what diversification strategies are and why they are important.

In investing, diversification means spreading risk by making investments across a variety of forms: small company stocks, large company stocks, bonds, money market instruments, banks, certificates of deposit (CDs), domestic and international companies, and on, and on. The hope is that by diversifying, the risk of a failure in any one type or size of investment is mitigated or at least reduced in impact on the entire portfolio of investments.

In business strategy, the meaning of diversification is similar, but the application and execution is different. Diversification strategies in business may be horizontal, in which expansion moves into similar product or service areas but in different geographic or price/specification market segments. Or the diversification strategy may be vertical (also called *vertical integration* or *backward integration*), whereby an organization acquires the suppliers of the raw materials, components, or goods and services it uses in its business or activities.

One of the latter forms of vertical diversification, called *vertical integration,* was very popular in the early 20th century, following the success of legendary giant Henry Ford, whose Ford Motor Company once owned everything from the iron ore mines to the steel mills that produced the steel and iron used in Ford automobiles.

Horizontal diversification became more popular in the mid-20th century with the creation of large conglomerates and financial holding companies. ITT under the leadership of Harold Geneen was one such noted conglomerate. These businesses diversified into many unrelated industry segments whose only common thread was financial ownership and central corporate management. Many failed because they lacked the breadth of management skills to effectively manage these large and diverse enterprises.

Later in the 20th century, companies such as Dover, Danaher, and Tyco attempted to capitalize on parts of the conglomerate-based horizontal diversification but to date their success has been mixed. The concept of concentric diversification was embodied in Tyco's purchase of CIT Financial, diversifying into an activity that surrounded its other business units and at least theoretically added value to the overall corporation. General Electric's success in diversifying both concentrically (via GE Capital) and as a conglomerate (aircraft engines, plastics, broadcasting, appliances, and so on) has been difficult for others to emulate successfully because of the range of management know-how and strategic skills needed to manage such widely diversified corporations.

Vertical diversification in other forms has met with moderate success. One primary example is that of producers also being retailers of the products they produce. Companies such as Hallmark Cards do the creative development of many items in their assortment, produce or procure those items, and then sell them through company-owned and -operated stores (as well as through leased departments and stand-alone retail sales to regular retailers). This requires a great breadth of product offering and skill in marketing to avoid channel conflicts in pricing and products.

Sears, Roebuck attempted vertical diversification somewhat more indirectly in the second half of the 20th century as it developed captive suppliers in which it owned major and often controlling positions. This assured a tightly linked supply of proprietary products, but it overlooked the risk of attack from widely different types of companies such as general merchandise discounters (Wal-Mart and Target), home centers (Lowe's and Home Depot), and soft-goods retailers (Kohl's), all sourcing better-value products from a variety of the best global suppliers.

Diversification strategies are a double-edged sword. Spreading the risk is a valuable concept, as is spreading the opportunity. The wider the spread—concentrically, vertically, or horizontally—the greater the challenge for the management. The more widely spread the diversified company, the more widely spread the know-how and market knowledge required for it to succeed.

Globalization has only accentuated the possibilities for diversification. Now a company that dominates a market in one country or on one continent can aspire to do so around the world. None are more representative of this than U.S. retailers Toys R Us, and Wal-Mart. Toys R Us diversified globally ahead of most specialty retailers. In doing so, it reaped many benefits in the form of toy sales in countries around the world. It also suffered the pain of learning the problems and complexity of doing business in many different countries and cultures.

The challenges of diversification are many, and done well (as personified by General Electric) the rewards can be great. But few have succeeded, whereas many have failed. The fundamental strategic issue with diversification, regardless of whether vertical, horizontal, concentric, or conglomerate based, is that there must be a set of core competencies and capabilities underlying the choice of where and how to diversify.

Core competencies are most simply defined as "what an organization is genuinely good at doing" and core capabilities are essentially "how an organization accomplished what it does better than competitors." If a paper company chooses to diversify backward into owning forests, it must develop the core competencies and capabilities required to be a competitor manager of forestry.

Auto companies have decided to abandon backward integration, selling off component divisions (Delphi and Visteon, to name just two), and choosing instead to diversify horizontally. DaimlerChrysler now also owns a major stake in Mitsubishi. Ford owns Volvo and Jaguar. General Motors now owns major interests in Saab, Fiat, and several second-tier Japanese auto companies. Peugeot and Nissan are part of the same entity. This is horizontal diversification on a massive global scale in one of the world's largest industries.

The competitive impetus for such horizontal diversification is scale and market presence. Whether it is strategically right or not remains to be seen, as Toyota, Honda, and BMW (with a minor exception of the confusing Rolls-Royce deal) have remained focused and independent and seem to be doing quite well. Honda's diversification is based on its engine design and production competency and that appears to be a soundly executed strategy.

Although this definition has attempted to clarify many forms of diversification, there is almost no limit to new ones that might emerge. Drug store companies such as Walgreen are selling groceries and some seasonal durable items. General merchants such as Wal-Mart and Target are becoming powerful grocery sellers. Gas stations now sell large quantities of a much more expensive liquid than gasoline—bottled water and soft drinks. And so diversification is limited only by the imagination of corporate decision makers and their ability to successfully gain the know-how and apply the management expertise required to make the new diversification successful.

—John L. Mariotti

See also Strategy

FURTHER READING

Business—the ultimate resource. (2002). Cambridge, MA: Perseus.

Porter, M. (1980). *Competitive strategy: Techniques for analyzing industries and competitors.* New York: Free Press.

Porter, M. (1985). *Competitive advantage: Creating and sustaining superior performance.* New York: Free Press.

DIVESTITURE STRATEGIES

Divestiture strategy considers how a firm made up of many individual business units can optimize its overall value and effectiveness through the thoughtful removal of specific business components. This concept is similar to that of an investment portfolio made up of individual stocks. The goal of the investor is to maximize the overall return of the portfolio while minimizing risk by adding promising stocks and selling stocks that fail to perform.

In a manner similar to the investor adding stocks to a portfolio, managers acquire business units in the hope that the resulting unit will yield benefits exceeding the purchase cost of the new business unit. Divestiture, or the sale of a business unit, is then seen by some managers as the mirror image of a business acquisition where distinct business components are removed from the firm rather than added. However, this is where the stock portfolio analogy falls short, because there are several unique and specific issues to consider when evaluating a divestiture strategy.

Managers, being human, typically enjoy the concept of acquiring a new business unit, because it represents growth, expansion, and ultimately, success. Conversely, divestiture may represent an admission of failure in that the business unit being sold did not yield the expected results. Because most managers would greatly prefer to focus on the exciting acquisition issues, the divestiture option is very easy to ignore. This same failure avoidance pattern is seen in investors who refrain from selling a losing stock position in hopes of its eventual recovery. Effective investment managers know this is a serious error and that to build overall portfolio value, investments should be made in the best possible stocks at this time. If there are losing investments that do not provide the best chance for future regard, they should be sold.

Company managers experience the same reluctance to "cut the cord" with a struggling business unit, and they avoid the expression of failure that is often associated with divestment. This reluctance is especially true if the business unit was purchased by the current company chief executive officer (CEO). Under these conditions, divestiture is usually seen as the managerial option of last resort and is delayed until the business unit is in dire condition, resulting in its removal at fire sale prices.

Newly appointed CEOs often bring a different managerial viewpoint and have no emotional attachment to a business unit purchased by the prior administration. As a result, it is very common for the new senior manager to immediately discard business units that should have been removed much earlier. It is also interesting to note that the new CEO undertakes very little risk with the divestiture option, because even if the divestment goes poorly, the former CEO usually shoulders the blame.

STRATEGIC FIT ISSUES

Effective managers attempt to rise above these issues of failure and frustration that cloud divestiture actions and to recognize the true role of divestiture in running an efficient and effective business. When a manager faces a divestiture decision, the key question is "Which business unit should we divest and when?" Divestiture decisions in the health care field are particularly difficult to reach, given the rapid rate of change and the need to constantly evaluate business units in light of expected future performance. In addition, although it is tempting to base the evaluation of business units on financial performance alone, there are also other important measures to consider, such as operating fit, strategic fit, managerial fit, and cultural fit.

These measures of corporate fit focus on how well a business unit meshes with the rest of the organization and can easily outweigh financial potential. If a business unit shows financial promise but does not fit strategically or culturally with the parent organization, the management effort needed to build the unit often vastly exceeds the potential financial reward. These business units are excellent candidates for divestiture, because their potential financial strength is attractive to a potential buyer.

A more difficult divestiture scenario involves a business unit with both "fit" problems and poor financial prospects. In these cases, it is natural for the unit operating managers to try to rebuild the operation, but such an effort invariably takes substantial resource allocations of time and money. This type of effort also tends to divert senior management's attention from the other successful core businesses, and as a result the entire organization suffers from poor performance. Effective senior managers therefore move aggressively and tend to eliminate units that do not display both strong financial promise and close managerial fit.

In summary, divestiture should be viewed as an important, routine managerial option that is used to build the overall strength and value of the firm. Although financial performance is one important indicator of divestment candidates, characteristics of managerial, strategic, operational, and cultural fit are equally important in weighing a divestment decision.

—Richard T. Christoph

See also Acquisitions, BCG Portfolio Analysis, Consolidation, Downsizing, Merger and Acquisition, Restructuring, Strategic Business Unit, Strategic Fit, Strategy

FURTHER READING

Bing, G. (1978). *Corporate divestment.* Houston: Gulf Publishing.

Dranikoff, L., Koller, T., & Schneider, A. (2002). Divestiture: Strategy's missing link. *Harvard Business Review, 80,* 5, 74–83.

Stahl, M. J. (1989). *Strategic executive decisions.* New York: Quorum Books.

DIVIDENDS

Dividends are a portion of a company's earnings distributed to the holders of its common and/or preferred stock. In other words, a dividend represents the shareholders' return on investment just as interest represents the return on investment on checking and money market accounts, certificates of deposit, bonds, and other fixed-rate debt investments. The company's board of directors declares the dividend on a "per share" basis, so the distribution to each shareholder is in direct proportion to the amount of stock the shareholder possesses. The dividend itself can be paid in cash, property, or additional shares of the company's own stock. Dividends received by the shareholders are generally considered fully taxable income by the Internal Revenue Service.

Whether or not a dividend is declared and paid depends on the type of stock held by the shareholder (that is, preferred stock or common stock). Dividends must be paid to holders of preferred stock before they can be paid to holders of common stock, although there is no legal requirement that the company pay dividends to common stock shareholders at all. The amount of dividends paid to holders of preferred stock depends on whether the preferred stock is cumulative or noncumulative. If a dividend was declared for cumulative preferred stock in a previous year, but not paid, then that dividend is considered in "arrears" and must be paid before any current or future dividends can be paid. If the preferred stock was noncumulative, then the current year dividend is all that is owed. If there is any cash, property, or stock available after the preferred shareholders are paid, the remaining amount can be distributed to the common stock shareholders.

There are three important dates to remember related to the payment of dividends: the date of declaration, the date of record, and the date of payment. The date of declaration is the date at which the board of directors actually declares a dividend is to be paid. The date of record is the date on which all shareholders of that date are paid the declared dividend. The date of payment is the date at which the dividend is paid. For example, on May 13, 200X, the board of directors of XYZ Corporation declares that they will pay a $2 per share dividend on June 15, 200X, to all individuals holding shares of their stock as of May 31, 200X. May 13 is the date of declaration, May 31 is the date of record, and June 15 is the date of payment.

From a financial statement standpoint, dividends declared are shown as a reduction in retained earnings on the statement of changes in stockholders' equity. If a cash dividend is paid, then it would be included as a cash outflow on from financing activities on the statement of cash flows. If the dividend was paid with property or stock, then the dividend is disclosed as a noncash item on the statement of cash flows. If the dividend has not been paid, the dividend payable is generally included as a liability on the statement of financial position (balance sheet).

—Edward Pershing

DIVISIONAL STRUCTURE

See Structure

DIVISION-LEVEL STRATEGIES

See Strategic Business Unit

DOUBLE-BLINDING

See Blinding

DOWNSIZING

See Contraction Strategy, Restructuring

DRUG COVERAGE

Prescription drugs play an increasing role in modern medicine. Their importance is indicated by their ability to improve health and quality of life and to replace surgery or invasive procedures. However, 23% of Americans under 65 and 31% of Medicare beneficiaries had no prescription drug coverage in 1996, and many others had inadequate coverage. Drug coverage varies in extent of coverage, participant contribution, and how benefits are obtained. The sources of coverage include employer sponsored (including union plans and worker's compensation), private/nongroup coverage, Medicaid, Medicare, and other federal or state programs.

Employer-sponsored health benefits are the single largest source of drug coverage, with managed care plans responsible for covering 89% of workers. Medicare does not cover outpatient prescription drugs, so supplemental coverage is commonly obtained through retiree health benefits, private Medigap policies, or Medicare + Choice plans. A Medigap policy is supplemental to Medicare and is offered by private insurers that include varied prescription drug coverage. Plans differ in deductible, percentage of drug costs covered, and maximum plan payment. Medicare + Choice plans are usually HMOs that receive a fixed monthly payment from Medicare to provide Medicare-covered services including drug coverage. Low-income Medicare enrollees may also qualify for Medicaid. Medicaid drug coverage is optional under federal law; however, all states provide this benefit for families and children enrolled. Federal and state programs include the Department of Veterans' Affairs (VA) and the Civilian Health and Medical Program of the Uniformed Services (CHAMPUS). Uninsured patients can receive certain drugs at no cost through indigent patient programs offered by drug manufacturers.

—Donna Sym

FURTHER READING

U.S. Department of Health and Human Services. (2000, April). *Report to the president: Prescription drug coverage, spending, utilization, and prices.* Washington, DC: U.S. Department of Health and Human Services.
www.phrma.org

DURABLE POWERS OF ATTORNEY FOR HEALTH CARE (DPAHC)

Durable powers of attorney for health care (DPAHC) are advanced health care directives in which individuals delegate decision making regarding their health care to another person(s). The individual delegating authority is called the "principal," and the individual so designated to have such authority is referred to as an "attorney-in-fact," "proxy," "agent," or "surrogate." Durable powers of attorney for health care are principals' statements of authority to their chosen attorneys-in-fact to speak for them concerning medical care, whenever they are unable to communicate for themselves.

The authority granted by a durable power of attorney for health care may be narrow, operating only for a limited time or for a particular circumstance. An example of such a limited power occurs when an individual gives authority to another to make medical decisions for that individual while under anesthesia for a certain surgery on a certain date. In contrast, durable powers of attorney for health care may be very broad and powerful, allowing the attorney-in-fact to make medical decisions that cover almost every conceivable question or situation that may arise. Under such a broad power of attorney for health care, a principal's agent can make medical care decisions as well as consult with health care providers to receive information and give informed consent. The agent also has the authority to sign medical consents, authorizations, or releases; to access any clinical records or other medical information; to apply for benefits; and to transfer an individual to or from a hospital, hospice, nursing home, or other care facility.

States providing for durable powers of attorney for health care have set forth in their statutes certain powers that may be granted to a proxy or attorney in fact, and such powers of attorney often include a reference to these statutory provisions when granting named agents their powers to act. However, to give some powers to the attorney-in-fact, such as the authority to make decisions regarding the withholding or withdrawal of artificially provided food or water, those powers must be specifically stated in the durable power of attorney for health care.

States' laws may also require certain language to be included in durable powers of attorney for health care to make the documents "durable" (a term that means the document is intended to continue in full force and effect even if the principal who originally executed the document becomes incapacitated). Under most circumstances, contracts made by an individual become ineffective on that individual's incompetence; however, the effect and authority of powers of attorney for health care executed in accordance with a state's statutes can, if desired, survive the incapacity of the principal, allowing the attorney in fact to continue to make health care decisions on behalf of the incompetent individual. By setting forth provisions and procedures for formalizing and executing durable powers of attorney for health care, state laws provide standards for these documents on which health care professionals can rely when asked to honor such documents for their patients.

Durable powers of attorney for health care are valid when the principal signs the document; however, they do not take effect until decisional or communicative incapacity begins. Therefore, although the documents are immediately recognized as legal documents, they are not invoked if a patient has sufficient ability to consider treatment options and give informed consent. Moreover, many state statutes provide that these powers can be revoked by the principal at any time, either orally or in writing, and often irrespective of mental capacity.

—Anne M. McKinney

See also Advanced Health Care Directives, Living Wills

FURTHER READING

Krohm, C., & Summers, S. (2002). *Advance health care directives: A handbook for professionals.* Chicago: ABA Publishing.

McKinney, A. M., & Berteau, J. T. (2002). *Estate planning in Tennessee* (2nd ed.). Knoxville, TN: Pro-Practice Press.

E

EARLY ADOPTERS

See Adopter Categories

EARNINGS BEFORE INTEREST AND TAXES (EBIT)

See Operating Cash Flow, Profit

ECONOMIC ORDER QUANTITY (EOQ)

The economic order quantity (EOQ) is the quantity of an item that should be ordered to minimize the relevant costs of placing orders and carrying inventory.

The EOQ is most appropriate for items used on a regular basis for which demand is relatively stable and independent. In a health care environment, the EOQ could help to minimize costs associated with providing basic items such as sanitary gloves, surgical masks, and bandages.

The basic idea of the simple EOQ model is that a cost is associated with placing an order for the item, and a cost is associated with carrying the item in inventory if more is ordered than is immediately needed. These two costs conflict and must be traded off to find the best ordering plan.

The EOQ assumes the order cost is fixed and is incurred each time an order is placed regardless of the order size. This cost is associated with administrative costs, transportation, and handling.

The annual inventory carrying cost per unit is usually estimated to be a percentage of the item cost. The percentage includes the cost of capital, representing the opportunity cost of having money invested in inventory.

EOQ makes the cost tradeoff as shown in the following example. Suppose a hospital uses 12,000 packs of sanitary gloves each year. The cost of each pack is $10, and the cost to process each order with the supplier is estimated to be $75. The annual carrying cost rate is 8%. The hospital currently orders 3,000 glove packs each quarter. The general form of the EOQ model, using the data just given, is

D = annual demand for the item in units (12,000)

O = fixed cost to place an order in dollars ($75)

C = unit cost of the item in dollars ($10)

I = annual carrying cost rate (8%)

Q = order quantity (to be determined)

Total cost = average annual ordering cost + average annual holding cost

$$(1) \text{ Total cost} = (D/Q * O) + (Q/2 * I * C)$$

We can use expression (1) to find the cost of the current policy, in which $Q = 3,000$:

$$TC (3,000) = (12,000/3,000 * 75) + (3,000/2 * .08 * 10) = \$1,500$$

The EOQ is the value of Q that minimizes expression (1). The general formula is found through differential calculus, resulting in the basic EOQ model shown in expression (2).

$$(2) \ Q = \text{v} [(2 * D * O) / (I * C)]$$

Plugging in estimates from the sanitary glove packs into the EOQ model in expression (2) shows that the best order quantity is 1,500 packs.

$$Q = \sqrt{(2 * 12{,}000 * 75) / (.08 * 10)} = 1{,}500$$

From expression (1), the total annual cost of ordering 1,500 packs with each order is $1,200, representing a savings of 20% over the current quarterly ordering plan.

$$TC\ (1{,}500) = [(12{,}000 / 1{,}500) * 75] + [(1{,}500/2) * .08 * 10] = \$1{,}200$$

In situations where the item unit cost varies with the quantity ordered, the total costs must include the purchase costs in addition to the order costs and carrying costs.

—R. Lawrence LaForge

FURTHER READING

Arnold, J. R. T., & Chapman, S. N. (2001). *Introduction to materials management* (4th ed.). Upper Saddle River, NJ: Prentice Hall.

Haksever, C., Render, B., Russell, R. S., & Murdick, R. G. (2000). *Service management and operations* (2nd ed.). Upper Saddle River, NJ: Prentice Hall.

ECONOMIES OF SCALE

Economies of scale exist when the average cost of production decreases as the quantity of output produced rises. In other words, output can be doubled for less than a doubling of cost.

This phenomenon is in contrast to diseconomies of scale, where the unit cost of production rises as output increases. Constant returns to scale occur when the unit cost of production remains constant as output increases. All three concepts can be illustrated in a graph of production costs against output produced. (See Figure 1).

Most production processes are believed to exhibit economies of scale at relatively low levels of output, followed by relatively constant returns to scale, then diseconomies of scale as output increases.

Economies of scale often occur in cases where production involves a substantial amount of fixed costs; costs that are fixed, regardless of the amount of output produced. For example, to bring a brand name drug to market, pharmaceutical companies must invest a fixed amount of money on research and development, regardless of how many prescriptions will be sold. An insurer may wish to advertise a new insurance policy using television or newspaper ads,

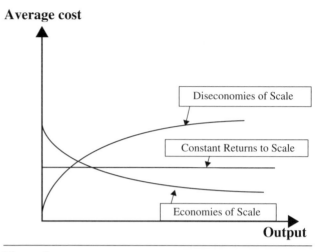

Average cost

Diseconomies of Scale

Constant Returns to Scale

Economies of Scale

Output

Figure 1

which represent mostly fixed costs, regardless of the number of new policyholders enrolled.

Where economies of scale exist, larger firms have an advantage over smaller firms.

—Vivian Ho

EFFECTIVE DOSE

The term *effective dose* is used in conjunction with drug dosing or radiation dosing. The exact meaning varies depending on the context.

In radiation safety, the term *effective dose* was coined by the International Commission on Radiological Protection. It does not refer to an exact quantity but is calculated by multiplying actual organ doses by weighted risk factors that are related to an individual organ's radiosensitivity for developing cancer. The sum of the products is called the *effective whole-body dose* or the *effective dose*. Tissue-weighting factors can vary from 0.01 for skin, or 0.05 for thyroid, to 0.20 for the gonads.

In reference to a pharmacologic agent, the effective dose of the agent is the dose that produces a response considered "effective" as defined by the study protocol or clinical response. It may represent a cure of a disease or a mitigation of symptoms.

When considering a "dose–response" curve, different effective doses can be defined. The effective dose (50), or ED50 is the effective dose in 50% of the patients or subjects. The ED95 represents the effective dose in 95% of patients or subjects.

Because each patient is unique in the way he or she responds to a given drug, to arrive at an effective dose researchers must consider many factors. The dose of a medication may need to be adjusted to compensate for age, gender, pregnancy, pharmacogenetic phenotype, kidney function, liver function, concurrent medications, concurrent diseases, and prior adverse drug reactions or drug allergies.

—Stephen A. Vitkun

FURTHER READING

Carruthers, S. G., Hoffman, B. B., Melmon, K. L., & Nierenberg, D. W. (2000). *Melmon and Morrelli's Clinical Pharmacology* (4th ed.). New York: McGraw-Hill.

Ginsberg, D. (1999). *The investigator's guide to clinical research* (2nd ed.). Boston: CenterWatch.

www.hps.org/publicinformation/ate/q1252.html

www.triumf.ca/safety/tsn/tsn_6_1/subsection3_2_7.html

EFFICACY

The term *efficacy* relates to the pharmacodynamic effectiveness of drugs. However, the terms *efficacy* and *effectiveness* are not exactly interchangeable. Efficacy is the maximal effect of an agonist (a drug or chemical that activates a specific receptor system). This occurs when the dose is taken at very high levels. The efficacy is determined primarily by the receptor system (the molecules in a biological system that interact with drugs to change the functioning of the system) and by the effector system (effectors are the molecules that translate the drug-receptor interaction into an actual change in the activities of the cell). Efficacy can be measured with a graded dose–response curve. A graded dose–response curve is a graphical representation of the response of a specific receptor–effector system measured against an increasing concentration of a specific drug. Traditionally, it is graphically represented as a sigmoid curve on semilogarithmic axes where efficacy is depicted by the plateau of the dose–response curve. The efficacy (maximum effectiveness) and potency (the dose causing 50% of the maximum effect) parameters can be derived from these data.

It is important to recognize that undesirable effects (side-effects) may limit the dose of a drug so that the concentration associated with its maximal desirable effect is not achieved. The therapeutic index of a drug represents the margin of safety. It is the difference between the dose of the drug that produces a desired effect and the dose that produces undesirable effects. The therapeutic index of a drug is often defined as the ratio between the median lethal dose and the median effective dose (LD50/ED50).

—Anthony J. Ippolito

See also Effective Dose

FURTHER READING

Stoelting, R. K. (1999). *Pharmacology & physiology in anesthetic practice* (3rd ed.). Philadelphia: Lippincott-Raven.

Trevor, A. J., Katzung, B. G., & Masters, S. B. (2002). *Katzung & Trevor's Pharmacology: Examination & board review* (6th ed.). New York: Lange Medical Books/McGraw-Hill.

E-HEALTH

The general term "e-health" has been used to refer to any health care services delivered over the Internet. However, the term more accurately describes an emerging field in which medical informatics, public health administration, and business intersect for delivery or enhancement of health services and information.

Electronic health care delivered over the Internet ranges from informational, educational, and commercial products to direct services offered by professionals, nonprofessionals, and businesses. These can be broadly characterized as

- Consumer information services that provide general health and wellness information or are targeted to specific populations, diseases, or issues. These services can be nonprofit or commercial.
- Support groups, including chat rooms, Web sites, e-mail, and newsgroups in which patients and families share information, feelings, or ideas. Some of these groups are moderated by a health professional, but most are unconstrained discussion groups for exchange of ideas and advice.
- Health-related products sales, including prescription and nonprescription drugs, medical devices, literature, and other products. Some sites require written prescriptions before filling orders for drugs, whereas others supply any requested medication or device regardless of physician's prescription or even regulatory approval.
- Medical diagnosis and advice can consist of basic answers to consumers' questions or more sophisticated diagnostic and treatment recommendations based on a patient's answers to specific questions. The latter consultations generally charge a fee, which may not be reimbursable by insurance.
- Contract health services are information and services for a closed set of consumers under contract with an insurance plan or employer. These sites may provide information about wellness and disease prevention as well as describing the health benefits program.

- Business support services to assist health care providers with billing, record maintenance, and database access.

In addition to these Web-based e-health services, e-mail is increasingly used by patients and health care providers to schedule appointments and procedures as well as for communication between patient and provider.

The goals of the e-health initiative have been to lower health care costs, provide high-quality health care information, and increase access. However, the rapid growth in the number of e-health sites, the volume of information, and consumer access to knowledge previously available only to professionals have raised concerns. Consumers are now able to access the same medical databases, libraries, and research publications as health care professionals and, as a result, have become empowered to take more responsibility for their own health care decisions and to rely less on individual practitioners. The increasing sophistication of health care knowledge by the public has the potential to make the relationship between patient and physician more egalitarian and requires adjustments on the part of both.

The relative lack of regulation of the Internet has also raised concerns about confidentiality, privacy, and security of personal health information. Health care professionals and the public rightly fear that breaches of security might limit insurance coverage and job opportunities, or prompt malpractice claims. Before any e-health applications that are intended to reduce costs, such as electronic health records, reduction of medical errors, and data collection and dissemination, can be widely adopted, consumers and providers need to be confident that data will not be shared or sold To address some of these issues, a number of professional and consumer groups have developed guidelines, codes of ethics, and seals of approval for e-health sites that require security measures and allow users to access and change any data they have submitted. Other measures include digital credentials to provide authentication for secure Internet transactions and encryption software to protect e-mail messages.

It was hoped that providing access to high-quality health care information and services would reduce the number of unnecessary office visits and lower costs. It has become apparent, however, that many underserved populations have not been able to benefit from electronic health services. The so-called digital divide refers to the gap in computer and Internet access between groups segmented by income, educational level, race/ethnicity, age, disability, and other parameters. Access can be improved by providing computers and Internet access in public areas such as libraries and schools, but site developers need to address issues of literacy, health practices, and content complexity as well.

Other issues related to e-health concern data standards, site content, evaluation of research studies, and integration of health services. Current data systems are proprietary and run on various operating systems and platforms. Translating software is often required. For e-health systems to become linked with health care information, data exchange standards need to be developed. Similarly, site content and e-health applications have been developed independently and frequently been driven by market forces rather than public need. Consequently, there are gaps and overlaps in the type of information and services available. Commercial interests foster development of areas such as clinical care support, health care transactions, and business applications, whereas other functions such as community health tools and population-based registries may not be offered. The traditional lack of communication among the fields of health care provision, public health, personal health, business, and technology is also present online. Functions such as health information and support, electronic recordkeeping, transaction processing, clinical and public health information systems, and disease management programs can all be provided online and, if properly integrated, can increase efficiency of health care delivery and improve continuity of care.

Emerging technology will continue to have an impact on e-health. Although predicting the future of e-health is not without risk, several trends have been identified as likely to have impact:

- Commercialization is expected to continue and perhaps increase.
- Increasing numbers of e-health resources will address global issues and audiences.
- Demand will increase for more immediate and constant access to online resources.
- There will be increasing provision and use of multimedia resources, including full-motion video.
- Non-PC access by personal data assistants (PDAs), Web-enabled phones, interactive TV, and other technologies will lead to development of e-health sites for a variety of access devices and formats
- Applications will be developed for personalization and tailoring of site content according to wants and needs of an individual user.
- E-health tools will be developed to store, interpret, and evaluate genetic knowledge in decision making on the part of consumers and clinicians.

Emerging technology is likely to have a great impact on future provision of health care and e-health services in particular. As yet it is unclear how rapidly advances will evolve into commercial applications or health care provision. Fundamental societal questions about ethical and legal implications, access, standards, and costs remain unanswered and will need to be addressed before the full potential of e-health services can be realized.

—Francois Nader and Judith Lackland

See also Access, Health Policy, Telemedicine

FURTHER READING

EHealth International. A guide to e-health for the health care professional: An introduction. *Journal of Applied Health Technology.* http://www.atmeda.org/ehealth/guide.htm.

Eng, T. R. (2001). *The ehealth landscape: a terrain map of emerging information and communication technologies in health and health care.* Princeton, NJ: The Robert Wood Johnson Foundation.www.rwjf.org

Eysenbach, G. (2001). What is e-health? *Journal of Medical Internet Research, 3*(2), e20.

ELECTROCARDIOGRAM (EKG OR ECG)

An electrocardiogram (EKG or ECG) is a printout of the electrical activity of the heart. Clinical information gained from this printout includes heart rate, rhythm, conduction abnormalities, myocardial ischemia (insufficient blood supply to the heart that may lead to a heart attack), or previous myocardial infarction (heart attack). The 3- and 5-lead EKG is commonly used as telemetry, a monitoring system for abnormal rates or rhythms. In a hospital setting, multiple patients each wearing a pocket-sized monitor can be observed from a central location by specialized nursing staff. Outpatients can be given a monitoring device that continually records cardiac activity over a 24-hour period. The 12-lead EKG is used primarily for diagnostics and is a key component in the evaluation of the nearly 5 million people per year that come to emergency rooms complaining chest pain. In the prehospital evaluation of the patient with chest pain, it has a sensitivity of 76% and a specificity of 88%. The in-hospital evaluation of a heart attack can involve serial (taken at predetermined intervals) EKGs as well as blood levels of cardiac enzyme markers (CPK MB and troponin). An EKG is also considered part of routine health screening by organizations such as the American College of Cardiology, which recommends an EKG for both men and women over the age of 40, for competitive athletes, and for individuals whose cardiovascular health is linked to public safety (such as firefighters). An EKG is also recommended as a preoperative screening test for women over age 50 and men over age 40.

—Daryn H. Moller

FURTHER READING

www.acc.org

ELASTICITY OF DEMAND

The quantity demanded of a good or service responds to changes in its own price, changes in the price of other goods or services, and changes in consumer income. Demand elasticities measure the responsiveness of the quantity demanded to changes in these factors. The own-price elasticity of demand equals the percentage decrease in quantity demanded, divided by the percentage increase in price of a given product or service. For example, the own-price elasticity of demand for hospital admissions has been estimated to be between −0.1 and −0.2. A 1% increase in the price of a hospital stay reduces demand for hospital admissions by 0.1%. If a 1% increase in the price of a product or service leads to more than a 1% decrease in quantity demanded, then demand is said to be price elastic. Conversely, if the absolute value of the own-price elasticity of demand is less than 1, then demand for the product or service is said to be price inelastic.

The cross-price elasticity of demand is equal to the percentage change in quantity demanded divided by the percentage change in price of another good or service. If this fraction is negative, then the two goods or services are complements. If the cross-price elasticity of demand is positive, then the two goods or services are complements. The income elasticity of demand is equal to the percentage change in quantity demanded, divided by the percentage change in consumer income.

—Vivian Ho

FURTHER READING

Santerre, R. E., & Neun, S. P. (2000). *Health economics: Theories, insights, and industry studies.* Orlando, FL: Dryden Press.

ELDER CARE

See Long-Term Care

ELECTRONIC BILLING

See Billing

ELECTRONIC CLAIMS

An electronic claim is a bill or statement of charges for health care services submitted to an insurance carrier or managed care organization using an electronic data interchange (EDI) medium. An EDI application allows information to be transferred between the computer of one organization and the computer of another organization, thus avoiding the need to prepare paper forms for mailing or to transmit electronically. Claims data can be entered into an electronic form, uploaded or downloaded from an electronic file, or transmitted by fax.

Electronic claims can significantly reduce the amount of time a health care organization or physician provider waits to be paid for services provided. Estimates suggest that electronic claims are paid in approximately half the time required for paper claims. Electronic submission not only decreases turnaround time for payment but also accrues benefits by eliminating paper, labor, and mailing costs and by reducing errors.

Although large health care organizations and systems typically collect, process, and transmit their own billing information for payment, smaller organizations such as physician practices may outsource the billing function to a commercial vendor.

The Health Insurance Portability and Accountability Act of 1996 (HIPAA), signed into law in August 1997, mandated development of standards for electronic health information transactions. Electronic transmission of financial and administrative transactions, including billing and electronic claims processing, were included in the provisions. Organizations whose data are not compliant with HIPAA standards may submit their data to a health care clearinghouse that transforms the data into standard elements and standard transactions.

—Donna J. Slovensky

See also Electronic Data Interchange (EDI)

FURTHER READING

Topel, K., & Mullen, H. (2002, February). At the speed of EDI: Physician practice converts to EDI and slashes both its claims turnaround and accounts receivable days. *Health Management Technology, 23*(2), 26.

ELECTRONIC COMMERCE

Electronic commerce or e-commerce is technically defined as electronic sharing of information at any point during a sales transaction. Large businesses have engaged in a form of electronic commerce called electronic data interchange (EDI) since the 1970s. However, not until the early 1990s and the invention of the World Wide Web (WWW) did electronic commerce proliferate. The WWW is the portion of the Internet that supports graphics, audio, and video as well as links to other documents. Accordingly, to conduct basic e-commerce on the WWW requires capital investments that are a fraction of those required previously. The relatively low cost and user friendliness of the WWW spawned numerous innovations in electronic business communications that quickly rendered too narrow the technical definition of electronic commerce.

In the late 1990s the term *electronic business (e-business)* was coined to refer more broadly to inter- and intraorganizational sharing of any type of information through electronic means. Although e-commerce and e-business differ technically, e-business progressed naturally from organizational investments in e-commerce, so the two terms are often used interchangeably.

E-business activities are commonly classified by their strategic design. At the highest level, the two most common strategic classifications are business-to-consumer and business-to-business, although there are additional categories such as business-to-government and consumer-to-consumer. The category with the greatest economic potential is business-to-business. Through economic ups and downs, businesses continue to migrate significant portions of their operations to the Web. According to the Gartner Group, business-to-business investments will reach 7.3 trillion (or 6.9% of the global economy) by 2004.[1] At the same time, by 2004 an estimated 35% of U.S. firms will bill customers online, saving on average $3.35 per transaction.

Some potential benefits of e-business investments include the following:

- Less administrative paperwork
- Streamlined business processes
- Dramatic long-term cost savings
- Improved customer service
- Improved cash management
- Ability to attract business from new markets
- Stronger relations with trading partners

Being tightly coupled to the Web also presents a number of complex challenges to the business community:

- Identifying appropriate practices for management, organization, and control of e-business activities
- Developing solutions to connect two or more companies with highly complex and very different organizational and technical infrastructures
- Identifying appropriate marketing strategies for products and services

- Governing the myriad activities in e-business, including complex challenges to accounting and legal institutions

Numerous e-business initiatives are currently applied in health care. Insurance companies, hospitals, and provider offices often consider investments in complementary e-business strategies as they invest in applications and infrastructure to become compliant with the Health Insurance Portability and Accountability Act of 1996. Examples of specific e-business efforts in health care include the following:

- Partnerships among providers and other health care companies to create health care content and communities targeted to specific audiences
- Web sites designed to facilitate physician–patient communication
- Creative employment of the Web for telemedicine applications

—Amy W. Ray

See also Health Insurance Portability and Accountability Act (HIPAA) of 1996

NOTE

1. Landergren, P. G. (2000, April 3). B-to-B e-sales will exceed B-to-C by tenfold next year. *Computerworld Online*

FURTHER READING

Goldstein, D. (2000). *E-Healthcare: Harness the power of Internet, e-commerce & e-care.* Gaithersburg, MD: Aspen.
Vegoda, P. (2001). *Integrating the healthcare enterprise.* HIMSS Target Issues Monograph. Health Information and Management systems Society. (www.himss.org)
Wisnosky, D., & Sones, A. (2000). Improving healthcare delivery with electronic transactions Napierville, IL: Wizdom Systems, Inc. (www.wizdomsystems.com)

ELECTRONIC DATA INTERCHANGE (EDI)

Electronic data interchange (EDI) is the electronic transfer of information among the various units of a business enterprise, or with its trading partners. In addition to benefits associated with paperwork reduction, EDI improves the efficiency of transaction processing by reducing data redundancy and improving data quality. Examples of business information transmitted electronically among health care organizations include insurance eligibility information, encounter data, claims for payment of medical services and products, and purchase orders and supplier invoices.

Electronic data interchange can occur effectively only in open systems, where exchange partners use data standards (common syntax, data structure, and editing conventions). The accepted standard for all types of electronic commerce is *ANSI ASC X12,* published by the ANSI (American National Standards Institute) Accredited Standards Committee. Various ANSI subcommittees develop standards related to specific types of data, such as the ASC X12N Health Care Claim (837), developed by the ANSI Health Care Task Group. This standard enables administrative processing of electronic claims for payment of health care services (medical, dental, and other provider encounters), and products such as pharmaceuticals and durable medical equipment. Another ANSI organization developing health care standards for clinical and administrative data, Health Level Seven (HL7), is addressing the administrative simplification requirements of the Health Insurance Portability and Accountability Act (HIPAA).

The Workgroup on Electronic Data Interchange (WEDI), a health industry coalition founded in 1991 to promote adoption of EDI technology and to provide leadership in health care standards development, consists of individuals and organizations representing payers, providers, government and standards agencies, vendors, and consumer groups. This organization has a particular focus on disseminating information about pending legislative and regulatory issues related to EDI.

—Donna J. Slovensky

See also Electronic Claims, Electronic Commerce

FURTHER READING

A useful EDI primer from the Accredited Standards Committee. (2001). *IT Health Care Strategist, 3*(4), 12.
www.hl7.org
www.wedi.org

ELECTRONIC MEDICAL RECORD

See Electronic Patient Record

ELECTRONIC PATIENT RECORD

In its simplest form, an electronic patient record is a medical document stored in a machine-readable format. Data are entered into the record via many different sources, including computerized entry and various document imaging systems. The record should include electronic documentation of information normally included in a paper record regarding a specific patient. The ideal electronic patient record should reflect the same information that is typically found in the classic paper record, with variance according to provider as well as patient. The record is typically stored on a computer or server and is accessible to anyone having access to the file. The key feature is accessibility via a machine such as a computer.

Data stored in an electronic record can be as simple as an image of the paper record such as is available through many different scanning utilities. Reasons one might consider a simple electronic representation of a paper record include such things as decreasing storage space, increasing security of the record, and ease of access to a specific record. This type of record, although useful, has obvious limitations and likely has associated cost that will not provide substantial return on investment. Increasing utility is achieved by adding searchable fields to the record, allowing the searcher to find specific elements in the record itself. Records that store data in specific fields capable of being indexed, tracked, and searched can dramatically improve care for the patient and increase return on investment. This potential improvement in care has led to an ever increasing interest in electronic medical records.

The advances in electronic records include systems that support users by storing data in databases that are coded and structured to allow easy retrieval by stakeholders for patient care delivery, management, decision support, and analysis. Some (including the Institute of Medicine) refer to these advanced records as *computer-based patient records.* The ideal electronic medical record is still being defined but should include minimum elements such as a complete recording of historical items related to a particular patient's care, stored in a database with defined values as opposed to narrative value that is not as searchable. It should also be easily accessible and improve efficiency of record taking. The ideal medical record will eventually be compatible with data management instead of just data collection and should be planned with management as the goal.

Data recording without management capacity will handicap the ability of health care to improve itself. All quality control efforts require application of scientific method to data rather than just to collection of data. Electronic patient record designs should allow investigators to evaluate groups of diseases and conditions with their various characteristics and treatments. This will allow more standardization of medical care, leading to more consistent and error-free care. To such end, all records should be planned with database evaluation as an ultimate goal.

Electronic patient records should provide an integrated view of information needed regarding a specific patient's care. There are presently so many providers of care to patients including ancillary services (laboratory, radiology, and so on), primary care, specialist care, and hospital or after-hours clinic care that it becomes nearly impossible to keep an integrated record of care provided to a patient without an electronic repository of information stored in a location accessible to all appropriate stakeholders. Any design of an electronic record should plan for integration with other potential electronic record sources.

The ability to record information about patients that is pertinent and accurate has become increasingly difficult through the years. The demand for types of information has increased with each additional stakeholder in patient care. Payers, caregivers, ancillary personnel, patients themselves, other physicians or caregivers, and even litigators all have different demands for recordkeeping. Government agencies also have a huge interest in the type and accuracy of information collected and stored about a particular patient. The more complex the information required becomes, the more appealing an electronic medical record becomes. The days of a medical record consisting of single-word entries for each visit have long since gone. The documentation now requested and required has become so complex as to necessitate a new, more efficient way of collecting and storing information regarding patients. Any electronic medical record that does not increase the efficiency and reduce the time involved for medical record taking should not be acceptable as a viable alternative to the paper record.

An important feature of electronic patient records is security. A well-designed electronic patient record includes at least one layer of security such as password protection. Indeed, expectations for at least two levels of protection should be standard. In the near future, biometric security devices such as thumbprints or retinal scans will become standard. An adequate security policy for an electronic patient record will protect the record from tampering by including a trail of all changes to the record as well as the originator of any record changes. It will have layers of accessibility based on need to know. It will ultimately protect patients' rights.

The record must be at least as incorruptible as the paper record and really should be held to a higher standard than paper records. One way this is achieved is by continuous or near-continuous backup of the record. There also needs to be an element of redundancy in any network that is built to host an electronic patient record, so that the record taking is not hampered or lost because of hardware failure. This need adds an extra facet to the security issues previously discussed but should be considered critical to any electronic patient record.

Barriers to acceptance of an electronic patient record include affordability. Another barrier to implementation and acceptance of electronic patient records is the process change involved in conversion to an electronic medical record. Regardless of the barriers, electronic patient records are becoming more and more expected by large stakeholders in patient care, including the government and payers. Real expectations are widespread use of electronic patient records in the future.

—Kenneth R. Robertson

FURTHER READING

Carter, J. H. (2001). *Electronic medical records: A guide for clinicians and administrators.* Philadelphia: American College of Physicians/American Society of Internal Medicine.

Committee on Quality Healthcare in America, Institute of Medicine. (2001). *Crossing the quality chasm: A new health system for the 21st century.* Washington, DC: National Academy Press.

EMERGENCY ROOM (ER)

An emergency room (ER) is defined as a hospital room or area that is equipped and staffed to deal with the treatment of people requiring immediate medical care. An emergency is a medical condition manifested by acute symptoms of sufficient severity that a layperson who possesses an average knowledge of health and medicine could reasonably expect the absence of immediate medical attention to result in placing the health of that person in serious jeopardy or serious impairment of bodily function. Emergency care applies to health services required for alleviation of severe pain or immediate diagnosis and treatment of unforeseen medical conditions, which could lead to disability or death if not treated quickly.

There are nearly 5,000 emergency departments (EDs) in the United States today. The number of EDs has been decreasing in the past decade, as a result of cost-cutting measures by hospitals as well as numerous hospital closings. EDs provide an essential public service, 24 hours a day, seven days a week. They are a vital part of the country's health care safety net and provide care to all individuals regardless of ability to pay. EDs represent less than 2% of the $1 trillion spent annually on health care.

EMTALA

In 1986, Congress enacted the Emergency Medical Treatment and Active Labor Act (EMTALA). It was designed to prevent hospitals from refusing to treat patients or transferring them to other hospitals because the patients were unable to pay for their care. This legislation has increased demand on EDs, because even those who come in without a true emergency must be treated. Some insurance companies have tried to alleviate this problem by refusing to pay for their subscribers to use the emergency room for nonemergency reasons.

HISTORY

The history of emergency medicine is unclear. The accident rooms of the past were poorly staffed and equipped to deal with severe illness or injuries. Emergency rooms as we now know them developed around the 1960s. As the family physician that made house calls became a thing of the past, people sought other ways to receive after-hours care. Also, with health insurance covering hospital care but not office care, ER visits quadrupled by 1970. During this time, the concept of intensive care units (ICUs) was beginning to develop as well.

People realized the need for standardized emergency care with a dedicated group of trained emergency physicians and staff. Pressure from an increasingly mobile society to have competent emergency care also encouraged the move toward developing emergency medicine as a specialty.

The first full-time group of physicians to provide exclusive emergency care consisted of four general medicine physicians who banded together in 1961. In 1968, 32 physicians from 18 states met and incorporated the American College of Emergency Physicians (ACEP). Then, in 1970, the University Association for Emergency Medical Services (UAEMS) was formed. The focus initially was on surgical emergencies and trauma. Also in 1970, ACEP drafted a training program for emergency medicine residents. The universities of Southern California and Louisville had the first two departments of emergency medicine in their medical schools by 1971. The American Medical Association (AMA) in 1976 approved a formal section in emergency medicine.

THE PRESENT

The emergency department generally consists of a number of different areas that treat specific diseases or injuries. Examples are trauma room, chest pain area, triage area, fast track area, and pediatric area. The French word *triage* is translated as "sorting." Triage for medical emergencies was developed on the battlefield during World War II. Mandated by the Joint Commission on Accreditation of Healthcare Organizations (JCAHO), the triage system evaluates patients based on the seriousness of their illness or injury. The most critical patients are seen first, as opposed to all patients being seen on a first-come, first-served basis. Because of managed care restrictions on hospital admission, more patients now receive all their treatment in the ED. For example, a patient tested for a myocardial infarction (MI, or heart attack) and found to be negative may be treated and released from the ED. If the hospital chooses to admit such a patient, it still may only be reimbursed at emergency room rates. The fast-track area is designed for treating minor injuries such as sprains or lacerations requiring stitches. Nurse practitioners or physician's assistants can treat these patients, who are moved more quickly through the system because they require fewer interventions. The trauma room is an area where patients who have been in an automobile accident or have been victims of violence, such as gunshot wounds or stab wounds, can be seen and treated by both emergency and surgical trauma staff. These staff are trained in the complications of trauma and are looking for signs that are precursors of such complications. Chest pain ERs are becoming very popular. Treatment of an acute myocardial infarction can mean the difference between life and death. Many potential complications can be averted if promptly treated by qualified staff. Because the care of pediatric patients is very different from adults, creating pediatric areas in the ED was necessary. Here, children can be treated by personnel who are familiar with medication dosages and treatments specific to the pediatric population.

With advances in technology of the auto industry (such as air bags) and public service announcements regarding the use of safety belts, a larger number of people are surviving automobile accidents that would otherwise have been fatal. The pressure on local law enforcement to stop drinking and driving has also contributed to the decrease in traffic fatalities. As a result, EDs now see a larger number of more severely injured clients. Trauma surgeons now deal with more severe orthopedic injuries, because such clients would once have succumbed to fatal head and chest injuries.

—Doreen T. Day

FURTHER READING

www.acep.org
www.ccems.org
www.emtala.com
www.saem.org

EMERGENT STRATEGY

Emergent strategies are patterns of activity created by an organization's employees as they carry out their daily tasks. Unlike deliberate strategies, which are carefully planned by top administrators, emergent strategies represent unexpected, bottom-up ideas. Once recognized, these fresh ideas may be formally adopted by management and may become part of the organization's official plan. As such, emergent strategies can play an important role in stimulating organizational change.

By definition, emergent strategies are not part of management's intended plans for the organization. Instead, these strategies arise when employees in one department or another experiment with new products or processes, attempt to solve problems, negotiate with suppliers, or listen to customers, patients, or clients, and so on. When employees are

given the flexibility to cope with their situations in this way, they often come up with approaches that work better than standard practices. In essence, they learn what works. Another level of learning takes place when management notices the innovation and chooses to adopt it as part of the organization's formal strategy.

Although this process of experimentation and learning may seem like a rather chaotic approach to strategic management, it is actually beneficial in several respects. First, openness to emergent strategy helps organizations to adapt to rapidly changing environments. Instead of rigidly following pre-established plans, managers can talk with front-line personnel to learn what works in a new situation. Second, observing employee actions can allow administrators to find strengths that were previously unrecognized, thereby opening new routes to competitive advantage. In essence, organizations that are open to emergent strategies gain agility, increased response times, and the opportunity for continued development of organizational competencies.

These advantages can be particularly important in an industry such as health care, which has been marked by significant environmental changes. To take advantage of such benefits, health care administrators should seek out emergent strategies across their organizations. This will require active, personal attention to the way things are being done in various hospital units. Whenever possible, administrators should discuss operational data and current initiatives with department heads and staff members on a face-to-face basis. In addition, they should ensure that good ideas are shared across departments so that they can be used more broadly. Openness to learning and responsiveness to new ideas are crucial.

A willingness to adopt emergent strategy can be an effective part of an ongoing strategic management process. But short-term responsiveness is not the whole picture. This responsiveness must be matched with a vision for the future and a framework for moving forward. Those emergent strategies that fit best within this proactive thinking should be easily adopted. Those that indicate a larger change in perspective may require more serious consideration. In the long run, short-term flexibility must be balanced against the larger vision.

—Barbara A. Spencer

See also Strategic Management

FURTHER READING

Mintzberg, H. (1978). Patterns in strategy formation. *Management Science, 24*(9), 934–948.

Mintzberg, H., & Waters, J. A. (1985). Of strategies, deliberate and emergent. *Strategic Management Journal, 6*(3), 257–271.

Osborne, C. S. (1998). Systems for sustainable organizations: Emergent strategies, interactive controls and semi-formal information. *Journal of Management Studies, 35*(4), 481–509.

EMPLOYEE ABSENTEEISM

Although *absenteeism* has been historically synonymous with *sick days,* employees are absent from work for numerous reasons. This has become increasingly expensive to organizations, because an employee's absence may entail a client not being served in a timely manner, a product not being made on schedule, and so on. According to a survey published by the Society of Human Resource Management (SHRM), absenteeism increased by 14% between the years of 1992 and 1996. This is particularly disturbing because companies are now using nearly 2% of their payroll to pay for unscheduled absences. In fact, on average, absenteeism costs organizations $755 per employee annually. Three main causes of absenteeism are physical health, stress, and motivation.

PHYSICAL HEALTH

Employers recognize that at some point all employees experience some illness and typically offer paid days to subsidize income to individuals who must miss work for health-related reasons. Because a sick day policy is easy to abuse, most companies have reduced the number of sick days allotted to employees. On average, most companies offer somewhere between four and eight sick days annually. Although there is not much employers can do to prevent employees from catching a cold, other health-related issues can be controlled. More specifically, employers can examine and decrease work-related injuries. For instance, an increasing number of absences because of lower back pain may indicate a need for ergonomic changes that will produce less stress to the back. Taking care of some of these issues beforehand can reduce work-related injury absences from 122 days to 42 days. As such, organizations should use industry data or medical professionals to identify trends common to a particular industry or position and to prevent any foreseeable injuries.

STRESS

An estimated 1 million people are absent from work each year because of stress-related reasons, and 80% of all employees report feeling stress in the workplace. Whereas many organizations currently use disciplinary action to reduce absenteeism (93%), human resource professionals suggest work-life programs that recognize both schedule demands as an alternative to decreasing absenteeism. They note that disciplinary action should instead be used as a last resort, particularly if work–family conflict and other life stressors are contributing to absenteeism. This is becoming increasingly important because in 2001, for example, 21% of employees attributed their unscheduled absence to stress.

Human resource professionals ranked flexible scheduling, working from home, and a four-day workweek as the most effective work-life programs to keep down stress-related absences.

Many organizations have found monetary results by accommodating employees' time constraints. The three programs currently used most by organizations, flexible scheduling, leave for school functions, and employee assistance programs, have shown marked improvements in absenteeism. For instance, Xerox reduced absenteeism by 30% by implementing a flexible scheduling program. A program initiated to assist mothers of young children saved the Arnold and Porter Law Firm $800,000 in 1993 alone.

MOTIVATION

A recent survey published by SHRM demonstrated that 32% of employees attribute their absences to personal illness, whereas another 21% are absent because of family issues. However, nearly 10% of absences are attributed to dissatisfaction and lack of motivation. A common theory used to outline this occurrence is equity theory. Employees want to be treated fairly, and they decide what is fair by comparing their input-to-outcome ratio with others. For instance, a physician's assistant with a master's degree and three years of work experience expects pay equal to another physician's assistant with similar background and experiences. When feelings of inequity arise, the individual attempts to redress the inequity. One way to do this is to put less effort into work or appear to work less often. Thus one important way to improve absenteeism rates is to address potential feelings of inequity among employees.

Regardless of the cause of absenteeism, companies should institute formal policies to ensure efficient operation. Although no policy should be applied across the board, successful absence programs have some similarities. Identifying the causes of increased absences in the company provides employers with the major focus for their program. Following that, policies should maintain reliable attendance while avoiding penalizing employees for situations beyond their control. Attendance policies should include some leeway for extenuating circumstances. Finally, companies can use positive incentives to discourage employees from using "sick days" while increasing employee satisfaction, minimizing stress, and decreasing absence.

—Jillian A. Peat

See also Employee Turnover

FURTHER READING

Fisher, C. D., Schoenfeldt, L. F., & Shaw, J. B. (1999). *Human resource management.* Boston: Houghton Mifflin

Robinson, B. (2002). An integrated approach to managing absence supports greater organizational productivity. *Employee Benefits Journal, 27*(2), 7–11.

Strategies for developing an effective employee absenteeism policy. (2001). *HR Focus, 78*(9), 5–6.

www.hrnext.com

www.shrm.org

EMPLOYEE ASSISTANCE PROGRAM (EAP)

An employee assistance program (EAP) is a collection of services designed to deal with a wide range of stress-related problems encountered by employees. These problems may include (but are not limited to) marital discord, financial difficulties, alcoholism or substance abuse, and behavioral or emotional difficulties. Although some of these problems may originate outside of the workplace environment, their effects can certainly affect employees' on-the-job performance. Services offered by EAPs range from diagnosis and short-term counseling for employees already experiencing problems, to educational programs aimed at equipping employees with methods to deal more successfully with potentially stressful situations. Organizations may have their own internally run EAP, or they may contract with an outside private firm to provide services. Employee participation in an EAP is voluntary. Employees may refer themselves to an EAP, or, on witnessing questionable or troubling behavior, their supervisors may refer them.

Although companies are not legally required to offer EAP services, the presence of EAPs within organizations has become more widespread over the past three decades. In a survey conducted by the Society for Human Resource Management (SHRM), 67% of all respondents across private and public organizations offered EAP services (SHRM, 2001). The increasing prevalence of EAPs is primarily due to the belief that good health among employees is ultimately for the good of the organization. Among the benefits cited by organizations implementing these programs are increased return on investment, decreased overall medical expenses, and reduced absenteeism among employees enrolled in an EAP (Drotos, 1999).

However, although the number of organizations offering EAPs has been rising, the number of employees using these available services remains low. Therefore, certain elements are critical to the success of an EAP. Employees are more likely to take advantage of services offered if they are first aware that such a program is available to them. Organizations should publicize these programs whenever possible and educate employees as to their capabilities.

Second, organizations must ensure that confidentiality is maintained. A lack of trust that services provided will remain private will most likely limit use of these services. Last, employees must believe that enrollment in an EAP will have no negative implications regarding, for example, job security or promotions.

—Elizabeth M. Smith

See also Wellness

FURTHER READING

Drotos, J. C. (1999). A management cutting edge tool: The EAP. *Behavioral Health Management, 19,* 48.

French, M. T., Dunlap, L. J., Roman, P. M., & Steele, P. D. (1997). Factors that influence the use and perceptions of employee assistance programs at six worksites. *Journal of Occupational Health Psychology, 2,* 312–324.

Harris, M. M., & Fennell, M. L. (1988). Perceptions of an employee assistance program and employees' willingness to participate. *Journal of Applied Behavioral Science, 24,* 423–438.

Hartwell, T. D., Steele, P. D., French, M. T., Potter, F. J., Rodman, N. F., & Zarkin, G. A. (1996). Aiding troubled employees: Prevalence, cost, and characteristics of employee assistance programs (EAPs) in the United States. *American Journal of Public Health, 86,* 804–808.

Society for Human Resource Management (SHRM). (2001). *2001 Benefits Survey.* Alexandria, VA: Author.

www.shrm.org

EMPLOYEE BENEFITS

See Employee Assistance Program (EAP), Employee Compensation, Employee Retirement Income Security Act (ERISA), Employee Stock Ownership Plan (ESOP)

EMPLOYEE COMPENSATION

World at Work, the American Compensation Association, uses the concept of total rewards to describe the broad view of how to attract, retain, and motivate a talented and productive workforce. Total rewards consist of three elements: compensation, benefits, and the work experience. These three elements may be analyzed separately, but they work together and to the extent that they work together and are consistent with each other, the organization will realize a synergistic impact. Compensation and benefits are discussed elsewhere in this encyclopedia, so this section focuses on the third element: the work experience.

The Corporate Leadership Council (CLC) has identified four concepts that describe the work experience and that contribute to employee retention. An organization that aspires to improve the work experience for its associates and thereby to retain them must consider these four variables: organizational commitment, job satisfaction, pay satisfaction, and external opportunities. Considering these variables within a large complex organization such as a hospital guides the development of multiple retention strategies for various units, job families, and pay grades within an organization.

The term *organizational commitment* refers to the relationship between the individual employee and the organization. Is the employer seen as a good organization in which to work? What does the employer do to promote a loyal workforce? Are the employees proud to be employees? Does the employer promote a balance between work and other life roles? Does the employer facilitate a satisfying relationship among coworkers? Do employees have a sense of job security? All these questions help assess the organizational commitment.

Job satisfaction has been extensively researched and frequently measured. However, it is important to note that there is no one-to-one inverse relationship between job satisfaction and intention to leave an employer. The strongest indicator of job satisfaction is an employee's relationship with his or her supervisor. The importance of the immediate supervisor is compounded by the fact that implementing employee retention programs depends on front-line supervisors. Job satisfaction includes the nature of the job itself, promotional opportunities, professional and personal development opportunities, coworker relationships, and work–life balance. Obviously, there is some overlap between job satisfaction and organizational commitment.

Pay satisfaction involves employees' perception of their pay relative to other comparable employees inside the organization (internal equity) and with competitors (market competitiveness). Pay satisfaction includes base pay, retirement, health benefits, and bonuses as a percentage of base pay. Data indicate that pay satisfaction is particularly important to high performers in industry.

External opportunities as perceived by employees are an increasingly influential variable on intention to leave. Increased awareness of options in the labor market leads to greater movement and growth in the percentage of the workforce that is effectively available to the market. Perception of external opportunities are now playing at least a role equal to job satisfaction in predicting turnover. The relationship between organizational commitment and external opportunities needs to be further explored to ascertain if the former acts as a counterweight to the latter. That is, an organization may find that increased emphasis on

building organizational commitment may reduce the impact of the external market.

It is clear from close studies of employee retention that organizations can be very successful by developing a retention strategy that is informed by employee surveys and that relies on pushing responsibility for retention down the organization. Therefore, organizations must focus their efforts to improve the work experience of their employees. Such efforts should involve a four-step process of diagnosing, planning, acting, and evaluating the changes that are designed to retain highly valued employees.

Describing and measuring the salient aspects of our work experience has been the subject of intensive research. The Gallup Poll has surveyed workplace perceptions of thousands of employees. The results provide tangible data that can constitute both an organizational baseline and a methodology for evaluating changes in an organization's work experience as perceived by its employees.

Researchers have analyzed voluminous data collected by the Gallup organization and have concluded that employees' perception about their work experience can be captured in 12 questions. These questions (referred to by the Corporate Leadership Council as Q12) are as follows:

1. I know what is expected of me at work.

2. I have the materials and equipment I need to do my work right.

3. At work I have the opportunity to do what I do best every day.

4. In the last seven days, I have received recognition or praise for doing good work.

5. My supervisor or someone at work cares about me as a person.

6. There is someone at work who encourages my development.

7. At work my opinions seem to count.

8. The mission and purpose of the organization makes me feel that my job is important.

9. My coworkers are committed to doing quality work.

10. I have a best friend at work.

11. In the last six months, someone at work has talked to me about my progress.

12. This last year I have had opportunities at work to learn and grow.

The sequence of these questions is important because if the analysis indicates problems in the lower-number items, those problems must be solved before problems in the higher-number items can be addressed. For example, if a group of employees do not know what is expected of them, then encouraging their professional development will not be helpful and, in fact, may be counterproductive. The authors of this scale (CLC) use the analogy of mountain climbing; you have to start at the base camp and systematically work your way up the mountain.

Questions 1 and 2 address defining expectations and are the fundamental starting point of defining the relationship between the individual and the organization. Questions 3 through 6 are questions about individual contribution to the organization. Basically the issues here are "Do I feel that I can contribute?" and "Do people in the organization recognize my contribution?" Questions 7 through 10 focus on congruence between individual and organizational values. Difficulty in this level of questions may indicate a need to refocus the group through a strategic planning effort or assessing that your performance management system is functioning appropriately. Finally, the last level of questions (11 and 12) is designed to assess teamwork and innovation in the workplace. These questions are particularly critical in organizations that are undergoing rapid change either as a result of internal reorganization or forces external to the organization. The bottom line in these questions is that individuals or units that fail to adapt to change run the risk of becoming irrelevant or useless to the organization and, therefore, eliminated. Difficulty at this level may require job redesign, skill training, team building, and/or staffing level changes.

It is important to note that these 12 questions give one insight into only one aspect of the employer–employee relationship. If there is a problem in one area of employee morale, it is not possible to say that the solution to that problem is always going to be the same. Identifying barriers to retention and productivity requires multiple sources of data on such variables as commitment to the organization, the external job market, enjoyment of the work itself, pay, and benefits. Identifying barriers is only the first step toward solving organizational problems. This diagnostic phase is followed by planning, action, and evaluation.

Answers to the Q12, along with other questions presented to employees in an organization, begin to define the problems that exist in an organization. This is the diagnostic phase of organizational intervention. The data from the questionnaires must be reviewed with other data that help provide insight into the organization as a whole. For example, a large hospital may discover that outpatient RNs are likely to disagree with the statements that their supervisors care about them as people and that their opinions seem to count. In addition, the hospital may learn that these people who feel undervalued expect to leave the hospital.

Now the next step is to develop a plan to correct this problem. The planning process should include brainstorming,

open communication, and effective and timely decision making. For the sake of our example, let's assume the hospital decides to improve its performance management system by including employee suggestions about how the unit's operation could be improved. Once a timetable and identification of responsibilities for implementation are established, the intervention moves to the implementation or action phase.

The action phase in our example would involve implementing the new performance management system. At this point, those responsible for implementation should anticipate resistance to change. Such resistance should be listened to carefully, and, where appropriate, improvements in the program should be made. Managers will be reluctant to devote the time necessary for the new performance management system, and employees will be skeptical that any recommendations will be taken seriously and may fear that management will resent their suggestions. Listening, communicating, and modifying are excellent responses to resistance. Abandoning the program should only be a last resort.

The final step in implementing an improvement in the work experience in an organization is evaluation. The keys to evaluation are to collect data from multiple sources and to view evaluation as an opportunity to uncover new problems. If we administer the Q12 questionnaire to RNs one year later and get essentially the same results, then we know that the intervention did not work and we must go back to the drawing board in planning a different intervention. In contrast, if we see improved responses to questions 6 and 7 and reduced turnover among RNs, then we can conclude the intervention is successful and can explore other ways to improve the work experience in the organization.

A comprehensive system of employee rewards can provide an organization with a competitive advantage. However, establishing and maintaining such a system is a complicated and difficult process. It requires understanding pay, benefit, and people issues. It also requires understanding the manner in which organizations change, and it requires frequent communication with all levels of the organization.

—Alan P. Chesney

FURTHER READING

Buckingham, M., & Coffman, C. (1999). *First, break all the rules: What the world's greatest managers do differently.* New York: Simon & Schuster.

Carsen, J. (2002). *Employee retention: Everything you need to know about creating an effective employee retention program.* Chicago: CCH Knowledge Point.

Collins, J. (2001). *Good to great: Why some companies make the leap and others don't.* New York: HarperCollins.

Corporate Leadership Council. (1998). *Employee retention: New tools for managing workforce stability and engagement.* Washington, DC: Corporate Executive Board.

Frieberg, K., & Frieberg, J. (1996). *Nuts! Southwest Airlines' crazy recipe for business and personal success.* Austin, TX: Bard Press.

Hochwald, L. (2002, July–August). The ten best companies for women. *Health.* pp. 10–12.

Levering, R., & Moskowitz, M. (1993). *The 100 best companies to work for in America.* New York: Doubleday.

Rosner, R., Halcrow, A., & Levius, A. (2001, August 6). Why you should update your management style. *Wall Street Journal.*

EMPLOYEE HEALTH

Health insurance and health promotion programs are part of an overall corporate strategy to retain the most productive employees. Employee health programs within health care organizations are a bit of an anomaly. In considering health services for its employees, hospitals and other health care organizations must shift their thinking from being providers to being consumers of health services. The role of the employer in employee health started in the United States during World War II. In an effort to attract women into the workforce to replace men who were in the armed services, industry began offering low-cost health insurance. This benefit proved so successful that it has become a cornerstone of employment in the United States. An indication of the importance of health insurance coverage to employees is that many rank it as a higher priority than pay in the decision to change jobs. Management's concern about health insurance costs was most graphically illustrated in the 1960s when General Motors (GM) announced that for every automobile that GM produced, it spent more money on health insurance than it did on steel. The crises in health care financing have reached a situation where M.D.s in West Virginia are striking in protest of malpractice insurance costs and workers at General Electric (GE) are striking in protest of a $200 annual increase in premiums. GE reports that in 2001 it spent $1.4 billion on its workers' medical needs. Today employers struggle with a dual agenda of providing a quality health benefit for employees at a well-managed cost.

Employers have several options available for reducing their health care costs. The most obvious one is to drop health care coverage as a benefit. Whereas this option is not realistic for large or midsize employers, it is realistic for small employers. The National Coalition on Health Care estimates that 10% of the small businesses that offer health insurance to employees will drop the coverage in 2002. Midsize and large employers do have the option of reducing health care costs by outsourcing services. Organizations that have outsourced custodial, food services, and other lower-paid jobs have found that a significant part of their cost savings is in health insurance premiums. As premiums continue to escalate, employers will find that a smaller proportion of their workforce is covered by health insurance, either because the employer has reduced the number of employees who are eligible, or because employees cannot afford their portion of the premium. If health insurance premiums escalate 15% over the next four years and wages escalate 5% per year over the same period, many families will see that a larger and larger portion of their paycheck is going toward health insurance. Many will decide to take the risk of dropping their health coverage. This phenomenon is already occurring among families whose income is between $50,000 and $75,000 per year.

The cost savings methods in the preceding paragraph are a result of reduced services. However, the challenge for many employers is to *improve* benefits while reducing costs. This goal is a much greater challenge. Organizations have learned that partnering with other organizations in health care coalitions can reduce costs and improve services. Health care coalitions, beginning with the Washington Business Group on Health, have demonstrated that well-informed business leaders working together can produce changes in health care that benefit employees (see *Coalitions* entry).

A new trend in health care benefit management is to increase employee involvement as a consumer of health care. Organizations are using a combination of higher deductibles and employer contributions to personal spending accounts to provide incentives to employees to be better consumers of health care. Organizations that solicit employee input into health benefits are more likely to have benefits that meet employee needs and to have better-informed employees. Health care organizations should not assume that all their employees are knowledgeable consumers just because they work in the health care field.

The challenge of managing costs while continuing to provide benefits to employees is substantial. Employers have developed various health services that are demonstrated to have a significant impact on the bottom line. Employee assistance programs, health promotion programs, and managed pharmacy benefit programs have all aided employees while providing significant return on investment. Employee assistance programs (EAPs) are focused on services to employees whose personal problems may be affecting their job performance. Typically EAPs involve brief counseling, referral, and educational programs for employees. EAP services may be provided in-house or outsourced. Most EAPs provide supervisory training programs to help supervisors identify troubled employees and refer them to the EAP. The EAP provides early identification of problems, referral to treatment, and return-to-work conferences where necessary. Research indicates that the return on investment of EAPs is approximately 3 to 1.

Employer-based health promotion programs focus on stress management, chronic disease management and prevention, and health education activities. Stress management focuses on the balance between the demands on a particular individual and his or her ability to cope with those demands. Obviously, one part of a stress management strategy is to reduce the demand side of the equation by clarifying expectations, providing necessary tools to do the job, providing social support, and so forth. Organizations are also involved in helping employees improve their ability to cope with stress through stress management classes, incentives for lifestyle improvements, and programs that foster a better work–nonwork balance, such as onsite child care.

Health education and disease management programs have proven very successful in enhancing employee health and organizational commitment. Services in this area include health screenings, diabetes education, physical fitness training, onsite exercise programs, healthy heart programs, behavioral weight loss programs, and smoking cessation programs. Many of these programs are relatively low cost and when targeted at high-risk employee groups can be very successful. As health care costs escalate approximately 15% per year in the next few years, these programs will become more and more attractive to employers. Many can be offered at low cost, and they have been successful in providing a significant return on investment.

Prescription drug costs is one of the fastest rising health care costs. As a result, it has become the focus of increased management efforts. Employers may reduce health care costs and provide better pharmacy services by providing a low copayment for generic drugs, providing mail-order pharmacy services, and monitoring use. Effective pharmacy benefit management can save 7% to 10% in pharmacy costs. Here again, educating employees about drug costs and quality issues is an important part of a successful program.

During the early part of the first decade in 2000, health care premiums are expected to have an annual growth of approximately 15%. No other area of business represents such an increased threat to the corporate bottom line. These predictions will encourage employers to develop creative and effective methods of controlling these costs. The implications for the health care industry are twofold. First, the impending economic crises may provide an opportunity for health care organizations to partner with employers to create more effective solutions. Second, health care organizations will be caught in the same situation as other employers, watching their health care costs escalate and threaten the organization's bottom line. Therefore, health care organizations should be in the forefront of solution generation. Issues of cost, access, quality, and responsibility must be considered simultaneously if progress is to be made. Solutions that reduce cost at the expense of quality or access may achieve short-term success but will fail in the

long run. Likewise, programs that do not balance individual and corporate responsibility for health will not be successful. The challenge is to create a dynamic balance in which cost, access, quality, and responsibility are given equal weight.

—Alan P. Chesney

FURTHER READING

Caudron, S. (2002, February). Health-care costs: HR's crisis has real solutions. *Workforce,* pp. 12–14.

Dressler, G. (1999). *Human resource management* (8th ed.). Upper Saddle River, NJ: Prentice Hall.

Employee Benefits Research Institute. (1997). *Data book on employee benefits* (4th ed.). Washington, DC: Author.

Employee Benefits Research Institute. (2002). *2002 Health Confidence Survey.* Washington, DC: Author.

Gentry, W. D. (1984). *Handbook of behavioral medicine.* New York: Guilford.

Henninger, D. (2003, January 10). Marcus Welby doesn't live here anymore. *Wall Street Journal.*

Miller, J. (2001, November). *A perfect storm: The confluence of forces affecting health care coverage.* Washington, DC: National Health Care Coalition.

EMPLOYEE ORIENTATION PROGRAMS

An employee orientation program is a method of socializing new employees into the organization by introducing individuals to information about the hiring organization and the employees' jobs. Facts about the company's mission and culture, as well as expectations for employee behavior, are conveyed in a standardized approach at the onset of the employment relationship. In addition, required personnel forms and procedures can be completed in a condensed manner instead of piecemeal. Organizations that conduct employee orientation programs may realize several benefits, including a decrease in the amount of time it takes for new employees to be productive, an increase in employee satisfaction, a reduction in employee turnover, and the strengthening of the company's culture.

Both organization-level information and department-level information may be provided during an employee orientation program. At the organizational level, employees receive information concerning the history of the organization, the products and services offered, a review of the organizational chart, and organizationwide human resource policies. At the department level, information is more job specific and includes information about departmental functions, a departmental tour, introduction to new coworkers, and an explanation of job duties and performance expectations.

Topics typically covered by new employee orientation in a medical setting may include the following:

- Organization's history and context
- Organizational chart
- Organization's mission, vision, and values
- Business of health care
- Corporate compliance
- Risk management
- Confidentiality issues
- Standards for patient assessment and care
- Employee benefits (such as insurance, retirement, credit union, employee discounts, tuition reimbursement)
- Compensation (such as overtime, holiday pay, time clock, pay day schedule)
- Human resource policies (such as attendance, work schedules, vacations, holidays, grievances, ID badges, dress code, leaves of absence, use of illicit substances, weapons)
- Physical facilities (such as layout, parking, cafeteria)
- Employee assistance services
- Sexual harassment prevention
- Computer orientation (such as medical records procedures, voice dictation)
- Union information (such as officials, joining procedure, affiliation, contract)
- Fire safety
- Hazard communications
- Infection control
- Radiation safety
- Oxygen safety
- Laser safety
- Incident reporting

New employee orientation programs are typically the responsibility of the human resource department. At a minimum, the HR department provides the hiring supervisor with an orientation checklist to review with a new employee. In health care settings with more involved orientation programs, HR conducts the program during scheduled days on a monthly or even weekly basis. In general, orientation programs are mandatory for all new employees and typically last one or one and one-half days. With the advent of computer-based learning, some organizations are shifting their orientation programs to an online, self-paced process that new employees must complete during the first few weeks of their employment. However, because of the complexity of some jobs and organizations, certain orientation programs may be conducted over a period of five days or longer. For example, a new nursing staff member may be required to attend a multiday session that reviews specific

position-related requirements and current established patient care procedures and protocols.

—E. Kate Atchley

See also Organizational Behavior Management (OBM)

FURTHER READING

Schettler, J., & Johnson, H. (2002). Welcome to ACME Inc. *Training, 39*(8), 36–43.

Wanous, J. P. (1992). *Organizational entry: Recruitment, selection and socialization of newcomers* (2nd ed.). Reading, MA: Addison-Wesley.

Wanous, J. P., & Reichers, A. E. (2000). New employee orientation programs. *Human Resource Management Review, 10*(4), 435–451.

EMPLOYEE RECRUITMENT

Recruitment is the process used by organizations to locate and attract candidates for employment. Depending on the job and purpose of the recruitment effort, companies attempt to attract large numbers of candidates, fill vacancies quickly, seek people who will perform well, or hire people who will stay with the organization for an extended period of time. As such, employee recruitment serves three primary purposes for the organization: (a) increasing selection rate by decreasing the number of poorly qualified applicants, (b) increasing number of job applicants at minimal cost, and (c) meeting legal obligations regarding demographic makeup of workforce.

SELECTION RATE

Once a company decides it needs additional employees, the recruitment process is just beginning. This decision gives no indication as to the necessary effort and extent of the search. For instance, a hospital seeking to hire three oncologists will need to ascertain the total number of applicants necessary to find three qualified individuals willing to accept a job offer. Based on past experience in similar situations, a recruiter can calculate the percentage of candidates that will pass through each stage. For instance, if 3% of individuals who have initial contact with the organization are eligible for and willing to accept a job offer, a hospital seeking three radiologists will need to make 100 contacts to meet the specified numeric goal. Previous experience data can also indicate the number of professional organizations to be contacted, or other recruitment strategies will be necessary to locate 100 applicants for such a position.

INCREASE APPLICANTS

Companies have many options when trying to fill vacancies. They can seek individuals internally and externally to replace employees who have retired, been promoted, or terminated. Internal recruitment involves an examination of workers already present in the organization and may be a fast and economical approach for the organization. The most common form of internal recruitment for lower-level positions is posting the position, pay rates, and qualifications in a common area in the workplace where employees are encouraged to apply for a position. Although this method may be effective for recruiting at lower levels, for upper-management positions another technique may be essential. Companies trying to fill these higher-level positions typically employ a managerial succession plan where managers' education, skills, experience, education, and location preferences are computerized, so that a list of qualified candidates can be easily produced and considered for new opportunities. Although the advantages to internal recruiting include working with individuals with known skills and abilities who have a pre-existing relationship with the organization, reasons for using external recruiting include bringing in individuals who have new ideas and viewpoints. As such, external recruiting may help organizations deal with rapid turnover without overusing inexperienced personnel who may not have the skills required for advanced positions.

In most medium- to large-size organizations with more than 50 employees, a separate human resources function is typically essential to carry out an external recruiting processes. The major sources for external recruitment include advertising, employment agencies, college recruitment, and walk-ins. Whichever method is used, recruitment efforts must match organizational goals (for example, decreasing turnover or hiring many employees over a short period of time). As such, when considering recruitment source, companies must examine the demographic mix of individuals sought. For example, a hospital recruiting an experienced oncologist might choose a trade journal, whereas a clinic recruiting for a more general position, such as registered nurse, might choose to advertise in the newspaper.

LEGAL OBLIGATIONS

Whichever format is used, most organizations create a system for tracking candidates as they go through the recruitment process, because they may need to calculate information regarding adverse impact. The essential statistics to be calculated include the ratio of blacks, other minorites, females, and applicants over the age of 40 in each job category. Such information may affect future recruiting efforts. More specifically, because whites use the Internet as a source for job searches more than other groups, a pharmaceutical company seeking to increase the number of minority employees can include advertisements on a billboard to supplement advertisements on the Internet and thus potentially increase minority applicants. Other sources for finding minority and female applicants include foreign- language newspapers, predominantly minority or female college campuses, and professional organizations (such as the Black Graduate and Professional Student Association and the Society of Women Engineers). Furthermore, advertisements must be structured so as not to convey stereotypes or preference for a particular gender or race. Such considerations influence the cost and range of recruitment sources used.

—Jillian A. Peat

See also Affirmative Action in Employment, Employee Selection and Hiring, Human Resource Management

FURTHER READING

Fisher, C. D., Schoenfeldt, L. F., & Shaw, J. B. (1999). *Human resource management.* Boston: Houghton Mifflin.
www.eeoc.gov
www.shrm.org

EMPLOYEE RETENTION

See Employee Turnover

EMPLOYEE RETIREMENT INCOME SECURITY ACT (ERISA)

The Employee Retirement Income Security Act (ERISA) of 1974 is a federal law that sets minimum standards for health plans provided by private sector employers in the United States. It does not, however, cover group health plans provided by government or churches for their employees. Moreover, there is no requirement in ERISA that employers provide health plans to their employees. ERISA requires health plan administrators for covered plans to provide covered employees with information about their health plan, including a summary plan description (SPD) that is provided to all employees at the time of their enrollment in the plan. ERISA also imposes fiduciary responsibilities on those responsible for administering a health plan.

There have been a number of important amendments to ERISA since its enactment in 1974. The Comprehensive

Omnibus Budget Reconciliation Act (COBRA) of 1986 amends ERISA to allow employees or their families who lose health coverage because of loss of a job, death of a spouse, or divorce to continue their group health coverage for a limited period of time. People exercising their right to continuation coverage under COBRA are ordinarily required to pay the full premium for this coverage. The Health Insurance Portability and Accountability Act (HIPAA) of 1996 amends ERISA to limit exclusion from coverage for pre-existing conditions, and prohibits discrimination against employees and their dependents based on health status. The Newborns' and Mothers' Protection Act of 1996 amends ERISA to require plans that provide childbirth coverage to allow at least a 48-hour hospital stay following a vaginal delivery and a 96-hour stay following a cesarean section. Finally, the Women's Health and Cancer Rights Act (WHCRA) of 1998 requires that health plans providing coverage for mastectomies also cover reconstructive surgery and treatment of certain physical complications from the mastectomy, including lymphedemas.

ERISA preempts state laws relating to employee benefit plans. ERISA also contains an insurance savings clause that reasserts state regulatory authority over health insurance. It further contains a clause that deems self-funded health plans provided by employers not to be insurance within the meaning of the insurance savings clause. These three clauses have resulted in a great deal of litigation. Self-funded employer health plans have been able to avoid the impact of state-mandated benefit laws by the combined effect of the preemption clause and the deemed clause. In contrast, employers that purchase coverage for their employees from a health insurer are subject to state-mandated benefit laws under the insurance savings clause. ERISA's preemption clause has also been construed to bar tort lawsuits in state court by beneficiaries against health plans for the denial of benefits. However, some courts have held that ERISA does not preempt state court tort actions against health plans for malpractice committed by plan physicians. And the U.S. Supreme Court recently upheld an Illinois statute requiring HMOs to provide independent review of disputes between primary care physicians. The act requires HMOs to cover services deemed medically necessary by the independent reviewer.

—Leonard J. Nelson, III

FURTHER READING

Mariner, W. K. (1992). Problems with employer-provided health insurance—The Employee Retirement Income Security Act and health care reform. *New England Journal of Medicine, 327,* 1682.

Mariner, W. K. (2000). What Recourse? —Liability for managed care decisions and the Employee Retirement Income Security Act. *New England Journal of Medicine, 343,* 592.

Rush Prudential HMO v. Moran. (2002). 122 S. Ct. 2151.

U.S. Department of Labor Pension and Welfare Benefits Administration. (1999, June). *Questions and Answers: Recent Changes in Health Care Law.* Washington, DC: U.S. Department of Labor Pension and Welfare Benefits Administration.

EMPLOYEE RIGHTS

The broad term *employee rights* is used to describe the rights accorded to employees by federal, state, or local laws and constitutions. Such rights are also created and defined through administrative agency regulations, interpretation, and court decisions. Federal statutes provide the source for most employment law activity; however, all states also have state civil rights statutes or fair employment practices, which should be consulted before making final determinations about employee rights.

Generally, these laws seek to prohibit discriminatory employment practices by state and private employers. The growing body of employment discrimination laws that have developed over the years prohibit bias in employment practices and harassment by employers and coworkers based on race, color, sex, religion, national origin, disability, and age. The application and interpretation of these laws by regulatory agencies and the courts provide the foundation for most employee rights. Each law is assigned to a federal (or state, in the case of state employment laws) agency for the creation of regulations and interpretation of the law. Traditionally, agency regulations and interpretation have been given significant weight by the courts; however, they are still subject to court review and acceptance. As an example, Equal Employment Opportunity Commission (EEOC) guidance for the Americans with Disabilities Act (ADA) suggested that an individual's disability should be examined without regard to the individual's use of mitigating measures such as hearing aids in determining whether that individual was substantially limited in a major life activity (as required by the definition for disability). The U.S. Supreme Court responded to this interpretation through a series of cases and ultimately decided that mitigating measures should be taken into account when determining the existence and effect of a disability. The EEOC guidance had an expansive view of employee rights, whereas the Supreme Court narrowed the interpretation of the law.

Employee rights may also be specified or outlined by employee contracts, employment agreements, or employee handbooks. Such documents provide the employee and the employer with the first source of information for determining an employee's rights in a given situation. For instance, an employee handbook may specify work rules and what process to follow if a rule is violated. An employer's failure to follow its own rules may be critical in an assessment of whether an employee's rights have been violated.

Some of the most comprehensive and important legislation creating employee rights include the Americans with Disabilities Act (ADA) of 1990, the Age Discrimination in Employment Act (ADEA) of 1967, Title VII of the Civil Rights Act of 1964, the Civil Rights Act of 1991, the Equal Pay Act (EPA) of 1963, and the Family Medical and Leave Act (FMLA) of 1993.

The Americans with Disabilities Act (ADA) prohibits discrimination on the basis of a physical or mental disability in employment, housing, transportation, access to public accommodations and services, education, and telecommunications. Further, an employer may have a duty to make reasonable accommodations for a qualified employee with a disability. The ADA is a complex statute that continues to undergo recent and current U.S. Supreme Court review for the interpretation of its provisions. The ADA has many implications for medical service providers, particularly in the treatment of patients and employees with diseases such as AIDS. This disease, and the complications thereof, is an example of the type of disability Congress intended to cover under the ADA. Services must be provided in accordance with best medical practice, without regard to an individual's disability. There are a few limited exceptions to the provisions of the ADA.

Health care providers may serve several functions anticipated by the ADA. As employers, such providers are required to follow the intent and purpose of the law. As medical professionals, health care providers often have a very active role in helping patients and employers determine and understand the nature of a disability, while engaging in an interactive process to develop appropriate and reasonable workplace accommodations.

The Age Discrimination in Employment Act (ADEA) prohibits employers from using age, when the individual is over 40, as a factor in the hiring process, and in the terms and conditions of employment. It also contains provisions regarding employee benefit, pension, and retirement plans. The ADEA applies to employers with 20 or more employees.

The Civil Rights Act of 1964, along with the Civil Rights Act of 1991, is the cornerstone legislation for determining many employee rights and for much employment law litigation. Title VII of the 1964 act makes it unlawful for employers to treat employees (or applicants for employment) differently in any respect because of race, color, sex, or national origin. The provisions that prohibit gender discrimination include those on pregnancy, childbirth, or related medical conditions. Importantly, gender discrimination also encompasses sexual harassment, making it illegal for employers to engage in or to allow sexual harassment at the workplace. Title VII applies to all employers who have 15 or more employees for each working day in each of 20 or more calendar weeks in the current or preceding calendar year.

The Equal Pay Act (EPA) is part of the Fair Labor Standards Act of 1938, as amended. This act prohibits covered employers from compensating employees differently because of their gender. Compensation includes wages, fringe benefits, and wage rates. (Pay that differs because of gender is also prohibited by Title VII of the Civil Rights Act of 1964.) The EPA was enacted to ensure that employees performing substantially similar jobs under similar circumstances and having similar qualifications are compensated equally regardless of gender. For the work to be considered equal, it must require equal skill, effort, and responsibility, and the working conditions must be similar. The jobs being compared need not be identical but must be substantially equal. As part of the Fair Labor Standards Act, the EPA applies to virtually all employers regardless of size.

The Family Medical Leave Act (FMLA) creates an employee right to take 12 weeks of leave during any twelve-month period for the birth or adoption of a child; for the care of a spouse, child, or parent with a serious health condition; or for the employee's own serious health condition. The leave may be paid or unpaid leave, depending on the employer's leave provisions. If the employer offers paid vacation leave or medical or sick leave, the employer may require the employee to apply the accrued leave to the 12-week period. Any portion of the 12-week period for which the employee has no accrued paid leave is unpaid leave (unless the employer agrees to other arrangements).

Not all employees are entitled to the rights provided by the FMLA, nor are all employers required to provide family leave under the act. An individual is not eligible for such leave unless he or she has been employed for at least 12 months by the employer from whom leave is requested. During that 12-month period, the employee must have at least 1,250 hours of service with the employer. In addition, the act does not cover employers with fewer than 50 employees at one worksite unless the employer has more than 50 employees within a 75-mile radius. Thus, small medical providers may not be covered by the act. Larger health care providers, medical corporations, and hospitals are required to follow the provisions of the FMLA.

The FMLA has specific guidelines for both employer and employee to follow. It contains, for instance, notice requirements on the part of the employer to inform the employee that leave is being assessed as FMLA leave. The act also allows the employer to require a certification by the employee's health care provider as to the commencement and probable duration of the serious health condition, and any appropriate medical facts regarding the condition. Further conditions to the certification are covered in the act itself.

As with the ADA, health care providers have a dual role with the FMLA. As employers, they may be required to provide their employees with the rights guaranteed by the act. As health care providers, they may be engaged in the certification and documentation process on behalf of their patients.

The statutes and laws mentioned in this article represent a small, but major, portion of the legislation that creates and affects employee rights.

—Jennifer L. Richter

See also Age Discrimination in Employment, Americans with Disabilities Act (ADA) of 1990, Civil Rights Acts of 1964 and 1991, Equal Pay Act, Family and Medical Leave Act (FMLA), Title VII of the Civil Rights Act of 1964

FURTHER READING

www.dol.gov
www.eeoc.gov
www.law.cornell.edu

EMPLOYEE SELECTION AND HIRING

Employee selection and hiring involves two processes. Recruitment is the process of attracting prospective employees and building a qualified applicant pool. The key element in recruitment is that all employer activities are directed to influence decisions made by the prospective employee, first to apply for the job, and eventually to accept an offer of employment. Employee selection is focused on decision making by the employer. Selection activities are all directed toward making "hire/no hire" decisions. Although in practice both of these processes occur simultaneously, it is important to recognize the important distinctions between the two.

RECRUITMENT

Generally recruitment has two purposes. First, recruitment is performed to attract or increase a qualified applicant pool while maintaining a reasonable cost to the employer. Usually a large applicant pool is desirable, because it allows for more selectivity in the selection process. Nevertheless, recruiting unqualified applicants only increases selection and recruitment costs without resulting in any real gain or potential gain for an employer. Focusing recruitment on sources appropriate for the job is much more effective than indiscriminate recruiting.

A second purpose of recruitment is to meet the social and legal obligations of the organization. Focused recruitment that tends to limit the number of applicants from protected demographic groups such as African Americans or women may cause problems when responding to affirmative action goals and timetables. Equal employment law prohibits using recruitment techniques that may limit equal access to employment on the basis of race, color, religion, national origin, or sex.

Numerous decisions are required of employers during the recruitment process. Principal among these decisions is the issue of source. Recruitment for jobs other than entry level can be strictly internal to the organization or may also involve seeking applicants from outside the organization. Promotion from within is a general policy for many organizations, whereas other organizations prefer seeking "new blood" for many positions. Whenever external recruitment is involved, decisions must be made regarding what external sources to use. Some of the common sources for external applicants include colleges and schools; professional or trade organizations; employee referral programs; walk-in applicants; direct advertising through newspapers, journals, the Internet, and other media; employment agencies; and Internet-based recruiting services. Often the choice of source is associated with the nature or level of the job. Care must be exercised when choosing sources, because different demographic groups use different sources at different rates. Using a very limited source or sources may result in unintended adverse impact on a group of prospective applicants.

Gender, age, and ethnicity can all affect applicants' perceptions of an organization, so care should be exercised regarding who performs recruitment tasks. Similarly, the apparent care and timeliness exercised by a company during the recruitment and selection process can influence applicant reactions and consequently can affect the overall success of the program.

Perhaps the most important recruitment question facing an employer is "What do we tell and show them?" Here the choice is clear. On the one hand, an employer can paint an ideal image of the job and the organization, in an attempt to attract more and better applicants. On the other hand, an employer can provide what is known as a "realistic job preview," where prospective applicants and applicants are presented with a two-sided view of the job—a preview of both the good and the bad elements associated with the job and the organization. The rationale for providing a realistic preview is that prospective applicants who would be unhappy on the job, and would therefore be more likely to quit in a short time, will self-select themselves out of the applicant pool.

SELECTION

Assuming that a reasonable recruitment process has taken place, the question facing an employer becomes, Whom do we hire? As long as the methods and results of the selection process are free from bias, an employer may generally select employees using any technique or process they see fit. There are, however, some legal limitations regarding what and when information can be gathered. For example, employers are precluded from using a polygraph during the selection process and can only obtain medical information after a tentative offer of employment has been made. The assumption of freedom from bias is, however, a major one. Whenever a selection program results in adverse impact against any group from a protected class of applicants (age, color, disability status, gender, national origin, race, religion), the selection program must be manifestly job related. That is, the means of determining whom to hire must be directly associated with the requirements of the job. Because it is typically impossible to predict with certainty that a selection program will not have adverse impact, it is always appropriate to develop a job-relevant selection program.

The purpose of any selection program is to hire the most qualified individuals possible in as cost-effective a manner as possible. Given this objective, job relevance plays a very important role in the selection process. Job-relevant selection programs improve the chances of selecting or promoting highly qualified individuals.

Assuring job relevance in selection generally begins with a job analysis. The organization must ask, What will the new employees be doing, and what knowledge, skills, and abilities (KSAs) are required to perform the job effectively? The systematic gathering of this information, referred to as a *job analysis*, generally results in a concise description of the job and a listing of the minimal and desired KSAs associated with the job. There are many types and forms of job analyses. Ranging from a rather molecular task analysis that breaks down a job into a set of tasks, to a very broad analysis of worker characteristics, numerous job analytic methods are available. The *Dictionary of Occupational Titles (DOT)*, from the U.S. Department of Labor, provides a very specific classification system that describes jobs as regards the degree of complexity associated with dealing with data, people, and things. Recently, *O*Net* has been developed as an Internet-based replacement for the DOT (online.onetcenter.org).

The actual process for screening applicants and determining who should receive a job offer typically proceeds in phases. If the applicant pool is very small, all phases may occur simultaneously, but generally screening consists of two or more decision-making hurdles. Accordingly, the original applicant pool is reduced to a short list of the most qualified candidates, from which the final selection decision is made.

The first phase of the selection process involves eliminating any applicants who are patently unqualified. This elimination occurs on the basis of candidates failing to possess one or more of the bona fide occupational qualifications (BFOQs) associated with the job. A physician must be licensed or immediately licensable; a therapist must

possess the appropriate certifications and license. The important distinction associated with a BFOQ is that it cannot be compensated for or replaced by some other characteristic. That is, possession of some other KSA or some other set of characteristic cannot overcome the BFOQ deficiency. Employers often incorrectly list highly desirable minimal qualifications that do not meet the criterion for being a BFOQ. At the end of this phase of selection, all remaining applicants are at least minimally qualified for the job. The task then becomes choosing the most qualified applicants.

Eliminating less qualified applicants is the second phase of the selection process. Randomly selecting a limited number of individuals from the qualified applicant pool generally yields employees who can do the job, but this method of selection provides little competitive advantage to an employer. More appropriately, some predictive instrument is used to suggest who will be the most successful on the job. For example, a test, behavioral sample, training or experience assessment, or interview may be administered and scored to yield a predictor of success. To increase the accuracy of the prediction, one or more of these instruments may be used at any given time.

Many instruments or tools are available for use in selection, but for any tool to be utilitarian it must be both reliable and valid. The term *reliability* refers to the consistency with which an instrument measures whatever it measures, and *validity* refers to the degree to which it accurately predicts performance. Unreliable measures cannot be valid predictors. When using published tests as predictors, employers should be able to obtain information regarding the reliability and validity of an instrument for a variety of jobs or circumstances. When relying on unpublished instruments, including in-house instruments developed by the employer, it is critical that the reliability and validity of the instruments be assessed whenever such assessment is feasible. A professional who is qualified to conduct such assessments (for example, an industrial and organizational psychologist) should conduct this assessment. The task of designing and using valid selection procedures is a complex one.

A very strong literature suggests that cognitive ability is an almost uniform predictor of job performance. That is, people who can think and reason clearly typically perform better than those who cannot. Although this might suggest that cognitive ability should always be used somewhere during a selection program, an equally strong literature suggests that measures of cognitive ability tend to have adverse impact on some groups of individuals (for example, on African Americans). Accordingly, relying heavily on cognitive ability tests may reduce the representation of those groups in an organization. Although this reduction may be legally defensible when validity can be demonstrated, it may also be counter to the social obligations of the employer. Numerous specific ability tests are available as alternatives to general cognitive ability tests, but most of these share some of the strengths and weaknesses of cognitive ability tests. Fortunately, numerous other predictors of performance also yield consistently positive validities.

Biographical or life history information (biodata) is one predictor that offers consistently strong prediction of performance over a wide variety of jobs. This information can typically be obtained using tests or scored application forms. The Internet is a particularly fertile means of assessing biodata.

Personality information obtained from tests is another form of data that can be very predictive of job success. Nevertheless, personality tests are often more complex than cognitive ability tests, and the validity of personality tests does not always generalize across jobs.

Behavioral assessment is a consistently valid predictor of success. Behavioral assessment attempts to sample behaviors through one or more simulations or work samples. Whenever the tasks closely resemble the job, validity is typically strong. An assessment center is perhaps the most thorough form of behavioral assessment. Multiple applicants participate in multiple behavioral exercises or simulations and are evaluated on multiple behavioral dimensions by multiple trained raters. All this information is combined with other data to provide a very comprehensive description of each applicant's job-relevant strengths and weaknesses. Assessment centers are very labor intensive and accordingly very costly but are particularly appropriate when small numbers of applicants are being assessed for critical jobs.

Some form of an interview is part of almost every selection program. Because almost all applicants expect to be interviewed sometime before being hired, interviews are important for both recruitment and selection purposes. Although some standard structured interview models are available, most employers use an interview constructed specifically for their use. Consequently, there is considerable variance in the reliability and validity of interviews. The effectiveness of interviews depends on the degree to which the interview is structured, the interviewers trained, and the questions tailored to be appropriate to the job. Panel interviews often reduce the effect of individual interviewers' biases. Some selection programs rely exclusively on interviews, whereas others use them for only the final set of the most highly qualified applicants.

—Robert T. Ladd

FURTHER READING

Gatewood, R. D., & Feild, H. S. (2001). *Human resource selection* (5th ed.). Mason, OH: South-Western.

Peterson, N. G., Mumford, M. D., Borman, W. C., Jeanneret, P. R., & Fleishman, E. A. (1999). *An occupational information system for the 21st century: The development of O*Net.* Washington, DC: American Psychological Association.

U.S. Department of Labor, Employment and Training Administration. (1991). *Dictionary of occupational titles* (4th ed.). Washington, DC: U.S. Government Printing Office.

EMPLOYEE STOCK OWNERSHIP PLAN (ESOP)

An employee stock ownership plan (ESOP) is an employee benefit plan that invests primarily in the stock of the sponsoring company. The notion of ESOPs was first introduced in the 1950s, and the U.S. Congress promoted the use of ESOPs in 1974 with the passage of the Employee Retirement Income Security Act (ERISA). The U.S. Department of Labor and the Internal Revenue Service regulate ESOPs. It is estimated that approximately 9 million U.S. workers are covered by more than 11,000 ESOPs, representing about $500 billion in assets. According to the National Center for Employee Ownership, several of America's largest businesses that are over 50% employee-owned represent health care industries, including two nursing home companies, a pharmaceutical manufacturer, and an ambulance service.

In addition to providing benefits to employees, there are other reasons a company may choose to establish an ESOP, including buying out an owner and financing expansion by borrowing money at a lower after-tax cost. If the owner of a closely held company sells 30% or more of his or her shares to the ESOP, he or she may defer capital gains taxes. In turn, the ESOP purchases the owner's shares with pretax money. In addition, a company may realize a tax advantage if it uses the ESOP to obtain a loan for capital investment purposes. In this case, a company may deduct the interest payments as well as principal on the loan.

The establishment of an ESOP is subject to complex regulations. In brief, a company sets up a trust, which then accepts tax-deductible contributions from the company to purchase company stock. The stock is then distributed to employees who hold individual accounts within the trust. The amount each employee receives is determined by a formula, usually involving annual salary, tenure, or a combination of these variables. There is typically a vesting period before employees are entitled to receive the stock; employees receive the vested stock when they leave the company, become disabled, or retire, and their beneficiaries receive their vested stock in cases of employee death. When employees reach the age of 55 and have 10 years of service with the company, the company must give them the option of diversifying 25% of their account; this diversification amount increases to 50% when the employee reaches age 60.

ESOPs were originally conceptualized as a method for increasing employee ownership. It was thought that encouraging employees to take an interest in the profitability of their company would increase their motivation and improve productivity; this improvement in productivity would increase profits, which in turn would benefit equity holders. In reality, studies have shown that ESOPs in themselves do not guarantee increased employee motivation. That is, for companies to realize improved performance, employee ownership must be coupled with a culture of participatory management. ESOPs can play a vital role in creating a corporate culture of participation and ownership mentality, which in turn can lead to higher organizational commitment by employees and improved firm performance.

—E. Kate Atchley

See also Employee Compensation, Employee Retirement Income Security Act (ERISA), Executive Compensation, Incentive Pay, Profit Sharing

FURTHER READING

Berger, L. A., & Berger, D. R. (1999). *The compensation handbook* (4th ed.). New York: McGraw-Hill.
www.esopassociation.org
www.nceo.org

EMPLOYEE TURNOVER

The term *employee turnover* is used to describe the exit of employees from an organization through resignations, retirements, layoffs, or firings. This phenomenon is part of a larger category of behaviors known as *employee withdrawal behaviors,* which includes events such as chronic absenteeism and employee disengagement (in which employees remain on the job but diminish their effort and contributions). Employee turnover is one of the most heavily researched topics in the organizational literature, and it has long been a major concern for managers and executives. Most research on employee turnover has focused on specific employee attributes (such as sex, age, and psychological traits of the employee). Turnover, however, is also affected by the changing nature of the employment relationship. During the past decade, commitment in the employment relationship has eroded. The focus for employers in the "new" workplace is "What can you do to earn your keep today?" Conversely, employees now tend to focus more on advancing their self-interests and careers, even if it means switching jobs frequently. According to the U.S. Department of Labor's *Futurework* report, the average 32-year-old has already held nine jobs. Similarly, a Federal Reserve Board study found that 2.7% of the U.S. workforce switched jobs in an average month during 1999.

TWO CATEGORIES OF TURNOVER

There are two categories of employee turnover: involuntary turnover and voluntary turnover. Involuntary turnover occurs when the organization takes the initiative to terminate or discharge an employee through firing, layoff, downsizing, or rightsizing (reorganizing employees to improve efficiency). Firings normally occur as the result of poor job performance or misconduct, whereas other forms of involuntary turnover are initiated for strategic or economic reasons. Managing involuntary turnover can be a complex process because of the legal, ethical, and public relations problems that often arise when organizations engage in massive layoffs, facility closures, or relocations.

Voluntary turnover occurs when an employee takes the initiative to leave the organization. Examples of voluntary turnover include resignations and retirement. Most resignations occur when an employee leaves an organization because of better employment prospects elsewhere. Because voluntary turnover usually has a more detrimental impact on the organization, it is not surprising that most research has focused on voluntary rather than on involuntary turnover. There are instances, however, when voluntary turnover serves a useful purpose, such as when a marginally performing employee resigns.

THE DYNAMICS OF VOLUNTARY TURNOVER

The literature on voluntary turnover describes the turnover process in terms of the employee rationally examining employment alternatives and selecting the one that provides the greatest economic and social utility. In reality, employees often compare job alternatives, and make the decision to leave an organization, based on incomplete or erroneous information. To the extent that this occurs, voluntary turnover harms both employee and employer.

Voluntary turnover is most likely to occur when two conditions are met: The employee (a) must want to leave the organization and (b) must have the ability to leave the organization.

The desire to leave an organization is a function of an employee's level of job satisfaction, life satisfaction, and commitment to the organization. A study of nurses, medical assistants, and laboratory technicians, for example, found that those who were dissatisfied with their jobs but had high overall life satisfaction were the most likely to resign (Judge, 1993). Job and life satisfaction, in turn, are a function of a multitude of factors such as pay, work environment, coworkers, family circumstances, and individual personality traits. Some employees quit their jobs even when their level of job satisfaction is high. This situation might occur, for example, when the employee desires to change careers, spend more time with family, increase leisure time, or accommodate a spouse's job change.

The employee's ability to leave an organization depends on labor market conditions; the knowledge, skills, and abilities possessed by the employee; contractual obligations to the organization, if any; and the employee's work history. "Tight" labor markets favor the employee, and low rates of unemployment in the economy are generally associated with higher levels of turnover. Nurses and other health care professionals with skills that are valued in the labor market typically have numerous employment opportunities. "Loose" labor markets, in contrast, favor the employer. During periods of high unemployment, employees may be forced to remain in an organization even when they would prefer to leave. A combination of a loose labor market and a dissatisfied employee may lead to high rates of absenteeism, disengagement, interpersonal conflicts, theft, sabotage, violence, or other counterproductive workplace behaviors.

COSTS ASSOCIATED WITH TURNOVER

Employee turnover can be costly to a health care organization. Both involuntary and voluntary turnover result in wasted recruitment, selection, and training expenditures. In the case of voluntary turnover, the organization must often spend additional money to hire and train a replacement. In addition, employees who resign may reveal competitive information that is useful to their next employer, or they may encourage clients or patients to follow them to their new health care facility. The aftermath of involuntary turnover includes costs such as severance allowances, increased unemployment compensation insurance premiums, and legal expenses associated with discrimination or wrongful termination suits. Involuntary terminations involving facility closings and mass layoffs can also create major public relations crises.

REDUCING VOLUNTARY TURNOVER

Health care organizations should make a concerted effort to manage and minimize employee turnover. Voluntary turnover can be reduced through

1. Careful employee selection (including background checks on an applicant's employment history to detect employees who chronically switch jobs).

2. Training and development programs that ensure employee socialization (understanding the organizational culture and the employee's role in that culture) and the development of necessary knowledge, skills, and abilities. (*Note:* One unintended consequence of training is that it can increase turnover by raising the employee's skill level, which makes the person more attractive to other employers).

3. Compensation programs that ensure both external (fair relative to the labor market) and internal equity (fair relative to other jobs and employees within the organization).

4. Benefit packages such as health care plans and retirement programs that "tie" employees to the organization.

5. A working environment that cultivates good communications, cooperative working and social relationships, high levels of job enrichment, and accommodations for the employee's family (such as flexible work schedules, child care and elder care, and personal holidays).

DEALING WITH INVOLUNTARY TURNOVER

Layoffs and facility closures must also be handled carefully to minimize the probability of legal and public relations problems. Gomez-Mejia, Balkin, and Cardy (2001) delineate a number of alternatives that can be used to avoid or soften the impact of involuntary turnover. Employment policies such as reduction through attrition, hiring freezes, eliminating part-time employees, moving subcontracted work in-house, reduced workhours, retraining employees, transfers, job sharing, and outplacement services are among the alternatives for dealing with the delicate issue of eliminating jobs and terminating employees. Health care organizations engaging in mass layoffs must also comply with the Worker Adjustment and Retraining Notification Act (WARN), which requires 60 days' notice for a facility closing or a layoff of 50 or more employees. (*Note:* WARN only applies to U.S. employers with 100 or more employees.)

—Terry Leap

FURTHER READING

Gomez-Mejia, L., Balkin, D., & Cardy, R. (2001). *Managing human resources* (3rd ed.). Upper Saddle River, NJ: Prentice Hall.

Judge, T. (1993). Does affective disposition moderate the relationship between job satisfaction and voluntary turnover? *Journal of Applied Psychology, 78,* 395–401.

EMPLOYMENT DISCRIMINATION

Employment discrimination is defined by federal equal employment opportunity (or EEO) laws prohibiting discrimination based on race, color, religion, sex, national origin, age, and disability. Among these laws, Title VII of the Civil Rights Act of 1964 offers the broadest protections.

Title VII prohibits discrimination based on race, color, religion, sex, and national origin in federal, state, local, and private entities with 15 or more employees. The prohibitions in Title VII cover terms, conditions, and privileges of employment (hiring, pay, training, promotion, benefits, and termination), segregation and classification, and retaliation. Claimants must first file with the Equal Opportunity Employment Commission (EEOC) to gain access to federal court. Title VII remedies include equitable relief (for example, reinstatement, back pay, lost benefits) and legal relief (compensatory and punitive damages) capped at $50,000 to $300,000 depending on the size of the company. Jury trials and legal relief were added to Title VII (and to other statutes) in the Civil Rights Act of 1991.

The most obvious violation in EEO law is facial (that is, up-front) discrimination, where protected groups are simply excluded (for example, "no women allowed"). Facial discrimination based on sex is defensible if the excluder can prove it is reasonably necessary to exclude all or most males or all or most females. This defense is termed *bona fide occupational qualification* (or *BFOQ*). For example, in *Dothard v. Rawlinson* (1977), being a male was deemed a BFOQ for prison guards in all-male maximum-security prisons. It is critically important to note that facial discrimination based on race or color is indefensible for any reason.

In most instances, facial exclusion is illegal and amounts to a "pattern or practice" of discrimination. For example, in *International Teamsters v. United States* (1977), minority bus drivers were segregated into shorter (and lower-paying) bus routes, and all longer (and higher-paying) bus routes were assigned to white employees. In another case, *Thompson v. Sawyer* (1982), men and women had substantially equal jobs, but men were classified as "bookbinders" (with higher pay) and women were classified as "bindery workers" (with lower pay).

The most common violation of Title VII (and other EEO laws) is "disparate treatment," or differential treatment based on group membership. For example, in *McDonnell-Douglas v. Green* (1975), a previously laid off employee was not rehired in a callback. Green claimed racial discrimination, but the company countered that his exclusion was based on illegal acts against the company he committed during the layoff. In this scenario, the burden of persuasion is on Green to discredit the employer's explanation or pretext. Note that harassment against any protected group member is a form of disparate treatment.

A final scenario to note is "disparate (or adverse) impact." For all intents and purposes, this scenario is unique to Title VII. Adverse impact occurs when an otherwise facially neutral test (or other selection factor) disproportionately excludes members of one group relative to another. For example, in *Griggs v. Duke Power* (1971), applicants were required to possess a high school degree and pass two IQ tests. These requirements excluded significantly more

blacks than whites. It is critically important to note that adverse impact is not, per se, illegal. However, the employer must show that any cause of adverse impact is job related and consistent with business necessity. Duke Power lost because the aforementioned requirements were deemed arbitrary.

In addition to being the broadest EEO law, Title VII has influenced all other EEO laws, including those that preceded it. For example, the due process clause of the Fifth Amendment has been used to challenge "reverse discrimination" in federal entities (*Adarand v. Pena,* 1995), and the equal protection clause of the Fourteenth Amendment has similarly been used against state entities (*Regents of the University of California v. Bakke,* 1978). Also, Section 1981, a Thirteenth Amendment statute, has been used to challenge disparate treatment and pattern or practice by private employers. Generally, constitutional amendments apply to smaller entities than Title VII, have uncapped legal relief, and may be used together with Title VII for increased remedies for the same violation.

The Equal Pay Act (or EPA) of 1963 is another law that preceded Title VII. The EPA covers discrimination in pay based on gender, a practice also covered in Title VII. Unlike Title VII, the EPA may be used against entities of any size. It may also be used together with Title VII to obtain remedies from both statutes.

The Age Discrimination in Employment Act (ADEA) of 1967 is the only statute covering age discrimination (age 40 and older). It has many Title VII features, including disparate treatment, pattern or practice scenarios, and the BFOQ defense. The most common complaints in the ADEA relate to layoffs and benefits. A 1990 law termed the Older Workers Benefit Protection Act was enacted to amend the ADEA with special protections in these major areas.

The Americans with Disabilities Act (ADA) of 1990, a successor to the Rehabilitation Act of 1973, protects individuals with physical or mental impairments that substantially interfere with major life activities. The ADA also protects individuals with a history of disability and individuals falsely regarded as being disabled. The ADA prohibits medical or psychological inquiries before a conditional job offer and requires reasonable accommodations to enable performance of essential job functions, unless employers can prove undue hardship or direct threat to workplace safety. The EEOC procedures and remedies from Title VII also apply to the ADA.

Finally, Executive Order 11246 (EO 11246) mandates affirmative action (primarily recruitment and training) when qualified and available minorities and women in the labor pool are underrepresented in the workforce. EO 11246 applies to federal contractors and to civilian employees in federal agencies. For contractors, failure to comply with EO 11246 may trigger sanctions and penalties such as fines, suspension, and in extreme cases, loss of contract privileges (disbarment). EO 11246 is discussed elsewhere in this encyclopedia. For present purposes, it is sufficient to know that EO 11246 does not require hiring or promoting unqualified or less qualified applicants, and it is not the sole source of affirmative action.

—Arthur Gutman

FURTHER READING

Adarand v. Pena. (1995). 115 S.Ct. 2097.

Dothard v. Rawlinson. (1977). 433 US 321.

Griggs v. Duke Power Company. (1971). 401 US 424.

International Brotherhood of Teamsters v. United States. (1977). 431 US 324.

McDonnell Douglas Corporation v. Green. (1973). 411 US 792.

Regents of University of California v. Bakke. (1978). 438 US 265.

Thompson v. Sawyer. (1982). D.C.Cir. 678 F.2d 257.

EMPLOYMENT INTERVIEW

WHAT IS THE EMPLOYMENT INTERVIEW?

The employment interview is a human resource selection method that involves an interviewer or panel of interviewers asking questions of job applicants (interviewees) whose responses, reactions, and so on, are used for determining applicants' suitability for employment. The employment interview is generally regarded as the most often used selection device in personnel selection. Because of its widespread use, the method has received a great deal of attention from personnel selection researchers and academicians. Although early interview studies concluded the interview was an unreliable, ineffective means for assessing applicants, recent research has shown that the interview, when properly implemented, is useful in predicting applicants' future job performance. More specifically, the interview has been found useful for assessing applicants' job knowledge, interpersonal skills, and employee characteristics such as dependability and conscientiousness. Consequently, the employment interview is a viable employee selection device that can be incorporated into almost any health care organization, large or small.

Although there are positive aspects of employment interviews, they are not without their problems. For example, interviewers are susceptible to a number of errors. Among the more common are the following:

- *Similarity error*: Interviewers are positively biased toward applicants exhibiting characteristics similar to them and are negatively disposed toward applicants who are different.

- *Contrast error*: Interviewers are likely to compare applicants to other applicants interviewed at about the same time.

- *First-impression error*: Interviewers often form first impressions that are resistant to change.

- *Overweighting information*: Interviewers are inclined to overweight negative information.

- *Stereotyping*: Interviewers may be more or less positive about applicants based on their personal characteristics (for example, age, race, or gender).

LEGAL ISSUES AND QUESTION TOPICS TO AVOID

As with any selection device, users of employment interviews should adhere to guidelines issued by the Equal Employment Opportunity Commission (EEOC) regarding the use of selection methods. When using employment interviews, it is critical that health care managers be knowledgeable of these guidelines; otherwise, the employing health care organization may be charged with employment discrimination.

One important source of employment discrimination can arise from the nature of the questions posed by an interviewer. Health care professionals should avoid asking job applicants any question associated with applicants' race, color, ancestry, age, sex, religion, physical handicap, marital status, or arrest/court record. For example, interview questions such as the following should not be asked:

- "What is your maiden name?"
- "What language do you commonly use?"
- "Does your religion keep you from working on weekends?"
- "Do you prefer being referred to as Miss, Mrs., or Ms.?"
- "Do you have any physical disabilities?"
- "Have you ever been arrested?"
- "When did you attend high school?"
- "Do you have any children?"

When an employment discrimination charge involving the employment interview has been made and gone to trial, research has shown that certain employment interview characteristics are associated with the outcome of the case. For instance, Laura Williamson and her colleagues found that employers were more likely to win the case when their employment interviews had certain characteristics: (a) Applicant behaviors rather than traits were assessed, (b) applicant interview performance was judged according to specific rather than general criteria, (c) interviewers had been trained in how to conduct the interview, (d) validity evidence was presented showing that interview performance was associated with job performance, (e) guides had been established on how to conduct the interviews, and

(f) predetermined, standardized interview questions were used with all applicants.

TYPES OF EMPLOYMENT INTERVIEWS

Generally, employment interviews are grouped into two categories: structured and unstructured. In defining structure, we refer to the definition provided by Michael Campion and his colleagues: Interview structure includes any enhancement of the interview intended to increase the interview's reliability and validity by increasing standardization or assisting the interviewer in determining what questions to ask or how to evaluate applicant responses.

Structured interviews are more likely to involve gathering information related to the knowledge, skills, and abilities (KSAs) required to effectively perform the job, with common information collected and scored for all applicants. Standardized collection, scoring, and evaluating of information makes the comparison among applicants easier and more legally defensible. Examples of structured interview characteristics include interviewers' use of preplanned questions, scoring formats, and decision rules for evaluating applicants' performance. In an unstructured interview, interviewers can ask any question they wish, regardless of its appropriateness. In addition, procedures for scoring and evaluating applicant responses are not used. Unstructured interviews have generally been found to be less predictive of applicant job performance and less defensible in court than structured interviews. In an unstructured interview situation, comparisons among applicants typically involve subjective processes susceptible to inappropriate interviewer biases.

HOW TO DEVELOP EFFECTIVE EMPLOYMENT INTERVIEWS

The development of a reliable and valid employment interview is critical to health care organizations. A number of steps can be taken to improve the employment interview. For further information, see the list of Further Reading for this entry. Some general recommendations are as follows.

Restrict the Use of the Interview

A major problem with employment interviews is users' attempts to employ them for multiple purposes. For example, during a typical one-hour interview interviewers may use the method as a medium to describe the organization's culture, as a recruitment vehicle to communicate organizational highlights, and as a selection device to evaluate applicants' job-related KSAs. However, the purposes of public relations, recruitment, and selection are not the same, and therefore these diverse human resource functions should not be addressed concurrently in one interview. If desired, these diverse purposes or objectives should be accomplished in separate interviews or by other means. Focusing the employment interview only on selection enhances its utility.

Restrict Use of Applicants' Preinterview Data

The personnel selection function ordinarily requires applicants to first complete an application blank or submit a résumé, subsequently followed by participation in one or more interviews. This preinterview information (for example, the application blank) is then made available to interviewers, and in many cases interviewers are encouraged to review the material before the interview, to assist them in formulating first impressions and interview questions. Although this approach has been commonly endorsed, recent research concludes that interviewers who reviewed preinterview data spent more time confirming their first impressions, were less reliable in evaluating applicants' performance during the interview, and were less accurate in describing applicants' personal characteristics than interviewers who did not have preinterview data available. This research suggests preinterview data (for example, other selection device scores, letters of reference) can interfere with the interview process by operating as a source of error and therefore should be withheld until after the selection interview is completed.

Use a Structured Interview Format

Generally, it is agreed that adding structure to the employment interview greatly improves its usefulness. When structure is imposed, interviewers have a set of pre-formulated questions related to the KSAs of the position, and these questions are asked of all applicants. The greatest strength of the structured interview concerns the standardization of questions and information gathered from each of the applicants, making comparisons among applicants much easier.

Use Job-Related Questions

Another employment interview concern involves the questions asked of the applicants. For example, developing a structured format is of little use to interviewers and hiring organizations if the designed questions are not directly related to the identified KSAs needed to effectively perform the job. Therefore, it is important to ensure that employment interview questions are specific and job related.

The most common type of interview question, job knowledge, involves the interviewer attempting to determine if applicants know specific information about the job.

For instance, if a medical group were interviewing candidates for a vascular surgeon position, appropriate questions might include the following:

- "What are your views on stent grafting of abdominal aortic aneurysms that are 4.5 to 4.9 cm in diameter in people less than 60 years of age?"
- "Can you tell me about vascular bypass, above the knee, for claudicators with occlusions of the superficial femoral artery less than 6 cm in diameter?"
- "How would you treat a 78-year-old patient experiencing renal failure with gangrene and severe tibial artery disease with no native veins? Assume the patient has multiorgan disease (congestive heart failure, poor eyesight, ambulatory with a walker, and so on)."

When using interview questions that concern job knowledge, a few important points are worth noting. Most important, the questions asked should be closely associated with the overall performance of the job. Second, the questions should not ask for information that is either easily learned on the job or is part of a training program. Third, the questions should assess important KSAs, not information that is better assessed using another selection device. Results of a thorough analysis of the job for which the employment interview is being used can be used to address such issues.

Adopt a Formal Scoring Format

In addition to structure, interview research has consistently shown that interviews that incorporate a formal, defined scoring format are more reliable, valid, and legally defensible than interview formats that do not include a scoring system. Commonly, the scoring format consists of rating scales with four to seven rating points. Each rating point has a number to reflect varying degrees of the characteristics being judged and a set of adjectives used to describe the differences among the points. The scoring format should also include a space for interviewers' comments. These comments provide not only additional information when evaluating applicants but also supporting documentation if the hiring decision is challenged in court.

Give Interviewer Training

As previously mentioned, a number of decision errors have been shown to bias interviewers' evaluations. One means found to overcome these errors is through interviewer training. When considering the costs associated with employment interviewing, it is interesting to note that a study conducted by Mary Connerley and Sara Rynes found only 69% of the interviewers reported having had formal training. However, this percentage was up from 41% in a study conducted 10 years earlier. When offered, interviewer training programs should focus at least on the following topics: (a) interviewers' listening skills, (b) interviewers' evaluation of the information received, and (c) improving interviewing behaviors.

—Michael S. Cole and Hubert S. Feild

FURTHER READING

Cable, D. M., & Gilovich, T. (1998). Looked over or over-looked? Prescreening decisions and post-interview evaluations. *Journal of Applied Psychology, 83,* 501–508.

Campion, M. A., Palmer, D. K., & Campion, J. E. (1997). A review of structure in the selection interview. *Personnel Psychology, 50,* 655–702.

Connerley, M. L., & Rynes, S. L. (1997). The influence of recruiter characteristics and organizational recruitment support on perceived recruiter effectiveness: Views from applicants and recruiters. *Human Relations, 50,* 1563–1586.

Dipboye, R. L. (1992). *Selection interviews: Process perspectives.* Cincinnati, OH: South-Western.

Eder, R. W., & Harris, M. M. (1999). *The employment interview handbook.* Newbury Park, CA: Sage.

Gatewood, R. D., & Feild, H. S. (2001). *Human resource selection* (5th ed.). Fort Worth, TX: Harcourt College.

Williamson, L. G., Campion, J. E., Malos, S. B., Roehling, M. V., & Campion, M. A. (1997). Employment interview on trial: Linking interview structure with litigation outcomes. *Journal of Applied Psychology, 82,* 900–912.

EMPLOYMENT LAW

Although laws regulating the actions of organizations predate the 20th century, regulation governing the relationship between employer and employee grew dramatically over the last 50 years. Unlike most previous legislation that addressed industry-specific problems, modern employment law affects all industries and all but the smallest employers. State and federal laws now regulate many human resource functions. This regulation takes many forms and offers many protections for both employees and organizations.

A MODEL FOR EMPLOYMENT REGULATION

Almost all employment laws are the result of either past abuses by employers or of developing social pressures in society. To meet their objectives, employers must hire, train, retain, compensate, promote, discipline, and terminate employees. Whenever those objectives or the means of furthering them are contrary to the objectives of society,

| **Problems** | **Laws** | **Agencies** | **Regulatory Actions** | **Management Responses** |

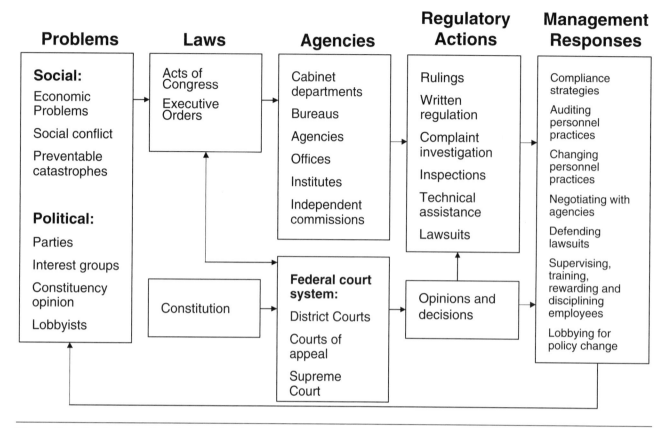

Figure 1   Employment Regulation Model

regulation occurs. Regulation limits and focuses the practice of business management.

James Ledvinka and Vida G. Scarpello (1991, p. 18) presented a regulatory model (Figure 1) that describes the process through which societal problems become employment policies and organizational actions. Their model proposes five components: social problems, laws and executive orders, regulatory agencies, regulatory actions, and management responses, each of which fulfills a unique function. First, political and social problems cause lawmakers to pass laws; these laws in turn direct and empower enforcement agencies to take actions; these actions require or prompt management responses. If management responses do not address the social problems that started the process, then the entire process is repeated.

The regulatory model has many implications. First, the problem that led to the passage of a law, and management's response to that problem are often separated by both time and multiple stages of interpretation. To successfully respond to any law, act, or regulation, it is often necessary to understand the problem driving the regulation and not just the policy or regulation. The system is also in a constant state of change, so interpretations at one stage of the process often affect several other stages. Finally, the court

system is the ultimate arbiter of disputes, laws, regulations, and action.

TYPES OF EMPLOYMENT LAW

Over the course of time, employment laws have addressed numerous problems. Early laws focused on fostering labor unions and collective bargaining, whereas later laws focus much more on employee rights and direct protection of each employee. Almost no domain of regulation is determined by only one law or executive order. Rather, the regulatory process usually results in several laws or orders that together determine the protection provided. Nevertheless, laws addressing a particular social problem are grouped together conceptually and known by the major law (often not the first) addressing the problem.

Equal employment opportunity (EEO) encompasses laws, regulations, and agencies that address the problem of discrimination on the basis of race, color, religion, national origin, sex, or age. These laws prohibit using any of these protected classes of information for employment purposes. These laws not only prohibit overt discrimination against a person of a given group (for example, women or African Americans) but also prohibit using policies or procedures that appear neutral but have discriminatory impact. The principal law associated with EEO is the Civil Rights Act of 1964, but this law has been amended and augmented by numerous other laws. Affirmative action is a requirement of federal employers and contractors; it requires special efforts to better incorporate into the workplace groups of individuals who have historically been underrepresented in certain segments of the workforce. The regulatory agency associated with affirmative action is the Office of Federal Contract Compliance. Affirmative action is not a law, but a policy of the government of the United States, established by Executive Order 11246.

Discrimination against qualified individuals with disabilities is one of the major elements of the Americans with Disabilities Act (ADA) of 1990. This comprehensive act also targeted access to public buildings and other impediments to a disabled person's opportunity to work and other major life activities. Employers are prohibited from discriminating against a qualified individual with a disability and are expected to provide reasonable accommodation for the individual's disability. Employers are not required to accommodate a person with a disability if that accommodation would cause the employer significant difficulty or expense. The courts are still considering many of the major issues regarding the regulation and enforcement of this act.

Labor laws foster the combination of employees and promote collective bargaining with employers; they counter antitrust laws that prohibit combination and cooperation of competitors and provide power to employees through the power of numbers. Most of these laws were created during the labor movement of the first half of the 20th century. Prior to these laws, which were created in response to the labor movement of the first half of the 20th century, employees had very few rights and almost no means of influencing employment policies. The principal agency associated with labor laws is the National Labor Relations Board (NLRB). This board had both regulatory and judicial power and is charged with certifying and decertifying unions to represent employees. One major concern for employers is a set of "unfair labor practices," which are acts deemed destructive of the balance of power between employer and union.

Pay laws are often associated with labor laws but occupy a distinctive role in the regulation of employment. Stemming from child labor abuses, worker exploitation by competition for jobs, and sweatshop working conditions, pay laws set minimum wages, define overtime work, set standards for pay, and prohibit or significantly limit child labor. The principal regulatory act associated with the regulation of pay is the Fair Labor Standards Act of 1938. The Equal Pay Act of 1963 is both a pay law and an EEO law. This act specifies that men and women doing the same work must receive equal pay. The act specifies numerous "affirmative defenses," or legitimate reasons for differences in pay, including experience and the quality and quantity of work performed. The concept of requiring equal pay for work of comparable value (comparable worth) has been debated and endorsed by many groups but has never progressed from problem to law.

Workers' compensation laws stem from a system of state laws designed to compensate employees for work-related injuries and illnesses. Generally, an employee who is accidentally injured on the job is afforded compensation for those injuries but gives up the right to sue the employer for accidental injuries. Both the employer and the employee are protected by these laws.

Occupational health and safety laws are a response to a prevalence of unsafe working conditions. Protected by state workers' compensation laws, employers often ignored unsafe conditions in favor of saving cost and time, and thereby increasing profits. The Occupational Safety and Health Act (OSHA) of 1970 provided federal regulation of working conditions by making accident prevention a requirement of all employers. Unlike many other employment laws, such as EEO and ADA, OSHA is a short law with enormous regulatory power granted to the various regulatory agencies. Although general knowledge of this act is useful, careful compliance requires attention to numerous detailed regulations.

Perhaps no employment law stems more directly from employer and union abuses than the law regulating employee benefit plans. Often very stringent qualification rules were applied to pension plan participation. Long-term employees who had contributed large sums to their pension plans found themselves without any retirement income; workers were terminated days before qualifying for benefits; pension funds were drained by an employer to finance operations. The societal impact of such actions was devastating to families and communities. The Employee Retirement Income Security Act (ERISA) of 1974 established uniform rules and standards for pension plans. The act established standards for the management of pension funds so that plan protection could extend beyond a company's closing, and provided tax protection for retirement plan contributions. Rules were established for *plan participation,* the process of contributing to a retirement account; *vesting,* the unforfeitable right to a retirement benefit; and *retirement,* the determination of when an employee can terminate employment and begin drawing retirement benefits.

Numerous other state and federal laws have shaped employment law. Certainly laws affecting employer liability and unemployment compensation are principal among these laws. From the Clayton Act of 1914, one of the first labor laws, which held among other things that humans are not commodities, to the present day, the world of work has been shaped by repeated regulation for the benefit of society.

—Robert T. Ladd

FURTHER READING

Deskbook encyclopedia of employment law (6th ed.). Rosemount, MN: Data Research Inc.

Gutman, A. (2000). *EEO law and personnel practices* (2nd ed.). Thousand Oaks, CA: Sage.

Ledvinka, J., & Scarpello, V. G. (1991). *Federal regulation of personnel and human resources management* (2nd ed.). Boston: PWS Kent.

EMPLOYMENT REFERENCES

Employment references are typically business-to-business communications between a former employer and a prospective employer regarding an applicant for employment. Superficially, soliciting and providing employment references would seem to be a simple and straightforward task. Certainly these communications are one of the oldest means of assessing a job candidate's qualifications. A former employer should be an excellent source of job-related information regarding an individual, and it would seem foolish for a prospective employer to ignore former employers as a source of a candidate's qualifications. Nevertheless, the litigious nature of today's society and the strong emphasis of the courts on individual rights require care and diligence in both providing and requesting information.

Generally, an employer has the legal right to ask about an applicant's former employment and may verify any claims of previous employment through communications with former employers. Employers are also protected as regards providing information to the police and other employers as long as the information is truthful, or is thought to be. These rights, however, are not rights granted by the U.S. Constitution but are often the result of numerous state and federal laws and court decisions regulating the employment relationship. Accordingly, before seeking or providing employment references all employers are advised to seek the advice of a competent attorney familiar with the state specific legal environment of employment.

PROVIDING EMPLOYMENT REFERENCES

A former (or current) employer who provides information to a prospective employer faces two major pitfalls, defamation and liability for negligence. Any negative information regarding an individual may be viewed by that person as harming her or his future employment opportunities and may therefore be regarded as defamatory. Legally, defamation, is not simply harming someone's reputation but is the "offense of injuring a person's character, fame, or reputation by false and malicious statements" (*Black's Law Dictionary*, p. 505). As long as the information provided by an employer is true, or is thought to be true, and is not intended to do harm, answering the charge of defamation should not be a problem, apart from the burden of answering any claims of defamation brought through the legal system. This burden, however, has been viewed by some employers to be so great as to require them to set policies targeted at reducing the probability that a former employee might file a defamation lawsuit. Generally, these policies specify that only minimal information should be provided to reference requests; this information typically includes job title, dates of employment, and perhaps job grade or wage information.

Providing only minimal information in response to reference requests is not always a good policy. Although such a policy may allay some of the burden of defending a defamation lawsuit, there are circumstances where a former employer must provide additional information. Failure to disclose certain information may lead to subsequent liability cases. These circumstances include disclosure of aggressive, violent, or negligent behavior that may endanger the public. This information is particularly relevant within the health care industry, where most employees significantly interact with the public. For example, if by policy a hospital provided only minimal information about a nurse who had demonstrated violent or aggressive behavior toward certain individuals and who had been terminated with cause for those actions, and that nurse later harmed someone through similar actions at a different hospital, then the second hospital could file suit against the former employer for negligently placing the public at risk by failing to disclose the information.

Numerous minor issues should limit the information provided by employers. These include union-related blacklisting laws, invasion of privacy protection, equal employment opportunity regulation, and liability for negligence. Although no general policy can be appropriate in all circumstances, employers should exercise care to provide only honest, objective information that is job relevant and in response to the specific requests of the requesting party. Employers should have a formal policy that limits who can respond to employment reference requests and that articulates what information those individuals can and cannot provide. Moreover, policies should be developed that prohibit an individual who has had a history of problems with an employee from answering any reference requests regarding that employee.

Perhaps the best protection against legal claims arising from providing employment references is to obtain written release from the employee authorizing release of information. Although this is not required, it is a good practice. The release can be obtained at the time of employment, at the time of termination, or indirectly through the inquiring party. Such releases have proven invaluable when released information did not meet with a former employee's expectations.

REQUESTING EMPLOYEE REFERENCES

Conducting a reasonable check of a prospective employee's references is almost always a good idea. Apart from the job-relevant information that can be obtained through employer references, several court decisions have concluded that it is a duty of employers to conduct a thorough check. This duty appears reasonably independent of the responsibilities associated with the job or the contact the person may have with the public. For example, in Florida a furniture company was found negligent when a man hired to deliver furniture subsequently attacked a person to whom he had delivered furniture. The man had been hired without obtaining employment references and without other exercise of care in employment selection; the company was required to pay in excess of $2 million in compensatory and punitive damages (*Tallahassee Furniture Co. v. Harrison,* 583 So.2d 744, 1991).

Diligence and care should be exercised when checking employment references. As noted, obtaining written authorization to conduct the reference check is always a good idea. Limit the information requested to job-relevant information, to avoid claims of privacy invasion and charges of discrimination. To protect all parties, requests should be made and received in writing. Finally, if discrepancies occur, explanations should be sought from both the prospective employee and the former employer.

—Robert T. Ladd

EMPLOYMENT TESTING

In its broadest sense, an employment test is any identifiable or quantifiable piece of information about applicants or employees used to make personnel selection decisions. Equally as broad is the definition of personnel selection decisions, which may include any term or condition of employment such as hiring, training, benefits, pay, promotion, and termination. In accordance with the *Principles for the Validation and Use of Personnel Selection Procedures* (or simply, the *Principles*), any of the following pieces of information constitutes an employment test:

Paper-and-pencil tests, performance tests, work samples, personality inventories, interest inventories, projective techniques, tests of honesty or integrity including polygraph examinations, assessment center evaluations, biographical data forms or score application blanks, interviews, educational requirements, experience requirements, reference checks, physical requirements such as height and weight, physical ability tests, appraisals of job performance, computer-based test interpretations, estimates of advanced potentials, or any other selection instrument, whenever any one or a combination of them is used or assists in making a personnel decision.

There are two good reasons for adopting these broad definitions. First, in making selection decisions human resources (HR) managers should seek any data associated with (or predictive of) job performance. Second, HR managers must also be mindful of the myriad of legal issues associated with federal laws such as Title VII of the Civil Rights Act of 1964 (as amended by the Civil Rights Act of 1991), the Americans with Disabilities Act of 1990, and various constitutional amendments. The major legal issues addressed as follows are (a) adverse impact on selection rates of minorities and women, (b) test items that constitute illegal inquiries into physical or mental impairments, (c) test formats that require reasonable accommodations for physically or mentally impaired applicants, and (d) test items that offend the right to privacy. Among these issues, adverse impact has received the lion's share of attention in federal court cases.

The concept of adverse impact is illustrated by society's post–Civil War reaction to the Thirteenth Amendment, which ended slavery, and the Fifteenth Amendment, which gave all (male) citizens the right to vote. Some states, unfriendly to such ideas, created barriers to this newfound right. Thus all citizens, to vote, had to own property, pay a poll tax, pass a reading test, and so on. Such practices were not completely outlawed until 1964 (in the Twenty-Sixth Amendment). Critically, the barriers to voting were not inherently discriminatory; indeed, on their face (or surface) they were neutral. In comparison, the prior policies were facially discriminatory, because whole classes of people were denied various rights and privileges, no questions asked. In short, although the barriers to voting did not facially exclude any group or class of citizens from voting, they had the *effect* (or impact) of excluding a much higher percentage of black voters than white voters.

Fast-forwarding 100 years to when Title VII was enacted to outlaw workplace discrimination based on race, color, religion, sex, and national origin, we see that some employers turned to facially neutral selection policies that proved as arbitrary for job performance as poll taxes were for voting. However, unlike the voting rights issue, which required a constitutional amendment, these arbitrary job policies were struck down in a landmark unanimous U.S. Supreme Court decision in *Griggs v. Duke Power* (1971).

Historically, Duke Power hired blacks for low-wage labor jobs, but not for higher-wage operations jobs. In 1955, entry into operations jobs was made contingent on possession of a high school diploma. Then, on July 2, 1965, the very day Title VII became law, all new operations employees were required to possess the diploma *and* to pass two cognitive tests (the Bennett and the Wunderlich tests). Those without diplomas (whites hired before 1955) could transfer to operations by passing the cognitive tests. Interestingly, before 1965 whites without diplomas were routinely promoted to operations. Thus ample evidence showed that the diploma and the cognitive tests were arbitrary requirements. The cognitive tests excluded 94% of black applicants as compared with only 42% of white applicants. The diploma had the same adverse impact, because the graduation rate in North Carolina was 34% for whites but only 12% for blacks.

Although both the diploma and testing requirements were struck down by the U.S. Supreme Court, the *Griggs* ruling focused primarily on issues related to standardized testing. Statutory language in Title VII made it legal to use "professionally developed ability tests," as long as such tests did not discriminate against classes protected under Title VII. According to the 1966 *EEOC Guidelines*, a "professionally developed ability test" was defined as one that

> [f]airly measures the knowledge or skills required by the particular job or class of jobs which the applicant seeks, or which fairly affords the employer a chance to measure the applicant's ability to perform a particular job or class of jobs.

The lower courts ignored this guidance, but Justice Burger, speaking for a unanimous Supreme Court, ruled that Title VII covers the "consequences of employment practices, not simply the motivation" of employers. He then wrote what arguably are the two most important words in adverse impact case law; that when adverse impact against a protected Title VII class occurs, the employer must prove that there is a "manifest relationship" between the challenged practice and the "employment in question."

Subsequently, in *Albermarle v. Moody* (1975), the company used the same two tests as in *Griggs* but hired an expert to correlate test scores with job performance ratings (that is, a criterion validity study). However, it was a hasty effort conducted shortly before trial. As a result, there were major defects in the study. Relying on the 1974 *EEOC Guidelines,* the Supreme Court defined how a manifest relationship should be proven.

The message of these *EEOC Guidelines* is the same as that of the *Griggs* case: that discriminatory tests are impermissible unless shown, by professionally acceptable methods, to be "predictive of or significantly correlated with important elements of work behavior which comprise or are relevant to the job or jobs for which candidates are evaluated" [29 CFR section 1607.4(c)].

Subsequently, the *Uniform Guidelines on Employee Selection Procedures* were adopted in 1978 to clarify how "professionally developed ability tests" should be validated in accordance with the *Griggs* and *Albermarle* rulings. It should be noted that as of this writing, both the *Guidelines* and the aforementioned *Principles* are under revision.

—Arthur Gutman

EMPOWERMENT (DELEGATION OF AUTHORITY)

Within a managerial context, empowerment is associated with actions that share power with others. Decentralization of decision making is central to sharing power, and has been associated with participative managerial techniques such as quality circles, management by objectives (MBO), and goal setting. Empowerment goes beyond simply delegation of tasks, to delegation of choice, based on implied competence and potential for impact.

Within a psychological context, empowerment is a source of heightened individual motivation associated with a sense of personal power. Underlying this motivation is the need most people share for self-determination, that is, to be in control of their own destiny. People feel more powerful when they believe their decisions will affect the outcomes of significant events and when they can adapt to situations as they arise. Conversely, people feel helpless when they believe their ability to adapt is unreasonably limited.

Empowerment involves establishing or changing four perceptions on the part of an individual. First, people must perceive the task they are performing as having value or meaning. They must also believe they are capable of accomplishing the task and must see their decisions and behaviors as being instrumental of task accomplishment. Finally, they must believe their actions will have significant positive impact. Managerial action focused on increasing these perceptions among employees empowers employees and accordingly is believed to increase employees' motivation to perform.

—Robert T. Ladd

See also Leadership

FURTHER READING

Conger, J. A. (1989). Leadership: The art of empowering others. *Academy of Management Executive, 33,* 17–24.

Conger, J. A., & Kamungo, R. N. (1988). The empowerment process: Integrating theory and practice. *Academy of Management Review, 31,* 471–482.

Thomas, K. W., & Velthouse, B. A. (1990). Cognitive elements of empowerment. *Academy of Management Review, 15,* 666–681.

ENCRYPTION

Encryption is the process of converting data into a secret code. Encryption is most often used to protect data as they are transferred from point to point over a network and also to scramble sensitive information residing in a database. The process of encoding data is called *encryption,* and the process of decoding data is called *decryption.* Unencrypted data are called *plain text,* and encrypted data are called *cipher text.*

In business, two major types of encryption are commonly used. Both methods employ "keys" or secret codes to "lock" or scramble data. Once a key is selected, a mathematical formula is applied to lock the data with the key. An easy way to visualize the role of the key, the data, and the formula is to compare encryption to home protection where the data represent the home contents and the mathematical algorithm is the type of lock used, which the key unlocks. One conceptual difference is that with encryption, the data being transferred often play a role in the actual locking process.

The first primary method of encryption uses just one key to both encode and decode data and is called *private key* or *symmetric key encryption.* Anyone with access to the key can read the message, so the intended recipient and the sender must ensure the security of the key to maintain message privacy. Commonly used symmetric keys include DES, IDEA, Skipjack, Triple DES, and Rijndael.

The second primary type of encryption employs a pair of keys to encode and decode data and is called *public key* or *asymmetric encryption.* Public key encryption requires each individual involved in a transaction to use a unique key pair. The algorithm employed is called a *one-way function,* meaning it is easy to perform in one direction, but very difficult and time-consuming to reverse. Commonly used asymmetric keys include RSA, Diffie-Hellman, El Gamal, and Elliptic Curve.

Asymmetric key encryption is inherently more secure, but symmetric key encryption is much faster than asymmetric—100 to 1,000 times faster. Symmetric keys should be used when a secure channel is available for key delivery, when encrypting large amounts of data, and when processing speed is important. Asymmetric keys are used when channels are insecure and when data being transferred are highly sensitive. Asymmetric keys are also used to create virtual private networks, or protected channels through untrusted networks such as the Internet, and to create digital signatures, which are used for authenticating individual parties involved in an electronic transaction.

In an effort to balance efficiency and security, companies often apply symmetric encryption to a plain text message but encrypt the symmetric key with an asymmetric key. Because the key is usually far smaller than the text message, this saves a great deal of processing time.

The level of secrecy achieved with encryption is a function of the strength of the algorithm, the length of the key, and the type of key management policies employed.

Encryption can play a vital role in protecting confidential information, including data, voice, and video, that is commonly exchanged among hospitals, physicians' offices, insurance companies, pharmaceutical companies, and other health care organizations.

—Amy W. Ray

See also Health Insurance Portability and Accountability Act (HIPAA), Electronic Commerce, Virtual Private Networks

FURTHER READING

Levy, S. (2001). *Crypto: How the code rebels beat the government—Saving privacy in the digital age.* New York: Viking Press.

Singh, S. (2000). *The code book: The science of secrecy from ancient Egypt to quantum cryptography.* New York: Anchor Books.

END-OF-LIFE CARE

See Hospice

ENROLLEE

An enrollee is a person who is eligible to receive or is receiving benefits from a health maintenance organization (HMO) or other insurance plan. This includes not only those who have subscribed to the plan but also the subscriber's eligible dependents. Eligible dependents may be a spouse, a child, an adult child who is disabled, or an elderly parent.

All enrollees must meet the health plan's eligibility requirements, be currently enrolled in the plan, and accept financial responsibility for premiums, copayments, and deductibles. Premiums are the annual or monthly payments made to the plan to have the health benefit. Copayments are the per-visit outlay for a service covered by the plan. Deductibles are the annual amount paid out of pocket before the plan starts coverage.

The benefit package is the list of covered services that an insurance company, HMO, or preferred provider organization (PPO) offers a group or individual in its health plan. Basic benefits are a set of basic health services specified in the member's certificate. Basic benefits are services that are required under applicable federal and state laws and regulations.

An enrolled group consists of individuals with the same employer or membership in an organization in common, who are enrolled collectively in a health plan. The health plan may stipulate that the group be of a certain size and that a certain percentage of that group must enroll before the coverage is made available to them.

—Doreen T. Day

FURTHER READING

www.casact.org

ENROLLMENT

The term *enrollment* can apply to more than one concept in a health insurance environment. First, it can represent the number of members in a health maintenance organization (HMO) or other insurance plan. Open enrollment is the annual period during which members can choose between two or more plans that are offered by a health plan. It also applies to the period during which a federally qualified HMO must make its plan available, without restriction, to individuals who are not part of a group. A federally qualified HMO is one that meets federally stipulated provisions aimed at protecting consumers. It must provide a broad range of basic health services, assure financial solvency, and monitor the quality of their care.

Second, it can represent the number of members assigned to a physician or medical group providing care under contract with an HMO. The enrollment area, also known as the *service area,* is the geographic region within a designated radius of the primary medical group (PMG) selected by the subscriber. This area can vary in size by the specific HMO.

Last, it can represent the process by which the health plan signs up individuals or groups as subscribers. The waiting period is the length of time that an individual must wait to become eligible for benefits for a specific condition after overall coverage has begun. The termination date is the date on which the group contract expires or an individual is no longer eligible for benefits.

Government legislation has been enacted to protect enrollees from loss of benefits. The Consolidated Omnibus Budget Reconciliation Act (COBRA) of 1985 is a statute that requires employers sponsoring group health plans to offer continuation of coverage under the group plan to employees and their dependents who lost coverage secondary to a qualifying event. A qualifying event may be a decrease in work hours, death, divorce, and many different types of termination of employment.

The Health Insurance Portability and Accountability Act (HIPAA) of 1996 is another legislative attempt to safeguard individuals from loss of health insurance coverage. The original legislation was intended to protect people who are covered under a group policy. The intent was to waive the exclusion of pre-existing conditions from coverage when a current employee leaves and goes to another employer. An enrollee or an enrollee's dependent with an expensive chronic condition could not be excluded from coverage by the new plan. This legislation has gone well beyond its original intention of achieving portability and now also involves privacy issues.

Enrollment protection is the practice of HMOs to protect contracted medical groups against part or all losses incurred for physician services above a specified dollar amount while caring for the HMO enrollees. The insurance company or HMO purchases insurance from another company to protect it from losses incurred in the process of honoring the claims of its policyholders. This practice is also known as *stop loss* or *reinsurance.*

—Doreen T. Day

FURTHER READING

www.academyhealth.org
www.casact.org
www.pohly.com/terms

ENTERPRISE RESOURCE PLANNING (ERP) IN HEALTH CARE

An enterprise resource planning (ERP) system is a business management system typically managed with computers. The goal of an ERP system is to integrate and coordinate a variety of business functions, including payroll, accounts payable, materials management, quality management, plant maintenance, sales and distribution, project management, and human resources management. ERP systems trace their origins to materials *requirement* planning (MRP) systems, which evolved in the early 1970s. The MRP system was designed to help manufacturing organizations plan their production and procurement operations and was originally conceived as a means of specifying what material should be ordered and when the order should be placed. Subsequently, MRP systems evolved to MRP II systems or manufacturing *resource* planning systems. These systems covered more aspects of business, including job costing and limited financial applications. ERP is the result of the continued push by developers of MRP II systems to cover more business applications. Now ERP can, in theory, integrate several different software applications to provide a user interface that does not require the users to navigate between disparate software/hardware platforms.

ERP software is complex and expensive, and companies often devote significant human resources to ERP projects, hiring consultants or systems integrators to help them implement them. Companies can conceivably spend millions of dollars and a number of years on ERP projects. The potential payback is, however, high. A carefully planned ERP system can provide an organization with a reliable, integrated database that can be used to manage businesses more effectively.

In the medical industry, ERP systems can keep track of patients' payment history, pay for supplies, ensure receipts of insurance reimbursements, and provide appointment reminders, to name a few applications. They can help speed the collection of data required to bill and collect from payers. The links between physician offices and the hospital help both parties maintain and update data required for billing. ERP can also handle purchasing and distribution functions. These applications allow doctors and nurses to free themselves from routing clerical recordkeeping that is often necessary in the health care industry and allows them to devote more time to managing patients or clients.

Even though ERP systems are finding increasing use in health care, the growth of ERP applications has concentrated on manufacturing systems. For instance, the ERP systems that have grown out of traditional MRP systems still focus on materials planning and better asset management. The health care industry has very different needs from manufacturing systems. For one, a health care system is primarily labor intensive rather than capital intensive. Even though health care providers would like to optimize their return on assets, their primary focus must be on managing staff and care processes. Therefore, health care ERP system must be designed with these functions in mind.

The recent trend toward consolidation in the health care industry provides another challenge for successful integration of ERP systems. Despite the challenges facing ERP implementation, there is great potential for these systems to facilitate consolidation efforts. "Currently available ERP systems can facilitate the creation of custom workflows for each patient by establishing common links among physician offices, the emergency department, the hospital admission process, and all other departments and entities throughout the care delivery system" (*FS Partners Newsletters,* 2001, p. 1).

FURTHER READING

www.fsforum.com/newsletter_09_01.html

ENTITLEMENT PROGRAMS

The terms *entitlement program, transfer program,* and *social insurance* are largely synonymous, each referring to systems of public benefits, in cash or in kind, for which a person is legally eligible based on a condition such as age, disability, or poverty. In the United States, federal entitlement programs include the Old Age, Survivors, Disability Insurance, and Supplemental Security Income (SSI) programs of Social Security, as well as Medicare, Medicaid, Unemployment Compensation, Earned Entitlements for Railroad Employees, Trade Adjustment Assistance, Temporary Assistance for Needy Families, Social Services Block Grants, Food Stamps, and the Women, Infants and Children (WIC) Program. Some "means-tested" programs (such as Food Stamps and Medicaid) require an individual to show sufficiently low income to qualify for benefits. Others (such as unemployment insurance) require a minimum period before benefits can be collected, during which the individual or an employer makes premium contributions. Entitlement programs typically involve a subsidy whereby funds are transferred from one group, such as general taxpayers or current workers, to another such as the retired or disabled. Entitlement programs are an important item in public spending. For example, in the *2000 National Income and Product Accounts* (available at the Web site of the U.S. Department of Commerce, Bureau of Economic Analysis), personal income was \$8,406.6 billion, of which transfer payments were \$1,070.3 billion. The rationale for entitlement programs is that they form a social "safety net" that protects individuals from risks for which private insurance may be too expensive. Critics argue that entitlement spending grows because each separate program creates a political constituency that favors it and because no one program is sufficiently large to arouse opposition from taxpayers.

—Stephen T. Mennemeyer

See also Access, Adverse Selection, Aid to Families with Dependent Children (AFDC), Health Insurance, Medicaid, U.S. Department of Health and Human Services (DHHS), Women, Infants and Children (WIC) Program

FURTHER READING

U.S. House of Representatives, Committee on Ways and Means, 106th Congress. (2000). *2000 Green Book, background material and data on programs within the jurisdiction of the Committee on Ways and Means* (pp. 61–710). Washington, DC: U.S. Government Printing Office. Available on the Web at aspe.os.dhhs.gov/2000gb/index.htm.

U.S. President. (2001). *Economic Report of the President transmitted to Congress.* Washington, DC: U.S. Government Printing Office. Available on the Web at w3.access.gpo.gov/usbudgetwww.auburn.edu/~johnspm/gloss

www.bea.doc.gov/bea

ENVIRONMENTAL ANALYSIS

Environmental analysis is the strategic planning process that attempts to understand issues in the external environment—including the general environment, the health care industry, and specific competitor strategies—to determine their implications for the organization. Environmental analysis is the broad look at the general external environment that once analyzed, should be followed by a more specific industry and service area competitive analysis to complete the picture. The results of the environmental analysis directly influence the development of the organization's mission, vision, values, goals, and strategy.

Environmental analysis is required when the external environment influences the capital allocation and decision-making processes or previous strategic plans have been scrapped because of unexpected changes in the environment. If unpleasant surprises have occurred, competition is increasing in the industry, or the service category is becoming more marketing oriented, environmental analysis is necessary. Further, when more—as well as different kinds of—external forces seem to be influencing decisions or management is unhappy with past forecasting and planning efforts, external analysis should be undertaken. The external environmental analysis process attempts to identify, aggregate, and interpret environmental issues. Environmental analysis seeks to eliminate many of the surprises in the external environment.

ENVIRONMENTAL ISSUES

An organization engaging in strategic management must try to sort out the general information being generated in the external environment and detect the major shifts taking place. Identifying and evaluating the issues in the general environment are important because the issues will accelerate or retard changes taking place within the health care environment and may affect the organization directly.

To develop awareness of changes taking place outside of their own organization, health care managers must thoroughly understand the other types of organizations that are creating changes as well as the nature of those changes. Governments, businesses, educational institutions, religious institutions, research organizations and foundations, and independent individuals generate important information within the general environment. Organizations and individuals in the general environment, acting alone or in concert with others, initiate and foster the macroenvironmental changes in society. These organizations and individuals generate technological, social, regulatory, political, economic, and competitive information that will, in the long run, affect many different industries (including health care). External organizations, engaged in their own

processes and pursuing their own missions, are developing new information that will affect other industries, organizations, and individuals.

A government organization that fosters changes in the general regulatory climate (new information) or a business that develops a breakthrough in computer technology (new information) contributes to macroenvironmental changes that, although perhaps not specifically related to health care, may have a significant and long-lasting impact on the delivery of health care. The organization itself may be affected directly by the technological, social, regulatory, political, economic, and competitive information initiated and fostered by organizations in the general environment.

After analyzing the general environment, strategic leaders should look at the health care environment more closely, with the intent of understanding the nature of the issues and changes taking place in a more specific context. For example, organizations and individuals within health care develop and employ new technologies, deal with changing social issues, address political change, develop and comply with regulations, compete with other health care organizations, and participate in the health care economy.

Change areas (information flows) facilitate the early identification and analysis of industry-specific environmental issues and trends that will affect the organization. The health care system may be generally grouped into five segments: organizations that regulate primary and secondary providers; organizations that provide health services (primary providers such as hospitals, physicians, and physical therapists); organizations that provide resources for the health care system (secondary providers such as health care insurers and medical education); organizations that represent the primary and secondary providers (American Medical Association, American Hospital Association, and so on); and individuals involved in health care and patients (consumers of health care services).

Changes that are more likely to have direct impact on the organization are those brought about by local competitors. The process of understanding competition is often referred to as *service area competitor analysis* (or *industry analysis*). It seeks to identify indirect competitors as well as direct competitors (those in a strategic group) that generate issues the organization will need to address. The decisions made by strategic competitors affect the organization far more than the activities of others that have similar service offerings but are not in the strategic group.

GOALS OF ENVIRONMENTAL ANALYSIS

There is an abundance of information in the external environment. For it to be meaningful, managers must identify the sources of information as well as aggregate and classify it. Although the overall intent of environmental analysis is to position the organization within its environment, there are a number of specific goals:

1. Classify and order information flows generated by outside organizations.

2. Identify and analyze current important issues that will affect the organization.

3. Detect and analyze weak signals of emerging issues that will affect the organization.

4. Identify speculations about the likely future issues that will have significant impact on the organization.

5. Organize information for the development of the organization's mission, vision, values, goals, internal analysis, and strategy.

In addition to identifying current issues, environmental analysis seeks to detect weak signals within the external environment that may portend a future issue.

Sometimes, based on a little hard data, managers attempt to identify patterns that suggest emerging issues that will become significant for the organization. Such speculative trends, if they continue or actually do occur, may represent significant challenges. Early identification aids in developing appropriate strategies. Strategic managers must go beyond what is known and speculate on the nature of the industry and the organization in the future. This process often stimulates creative thinking concerning the organization's present and future products and services. Such speculation is valuable in formulating a guiding vision and developing mission and strategy.

The environmental analysis process should foster strategic thinking. When strategic leaders—top managers, middle managers, and front-line supervisors throughout the organization—are considering the relationship of the organization to its environment, innovation and a high level of service are likely. Strategic thinking within an organization fosters adaptability; organizations that "adapt best will ultimately displace the rest."

THE LIMITATIONS OF ENVIRONMENTAL ANALYSIS

Although environmental analysis receives considerable emphasis in strategic management, it has important limitations. Environmental analysis cannot foretell the future, and managers cannot see everything. Sometimes pertinent and timely information is difficult or impossible to obtain. Delays occur between the occurrence of external events and management's ability to interpret them. Often the organization's inability to respond quickly enough means that management cannot take advantage of the issue or issues detected. Finally, managers' strongly held beliefs sometimes inhibit their ability to detect or interpret issues. Despite the limitations, environmental analysis benefits strategic thinking.

CONDUCTING ENVIRONMENTAL ANALYSIS

Regardless of the approach, to conduct an environmental analysis four fundamental processes are common: scanning, monitoring, forecasting, and assessing. Scanning attempts to identify signals of environmental change. Monitoring attempts to keep track of the identified issues. Forecasting seeks to predict the changes in the future direction of the issues, and assessing seeks to explain the organizational implications of the issues. Some of the organizations and individuals in the external environment have little direct involvement with the health care industry, whereas others are directly involved. These organizations and individuals, through their normal operations and activities, are generating information that may be important to the future of other organizations. Information in the general environment is always "breaking through" to the health care environment, as when laser technology was developed outside of the health care industry and was quickly adopted within the industry. General environment information flows may have a direct impact on any one health care organization if it is the member of the health care industry that most immediately sees an application for the information.

SCANNING THE ENVIRONMENT

Managers engaged in environmental scanning view external environmental information, organize external information into several desired categories, and identify issues within each category. Strategic issues are trends, developments, dilemmas, and possible events that affect an organization as a whole and its position within its environment. The scanning function is a process of moving the lens across the array of external organizations in search of current and emerging patterns of information. The manager focuses on diverse and unorganized information generated by external organizations and individuals, compiling and organizing it into meaningful categories. Thus information generated in the external environment is organized through the scanning process.

MONITORING THE ENVIRONMENT

The monitoring function is the tracking of trends, issues, and possible events identified in the scanning process. Monitoring researches and identifies additional sources of information for specific issues delineated in the scanning process, adds to the environmental database, attempts to confirm or disprove issues (trends, developments, dilemmas, and the possibility of events), and seeks to determine the rate of change within issues.

The monitoring process investigates the sources of the information obtained in the scanning process; it has a much narrower focus than scanning. The objective is to accumulate data around an identified issue to eventually confirm or disconfirm the trend, development, dilemma, or possibility of an event and to determine the rate of change taking place within the environment.

FORECASTING ENVIRONMENTAL CHANGE

Forecasting environmental change is a process of extending the trends, developments, dilemmas, and events that the organization is monitoring. The forecasting function attempts to answer the question "If these trends continue, or if issues accelerate beyond their present rate, or if this event occurs, what will the issues and trends 'look like' in the future?" Assessing environmental change is a judgmental process that includes evaluating the significance of the extended (forecasted) issue on the organization and identifying the issues that must be considered in formulating the vision, mission, internal analysis, and strategic plan.

ASSESSING THE CHANGE

The assessment process is not an exact science, and sound human judgment and creativity may be bottom-line techniques for a process without much structure. The fundamental challenge is to make sense out of fuzzy, ambiguous, and unrelated data. Environmental analysis techniques that identify and assess trends and issues in the external environment include simple trend identification and extrapolation; solicitation of expert opinion through Delphi technique, nominal group technique, brainstorming, and focus groups; stakeholder analysis; dialectic inquiry; and scenario writing and future studies.

SELECTING THE TECHNIQUE

The intent of environmental analysis is to identify and understand the issues in the external environment. The technique selected for environmental analysis depends on such factors as the size of the organization, the diversity of the products and services, and the complexity and size of the markets (service areas). Organizations that are relatively small, do not have a great deal of diversity, but do have well-defined service areas may opt for simple techniques that may be carried out on an in-house basis, such as trend identification and extension, in-house nominal group technique or brainstorming, or stakeholder analysis. Such organizations may include independent hospitals, HMOs, rural and community hospitals, large group practices, long-term care facilities, hospices, and county public health departments.

Health care organizations that are large, have diverse products and services, and have ill-defined or extensive service areas may want to use techniques that draw on the knowledge of a wide range of experts. As a result, these organizations are more likely to set up Delphi panels, outside nominal and brainstorming groups, or to engage in scenario writing. Such techniques are usually more time-consuming, fairly expensive, and require a great deal of extensive coordination. Organizations using these techniques may include national and regional for-profit health care chains, regional health systems, large federations and alliances, and state public health departments.

ENVIRONMENTAL ANALYSIS AS FOUNDATION

For the foreseeable future, the general environment as well as the health care environment will continue to generate numerous complex issues. Managers of health care organizations should assess these issues and others unique to their organizations in order to provide a foundation for understanding the complexity of health care delivery and to furnish a backdrop for developing strategy.

—Linda E. Swayne

See also General Environment, Health Care Environment, Sales Forecasting, Service Area Competitor Analysis, Strategic Group

FURTHER READING

Fahey, L., & Narayanan, V. K. (1986). *Macroenvironmental analysis for strategic management.* St. Paul, MN: West.

Fottler, M. D., Blair, J. D., Whitehead, C. J., Laus, M. D., & Savage, G. T. (1989). Assessing key stakeholders: Who matters to hospitals and why? *Hospital and Health Services Administration, 34,* 4, 527.

Ginter, P. M., Swayne, L. E., & Duncan, W. J. (2002). Understanding and analyzing the external environment. In P. M. Ginter, L. E. Swayne, & W. J. Duncan, *Strategic management of health care organizations* (4th ed.). Oxford, UK: Blackwell.

Jain, S. C. (1984). Environmental scanning in US corporations. *Long Range Planning, 17,* 125.

Jennings, M. C. (2000). *Health care strategy for uncertain times.* San Francisco: AHA Press/Jossey-Bass.

Kovner, A. R., & Jonas, S. (1999). *Jonas & Kovner's health care delivery in the United States* (6th ed.). New York: Springer.

Longest, B. B., Jr. (1990). *Management practice for the health professional* (4th ed.). Norwalk, CT: Appleton & Lange.

Mesch, A. H. (1984). Developing an effective environmental assessment function. *Managerial Planning, 32,* 17–22.

Thomas, J. B., & McDaniel, R. R., Jr. (1990). Interpreting strategic issues: Effects of strategy and the information-processing structure of top management teams. *Academy of Management Journal, 33,* 2, 288.

ENVIRONMENTAL HEALTH SCIENCE

Environmental health is the study of the effects of environmental factors on human health. Factors such as ultraviolet light, chemical substances, and pharmaceutical products are needed to sustain life but at the same time may produce harmful and adverse effects on susceptible individuals and unprotected employees. Environmental health study has become an important research topic and an important source of revenue as companies strive for better and safer ways to dispose of chemical, toxic, and biohazardous materials. Solid waste disposal is a major burden for leaders of developed countries.

Environmental health has been the source of important legislation in both the national and the international arena. Legislation has been approved for the protection of our nation's natural resources (the Clean Air and Clean Water acts) and for the protection of its workforce with adequate gear and training. Health issues related to the environment frequently become problematic in negotiations between management and labor and between businesses and communities. Every manager in the health care industry needs to be knowledgeable about the laws and regulations governing the appropriate implementation of programs to protect employees and the proper disposition of toxic or contaminated materials. The Occupational Health Safety Agency (OSHA) and Environmental Protection Agency (EPA) guidelines should be followed at all times. OSHA and EPA have very strict regulations and impose significant fines for violations. Environmental health science will continue to be a major determinant of the way that the health care industry performs its duty in the future.

—Raúl F. Montalvo

See also Bioterrorism, Employee Rights, Federal Regulating Agencies

FURTHER READING

Lack, R. W. (Ed.).(2001). *Safety, health and asset protection: Management essentials* (2nd ed.). Boca Raton, FL: Lewis.

Molak, V. (Ed.). (1996). *Fundamentals of risk analysis and risk management.* Boca Raton, FL: Lewis.

EPIDEMIOLOGY

Epidemiology studies the frequency, distribution, and determinants of health events in human populations and applies this knowledge to design, implement, and evaluate interventions for preventing and controlling health problems.

One of the main applications of epidemiology is to identify populations at risk of disease or death and implement early preventive or curative interventions. Epidemiological findings have demonstrated that there is significant variation in the frequency, distribution, and importance of risk factors between different populations, that some groups may share similar risk factors, and that we can devise interventions specific to behavior and to health. Decision makers need reliable data to be able to identify areas and populations with health needs and to use those data to develop specific responses. Researchers estimate that these health needs are associated with geographic positioning in 80% of the cases.

BASIC CONCEPTS

The following are basic concepts in epidemiology:

Probability provides the foundation for statistical inference.

Statistical inference draws conclusions about an entire population based on a sample from that population.

Statistical data are understood better when graphical representation is used, because visual presentation helps to identify variations and examine the shape of the distribution. A *histogram* is used to demonstrate a graph of a frequency distribution.

Frequency distribution has certain characteristics; data may show a *central tendency* or *variation (dispersion).*

Average and *median* are measures of central tendency, whereas *range, variance,* and *standard error* are measures of dispersion or variation. Given a set of *n* measurements normally distributed, on average 68.3% of measurements are within 1 standard deviation of the mean, 95.5% are within two standard deviations of the mean, and 99.7% of measurements are within 3 standard deviations of the mean.

Proportion measures relate the number of events occurring in a given place at a given time with a reference population.

Prevalence, the number of existing cases of a disease, is used with chronic diseases and those of long duration.

Incidence, the number of new cases over a specific period of time, is used mainly with infectious diseases and those of short duration.

Ratios are measures that relate two events in different populations and areas, such as mortality ratio.

Rates, in epidemiology, are incidence density measures, where the numerator is the number of new cases and the denominator is person-time (i.e., per person per time period).

APPLICATIONS

The study of the distribution of diseases began with the analysis of the causes of infectious diseases and actually involves the study of the distribution of all diseases.

Lifestyle, environmental or toxic exposures, and even bioterrorism are factors well documented in modern epidemiological studies.

The analysis of risk factors and relative risks ratios are important measurements in the study of the distribution of diseases. The risk for heart disease is increased in people who have high cholesterol and also in people with arterial hypertension but is further increased for a person who has the two risk factors, high cholesterol and high blood pressure, at the same time. Against this background of basic information, this section seeks to explain the significance of what it means to properly implement epidemiological findings. Epidemiology in a pure sense has been reserved as a science for people with special mathematical training and knowledge but with limited impact on decision making. It is thus explainable why we accumulate important information that frequently is missed when managers and government officers in the health care industry implement public health strategies.

The health care industry confronts several constraints that influence decision making:

- Lack of standardized processing
- Fragmentation of data
- Miscommunication (such as among planners, managers, and providers)
- Emphasis on cost containment instead of on evidence-based medicine
- Limited technological resources and availability
- Limited financial resources

Every manager in the health care industry needs to be familiar with the epidemiological concepts of incidence and prevalence of the diseases affecting the population served. The role of epidemiology has changed with the advent of technological innovation. The Internet and the availability of powerful analytical computer programs permit the rapid distribution of information and provide data for decision support. Epidemiology has become an agile science that can be used not just for analysis of past events but also as a resource for predicting future occurrences.

The application of geographic information systems (GISs) has permitted great improvement in understanding the distribution of diseases in the United States and many other countries. Digitized maps are invaluable resources to demonstrate in a very powerful fashion the impact of diseases in any given region. GISs provide an additional tool to simplify the representation of highly complex mathematical processes in a way that people with minimal training can understand. The World Health Organization and the Pan-American Health Organization are working very actively with governments to improve sanitary conditions, to immunize populations, and to apply insecticide in high-risk areas based on information obtained by epidemiological studies with GIS representation. GISs are very useful for supporting public health surveillance and monitoring. The application of these systems permits the identification of the specific areas with the highest incidence of cases of a particular disease or infection. The information obtained is used to estimate the resources needed for planning and implementing successful interventions. All these achievements are possible because of the technological advance in the science of epidemiology and the integration of government officers, epidemiologists, and health managers working together to find appropriate solutions.

The term *managerial epidemiology* is given to the emerging discipline that integrates health management and epidemiology. As we move to a more regulated health care industry, managers need to master administrative skills that apply epidemiological concepts and models to provide the solutions the market demands.

As health care managers and executives look for solutions in the challenging environment of cost containment and technological innovation, managerial geoepidemiology emerges as the logical dynamic approach to be the cornerstone of public health policy, to provide guidance and direction to the health care industry. The integration of geographic information systems as standardized, generic, friendly tools for data collection represents a potential solution to actual dislocated health care systems environments.

—Raúl F. Montalvo

See also Common Cause Variation, Evidence-Based Medicine (EBM), Geographic Information System (GIS), Public Health, Special Cause Variation, Statistical Thinking, World Health Organization

FURTHER READING

Salgado, C. C. (2000). *Geographic information systems in health: Basic concepts.* Washington, DC: Pan American Health Organization.

EPISODES OF CARE

The concept of episodes of care emanates from efforts by payers and providers to better understand and control resource allocation and costs in the delivery of health care services. A number of approaches have been designed over the years to describe the delivery of health services, such as the use of ICD-9 and CPT-4 codes, diagnosis-related groups (DRGs), and resource-based relative value scales, but these approaches often are inadequate to account for the variation in the care of a particular patient treated by a particular physician during a defined time period for a particular disease. Health care analysts find these methods of analysis prove useful in certain applications but fail to provide information about specific "best practices" for determining the quality and cost of care for a clinical condition. Episodes of care are designed to provide a comprehensive structure within which the value of health care (that is, the cost and quality) can be examined.

For any disease, specific time periods in the course of the disease can be classified according to some criteria, for example, a known complication such as diabetic ketoacidosis; a particular period of an illness such as the febrile period of streptococcal pharyngitis; a lab value, such as a low sodium value during an episode of hyponatremic dehydration; or any of several other criteria related to the disease or treatment. For example, a managed care organization may want to define an episode of care by some financial issues rather than by clinical conditions. A hospital may want to focus on procedures as the basis for defining an episode of care. The key to effectively using the "episodes of care" concept is to involve experts in designing the measurement system used to define the episode, using a clinical framework appropriate for the clinical condition and the environment of care.

Episodes of care provide a useful way of evaluating patterns of care. For example, O'Reilly evaluated nursing practice and hospital resource allocation for the perioperative period in patients undergoing total abdominal hysterectomy (O'Reilly, 2001), in which the definition of an episode of care helped define the boundaries of care so that best practices and resource allocation could be analyzed. Another example of effectively using the episodes-of-care concept was published by Pine (2001), who risk-stratified 100,000 episodes of care for nonsurgical coronary revascularization to evaluate quality and cost. The information gleaned from that study can help payers determine the value of specific procedures performed by providers. Evaluation of episodes of care can then be analyzed among providers to determine those who produce the greatest value in terms of quality and cost.

Episodes of care have been evaluated in a number of ways. For example, an inpatient hospital stay may be the defined episode of care, and the patient record may be the source of quality data, whereas the administrative data may be contained in the bill generated by the hospital at the time of patient discharge. These episodes may be grouped by procedure or diagnosis code, or by particular resource use patterns, or some other parameter of interest. However, the creation of an episode of care starts with the first service or patient encounter and ends when the patient's clinical condition has resolved or transition to another care environment has occurred. For example, systems of analysis that use administrative (health care claims) data, these starting and ending points may be easily identified by dates or places of service codes. Another method of analysis that has been created uses a model termed Episode Treatment Groups™ or ETGs, developed by Symmetry Health Data Systems Inc. in Arizona (www.symmetry-health.com). ETGs have been formulated to be similar to DRGs, in that

each ETG belongs to a major practice category (MPC), just as each DRG belongs to a single major diagnostic category (MDC) defined by body system. Each MPC represents a body system and/or a particular physician specialty, such as endocrinology or urology or infectious diseases. ETGs have some unique characteristics that differentiate them from DRGs:

- *ETGs are adjusted for case mix,* such as age, complicating conditions, comorbidities, and surgical procedures.
- *ETGs are clinically homogeneous* regarding clinical condition and treatment requirements.
- *Episodes incorporate inpatient and outpatient care,* as well as pharmaceutical services and medications. Software using this methodology captures clinical and administrative information until the episode ends, signified by a period in which no treatment is rendered or the clinical condition is identified as resolved.
- *ETGs can measure concurrent and recurrent episodes,* by coding for specific clinical conditions, even if they occur simultaneously. Recurrences can be tracked using software systems that identify new episodes of the same ETG, providing information about the progression and management of chronic diseases.
- *As patients improve or deteriorate, ETGs may change to reflect changes in the underlying condition.* Thus a patient's required level of care should accurately be reflected by the ETG classification.

To date, 574 ETGs have been defined. An overview of ETGs can be found at www.symmetry-health.com/ETGTut_Desc1.htm.

This framework provides another method of analyzing cost and quality of care, and in many circumstances can provide more information about patterns of care when compared to traditional approaches using diagnosis or procedure codes, or even DRGs. As health care continues to be scrutinized for quality, this approach will prove useful to analysts and planners for continually improving the system.

—David L. Gossage

See also Patterns of Care

FURTHER READING

Emery, D. (1999). *Global fees for episodes of care: New approaches to the purchasing of healthcare.* New York: McGraw-Hill.

Lighter, D., & Fair, D. (2000). *Principles and methods of quality management in health care.* Gaithersburg, MD: Aspen.

O'Reilly, D. (2001, September). An analysis of perioperative care. *British Journal of Perioperative Nursing, 11*(9), 402–511).

Pine, M. (2001, Summer). Episodes in action: Linking the cost and quality of nonsurgical coronary revascularization. *Managed Care Quality, 9*(3), 25–33.

EQUAL EMPLOYMENT OPPORTUNITY COMMISSION (EEOC)

The EEOC is charged with interpreting and enforcing federal equal employment opportunity laws, the dominant ones being Title VII of the Civil Rights Act of 1964, the Equal Pay Act of 1963, the Age Discrimination in Employment Act of 1967, the Americans with Disabilities Act, and the Civil Rights Act of 1991. The EEOC also has responsibility for coordinating all federal equal employment opportunity policies and regulations, offering outreach and educational programs, and processing employment discrimination complaints. Any person who believes he or she has been discriminated against in an employment setting may file a complaint with the EEOC; on an annual basis, approximately 75,000 complaints are submitted to the commission. When a complaint is received, the EEOC investigates the charge and establishes if there is reasonable cause to believe discrimination occurred. If reasonable cause is found, the commission strongly encourages a negotiated voluntary resolution between the employee and employer. Remedies may include hiring, reinstatement, back pay, promotion, or reasonable accommodation. If a satisfactory outcome cannot be reached, the commission may choose to file a federal lawsuit on behalf of the plaintiff or issue a "right-to-sue notice" to the plaintiff, which allows the plaintiff to begin a court action without the commission's involvement.

—E. Kate Atchley

See also Age Discrimination in Employment, Americans with Disabilities Act (ADA) of 1990, Civil Rights Acts of 1964 and 1991, Equal Pay Act, Title VII of the Civil Rights Act of 1964

FURTHER READING

Guttman, A. (2000). *EEO law and personnel practices.* Thousand Oaks, CA: Sage.
www.eeoc.gov

EQUAL PAY ACT

The Equal Pay Act of 1963 requires organizations to provide equal pay for equal work, regardless of the gender of the employee. *Equal work* is defined as that which requires equal skill, effort, responsibility, and working conditions. *Skill* pertains to experience, ability, education, and training required to perform the job. *Effort* refers to both physical and mental exertion required. *Responsibility* is measured by the degree of accountability or decision making authority inherent in the job. Finally, *working conditions* are the physical surroundings and hazards present when the job is performed.

In essence, the Equal Pay Act requires compensation for a particular job to be based on job content rather than on the sex of the person. Employers may not assign different job titles to men and women who accomplish the same tasks and then use these labels to justify pay differentials on the basis of gender. In other words, the use of two job titles for the same job, such as "office assistant" for a male and "receptionist" for a female, is illegal when used as justification for paying less for one job title than for another.

As with most federal employment laws, some exceptions to the Equal Pay Act exist. Organizations may pay workers on the basis of a seniority system, differences in the quality of performance, or differences in productivity, even though these practices may create average salary differentials between men and women. For example, a hospital's average wage for men holding the job of lab technician may be higher than that of women simply because the women in the lab technician position have been more recently hired. Because this pay differential is based on a seniority system, the organization is not in violation of the Equal Pay Act.

The Equal Pay Act is administered by the Equal Employment Opportunity Commission (EEOC). Claims under the Equal Pay Act, however, have historically accounted for less than 2% of EEOC complaints in a given year.

Related to the concept of equal pay is that of comparable worth. Although the constraints contained within the Equal Pay Act consider subject to equal pay only those jobs that are substantially *equal,* proponents of comparable worth argue that jobs that are *comparable* in skill, effort, and responsibility should be paid equally. The notion behind comparable worth is that women and men fill roles in society that are somewhat different, albeit equally important. To overcome wage differentials between women and men that are caused by disparate participation in societal roles, proponents argue that jobs should be compensated on the basis of their value to society. Teachers are a prime example of such an occupation, because teaching is a field that attracts many women but is widely believed to be undercompensated. Although some states have passed comparable worth laws for state employees, the federal legislature has not passed any of the many bills that have been introduced that embrace comparable worth. Furthermore, federal courts have been generally unsympathetic to comparable worth claims.

—Jennifer R. D. Burgess

See also Equal Employment Opportunity Commission (EEOC)

FURTHER READING

Fisher, C. D., Schoenfeldt, L. F., & Shaw, J. B. (1999). *Human resource management* (4th ed.). Boston: Houghton Mifflin.

Patten, T. H. (1988). *Fair pay*. San Francisco: Jossey-Bass.

www.eeoc.gov

EQUITY

As an accounting and financial term, *equity* is defined by the Financial Accounting Standards Board in Statement of Financial Accounting Concepts No. 6, *Elements of Financial Statements*. In its most basic conceptual form, equity represents the net assets of an organization; that is, the residual interest in the assets of the organization less its liabilities. The fundamental difference between a liability and equity lies in the nature of the claim against assets. Generally, liabilities have a definitive claim, whereas the equity claim is residual in nature.

Although conceptually the same across organizations, equity takes on different names based on the nature of the organization. In most business entities that are organized as taxable, for-profit entities with ownership based on shares of common stock, equity is broadly defined as stockholders' equity. There are several components to shareholders' equity, as discussed further. In the language of not-for-profit organizations, which do not have ownership interest as such represented by shares of stock, equity is known as *net assets*. These are categorized into several classes depending on the nature of any donor restrictions. Although the components of net assets of not-for-profit organizations are not discussed here, the basic concept of assets less liabilities remains the same.

Stockholders' equity consists of several distinct components, each with its own origin and its own purpose and nature. The stockholders' equity section of an organization's balance sheet must clearly disclose these components. In complex equity situations, such as where there are several classes of ownership interests, the rights and preferences of the different classes of ownership interest must also be disclosed.

The fundamental element of stockholders' equity for an organization is its capital stock. Most commonly, the ownership of an organization consists of common stock. Such stock may have a par or stated value, which historically has been related to the legal capital that a state requires to be available. Certain common stock in some jurisdictions may be no-par and, therefore, there is no distinction between a par value and amounts that may be paid in to the corporation in excess of par. Any amounts that are paid in excess of par constitute additional paid-in capital, which may be returned to stockholders in the form of a distribution. As indicated, there could be several classes of common stock in more complex corporations, and the rights and preferences of each may differ. However, one class of common stock owner has first claim to the assets and, therefore, the greatest ownership risk.

Preferred stock owners represent a class of ownership who have certain rights and preferences, with regards to claims on earnings or on assets, that are above those of common stockholders. These preferences may include first rights to earnings in the form of a stated dividend and preferential rights to assets in the event of a liquidation. Dividends may be cumulative and accumulate in arrears, or they may be noncumulative. The preferred shares may also have additional earnings participation features or may be convertible to common stock as specified in the preferred stock agreements.

Another element of stockholders' equity, in this case a reduction of such equity, is treasury stock. Corporations may buy back their own stock with the intent of either eventual cancelation, subject to any legal capital requirements, or of reissuance. In any event, this stock generally does not represent an asset of the corporation; rather, it is reported as a deduction in the stockholders' equity section of the balance sheet. Although there are several methods of accounting for treasury stock, which vary in their effect on the components of stockholders' equity, the fundamental nature of treasury stock does not change.

A major component of stockholders' equity is the accumulated earnings, or losses, which are retained in the corporation. Generally speaking, these retained earnings are available for future use by the corporation or for dividend distribution to stockholders.

Just as equity is viewed as ownership interests from the perspective of the corporation, the term *equity* has specific meaning from the perspective of the owner, or investor. Equity investments are those with which the owner may exercise a degree of influence over the investee. The degree of that influence dictates the accounting treatment for those investments in the financial statements of the investor. Equity investments are those for which the investor expects some degree of return, either in the form of dividends, or capital appreciation, or both. Clearly, they are by nature riskier than debt investments.

Equity securities are generally carried at a fair market value in the financial statements of the investor. Although the rules vary in the approach and financial statement presentation and disclosure, the fair value concept for equity investments applies to both for-profit and not-for-profit investors. Gains or losses from adjustments to fair value are considered unrealized but are still recognized in the financial statements. Realized gains and losses are recognized when the investment is sold.

However, in situations where the investor is deemed to exercise a significant influence over the investee, investments are reported under the equity method of accounting in the financial statements. This method requires the investor to recognize its underlying share of an investee's income or loss or other changes in the investor's financial statements. Significant influence for the equity method is generally deemed to be at least a 20% interest.

The fundamental concept of equity is not unique to any particular industry or type of organization. Therefore, health care organizations recognize equity, or net assets in the case of not-for-profit organizations, and equity interest in their financial statements, consistent with organizations in other industries.

—Edward Pershing

EQUITY CAPITAL

See Dividends, Equity, Return on Owner's Equity

ETHICAL CODE

See Code of Ethics

ETHICAL DRUGS

See Drug Coverage

ETHICAL ISSUES FACED BY MANAGERS

Ethical issues are present even in routine daily decisions of a manager. Managing involves ethics at every level from small personal decisions to large public policies. It may be appropriate to regard most managerial decisions as being permeated by ethics, rather than as being tangential issues. Because managers have power that affects people's lives, they have the potential for acting in good or evil ways. Managers who make incorrect decisions to promote their own interests are unethical. In addition, any situation that is less favorable than it could have been is ethically compromised. Managers should attempt to distribute resources in a fair manner; however, a fair distribution is not always an equal distribution. Managers design and enforce organizational rules. Their ethical responsibility is to produce a system of shared values and expectations that is realistic and fair. Managerial decisions may be ethical because they may test the manager's personal values. These types of conflicts involve discrepancies between personal and organizational values. Managers act as the link between organizational success and the lives of the people they manage.

Ethical behavior may be encouraged by designing organizations with optimal distribution of power and minimizing pressures that might encourage unethical behavior. Managers should attempt to create a corporate culture of openness and cooperation. Efforts should be made to understand the factors in organizations that enhance or distort human values and behavior.

Here are four examples of ethical issues for managers:

External Effects

- Unsafe consumer products or services
- Arrogance in dealing with foreign people—those different from ourselves

Internal Conflicts

- Negligence in guaranteeing the health and safety of employees
- Foot-dragging among members with regard to affirmative action
- Foot-dragging among members regarding equitable promotions

Conflicts

- Decision to shut down a profitable unit, leaving local individuals and managers to handle the fallout
- Rushed schedules that jeopardize health and safety regulations

Stakeholder Value Conflicts (Examples)

- Issues related to placement of an MRI unit
- Possible safety hazards, costs, resource depletion
- Return on investment and long-term health of the company

Health Care Organizational Issues

Obvious organizational issues that present opportunities for physician leaders to lead with ethics include the following:

- Employee rights: due process, privacy
- Sexual harassment
- Whistle-blowing
- Misuse of power
- Discouraging intrinsic motivation
- Selection and placement
- Corporate culture
- Corporate social responsibility
- Agreed-on incentive system versus actual system
- Terminations
- Organizational structure, design, and politics
- Performance appraisals
- Drug testing and physical exams for employees
- Diversity and discrimination
- Planning, policy, and control issues
- Government relations
- Safety and health issues
- Technical development
- Foreign payments
- Environmental protection
- Product safety and reliability
- Quality management
- Purchasing (gifts, bribes)
- Automation and robotics
- Confidentiality
- Inappropriate requests
- Intellectual property
- Truth in claims
- Organizational versus individual needs
- Customer and user participation
- Conflicts of interest
- Personal biases
- Individual and population differences
- Appropriate interventions
- Intervention consequences
- Pricing fairly

—Peter J. Dean

ETHICS COMMITTEE

See Ethical Issues Faced by Managers, Ethics Officer

ETHICS OFFICER

The standards for ethical practice to be upheld by professional ethicists include the following:

Integrity. Professional ethicists are honest and play fair while acting in good faith to others in all dealings for the company. They seek to know their own preferred belief systems, values, needs, and limitations, to know how their systems, values, needs, and limitations might differ from those of others, and to be conscious of the potential effect of these differences on their work. They refrain from making false, misleading, or deceptive statements, and they provide accurate information. They avoid conflict-of-interest relationships as well as expensive gift giving, bribery, nepotism, and abuse of government relationships. They clarify to all parties the exact nature of their performance and function. Professional ethicists act in the expectation that each exchange in business is in effect one of many more to come. They act with the intent of a long-term business relationship.

Productivity. Professional ethicists are expected to be knowledgeable about all aspects of their profession and to perform their work in an exemplary fashion. They exercise careful judgment to protect those for whom they are responsible. They use appropriate information, resources, incentives, research, and applications to secure the best service for each stakeholder. They are aware of cultural, individual, and role differences involving age, sex and gender, race, ethnicity, national origin, religion, sexual orientation, disability, language, and socioeconomic status. They work continuously to eliminate the effect on work in the company of biases based on the preceding differences. They do not condone or participate in unfair discriminatory practices of any kind. They strive to advance individual and organizational learning, performance, and development while mitigating the causes preventing stakeholder welfare. They comply with laws and social policies that serve the interests of stakeholders, the public, society, and the environment. Moreover, they should possess skills in the following:

- Establishing and managing client relationships
- Conducting analyses
- Identifying root causes of conflicts
- Building partnership within the firm
- Negotiating
- Conflict resolution
- Handling technical issues
- Building consensus and commitment
- Project management
- Speaking
- Facilitating the leadership, implementation, and management of change

Responsibility. Professional ethicists uphold the law and these ethical standards and prevent harm to any stakeholder. They consult with colleagues and clients regarding the ethical compliance of their professional duties. They engage in proper business conduct to prevent unethical dilemmas. They share credit for work accomplishments when appropriate and are worthy of trust as a professional ethicists. They serve the company by honoring all contracts, promises, and any commitment agreed on. Moreover, they are aware of their professional responsibility to the community in which they work and live, to the society to which they belong, and to a livable planet. They understand there is a necessary confluence of a healthy ecosystem, stable governments, a healthy economy, and healthy organizations. Professional ethicists have an obvious responsibility not to bring harm to another individual, department, division, company, community, or any other element in society.

Respectfulness in Relationships. Professional ethicists recognize, respect, and are concerned about the intrinsic worth of individuals, their interactions with each other, as well as their rights to privacy, confidentiality, and self-directedness within the context of fundamental dignity, financial information, and worth of all people. They advocate that the restricting of the rights of individuals by managers at work should be limited and used only with clear business justifications. They are alert to the fact that legal obligations manifested as compliance policies and procedures may lead to inconsistency and conflict with the exercise of the rights of individuals. When conflict does occur among stakeholders' obligations, concerns, and rights, they attempt to resolve these conflicts in a responsible and ethical manner, avoiding or minimizing harm to others. They are sensitive to power differences among all stakeholders and do not mislead or exploit other people before, during, or after professional work exchanges. Respectfulness in relationships creates confidence among stakeholders.

Physician leaders are uniquely positioned to influence ethical awareness in the workplace. Understanding the basic underpinnings of ethical theory and empirical research in ethics gives physician leaders a grounding in the ethical implications of their decisions.

Here are some things a physician leader should *not* do:

- Violate professional, academic, or business ethics by being less than honest in billing or submitting low proposal bids and higher final bills.
- Promise that solutions will work when the opposite may be true.
- Make false return-on-investment (ROI) claims.
- Use client information for personal gain.
- Falsify data.
- Compromise the technology for any personal or political gain by providing interventions that are acceptable to the client but incorrect for the context.
- Take credit for the work of another.

- Make false claims about any professional's behaviors or potential accomplishments.

—Peter J. Dean

FURTHER READING

Dean, P. J. (1992). Making codes of ethics "real." *Journal of Business Ethics, 11*(4), 285–291.

Dean, P. J. (1993). A selected review of the underpinnings of ethics for human performance technology professionals, Parts 1 and 2. *Performance Improvement Quarterly, 6*(4), 3–49.

Dean, P. J. (1994, November–December). Some basics about ethics. *Performance and Instruction, 33,* 42–45.

EVIDENCE-BASED MEDICINE (EBM)

WHAT IT IS

Evidence-based medicine (EBM) is a component of the scientific arm of the practice of medicine. It is an active process in which health care providers conscientiously, explicitly, and judiciously seek out, interpret, and use the current best evidence from clinical care research to determine the management of individual patients. EBM is a tool that functions to bridge the gap between medical research and the practice of medicine. By using diagnostic tests and therapeutic interventions that are accurate, safe, and as efficacious as possible, EBM promotes optimal health care solutions for individual patients.

The practice of EBM necessitates the integration of clinical expertise and knowledge of patient values and preferences in the decision-making process. To employ one without the others may result in unbalanced and poor medical decisions. Without current best medical evidence, a provider runs the risk of practicing antiquated medicine to the detriment of his or her patients. Without clinical expertise a provider may become obsessed with evidence that may be inapplicable or inappropriate for an individual patient. Evidence per se does not make clinical decisions; it only reveals consequences of alternative actions. Without attention to patient values and preferences, adherence to a given medical regimen is likely to be compromised.

The process of EBM begins and ends with the patient. The first step usually involves a patient encounter that generates a focused clinical question. A well-constructed clinical question contains three elements: (a) a patient or problem, (b) an intervention and if necessary a comparison intervention, and (c) expected outcomes. Once the clinical question is formulated, current medical databases are searched and filtered to find the best available evidence. This evidence is then critiqued for its validity and utility. To aid practitioners in this process of information mastery, two instruments have been developed. One is called POEM, which stands for "patient-oriented evidence that matters." The other is called CAT, meaning "critically appraised topic." These two instruments assess the validity or correctness of the medical information as well as its usefulness in a clinical setting. Next, the results of the search are discussed with the patient and a treatment plan is initiated. The final step in the process is to evaluate the performance or outcome of the patient.

WHAT IT IS NOT

EBM is not "cookbook" medicine. Because it begins with the patient, it requires a bottom-up approach to the medical decision process. This distinction separates it from "top-down" recipes to medical care that apply general medical information about a given disease or disorder to a broad population. EBM encourages the blending of scientific data with clinical expertise and patient values and preferences when arriving at a clinical decision.

Contrary to some beliefs, EBM is not "old hat." Although in the past clinicians have used the medical literature to guide their decision making, EBM now processes and filters the literature so that decisions are based on systematically reviewed "strong" evidence.

Randomized, controlled, double-blind clinical trials serve as the "gold standard" in addressing many clinical questions. However, critics of EBM argue that such studies may not be available for every clinical question. They worry this lack of information might paralyze the medical decision process. In those cases, EBM considers data from the next best level of evidence. Conceding a lower level of certainty, EBM may still make meaningful recommendations.

Some critics of EBM fear that purchasers and managers of health care will use this new decision-making process as a cost-cutting tool. In its purest form, EBM leads health care providers to identify and apply the most efficacious interventions to maximize quality and quantity of life for individual patients. This model may actually raise the cost of care rather than lower it. In contrast, evidence-based health care (EBH), an extension of EBM, focuses on evidence-based medicine, available resources, and values. Participants in EBH include all health care professionals as well as purchasing and management personnel. Because of the business influence of EBH, it is conceivable that different medical solutions could be obtained when comparing EBM with EBH.

Despite its critics, EBM is a paradigm in medical decision making that is gaining worldwide acceptance in medical communities. A daunting challenge for many providers with regard to EBM is the continual demands of searching the literature for the best evidence. Millions of published reports, journal articles, correspondence, and studies are available to providers, making it hard for them "to see the forest for the trees." The use of computerized, Internet-based searches may simplify this task. Large databases such as PUBMED provide access to the primary literature. Secondary sources that present assessments of original studies include the American College of Physicians Journal Club, POEMS, and *Clinical Evidence;* the last is published by the British Medical Journal. The Cochrane Library provides access to evidence-based systematic reviews that summarize the results from a number of studies on select medical subjects.

—David L. Gossage

FURTHER READING

Greenhalgh, T. (1997). How to read a paper: The Medline database. *British Medical Journal, 318,* 180–183.

Sackett, D. L., Rosenberg, W. M. C., Gray, J. A. M., Haynes, R. B., & Richardson, W. S. (1996). Evidence-based medicine: What it is and what it isn't. *British Medical Journal, 312,* 71–72.

Sackett, D. L., Straus, S. E., Richardson, W. S., Rosenberg, W., & Haynes, R. B. (Eds.). (2000). *Evidence-based medicine: How to practice and teach EBM.* New York: Churchill-Livingstone.

Smith, R. (1996). What clinical information do doctors need? *British Medical Journal, 313,* 1062–1068.

EXCESS CAPACITY

Excess capacity in health care is when available resources exceed patient demand for them. Most often this term refers to more beds in health care facilities than needed to care for the patients seeking care. It may also refer to having more health care providers than required to care for patients seeking care, more operating rooms, procedure times, or testing than required to perform the necessary operations, procedures, or tests.

Hospital and health care facilities track their admissions/discharges and their patient days to evaluate the supply and demand for their services. In general, as technology, medical advances, and economic pressures drove down the demand for services, excess capacity was found in existing facilities. Beds, operating rooms, and sometimes whole facilities closed. Running counter to this trend is the increasing demand of an aging population for health care. Some medical specialty boards that had reduced training positions faced with excess capacity predictions, are now increasing positions to address shortages that have arisen.

—Kathleen Ferrara

EXCESS LIABILITY COVERAGE

Excess liability coverage provides additional limits above the primary medical malpractice insurance. It expands the limits of liability in case of a high-severity loss. (The majority of policies provide liability limits of at least $1 million per claim and $3 million in the aggregate per policy period.) Excess coverage usually is purchased at the same time and covers the same policy term as the primary policy. Unless excess insurance is purchased, a physician will be personally liable for all amounts paid in settlement or following an adverse verdict in excess of the stated policy limits. Gaps in coverage should be avoided by ensuring that all liability policies have the same policy-effective dates.

An excess insurance policy may be written by a different insurance carrier. Excess coverage should be carefully selected, because it entails a new policy of insurance that includes its own set of limitations, exclusions, and endorsements, some of which may affect the handling of a particular claim that threatens to tap into the excess coverage. For example, excess insurers typically prefer that claims are settled within the limits of the underlying primary liability policy. The excess insurance policy may contain provisions to facilitate such settlement. Likewise, in some high-risk cases the primary policy may advance the entire policy limit, leaving the excess carrier to defend the remainder of the claim. This may involve litigation over how much the plaintiff should recover in excess of the amounts already paid as a settlement.

FURTHER READING

Harpster, L. M., & Veach, M. S. (Eds.). (1990). *Risk management handbook for health care facilities.* American Society for Healthcare Risk Management.

EXCESS OF REVENUES OVER EXPENSES

See Operating Cash Flow, Profit

EXCLUSION CRITERIA

Exclusion criteria are factors from the subjects' medical history, physical examination, or laboratory tests that are used to eliminate, from a clinical trial, certain people within the target populations. The exclusions may be made for safety reasons or because researchers suspect the intervention will not be effective. For example, minors, the elderly, pregnant women, terminally ill patients, and those unable to understand the clinical trial or give informed consent are commonly excluded from trials, especially early in clinical development of a new intervention.

The exclusion criteria should be as few as possible, to improve the external validity of a clinical trial. It is not uncommon for investigators, who see a broad spectrum of patients who may have a legitimate medical need for a drug, to want to minimize exclusion criteria, whereas a pharmaceutical drug sponsor may want many exclusion criteria, to try to get a "homogeneous" study patient population.

—Steven C. Quay

EXCLUSIVE DISTRIBUTION

Exclusive distribution is one of three levels of distribution intensity that companies may choose from as they develop their marketing channels. Intensive and selective distribution are the other two levels of intensity. Manufacturers must decide the extent to which the consumer has access to their products. In other words, each manufacturer must determine the extent of market coverage it considers adequate. This coverage decision is affected by a number of factors, including how much control over the channel's members the manufacturer wants, the type of product being distributed, and the target markets (consumer segments) being pursued.

For example, a product such as milk is purchased frequently by consumers, in part because it is perishable. Dairy producers thus want to have their markets thoroughly covered, so these products are available in grocery stores, convenience stores, and many other retail outlets. This is intensive distribution. Other products are bought less frequently, involve more risks (financial, psychological, social, and physical), and require that consumers spend more time in the decision-making process.

Exclusive distribution is used for products that are very expensive, have a high degree of brand loyalty, and are important enough for consumers to spend extensive time searching for them. There's also more risk involved in these purchases. There is financial risk, because consumers are paying a high price for the product and want assurances that the quality and value they receive from the product are worth the cost. Psychological and social risks may be involved, because consumers may worry about what their friends and family members may say or think about their purchases. In the case of health care products, there is a strong chance for physical risk to be involved as well. Consumers dealing with cancer or heart disease are concerned about the quality of treatment received for the amount of money being spent; that is, "Will the treatment cure the disease and prolong my life in a meaningful way?"

A medical equipment manufacturer that allows only one hospital in a broad geographic region to bring in its specialized piece of equipment to treat a special disease, while excluding other hospitals in the region from offering the treatment with the specialized equipment, is practicing exclusive distribution. Consumers must be willing to fly or drive hours to the one hospital's location for their specialized health care treatment needs.

—Jeffrey W. Totten

See also Intensive Distribution, Selective Distribution

FURTHER READING

Boone, L. E., & Kurtz, D. L. (2002). Distribution channels and logistics management. In L. E. Boone & D. L. Kurtz, *Contemporary marketing 2002* (Chapter 13). Cincinnati, OH: Thompson Learning.

Kotler, P., & Armstrong, G. (2001). Distribution channels and logistics management. In P. Kotler & G. Armstrong, *Principles of marketing* (9th ed., Chapter 12). Upper Saddle River, NJ: Prentice Hall.

EXCLUSIVE PROVIDER ORGANIZATION (EPO)

An exclusive provider organization (EPO) is a health care plan that reimburses its members or subscribing patients only when a provider participating in its designated network provides service. If patients choose to see an out-of-network provider, no benefits will be paid. An EPO has similarities to a health maintenance organization (HMO) and a preferred provider organization (PPO). With an EPO, an individual chooses a primary care physician through the network and that physician is responsible for coordinating all care received by that patient. Similar to a PPO, the EPO provider agrees to be compensated as a fee-for-service provider. Members of an EPO who go out of network for care are not reimbursed. The PPO rules for out-of-network care are less stringent than the EPO rule. In HMOs individuals who work for the HMO provide all care. Only on the recommendation of the HMO may a patient receive HMO-paid service by a provider not on the panel or in the network of the HMO.

—Thomas Biancaniello

EXECUTIVE COMPENSATION

In the aftermath of huge corporate scandals at Enron, Global Crossing, WorldCom, Adelphia, and others, there is new pressure for corporate accountability and calls for review of executive compensation. Many are concerned about how a CEO can make tens of millions of dollars per year and yet also take a company into bankruptcy. Larry Ellison of Oracle Corporation took home $706 million in 2001 when he exercised stock options as Oracle's stock price began to fall. It appears to the average stockholder that CEO pay is not based on company performance but rises continuously at a rate greater than inflation. In 2001, CEOs experienced their first double-digit decline in pay in seven years (16%). Even in these past three years of economic downturn, many CEOs experienced substantial increases in total compensation. These events have led *Business Week* to call for a change in how executive pay is calculated. To understand this situation better, let's explore three theories of executive compensation.

The first theory is social comparison, which basically argues that executive compensation should be set in relationship to other salaries. In this approach to executive compensation, arriving at a relevant comparison group is a major challenge. Some argue that the appropriate peer group is other CEOs of similar organizations. These comparisons are market driven, and in the case of hospitals comparisons to CEO salaries in other hospitals would control for size and location of the hospital. Another approach is to compare the CEO salary with that of the lowest-paid employee. Ben and Jerry's Ice Cream became the most famous example of this methodology by setting the CEO salary at seven times the salary of the lowest-paid employee. This comparison demonstrates how the CEO salary has risen much faster than ordinary wages. In 1980 the average CEO was paid a salary that was 42 times the wages of ordinary workers. By 1990 that factor more than doubled, rising to 85 (Milkovich & Newman, 1996). However, because employee salaries vary widely among industries, it is not advisable to establish a uniform rate for all CEOs. Review of this type of data is relevant for compensation committees that set the salaries of CEOs. Organizations that have a pay structure where the CEO makes 85 to 100 times that of the lowest-paid employee run the risk of disgruntled, unproductive employees. Within the health care field, the social comparison theory has added the dimension of comparing salaries to potential services rendered. In California, the State Nurses Association has called on Tenent Healthcare to reallocate profits and executive wealth to help resolve the public health care crises in Los Angeles.

A second theoretical perspective on executive salary is economic. Here the basic question is, How well is the company performing? The idea is to tie CEO compensation to corporate success. This is easier said than done: Even in the for-profit sector of health care, the economic model does not appear to be a major factor in an economic downturn. In 1999, the compensation of CEOs of 17 publicly traded HMOs rose by 14% while the company's stock declined by an average of 15%. Traditionally, corporate success has been measured by stock market prices, but this perspective emphasizes short-term gains. Although defining a well-run (successful) organization is increasingly complicated, it is not impossible. Including indicators of customer satisfaction and loyalty, employee retention rates, and market share into a CEO's performance scorecard would help develop a more balanced assessment of the organization. The pay then would depend on whether or not the organization met pre-established goals. One problem in this methodology is that the CEO may be able to manipulate the data to demonstrate success in the short run, at the expense of long-term success. This model of executive pay has been used most frequently in establishing the bonus portion of executive compensation.

Many corporations include stock options, or phantom stock options, to motivate a CEO to act in the interests of stockholders. The theory is that if a CEO is invested in the company, he or she will act in its best interests. However, there are two problems with this logic. First, the CEO may sell stock whenever he or she desires, and we have seen numerous examples where executives have unloaded stock just as the stock price took a precipitous fall (for example, Oracle, Enron, Cisco, Tyco, and IBM). A second problem with acquiring stock options is that there is no way an executive can lose money; it is comparable to "Heads, I win/ Tails, we flip again." One solution would be to require executives to buy and hold the stock during their tenure and for some period of time after they leave the organization. Another problem is that in the boom economy, stock options became the primary source of income for the top management in an organization. Options now account for 80% of the executives compensation package. The other two components of executive compensation (salary and bonuses) have become an afterthought. Rebalancing the components of executive pay may therefore be another solution.

The third theory is agency theory, which suggests that CEOs make decisions in their own self-interest and for their own self-protection. Therefore, they ensure their own high compensation by bringing in a compensation consultant to review executive salaries. The consultant recommends a salary increase under one of three scenarios: Executives are underpaid relative to market, executives are in a successful company and should be paid above market, or the company is struggling and should provide better salaries to retain its current executives. An organization's governing board must carefully examine the role of executives in setting their own compensation. To convince the public they are acting responsibly, boards and their executive compensation committees must accept closer public scrutiny of their decisions.

Executive compensation appears to be spiraling out of control. However, the situation is not hopeless. Organizational changes that make board decisions more public, that tie executive salaries to organization outcomes, and that examine executive salaries in relationship to other employees in the organization will result in a more effective compensation system for top executives. Recent developments indicate that large health care organizations are responding to concerns expressed by both employee groups and shareholder groups. In Seattle, when the Group Health Cooperative was forced to cut its budget by $30 million, the CEO took a voluntary 20% pay cut and eight other executives took a 10% pay cut. Organizations that use the same model for establishing all employee pay seem to be quite successful. Companies that have cut back executive pay when the organization is losing its market share or laying off employees seem to have more credibility with their own employees, shareholders, and customers.

—Alan P. Chesney

FURTHER READING

Dressler, G. (1999). *Human resource management* (8th ed.). Upper Saddle River, NJ: Prentice Hall.

Lavelle, L. (2002, April 15). Executive pay. *Business Week.*

Milkovich, G., & Newman, J. (1996). *Compensation* (5th ed.). Chicago: Irwin.

EXECUTIVE ORDER 11246 ON AFFIRMATIVE ACTION

Executive Order 11246 (or EO 11246) was issued by President Johnson in 1965; it is the end product of a series of prior executive orders written by presidents Roosevelt, Truman, Eisenhower, and Kennedy. Amendments were subsequently added by Johnson himself and by Nixon and Carter. In its current form, EO 11246 applies to (a) federal agencies, (b) procurement contractors, and (c) construction contractors. Participation for federal agencies is mandatory and is administered by the Equal Employment Opportunity Commission (EEOC). Participation for outside contractors is termed "voluntary," but contracts for $10,000 or more are subject to rules written by the Office of Federal Contract Compliance Programs (OFCCP) of the (U.S. Department of Labor (DOL), under penalty of forfeiture of the right to contract with the federal government. The following discussion focuses on the contractors.

Unlike nondiscrimination laws such as Title VII, which protect minorities and nonminorities as well as men and women, EO 11246 applies only to minorities (blacks, Hispanics, Native Americans, and Pacific Islanders) and to women. The key requirement is the affirmative action plan (AAP) to correct underutilization, defined as a statistical disparity between percentages of minorities and women in the contractor's workforce as compared to percentages of qualified and available minorities and women in the labor pool. The OFFCP has broader powers to administer EO 11246, as compared, for example, to the EEOC's role regarding Title VII of the Civil Rights Act of 1964 and other similar statutes. For example, in Title VII, the employer must lose in federal court before submitting to remedies; in EO 11246, the OFCCP may impose remedies such as suspension and/or cancelation of the right to contract, and even affected class rulings (payments to individual victims). To challenge such rulings, the contractor must first appeal (and lose) to the U.S. Secretary of Labor and then submit to the remedies before receiving a hearing in federal court. Consequently, there have been very few court challenges to OFCCP rulings; see, for example, *United States v. Duquesne Light Co.* (1976) and *St. Regis Paper v. Marshall* (1979).

Under most conditions, the OFCCP rules dictate that contractors conduct the availability analysis and write written AAPs with goals and timetables to correct underutilization (or decrease disparities between workforce versus labor pool percentages). The OFCCP also has "imposed plans" for contracts of $1 million or more, so-called hometown plans, written by various contractors in anticipation of OFCCP requirements (see, for example, the "Boston Plan" in *Contractors Association of Eastern Pennsylvania v. Secretary of Labor* (1971), and the so-called standard clause, for preapproval on a per contract basis by any contractor. Regardless of how the AAP is formed, the OFCCP has a monitoring system that includes compliance reviews. If the OFCCP finds noncompliance, it may then order the remedies just cited.

There are two critical misconceptions about EO 11246. First, it is not the only form of affirmative action (AA). Second, EO 11246 itself does not require what nondiscrimination laws such as Title VII and the constitutional amendments prohibit.

Regarding the first misconception, EO 11246 is one of four sources of AA. The other three include (a) court-ordered affirmative action as a remedy for committing egregious discriminatory acts such as a pattern or practice of discrimination (*see United States v. Paradise,* 1987); (b) court-approved consent decrees in lieu of (or to head off) litigation in pattern-or-practice cases (see *Local 93 v. Cleveland,* 1986); and (c) government set-aside programs for MBEs or minority business enterprises (*see City of Richmond v. Croson,* 1989) and for DBEs or disadvantaged business enterprises (see *Adarand v. Pena,* 1995). Challenges to any form of AA are made in so-called reverse

discrimination claims under Title VII and/or constitutional amendments. Included among these are challenges to programs conducted under EO 11246 itself (see *Regents v. Bakke,* 1979, *United Steelworkers v. Weber,* 1979, and *Johnson v. Transportation,* 1987). However, critically, there is no mechanism for alleged victims to challenge an employer's failure to abide by EO 11246; this power is reserved exclusively for the OFCCP.

Regarding the second misconception, under most normal circumstances there is a bright line between what EO 11246 requires and what the nondiscrimination laws prohibit. North of this bright line (legal under the nondiscrimination laws) are actions such as (a) targeted recruitment and outreach when there is underutilization, (b) training of otherwise unqualified applicants and employees, as long as training is offered to all who are unqualified, (c) identification and elimination of existing discrimination within the company, and (d) altering or replacing tests or other selection requirements that produce adverse impact. It is critically important to understand that no requirement with EO 11246 itself demands preference in any selection decision, including hiring, promotion, and/or discharge. Therefore, it is a mistake to believe that employers must select unqualified applicants, or even less qualified applicants based on minority status and/or gender. Indeed, selection based solely on race or gender is a likely loser in a reverse discrimination challenge. Therefore, in short, EO 11246 says recruit, train, and eliminate existing causes of discrimination, but do not use AA principles to hire, promote, or discharge.

A final point to note about affirmative action is a concept that it is evolving in two important domains. First, there is debate to change the protected classes in EO 11246 from minorities and women to socially or economically disadvantaged individuals or employers (see *Adarand v. Slater,* 2000). The notion here is that traditional definitions lead to both overinclusion (minorities and women who are not in need of AA) and underinclusion (nonminorities and men who do need AA). A second issue that has emerged in recent years is the notion of diversity as a means of improving business operations. This movement is most evident in colleges and universities, who argue that a diverse student population is necessary for a good education, and in police forces, where it argued that minority and nonminority citizens need to see minority and nonminority law enforcement officers acting in harmony, particularly when there is civil unrest.

—Arthur Gutman

FURTHER READING

Adarand v. Slater. (1999). CA10 169 F.3d 1292.

Adarand v. Pena. (1995). 115 S.Ct 2097.

City of Richmond v. Croson. (1989). 488 US 469.

Contractors Assoc. of Eastern Pa. v. Secretary of Labor. (CA3 1971).

Johnson v. Transportation Agency, Santa Clara County, Ca. (1987). 480 US 616.

Local #93, Int. Assoc. of Firefighters v. City of Cleveland. (1986).

Regents of University of California v. Bakke. (1978). 438 US 265.

St. Regis Paper Co. v. Marshall. 1979). CA10 591 F.2d 612.

United States v. Duquesne Light Co. (1976). W.D. Pa. 423 F.Supp 507.

United States v. Paradise. (1987). 480 US 149.

United Steelworkers etc. v. Weber. (1979). 443 US 193.

EXPANSION STRATEGIES

Expansion strategies seek to increase the size and scope of an organization. If expansion is selected as the best way to perform the mission and realize the vision of the organization, several alternatives are available. Expansion strategies include diversification, vertical integration, market development, product development, and penetration.

DIVERSIFICATION

Diversification strategies are selected because opportunities have been identified outside of the organization's core business that offer potential for growth. Often an organization that selects a diversification strategy is not achieving its revenue goals within its current service area or product offerings. Other organizations diversify to achieve growth in less regulated markets such as specialty hospitals, long-term care facilities, or managed care.

Diversification can be a risky alternative, because the organization is entering a relatively unfamiliar market or offering a product or service that is different from its current products or services. Organizations have found that the risk of diversification can be reduced if complementary markets and products are selected.

VERTICAL INTEGRATION

A vertical integration strategy is a decision to grow along the channel of distribution of the core operations. The growth of an organization along the channel of distribution toward its suppliers (upstream) is called *backward vertical integration*. The growth of an organization toward the consumer or patient (downstream) is called *forward vertical integration*.

A vertically integrated health care system offers a range of patient care and support services operated in a functionally unified manner. The expansion of services may be arranged around an acute care hospital and include preacute, acute, and postacute services or may be organized around specialized services related solely to long-term care,

mental health care, or some other specialized area. The purpose of vertical integration is to increase the comprehensiveness and continuity of care, while simultaneously controlling the channel of demand for health care services.

Vertical integration can reduce costs and thus enhance an organization's competitive position. Cost reductions may occur through lower supply costs and better integration of the "elements of production." With vertical integration, management can better ensure that supplies are of the appropriate quality and delivered at the right time. For instance, some hospitals have instituted technical educational programs (nursing, physical therapy) to develop their own health professionals (the major element of production in health care) because many workers are in critically short supply.

Because a decision to vertically integrate further commits an organization to a particular product or market, management must believe in the long-term viability of the product/service and market. As a result, the opportunity costs of vertical integration must be weighed against the benefits of other strategic alternatives such as diversification or product development. Examples of vertical integration are a hospital chain acquiring one of its major medical products suppliers (backward integration) or a drug manufacturer moving into drug distribution (forward integration).

Numerous extensive health networks are the result of integration strategies over the past 20 years. The major reason why hospitals join networks and systems is to help secure needed resources (financial, human, information systems, and technologies), increase capabilities (management and marketing), and gain greater bargaining power with purchasers and health plans. More recently, some "disintegration" has occurred, with health care systems divesting health plans, physician groups, or home health care companies.

MARKET DEVELOPMENT

Market development is a strategy used to enter new markets with present products or services. Specifically, market development is designed to achieve greater volume by expanding geographic service area or by targeting new market segments within the present area. Typically, market development is selected when the organization is fairly strong (often with a differentiated product), the product's demand is growing, and the prospects are good for long-term growth. A market development strategy requires strong support from the marketing, financial, information systems, and human resources functions. An example of a market development strategy would be a chain of outpatient clinics opening a new clinic in a new geographic area (present products and services in a new market).

Horizontal integration is a type of market development used to obtain growth across markets by acquiring or affiliating with direct competitors rather than using internal operational/functional strategies to take market share from competitors. Many hospitals and medical practices engaged in horizontal integration throughout the 1980s and early 1990s creating multihospital systems expecting to achieve increased access to capital, reduced duplication of services, larger economies of scale, improved productivity and operating efficiencies, improved patient access, better quality, and increased political power. However, many of these benefits did not materialize; the growth of horizontal integration strategies slowed in the late 1990s.

Another type of market development, the market-driven or focused factory strategy, is based on the fundamental principle that an organization that focuses on only one function is likely to perform better. This strategy involves providing comprehensive services across multiple markets (horizontal integration) for one specific disease such as diabetes management or one surgery such as heart surgery.

Focused factories become so effective (high quality, convenience, and so on) and efficient (less costly) that other providers are "forced" to use their services. Providers obtain higher-quality services at less cost by outsourcing to the focused factory. In turn, the focused factory commands a place in the payment systems.

PRODUCT DEVELOPMENT

Product development is the introduction of new products/ services to present markets (geographic and customer segments). Typically, product development takes the form of product enhancements and product line extension. Product development strategies are common in large metropolitan areas where hospitals vie for increased market share within particular segments of the market, such as cancer treatment and open-heart surgery. Another good example of product development is in the area of women's health. Many hospitals have opened clinics designed to serve the special needs of women in the present market area.

PENETRATION

An attempt to better serve current markets with current products or services is referred to as a *market penetration strategy*. To increase volume and market share with the same products in the same markets, a market penetration strategy requires aggressive functional strategies, particularly within marketing. Market penetration is centered on promotional, distribution, and pricing strategies.

—Linda E. Swayne

See also Diversification Strategies, Horizontal Integration, Strategic Management, Vertical Integration

FURTHER READING

Bazzoli, G. J., Shortell, S. M., Dubbs, N., Chan, C., & Kralovec, P. (1999). A taxonomy of health networks and systems: Bringing order out of chaos. *Health Services Research, 33,* 6, 1683–1717.

Ginter, P. M., Swayne, L. E., & Duncan, W. J. (2002). Developing strategic alternatives. In P. M. Ginter, L. E. Swayne, & W. J. Duncan (Eds.), *Strategic management of health care organizations* (4th ed., Chapter 6). Oxford, UK: Blackwell.

Mick, S. S., & Conrad, D. A. (1988). The decision to integrate vertically in health care organizations. *Hospital and Health Services Administration, 33,* 3, 352.

Palich, L. E., Cardinal, L. B., & Miller, C. C. (2000). Curvilinearity in the diversification- performance linkage: An examination of over three decades of research. *Strategic Management Journal, 21,* 2, 155–174.

EXPECTED RATE OF RETURN

The expected rate of return is a collaboration of calculations that show what the return might be on an investment. It is calculated before investing, to yield another piece of decision-making information to those looking at an investment.

It is most commonly discussed in a conversation about the model of return-on-investment (ROI) rate. This model is used to provide information on decisions affecting business operations. Business conversations initiated aboout the impact may ask, How much will it decrease costs? How much will it increase revenue? What will it cost to implement? How long before we see a "return"? What is the "expected rate of return" on the investment? All these factors help predict, with reasonable accuracy, the "rate of return" on an investment.

To complete the process, the expected rate of return considers many variables. Some examples are decreasing costs by reducing labor, increasing revenues with new abilities provided by the investment, impact on employees, impact on others outside the enterprise, impact cost on utilization of resources considering existing capacity, impact on inventories and accuracy, capital costs, operational costs, impact on quality, growth rate, current size of enterprise, degrees of change, and others.

Typically a target is established that the expected rate of return should meet for the investment to be considered successful. For example, if the expected rate of return is to have the investment pay for itself in three years, then the return should show a 100% payback in three years, considering the time value of money.

If a enterprise made an investment of $100,000 in its investment portfolio and this investment paid an annual dividend of $10,000 a year, the expected return would be 10% (expected rate of return = $10,000/$100,000 = 10%).

The advantages of calculating the expected rate of return lie in estimating future cash flows and financial impact. The disadvantages are that even though analysts are blessed with enormous amounts of historical data, the analysts assume that the future will be like the past.

—Terry Moore

See also Investment, Return on Assets (ROA), Rate of Return (ROR)

FURTHER READING

Freidman, J. P. (2000). *Dictionary of business terms.* Hauppauge, NY: Barron's.

Gepenski, L. C. (2001). *Healthcare finance: An introduction to accounting and financial management.* Chicago: Health Administration Press.

Zelman, W., McCue, M. J., & Millikan, A. R. (1998). *Financial management of healthcare organizations: An introduction to fundamental tools, concepts and applications.* Malden, MA: Blackwell.

EXPOSURE

Exposure is the risk of financial loss. There are different types of exposure for health care operations. An exposure is the total value of what is covered under a policy of insurance. Directors' and officers' coverage, property insurance, and product liability can be particularly expensive sources of health care operations loss. Director's and officer's insurance covers the board of directors and officers of a health care organization for administrative activities such as medical staff appointment approval and decisions made by the board to act in the best interests of the institution.

Litigation and claims history of a health care entity can be used to project pending losses that exceed coverage limits or reveal gaps in coverage. The other area of exposure requiring evaluation is the potential for inheriting personnel problems from workers compensation losses, EEOC litigation, or Occupational Safety and Health Administration (OSHA) regulation violations. More recent types of exposures are related to expansion of services away from the primary health care site to broaden services and compete with large health care systems. Off-premises liability may involve contracted services and personnel to supplement existing resources and staff. In each type of exposure, quality issues may arise that may represent liability that is not anticipated, funded, or insured.

—Kathleen Ferrara

FURTHER READING

Youngberg, B. (1998). *Risk manager's desk reference* (2nd ed., Chapter 13). Gaithersburg, MD: Aspen.

EXTENDED PRODUCT PORTFOLIO MATRIX

See BCG Portfolio Analysis

EXTERNAL CAPITAL

See Capital Structure

EXTERNAL ENVIRONMENTAL ANALYSIS

See Environmental Analysis

FACILITIES MANAGEMENT

Facilities management is the practice and art of coordinating the people and work processes of an organization with the physical facilities. This coordination may be as simple as providing core support services to the organization (housekeeping, building maintenance, security services) or as complex as incorporating the provision of physical facilities into the overall strategic planning process. Involvement in the strategic planning process elevates facilities management from a basic administrative function to a core business process in many organizations. Successful facilities management allows organizations to adapt the physical working environment to the needs of the workforce and remain flexible in dynamic, changing work environments. In the case of health care facilities management, regulation dictates strict adherence to treatment protocols that require very specific facility designs and an elevated level of routine maintenance. In a complex health care facility, the role of facilities management can affect the outcome of patient treatment and in many cases be the difference between life and death. A broad spectrum of services falls within the realm of facilities management and may include such diverse functions as facility planning and forecasting; the management of space, security, and life safety operations; general administrative services; and involvement in the strategic planning process.

At the heart of every successful facilities management operation is the facility manager. This person orchestrates the multitude of facility management functions that are conducted simultaneously in any dynamic organizational environment. The facility manager wears many hats and is responsible for not only people but also the systems and equipment the organization needs to create products and provide services. The International Facility Management Association (IFMA) has identified a number of major functional areas for which facility managers are responsible, including basic and routine maintenance, the acquisition of real estate, financial planning for facility operations, the coordination of new construction, integration of telecommunications and security services, and long-range planning. The sophistication of facilities management in complex health care environments requires managers who are more than operations and maintenance foremen. The facilities management function requires the ability to integrate state-of-the-art management processes with traditional maintenance operations. Health care facilities management has the potential to determine the success of most health care organizations.

The rise in complexity of the facilities management function has fostered a trend referred to as *outsourcing*. This approach entails hiring someone who is not directly employed by the organization (usually under contract) to perform certain aspects of the facilities management function. Outsourcing may be as broad as contracting with an organization to manage the entire spectrum of the facilities management function or may be as narrow as hiring someone to take care of the grounds. The benefit of outsourcing is the flexibility it provides to organizations and facility managers, who are trying to provide services in the most cost-effective manner possible. In health care facilities, outsourcing is used for such functions as housekeeping and security services. Even with the advent of outsourcing, facilities management remains one of the most complex and challenging functions within any contemporary health care organization.

—Kevin LaFrance

FURTHER READING

Cotts, D. G. (1998). *The facility management handbook.* New York: AMACOM.
IFMA. (2002). *International Facility Management Association.* www.ifma.org

Lewis, B. T. (1999). *Facility manager's operation and maintenance handbook.* San Francisco: McGraw-Hill Professional.

Smith, P. R., et al. (2000). *Facilities engineering and management handbook: Commercial, industrial, and institutional buildings.* San Francisco: McGraw-Hill Professional.

Tompkins, J. A. (1996). *Facilities planning.* Indianapolis, IN: Wiley.

FACTORING OF ACCOUNTS RECEIVABLE

An account receivable is money that is owed to the business but hasn't yet been paid. For example, when a patient is billed for an insurance copayment of $50, an account receivable of $50 is created. When the patient's insurance company is billed its portion, $500, a different account receivable is created. When the patient pays the $50 bill, the account receivable is reduced by $50.

Sometimes a business does not want to wait for its customers to pay their bills. This may happen when the business needs cash very badly or customers are slow in paying. In these cases a business might sell its accounts receivable to a third party at a discount in return for immediate payment. So, for example, if John Smith owes $100 to Urology Associates, PC, then the business may sell this account to another company, Factors Intl., for $85. Urology Associates receives the $85 immediately, rather than having to wait until Mr. Smith pays.

Depending on the arrangement, Mr. Smith may either pay Factors Intl. the $100 he owes, or he may pay Urology Associates, who then turns over the entire $100 received to Factors Intl.

The advantage of factoring is that Urology Associates gets the use of the funds immediately rather than having to wait until Mr. Smith pays. And if Factors Intl. has taken over all collections duties for the account, then Urology Associates can avoid all expenses associated with billing and bad debt collection associated with the account.

—Phillip R. Daves

FURTHER READING

Brigham, E. F., & Daves, P. R. (2002). *Intermediate financial management* (7th ed.). Mason, OH: South-Western.

FAIR EMPLOYMENT AND PUBLIC POLICY

It is the policy of the U.S. government that the privilege and conditions of employment should be fair and without regard to any individual's age, color, disability, national origin, race, religion, or sex. Many other nations have similar policies. When making employment decisions, employers are enjoined from decisions that stem from any of these demographic characteristics of individuals. Although the concept of fairness is ancient, and issues involving fairness in employment can be tracked to the industrial revolution, child labor concerns, the labor movement, and concerns with occupational safety, the modern concept of employment fairness stems directly from the post–World War II civil rights movement and concern for the plight of African Americans.

The Civil Rights Act of 1964 was the monumental step that elevated fair employment from public debate to public policy. After more than 80 days of debate, Congress passed the law, granting broad, sweeping rights to all people. Title VII of the act, addressing employment, prohibited discrimination or segregation of employees or prospective employees on the basis of their race, creed, color, national origin, or sex. President Johnson signed the act into law on the day it was passed, and summarized the tenets of moral conscience that the law embraced, saying,

> We believe that all men are created equal—yet many are denied equal treatment. We believe that all men have certain inalienable rights. We believe that all men are entitled to the blessings of liberty—yet millions are being deprived of those blessings, not because of their own failures, but because of the color of their skins.
>
> The reasons are deeply embedded in history and tradition and the nature of man. We can understand without rancor or hatred how all this happens. But it cannot continue. Our Constitution, the foundation of our Republic, forbids it. The principles of our freedom forbid it. Morality forbids it. And the law I sign tonight forbids it. (www.congresslink. org/civil/essay.html)

Two concepts or models of fairness underlie most public policy in the United States. The first of these is typically associated with the Civil Rights Act of 1964. This model asserts that race, color, sex, or any other of the protected classes just listed should not have any bearing on employment decisions. In short, as regards color, employers should be color-blind; as regards sex, they should be sex-blind. With only minor exceptions, this is the model of fairness associated with all equal employment opportunity (EEO) laws and regulations. For the most part, adherence to these principles is the obligation of all but the smallest employers.

The second model of fairness seeks remedy for past discrimination. This model holds that certain classes of individuals, such as African Americans, Hispanic Americans, and women, have been underrepresented in segments of the workforce and accordingly deserve special accommodations, or affirmative action (AA), to increase their representation in a reasonable period of time. This model of fairness is the employment policy of the federal government, is required of government contractors, and is administered by the Office of Federal Contract Compliance Programs (OFCCP) of the U.S. Department of Labor.

At first glance, EEO and AA may appear incompatible with each other. It is impossible to treat all individuals the same while at the same time affording some corrective advantage or privilege to a subset of individuals. Nevertheless, although these two models of fair employment are incompatible as regards operation, they are compatible in spirit and intent. The U.S. Supreme Court focused on this common intent when considering the monumental case *United Steel Workers of America v. Weber* (443 U.S. 193), reconciling these two models. They concluded that affirmative action is warranted when it is temporary, "not intended to maintain racial balance, but simply to eliminate a manifest racial imbalance," does not unnecessarily harm the interests of the majority, and does not create an "absolute bar to advancement" for those not receiving the affirmative action. In summary, reasonable corrective action in the form of affirmative action is consistent with the policy of the U.S. government.

Since 1964, numerous changes have occurred in equal employment law. Supreme Court decisions, acts of Congress, and executive orders have all shaped the landscape of fair employment. Although racial inequality was the principal focus of early actions, numerous other classes of individuals have been protected. Older workers were added to the list of those protected by the Age Discrimination in Employment Act (ADEA) of 1967. Although sex was among the classes protected by the Civil Rights Act, not until the Pregnancy Discrimination Act of 1978 was this inclusion given full protection. As the courts have interpreted congressional acts, Congress has changed the law to reflect renewed conscientiousness and concern for expanding models of fair employment.

The most significant addition to fair employment policy came in 1990 with the passage of the Americans with Disabilities Act (ADA) of 1990. Recognizing that society has historically tended to segregate and isolate individuals with disabilities and that these people have been discriminated against in employment, education, health service, transportation, and access to public buildings, the ADA was crafted "to provide a clear and comprehensive national mandate for the elimination of discrimination against individuals with disabilities." Like the Civil Rights Act of 1964, this act stopped short of requiring affirmative action but does "provide clear, strong, consistent, enforceable standards addressing discrimination against individuals with disabilities."

Given the diverse ideology and constitutional foundations of the United States, continued development in fair employment law and policy is inevitable. Presently, social pressure is building to protect individuals from discrimination on the basis of sexual orientation and to afford additional rights to contingent workers, including subcontractors, temporary employees, and individuals in part-time jobs. Whether either of these issues develop to the point of becoming public policy is a matter for which only time will provide an answer.

—Robert T. Ladd

FURTHER READING

Dirksen Congressional Center. (2003). A case history: The Civil Rights Act of 1964. www.congresslink.org/civil/ essay.html

Equal Employment Opportunity Commission (EEOC). (2000). *35 years of ensuring the promise of opportunity.* www.eeoc.gov/35th/index.html

Ledvinka, J., & Scarpello, V. G. (1991). *Federal regulation of personnel and human resources management* (2nd ed.). Boston: PWS Kent.

FALSE CLAIM

See Billing

FAMILY AND MEDICAL LEAVE ACT (FMLA)

The Family and Medical Leave Act (FMLA) of 1993[1] was the result of Congress's reaction to dramatic changes that had taken place in the workforce of the United States over the past 40 years, intended to "balance the demands of the workplace with the needs of families." The Senate Report that accompanied the FMLA noted, for example, that the number of female workers in the civilian labor force had increased by over 200% in that period. In addition, the American population generally was aging, leading to predictions that a large percentage of workers would have some caregiving responsibilities for an older family member. Finally, the number of single-parent households had increased substantially, because of increases in the number of unwed mothers and in rates of separation and divorce. Between 40% and 50% of the nation's workforce are estimated to be covered by FMLA.[2]

Employers are covered by FMLA if they employ 50 or more employees for each working day during twenty or more weeks in the preceding or current calendar year. FMLA incorporates the definition of "public agency" as defined by the Fair Labor Standards Act, so that "the government of a State or political subdivision thereof, a State, or a political subdivision of a State" also are included as employers. Claims under FMLA are not preempted by collective bargaining agreements that have arbitration provisions.

An "eligible employee" is an individual who has "been employed . . . for at least 12 months . . . for at least 1,250 hours . . . during the previous 12-month period," that is, before the leave is requested. Eligible employees are entitled to up to 12 weeks of unpaid leave during a twelve-month period. If both a wife and husband have the same employer, only a total of 12 weeks leave may be taken. The employer may require, or the employee may elect, to substitute accrued paid personal leave, family leave, or vacation leave for part of the 12-week period. Continuation of health insurance coverage must be provided by the employer during the period of leave, and the employee is entitled to restoration of the original position or an equivalent one after returning from leave.

Leave may be taken for one or more of the following reasons: when the requested leave is due to (a) the birth of an employee's son or daughter, (b) placement of a child with the employee for foster care or for adoption, (c) the employee's own serious health condition, or (d) the serious health condition of a member of the employee's immediate family (spouse, son, daughter, or parent).

"Serious health condition" is defined as "an illness, injury, impairment, or physical or mental condition [requiring] inpatient care . . . [or] continuing treatment by a health care provider." Cosmetic or voluntary treatments not medically necessary may qualify if they require "inpatient hospital care." Determination of a serious health condition is fact intensive. For example, if sufficiently severe, carpal tunnel syndrome may qualify as a serious health condition.[3] However, an employee's heart arrhythmia and hypertension was judged not a serious medical condition where his doctor cleared him for work and he could obtain medical treatment without missing work.[4] Terminating an employee because she was absent from work for four days to take care of her son, who had an ear infection, was not a violation of FMLA because the son's illness was not a serious health condition.[5] In contrast, a teacher's mother who fell, was incapacitated, and was unable to take care of her basic needs for several days (in addition to other chronic health conditions) was considered to suffer a "serious health condition."[6]

Several diagnoses, none of which alone is a serious health condition but which are temporally linked, may rise to that level when taken together.[7] The employer may require that the employee support a request for leave with certification from the health care provider of the employee,

spouse, child, or parent on whose behalf leave is requested. The employer may require an opinion from a second provider, at the employer's expense. Conflicting opinions may be resolved, at the employer's expense, by the opinion of a third health care provider, jointly approved by the employee and employer.

Under some circumstances, leave may be taken intermittently, or on a "reduced leave schedule" if the employee and employer agree.[8] If such leave is requested because of the employee's own health condition or that of a family member, the employer may require the temporary transfer of the employee to an alternative position, with equivalent benefits and pay, that is available. The employee is required to give the employer 30 days or more notice before the requested leave is to begin, if the need for the leave is known ahead of time. Implementing regulations require the employer to provide information on FMLA rights and responsibilities to the employee, either in an employee handbook (if one is provided) or other written guidance.

At the time of this writing, it is unsettled whether states, as compared with local governments, are subject to the FMLA. A majority of the circuit courts of appeal have held they are not. The U.S. Supreme Court has granted certiorari to resolve the issue during its October 2002 term.[9]

—Arthur Gutman

NOTES

1. Pub. Law No. 103–3, Titles I and II, 107 Stat. 6 (codified as 29 U.S.C. 2601 et seq., and 5 U.S.C. 6381 et seq., respectively).

2. This excludes most federal workers. Title I covers state and local governments, and private employers. Federal employees are covered by Title II. This entry focuses on Title I.

3. *Price v. Marathon Cheese Corp.* (1997), 119 F.3d 330 (5th Cir.)

4. *Hodgens v. General Dynamics Corp.* (1997), 963 F. Supp. 102 (D.C. R.I.).

5. *Seidle v. Provident Mutual Life Insurance Co.* (1994), 871 F. Supp. 238 (E.D. Pa.).

6. *Ozolins v. Northwood-Kensett Community School District* (1999), 40 F. Supp. 2d 1055 (N.D. Iowa).

7. *Price v. City of Fort Wayne* (1991), 117 F. 3d 1022 (7th Cir.).

8. "Intermittent leave" is taken in different blocks of time, because of a single injury or illness, and may vary from an hour to several weeks. "Reduced leave schedule" reduces hours per workday or per workweek.

9. The Court will review *Hibbs v. HDM Department of Human Res.* (2001), 273 F.3d 844 (9th Cir.), which held that FMLA did validly abrogate the states' Eleventh Amendment immunity from suits by individuals.

FAMILY-ORIENTED CARE

Family practice is a medical specialty that which provides comprehensive and continuing health care for the individual and the family. It integrates the biological, behavioral, and clinical sciences into one discipline. It encompasses all ages, both sexes, all organ systems, and every disease entity. The goal is to achieve optimal physical and mental health through accessible, cost-effective care. Family-oriented care is like other medical disciplines in that it is based on best evidence. It differs in that it is responsive to the needs of patients and respectful of family, personal values, and beliefs.

Family practice is the current expression of the historical family doctor that made house calls. For thousands of years, physicians were generalists. They diagnosed and treated illness, performed surgery, and delivered babies. With the advancement in technology, many physicians chose to limit the scope of their practice. During the time of World War II, specialists began to flourish. For two decades the number of generalists decreased as specialists increased. As the public complained about fragmented health care, family-oriented care was reborn. Family practice became medicine's 20th specialty.

Medical knowledge and skill are the same as with other disciplines, but the process of family practice is what makes it different. Family physicians are the first line of entry into the medical arena. They are positioned to form a close relationship with the family. They see the family members as well beings and promote disease prevention.

—Doreen T. Day

See also Family-Oriented Care

FURTHER READING

www.aafp.org

FAVORABLE SELECTION

See Risk Adjustment, Risk Selection

FEASIBILITY STUDY

A feasibility study is basic research on whether a projected plan will work and be of benefit to the group or business that is considering the action. In many businesses, the need to project what is likely to happen is a usual activity before proceeding. The study involves gathering information, analyzing, and evaluating. The information should be used to answer the question "Should we move forward with Plan X?"

Steps to take include the following:

- Define the specifics and objective of the plan (number, location, and so on).
- Determine the stakeholders in the change.
- Study community feedback, concerns, and issues.
- Answer the question, Is it a reasonable change?
- Define and study the demographics.
- Establish a financial plan with projections of cost, revenue, and losses.

Certain basic issues need to be considered. The range depends on the program, the costs involved, and finally the manpower needed to support the program. A good example might be the consideration to increase the size of the neonatal intensive care unit (NICU) at a university hospital.

The first step is to identify the present census of the NICU and the demand for use. If the unit is rarely full and you can take all cases, you may not need to pursue additional beds. If, in contrast, your unit is the only NICU in an entire county of 1 million lives and you are unable to keep up with the demand, you need to proceed. Data from the information systems (ISs) should be able to provide the necessary information to answer these questions.

The second step is to identify the population and define who is in the geographic area for these beds. A demographic review may determine if sufficient people will potentially need the service.

For example, you might expect an area with the median age of 33 years to have a greater need for these services than where the median age is 55. In the first area, additional NICU beds might be useful, but in the other, perhaps additional medical intensive care unit (MICU) beds might be needed instead.

Once these questions are answered, you will know if you should proceed.

Look at the estimated volume of beds needed to satisfy the demand, being careful not to have too many beds that lie vacant. Estimate costs per bed for staffing and equipment, length of time to make the additions, interference with routines, costs associated with the additions, and potential costs of lost business while the changes take place. Staffing requirements may be dictated by state mandates and, as one of the most costly elements of such a change, need to be factored into the entire study. New systems may be required to support the added beds, and technology and upgrades may also be factors to include.

The business plan should be completed and discussed with those affected. Meetings should be held with the executive administrators who deployed the study and consultants who performed the study (if applicable). Major players, such as representatives of nursing, information technology, dietary, housekeeping, infection control, architects, construction, social work, and public relations should be at the discussion table to complete the study.

In some states these changes must undergo additional scrutiny in the form of a certificate of need (CON), supplied by the state. This CON is a review of your feasibility study, and outcomes and a determination are made based on your study and business plan.

If it is determined that there is an established need for the community served and there appears to be a thorough review of the issues with provisions, implementation plan, and costs addressed, the state may grant you the CON. You will then be allowed to proceed. This may appear an extraordinary extra step, but it has proven an excellent way to regionalize care and prevent duplication. A salient example might be the purchasing of a computerized tomography (CT) scan machine. In the 1980s when the CT scan was the latest technology to assist in diagnosis for strokes, tumors, and other diseases, CT scan equipment proliferated to almost every hospital. The actual need was established as one CT scan for every 5,000 lives covered. If you had two CT scan machines in a demographic area of only 7,000 lives, you actually were underutilizing the technology, the costs were not appropriate, and the skill of the technician and the physician were not utilized to the fullest. Thus a certificate of need can prevent the use of resources unnecessary to a region.

—Edna Lee Kucera

FURTHER READING

www.ceds.gatech.edu
www.liraz.com

FEDERAL REGULATING AGENCIES

Federal regulating agencies are those federal government agencies established to administer regulative laws (laws that control individual and organizational behavior) in certain fields. They are responsible for overseeing state and local agencies in that field. Federal regulatory agencies that oversee health care are primarily arms of the U.S. Department of Health and Human Services (DHHS). The regulatory agencies that are concerned with the health care field are discussed in the following sections.

CENTERS FOR DISEASE CONTROL AND PREVENTION (CDC)

The Centers for Disease Control and Prevention (CDC) is recognized as the primary federal agency for protecting the safety and health of people in the United States. The CDC forms partnerships throughout the United States and the rest of the world to protect and promote wellness. It employs 8,500 people in 170 occupations and consists of 12 centers. The CDC mission is to promote health and quality of life by preventing and controlling disease, injury, and disability. Established in 1946 as the Communicable Disease Center, the CDC now has an annual budget of $3.7 billion. Working with the states and other partners, the CDC provides a system of health surveillance to monitor and prevent disease outbreaks, including bioterrorism. The CDC implements disease prevention strategies and maintains national health statistics.

CENTERS FOR MEDICARE AND MEDICAID SERVICES (CMS)

Formerly known as Health Care Financing Administration (HCFA), Centers for Medicare and Medicaid Services (CMS) runs Medicare and Medicaid, two national health care programs that benefit approximately 75 million Americans. In conjunction with the Health Resources and Services Administration (HRSA), they also run the State Children's Health Insurance Program (SCHIP), which is expected to cover nearly 10 million uninsured children. CMS regulates all but research laboratory testing in the United States. Each year $360 billion is spent on Medicare, Medicaid, and SCHIP. CMS, established in 1977, had a 2002 budget of $374.7 billion and over 45,000 employees.

JOINT COMMISSION ON ACCREDITATION OF HEALTH CARE ORGANIZATIONS (JCAHO)

The Joint Commission on Accreditation of Health Care Organizations (JCAHO) is an independent, not-for-profit organization established over 50 years ago. Its governing board includes physicians, nurses, and consumers. JCAHO sets the standards by which health care quality is measured in the United States and around the world. Its mission is to improve quality and safety of the care provided to the public by evaluating more than 17,000 health care organizations at least every three years. JCAHO provides health care accreditation and related services that support performance improvement in health care organizations.

NATIONAL INSTITUTES OF HEALTH (NIH)

The NIH is one of the foremost medical research centers in the world. It began in 1887 as the Laboratory of Hygiene. Its mission is to pursue knowledge on all living systems and to transfer that knowledge into the extension of healthy life and to reduce the effects of disability and illness. NIH both conducts and supports research as well as developing and supporting medical libraries. NIH supports around 35,000 research projects, employs over 17,000 people, and has an annual budget of nearly $21 billion.

FOOD AND DRUG ADMINISTRATION (FDA)

Established in 1906, the work of the U.S. Food and Drug Administration (FDA) is a blend of both science and law. The FDA's mission is to protect and promote the public health by assisting safe and effective medical products to reach the market in a timely fashion. The FDA also monitors these products for continued safety after they are in use. The FDA assures the safety of foods, cosmetics, pharmaceuticals, and biological products. The annual budget is over $1 billion, and the agency employs nearly 10,000 people.

ADMINISTRATION FOR CHILDREN AND FAMILIES (ACF)

The Administration for Children and Families (ACF) is responsible for some 60 programs that promote the economic and social well-being of families, children, and communities. It administers Temporary Assistance to Needy Families (TANF, the state and federal welfare program), the National Electronic Child Support Resource System (NECSRS), and the Head Start program. ACF provides funds so that low-income families can pay for child care and to support programs to prevent child abuse and domestic violence. Established in 1991, it brought together several programs that already existed. It employs around, 1,500 and has an annual budget of $44.6 billion.

ADMINISTRATION ON AGING (AoA)

The Administration on Aging (AoA) administers federal programs mandated under the Older Americans Act. Many of these programs allow older Americans to remain in their homes by providing supportive services such as Meals on Wheels, which delivers prepared meals to the home. The AoA is the focal point and advocate agency for older people and their concerns. Other programs offer older Americans the opportunity to enhance their health and to be active contributors to their communities.

AGENCY FOR HEALTHCARE RESEARCH AND QUALITY (AHRQ)

The Agency for Healthcare Research and Quality (AHRQ) is the health services research arm of DHHS and the nation's lead federal agency for research on health care quality, costs, outcomes, and patient safety. It complements the biomedical research of NIH. AHRQ works with both the public and private sector to find out what does and does not work in health care and then to translate this knowledge into policy and practice. The 2002 budget for AHRQ was $91 million, and about 300 people were employed.

SOCIAL SECURITY ADMINISTRATION (SSA)

The Social Security Administration (SSA) was part of the DHHS until 1995, when it became an independent agency. The SSA continues to work closely with DHHS departments. The SSA was created by the Social Security Act, which was signed into law in 1935. SSA activities include several programs for general welfare, the most important being the social insurance program to pay retired workers 65 or older. There have been many legislative changes to the Social Security Act over the years, to include the disabled and surviving spouses and children. Today, one in seven Americans, approximately 44 million people, receive benefits.

SUBSTANCE ABUSE AND MENTAL HEALTH SERVICES ADMINISTRATION (SAMHSA)

The Substance Abuse and Mental Health Services Administration (SAMHSA) works to improve the quality and availability of substance abuse prevention, addiction treatment, and mental health services. It provides federal block grants to support these state programs. SAMHSA funds programs nationwide that have been shown effective and encourages the use of these methods elsewhere. SAMHSA has over 600 employees and a $3 billion budget.

—Doreen T. Day

FURTHER READING

www.acf.dhhs.gov
www.ahcpr.gov
www.cdc.gov
www.fda.gov
www.hhs.gov
www.jcaho.org
www.nih.gov
www.ssa.gov

FEE-FOR-SERVICE (FFS) PAYMENT

Fee-for-service (FFS) payment is the way that professionals in the United States have historically been paid. In the industrial sector, it would be called *piecework*. The professional develops a fee schedule with a unit price for each service provided and then bills the patient or insurer according to that schedule for each specific service delivered. The provider does not necessarily receive all that is billed, because the insurer may command a percentage discount or substitute a negotiated fee schedule, or the provider may not be able to collect the full amount from the patient. The key attribute of FFS is that the payment to the provider increases whenever more procedures and services are performed and billed.

Alternatives to FFS payment in the United States and elsewhere include capitation and salaried employment by the government or HMOs, as well as mixtures of all three forms. Capitation involves a flat periodic payment for providing coverage whether or not the services are demanded. Government employment provides one's primary compensation in countries with a tax-supported universal health service. In most countries with a government health service, however, physician income lags behind comparable professional incomes and does not support a middle-class standard of living for the doctor's family. Therefore, physicians often have fee-paying private patients on the side in order to maintain a reasonable standard of living, regardless of whether or not such practices are legal.

The advantage of fee-for-service payment is that it provides an incentive to see as many patients as one likes or has available. The downside is that it can encourage overutilization in terms of visits, admissions, and procedures. Because physicians tend to perform mostly reimbursed services, their efforts become focused on acute illness and not on prevention. (Note, however, that that has been a function of what insurers chose to pay for, not necessarily an intrinsic characteristic of fee-for-service delivery.) The downside of capitation or tax-supported salaries is that there is little or no financial incentive for increased productivity. The upside of capitation is that it bypasses all the paperwork and debate over the appropriate payment for each visit or procedure. Because there are variable costs to the provider of giving a service, capitation may motivate underutilization of care. In government-provided health care, the paperwork for each visit is less important, but public-sector accountability requirements usually impose heavy paperwork requirements anyway.

These three methods of payment also vary in terms of who carries the risks. In the FFS system, the insurer is at risk for service costs that exceed expectations. The income of the provider continues to rise as more and more services are delivered. In the capitation system, the provider is at risk for any unexpected costs, and with salaried providers the government or HMO is at risk. What one sees in the United States is a hybrid system that is mostly FFS but has additional features that spread or limit the risk. Both primary insurers and capitation providers (including HMOs) may purchase stop-loss insurance for catastrophic cases. Providers may take on the mixture of FFS and capitation contracts with insurers and health maintenance organizations

that represent their relative willingness to accept risk and their negotiating power in the marketplace. Increasingly the risks are shifted to the patients and their families by rising copayments tied to the services provided and by deductibles that make some initial portion of one's annual claims the patient's responsibility. Governments reduce their risks either by budget constraints, paying only so long as the appropriation has not been consumed, or by ratcheting down their substitute fee schedules to match the budgeted amount against the demand for services. Insurers reduce their risks under both FFS and capitation by underwriting decisions that exclude or increase premiums for high-risk patients and by dropping high-cost providers.

Many other direct and indirect controls are operating in the fee-for-service environment. These include alternative, deeply discounted fee schedules used by private insurers, Medicare, and Medicaid; concurrent review of hospitalized cases; prior approval for some services and prescriptions; retrospective claims review (including peer review); and carve-outs.

There are also risk-sharing arrangements with primary care providers (PCPs), involving withholding some of the capitation payments to cover overbudget average expenses and returning the unused portion to the PCPs if use and costs are below targets. Occasionally these risk-sharing schemes are applied to specialists as well, including obstetrician-gynecologists (OB-GYNs).

Other countries that use a constrained fee-for-service system include Canada, Japan, and Germany. However, those countries have much lower costs of care, with similar health outcomes. Hospitals in Canada receive a global annual budget to service their region. U.K., Japanese, and German hospitals are paid on a regulated or negotiated fee-for-service basis. Great Britain has a mixed physician payment system with capitated gatekeepers, again with lower average costs. All these countries have much lower average physician incomes, less use of technology, less aggressive treatment of the terminally ill, and often reduced access to services and procedures, especially among the elderly. Even among the United States and these four countries, there are wide differences in doctor and hospital use patterns, attributable to the payment and incentive systems in place.

—Curtis P. McLaughlin

See also Deductibles, Health Insurance

FURTHER READING

Bodenheimer, T. S., & Grumbach, K. (2002). *Understanding health policy: A clinical approach* (3rd ed.). New York: Lange Medical/McGraw-Hill.

Feldstein, P. J. (1999). *Health care economics* (5th ed.). Albany, NY: Delmar.

Herzlinger, R. (1997). *Market driven health care.* Reading, MA: Addison-Wesley.

Phelps, C. E. (1997). *Health economics* (2nd ed.). Reading, MA: Addison-Wesley.

FINANCIAL PERFORMANCE INDICATORS (FPIS)

The way to determine if a health care organization is operating in an effective and efficient manner is through the use of financial performance indicators (FPIs). The review of the balance sheet, income statement, and cash flow statement is an essential and fundamental task to analyzing the financial performance of any health care organization. But this is only the beginning for successful financial management and analysis. The number and types of users of a health care organization's financial statements include management, board of directors, creditors, investors, government bodies, grant-making agencies, and the general public. Unless a user is well trained in finance or business administration, the financial information found in these statements may seem an endless array of numbers with little meaning.

An analysis of FPIs gives the user a measure of the organization's performance. The primary sources of data for calculating these indicators come from the basic income statement, balance sheet, and cash flow statement. However, FPI analysis is not just comparing different numbers from the balance sheet, income statement, and cash flow statement. It is comparing the numbers against previous years, other peer health care organizations, the industry, or even the economy in general. FPIs look at the relationships between individual values and relate them to how a health care organization has performed in the past and might perform in the future. For example, current assets alone do not tell a lot, but when they are divided by current liabilities, a user can determine whether the organization has enough assets to cover short-term debts. FPIs may provide the very important early-warning indications that allow financial and other business problems to be identified, thus allowing early corrective action by management.

FPIs can be classified into several major categories, including profitability indicators, liquidity indicators, capital structure indicators, asset efficiency indicators, and other financial indicators.

Profitability indicators are an important concept in any industry or any organization. Few health care organizations could remain financially viable without a profit (or excess of revenues over expenses), especially over a long period of time. For instance, cash flow would not be sufficient to meet normal cash requirements such as debt principal repayment and investment in fixed or current assets. The presence or absence of profit has a pervasive effect on most other FPIs. Low values of profit may adversely affect liquidity indicators and reduce debt repayment ability.

Examples of FPIs that measure profitability include the following:

Total margin (the desired trend is an increasing value) = excess of revenues over expenses / total revenues

Return on equity (the desired trend is an increasing value) = excess of revenues over expenses / net assets

Economic value added (EVA) (the desired trend is an increasing value) = net operating profit after taxes (NOPAT) / NOPAT – cost of capital

Liquidity indicators measure the ability of an organization to meet its short-term obligations. Most organizations experience financial problems because of a liquidity problem, which is when they are unable to pay current obligations as they become due. A worsening liquidity position may be the first indication that the organization has serious underlying problems.

Here are examples of FPIs that measure liquidity:

Current ratio (the desired trend is an increasing value) = current assets / current liabilities

Days in patient accounts receivable (the desired trend is a decreasing value) = net patient accounts receivable / net daily patient service revenues

Days cash on hand (the desired trend is an increasing value) = cash + short-term investments / [(total expenses – depreciation) / 365]

Capital structure indicators are used to determine an organization's ability to increase its amount of debt financing. Many long-term creditors and bond-rating agencies are particularly interested in capital structure indicators. The values for these may ultimately affect the amount of funding available to a health care organization, and this could directly affect its rate of growth.

Examples of FPIs that measure capital structure include the following:

Equity financing ratio (the desired trend is an increasing value) = net assets / total assets

Capital expense ratio (the desired trend is a decreasing value): = interest expense + depreciation expense / total expenses

Cushion ratio (the desired trend is an increasing value) =
(cash + short-term investments
+ long-term investments) / (principal
payments + interest expense)

Asset efficiency indicators measure the relationship between revenues and assets. The numerator is revenues, which is considered a proxy for output. The denominator is investment in some type of asset and is considered a measure of input.

Examples of FPIs that measure asset efficiency include the following:

Total asset turnover (the desired trend is an
increasing value) =
total revenues / total assets

Fixed asset turnover (the desired trend is an
increasing value) =
total revenues / net fixed assets

Inventory ratio (the desired trend is an
increasing value) =
total revenues / inventory

Other financial performance indicators provide additional information that can lead to a more comprehensive picture of the financial position of a health care organization.

Examples of these FPIs include the following:

Average age of plant (the desired trend
is a decreasing value) =
accumulated depreciation / depreciation expense

Depreciation rate (the desired trend is
neutral or stable) =
depreciation expense / gross property, plant, and equipment

Working capital absorption (the desired trend
is a decreasing value) =
increase in net working capital (excluding cash) / (excess
of revenues over expenses + depreciation)

Once you have completed your health care organization's analysis of its financial performance indicators, you will come away with a better understanding of the organization's strengths, weaknesses, and areas of concern. This will allow you to begin the process of implementing the necessary steps that must be taken to ensure your organization's long-term health.

—Richard Clarke

FURTHER READING

Aspen. (2001). *The benchmark in hospital receivables (HARA).* Frederick, MD: Author.

Czarnecki, T. M. (1994). *Benchmarking strategies for health care management.* Gaithersburg, MD: Aspen.

Ingenix. (2001). *2002 almanac of hospital financial & operating indicators: A comprehensive benchmark of the nation's hospitals* (Book with CD-ROM). Salt Lake City, UT: Ingenix, Inc.

Ingenix. (2002, October 1). *HospitalBenchmarks.com.* www.hospitalbenchmarks.com

Interstudy. (2002). *The 12.1 competitive edge HMO industry report.* St. Paul, MN: Interstudy Publications.

Lutz, S., & Gee, P. E. (1997). *Financial and clinical benchmarking: The strategic use of data.* Baltimore, MD: HCIA and Healthcare Financial Management Association.

FINANCIAL STATEMENTS

A standard set of financial statements includes the balance sheet, income statement, statement of cash flows, and associated footnotes. These statements can be issued on a daily, monthly, quarterly, or annual basis. Additional statements may include, for example, the analysis of stockholders equity section. If accounting is the basic language of business, then financial statements are the fundamental scorecards that report organizational performance. Every paradigm has its own particular language and set of rules, especially the medical field, and to play in this arena health care professionals need to understand both. Do individuals need to understand detailed accounting constructs such as debits or credits? No, but they do need to understand how financial statements are developed, how the income statement, balance sheet, and statement of cash flows articulate with one another and some of the underlying assumptions that are used to develop the financial statements.

Accounting is not an exact science. Although financial statements are produced under the authoritative guidelines of generally accepted accounting procedures (GAAPs), health care professionals should understand some fundamental concepts and assumptions about financial statements. First, almost all the numbers in financial statements are based on managerial estimates. Yes, that is right. Probably the only really firm number on the financial statements is cash. It is like a group of people looking at Sears Tower, asking, How tall is this building? How many different guesses would you receive? On average the group would probably be pretty close but not exact. To become more precise, the group would have to exert more time and energy. The same is true of financial statements. There is always a tradeoff between more accurate information and the cost to produce such information.

Another assumption is that GAAP financial statements are based on materiality thresholds. If you examine an audit opinion, you will see that the auditors usually say something like the following: "In our opinion, the financial statements referred to above present fairly, in all material respects, the consolidated financial position of company and subsidiaries at December 31, 2008, and 2007, and the consolidated results of their operations and their cash flows for each of the three years in the period ended December 31, 2008, in conformity with generally accepted accounting principles." So are numbers included in financial statements 100% accurate? No, they are *materially* correct.

GAAP financial statements are also prepared under the principle of conservatism. For example, organizations cannot include the intellectual capital of employees on their balance sheets. Organizations also cannot show, for the most part, the appreciated market value of their assets. Why is this? Well, how much value can one place on employee knowledge? Would an independent third party ascertain the identical value you placed on the asset? Thus intangible assets do not appear on financial statements unless someone (or some company) buys the assets in an actual transaction. The same is true for appreciating assets. Because market values are difficult to determine, accountants usually use historical cost transactions to develop the financial statements.

Although many other accounting assumptions influence the way financial statements are developed, it is important to understand that although accounting financial statements provide valuable information, health care professionals need to be aware of the assumptions used to prepare them. Accounting financial statements still provide valuable data that are reliable, comparable, and consistent. In addition, financial data must be timely to provide people with the ability to assess future cash flows and assist in decision making (an information role) and to monitor debt covenants and bonus arrangements (a stewardship role).

How can a health care professional understand how financial statements articulate with one another without taking five years of accounting and without learning all the vernacular such as *debits* and *credits*? You can approach understanding through simple mathematical equations. Almost everyone can understand the basic mathematical laws of addition and subtraction. If you can handle this, you can understand the miracle of accounting. Let us start by looking at the balance sheet as an equation at the end of a period:

$$\text{Assets} = \text{liabilities} + \text{owners' equity}$$

Most of us can grasp what an asset is: something the company owns that has a monetary value such as cash, equipment, and buildings. What this equation says is that all company assets accumulated throughout the years are owned (or claimed) by someone. A portion of the assets are claimed by creditors (liabilities), and some of the assets are claimed by the owners (owners' equity). So if assets equal $100,000, liabilities equal $30,000, and owners' equity equals $70,000, then this equation should be in balance. Is it?

$100,000 = $30,000 + $70,000? Yes, looks good so far! But does this equality always hold?

If we expand the owners' equity portion of this equation, we can now include the summary result of the income statement (net income):

$$\text{Owners' equity (ending)} =$$
$$\text{owners' equity (beginning)} + (\text{net income} - \text{dividends})$$

and because

$$\text{Net income} = \text{revenues} - \text{expenses}$$

we now have an equation that can demonstrate how the financial statements are linked together:

$$\text{Assets} =$$
$$\text{Liabilities} + (\text{owners'}$$
$$\text{equity} + \text{revenues} - \text{expenses} - \text{dividends})$$

If beginning owners' equity is $60,000, revenues are $300,000, expenses are $270,000, and dividends $20,000, does this equality balance? ($100,000 = $30,000 + $60,000 + $300,000 − $270,000 − $20,000) Yes, it does—a simple approach to understanding financial statements.

—Bruce Behn

FURTHER READING

Cleverley, W. O., & Cameron, A. E. (2002). *Essentials of health care finance* (5th ed., pp. 118–134). Gaithersburg, MD: Aspen.

FIRST-MOVER ADVANTAGE (FMA)

The concept of first-mover advantage (FMA) refers to the supposed advantages a company gains by becoming the first significant entrant into a particular market segment. The term has been popularized with the advent of Internet-related businesses and correlates somewhat with the term "first to market" for traditional businesses. Businesses employing FMA as their major strategy may be seeking to emulate unstoppable market domination as displayed by such companies as Amazon.com and eBay.

There are a number of ways in which FMA strategy allows for at least the potential for domination: the possibility of setting the particular industry segment's standardizations, popularizing a new technology or method, branding a particular service, and establishing a loyal base of customers and vendors. Another FMA is the so-called network effect, in which a multiplying number of users advantageously use the new technology or service, rapidly expanding the FMA company's market and further bonding the customer base to the first mover.

In an attempt to preempt challengers, a hospital may employ FMA strategy to open several urgent care centers in and even beyond its traditional service market, seeking sustainable competitive advantage in branding, loyalty, economies of scale, inpatient and ancillary utilization, and insurer contracting.

The FMA concept has often proved illusory, because of its many inherent uncertainties, such as overestimation of market desire or irreversible investment in technologies that quickly become outmoded. "Fast followers" and "second-mover advantage" strategies, as their names imply, employ purposeful waiting to learn from first-mover successes and failures before launching a new venture.

—Barry Henderson

See also Expansion Strategies, Market Entry Strategies, Service Area Competitor Analysis, Strategy

FURTHER READING

Tellis, G. J., & Golder, P. N. (2001). *Will and vision: How latecomers grow to dominate markets.* New York: McGraw-Hill.

FIXED COSTS

Fixed costs are costs that do not directly change as patient volumes increase or decrease. This definition assumes that costs will be fixed within an expected range of activity or volume for a specified time period. Alternatively, costs will not remain constant if there are extreme fluctuations in patient volumes.[1] A hospital may estimate that patient days in the coming year will range from 30,000 to 45,000. If it is unlikely that utilization will fall outside of this estimate, the range serves as the hospital's relevant range.[2]

Examples of fixed costs include those related to facilities and equipment, certain salaries, and other costs such as information systems. Assets intended to serve a long-term purpose remain fixed in the short term, regardless of volume. However, no costs remain fixed over the long term, because patient volumes generally continue to increase over time. With this trend, fixed costs increase as health care organizations acquire additional property and equipment, labor, and other assets. Conversely, if patient volumes decrease significantly, fixed costs will decrease to reflect a reduction in fixed assets.[3]

Fixed costs do not represent the total costs incurred by a health care organization. Total costs consist of both fixed and variable costs. Whereas fixed costs do not directly change in relation to the number of patients, variable costs, such as medical supplies and pharmaceuticals, are directly related to patient volumes. Although variable costs change directly with a change in volume, the variable cost per unit is expected to remain relatively constant. In contrast, fixed costs per unit change inversely with volume. As patient activity increases, fixed costs decrease at a decreasing rate, as illustrated next. The fixed cost is shared across a greater number of patients, and as a result the assets are used more efficiently.[4]

FixedCost	Patient Days	Fixed Cost per Unit
$900,000	30,000	$30
$900,000	45,000	$20
$900,000	60,000	$15

Health care organizations may also categorize costs as semifixed or step-fixed. Semifixed costs are defined as costs that are fixed within a certain volume range; however, there may be several semifixed ranges within an organization's overall relevant range. If current hospital staffing can only accommodate 40,000 patient days, additional labor is required to staff 45,000 patient days. Labor costs would then be fixed from 30,000 to 40,000 patient days and then from 40,000 to 45,000 patient days, but they are not fixed over the entire relevant range.[5]

Individual organizations differ on how to categorize fixed and variable costs. Labor costs or salaries serve as an example. The labor cost required to perform a CT scan may be considered variable, because more patients requiring the test will increase the cost of the service. However, a nurse supervisor salary may be fixed over the relevant range. It does not change in the short term but will change in the long term as patient volumes shift or the facility reorganizes. Despite the different classification methods, fixed costs represent a significant portion of the health care organization's total costs and operating structure.[6]

—Edward Pershing

NOTES

1. S. A. Finkler (1994), Cost accounting for health care organizations: Concepts and applications (Gaithersburg, MD: Aspen), p. 35.

2. L. C. Gapenski (2002), Healthcare finance: An introduction to accounting and financial management (2nd ed.). Chicago: Foundation of the American College of Healthcare Executives), p. 131.

3. Gapenski (2002), p. 131.

4. M. J. McCue, A. R., Millikan, & W. N. Zelman (1998), Financial management of healthcare organizations: An introduction to fundamental tools, concepts, and applications (Malden, MA: Blackwell), pp. 248–251.

5. Gapenski (2002), pp. 134–135.

6. R. R. Roberts, P. W, Frutos, G. G. Ciavarella, L. M. Gussow, E. K. Mensah, L. M. Kampe, H. E. Straus, G. Joseph, & R. J. Rydman

(1999, February 17), Distribution of variable vs. fixed costs of hospital care, JAMA (Journal of the American Medical Association), 281(7).

FLEXTIME

Flextime is a flexible work arrangement where employees have the opportunity to set their own individual start and stop times for work. In most cases, the employer designates a block of five or six hours where all employees are required to be at work. These are frequently referred to as *core hours*. Core hours should span the portion of the day where peak work activity occurs (the portion of the day that necessitates the maximum availability of employees).

Once the core hours are established, employees are allowed to set their own start and ending work times. For example, the administrative office in a hospital may typically be open between 8 A.M. and 5 P.M., but the office receives most of its inquiries between 9 A.M. and 3 P.M. However, if the office could open before 8 A.M. and stay open later than 5 P.M. there would be the opportunities to better serve hospital staff and customers. Therefore, this administrative office might choose to set core hours of 10 A.M. to 3 P.M., allowing employees the ability to start their workday as early as 6 A.M. and end their workday as late as 7 P.M. All employees are required to work an 8-hour shift, with consistent but individual start and end times; thus service hours of the administrative office are extended.

It is recommended that managers remain active in the evaluation and approval of individual requests for flexible scheduling, to avoid any gaps in office coverage. A well-managed office, however, has the strong possibility of not only accommodating the individual needs of employees but also substantially extending the hours of service delivery.

Flextime is one of several work-scheduling alternative an employer may want to consider. Other options include compressed workweeks and telecommuting. When allowing employees to pursue flexible work scheduling, it is advisable to have employees commit to the alternative schedule for a fixed amount of time, such as three months, so the success of the different work schedule can be appropriately evaluated.

—Laura Gniatczyk

See also Compressed Workweeks, Telecommuting

FURTHER READING

Capowski, G. (1996). The joy of flex. *Management Review, 85,* 12–19.

Gale, S. F. (2001). Formalized flextime: The perk that brings productivity. *Workforce, 80,* 38–42.

Solomon, C. M. (1996). Flexibility comes out of flux. *Personnel Journal, 75,* 34–41.

FLOAT MANAGEMENT

See Average Collection Period (ACP), Factoring of Accounts Receivable

FLOWCHART

A flowchart, or flow diagram, is a graphical representation of a process and depicts either an actual or an ideal sequence of steps. These steps are portrayed through the use of geometric shapes that represent actions (rectangles), decision points (diamonds), and terminal events (rounded rectangles). Arrows, or flow lines, are used to represent the flow of material, information, and events that occur within the process. A flowchart can be very simple or highly intricate, depending on the complexity of the process being studied.

Members of quality control circles initially used flowcharts in the manufacturing industry in Japan. In these voluntary circles, factory workers studied the quality control process. Quality expert Kaoru Ishikawa assisted circle members by providing guidance on a number of problem-solving techniques. From his work in the quality arena, seven basic problem-solving tools have emerged to include the flow diagram, the cause-and-effect chart, the Pareto chart, the run chart, the histogram, the scatter diagram, and the control chart.

Flowcharts are particularly useful in the health services industry because of the many health care processes involving complex interactions and unseen steps. One example of the usefulness of flowcharting is in the area of patient safety. When a medical error or a near miss occurs, a root cause analysis is conducted to determine the most basic cause of the problem and prevent its recurrence. The flowchart is an essential component of this analysis and serves to provide all members of a quality team with a common understanding of the process. By thoroughly and systematically documenting all the steps in a given process, inefficiencies, redundancies, disconnects, and flaws can be readily identified.

The flowchart can be used in either a prospective or a retrospective process analysis. In a prospective analysis, it serves as the basis for brainstorming sessions that seek an ideal process design or a best practice model. In a retrospective analysis, it provides a launching point for clarification, discussion, and further analysis of an existing process that needs improvement. Often, quality teams use both types of analysis and then conduct a gap analysis that compares the ideal process flowchart with the process as it actually occurred.

Flowcharts are perhaps the most frequently used quality improvement tool. Their usefulness lies in their flexibility and their fundamental purpose: ensuring a thorough and systematic understanding of all the steps in a process so that meaningful dialog and process improvement can occur.

—Shonna L. Mulkey

See also Plan–Do–Study–Act Cycle, Quality Improvement Cycle

FURTHER READING

Carey, R. G., & Lloyd, R. C. (1995). *Measuring quality improvement in healthcare: A guide to statistical process control applications.* New York: Quality Resources.

Ishikawa, K. (1982). *Guide to quality control.* White Plains, NY: Kraus International.

Juran, J. M. (1999). *Juran's quality handbook* (5th ed.). New York: McGraw-Hill.

Walton, M. (1990). *Deming management at work.* New York: Putnam.

FOCUS STRATEGIES

See Generic Strategies

FOOD AND DRUG ADMINISTRATION (FDA)

The Food and Drug Administration (FDA) is a federal government agency responsible for regulating foods, drugs, medical devices, biologics such as vaccines and blood products, animal feed, cosmetics, and radiation-emitting devices. The FDA is a subdivision of the U.S. Department of Health and Human Services and is itself subdivided into eight offices based on regulatory subject. The FDA has over 9,000 employees in 167 field offices throughout the country. For the 2003 fiscal year, the FDA has a proposed budget of almost $1.73 billion, which is an increase of nearly 8% over fiscal year 2002.

Historically, the FDA can trace its origins to the U.S. Department of Agriculture in 1862, but the modern FDA began in 1906 with the passage of the Federal Food and Drugs Act. This early legislation was focused on the labeling of foods and medications by the manufacturer to reveal their contents and additives. In 1938, Congress passed the Food, Drug, and Cosmetic Act, which brought cosmetics and medical devices under the control of the FDA and required that drugs be labeled with adequate directions for safe use. Moreover, it mandated premarket approval of all new drugs: A manufacturer would have to prove to the FDA that a drug was safe before it could be sold.

Despite numerous laws and organizational changes, this feature has remained a prime focus of the FDA. Currently, certain things are not officially regulated by the FDA, such as dietary supplements, pesticides, and "street" drugs. In 1994 Congress passed the Dietary Health and Education Act, allowing dietary supplements to be marketed with statements regarding their role in health, provided that the packaging had a disclaimer that the FDA had not evaluated the statements of the product's efficacy. Pesticide sale and use are directly controlled by the Environmental Protection Agency (EPA), but foods are tested by the FDA to determine if these compounds are present in unacceptable amounts. "Street" or illicit drugs are controlled by the Drug Enforcement Administration (DEA) and not the FDA. However, if an illicit drug were to be used for a legitimate therapeutic medical purpose, the FDA would treat it as an investigational drug. Prescription drugs that are controlled by the FDA for medical usages but are used as "street" drugs are under the jurisdiction of the DEA.

One of the divisions of the FDA is the Center for Drug Evaluation and Research (CDER), which has the responsibility of ensuring that safe and effective drugs are available for consumption. During development of a new pharmaceutical, the FDA is involved at several key times. After preclinical development and testing, a sponsor or manufacturer must submit an Investigational New Drug (IND) application, which includes information on the manufacture process, stability and composition of the new drug, animal pharmacology and toxicology, and clinical protocols for human trials. After clinical human trials (Phase I, II, III), a New Drug Application (NDA) must be submitted for evaluation containing statistical, pharmacokinetic, and adverse event data encountered during the clinical trials. The FDA has the option of seeking the advice of outside agencies or individuals at this point in the process, via advisory committees. An "action package" and letter are created, containing the information from the sponsor, research, and advisory committees. If approved by the division director or office director, the pharmaceutical is then legal for marketing in the United States. The approval process can be shortened via an accelerated development or parallel track. These processes, developed for approving medications to treat HIV/AIDS, allow rapid development of promising new drugs for life-threatening conditions.

The FDA is responsible for regulating cosmetics. Under the federal Food, Drug, and Cosmetic Act, cosmetics are not required to undergo premarket testing of safety, provided the package is labeled "WARNING: The safety of this product has not been determined." However, the Fair Package and Labeling Act requires that all ingredients in a product be listed in descending order of quantity. Occasionally, a product may be claimed to prevent a disease, for example, a dermatological condition. However, the active ingredient as listed on the packaging must still be tested and proven safe for its intended use.

The FDA is also charged with the regulation of radiation-emitting devices, to prevent unnecessary exposure. These devices can either emit radiation as their primary purpose, as with medical imaging equipment, or as a consequence of their normal function (as with cell phones, microwave ovens, and so on). The FDA does not review the safety of radiation-emitting consumer products prior to their sale, as it does with medications or medical devices. For cell phones, the FDA is part of a multiorganizational group (including the Federal Communications Commission, Occupational Safety and Health Administration, National Institute for Occupational Safety and Health, and the Environmental Protection Agency) that is designed to ensure radio-frequency energy safety and guidelines for exposure.

The Center for Biologicals Evaluation and Research (CBER) is assigned the task of ensuring the safety of the nation's blood supply, vaccines, recombinant DNA technology, and cellular and gene therapy. This division works closely with the federal Public Health Service and Centers for Disease Control (CDC).

The FDA is continually monitoring both new products and those already being marketed. One method of ensuring consumer safety is via a recall, which can be initiated by the manufacturer independently or at the request of the FDA. The FDA can also initiate a recall under its own authority. Recalls are divided into classes: A Class III recall is used when exposure to the product in question is unlikely to cause adverse health consequences; a Class II recall is associated with the probability of a temporary or medical reversible injury or where serious health risk is possible but remains remote. In a Class I recall there is reasonable probability that exposure to a product will either result in serious adverse consequences to one's health or in death. A product can also be removed from circulation via a market withdraw, which is considered a minor violation and not subject to FDA legal action.

The FDA is also continually seeking information regarding adverse events from prescription and over-the-counter medications as well as from devices. Consumers submit formal complaints to the FDA via the MedWatch Program (at 800/FDA-1088 or electronically via the MedWatch Web site).

—Daryn H. Moller

See also Clinical Trials, Phase 1 Study (Phase 1 Clinical Trial), Phase 2 Study, Phase 3 Study, Phase 4 Study

FURTHER READING

Association of Clinical Research Professionals. (2002). *Certification examination review for clinical research coordinators.* Alexandria, VA: Author.

Chow, S.-C., & Liu, J.-P. (1998). *Design and analysis of clinical trials: Concepts and methodologies.* New York: Wiley.

www.fda.gov

FORECASTING

See Sales Forecasting

FORMULARY

Originally, the word *formulary* referred to a book listing the ingredients and formulae for making medicines. As the pharmaceutical companies took over the manufacturing task from the pharmacists, the term was used to refer to a list of those drugs that a hospital or other health care organization planned to carry in inventory. As drugs became more numerous and more effective and made up a greater portion of the health care budget, institutions and payers began to exert greater control over what did or did not go into that list. They became increasingly insistent that prescribers on their staff pay attention to that list. The hospital pharmacy and therapeutics (P&T) committees that make inclusion decisions became an important part of its governance process. Now formularies are a normal adjunct to the managed care process. Hospitals have them, health plans have them, and so do their pharmacy benefit managers (PBMs).

Employers and insurers often contract out (outsource) prescription drug management to one of a number of national PBM companies who also provide their own formularies. Physicians are expected to use the drugs on the list unless there is a good medical reason for not doing so. Often there is a separate formulary for each health plan that a physician's patients belong to. Most primary care physicians' offices have hard copies (printouts) of the list from each payer, but the lists may or may not be up-to-date, and each has its own format. The result is that the prescriber is usually confused and angry about this complex constraint on professional autonomy and the doctor–patient relationship. The patient probably does not have the formulary information either, although it is usually available on the Internet. Patients become aware of it only when the pharmacy informs them of whether or not the patient's medical insurance will pay for it and what tier it falls into for copayment purposes.

TIERED FORMULARIES

Most formularies are divided into tiers for reimbursement and copayment. Many programs use a three- or four-tiered program with generic substitutes requiring the lowest copayment, preferred drugs without accepted substitutes have a somewhat higher copayment, whereas nonpreferred drugs and branded drugs for which a substitute is available but not dispensed carry a much higher copayment. The fourth tier involves denial of payment because the drug is not medically necessary or not covered for some other reason without prior approval.

CONTROVERSIES

Formularies are becoming increasingly controversial as managed care pharmacy benefits management covers more transactions, and there is increasing litigation as exclusion becomes more critical to the pharmaceutical manufacturer's profitability. Recently, litigation has centered on the efforts of states and other payers to use inclusion or exclusion in a health plan's formulary as a bargaining chip in negotiating price discounts. The individual states play a major role here because Medicaid programs do carry drug benefits, and the states have become increasingly aggressive trying to control drug costs.

Those who make formulary decisions should consider more than cost. The dominant membership of the P&T committee is usually physicians and pharmacists with representatives from nursing, other relevant professions, administration, and occasionally lay health plan members. The primary objective should be to provide the most cost-effective care for the patient, so efficacy and effectiveness are major concerns. Where more than one treatment is available, the committee must consider the comparative effectiveness of the contenders. As substitutes become available, it is important to consider equivalency based on pharmacologic, pharmacokinetic, pharmacoeconomic, and safety information. Efficacy data are typically available from studies submitted to the Food and Drug Administration for drug approval. Where possible, these are based on double-blind randomized controlled experiments. However, these experiments do not always approximate the way the approved drug performs under less controlled clinical conditions. Therefore, some argue that the P&T standard should be use effectiveness, which takes into account patient compliance and adherence and revealed preferences of physicians and patients. A number of guidelines are available for P&T committees to use in requesting and interpreting clinical and economic information from vendors. One widely used one is available from the Academy of Managed Care Pharmacy.

The biggest controversies will always surround tradeoffs among efficacy, effectiveness, and cost and take place over the point of view to be taken in the analysis. If a drug reduces the medical necessity for emergency room visits as shown in clinical trials, should the pharmacy benefits manager give that precedence over the costs of drugs (after price discounts, rebates, and copayments)? If so, how much? The point of view and hence the recommendations may vary considerably, depending on whether one is a PBM, the hospital, the insurer, or the patient. Point of view is important.

Another area of controversy concerns any rewards and sanctions attendant on complying or not with the use of preferred drugs. The choice may also be linked with complying or not complying with other protocols that may call for using specific classes of drugs, such as ACE inhibitors to control blood pressure after heart attacks. These may even affect the institution's quality ratings with organizations such as National Committee for Quality Assurance (NCQA). Because the patient and the insurer pay for the drugs, no incentive is involved for the prescriber. However, utilization review by the health plan or the hospital can lead to sanctions, if the physician repeatedly orders expensive drugs. Patients may also begin to hold their physicians responsible when the insurer points out a less expensive or more effective alternative that was not discussed.

Where electronic prescribing is in use, electronic formulary information can be made immediately available to the prescriber. This has already been shown to increase prescriber compliance with guidelines. As this mode of entry is mandated by more and more institutions and health plans, some of the information updating and availability of information problems with formularies may be alleviated. The provider may even be able to include the patient's preferences and attitudes based on copayments in the decision-making process.

—Curtis P. McLaughlin

See also Efficacy

FURTHER READING

Academy of Managed Care Pharmacy. (2002, July). *Format for formulary submissions.* www.amcp.org/publications/format.pdf

Navarro, R. P. (Ed.). (1999). *Managed care pharmacy practice.* Gaithersburg, MD: Aspen.

FOR-PROFIT HOSPITAL

See Hospitals

FORWARD VERTICAL INTEGRATION

See Vertical Integration

FRANCHISING

Franchising is a contractual arrangement between two parties that is found both in retailing and in international markets. This form of licensing has grown tremendously in the last 10 years or so (Lamb, Hair, & McDaniel, 2002, p. 113). The typical type of franchising found in health care is that of business format franchising. The originator of the business format, such as Interim HealthCare and its health care staffing services (Brown, 2002, p. 3), grants the rights to operate the format to an entrepreneur who wants to manage a business with some ongoing training and support. The originator is called the *franchiser,* and the entrepreneur who is granted operating rights is called the *franchisee.*

A person or business looking to be a franchisee can expect to pay approximately $150,000 in initial costs (Brown, 2002, p. 1). Royalty fees are also charged on a monthly, or more frequent, basis. These fees usually range from 3% to 7% of a franchisee's gross revenues. Additional fees vary from franchiser to franchiser. Other requirements and expenses to be carried by the franchisee include advertising expenses; equipment purchases; inventory purchases and maintenance; hiring, training, and evaluation of employees; building layout and signage; and attendance at conventions and training seminars (Lamb et al., 2002, p. 440). Again, these expectations vary from franchiser to franchiser.

A franchise is a legal, contractual agreement between the two parties, and if the franchisee fails to abide by the terms of the contract, the franchiser can take away the franchising rights. For example, if one notices the sudden closing of several fast food restaurants in one chain in a large city, most likely what has happened is that the franchisee failed to fulfill the terms of the franchise agreement and thus lost the right to operate those restaurants in that city.

Care of seniors in the home and medical staffing are two key service areas of health care that are projected to grow exponentially in the years to come (Brown, 2002, p. 3; Smith, 2002, p. 1). In fact, the health category had a 62.8% increase in the number of franchise units from 2000 to 2001, according to *Entrepreneur* magazine (Smith, 2002, p. 2). Franchising opportunities are available in these and other areas of health care services. Resources are available to anyone who is interested in becoming a franchisee. The industry trade group, the International Franchise Association, offers many resources online at www.franchise.org. Other sources available to potential franchisees include *Franchise* (www.franchisetimes.com), the Franchise Network (www.bison1.com), and FranCorp, a large franchising consulting group (www.francorp.com) (Brown, p. 2).

—Jeffrey W. Totten

See also Licensing, Market Entry Strategies

FURTHER READING

Brown, C. M. (2002, May). Franchising: An entrepreneurial opportunity. *Black Enterprise, 32,* 101(3). www.infotrac.galegroup.com

Lamb, C. W., Jr., Hair, J. F., Jr., & McDaniel, C. (2002). *Marketing* (6th ed.). Cincinnati, OH: South-Western/Thompson Learning.

Smith, D. (2002, January). Coming on strong: Don't call them also-rans. These 5 franchise industries are burning up the track. *Entrepreneur, 30,* 111(2). web2.infotrac.galegroup.com

Whittemore, M. (1991, December). Filling niches in health care. *Nation's Business, 79,* 54(2). web4.infotrac.galegroup.com

FREE CASH FLOW

See Discounted Cash Flows

FULL PRICE OF MEDICAL CARE

Relatively few individuals are aware of the full price of their medical care, and even fewer are aware of the full costs associated with that care. Many people use the term *cost of care* very loosely. What they refer to much of the time is the price they personally pay for a service, usually something less than either the full cost or the full price of their care because of insurance and other applicable third-party payments. However, some may be overstating the full cost of their care, because they are unaware of the discounts taken by payers, which may be on the order of 40% to 60%.

Payment for medical care is highly fragmented in the United States, especially among the elderly. For example, let us say a 68-year-old male has prostate surgery. He is a former professor at a state university and a Medicare enrollee. His initial doctor visits are covered by Medicare Part B and paid according to a discounted fee schedule by the private insurer who handles that program. He has already paid a separate $50 monthly premium for that. The hospital admission is covered by Medicare Part A, but he has to pay a $792 deductible on that bill, with Medicare paying the rest. The surgeon is paid through Medicare Part B. In-hospital drugs are part of the cost covered by Medicare Part A, as is a brief recovery period (up to 20 days) in a skilled nursing facility (nursing home). Medications purchased directly by this person for use at home during the recovery period are not covered by Medicare but may be covered by the drug benefit under a major medical policy provided by his former employer. So may some of the other costs not covered by Medicare, depending on the major medical policy. In the case of the drugs, the retiree may see only the cost of the copayment and not know the amount actually paid by the former employer's insurance plan. He may not know the amount actually paid by either insurer to the hospital and the doctors, because he may only see a bill for charges, rather than actual payments. Certain medical supplies to use during the recovery period may not be paid for by any insurance. The retiree sees only what the Social Security Administration deducts from his monthly check for the Part B premium, the deductible for the hospital visit that is not covered by the major medical policy, the copayments for drugs purchased, and the full cost of the supplies not covered by insurance.

It is unlikely that the hospital knows what it actually cost to treat the case, knowing only the average costs, including allocated overheads, attributed to that DRG (diagnosis-related group) and not the time and materials that went into each specific case. If the case was treated in an academic medical center, the payments for the doctors (surgeon, anesthesiologist, pathologist) were probably pooled with other payments to other members of each doctor's clinical department, including research and teaching revenues. Whether teaching and research costs show up in the reported costs of care is a frequently asked question that can be answered only by a detailed review of the individual accounting system used. Residents and interns who worked on the case were probably paid by the hospital out of its budget with money generated by the admission and length of stay.

If the patient develops major ambulatory or self-care problems and has to stay in a nursing home for more than 60 days, the remaining cost of that nursing home care is not covered by the insurance already mentioned. If the patient has long-term care insurance, that will pay about half of the costs and the patient will be responsible for the rest. In the absence of such insurance, the patient will have to pay the nursing home costs, until he becomes medically indigent, at which time Medicaid begins to cover the nursing home bill. Medicaid costs are split among the federal government and the state and local governments, under arrangements that vary from state to state.

Despite the huge expenditures on Medicare cases, insurance pays only about half the direct cost of health care for the elderly. There are also indirect costs associated with medical care that are seldom captured. These include cost of travel to receive treatment, wages lost because of illness and seeking care, and income lost for those who stay out of the workforce to care for their relatives or friends.

—Curtis P. McLaughlin

See also Deductibles, Health Insurance

FURTHER READING

Bodenheimer, T. S., & Grumbach, K. (2002). *Understanding health policy: A clinical approach* (3rd ed.). New York: Lange Medical / McGraw-Hill.

Kongstvedt, P. R. (2001). *Essentials of managed health care* (4th ed.). Gaithersburg, MD: Aspen.

FULL-TIME EQUIVALENT (FTE)

Full-time equivalent, or FTE, is a percentage value used to compare the number of hours required by a position to the hours of a full-time position. "Full time" can be defined differently by different organizations; typically, a full-time position means 8 hours of work per day, 40 hours per week, and 2080 hours per year. An FTE value is always represented by a whole percentage (such as 75%, 50%, or 25%) and is calculated by dividing the number of working hours assigned to a position by the amount of time assigned to a full-time position. For example, a part-time medical transcription position that requires an individual to work 20 hours per week would equate to a 50% FTE (that is, 20 hrs/40 hrs = .50). FTE values are frequently used to determine which benefits are available to employees. For instance, many hospitals require an employee to be in a position that is at least a 75% FTE in order to qualify for health insurance and paid vacation. FTE values are also used to calculate staffing requirements, resource needs, and various metrics that allow comparison across different departments, subspecialties, or organizations, and to track trends over time. For example, a family practice group may monitor "revenue per FTE physician" to ascertain productivity over time, or "number of in-house radiology procedures per FTE physician" to track utilization of specialized services and equipment.

—E. Kate Atchley

See also Employee Assistance Program (EAP), Employee Compensation, Employee Health, Employee Retirement Income Security Act (ERISA)

FURTHER READING

Myers, D. W. (1992). *Human resource management: Principles and practice* (2nd ed.). Chicago: Commerce Clearing House.

FUNCTIONAL STRUCTURES

See Structures

FUND BALANCE

The accounting term *fund balance* is usually reserved for government units, including government hospitals, which are typically a proprietary fund of a government entity such as a county or city. It is similar to *equity* as that term is used by for-profit entities and to *net assets* as that term is used by not-for-profit organizations. Fund balance, simply stated, is the surplus of assets of a fund over its liabilities. Fund accounting is the process of segregating activities into identifiable units enabling management to better understand what assets have been allocated to the fund, how much has been spent from the fund, and the quantity of unspent funds that remain. Fund balance for general governmental units is divided into two categories: reserved and unreserved.

Reserved fund balances are resources that have been set aside for a specific purpose. They represent a portion of the fund balance that cannot be used for any purpose other than the one for which it was legally intended. An example of a situation requiring the need for reservation of fund balances is a payable or commitment to a third party existing at the balance sheet date that has not yet come to fruition but that the organization knows will materialize in the near future. Another situation requiring reservation of fund balances exists when the asset in question is not available for current appropriation. An example of this situation is when the organization has assets on the books, such as noncurrent receivables, and where the organization expects to receive this money in the future. However, at that point in time, the funds are not readily available to satisfy current liabilities.

Unreserved fund balances are further broken down into two subcategories: designated and undesignated.

Designated, unreserved fund balances are funds that are tentatively earmarked for particular expenditures. These designations may never be legally authorized or needed by the organization. In other words, the funds may never be used for their designated purpose. An example of this situation is money budgeted for unforeseen expenditures relating to a future construction project that are never expended. Designating unreserved funds differs from reserving fund balances because the designation of unreserved funds is not an allocation of funds that is required to be legally authorized by the governmental unit. Reserved fund balances are established to legally reserve a portion of the fund balance. Designating unreserved fund balances is more of a budgeting process conducted by management.

Undesignated, unreserved fund balances are basically the funds left over after the reserves for fund balance and the designation of unreserved fund balances. These funds are not set aside for a specific purpose and are readily available for all other expenditures that might arise.

Fund accounting is not limited to governmental units in that it is also used by not-for-profit organizations. Where governments are required to use fund accounting, not-for-profits are not. According to the Financial Accounting Standards Board in Statement of Financial Accounting Standards No. 117, not-for-profit organizations are not required to use fund accounting, but they are required to categorize their net assets into three distinct classes: unrestricted, temporarily restricted, and permanently restricted.

Temporarily restricted net assets are assets donated to an organization with restrictions set forth by the donor. The two types of restrictions on temporarily restricted net assets are those based on time and those based on purpose. An example of a restriction based on time is one in which a donor has given the organization a sum of money that is to be spent in predetermined amounts over a predetermined number of years. Each year, the amount of money allocated to be spent in that year is no longer considered to be temporarily restricted. In other words, the restriction on time has been satisfied and the organization is now allowed to consider the funds released from restriction. An example of a restriction based on purpose is one in which a donor gave an organization a sum of money to finance scholarships for deserving high school students. Each time a scholarship is awarded, the organization has fulfilled the requirement set forth by the donor and the funds needed to finance the scholarship are now available to the organization.

Permanently restricted net assets are those donated to the organization under which restrictions can never be satisfied by time or purpose. The organization has ownership of these assets and can use, but never extinguish, them. These net assets typically consist of endowments and other vehicles where the principal is to remain intact. Examples of permanently restricted net assets are property donated by an individual that is never to be sold by the organization or money donated to an organization that can never be spent by the organization. The way these assets are used by the organization can still be very profitable. For instance, the donated property can be used to house the organization or the organization could decide to lease the property out to provide a steady flow of income. Donated cash or investments would earn interest that, barring any other donor restrictions, could be used by the organization.

Unrestricted net assets represent resources that have no donor restrictions. They may be donated without restrictions or may be generated by the organization's activities. The organization can generally use these resources for any purpose consistent with the mission of the organization. Temporarily restricted net assets are reclassified to unrestricted net assets once the donor-imposed restriction has been satisfied. Reclassification between temporarily restricted and unrestricted net assets has no net effect on total net assets.

—Edward Pershing

FUNDRAISING

See Philanthropy in Health Care

FUTURE VALUE

See Time Value of Money

GATEKEEPERS

See Managed Care Organization, Managed Care Plans

GENERAL ENVIRONMENT

See Environmental Analysis

GENERALLY ACCEPTED ACCOUNTING PRINCIPLES (GAAPS)

Generally accepted accounting principles (GAAPs) are used by accountants and organizations as a guiding framework to formulate financial statements. Each country has its own set of GAAPs; however, there is a push toward harmonizing these various national GAAP systems into one international GAAP regime. In the United States, in the past, these principles were developed from best industry practices; however, now GAAPs are promulgated by authoritative bodies such as the Financial Accounting Standards Board (FASB). The FASB is an independent body that formulates the new accounting rules (for example, statements) that are to be adhered to by the accounting profession and practicing health care accountants. Other institutions have issued accounting guidelines over the years, and therefore there are different sources of GAAPs, collectively referred to as the GAAP hierarchy. It is important for health care accounting practitioners to understand the different levels of the GAAP hierarchy.

GAAPs are not "black and white" rules that define what should be done in every conceivable situation but rather guideline sets (or frameworks) to determine what is the proper treatment of an organizational transaction. In fact, GAAPs usually provide different options practitioners can use and still conform. For example, GAAPs allow a number of different ways for organizations to properly depreciate assets (for example, straight-line methods, accelerated methods, and so on). The same is true for inventory valuations, for example, last in, first out (LIFO); first in, first out (FIFO), and so on. The purpose of these alternatives is to give organizations the opportunity to choose the reporting option that best reflects the economic reality of the underlying transactions.

—Bruce Behn

FURTHER READING

Williams, J. R., Carcello, J. V., & Weiss J. (2002). *2002 Miller GAAP practice manual.* Gaithersburg, MD: Aspen.

GENERIC DRUGS

As per the Office of Generic Drugs (OGD) of the U.S. Food and Drug Association, a generic drug is "identical, or bioequivalent to a brand name drug in dosage form, safety, strength, route of administration, quality, performance characteristics and intended use. Although generic drugs are chemically identical to their branded counterparts, they are typically sold at substantial discounts from the branded price." To provide protection for the person or entity that incurred the initial expense (including research, development, and marketing expenses) to develop the new drug, brand name drugs are generally given patent protection for

20 years from the date of submission of the patent. When the patent expires, other drug companies can introduce competitive generic versions, which have to be thoroughly tested by the manufacturer and approved by the FDA before release.

Patents granted after June 8, 1995, now have a 20-year patent life from the date of the first filing of the patent application. Before June 8, 1995, patents were granted for 17 years. However, the effective patent term is frequently less than 20 years, because patents are often obtained before products are actually marketed. Many factors influence the length of the effective patent term, including the requirements in the federal Food, Drug, and Cosmetic Act and in the Public Health Service Act that certain products receive FDA approval before marketing. Before the FDA will approve the product for marketing, new drug products for humans generally must undergo extensive testing in both animals and humans to show that the drugs are both safe and effective. Consequently, to stimulate product development and innovation, Congress in 1984 enacted Title II of the Drug Price Competition and Patent Term Restoration Act (Public Law 98–417) to extend patent life to compensate patent holders for marketing time lost while developing the product and awaiting government approval. A maximum of 5 years can be restored to the patent. In all cases, the total patent life for the product with the patent extension cannot exceed 14 years from the product's approval date, or in other words, 14 years of potential marketing time. If the patent life of the product after approval is 14 or more years, the product would not be eligible for patent extension. To get an extension, the application for patent extension must be filed within 60 days of FDA approval of the drug product, even if the product cannot be commercially marketed at that time.

Just as there is a process to approve new branded drugs on the marketplace, the FDA also has a rigorous approval process for generic drugs. The application process for generic drugs is much more abbreviated, because preclinical data from animal studies or preliminary human data are not required (this was already provided by the branded medication and would only be redundant). Instead, the principle of bioequivalence is used by measuring the time it takes the generic drug to reach the bloodstream in 24 to 36 healthy volunteers. This gives the rate of absorption, or bioavailability, of the generic drug, which can then be compared with that of the branded drug. The generic version must deliver the same amount of active ingredients into a patient's bloodstream in the same amount of time as the innovator drug.

Under the Drug Price Competition and Patent Term Restoration Act (the Hatch-Waxman Act), a company can seek approval from the FDA to market a generic drug before the expiration of a patent relating to the brand name drug on which the generic is based. The first company to submit an Abbreviated New Drug Application (ANDA) with the FDA has the exclusive right to market the generic drug for 180 days. To begin the FDA approval process, the generic applicant must (a) certify in its ANDA that the patent in question is invalid or is not infringed on by the generic product (known as "paragraph IV certification"), and (b) notify the patent holder of the submission of the ANDA. If the patent holder files an infringement suit against the generic applicant within 45 days of the ANDA notification, FDA approval to market the generic drug is automatically postponed for 30 months, unless, before that time, the patent expires or is judged to be invalid or not infringed. This 30-month postponement allows the patent holder time to assert its patent rights in court before a generic competitor is permitted to enter.

These regulations were intended to reduce the time to market for generics; however, at times the automatic 30-month stays have served to allow pharmaceutical companies to extend protection of their branded drugs. As a result, lobbying organizations have developed such as the Coalitions for a Competitive Pharmaceuticals Market (CompetitiveRx.com) to further facilitate and encourage introduction of generics into the marketplace.

According to the Congressional Budget Office, generic drugs save consumers an estimated $8 to $10 billion a year at retail pharmacies. Even more billions are saved when hospitals use generics. The Generic Pharmaceutical Association states that "generic drugs typically cost 50% or less than 'brands.' Generics often enter the market at prices 25% less than brands, then drop to 60% off the brand price after two years." Given the rapidly escalating cost of pharmaceuticals, there has been great pressure to bring generics to market. Recently, however, it has been noted that generic prices are also climbing. With the advent of the Internet and World Wide Web, some people are also seeking generic versions of medications from abroad, creating problems not unlike the ones the music industry faces in defending their intellectual property from people making illegal copies.

This has been of particular import in developing countries, where HIV infection is widespread and yet medications remain very expensive and therefore not accessible. Sometimes even foreign governments have sanctioned the violation of patents in hopes of improving access to such expensive yet life-saving drugs.

—Miguel A. Nuñez, Jr.

FURTHER READING

www.competitiverx.com

www.fda.gov/cder/ogd

www.gphaonline.org/about/index.phtml

www.phrma.org

GENERIC STRATEGIES

Generic strategies are basic strategies that can be used by organizations in all kinds of industries. Michael Porter's 1980 book *Competitive Strategy* established a framework based on three distinct generic strategies: cost leadership, differentiation, and focus. This framework is based on the premise that organizations can use any one of these strategies to achieve a competitive advantage and to outperform competitors in their industry. Conversely, organizations that lack a coherent strategy may become stuck in the middle, a position associated with poor performance.

Overall cost leadership is a strategy in which organizations attempt to increase market share by emphasizing low costs relative to competitors. This strategy is suited to relatively large organizations that can control their costs by taking advantage of economies of scale, obtaining greater access to resources, and streamlining their processes to enhance efficiency. An effective cost leader can charge the same prices as the competition, and generate above-average profit margins because of its low-cost position.

Cost leadership is a very viable strategy in the health care industry, where consumers are highly concerned about the cost of quality care. For instance, a community hospital can streamline its administrative processes, outsource certain services, and cut back on more expensive, but seldom-used medical specialties. To fulfill all patient needs while keeping costs low, it may choose to form a partnership with a nearby research hospital.

Organizations following a differentiation strategy seek to create a product or service that is perceived by customers as unique. This uniqueness can take many forms. For instance, an organization may differentiate itself based on its level or type of service, its product features, its reputation, its location, and so on. The key is to provide features that customers want and are willing to pay for. This is critical, because it may be expensive to develop products or services that exceed the norm. Hence, even differentiated organizations must be concerned about their costs. They should expend extra resources on those things that contribute to their differentiation but be conservative in areas that do not. By following these guidelines, they can set themselves apart from competitors while still generating comfortable profits.

Health care providers can differentiate themselves in a variety of ways. Some large tertiary care institutions have established worldwide reputations for their unsurpassed quality in areas ranging from heart transplants to children's care. A chain of long-term care facilities could develop a national reputation for its excellent nursing services. A regional hospital could become known for its wellness center, by offering flexible hours, excellent training, and customized exercise programs.

The third generic strategy is the focus strategy. With this alternative, an organization directs its efforts to the unique needs of a small target market or a narrowly defined geographic market and attempts to achieve a cost advantage or a product or service advantage. The objective is to serve a particular market segment better than any other competitor serves it. For a focus strategy to work, there must be a significant difference between the needs of the target market and those of other segments in the market. The organization makes its products or services attractive to these customers by providing something they desire but cannot find elsewhere. An alcohol and drug rehabilitation center that serves a wealthy clientele is following a focus strategy, as is a psychiatric center that specializes in serving young females with eating disorders.

The major difference between the focus strategy and the low-cost and differentiation strategies is the scope of the target market served. Focus strategies are based on narrowly defined market segments; in fact, another term for such a strategy is a *niche strategy*. In contrast, cost leaders and differentiators define their markets broadly.

Organizations that attempt to implement both cost leadership and differentiation strategies, instead of doing one or the other, may become "stuck in the middle" (Porter, 1980). The concern is that cost leadership and differentiation are inconsistent with each other, because one requires activities that increase costs, whereas the other attempts to decrease costs; trying to do both may yield poor results. Some scholars disagree with this idea, however. In fact, some researchers have speculated that certain strategic accomplishments, such as quality improvements or process innovations, may simultaneously lower costs and increase differentiation. Others have contended that organizations using elements of both generic strategies may be more flexible and adaptive, and less vulnerable to imitation.

When choosing whether to implement a pure generic strategy or a combination approach, health care administrators must consider several things. First, who is the target market and what are its needs? Second, does the organization have the capabilities needed to meet those needs better than other competitors? The answers to these questions can help managers choose strategic actions that make sense for the organization and its clientele.

—Barbara Spencer

See also Niche Strategies

FURTHER READING

Miller, A., & Dess, G. G. (1993). Assessing Porter's (1980) model in terms of its generalizability, accuracy and simplicity. *Journal of Management Studies, 30*(4), 553–585.

Miller, D. (1992, January–February). The generic strategy trap. *Journal of Business Strategy, 26*, 37–41.

Porter, M. E. (1980). *Competitive strategy.* New York: Free Press.

GENOMICS

The terms *genomics* and *genetics* are often used interchangeably. Technically, genetics is the study of the unique DNA and RNA codes of individuals, whereas genomics is the technologies for dealing with groups of individuals or batches of genetic information. First used in 1986, the term *genome* referred to the mapping of the full sequence of mammalian genes. Since then, the usage for *genomics* has broadened to include the infrastructure necessary to exploit these research results.

What has enabled the widening influence of genomics research on health care has been the development of high-capacity information systems for processing genetic information on coding and sequencing and increased ability to use that information to associate clinical symptoms with the expression of individual and multiple genes. Although genotyping is currently expensive, costs per gene studied are dropping very rapidly, exhibiting the type of cost curves that have characterized microelectronics and computers. Because current disease definitions are based on signs and symptoms rather than on genetic classifications, it is likely that many current diseases will turn out to have multiple genetic variants. New gene-based classifications will make diagnosis and treatment much more specific, but the populations involved with each unique genetic variant will be much smaller. Clinical trials that failed may have done so because they involved patients with common symptoms but a mixture of genetic anomalies, not all of which would respond the same way to an experimental drug treatment. Although more focused Phase II trials based on genetic classification will require fewer participants and thus cost less, the likelihood of finding "blockbuster" drugs, drugs with very high market volume, is reduced, because of the smaller populations involved. Therefore, pharmaceutical companies may be less willing to incur the costs of developing them and achieving Drug Enforcement Administration (DEA) licensure.

Even when the genetic information is available, it is unlikely that simple genetic laws based on the presence or absence of a single gene will apply. More likely the findings will be probabilistic. For example, the presence of one variant of a gene may lead to a disease state 30% of the time. This could be because multiple gene combinations are involved in presentation of a disease or because multiple factors affect the type of and intensity of a gene's expression. The impact of genes interacts with the impact of environmental factors. One aphorism used in the biotechnology industry is that "genetics loads the gun, but environment pulls the trigger."

UTILIZATION

Two other factors affecting the usability of genomics discoveries in medicine are (a) the patenting of gene discoveries, and (b) the difficulties inherent in developing and expanding biotechnology manufacturing processes. Most pharmaceuticals on the market are referred to as "small-molecule drugs." Drugs likely to be associated with genomics research are proteins and their derivatives. These tend to be much more complex to make and control. Some observers suggest that genomics will lead to another class of discoveries called *proteomics* once the genetic code information can be associated with specific protein systems and processes that in turn are associated with specific disease states.

The patenting of genes could limit access to genomic information and research, either economically or physically, despite the material occurring in nature. Questions are also being raised about the residual legal rights of the original DNA donors in these cases.

LEGAL AND ETHICAL ISSUES

A host of legal and ethical issues are yet to be resolved before the results of genomic research and genetic engineering can be fully implemented. These include the following:

- Who can use genetic information, and when? Should we exclude employers and insurers?
- How do we assess the safety of genetically modified materials? Do they threaten natural species? Could they trigger new diseases? Epidemics?
- Should be we avoid modifying germ lines of any species on religious grounds? Is it proper to interfere with the natural processes of either a Creator or natural selection?
- Does genomic research deal effectively with the diversity of genetic information? Any experimental data are specific to an individual. Are the right variants represented? Can some individuals or groups opt out of the process?

Genomics methods are amassing genetic information very rapidly, using some of the world's largest computer systems. However, our legal, ethical, commercial, and health care systems will have to make many adjustments to its impacts before those impacts can be fully controlled or implemented.

—Curtis P. McLaughlin

See also Clinical Trials

FURTHER READING

Fitzgerald, C. Q., & McLaughlin, C. P. (2001). Medicine for the masses. *Pharmaceutical Executive, 21*(12), 64–68.

Keller, E. F. (2000). *The century of the gene.* Cambridge, MA: Harvard University Press.

Miller, P. (2002, February). Analyzing genetic discrimination in the workplace. *Human Genome News, 12*(1,2). www.ornl.gov/hgmis/publicat/

Pang, T. (2002). The impact of genomics on global health. *American Journal of Public Health, 92*(7), 1077–1079.

Ridley, M. (1999). *Genome: The autobiography of a species in 23 chapters.* New York: HarperCollins.

Robertson, J. A., Brody, B., Buchanan, A., Kahn, J., & McPherson, E. (2002). Pharmacogenetic challenges for the health care system. *Health Affairs, 21*(4), 153–167.

Roses, A. D. (2002). Genome-based pharmacogenetics and the pharmaceutical industry. *National Review of Drug Discovery, 1*(7), 541–549.

Tollman, P., Guy, P., Altshuler, A., Flanagan, A., & Steiner, M. A. (2001, November). *Revolution in R&D: How genomics and genetics are transforming the biopharmaceutical industry.* New York: Boston Consulting Group.

GEOGRAPHIC BOUNDARIES OF SERVICE AREA

See Service Area Competitor Analysis

GEOGRAPHIC INFORMATION SYSTEM (GIS)

A geographic information system (GIS) is a computer-based platform for managing, displaying, and analyzing location-specific (*spatial*) data related to a business. Data can be either organization specific, such as those concerning facilities, existing customers, or competitor locations, or they can be more generally available data such as those concerning population demographics, political boundaries, landmarks, and transportation networks. With both kinds of data, a GIS facilitates spatial analysis, the ability to display data or relationships in a geographic context in order to discover patterns, assess coverage, and understand system logistics. For example, in health care systems a GIS can easily generate a map of patient locations relative to health care facilities.

Business applications of GIS include natural resource management, facilities management, location analysis, sales territory management, network planning, transportation, and route planning. Within the category of *location analysis,* the most common application of GIS involves service area analysis. Service area analyses usually use either publicly or commercially available demographic data to identify population proximity to service resources. Within a GIS, service area analyses usually involve constructing *thematic maps* to display demographic data, such as age-stratified population figures, at the levels of the 5-digit zip code, county, 3-digit zip code, or state. Typical display techniques used in thematic maps include color shading, dot-density representations, and variable sizing of symbols. For example, a GIS can display geographic population densities using a dot-density representation as well as show the geographic distribution of average income levels using a combination of the display techniques. For organizations with existing customers in a study area, the analysis can be enhanced by constructing thematic maps showing customer density or customers per population as a proxy for market penetration or market share. Given the significant role of proximity in health care customer choice, the most common applications of GIS in health care settings have been in locating new facilities and evaluating coverage of public or private health care networks.

—Charles. E. Noon

See also Health Care Service Operations, Service Operations

GLOBAL BLOOD SAFETY PROJECTS

Assuring worldwide safety and availability of blood is a major public health need. The main issues of blood safety are increasing volunteer donation, improving laboratory resources and testing, avoiding inappropriate use of resources, and organizing national and regional resources. Volunteer donors have a markedly lower risk of infectious diseases and many countries cannot afford the training or testing to test blood for transmissible diseases. Several international agencies constructed projects to address these needs.

The Global Blood Safety Initiative developed out of meetings designed to combat the spread of the human immunodeficiency virus (HIV), the viral infection responsible for acquired immunodeficiency syndrome (AIDS). About 10% of HIV cases are related to blood transfusions. This project coordinates global blood-banking practices to identify and avoid transfusion of HIV-infected blood. The World Health Organization (WHO) has formed the Global Collaboration for Blood Safety (GCBS). This group promotes the blood safety initiatives of WHO, specifically addressing the needs for developing countries. The Pan American Health Organization as well as other regional organizations have made similar issues a priority.

Several U.S. agencies are also addressing global blood safety issues: The Centers for Disease Control has collaborated in Africa through a program called "Leadership and

Investment in Fighting the Epidemic." Other agencies such as the Food and Drug Administration the American Red Cross, and the American Association of Blood Banks are coordinating global efforts on many levels.

The WHO GCBS (www.who.int) has developed a database to follow and report on these initiatives.

—Brian J. Daley

FURTHER READING

www.cdc.gov
www.os.dhhs.gov
www.who.int

GOAL

See Objectives, Vision

GOAL SETTING

See Objectives

GOOD CLINICAL PRACTICES (GCPs)

Clinical research must be conducted in accordance with standards that are formalized through many international guidelines and regulations. The ultimate goals of good clinical research are the protection of all research participants and the assurance that only worthwhile treatments are approved for clinical use on future patients. To achieve this goal, the adaptation of and adherence to good clinical practices (GCPs) are necessary. These principles provide the framework for conducting GCP-compliant clinical research.

Many systems and procedures must be established and put into place before the start of a clinical trial study. This practice ensures that the standards for conducting the study, and the methods for determining if these standards are being met, are known to all interested parties. Documentation must clearly indicate compliance with the systems and procedures. This documentation must be of such high caliber that an independent reviewer could verify that the research was conducted as the researchers reported it was.

The implementation of the following systems and procedures ensures compliance with GCP requirements:

planning (studies are conducted for valid ethical and scientific reasons); standard operating procedures (see entry in this encyclopedia); qualified personnel (all personnel must be appropriately experienced and qualified to perform assigned tasks, and documentation of these qualifications must be readily available); review and approval from an ethics committee or independent review board (IRB) prior to study start as well as continuing review (assesses study participant risks); informed consent (see entry for this key word); well-designed study (protocol documents, valid study design, and data collection plans that can be reviewed by all interested parties); monitoring (clinical study quality control performed by sponsor/CRO (Contract Research Organization); control of study medications and devices (management of study product to ensure subject safety as well as documentation indicating full accountability of same); data integrity (must be honest and reviewed by site personnel, monitors, and transcribers); quality assurance (quality checks must be established and followed at all study stages); and archives (secure retention of research activities documentation provides evidence of said activities).

—Linda M. Cimino

See also Informed Consent, Institutional Review Board (IRB), Quality Assurance, Standard Operating Procedures (SOPs)

FURTHER READING

Bohaychuk, W., & Ball, G. (1999). *Conducting GCP-compliant clinical research.* Chichester, UK: Wiley.

Chow, S.-C., & Liu, J.-P. (1998). *Design and analysis of clinical trials: Concepts and methodologies.* New York: Wiley.

Glossary: Clinical research terminology. (2001, December). *Applied Clinical Trials.* 36–48.

Kolman, J., Meng, P., & Scott, G. (1998). *Good clinical practice* (pp. 2–3). Chichester, UK: Wiley.

Wittemore, R., & Grey, M. (2002, Second Quarter). The systematic development of nursing interventions. *Journal of Nursing Scholarship,* 115–120.

GOODWILL

Goodwill is a residual consequence of excess consideration given for the fair market value of readily identifiable tangible assets and liabilities acquired or assumed in a purchase transaction between two or more unrelated companies. The excess purchase price represents the intangible value for such items as reputation, brand recognition, technical skills, and other intellectual capital an acquiring company believes is inherent in the acquired company.

For example, assume ABC Medical Center purchases XYZ Hospital for $10 million although the net assets of XYZ Hospital have a fair market value of $9 million. ABC Medical Center would record, as a long-term asset, $1 million in goodwill.

When goodwill emerges as a result of a business combination, the initial recognition and subsequent treatment, including impairment recognition parameters, are governed in the United States primarily by the Financial Accounting Standards Board (FASB) in Statement of Financial Accounting Standards No. 142. Under the provisions of Statement No. 142, goodwill is no longer subject to amortization as it was under previous authoritative guidance. Rather, companies must annually reassess the value of their recognized goodwill and, if certain conditions or indications of impairment are present, write the recorded goodwill down to the current fair value. Any writedown that occurs because of impairment may not be restored at a future date in the event of a recovery in value.

—Edward Pershing

GOVERNANCE

See Boards of Directors

GOVERNING BOARDS

See Boards of Directors

GRADUATE MEDICAL EDUCATION (GME)

The requirements of graduate medical education (GME), or the training of physicians in a surgical/medical specialty, vary from country to country. In the United States, oversight for GME is vested in the Accreditation Council for Graduate Medical Education (ACGME), which is responsible for residency training programs. Accreditation is based on published standards and guidelines, and is established through a process of peer review. To be accredited, a program must have a primary sponsoring institution, which establishes and ensures standards both for itself and any participating institutions. Participating institutions must have a written agreement with the sponsoring institution that outlines the educational benefits and goals the

participating institution brings to the program. There must be a program director, board certified in the specialty or possessing qualities otherwise acceptable to the residency review committee (RRC), whose primary responsibility is to assure that the program abides by its own rules and the written requirements of the ACGME and RRC in each specialty. There must be a physician faculty, all of whom are board certified or possessing qualifications acceptable to the RRC, of sufficient number to provide the required training to all the residents in the program, and who provide timely and periodic evaluations to all the residents. A residency program must have sufficient support personnel to ensure the academic, educational, and administrative requirements of the program. All residency programs must ensure that their residents are trained in compassionate, professional patient care; provide an exposure for scholarship and research; provide periodic evaluation of the residents' progress; provide an opportunity for the residents to evaluate the quality of their own instruction; and abide by rules limiting work hours, working conditions, and upholding due process and an opportunity for fair expression of grievances on the part of residents.

—Robert I. Katz

FURTHER READING

www.acgme.org
www.ecfmg.org/index.html

GROSS DOMESTIC PRODUCT (GDP)

Gross domestic product (GDP) is the total value of all final goods and services produced within a country during a particular period valued at prices in that period. This important indicator of the way in which an economic system is functioning can be divided into four broad components, based on who purchases the goods and services. Components of GDP include personal consumption expenditures, gross private domestic investment, government purchases, and net exports.

Personal consumption expenditures measures the value of durable and nondurable goods and services purchased by households during a given time period. Examples of durable goods include motor vehicles, furniture, and household equipment. Nondurable goods include such items as food, clothing, gasoline, and fuel oil. Housing, transportation, and medical care purchases are important service transactions. Production of consumer goods and services accounts for more than two thirds of GDP. Medical care purchases account for 14% of GDP and more than 20% of all consumer service expenditures.

The term *gross private domestic investment* refers to the value of all goods produced during a period for use in the production of other goods and services. Economists restrict this spending category to activities that increase the economy's stock of productive capital. Fixed investment in nonresidential and residential structures, tools and equipment, software, and changes in private inventories are important components of private domestic investment. Inventory changes are included to account for production in the period in which it occurs. Gross private domestic investment makes up about 16% of GDP.

Government purchases are purchases of goods and services from firms by government agencies, plus the total value of output produced by government agencies themselves during a period of time. Only government purchases that reflect production of a good or service are included in GDP. For example, transfer payments such as Social Security and unemployment compensation do not enter GDP calculations, because they do not require the recipient to produce a good or service. Government purchases make up about 18% of GDP.

The term *net exports* refers to sales of a country's goods and services to buyers in the rest of the world during a given time period (exports), minus purchases of foreign goods and services by the home country's residents during a period (imports). Subtracting imports, or the value of goods and services produced abroad that are consumed at home, from exports, or the value of goods and services that are produced at home but are consumed abroad, provides a measure of the net effect of global trade on the home country's production. Net exports are positive when exports exceed imports, and negative when the reverse holds.

GDP can be measured in nominal terms, using current dollar prices, or in real terms, by adjusting nominal GDP figures each year to eliminate the effect of changes in prices. A price index called the *GDP implicit price deflator* is used for this purpose. Figures on nominal and real GDP are reported at www.bea.doc.gov.

—Don P. Clark

FURTHER READING

Folland, S., Goodman, A. C., & Santo, M. (2001). *The economics of health and health care* (3rd ed.). Upper Saddle River, NJ: Prentice Hall.

Hall, R. E., & Lieberman, M. (2001). *Economics: Principles and applications.* Cincinnati, OH: South-Western.

GROUP BEHAVIOR

See Group Performance

GROUP NORMS

Group norms are beliefs and habits shared in common among members of a group, and include spoken and unspoken rules of conduct members expect one another to follow as well as shared perceptions. Norms are a group's normal ways of behaving and interacting, and prescribe to members what they ought to do in certain situations. Norms are implicitly understood ranges of behavior and reflect the group's consensus about what behaviors are acceptable. Examples of norms in a medical treatment group might include arriving on time for group meetings, using humor in stressful situations, and speaking critically about other members only within the group.

Norms can develop early and quickly or can emerge gradually over a group's life span. Norms for interaction behaviors are often created in the group's first meetings and can set the tone for the group's productivity and interactions internally and externally. One classic laboratory study that demonstrates how quickly norms can be formed found that when groups of strangers saw an ambiguous visual stimulus every few minutes, they at first disagreed on what it was, but after three or four trials their judgments typically converged to a *perceptual norm.* Another study of college students living in one dormitory showed that over an academic year, their political beliefs converged.

Individuals tend to *internalize* group norms, to adopt them as personal beliefs and habits that guide their thinking and action—even away from other group members. Individuals also tend to affiliate with groups whose members have beliefs and habits compatible with their own. Consistent with both tendencies, a study of eating disorders found unusually high rates of bulimia among cheerleading squads, sports teams, and sororities. Members of these groups who did not have the habit when they joined demonstrated an increasing tendency to adopt bulimia the longer they remained. This result illustrates the well-established finding that groups can maintain norms that oppose those of the larger social unit or community.

Group norms can include shared *stereotypes,* or generalized beliefs about the attributes of those who belong to certain identifiable groups or social categories. For example, a group of nurses might develop a stereotype concerning local physicians, either favorable ("Docs here really care about patients") or unfavorable ("Our docs have rotten bedside manners") or both. Intergroup cooperation or hostility can accompany such stereotypes.

Individuals typically conform with group norms—even concerning matters irrelevant to group goals—in part because groups tend to enforce certain norms through subtle or even harsh sanctions of deviants. A study of discussion groups found that those who espoused decisions contrary to group consensus and who refused to be persuaded by their groups, tended to be excluded from later discussion. Another example concerned groups that formed among workers in the Hawthorne Studies at the Western Electric Company, who agreed to be observed in a special work room where they assembled telephone-switching equipment. Two informal groups formed in the same room. One developed a norm for high production; the other developed norms for lower output. Members of this second group who exceeded or fell short of their quotas—"ratebusters" or "chiselers," respectively—experienced "binging," in which other members took turns slugging them hard on the shoulder. Work groups routinely develop and enforce norms concerning collective output, or production, even at odds with their host organizations.

Conformity with norms concerning production and other topics increases with group *cohesion* (the extent to which a group's members feel attracted to their group and value their membership in it). Conformity also increases with the ambiguity of the group's situation or task. Conformity by a lone dissenter becomes more likely as group size increases. However, the presence of two or more mutually supportive dissenters—or a *coalition*—greatly increases their resistance to conformity, regardless of group size.

Norms tend to reinforce existing practices and create resistance to change. For example, a surgical team that favors a particular technique may find it difficult to embrace a new procedure, especially one that requires redefinition of members' roles and relationships.

Individuals with higher rank or status in a group have relatively powerful influence on the development and enforcement of norms, and yet have greater latitude than other members to deviate from those norms. A group's leader may even be expected to initiate new norms. In new groups, the leader and members establish norms, which often grow out of their individual personalities, preferences, and skills. As membership changes, norms can persist even when no longer helpful. New members may be selected more for compatibility with the existing norms than for their characteristics that could improve group performance. Conformity with norms increases with a decentralized style of leadership, ambiguous tasks or situations, and group cohesion.

—Elaine Seat and Eric D. Sundstrom

See also Group Performance, Groupthink

FURTHER READING

Allen, V. L. (1975). Social support for nonconformity. *Advances in Experimental Social Psychology, 8,* 2–43.

Crandall, C. S. (1988). Social contagion of binge eating. *Journal of Personality and Social Psychology, 55,* 588–598.

Forsyth, D. (1999). *Group dynamics* (3rd ed.). Belmont, CA: Wadsworth.

Homans, G. C. (1950). *The human group.* New York: Harcourt, Brace & World.

McGrath, J. E. (1984). *Groups: Interaction and performance.* Englewood Cliffs, NJ: Prentice Hall.

Newcomb, T. M. (1943). *Personality and social change.* New York: Dryden Press.

Schachter, S. (1968). Deviation, rejection, and communication. In D. Cartwright & A. Zander (Eds.), *Group dynamics* (3rd ed., pp. 165–181). New York: Harper & Row.

Sherif, M. (1936). *The psychology of social norms.* New York: Harper & Row.

GROUP PERFORMANCE

Group performance represents the extent to which a group's products or services meet the expectations of those who use, receive, or evaluate them. Expectations concerning performance derive from the group's *mission* or *role* as defined by the group's primary counterparts: the manager responsible for assigning and supervising the group's work; customers who receive the group's output; and possibly others with an interest in the group's practices, processes, or results, such as professional peers, regulators, stakeholders, or support staff.

Defining and clarifying the group's role are critical for group performance. Usual sources of role definition include the group's manager (for example, in a new product team), members (for example, physicians in a medical practice), and their individual roles in the larger organization (for example, a surgical team). Clarifying a group's role in the workplace calls for specifying the group's responsibility for negotiating and organizing its work, based on the combination of members' knowledge, skills, abilities, and preferences. Role specification also focuses on the group's responsibilities, timelines, work standards, and methods for measuring performance. Objective criteria of performance—based on counts of output—are ideal, although not always available. Reports or ratings of satisfaction by customers or managers are more common, and are best when specific.

Group effectiveness encompasses group performance plus *viability,* or long-term, continuing capability of performing as a group in the future. Because a group can burn out, fall apart, or otherwise lose its capacity to perform, effectiveness requires more than performance. Viability depends on the extent to which (a) working in the group continues to meet the members' needs, (b) members maintain the necessary individual expertise and collective capacities for coordinated effort, and (c) members maintain positive interpersonal relationships and willingness to continue working together in the future. For example, an effective ER team not only provides excellent emergency services, but its members also maintain and update their individual, specialized skills; the group maintains its team-work skills; and members like and respect one another well enough to continue working together.

Psychologist Ivan Steiner (1972) proposed an equation to describe group productivity, a form of performance (output produced with available resources):

Actual productivity = potential productivity − process losses + process gains

In this equation, group performance (productivity) depends on (a) *potential productivity* expected in view of its resources—especially members' expertise—and constraints; (b) *process losses,* or failures to apply the resources to the mission, through faulty interaction processes; and (c) *process gains,* or increments in performance beyond the expected potential, gained through interaction in which members' collaborative results exceed the expected sum of their separate, individual efforts.

The following sections describe the terms on the right-hand side of the equation and identify factors related to process losses and gains.

POTENTIAL GROUP PRODUCTIVITY OR PERFORMANCE

A group's potential performance depends on the fit of its resources—especially members' knowledge, skills, abilities, and other traits—with the group's role, including specific responsibilities and constraints. Resources also include budget, tools, equipment, technology, facilities, and work time. Constraints can include reporting relationships, acceptable procedures, and work standards, among others. Ideally a group's members collectively possess all necessary capabilities and resources. If so, the group's potential performance is 100%.

PROCESS LOSSES

Groups' interaction processes can lead actual performance to fall short of potential performance through failures to fully apply members' capabilities. Common sources of process loss involve *coordination,* as in a tug-of-war with people tripping over one another; or *motivation,* not pulling hard enough; or *direction,* as when a leader instructs people to pull in different directions.

Some well-established group dynamics commonly produce process losses: groupthink, conflict, and others. Process losses become more common as group size increases, and as coordination becomes more difficult. Process losses can stem from a mismatch of the leader's style, the group's composition, the situation, and/or the mission.

PROCESS GAINS OR *SYNERGY*

Process gains occur when interactions among group members build on or extend the combination of individual contributions for better-than-expected outcomes. The term *synergy* describes such interactions, in which the collective result substantially exceeds the sum of results expected from the same individuals working separately. For instance, a new product team may conduct a "brainstorming" session and identify several new product ideas, all worthy of development, none of which the members might have conceived while working alone. Gains via interaction processes can come from innovative ways of combining members' complementary skills, new work technologies, refinements in procedure, or simply coincidence. For example, a new orthopedic cast replacement was created when materials experts and orthopedic surgeons assembled to manufacture new sizes of an existing product. Similar gains can occur when a group finds a better way (or "breakthrough") to accomplish a well-defined mission.

FACTORS IN GROUP PROCESS LOSSES AND PROCESS GAINS

Group Size. Experts recommend forming groups of the smallest size that incorporates the needed expertise. Relatively small groups allow comfortable, efficient interaction among members. As group size increases, potential productivity rises at a decelerating rate, whereas potential problems in coordinating the members' efforts increase at an accelerating rate, along with prospects for process losses.

Group Composition. Research has found that group performance is related to group composition, the particular combination of individual ability and personality among members. For example, group average cognitive ability correlates positively with group performance for most tasks studied. Some research shows process gains in homogeneous, high-ability groups. Composition on some personality traits, especially average conscientiousness and agreeableness, relate to group performance of some kinds of work.

Heterogeneous groups—those with relatively diverse personalities—experience more conflict than other groups, and if they manage it well, may generate more creative solutions. In contrast, homogeneous groups tend to be more cohesive, less prone to process losses, and possibly less creative. Experts recommend staffing teams on the basis of complementary, work-related *expertise,* and not on personality. Diverse teams may need extra training in teamwork skills for managing individual differences.

Cohesion. Group cohesion, the extent to which members feel attracted and committed to their groups, tends to magnify the influence of *group norms.* In groups whose norms favor high performance, cohesion correlates positively with performance. In groups whose norms do not favor productivity, cohesion correlates inversely with performance. Cohesive groups tend to remain intact for relatively long periods, and generally perform well. Under certain conditions, however, cohesive groups can become susceptible to process losses from *groupthink* (a dysfunctional approach to decision making that involves a false perception of unanimity).

Goals and Goal Setting. Groups that adopt specific, moderately difficult goals perform better, on average, than groups with no goals, vague goals, or apparently impossible goals. The gain in performance from setting specific, moderately difficult goals generally improves when members participate in setting the goals, or set the goals themselves.

Performance Measurement and Feedback. Groups whose members have timely access to measurements of their performance—that is, immediate feedback—tend to improve their performance more rapidly than do groups that receive no feedback. Some research has found dramatic gains from measuring group performance and providing timely feedback.

Motivation. Among the most powerful motivators for group performance are contingent rewards or incentives, particularly pay systems that incorporate *team compensation,* or rewards for collective performance by groups. Other sources of motivation include professional awards, public recognition, and evaluation by professional peers. Highly motivated groups tend to demonstrate process gains.

Leadership. Leadership roles, both internal and external to a group, include responsibility for (a) facilitating external communications and work linkages, (b) providing direction and coordination within the group, and (c) facilitating the development of positive interpersonal relationships among members to enable long-term group viability.

A leader whose approach complements the group's mission and composition can produce process gains, and a leader who uses a mismatched approach can create process losses. For example, a study at a health care facility found poorer participation and performance among groups whose leaders used an autocratic approach that overrepresented physicians' opinions and underrepresented the views of other professionals. In contrast, many situations involving groups in health care settings call for decision making by *consensus* (agreement by all members to support the group's decision). Research has consistently found process gains from consensus decision making, which takes more time than other methods of decision making and is best used for key decisions.

Conflict. Groups with interpersonal conflict—concerning personal differences—tend to perform poorly, at least in part because they spend time addressing relationship-focused conflicts that they could spend on their work. In contrast, well-managed task conflict—concerning alternative ways of approaching the group's work—tends to bring process gains. However, task-related conflict can become detrimental to performance when members refuse to compromise or adapt to one another's views and approaches. Best-performing groups have a moderate amount of well-managed conflict focused on the group's work and minimal conflict concerning interpersonal relationships.

Teamwork Skills. Specific skills needed for effective teamwork, such as consensus decision making and conflict management, are taught as part of the standard training in teamwork skills offered by many successful team-based organizations.

—Eric Sundstrom and Elaine Seat

See also Group Norms, Groupthink, Team-Based Compensation, Teamwork

FURTHER READING

Cohen, S. G., & Bailey, D. E. (1997). What makes teams work: Group effectiveness research from the shop floor to the executive suite. *Journal of Management, 23*(3), 239–290.

Hackman, J. R. (1990). *Groups that work (and those that don't): Creating conditions for effective teamwork.* San Francisco: Jossey-Bass.

Pritchard, R. D., Jones, S., Roth, P., Stuebing, K., & Ekeberg, S. (1988). Effects of group feedback, goal setting, and incentives on organizational productivity. *Journal of Applied Psychology, 73*(2), 337–358.

Steiner, I. D. (1972). *Group process and productivity.* New York: Academic Press.

Stewart, G. L., Barrick, M., Neubert, M. J., & Mount, M. K. (1998). Relating member ability and personality to work-team processes and team effectiveness. *Journal of Applied Psychology, 83*(3), 377–391.

Sundstrom, E., De Meuse, K., & Futrell, D. (1990). Work teams: Applications and effectiveness. *American Psychologist, 45,* 120–133.

GROUPTHINK

The term *groupthink* refers to a type of failure in group decision making where a highly cohesive group only considers limited options and arrives at a faulty decision even though other information was available. Groupthink happens when members develop a strong bond to the group and the focus shifts from objectively evaluating options to maintaining group conformity and identity.

The concept of groupthink was first proposed in a 1971 book by social psychologist Irving Janis. He analyzed political decisions by groups, such as the 1961 decision by President Kennedy and his advisers to invade Cuba at the Bay of Pigs. Many advisers knew the invasion would fail, yet kept silent, incorrectly perceiving themselves as lone dissenters.

Other examples of groupthink include the decision by Nixon's White House advisers to authorize a wiretap in the Watergate Hotel, the business decision by Beech-Nut to purchase poor-quality apple juice, the early 1990s Salomon Brothers Treasury auction scandal, and the decision at NASA to launch the space shuttle *Challenger.*

Groupthink can occur in medical decision making. For example, a group of physicians may prematurely adopt a new medication, or cover up a mistake in surgery, or reject a promising but risky treatment.

Groupthink incorporates the tendencies of groups to develop norms (shared habits and beliefs) and to demonstrate conformity. An example of a norm that might enable groupthink is deference to the leader. Pressures toward conformity strengthen with increasing group cohesion. Groupthink is no single flaw but instead describes a flawed decision-making process set up by skewed communication processes. These flawed decisions are often made under time constraints where the group uses what time it has to further discuss facts and opinions that continue to support its decision, rather than to seek out and evaluate options. The basis for the decision often shifts from "Prove why we should do this" to "Prove why we *shouldn't* do this."

Groupthink may pose problems in virtual groups whose members interact electronically from remote locations via telephone, e-mail, or computer. Because much interpersonal communication involves nonverbal messages—from facial expressions, gestures, posture, and tone of voice—their relative absence in virtual interaction can add to the likelihood that members mistake silence for support.

Researchers disagree about the usefulness of the concept of groupthink. Although some see it as a helpful way of describing a common syndrome, others point out that it merely renames a combination of well-known group dynamics.

SYMPTOMS OF GROUPTHINK

Groupthink has nine contributing factors:

1. An *illusion of invulnerability* where the group overestimates its expertise and becomes overly optimistic.

2. The stress of a perceived threat—usually a deadline or time pressure to make a decision.

3. Collective rationalization of some facts and opinions while discounting alternatives.

4. Confidence in the inherent morality of the group's position, even in defiance of prevailing ethics or laws.

5. Derogatory and stereotypical descriptions of dissenters, to discount those who disagree.

6. Pressures by the group majority to conform.

7. Censorship of individual's own differing opinions, because the group appears to have consensus. Silence is taken as approval.

8. A false perception of unanimity based on overemphasis of points of agreement and on underemphasis of differences.

9. Self-appointed *mind guards* protecting the group from adverse information. Mind guards prevent outsiders from addressing the group and withhold alternate information.

PREVENTING GROUPTHINK

Prevention of groupthink is part of the leadership role. Because groupthink involves a failure to incorporate members' knowledge into group decisions, avoiding it can depend on the extent to which the leader encourages members to offer their ideas. Because groupthink can represent a rush to judgment, avoiding it can depend on the extent to which a leader slows deliberation at critical times. And because groupthink arises in isolation, avoiding it can depend on the extent to which a leader links the group externally.

To prevent groupthink, a leader can

1. *Openly discuss the group's decision processes, leader role, and kind of input—if any—invited from members.* Sometimes a leader decides on a course of action without input. Examples include time-urgent crises in which the leader has expert knowledge or unique information needed to direct a group response, as in emergency surgery. In other situations—especially when members have special knowledge or information the leader lacks—the best decision process involves members' input or active participation in reaching consensus. Ideally a group discusses its decision-making processes in advance of confronting a crisis.

2. *Legitimize and promote conflict.* Mechanisms include holding round-robin forums in which members take turns expressing viewpoints; appointing a devil's advocate, or designated critic, whose task is to raise drawbacks; assigning subgroups to explore specific options and present pros and cons; and holding mock debates in which assigned advocates argue for various options.

3. *Delay expressing an opinion until all other members have expressed their ideas about the group's options.*

4. *Encourage external interaction.* Mechanisms include inviting outside experts to speak at group meetings, encouraging members to obtain expert reviews or consultations concerning their work, and assigning members to do reports.

A group can also avoid groupthink through developing norms. One example is checking with all members before adopting a decision. Another is allowing a *one-minute commercial* by any member in a meeting, any time, without interruption.

—Elaine Seat and Eric Sundstrom

See also Group Norms, Group Performance, Leadership

FURTHER READING

Janis, I. L. (1971). *Victims of groupthink: A psychological study of foreign policy decisions and fiascos.* Boston: Houghton Mifflin.

Janis, I. L. (1983). *Groupthink: Psychological studies of policy decisions and fiascoes* (2nd ed.). Boston: Houghton Mifflin.

Moorhead, G., Ference, R., & Neck, C. P. (1991). Group decision fiascoes continue: Space shuttle *Challenger* and a revised groupthink framework. *Human Relations, 44*(6), 539–550.

Park, W. W. (1990). A review of research on groupthink. *Journal of Behavioral Decision Making, 3,* 229–245.

Sims, R. R. (1992). Linking groupthink to unethical behavior in organizations. *Journal of Business Ethics, 11,* 651–662.

Special issue on groupthink. (1998). *Organizational Behavior and Human Decision Making Processes, 73*(2–3).

GROWTH STAGE OF PRODUCT LIFE CYCLE

See Product Life Cycle (PLC) Analysis

H

HACKER

A hacker hacks away into the intricacies of complex computer systems to uncover sources of operating problems, design quick remedies, and implement effective solutions. These computer enthusiasts are usually adept at several programming languages and can use these skills to uncover computer code of secure systems, thereby giving them the ability to break into proprietary systems to steal valuable information. Unfortunately, hacker attacks are rarely reported, for fear of negative publicity (Bradner, 2002).

The more popular use of the word "hacker" is derogatory—computer experts who use their skills for malicious purposes. People in the computing profession like to refer to them as "crackers." These expert computer enthusiasts break into secure systems and cause systems to break down, steal valuable and sensitive data, or modify code so that systems malfunction.

The security threat posed by hackers (crackers) can be potentially devastating. The most common reason for breaking into an organization's computer systems is to steal sensitive business and personal information so that it can be sold to competitors and marketing firms. Organizations are spending a significant proportion of their information technology (IT) budgets to prevent unauthorized security breaches by hackers. Several laws are in place so that organizations protect the privacy of their customers and employees.

One such law, the Health Insurance Portability and Accountability Act of 1996, mandates that hospitals and their business partners secure their business networks and patient registry information systems (Tieman, 2001). A hacker can potentially break into a hospital's database and retrieve sensitive and personal information on patients. This information can be used in many ways, ranging from relatively benign marketing programs to more damaging activities such as credit card theft. On the business side, a hacker can disrupt a hospital's ordering and scheduling systems, thus disrupting supplies and operations. Unfortunately, hacker attacks are rarely reported, for fear of negative publicity (Bradner, 2002).

The American Hospital Association, with 4600 member organizations, is designing a hub to manage business networks of hospitals and their business partners. These "hacker proof" network and e-commerce services will help health care organizations protect their patient, clinical, and business information (Tieman, 2001).

Hackers are expert computer programmers or users who possess skills that can be used for productive or desirable purposes. The correct term for the person who uses these skills for malicious reasons is "cracker." This distinction is made clear in a news story on efforts to break into the communication networks of terrorists. After the World Trade Center tragedy, a top-secret U.S. security agency recruited a 16-year-old hacker from New Delhi. He is a security expert with expertise in deciphering messages hidden in Web pages. His expertise is being used to make it harder for crackers to communicate (Mackler, 2002).

—Alok Srivastava

See also Information Technology

FURTHER READING

Bradner, S. (2002). Your confession is good for us. *Network World, 15,* 30.

Mackler, C. (2002). Hacker vs. crackers. *Teen People, 5,* 136.

Tieman, J. (2001). AHA tries to make a sale. *Modern Healthcare, 46,* 9.

HARVESTING STRATEGIES

The term *harvesting strategies* describes the process of deciding to remove and then removing an organizational unit by selling it for the best possible return or by pricing its goods and services as high as possible to maximize profitability with little regard for longer-term consequences. Just as the farmer harvests a live crop to sell for cash and profit, businesses and other organizations "harvest" business units for a variety of reasons.

Organizations often face dilemmas of where to focus their efforts and resources. To determine this, the organization's management must consider the various elements as if they were parts of an investment portfolio. Some are great performers. Others are terrible. Still others have great potential for growth but require heavy investments to realize that potential. Finally, there may be a group that is performing quite well but whose future is uncertain.

The future uncertainty may be due to many different situations: market position, conditions, competition, technology, and so on. The reason is immaterial to this definition. Once a company or an organization has determined that it would be best served by removing a unit from its "portfolio," it moves into a harvesting strategy. At this stage, some investment may still be required to maximize the result of a sale. Just as the farmer must pick a crop, perhaps sort it, and transport it to market, a business or other organization must prepare a unit for harvesting.

The process of deciding when to dispose of a unit and doing so is known as a *harvesting strategy*. Such strategies are usually employed in business when the unit still has strong cash flows but little prospect for growth, or doesn't fit the future strategic direction of the parent organization.

—John L. Mariotti

See also BCG Portfolio Analysis, Strategy

FURTHER READING

Porter, M. (1980). *Competitive strategy: Techniques for analyzing industries and competitors.* New York: Free Press.
Porter, M. (1985). *Competitive advantage: Creating and sustaining superior performance.* New York: Free Press.

HEALTH

The term *health* has been defined in many different ways but generally refers to individual wellness, indicating the sum of an individual's state of being, that person's optimal physical and mental functioning within the context of the living environment (home, work, community). The term *health* may also refer to a group of people, as a summary indication of the group's functional state.

Standard dictionary definitions of health present two concepts: (a) the absence of disease or disability, and (b) optimal wellness, where a person is functioning at a personally defined maximum capacity in a certain set of environmental constraints. These two concepts, illness and wellness, are not necessarily connected in a continuum; that is, individuals can feel ill in the absence of illness or disability.

In 1948, as part of the World Health Organization (WHO) constitution, health was defined as "a state of complete physical, mental, and social well-being and not merely the absence of disease or infirmity." In 1978 in the Declaration of Alma Ata, WHO reaffirmed its definition of health and declared that health is a fundamental human right. A revised definition called for a level of health that will permit people to lead socially and economically productive lives. In 1984, WHO advanced a revised statement that any measure of health must take into account "the extent to which an individual or a group is able to realize aspirations and satisfy needs, and to change or cope with the environment."

The Institute of Medicine's Committee on Using Performance Monitoring to Improve Community Health in 1997 defined health as "a state of well-being and the capability to function in the face of changing circumstances. Health is, therefore, a positive concept emphasizing social and personal resources as well as physical capabilities."

HEALTH VIEWED THROUGH HISTORY

Early civilizations had many practices purported to be protective of health. Some of these were religious prescriptions or laws, for example, related to food, personal and societal cleanliness, and disposal of human waste. Other practices were described in legal systems or in early scientific explorations. Desired behaviors or interventions were based on religious beliefs or on early ideas about the anatomy and physiology of illness. Most early ideas of health were negative, because communicable disease epidemics were common and exerted the most visible effects on health.

Many of the most serious early threats to health had their origin in community living. Infectious diseases have remained a major cause of global morbidity and mortality despite the discovery of antibiotics and the method of disease transmission. In the past 50 years, there is increasing evidence of the effect of broader factors on individual and population health such as the social and economic environment.

MEASUREMENT OF HEALTH

There are no direct measurements of health. Although one can measure the physiologic parameters of the body's organ systems, this is only an indirect indicator of "healthiness." There is still debate on the best methods of measurement of overall health, reflecting the complexity and abstractness of the idea of health. Indicators of health can be selected and measured for individuals and for populations. Numbers are assigned to objects or events and are represented by a wide range of objective and subjective types. For example, a laboratory measurement of blood lead levels is one type of measurement of health, and a self-reported question on how well the respondent is functioning is another. Indicators are frequently chosen to represent health problems of social concern and to focus public attention on a particular health issue.

Morbidity and mortality are frequently used as population measurements of health. Years of life lost (YLL) and years lost due to disability (YLD) describe years lost due to premature mortality and disability of an index condition. Disability-adjusted life-years (DALY) have been developed to describe the burden of disease in a population; this burden is represented by a lost year of healthy life. These indices represent a "quantity" measurement of health. Newer indices of health have been devised to describe the "quality" of life, including the quality-adjusted life-years (QALY).

Indices measuring individual health have been developed to cover most aspects of daily functioning, assessing the entire person within their individual living environment. Subjective health measurements record general feelings of well-being or symptoms of illness, or they may focus on the adequacy of an individual's functioning.

Data reflecting health status are found in a variety of different sources, including vital statistics documents, medical documents in health care systems, or insurance records. Here are some specific health data sources, named in Turnock's *Public Health: What It Is and How It Works* (1997): mortality statistics, medical data from birth records, reportable disease statistics, mass diagnostic and screening surveys, disease registries, morbidity surveys of the general population, health insurance statistics, life insurance statistics, hospital inpatient statistics, hospital outpatient statistics, data on disease treated in special clinics and hospitals, data from public health clinics, data from records of physician practices, absenteeism data from work or school, data from school health programs, statistics on morbidity in armed forces, statistics on veterans, Social Security statistics, U.S. Department of Labor statistics, and census data.

INFLUENCES ON HEALTH

Some factors have been linked by epidemiologic studies to be more directly associated with the major health problems in the United States. For example, it is well-known that smoking, high blood pressure, obesity, and diabetes have a strong relationship to heart disease. The National Center for Health Statistics as part of the Centers for Disease Control and Prevention (CDC) in the U.S. Department of Health and Human Services maintains several ongoing surveys of the U.S. population that measure physical health parameters and potential risk factors. State health departments participate in an annual CDC survey of behavioral risk factors.

The factors that are linked with specific health problems as in the preceding example are often termed "risk factors." Those risk factors most closely associated with a disease entity are termed "determinants." Risk factors that are further removed in the chain of causation are called "direct and indirect contributing factors" and can be described at either an individual or population level.

Bunker and colleagues in 1995 found that of the 30-year increase in life expectancy achieved in this century, only about 5 years can be attributed to health care. The most prominent contributors to mortality in the United States in 1990, as identified in a *JAMA* article on the actual causes of death, were tobacco, diet and activity patterns, alcohol, microbial agents, toxic agents, firearms, sexual behavior, motor vehicles, and illicit use of drugs. Socioeconomic status and access to medical care are also important contributors but are difficult to quantify independent of the other factors cited.

Considerable evidence indicates that socioeconomic status, social inequality, and income disparity are key underlying determinants of health. Stress has been shown to be a key factor in health disparities based on socioeconomic status; both experts and the public identify the stress of daily life as a factor that promotes unhealthy choices. Some experts have identified social isolation and the loss of community as important underlying determinants of health.

In the 1970s, Henrik Blum, at the University of California at Berkeley, grouped the factors influencing health into four principal forces: environment, heredity, lifestyles, and health care. A Canadian government White Paper, the *Lalonde Report,* brought wider attention to this way of thinking about factors influencing health. More recently, Evans and Stoddart (1994) proposed an expanded version of this model that identified both the major influences on health and well-being and the dynamic relationships among them: (a) social environment, (b) physical environment, (c) genetic endowment, (d) individual response (behavior and biology), (e) health care, (f) disease, (g) health and function, (h) well-being, and (i) prosperity.

PRINCIPAL U.S. HEALTH ISSUES

Major mortality has changed in the United States over the past 100 years, from deaths because of infectious diseases such as infant diarrhea and tuberculosis, to chronic diseases such as heart disease and cancer caused by heredity, lifestyle behaviors, and environmental factors. Life expectancy increased from 47 years at birth in 1900 to 73.1 years in 1996.

The DHHS publication *Health, United States, 2001* (see Further Reading) relates current morbidity and mortality data from national survey information. A common historic measurement, infant mortality, approximately 7 per 1000 live births in the United States in 1998, measures the number of deaths of children before age 1 and is a reflection of the health of the mother and access to prenatal and perinatal health services. Almost 70% of deaths in children and young adults (1 to 24 years of age) are due to injuries and are therefore preventable. Deaths among people 25 to 65 years accounted for 22% of all deaths in 1998. The three leading causes of death for working-age adults are cancer, heart disease, and unintentional injuries, with lung cancer the leading cause of cancer mortality. Three quarters of all deaths in the United States occur among people age 65 and over. The top five causes of death for elderly Americans are heart disease, cancer, stroke, chronic obstructive pulmonary disease, and pneumonia. Provision of appropriate and timely health services can help the elderly prevent, treat, and manage chronic illnesses, thus enhancing quality of life and preventing premature death.

GLOBAL HEALTH

A few health indices provide perspective on the current health status of the world's population. Despite an average life expectancy of 68, two fifths of all deaths in the world can be considered premature in that, in 1998, 20 million people died before the age of 50, half of them children under 5 years of age. Half of all deaths in the developing world are due to infectious diseases and parasites, with a major burden of mortality being HIV/AIDS. As of 2002 the global population, about 5.8 billion people, is projected to increase to about 8 billion by 2025, with an increasing proportion of people over 65 and a decreasing proportion of young people under age 20. In 1955 about 68% of the global population lived in rural areas and 32% in urban areas. In 1995 the ratio was 55% rural and 45% urban, and by 2025 it is projected to be 41% rural and 59% urban.

Health indices of all nations worldwide show considerable variation. Given the variation in sociocultural, political, and economic systems, and environmental conditions, it is difficult to make any generalizations about underlying determinants of health in comparing one country with another. Some international epidemiologists argue that the major threats to health in both the developed and developing world are the "3 P's" of pollution, population, and poverty. Although these factors might appear to be directly related to national wealth, national health status and per capita income are not linked in a direct way. In general, factors such as literacy rates, economic conditions, and social welfare policies have more to do with improved health status than with specific preventive interventions.

STRATEGIES FOR IMPROVING HEALTH

It is possible to target various determinants of health to produce change at an individual level, a population level, or

both. In the past, strategies to improve health have been based on specific disease entities or behaviors. Research connecting broader socioeconomic factors with health suggests that a wider range of intervention targets may be more effective. Health improvement efforts, whether focused on a specific disease or broader determinants, should use evidence-based methods of effectiveness and should have clear causal linkages between risk factors and health.

—Ray M. Nicola

See also Community Health, Community Health Status Indicators, Epidemiology, Health Behavior, Health Care, Health Policy, Health Promotion, Health Status Indicators, Healthy People 2010, Morbidity, Mortality, Public Health, Public Health Core Disciplines, Wellness

FURTHER READING

Bailey, L. A., Durch, J. S., Stoto, M. A., & Institute of Medicine Committee on Using Performance Monitoring to Improve Community Health (B. Berkowitz & T. Inui, Cochairs). (1997). *Improving health in the community: A role for performance monitoring.* Washington, DC: National Academy of Sciences Press.

Bunker, J. P., Frazier, H. S., & Mosteller, F. (1995). The role of medical care in determining health: Creating an inventory of benefits. In B. C. Amick, S. Levine, A. R. Tarlov, & D. C. Walsh (Eds.), *Society and health.* New York: Oxford University Press.

Detels, R., Holland, W. H., McEwen, J., & Omenn, G. (Eds.). (1997). *Oxford textbook of public health: Vol. 1. The scope of public health.* New York: Oxford University Press.

Evans, R. G., & Stoddart, G. L. (1994). Producing health, consuming health care. In R. G. Evans, M. L. Barer, & T. R. Marmor (Eds.), *Why are some people healthy and others not? The determinants of health of populations.* New York: Aldine De Gruyter.

McDowell, I., & Newell, C. (1987). *Measuring health: A guide to rating scales and questionnaires.* New York: Oxford University Press.

McGinnis, J. M., & Foege, W. (1993). Actual causes of death in the United States. *JAMA, 270,* 2207–2212.

Murray, C. J. L., Salomon, J. A., Mathers, C. D., & Lopez, A. D. (Eds.). (2001). *Summary measures of population health: Conceptual, ethical, technical and measurement issues.* Geneva: World Health Organization.

Preamble to the Constitution of the World Health Organization as adopted by the International Health Conference, New York, 1946, June 19–22; signed on July 22, 1946 by the representatives of 61 states (*Official Records of the World Health Organization,* no. 2, p. 100) and entered into force on April 7, 1948.

Rosen, G. (1958). *A history of public health.* New York: MD Publications.

Turnock, B. (1997). *Public health: What it is and how it works.* Gaithersburg, MD: Aspen.

U.S. Department of Health and Human Services, Centers for Disease Control and Prevention, National Center for Health Statistics. (2001, September). *Health, United States, 2001, with urban and rural health chartbook.* Hyattsville, MD: Author.

World Health Organization. (1998). *The World Health Report, 1998: Life in the 21st century, a vision for all.* Geneva: Author.

HEALTH BEHAVIOR

See Wellness

HEALTH CARE

The term *health care* refers to services that produce health. Physician visits, for example, certainly fall under this definition. Such services are frequently thought of as "health care" because they can exert a relatively direct influence on health. Other services (such as wellness programs) may exert a less direct, but perhaps greater cumulative, influence on health. Broadly defined, these services too would thus constitute health care.

An important debate among health policy scholars is how to distribute *limited* public resources to health care's various components in a manner that optimizes population health. Understanding how health care's components relate to health can advance this debate.

Consider, for example, the case of health insurance. To the extent that health insurance improves health, it falls under the present definition of "health care." Because public resources are limited, however, a policy that maximizes health insurance would not maximize health. Inputs to any production process tend to exhibit "decreasing returns"; that is, holding other factors constant, the rate at which they increase output eventually decreases. Insurance is no exception—it is, quite simply, an input to the production of health. Consequently, although initial levels of health insurance may be very productive with respect to influencing health (for example, they may cover catastrophic illnesses), higher levels necessarily cover health care components that tend to be less productive (such as eyeglasses).

The point here is not that glasses cannot improve health—they certainly can. Rather, on average, glasses are probably a less productive input to health's production than is bypass surgery (especially if one employs a coarse measure of health, such as mortality rates). Indeed, unless one has access to such surgical services, one may never demand glasses again. In this manner, insurance exhibits decreasing returns. As a consequence, policies that allocate scarce resources to expanding health insurance, especially if coverage is already relatively high, may be inefficient if one's objective is to maximize the production of health.

Whether the marginal product of any particular health care component is sufficient to warrant additional resources is thus an important empirical question. Perhaps the most famous study addressing such questions took place in the 1970s when RAND Corporation researchers conducted a remarkable (by social science standards) health insurance experiment. In short, RAND researchers randomly assigned individuals to insurance plans that differed in their coverage tenure (from three to five years) and benefit levels. Somewhat surprisingly, they found that individuals' health did *not* vary considerably across the different plans.

Rather than implying that health insurance (and thus "health care," traditionally defined) does not significantly influence health, the RAND study suggests that *marginal* resources allocated in this direction may have a relatively small health impact. In other words, when evaluated at relatively high levels, health insurance may produce small health improvements. In this case, policy resources may, at the same or lower cost, be allocated to a more productive element of health care and thus create relatively large health improvements.

Within this context, some researchers and policymakers are turning their efforts toward understanding the potential for health care's less obvious components to improve health. The idea here is that, to the extent policy has exhausted the productivity of conventional inputs to health's production, allocating resources to "unexploited" health care elements can create relatively large health gains at relatively small resource cost.

Education may be one such element. Empirically, it exhibits a strong association with health and may cause health by, say, affecting one's capacity to transform pharmaceutical or behavioral prescriptions into health. It may also affect health by influencing one's "life chances" and thus one's socioeconomic status. Accumulating evidence, in turn, suggests that socioeconomic status (both relative and absolute) can significantly and independently influence health. In any event, to the extent that education is a relatively untapped source of health improvements, the rate at which it can be transformed into health is probably greater than that at which goods and services more commonly understood as "health care" can be transformed into health.

Extending the definition of health care may thus have a real potential to improve population health. "Health care," narrowly defined, frequently acts as an intermediate policy objective. If the ultimate objective is to improve health, however, then allocating resources to less obvious components of health care can produce a relatively rapid health improvement. This prospect can be especially significant for societies that have already exhausted the productivity of conventionally defined health care. In short, although allocating marginal resources toward traditional health care components can certainly improve health, allocating those same resources to health care's less obvious components (such as those that do not involve a physician but nevertheless significantly influence health) may produce greater improvements for the same resource cost. Understanding "health care" as the relatively diverse set of elements that produce health, as opposed to the relatively small set of direct health inputs, may facilitate the recognition of such welfare gains.

—Dino Falaschetti

FURTHER READING

Feldstein, P. J. (1999). *Health care economics* (5th ed.). Albany, NY: Delmar.

Phelps, C. E. (1997). *Health economics* (2nd ed.). Reading, MA: Addison-Wesley.

HEALTH CARE AGENT

See Durable Powers of Attorney for Health Care (DPAHC), Living Wills

HEALTH CARE AS LUXURY GOODS

For a luxury good, the ratio of the increase in demand for that good to any attendant increase in income will exceed unity. This ratio, that is, the percent increase in quantity of a good demanded divided by the percent increase in income, is termed the *income elasticity of demand* (E_i). In essence, E_i provides a measure of the responsiveness of demand for, or expenditures on, a good or service, to a change in the income of a given group or individual. When this demand is highly responsive to changes in income, the group under consideration is displaying income elasticity, whereas a lack of change in demand concomitant to a change in income reflects income inelasticity.

Using the income elasticity of demand, four types of goods (or services) can be identified:

1. *Normal good*—By definition, E_i for a normal good is greater than zero; that is, the demand for a normal good varies directly with income. As the income of the group under consideration increases, the demand for a normal good will increase.

2. *Inferior good*—E_i for an inferior good is less than zero; that is, the demand for an inferior good actually decreases as income increases; that is, demand and income vary inversely.

3. *Luxury good*—E_i exceeds unity; the demand for a luxury good increases out of proportion to any increase in the income of the individual or group being studied.

4. *Necessity*—E_i is less than unity; the more basic or essential the product, the lower the income elasticity. This is because a basic or required good needs to be purchased irrespective of any change in income.

There is ongoing debate as to whether health care constitutes a "luxury good"; that is, does the E_i for health care goods and services exceed unity? In fact, E_i will vary depending on the specific type of health care service or good being purchased. Furthermore, E_i will also change as a function of the boundaries of the transaction; that is, the specific group funding or purchasing the health care service or product.

For an individual, or individual household that is covered by insurance that does not require a copayment, E_i will be close to zero or may even be less than zero if there is a perception on the part of the insured that there is an entitlement to health care services and goods without any out-of-pocket expense beyond the insurance premium (which may even be paid for in full by the employer). In fact, one purpose of insurance is to make the individual more income inelastic (although the insurance plan, purchasing cooperative, employer, or entity actually funding or paying for the enrollee's health care will, of necessity, need to be both income and price elastic). If the plan involves copayments, the income elasticity of the enrollee would be expected to increase. Interestingly, and not surprisingly, examination of data regarding income elasticity in the pre-1960 era, during which many health care services were paid for out-of-pocket, indicates that consumers were income elastic.

Examination of health care expenditures as a function of income, at the national level, indicates an income elasticity that exceeds unity. In addition, the income elasticity for certain health care services, such as plastic surgery, dental services, counseling, eyeglasses, and so on, also exceeds unity. Hence, these types of health care services can be considered luxuries, as can health care when considered at the macro, national level.

To summarize, income elasticity is the change in demand for a good or service as a function of a change in income. A luxury good has an income elasticity that exceeds unity, such as a meal in an expensive restaurant. In the case of health care, the financial boundaries of the health care purchase transaction, as well as the specific type of health care service or good being consumed, will determine whether or not the microeconomic criteria for designation as a luxury good are met. Considered at the national level, health care appears to be a luxury good. At the level of the individual, health care behaves more like a necessity or normal good depending on the role of the individual in the health care purchase transaction.

—Darren S. Kaufman

FURTHER READING

www.sbm.temple.edu/~tgetzen/LUXURY.doc

HEALTH CARE ENVIRONMENT

See Health Policy, Strength-Weakness-Opportunity-Threat (SWOT) Analysis

HEALTH CARE GOODS AND SERVICES CONTINUUM

The U.S. health services system is respected throughout the nation and the world. It is a comprehensive system that includes goods and services from "womb to tomb." It begins with prenatal care for pregnant women and closes out with services such as hospice/palliative care for the terminally ill. In between those two ends lie the goods and services that make up the health care system.

The system begins with prenatal care and healthy birth services, proceeds to health promotion, primary disease prevention, diagnosis of disease, treatment of acute disease, secondary disease prevention, tertiary disease prevention, treatment of chronic illness or disease, rehabilitative care, and long-term care, and ends with palliative care. All providers of the services in this continuum must address and manage the same issues: availability, accessibility, and affordability.

Prenatal care designed to ensure perpetuation of the species has long been the norm within the health care system. Modern medicine has afforded sophisticated interventions to ensure that such care continues.

Health promotion, the next step in the continuum, seeks to preserve and enhance health status. This step has only recently been a focus within the system, which typically has been oriented to curative care. Healthy behaviors and lifestyles as a deterrent to disease have been known for some time, but little had been done to promote that idea. Health promotion focuses on physical activity and fitness, nutrition, eliminating tobacco use, controlling the use of alcohol and other drugs, family planning, support of mental health and detection of mental disorders, addressing violent and abusive behavior, and sponsoring educational and community-based programs.

Health protection is an extremely important function in the continuum of services. It seeks to preserve a safe and healthy environment, and without it the other parts of the system would fail. However, sometimes protection is not recognized as a part of the continuum.

Disease prevention can be divided into three levels: primary, secondary, and tertiary. To be effective, primary disease prevention in the continuum of services arena requires providers to offer testing, counseling, and health screenings. Public clinics and physician officers are the usual places of service. If disease cannot or has not been prevented, the secondary level is initiated, including early detection and treatment to cure or control the disease process. These services typically are provided in physicians' offices or hospitals. Finally, tertiary care is designed to ameliorate the seriousness of disease by decreasing disability or the dependence resulting from it. It seeks to maintain the individual's physical and functional abilities and independence.

The U.S. health care system continuum provides goods and services for chronic illnesses such as cancer, asthma, arthritis, kidney disease, and other long-term conditions. At this end of the continuum, services are extremely expensive both for providers and patients.

Palliative care provides end-of-life services to ease pain and suffering when no medical or surgical interventions are expected to further the life of the patient. It can be provided in any number of settings, including the patient's home.

—Patti Elaine Griffin

FURTHER READING

Barton, P. L. (1998). *Understanding the U.S. health services system.* Chicago: AUPHA Press/Health Administration Press.

Editor. (2001, June 13). A Northern Light special collection document. *Christian Science Monitor, 17,* 22.

Editor. Healthy communities initiatives. South Carolina Hospital Association. www.scha/org/Public/Health/Comm/hlthComm.htm

Editor. Manage your healthcare . . . Visiting Nurse Service of New York. wysiwyg://198/www.ynsyn.org/whopays.html

Editor. Population-based planning. HDR. wysiwyg://201/www.hdrinc.com/information

Long, M. J. (1998). *Health and healthcare in the United States.* Chicago: AUPHA Press/Health Administration Press.

HEALTHCARE FINANCIAL MANAGEMENT ASSOCIATION (HFMA)

The Healthcare Financial Management Association (HFMA) is the nation's leading personal membership organization for health care financial management professionals. HFMA brings perspective and clarity to the industry's complex issues for the purpose of preparing members to succeed. Through programs, publications, and partnerships, HFMA enhances the capabilities that strengthen not only individual careers but also the organizations from which its members come.

HFMA members include nearly 32,000 health care financial management professionals employed by hospitals, integrated delivery systems, managed care organizations, ambulatory and long-term care facilities, physician practices, accounting and consulting firms, and insurance companies. Members' positions include chief executive officer, chief financial officer, controller, patient accounts manager, accountant, and consultant.

HFMA continually evaluates, interprets, and clarifies the work of government and industry policymakers and, in doing so, has become a trusted resource for providing expert insights and relevant approaches to current health care finance issues. HFMA's educational and professional development programs, practical information, and technical data provide members with practical and timely tools and solutions. Members receive career-long support through networking, idea sharing among peers, and mentoring relationships. For many members, HFMA is a primary vehicle for maintaining awareness of how their professional contributions make a difference in the lives of patients and in the health of communities.

—Richard Clarke

FURTHER READING

www.hfma.org

HEALTH CARE FINANCING ADMINISTRATION (HCFA)

See Centers for Medicare and Medicaid Services (CMS)

HEALTH CARE IN CHINA

According to the Ministry of Health, per capita health care expenditures in China reached $51.40 in 2001, compared with $45.40 in 2000, which displayed in turn an increase of 13.5% over 1999. Annual growth in China's total health care expenditures since 1999 has been rising faster than national economic development, at an average of 13% for the former compared to 7.5% for the latter. China will

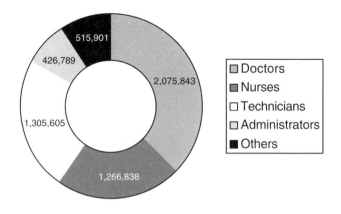

Figure 1   Health Care Personnel in China, 2000
Source: Ministry of Health, PRC

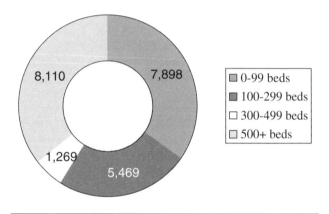

Figure 2   National-Level Hospitals in China, 2000
Source: Ministry of Health, PRC

need an estimated 5.8 million extra hospital beds and 1.2 million extra doctors if its health care services continue to expand at current rates. Revenues from medical treatment services in 2000 rose to 351 billion renminbi ($42.4 million) from 311 billion renminbi in 1999. Under its agreement with the World Trade Organization (WTO), by 2003 China will fully open its health care sector to foreign direct investment.

Figure 1 shows the number of health care personnel in China in 2000. In 2000, Chinese health care institutions, including national-level hospitals as well as treatment centers, sanitariums, and health centers, had a total of 3,137,532 beds. Figure 2 indicates the number of national-level hospitals by beds in China.

Since the 1980s, the People's Republic of China (PRC) government has dismantled China's universal health care system, a landmark of the socialist system; the current system shows the stresses of rapid change. Currently, about 25% of China's 1.3 billion population has health insurance coverage. Health care financing in China includes the following:

- *Insurance for government employees:* Public service medical care covers about 30 million employees and reimburses 100% of health care costs. It includes government workers; labor unions' officials; youth and women's leagues; cultural, educational, health, and research institutes' staff; and approved college and university students.
- *Insurance for state-owned and collective enterprises' employees:* Insurance for state-owned enterprises (SOEs) and collectives covered about 140 million workers and 60 million family members in 1997. This insurance reimburses 100% of employees' health care costs and 50% of family members' costs.
- *Cooperative insurance plans for rural areas:* Cooperative medical system (CMS) plans cover about 120 million farmers and town-and-village enterprise employees. Local governments, collectives, and individuals fund these plans and reimburse participants for 20% to 80% of health care costs, depending on funds. In 1997, 12% of all farmers participated in CMS plans.
- *Self-payment:* Health care financing ignores over 900 million farmers, private sector employees, and self-employed individuals who must pay the entire cost of health care themselves.

Foreign-invested enterprises have to provide health insurance. For example, for multinational corporations' employees in Beijing hired through the Foreign Enterprises Service Corporation (FESCO), the corporations pay FESCO, which then buys insurance policies for the employees.

The government plans to allow private companies to cover about 50 million uninsured urban people and has welcomed experiments from multinational corporations. For example, Shanghai Medical University and Kaiser Permanente International produced a feasibility study for a health maintenance organization (HMO) with the Shanghai Petroleum Company.

Historically, Chinese hospitals supplied both medical care and medicines. Through the 1980s, hospitals relied on government funds and operational revenue to finance these services. The governments generally set diagnostic and nonpharmaceutical services' prices far below costs and reimbursed hospitals on fee-for-service bases. Only pharmaceutical services could produce a profit, typically 15% of total sales. Hospitals used government funds and pharmaceutical revenues to offset the losses incurred from nonpharmaceutical services.

Since the late 1980s, the governments have reduced their investments in hospitals. From 1978 to 1996, government investments as a share of hospital revenues decreased by 50% nationally. Simultaneously, the governments have raised prices above costs for new services, such as magnetic resonance imaging (MRI) scanners, and nonpharmaceutical services, such as surgery and hospital rooms. Charges for most traditional services still remain below costs. To compensate for reduced government financing, hospitals often buy the most advanced equipment and sell as much medicine as possible. Many experts believe that hospitals' heavy dependence on revenues from medicines and high-technology services has contributed significantly to soaring health care costs.

The governments use three major forms of payment to hospitals: (a) *Average payment,* where they reimburse hospitals according to average daily-patient charges, regardless of costs. (b) *Capitation,* where they provide hospitals with fixed payments for patients' care for specific periods. If the hospitals spend less than the payments, they may retain the rest as profits. (c) *Global budgeting,* where they determine the maximum growth rate in hospitals' revenues, confiscate revenues over the limits, and may even fine hospitals that exceed growth rates. Simultaneously, they set ceilings for pharmaceutical services' revenues and nonpharmaceutical services' price increases.

In the past, government health insurance reimbursed 100% of all drug expenses. But in 1992, the PRC Ministry of Health began developing a national essential drug list (NEDL) to reimburse customers for medicines under state insurance plans. Selection criteria included clinical necessity, effectiveness, safety, and consistency between price and effectiveness. The list covers about half the medicines currently available in China. Local governments have drawn up drug reimbursement lists based on the NEDL, and the central government has done the same for public service medical care. Pharmaceutical producers grant great importance to these national and local lists, as state insurance will only reimburse listed drugs.

Pharmaceutical costs account for over 50% of health care expenditures and constitute the largest single category of medical spending. From 1990 to 1995, total drug sales grew at an average rate of over 20% per year, and sales of imported and joint venture drugs in Shanghai and Beijing grew over 30% per year, according to the Chinese Pharmaceutical Association. The number of retail pharmacies, roughly 60,000 in 1996, is also growing rapidly. As state insurance no longer covers many imported drugs, more insured patients are buying from retail pharmacies. Under capitation and global budgeting, hospitals also have financial incentives to sell as few drugs as possible. The sales of over-the-counter (OTC), imported, and expensive drugs will likely shift from hospitals to retail pharmacies.

—Usha C. V. Haley

FURTHER READING

Bloom, G. (1997, March). *Primary health care meets the market: Lessons from China and Vietnam.* IDS Working Paper 53. Institute of Development Studies, University of Sussex, Brighton, UK.

Haley, G. T., Haley, U. C. V., & Tan, C. T. (2003). *Asia's Tao of business: The logic of Chinese business strategy.* New York: Wiley.

Li, X., & Schweitzer, S. O. (1998, November). The health market. *China Business Review, 25*(6), 20.

HEALTH CARE IN EASTERN EUROPE

THE HEALTH CARE SECTOR BEFORE THE REFORMS

Rapid economic growth, expansion in the social sectors, including health care, and secure employment led to significant improvements in living standards and health status in many of the eastern European countries during the early years of central planning. Infant mortality rates fell by nearly half in the communist countries, and life expectancy at birth increased by around five years. During the following decades, health status in eastern European countries stagnated or deteriorated, whereas in the Organization for Economic Cooperation and Development (OECD) countries it showed a steady improvement.[9,14]

Entitlement by the entire population to a full range of health services was one of the main achievements of the communist system in eastern Europe. Structurally integrated networks of hospitals, polyclinics, and other medical organizations, secured universal access to health care services. National specialist institutes capable of providing advanced medical treatment were established. Accessibility to the health care system was high, as there were few financial barriers.

Yet the political leadership in the communist period gave different priorities to the different branches of the economy. For example, the highest priority went to heavy industry, especially the military sector, whereas the health care sector was considered to be among the low-priority branches. Although the total resources devoted to the health care sector increased as the economy grew, its share in the total allocation remained consistently low.

Under communism, all institutions providing medical care were state owned. All those who worked in the health care sector were state employees, and their salaries were determined centrally. Besides, all buildings and equipment related to health care were owned by the state. The decision making about investment projects was centralized. In fact, decisions about how much of the total resources of the economy to allocate to the health care sector were made at the highest political level. Moreover, those decisions were not based on economic cost–benefit analysis. Ordinary citizens had no say in those important decisions at all.

Rigid, overcentralized structure with an overemphasis on institutional care and the use of arbitrary statistical norms resulted in many imbalances in the health care sector in eastern Europe. Narrow overspecialization and isolation prevailed, as graduate education was isolated from universities and research was isolated from teaching. International isolation in training, research, and technology was characteristic of all eastern European countries. Poorly managed investments led to an excessive specialization at the expense of primary care. The rigid and overcentralized system of health care was associated with significant overlaps and gaps.

One of the symptoms of economic weaknesses under the communist system was that shortages and surpluses existed side by side throughout the economy. The health care sector did not make an exception. For example, it is a fact that relatively poor countries, such as Bulgaria or Slovakia, had more doctors or hospital beds per capita than the OECD countries on average. One should also note the establishment of a relatively comprehensive system of basic public health care services. At the same time, doctors' waiting rooms, clinics, and hospitals were overcrowded, and waiting lists for examinations, treatments, and long-postponed surgeries constituted a norm. Neither physical nor human capital were used effectively. The fact that all citizens were entitled to free medical care led to economic inefficiency, as patients had no incentive whatever to moderate their demands.

State monopoly, bureaucratic centralization, and the shortage economy were the forces that most crucially influenced the health care sector in eastern Europe under communism. The most conspicuous results were poor health status of the general population, low quality of medical care, and sluggish technological developments.

Mortality, especially among adult men, and morbidity were relatively high at the end of the 1980s. There was a lack of responsiveness to local needs, as well as a weak management of health care.[13,14] Flows of information in tracking and evaluating health trends were ineffective. Incentives to efficiency were virtually nonexistent, either to motivate patients to use scarce resources responsibly or to encourage health care practitioners and institutions to improve the quality of service. Family planning under the communist regime was grossly inadequate throughout eastern Europe, leading to many unwanted pregnancies, frequent and expensive hospital abortions, and dangerous illegal terminations of pregnancies.[14] Medical services were financed almost entirely from the central budget by using general revenues. That left the health sector in eastern Europe at the mercy of political interests.

REFORMS IN THE HEALTH CARE SECTOR

The main emphasis of the transformation in eastern Europe is to promote individual freedom, increase living standards, and create a strong safety net for the less fortunate members of society. Many eastern European governments are giving a very high priority to policies in the health care sector aimed at achieving a general balance. These policies are of two broad forms: (a) policies to limit public expenditure on health care in an effort to correct economic imbalances and protect the newly growing private sector and (b) policies to mobilize nonbudgetary resources for health care.[13,14] Consequently, market-oriented reforms have been introduced to deal with the systemic failure of excessive government involvement. They include a search for a more efficient allocation of resources through market mechanisms, promoting greater individual freedom in choosing the highest-quality health care services one can afford, and liberalization of the demand for and the supply of medical services.

Several eastern European countries have removed certain health care services, such as dental care, from the scope of free medical care. Essentially, these countries have started distinguishing between basic care available free (or almost free) under the social insurance schemes and supplementary health care. All countries have introduced copayments, to supplement the social insurance contributions and to curb the excessive use of the available scarce resources.

However, in most cases the reforms have been inconsistent.[8,10,13] For example, profit-maximizing owners would not tolerate a situation in which the compensation for their services did not cover depreciation and provide the funds for renewal and development. The health care institutions of eastern Europe are, however, forced to tolerate this. Their compensation is set in a manner that makes it possible to cover only the provider's operating costs. Notably, it does not cover the costs of renewing and developing fixed assets. The settlement arrangements do not take into account depreciation, either. Furthermore, the development and functioning of market mechanisms in health care in eastern Europe have been obstructed by various forms of government intervention.

THE DEMAND SIDE

At present, patients are becoming active consumers of health care, in contrast with their passive role under the old system in eastern Europe. For example, patients have gained increased freedom to choose their doctor in the Czech Republic and Bulgaria. To facilitate patients in their search for medical help, all eastern European countries have adopted settlement mechanisms, which critically depend on the role of a social insurance fund. As a matter of fact, the social insurance fund has become the main source of financing for the health care sector in eastern Europe. That fund has its own, separate source of revenue, consisting of contributions that employers and employees are legally obligated to pay for the purpose. The size of these contributions and the nominal split between employers and employees, however, varies from country to country. These compulsory contributions form the main source of revenue for the social insurance fund. The fund, then, stands as a purchaser paying money to the providers. In Hungary, for example, the social insurance fund has acted as an independent purchaser since 1991. The fund was autonomous until mid-1998, and since then it has been subordinated to the government.[8,9] The Czech Republic, Poland, Slovenia, Croatia, Russia, Bulgaria, and other countries have introduced similar settlement mechanisms.[18]

In fact, the postcommunist health care sector in eastern Europe has largely followed the German model.[8,10] That model essentially stipulates that health care expenditures should be controlled through a complex process of managed price fixing and that prices should be determined through negotiated agreements among the government, the social insurance fund, and the medical practitioners. The central state budget continues to finance public health care, and it still actively subsidizes large, specialized national institutions, much of the medical research, and medical training.[1,5,6,7,11,13,16]

Voluntary insurance has also been introduced in almost all eastern European countries. Private for-profit and not-for-profit organizations, offering medical insurance, have become popular.[9,10,18] Private insurance coverage is mostly purchased by those who do not qualify for social insurance and by those who want to cover supplementary services not funded by health insurance.

Moreover, all eastern European countries have introduced systems of copayments.[5,6,7,18,19,20] The principle that patients should make certain contributions to the costs of health care services has been widely implemented in practice. Notably, the copayments are quite high in some countries, such as Bulgaria, Hungary, and Slovenia.[12,16,18,21] However, it is worth emphasizing that the introduction of copayments in the health care sectors of individual countries is still applicable only to a small proportion of health services.

THE SUPPLY SIDE

As far as ownership relations are concerned, the vast majority of the institutions providing health care services have remained owned by the public even in the countries where the reforms are most advanced.[1,2,7,16,21] However, the role of hospitals, polyclinics, and other medical, publicly owned institutions has changed considerably in the postcommunist period.

A peculiar hybrid of centralized bureaucratic control and market coordination has emerged. Health care providers have won a certain degree of independence, but there still remains a dependency on central, state-controlled organizations. Institutions representing the state essentially decide on capital investment in the health care providers.[8,10] Moreover, government organizations or the social insurance fund actively participate in determining the budget for current expenditures.

In most countries, physicians working in public hospitals and other health care organizations qualify as public servants, and their salaries critically depend on the budget allocations to health care.[3,4,15] It is stipulated that health care providers have no right to exceed their budget allocations. In practice, this happens constantly. The outcome is usually a bailout, in which the deficit is covered out of the central or local state budget.[8,9]

Nonpublic hospitals, polyclinics, and other similar health care providers have already appeared in most eastern European countries (such as Poland, the Czech Republic, Hungary, Russia, Slovakia, Bulgaria, and Slovenia). Some nonpublic providers are owned by churches and private foundations and operate on a not-for-profit basis. Others are commercial, for-profit organizations. In the eastern European region as a whole, the share of the nonpublic sector in the total volume of health care services is estimated to be relatively small. However, there are exceptions. In particular, the privatization of dental care and pharmacies is quite extensive in most eastern European countries. There are also many individual practitioners working on a private basis at present.

Comprehensive data for the whole region are not readily available, but the information obtained suggests that the proportion of health services provided through legal private practice has greatly increased in most countries. Although most large, hospital-scale activity remains in public ownership, privatization of health services provided by small-scale organizations has been quite extensive. For example, relatively small private pharmaceutical companies have been provided with incentives to produce desired medical supplies, drugs, and vaccines in Russia, the Czech Republic, Hungary, and Poland.

Another important aspect of the reforms in the health care sector in eastern Europe is that the pay of doctors, especially those employed by public institutions, is still disproportionately (to U.S. doctors) low.[4,5,12,15,18,22] This situation understandably embitters physicians and other practitioners. The depressed state of physicians' official pay seems to them less and less acceptable as the development of the market economy has led to a significant differentiation of earnings in other areas.[15,17,19,20,21,22] As a result, semilegal payments to doctors are very widespread in Hungary, Romania, Poland, and Bulgaria. They seem popular, although to a much smaller degree, in the Czech Republic, Slovakia, Croatia, and Slovenia. The amount of "gratuities" doctors receive in most eastern European countries is roughly equivalent to their official gross salary. In some countries, total "gratuity" received by practicing physicians is more than 1.5 times bigger than their official aggregate earnings.[8,10] Although many medical practitioners sit on influential legislative committees, there has apparently been little self-regulation of the health care providers.

CONCLUSIONS

In summary, the reforms have brought about substantial changes in the health care sector in eastern Europe compared with the situation during the communist period. Some countries have made great strides, whereas others have not proceeded so fast. Generally, there is an apparent need for continuation of the reforms, as the results everywhere have been more or less inconsistent.

Economic liberalization in the health care sector in eastern Europe seems to have gone too far too fast. Rapid introduction of unregulated competitive markets have already led to the emergence of significant market failures. For example, the original annual budget of the newly created social insurance fund in the Czech Republic was more or less exhausted within six months of its establishment. Unrestrained privatization within an excessively relaxed regulatory framework has also led to unscrupulous profiteering by some health care providers.

An excessive reliance on individual autonomy and self-interest has dangerously obscured concerns for collective protection and equity. The rapid restructuring has resulted in a breakdown in referral networks in countries such as Bulgaria, the Czech Republic, Hungary, and Slovakia, which has already led to expensive overlaps. Future reforms in the health care sector are expected to include measures to raise standards of living, to promote healthier lifestyles, to protect the environment, to diversify the supply side of the sector, and to ensure quality of medical services.

Governments in eastern Europe have already discovered that market forces are an excellent way to improve efficiency and quality in health care, but only if they are accompanied by adequate legislative measures, a new public–private partnership in the financing and provision of health care services, a carefully designed blend of market mechanisms and government intervention, and internally consistent implementation of the reform measures.

—Detelin Elenkov

REFERENCES

1. Central Bureau of Statistics. (2002). *Statistical yearbook of the Republic of Croatia 2001*. Zagreb: Author.

2. Central Statistic Office. (2002). *Statistical yearbook of the Republic of Poland 2001.* Warsaw: Author.

3. Czech Statistical Office. (2002). *Structure of earnings survey 2001.* Prague: Author.

4. Delcheva, E., Balabanova, D., & McKee, M. (1997). Under-the-counter payments for health care in Bulgaria. *Health Policy, 42,* 89–100.

5. Health Insurance Institute of Albania. (2002). *Statistical indicators for 2001.* Tirana: Author.

6. Health Insurance Institute of Slovenia. (2001). *Annual report of the Health Insurance Institute of Slovenia for 2000.* Ljubljana: Author.

7. Institute of Health Information and Statistics of the Czech Republic. (2002). *Czech health statistics yearbook 2001.* Prague: Author.

8. Kornai, J., & Eggleston, K. (2001). Welfare. *Choice, and solidarity in transition: Reforming the health section in eastern Europe.* Cambridge, UK: Cambridge University Press.

9. Kornai, J., & McHale, J. (2000). Is post-communist health spending unusual? A comparison with established market economies. *Economics of Transition, 8,* 359–399.

10. Kornai, J., Haggard, S., & Kaufman, R. R. (Eds.). (2001). *Reforming the state: Fiscal and welfare reform in post-socialist countries.* Cambridge, UK: Cambridge University Press.

11. National Statistical Institute. (2002). *Statistical yearbook of Bulgaria 2001.* Sofia: Author.

12. National Statistical Institute. (2002). *Statistical reference book of the Republic of Bulgaria 2001.* Sofia: Author.

13. Phare. (1998). Recent reforms in organization, financing and delivery of the health care in Central and Eastern Europe in the light of accession to the Europe Union. Brussels, Belgium, Phare Conference, May 24–25, 1998. Available at http://europa.eu.int/comm/enlargement/pas/phare/intro.htm#11

14. Preker, A. S., & Feachem, R. G. (1995). *Market mechanisms and the health sector in central and eastern Europe.* Washington, DC: World Bank.

15. Romania National Commission for Statistics. (2001). *Romanian statistic yearbook 2000.* Bucharest: Author.

16. Statistical Office of the Republic of Slovenia. (2001). *Statistical yearbook of the Republic of Slovenia 2000.* Ljubljana: Author.

17. Statistical Office of the Slovak Republic. (2002). *Statistic yearbook of the Slovak Republic 2001.* Bratislava, Slovak Republic: Veda.

18. World Health Organization. (1999). *Health for all database.* Copenhagen: WHO Regional Office for Europe.

19. World Health Organization. (1999). *Health care system in transition: Bulgaria.* Copenhagen: WHO Regional Office for Europe.

20. World Health Organization. (1999). *Health care system in transition: Croatia.* Copenhagen: WHO Regional Office for Europe.

21. World Health Organization. (1999). *Health care system in transition: Hungary.* Copenhagen: WHO Regional Office for Europe.

22. World Health Organization. (2000). *Health care system in transition: Russia.* Copenhagen: WHO Regional Office for Europe.

HEALTH CARE PROVIDER

The broad term *health care provider* can apply to various individuals, groups, or entities in the health care field. A health care provider is a person or place that is trained and licensed to give health care.

INDIVIDUALS

Physicians are members of the health care provider group. They can be primary-care M.D.s, surgeons, or a number of specialists such as cardiologists or neurologists. Physician extenders are individuals trained to do some of the physicians' functions. These individuals are nurse practitioners or physician's assistants.

Other health care providers are therapists such as physical and occupational therapists. These individuals, under doctors' orders, can treat patients in their specialty areas. These services can be provided in the hospital setting, in the community, and at home.

Nurses are also licensed and trained to give health care services. They not only can provide hospital care but also can perform many health care functions in the community.

Social workers provide services to clients both in and out of the hospital. They can assist a patient and family with short- or long-term placement, hospice care, future planning, or provide them with counseling.

FACILITIES

Hospitals are considered health care providers. They provide health care services to individuals for acute illness or injury. Nursing homes provide a wide variety of services. They can provide long-term care for the elderly. Some nursing homes provide restorative and rehabilitative therapy for people who will eventually be discharged back to their homes. Some hospitals also provide restorative therapy to individuals who can handle more intensive therapy. These facilities are called *acute rehabilitation centers.* Inpatient hospice facilities are there to provide care to those who are terminal and unable to be cared for at home.

Some assisted living facilities can also be considered health care providers. They can provide a full range of care from independent living through nursing home care for their residents. The patients in these facilities can move in either direction from a higher to lower level of care, depending on their needs.

GROUPS

Home health agencies are also considered health care providers. They can provide a wide variety of services at home that were once restricted to the hospital setting. Given increased pressures to decrease the length of hospital stays, home health care is a viable alternative. Hospice services can be provided to those who are terminally ill, to allow them to die at home. Hospice also provides some respite for the families of the dying so they can have time away from the home.

Another group of health care providers are the durable medical equipment (DME) companies. These companies supply clients with oxygen equipment as well as hospital beds, commodes, and an array of items needed to assist with the patient's functions at home. They provide respiratory therapists that assist the client with the use of oxygen equipment and nebulizer treatments and teach the client and family regarding safe use of oxygen in the home.

—Doreen T. Day

See also Federal Regulating Agencies

FURTHER READING

www.bricker.com/attserv/practice/hcare/hipaa
www.Medicare.gov

HEALTH CARE PROXY

See Durable Powers of Attorney for Health Care (DPAHC), Living Wills

HEALTH CARE REFORM

Health care reform constitutes the process by which the social policies that regulate health care are created and modified. Health care reform, therefore, represents a subset of health care policy. In essence, health care reform is driven, to a large extent, by regulatory reform. However, it is important to recognize nonregulatory drivers of health care reform such as the impact of market forces on the level of

quality of care, as with the Leapfrog group, and the recent report from the Institute of Medicine regarding medical errors. Health care reform can lead to changes in the degree to which the government controls and manages access of the population to health care and the way in which health care is financed. Disparate societal philosophies regarding the role and responsibility of the government in providing health care services, and the underwriting of such services, such as can be seen in the United States and Canada, do not preclude health care reform from having a profound impact on patients, the public, providers, and payers of these very different systems.

The process of health care reform has led to diminished independence of the medical profession. This, in turn, has resulted in the current system by which health care providers are reimbursed for the services and resources that they provide. At one time, the medical profession controlled entry into the health care system and set the prices that would be charged for the delivery of their services. In addition, the medical profession determined which hospital a patient would be admitted to, which laboratory a patient would utilize, and where a patient would go for other radiological and ancillary services. Pricing was led by the costs incurred by the provider. To determine pricing, the provider determined its costs and the desired profit margin. Regulation of health care, at that time, was focused on the licensing and accreditation of health care providers. However, in the 1970s, driven by economic recession and inflation, health care reform became, in essence, a process focused on health care cost containment. Primacy was given to the development of reimbursement policies that would act to influence the behavior of providers such that utilization of health care services, and the attendant medical costs, would be reduced.

MEDICARE REFORM

Medicare, which is underwritten by the U.S. federal government, provides health insurance for more Americans than does any other payer. Hence, changes in Medicare reimbursement policies constitute a significant component of health care reform.

Early Medicare reimbursement policy allowed Medicare payments to be based on costs rather than a formalized fee schedule. Even noncash costs, such as depreciation of capital equipment, were included in payment formulas, resulting in higher prices for health care services and equipment. The adoption of fee schedules such as reimbursement for inpatient services based on diagnosis-related groups, or DRGs, has helped trim the health care costs that would have otherwise grown. The Balanced Budget Act of 1997 has led to the adoption of additional changes in Medicare reimbursement policy.

MANAGED CARE

The elimination of regulations that made HMOs non-competitive has allowed these types of health care plans to flourish. Because of the increasing penetration of managed care into the U.S. health care marketplace, increasing linkages between the financing of health care, on the one hand, and access to and the delivery of health care services, on the other, are evolving. Regulatory policies, market forces (the need for employers to provide adequate coverage to be able to attract talented employees versus the need for the employer to contain costs related to the provision of such coverage), and an increasing focus on providing high-quality care, the mitigation of medical errors, and plans that allow consumers to chose their provider, are the forces that are currently shaping the face of managed care and health care reform. Efforts to shift disadvantaged people into managed care plans, such as Medicaid managed care, are having an impact on this population's access to health care services.

THE DILEMMA OF THE UNINSURED

Despite the aforementioned impact on the U.S. health care system, the process of health care reform to date has not had a salutary impact on the issue of providing uninsured people with unfettered access to health care services. In the future, it is possible that the government may underwrite more of the cost of health care services provided to the uninsured. However, the path of health care reform in the United States has steered clear of the adoption of a Canadian-style single-payer system.

—Darren S. Kaufman

FURTHER READING

Crane, M. (2001, August 6). The new IOM report: Will it change your practice? *Medical Economics, 15,* 32–34.

Finger, A. (1999, December 20). Caring for the uninsured. Will the problem ever be solved? *Medical Economics, 24,* 132–135.

Guglielmo, W. (2000, August 21). Managed care reform? Sure—but don't look to Washington. *Medical Economics, 16,* 40–41.

Guglielmo, W. (2002, January 25). Action on health care in 2001? *Medical Economics, 2,* 22–23.

http://cfmresearch.tripod.com/healthcare/index.html

http://tcf.org/Publications/Basics/Medicare_2001/index.html

Terry, K. (2000, April 10). Where's managed care headed? *Medical Economics, 7,* 244–247.

HEALTH CARE SERVICE OPERATIONS

Business operations are the systems and resources that enable a transformation process. The classic view of the transformation process is that of inputs passing through an operation, whereby the inputs undergo a transformation and thus emerge as outputs. Health care service operations create value through transformation processes that may be physiological, psychological, informational, or educational. An example of a *physiological transformation* process is a surgery center. The inputs are a facility, a skilled workforce, equipment, medical supplies, and a patient who needs surgery. The output is the patient with improved health as a result of the physiological changes occurring during surgery. Psychiatric hospitals facilitate a psychological transformation *process* through counseling and treatment, with output in the form of patients with improved mental health. Mammography centers facilitate *informational transformations* through examination and diagnosis, the output being a more informed and advised patient. Urban clinics may facilitate an *educational transformation process* by providing instruction in nutrition, AIDS prevention, and family planning. The output is a more educated and potentially safer individual.

The management of health care service operations involves decisions that are characterized as strategic, tactical, or operational. *Strategic decisions* represent long-term decisions focused on how the operations will ultimately create value. Such decisions are often expensive and time consuming to implement and/or change. In health care, strategic decisions begin with a careful definition of the mix and scope of service offerings. The remaining strategic decisions concern the resources, relationships, and processes to provide the service offerings. These decisions include the service delivery system design, facility location and capacity, supply and service chain partnerships, outsourcing decisions, and large-scale technology decisions. For example, the strategic decisions for an outpatient surgery center include a clear definition of the level of care and the range of procedures that can performed, approximate facility location, and size, and primary affiliations. *Tactical decisions* are considered medium-term decisions mostly concerned with planning. These decisions include planned levels and skills of workforce, physical capacity planning, materials/services acquisition planning, and equipment maintenance and replacement decisions. For the outpatient surgery center example, tactical decisions would include a specific plan for staffing, facility size and layout (number of suites, number of recovery beds), and vendor selections for supplies and equipment (lease/own, maintenance, and so on). *Operational decisions* (also referred to as *control decisions*) are short term in nature and include the management of supporting materials, workforce scheduling, task assignment and scheduling, and patient flow management. For the surgery center example, operational decisions concern the coordination of all activities leading up to, during, and after the surgical procedure (patient information, test results, surgical suite preparation, medical supplies, equipment, personnel).

The nature of the health care services makes them difficult to manage. The services have a high degree of customer interaction. This means the quality of the processes, workforce training, and facility are readily visible to customers. Furthermore, the services are directed at the customers themselves, which means that a service delivery failure will be annoying at best (waiting time) and dangerous or even fatal at worst (wrong medication given). At the same time, it is difficult to define what constitutes a "quality" health care service encounter, because many of the contributing factors are difficult-to-quantify, even emotional, elements. Also, customers have their own particular preferences about what contributes to a quality service encounter. For example, some patients greatly value spending time with providers, whereas others may see such time as wasteful. Even the duration and depth of customer relationships can vary considerably, from a one-time episode of care to a series of treatments for lifelong conditions. Customer needs can either be handled in a reactive fashion, or future needs can be influenced by current activities. For example, proactive regular checkups can sometimes prevent or provide an early detection advantage for conditions that would otherwise have progressed and gotten much worse.

Health care service operations are also challenging because of the multistage nature of customer flow and the degree of operational complexity. Even a simple office visit for a checkup involves interfacing with in-house "servers" (receptionist, nurse, physician, payment clerk) as well as a number of external servers (lab, insurance). At each stage of the process, the customer may experience waiting time, one of the more problematic aspects of health care operations. Waiting time occurs when customer service requests arrive at a rate faster than the server can provide the service. In general, a queuing system is a situation in which customers "arrive" for service and must be processed by a server with limited capacity. Queuing systems abound in health care, both within and between organizations. The level of variation in the arrival process and the level of variation in providing the service contribute to poor performance in terms of unpredictable and excessive waits. Many customer arrivals in health care occur in a random fashion. Emergency room arrivals are obviously random, but also the arrivals in some stages of appointment-based systems can appear to be random. In the office visit example, the timing of arrivals to the last stage (payment clerk) will be quite unpredictable. The result is that some degree of waiting is inevitable in health care service operations and must be managed carefully, both in terms of waiting time and customer perceptions of waiting. Because some health care needs cannot safely tolerate waiting (births, for example), health care service operations must often build in excess capacities that may often be idle.

Health care service operations are challenging to manage, because of the degree of interorganizational interactions and relationships. The personnel who play a role in performing a typical surgical procedure differ considerably in terms of their employment arrangement and incentives. As a result, one's ability to manage and improve such processes may be limited. Added to that is the fact that in today's managed care environment, the buyer of health care services is not the individual actually receiving the care. This confuses the question of "who is our customer?" and further creates situations where objectives and expectation may not be aligned.

—Charles E. Noon

See also Operations Management, Queuing, Service Operations, Waiting Time

HEALTH CARE SERVICES

Health care services are the activities performed by health care organizations that aim to generate "health" as an output. The precise definition of health, per se, is broad and somewhat vague, but a working, managerial definition can include the following, depending on the precise setting:

- *Disease-free state:* cure, prevention such as cancer screening, vaccines
- *Symptom-free state:* for example, pain management
- *Reduction in disease severity:* for example, palliation, chronic disease management

The term "health care organization" used in the preceding definition is limited to

- Physician practices, including the nonphysician providers and nurses in their employ
- Hospitals
- Nursing homes
- Hospices
- Home health agencies

CHARACTERISTICS OF HEALTH CARE SERVICES

Health care services display many of the characteristics of other types of services such as financial services, insurance, and consulting firms. This is important in that many of the generic principles of service operations management are applicable to the management of health care services. Such shared characteristics include the following:

- *Intangibility.* A patient is purchasing the efforts toward resolving a health problem such as diagnosing and treating a cough or high blood pressure. The patient is not purchasing the physical goods attendant to the diagnosis and treatment, which are referred to as "facilitating goods."

- *Can't be inventoried.* The provision of a health care service and its consumption by the patient occur simultaneously. The recognition of this characteristic is crucial to the management of health care service organizations. For instance, the number of beds in a hospital, or the number of exam rooms available in a physician's office practice determine the service capacity. Any mismatch between the demand for service and the capacity to provide the service will affect revenues, service quality, and patient satisfaction. As with any service entity, capacity decisions are crucial to health care services.

- *Service production and consumption occur in the same location.* As with many service entities, health care services are produced on site, with a high degree of interaction with the "customer." This has important implications for the marketing of health care services, as well as quality control. For instance, in a manufacturing operation, quality control can occur at identified points along the production line or at the level of the finished product. The customer, in the case of health care services, can view, and literally, experience, each step in the health care delivery process. A high-quality (both technical and customer service quality) health care service operation is key to maintaining demand for that entity's services. Hence, there is no clear boundary that divides the marketing and operations functions of a health care service entity.

HEALTH CARE SERVICES: FINANCIAL ENVIRONMENT

Ultimately, health care organizations are subject to fiscal reality. Business considerations, therefore, have a heavy impact on the design and implementation of health care services. For the health care organization to survive, over the long term, total revenues, plus other sources of financial support, such as research grants, contributions, and endowments, must exceed total costs. Most health care organizations receive the bulk of their funds via payments from third parties for the provision of health care services. Moreover, given the pricing schema used for third-party payments, such as diagnosis-related groups (DRGs) for reimbursement for health care services provided by hospitals, managed care contracts specifying reimbursement for specific levels of outpatient care, and so on, cost control is key to the financial viability of health care service entities.

HEALTH CARE SERVICES: COMPETITIVE ENVIRONMENT

Entities within the health care service industry are subject to a variety of competitive forces. The relative impact of these forces has evolved as the result of managed care, the making of health care services into commodities, and changes in legislation.

- *Buyer power.* The various purchasers of health care, including individual patients, health care plans and purchasing cooperatives, employers, and the government, exert control over how health care services are delivered. This influence has begun to extend beyond pricing and reimbursement. Some groups, such as the Leapfrog Group, are mandating that certain quality standards, such as the availability of computer order entry systems and intensivist-run intensive care units at hospitals, be available in order for the services of that facility to be utilized by their enrollees.

- *Supplier power.* As new technologies and pharmaceuticals become available, the companies that develop and distribute these resources can exert influence over how their products are used in providing health care services. For example, marketing new pharmaceuticals to individual providers can influence the adoption of these products and their inclusion on hospital formularies. This phenomenon is of particular import to health care organizations such as hospitals, because the early, widespread adoption and utilization of new agents, which have no documented benefit over and above existing agents, can increase the cost of health care services.

- *New entrants/substitute products.* Within a given marketplace, health care organizations and the providers of health care services are subject to rivalry. In fact, such internal rivalry provides significant impetus for such organizations to maintain and constantly improve service quality. However, the making of health care services into commodities has allowed the entry of new players into the health care service arena, including alternative medicine providers, disease management programs based in drug companies, information technology firms, and so forth. The barriers to entry for some of these types of services are not prohibitive, whereas the entry barriers for new, traditional health care service operations, such as hospitals, nursing homes, or even physician practices, are formidable.

—Darren S. Kaufman

FURTHER READING

Cleverley, W. (1997). *Essentials of health care finance.* Gaithersburg, MD: Aspen.

Enzmann, D. (1997). *Surviving in health care.* St. Louis, MO: Mosby-Year Book.

Porter, M. (1980). *Competitive strategy.* New York: Free Press.

Schmenner, R. (1995). *Service operations management.* Upper Saddle River, NJ: Prentice Hall.

HEALTH CARE UTILIZATION

Health care utilization is the use or consumption of health care services and supplies. Operationally, measurement of health care utilization involves the quantification of the expenditure attendant to the use of health care services and supplies for a given population at risk, over a specified period of time. Utilization data are typically stratified to reflect the type of service or supply, such as pharmaceuticals, doctor's office visit, or hospital admission, that is being rendered or used. Such data are employed, particularly in the managed care setting, to identify cost variances related to changes in utilization of services related to health care . The process by which peer groups, public agencies, or health plans review the appropriateness of health care utilization is termed *utilization review*. The active management of health care utilization by such third parties constitutes an important component of what has been termed *managed care*.

THE MEASUREMENT OF HEALTH CARE UTILIZATION

The utilization of health care services and supplies can be expressed as the rate of usage of a given service or supply per unit population at risk for a given period of time. In a capitated system, the denominator reflects the total population of the system, yielding data expressed as per member per month, or PMPM. Importantly, the type or location of service needs to be defined, such as hospital admissions, office visits, drug prescriptions, or lab tests, for instance, the number of office visits per enrollee of a given health plan, per annum. As noted earlier, to identify cost variances, utilization data are oftentimes converted into a dollar cost amount. This is done by multiplying the utilization rate by the cost per unit of service; for example, 5 office visits per enrollee per annum times $50 cost per visit = $250 per annum. In this case, one could go on to isolate the component of the total cost variance attendant on the disparity between the actual and budgeted office visit utilization, using the following formula:

Office visit cost variance = [visits per enrollee (actual) – visits per enrollee (budgeted)] × number of enrollees in plan × cost per visit

To be strictly correct, the preceding figure needs to be multiplied by the budgeted office visit case mix index, which reflects the severity of illness of the population being analyzed. This is important because failure to appropriately adjust for severity of illness and comorbidities in the population at risk leads to a failure to recognize cost variances caused by changes in the population case mix over time and may result in an over- or underestimation of utilization cost variance.

If a material cost variance caused by health care utilization is identified, the organization involved (hospital, health plan, or so on) will need to further analyze the appropriateness of its health care utilization. When this process is undertaken in a formalized, systematic fashion, it is termed *utilization review*. The limitation or active control of health care utilization by a third party is termed *utilization management*. Utilization management is an important component of managed care.

UTILIZATION REVIEW/UTILIZATION MANAGEMENT

By definition, an important component of managed care is the limitation of health care utilization to services that are deemed appropriate based on the adopted policies of the managed care organization. This may involve excluding or limiting delivery of services by out-of-network providers and can also include third-party review of services. For instance, to decrease hospital length of stay a "current review" may take place on an ongoing basis during a patient's hospitalization, to ensure that continued hospitalization is required. Thoughtful discharge planning is an important way to appropriately limit health care utilization. Representatives of the health plan may interact directly with the provider to see if the patient can receive commensurate care in a less acute setting. Some health care plans require the provider to have expensive lab tests and imaging studies, hospital admissions, and surgical procedures "precertified" by the plan in order for the service to be paid for by the plan. Although the practice has been falling out of favor, some plans require some or all services to be ordered by the patient's primary care provider (PCP). In this setting, the PCP acts as a "gatekeeper" who controls the patient's access to health care services. Because of patient and physician dissatisfaction with the gatekeeper model, and questionable usefulness of this practice with regard to cost containment, many plans now allow access to a variety of services and to specialist consultation without the need to go through a gatekeeper.

UTILIZATION TARGETS AND CAPITATION

Capitation is a payment system in which the health care plan reimburses the provider a fixed amount per enrollee over a given time period. For instance, a primary care provider might enter into a contract whereby $20 per covered member per month is paid to the provider. Fee for service is at the other end of the spectrum of payment systems. With a fee-for-service model, the provider is paid for each billable event, such as an office visit, consultation, and so on. It is readily apparent that providers operating in a capitated system stand to benefit when utilization of health care services is well managed. Conversely, capitation places the provider at financial risk should utilization exceed expected targets.

The aforementioned utilization targets are key to the development of projected cost data, which in turn are requisite to the formulation of capitated payment rates. Utilization targets are a function of the degree of management of health care utilization. In a system in which utilization is aggressively managed—that is, all the health care services provided are necessary—utilization is less, with concomitant reductions in expected costs and higher capitated payments.

UNDERUTILIZATION

An appropriate degree of utilization management reduces health care costs while maintaining quality of care and the expected level of favorable outcomes. However, when utilization is managed to the point that requisite health care services are not provided, quality of care and outcomes can be adversely affected. Overzealous limitation of health care utilization is termed *underutilization*. To prevent underutilization, the federal government as well as several states have adopted legislation regulating "physician incentive plans" that seek to limit health care utilization. For example, a 1990 amendment to federal Medicare and Medicaid law precludes payment to providers to reward decreased utilization and mandates that HMOs provide stop-loss protection to providers who are exposed to financial risk should the utilization of services exceed the expected utilization targets. Any incentive arrangement between the HMO and the provider must be disclosed to Center for Medicare and Medicaid Services (CMS), formerly Health Care Financing Administration (HCFA). Many states require enrollees to be informed regarding the provisions of provider compensation agreements so that enrollees can make their own assessment regarding the potential for such an agreement to have an impact on the provider's fiduciary interest in their care.

Several state medical boards now consider utilization management to constitute the practice of medicine on the part of the medical director of the health care plan. Previously, the medical director was not viewed as an agent apart from the managed care organization and the medical director's decision to deny payment for a given service was not viewed as "practicing medicine," because the patient's attending physician was still free to act in the best interest of the patient. However, the medical licensing boards of states that view utilization management as a form of medical practice will initiate disciplinary hearings against medical directors if the enrollee of a health plan makes a complaint.

PHARMACEUTICAL UTILIZATION

Health care expenditures related to prescription drugs are a function of the price for each prescription and the number of prescriptions written, that is, utilization. The number of prescriptions written is itself a function of the number of plan enrollees studied and the number of prescriptions per enrollee. The relative contribution of price and utilization varies for each drug class.

The utilization of prescription drugs is increasing. This may be due to an increase in the number of people taking medication, an increase in the number of drugs prescribed per person, and the availability of new, more effective medications such as proton pump inhibitors for the treatment of gastrointestinal disease, nonsteroidal anti-inflammatory drugs (NSAIDs) for arthritis, and cholesterol-lowering medications such as HMG CoA reductase inhibitors. In addition, demographic factors, such as the aging of the population, and marketing practices, such as aggressive marketing to physicians and direct-to-consumer advertising, also play a role in driving prescription drug utilization. Some health care plans seek to limit prescription drug utilization by shifting some of the cost of such utilization onto the consumer via tiered copayment programs and by the use of "prior approval" policies for costly medications. Managed care companies manage drug utilization further by implementing closed drug formularies, physician and patient education programs, over-the-counter substitution, preferred drug programs, and disease management programs. In addition, some hospitals have developed and adopted guidelines that dictate the inpatient use of certain high-cost medications in an effort to eliminate unnecessary drug utilization. For example, the drug epoetin alfa is routinely administered to patients with advanced kidney failure to treat the anemia that is associated with this condition. For this drug to be effective, the patient must have adequate iron stores in the body, because the drug works by stimulating the production of red blood cells, which contain iron. By adopting and implementing a guideline that requires the hospital pharmacist to question an order for epoetin alfa in a patient who is not iron replete, the hospital can appropriately limit drug utilization and improve outcomes by ensuring that iron be administered to the patient.

GATEKEEPING

The gatekeeping model has, historically, been an important utilization management tool for managed care organizations. The "gate" is the point of entry into the health care system, and the "gatekeeper" controls the enrollee's access to the system. In a managed care organization, the "gatekeeper" is typically the plan member's primary care physician (PCP). However, in some managed care organizations the PCP is beholden to a case manager. Depending on the particular plan, the gatekeeper has various degrees of control over the plan member's access to health care services. At one end of the spectrum, the gatekeeper must order all nonemergency services, such as referral to a specialist. Other types of plans, such as preferred provider organizations (PPOs), allow enrollees to have access to specialist care without the need for a referral.

By interposing a gatekeeper between the enrollee and health care services, the managed care organization seeks to avoid unnecessary utilization, control costs, and optimize the interaction between the PCP and specialists. Because of market forces, customer satisfaction issues, and a growing awareness that health care utilization is not materially affected by the gatekeeping process, many plans are eliminating or liberalizing their gatekeeper models.

HEALTH CARE UTILIZATION: ETHICAL ISSUES

In an ideal health care environment, the care rendered to every patient is evidence based and is directed by a provider with a fiduciary interest in the patient's welfare. Such a system would obviate the need for utilization management, because "overutilization" would be mitigated by evidence-based practice and "underutilization" would be proscribed by the provider's fiduciary relationship with the patient. However, in reality, factors such as economic credentialing, physician incentives, fear of malpractice, and lack of data from prospective, double-blinded, controlled studies regarding diagnosis and treatment of many diseases all intrude on the ability of providers to practice cost-effective and evidence-based medicine, on the one hand, and the ability of health care plans to accurately measure true quality of care, on the other hand. The health care system, under the influence of prevailing economic conditions, market forces, the development of new technologies and drugs, as well as changes in tort and public health policy, can be expected to evolve with concomitant changes in the way health care utilization decisions are monitored, regulated, and implemented.

—Darren S. Kaufman

FURTHER READING

Cleverley, W. (1997). *Essentials of health care finance.* Gaithersburg, MD: Aspen.

Couch, J. (1997). *The physician's guide to disease management.* Gaithersburg, MD: Aspen.

Enzmann, E. (1997). *Surviving in health care.* St. Louis, MO: Mosby.

Kirz, H. (1999). *Thriving in capitation.* Tampa, FL: American College of Physician Executives.

HEALTH ECONOMIES

See Health Care, Health Policy, Spending on Health Care

HEALTH INFORMATION SYSTEMS MANAGEMENT

Health information systems management is the design, analysis, implementation, and support activities related to information systems focused on health and health data. Managing information through information technology is a core business process across all industries and the health care industry is particularly positioned to benefit significantly from its potential. Health information systems have a tremendous capacity to improve health and enhance the value of limited health care dollars of health care direct care delivery and delivery support.

Many unique issues and opportunities are influencing the management and development of health information systems, and the health administrator is often the dominant leader. The administrator is relied on to accurately collect and then transform data into information and knowledge necessary to achieve strategic business goals and objectives. The core business processes used in this management effort are planning, systems design, analysis, selection processes, implementation, and support. Surrounding these core processes are dynamic, systemwide issues and opportunities where health information systems is a dominant player: the continuous pursuit of quality in a perpetually changing health delivery system; security, privacy, and data quality; and the newest medium for health innovations, the Internet.

CORE FUNCTIONS

- *Systems planning* is the strategic linking of information systems applications with enterprisewide strategic business goals and objectives. The information systems manager is responsible for ensuring that information systems projects are planned and executed in a manner that furthers the strategic priorities of the organization. In most organizations, the chief information officer reports directly to the chief executive officer and they jointly plan the information systems architecture to match systems with operational requirements.

- *Systems analysis* is the evaluation of current and future business function requirements, the current information systems response, and the identification of new information systems requirements to support the future business function requirements. This is often the first step in developing a new information systems application. Success in this step is dependent on the accurate capturing of the elements of the business function, the user environment, and the information technology capabilities.

- *Systems design,* informed directly by the systems analysis, is the process of translating information systems requirements into new information systems application specifications. Successful systems design management includes a clear linking of the new application to strategic business goals or objectives, user participation in input and output expectations, and the identification of necessary technical enterprisewide systems compatibility.

- *Systems selection* is the identification of the appropriate application provider and application to meet the required systems specifications. Successful management of the selection process includes consideration of the advantages and disadvantages of in-house development or contract development and the choice of an industry standard or proprietary application coding structure. Evaluation of the potential solutions should include technical compliance with the identified systems requirements and successful application testing by end users.

- *Systems implementation and support* is the continuum of information systems management activities from purchasing the selected application, through facility preparation, application installation, data conversion, systems testing, and user training, to operational and maintenance support. Because of the serious consequences inherent in supporting most health care operations, testing new applications prior to going operational is the most critical phase in systems implementation. The highest consequence health operations may require simultaneous operations of both old and new applications until all implementation issues are addressed. Of equal importance after implementation is the training of support personnel to immediately respond to and fix systems breakdowns.

KEY ISSUES AND OPPORTUNITIES

Continuous Quality Improvement

Staying abreast of advancing information systems technologies and their potential impact on the quality of health care delivery is becoming a core competency of a successful health administrator. Perpetual advancements in health care delivery and delivery support drive the health administrator to seek ways to continuously improve the quality of the health delivery experience. Innovative health information systems applications are often central in evaluating the need for and supporting these new delivery and delivery support opportunities. These systems have significantly influenced administrative, clinical, and community health operations.

Administrative information systems technologies have dramatically reduced the percentage of the health care dollar spent on health delivery support expenditures. Often the first area of health operations to introduce information systems solutions, administration functions are a natural fit with the automation strengths of new systems applications.

Typical administrative functions that are served best by information systems applications include decision support, managed care, finance and accounting, human resources, logistics, material, facility management, scheduling, and practice management.

Clinical information systems technologies are advancing both the art and science of medicine. Electronic medical records preserve vital information for both future static review and continuously available cross-referencing over a patient's lifetime of care. The real-time posting of ancillary service results and automated provision of clinical reminders, warnings, and care guidelines have dramatically decreased errors at the point of service. Clinical decision support systems provide immediate clinical advice, allow for the advancement of informed decision making, and reduce unnecessary variations in clinical practice.

Systems established to support health enterprise operations can also serve the health needs of a community. Community health information systems are designed to provide community-accessible health information infrastructures linking information from the formal health care delivery system to information relating to community behavioral and environmental issues. The success of these efforts is founded on commitments made by community stakeholders to cooperatively develop the desired community applications. Elements of a successful community health information system include accessibility across socioeconomic strata, agreed-on standards and protocols, systems security, and uncompromising procedures for patient and organizational privacy.

Security, Privacy, and Data Quality

Health information systems have advanced health in direct parallel with the industry's ability to improve security, privacy, and data quality. The Health Insurance Portability and Accountability Act (HIPAA) of 1996 established many of the objectives underpinning these major improvements.

Security of information systems includes the protection of information and the control of access to that information through administrative procedures, physical safeguards, and technical security measures. Administrative procedures focus on the measures to select and manage security processes and the management of the conduct of personnel involved with health data. These procedures include contingency planning, access controls, security management procedures, and training. Physical safeguards attempt to protect the physical computer and the surrounding environment from damage or intrusion. Security of information systems also includes technical safeguards to protect access, authenticate data and users, and guard against damage or intrusion into the communication networks carrying health data.

Patients have the right to keep the information about themselves from unauthorized disclosure to others. This expectation of privacy, founded in the Hippocratic Oath of the 4th century BCE, is a balance between individual privacy and the requirement to share patient information for optimal patient care. Patient consent for disclosure often includes agreement on when disclosure authorization is required, notices of the minimally necessary health personnel who may have access to the protected information, and procedures for de-identification of records. Management of health information systems includes the requirement to protect the privacy of patient data.

Trust in health information systems is developed from the expectation that the data are complete, timely, accurate, and fit for their intended use. Known generally as *data quality*, this expectation is met through effective processes, policies, and leadership. The process of inputting data is the weakest point in the systems process for data quality. User–system interfacing is a complex communication process, and managers must strive to simplify the input process and take steps to ensure this step provides added value to patient outcomes. System policies often improve data quality when they identify the most efficient methods for data collection and handling and encourage all stakeholders to provide input. Finally, trust of the health information is sustained when enterprise leadership articulates the importance of data quality in the provision of effective health care and the attainment of enterprise goals and objectives.

The Internet

The Internet is a medium for health care managers to more conveniently meet the health information needs of patients in varying settings both inside and outside the physical location of health care operations. Health administrators face forces, from employers and patients, that demand they make optimal use of this medium to provide health information services. The response to these forces can be categorized as e-health content, commerce, connectivity, care, and community.

Employers are a major force in the health administrator's response strategies in the online provision of health information. Health care entitlements are increasingly growing as a percentage of operating costs, and employers seek more health information to make informed choices. Employers seek comparative quality indicators among hospitals and health plans—as the cost of this employee benefit rises, this is an economic viability issue.

Patients are also a force behind the drive to have health information provided online. Paradoxically, patients seeking a more personal involvement in their health embrace the "impersonal" venue of the Internet. The typical health consumers online are educated and interested in engaging in

decisions affecting their own health. Health administrators respond to this interest by providing health information through e-health offerings on the Internet.

- *E-health content* is the electronic exchange of health information and is the most common online offering by health enterprises. Administrative linkages to appointment systems, lab results, and even claims management are services offered beyond the simple "brochure" information (directions, contact information, hours) typically sought by patients. Health administrators attain strategic advantage when they provide interesting and meaningful content, make it local and detailed, and link the information to commerce and care offerings.

- *E-health commerce* is the researching of and purchasing of health products online. Spanning from the purchase of publications to health and beauty products, this online activity attempts to connect the delivery of health information with the business of providing products and services to meet the needs generated by that information. Successful strategies for administrators include making the link to products and services convenient and clearly delineated from the noncommercial health information.

- *E-health connectivity* encompasses the Internet-based health information systems that link all the players in the health care marketplace. Patients have expectations of a seamless connection between the care they need, access to the provider qualified to provide it, and approval and funding by their health insurer. The Internet can provide that connection wherever the point of service is needed. Health administrators attain strategic advantage when they provide their patients this connectivity as seamlessly as possible.

- *E-health care* is the use of Internet capabilities to extend clinical capabilities and outreach between health providers and their patients. This type of care has evolved from information-rich bedside services to virtual health services. Health administrators attain strategic advantage in this area when they enable care innovations simultaneously with connectivity innovations.

- *E-health community* involves leveraging Internet capabilities to improve the health of populations and link key health stakeholders in communities. This includes both linking care provision across community health services and data collection for epidemiologic health assessment. Strategic advantage can be gained by health administrators in this area by using the Internet to enhance their participation in the improvement of overall community health.

—James F. Meyers

FURTHER READING

Austin, C. J., & Boxerman, S. B. (1998). *Information systems for health service administrators.* Chicago: Health Administration Press.

Duncan, K. A. (1998). *Community health information systems lessons for the future.* Chicago: Health Administration Press.

Meyers, J. F., Van Brunt, D., Patrick, K., & Greene, A. (2002). Personalizing medicine on the Web: E-health offers hospitals several strategies for success. *Health Forum Journal, 45*(1), 22–26.

Middleton, B. (1999). *Clinical decision support systems (special edition). Journal of Healthcare Information Management, 13*(2), 1–120.

Nicholson, L. (1999). *The Internet and healthcare.* Chicago: Health Administration Press.

Rognehaugh, R. (1999). *The health information technology dictionary.* Gaithersburg, MD: Aspen.

Tan, J. K. H. (1998). *Health decision support systems.* Gaithersburg, MD: Aspen.

Worthley, J. A. (2000). *Managing information in healthcare: Concepts and cases.* Chicago: Health Administration Press.

HEALTH INSURANCE

Health insurance is a contractual relationship in which the insurer, in exchange for a premium, agrees to provide or to reimburse for the costs of medical care provided to the insured in the event of losses resulting from illness or injury.

The history of private health insurance in the United States largely began with the Great Depression. In 1929 Justin Kimble of Baylor Hospital provided 21 days of hospital care per year at his hospital in exchange for fifty cents per month premium. The American Hospital Association soon began approving these plans and assigning marketing areas; the plans became known as Blue Cross. Indemnity payment plans for physician services emerged in 1934 and were approved by the American Medical Association. They became known as Blue Shield plans. Prepaid health plans, the forerunners of health maintenance organizations (HMOs), also had their inception in the early days of the Depression. The Ross-Loos Health Plan was established in California in 1929, and group health plans were subsequently established in many major cities (Starr, 1982).

Insurance coverage was spurred during World War II because it was a form of compensation paid to workers that was not subject to wartime wage and price controls. The Taft-Hartley Act of 1947 made health insurance a working condition subject to collective bargaining. Tax treatment further encouraged the growth of employer-sponsored health insurance. The Internal Revenue Service excluded employer-sponsored health insurance from federal individual income taxes in a special ruling in 1943. Congress codified this in 1954 (Helms, 1999).

The demand for health insurance exists because individuals are willing to pay more than the expected loss to avoid the consequences of variable and uncertain potential losses. The theory of insurance argues that more health insurance will be purchased when people are risk averse; when the size of the potential loss is large; when the probability of loss is neither too large nor too small; and when family income is smaller. The income–insurance relationship is perhaps counterintuitive but reflects the ability of higher-income families to self-insure larger medical expenses.

It is estimated that in 2000, 84.2% of the U.S. nonelderly population had health insurance coverage. Approximately two thirds of these have coverage through employer-sponsored coverage. Of those with insurance, 6.6% purchase coverage individually, and 14% have coverage through public programs, largely Medicaid. In addition, virtually all those aged 65 and over have coverage through Medicare (Employee Benefit Research Institute [EBRI], 2001).

There are four forms of health insurance typically offered by employers. First, conventional coverage offers coverage for care from virtually all hospital and physician providers in the community and typically throughout the country. Prescription drug coverage is often included. Subscribers typically face a deductible of $200 and, once the deductible has been satisfied, pay a share (often 20%) of the hospital, physician, or pharmacist bills. Second, HMOs offer similar benefits but only at a relatively small set of providers in the community with whom it has contracted to provide care. Subscribers often copay $10 to $20 per physician visit but are responsible for the entire bill if they use providers that are not part of the HMO's network. Subscribers typically choose a primary care physician who is responsible for their care and who must authorize referrals to specialists. Third, preferred provider organizations (PPOs) offer coverage at a narrow set of providers, and subscribers are subject to copayments as in an HMO. However, PPO subscribers also may use a wider set of providers in the community and pay a somewhat larger share of the bill when they do so. Unlike conventional plans or HMOs, PPOs often do not bear insurance risk. Rather, they arrange and manage a set of contracts between health care providers and self-insured employers. Finally, point-of-service plans (POSs) are a hybrid of HMO and PPO features. They offer the ability to use covered providers outside the narrow network as does a PPO, but they require a primary care provider like an HMO. As of 2002, 5% of workers with employer-sponsored coverage were in a conventional plan, 26% were in an HMO, 52% in a PPO, and the remaining 17% in a POS (Gabel et al., 2002).

Premiums differ rather substantially across plan types. A 2002 national survey of employers found that single/family monthly premiums were $299/$707 for conventional coverage, $265/$681 for POS plan coverage, $260/$670 for PPO coverage, and only $230/$628 for HMO coverage (Gabel et al., 2002). The differences reflect both adverse selection into conventional (and possibly POS and PPO) plans and the ability of managed care plans, generally, to negotiate lower prices from health care providers.

Virtually all firms with 200 or more workers offer employer-sponsored health insurance. However, only 55% of firms with 3 to 9 workers offered coverage in 2002 (Gabel et al., 2002). Part-time and temporary workers are much less likely to be eligible for coverage than are full-time workers. Smaller firms tend to offer a single health insurance option. The number of plans offered increases with firm size. Half of firms with 200 to 999 workers offer more than one plan. Only 17% of firms with over 5000 workers offer a single plan; 72% offer three or more. Larger employers also tend to self-insure their conventional, PPO, and POS plans rather than buying coverage from an insurer. By 1998, 58% of workers in firms with 200 or more workers were covered by a self-insured plan (KPMG Peat Marwick, 1998).

Health insurance, although often provided by an employer, is thought to be paid for by the worker. The economic argument is straightforward. Workers are paid what he or she is worth, that is, her marginal revenue product. The compensation can take many forms, including money wages, pensions, and vacation time. If health insurance is added to compensation bundle, something else must be removed or the employer is paying more than is needed to attract workers of the desired skill levels. Thus, workers pay for health insurance in the form of lower wages or fewer other benefits. Rigorous tests of this tradeoff are difficult to construct, and the empirical evidence is mixed (Morrisey, 2001).

Of the population under age 65 in the United States, 6% to 7% have health insurance purchased in the individual market. Compared with those who get coverage through an employer, individual purchasers tend to have lower incomes and do not choose HMOs. Among this cohort, the probability of buying coverage increases with income and age, and modestly with better health status. Individually purchased insurance is relatively expensive. Loading costs are the amounts, in addition to claims expenditures, making up the health insurance premium. These include administrative costs, reserves, and profits. Loading costs in employer-sponsored plans tend to be 15% to 20% of claims paid. The loading costs of individual-purchased insurance tend to be 50% to 66% of claims (Pauly & Percy, 2000). Such coverage is increasingly available for purchase on the Web.

The major forms of public health insurance in the United States are Medicare and Medicaid. Both were enacted in 1965, as amendments to the Social Security Act, and both were extensions of earlier and smaller programs. Medicare provides coverage to those over age 65 and to the disabled. In 1999, 40 million people were covered. Medicare Part A covers institutional care (largely hospital care) and is paid for from payroll taxes the Federal Insurance Contributions

Act (FICA) assessed on people currently working. Citizens and permanent residents typically become eligible by having 10 years of Medicare-covered employment or being married to someone who does. Traditional Medicare is a conventional insurance plan requiring an $812 hospital deductible (in 2002) per 90-day spell of illness. Per diem copayments are required after 60 days. Virtually all beneficiaries obtain voluntary Medicare Part B coverage for professional services. In 2002 they paid a monthly premium of $54. Of the total Medicare Part B costs, 25% is paid for by the monthly premium; the remainder is paid from general federal tax revenues. Medicare does not cover prescription drugs or nursing home care beyond 100 days in a skilled nursing facility.

Of Medicare beneficiaries, 13% are enrolled in a Medicare HMO. However, enrollment is very skewed, with Medicare HMOs enrolling one quarter to one third of Medicare beneficiaries in Arizona, California, Colorado, Oregon, Pennsylvania, and Rhode Island. Medicare HMOs are to provide the same benefits as traditional Medicare without imposing additional costs. Plans with costs below the Medicare payment level are required to provide additional benefits. Plans may also provide additional benefits for an additional premium. Of Medicare HMO beneficiaries, 71% have prescription drug coverage, typically with specified dollar limits on total covered drug expenditures. Of Medicare HMO beneficiaries, 40% pay no additional premium, one third pay premiums of $50 per month or more (Kaiser Family Foundation, 2002).

The vast majority of Medicare beneficiaries obtain private coverage to supplement Medicare. As noted, 13% are enrolled in Medicare HMOs. Further, 35% have retiree coverage from a former employer, 25% purchase a Medigap plan, and approximately 14% have Medicaid coverage (Kaiser Family Foundation, 2001). Retiree coverage closely resembles the coverages offered by employers to active workers. Medigap plans tend to cover the deductibles and coinsurance associated with conventional Medicare but seldom include additional benefits.

Medicaid is a jointly funded, federal-and-state health insurance program for certain low-income and needy people. It covers approximately 36 million individuals, including children; the aged, blind, and/or disabled; and people who are eligible to receive federally assisted income maintenance payments. The costs of the program are shared between federal and state governments using a formula based on the ratio of state to federal per capita income. States exercise considerable flexibility in the nature and extent of coverage, and therefore the program eligibility and benefits differ substantially across states. Medicaid is typically the second largest source of state government spending after elementary and secondary education. Historically children have represented the largest group of covered individuals. Program expansions in the 1980s contributed to this. In 1998, 20.2 million children were covered. Over 11% of Medicaid enrollees are age 65 or older, and another 18% are blind and disabled. These groups, however, constitute 71% of Medicaid expenditures, largely for nursing home care (Centers for Medicare and Medicaid Services [CMS], 2000).

—Michael A. Morrisey

FURTHER READING

Employee Benefit Research Institute (EBRI). (2001, December). Sources of health insurance and characteristics of the uninsured: Analysis of the March 2001 current population survey. *EBRI Issue Brief,* no. 240. Washington, DC: Author.

Gabel, J., Levitt, L., Holve, E., et al. (2002). Job-based health benefits in 2002: Some important trends. *Health Affairs, 21*(5), 143–151.

Helms, R. B. (1999). The tax treatment of health insurance: Early history and evidence, 1940–1970. In G.-M. Arnett (Ed.), *Empowering health care consumers through tax reform* (pp. 1–26). Ann Arbor: University of Michigan Press.

http://cms.hhs.gov/charts/medicaid/2tchartbk.pdf

Kaiser Family Foundation. (2001, February). Medicare at a glance. *The Medicare Program.* Menlo Park, CA: Kaiser Family Foundation.

Kaiser Family Foundation. (2002, June). Medicare + Choice. *The Medicare Program.* Menlo Park, CA: Kaiser Family Foundation.

KPMG Peat Marwick. (1998, June). *Health benefits in 1998.* Arlington, VA: Author.

Morrisey, M. A. (2001). Why do employers do what they do? Compensating differentials. *International Journal of Health Care Finance and Economics, 1*(3–4), 195–202.

Pauly, M. V., & Percy, A. M. (2000). Cost and performance: A comparison of the individual and group health insurance markets. *Journal of Health Politics, Policy and Law, 25*(1), 9–26.

Starr, P. (1982). *The social transformation of American medicine.* New York: Basic Books.

HEALTH INSURANCE PORTABILITY AND ACCOUNTABILITY ACT (HIPAA)

The Health Insurance Portability and Accountability Act (HIPAA) was enacted in 1996 and includes five primary sections or "titles":

- *Title I:* Health Care Access, Portability, and Renewability
- *Title II:* Preventing Health Care Fraud and Abuse; Administrative Simplification
- *Title III:* Tax-Related Health Provisions
- *Title IV:* Application and Enforcement of Group Health Plan Requirements
- *Title V:* Revenue Offsets

Title I provides new protections for Americans against loss of insurance coverage because of illness or change in employment. Specific protections include the following:

- Limits on health care coverage exclusions because of pre-existing conditions
- Guarantees that individuals and certain small employers have the right to purchase health insurance when other health coverage is lost
- Guarantees that employers or individuals can renew health care coverage regardless of health conditions, in most cases

Title II of HIPAA addresses administrative simplification of health care transactions and includes a detailed discussion of required standards for electronic transmission of health information. This has been the most complicated and controversial portion of HIPAA. There are four major sections of Title II, including:

- Electronic Health Transactions Standards (final deadline for compliance is October 16, 2003)
- Unique Employer Identifiers (compliance required by August 1, 2005, for small health plans, July 30, 2004, for all other covered entities)
- Security & Electronic Signature Standards (compliance required by April 21, 2006, for small health plans, April 21, 2005, for all other covered entities)
- Privacy & Confidentiality Standards (compliance required by April 14, 2004, for small health plans, April 14, 2003, for all other covered entities)

Specific details for Title II have been delivered in phases.

The first two major sections of Title II on electronic health transaction standards and unique identifiers were motivated by the spiraling health costs. Administrative health care costs in the United States are estimated to be 25% of all health care costs. One contributing factor is the growing number of claims filed each year, with relatively few being filed electronically. The existence of over 400 different formats for filing claims is another factor. The U.S. government estimates that cost savings from compliance with Title II will be approximately $9 billion per year.

The privacy and confidentiality standards under Title II are designed to protect personal health information accessible through health plans, health care providers, and health care clearinghouses. All forms of data, including electronic, paper, and verbally communicated data, are covered under the HIPAA. The specific concern is for protection of individually identifiable health information (IIHI), including the following:

- Demographic information
- Information created or received from a health plan, health care provider, or health care clearinghouse
- Information related to the past, present, or future physical or mental health or condition of individuals, the provision of care to individuals and the past, present, or future payment for provision of health care

In general, Title II has several important implications for the health care community. First, there is a relatively short time frame for compliance with standards once they are put into place. Specifically, organizations generally have two to three years to comply with new regulations as they become available. Title II legislation has a broad scope: All functions, processes, and systems that store, handle, or generate health information are affected, making quick compliance even more challenging. Because Title II mandates standard formats for the most common transactions among health care organizations and also requires health care organizations to rethink how they protect the security and privacy of patients and consumers, many health care organizations will need to replace or substantially change current systems and processes to comply.

Title II carries with it stiff penalties for noncompliance, including the following:

- General civil penalty for failure to comply no more than $100 per violation per person, not to exceed $25,000 in a year
- Penalty for knowingly and wrongfully disclosing individually identifiable health information:
  - Up to $50,000, 1 year imprisonment, or both for simple offense
  - If committed under false pretenses, up to $100,000, 5 years imprisonment, or both
  - If committed with intent to sell, transfer, or use individual identifiable health information for commercial advantage, personal gain, or malicious harm, up to $250,000, 10 years imprisonment, or both

It is also important to note that health care organizations can take advantage of new business opportunities through HIPAA compliance and related investments. Compliance itself will ultimately result in huge long-term cost savings for organizations and will reduce administrative hassles. The required standardization of processes along with assurance of transaction privacy and security provides organizations with the potential to play in new markets and utilize new electronic business models. Being HIPAA compliant also provides a good platform for developing new forms of customer service.

Titles III through V have generated much less controversy. Title III on tax-related health provisions includes the following:

- An amendment to the Internal Revenue Code to allow a deduction for limited amounts paid to a medical savings account (MSA)
- Increases in the deduction for medical insurance expenditures by self-employed individuals
- Provisions for treatment of long-term care services and contracts
- Provisions for treatment of accelerated death benefits
- Exemptions from taxation for certain state-established membership organizations
- Provisions for organizations subject to Section 833 of the Internal Revenue Code
- Provisions for penalty-free distributions from IRA accounts to pay health insurance
- Direction to include organ and tissue donation information with tax refund payments where practicable

Title IV is similar to Title I but provides rules specifically for group health plans. Title IV permits a group health plan to impose pre-existing condition exclusion only if very specific conditions are met. Title IV also prohibits group health plans from refusing to enroll, subject to exceptions, an individual because of the individual's health status, medical condition, claims experience, receipt of health care, medical history, genetic information, evidence of insurability, or disability. Title IV also provides for guaranteed renewability in multiemployer plans and certain multiple employer welfare arrangements, subject to certain exceptions, including nonpayment of premiums, fraud, or the plan ceasing to cover a geographic area.

Finally, Title V on revenue offsets revises provisions prohibiting a deduction for interest on loans with respect to company-owned life insurance, including a revision that prohibits a deduction for interest on loans with respect to company-owned endowment or annuity contracts. Title V also addresses treatment of individuals who lose U.S. citizenship.

—Amy W. Ray

See also Electronic Commerce, Encryption, Virtual Private Network

FURTHER READING

http://aspe.os.dhhs.gov/admnsimp

Medicode. (2003). *2003 HIPAA desk reference: A physicians' guide to understanding the administration simplification provision.* Salt Lake City, UT: St. Anthony Publishing.

www.ahima.org/hot.topics/hipaa.html

HEALTH INSURANCE PURCHASING COOPERATIVE (HIPC)

A health insurance purchasing cooperative (HIPC) is an entity that purchases health insurance for individuals as well as employers. By belonging to the cooperative, individuals and employers are provided access to more affordable health insurance as a result of the HIPC's increased purchasing power. Health insurance purchasing cooperatives represent a subset of purchasing cooperatives, in general. Individuals and employers in many business sectors seek membership in purchasing cooperatives that allow access to a variety of resources, services, and insurance types. For example, purchasing cooperatives can provide access to health insurance, property and liability insurance, telecommunications, payroll services, office supplies, auto and home insurance, 401(k) programs, and so forth.

HOW DO HIPCS DECREASE INSURANCE COSTS?

By definition, the HIPC is a pool of individuals and employers. Hence, the underwriter of the insurance is able to spread risk among a greater number of people with a concomitant reduction in risk premiums. In addition, because the insurer can deal uniformly with a large group, this creates economies of scale and reduced administrative costs. And finally, as noted, the larger the pool, the greater the purchasing power, resulting in the ability to negotiate lower rates for a given scale and scope of covered health care services.

TYPES OF HIPCS

Active HIPC

An active HIPC (also referred to as a *health alliance*) provides a scope of services beyond simply contracting for health insurance. A health alliance participates in managerial and regulatory affairs such as quality-related services, cost control, and risk assessment.

Passive HIPC

A passive HIPC subserves no regulatory or managerial function. The passive HIPC's role is limited to contracting for health insurance and the attendant functions of premium collection and disbursement.

BENEFITS OF HIPC MEMBERSHIP

As discussed, membership in a purchasing cooperative leverages the purchasing power of the individual or employer by allowing the member to negotiate the price of insurance coverage or other services, as part of a large pool of members.

When considering the attractiveness of employment with a given employer, many potential employees give primacy not only to salary but also to the health care benefits offered by the employer and to the cost of these benefits. As a member of an HIPC, a smaller employer can compete with larger firms, such as Fortune 500 companies, for access to talented and experienced workers. Hence, HIPC membership is an important recruiting tool for smaller employers in business sectors with limited numbers of qualified and experienced workers.

FORMING A HEALTH INSURANCE PURCHASING COOPERATIVE

The regulations governing the formation of health insurance purchasing pools vary from state to state. However, certain generic issues need to be addressed when forming such entities:

1. The type of health insurance coverage that will be provided, such as a comprehensive plan versus more limited coverage (the HIPC will need to assess the demographics and health care needs of its members)

2. The provider pool that the members will have access to, such as a health maintenance organization (HMO), a preferred provider organization (PPO), an indemnity plan, and so forth

3. The "portability" of the plan; that is, does coverage continue when the member moves or travels to another locale?

—Darren S. Kaufman

FURTHER READING

www.ianr.unl.edu/pubs/consumered/nf263.htm

HEALTH INTERVENTIONS

See Health

HEALTH MAINTENANCE ORGANIZATIONS (HMOs)

The health maintenance organization (HMO) is defined as an organized health care delivery system that incorporates both a financing and a delivery mechanism. The system is managed by a single administrative entity and provides a wide range of health care services to an enrolled beneficiary population. In effect, HMOs are both insurers and health care providers. HMOs create networks through the development of contracts with health care providers in different specialties. These providers include individual physicians, physician groups, and hospitals that agree to provide care for a specified population under a discounted, fixed-fee arrangement. Because members of an HMO are required to seek care within the network, providers often experience an increased volume of patients. Typically HMOs concentrate on cost, access, and quality in managing their organizations. They must control costs within the context of any fixed-fee arrangement, they must provide access to their patients for covered services, and most HMOs are responsible for the quality of health care service provided to their enrolled populations.

HMOs are not a new concept within the health care delivery system. In fact, HMOs are thought to have predated indemnity or fee-for-service insurance plans by a number of years. The first HMO-like organization can be found as early as 1929. Dr. Michael Shadid is credited with starting Farmers' Union-Cooperative Health Association for farmers and supply cooperatives, the first prepaid group medical practice in the country. From these early beginnings, the role of prepaid health insurance continued a slow growth. The Kaiser Foundation Health Plans of California and the Group Health Cooperative of Puget Sound are examples of early prepaid health plans. The impact of prepaid health plans was relatively small until Congress and President Nixon focused attention on HMOs with the passage of the Health Maintenance Organization Act of 1973. The primary purpose of this act was to provide resources for the development and start-up of HMOs across the country. The development of HMOs was the cornerstone of President Nixon's "National Healthcare Strategy." He saw HMOs as playing a vital role in providing equal access to health care for all citizens, creating efficiencies within the existing health care system and dealing with the economic impact of supply and demand on the health care market. The development of a national health care strategy was thought to be a necessary approach to dealing with the rising costs of health care and improving access for many underserved populations. The primary features of the HMO Act included government-sponsored funding for the expansion of existing HMOs into broader service areas and the

creation of new HMOs in different markets throughout the country. In addition, the act exempted HMOs from state insurance mandates that restricted or prohibited the operation of HMOs within state boarders as long as the HMO met federal standards for the conduct and operation of HMOs. The act also required employers that offered fee-for-service health care coverage and had more than 25 employees to offer the choice of an HMO as well. The ultimate result of the HMO Act of 1973 was a moderate and steady growth of HMOs within the health care industry. The number of HMOs has risen from less than 150 plans in the mid 1970s to more than 500 individual HMO health plans in today's marketplace.

Even with the phenomenal growth of HMOs, the primary philosophy and goals of each organization has remained the same. HMOs have strived to provide an alternative to traditional fee-for-service plans and introduce the concept of choice in the health care delivery and insurance system that was not present prior to their arrival. In addition, HMOs attempt to control cost through such mechanisms as provider incentives, utilization review, and greater patient involvement in the health care process. A philosophical orientation to primary care as the portal for entry into the system has allowed HMOs to manage the full spectrum of care for any individual patient. Risk-sharing arrangements with primary care providers create an incentive to be efficient and diligent in the delivery of care. This is an outcome not typically seen in the fee-for-service system. Whether HMOs have been successful in meeting these goals is a contentious issue. What most people agree on is the fact that HMOs have been able to slow the growth of health care costs and provide greater access to a wide range of health care offerings.

In the beginning HMOs were relatively simple organizational entities that were relatively similar from organization to organization. Over the years, as the presence of HMOs in the marketplace has become more prominent, a continual transformation in the structure of heath maintenance organizations has occurred. Currently there are nine widely accepted "types" of HMO organizational structures, including the staff model, group model, network model, independent practice association (IPA), direct contract model, and a number of hybrid models that capture certain aspects of the health care delivery system not fully covered in one of the five main models. These different types of HMOs vary in their complexity, provider arrangements, and control of the aspects of care. The five most prominent types of HMOs are as follows.

STAFF MODEL

The defining aspect of a staff model HMO is that the physicians who provide medical services to the enrolled beneficiary population are employed by the HMO. The physicians are most often compensated on a salary basis and are typically provided monetary incentives for keeping health care treatment costs down. Staff model HMOs hire primary care and specialty physicians in order to offer the full spectrum of health care. Staff model HMOs own and operate their own facilities; therefore, they incur the associated overhead and maintenance costs. This provides a challenging environment in which to control costs and maintain quality. The advantage of the staff model is that the organization has significant control over the inputs of production. Every attempt is made to treat patients efficiently, which in turn creates opportunity for the physicians to be as productive as possible.

Staff model HMOs are sometimes referred to as *closed-panel HMOs,* because physicians who are not directly employed with the HMO do not have access to the enrolled patient population. For specialty services that are not frequently used, the HMO contracts with local providers for the services on an as-needed basis. Typically patients in a staff model HMO are assigned to a specific primary care physician who evaluates them initially on every episode of care. If specialty intervention is needed, the primary care physician refers to a specialist within the organization and continues to monitor the patient throughout the diagnostic and treatment process. For the majority of people enrolled in a staff model HMO there is little or no copayment for covered services. Traditionally, staff model HMOs provide a "one-stop" health care experience within the confines of a tightly controlled health care delivery system.

GROUP MODEL

In the group model HMO design, physician groups contract directly with the HMO to provide health services to the enrolled beneficiary population. These physician groups are more often than not composed of primary care and specialty physicians who are capable of providing a wide spectrum of health care services. Two types of group models exist: the captive group and the independent group. In the captive group model, the physician organization exists solely to provide services to the HMO. These groups are often developed by the HMO for the purpose of providing direct patient care support. Typically, the captive group model provides a greater degree of control over the physicians than does the independent. An example of a captive group HMO is the Kaiser Foundation Health Plan. In the independent group model the physician group provides services to the HMO-enrolled patient population but also provides services to patients outside of the HMO. In either case the captive and independent group model HMOs are considered closed-panel groups, because physicians who are not part of the group do not have access to the enrolled HMO population. One significant advantage of the group

model is the ability to monitor and control utilization. Because all physicians are members of the group, the group administration has significant leverage to identify any existing weaknesses in utilization and fix the deficiencies at the individual provider level. This is all accomplished in the same manner that staff model HMOs function, without the associated cost of physician salaries.

NETWORK MODEL

In the network model design, HMOs contract with provider groups for direct patient care support services. These medical groups may be spread out over a wide geographic region and may be based on a multispecialty or a primary care model. If the provider group is multispecialty, then the network model HMO is a close representation of the staff model HMO without the HMO "owning" the physicians. In a primary care network arrangement, the group or groups that are contracted with provide basic primary care and are responsible for all referrals made to specialty physicians. Under the network model arrangement, HMOs are able to offer a greater choice of physicians to their enrolled beneficiary population because of the wider geographic dispersion and total number of physicians. Because the medical groups contracted with are independent, the associated physicians are allowed to see both HMO and non-HMO patients. The network model does not afford the HMO as much control as the staff or group model; therefore, the HMO must continue to conduct utilization review in order to monitor costs, efficiency, and quality.

INDEPENDENT PRACTICE ASSOCIATION (IPA)

The independent practice association (IPA) is composed of individual physicians who contract with the IPA to provide services to a particular HMO. These individual physicians often run private practices in addition to their association with the IPA. The HMO in turn contracts with the IPA for health care services. HMOs typically reimburse the IPA on an all-inclusive capitated basis. The IPA is then responsible for compensating the individual physicians that are part of the organization and this may be done through a capitated arrangement or on a fee-for-service basis. IPAs are typically multispecialty, with a large primary care base. The large primary care base is attractive to prospective HMOs and provides greater choice to the consumer. The presence of IPAs varies greatly from location to location. In some areas multiple IPAs may exist and be in direct competition for HMO business. Some areas may have only one IPA for HMOs to choose from. IPAs are considered open-panel HMO arrangements, because any physician has access to the network of enrolled HMO participants as long as they meet the IPA and HMO requirements for inclusion in the organization.

DIRECT CONTRACT MODEL

In the direct contract model design, the HMO contracts directly with individual physicians in order to provide care to their enrolled beneficiaries. This allows the HMO to provide broad geographic coverage and a variety of primary care and specialty services. Because each physician in the direct contract model operates independently, it can be difficult for the HMO to control utilization. Under the direct contract model, primary care physicians are often utilized as "gatekeepers" to monitor the entire episode of care for any particular patient. If specialty care is necessary, the primary care physician makes a referral to one of the specialty physicians who are also part of the direct contract network. In this way there is some control of utilization, but each primary care physician's treatment and referral habits must be tracked independently. Therefore, the management of each individual contract and the requirement to track individual utilization significantly increases the administration overhead for the HMO.

Additional HMO organizational variations exist, but most are hybrids that vary in their compensation mechanisms, physician arrangements, or service offerings (vision, dental, and so on). As a group, they compose the smallest portion of the overall HMO offerings in the managed care marketplace. Regardless of HMO type, all HMOs attempt to reduce costs, improve access, and provide quality health care to their enrolled populations.

—Kevin G. LaFrance

See also Health Insurance, Integrated Delivery System, Preferred Provider Organization (PPO), Utilization Review

FURTHER READING

Cafferky, M. E. (1997). *Managed care & you: The consumer guide to managing your health care.* Los Angeles: Health Information Press.

Coleman, J. R., & Kaminsky, F. C. (1977). *Ambulatory care systems.* Lexington, MA: Lexington Books.

Knight, W. (1997). *Managed care contracting: A guide for health care professionals.* Gaithersburg, MD: Aspen.

Kongstvedt, P. R. (2001). *Essentials of managed health care.* Gaithersburg, MD: Aspen.

Shouldice, R. G. (1991). *Introduction to managed care: Health maintenance organizations, preferred provider organizations, and competitive medical plans.* Arlington, VA: Information Resources Press.

HEALTH OFFICER AND HEALTH COMMISSIONER

The "state health officer or commissioner" is the elected or appointed head of the main health agency, reporting to the governor or legislature, with primary responsibility for leading the state's lead health agency (Centers for Disease Control and Prevention, 1992; Ford, Duncan, & Ginter, 2003). The agencies that different state health officers oversee, and requirements for the job, can vary greatly from state to state.

State health agency structures differ in two dimensions. The first dimension is the nature of the agency's oversight or reporting requirements. In most states, agencies are a part of the executive branch with the state health officer reporting directly to the governor. An alternative model has the state health agency supervised by a health commission or board, with the commissioner reporting to either the legislative or executive branch of government. The latter arrangement is rapidly disappearing, along with the state health commissioner title, as the scope of agency duties is continually being rearranged.

The second structural difference is the scope of duties within an agency. Numerous agencies in every state have some responsibility for health activities. The simplest means of identifying the lead agency is by going to the Association of State and Territorial Health Officers' Web page. A growing number of state health agencies are part of a multipurpose human service "superagency" that includes various social services. About one third of the states have adopted this model. As the nature of the agencies change over time, so do the job qualifications of the state health officer.

Traditionally, and by law in many states, the health officer has been a physician. This paradigm is gradually shifting toward a model without this tradition or restriction. The CDC and other organizations are promoting a health agency leadership model favoring candidates who are formally trained in public health practice and possess relevant work experience.

—Eric W. Ford

FURTHER READING

Centers for Disease Control and Prevention (CDC). (1992). Leadership development survey of state health officers—United States, 1988. *Morbidity and Mortality Weekly, 41*(13), 221–223.

Ford, E. W., Duncan, W. J., & Ginter, P. M. (2003). The structure of state health agencies: A strategic analysis. *Medical Care Research and Review, 60*(1), 31–57.

http://astho.org

HEALTH PLAN

See Health Insurance

HEALTH PLAN EMPLOYER DATA AND INFORMATION SET (HEDIS)

HEDIS® (Health Plan Employer Data and Information Set) is an assessment tool for purchasers of health care plans to facilitate comparison of products, services, and providers. The tool is based on a standard protocol of performance measures. The National Committee for Quality Assurance (NCQA), a collaboration of health plans, public and private employers, organized labor, and public officials, developed HEDIS for measuring managed health care plans beginning in the late 1980s. NCQA is an independent not-for-profit organization with a mission to improve health care quality.

Data are collected through self-report, audits, and onsite surveys. In 2001, half of all HMOs (372) participated in HEDIS and 90% of all health plans used HEDIS to measure performance. The statistics represent 63 million covered lives. HEDIS has evolved, responding to criticisms of scope, accuracy, and utility. The changes have included increasing the number of participating HMOs and health plans, efforts to enhance validity, expansion of measures beyond prevention and process measures, and introduction of a user-friendly database, the Quality Compass. Onsite surveys have improved the reliability of the data. Among Fortune 500 companies, 53% include HEDIS results in their purchasing decision, and half require NCQA accreditation of their health plan.

The current version, HEDIS 2003, collects information regarding clinical access and utilization, details of care in the areas of behavioral, cardiac, child and adolescent, maternity, and surgery, plus issues of living with illness and getting better, as well as member satisfaction. The goal of providing measures for comparison between health plans takes precedence over measures of quality improvement of any one plan. The measures seek these desirable attributes: relevance, scientific soundness, and feasibility. The attribute of relevance addresses meaningfulness to purchasers from the standpoint of scope and variability among health plans, quality, and cost-effectiveness. Scientific soundness is concerned with issues of clinical evidence, case mix and risk adjustment factors, and reproducible results. The attribute of feasibility focuses on clarity of definitions, reasonable cost, patient confidentiality, logistics, and ability to audit.

In 2002, NCQA published the fifth annual edition of *State of Managed Care Quality,* containing results for 2001. The report reflects trends in quality within the managed care industry. Incremental across-the-board improvements were noted in breast cancer screening and efforts to discourage smoking. Sharp increases were noted in childhood immunization rates and diabetic care. Decreasing variability

between low-performing health plans and high-performing plans was observed in the use of beta blockers after heart attacks, cervical cancer screening, cholesterol management, and 30-day follow-up after hospitalization for mental illness.

In this publication, NCQA introduced an economic model that presents the business case for quality. The model is based on research that demonstrates how the cost to promote health care quality can be compared against the resulting savings. The model, called the Quality Dividend Calculator, can actually be used online. The calculator is based on several specific medical conditions, including asthma, heart disease, depression, and high blood pressure. It utilizes absenteeism and low productivity days, the firms' average revenue and wage per employee, then produces calculations of savings when health plans reduce the economic impact of these illnesses. The economic difference between high- and low-quality health plans can be compared.

—Jerry Burgess

FURTHER READING

Corporate health care purchasing among the Fortune 500. (2001, May). National Health Care Purchasing Institute. www.nhcpi.net

State of managed care quality report. (2002). National Committee for Quality Assurance. www.ncqa.org

HEALTH POLICY

Most of us are clear on what *health policy* is about. It addresses collectively and individually questions such as, Where are we with respect to the quality, cost, availability, and equity of health care? What is an individual's right to health care? How did we get where we are? Do we want to be there? What other alternatives are there throughout the world? What is likely to work in the future and how well? How do we prepare for that future, given our political process? What laws, expenditures, incentives, and organizational structures are necessary to achieve our desired results? What are the likely roles of health professionals and ordinary citizens in this process? What are their appropriate roles? Because health policy decisions are part of complex economic and political processes and are tied to basic ethical and religious values, there is seldom agreement on the answers. However, effective policy analysis can enlighten the debate considerably.

Health policy is a thorny problem for the United States. No government agency or other social institution has been assigned the role of developing or implementing a national health policy. Most decision making in this society is done in or by the marketplace. Furthermore, the U.S. Constitution is silent on the subject of health and health care. Although its preamble promises "to promote the general Welfare," the Tenth Amendment to the Constitution contains the following wording: "The powers not delegated to the United States by the Constitution, nor prohibited by it to the States, are reserved to the States respectively, or to the people." Neither education nor health care are specifically allotted to the federal government in the Constitution. However, omission of health in the Constitution cannot be attributed solely to the intent of the framers. They lived in a world in which one talked of "evil humours" and visited "barbers and churgeons."

Consequently, there are essentially 50 or more health systems in the United States, providing a number of laboratories for health policy research. Therefore, U.S. policy making for health care is highly dispersed, and any discussion of health policy must take into account policy choices that appear at the multiple levels of the following:

- National government
- State and local governments
- Institutions
- Employers
- Private sector providers

CENTRALIZATION VERSUS DECENTRALIZATION

Many countries where there is a national health service have recently chosen to decentralize that system service to make it more responsive to local needs and to tap revenues available at the regional and local levels. Sometimes this transfer of decision-making power carries with it a privatization component, as in the United Kingdom. Institutions can be transferred from the public to the private not-for-profit or to the for-profit sectors and back again. When decentralization happens, the government may or may not encourage the entry of new institutions into the health sector to generate competition among providers. Therefore, each country, political subdivision, health care institution, and citizen must at some level, and often at multiple levels, participate in the development and implementation of health care policy.

It is important to understand that high-sounding goals, such as the World Health Organization's 1978 Alma Ata Conference's declaration of "Health for All by the Year 2000," turned out to be a slogan and not a policy. Although sounding good, it was not backed up by detailed plans, adequate resources, or firm commitments to generating change, and in 1998 it was replaced by "Health for All in the 21st Century." Yet individual developed countries, such as Canada, Germany, Japan, and the United Kingdom, have taken rather different routes to more or less successful health care systems. These results have been achieved over

decades, and their systems have had time to adapt to the cultures of those countries. No one is going to change an entire health system overnight, least of all the United States.

HEALTH CARE POLICY TERMINOLOGY: CONFUSING MULTIPLE DEFINITIONS

Can we expect experts on health policy to agree on the answers to those questions? Of course not. Their interests are often in conflict, and their background disciplines often use the same terms differently. Academic departments concerned with health policy tend to build on the disciplines of economics, political science, management, and public administration. Consequently, the literature can introduce considerable confusion into the usage of health policy terms. The term *health* can be used two ways. One definition is the restoration from illness. The second definition is one of wellness, a positive state of being, not entirely grounded in medical status. Increasingly, however, the second meaning is being designated by *wellness*. It is important in discussing policy matters to be clear about the end state that one is committed to achieving. This end state should focus on outcomes and the distribution of those desired outcomes throughout the population.

There are also multiple meanings of the words, as with *strategy* and *policy, manager* and *administrator,* and *goals* and *objectives.* In the business literature, strategy is the big picture, the framework within which the details are worked out using the subsequent tactics and policies adopted by management. In that sense the business literature parallels the military usage in which the generals plan strategies and the field commanders implement strategy through tactical decisions within the policies (and constraints) sent down by their superiors. In such settings, the term *policy* may be reduced to highly detailed responses as in a "policy and procedures manual." In contrast, the literature of public administration refers to a strategy as a means of getting from A to B after the big picture has been established by "policymakers." The health care field is especially subject to confusion, because the hospital administration field has been steadily moving from public administration toward a business model, with consequent changes in the use of terms. Many trustee boards are now called *directors,* and the administrator is increasingly the *chief executive officer (CEO)* or even *president.* In the management literature the manager oversees the administrator, but the opposite is true in public administration.

The terms *goals* and *objectives* are also hopelessly intertwined. Whichever hierarchically drives the other is strictly up to usage of the writer. Be very careful, in reading the literature, to discern the intent of the individual presenter when using these terms.

QUANTITATIVE ANALYSIS

Cost–benefit analysis and cost-effectiveness analysis are basic tools in health policy analysis. Mathematically, these techniques are similar to the return-on-investment calculations used to make private sector investment decisions. These allow comparisons of alternatives based on the ratio of benefits related to the outcomes produced to the resources consumed. In the health care literature, cost–benefit analysis uses dollars as the common metric, whereas cost-effectiveness uses some other metric such as lives saved or quality-adjusted life-years. Economists are more likely to describe cost–benefit analysis as maximizing the benefits of a given resource base, whereas cost-effectiveness seeks to find the minimum cost approach to achieving a given set of benefits. Results for any given situation can vary widely depending on the time-adjusted values assigned to streams of costs and savings, the time horizon used, and the points of view of the stakeholders represented.

Small-area studies and outcomes studies are two significant investigative tools of health policy analysis. Small-area studies look at differences in disease rates, patterns of care, and health outcomes between specific geographic areas. For example, rates of surgery and outcomes assessments vary considerably from locale to locale, and this information is useful for both quality and cost analysis purposes. Outcomes studies use proven clinical trials methods to compare the outcomes from using alternative approaches to treatment and prevention. They measure the effectiveness and cost of specific alternatives under controlled conditions, providing (one hopes) information on best practices under controlled and financially neutral conditions. Outcomes studies are the primary evidence in evidence-based medicine.

QUALITATIVE ANALYSIS

Beyond the quantitative, policy analysts must be concerned with issues such as public acceptability and political feasibility, impact on access to care, method of financing, incentives used and their effects on productivity, allocating resources between treatment and prevention, reaching underserved populations in rural areas and inner-city neighborhoods, rationing care when resources are constrained, where to focus government investments in medical research and in training health care professionals, and controlling those health care costs that grow at rates considerably higher than growth of individual incomes and government revenues.

POLITICAL PROCESSES

Because the federal government is by far the largest purchaser and insurer of health care, health care issues are still addressed in its political processes. Medicare, Medicaid,

the Department of Defense, and other government agencies purchase care for their clients, enrollees, and their employees and dependents. Dissatisfaction with access to care, such as the cost of prescription drugs or parity in insurance for mental health treatment, leads to demands that government do something. However, the political process also means that interest groups all have their chance to have their say, directly or through paid lobbyists, both at the federal and state levels. Thus policy analysis is but one input to the decision-making process, yet an important one.

—Curtis P. McLaughlin

See also Access, Centers for Medicare and Medicaid Services, Cost–Benefit Analysis (CBA), Cost Effectiveness, Medicaid, Outcomes Research

FURTHER READING

Bodenheimer, T. S., & Grumbach, K. (2002). *Understanding health policy: A clinical approach* (3rd ed.). New York: Lange Medical/McGraw-Hill.

Herzlinger, R. (1997). *Market driven health care*. Reading, MA: Addison-Wesley.

Kissick, W. L. (1994). *Medicine's dilemmas: Infinite needs versus finite resources*. New Haven, CT: Yale University Press.

Lathrop, J. P. (1993). *Restructuring health care: The patient-focused paradigm*. San Francisco: Jossey-Bass.

Redman, E., & Neustadt, R. (2001). *The dance of legislation* (2nd ed.). Seattle: University of Washington Press.

Schwartz, W. B. (1998). *Life without disease: The pursuit of medical utopia*. Berkeley: University of California Press.

Weimer, D. L., Vining, A. R., & Vining, A. (1998). *Policy analysis: Concepts and practice* (3rd ed.). Upper Saddle River, NJ: Prentice Hall.

HEALTH PRODUCTION FUNCTIONS

Health production functions relate end result measures of health (for example, morbidity rates, mortality rates, self-rated health status, or functional health status) to such health inputs as medical care services, diet, exercise, recreation, cigarette smoking, and alcohol use. Because the consumer's time is required to obtain medical care and to engage in exercise and recreational activities, his or her own time also is a relevant input. The multivariate nature of this function suggests that many factors in addition to medical care determine health levels. Indeed, there is evidence that these factors play more important roles in health outcomes than the quantity of medical care in the United States and other developed countries. Of course, technological advances in the treatment of illness and the introduction of new drugs have led to dramatic increases in longevity over long periods of time.

HEALTH AND MEDICAL CARE

The relationship between health and medical care reflects causality in both directions. On the one hand, more medical care leads to better health. On the other hand, sicker people demand more medical care services, and physicians and hospitals may be more numerous in areas where the health of the population creates a strong demand for their services. Economists use the statistical technique of instrumental variables to estimate the causal impact of medical care on health. Suppose that different consumers pay different prices for medical care services, perhaps because some have more generous health insurance than others. If consumers are grouped according to these prices, medical care and health will vary among these groups solely because of variations in prices and not because initial illness levels differ. Hence, group differences in health and medical care reflect the causal impact of medical care on health.

Technically, the price of medical care serves as an instrument for medical care. It is correlated with medical care but not correlated with initial illness levels. Using this technique, researchers have demonstrated that women who begin prenatal care within the first trimester of their pregnancies give birth to heavier infants who are much less likely to die within the first month of life. They also have shown that heart attack victims are more likely to survive if they are treated in a hospital with the capacity to provide intensive cardiac treatment.

HEALTH AND SCHOOLING

Because the consumer's time is required to produce health, his or her personal characteristics may influence health outcomes. Many studies suggest that years of formal schooling completed is the most important correlate of good health. This finding emerges whether health levels are measured by mortality rates, morbidity rates, self-evaluation of health status, or physiological indicators of health and whether the units of observation are individuals or groups. There is much less consensus as to whether this correlation reflects causality from more schooling to better health. A number of investigators have argued that omitted "third variables" such as a future orientation may cause both schooling and health to rise. Very recent research has established the causal nature of the schooling effect by examining groups exposed to different compulsory schooling laws or differences in the availability of college.

—Michael Grossman

FURTHER READING

Fuchs, V. R. (1974). *Who shall live? Health, economics, and social choice.* New York: Basic Books.

Grossman, M. (2000). The human capital model. In A. J. Culyer & J. P. Newhouse (Eds.), *Handbook of health economics* (Vol. 1A). Amsterdam: North-Holland.

McClellan, M. B., McNeil, B. J., & Newhouse, J. P. (1994). Does more intensive medical treatment of acute myocardial infarction in the elderly reduce mortality? *JAMA, 272*(11), 859–866.

Rosenzweig, M. R., & Schultz, T. P. (1983). Estimating a household production function: Heterogeneity, the demand for health inputs, and their effects on birth weight. *Journal of Political Economy, 91*(5), 723–746.

HEALTH PROMOTION

See Wellness

HEALTH STATUS INDICATORS

Health status indicators are a series of standardized measurements and parameters that define the health level of a population or a nation. The rising costs of health care, the fragmentation of health status information, and public demand have been important factors in the development of strategies and initiatives by the government, not-for-profit organizations, and private corporations to assess the health status of populations, groups of employees, and patients with special needs.

The Healthy People 2010 Initiative has been developed to guide health care organizations, providers, and the community in general to focus in a predetermined set of measurements and parameters in order to improve health by accomplishing specific objectives by the year 2010. The federal government leads this effort, with the participation of agencies from all lines of government and the private sector. The leading health indicators for 2010 are as follows:

1. Physical activity

2. Overweight and obesity

3. Tobacco use

4. Substance abuse

5. Responsible sexual behavior

6. Mental health

7. Injury and violence

8. Environmental quality

9. Immunization

10. Access to health care

The leading health indicators for 2010 represent the major causes of concern for the government. Each leading indicator may contain one or more objectives to be accomplished. These indicators are not just measures to be taken; they are drivers of public policy for government and direction to health care organizations. Health status indicators provide the road map for clinicians, colleges, universities, local governments, and associations to focus their efforts in disease prevention and health promotion, in an organized and coordinated attempt to accomplish the preset objectives. For example, in access to care, one of the objectives is to have 100% of the population covered with health insurance by the year 2010. To fulfill the objective, government must produce legislation to offer insurance to all in the next eight years.

The Health Employers Data Information Set (HEDIS®) criteria sponsored by the National Committee on Quality Assurance (NCQA) are the best known set of health indicators. The HEDIS® criteria are used to compare providers and managed health plans. The main purpose of this measurement system is to improve the quality of care we practice in America by providing guidelines to physicians and a reference to the general public.

Health status indicators constitute a rich database on which important interventional strategies have been construed. Education and promotion of a healthy lifestyle focused on preventive initiatives emphasizing immunizations, maintenance of a reasonable body weight, and accident prevention (safety belts for all car occupants, car seats for infants, adequate gear in the working areas, and so on) are just a few examples.

There is also growing evidence of the benefit of the implementation of coordinated interventional strategies for chronic diseases such as diabetes mellitus, bronchial asthma, and congestive heart failure. The utilization of a comprehensive multidisciplinary approach based on the information obtained by this systematic assessment can reduce morbidity and mortality, at the same time decreasing the costs associated with the management of chronic illnesses.

—Raúl F. Montalvo

See also Access, Community Health Status Indicators, Health Plan Employer Data and Information Set (HEDIS), Health Promotion, Healthy People 2010

FURTHER READING

www.health.gov/healthypeople

www.ncqa.org

HEALTHY PEOPLE 2010

Healthy People 2010 is a national effort by a broad government-led consortium to use specific 10-year health objectives for the year 2010 to improve the health status of the U.S. population.

The United States first developed specific national health objectives in 1979 with *Healthy People: The Surgeon General's Report on Health Promotion and Disease Prevention*, which was followed in 1990 by *Healthy People 2000*.

There are two overarching goals for Healthy People 2010: (a) Increase quality and years of healthy life, and (b) eliminate health disparities. In January 2000, 467 objectives in 28 focus areas were published in *Healthy People 2010*, after several years of development and an extensive public input process.

The Healthy People Consortium consists of over 400 national membership organizations, including most health care provider associations and medical specialty societies, all state and territorial public health agencies, mental health, substance abuse, environmental agencies, and national associations of public health officials who meet annually to review progress in meeting national health goals. The Secretary's Council on National Health Promotion and Disease Prevention Objectives for 2010, chaired by the Secretary of the U.S. Department of Health and Human Services (DHHS), and composed of the Surgeon General and the former Assistant Secretaries for Health, advises the national initiative. A Healthy People Steering Committee composed of DHHS agency representatives is charged with leading the implementation of Healthy People 2010.

Many states have developed "healthy people" initiatives. As of summer 2001, 15 states had developed Healthy People 2010 state plans.

Ten "Leading Health Indicators" were chosen to monitor the nation's health and to track progress: physical activity, overweight and obesity, tobacco use, substance abuse, responsible sexual behavior, mental health, injury and violence, environmental quality, immunization, and access to health care. Specific objectives from Healthy People 2010 will be used to measure each of the Leading Health Indicators.

Focus areas for Healthy People 2010 include access to quality health services; arthritis, osteoporosis, and chronic back conditions; cancer; chronic kidney disease; diabetes; disability and secondary conditions; educational and community-based programs; environmental health; family planning; food safety; health communication; health disease and stroke; HIV; immunization and infectious diseases; injury and violence prevention; maternal, infant, and child health; medical product safety; mental health and mental disorders; nutrition and overweight; occupational safety and health; oral health; physical activity and fitness; public health infrastructure; respiratory diseases; sexually transmitted diseases; substance abuse; tobacco use; and vision and hearing.

—Ray M. Nicola

See also Community Health, Community Health Status Indicators, Health, Health Promotion, Health Status Indicators, Wellness

FURTHER READING

Public Health Foundation. (1999). *Healthy People 2010 toolkit: A field guide to health planning.* Washington, DC: Public Health Foundation.

U.S. Department of Health and Human Services. (2001). *Healthy people in healthy communities.* Washington, DC: U.S. Government Printing Office. www.health.gov/healthypeople

HIPPOCRATIC OATH

Little is actually known about the life of the Greek physician Hippocrates, thought to have been born on the island of Cos between 470 and 460 BCE. His father and grandfather were both physicians. Hippocrates left behind a series of writings that comprose the earliest known Greek medical texts. Few of these texts, however, have survived to the present, and doubt has been cast on the authenticity of many. Of those regarded as genuine, the most famous is the "Hippocratic Oath."

In its original form, the oath begins with an affirmation of Apollo and the various other gods and goddesses. The apprentice physician then swears to support his teachers financially and in turn to teach their male children the medical art without fee or payment. He swears to keep medical knowledge secret from those who are not physicians and who have not themselves taken the oath. Following are a series of rules regarding conduct with patients: to work for their benefit, to keep them from harm and injustice, to perform no abortions, to give no deadly drug, to leave surgical procedures to those who are trained to perform them, to remain free of intentional mischief—including sexual relations—in whatever house he may visit in his capacity as a physician, and to keep his patients' confidentiality.

A reading of the oath could lead one to assume that the medical profession had an organized structure at the time of Hippocrates, with accepted rules of deportment and behavior. Some authorities, however, have concluded that Hippocrates was to some extent a rebel and that the oath was an attempt to codify a reformist code of medical ethics. Certainly, at the time of Hippocrates infanticide (and, by inference, abortion) as well as suicide were generally accepted in Greek society. The oath has undergone many revisions over the years, and many of its original precepts are regarded as outmoded. Certainly, few physicians today would consider it appropriate to swear by Apollo and the other Greek gods and goddesses, and the practice of medicine is no longer limited to males. In addition, the forswearing of abortion is deleted from most modern versions of the oath, and the current controversy over such topics as physician-assisted suicide and euthanasia has made this passage problematic as well.

The Hippocratic Oath has waxed and waned in popularity, with many critics considering it more a series of "guild rules," whose primary purpose is to protect and promote the interests of the medical profession in society, rather than a set of moral precepts guiding proper physician action toward patients. In February 2002, a Charter on Medical Professionalism was published simultaneously in the *Lancet* and *Annals of Internal Medicine*. The charter does not claim to be a direct revision of the oath. Nevertheless, it contains many of the same precepts, and addresses many of the same issues. Most medical students today are required to study both the original and modern versions of the Hippocratic Oath, and many medical schools have incorporated it, in one form or another, into graduation, and in some cases, into induction ceremonies.

—Robert I. Katz

FURTHER READING

www.pregnantpause.org/ethics/medprof.htm
www.rts.edu/quarterly/winter98/hippocratic.html

HOME HEALTH CARE

The delivery of home health care includes professional caregivers, volunteers, and untrained assistants who give medical and nursing care to the acutely or chronically ill in private homes and retirement communities. The goal of home care is to provide necessary services in the comfort and convenience of the patient's home environment. Additional goals include avoiding the cost and risk of hospitalizations and nursing home placement, and providing relief for family caregivers.

Services that in the past could only be given in a hospital can now be given at home. Examples include intravenous antibiotics and ventilator machines for patients unable to breathe on their own.

Professional caregivers are usually obtained through a home health agency. These agencies employ or contract with nurses, nursing assistants, physical therapists, occupational, respiratory, and speech therapists, and social workers.

Many agencies also provide home health aides who assist with bathing, meal preparation, and basic housekeeping. Home health agencies also facilitate the purchase and use of respiratory and durable medical equipment that is needed in the home. Examples include oxygen, nebulizer machines, wheelchairs, and grab bars for the bathroom.

In the United States, home health agencies are strictly regulated, and a detailed initial evaluation of each patient must be completed by a nurse and updated periodically. If the services of a home health agency are required for an acute, short-term illness, the costs are often paid by private insurance or Medicare. Most health insurance does not cover the costs of home care for a chronic or long-term illness. Some individuals purchase long-term care insurance to cover these potential costs.

Examples of acute care that would be covered by most insurance plans include (a) home physical and occupational therapy after a stroke or joint replacement, or (b) nursing care to monitor the effects of a new medication or to care for a wound. Examples of chronic care that would not be covered by most medical insurance plans in the United States include (a) assistance with bathing, toileting, and feeding for a person who suffered a stroke and has permanent disability or (b) monitoring and administering medication that is taken on a long-term basis.

Some managed care companies and health systems have recognized that providing home care for the chronically ill saves money by reducing hospitalizations. At no extra cost to the individual, these companies may provide the following for selected high-risk individuals: home nursing visits, telephone monitoring, the services of a social worker or case manager, and caregiver and patient education.

Volunteers often provide companionship, transportation, and meals. In many communities, the volunteers are organized and trained by churches and synagogues, hospitals, long-term care organizations, service organizations, or county offices of aging. Other volunteers are people who are neighborly and will assist a frail older person or a disabled person with chores, transportation, or meals.

Many times home health care for the chronically ill is provided by a family member or by a person whom the family member hires. The abilities and training of these caregivers are variable. It is estimated that 80% of the home care given in the United States is provided by unpaid and untrained caregivers. The economic, emotional, and physical strain on these caregivers is substantial.

An interesting aspect of home care that is beginning to demonstrate its potential is the use of electronic and video systems to facilitate communication among patients, caregivers, and families. Examples include patients who transmit daily weights and blood pressure measurements to a congestive heart failure nurse specialist, or asthmatics who transmit daily information on peak breathing flow rates. In addition, video conferencing can allow specialist physicians to evaluate patients in the home. This is already being used in some rural areas, with success demonstrated in psychiatry and dermatology. As our population has become more mobile, great distances often separate the disabled or elderly from other family members. Electronic innovations such as video monitoring and e-mail to caregivers may help to bridge some of these gaps.

End-of-life care can also be provided in the home with the assistance of hospice programs. Hospice programs are often subsidiaries of home health agencies or health systems. Their services include visits from nurses, home health aides, and social workers. Family education, chaplain services, and bereavement counseling are included in hospice services.

Challenges for the future include finding ways to finance and train the many caregivers that will be needed as the population ages and chronic diseases become more prevalent. Barriers to effective home care need to be identified and removed. In addition to financial and training issues, many individuals and ethnic groups are hesitant to allow outsiders into the home. An often-unrecognized barrier is an older person's reluctance to allow home care because of fear that vulnerabilities will be exposed, prompting transfer to a nursing home.

Although currently rare in the United States, physicians who make house calls are becoming more available. The development of portable diagnostic equipment and more equitable Medicare payments for physician home visits have made this a realistic option. Some physicians devote their practices solely to house calls. A physician visit to the home facilitates optimal coordination of all aspects of home health care.

—Jean Stretton

See also Home Health Care Agencies, Hospice

FURTHER READING

Boling, P. A. (2000). The case for medical home care. *Annals of Long-Term Care, 8,* 27–30.

Hughes, S. L., Weaver, F. M., & Giobbie-Hurder, A. (2000). Effectiveness of team-managed home-based primary care: A randomized multicenter trial. *JAMA, 284,* 2877–2885.

O'Hara, D. (2000, September 17). How can you care for the invisible caregiver? *American Medical News,* 25–27.

www.aahcp.org

www.ama-assn.org

HOME HEALTH CARE AGENCIES

Home health care agencies provide nursing, therapy, and social services in an individual's home. These agencies can be for-profit or not-for-profit. They can be independent but often are subsidiaries of a hospital, health system, or long-term care organization. During the 19th century, visiting nurse associations were founded in many communities to provide home nursing for those who could not afford private nurses. Some of these voluntary services have evolved into the home health agencies of today.

Keeping abreast of financial and regulatory issues is essential to the success of a home health care agency. These agencies are rigorously regulated in the United States. For a patient to receive Medicare home care benefits, a physician must certify that the patient is homebound and that the services are medically necessary. A detailed physical and psychosocial evaluation of the patient must be completed by a nurse and submitted with the bill for services. The Balanced Budget Act changed the payment methodology for home care services. Home health agencies were previously reimbursed for their costs. They are now paid on a per case basis, with some adjustment for the complexity of the problems that are being managed.

Traditional Medicare coverage pays for home health care only after an acute illness or injury. Medicare's home health coverage ends when the patient's condition has reached a plateau. Medicaid, which is administered somewhat differently by each of the 50 states, provides medical insurance for individuals with low incomes. Medicaid may cover some of the costs of care in the home for low-income people with chronic illnesses.

—Jean Stretton

See also Home Health Care Agencies, Hospice

FURTHER READING

Benjamin, A. E. (2001). Consumer directed services at home: A new model for persons with disabilities. *Health Affairs, 20,* 80–95.

Feder, J., Komisar, H. L., & Niefeld, M. (2000). Long-term care in the United States: An overview. *Health Affairs, 19,* 40–56.

HORIZONTAL INTEGRATION AND DIVERSIFICATION

The term *horizontal diversification* refers to the unrelatedness or diversity of the organization's products and markets. A conglomerate is a widely diversified firm with unrelated products and markets.

Conversely, the term *horizontal integration* refers to the relatedness of the organization's products and markets. A highly concentrated organization, or one built on pure concentration, offers similar products or services in narrow markets.

To insulate the organization from risk of downturns in one product or market, or to spread financial risk, some organizations diversify horizontally into products or markets that are not closely related to its core business. For example, a chemical company that acquires a pharmaceutical company finds itself interacting with new products with new kinds of employees in new markets with new kinds of customers. An acute care hospital that acquires a home health agency must become expert at delivering new forms of health care services in new distribution channels away from the core hospital. To diversify financial variability, the organization enters into many unrelated markets with different earnings streams. In financial theory, this evens out the fluctuations in the corporate earnings by reducing the variability of the total earnings stream. Such an organization finds itself in unrelated industries in which it has limited core competence. A hospital that starts a restaurant or parking garage is diversifying away from its core competence of health care. Many hospitals contract out food services or parking services, because few hospitals have competencies in those areas.

The organization facing diversification needs to ask itself two very important questions. First, how important is it to be expert in its business lines? If its reputation for excellence is part of its culture and strategy, then it may wish to contract out the noncore operations and focus on the core processes, products, and services. Management and staff energy can then concentrate on the chosen business, products, and customers. Second, how important is it to smooth out earnings variability? If the organization can manage variability of cash flow with strong market positions in core competencies, then the organization may not need the diversity of earnings streams offered by diverse products and services.

—Michael J. Stahl

See also Acquisitions, Diversification Strategies, Divestiture Strategies, Merger and Acquisition

FURTHER READING

Ginter, P. M., Swayne, L. M., & Duncan, W. J. (1998). *Strategic management of health care organizations.* Malden, MA: Blackwell.

Pitts, R. A., & Hopkins, R. (1984). Firm diversity: Conceptualization and measurement. *Academy of Management Review, 7,* 620–629.

Porter, M. E. (1987, May–June). From competitive advantage to corporate strategy. *Harvard Business Review, 65,* 43.

Stahl, M., & Grigsby, D. (1997). *Strategic management* (Chapter 5). Oxford, UK: Blackwell.

Venkatraman, N., & Camillus, J. (1984). Exploring the concept of fit in strategic management. *Academy of Management Review, 7,* 513–525.

HOSPICE

Hospice is a comprehensive health care program that provides end-of-life care to patients with terminal illnesses defined by a life expectancy of six months or less. The program provides full-time medical and nonmedical services aimed at helping the patient and caregivers cope with physical and psychological end-of-life issues associated with a terminal disease. Central to the mission of hospice is the belief that people in the final stage of an incurable disease have the right to die with dignity and be free from controllable pain. Accordingly, the medical objective of hospice is focused on providing palliative management of symptoms related to the terminal illness with emphasis on pain control and preservation of physical functions rather than attempting to cure.

The nonmedical services include emotional, spiritual, and respite support for the patients and their primary caregivers.

An interdisciplinary team delivers medical, nursing, social, volunteer, bereavement, respite, and inpatient services. The hospice staff is typically composed of a primary care physician, hospice medical director, primary care nurse, personal care provider, social worker, pastoral care provider, and volunteers. Hospice care can be administered at home by the patient's primary caregiver with 24-hour, 7-days-a-week support by the professional hospice staff. Depending on an individual patient's needs, services can also be provided by free-standing hospice facilities, hospitals, and long-term care facilities such as nursing homes.

Enrollment into a hospice program requires (a) a signed statement from the patient documenting a self-arrived-at decision to elect noncurative care rather than treatment for the terminal illness, and (b) certification of terminal status by the patient's physician and the hospice medical director.

Reimbursement for hospice services can be covered by Medicare (Part A, Hospital Insurance), Medicaid, and private insurance with hospice benefits. Not-for-profit hospices are also entitled to solicit and receive charitable donations to fund services provided to patients who lack insurance or financial means to pay for their care. For-profit programs can only receive but not solicit donations.

Hospices are reimbursed by payers on a per diem basis that depends on the number of days a patient is enrolled in the program rather than on the amount of services the patient receives. An exception is 24-hour home nursing care that is reimbursed on an hourly basis. Under Medicare, hospice coverage is provided for two 90-day periods. If needed, an unlimited number of 60-day periods can also be added. At all times, the patient retains the power to cancel hospice care and switch to standard Medicare coverage for curative treatment. If necessary, return to hospice coverage is also allowed.

In a situation where the patient survives beyond four benefit periods, a recertification of terminal status is required for continual enrollment in a hospice program and Medicare coverage.

—Bernard T. Ng

See also Health Insurance, Centers for Medicare and Medicaid Services, Medicaid, Not-for-Profit Organization

FURTHER READING

www.americanhospice.org

www.hospiceinfo.org/index.cfm?webURL=/public/articles/index.cfm?cat=2

HOSPITAL COMPETITION

See Hospitals

HOSPITALS

Over the course of the 20th century, hospitals in the United States changed from unsophisticated institutions that offered palliative care to people suffering from severe, frequently terminal illnesses, into facilities that provide the most sophisticated services available to correct almost all health or physical problems and to prevent, or at least significantly delay, death. Over the short course of 100 years, primary causes of death changed from infections such as tuberculosis, pneumonia, polio, and diarrhea to chronic diseases, heart disease, cancer, stroke, and accidents. The phenomenal 20th-century advances in science permitted a belief that science could solve almost any physical health problem, and hospitals became the institutions that provided the solutions of science to the people.

At the beginning of the 21st century, a hospital is defined by the Joint Commission on Accreditation of Healthcare Organizations (JCAHO) as "a health care organization that has a governing body, an organized medical staff and professional staff, and inpatient facilities and provides medical, nursing, and related services for ill and injured patients 24 hours per day, seven days per week. For licensing purposes, each state has its own definition of a hospital." Over 5000 hospitals are currently in business in the United States.

TYPES OF HOSPITALS

Generally speaking, there are seven types of hospitals in the United States:

- *Academic medical centers (AMCs)* are hospitals intimately affiliated with medical schools. Such facilities typically have teaching and research missions in addition to providing clinical inpatient care. Clinical services in such centers usually include a complete array of services and the ability to provide care to individuals who have the most rare physical problems. These facilities are usually owned by the associated academic institution.

- *Veterans Administration (VA) hospitals* are facilities across the United States designed and maintained to provide care to veterans of the various U.S. uniformed services who seek care through these institutions. Clinical services in these hospitals are designed to meet the needs of veterans and do not include obstetric, newborn, or pediatric care. Physicians affiliated with VA facilities typically are employed by the institute either on a full-time or part-time basis. These hospitals are owned by the Veterans Administration.

- *Public hospitals* are typically large, inner-city facilities that are supported by local taxes. Such institutions frequently are affiliated with medical schools that provide the majority of the institution's medical staff. These facilities were originally developed to provide charity care to individuals with limited financial resources. Public hospitals are usually owned by local government.

- *Not-for-profit community hospitals* are the most common type of facility. These facilities agree to provide a minimal level of community service in exchange for not-for-profit status, which excludes these facilities from property and business taxes. Most not-for-profit community hospitals have open medical staffs. Physicians who practice medicine in the community apply for clinical privileges at the community hospital and are granted such privileges after review of their training credentials and experience. Not-for-profit hospitals are tax exempt and are owned by their respective not-for-profit foundations.

- *For-profit community hospitals* are basically the same as not-for-profit institutes except for their tax status. These institutions have access to public markets in order to raise capital, as opposed to bond markets, which are used by not-for-profits. Medical staff in for-profit facilities typically are physicians in the community who apply for privileges based on their training and experience. For-profit facilities are owned by a public company.

- *Rural hospitals* are facilities located in counties outside standard metropolitan statistical areas. These facilities may be for-profit or not-for-profit and attract medical staff from their area to apply for privileges based on their training and experience. Rural hospitals are so designated by the U.S. Public Health Services and are recipients of federal support to assure their continuation. Rural hospitals may be not-for-profit or for-profit and owned either by a not-for-profit foundation or a for-profit company, respectively.

- *Specialty hospitals* have existed in the fields of obstetric/newborn, pediatric, and orthopedic care for many years. These facilities may be not-for-profit or for-profit, and services are limited to their particular area. Medical staffs are typically specialists in the hospital's fields who practice in the community and apply for privileges based on their training and experience. Recently, other types of specialty hospitals have emerged. These have been heart hospitals or other specialty areas that are owned, in part, by physicians. These hospitals' medical staff typically is composed of physicians who have an equity position in the facility. Pediatric hospitals in the United States tend to be affiliated with medical schools and may be owned by the academic center. Ownership of other specialty facilities may vary as suggested earlier.

SCOPE OF SERVICE

The scope of service at America's hospitals varies considerably. Generally most academic medical centers offer essentially all approved services. These facilities also tend to participate in significant numbers of research programs, thereby offering some treatments that have not yet received FDA approval.

Community hospitals, both not-for-profit and for-profit, usually offer multiple services, including emergency, obstetric/newborn care, urgent care, general medicine, general surgery, and an array of medical and surgical subspecialties. Many hospitals offer open-heart surgery, but more than 50% do not.

Rural hospitals are usually small in size and limited in scope of services. Most include emergency care, obstetric/newborn care, as well as general medicine and general surgery.

In the 1970s, federal legislation required all states to implement Certificate of Need (CON) requirements for all hospital expenditures or for additional hospital services. These laws were designed to control the increase in costs of health care and were based on the belief that if the state controlled hospital expansions, the cost of care would be "controlled." In 1972, health care in the United States was about 7.5% of the gross national product.

During the 1990s, CON laws were repealed in a number of states and revised in others. In 2002, generally speaking, states east of Mississippi retained CON laws and western states repealed them.

PAYMENT FOR HOSPITAL SERVICES IN THE UNITED STATES

During the early 1980s, two significant changes occurred that altered payment for hospital services. In 1983, the federal medicine program changed from charge-based reimbursement to payment by diagnosis-related groups (DRGs). Thus, hospitals were paid based on the patient's diagnosis, regardless of length of stay or resource utilization. This system greatly reduced the length of stay for Medicare recipients.

Also during the early 1980s, HMOs became a significant factor in hospital reimbursement for employed, non-Medicare populations. The HMO's policies of strict utilization management, including precertification requirements for hospital admissions, and incentive payments to physicians to reduce hospital use, resulted in dramatic decreases in admission rates for the under-65 population.

Admission rates to American hospitals decreased throughout the 1980s and early 1990s. Since 1996 (the year "baby-boomers" began entering their fifties) these trends have reversed and admission rates have began to increase.

For the past decade hospital costs in the United States have represented about one third of all health care costs. These costs are financed by governmental programs, federal, state, and local, private insurance, and individual payments. In a typical community hospital, Medicare and Medicaid payments will be about 50% of the facility's revenue stream. "Managed care" insurance plans will represent about 30% to 35%, other insurance about 5%, and self-pay or no pay about 10%. Interestingly, very little of the costs are paid directly by a patient to the hospital.

During the 1990s hospitals in the United States, because of managed care plans, especially HMOs, assumed increasing levels of risk for the cost of care they provided. This risk took the form of prepayment or per diem payment schemes. The prepayment or full-risk scheme caused the hospitals to move toward becoming "integrated delivery systems." In other words, hospitals began buying physicians' practices, home health agencies, and other health care delivery elements so that, in theory at least, the system could control costs and thereby be profitable under per payment or capitation arrangements.

During the late 1990s, for a number of reasons (continual efforts on the part of HMOs to lower capitation payments, hospital systems' inability to control costs, failure of managed care plans to channel business volumes, and the desire for choice of providers by the American public), integrated delivery systems were recognized as failures.

Over the past few years, hospitals have tended to sell all elements of health care except inpatient and outpatient services, and capitation as a payment modality has largely disappeared.

HOSPITAL ACCREDITATION

In 1917 the American College of Surgeons developed its "Minimum Standard for Hospitals" and the following year began inspecting hospitals. In 1951, the American College of Physicians, the American Hospital Association, the American Medical Association, and the Canadian Medical Association all joined with the American College of Surgeons to establish the Joint Commission on Accreditation of Hospitals. The JCAHO's stated goal was to provide voluntary accreditation to hospitals. When Congress established Medicare in 1965, the law included the provision that JCAHO-accredited hospitals were "deemed" to be in compliance with "Conditions of Participation." With this Medicare proviso, the commission became increasingly important in and to American hospitals.

Today JCAHO accreditation is a formal survey process that occurs every three years in most all hospitals. The purpose of accreditation is to assure the quality of a hospital. Because the JCAHO process is standards based and occurs only every three years, increasing demands have developed in recent years to develop more timely and outcome-related processes of assurance. The 1999 Institute of Medicine Report suggested that medical errors account for 44,000 to 98,000 deaths in the United States each year and that in 1999 the most common of these errors were medication errors in hospitals. This report has resulted in growing demands for new quality assurance measures for hospitals. The employee group Leapfrog, for example, is calling for computerization of hospital medication ordering, volume-based referral, and the use of intensivists in ICUs (intensive care units). It is anticipated that such external demands will result in additional requirements being placed on hospitals as conditions for participation in Medicare.

PHYSICIAN–HOSPITAL RELATIONSHIPS

Physician–hospital relationships have changed significantly over the past century. Prior to World War I, hospitals had very little to offer to patients other than surgery using ether drip anesthesia. With the advent of sterilization technologies, improved anesthesia, and antibiotics, hospitals evolved from facilities of last resort to institutions designed to improve health. With the widespread use of penicillin after World War II, this perspective became firmly entrenched.

Physicians, following World War II, became likewise much more capable of providing positive measures to return people to health, and the most sophisticated of these measures were provided in the hospitals from surgery, to obstetrics, to treatment of cancer.

To assure consistency in the provision of inpatient services, standards were developed with the JCAHO to define medical staff relationships with hospitals. These standards included bylaw requirements for voluntary medical staffs to require physician credentialing for hospital privileges and peer review activities to assure quality.

Over the past two decades, because of DRG and HMO influences, as well as improved technology, many procedures have moved from inpatient to outpatient settings. However, new technologies have also resulted in more advanced procedures that require inpatient capabilities. These changes have placed increased importance on credentialing and peer review and the responsibility of the hospital to assure that these measures are effective.

HOSPITALS AS EMPLOYERS

With the dramatic growth in the capabilities of medical care over the past 75 years, hospitals frequently are the largest employer in their community. Today, hospitals are the largest employer of nurses in the United States and a major employer of all allied health professionals. Most costs in hospitals are for labor. Thus the industry is very sensitive to the periodic shortages that occur in the health professions. Clinical staffing is an ongoing challenge in all hospitals, which must maintain adequate numbers of qualified clinicians to meet the care needs of patients and do so within the reimbursement constraints of third-party payers.

—Frank Houser

FURTHER READING

www.hospitalconnect.com
www.jcaho.org

HUMAN GENOME PROJECT

See Genomics

HUMAN RESOURCE MANAGEMENT

Human resource (HR) management (also known as *personnel management*) focuses on the management of an organization's employees. HR management is especially critical to the core competencies of health care organizations, which rely heavily on attracting and retaining quality personnel.

THE ROLE OF HR MANAGEMENT

HR management is a *staff function* because it provides support to a health care organization's managers. Unlike some organizational functions such as purchasing or legal that are almost entirely self-contained, many of the HR functions are the *joint* responsibility of the HR department and managerial or supervisory personnel. When a nurse is hired, for example, the hospital HR department typically

provides support activities such as processing the written application, scheduling an interview, and ensuring that the necessary tax and benefit paperwork have been completed. The actual hiring decision, however, is usually left up to the nursing supervisor who will be working directly with the new hire. The HR department also formulates and implements a variety of HR policies (for example, the hospital's affirmative action plan).

The HR function has four essential functions:

1. To help the health care institution to acquire the best employees (through job analysis, job design, recruitment, and selection)

2. To maximize employee contributions to the health care organization's mission and strategies (through performance appraisal, training, and development)

3. To enable the health care organization to identify and retain competent employees and get rid of incompetent or counterproductive employees (through performance appraisal, compensation management, employee discipline, and control)

4. To ensure that the health care organization complies with relevant legislation (equal employment opportunity, health and safety, compensation and benefit, and other laws)

THE HR MAJOR FUNCTIONS

HR management typically entails the following highly interrelated functions:

• *Job analysis and design* involves systematically gathering information on the job (job description), determining the knowledge, skills, and abilities needed to perform the job competently (job specification), and designing a job that can be performed efficiently and competently by a qualified employee.

• *HR planning* is the process of balancing a health care organization's HR supply and demand so that shortages or excesses of certain personnel are avoided. HR planning, for example, might involve determining how many additional physicians, nurses, therapists, and support technical personnel will be needed to staff an expanded sports medicine center in a large suburban hospital.

• *Employee recruitment* involves assembling a pool of job applicants from which the health care organization can draw. Recruitment involves identifying and using various recruitment sources (for example, a private employment agency, temporary help agency, university placement office). HR managers recognize that recruitment sources vary with respect to the type and quality of applicant that they yield and the expense that they involve.

- *Employee selection* involves identifying and hiring the best applicants from the recruitment pool. The selection process involves the intelligent use of selection predictors (devices used to gather information to "predict" whether an employee will perform competently) such as application blanks, interviews, background checks, personality and integrity tests, and knowledge tests, among others. One selection predictor that has become increasingly important is a background check to verify previous employment and to check an applicant's criminal, driving, and credit history. The use of selection predictors often requires consulting with a qualified industrial psychologist.

- *Training and development* is used to provide employees with the knowledge, skills, and abilities needed to perform their jobs, stay abreast of the latest developments in their field, and enhance their careers. This HR function may be performed in-house using HR staff or externally using consultants and experts. Training and development activities include identifying training needs, establishing training program goals, selecting employees for training, designing training programs, conducting the programs, and evaluating the effectiveness of the programs.

- *Performance appraisal* is the process of determining how well an employee is doing the job. Typically, the HR department designs the performance appraisal instrument, and the supervisor or manager administers the instrument on a periodic basis. The performance appraisal process should include a postappraisal interview for employee feedback.

- *Compensation and benefit management* entails administering salary surveys, performing job evaluation, designing pay structures and benefit packages, and ensuring the proper administration of the compensation and benefit program. Compensation and benefit management is probably the most complex HR function because of the myriad of laws affecting pay and benefits as well as the economic, social, and psychological factors that affect employee perceptions of pay.

- *Health and safety* is a critical issue in many health care institutions. Although supervisors are clearly responsible for workplace safety, the HR department usually monitors compliance with federal (Occupational Safety and Health Administration, or OSHA) and state health and safety laws.

THE PROFESSIONALISM OF HR MANAGERS

Historically, HR managers have ranked below accounting, financial, marketing, and other managers in terms of pay and prestige. In recent years, however, the importance and recognition of HR managers has grown as organizations have become cognizant of the critical importance that

human resources play in the success of an organization. The major professional organization for HR managers is the Society for Human Resource Management (SHRM). It provides a variety of educational and certification opportunities for HR managers. The organization also keeps HR managers up to date on developments in the field.

The two professional tracks for HR managers are the HR generalist and the HR specialist. HR generalists, such as a medical center HR director, are in charge of an entire HR function. They oversee a staff that performs the HR functions described earlier. A generalist may have a business degree such as an M.B.A. or master's degree in human resource management. An HR specialist focuses on a specific aspect of HR management such as discrimination law, health and safety, or benefit programs and may work as a consultant or at the headquarters of a large organization. HR specialists may have master's, doctoral, or law degrees, and they may have spent a considerable amount of time becoming experts in a relatively well-defined HR area.

—Terry Leap

FURTHER READING

Gomez-Mejia, L., Balkin, D., & Cardy, R. (2001). *Managing human resources.* Upper Saddle River, NJ: Prentice Hall.

Pfeffer, J. (1998). *Human equation.* Boston: Harvard Business School Press.

HUMAN RESOURCE PLANNING

Human resource planning is an activity undertaken by the human resource function within an organization to assure that human resource actions and activities are properly aligned with the overall business or organization strategy. Traditionally, the term *human resource planning* referred solely to the practice of examining the number of anticipated openings, comparing that with the labor market trends and ensuring that the appropriate actions were taken to fill those positions. Human resource planning in the 21st century is a much more comprehensive set of analyses and examinations to ensure that the human resource function optimally contributes to the organization's overall business success.

As the human resource function transitions away from a primarily transactional or administrative function and strives toward creating stronger business partnerships within the organization, the need for thorough and accurate human resource planning increases. The process of human resource planning is likely to be unique to each organization; however, the most common steps to human resource planning are as follows:

- Thorough analysis of both the internal and external environment, which includes an analysis of the current state and the anticipated future state
- Examination of the internal and external analysis and determination of the human resource implications
- Creation and implementation of a human resource strategy to support business endeavors
- Monitoring and evaluation of the appropriateness and effectiveness of the human resource strategies

Each of the aforementioned steps is reviewed in more detail next.

ANALYSIS OF INTERNAL FACTORS

Thoroughly examining information internal to the business or organization is a critical first step to human resources being seen as a viable business partner. This examination should begin with a review of the business goals, both long and short term. Only after truly understanding the changing nature of the business goals can human resources be prepared to support the business with these new objectives.

The internal factors examination should also look to anticipate the future personnel that will be needed to help the organization achieve its business goals. When considering future personnel needs, it is important to focus on skills and abilities needed in additional or shifting resources, not just on raw numbers of individuals needed.

The internal analysis could also focus on the current internal environment through the gathering of employee opinions via survey and/or actively maintaining a turnover analysis, to better understand how many and what type of employees are leaving the organization, and for what reasons. In addition to an environmental or culture analysis and/or turnover analysis, the human resource team should examine critical talent within the organization and the succession plans to determine if indeed the organization has the internal manpower needed to achieve the business goals.

In sum, the internal analysis should include an examination of the current state of the business and, more importantly, the future business goals and direction. After understanding the context provided through the business goals, a closer analysis should be made of the organizational environment and the personnel available and needed for future success. This information should then be coupled with the external or environmental analysis findings before devising a human resource strategy.

ANALYSIS OF EXTERNAL FACTORS

The external analysis, also known as an *environmental scan,* helps provide the appropriate context for the internal analysis. This analysis often includes an examination of the economic conditions of the country or region of the business, a labor market analysis, and a consideration of any new governmental regulations that may have implications for the business. Moreover, the external scan is particularly useful to better understand the labor market status, such as the unemployment rate and the changing demographics of the workforce. This analysis should aid the organization in anticipating whether or not the employees needed for the future success of the organization can be recruited to the organization or if they will need to be developed within the organization. Lastly, the environmental scan should pay special attention to any social trends that may have implications for business goals or personnel availability.

DETERMINING THE HUMAN RESOURCE IMPLICATIONS

The compilation of the information from the internal and external analysis should help to inform what role the human resources function needs to fill in the coming years. For example, if the labor market is very tight and only a limited number of new college graduates have the skills needed to help the organization achieve its business goals, the human resource function may need to shift attention from the recruiting of new talent, to systematically developing the skills of existing employees. If, in contrast, the business objectives suggest that fewer employees will be necessary in the future to meet the business objective, the human resource function may shift to enhancing the performance appraisal strategy within the organization, so that wise outplacement decisions can be made. Whatever the internal and external scan suggest, there will be human resource implications, and understanding those implications will be critical to crafting the appropriate human resource strategy.

CREATING AND IMPLEMENTING A HUMAN RESOURCE STRATEGY

The human resource function then needs to implement the appropriate programs, policies, and practices to align the human resource services with the needs of the business, taking into consideration the internal and external information. These programs should address short-, mid- and long-term business needs. Moreover, they should all be aligned to an overarching human resources strategy.

MONITORING AND EVALUATING

As the human resource function begins to actively plan and implement changes throughout the organization, the effectiveness of such initiatives needs to be evaluated. The process for evaluation can take many forms, and far surpasses the scope of this entry. In brief, some methods for monitoring or evaluating the effectiveness include follow-up employee opinion surveys (looking for change in the results), and measurable progress on critical human resource metrics used to evaluate services and practices (such as reduction in the voluntary turnover rate, and increased number of viable applicants for each open position). In addition, a human resource function may choose to conduct an internal customer satisfaction survey aimed at getting feedback from internal customers and business partners to evaluate the effectiveness of the human resources function.

The basic steps for human resource planning, reviewed earlier, provide a process for regular and consistent planning within the human resource function. This process can be aided or even simplified with the implementation of a human resource information system (HRIS), which serves as a database repository for personnel data and transaction tracking.

Human resource departments that align their activities with the needs and changing direction of the business have great potential to make a significant impact on the bottom line success of the overall organization. This shift from a provider of transactional services such as benefits enrollment and processing of employment status changes to that of a function that is actively working on improving both the quality and effectiveness of the human resource function will aid in the overall success of the organization.

—Laura Gniatczyk

See also Succession Planning

FURTHER READING

Becker, B. E., Huselid, M. A., & Ulrich, D. (2001). *The HR scorecard: Linking people, strategy, and performance.* Boston: Harvard Business School Press.

Jarrell, D. W. (1993). *Human resource planning: A business planning approach.* Englewood Cliffs, NJ: Prentice Hall.

Miklovich, G. T., & Bourdreau, J. W. (1993). *Personnel: Human resource management* (7th ed.). Homewood, IL: Irwin.

Schuler, R. S., & Jackson, S. E. (1996). *Human resource management: Positioning for the 21st century* (7th ed.). Minneapolis/St. Paul: West.

HYPERCOMPETITION

HYPERTURBULENCE AND HYPERCOMPETITION

The pace of change in the health care industry has been accelerating. An aging population, complex regulations, new drugs and technologies, inflation, provider shortages, and a host of other environmental factors create a marketplace that is hyperturbulent. In a hyperturbulent market, organizations operate under conditions of constant uncertainty and competitive disequilibrium.

As a means of adapting to hyperturbulent environments, health care organizations are engaged in rapidly changing competitive paradigms based on "price-quality positioning, competition to create new know-how and establish first-mover advantage, competition to protect or invade established product or geographic markets, and competition based on deep pockets and creation of even deeper pocketed alliances" (D'Aveni, 1995). Such strategic maneuvering is hypercompetition. Where Porter's (1980) five forces model focused on how to build defensive barriers, hypercompetition puts companies on the attack, eroding, circumventing, and hurdling such barriers so no company enjoys a sustainable advantage. Even in environments where an organization has few direct competitors, suppliers and customers work to erode any competitive advantage that creates a profit. The net effect of this paradigm is that organizations need to recognize and exploit temporary advantages.

The key to exploiting transient advantages and surviving in a hypercompetitive environment is to build a flexible organization with a high degree of adaptive capacity. Flexibility is the effective search for an optimal fit or opportunity to change the environment that flows from organizational members' "strategic thinking." Adaptive capacity is the ability to act on new opportunities and is a characteristic of "learning organizations" that allows them to change themselves in an effective and orderly manner.

—Eric W. Ford

See also Learning Organizations, Strategic Thinking

FURTHER READING

D'Aveni, R. A. (1995). Coping with hypercompetition: Utilizing the new 7S's framework. *Academy of Management Executive, 9*(3), 45–60.

Porter, M. E. (1980). *Competitive strategy: Techniques for analyzing industries and competitors.* New York: Free Press.

I

IMMIGRATION REFORM AND CONTROL ACT OF 1986 (IRCA)

The Immigration Reform and Control Act (IRCA) of 1986 prohibits employers both from discriminating on the basis of national origin or citizenship and from hiring illegal aliens. The Immigration and Naturalization Service (INS) is the U.S. regulatory body charged with the enforcement of IRCA. The INS may impose monetary fines of up to $10,000 for non-compliance and may impose incarceration penalties of up to 6 months for sustained patterns of illegal hiring. To comply with the IRCA, all employers, regardless of size or sector, must verify job applicants' U.S. citizenship or eligibility to work in the United States by completing an INS I-9 form and examining documents that establish the identity and employment eligibility of the employee. To avoid discrimination on the basis of national origin, applicants' documents should be examined after the hiring decision is made. Permissible documents for proving identity and employment eligibility differ, depending on circumstances of the job applicant (such as U.S. citizen, permanent resident, or naturalized citizen); all I-9 forms contain a listing of acceptable documentation. Employers are not required to verify the authenticity of documents furnished by job applicants. Records should be maintained for three years after the hiring date or one year after termination of an employee. The INS or U.S. Department of Labor may inspect these records with three days notice and may impose fines for law violations or lax recordkeeping.

—E. Kate Atchley

FURTHER READING

Guttman, A. (2000). *EEO law and personnel practices.* Thousand Oaks, CA: Sage.
www.bcis.gov

IMPROVING EMPLOYEE PRODUCTIVITY

Improving employee productivity is a critical goal for today's organizations. Increasing employee output, decreasing costs, improving quality, and reducing absenteeism have a direct effect on the bottom line. Companies seeking to improve employee productivity need to ensure that they have highly able and motivated employees and that obstacles to high performance are removed.

Ensuring that employees are motivated and able begins with the company's recruitment and selection practices. Finding and promoting the right people, and placing them in jobs that interest and challenge them, is key to high productivity. During recruitment, employees should be oriented to the type of work they will perform and the type of culture in which they will work. To select employees, organizations should use reliable and valid assessment tools, such as structured interviews, work samples, assessment centers, and personality inventories.

Companies can also improve productivity by giving employees clear and specific descriptions of their job, roles, responsibilities, performance expectations, and job requirements. When employees are left to ask, "What am I supposed to do?" then productivity will likely be low. For employees to improve productivity, they need to first know what is expected of them and for what outcomes they will be held accountable.

Within the health care industry, new insurance practices and regulations, new diseases and viruses, new medicines, new equipment and techniques, and changing customer expectations have created a situation where change is the only constant. For employees to increase their productivity in this environment, they need to receive continuous training and development. In-service training, projects and assignments, professional seminars, coaching, and mentoring are activities that can improve an employee's abilities.

For current employees whose performance has slipped because their jobs have outgrown them (as was sometimes the case when computer technology revolutionized the way people work), further skills training is essential to improve productivity. Otherwise, alternative job placements may be necessary to improve the productivity of a once-productive employee. Many companies also use performance management systems to evaluate employee performance and provide feedback. Regular, ongoing feedback is a tool that employees can use to gauge their efforts and target activities to improve their productivity.

Companies also make several types of efforts to motivate their workforce. Current employees who are bored or complacent can be given new assignments, increased responsibility, more challenge, or a new position. Assuming they are qualified to handle the changes, such changes can reignite employees' motivation, increasing their productivity. Another way to increase productivity is to create a more satisfied workforce. Employee opinion surveys and focus groups can help companies measure employee satisfaction and identify solutions to improve satisfaction.

Managers often use goal-setting techniques and programs, such as management by objectives, to improve employee productivity. Setting challenging, relevant, and achievable goals has been shown to increase efforts and results. Companies also use reward and recognition systems to increase productivity. Rewards may include salary increases, profit sharing, incentive pay, bonuses, plaques and trinkets, extra vacation days, and letters of recognition. Supervisors should not underestimate the power of regular praise and positive feedback for motivating employees. The underlying assumption behind the use of rewards is that desired behavior (good performance) is strengthened when paired with a desired consequence (reward and recognition).

Progressive companies should continuously look inward to identify barriers to improving productivity. Such barriers could include outdated human resources policies and procedures, lack of proper equipment and tools, organizational bureaucracy and micromanagement (overcontrol, or too much supervision), poor workplace layout and design, restrictive work arrangements, or lack of employee empowerment. Such practices can often decrease an employee's motivation. In response to these barriers, many organizations have implemented innovative work arrangements and designs, including self-managed work teams, flextime, and telecommuting. By removing such barriers, companies go far toward ensuring that employees' efforts are more directly tied to increased productivity.

—Mark L. Poteet

See also Compensation Systems, Employee Compensation, Employee Selection and Hiring, Job Design, Job Satisfaction, Organizational Behavior Management (OBM), Performance Management, Productivity

FURTHER READING

Hiam, A. (2002). *Motivational management: Inspiring your people for maximum performance.* New York: AMACOM.

Landy, F. J. (1989). *Psychology of work behavior* (4th ed.). Pacific Grove, CA: Brooks/Cole.

Langdon, D. G. (1999). *Aligning performance: Improving people, systems, and organizations.* New York: Wiley.

Langdon, D. G., Whiteside, K. S., & McKenna, M. M. (1999). *Intervention resource guide: 50 performance improvement tools.* New York: Wiley.

McAdams, J. L. (1996). *The reward plan advantage: A manager's guide to improving business performance through people.* San Francisco: Jossey-Bass.

INCENTIVE PAY

Many businesses have adopted an incentive pay or pay-for-performance approach, because of its links to increased productivity. More specifically, studies show nearly 80% of U.S. corporations rank linking rewards to performance as an important organizational objective. The increase in use of incentive pay may be attributed to the expected motivational impacts; that is, research has found that pay contingent on performance results in greater productivity and retention than when that contingency is not present. Organizations have many choices for reward programs, including piece rate pay, commissions, bonuses, skill-based pay, and merit pay. Organizations can also choose to implement programs at an individual or group level. Individual performance should be rewarded when it is identifiable and measurable; otherwise, group performance is important in situations requiring employee cooperation and coordination. Although these programs seem straightforward, there are difficulties in implementing incentive pay programs. To be specific, the pay system should take into consideration the employees' task and activities that can be controlled by the employee. Second, the system should incorporate performance standards that can be measured accurately and with precision. Third, the reward needs to be significant. Studies show that approximately a 10% increase over base salary is needed to motivate employees. Finally, managers should not limit incentives to monetary rewards. Other rewards that may be important to health care personnel include amount of patient contact, research and grant funding, health benefits, personal days, and continuing education assistance.

—Jillian A. Peat

See also Employee Compensation

FURTHER READING

Bureau of National Affairs. (1991). *Non-traditional incentive pay programs.* Washington, DC: Bureau of National Affairs.

Wilson, T. B. (1995). *Innovative reward systems for the changing workplace.* New York: McGraw-Hill.

INCIDENT

The term *incident* is generally accepted to mean any happening not consistent with the routine operation of the facility or the routine care of a particular patient. Subsequent to an incident, an incident report may be generated. The report is a tool that was borrowed from the insurance industry and made part of hospital management operations. It has been most effective in identifying trends relating to occurrences and outcomes such as patient falls, medication problems, and equipment failures. It has also been a useful tool in the reporting and follow-up of employee injuries for workers' compensation purposes. The reluctance to actively use such a system stems from the incorrect assumption that such reports indicate negligence rather than serve as a mechanism for loss prevention.

—Kathleen Ferrara

FURTHER READING

American Society of Healthcare Risk Management (ASHRM). (1990). *Risk management handbook for healthcare facilities.* (p. 255). Chicago: Author.

INCLUSION CRITERIA

Inclusion criteria are the factors from a subject's medical history, physical examination, or laboratory tests that are used to qualify a subject for entry into a clinical trial. A clinical trial is a prospectively designed study of an intervention in a target population. Participant eligibility criteria can range from general (age, sex, type of illness) to specific (prior treatment, stage of disease, organ function, such as liver or kidney). Eligibility criteria may also vary with trial phase. In Phase 1 and 2 trials, the criteria often focus on making sure that people are not put at risk who might be harmed because of their abnormal organ function or other factors. Phase 2 and 3 trials often add criteria regarding disease type and stage, and number of prior or current treatments. Eligibility criteria may be very detailed if researchers think that a drug will work best on a specific type of cancer or a particular manifestation of a condition

in the population. Trials with narrow eligibility criteria may be complicated to conduct and may produce less widely applicable results.

Researchers therefore attempt to include as many types of people as possible in a clinical trial without making the study population too diverse to tell whether the treatment might be as effective on a more narrowly defined population. The more diverse the trial's population, the more useful the results could be to the general population, particularly in Phase 3 trials. Results of Phase 3 trials should be as generally applicable as possible in order to benefit the maximum number of people. The trend today is toward broadening eligibility criteria for Phase 3 clinical trials. Less restrictive criteria may enable more researchers and people to participate in these trials. With more participants, the disadvantages of having a more diverse population are outweighed by the results applying more generally to the population.

—Steven C. Quay

INCOME

See Revenues

INCOME STATEMENT (IS)

The income statement (IS) is one component of the financial statements. A standard set of financial statements includes the balance sheet, income statement, statement of cash flows, and associated footnotes. These statements can be issued on a daily, monthly, quarterly, or annual basis. If accounting is the basic language of business, then financial statements are the fundamental scorecards that report organizational performance, and the income statement depicts the net result of organizational activities, using accrual accounting, over a period of time (for example, organization X's income statement for the year ending December 12, 2008). Accrual accounting differentiates itself from cash accounting in that revenues and expenses are matched with the time period and underlying economic transaction, rather than with when cash is received or paid. The balance sheet, in contrast, is the operational snapshot of an organization's financial situation at a particular point in time (such as organization X's balance sheet as of December 31, 2008). The statement of cash flows depicts organizational activities over a period of time using cash basis accounting.

A typical income statement is composed of four basic components: revenues, operating expenses, other income and expenses, and special accounting transactions. Revenue usually includes amounts earned for patient services, other (nonpatient) services, and nonoperating gains and losses. Operating expenses are items such as salaries, fringe benefits, rent, professional fees, and depreciation incurred to earn these associated revenues. Other income and expenses could include items such as interest income and expenses and equity gains or losses. Special accounting events can be usually classified into three groupings (DEC): discontinued operations (D), extraordinary items (E), and cumulative effect of accounting changes (C). Discontinued operations include the income statement effects of operations the organization intends to discontinue or has already discontinued. Extraordinary items include the effects of transactions that are both unusual in nature and infrequent. Cumulative effect of accounting changes includes the effects of changing from a generally accepted method of accounting to another generally accepted method of accounting.

A typical income statement has these previously discussed components ordered as follows:

1. Total revenues minus total operating expenses equals income (loss) from operations

2. Income (loss) from operations plus (minus) total other income (expenses) equals net income (loss) before special accounting (DEC) items

3. Net income before special accounting (DEC) items plus (or minus) DEC items equals bottom-line net income (or loss)

Although financial statements, including the income statement, are based on a number of different assumptions, it is important for health care professionals to understand that accounting financial statements provide valuable data that are reliable, comparable, and consistent. In addition, financial statements provide timely data that enhance the ability to assess future cash flows, to assist in decision making (an information role), and to monitor debt covenants and bonus arrangements (a stewardship role).

—Bruce Behn

FURTHER READING

Cleverley, W. O., & Cameron, A. E. (2002). *Essentials of health care finance* (5th ed., pp. 130–134). Gaithersburg, MD: Aspen.

INDEMNIFICATION

Indemnification is one party's agreeing to reimburse another party for an actual loss sustained. The professional liability insurer has the obligation, within the terms of the particular policy, to defend the health care provider and to pay or indemnify him or her for any settlement or judgment rendered in favor of the plaintiff for an amount up to the policy limits. The insurer may be authorized under the policy terms to settle claims without the consent of the insured policyholder, but the defendant is customarily consulted concerning this important decision.

—Kathleen Ferrara

FURTHER READING

Shilling, D. (2000). *Lawyer's deskbook* (11th ed., pp. 24–25). Upper Saddle River, NJ: Prentice Hall.

INDEMNITY HEALTH CARE INSURANCE

See Health Insurance

INDIGENT HEALTH CARE

Indigent health care is care provided to individuals who are uninsured or underinsured and unable to pay for their medical care. There are an estimated 43 million Americans without health insurance and an additional 29 million who are underinsured. Nearly 1 in 5 Americans under the age of 65 is uninsured, and that number increases to 30% for those aged 18 to 24. And these numbers don't address the scores of undocumented aliens in this country.

Indigent health care does not apply to those who are eligible for Medicaid or other government benefits. Many are Americans who work and who don't qualify for Medicaid because of their salaries. Even though they make too much to qualify for Medicaid, they have jobs that don't offer benefits and the cost of paying for health insurance is prohibitive. Others have some health insurance, but the coverage is limited or their copayments are very high.

The fastest growing segment of the uninsured is middle-income working families. Low-income adults comprise 27% of the population but 60% of the adult uninsured. Moreover, 10 million children are uninsured, as are an estimated 5 million illegal immigrants.

The rationale for treating the undocumented illegal immigrants is as follows. To protect the public health, we must address the issue of communicable disease, which runs rampant in the close quarters occupied by illegal aliens. Discrimination against illegal aliens is forbidden in emergency circumstances. Some of the emergency care can be avoided by providing primary and preventive care to these populations. Administrative costs incurred by trying to screen out illegals is enormous.

The lack of insurance contributes to poor health, because uninsured individuals are more likely to delay seeking care. They are more likely to receive less or no cancer screening, which delays diagnosis and treatment and leads to premature death. They tend to go without regular follow-up for chronic diseases such as diabetes, which results in greater morbidity. They don't take their prescribed medications, which also increases morbidity.

Many hospitals and physicians provide charity care at no or reduced charge. This care does impose a cost on society. It gets paid for indirectly by insured patients, whose charges are increased as a result. Taxpayers also pay the cost through federal and state subsidies to the providers that serve them. Health care safety nets include emergency departments, community health centers, public hospitals, charitable clinics, and teaching and community hospitals. These providers are incurring billions of dollars in uncompensated care costs.

In February 2002, several national business and labor organizations united to form CoveringTheUninsured.Org, a coalition designed to increase awareness of the challenges facing the millions of uninsured Americans. The group consists of the Robert Wood Johnson Foundation and 12 major national organizations, including the American Association of Retired Persons (AARP) and the AFL-CIO. They are sponsoring an educational campaign to publicize the extent of the problem and make Americans aware. Then perhaps solutions to this problem can be found.

—Doreen T. Day

FURTHER READING

www.acep.org
www.bcbshealthissues.com
www.coveringtheuninsured.org
www.cppp.org

INDIVIDUALS WITH DISABILITIES EDUCATION ACT (IDEA)

The entitlement of every child to a tuition-free education, through graduation from high school, is a hallmark of the American public education system. In 1974 and 1975, with numerous "right to education" cases pending in the courts, Congress passed the Individuals with Disabilities Education Act (IDEA)[1] to ensure that access

to public education extended as well to children with disabilities. IDEA promotes access by providing financial support for states that establish special education programs that meet the federal standards created by the act.[2] Various estimates suggest that as many as 10% of students in the United States meet the requirements of the services provided under the IDEA. All the states now participate.

A "child with a disability" may have "mental retardation, hearing impairments . . . , speech or language impairments, visual impairments . . . , serious emotional disturbance . . . , orthopedic impairments, autism, traumatic brain injury, other health impairments, or specific learning disabilities." The key concept of IDEA is "free appropriate public education" (FAPE). This is defined in the statute to mean "special education and related services . . . provided at public expense, under public supervision and direction, and without charge; . . . [that] meet the standards of the State educational agency; . . . include an appropriate preschool, elementary, or secondary education [and] provided in conformity with the individualized educational program [IEP] [that is required]." *Special education* means "specially designed instruction, at no cost to parents, to meet the unique needs of a child with a disability, including . . . instruction . . . in the classroom, in the home, in hospitals and institutions, and in other settings; and . . . physical education."

What is required to achieve a free appropriate education is governed by the IEP, which is tailored to meet the disabled child's unique needs. The IEP is a written statement that includes "a statement of . . . present levels of performance [and how the disability affects performance]; a statement of measurable goals . . . ; a statement of the special education and related services . . . and program modification [that will be required]; [and] the extent of participation with nondisabled children in regular class activities." The IEP is prepared by a "program team" that includes the disabled child's parents, a regular teacher of the child, a special education teacher, representative of the local school district, and a person trained in interpreting test evaluations. The disabled child may also participate, when deemed appropriate, as well as others having specialized knowledge or expertise. Preparation of the IEP emphasizes the role of the parents on the team and is reviewed at least once annually. When school officials and the parents cannot agree, an impartial due process hearing may be held, conducted by the local or state educational agency, with issues sometimes ultimately decided by the courts.

IDEA is silent as to the substantive standard of education that is to be achieved. The U.S. Supreme Court has rejected, however, that the standard is to "maximize the potential of handicapped children 'commensurate with the opportunity provided to other children.'"[3] Under the requirement to provide "related services," schools are required to provide assistance to care for the physical needs of the disabled child while in school.[4]

School districts are allowed to pay for disabled children to attend private schools and have been ordered to do so.[5] It is not per se a violation of the establishment clause of the U.S. Constitution to provide support for disabled children attending religious schools.[6] Parents who choose to home-school their children may not be able to avail themselves of IDEA financial support.[7]

The IDEA requires that "To the maximum extent appropriate, children with disabilities . . . are educated with children who are not disabled." This mandate is variously referred to as *mainstreaming, inclusion,* or requiring the *least restrictive environment.*[8] If necessary, school districts may be required to hire teacher's aides to assist participation in classroom activities. If the disabled child exhibits disruptive behavior that generally would call for disciplinary action, the child may be placed in an "alternative educational setting" or suspended for not more than 10 days.[9] Schools are required to conduct a "manifestation determination review" within 10 days to determine if the disruptive behavior was a manifestation of the disability. If determined not to be a manifestation of the disability, the same disciplinary procedures may be followed as with a nondisabled child. If the behavior is a manifestation, discipline or removal from the school may not be imposed.

—Donald L. Zink

NOTES

1.   Congress first passed the Education of the Handicapped Act of 1974, and then the Education for All Handicapped Children Act of 1975. IDEA has been significantly revised and added to over a dozen times, most recently in 1997, Pub. Law 105–17, Title I, and is codified as 20 U.S.C. 1400 et seq.

2.   In some instances, IDEA may overlap with Section 504 of the Rehabilitation Act, and with Title II of the ADA (Americans with Disabilities Act). IDEA, however, considers every child as "qualified" for school; the concept of "otherwise qualified" does not apply. The underlying rule of IDEA has been described as "zero reject."

3.   *Board of Education of the Hendrick Hudson Central School District v. Rowley* (1982), 458 U.S. 176. The Court found it sufficient, if the child's education comported with the IEP, that the child achieved passing marks and was advancing in grade level.

4.   *Cedar Rapids Community School District v. Garret F.* (1999), 526 U.S. 66. The student was quadriplegic and required bladder catheterization, suctioning of his tracheotomy tube, assistance with eating, and other assistance. "Related services" do not include "medical services," which must be provided by a licensed physician.

5.   *Florence County School District 4 v. Carter* (1993), 510 U.S. 7. Because the IEP was inadequate and did not meet the child's needs, the parents had a unilateral right to withdraw their child from a public school setting.

6.   *Zobrest v. Catalina Foothills School District* (1993), 506 U.S. 1. It was held permissible to provide a sign language interpreter for a deaf student attending classes at a Catholic high school. The Court reasoned that the IDEA was a neutral program, providing aid to disabled children, not to schools, and thereby avoided establishment clause problems.

7.   *Hooks v. Clark County School District* (2000), 228 F.3d 1036 (9th Cir.).

8.   IDEA does not specify, and courts have not agreed on, standards as to when "inclusion" is the appropriate setting. Some have suggested that more parents now are requesting special curricula or tutoring instead.

9.   A period of 45 days is permitted if weapons or drugs are involved.

INDUSTRY ANALYSIS

All organizations compete for customers and revenues with other competitors within an industry. Yet these industries vary widely in terms of their size, extent of rivalry, overall attractiveness, and rate of change. As a result, industry analysis is an important part of environmental analysis and of the overall strategic management process. Industry analysis involves a thorough examination of the scope, trends, forces, and competitive positions characterizing an industry at one point in time, and an attempt to understand how changes in these components will affect industry customers and competitors in the future.

When analyzing an industry, strategists ask four major questions: (a) How attractive is this industry overall; that is, is this a desirable playing field for our organization? (b) What trends or forces are causing the industry to change? (c) How are our competitors positioned within the industry? and (d) What are the key success factors for the industry? Answers to these questions are incorporated into administrators' decisions concerning the organization's mission, vision, and strategy.

INDUSTRY ATTRACTIVENESS

Industries vary in their attractiveness, or long-term profit potential, based not only on their overall size and growth rate but also on the extent of rivalry exhibited by competitors. As a result, the first step of an industry analysis is to evaluate total market size and growth rates and to assess competitive rivalry. Market size is typically measured by determining the total revenues generated by relevant industry competitors. Depending on the organization, the market could be defined regionally, nationally, or even globally. Most health care organizations compete mainly with other local entities and hence would seek information on market size within the region. In contrast, some prestigious medical institutions offer highly specialized services drawing patients from all over the world. The market for heart transplants, for example, is defined globally.

Market growth rate is another key indicator of industry attractiveness. Most organizations seek at least moderate growth in revenues, but this is difficult to come by in a stagnant or declining industry. Moreover, knowing whether industry revenues are growing helps administrators to make sense of their own revenue gains. Revenue growth of 3% might appear an adequate outcome for an organization, but perhaps not if the industry has grown by 6%. A 13% decline in sales could be acceptable (at least in the short run) if industry revenues have declined by 18%.

Excessive competition can make matters worse by reducing the earnings associated with hard-earned revenues. In his book *Competitive Strategy* (1980), Michael Porter showed that the intensity of competition within an industry is a function of five basic structural forces. These include the threat of new entrants, buying power of customers, buying power of suppliers, threat of substitutes, and rivalry among existing firms. The collective strength of these forces determines the overall profit potential, and therefore the attractiveness, of an industry.

By carefully analyzing the strength of these forces within an industry, administrators can determine how to position their organizations to defend against these forces or how to influence these forces in their favor. In addition, they can decide whether further investment in an industry is warranted or whether another market might yield more substantial returns in the long run.

The first force, threat of new entrants, poses a danger to industry competitors, because when entry is easy increased rivalry and decreased prices are the likely result. New entrants are probable when the following conditions exist: (a) economies of scale are low, (b) product or service differentiation is limited, (c) amount of capital requirements needed to compete is low, (d) cost to customers of switching from one service provider to another is low, (e) distribution channels are easily accessible, (f) established firms have few cost advantages not replicable by potential entrants, (g) no government policies restrict newcomers from entering the industry, and (h) current competitors are not expected to retaliate strongly against newcomers. Entrants to the health care industry must meet strict government standards and must compete with some highly differentiated institutions. Yet research often opens up new specializations and technologies, allowing newcomers to establish themselves in emergent niches.

Powerful buying groups decrease industry profitability by forcing down prices, bargaining for higher quality, or playing competitors against each other. Buyers gain power when (a) they are concentrated or purchase in large quantities, (b) they are price sensitive because the products they

are purchasing represent a significant fraction of their costs, (c) they face few switching costs, (d) the products they are buying are undifferentiated, (e) they could easily make the product themselves, or (f) they have full information. In the health care industry, some buyers gain power by working through organized groups such as the American Association of Retired Persons (AARP), whereas others are hampered by their lack of knowledge about medical procedures and techniques.

Powerful supplier groups negatively affect long-term industry results by raising prices on inputs. Suppliers gain power under the following conditions: (a) the supplier industry is dominated by a few large companies, (b) there are few substitute products, (c) the quality of the supplier's product is very important, and (d) the supplier's products are differentiated or have built-up switching costs. Health care organizations may confront powerful suppliers for specialized equipment or high-demand medications. However, the growth of standardized, generic drugs has reduced at least some of this power.

The presence of substitute products or services limits potential returns to an industry by restricting the prices that industry members can charge. Alternative therapies such as acupuncture and colon cleansing, or alternative care providers such as chiropractors and midwives may be chosen as substitutes for prescription drugs or medical doctors. Should any of these alternatives become more well accepted, some traditional care providers could feel pressure to lower their prices.

Finally, the extent of rivalry among current competitors has potential to harm industry profits. Price cuts, discounts, extensive advertising, and other competitive behaviors cut into earnings. These behaviors tend to increase when industry growth is slow, competitors are numerous, differentiation is low, and exit barriers are high.

Once these five structural forces have been diagnosed, organizational administrators can see how the organization is situated relative to the forces and can choose where to confront competition and where to avoid it. The next step in industry analysis is to examine current trends characterizing the industry to look for those forces that are driving change.

INDUSTRY TRENDS AND FORCES

Many aspects of an organization's industry environment change over time, thereby affecting customer demand and competitors' actions. Technology developments, new product or service offerings by competitors, innovative marketing approaches by competitors, new government standards, and many other trends can affect long-term industry growth and decline. When analyzing the industry, health care administrators should identify as many changes as possible and attempt to predict their potential long-term effects on both the organization and the industry. In general, these trends serve as valuable opportunities for industry competitors or as threats to be avoided.

When studying current trends, it is crucial to search for changes in consumer attitudes and behaviors toward the product or service. Societal changes, demographic shifts, and lifestyle evolutions are all part of this analysis. In addition, organizational managers should study both current customers, to assess their likes and dislikes, as well as noncustomers. It is important to know why some people choose *not* to do business with the focal institution. What needs do they have that the organization cannot accommodate? And are these needs symptomatic of a shift in customer demand?

As these questions show, at any given time some trends may emerge as key drivers of change within the industry. These drivers deserve special attention when formulating strategy because they are helping to reshape the industry in some fundamental way. Important drivers of change in the health care industry today include the rising cost of medical malpractice insurance, the aging of the population, and the push for lower costs by insurance companies and consumer groups.

KEY COMPETITORS

The observation and evaluation of key competitors is another important step in industry analysis. Industry competitors are striving to build their own customer bases within the industry. It is important to understand how they are trying to compete for customers, and what they might do in the future. Analysts should ask, What strengths and weaknesses do they possess? What types of clients do they attract and why? How have they historically reacted to change? What are their objectives? By seeking answers to these questions about their competitors, analysts will be better prepared to cope with competitive challenges.

One way to get a good sense of where an organization fits in the industry arena is to create a strategic map of the industry showing the different ways in which industry competitors are positioned. That is, do they serve a broad or narrow range of customers? Do they offer a broad or narrow mix of services? Are they differentiated or low-cost providers? Strategic positions in an industry can be mapped by plotting the locations of industry competitors relative to any two of these strategic characteristics. Organizations with similar strategies tend to clump together on such a map. Organizations with similar strategic positions tend to compete more intensively with each other for the same customers.

Administrators can learn different things by studying competitors in different strategic positions. For instance, by observing competitors that are most similar to their own organization, they can gain a better perspective on their own capabilities and limitations. Not only can they avoid blind spots and counter upcoming competitive moves, but they can also enhance their own position by building on strengths that other close competitors lack. By observing very different types of competitors, they might identify new ideas for products or processes that would help to serve their own customers better. Effective strategies are built from imaginative blends of imitation, innovation, and implementation but should be based on careful observation and assessment of what works.

KEY SUCCESS FACTORS

Key success factors are defined as those things that every competitor in an industry must do in order to survive. Convenience stores cannot survive unless they are in an easily accessible, high-traffic area. Hospitals cannot survive unless they can secure competent physicians and provide quality care.

Like everything else, the key success factors in an industry are constantly changing. Today, most hospitals have had to expand their range of services to include special birthing rooms and wellness centers. Such amenities do not provide a competitive advantage, however; they simply allow the institution to stay in the game.

SOURCES OF INFORMATION

Conducting an industry analysis is a time-consuming task. To be meaningful, the analysis should be based on solid information about industry processes, competitors, technologies, trends, and customers. Where is this information acquired?

In the health care industry, quantitative information on industry competitors is easily accessible through industry association databases. This should be supplemented with ongoing surveillance of competitors, customers, and other stakeholders. General information on industry trends can be obtained from a variety of sources, including patients, suppliers, physicians, subordinates, competitors, conferences, meetings, trade publications, and personal observation. In addition, information on industry competitors can be gleaned from their annual reports, advertisements, Web sites, and customers. The more sources used for gathering data, the more likely that meaningful information will be gleaned. The use of multiple sources is important in assessing data for establishing consistency and ensuring validity.

—Barbara Spencer

See also Environmental Analysis, Strategic Management

FURTHER READING

Ghoshal, S., & Westney, D. E. (1991). Organizing competitor analysis systems. *Strategic Management Journal, 18,* 149–157.

Porter, M. E. (1980). *Competitive strategy.* New York: Free Press.

Zahra, S. A., & Shaples, S. S. (1993). Blind spots in competitive analysis. *Academy of Management Executive, 8*(2), 7–28.

INFANT MORTALITY

The neonatal mortality rate (NMR) is a calculation of the number of deaths that occur between birth and 28 days of age. The calculation of the rate is simply

NMR = (number of deaths from birth through 27 days, 23 hours, 59 minutes of age × 1000) / (number of live births during the same period of time)

In contrast, the postneonatal mortality rate covers deaths from 28 days of age up to 1 year of age. Combining neonatal mortality and postneonatal mortality creates the infant mortality rate (IMR). Both NMR and IMR are key measures of efforts aimed at improving public health outcomes.

The United States and other developed countries made great strides at reducing the IMR during the 20th century. The Centers for Disease Control (CDC) have hailed these strides as one of the 10 great medical achievements of the century. Between 1900 and 1999, the IMR decreased from 100 deaths per 1000 live births to 7/1000 live births in the United States. There has been a somewhat disparate improvement, as evidenced by a rate of 5.8/1000 among white births and 14/1000 in the black population. Despite these strides, the United States still lags behind more than 20 other countries in IMR. This is thought to be attributable to low early access and/or use of perinatal care for certain high-risk pregnancies. Further improvement continues to be a high priority sought by many public and private health initiatives. Currently the main focus of these efforts is to continue to reduce teen pregnancies while improving the early initiation of care during pregnancy.

—Charles T. Hankins

See also March of Dimes, Neonatal Care

FURTHER READING

Centers for Disease Control. (1999). Healthier mothers and babies. *Morbidity and Mortality Weekly Report, 48*(38), 849–858.

Centers for Disease Control. (1999). Ten great public health achievements—United States 1900–1999. *Morbidity and Mortality Weekly Report, 48*(12), 241–243.

INFORMATION SYSTEMS

See Information Technology

INFORMATION TECHNOLOGY

The broad term *information technology* (IT) is used to describe computer-based tools, techniques, and methods used for the storage and delivery of information. IT covers equipment (hardware), processing capabilities (software), and communication methods (networks) for the delivery of information.

IT has become a household technology to retrieve information from the Web and for communication between users using e-mail. However, business users constitute the largest group of consumers of IT. Business uses of IT cover the areas of enterprise resource planning (ERP), customer relationship management (CRM), and supply chain management (SCM). The key element that is the foundation for all IT applications is data warehousing, which makes it possible to retrieve and process data for the production of useful and meaningful information for reporting and decision making.

ERP applications in a health care organization can include financial planning, accounting, patient registry, staff scheduling, assignment of personnel, and management of inventories. Management and procurement of supplies with business partners is accomplished through SCM applications. CRM applications are designed to create superior value for the customer. Such applications in the health care industry may cover efficient promotion, sales, marketing, and services to patients and potential patients. CRM applications are designed for effective customer acquisition and retention through superior management of communication with customers. Hence ERP applications cover information requirements within an organization, SCM applications manage information transactions with suppliers, and CRM applications deliver a more meaningful interaction with current and potential customers.

Health care organizations can benefit greatly from IT in improving the delivery of services. In a recent report in the *Wall Street Journal,* the most IT-enabled hospitals scored better than the national averages in terms of lower mortality and fewer medical errors (Landro, 2002). Several laws (such as the Balanced Budget Act of 1997) and reports (Institute of Medicine reports of 2000 and 2001) are making it mandatory for hospitals to reduce medical errors and deliver safer, high-quality service (Williams, 2002). In response to such concerns, a medical consortium called Leapfrog plans to implement its computer physician order entry (CPOE) systems in over a thousand hospitals by 2004 (Brewin, 2002). Such trends in the adoption of IT can result in cost-effectiveness and superior quality of services, thus aiding both the business, clinical, and patient dimensions of health care.

Several hospitals are pioneering in the use of IT and are able to save money, provide better care, and use staff more efficiently (Joch, 2002). Kaiser Permanente's use of data warehousing technology was very effective in dealing with the anthrax crisis in Washington, D.C. (McGee, 2001). There is also a move in the pharmaceutical industry to automate the delivery of information and ordering of prescriptions through IT applications. Pfizer and Merck have teamed up with major IT vendors to market a wide range of applications to 650,000 physicians (Romano, 2001). Other applications that are being adopted cover management of business transactions with suppliers and effective communication with patients, enhancing the overall service provided by physicians, clinics, and hospitals.

—Alok Srivastava

See also Decision Support Systems, Health Information Systems Management

FURTHER READING

Brewin, B. (2002). Health care group: Lack of IT leads to deaths. *Computerworld, 17,* 8.

Joch, A. (2002). Most wired on a budget. *Hospitals & Health Networks, 1,* 14–19.

Landro, L. (2002, June 10). Who leads the online race: A look at the hospitals that are out in front in the drive to bring information technology to health care. *Wall Street Journal,* p. R7.

McGee, M. K. (2001). Get well, fast. *InformationWeek, 864,* 52–58.

Romano, M. (2001). Drugmakers seek gold in doc IT. *Modern Healthcare, 44,* 6–8.

Williams, T. G. (2002). IT investments can add business value. *Healthcare Financial Management, 5,* 34–39.

INFORMED CONSENT

Informed consent is a process whose purpose is to provide information to potential study subjects to enable these individuals to make an informed decision as to whether or not to participate in a research study. It also ensures that a subject's rights are protected and that subjects understand that participation is voluntary. An investigator may not involve an individual in a clinical study without first obtaining an informed consent from the individual. Informed consent is a part of the recommendations included in procedures required to ensure subject safety in clinical trials. This was described in a set of ethical guidelines for the conduct of research on humans. This was first agreed to in 1964 by the World Medical Association in Helsinki, Finland, and was part of the Declaration of Helsinki.

There are conditions of informed consent. An individual must be given sufficient opportunity to decide whether to participate, without undue pressure or influence from the investigator. Informed consent may be obtained from an individual study participant or a legally authorized representative. If informed consent is to be obtained for the participation of a minor, the minor's consent must be obtained in addition to the informed consent of the minor's legal guardian. Informed consent must also be obtained before entry into a clinical trial or before procedures are to be performed. The language that must be used to obtain informed consent must be understandable. This entails that the language be in layperson's terms. On the informed consent document must appear the signature of the subject or representative, witnessed by the clinical trial personnel. A copy of the informed consent document should be given to the subject.

The process of obtaining informed consent has several basic elements. First, it requires a statement that the study involves research, an explanation of the purposes of the research, the expected duration of the subject's participation, a description of the procedures to be followed, and identification of any procedures that are experimental. Second, informed consent should have a description of any reasonably foreseeable risks or discomfort to the subject. Third, there must be a description of any benefits to the subject or to others that may reasonably be expected from the research. Next, there should be a disclosure of appropriate alternative procedures or courses of treatment that might be advantageous to the subject. Then, informed consent should include a statement regarding the extent to which confidentiality of records identifying the subject will be maintained and that notes the possibility that the Food and Drug Administration may inspect the records. Moreover, for research involving more than minimal risk, there should be an explanation regarding compensation and an explanation as to whether medical treatments are available if injury occurs and, if so, of what they consist or whether further information may be obtained. In addition, informed consent should provide an explanation of who is to be contacted for answers to pertinent questions about the research and research subject's rights, and in the event of a research-related injury to the subject. Last, a statement should be included specifying that participation is voluntary, refusal to participate is allowable without penalty or loss of benefits to which the subject is entitled, and a subject may discontinue participation in the study at any time with impunity and without loss of benefits to which the subject is entitled. Informed consent is a vital part of the research process. It protects the rights of research subjects, and it allows them to question "what they're getting into." Informed consent procedures help ensure that subjects are treated in an informative and humane manner while they undergo a research study.

—Anthony J. Ippolito

See also Clinical Trials, Declaration of Helsinki Laws, Good Clinical Practices (GCPs)

FURTHER READING

Association of Clinical Research Professionals. (2002). *Certification examination review for clinical research coordinators.* Washington, D.C: Author.

Day, S. (1999). *Dictionary for clinical trials.* Chichester, UK: Wiley.

INITIAL PUBLIC OFFERING (IPO)

An initial public offering (IPO) is the first-time selling or issuance of a firm's securities (such as stock) in an open, public market. Examples of open, public markets include the New York Stock Exchange, the American Stock Exchange, and the NASDAQ. The offering of these new securities is referred to as "going public." The trading of IPO stocks is referred to as the new issues market. Through an IPO, health care firms may be able to raise capital to which they previously did not have access. Recent examples of health care IPOs include Applied Imaging Corporation, Laser Vision Centers Inc., and Universal Hospital Services Inc.

To issue an IPO, an organization must first register with the Securities and Exchange Commission (SEC). The SEC, however, is concerned not with the merits of the offering (is it a good investment?), but rather with the adequacy of the information disclosed to all potential investors. The SEC requires firms to disclose information that privately held firms may not otherwise have to make known. This information includes its business and associated business risks (including its competition), audited financial statements, its officers' and directors' identity and their compensation, material transactions between the company and its officers and directors, material legal proceedings involving the company or its officers and directors, its securities distribution plan, and the intended use of the proceeds of the initial public offering. Not until the SEC declares its registration statement effective can a firm sell securities associated with its IPO in an open, public market.

—David R. Williams

FURTHER READING

Aggarwal, R., & Rivoli, P. (1991). Evaluating the costs of raising capital through an initial public offering. *Journal of Business Venturing, 6,* 351–361.

Bouillet-Cordonnier, G. (1992). Legal aspects of start-up evaluation and adjustment methods. *Journal of Business Venturing, 7,* 91–101.

INPATIENT SERVICES

Inpatient services are medical care provided to patients confined within a hospital setting as opposed to those provided by ambulatory/outpatient facilities. Although these services are most typically provided in an acute care setting, they are not necessarily provided within an acute care general hospital. They may be provided in other, more specialized facilities such as psychiatric institutions or other long-term care settings.

Inpatient services as defined by federal regulators are those requiring admission to the hospital. The definition is not dependent on the complexity of the services provided. These admissions may be broken down into short-stay and long-stay varieties. A short stay in U.S. hospitals is typically considered to be less than 24 hours, although other North American health care systems such as Canada's may define a short stay to be as long as 59 days.

A trend developed in the 1980s and 1990s whereby many services previously provided on an inpatient basis were shifted to the ambulatory setting, usually driven by the fact that they could be provided there at lower costs. The changing demographics of the North American population, however, will cause increasing demand for inpatient services throughout the early part of the 21st century.

The population's aging brings with it more chronic, long-term illness and medical admissions. The shift toward these types of admissions and away from procedural and surgical admissions will result in more admissions with longer average length of stays, resulting in an effective increase in inpatient census. This increase will require the development of additional inpatient beds and capacity in many parts of the nation in contrast to the previously perceived excesses of the 1980s.

See also Acute Care, Aging Society, Ambulatory Care, Bed Occupancy, Capacity and Capacity Utilization, Demographics, Health Care Utilization, Hospitals, Length of Stay (LOS)

FURTHER READING

www.umanitoba.ca/centres/mchp/concept/thesaurus/thesaurus_I.html

INSTITUTE OF MEDICINE (IOM)

The Institute of Medicine (IOM) is an independent, private, nongovernmental organization associated with the National Academy of Sciences, based in Washington, D.C. The National Academy of Sciences was created by the federal government to be an adviser on scientific and technological matters. These organizations do not receive direct federal appropriations for their work. Most studies carried out by the Institute of Medicine are done at the request of government agencies. The IOM uses unpaid volunteer experts to author most reports. Each report must go through an institutional process that assures a rigorous and formal peer review process. The process requires that findings and recommendations be evidence based whenever possible and noted as an expert opinion where that is not possible. Because the IOM is a nongovernmental organization, experts and committees have a greater variety of options for conducting studies. Although their work may be conducted in a public forum, the committee may deliberate privately as a group. Peer review occurs independent of the deliberations of the authoring committee. The committee process is designed to reach consensus on the evidence base and its implications.

The Institute of Medicine was established in 1970 by the National Academy of Sciences to secure the services of eminent members of appropriate professions in the examination of policy matters pertaining to the health of the public. The institute acts under the responsibility given to the National Academy of Sciences by its congressional charter to be an adviser to the federal government and, on its own initiative, to identify issues of medical care, research, and education.

In 1998 the IOM launched the Committee on Quality of Health Care in America. The committee was charged to provide the nation with a road map for changes that could transform the health care system into one that is safe, efficient, and consumer centered. One of the major objectives is to provide a better working environment for physicians and other health care professionals and to the degree possible, help patients direct the care that they receive. The committee's first report, *To Err Is Human: Building a Safer Health System,* argues that safety or freedom from accidental injury during medical treatment is a critical first step toward improving the quality of health care. The report takes a comprehensive approach to identifying preventable errors in the health care delivery system, in an effort to break the cycle of inaction on medical errors. The charge of the committee was to develop a long-term national strategy to effect a 50% reduction in errors over 5 years. This report has triggered patient safety initiatives by regulatory agencies, health care providers, consumer groups, and the general public.

—Kathleen Ferrara

FURTHER READING

www.iom.edu

INSTITUTIONAL REVIEW BOARD (IRB)

An institutional review board (IRB) is a committee that is charged with the responsibility of protecting the rights and welfare of human subjects who participate in research activities. It carries out this responsibility via in-depth initial and continued review of all research activities involving human subjects within its jurisdiction. The establishment of this committee is required at institutions that receive federal funding for research involving human subjects. However, sites that do not receive such funding are encouraged to voluntarily establish such a board, to demonstrate their intent to protect human subjects, in accordance with federal regulations governing human subject protections (Code of Federal Regulations at Title 45 [Public Welfare], Part 46, Protection of Human Subjects; 45 CFR 46).

IRB constitution, functions, operations, criteria for study approval, and requirements for IRB recordkeeping are specified at 45 CFR 46, subpart A (also known as the "Common Rule," as it has been adopted by several other federal agencies. Further, the federal regulations at 21 CFR 50 and 56 codify the Common Rule for drug, biological, and device research that is under the jurisdiction of the Food and Drug Administration.

The constitution of a federally recognized IRB includes at least five members, with combined expertise and sufficient diversity (in terms of race, gender, and so on) to allow for appropriate safeguarding of the subject populations that may participate in the research under its jurisdiction. Required membership includes at least one member whose interests are scientific, one member whose interests are nonscientific, and one member who is not affiliated with the institution in any way outside of membership on the IRB. A meeting of the IRB cannot be convened without the presence of a nonscientific member.

In reviewing proposed studies, an IRB must ensure that many criteria are met. An analysis of the foreseeable risks and benefits must take place, such that risks are minimized and benefits are maximized. The proposed recruitment and consent process must be acceptable, as well as the forms through which consent will be documented (note that waivers of consent, or the documentation thereof, are allowable, if certain criteria are met, per 45 CFR 46). Inclusion and exclusion criteria must be reviewed to ensure the equitable selection of subjects.

In addition to the mandate to safeguard the rights and welfare of research subjects, IRBs play a critical role in ensuring that additional protections are in place if vulnerable subject populations are included in the research activity. There are many types of vulnerable populations, including adults who are unable to consent for themselves, minors, the elderly, the economically or educationally disadvantaged, pregnant women, and women of child-bearing potential. For example, in the case where minors are deemed acceptable for inclusion in the research activity, an IRB will assess the need to obtain parental permission and the assent of the minor subject.

Continuing review of research activities that have been approved by an IRB is an important part of protecting human subjects. Review of proposed amendments to approved protocols, of unanticipated problems, and of adverse events is important in the continuing assessment of whether or not a study continues to be safe and ethical for inclusion of human subjects. Therefore, communication between the investigator and the IRB is a critical aspect to the success of any program involving the protection of research subjects.

—Judy Matuk

See also Belmont Report, Office for Human Research Protections (OHRP), Vulnerable Research Subject Populations

FURTHER READING

http://ohrp.osophs.dhhs.gov
http://ohrp.osophs.dhhs.gov/irb/irb_guidebook.htm
www.access.gpo.gov/nara/cfr/waisidx_99/45cfr46_99.html
www.fda.gov/oc/ohrt/irbs/default.htm

INTEGRATED DELIVERY SYSTEM

Integrated delivery systems combine and own or closely coordinate multiple stages of health care delivery. Economists call them *vertically integrated systems.* The integration usually includes many steps in the full spectrum of health services delivery, including physicians and hospitals and long-term care facilities. Some observers use the term *integrated delivery system* to refer to a managed care organization in which physicians are salaried and in which the practices, hospital, and long-term care facilities are under common ownership. If the integrated system does not own its own health plan (insurance program), it is closely aligned or partnering with a health plan, so the bulk of the monies flow through a single entity. The concept of integrated delivery has held great promise for overcoming the problems of poor coordination that plague so much of health care. Inappropriate referrals, medical errors, self-referrals, indiscriminate use of emergency rooms, excessive hospital lengths of stay, unnecessary admissions, and duplication of tests and procedures—all have been attributed in part to poor coordination of care.

U.S. government policies supporting health maintenance organizations were based on the early successes of integrated health maintenance organizations such as Kaiser Permanente. That California group established ownership of the insurance function (capitation) and control of delivery through "staff model" closed physician panels and company-owned hospitals. Physicians were on salary, with a modest potential for bonuses. Over time such closed-panel practices have become less popular and have given way to more loose relationships with independently practicing physicians (see also the entry for *Integrated Service Network*). Staff model practices have tended to be concentrated in a few limited geographic sites and have trouble rapidly adjusting their capacities to meet shifting market allegiances. Patients have often shown reluctance to abandon their primary care providers and shift their care to the providers in the closed panel. Owned hospitals became a financial burden as occupancy rates fell under managed care.

ORGANIZATIONAL FORMS

Integrated health care systems now come in many varieties, from common ownership of health plan, physician practices, hospitals, nursing homes, and other providers to loosely linked networks of providers who agree to exchange patient information and contract for referrals and other services from affiliated groups. See also the entry for *Integrated Service Network.*

A key element of any integrated delivery system is a primary care provider network incorporating the physicians who practice at the affiliated hospitals but covering sufficient geographic area to generate the needed work for the system's specialists, hospitals, and other units. Geographic dispersion is also necessary so that fewer patients have to change their primary physician to participate in the plan. A second key element is an incentive system such that these primary care "gatekeepers" are motivated to contain the use of specialists and hospitals to situations of true medical necessity.

A variety of governance arrangements have been implemented to integrate systems. Many are a natural outgrowth of preferred provider organizations (PPOs), networks established by insurers to serve patients in areas with high enrollee concentrations. There is a wide variety of less formal arrangements available such as provider service organizations (PSOs), which can also achieve some of benefits of integration without the problems of conflicts between professional autonomy and corporate governance. Other networks have been funded by independent practice associations (IPAs), groups of physicians who undertake some insurance risks and then want to achieve more control over markets and costs. Hospitals may also be drivers in integration by expanding the networks that they have developed, to recruit and support the physicians who feed patients into their facility. In the 1990s many hospitals purchased physician practices to assure a steady supply of patients and to dominate their markets. A decade or so later many of these same hospitals are divesting themselves of those practices because they have been unable to maintain sufficient physician productivity. Where competition is already limited, attempts at integration have also run afoul of state and federal antitrust constraints.

ALIGNMENT

True alignment of incentives in an integrated system usually requires the close participation of the insurer, the health plan. If the system consists solely of providers, the tendency is likely to maximize provider revenues, by-passing goals of cost control and competitive premium prices. Although the inclusion of the insurer adds another major player whose goals may differ from those of physicians and hospitals, it is unlikely that a disciplined, cost-competitive, *and* collaborative culture can be established without the leverage that its resources can provide. Because health plans must pool many covered lives and are moving away from provider ownership, collaboration with the health plan is more likely than full assumption of all the financial risks by the system. Then the plan can spread the risk across many different geographic markets.

Ownership of the health plan, however, may enhance access to capital, because one then has a more reliable source of revenue in premium income. Some of the presumed advantages of size are called *economies of scale,* one of which is the ability to access financial markets in volume. Another advantage is the pooling of risks. Each stage of delivery of health care has its own risks, but by engaging in delivery at multiple stages some of these can be smoothed out. However, the most notable bankruptcies in health care have been those of health plans that were unable to withstand short-run underwriting losses in a period of rising costs and intense price competition.

CULTURAL BARRIERS

Unfortunately, the promises of efficient services delivery have not been fulfilled in many communities, because of the differing cultures and interests of the providers involved. Hospitals have one set of interests, and most physicians another.

Attempts at integration involving physicians are not likely to work well if the parties do not work out issues of professional autonomy and related issues of physician control and physician incentives to everyone's satisfaction. Many mergers lost sight of the objective of improved patient care and focused on corporate restructuring and unitary ownership of assets. More recently, virtual integration—using contractual methods, common methods and standards, and interacting information systems but not unitary ownership of bricks and mortar—have experienced success. See also the entry for *Integrated Service Network.*

Integrating organizations appear to have to achieve three stages or levels of integration: managerial (functional), physician, and clinical (Shortell et al., 2000). How this takes place must be tailored to the local institutions and health care marketplace. Shortell et al. suggest that

successful managerial integration involves development of a common business strategy and a common information technology together with organizationwide incentive systems and quality improvement efforts. The integration of physicians into the organization seems to require strong physician leadership and acceptance of incentive systems that align physician interests with overall organizational goals as well as to require successful managerial integration. Note, however, that a further level of integration, clinical integration, is necessary to address effectively the ills of poor coordination cited in the first paragraph of this entry. That level requires that the organization have the will to achieve coordination at the level of the individual patient across providers, payers, and institutions. The first requirement here is commitment to this central task, supporting it with information technology design, technology assessment methods, commitment to cultural change, personnel training, population-based planning and assessment, and performance assessment and incentive systems. Short of that, one might achieve some improvements in efficiency, but not much in terms of both efficiency and effectiveness.

CAPACITY FLEXIBILITY

The Achilles heel of integrated delivery systems is that they often assume very high fixed costs. They have large fixed assets in their hospital and long-term care components, and they often end up building or leasing space for their physician practices. With physicians on salary, they find it difficult to respond rapidly to enrollment shifts caused by market forces. When they book many new members, they find that their staff is overburdened and that increases in telephone-answering and appointment waiting times quickly lead to patient dissatisfaction. When another health plan captures the employees and dependents of a major local employer, they end up with idle capacity. Because the physicians that accept employment on salary do so primarily for job security and lifestyle reasons, lay-offs can make it very hard to recruit good people in the future to deal with attrition and further growth. Therefore, HMOs tend to be quite slow to let surplus physicians go, preferring to hang on in hopes of an upturn. This problem is not unique to health care. National productivity generally drops off rapidly during a downturn and rises rapidly in an upturn as hiring is postponed to make sure that the observed demand increases will continue. If the provider is undercapitalized, the poor productivity associated with periods of market losses can quickly lead to bankruptcy.

—Curtis P. McLaughlin

See also Information Systems, Integrated Delivery System

FURTHER READING

Burns, R. L., & Pauly, M. V. (2002). Integrated delivery networks: A detour on the road to integrated health care? *Health Affairs, 21*(4), 128–143.

Burns, R. L., Walston, S. L., Alexander, J. A., Zuckerman, H. S., Andersen, R. M., Torrens, P. R., & Hilberman, D. (2001). Just how integrated are integrated delivery systems? Results from a national survey. *Health Care Management Review, 26*(1), 20–39.

Coddington, D. C., Moore, K. D., & Fischer, E. E. (1996). *Making integrated health care work.* San Francisco: Jossey-Bass.

Phelps, C. E. (1997). *Health economics* (2nd ed.). Reading, MA: Addison-Wesley.

Satinsky, M. A. (1998). *The foundations of integrated care: Facing the challenges of change.* Chicago: American Hospital Publishing.

Shortell, S. M., Gillies, R. M., Anderson, D. A., Erickson, K. M., & Mitchell, J. B. (2000). *Remaking health care in America: The evolution of organized delivery systems* (2nd ed.). San Francisco: Jossey-Bass.

Wan, T. T., Liu, B. Y., & Ma, A. (2002). Integration mechanisms and hospital efficiency in integrated health care delivery systems. *Journal of Medical Systems, 26*(2), 127–143.

INTEGRATED MARKETING COMMUNICATION (IMC)

The term *integrated marketing communication* (IMC) has been described in multiple ways to include consideration as an overall philosophy of communication, to a more specific communication strategic focus, to a set of specified practices. Regardless of how it is positioned, IMC ultimately reflects the notion of integrating message, media, and audience. Perhaps IMC can best be understood by taking into account four basic principles of an IMC strategy. First and foremost, an effective IMC strategy must adopt an audience perspective. It must consider the communicated message as interpreted by the receiver, not the sender. A strong IMC strategy seeks to facilitate relationships with various relevant audiences to gain knowledge and respect for audience needs, desires, preferences, and response patterns. In doing so, IMC strategy must consider multiple consumer groups with differing levels of involvement with the category or brand, as well as nonconsumer audiences (employees, retailers, government, community). IMC relies heavily on accurate audience research. For example, several years ago the Centers for Disease Control (CDC) conducted significant research to determine how rural populations would best receive a communicated message meant to encourage and reinforce condom usage as an important AIDS preventive.

Second, an IMC strategy must identify all potential opportunities to reach the varied audiences at numerous points in the influence or purchasing process. These are termed *points of contact*. Every possible point of contact with the audience should be considered: where they live, what they read, listen to, and view, where they go during a typical day, their work and leisure activities, group memberships, and so forth. For example, in targeting a teenage audience for a campaign to reinforce the designated driver initiative, points of contact could include schools, youth clubs, after-school activities, books and magazines, television programs, computer Web sites, and shopping malls.

Third, these points of contact must be considered in terms of *integrating message and media*. What is the main message that needs to be communicated to the audience and that will be received favorably? What are the points of contact with this audience? What are the specific media forms that can be used at each point of contact? Media forms may include the traditional media of broadcast (television, radio) and print (newspaper, magazines, signage), but could also consider the newer media forms such as targeted broadcasting (for example, televised programming viewed in doctors' offices, hospitals, schools, retail establishments, airports), print (such as point-of-purchase signage, changing billboards, restrooms), electronic media (computers, PDAs, cell phones), and direct communications (such as telemarketing, direct mail). As new communication forms present themselves, new opportunities will emerge for IMC strategy.

Finally, IMC strategy depends on an evaluation of outcomes. Advances in technology, such as scanners and databases, make it possible to measure, monitor, and evaluate outcomes of integrated marketing communication strategy and tactics. By keeping records of audience activity, promoters can better target future promotion. For example, subscribers of *Prevention Magazine* are automatically sent general direct mail flyers for a series of newly published books on health-related topics. Once a person actually buys a promoted book, that individual is bombarded with fliers on other books or tapes on the topic as well as materials on related topics. This is similar to the database strategy Amazon.com employs that keeps a record of every person's order and provides periodic updates on new books or tapes on the same topic.

IMC should be viewed as *continuous* rather than an either/or selection. In other words, strategies may differ to the extent to which they adopt the audience perspective, include all potential points of contact, integrate message and media, and link communication objectives to outcomes. It is therefore important to consider IMC in terms of degrees rather than being present or absent. The degree of integration can be thought of as a continuum anchored by some basic coordination to a total synergistic effort.

Integration can occur on six measurable dimensions. It may be helpful to use the example of a hospital introducing a new service to the community. Each dimension will be described briefly, with an example. First, *integration across target audiences* occurs when the perspectives of multiple audiences are considered and conflicting preferences are balanced in the development of communication strategies (perspective of physician specialists, potential patients, insurance companies, government regulators, and so on). Second, because consumer response to marketing communications changes as information search, decision making, purchase, and postpurchase evaluation occurs, coordination of communication strategies across these behaviors reflects *integration across stages in the buying process* (for example, communication with a patient from an initial visit with the primary physician, the referral to the hospital, communication with hospital officials regarding the new service, communication by the acting physician regarding the new service, and postservice evaluation). Third, *integration across points of contact* represents the breadth of interactions between the company and the individuals that are considered (promotion of the service through public relations, workplace flyers, television and newspaper advertising, direct mail, billboards, and so on). For example, at any given time a company may communicate with consumers over different stages of the buying process, within stages of the buying process, and with individuals who are members of multiple target audiences (such as a consumer who is also an employee). Knowing the various combinations of interactions that individuals may have with the company facilitates integration across points of contact. Fourth, coordination of message content across points of contact can be termed *integration of messages* (introducing the service to a patient, first in general terms through advertising, subsequently increasing the depth of knowledge as a patient needs the service). Fifth, integration between the audience and the company occurs when audience response to IMC strategies is *measured and evaluated* (patient satisfaction surveys concerning the new service). Finally, overall integration provides a *global indicator of performance* across the first five dimensions (for example, performance indicators might include physician referrals, the reputation of the service within the physician profession, and the financial return on investment of the IMC strategy). Measures of a company's performance on these six dimensions indicates the extent to which it has implemented IMC.

—David W. Schumann

FURTHER READING

Belch, G. E., & Belch, M. A. (2000). *Advertising and promotion: An integrated marketing communication perspective.* New York: McGraw-Hill.

Cathey, A., & Schumann, D. (1996). A process model of integrated marketing communication. In G. B. Wilcox (Ed.), *Proceedings of the American Academy of Advertising.* Austin: University of Texas.

Pickton, D., & Broderick, A. (2001). *Integrated marketing communication.* Upper Saddle River, NJ: Prentice Hall.

Schultz, D. E. (1996). *The new marketing paradigm: Integrated marketing communications.* New York: Contemporary Books.

Schultz, D. E. (2000). *Communicating globally: An integrated marketing approach.* New York: McGraw-Hill.

Shimp, T. A. (1997). *Advertising, promotion, and supplemental aspects of integrated marketing communications* (4th ed.). Orlando, FL: Dryden Press.

INTEGRATED SERVICE NETWORK (ISN)

Integrated service networks (ISNs) combine or coordinate several stages of health care delivery. Economists call them *vertically integrated systems.* The integration usually includes several stages in the complete chain of services delivery, including physicians and hospitals and long-term care facilities. If the integration includes ownership of practices, hospital bricks and mortar and a health plan (insurance program), or is partnering very closely with a health plan, it is called an *integrated delivery system* (see entry). The concept of integrated delivery has held great promise for overcoming the problems of poor coordination that plague so much of health care. Inappropriate referrals, medical errors, self-referrals, indiscriminate use of emergency rooms, excessive lengths of hospital stay, unnecessary admissions, and duplication of tests and procedures, all have been attributed in part to poor coordination of care.

The use of the word *network* implies that the system is not integrated through common ownership and is linked through a number of coordinating mechanisms, such as contracts, information systems, personal relationships, and mutually supportive strategies and values.

The network may be developed for a number of reasons, including improved delivery of care, greater bargaining power with purchasers of care, and the hope of ultimately becoming a health plan and an integrated delivery system. The core membership of an integrated service network is a group of physicians, usually a local IPA, and one or more hospitals and long-term care facilities.

VIRTUAL INTEGRATION

Virtual integration is the opposite of common ownership of assets and practices. Three elements are necessary for a functional virtually integrated system:

- Contracts and agreements covering patient referrals and management
- An information system that transfers information and tracks events and outcomes
- Financial incentives that are aligned to support and integrate the activities of the various actors, including patients

One advantage of virtual integration is that each provider maintains its ownership interest and has an incentive to make its portion of the enterprise productive and efficient, while striving to meet the overall goals of the network's governing body.

If the network is going to undertake risk contracting, such as capitation, it must also have mechanisms that capture actual costs, monitor utilization, disseminate best practices, and motivate system and unit improvements, as well as coordination of patient care. The network must be large enough to have a sufficient patient pool to make risk-taking effective and a data-tracking system to support its underwriting and rate-setting functions.

GOVERNANCE

Reaching economic decisions that stand up in the marketplace over time is difficult for networked organizations. The interests of primary care physicians, specialists, and hospitals can be at odds with each other. Where there is no executive in charge with the power to hire and fire and no external board of directors to evaluate CEO performance, conflicts are difficult to resolve. Strong physician leadership and good information systems are keys to effective management. Partnerships are not easy to manage, but a network is not even a partnership. There may not be a common bottom line. There has to be a give and take among the bottom lines of all the network members mediated by payment systems and by committee structures that consider key issues and make recommendations that network members must be willing to live with. Key committees must deal with membership and credentialing, revenue allocation among providers, contract negotiation, quality assurance, utilization review, and medical management.

PHYSICIAN LEADERSHIP

Most networks will have a professional nonphysician administrator. The role of physician leadership is not merely to represent physician viewpoints and interests but also to mediate among all interests including those of physicians and especially to build consensus and respect among the physicians and physician groups that must collaborate. Most networks are not established *de novo*. They come into being in communities where the same physicians may have practiced for years, competed tooth and nail, been partners and broken up, and so on. Vestiges of these

interactions will continue, and physician leadership must work hard to keep the physician participants focused on their common objectives rather than reliving old grievances.

FLEXIBILITY ADVANTAGE

One advantage of the network approach to vertical integration through ownership is flexibility. The network does not typically go into debt to acquire assets. The assets remain with the members, and they can access patients and revenues from a variety of health plans and individuals. Capacity can be expanded rapidly by adding new participating providers or downsized merely by reducing payments to members as business falls. Usually a network contracts on a capitated basis but pays its members in proportion to the services rendered. If demand falls, those payments automatically fall. Organizations with employed physicians find it difficult to reduce staff, except by attrition, because of concerns about their reputation and their ability to recruit good people in the future.

Burns and Pauly (2002) offer four suggestions to overcome the past integration failures in hospital-based networks and still provide better coordination of care. They are (a) to provide disease management and case management programs to coordinate care for chronic disease cases; (b) to co-locate (locate in the same place) services, including primary care providers and specialists used by patients with common problems; (c) to integrate patient records using a common information technology system; and (d) to involve patients in the integration of their own care, including giving them possession of their own electronic medical records and authority to self-refer among a specific panel of specialists.

—Curtis P. McLaughlin

See also Integrated Delivery System, Vertical Integration

FURTHER READING

Burns, L. R., & Pauly, M. V. (2002). Integrated delivery networks: A detour on the road to integrated health care? *Health Affairs, 21*(4), 128–143.

Kongstvedt, P. R. (2001). *Essentials of managed health care* (4th ed.). Gaithersburg, MD: Aspen.

Kralewski, E. J., deVries, A., Dowd, B., & Potthoff, S. (1995). The development of integrated service networks in Minnesota. *Health Care Management Review, 29*(4), 42–56.

Schaefer, L. D., & McMurtry, D. E. (1997). Virtually integrated health care systems. In K. A. Miller & E. K. Miller (Eds.), *Making sense of managed care: Vol. 1. Building blocks and fundamentals* (pp. 126–136). San Francisco: Jossey-Bass.

Shortell, S. M., Gillies, R. M., Anderson, D. A., Erickson, K. M., & Mitchell, J. B. (2000). *Remaking health care in America: The evolution of organized delivery systems* (2nd ed.). San Francisco: Jossey-Bass.

INTEGRATIVE MEDICINE

See Alternative Medicine (Complementary Medicine, Integrative Medicine, Unconventional Medicine)

INTENSIVE DISTRIBUTION

Businesses try to distribute their products in three different ways: intensive, selective, and exclusive distribution. When a company tries to make its product available in as many outlets (such as retail stores) as possible so that it can serve customers easily and saturate the market, the method or strategy of distribution employed is termed *intensive distribution.* Firms choose this strategy when customer switching of brands is common. For example, if customers feel indifferent about a headache remedy, a marketer of this kind of product attempts to make its product present in the shelves of pharmacies, supermarkets, and other retail outlets where consumers regularly shop.

In the health care industry, most consumers are brand loyal, meaning that they are likely to buy the brand name products they have used and benefited from before. If a consumer has used the Mayo Clinic for health care and was happy with the service, this consumer is likely to search for a Mayo Clinic when he or she moves to a new location in the United States. This is because the consumer is brand loyal. If a Mayo Clinic is not available in the new location that the consumer moves into, the consumer will have to search for a new medical service provider. This is why the Mayo Clinic is available in more than a single location. However, because of the high cost of capital in the health care industry, the intensive distribution strategy is rarely used. Keep in mind, however, manufacturers of most over-the-counter products utilize intensive distribution strategy, because if the product is not available, consumers are likely to switch to a different brand (such as Tylenol as opposed to Advil or Bufferin).

Medical doctors commonly use an intensive distribution strategy. Many doctors provide services in multiple locations in a variety of medical facilities including hospitals, clinics, and medical office buildings. However, this practice is not the same as distribution of products. Although many products distributed by an intensive strategy can be available even in vending machines, a doctor's care cannot be provided through a vending machine.

Most products distributed intensively are available in convenient locations for consumers to see and purchase. Checkout counters in retail stores are examples of this strategy. At checkout counters, consumers see and purchase many products that they did not plan to purchase. Often products distributed utilizing this strategy are purchased on impulse while the customer is waiting in line at a checkout counter.

Although it is costly and sometimes uncommon to use the intensive distribution strategy in the medical field, companies attempt to come close to using this strategy by trying different methods. For example, giving free samples of medicines to medical doctors to distribute to their patients is a good example of the intensive distribution strategy in practice. As the health care industry grows, we are likely to see this strategy being utilized more and more.

—Fahri Karakaya

See also Competitive Strategy and Groups, Marketing Mix

FURTHER READING

Perrault, W., & McCarty, J. (2002). *Basic marketing* (14th ed.). Boston: Irwin McGraw Hill.

INTERMEDIATE CARE FACILITY (ICF)

An intermediate care facility (ICF) is a health care facility for individuals who are disabled, elderly, or not acutely ill, and who require less intensive care than that of a hospital or skilled nursing facility (SNF). These facilities, sometimes known as *subacute facilities,* are used extensively both by the managed care companies as well as by hospitals to assure that the care is at the most appropriate level for patient needs. A subacute facility may be housed in a SNF or a hospital but is separated for both reimbursement and level and intensity of care.

In recent years the ICF or subacute facility began cropping up when health care benefits began to be "cut back" on what was covered in the hospital as well as in the home. In the 1980s and early 1990s home care for IV therapy for antibiotics and pain management was an accepted practice and was provided in both venues. When the costs of health care continued to escalate, the federal government began to limit coverage for these "nonacute" services in the hospital. At the same time, coverage for IV antibiotics in the home was no longer available. The need for health care in an alternate setting addressing these issues was identified. In addition, many seniors and other individuals with disabilities did not fit the Medicare/Medicaid requirements for acute rehabilitation. That is not to say that they did not require physical, occupational, or speech therapy, but rather that they were not able to tolerate the vigorous three hours of therapy each day. The ICF was the ideal facility for these types of patients and filled the need.

As you might imagine, the ICF requires less staff at all levels. In the acute care setting you may need one RN with specialized training for every two patients in the intensive care setting (per shift) and perhaps one RN for every eight patients per shift in other areas. The support staff, clinical assistants (nurse assistants), and unit clerks (unit secretary) as well as transporters and others are also needed to take care of the patients in acute care. These staffing levels must be maintained whether or not the hospital is at a predetermined occupancy level. Hospitals are expected to provide the full range of services, including acute rehabilitation services, and therefore are required to have a full complement of physical, occupational, and speech therapy for the patient.

These services must be provided until the patient is transferred to another facility. In the ICF the ratio for patients is significantly less. The patient does not require the same surveillance by an RN, nor does the patient require the same intensity of physical, occupational, and speech therapies. The requirement for these therapies in an ICF is that the patient be able to tolerate as little as one or two hours a day.

In the acute rehabilitation setting, the patient is on a fast-paced and intensive program, which must be a minimum of three hours a day. Managed care companies offer this extended care in ICF as part of their benefit package. The companies request concurrent reviews from the utilization review departments in the hospital and then make a determination as to when acute care stops and subacute care begins. It is at this decision point that the patient is prepared to transfer to one of the covered facilities for the required care. Discharge planning takes place throughout the patient's stay from day of admission. These activities, as well as the concurrent reviews, make the identification and transition smooth for the patient and the family.

At times the health care team in the acute care setting makes a recommendation as to the "next step" for the patient that differs from that of the payer, in this case the managed care company. For example, the physical therapist, physician, and nursing and RN case manager at the hospital evaluate the patient's abilities and determine that the most appropriate posthospital care is that of an acute rehabilitation facility. The managed care company may disagree and deny this placement. The patient has the right, and is encouraged to exercise that right, to an expedited review of the care given and care identified as needed for posthospital care. This expedited review allows the patient and the provider an opportunity to appeal the payment issue. The response from the managed care company must be completed within 72 hours so as not to prolong the process or interrupt the necessary care for the patient's well-being. Once the determination is made, the patient has another opportunity to challenge the decision if it is a negative decision. This second appeal is sent to a unbiased, independent review group that will make a binding determination based on the medical record and other data. This response must also be provided within 72 hours.

Intermediate care facilities have filled an important health care need to support the ever changing and high costs of health care in the country today.

—Edna Lee Kucera

FURTHER READING

www.cms.gov
www.ipro.org

INTERNAL CAPITAL

See Operating Cash Flow

INTERNAL ENVIRONMENTAL ANALYSIS

Internal environmental analysis is the conscious and objective search for the organizational strengths and weaknesses that are likely to provide a competitive advantage or disadvantage. Within the strategic management process, three important questions must be answered: (a) What should we do? (b) What can we do? and (c) What do we want to do? The answer to the first question is provided by an analysis of the external environment. What we want to do is provided by the mission, vision, and values. Internal environmental analysis addresses the question of what we can do.

Internal environmental analysis is an integral part of situation analysis, the first stage of strategic planning. The goal of situation analysis is, as the name implies, to help strategic planners understand the present situation. Therefore, situation analysis is essentially a process of data gathering and analysis, so internal environmental analysis involves collecting and analyzing information about an organization's strategic capacity. The process of internal environmental analysis requires that planners look inside their organization and identify the organization's strengths and weaknesses. This information, in association with other types of data (external strategic issues, mission, vision, and so on), is collected and analyzed as part of situation analysis and becomes the basis for strategy formulation. In all likelihood, the strategy formulated will require that changes be made. Any assessment of the probable success of the strategy requires a thorough understanding of the organization's strengths and weaknesses.

IDENTIFYING STRENGTHS AND WEAKNESSES

The first step in internal environmental analysis is the identification the organization's strengths and weaknesses.

There are two important considerations in this step. First, one must determine how to conduct the search. The most commonly used approach is to think of the organization in terms of a number of functional subsystems such as clinical operations, marketing, community relations, human resources, finance and accounting, information systems, and so on. The organization's value chain can also be used for organizing the search. Customarily, once the subsystems are identified a list of strengths and weaknesses for each subsystem is developed.

The second consideration relates to the "depth of the probe" or the extent to which each subsystem is searched. Using a radar screen analogy, we first scan the various subsystems looking for possible strengths and weaknesses. When we identify possible strengths and weaknesses, it is necessary to probe deeper to see which strengths have the potential to make us effective competitors in our market and which weaknesses must be corrected if we are to remain competitive. When these competitively relevant strengths and weaknesses are identified, each one must be carefully evaluated and we must decide the best way to maximize the competitive potential of the strengths and the best way to minimize the disadvantage created by the weaknesses.

SOME IMPORTANT CAUTIONS ABOUT INTERNAL ENVIRONMENTAL ANALYSIS

Internal environmental analysis creates several important challenges for strategic planners. First, internal analysis requires an open mind. It is difficult for leaders and employees who believe strongly in their organization to objectively assess "what we do well and what we do not do well." It is equally difficult for demoralized leaders and employees to see the good things that take place in the organization. Effective internal environmental analysis requires that organizational members step back and take an objective look at strengths and weaknesses so they can focus on the actions needed to capitalize on strengths and minimize the adverse affects of weaknesses.

Second, internal environmental analysis is an exercise in data gathering and analysis. The intent is to obtain information that can be used in strategy formulation. Strategic planners are sometimes tempted to try to formulate strategies around strengths and weaknesses without integrating the information with the results of external environmental analysis and mission, vision, and values. Strengths and weaknesses are only one part of situation analysis and must be carefully considered as part of the bigger picture of strategy formulation.

Third, it is important not to be paralyzed by analysis. Data collection and analysis are critical aspects of effective internal environmental analysis. However, planners should not be hesitant to use their intuition as well as the objective data. Experience, intuition, surveys, interviews, and so on are all important sources of information about the organization

and its strategic capacity. It is important not to be paralyzed by the need for additional information.

Strategic decision makers never have all the information they need to make decisions. This is why strategy is an example of decision making under conditions of ambiguity and uncertainty. At some point the decision maker must make a judgment—do I have enough information to make an informed decision, or should I continue data gathering and analysis? When the cost of additional information search exceeds the likely value, the strategic leader must act even without the benefit of perfect information.

—W. Jack Duncan

See also Environmental Analysis, Mission, Strategic Planning, Values (Guiding Principles), Vision

FURTHER READING

Fleisher, C. S., & Bensoussan, B. E. (2003). *Strategic and competitive analysis: Methods and techniques for analyzing business competition.* Upper Saddle River, NJ: Prentice Hall.

Grant, R. M. (2002). *Contemporary strategy analysis: Concepts, techniques, applications.* Malden, MA: Blackwell.

Pitts, R. A., & Lei, D. (2003). *Strategic management: Building and sustaining competitive advantage.* Mason, OH: South-Western.

INTERNAL RATE OF RETURN (IRR)

The internal rate of return (IRR) is what you get back (increase or decrease) for what you put in, in this case internally over a defined period of time. You may not have heard this definition from an economist or accountant, but in its true form it is accurate.

The term *internal rate of return* is most commonly used in business, understanding that return considering cash flows based on an "internal" investment of "capital" (money, resources, time, and so on). This is a very common method of analyzing a major investment (such as a capital project, reallocating resources, or change of a process), allowing you to consider the multiple variables. Most commonly, you find the investment rate (interest rate) that is equivalent to the dollar value return you expect from the investment. Once you have calculated the "rate," you can compare the rates you could earn from other investments of the same resources. It allows you to find the interest rate that is equivalent to the dollar returns you expect from your project, taking into consideration the time value of money.

There are various definitions for internal rate of return used, but the way this term is used in today's business world takes into account various characteristics. When someone starts out, "The internal rate of return is . . . ," begin to think about the variables that follow and questions you would ask in order to understand them.

A fairly common definition might read thus: The realized return for an internal investment taking into consideration the time value of money, over a defined period of time (usually annually).

Here is a simple example: If you invested $100 and earned 10% on an annual basis, your rate of return would be $10 or 10%, if there were no inflation or deflation associated with the investment.

If you invested $10 and earned 10% on an annual basis but inflation was 3%, then your rate of return annually would be $7, or 7% (10% − 3% = 7%).

Let's suppose the investment deals with medical equipment. If the "internal rate of return" (percentage) is less than the cost of borrowing (interest rate or percentage of cost of capital) used to fund your project, the project will clearly not be a good investment in monetary terms. A common practice in health care evaluations is that a purchase or investment will have a projected IRR that is at multiple percentage points higher than the cost of the acquisition, to make up for its risk and other factors associated with the project. There may be nonmonetary factors included in the evaluations such as lost opportunity cost (what will happen if we do not invest?), quality of care issues, and additional resource retention or recruitment.

Here is a simple example of how this IRR might work in health care:

Let's propose you are about to purchase a large piece of medical equipment, and the total cost to own this piece of equipment is $1.5 million. You expected to increase your revenues (cash flow) over a five-year period by $700,000, $600,000, $300,000, $200,000, and $100,000 a year respectively, or $1.9 million (five years of cash flow) in total, because of the investment. With all factors considered (depreciation, cost of operation, taxes, and so on), let's estimate the desired internal rate of return for the project would be approximately 12%.

If your cost of borrowing or reallocation of dollars for the investment is less than 12%, the project may be worthwhile. If the cost of borrowing or reallocation of dollars for the investment is 12% or greater, it will not make sense financially to do the project. This is part of an analysis that every organization reviews on projects, called *return on investment* (ROI), which can take into consideration the IRR calculations, costs, benefits, alternative financing, and so forth. In health care many times the IRR is used to look strictly at the cash flow analysis of an investment.

Questions you might ask are as follows:

- What would I do with the $1.5 million if I did not invest in this project?
- What did it take to make the $1.5 million?

- Can I protect the investment from inflation?
- Are there other investments that can return better than 12%?
- What are the risks associated with the 12% return?

IRR is one of several metrics that expresses the dollar returns expected from a project as an interest rate. Once the rate is established, you can compare it to rates you would earn by investing in other projects, in this instance those that would return greater than 12%. IRR is calculated to see if it meets an organization's "hurdle rate" for an investment, because it's usually the lowest rate of return that management will accept. Typically, a project must earn an IRR that is several percentage points higher than the cost of borrowing, to compensate the company for its risk exposure and time.

To compute a simple IRR, find a good financial calculator. If you do not have one, then find a copy of some net present value tables. You can then find the projected rate of return by using them. Once you have the tables, divide the cost of the investment by the annual projected cash flow generated by the investment. The result is a ratio that you can match to the tables, taking into consideration the time period you are calculating to.

An advantage of IRR is that it includes the cash flow related to a project and considers the time value of money. The internal rate of return of a cash flow creates the interest rate that makes the present value of a cash flow equal to zero. Two disadvantages are that IRR is cumbersome for simply calculating interest rates when cash flows vary widely year to year and that it assumes cash flows are reinvested.

The internal rate of return is used quite frequently in looking at future investments and in evaluating the past performance of an investment. When considering the internal rate of return as a simple straightforward calculation, you can take a quick snapshot of the projected value of the investment. In your effort to make a final decision or evaluation on that investment, you can then add or subtract the risk factors that may be involved.

—Terry Moore

See also Investment, Rate of Return, Return on Assets (ROA)

FURTHER READING

Freidman, J. P. (2000). *Dictionary of business terms.* Hauppauge, NY: Barron's.

Gepenski, L. C. (2001). *Healthcare finance: An introduction to accounting and financial management.* Chicago: Health Administration Press.

Helfert, E. A. (1994). *Techniques of financial analysis.* Boston: Irwin.

INTERNALLY GENERATED CASH FLOW

See Operating Cash Flow

INTRODUCTORY STAGE OF PRODUCT LIFE CYCLE

See Product Life Cycle (PLC) Analysis

INVESTIGATIONAL NEW DRUG APPLICATION (IND)

A "Notice of Claimed Investigational Exemption for a New Drug" (IND) is required under law to be submitted for any new chemical entity, biological, or antibiotic, before it is to be clinically evaluated in human subjects. Section 505 (a) of the federal Food, Drug, and Cosmetic Act states, "No person shall introduce into interstate commerce any new drug unless there is for that drug an approved New Drug Application or an effective IND."

There are three types of INDs:

1. A *research IND* is submitted by a physician, who both initiates and conducts investigations.

2. An *emergency use IND* allows the FDA to authorize use of an experimental drug in an emergency situation.

3. A *treatment IND* is submitted for an experimental drug showing promise in clinical testing for serious or immediately life-threatening diseases.

The organization of an IND is based on Form 1571, which serves as the cover sheet for the IND and therefore outlines the content requirements in the order in which it should be presented to the FDA. See FDA Form 1571 for a detailed description of the required information of an IND and the FDA guidance document "Content and Format of IND for Phase 1 Studies of Drugs, Including Well-Characterized Therapeutic, Biotechnology-Derived Products." In addition, a pre-IND meeting with the FDA is also recommended.

The IND must contain animal pharmacology and toxicology studies, manufacturing information and clinical protocols, and investigator information.

The mechanics of the IND are as follows:

- The inclusion of an introduction to provide a brief description of the study drug, the purpose of the IND, the disease state to be treated, and the benefits to be derived.
- Description of the chemistry, manufacturing procedures, and quality control testing methods including the chemical name of the drug, how it will be administered, and the components and quantitative composition of the drug product.
- Safety statement to assure that the study drug will not be of any risk to the subjects and pertinent preclinical and clinical experience. Informational material should be presented, such as labels, labeling, directions for use, and a clinical investigational brochure.
- A description of the investigator's qualifications for the phase of the studies.
- Identification of the investigators and signed commitments to follow the protocol. Copies of Form FDA 1572/1573 and copies of curriculum vitae.
- Signed clinical investigation protocol and case report forms. A copy of patient informed consent and written IRB approval.
- Outline of the Phase 1 study and planned investigations.
- Sponsor's agreement to notify the FDA or investigators if the clinical study is discontinued.
- An agreement that all investigators will be notified if a new drug application is approved.
- Statement by the sponsor that the test product will not be sold during the clinical trials.
- Statement that the sponsor understands that the studies will not be started until 30 days after receipt of the IND by the FDA and that the FDA hasn't put the IND under clinical hold within 30 days after submission.
- U.S. Environmental Protection Agency impact analysis report.
- Statement that the preclinical trials will be conducted according to good laboratory practices regulations.

—Anthony J. Sileno

See also New Drug Application (NDA)

FURTHER READING

Cato, E. C. (Ed.). (1988). *Clinical trials and tribulations.* New York: Marcel Dekker.

Center for Drug Evaluation and Research and Center for Biologics Evaluation and Research. (1995). *Content and format of investigational new drug applications (INDs) for Phase 1 studies of drugs, including well-characterized, therapeutic, biotechnology-derived products.* Rockville, MD: Author.

Guarino, R. A. (Ed.). (1987). *New drug approval process.* New York: Marcel Dekker.

INVESTIGATOR (PRINCIPAL INVESTIGATOR)

An investigator is the person who is responsible for an investigation (or study or clinical trial). In a situation where several individuals are working collectively to conduct a study or trial, one individual is designated as the *principal investigator.* The other investigators are sometimes referred to as subinvestigators or coinvestigators. The roles and responsibilities of principal investigators and subinvestigators or coinvestigators are usually clearly defined.

A principal investigator has the overall responsibility for the study but may not have specific responsibility for the well-being of participants who are treated by other investigators (subinvestigators) who are taking part in the study.

Investigators in clinical studies are most commonly medical doctors but scientists and dentists may also be investigators (principal or subinvestigators) depending on the type of study.

The Food and Drug Administration specifies that an investigator should be qualified by education, training, and experience to assume the responsibility for the proper conduct of a clinical study. The investigator must provide the FDA with evidence of qualifications through an up-to-date CV (curriculum vitae) or other documentation that may be required by the sponsor (a pharmaceutical company, a government agency such as the National Institutes of Health, a foundation, or others), the institutional review board, or regulatory authorities.

The investigator has an obligation to be familiar with the investigational products, the protocol, and the current investigator's brochure. The investigator should conduct the study using good clinical practices and regulatory requirements. With rare exceptions, an informed consent must be obtained from study participants prior to entry into the study.

The investigator also has the responsibility to work with auditors from the sponsor and/or regulatory authorities. The principal investigator should maintain a list of qualified people who are involved with the study as well as their delegated trial-related duties. A qualified physician (or dentist) who is an investigator should be responsible for all trial-related medical or dental decisions. The investigator should also ensure that adequate medical care is provided to participants for any adverse events, including clinically significant laboratory values related to the trial. The investigator may also inform the subject's primary physician about the patient's participation in the study.

The investigator should also assure that the trial is conducted in compliance with the protocol, as well as report deviations from the protocol. The investigator is also responsible for accountability for study product(s).

At least annually the investigator (or institution) must provide a written report to the institutional review board or institutional ethics committee. In general, the investigator is responsible for reporting adverse events (AEs) or serious adverse events (SAEs) to the institutional review board or institutional ethics committee, the sponsor, and possibly the Food and Drug Administration or other regulatory authority.

The role of an investigator is multifaceted. The investigator not only is responsible for understanding the science and study design but must also be familiar with other aspects of the study as well as with the principles of informed consent, good clinical practice, and communicating with the institutional review board or institutional ethics committee, the sponsor, and other regulatory authorities.

The investigator may find the following organizations helpful to determine guidelines and responsibilities:

European Union (EU; www.europa.eu.int)

Food and Drug Administration (FDA; www.FDA.gov)

International Conference on Harmonization (ICH; www.ICH.org)

National Institutes of Health (NIH; www.NIH.gov)

U.S. Department of Health and Human Services (DHHS; www.os.dhhs.gov)

World Medical Association (WMA; www.WMA.net)

—Steven A. Vitkun

See also Clinical Trials, Food and Drug Administration (FDA), Informed Consent, Institutional Review Board (IRB), Subinvestigator

FURTHER READING

Day, S. (1999). *Dictionary for clinical trials.* New York: Wiley.

Federal regulations and guidelines reference manual. (2002). Association of Clinical Research Professionals. Washington, DC:

INVESTMENT

The basic driving force of business, including health care, is investment.

Often organizations use the word "investment" in various situations. The word refers to the acquisition or allocation of a specific type of resource for the purpose of increasing in value. That resource could be time, money, people, ownership, equipment, property, research, and so on, and the commitment of it for a purpose of an increased return over a period of time. The result of a "good investment" would be an increase in the value of time, money, or other resources.

Investment management is key to basic investment fundamentals. You may want to establish your investment strategy before you begin investing assets and their allocation. Strategies are based on a foundation of acceptable risk and desire of a defined minimum return.

Timing is the most critical element in deciding what or when to invest. The criteria for a decision to invest are based on a risk management strategy the enterprise subscribes to. In health care, today's challenges that impact health care professionals are issues such as rising medical costs, health care access, a weak economy, and reimbursement, to name just a few.

The investments most familiar to individuals are monetary, such as savings accounts, stocks, bonds, mutual funds, certificates of deposit, mutual funds, property, and so on. These are important to business as well. There are other personal investments we can make in our own health such as investing time to perform physical activity to result in a healthier lifestyle, so investments are not always "monetary."

Health care investment is considerably different from personal investments. There can always be the temptation to devise a set of static rules to evaluate investment decisions, but evaluation is not always that straightforward. Health care enterprises must also consider the human, societal, technical, competitive, and other challenges that will affect the strategic content of the investment being evaluated, not just the tangible costs and benefits. Investments in health care take the form of buildings, equipment, doctors, nurses, employee benefits, procedures, insurance, and so on. Some of these investments may not "make money." Others will if the enterprise manages a balanced portfolio that allows the health care organization to provide the desired quality of its intended services.

A health care enterprise's business investments comprise an investment portfolio targeted to produce a profitable result based on an organization's operational and financial objectives. By reviewing the industry environment and implementing best practices in operations, an enterprise can maximize returns and manage risk effectively. Many tools are used to help select and make decisions on investments, such as rate of return (such as return on assets and return on investment) and present values (such as net present value, internal rate of return, and discounted payback). Strategies used in determining the direction for investments use processes involving portfolio management, capital budgeting, emphasis, and deployment and divestiture.

—Terry Moore

See also Rate of Return, Return on Assets (ROA)

FURTHER READING

Freidman, J. P. (2000). *Dictionary of business terms.* Hauppauge, NY: Barron's.

Gepenski, L. C. (2001). *Healthcare finance: An introduction to accounting and financial management.* Chicago: Health Administration Press.

Nowicki, M. (2001). *The financial management of hospital and healthcare organizations.* Chicago: Healthcare Financial Management Association and Healthcare Administration Press.

IN VITRO TESTING

The term *in vitro testing* refers to experimentation and research done in nonliving models. "In vitro" comes from the Latin word meaning "in glass" Thus, in vitro testing provides alternative test methods to testing on living models. Such nonanimal research and testing services effectively reduce animal use.

In vitro testing can be used for many purposes, including for acute toxic responses such as eye or skin injury that may occur from products. With in vitro testing, many nonanimal methods can replace the use of live animals in research and testing. Thus companies can test the safety and efficacy of their products using methods that do not cause pain and distress to animals.

Manipulation of tissue culture and cell physiology makes in vitro testing possible. Cell cultures can be nurtured and allowed to develop in a glass dish. By adding or subtracting nutrients and other media, the cell cultures can be altered. These changes are carefully observed, recorded, and documented. Propagation and transformation of cell cultures can be assessed so that a substance added to the glass dish can be identified as a growth factor, a mutagen, or a poison. Moreover, this type of testing can be performed in a controlled environment under pristine conditions. As long as aseptic technique is practiced, the effect of a substance on a group of cells can be carefully monitored. Hence, in vitro testing will continue to be popular among the scientific community.

—Anthony J. Ippolito

See also In Vivo Testing

FURTHER READING

Chow, S.-C., & Liu, J.-P. (1998). *Design and analysis of clinical trials: Concepts and methodologies.* New York: Wiley.
www.iivs.org

IN VIVO TESTING

Simply stated, in vivo testing is the testing of an investigational drug or device in a living system. This is in contrast to in vitro testing, in which the testing is carried out in a "test tube" (nonliving) system. One way to learn how a drug or device may affect people is to understand their effects in appropriate animal models. In vivo testing systems may include specific genetic animal models. These specific models may be used to evaluate neoplastic (cancer), neurologic, cardiovascular, immune, metabolic, infectious, and endocrine diseases.

Unlike in vitro analysis, in vivo testing requires that the drug or device be able to overcome barriers between the initial location (perhaps an intravenous injection) and the target. These barriers may include vascular endothelium, basement membranes, cell membranes, and intracellular organelle membranes. Pharmacokinetic effects may also have an important role in an in vivo system. The absorption, distribution, metabolism, and excretion of a drug can dramatically affect how it interacts with the target organ or receptor–effector system. In vivo testing can help establish the most effective routes of administration as well as side effects and toxicities that cannot be directly evaluated in vitro. In vivo testing is regulated by the U.S. Food and Drug Administration (FDA), and approval for research in animals must be sought. An institutional review board (IRB) must approve the study, and good clinical practices (GCPs) in accord with the FDA and the International Conference on Harmonization (ICH) must be followed.

—Anthony J. Ippolito

See also Food and Drug Administration (FDA), Good Clinical Practices (GCPs), Institutional Review Board (IRB), In Vitro Testing

IRREGULAR DEMAND

See Services

J

JOB ANALYSIS

Job analysis is the process of collecting information about jobs, including the observable activities performed; the tools and equipment necessary for the job; the context of the surrounding work environment; and the knowledge, skills, and abilities (KSAs) required to perform the job. From this process, organizations can produce two key written documents. The first, a job description, details the tasks performed by a jobholder. The second document is a job specification, which lists the KSAs deemed necessary for the job. Job analysis is a critical prerequisite to almost all personnel and organizational management processes. For example, to select the appropriate candidate for a particular open position, the organization must first determine what the job will require. In this instance, job analysis is a legal necessity, as the KSAs deemed necessary to perform the job successfully must be established as relevant to the job. Moreover, in the case of performance appraisal, employees should be evaluated on their completion of activities that are actually related to successful performance of their jobs.

The manner in which a job analysis may be conducted varies greatly. Some approaches are more job oriented; that is, they focus on the nature of the tasks performed. A task analysis inventory is an example of such a technique, as it breaks down jobs into the tasks that compose them. Other methods are worker oriented, in that they focus on the human talent required to perform the job; these processes generally place an emphasis on the necessary KSAs. A common example of this approach is the position analysis questionnaire, or PAQ. Organizations should consider using instruments from both types of approaches, enabling the formation of linkages from the tasks performed to the KSAs. For example, one of the tasks performed by a nurse supervisor may be to disseminate information regarding patients and procedures to other nurses. In this instance,

oral communication ability will be critical to performing the job successfully.

Job analysis methods also differ in the manner in which information is obtained. Information about the job in question can be gathered from multiple sources, usually referred to as subject matter experts (SMEs). These sources include job incumbents, their supervisors, and trained job analysts. Although incumbents have the most knowledge of their jobs, they may tend to embellish the critical nature of their tasks. Therefore, supervisors and analysts are often used to provide a more objective picture. The SMEs may be interviewed about the nature of their work, or incumbents may be observed performing their job duties. In addition, SMEs may complete questionnaires or inventories pertaining to their job activities; these instruments often require SMEs to indicate the relevance of various tasks to their jobs. All techniques have advantages and disadvantages, and not all are appropriate for all jobs. For example, although direct observation allows for a detailed picture of the work performed, the practice can often be obtrusive to current employees. Organizations should consider these matters of practicality, and should use multiple techniques to combat the disadvantages of each.

—Elizabeth M. Smith

See also Employee Selection and Hiring, Employment Law, Job Design

FURTHER READING

Brannick, M. T., & Levine, E. L. (2002). *Job analysis: Methods, research, and applications for human resource management in the new millennium*. Thousand Oaks, CA: Sage.

Harvey, R. J. (1991). Job analysis. In M. D. Dunnette & L. M. Hough (Eds.), *Handbook of industrial and organizational psychology* (Vol. 2, pp. 71–163). Palo Alto, CA: Consulting Psychologists Press.

Landy, F. J., & Vasey, J. (1991). Job analysis: The composition of SME samples. *Personnel Psychology, 44,* 27–50.

McCormick, E. J. (1976). Job and task analysis. In M. D. Dunnette & L. M. Hough (Eds.), *Handbook of industrial and organizational psychology* (Vol. 1, pp. 651–696). Chicago: Rand McNally.

JOB DESIGN

Job design pertains to the allocation and arrangement of organizational work activities and tasks into individual jobs. The process seeks to specify three aspects: the number and variety of tasks to be performed; the discretion or independence with which an employee may perform the job; and the relationships that will need to be maintained to perform the job successfully. For example, in the health care industry, anesthesiologists may enjoy a great deal of discretion over job activities, yet the range of tasks they perform may be fewer than those performed by other physicians. In contrast, although nurses may perform a wide range of job duties, their input into how their jobs are structured or performed may be limited. At its core, job design attempts to increase employee motivation, the belief being that employees will be more likely to work efficiently and effectively if their jobs are structured in a way that facilitates those goals. However, in designing jobs for their organizations, employers should bear in mind that the needs of both the employee and the organization should be taken into account. What might work for one organization will not necessarily be beneficial in another; similarly, one employee might respond better to a certain job structure than might another. Keeping these considerations in mind, organizations may want to explore various types of job design strategies.

One common strategy is job enlargement, which increases the number and variety of tasks performed by employees. Another strategy is that of job enrichment, involving the increase in control over the planning and performance of a job. For example, employers may allow individuals to schedule some part of their work or to be personally accountable for work outcomes.

Furthermore, another popular approach is based on the job characteristics model, which essentially integrates the job enlargement and job enrichment strategies. This model describes five core dimensions of all jobs. Skill variety entails the number of tasks or activities that the job requires. The term *task identity* refers to the degree to which a job requires completion of an entire piece of work (doing a job from beginning to end). Task significance measures the impact the job has on other people, either from within the organization or outside of it. The term *autonomy* refers to the discretion that employees maintain in determining job procedures. Finally, task feedback entails whether the work performed results in clear information regarding the employees' effectiveness. These dimensions were originally thought to affect three psychological states of employees: experienced meaningfulness of work, experienced responsibility for work outcomes, and knowledge of results. These psychological states were then theorized to lead to desired work outcomes, such as increased worker motivation, performance, and job satisfaction, and lower absenteeism and turnover. Although research has generally not supported the role of psychological states as originally hypothesized, studies have supported the correlation between an increase in the core job dimensions and higher job satisfaction, employee performance, and attendance.

Finally, alternative job design strategies have been growing in popularity. Three of the most common such strategies are flextime, job sharing, and telecommuting. The term *flextime* refers to the notion of flexible working hours. This arrangement allows employees to determine when they will start and finish their workday, contingent on having worked a certain required number of hours. With job sharing, two or more employees share the same job. Last, telecommuting allows employees to work from home or other places outside the office. Advances in technology continue to make this option ever more feasible.

Again, it should be emphasized that the process of job design does not take place in a vacuum; other areas of the organization will more than likely be affected. Thus, a great deal of planning and consideration must go into the process, especially if a current job is being redesigned. In such a case, the organization should first identify the need for a behavioral intervention. The change in question should be not only economically feasible at the time, but it should produce desired results among employees; it is inadvisable to attempt a major change if employees will not support such a move. The organization should then conduct a job analysis to identify the tasks and activities that comprise the jobs in question. In addition, these activities should be measured according to the core job dimensions described previously. For example, how much autonomy should employees enjoy over certain tasks? After specifying an appropriate intervention, the organization needs to evaluate the effectiveness of such a change. In so doing, it must specify the criteria on which the change will be evaluated; is an increase in efficiency more important, or is a reduction in turnover a more appropriate criterion? Last, the organization should bear in mind that such a change is long range in focus. Results will not be immediate, and may take months or even years to appear.

—Elizabeth M. Smith

See also Flextime, Job Analysis, Organizational Design and Discontinuous Change, Organizational Structure, Telecommuting, Work Design

FURTHER READING

Aldag, R. J., & Brief, A. P. (1979). *Task design and employee motivation.* Glenview, IL: Scott, Foresman.

Campion, M. A., & McClelland, C. L. (1993). Follow-up and extension of the interdisciplinary costs and benefits of enlarged jobs. *Journal of Applied Psychology, 78,* 339–351.

Fried, Y., & Ferris, G. R. (1987). The validity of the job characteristics model: A review and meta-analysis. *Personnel Psychology, 40,* 287–322.

Hackman, J. R., & Lawler, E. E. (1971). Employee reactions to job characteristics. *Journal of Applied Psychology, 55,* 259–286.

Hackman, J. R., & Oldham, G. R. (1976). Motivation through the design of work: Test of a theory. *Organizational behavior and human performance, 16,* 250–279.

Parker, S. K., & Wall, T. D. (1998). *Job and work design: Organizing work to promote well-being and effectiveness.* Thousand Oaks, CA: Sage.

JOB EVALUATION

See Job Analysis

JOB SATISFACTION

Job satisfaction is an attitude, the attitude people have about their work. The term *job satisfaction* refers to the feelings people have about their jobs. These feelings exist among both nursing staff and physicians, the two groups of hospital employees most involved in the delivery of patient care. It has become an important concept in health care management for the past forty years. The assumed link between job satisfaction and job behavior led to the "happy worker" hypothesis—a happy worker was a productive worker. As a result, hospital management became interested in improving the job satisfaction of employees. However, forty years of accumulated research findings have indicated that the "happy worker" hypothesis was overly simplistic. While the relationship between job satisfaction, job performance, and productivity had been found to be generally positive and often statistically significant, the strength of this relationship has been shown to be modest. Satisfaction with some aspects of organizational policy such as fringe benefits are so far removed from one's job behaviors that it will not be related directly or strongly to performance.

Job satisfaction is a reflection of the perceived characteristics of a job in relation to the person's frame of reference (alternatives, expectations, experiences).

An individual's feeling of job satisfaction is influenced by his or her frame of reference; the latter in turn, is affected by all the situations and experiences the person has had and the possible alternatives available to the individual (best and worst jobs one can imagine).

One can consider the concept of job satisfaction in terms of time perspective (long term versus short term), absolute versus relative standards, and descriptive versus evaluative dimensions. A short-term perspective considers one's day-to-day experiences and reactions; a long-term perspective considers the job in the context of one's lifetime aspirations. The term *absolute evaluation* refers to an internal standard; relative evaluations are made in reference to an external standard in a given situation. Descriptive measures tap concrete, specific aspects of the job; evaluative measures address the issue of how "good," or satisfied the individual is, with a particular aspect of the work.

Unless a particular job is one that the employee has a reasonable chance of holding, it is unlikely that this person will use this job as a standard. A janitor in a hospital will not use the job of the director of nursing services, though he or she knows about it, as a basis for comparing and evaluating his or her present job.

In addition, employees can have different feelings corresponding to different aspects of their jobs (pay, supervision, and so on). Studies have shown there are many distinguishable areas of job satisfaction. These areas have been found to be more clearly differentiated by using descriptive instead of evaluative measures.

Job satisfaction has been found to comprise at least five factors. These factors are also likely to be positively correlated. Commonly found factors include the work itself, pay, promotions, supervision, and coworkers. Various aspects of job satisfaction should be considered separately. Different areas of satisfaction have been found to relate to different situational characteristics. A global measure, although perhaps adding additional information, does not simply substitute for specific job factors. In addition, the behavioral correlates of the various satisfaction factors are also likely to be different.

It is important to consider the effects of moderating variables in understanding the consequences of job satisfaction. For example, data from women and men should be considered separately until analyses have been undertaken showing similarity of findings. Women may have different mean levels on particular job satisfaction factors, different mean levels on situational characteristics, and different frames of reference.

Job satisfaction factors are also likely to relate to job behaviors in different ways depending on the context. Dissatisfaction can be expressed in a number of different ways depending on the situation (and possible alternatives): absenteeism, quitting, specific on-the-job behaviors.

It is critical that job satisfaction be considered in terms of the interrelationships of a number of variables. These include the objective characteristics of the job, individual abilities and experiences, alternatives available in the organization and larger community, and individual values—all of which influence both job satisfaction and performance and productivity.

There is evidence that levels of job satisfaction among both nursing staff and physicians have declined over the past decade. Both nurses and physicians believe they have been adversely affected by financial pressures resulting from reduced levels of support by governments in many countries as well as from health insurers. Declines in nursing staff and physician job satisfaction have been shown to be associated with declines in patient satisfactions as well. Patient care is fundamental to nurse and physician satisfaction. The ability to provide good patient care is important to their job satisfaction.

There has been during this time a change in the role of nursing staff and physicians. Both occupations have played many roles, as professionals, suppliers, and caregivers. Now the worker role has been added; more physicians are now holding jobs and working for organizations, resulting in a loss of autonomy and control.

Physicians typically report relatively high levels of job satisfaction, reflecting their incomes, the prestige of their occupations, and the autonomy many find in their jobs. Nursing staff generally report lower levels of job satisfaction than do physicians, again reflecting some of these same factors.

NURSING STAFF JOB SATISFACTION

Table 1 shows some antecedents and consequences of nursing staff job satisfaction that have been considered in the published literature (Blegen, 1993; Irvine & Evans, 1995). Antecedents have been organized into various categories: personal demographics, work situation characteristics, workplace factors, and professional experiences. Although each of the specific examples in these four categories has been found to influence levels of job satisfaction of nursing staff, workplace factors have shown the strongest and most consistent influences.

Job satisfaction of nursing staff has also been shown to have important individual, family, work, and professional consequences. Job satisfaction has been found to be related to nursing staff burnout, psychological distress, and physical health symptoms (Newman, Maylor, & Chansarkar, 2001). Not surprisingly, because 95% of nursing staff are women, job satisfaction has an influence on work–family issues, particularly the spillover of negative workplace emotions into family life. Job satisfaction of nursing staff is ultimately translated into workplace behaviors such as absenteeism and tardiness and patient care activities such as performing necessary tasks to ensure comfort and recovery. Finally,

Table 1   Nursing Staff Job Satisfaction

Antecedents	*Consequences*
Personal	*Work*
Age	Absenteeism
Family structure	Intent to quit
Education	Job future insecurity
Urban/Rural	Citizenship behaviors
	Job involvement
Situational	
Nursing unit	*Family*
Work status	Work-family conflict
Shift length	Family-work conflict
Patient-to-nurse ratio	Family satisfaction
Work environment	*Individual*
Supervision	Psychological well-being
Pay and benefits	Lifestyle behaviors
Job design	Physical health
Organizational structure	Burnout
Training and development	
Demands/stressors	*Unit/hospital*
Paperwork	Coordination
	Errors/injuries
Profession	Quality of patient care
Care	
	Profession
	Attraction
	Motivation
	Retention
	Militancy

nursing staff job satisfaction has an influence on the vitality of the nursing profession as a whole.

Considerable concern is being expressed about a potential crisis in the nursing profession. Fewer young women and men are entering the profession. There is currently a shortage of nurses. Those nurses still working in the profession are aging. More nurses are leaving the profession for a variety of reasons.

Aiken et al. (2001) report data collected from 43,000 nurses at more than 700 hospitals in the United States, Canada, England, Scotland, and Germany in 1998–1999. Although these five countries represent distinctly different health care systems, high nurse job dissatisfaction and uneven quality of hospital care was evident in each. The percentages of nursing staff dissatisfied with their present jobs were 41% (United States), 38% (Scotland) 36% (England), 33% (Canada), and 17% (Germany). The percentages of nurses planning to leave their present jobs in the next year were 39% (England), 30% (Scotland), 23% (United States), and 17% (in both Germany and Canada). These percentages were at least 10 points higher in each country among nurses under 30 years of age. In each country

Table 2   Physician Job Satisfaction

Antecedents	Consequences
Personal	*Work*
Age	Intent to quit
Family structure	Decrease work hours
Sex	Change specialty
Urban/rural	Leave direct patient care
Situational	*Family*
Type of practice	Work-family conflict
Hours worked	Family-work conflict
Income	Family satisfaction
Medical specialty	
	Individual
Work environment	Psychological well-being
Practice structure	Lifestyle behaviors
Supervision	Physical health
Bureaucratic hassles	Burnout
Demands/stressors	
Continuing education	*Organization*
Paperwork	Errors, malpractice
	Quality of patient care
Profession	
Professional values	*Profession*
Autonomy	Attraction
	Motivation
	Retention
	Militancy

nurses had concerns about staffing levels, support services, workforce management, opportunities for advancement, salaries, workload increases, and low-quality patient care.

There are, however, examples of hospitals that are associated with high levels of both nursing staff job satisfaction and patient care (Aiken, Smith, & Lake, 1994). These "magnet" hospitals were characterized by flat organizational structures within the nursing departments, nurse autonomy to make clinical decisions, nurse control of the practice environment, organization of nursing jobs to promote accountability and continuity of care, and an established culture signifying nursing's importance in the overall hospital mission (Coile, 2001).

PHYSICIAN JOB SATISFACTION

Table 2 lists some antecedents and consequences of physician job satisfaction examined in the literature. Although the broad categories are identical to those shown for nursing staff in Table 1, some of the specific items within each category reflect unique aspects of physicians' jobs. Once again, workplace factors emerge as the strongest

and most consistent predictors of physician job satisfaction (see Williams et al., 2002). In addition, physician job satisfaction has been associated with the same categories of consequences.

Williams et al. (2002) studied the impact that physician, practice, and patient characteristics had on physician stress, satisfaction, and mental and physical health ($N = 1411$ primary care physicians). Practice characteristics, and to a lesser extent physician characteristics, influenced job satisfaction, whereas only practice characteristics influenced job stress. Patient characteristics had little influence. Job stress had strong association with job satisfaction and with physical and mental health.

There is some evidence that physician job satisfaction has declined over the past decade. Burdi and Baker (1999) compared levels of satisfaction and autonomy among California physicians using data from a 1991 survey of physicians and a 1996 survey of California physicians. The surveys measured physicians' perceived freedom to undertake eight common activities that may be threatened by marketplace changes, satisfaction with current practice, and inclination to attend medical school again. Young physicians in 1996 were significantly less likely to report that they were able to spend enough time on the eight identified patient care activities. They were also significantly less satisfied with their current practice and less likely to say they would go to medical school again. Satisfaction also declined for older physicians between 1991 and 1996.

Changes in the health care marketplace have reduced physician outcomes (central reviews, organizational rules, treatment protocols): (a) competition and financial pressures from health insurers and physician-run health plans; (b) use of financial incentives that pit patients' interests against physicians' financial interests; (c) less freedom to make independent decisions about the care of patients, lower quality of patient care; (d) declining autonomy in a profession that has historically enjoyed a high degree of it may have reduced satisfaction; (e) the increased hassle and anxiety of a competitive marketplace, more difficult dealings with managed care plans, and declining incomes of some physicians. Physicians are caught in the bind between the need to lower health care costs and providing a higher quality of patient care. Declines in physician satisfaction have been shown to be associated with declines in patient satisfaction.

—Ronald J. Burke

NOTE

Preparation of this contribution was supported in part by the School of Business of York University and by the Social Sciences and Humanities Research Council of Canada. Louise Coutu prepared the manuscript. Joe Krasman assisted in collecting relevant literature.

FURTHER READING

Aiken, L. H., Clarke, S. P., Sloane, D. M., Sochalski, J. A., Busse, R., Clarke, H., Giovanneti, P., Hunt, J., Rafferty, A. M., & Shamian, J. (2001). Nurses' reports on hospital care in five countries. *Health Affairs, 20,* 43–53.

Aiken, L. H., Smith, H. L., & Lake, E. T. (1994). Lower Medicare mortality among a set of hospitals known for good nursing care. *Medical Care, 32,* 771–787.

Blegen, M. A. (1993). Nurses' job satisfaction: A meta-analysis of related variables. *Nursing Research, 42,* 36–41.

Burdi, M. D., & Baker, L. C. (1999). Physicians perceptions of autonomy and satisfaction in California. *Health Affairs, 18,* 134–145.

Coile, R. C. (2001). Magnet hospitals use culture, not wages to solve nursing shortage. *Future Trends, 46,* 224–227.

Irvine, D. M., & Evans, M. G. (1995). Job satisfaction and turnover among nurses: Integrating research findings across studies. *Nursing Research, 44,* 246–253.

Newman, K., Maylor, V., & Chansarkar, B. (2001). The nurse retention, quality of care and patient satisfaction chain. *International Journal of Healthcare Quality Assurance, 14,* 57–68.

Williams, E. S., Konrad, T. R., Linzer, M., McMurray, J., Pathman, D. E., Gerrity, M., Schwartz, M. D., Scheckler, W. E., & Douglas, J. (2002). Physician practice and patient characteristics related to primary care physician physical and mental health: Results from the physician worklife study. *HSR: Health Services Research, 37,* 121–143.

JOINT COMMISSION ON ACCREDITATION OF HEALTHCARE ORGANIZATIONS (JCAHO)

The Joint Commission on Accreditation of Healthcare Organizations (JCAHO) started as the Joint Commission on Accreditation of Hospitals (JCAH) in 1952, an outgrowth of the American College of Surgeons' accreditation program. The underlying concept of JCAHO began in 1910 when Dr. Ernest Codman proposed a system of evaluation for hospitals that entailed tracking a patient long enough after a hospitalization to determine if the treatment rendered was successful. When the American College of Surgeons was formed in 1913, Dr. Codman's idea became one of the core tenets of the organization's charter. The ACS established accreditation standards for hospitals in 1917 and continued to accredit hospitals until 1952, when the accreditation process was transferred to the Joint Commission of Hospitals. As the organization's mission evolved to one of quality improvement for all health care enterprises, JCAH became JCAHO.

JCAHO's mission is "to continuously improve the safety and quality of care provided to the public through the

Table 1   Types of Health Care Organizations Accredited by JCAHO in 2002

Hospitals—general, psychiatric, children's, rehabilitation	Integrated delivery networks
Health maintenance organizations	Preferred provider
Managed behavioral health organizations	Home care organizations
Home infusion and pharmacy services	Durable medical equipment services
Hospice services	Nursing homes
Long-term care facilities	Long-term care pharmacies
Assisted living facilities	Behavioral health organizations
Ambulatory facilities	Outpatient surgery facilites
Rehabilitation centers	Infusion centers
Group practices	Clinical laboratories

provision of health care accreditation and related services that support performance improvement in health care organizations" (www.jcaho.org/about+us/index.htm). Hospitals must be JCAHO accredited to receive Medicare and Medicaid funds, so the organization has great importance in the health care delivery system.

In the last two decades of the 20th century, JCAHO expanded its scope of influence to include all the health care organizations in Table 1.

JCAHO is governed by a 28-member board of commissioners that includes nurses, physicians, consumers, medical directors, administrators, providers, employers, labor representatives, health plan leaders, quality experts, ethicists, health insurance administrators, and educators. Corporate members include the American College of Physicians, the American Society of Internal Medicine, the American College of Surgeons, the American Dental Association, the American Hospital Association, and the American Medical Association.

JCAHO has over 1000 surveyors who have experience in each type of organization reviewed, and has offices in Oakbrook Terrace, Illinois, and Washington, D.C. The surveyors review approximately 17,000 health care organizations in the United States, and the JCAHO is expanding operations to several countries overseas. To receive and retain accreditation, an organization must go through an on-site survey by a JCAHO survey team at least every three years. Laboratories must be surveyed every two years. The survey involves a thorough inspection of the facility, not only for adequacy of the facilities but also for the quality of organizational processes and attention to patient safety. The reviewers use a systematic scoring system, and the scores and critiques are provided to the institution for improvement (www.jcaho.org/ebcu/unions/standards.htm). If a health care organization is found to have specific types of problems in the facilities or organizational process, it may be resurveyed in less than three years. So-called Type 1 recommendations require follow-up and correction in one to six months following the survey for the organization to avoid losing accreditation.

One of JCAHO's initiatives involves improving patient safety. A seminal work by the Institute of Medicine in 1999, *To Err Is Human* (National Academy Press), indicated that patient safety in U.S. health care organizations was far below the level expected by society and payers. JCAHO set goals to reduce errors in hospitals and other health care institutions through programs to anticipate and prevent errors, rather than react to issues after patients have been harmed. In addition, JCAHO requires health care institutions to track and improve certain performance measures as part of the accreditation process.

—Donald E. Lighter

FURTHER READING

Barnard, C., & Eisenberg, J. (2000). *Performance improvement: Winning strategies for quality and JCAHO compliance.* Kansas City: Opus Communications.

Chamberlain, K., & Hamner, C. (2002). *The JCAHO mock survey made simple.* Kansas City: Opus Communications.

Lighter, D., & Fair, D. (2000). *Principles and methods of quality improvement in health care.* Gaithersburg, MD: Aspen.

www.jcaho.org

JUDGMENT

A decision by a court or competent tribunal on the facts presented to it and/or the law in question is known as a *judgment*. A judgment is arrived at after a full hearing in a particular case, and is crafted by the court or tribunal based on the facts and/or law and the circumstances at issue. To decide a particular case, the judgment applies common law or statutory law to the facts. Judgments can be either interlocutory or final. An interlocutory judgment is one made by a judge with the court's specific intention that there be time for appeal to a higher appellate court before final judgment is made. A final judgment is the final rendered decision after all parties have presented their cases before the court.

Each judgment determines the rights and duties of the parties to a lawsuit. A judgment may include an injunction, which is an order that directs a party to specifically do something, as compared with simply deciding a monetary penalty or ownership rights.

A judgment is only effective if it is made after the completion of legally mandated proceedings (after due deliberation and inquiry). Therefore, in the event a court did not

have jurisdiction in a case or failed to hear all the facts in a case, its judgment could be nullified as inappropriate and/or premature.

Judgments apply only to the litigants (the parties) in the case and do not extend to others. Laws affecting nonparties are generally relegated exclusively to legislatures, and not to courts.

There are two basic types of judgments in civil (noncriminal) cases:

1. When the facts are admitted by the parties and only the law is in dispute, the resulting decision is a judgment on demurrer.

2. When the law is admitted and only the facts are disputed, the resulting decision is a judgment on a verdict.

A summary judgment is a specific form of judgment where the defendant (the party being sued or prosecuted) asks the court to decide in its favor because the plaintiff (the moving party or accuser) has not presented enough facts or law on which the lawsuit or prosecution could be decided. A motion for summary judgment is generally made immediately after a court has received all initial papers on a case and is decided prior to a trial. If the defendant wins its summary judgment motion, then he or she wins the case and the lawsuit or prosecution is ended.

—Kenneth Steiner and Stuart Hochron

JUST IN TIME AND HEALTH CARE MANAGEMENT

Just In Time (JIT) is a term popularized by the manufacturing industry in the 1980s. In a manufacturing context, it refers to the practice of an upstream process delivering materials required by a downstream process just when the latter process requires it. If every process in the manufacturing supply chain manufactures and delivers products just in time, then the entire supply chain can operate with fewer inventories. JIT calls for frequent and uninterrupted deliveries of material in small batch sizes and requires careful coordination among the various participating organizations in the supply chain.

Lower inventories are associated with a variety of benefits, a primary one being quicker response times. Simply put, a manufacturing process that has very little raw material to process will be able to respond to a new order from a customer much more quickly than would a process that has a lot of raw material piled up in front of it. Lower inventories also reduce costs through potential shrinkage, obsolescence, and spoilage.

These benefits have not gone unnoticed by the increasingly competitive medical industry. However, the idea of minimal inventories, smaller and uninterrupted deliveries, and the reliance on computer-driven order systems has brought about considerable debate regarding its application in health care management. The misgivings stem from the potential damages incurred if any aberration within the system results in a shortage or stock-out.

Despite these misgivings, many medical organizations are attempting to install JIT systems. As a consequence of successful JIT implementation, a number of hospitals have reported cutting more than half a million dollars in inventory carrying costs without compromising health care.

—M.M. Srivanasan

KEFAUVER-HARRIS AMENDMENTS

The impetus for the 1962 Kefauver-Harris Amendments to the Food, Drug, and Cosmetic Act was thalidomide-induced birth defects that affected more than 300 infants born between 1960 and 1961 in the United States. The thalidomide tragedy had its origins in western Europe, where it was introduced as a new sleeping pill. The drug was found to have been the cause of birth defects in thousands of babies there. Public support for stronger drug regulation was the result of media coverage of the steadfast stance taken by then FDA medical officer Dr. Frances Kelsey to keep this drug off the U.S. market.

In the past, FDA regulations often were the result of a tragedy, a reactive rather than a proactive response. These amendments mandate that drug manufacturers adhere to new requirements regarding test products' purity, safety, and effectiveness. Product efficacy must be established. These determinations of purity, safety, and effectiveness must be established before marketing.

Sponsors are now also required to submit results of two well-controlled double-blind trials as part of a new drug application (NDA) or 510k submission. These amendments require sponsors to obtain informed consent from research subjects. Sponsors must accurately and ethically advertise and recruit study subjects to comply with these amendments.

—Linda M. Cimino

See also Clinical Trials, Food and Drug Administration (FDA), Informed Consent, New Drug Application (NDA)

FURTHER READING

Chow, S.-C., & Liu, J.-P. (1998). *Design and analysis of clinical trials: Concepts and methodologies.* New York: Wiley.

Glossary: Clinical research terminology. (2001, December). *Applied Clinical Trials,* 36–48.

Kolman, J., Meng, P., & Scott, G. (1998). *Good clinical practice* (pp. 2–3). Chichester, UK: Wiley.

Wittemore, R., & Grey, M. (2002, Second Quarter). The systematic development of nursing interventions. *Journal of Nursing Scholarship,* 115–120.

KEY PERFORMANCE AREAS

See Critical Success Factors

KICKBACKS

The federal antikickback law (the Fraud and Abuse Statute) prohibits anyone (entities or individuals) from soliciting or receiving, offering, or paying any remuneration to induce business for which payment may be made under a federal health care program. Remuneration may be a bribe, rebate, kickback, or any other form of inducement or reward for referrals, purchases, leases, or arrangement for goods, facilities, or services. The antikickback law is a double-pronged statute that targets both parties to the illegal agreement. In addition to the federal law, most states have antikickback statutes as well, and these laws are often more restrictive than the federal law.

The antikickback law is one of many fraud and abuse laws passed to protect the integrity and financial viability of the U.S. health care system. A free market system endorses the philosophy that unfettered competition ensures the lowest prices and the highest quality. When health care decisions are based on financial incentives, these incentives can affect utilization, competition, and patient choice. Where referrals are governed by financial incentives, the medical marketplace suffers, because new competitors can no longer win business with superior quality, service, or price. Therefore, health care laws prohibit kickbacks, payments, or favors given to induce referrals.

The antikickback law makes it a crime to knowingly or willfully offer or solicit, pay or receive anything of value to induce referrals. Courts have struggled in trying to define the level of knowledge required to satisfy the statute. Generally, one who acts voluntarily and intentionally will be deemed to satisfy the "knowing" requirement for the statute. In addition, when employees of an entity engage in prohibited referrals, the entity also can be found criminally liable if the employees were acting within the scope of their employment and the acts were at least partially intended to benefit the employer. Given the collective knowledge of its employees, the entity is deemed to have acted "knowingly."

Violation of the kickback statute constitutes a felony. Penalties, which include a prison term of up to 5 years and/or a fine of up to $25,000, are assessed for each offense. Conviction also carries a mandatory exclusion from government health care programs. This means that any person or entity convicted under the statute cannot legally submit a claim for payment to government health care programs for services rendered. This exclusion extends not only to the excluded individual or entity but also to anyone doing business with that excluded provider. For instance, if an excluded provider admits a Medicare patient to the hospital, neither the hospital nor the provider will be allowed to seek Medicare reimbursement for the provision of services or supplies. This provision places a special burden on all health care entities to ensure that none of their referrals come from an excluded provider. The government maintains a list of providers that have been excluded from Medicare/Medicaid programs. In today's health care marketplace, exclusion is a virtual death knell for providers, because government-subsidized health care consumers comprise such a large part of the market.

One problem with the antikickback statute is that the broadly drafted prohibitions technically encompass many activities that are common practices in health care. Courts also have historically interpreted the antikickback statute broadly. For example, many courts have adopted the "one purpose" test in determining the legality of certain practices. Under this test, if one purpose of the business arrangement is to induce referrals the statute has been violated, regardless of other, legitimate purposes for the arrangement. For instance, if a hospital recruits physicians to its community and pays certain incentives to entice them to open or join practices in the community, is this an illegal kickback? Arguably, there would be legitimate reasons for bringing a new physician into the community, such as a shortage of physicians in that specialty. But at least one reason for offering the incentives would be the anticipation of future referrals. As a practical matter, it is fairly commonplace for hospitals to offer limited incentives to physicians to come to their community and join their medical staffs. Recruitment incentives are not generally deemed illegal kickbacks if structured properly. Certainly the incentives cannot be tied in any way to the volume of referrals or offered in exchange for a specific requirement that the physician refer to that hospital.

To clarify how certain business arrangements must be structured in order to be legal, the U.S. Department of Health and Human Services' Office of Inspector General (OIG), the federal agency in charge of oversight of the federal health care system, has created safe harbors for certain activities. Safe harbors describe certain financial arrangements that fall outside the reach of the antikickback statute. The safe harbors are narrowly drafted, and arrangements that satisfy all the elements of a particular safe harbor are protected. The OIG emphasizes that compliance with a safe harbor is voluntary and failure to satisfy all the requirements does not by definition constitute illegal conduct. Activities falling outside a safe harbor will be scrutinized on a case-by-case basis. Guidance from the OIG is also available through the request of an advisory opinion. A person who is a party to an existing or pending business arrangement can submit a description of the arrangement, and the OIG will render a written opinion as to the legality and risks of the arrangement. These opinions are binding only on the parties and specific facts described in the request, but they are instructive as to how the OIG analyzes the legality of various practices. Fraud Alerts and Advisory Bulletins are yet another means through which the OIG informs providers about practices that it views with suspicion. The Fraud Alerts and Advisory Bulletins serve as warnings, describing certain conduct or practices that the OIG views as suspect or impermissible.

Despite the OIG's various attempts to offer guidance about the risks or acceptability of financial and business arrangements, there is still considerable uncertainty as to what arrangements may violate one or more of the fraud and abuse statutes or constitute a prohibited referral. Because the consequences of violations are so severe, providers must take great care to understand the law and avoid prohibited practices. Vigorous enforcement of the fraud and abuse laws is seen as the best means of protecting government health care programs. Thus providers and their business practices will continue to be scrutinized to ensure that health care decisions are based on concerns for quality and patient care and not on financial incentives.

—Cheryl S. Massingale

FURTHER READING

Fraud and Abuse Statute. (1977). 42 U.S.C. § 1320a-7b(b).
http://oig.hhs.gov.fraud/exclusions.html
Polk County v. Peters. (1992). 800 F.Supp. 1451 (E.D. Tex.).
United States v. Greber. (1985). 760 F.2d 68 (3rd Cir.).

LABOR MARKETS

A labor market is the geographic area from which an employer recruits applicants qualified to fill a particular position. The size of the geographic area often changes depending on the nature of the skills needed for that position. For lower-level administrative or laborer positions, the labor market typically consists of the immediate surrounding area. However, for highly technical positions, positions that require specialized skills, or those that necessitate advanced education, a wider geographic area is often needed to obtain qualified applicants. Applicants are willing to relocate or commute for these types of positions, so the labor market can be regional, nationwide, or even international in some cases. Labor markets are often described as either "loose," meaning that several qualified applicants are available to fill the particular job, or "tight," meaning that few qualified applicants are available to fill the job.

Human resource professionals in organizations keep track of the number of qualified individuals available to fill positions for two key reasons. First, labor market data are used for strategic decision-making purposes. When the labor market is tight, organizations are competing for a small number of qualified applicants. Accordingly, they may choose to start the recruitment process for job openings sooner and offer appealing compensation and benefits packages to attract the best workers. In extreme situations, organizations may need to provide remedial training to newly hired workers if the labor market is so tight that no qualified applicants can be found. In contrast, when the labor market is loose, organizations typically have a broad array of applicants to choose from. As such, competition for these applicants is lessened and may lead to reductions in efforts to attract applicants.

The second reason why organizations monitor labor market data deals with legal compliance. In affirmative action plans, labor market data are used as a standard to determine if organizations employ appropriate proportions of workers from various race and gender categories. If the proportions of the race and gender of those employed do not closely match the proportions available in the relevant labor market, corrective action must be taken as specified in the affirmative action plan. Similar comparisons are made in adverse impact court cases and Equal Employment Opportunity Commission (EEOC) claims when determining if a company has discriminated against a certain protected class of workers. Discrepancies found when making these comparisons between the organization and the relevant labor market are often sufficient evidence for a case to move forward.

Labor market data are often available for each state and its regions through the state department of labor, and an extensive report based on national census data is generated and managed by the EEOC. Although these reports typically provide sound information on the number of workers available in a geographic area, it is much harder to determine the number of individuals who can be considered "qualified" to fill a particular position in a particular industry. For this reason, determining the state of the labor market for a particular job is often a subjective process.

—Jennifer R. D. Burgess

See also Adverse Selection, Affirmative Action in Employment, Equal Employment Opportunity Commission (EEOC), Title VII of the Civil Rights Act of 1964

FURTHER READING

Fisher, C. D., Schoenfeldt, L. F., & Shaw, J. B. (1999). *Human Resource Management* (4th ed.). Boston: Houghton Mifflin.
Hazelwood School District v. United States. (1977). 433 U.S. 299.
www.eeoc.gov

LABOR UNIONS

Labor unions are organizations of individual workers who by their collective action seek to negotiate with their employer(s). Negotiation topics include wages, hours, and working conditions. The object of labor unions is to enhance the workers' lot by means of collective action. Simply stated, labor union members recognize strength through numbers when dealing with their employer. By withholding or threatening to withhold the labor supply, labor unions seek to drive up the price of the labor factor of production.

Although there were labor unions prior to passage in 1935 of the National Labor Relations Act (NLRA, also known as the "Wagner Act"), this federal statute sets out a mechanism for peaceful union recognition of an employer's workforce through representation elections. The National Labor Relations Board (NLRB), also established by the NLRA, supervises the representation elections.

The NLRA also created a new type of "wrong" in the area of employer–employee relations: the "unfair labor practice" or "ULP," which could only be committed by an employer. In 1947 the Taft-Hartley Act amended the NLRA to include ULPs that could be committed by unions.

—Bruce D. Fisher

FURTHER READING

Fisher, B. D., & Phillips, M. J. (2004). *The legal, ethical, and regulatory environment of business* (8th ed., Chapter 17). Mason, OH: Thomson-South-Western.

LEADERLESS GROUP DISCUSSION

A leaderless group discussion is a situational exercise commonly used in assessment centers, one of the most widely used and heavily researched tools for managerial selection and development. A typical assessment center is composed of situational tests designed to elicit specific managerial behaviors. The exercises used are representative of situations that participants may actually encounter in a job. For example, in a leaderless group discussion candidates participate in a job-related discussion in which no spokesperson or leader has been named. They are presented with a scenario containing multiple problems that they must attempt to resolve in an allotted period of time, usually around one hour. For example, candidates for an executive-level position within a health care organization may be directed to recommend solutions to personnel or financial issues facing a fictional but similar organization. Participants are directed to discuss the presented issues and to arrive at recommendations on which they all agree by the end of the allotted time. Trained assessors observe participants in this exercise and evaluate demonstrated performance across a variety of skill dimensions determined to be relevant for the particular job in question. Dimensions commonly assessed in a leaderless group discussion include judgment, leadership, and teamwork orientation. Performance in this exercise is then typically considered with performance in other exercises (often including role-playing simulations and assorted written exercises) to arrive at final ratings of effectiveness. These ratings are then used to predict future managerial performance.

—Elizabeth M. Smith

FURTHER READING

Thornton, G. C. (1992). *Assessment centers in human resource management*. Reading, MA: Addison-Wesley.

LEADERSHIP

Leadership is the ability to convince people to follow a path they have never taken, to a place they have never been—and, on finding the journey successful, to do it over and over again.

The term *leadership* also describes the individual or group of individuals who lead, and although the word has two different but closely related meanings, both describe the ability to get results through the efforts of others.

To clarify what leadership is in more depth requires an understanding of the roles and responsibilities of a leader, and the characteristics of strong leaders and leadership. Perhaps of equal importance to the definition of leadership is understanding the consequences of strong leadership—or the the consequences of weak or no leadership. After all, leadership is about getting results through the efforts of others.

For any organization to be successful, the one ingredient that is not optional is strong leadership. Leadership starts with a single leader at the top—usually with a title like chairman, managing director, president, or CEO. If a weak leader holds this position, the leaders in other parts of the organization will become frustrated, demotivated, and often leave the organization. Without a strong leader at the top, the organization that has strong leaders in other positions will be pulled hither and yon as each pursues his or her own direction, taking along some part of the organization.

To start, what is the role of a leader, and hence of leadership, and what is the most important aspect of leadership? The answer is "To take people to places they would be afraid to go alone." To do that, a leader must understand the roles and responsibilities of leadership. The role of leadership is

- To create a clear understanding of the current reality, and a healthy dissatisfaction with the current situation
- To help develop a shared vision of a more desirable future situation or objective
- To create the belief that there is a viable path from the former to the latter
- To create an environment in which people are motivated to embark on the journey to achieve that future

The responsibilities of leadership are as follows:

- To help the organization remove or overcome obstacles on the journey
- To assure that the resources needed for the journey are available or can be obtained
- To provide encouragement, honest feedback (positive or negative), and continued support during the journey
- To take part in the journey

But is it true that "leaders are born, not made"? Is leadership something the leader has in his or her genetic makeup, or can leadership be taught or learned? The answer is that leadership cannot be taught per se, but leadership can be role-modeled and emulated.

Is there much "unrealized leadership" in most people? The amount varies, and the circumstances under which it emerges (if ever) depend on whether it is needed, the other potential leaders available to act as role models or to assume the leadership role and responsibilities, and the risks involved in assuming a leadership role.

To learn about this, it is appropriate to observe the characteristics exhibited by great leaders. Great leaders ultimately can achieve only limited results alone. They need one ingredient more than anything else—*great followers.* Those followers are all leaders in their own right, but they lead only a few people and sometimes they lead only one person—themselves.

Leadership is all about helping followers decide where they are going, why, and how they will get there. Then leadership keeps the group on course during the journey as unexpected obstacles and pitfalls are encountered. When leaders assume their roles properly and take their responsibilities seriously, followers almost always respond—and usually successfully.

Leadership has an inherent assumption in its definition: that some group wants to achieve its goals. To this end, leadership is an enabler through which the group can achieve more collectively than they could achieve individually.

If leadership is about enabling a group of "followers" to achieve goals, then what are the characteristics of great leaders—and thus the characteristics of great leadership?

Great leadership must have *integrity*—it is the foundation on which everything else is built. It is invisible, but people can feel it more than see it. Great leadership must have *vision* to see the possibilities in the future, and *optimism* to know they are there when they aren't quite visible.

To be a great leader, one must have the *spirit* to inspire others and be able to infect them with *enthusiasm* for the challenges and opportunities ahead. A great leader demands great preparation.

To be a great leader, one must have the *toughness* to stay the course and accept nothing less than *excellence,* even when the going is very tough. A great leader must have *persistence* to never give up, yet have a *sense of humor* to be able to laugh at the little upsets.

To be a great leader, one must have *heart and soul.* Heart to care and share with others, and soul to keep the faith and hope, with charity. A great leader must *love*—both life and people—and it must be evident. A great leader attracts other great people.

Last, but certainly not least, to be a great leader one must have *passion,* an *indomitable spirit,* a *will to win,* and the *confidence* in the team to emerge victorious. Above all, a great leader realizes that leaders don't win, the team of great followers does.

There is an almost tangible aura around great leadership. One can sense it. It emanates from somewhere deep within them, and makes people want to follow them. In that sense, Warren Bennis, who has studied and written extensively on leadership, says it very well: "Leadership is like beauty, it's hard to define, but you know it when you see it."

Not everyone can lead large groups of people, yet everyone is a leader in a very personal sense. Perhaps the real secret of great leadership is the feeling of purpose and self. Many of the greatest leaders were people of great character like Sam Walton. They were not pretentious or phony. Rather, they were genuine and sincere—and they were usually "servant leaders" seeking to enable their followers to achieve their goals.

There may be many other aspects of leadership worthy of mention, but these thoughts are the best way to begin. Great leaders don't just "talk the talk" of leadership—they "walk the talk," and indeed, they "live the talk," always remembering that the success of leadership is measured in the results achieved not by the leader, but by the followers. That is the true definition of leadership—the ability to see those who follow it, succeed.

—John L. Mariotti

FURTHER READING

Bennis, W. (1989). *On becoming a leader.* Cambridge, MA: Perseus.

Drucker, P. F. (1967). *The effective executive.* New York: Harper & Row.

Graham, P. (Ed.). (1995). *Mary Parker Follett: Prophet of management—A celebration of writings from the 1920s.* Boston: Harvard Business School Press.

Tichy, N. M., & Cohen, E. (2000). *The leadership engine: How winning companies build leaders at every level.* New York: Harper Business.

LEARNING ORGANIZATIONS

A learning organization is a conceptual model of an organization, which is characterized by a flat structure, openly communicative processes, an inquisitive, customer–focused culture, and collaborative relationships that are built on a shared vision that uses the curiosity, commitment, and cooperation of the participants (employees).

Chris Argyris and Donald Schon proposed the concept of learning organizations as part of their work on organizational learning in the late 1970s. They wrote about two forms of organizational learning: adaptive learning and generative learning.

Adaptive learning (sometimes called *single-loop learning* in earlier works by Chris Argyris) only occurs within a set of recognized and unrecognized constraints called the *learning boundaries.* Within these learning boundaries, organizational competitive progress may be made, but if competitors are developing their thinking and learning outside the boundaries, this progress will not be sufficient for market success.

Generative learning, in contrast, yields a more powerful type of solution. Argyris describes this as "double-loop thinking." In double-loop thinking, the organization is willing to question long-held assumptions about its mission, customers, competencies, and strategies. It is in questioning these assumptions that the true power of learning and unlearning can be realized.

Almost two decades later, learning organization theory gained attention on a much broader scale in the early 1990s as a result of Peter Senge's work described in his book *The Fifth Discipline.* Senge's premises built on Argyris and Schon's but went further: A learning organization is one that is willing to shift from viewpoints inherent in traditional, hierarchical organizations and to move toward a perspective in which all employees have the ability to challenge the prevailing thinking and provide new insights.

In *The Fifth Discipline,* Senge spent considerable attention on circular diagrams called *causal loops,* which map typical behaviors and organizational problems that he calls *system archetypes.*

Senge's work describes five elements of a learning organization:

- Mental models
- Personal mastery
- Systems thinking
- Shared visions
- Team learning

Through the use of left- and right-hand column exercises, Senge contends that organizations can identify what they really think (the left-hand column) and what they say (the right-hand column). Argyris has written extensively about the dilemma of organizations that confuse the behavior espoused (talk) with the behavior in use (actions). This exercise allows analysis and dialogue about the personal and organizational prejudices and misconceptions that impede progress.

Finally, Senge uses what he calls a *ladder of inference* to help discover why we behave the way we do. This approach helps avoid jumping to dangerous or misdirected conclusions:

I take ACTIONS based on my beliefs;

I adopt BELIEFS about the world;

I draw CONCLUSIONS;

I make ASSUMPTIONS based on the meanings added to my mental models;

I add MEANINGS (cultural and personal);

I select DATA from what I observe;

I OBSERVE data and experiences.

Source: Senge, 1990, p. 59

Some of the important tools for developing and succeeding with learning organizations are provided by Senge's "Fieldbook," which followed his original work and was based on challenges he met in trying to actually help organizations implement his ideas and discoveries.

If learning organizations are so potentially powerful, why are they not more prevalent? Despite the apparent power of learning organizations to achieve at unprecedented levels, they are still the exception, because their open, risk-tolerant cultures are in conflict with long-standing conservative corporate cultures. Most organizations are designed to resist learning, rather than facilitate it.

Learning is hard to do. It requires the real work of thought. It challenges the status quo and threatens the command and control mentality of traditional, hierarchical organizations and their leaders. Leaders have a key role to play in developing and sustaining learning organizations. But these types of organizations require very secure leaders, and in these turbulent times, many leaders are far from secure.

Some of the most important leadership tasks in learning organizations are as follows:

- To help create the shared vision, and to understand the purpose of the organization
- To maintain alignment, constancy, and focus
- To become a role model and a strong sponsor of the learning efforts
- To develop a strategy that best utilizes the power of a learning organization

An additional problem leaders face is that learning is difficult for well-educated professionals and executives. Smart people leap to solutions without considering previously unfamiliar options, and a learning organization frowns on such prescriptive thinking. Well-educated people are taught the "right" answers and the way to get to them, and breaking such entrenched habits of thought is very difficult.

The problem of unlearning is a serious obstacle to success in creating and capitalizing on learning organizations. In an era of increasing complexity and change, the need to learn, evolve, and adapt is as basic as the battle for survival in nature. Only the fittest survive, and only those who can learn, can remain the fittest. Making new learning and learning organizations the drivers for the new behaviors and actions is only successful if the old, outdated ways are unlearned and discarded!

What exactly do people in organizations have to "unlearn" in order to learn?

- People must unlearn their worldviews, because the old or current models are no longer working, due to changes in the environment.
- They must shed their conditioning—years of command and control—"hired hand" mentality.
- People must realize they no longer know what specific responses to make and actions to take to deal with these different demands or problems.
- People must unlearn old behaviors, limits, constraints, and work habits.
- They must toss out obsolete measure and reward systems, and the behaviors required to achieve them.
- People must think about a diverse set of problems that affect the entire organization, not just their own situation.
- They must discontinue leadership practices developed over years and ingrained in generations of management.

Under pressure there will be relapses, in which people and organizations revert to the old ways. The old ways worked in the past, but the problems and opportunities of the future are different from those of the past, so new, different solutions and approaches must be employed. The old must be unlearned to make way for the new—over and over again—to remain the fittest who will survive and succeed.

Some organizational characteristics are more conducive to unlearning, and thus prerequisite to becoming a learning organization:

- Openness to new experiences
- Good communications
- Cross-functional empathy and humility
- Internal and external borders permeable to new ideas
- Encouragement of responsible risk taking
- Ability to acknowledge and learn at least as much from failure as from success
- High trust levels
- Willingness to admit mistakes
- Pride and organizational memory (can both be pluses or minuses)

In summary, many kinds of learning are necessary for learning organizations to help their companies achieve and sustain a competitive advantage. Continuous learning is critical. Adaptive and generative thinking are both required. An enterprise that becomes a learning organization benefits from the vital knowledge and ideas of its people.

—John L. Mariotti

FURTHER READING

Argyris, C. (1990). *Overcoming organizational defenses.* Englewood Cliffs, NJ: Prentice Hall.

Argyris, C., & Schon, D. (1978). *Organizational learning: A theory-in-action perspective.* Reading, MA: Addison-Wesley.

Senge, P. M. (1990). *The fifth discipline.* New York: Doubleday-Currency.

LENGTH OF STAY (LOS)

Length of stay (LOS) is also known as the average length of stay (ALOS) or the arithmetic mean of length of stay (AMLOS). It is the average number of days patients stay in the hospital for a specific DRG (diagnosis-related group). The lower the number of days a patient stays in a hospital for a specific disease, such as pneumonia, the more efficient the hospital. To achieve this, it requires the hospital to have excellent coordination among several areas and departments, namely, preadmission screening, utilization management, discharge planning, case management, home care coordination, and social worker involvement. In many instances, CMS (Centers for Medicare and Medicaid Services) uses LOS to determine payment for cost outlier cases.

Geometric mean of length of stay (GMLOS) is another method that CMS uses to determine payment to the hospital.

It is a statistically adjusted value for all cases for a given DRG by subtracting the outliers. GMLOS is usually lower than AMLOS.

Utilization managers use LOS data for preadmission authorization, bed need assessment, concurrent review and discharge planning, and reimbursement review and adjustment. It is frequently used by managed care organizations, hospitals and HMOs to identify and select the hospitals with the best practices.

Some organizations, such as Milliman & Robertson, have also developed the length-of-stay efficiency index. It seeks to identify best-performance hospitals in managing inpatient length of stay for routine, uncomplicated cases. The objective of the LOS efficiency index is to measure the results of the hospitals that actually perform best and how close they are to achieving the goals.

—Jack S. L. Liao

FURTHER READING

Ingenix Publish Group. (2002). *DRG Expert: A comprehensive reference to the DRG classification system* (18th ed.). Salt Lake City, UT: Author.
www.milliman.com/health/tools_and_models

LETTER OF CREDIT

See Line of Credit

LIABILITIES

Liabilities represent an obligation to provide resources at some point in the future. These obligations can entail a wide variety of items, including amounts owed to suppliers, amounts due to employees for compensation earned, withholdings from employees' wages and salaries, various amounts owed to other third parties, debts from borrowings, deferred income taxes, and a number of complex financing arrangements. The Financial Accounting Standards Board (FASB) has defined liabilities as "probable future sacrifices of economic benefits arising from present obligations of a particular entity to transfer assets or provide services to other entities in the future as a result of past transactions or events." The FASB also commented that all liabilities appearing on the balance sheet should have three characteristics in common: (a) They should be present obligations that entail settlements by probable future transfers or uses of cash, goods, or services; (b) they should be unavoidable

obligations; and (c) the transaction or event obligating the enterprise must have already happened.

Current liabilities are obligations that must be satisfied within one year. They are expected to require the use of current resources or the creation of other current liabilities. Current liabilities can include a variety of items including accounts payable, short-term debts (due within one year from the balance sheet date), current maturities of long-term debts, dividends payable to stockholders, deferred revenues (services yet to be performed that are expected to require the use of current resources), and various accruals for items such as wages and salaries.

Liabilities can be specified by formal contract or by informal agreements, but they generally involve future cash outflows. Present value methods may be used to value certain liabilities on the balance sheet. In the case of current liabilities, however, the time period between present value and the time that the actual cash payment is due or the face value is normally immaterial; therefore, most current liabilities are recorded at their face value. Other long-term liabilities that do not bear interest may be discounted at an appropriate interest rate.

Long-term liabilities are obligations that will be due at some point beyond one year from the balance sheet date. These long-term obligations typically include notes payable, bonds payable, and capital lease obligations. Long-term liabilities are normally supported by written formal agreements. These formal agreements underlying such agreements typically specify the principal amount of the obligation, the periodic interest payments, the time over which the interest and principal are to be paid, collateral provisions, and, if applicable, covenants to protect the interests of the lender.

Long-term liabilities often arise from a company financing the purchase of real property and/or operating equipment for the business. When a company executes a formal agreement with a financing institution to borrow funds, in most instances the lender will provide an amortization schedule that will indicate the amount of principal and interest due for each period until the maturity date of the agreement. The amortization schedule enables the company to evaluate their ability to service the debt as it comes due. The portion of principal payment due in one year or less should be classified as a current liability on the company's balance sheet, as discussed earlier. The portion of principal that will be due over the remaining term of the agreement should be classified as long-term debt on the company's balance sheet. Certain types of bonded indebtedness may require a company to periodically set aside funds into a reserve or sinking fund account. These sinking funds will be used to service the debt as it comes due and are intended to provide the lender with a higher degree of confidence that the company will be able to meet the debt service requirements as they come due.

Also common in long-term financing agreements are debt covenants. Debt covenants may require a company to meet certain criteria during the term of the debt agreement. If a company fails meet one or more of the established debt covenants in a given year, the lender may reserve the right to call in the remaining balance of the liability immediately. At that point, the debt is considered current unless the lender waives its rights. As discussed, a company normally evaluates its ability to service debt over the term of the agreements and as they come due; however, that company may not have the ability to repay the remaining balance of a liability in full if called in by the lender. Therefore, it is extremely important for a company to understand all debt covenants before entering into a debt agreement. In addition, a company should consider all debt covenants in the planning and budgeting process on an ongoing basis.

The primary concern with liabilities is the identification of all liabilities and reporting them on the balance sheet. This can be particularly difficult with regard to contingent liabilities. Contingent liabilities are generally not recorded on the balance sheet unless certain criteria are met. For example, when a company is faced with litigation it may be difficult to determine whether the case will be resolved in the company's favor. However, if the company, perhaps with assistance from legal counsel, can determine that it is probable that the company will have to pay a cash settlement and that amount can be reasonably estimated, it may be necessary to record the corresponding liability. Financial Accounting Standard Number 5, *Accounting for Contingencies,* states, "An estimated loss from a loss contingency shall be accrued by a charge to income if both of the following conditions are met: (1) Information available prior to issuance of the financial statements indicates that it is probable that an asset had been impaired or a liability had been incurred at the date of the financial statements. It is implicit in this condition that it must be probable that one or more future events will occur confirming the fact of the loss. (2) The amount of loss can be reasonably estimated."

—Edward Pershing

LIABILITY IN MEDICAL MALPRACTICE

See Malpractice

LICENSING

Licensing is a contractual agreement between two parties, the licensor and the licensee. The process involves the licensor granting the rights to brand names and trademarks, manufacturing techniques, services, or other confidential knowledge to the licensee in exchange for an agreed-on royalty or fee payment. Licensing is used in U.S. and international retailing, the most common form being the franchise. Licensing is also one of several market entry strategies a company may choose from in entering a particular market, whether domestic or foreign.

Licensing offers a business, as a licensee, a way to quickly access technology that has been proven in the marketplace while reducing exposure to financial risks. However, the business as licensee still must have some strong, internal strengths (competencies) to draw on, and the licensing rights can be taken away by the licensor. The licensee also is dependent on the licensor for information, training, and ongoing support (Duncan, Ginter, & Swayne, pp. 238, 245).

In the field of health care management, an example of licensing is a computer software manufacturer granting a local hospital the right to use its health care-tailored software, such as customized patient billing and tracking, in return for a yearly fee. This is similar to a university contracting with SPSS (Statistical Package for the Social Sciences) to use its statistical software package on campus, in computer labs and faculty members' offices, for an annual fee. More information about licensing can be found at www.licensing.org, the Web site of the Licensing Industry Merchandisers' Association (LIMA).

—Jeffrey W. Totten

See also Franchising, Market Entry Strategies

FURTHER READING

Duncan, W. J., Ginter, P. M., & Swayne, L. E. (1995). Developing strategic alternatives. In W. J. Duncan, P. M. Ginter, & L. E. Swayne, *Strategic management of health care organizations* (2nd ed., Chapter 6). Cambridge, MA: Blackwell.

Lamb, C. W., Jr., Hair, J. F., Jr., & McDaniel, C. (2002). Developing a global vision. In C. W. Lamb, Jr., J. F. Hair, Jr., & C. McDaniel, *Marketing* (6th ed., Chapter 4). Cincinnati, OH: South-Western/Thompson Learning.

LIFESTYLE SEGMENTATION

See Segmentation

LIFETIME VALUE (LTV)

See Net Present Value (NPV)

LIMITED LIABILITY COMPANY (LLC)

A limited liability company (LLC) is a legal entity formed under state law with similar characteristics as a corporation. Businesses choosing the LLC option for their entity achieve the goals of limiting the liability of their owners, creating management by their owners, and reducing company taxes. The beneficial owners of interests in an LLC are called "members." Like shareholders in a corporation, LLC members share in the LLC's profit and loss. Members control the LLC with voting rights. Operations of an LLC are usually directed by "managers" who may or may not also be members. The LLC is created by filing articles of organization with the state's secretary of state. The document governing the relationship between the members and the entity and between the entity and the managers is called the *operating agreement*. The typical operating agreement contains provisions regarding management of the LLC, voting rights of members and managers, contributions and distributions, admission of members and assignment of membership rights, and dissolution.

—Theresa DiMartino

LIMITED LIABILITY PARTNERSHIP (LLP)

A limited liability partnership (LLP) is a general partnership that elects LLP status under state law. Most state LLP statutes limit formation of LLPs to certain professions (for example, California limits LLPs to accountants, attorneys, and architects; New York limits LLPs to the professions defined in New York's education law, including the practice of law, dentistry, medicine, accounting, and architecture, among others). The most significant benefit of LLP status in certain states (including New York) is liability protection for the partners. Unlike a general partnership, where the general partners are liable for the debts and obligations of other general partners, partners in an LLP in a state such as New York are given protection from all types of liability (with the exception of their own misconduct or negligence) merely by reason of the status of their partnership as an LLP. Many states do not offer such blanket liability protection, instead offering "partial shield" liability protection. In such states, choosing the LLC as the form of entity is most likely the wiser course.

—Theresa DiMartino

LINE OF CREDIT

By definition, a line of credit is a prearranged loan between an organization and a lender, from which an organization can borrow at will up to a maximum loan amount.[1] Terms of the line of credit vary from case to case but are often short in duration, with repayment of principal and interest accrued within a year. A line of credit is often used to shelter the organization from short-term drops in revenue or periodic spikes in operating expenses. Under such conditions, "drawing down" the line of credit allows an organization to continue normal operations by funding fixed and variable operating expenses despite a scarcity of available cash.

For instance, a hospital may have a short-term drop in revenue collections caused by change in insurance providers for a major employer within its patient service area. If the hospital is unable to reduce its costs in a timely manner, a shortfall in available cash may result. This situation may provide optimal use of a line of credit to fund normal operating costs until reimbursement for patient services returns to normal or changes in the organization can reduce operating expenses to a point that generates a positive cash flow. However, if the hospital borrows the maximum amount under the line of credit or revolving credit agreement, the lender may chose to deny the hospital an extension of credit under the prearranged agreement until the balance is paid. This scenario may force the hospital to search for alternate means to finance operations.

A line of credit is assigned to financial statements as a note payable and is thus considered a liability for the organization. Large organizations such as health systems and medical insurers may often need to utilize a line-of-credit hedge against sizable swings in cash flow. Large lines of credit are often called "revolving credit" or a "revolver." Under circumstances where a large "revolver" is outstanding, a syndication of financial institutions may fund a portion of each draw. Therefore, the risk of a large drawdown will be spread among a number of financial institutions, leaving no one institution at risk for the full amount.

As a rule of thumb, the interest rate on a revolver or line of credit is pegged to the prime rate, a specified Treasury bill rate, or other common interest rate indicators.[1] Under each arrangement, the interest rate is delineated as fixed, variable, or otherwise determined by the amount of borrowings. An important difference between a revolver and a line of credit is that the revolver is a legal obligation of the bank, whereas a line of credit is not. In addition, a line of credit may have a "cleanup clause" stating that the account must carry a zero balance for a cumulative term over the life of the agreement. This cleanup clause ensures that this financing vehicle will not become a permanent source of funds for the organization.[2]

Although a line of credit allows flexibility for an organization to manage cash flows, it may also leave an organization at risk. Variable interest rates often fluctuate in response to general economic conditions. If economic conditions deteriorate over a period for which an organization has drawn on its line of credit, then the interest rate may rise on the organization's outstanding balance. If the organization is experiencing financial difficulties during this time, and the organization has a great deal of outstanding debt, then a large increase in short-term interest rates could force a company into bankruptcy.

—Edward Pershing

REFERENCES

1. L. M. Fraser & A. Ormiston (2001), *Understanding financial statements* (6th ed.), (Upper Saddle River, NJ: Prentice Hall), p. 259.
2. E. F. Brigham, L. C. Gapenski, & M. C. Ehrhardt (1999), *Financial management: Theory and practice* (9th ed.). (Orlando, FL: Dryden Press), p. 847.

LIQUIDATION

See Retrenchment Strategies

LIQUIDITY RATIO

See Ratio Analysis

LIVING WILLS

Living wills are advanced health care directives that instruct attending health care professionals of an individual's wishes in the event the individual has a terminal condition from which there is no reasonable medical expectation of recovery and that, as a medical probability, will result in the individual's death regardless of the use or discontinuance of medical treatment implemented for the purpose of sustaining life or the life processes. When an individual is diagnosed as having such a medical condition and the individual is unable to communicate, a living will sets forth the individual's directions regarding death-delaying procedures and end-of-life care.

Living wills, unlike other advanced health care directives, operate only under very limited circumstances. They contain an individual's explicit instructions regarding procedures to be performed or withheld in the event the individual has a terminal condition and is facing certain death unless life-prolonging procedures are performed. Living wills instruct attending health care professionals to use or not to use life support, whether to continue or not to continue hydration and/or nutrition, and whether organ donation is desired. They may also set forth the individual's specific burial or cremation instructions after death.

Living wills typically do not give direction regarding any other health care procedures, treatments, or decisions. In states providing for living wills, state law usually defines the medical conditions in which the health care professional must consider and implement an individual's living will. These laws often set forth the actual provisions of living wills as well as the procedures and requirements for their execution and effectiveness, and strict compliance with such statutes is normally required.

If a health care professional is unwilling to comply with the living will of an individual, the health care professional is usually required to make a reasonable effort to transfer the patient to another health care professional who will follow the individual's instructions in the living will. Living wills can typically be revoked at any time by the maker of the living will until the individual is no longer able to communicate such revocation, and the revocation may either be made orally or in writing.

—Anne M. McKinney

See also Advanced Health Care Directives, Durable Powers of Attorney for Health Care (DPAHC)

FURTHER READING

Krohm, C., & Summers, S. (2002). *Advance health care directives: A handbook for professionals.* Chicago: ABA Publishing.
McKinney, A. M., & Berteau, J. T. (2002). *Estate planning in Tennessee* (2nd ed.). Knoxville, TN: Pro-Practice Press.

LOCAL PUBLIC HEALTH AGENCIES

Local public health agencies (LPHAs) are those agencies that deal with health issues of the individual cities, counties, districts, and tribes. Public health is dedicated to preventing disease, prolonging life, and promoting health through organized community efforts.

The major functions of LPHAs are threefold. First, they assess by monitoring the health of the communities and populations at risk to identify health problems and which are to be their priorities. Next, they develop public policies with community and government leaders to attempt to solve the local and national priorities. Last, they assure that all populations have access to appropriate and cost-effective care. This includes health promotion and disease prevention. They must also evaluate the effectiveness of care and adjust the care as needed.

Examples of the types of activities that LPHAs engage in are numerous. They perform immunizations and health screenings. Prevention programs aimed at the control of chronic diseases are one of the focuses of LPHAs. They monitor for contamination of air and water. They are at the forefront of efforts to educate the public on the dangers of smoking. LPHAs conduct programs that focus on healthy births and children. Disease prevention is another area where LPHAs focus their attentions, as in the outbreaks of West Nile virus.

The National Association of County and City Health Officials (NACCHO) is the national organization representing local public health agencies. It is a nonprofit membership organization serving all of the nearly 3000 local health departments. NACCHO provides education, information, research, and technical assistance as well as facilitates partnerships among local, state, and federal agencies in order to promote and strengthen public health.

—Doreen T. Day

FURTHER READING

www.naccho.org

LONGITUDINAL STUDY

Longitudinal studies follow the same subjects or a population over time. Because the same population is followed over time, changes collected from different observations can be attributed to individual changes rather than different samples of subjects.

Subjects in longitudinal studies are followed over various period of time, sometimes for decades. Such studies can relate incidence of cancer in a given population to certain population variables.

Groups of subjects are followed, one exposed to certain risk factors and the unexposed control. The groups are followed and the incidence rates are followed, thus attributing the disease to certain risk factors. Longitudinal research studies can evaluate biological and physiological processes associated with aging.

The problem with using longitudinal study design is that large numbers of patients must be followed for long periods of time to give statistically meaningful results. In addition, long-term commitment of funds and resources must

maintain the study. This can be an issue if the disease, such as cancer, has a long induction period from exposure from the hazard to the symptomatic disease.

An advantage of the longitudinal method is that historical controls can be used in order to follow populations that have been exposed to a certain risk factor and to accumulate data through intensive documentation of growth and change on the same individuals.

—Anthony Sileno

FURTHER READING

Portney, G. L., & Watkins, P. M. (2000). *Foundations of clinical research applications to practice.* Upper Saddle River, NJ: Prentice Hall Health.
www.bmj.com/epidem/epid.7.html
www.cls.ioe.ac.uk

LONG-RANGE PLANNING

Long-range planning focuses on forecasting the future. The objective of the forecast is to predict for some specified time in the future the size of demand for an organization's products and services and to determine where that demand will occur. Long-range planning developed in many organizations because operating budgets are difficult to prepare without some idea of future sales and the flow of funds. In addition, post–World War II economies were growing and demand for many products and services was accelerating. Long-range forecasts of demand allowed mangers to develop detailed marketing and distribution, facilities expansion, human resource, and financing growth plans for their organizations. Many hospitals have used long-range planning to determine facilities expansion. In the mid 1980s, as the health care industry became more volatile, long-range planning was replaced by strategic planning in most health care organizations.

Long-range planning is different from strategic planning in its underlying assumptions. Long-range planning assumes that the organization will continue to produce its present products and services; thus matching demand to production capacity is the critical issue. The assumption underlying strategic planning is that so much economic, social, political, technological, and competitive change is taking place that the organization must evaluate whether it should even be producing its present products and services, whether it should start producing different products and services, or whether it should be producing and marketing in a fundamentally different way.

—Peter M. Ginter

See also Strategic Management, Strategic Planning, Strategic Thinking

FURTHER READING

Ackoff, R. L. (1970). *The concept of corporate planning.* New York: Wiley.

Andrews, K. R. (1971). *The concept of corporate strategy.* Homewood, IL: Irwin.

LONG-TERM ASSETS

See Assets

LONG-TERM CARE

Long-term care is a set of services delivered over a sustained period of time to people who lack some degree of functional capacity. Put alternatively, long-term care is the help needed to cope, and sometimes to survive, when physical and cognitive disabilities impair the ability to perform activities of daily living, such as eating, bathing, and toileting. Unlike the provision of general health services that are targeted toward acute medical problems, long-term care must be continually provided and is, thus, continually expensive.

Long-term care services are needed by a diverse set of individuals who receive care from an equally wide array of providers. As the result of their diminishing abilities, older individuals—especially the very old—are the primary recipients of long-term care services, but younger individuals with physical or mental limitations also require services in some instances. The primary providers of long-term care services within the United States are "informal" providers such as family members and friends. Formal providers include nursing homes, board and care homes, home health care agencies, assisted living facilities, adult foster and day care homes, and continuing care retirement communities. Across these different formal providers, there are a number of different payer types, including out-of-pocket, public insurance, and private insurance. Because consumers are often thought to lack information regarding the quality of services provided, there is an immense amount of government regulation within the long-term care industry.

Important health care management issues arise in the provision and delivery of long-term care including the fragmented system of providers and payers, the reliance on human resources, the relationship with the acute health care system, recent organizational changes such as horizontal and vertical consolidation, the role of quality assurance and regulatory compliance, and the fact that many long-term care administrators lack management training.

WHO NEEDS LONG-TERM CARE?

The key to long-term care is functioning. Unlike acute health care where a number of highly technical medical services are typically provided to patients, the bulk of long-term care recipients do not necessarily receive medical care; rather, they receive assistance with daily tasks of living. Long-term care personnel have divided these tasks into (a) activities of daily living (ADLs) such as eating, toileting, dressing, bathing, and locomotion and (b) instrumental activities of daily living (IADLs) such as cooking, cleaning, doing laundry, handling household maintenance, transporting themselves, reading, writing, managing money, using equipment such as the telephone, and comprehending and following instructions. Clearly, the need for assistance with multiple ADLs might necessitate entry into some form of institutional care, whereas the need for assistance with one or two IADLs may potentially be addressed by a family member or friend.

Most elderly people are physically active, able to care for themselves, and not in need of long-term care. However, the prevalence of disability rises steeply with age. For example, only about 1 in 10 individuals aged 65 to 74 are disabled, but roughly 7 in 10 individuals aged 85 and older are disabled. In addition, not all disabled people are old. For example, individuals under age 65 with spinal cord injuries, advanced multiple sclerosis, traumatic brain injuries, developmental disabilities, and mental illnesses may all require some form of long-term care.

WHO PROVIDES LONG-TERM CARE?

Although most laypeople associate long-term care with nursing homes, the predominant provider of long-term care is the family. The predominant providers of care within the family have historically been spouses and adult children of elderly individuals, and parents of younger individuals in need of services. Although several recent societal trends have worked against informal provision of services (for example, the increased participation of women in the labor force and the geographic dispersion of families), this is still the dominant type of long-term care.

Elderly individuals almost universally prefer receiving care in their homes from family members. However, health, familial, and financial issues often precipitate the need for care from a formal provider. There is a broad continuum of services that constitute long-term care. Although nursing homes serve less than a quarter of the disabled elderly, they are certainly the most expensive long-term care option and the most thoroughly studied. In the United States, there are roughly 1.6 million residents living in nearly 17,000 nursing homes. About two thirds of all nursing homes are investor owned, about a quarter are not-for-profit, and the remaining are government-owned facilities. Roughly half of all nursing homes are members of a chain, and about 6% are hospital-based facilities. The average-sized facility has around 100 residents, and the overall occupancy rate is approximately 88%. Historically, occupancy rates have been much higher within this industry due to the presence of supply constraints such as certificate-of-need (CON) laws and construction moratorium laws that attempt to limit the growth in beds in an effort to hold down Medicaid expenditures. However, the recent growth in competing alternatives to nursing home care has likely drawn away some of the "healthier" nursing home residents to other care settings and lowered nursing home occupancy rates.

For individuals who can still live on their own, home care can range from periodic help with shopping and cleaning to full-time nursing help. There are also social support services, such as Meals on Wheels, adult foster care, and adult day care, which may enable individuals in need of long-term care to remain in the community. Assisted living facilities (also known as *board and care homes*) are residential settings that provide more supportive services than boardinghouses but less medical care than a nursing home. Assisted living may provide lodging, meals, protective oversight, activities, and some assistance with medications, personal care, and activities of daily living.

From a management perspective, one intriguing development within long-term care has been the blurring of the roles of provider and insurer with the growth of continuing care retirement communities (CCRCs). Under this model, residents pay a large initial fee on entry and rent an apartment for an additional monthly fee in a community setting designed specifically for elderly individuals. As health declines, the individual may make a transition from the independent living section of the CCRC to onsite assisted living and onsite nursing home care for additional charges.

WHO PAYS FOR LONG-TERM CARE?

Similar to acute health care services, long-term care is paid for by a number of sources. What is most striking about this sector, relative to the acute health sector, is the lack of private insurance coverage. Only about 1% of all long-term care expenditures are paid for by private insurance. Individuals who use long-term care pay for it out of their own (or their family's) income and assets, or they must qualify for public coverage. Thus, long-term care (along with prescription drugs) represents the largest source of catastrophic costs for the elderly. Although Medicare does cover some rehabilitative (or short-stay) nursing home care, the primary payers of long-term care services are the state Medicaid programs. Medicaid accounts for about half

of all expenditures on nursing home services, which amounted to about $44 billion dollars nationwide in 1998. Individuals must qualify for Medicaid by meeting income and asset criteria at the time of nursing home entry or by "spending down" during their stay.

Although home- and community-based services (HCBS) have been found to be associated with lower expenditures for individuals with certain care needs, most state Medicaid programs are more generous in covering nursing home services because there is a perceived moral hazard problem. That is, the very fact that an individual is insured tends to increase utilization of covered services. Because the elderly prefer HCBS to nursing home services, it is generally thought that the presence of HCBS will "crowd out" the existing provision of care by family members and friends. Thus, in recognition of this potential moral hazard, states are more likely to cover nursing home services relative to HCBS.

Note that currently no payment is available for informal care provision by family members and friends. Although such services are not reflected in the national health accounts, never trigger a payment from an insurer, do not inflate the federal deficit, and are rarely included in any calculation of the overall cost of long-term care, they nonetheless represent a genuine opportunity cost burden. For example, if an adult child is taking care of an elderly parent, this individual is forgoing other work and leisure opportunities. Recent proposed legislation has considered tax rebates and refunds to informal caregivers as a means of keeping individuals from requiring Medicaid coverage for long-term care services.

GOVERNMENT REGULATION OF LONG-TERM CARE

In the case of the nursing home industry, the government is not only a payer of long-term care services, but also a regulator of care in placing a number of restrictions on the industry. Although difficult to substantiate, industry officials often claim that the nursing home sector is the most heavily regulated industry in the U.S. economy after nuclear energy. The reason for the high degree of government intervention and oversight is often thought to relate to the inability of many nursing home consumers to effectively monitor quality. Dating back over three decades, there have been a number of reports and studies documenting low quality care within this industry. Although nursing home care is fairly nontechnical in nature, monitoring of care can often be difficult, and the quality learning period may be nontrivial relative to the length of stay in some instances. The nursing home resident is often neither the decision maker nor able to easily evaluate quality or communicate concerns to family members and staff. Furthermore, elderly individuals who seek nursing home care are disproportionately the ones with no informal family support to help them with the decision process. Finally, there are relatively few transfers from nursing home to nursing home. Movement among homes may be impeded by tight markets because of supply constraints such as certificate-of-need and construction moratorium laws and health concerns regarding relocation (termed "transfer trauma" or "transplantation shock"). Thus, consumers may not be able to "vote with their feet" by taking their business elsewhere.

To address this perceived lack of consumer information, the government has placed a number of restrictions on the industry. For example, the Nursing Home Reform Act (NHRA) of 1987 mandated that nursing facility care should be more consistent with expert recommendations for assuring quality care. These recommendations included reduction in the use of physical restraints, prevention of pressure ulcers, reduction of psychoactive medications, and some minimal staffing standards including the stipulation that a registered nurse must be on duty 24 hours a day and all nurses' aides must be certified.

The government is also an overseer of care via the survey and certification process. To accept Medicaid and Medicare recipients, a home must be annually certified via a Centers for Medicare and Medicaid Services (CMS) survey. Several alternative remedies may be imposed on facilities that receive a high number of deficiencies. These punishments include civil money penalties of up to $10,000 a day, denial of payment for new admissions, state monitoring, temporary outside management, and immediate termination. In addition to this survey process, certified homes must fill out minimum data set (MDS) assessments for every resident on a quarterly basis. Thus, the government generates an immense amount of quality information at a substantial cost. It was recently estimated that the survey and certification process costs the government nearly $400 million annually, which equates to about $22,000 per nursing home or $208 per nursing home bed. And this does not include the indirect costs to the facility of the certification process such as interacting with the regulatory agency, preparing for and hosting survey visits, gathering and providing data, and responding to complaint investigations. Experience from other sectors of the economy suggests that the indirect costs of the certification process to the nursing home are likely greater than the direct costs to the government.

MANAGEMENT ISSUES IN LONG-TERM CARE

A number of important management issues and challenges arise in the long-term care industry. First, the industry is marked by a constantly changing, fragmented system of health, housing and social services, and a wide array of financing and payment systems. Second, the nontechnical nature of long-term care entails that human resources are the primary input in the production of care. Nursing home directors must recruit and retain quality personnel in the face of shortages of nurses and high turnover of support staff, who often work in extremely stressful environments. Third, long-term care providers do not operate outside of the broader continuum of care. They must maintain relationships with hospitals and other providers as both a source of potential referrals and as a place to refer patients in need of acute health services. Fourth, there have been a number of organizational changes within the long-term care sector in recent years, including the growth of nursing home chains through mergers and acquisitions, vertical integration between various long-term care providers, the emergence of managed care as a payer of services, and the closure of many long-term care providers. Fifth, given the strong government involvement within this sector, providers must constantly interact with government officials to verify compliance with regulatory standards. Sixth, quality assurance and quality improvement activities are particularly important in this industry, given a long history of quality problems and the level of government oversight.

Given these unique health care management issues within the long-term care sector, it is somewhat ironic that there is a substantially smaller amount of management expertise in long-term care relative to the acute health care sector. Historically, long-term care administrators have often lacked management training and have taken on the role of primarily "putting out fires" rather than thinking about the strategic management of the firm. As the long-term care sector continues to grow in importance within the broader economy, there will be an increased role for the tools of health care management.

—David C. Grabowski

See also Home Health Care, Intermediate Care Facility (IFC), Medicaid, Medicare, Moral Hazard, Quality Management, Subacute Care

FURTHER READING

Evashwick, C. (Ed.). (2001). *The long-term continuum of care* (Vol. 2). Albany, NY: Delmar.

Grabowski, D. C. (2001). Medicaid reimbursement and the quality of nursing home care. *Journal of Health Economics, 20*(4), 549–569.

Infeld, D. L., & Kress, J. R. (1995). *Cases in long-term care management* (Vol. 2). Ann Arbor, MI: Health Administration Press.

Kane, R. A., & Kane, R. L. (1987). *Long-term care: Principles, programs, and policies.* New York: Springer.

Norton, E. C. (2000). Long-term care. In A. J. Cuyler & J. P. Newhouse (Eds.), *Handbook of health economics* (Vol. 1, pp. 955–994). Amsterdam: Elsevier Science.

Wiener, J. M., Illston, L. H., & Hanley, R. J. (1994). *Sharing the burden: Strategies for public and private long-term care insurance.* Washington, DC: Brookings Institution.

LONG-TERM DEBT

See Balance Sheet

LONG-TERM DEBT TO EQUITY

See Ratio Analysis

LONG-TERM INVESTMENTS

An investment is a resource with a value that is acquired or used for the purpose of increasing value. A long-term investment can take on many perspectives depending on the investment and the situation. Let's think of a long-term investment as a specific asset that may be held for an extended period of time.

A extended period of time for a human is maybe 80 to 90 years; a stock maybe 1 year; for a fourth-grade student it's a nine-month school year; for an insect it's maybe one day (a lifetime); for a surgeon, a few hours. A long term is relative to the time related to the purpose of increasing value for that asset.

An investment strategy determines what term is defined as a long-term choice. Choices include elements such as risk, flexibility of terms, timing, management preferences, control, environment, and so forth.

Four common elements that are reviewed to some degree for each business (including health care) investment consist of risk, flexibility, timing, and control. Risk in a financial sense includes cost of commitment, leverage of performance, interest rates, and competitive pressures. Flexibility is defined as viewing future options that may be made available because of the type of investment under review. Timing can be thought of in the context of a transaction, which may include movement in shifting business conditions. Control is very important on evaluating the investment's environment. Is the investment dependent on resources under the investor's control, or controlled by an outside source after the investment is committed to?

Long-term investments in the health care industries may consist of expenditures for facilities, technology, or equipment that may have a life expectancy of 10 or more years. These types of investments take a special set of criteria in the decision-making process that will connect the long-term commitment to shorter-term decisions that will affect the entire enterprise environment.

Terms employed in making long-term types of financial investment decisions are long-term debt, long-term financing, long-term liabilities, leasing, bonds, warrants, capital structure, depreciation, cash flow, breakeven analysis, rate of return, return on investment, and many others.

Long-term investments are key to the success of any business. Management of these investments, the terms and their performance can mean success or failure in the strategic use of assets.

—Terry Moore

See also Investment, Return on Assets (ROA)

FURTHER READING

Freidman, J. P. (2000). *Dictionary of business terms.* Hauppauge, NY: Barron's.

Gepenski, L. C. (2001). *Healthcare finance: An introduction to accounting and financial management.* Chicago: Health Administration Press.

Nowicki, M. (2001). *The financial management of hospital and healthcare organizations.* Chicago: Healthcare Financial Management Associations and Healthcare Administration Press.

LOYALTY IN HEALTH CARE CONSUMERS

Having adopted a marketing approach to patients only about 25 years ago, and slowly, sometimes grudgingly at that, health care has tended to be well behind the curve compared with other industries. But it has readily adopted a focus on consumer loyalty, because loyal patients are a blessing for individual physicians as well as for hospitals and other health care organizations (HCOs). Patients not only deliver benefits of repeated use of health services; they may also volunteer their help and donate money to assist HCOs, and refer their family and friends to both HCOs and physicians to whom they are loyal.

There are three distinct foundations for consumer loyalty in health care: (a) the features and attributes characterizing providers of care and their brand image that cause consumers to choose them in the first place, (b) the quality of the experiences consumers have when they use *those* providers, and (c) the differences that a continuing relationship with those providers makes on their health and lives. HCOs and physicians have concentrated their management and marketing efforts on their own characteristics in most instances, and for the longest time. They have recently given increasing attention to the experiences that patients have, improving both the healing environment, convenience, and comfort of their interactions with patients, including phone and online contacts, to improve patient satisfaction. It is likely that providers will increase their focus on the differences they make to consumers' lives, because consumers are finding many nontraditional products and providers who are meeting their growing demands for such differences.

Health care makes differences to the quality of life of consumers, as well as to the success of employers, health plans, and society at large, in every category of its use. Health promotion improves strength, stamina, and flexibility, reduces injuries, and increases energy and well-being. Health risk reduction and prevention can reduce the incidence and prevalence of a wide range of disease and injury conditions. Acute and chronic condition management can address the full impact of such conditions, and enable consumers and their families to recover from or cope with their conditions with the least intrusion into their lives. Life stage health management can improve both the experience and impacts of child development and adolescence, pregnancy and parenting, menopause and aging, and even the end of life.

Because loyalty involves a continuing relationship between consumers, as individuals and members of families, and health care providers, it makes sense that such relationships deliver their own kind of value to consumers, in addition to satisfying experiences with and admirable qualities of providers. As HCOs and physicians join other industries in striving for loyalty among consumers, those that focus on the differences they make in consumers' lives will have a distinct advantage over those that focus only on their own admirable traits and the occasional experiences of hospital stays and office visits. And because health care can and does make significant, often dramatic differences in the lives of consumers, it provides a far stronger basis for loyal relationships than do most other industries.

—Scott R. MacStravic

See also Customer Relationship Management (CRM)

FURTHER READING

MacStravic, S. (1998). *Creating consumer loyalty in health care.* Chicago: Health Administration Press.

Reidenbach, E., & McClung, G. (1999, Spring). Managing stakeholder loyalty. *Marketing Health Services, 19*(1), 20–29.

M

MACROENVIRONMENTAL ANALYSIS

See Environmental Analysis

MAINTENANCE OF SCOPE

Often organizations pursue maintenance-of-scope strategies when management believes the past strategy has been appropriate and few changes are required in the target market or the organization's products or services. Maintenance of scope does not necessarily mean that the organization does nothing; rather, management believes the organization is progressing appropriately. The maintenance-of-scope strategies include enhancement (doing better what is currently being done) and status quo (attempting to stabilize).

ENHANCEMENT

When management believes that the organization is progressing toward its vision and goals but needs to "do things better," an enhancement strategy may be used. Neither expansion nor contraction of operations is appropriate but "something needs to be done." Enhancement strategies include quality programs, such as continuous quality improvement (CQI) and total quality management (TQM), directed toward improving organizational processes, cost reduction programs designed to render the organization more efficient, or innovative management processes designed to speed the delivery of the products or services to the customer and add flexibility to the design of the products or services (marketwide customization). For example, a Milwaukee hospital made a commitment to total quality management by having physician directors lead colleagues and department managers through, TQM process, using various tools to make improvements throughout the organization.

After an expansion strategy, an organization often engages in maintenance enhancement strategies. Typically, after an acquisition, organizations initiate enhancement strategies directed toward upgrading facilities, reducing purchasing costs, installing new computer systems, enhancing information systems, improving the ability to evaluate clinical outcomes, reducing overhead costs, or improving quality.

STATUS QUO

Based on the assumption that the market has matured and periods of high growth are over, an acceptable market share must be defended against competitors. In a status quo strategy, the goal is to maintain market share—not necessarily an easy goal to achieve in the turbulent health care environment. Additional resources may be required as management attempts to prolong the life of the product or service for as long as possible. Other competitors may be fighting for survival, requiring an organization to invest significant management time, financial resources, and marketing expertise to maintain market share. An example of this strategy would be a full-service hospital investing heavily in marketing to prevent market share erosion for inpatient services.

To better utilize limited resources, organizations attempt a status quo strategy in some areas while engaging in market development, product development, or penetration strategies in other areas. For instance, a hospital may attempt to hold its market share (status quo) in slow-growth markets such as cardiac and pediatric services and attempt market development in higher-growth services such as renal dialysis or intravenous therapy.

In mature markets, consolidation occurs as organizations attempt to add volume and reduce costs. Therefore, managers must be wary of the emergence of a single dominant competitor that has achieved a significant cost differential. A status quo strategy is appropriate when there are two or three dominant providers in a stable market segment, because in this situation market development or product development may be quite difficult and extremely expensive.

—Linda E. Swayne

See also Continuous Quality Improvement (CQI), Expansion Strategies, Strategic Management, Total Quality Management (TQM)

FURTHER READING

Breindel, C. L. (1988). Nongrowth strategies and options in health care. *Hospital and Health Services Administration, 33,* 1, 42.

Ginter, P. M., Swayne, L. E., & Duncan, W. J. (2002). Developing strategic alternatives. In P. M. Ginter, L. E. Swayne, & W. J. Duncan. *Strategic management of health care organizations* (4th ed., Chapter 6). Oxford, UK: Blackwell.

Herzlinger, R. E. (1997). *Market-driven health care: Who wins, who loses in the transformation of America's largest service industry.* Reading, MA: Addison-Wesley.

MALPRACTICE

The practice of medicine centers on a physician making a judgment given the many similar patients in the past. Medical malpractice is neither failure to make a proper diagnosis nor even failure to provide curative treatment. Medical malpractice is professional negligence. Professional negligence is the failure to use reasonable care in providing medical treatment, resulting in harm to the patient. The distinction is important, in that some patients will have undesirable outcomes despite proper diagnosis and care (for example, massive trauma, cardiac arrest, and so on), but such sad and unfortunate results do not constitute malpractice. It is only when the physician or other medical professional deviates from the usual, widespread, generally perceived standard of care and the patient is harmed by that departure that malpractice occurs.

Despite the preceding definition of malpractice, the number of medical malpractice lawsuits and the size of dollar awards granted to patient plaintiffs have risen dramatically in recent years. The recent increased frequency and size of malpractice cases has a variety of causes. These include (a) a general public perception that medicine is, in fact, very good in the United States and therefore bad outcomes are not expected; (b) health care is very expensive and the system is often difficult to "navigate" for the patient, so emotions are often high, especially in critical cases; (c) plaintiff attorneys are increasingly adept in handling these cases; (d) an increasing number of physicians are actively working as "expert witnesses" to assist those attorneys; (e) juries in all types of cases have begun to award astronomical awards to plaintiffs through punitive damages in an attempt to provide some relief for plaintiffs in dire straits (for example, the recent multibillion-dollar tobacco settlement); and (f) a perception by juries that "it's just the insurance company's money anyway."

In any potential malpractice case, however, a high burden is placed on the patient plaintiff and his or her attorney. It has been said that anyone can sue over anything in this country but to be successful in a typical medical malpractice case, the attorney must convince the jury that the following existed or occurred:

- There was a doctor–patient relationship.
- There was deviation from the standard of care (that is, negligence).
- The patient suffered harm or damages.
- The actions of the physician caused the harm or damages.

Each of these elements must be proven in a medical malpractice case, to the satisfaction of a jury.

The first element listed, the existence of a doctor–patient relationship, seems obvious but it isn't always so. For instance, a physician who is asked by another physician to see a patient in consultation but who has not yet done so, does not have an established doctor–patient relationship, nor does a physician who happens to be in the hospital when a cardiac arrest announcement is made over the hospital intercom (usually in some cryptic language), if those physicians have not been involved in the care of the patient. In reality, although it is not unheard of for such physicians to originally be named in a malpractice case, the existence of a doctor–patient relationship is usually clear-cut and few cases proceed without such obvious facts.

The second element of a successful malpractice suit, deviation from the standard of care, is usually the most critical and difficult part of a malpractice lawsuit. The plaintiff's attorney must convince the jury that the physician, nurse, or other medical professional failed in some way to evaluate, diagnose, and treat the patient in a way that other competent clinicians would. The attorney generally tries to do so in a variety of ways, the most powerful of which is to have other medical professionals testify that the doctor did, in fact, deviate from the usual standard of care in one or more ways. The doctor's attorney tries to refute that position, usually by stressing the doctor's training, experience, prior practices and by presenting his or her own group of medical professionals to assert that the doctor's care was within the standard of care. These witnesses for the plaintiff and for the doctor are called "expert witnesses" and are usually paid to testify. Medicine is not a perfectly exact science; there can be legitimate differences of opinion among experts. It is also common to challenge the integrity of some experts. But ultimately the jury must decide whom to believe and must act accordingly.

The third element is harm or injury or damages. For any malpractice to have occurred, the patient must have suffered some injury. For instance, if a hospital employee accidentally sends the wrong patient to the radiology department for an X-ray that was intended for another patient, it is highly unlikely that a jury would grant a malpractice award to the patient, in that no demonstrable harm came from the error. Practically speaking, few malpractice cases go forward without injury being apparent or at least plausible. Some cases, however, center on proving the existence of real injury, and many expert witnesses may be called to convince the jury one way or another on this point alone. "Whiplash" claims from rear-end auto collisions are among the most well-known such cases.

The final element is "causation." The error of the physician must be the proximate cause of the injury for malpractice to have occurred. For example, some patients in automobile accidents are so critically injured that they expire even with perfect care. If a physician makes an error in such a case, it is difficult to prove that the error resulted in the death of the patient. Proving causation, however, can be pivotal when the patient has a bad or imperfect outcome. The plaintiff's attorney will try to show that the patient's obvious pain or economic hardship was caused by the doctor's failure to use the proper standard of care. The doctor's attorney will try to show that in spite of all reasonable care the patient had an undesirable outcome. In the final analysis, the jury must believe that there was a doctor–patient relationship, that the patient was injured in some way, that the doctor departed from the standard of care, and that the departure actually caused the injury or damages. Many cases are dropped or settled out of court before going to trial. If it becomes apparent that the case will not prevail, the plaintiff may choose to drop the case rather than incur the additional time and expense of going to trial. If the outcome is questionable, the parties may choose to "settle." This simply means that the parties agreed to some (usually confidential) settlement amount before the case goes to trial.

Statistically, most medical malpractice suits are won by the defendant doctor or dropped before trial. Those that are settled with monetary payment to the plaintiff before trial are usually settled for an amount paid by the doctor's malpractice insurance company. Those that go to trial by jury increasingly result in very high awards to the patient, often in excess of the amount of the doctor's insurance, putting the personal assets of the physician at risk. This risk of extremely large awards added to the costs in both economic and emotional terms are a large portion of the reason that cases are often settled prior to going to trial.

Due to the increasing frequency of these lawsuits, the rising dollar value of settlements, and very large jury awards, medical malpractice insurance premiums are rising dramatically. Many companies have stopped writing malpractice insurance coverage entirely, and a growing number of physicians are leaving states that have placed no caps or limits on malpractice awards. In many states the situation is so severe that the shortage of doctors in some specialties is reaching the crisis point and threatens the health and welfare of the patient population in this country. In recognition of the crisis, many states have passed laws to limit punitive damages in medical malpractice suits.

—Cheryl S. Massingale

FURTHER READING

Becker, S. (1999). *Physician's managed care success manual: Strategic options, alliances, and contracting issues.* Philadelphia: Mosby.

MANAGED CARE

Managed care may be defined as a comprehensive attempt to control care and costs in the health care industry by controlling access to care. Thus both dimensions of the cost of care and access to care need to be understood.

Many would argue that the root cause of managed care has been the accelerating costs of health care. Those costs have outstripped the general rate of inflation in the United States for many years. Indeed, in the early 1990s and in the early years of the next decade, many employers saw their health care costs increase between 10% and 20% per year. On a national basis, such increases led to forecasts that health care costs would represent 18% of the entire U.S. economy, and $3 trillion in expenditures, by the year 2012. In an attempt to control those nonsustainable cost increases, many employers joined forces with insurance companies to rein in the cost of care.

That attempt to manage cost by reining in the use of care became known as managed care. In the old fee-for-service or cost reimbursement model, providers were paid fees for health care services and the providers decided what services were needed. Under that model, there were allegations of overutilization of health care services. Access to health care services was almost unlimited for those with fee-for-service health insurance coverage. Partly in reaction to allegations of overutilization of health care services, the initial theme of managed care was controlling cost by controlling access to health care services.

One way to control access was through a gatekeeper model. In some cases, the gatekeeper was a nurse at a health insurance company who precertified the need for referral to a specialist, for a pharmaceutical product, or for a health care procedure. Such a precertification process by a nurse angered many physicians, who viewed the process as curtailing their autonomy to practice medicine.

Controlling access also took the form of limited panels of providers with a requirement to see a designated primary care physician such as a pediatrician or family practitioner on the panel of preapproved providers. Such approved providers on a panel often accepted lower fees, because they anticipated higher volumes of patients or because the providers feared the negotiating power of the insurance companies. A visit with an approved panel primary care physician may have been required before seeing a specialist or before requiring detailed tests or diagnostic procedures. Thus, only physicians designated on the panel of providers given by the insurance company could be used if reimbursement was desired. Certain pharmaceutical products were also denied if they were not on the approved list or formulary. In some instances, the pendulum may have swung from overutilization to underutilization of health care services. This limited choice of physicians, hospitals, and pharmaceutical products angered many patients, because they wanted the choice of providers and pharmaceutical products. These practices were implemented fully by organizations known as health maintenance organizations, or HMOs.

Given the dislike among physicians, other providers, and patients for the strong gatekeeper or HMO model, and a dislike for the precertification process among providers, patients expressed a need for choice among providers and for authorization of procedures by their physician. Thus, a health plan with broader panels of providers and more liberal reimbursement for out-of-panel providers and pharmaceutical products became known as a preferred provider organization (PPO). A point-of-service (POS) plan was a compromise between an HMO and PPO in terms of how narrow to make the approved panel of providers and the precertification process.

HMO growth may have peaked around the year 2000 with 80 million U.S. members, whereas PPO and POS plans were growing rapidly, with over 100 million members between them. A POS plan may be 20% to 25% more expensive than a pure HMO plan, and a PPO plan may be another 20% to 25% more expensive. However, growing numbers of patients were paying the extra premiums for the sake of choice of preferred providers and pharmaceutical products.

The preceding trends played out at different speeds in different parts of the country. California was viewed as the birthplace of the HMO movement, whereas small rural towns lagged behind the managed care movement in other parts of the country. Thus there were different stages of managed care in different parts of the country with different strategies used by providers and insurance companies.

In an early stage, with only a few percent of patients represented by an HMO, providers might fight the existence of managed care and refuse to join restrictive panels of physicians and the precertification process. In more advanced stages of managed care, with a majority of patients in managed care plans, physicians might merge practices so that large practices could negotiate with large managed care contracts.

Because of the reduced choice of providers and stories of denied care, the term HMO had such a distasteful connotation at the time of this writing that the HMO may disappear. However, in the name of managing costs, it appears there will continue to be some form of managed care, whether known as a PPO, a POS, or some yet-to-be-designed term. With a forecast of $3 trillion in health care expenditures by the year 2012, both employers and the government will make repeated attempts to control the rate of cost growth in the health care industry.

—Michael J. Stahl

See also Fee-for-Service (FFS) Payment, Formulary, Health Maintenance Organizations (HMOs), Point-of-Service (POS) Arrangements, Preferred Provider Organization (PPO)

FURTHER READING

Coile, R. C. (1997). *The five stages of managed care.* Chicago: American College of Healthcare Executives.

Coile, R. C. (2000). *New century healthcare.* Chicago: American College of Healthcare Executives.

Elipoulos, P. (Ed.). (1999, March). *Managed care: Facts, trends and data: 1998–99.* Vol. 4, no. 3. Washington, DC: Atlantic Information Services, Inc.

Health-care spending rises 8.7%, fastest expansion in 10 years. (2003, January 8). *Wall Street Journal*, D2.

Health spending is likely to slow but still exceed economic growth. (2003, February 7). *Wall Street Journal*, A2.

MANAGED CARE CONTRACTING

See Managed Care

MANAGED CARE ORGANIZATION

A managed care organization is a type of health insurance that combines (a) the collection of insurance premiums to pay for covered benefits with (b) methods that influence the cost and use of health services. A managed care organization uses methods to deliver health services and to pay hospitals and physicians that attempt to control or coordinate the use of services in order to contain expenditures, improve quality, or both.

A managed care organization is normally offered to potential enrollees as an alternative choice to traditional fee-for-service health insurance, which does not use methods to influence the cost and use of health services.

A managed care organization will have (a) a restricted network of hospitals and physicians, (b) administrative methods for utilization review, prior authorization, and quality assessment and improvement, and (c) financial incentives for enrollees to use the restricted network of hospitals and physicians.

Managed care organizations are primarily a U.S. phenomenon, although more managed care companies have been appearing in other countries over the last 10 years. The reason managed care organizations arose in the United States is because of the employment-based coverage of U.S. health insurance.

Most health care costs in the United States are paid by private health insurance plans. Most Americans, under the age of 65 years, are offered a health insurance plan through their place of employment. The employer pays more than half the cost of private health insurance when it is offered at the place of employment. Employer concern about the cost of health care for their employees led to establishment of health plans that attempted to control costs and improve the coordination of care after World War II.

The first managed care organization was the Kaiser Foundation Hospitals and Health Plan. It illustrates the influential role of employers over managed care organizations, because of the active role of Henry Kaiser, Sr., a prominent American industrialist and shipbuilder. He wanted his employees to have access to reasonable-cost, high-quality health care and pushed for the development of a form of health insurance in which administrators took over the management of service delivery to allow the physicians to only practice high-quality medicine. His original concept grew to be Kaiser Permanente, which today is America's largest not-for-profit managed care organization, serving 8.1 million members in nine states and the District of Columbia.

There are several types of managed care organizations. A health maintenance organization (HMO) is a type of managed care organization that accepts all the risk for covered services. A predetermined health insurance premium is paid for the managed care organization to provide the covered services within the budget supported by the premium—absorbing any financial loss or retaining any financial gain.

This type of managed care organization saw rapid growth in the 1970s and 1980s after the passage of the Health Maintenance Organization Act of 1973. Employers with more than 25 employees had to offer at least one HMO to their employees. To be approved by the federal government, HMOs had to expand their benefit package beyond hospital and physician services, offering mental health benefits and many other services. As a result, managed care organizations are often associated with comprehensive benefits. In 1985, the managed care organization was introduced to elderly Medicare beneficiaries when the federal government offered an alternative to paying only on a fee-for-service basis, by also paying HMOs through risk-based contracts. Approximately 5 million Medicare beneficiaries are enrolled in HMOs. In the 1990s, many states sharply expanded enrollment in HMOs for low-income and disabled people on Medicaid.

Another type of managed care organization is a preferred provider organization (PPO), which normally does not accept full risk for covered services. Rather, it consists of physicians, hospitals, or other providers, who provide health care services at a reduced fee. Patients face higher fees if they do not use the network of preferred providers.

Federal household survey data from 1997, the most recent available, indicate that 188 million Americans had private health insurance and 76.5 million (41%) were members of health maintenance organizations. InterStudy, a leading source of data on managed care organizations, reports that there are nearly 600 HMOs. The American Association of Preferred Provider Organizations estimates over 100 million persons belong to this type of managed care organization.

—Louis F. Rossiter

See also Health Maintenance Organizations (HMOs), Preferred Provider Organization (PPO)

FURTHER READING

Interstudy Publications. (2001). *HMO industry report.* St. Paul, MN: Author.

Levit, K., Smith, C., Cowan, C., Lazenby, H., & Martin, A. (2002, March–April). Inflation spurs health spending in 2000. *Health Affairs, 21*(1), 1–2.

www.aahp.org

www.aappo.org/about.html

MANAGED CARE PLANS

Managed care is a health care system that coordinates the health care services for a select group of covered individuals and integrates the financing for these services. These systems most often include payment arrangements with the providers, hospitals, and specialists on a predetermined fee schedule. Managed care plans include a wide variety of organizational structure and payment methodologies. There are three basic types: health maintenance organizations (HMOs), preferred provider organizations (PPOs), and point-of-service (POS) plans.

There are four types of HMO models. In independent practice associations (IPAs) a separate, legal entity contracts with the HMO for a predetermined, negotiated fee. This type of arrangement is usually part of a practice where practitioners continue to provide care to the patients within their own practice and to the IPA as part of their business practice. The staff model, in contrast, is a model where the providers practice as employees of the HMO, are paid a salary, and do not generally have a private practice. The group model differs from the staff model and the IPA, as the contract with the HMO includes a group of multispecialty practitioners to provide care to the plan members. They are employed not by the HMO but by the group practice, and paid at a negotiated rate by the group practice. Last, the network model is one where two or more IPAs provide services and are paid a predetermined, fixed rate per covered life.

Preferred provider organizations (PPOs) are managed care plans that directly contract with independent providers for a negotiated fee for service, usually at a reduced or discounted rate. Although there are significantly better benefits for the services with little or no additional cost using the PPO, most of these plans allow benefits to the nonparticipating providers, but the benefits are fewer and not as broad, and the costs for copayments higher.

Point-of-service plans are open-ended benefit plans where the enrollee has the choice of either using the managed care program or going outside the plan for services. Their costs are generally much higher, including the monthly premiums, higher deductible, and coinsurance if they select outside the contracted providers. They may make their selection each time they access their health care benefits.

Usually managed care plans have a "gatekeeper" who is the first point of contact and generally drives the care of the patient. The need for hospital inpatient services, testing at laboratories, X rays, medication, and referrals to a specialist are determined by this practitioner. The "gatekeeper" is usually the primary care practitioner who is contracted with the managed care company. In most cases, this individual is an M.D. or D.O., but advanced practice RNs (nurse practitioners) and physician assistants (PAs), employed by the physician, can be used to provide care in the physician office. This primary care is considered the most efficient way to manage scarce health care dollars.

In recent years the federal government has encouraged that Medicare and, in some cases, Mandated Medicaid services be managed by managed care plans. This was seen as a necessary next step to manage the escalating numbers of the uninsured or the underinsured and the costs of health care. The burden to individuals, businesses, and the government was overwhelming and needed to be addressed.

Many Medicare beneficiaries have determined that making the switch to managed care is in their best interest. These individuals "sign over" their benefits to the managed care company and the federal government pays the company on a predetermined rate (by diagnosis-related group, or DRG). The managed care company in turn provides the Medicare beneficiary the health care required. One of the important reasons why the Medicare beneficiary makes the switch is that the copayment of 20% that is typical in the Medicare program is waived and medication benefits are included in managed care plans and not in Medicare. One issue that quickly became apparent to the managed care companies is that the costs were high, with little benefit to the companies. Many managed care companies have stopped taking seniors (most of the Medicare population) as a result.

—Edna Lee Kucera

FURTHER READING

www.cmwf.org
www.ipro.org
www.managedcaregroup.com

MANAGED COMPETITION

Managed competition is an oxymoron. Although competition requires freedom for actors to negotiate prices and volumes of their goods and services, regulation seeks to restrain that freedom. Yet countries as culturally and institutionally diverse as Israel and Colombia are reorganizing their heath care systems with the aim of allowing more market incentives and more responsibilities for market actors. In the United States, managed competition allows competing health insurance agencies to selectively contract providers on behalf of their insured, under narrowly defined rules set by the government.

Economists since Kenneth Arrow have argued that the market for health care differs from other markets for products and services. This market displays several imperfections including moral hazard, supplier-induced demand, and X-inefficiencies. *Moral hazard* exists when insurance increases the possibility of incurring a covered loss or enhances the covered loss's size. Moral hazard implies that rational, insured people use more health services than people with no or limited insurance. This rational economic behavior leads to welfare losses as people demand services, which contribute less to their individual utility and more to social costs. *Supplier-induced demand* indicates that providers of highly specialized services induce demand among their patients for their services, which third-party insurers have to pay. *X-inefficiencies* occur due to imperfect information that individual patients have about their individual providers. Because of imperfect information about them, inefficient providers continue to operate in the market.

In 1978, Alan Enthoven, a Stanford University professor and former U.S. assistant secretary of defense, wrote an important article on managed competition in the *New England Journal of Medicine;* he elaborated on and amended his ideas in subsequent articles. With a managed competition model in place, Enthoven argued, market actors have incentives to behave as if they operated in perfectly competitive environments. Price signals and competitive pressures let cost-conscious consumers, and profit-seeking providers, as well as insurers, interact. Specific incentives and instruments, as well as particular institutions, obviate moral hazard, supplier-induced demand, and X-inefficiencies.

In managed competition, new market actors, or sponsors, act as purchasing agents for pools of consumers, define the basic rules for competition among insurers and providers, supply consumers with information, and monitor insurers' behaviors to prevent risk selection. Insurers offer potential consumers contracts at or above standardized ranges of health services at community-rated premiums. Consumers can freely switch between plans periodically. Ideally, sponsors collect premiums and distribute these premiums on risk-adjusted bases to individual insurers. In addition, sponsors provide consumers with information on price, quality, levels of coverage, and coinsurance schemes of the insurers. Insurers can contract selectively with providers, or even integrate with them. Moreover, they have to bear the financial risks of acting in the market. Thus, insurers have to monitor health care delivery as they compete for the insured, and providers have to increase technical efficiency as they compete for contracts with insurance agencies. Insurers compete for consumers with the levels of their premium, the range of the services they cover, and the quality of the services they offer. Effective policy on competition ensures a high degree of competition in both the insurer and the provider markets. Free-market access for providers and insurers enhances competition.

The managed care model controls for the three imperfections of health care markets. The introduction of deductibles or coinsurance reduces moral hazard. As providers will lose market shares if they position their unit costs too high, X-inefficiency falls. As insurers closely monitor the delivery of services, overconsumption caused by supplier-induced demand becomes unlikely.

In the United States, many large employers such as the California Public Employee Retirement System (CALPERS) provide managed competition in health care. Under managed competition, health plans have to provide uniform plan structures that the employers define. Employees then choose from several health plans based on their perceptions

of quality. In some cases, employers publish report cards comparing the plans based on employees' satisfaction surveys and how well they rate under the Health Plan Employer Data & Information Set (HEDIS) developed by the National Committee for Quality Assurance.

Managed health care systems such as health maintenance organizations (HMOs) have brought affordable health coverage to a wide range of consumers. However, critics have argued that these systems also cut costs by limiting treatment options and patients' choices. Doctors (including the American Medical Association) and patients (including the American Association of Retired Persons) increasingly have asked Congress to regulate managed care by giving patients new rights, including the right to sue their health plans. Not surprisingly, the health plans (including the Health Insurance Association of America) have staunchly opposed further regulation.

Theoretically, managed competition appears extremely attractive to systems with social health insurance, such as Germany and the Netherlands. First, it promises to increase efficiency. Second, it assures high standards of equity by implementing regulation to avoid risk selection by insurers and by safeguarding reasonably equal access to health insurance and health care. Finally, managed competition shifts the responsibility for cost control from governments to market actors. Consequently, despite potential problems, managed competition in some form exists in several countries besides the United States, including Germany, Brazil, and the Netherlands.

—Usha C. V. Haley

See also Competitive Strategy and Groups, Health Maintenance Organizations (HMOs), Strategy

FURTHER READING

Arrow, K. J. (1963). Uncertainty and the welfare economics of medical care. *American Economic Review, 53,* 941–973.

Enthoven, A. (1978). Consumer Choice Health Plan: A national health insurance proposal on regulated competition in the private sector. *New England Journal of Medicine, 298,* 709–720.

Enthoven, A. (1993). The history and principles of managed competition. *Health Affairs, 12*(Suppl.), 24–48.

Gress, S., Okma, K., & Hessel, F. (2001, May). Managed competition in health care in the Netherlands and Germany— Theoretical foundation, empirical findings and policy conclusions. Discussion Paper 04/2001. Institute of Health Care Management, University of Greifswald, Germany.

MANAGEMENT DEVELOPMENT

The broad term *management development* describes both the process of and the associated content used in creating, enhancing, and developing the skills of individual managers and groups of managers in an organization.

Management development incorporates both on-the-job learning and formally structured education and training. The on-the-job learning aspects of management development usually include assignments of a short- or medium-term nature, which provide learning opportunities for managers. Structured management development usually involves the assessment of the strengths and weakness of individual managers and/or groups of managers, followed by a program chosen/designed to enhance the managerial skills and knowledge of both individuals and the group.

Learning from education often deals with the "what and why" of management job content. Training more often deals with the "how" of specific aspects of jobs and responsibilities. General technical knowledge, job-related education, specific training, and interpersonal skills development are typical components of a management development process/program.

Coaching and mentoring are other aspects of management development, which involve personal interaction with experienced people who have either held similar jobs or are responsible for groups of managers working in similar jobs. Coaches can be both personally and professionally oriented and often help managers learn to deal with the nontechnical portions of their jobs.

A good management development process makes opportunities available to managers but relies on the initiative of those managers to seek out and use the content of the management development process. A frequent error is to "send someone" to a management development program or to "put them through" a process without ever first determining that the manager wanted to "be developed." Such processes are usually wasteful and unsuccessful.

Another part of a management development process deals with the larger issue of organizational development and succession planning. Although it is easy to think of management development as a one-person process, *management* is a plural effort in most instances. Groups of managers must work together in a collaborative and complementary manner to achieve the objectives of the organization. Doing this requires diversity in perspectives, skills, talents, and experience. It also requires the willingness to work together and the presence of a leader—with a plan—to make the management group cohesive and effective.

As in most processes leading to programs, planning is a critical element. Creating a management development plan is usually the assigned job of the human resource function but in fact is actually the job of the leader, whether hisor her title is director, vice president, president, chief organizational officer, chief executive officer, chairman, or whatever. Unless the leader has strong input into and ownership of the management development plan, it will be mediocre at best and a failure at worst.

The most important reason for the leader's critical role is that many elements of management development can be postponed, deferred, and canceled whenever there is the slightest pressure on earnings. Training programs are considered discretionary expenses, although good ones should be considered strategic investments. Expenses get cut in difficult times, and some get trimmed even in good times.

Without the leader's ownership, the critical on-the-job learning that comes from rotating assignments, project team roles, and so forth don't happen at all or happen only infrequently. Strong management groups understand how different jobs within the group contribute to the overall success of the management as a whole. The best way to gain this understanding is to work in several related areas and develop managerial skills and know-how from different perspectives.

Finally, to be most successful management development must follow a series of steps.

ASSESSMENT AND PLANNING

The order of these steps may vary in different situations, but the first three must be done first and then repeated at intervals as the development steps proceed:

- *Assessment*—of the individual manager's current skills, knowledge, experience, and aptitude
- *Evaluation*—of the job performance in past assignments, including feedback
- *Development plan*—consider the individual's wishes and potential

DEVELOPMENT

- *On-the-job training*—through short- or medium-term assignments, job rotation, project work, and so on
- *Specialized training*—in areas specifically related to current and planned assignments
- *General education*—in the principles and practices related to the manager's development plan
- *Interpersonal skills*—needed to succeed as a supervisor, leader, and manager
- *Mentoring*—in the unique combination of hard and soft, social and political nuances encountered
- *Coaching*—in the realistic awareness of the manager's potential and career path aspirations
- *Career planning*—for the manager and the organization to maximize the chance of mutual success

Management development can be a bad cliché, or it can be a powerful real-world tool of an organization that wishes to maximize its success through the efforts of the people who are its managers. Which way this turns out depends heavily on the leader's belief and personal investment in or ownership of the process of management development.

—John L. Mariotti

FURTHER READING

Carnegie, Dale, et al. (1995). *The leader in you: How to win friends and influence people and succeed in a changing world.* New York: Pocket Books.

Winterton, J., & Winterton, R. (1990). *Developing managerial competence.* New York: Routledge.

MANAGEMENT SERVICES/SUPPLY ORGANIZATION (MSO)

A management services/supply organization (MSO) is an entity that is owned by physicians, hospitals, or private investors, individually or in combination. The goal of MSOs is to provide physicians with contract management and the appropriate infrastructure to improve practice performance. The MSO provides to the physicians some or all of the following: facilities, equipment, personnel, management services, and capital for expansion. In highly developed managed care markets, MSOs tend to focus on contract management services, whereas MSOs in less developed markets often focus on practice management services.

MSOs typically offer two distinct categories of services. In one type, the MSO is totally responsible for the entire operation of the practice. The MSO could be a PPMC (physician practice management company); a hospital that has purchased a group of practices and is responsible for their management; or an MSO that signs a full management contract with an independent practice. The second type of MSO offers services to groups on an a la carte (separable) basis. These may include any or all of the following: billing, collections, marketing, facilities management, human resources, and HIPAA or coding compliance.

MSOs were first developed in California in the 1980s as a response to managed care, with the primary intention of increasing negotiating leverage with the managed care organization. Initial capitalization requirements for MSOs range from $1 million for small MSOs to hundreds of millions of dollars for MSOs operating in multiple regions or nationally. The number of MSOs peaked in the mid 1990s, with approximately 1200 in existence across the country. This number has begun to decrease because the industry has consolidated and many MSOs have failed.

—Donald Levick

www.mgma.com/acmpe

MANAGEMENT VERSUS LEADERSHIP

See Leadership, Managing Organizational Change

MANAGING ORGANIZATIONAL CHANGE

Managing organizational change is the process of making the plans and decisions, then taking the actions required to implement those plans and decisions to bring about a new, different set of behaviors in a group of people working together in an organization. This is no simple task.

To manage organizational change, first a set of goals and objectives must be established. This is necessary to provide unified criteria for success once achieved. Next a plan must be made in sufficient detail to describe what steps must be taken and how those actions must be implemented to move the organization toward the achievement of its goals and objectives.

Although the preceding steps seem clear and straightforward, they are not. Often people—management and companies—do not understand how to effectively manage, because the causes and effects of their actions are separated by so much time that the relationship between them is obscured and no learning results. To effectively manage organizational change, four points must be accepted as valid:

- There is much to be learned from studying the past—or many mistakes will be repeated.
- People are the most important factor in success, yet we often mistreat them and seldom value them enough.
- Technology is essential but not sufficient for success without the involvement and cooperation of people.
- Knowledge is power. Education and information combined with experience is the source of knowledge. *(This is the basis for a new competitive advantage.)*

In organizations today, getting people to change is still the greatest obstacle to managing organizational change. It is often necessary to move people out of their "comfort zones" before they will even consider changing. Consider the following groups of people.

Frequently the largest challenge is to get executives to understand that the leaders must change or the whole initiative will fail because it lacks their understanding and support when things get tough.

Middle management ranks often face the most difficult dilemma in managing organizational change, because they are caught in the middle between hourly employees who aren't sure why they should change in the first place and top management who thinks it doesn't really need to change if everyone else will.

Professionals—doctors, nurses, technicians, engineers, and so on—watch this drama unfold, perplexed by the fact that none of these groups understands anything nearly as well as they do.

Because of this resistance to change, the best place to start in managing organizational change is to recognize and deal with resistance to change. There are three distinct levels of resistance to change, and understanding these levels is important.

Level 1. *"I don't understand it."* Resistance is based on lack of information or on honest disagreement over the facts. Everything is on the table; there are no hidden agendas.

Level 2. *"I don't like it."* Personal and emotional resistance occurs because people are afraid. They fear that the change may cost them their jobs, reduce their control, or cause them to lose face. We often treat all resistance as if it were Level 1 and consequently miss the mark in managing organizational change, using slick visual presentations to explain the change when what people really want to hear is an answer to the question "What does this mean to me?"

Level 3. *"I don't like you—and I don't trust you."* This deeply ingrained resistance to change is the most difficult to deal with. Management techniques fall short of altering such an emotional and personal form of resistance.

Not only does resistance to organizational change occur at different levels; it manifests itself in different ways. Understanding how resistance to change appears is the first step to dealing with it—and that is an essential part of managing organizational change.

Resistance to change manifests itself in many ways. There are eight primary forms of resistance:

- *Confusion* (a fog that makes it hard for people to hear that change is going to happen)
- *Immediate criticism* (before people hear the details, they are against it)
- *Denial* (people refuse to see or accept that things are different)
- *Malicious compliance* (they smile and seem to go along, only to let people discover later that they don't)
- *Sabotage* (actions taken to inhibit or kill the change)
- *Easy agreement* (people agree without much resistance but may not realize what they are agreeing to)
- *Deflection* (change the subject, and maybe it'll go away)
- *Silence* (hard to deal with because there is no input)

How *not* to react to this resistance is important. Here are some typical wrong reactions to resistance, and their consequences:

- Use power to overcome it (this increases the resistance)
- Manipulate those who oppose (tricks don't work for long)
- Apply force of reason (this one is very common and can easily deteriorate into one of the others)
- Ignore resistance (but it won't go away)
- Play off relationships (friends may go along until they see the cost or tradeoffs)
- Make deals (if the resistance is low and the deal is good, maybe this works)
- Kill the messenger (many executives use this one—just get rid of the opposition, or banish them to Siberia)
- Give in too soon (and have a half-baked or mediocre success if any)

Now that the area of resistance to change is better understood and the forms of resistance recognized, it is time to move on to what to do to manage organizational change:

1. *Develop a vision, mission, strategy, and operating plan* that provides the business the greatest potential for success. Involve all organizational levels in the planning process, and communicate the results in varying detail. Allow them to question and to gain equity in the final plan.

2. *Set high expectations with specific goals and objectives*, but not unrealistic or unachievable ones. Communicate these along with their rationale. Don't apologize for difficulty. Embrace those people who resist, and consider their reasons carefully.

3. *Build trust.* Start by being totally honest, fair above reproach (even when painful), and trustworthy. Go more than halfway anytime there is doubt. Regularly assess how it's going with people who are not a part of the normal "inner circle." Use anonymous surveys to find out if trust is truly building. Without it, nothing else works.

4. *Define each person's roles and responsibilities* relative to the whole business. Keep it simple: What are they expected to *do,* (day-to-day roles), and what are they expected to *get done?* Ask for their help, and remember to say "please." Put the outcomes in writing, and revise them as needed. Give people as much influence as possible over their areas of responsibility.

5. *Establish agreed-on measures* so people can track how they (and the business) are doing. Post these openly, and frequently refer to them. Revise them when they change. Identify boundaries and limitations so they are known and understood. Relate the measures to external benefits, and back to the strategic and operating plans.

6. *Provide frequent, balanced feedback,* and lots of information about external conditions and "how things are going." Provide opportunities for people to use their ideas in things not going as hoped/planned. Use collaborative problem solving. Be sure the necessary resources and technology are available.

7. *Continuously update people on changes* in the external situation—customers, markets, competition, and so forth. Involve them in gathering this information, and sharing it. Repeat the vision, mission, and strategy over and over. Tell the people about important "news" before they read it in the media, or hear it on the grapevine.

8. *Recognize and praise success. Identify and critique failure.* Enlist people's help in building on success and identifying and remedying the root causes of the failures. Encourage action, discourage inaction. Criticize results and methods, not people. If some people are not willing or able to perform at the levels needed, make sure they know of the problem and then either help them improve *or remove them from the organization.* (Remove the minority who just won't make it—before they infect the rest.)

9. *Reward success and the desired behavior,* both psychologically and financially. Find a means of providing ownership, and share the wealth created by good financial results. Tie rewards as closely as possible to things over which the people have direct control. As in building trust, go more than halfway. Don't forget to say "thank you."

10. *Finally, celebrate successes (and grieve over setbacks)*—together. Resolve to correct errors, do better, and succeed the next time. Maintain an environment of enthusiasm, positive attitude, cooperation, collaboration, and sharing. Meet often in one-to-one's

and small groups. Create easy, informal interaction. Knock down walls of bureaucracy, and penalize political nonsense. *Emphasize getting the job done, taking care of the customer, beating the competition, and doing it—together.*

These 10 steps may not be perfect, but they provide a good starting point.

There is a final point to remember in managing organizational change. An old saying describes the essence of it: *"I hear and I understand; I see and I believe; I do and I know!"* Too many managers and leaders either cannot or will not show people what to do and then let them learn to do it, supporting them and correcting their mistakes until they get it right. Role modeling with feedback and coaching is a powerful way to facilitate and manage organizational change.

In conclusion, to successfully manage organizational change, first set goals and objectives. This provides a clear definition and measure for success. Next, make a plan in sufficient detail to describe the steps to be taken and how new and different actions must be implemented to move the organization toward its goals and objectives. Finally, remember the forms of resistance to change, the 10 steps, and the practice of using role modeling as a leadership tool.

—John L. Mariotti

FURTHER READING

Maurer, R. (1996). *Beyond the wall of resistance.* Austin, TX: Bard Press.
Maurer, R. (2002). *Why don't you want what I want?* Atlanta, GA: Bard Press.

MANAGING TEAMS

See Team-Based Compensation, Team Building, Teamwork

MANDATED COVERAGE

The term *mandated coverage* refers to services provided by insurance companies and instructs insurers on what benefits they must provide for their insured. Many states require coverage mandates of health plans in order to be eligible to sell their health insurance products in those states. In 1965, there were only 8 mandated health insurance benefits laws in the United States; in 1970 there were 30. The number grew to 1081 in 1992. These mandates cover a wide variety of coverage issues, including alcohol treatment, infertility, mental illness, hairpieces, and liver transplants. The mandates are imposed by law. These laws have been established in an attempt to force insurance companies to provide broader coverage to members for certain services and to constrain insurance company denials for payment of some services. Federal law mandates primarily affect hospitals and health centers that are in part or wholly funded by federal dollars.

In response to the imposed mandates, third-party payers have been forced to provide additional covered services. The effect has ultimately been to adversely affect the insured. There has been a significant increase in the number of uninsured as a result of mandates, because the costs of premiums for coverage have escalated. Because of this, some states have moved to limit mandates for small businesses; however, the outcome has frequently been to financially punish small businesses providing health care coverage, because of increased health care premiums paid, instead of to allow these companies to opt out of high-cost benefit plans. According to one study, mandated insurance coverage for dental services alone increases premiums by 15%. Another study states that one out of every four uninsured people has been priced out of the market by state-mandated benefit laws. The costs of copayments have also increased significantly as a result of the mandates.

State legislatures, nonetheless, continue to pass mandates for different "benefits" in an attempt to assist the insured. Wyoming has submitted coverage for all diabetes care, including equipment, and prohibits exclusion of coverage for newly diagnosed members. New Jersey, New York, and four other states have now mandated coverage for breast cancer treatment, chemotherapy, and prosthetic devices. As mandates increase, the costs of premiums continue to escalate, and the number of uninsured rises.

The most widely known federal mandates are COBRA and a section of this act called EMTALA.

The Consolidated Omnibus Budget Reconciliation Act (COBRA) of 1985 contains a segment that mandates continued coverage of employees after termination from their existing job. This act is designed to levy severe penalties on companies that do not facilitate continuity of health care benefits on dissolution of employment. The regulation, however, placed no restriction on the additional premium cost to the employee following termination. It is not uncommon for an employee to have his or her health care premium increase more than 40% at the time of enactment of COBRA compared with the monthly premium prior to discharge from the employer.

Another section of the COBRA mandate requires care of patients when they arrive to receive emergency medical care. The recipient hospital emergency room is mandated to provide usual care regardless of the patient's ability to pay, or the brand of the patient's insurance. This law has received great attention recently. It is called Emergency Medical Treatment and Active Labor Act. EMTALA is designed to prevent transfer of a patient because of his or her inability to pay for medical services. This indirectly affects paying patients by shifting expenses from those patients that cannot be transferred but are unable to pay, to those in the hospital system who are able to pay.

—Curtis Alex Mock

FURTHER READING

www.geocities.com/CapitolHill/5974/
www.ncpa.org/~ncpa/ea/eama93/eama93o.html
www.ncpa.org/w/w23.html
www.thompson.com/libraries/benefits/heal/index.html

MARCH OF DIMES

The March of Dimes is the hallmark of successful not-for-profit 501(c) corporations in the area of linking public health needs and scientific research. The long-standing success of this organization is based on the development of grassroots support at the local community level.

In 1938, President Franklin D. Roosevelt established the National Foundation for Infantile Paralysis in response to the epidemic nature and devastating effects of the poliovirus. Comedian Eddie Cantor became involved in the Depression-era fundraising by asking radio listeners across the land to send their spare dimes directly to the White House. This was such a success that the term "March of Dimes" soon became the official name of the foundation. Dr. Jonas Salk was recruited to lead the battle against polio. In 1954, approximately 2 million schoolchildren were vaccinated in "field trials." This effort depended on the largest mobilization of peacetime volunteers recorded, and further cemented the foundation as a mainstay in American culture. In 1958, the March of Dimes expanded its focus to include any cause of birth defects or infant mortality. It is with this mission that the foundation still operates today.

The March of Dimes continues to experience successes, which include the importance of folic acid in pregnancy, artificial surfactant effects, and nitric oxide efficacy, as well as many other initiatives that are having a positive effect on infant care. These initiatives have expanded to include education and legislation. These efforts have proven a catalyst to keep the volunteer spirit active, assuring ongoing successes for this organization.

—Charles T. Hankins

See also Neonatal Care

FURTHER READING

www.marchofdimes.com

MARGINS

See Income Statement (IS), Profits

MARKET ENTRY STRATEGIES

The selection of expansion or maintenance of scope strategies suggest that the next decision to be made is which of the market entry strategies to pursue. Because the expansion strategies specify entering a new market and the maintenance-of-scope strategies call for obtaining new resources, the next decision entails how the organization will enter or develop the market. However, if contraction is selected, no market entry strategies are needed.

The three major methods to enter a market include purchasing into the market, teaming with others by using cooperation, or using an organization's own resources to develop products and services. Keep in mind that market entry strategies are not ends in themselves but rather a means to expand or maintain scope.

PURCHASE STRATEGIES

Purchase market entry strategies enable an organization to enter a market quickly. The three purchase market entry strategies include acquisition, licensing, and investment. Acquisition entry strategies expand the organization through the purchase of an existing organization, unit of an organization, or product or service. Thus acquisition strategies may be used to achieve diversification, vertical integration, market development, or product development. Licensing avoids the financial, time, or market risks of new technology or product development and avoids acquiring a complete company. License agreements provide rapid access to proven technologies, generally reduce risk for the organization, and spread licensing fees over time. Venture capital investments offer an opportunity to enter or "try out" a market with lowered risk. Typically, venture capital investment is used to participate in the growth and development of a small organization that may potentially develop a new or innovative technology.

COOPERATION STRATEGIES

Probably most used and certainly the most talked-about strategies of the 1990s were cooperation strategies that supported diversification, vertical integration, and product and market development strategies. Cooperation strategies include mergers, alliances, and joint ventures. Similar to acquisitions, mergers combine two organizations through mutual agreement to form a single new organization, often with a new name. In health care, mergers have been used most to combine two similar organizations (horizontal integration) in an effort to gain greater efficiency in the delivery of health care services, reduce duplication of services, improve geographic dispersion, increase service scope, restrain pricing increases, and improve financial performance. Strategic alliances are loosely coupled arrangements among organizations. Federations, consortiums, networks, or systems are designed to achieve long-term strategic purpose not possible by any single organization. A joint venture combines the resources of two or more separate organizations to accomplish a designated task. It involves a pooling of assets or a combination of the specialized talents or skills of each organization.

DEVELOPMENT STRATEGIES

Internal development or internal ventures achieve diversification and vertical integration as well as market development and product development, although at a slower pace than acquisition. (However, the costs may be lower.) Internal development uses the existing organizational structure, personnel, and capital to generate new products or services or distribution strategies. Internal ventures are typically separate, relatively independent entities. Initial efforts by a hospital to develop home health care may be accomplished through an internal venture.

—Linda E. Swayne

See also Acquisitions, Alliances, Expansion Strategies, Horizontal Integration and Diversification, Licensing, Merger and Acquisition, Venture Capital Investment

FURTHER READING

Ginter, P. M., Swayne, L. E., & Duncan, W. J. (2002). Developing strategic alternatives. In P. M. Ginter, L. E. Swayne, & W. J. Duncan, *Strategic management of health care organizations* (4th ed., Chapter 6). Oxford, UK: Blackwell.

Hitt, M. A., Harrison, J. S., & Ireland, R. D. (2001). *Creating value through mergers and acquisitions.* Oxford, UK: Oxford University Press.

Weil, T. P. (2000). Management of integrated delivery systems in the next decade. *Health Care Management Review, 25,* 3, 9–23.

Zuckerman, H. S., & Kaluzny, A. D. (1991). Strategic alliances in health care: The challenges of cooperation. *Frontiers of Health Services Management, 7,* 3, 4.

MARKETING CONCEPT

The marketing concept combines the concepts of customer focus, profitability, and the integration and coordination of marketing with the other major functional areas of the organization, such as finance, human resources, logistics, purchasing, and operations. This approach evolved from conditions that existed immediately after World War II, when rationing of goods for the war effort left the consumer (end user) feeling deprived of products beyond the basic, from basic foodstuffs such as sugar and flour, to shoes and clothing, to automobiles and appliances. As a result, in the late 1940s and into the 1950s consumers would buy almost any product that came on the market, regardless of lack of assortment or quality. The focus in the firm was thus on production rather than the consumer, with profits being obtained through cost controls and efficiencies in the manufacturing and delivery process.

In the late 1950s and early 1960s, after the Korean War, consumers became more discriminating, having satisfied their pent-up demand. Firms then concentrated on the sales force, working under the assumption that aggressive selling would produce the volume of sales necessary to sustain profitability. This assumption proved false as the consumer became increasingly discriminating on a quality basis.

In the 1970s and 1980s the techniques of Deming and Juran were applied in Japan. The upgrading of Japanese goods to demonstrably superior quality over those produced in the United States resulted in the dominance of a number of Japanese products in the marketplace. U.S. firms realized that to compete, they would not only have to match quality with the Japanese firms, but would also have to understand what both intermediaries such as wholesalers and retailers, as well as consumer end users, wanted from a product or service. They would have to improve their industries in order to survive the Japanese, and later German, top level of quality and customer orientation.

This quality approach, even when combined in the United States with research to understand end user (particularly) and intermediary wants and needs, did not produce the desired profit levels. Companies had evolved in functional "silos," in which each functional area operated almost independently of others in the firm. This resulted in a lack of communication and interaction that made efficient, effective business practice problematic. The impetus toward profitability thus added the last element to the marketing concept, that being the integration and coordination of marketing and other functional areas of the firm.

The marketing concept is now becoming increasingly relevant in health care, particularly with the declining profitability produced by the pricing and margin restrictions inherent in managed care in areas such as physician practice, hospital management, and the pharmaceutical industry. Specifically, there is an increasing understanding in health care that to maintain profitability, a focus on the needs and wants of customers such as patients and referring physicians is central to success. In addition, for health care organizations to be most efficient, different functional areas of those organizations that had been competing and separate must work together in order to make operations smooth, efficient, and cost effective.

—Richard C. Reizenstein

See also Customer Value, Functional Structures, Managed Care, Matrix Structure, Quality Management, Six-Sigma Program

FURTHER READING

Armstrong, G., & Kotler, P. (2003). *Marketing: An introduction.* Upper Saddle River, NJ: Prentice Hall.

Boyd, H. W., Walker, O. C., Jr., Mullins, J., & Larreche, J.-C. (2002). *Marketing management.* New York: Irwin McGraw Hill.

Perreault, W. D., Jr., & McCarthy, E. J. (1999). *Basic marketing: A global-managerial approach.* Boston: Irwin McGraw Hill.

MARKETING MIX

Marketing mix includes four major elements of marketing: product, place, promotion, and price; often marketers also refer to these elements as the four P's. They are usually controllable by marketing managers. The marketing mix variables are adjusted around target markets or segments, to maximize customer satisfaction and create competitive advantage.

The product is what a firm offers to customers in the form of a tangible good or intangible good. Medications administered to patients in hospitals are physical products, whereas the process of administration is an intangible product or service. There are varieties of products in consumer markets, which also apply to the health care industry. Marketers categorize these products as convenience, shopping, specialty, and emergency goods. Customers spend very little time for convenience goods and these products are widely available using intensive distribution (such as aspirin). Customers shop around comparing product quality and price before making a purchase for shopping goods (such as furniture). Buyers go out of their way to spend time and effort in purchasing specialty goods (such as expensive jewelry). Consumers often do not think of emergency products ahead of time, and the need for them usually arises in case of emergency (such as ambulance, hospital emergency room). The preceding product categories briefly discussed apply to the health care industry as well, as noted from the emergency products example. Patients do compare doctors, hospitals, and medications and do shop around if no emergency exists. Similarly, patients conduct much research to find specialists in medicine and seek treatment from far away. For example, many patients located abroad come to the United States for medical treatment. Similarly, some U.S. patients insist on being treated by specialists located outside of their home states.

The place element of the marketing mix is related to distribution and availability of products and services to customers. Location of a hospital or medical clinic or availability of ambulatory care services is based on proximity of these services to population centers. Similarly, ambulances are placed in close proximity to highways and streets where the likelihood of accidents is high.

Promotion deals with providing information to current and potential customers about products and services a company has to offer. It includes three major methods: personal selling, mass selling including advertising and publicity, and sales promotion. Personal selling is face-to-face communication between buyers and sellers. In the health care industry, almost all pharmaceutical firms use personal selling, attempting to convince medical doctors to prescribe a specific brand of medicine to patients. Mass selling means communicating with large numbers of current and potential customers and includes the use of television, radio, newspapers, magazines, and sometimes billboards. Although the cost of utilizing this type of media is very high, it is an often efficient way of reaching customers. In using the mass selling method, the pharmaceutical industry also uses television and other mass media to provide information about their products and persuade consumers to ask their doctors to prescribe a specific brand of medicine. This "pull" strategy is very effective.

Price is the amount of money consumers have to pay for a service such as a surgery or medicine. There are three major considerations in setting a price: (a) cost, (b) competition, (c) customers' ability to pay, and (d) ethics. Of course, one should not forget the supply-and-demand relationship. When supply is limited, prices are high or increase. When demand is low, prices are low or decrease.

—Fahri Karakaya

See also Competitive Strategy and Groups, Marketing Plan, Product

FURTHER READING

Cravens, D. (2001). *Strategic marketing*. Boston: Irwin McGraw Hill.

Perrault, W., & McCarty, J. (2002). *Basic marketing* (14th ed.). Boston: Irwin McGraw Hill.

MARKETING PLAN

A *marketing plan* is the road map that guides an organization in its efforts to achieve its objectives in its marketplace. Marketing plans should be specific to a particular brand or product or service category and should be consistent with the firm's overall strategic plans. For example, a pharmaceutical company should have a marketing plan for each major category of drugs that it markets, and in some cases, a separate marketing plan for each branded drug. A good marketing plan consists of the following seven elements:

1. *Current market situation:* Describes the current target markets and the organization's position in those markets. This situation analysis should include
   - A market description that defines the market and its major segments
   - A product review that describes the company's current major product lines
   - A review of major competitors, including assessment of their current market positions
   - A review of the current distribution structure

2. *Threats and opportunities analysis:* Assesses major threats and opportunities that major product lines may face in the short and long terms.

3. *Objectives:* States the marketing objectives that the company would like to attain. These objectives should be measurable and exist within a particular time frame. For example, a pharmaceutical company might set an objective of 30% market share for a particular drug within a one-year planning horizon.

4. *Marketing strategy:* Describes the logic that will drive the organization to achieve its objectives. The marketing strategy should include
   - Specifics of which defined market segments are to be targeted
   - How the brand will be positioned within each targeted segment
   - How each element of the marketing mix (product development, pricing, distribution, and integrated marketing communications) will be coordinated to respond to the threats and opportunities discussed previously

5. *Action plan:* Describes the specific tactics that will be employed to implement the strategy just described. Answers the questions about *what* will be done, *who* is responsible for getting it done, *when* it will be completed, and *how much* it will cost.

6. *Budgets:* Details a marketing budget, which is a projected profit-and-loss statement for the products or

services that are covered in the marketing plan. It should show expected revenues and projected costs, including all marketing expenditures necessary to achieve the revenue goals.

7. *Controls:* Describes the process that will be used to monitor the implementation of the marketing plan, along with alternative strategies should marketing objectives not be met.

A marketing plan should be updated as often as necessary, to ensure that current objectives, strategies, and tactics are consistent with organizational goals and the external environment. This frequency will vary, depending on the volatility of the marketing environment. For example, a company in the business of disposable hospital supplies might be able to update its various marketing plans annually. However, a pharmaceutical company that competes in a rapidly changing marketplace may need to update its marketing plans much more frequently.

—Mark A. Moon

FURTHER READING

Armstrong, G., & Kotler, P. (2003). *Marketing: An introduction* (6th ed.). Upper Saddle River, NJ: Prentice Hall.

Parry, M. E. (2002). *Strategic marketing management.* New York: McGraw-Hill.

MARKETING RESEARCH

Marketing research is the systematic gathering, recording, analyzing, and interpretation of data related to marketing problems. Successful planning, implementation, control of marketing strategies, and solving marketing problems requires information about current and potential customers and is a crucial element of successful marketing strategy. However, because of cost and time constraints, most managers often rely on their intuitions in making marketing decisions. Although smaller firms conduct very little marketing research, many large corporations have their marketing research teams or rely on major marketing research firms or syndicated services that continuously supply marketing research data.

Marketing research steps include the following:

1. Problem definition

2. Situation analysis

3. Research design

4. Data gathering

5. Processing data

6. Analysis

7. Reporting

Problem definition is one of the most important steps in marketing research, because it provides direction to the kind of research to be conducted and the type and quantity of data to be gathered. One needs to be careful not to define the symptom of a problem, but to identify the possible causes of a problem. Therefore, decision makers often make educated guesses of formal hypotheses that need to be tested.

The second step, *situation analysis,* involves gathering of secondary data or informally talking to people who can provide information relating to the problem. Secondary data is information that is already available inside or outside the company. For example, company records and reports as well as knowledgeable people within an organization can be good sources. Similarly, the Internet, public and university libraries, government agencies, and marketing research and advertising firms all provide secondary data. The major advantages of using secondary data are that they are readily available and are not as expensive as primary data. However, secondary data may not be appropriate for solving specific problems. One should use secondary data with caution because of possible data reliability and validity problems. Sometimes, marketing problems are solved through gathering secondary data only and the marketing research process ends with the interpretation of these data.

If the marketing problem is not solved through gathering secondary data, the next step is research design. Before designing a formal marketing research study, organizations should define information needed to solve the problem(s) and decide on the type of data needed. This process often determines the type of study needed to gather data and is explained together with data-gathering methods. There are two major types of data: qualitative and quantitative.

Qualitative data do not contain any numbers and include focus group interviews, in-depth personal interviews, and in-depth, open-ended responses in surveys. Sometimes qualitative data gathering is also performed in the situation analysis stage, because the goal might be developing hypotheses to be tested. In qualitative research, the number of respondents is usually small, and it is difficult to conduct statistical analysis of the responses. However, qualitative data usually cost less, can be gathered in a short period of time, and can be as valuable as quantitative data.

Gathering *quantitative data* involves the use of structured questions that allow analysis and reporting in numbers. Questions are designed in such a way that responses may explain relationships among variables and the frequency of occurrence. Therefore a variety of statistical techniques can be used to make inferences. However, this requires having a fairly large sample size and responses so that appropriate statistics can be calculated.

Gathering quantitative data methods includes surveys, and experimental designs. There are three major surveys and each has advantages and disadvantages. Personal survey or mall intercept (conducted at shopping malls) has the advantage of having a large response rate and the trained marketing research personnel conducting the survey. If respondents have difficulty in understanding questions, the marketing research personnel can explain the questions and assist respondents. However, personal surveys can be costly and can take a long time to conduct. In addition, marketing research firms need to provide incentives for respondents to participate in surveys usually in the form of money. Mail surveys usually have low response rate (average of 15%), but if they are anonymous, sensitive information can be gathered. Telephone surveys can be performed rather quickly and are mostly appropriate for short questionnaires. They may be as costly as the personal surveys, and the response rate can be low or biased, because people often fear that telephone surveys are sales calls by direct marketers. In any survey, the goal should be to obtain responses from a sample that is representative of the population. When respondent or sample size increases, so does the reliability of the survey. As mentioned, response rates can often be increased by providing incentives for completing the survey, making it easier for respondents to participate in the survey (for example, short and pretested surveys), and clarifying that the survey is conducted to help serve customers better.

In gathering quantitative data, marketers often use experimental designs that provide somewhat more scientific or more reliable results. Some of these experiments are simple, although others are very complex. In most experimental designs, the intent is to determine cause-and-effect relationships. Thus, the experiment is controlled and the experimental variable, the variable for which one attempts to determine the effect (such as influence of advertising on sales), is manipulated. Some of the more commonly used experimental designs include the pretest-posttest control group, Solomon four-group, and control group with posttest only. There are also more complex designs called *quasi-experimentation,* including completely randomized, randomized block, Latin square, and factorial designs (see Further Readings). Although experimental designs provide valuable information, they can be costly.

Once data are gathered, if quantitative they must be coded, edited, and entered into a computer so that statistical tests can be performed. Through preliminary analysis, researchers need to identify the outliers and the invalid responses. In most cases, outliers and invalid responses are discarded; however, some researchers decide to include them in analysis and interpret the results with caution.

The next step in marketing research is data analysis, which includes the application of a variety of statistical techniques. In selecting the appropriate statistical procedures, one must carefully examine the type of data scale (that is, interval versus categorical). Indeed, this step requires statistical expertise and should only be performed by qualified personnel.

The final step is interpretation and reporting of data, which usually include the use of tables and chart. Of course, recommendations are made and supported by the findings of the research study. One last, important item that is not a step in marketing research is the follow-up. This is necessary for control purposes.

—Fahri Karakaya

FURTHER READING

Churchill, G. A. (2002). *Marketing research: Methodological foundations.* Chicago: Dryden.

MARKET OPPORTUNITY ANALYSIS

Market opportunity analysis (MOA) is a systematic approach to understanding a market opportunity through gathering and analyzing information that is available through existing secondary sources as well as to primary research targeted at the specific opportunity under investigation. A market opportunity analysis should be conducted prior to an organization making any major commitments to a new product or service, to a modification or repositioning of an existing product or service, or to the termination of a product or service that appears to be in decline.

MOA reduces the risk of investment due to a lack of knowledge of the market, facilitates effective strategic planning, and provides a better, more informed means of estimating demand.

STAGES IN THE MOA PROCESS

An analysis of the external macroenvironment is the first stage in the MOA process. This includes an assessment of such areas of the macroenvironment as geographic conditions, general economic trends, demographic factors, technological changes, the economy, political forces, the political/regulatory environment, and social and cultural events and change.

The end user market must then be defined, because the needs of the end user are what create demand. This critical stage provides focus on those customers and entities in which opportunity may reside, from broad generic markets (such as health care) to narrower product/service markets (such as hospitals, clinics, and private practices) to branded markets, or the individual brands within a particular product market.

After the end user market is defined, the values of the end users must be assessed. These include what these end users are like as firms or people (including areas such as needs, interests, and demographics), how end users decide to buy, and what factors (macroenvironmental and other) affect purchase.

Identification and analysis of key (or potential key) competitors is also critical at this point. These are the companies or entities competing for the same markets or targets who are most likely to be, or are, most successful. In-depth information should be collected, including financial size and strength, marketing strategies, and anticipated changes in products or services or market approaches of this potential competition.

Other essential information is obtained through supplier analysis and channel analysis, both necessary to a complete MOA to ascertain the feasibility of the potential opportunity. The supplier analysis investigates key characteristics and requirements of manufacturers and resellers who are critical suppliers for materials or components necessary for the firm conducting the MOA to be able to successfully deliver its product or service to the end user. The channel analysis assesses types of firms in the channel from suppliers, including intermediaries, as well as those entities (if any) further toward the end user than the organization conducting the MOA. Included are areas such as types of cooperation required by the channel (such as maintenance of inventory), incentives required (price discounts, delivery terms), and normal operating procedures (typical order cycle, terms of trade).

The MOA is concluded with a strength-weakness-opportunity-threat (SWOT) analysis. This is a realistic assessment of internal strengths and weaknesses of the entity conducting the MOA as well as an examination of external opportunities and threats revealed by prior stages in the MOA and a thorough analysis of the industry in question.

—Richard C. Reizenstein

See also Customer, Customer Value, Industry Analysis, Strength-Weakness-Opportunity-Threat (SWOT) Analysis, Supply Chain Management (SCM)

FURTHER READING

Cadotte, E. R., & Bruce, H. J. (Eds.). (2003). *The management of strategy in the marketplace.* Mason, OH: South-Western.

Woodruff, R. B., & Gardial, S. F. (1996). *Know your customer.* Cambridge, MA: Blackwell.

MARKET SEGMENTATION

Marketing segmentation is dividing a market into submarkets in which each submarket has different needs and wants and targeting these submarkets with different products. Sometimes products aimed at diverse segments are only slightly different, but enough to make buyers feel that they are purchasing products to satisfy their needs and wants better than an average product. For example, Tylenol, Advil, Bufferin, Aleve, and similar over-the-counter products are essentially the same, with some variations aimed at different target markets. Similarly, there are hospitals that specialize in different kinds of surgeries and treatments. Some hospitals target patients for treatment of cancer, general surgery, or eye and ear care and surgery, whereas others focus on internal medicine. This is also true for medical doctors specializing in many different areas of medicine. There are even hospitals and outpatient care facilities aimed at treating mentally ill patients and substance abuse patients.

In general, there are five major ways of segmenting markets, which include the following:

1. Demographic segmentation

2. Geographic segmentation

3. Psychographic segmentation

4. Usage segmentation

5. Benefit segmentation

Demographic segmentation is when firms utilize demographic variables such as age, income, gender, education, occupation, ethnic background, race, family size, and family life cycle. The goal is to satisfy the needs of market segments that have different needs and wants. For example, people in different age-groups such as young, middle aged, and old (seniors) need different kinds of medical care. Whereas many young people may need sports medicine, most elderly may need health care in internal medicine and age-related illnesses. Similarly, there are different types of over-the-counter medications or even hospital services aimed at children (for example, children's hospitals) and the elderly (such as nursing homes). Therefore, age is a very important and natural segmentation variable in the health care industry. Gender is also a good segmentation variable, because males and females differ in health care needs. Indeed, there are medical specialists serving each segment of the population. If patients have medical insurance, income may not be a good segmentation variable, but the types of insurance can be used for segmenting. Indeed, this classification mode is already being used by insurance companies offering different types of health insurance coverage. Family life cycle includes stages of life that people go through such as bachelorhood, new marriage, full nest, empty nest, and the final dissolution stage. This segmentation variable is related to age. Therefore, people in different life cycle stages have different types of health care needs.

For example, in a full nest stage couples have one or more children and their health care needs increase for children as well as for mothers. Often, when marketers use the demographic segmentation dimension, they combine two or more of the demographic variables (such as age and gender).

Geographic segmentation includes neighborhoods, towns, cities, counties, states, or countries. The rationale for using such segmentation is that people living within various boundaries may share common income levels, cultures, climates, and values. A simple example is people living in the northern United States in colder climates, who tend to have more colds or episodes of flu than do those living in warmer climates.

Psychographic segmentation groups people into submarkets according to similarities in lifestyles, which include activities, interests, and opinions. People with similar lifestyles are likely to have the same type of health-related problems. The process of segmentation for this dimension is rather complex and employs statistical techniques such as factor and cluster analysis. Stanford Research Institute has been collecting psychographic data for many years, and it identifies market segments based on people's lifestyles.

Usage segmentation involves dividing a market into submarkets based on how people use a product or service. For example, this segmentation dimension classifies people as heavy, medium, and light users for products. The goal is to develop different or slightly different products or services to satisfy customers. For example, many over-the-counter products are packed in different sizes. Other ways of using this segmentation dimension include classifying consumers as potential, nonusers, ex-users, regulars, first-time users, brand loyalists, and brand switchers.

Benefit segmentation is based on the kinds of benefits people derive from using products or services. People seek different benefits from using different health care facilities and different health care products. For example, people inquire about preventive medicine in order to enjoy the future benefits of being healthy. Similarly, there are medical procedures that are absolutely necessary, and the benefit of such procedures may indeed be extremely important to people. However, there are also elective or cosmetic medical procedures from which people seek benefits that are not as essential as the medically necessary procedures.

It important to consider the size of market segments because one can easily oversegment and have very small groups of customers to target. This results in cost increases and higher prices for customers and may not be a good competitive strategy. When segments are very small or not cost-effective, firms combine segments that are most similar to one another. For example, in the health care industry, we see medical doctors specializing in ear, nose, and throat. Mass marketers attempt to combine many different segments with the goal of increased sales and lower costs. Wal-Mart is a good example of a mass marketer that appeals to a broad range of people needing different products.

Once a firm identifies a number of market segments, it is important to evaluate them based on several factors such as size, likelihood of purchase by the market, and competition. Large market segments are often more competitive but are also more profitable.

—Fahri Karakaya

See also Competitive Strategy and Groups

FURTHER READING

Cravens, D. (2001). *Strategic marketing*. Boston: Irwin McGraw Hill.

Perrault, W., & McCarty, J. (2002). *Basic marketing* (14th ed.). Boston: Irwin McGraw Hill.

MARKET VALUE

To the residential real estate agent, market value is the price at which a house will sell in 60 to 90 days. To the financial analyst, market value is the sum of a company's total shares of stock outstanding multiplied by the per share price of that stock at a given point in time. To the small business owner, market value is what his or her business may be worth to a prospective buyer based on the business's combined tangible (inventory, buildings, equipment, and so on) and intangible (brand value, customer loyalty, goodwill, and so on) assets.

To the health care marketing professional, market value is no less important but often more difficult to define. Although a financial definition of market value can certainly apply in the health care setting—the value of a health care company's stock or the selling price of a local not-for-profit hospital, for example—when applied to the discipline of marketing, the term *market value* is generally thought of in terms of the intangible assets of the organization or brand that appeal to customers rather than a whole business valuation.

Market value can be thought of as a collection of strengths or attributes consumers use to differentiate one brand from another or the total value consumers place on a particular brand. This value may be quantified objectively in terms of measurable attributes (price, service, quality, clinical outcomes) or subjectively in terms of perceptions or feelings. Put another way, market value is the potential of a product or service to satisfy customers' needs and wants.[1]

Although an organization may attempt to define the appropriate attributes of its market value and even influence consumer's awareness, understanding, and acceptance of those attributes, ultimately the marketplace decides what the market value is for a given industry or product. Marketers cannot create market value in a vacuum.

For example, the rapid growth of outpatient diagnostic and treatment options is resulting in a shift of consumers' awareness and desire for ambulatory care services versus traditional inpatient services. Although much of this is fueled by new technologies and changes in how medicine if performed, the rate of change is also being accelerated by the demand sustained by educated health care consumers.

Value analysis is a popular research method for determining a particular product's value equation and a specific brand's value proposition among key customer groups. Value analysis is an important tool for understanding what value characteristics consumers use to choose a specific service or product and mapping these attributes against competing products. For a business to succeed, it must deliver superior customer value, which requires an emphasis on the competitors who set the performance standard.[2]

It is important to note that market value is typically dynamic and often changes over time as a result of changes in the marketplace, changes in consumers' needs, competitors introducing new or different products, and new technologies. What may be important or thought of as valuable today for consumers may not be in 10 years. Value analysis can also be an effective tool for tracking changes in consumers' perceptions of market value for an industry, a specific product or a given company.[3]

For instance, a health plan may find that total cost savings or the breadth of their provider network is most important when defining its market value for business owners. In turn, a hospital may need to appeal to consumers through its patient satisfaction scores, medical outcomes numbers, or simply its location and convenience.

Once market value has been defined by the organization, marketers can work to build and enhance their organization's market value through a variety of business strategies including product or service offerings, product design, pricing, distribution channel options, service strategies, advertising, and promotions.

—Daniel Fell

REFERENCES

1. Sheth, J. N., Banwari, M., & Newman, B. I. (1999). *Consumer behavior: Consumer behavior and beyond.* Fort Worth, TX: Dryden.
2. Day, G. S. (1990). *Market driven strategy: Processes for creating value.* New York: Free Press.
3. Ragland, T. (2002). *The four things your customers want to tell you.* Memphis, TN. Unpublished manuscript.

MASS CUSTOMIZATION

Mass customization is a process that offers a variety of products or services designed to meet on demand a wide range of consumer needs without losing the economies associated with the limited choices inherent in the methods of mass production. The term was introduced by Stanley M. Davis in his book *Future Perfect* (1987) and is receiving increased attention in the health services management literature.

Mass customization is the logical consequence of the ongoing industrialization of products and services. Health care organizations are presently evolving through that process. Historically, providing individualized and customized care within the context of the traditional doctor–patient relationship, the realities of cost, and the emergence of managed care has moved the industry into the mass production phase of the industrialization process. However, patient and provider variability and the expectation that treatment must adapt to individual differences have forced health care organizations to meet on demand a wide range of consumer needs without losing the economies inherent in a mass production system.

Advancing scientific knowledge of the underlying mechanisms of health and disease increase has reduced acceptable levels of clinical ambiguity and thus has reduced variation in practice patterns and their attendant costs. The revolution in genetics, for example, is increasing, and will continue to increase, the proportion of health care activities supported by science, reducing the proportion of patient care processes subject to artistry and craft. Highly reliable processes supported by information technology and modularization can provide the potential for mass customization. This development promises individualized treatment at reasonable cost.

Figure 1 shows a diagram of the four states of industrialization identified by Victor and Boynton (1998) with two possible paths. Path A shows the traditional path of industrialization in the production of goods and services. Once the dominant design of a product or service emerges in the marketplace, the process is rationalized and mass production takes place with low product and process variability. Modern quality improvement techniques are then used to continuously modify (and improve) the process, leading to opportunities for mass customization.

Path B shows the route being taken in many health care organizations where the mass production stage has been bypassed or at least minimized. The provision of health care has moved from a craft to process enhancement, in which the focus has been on quality-enhancing efforts such as continuous quality improvement, evidence-based medicine, best practices consortia, treatment protocols, and case management. These efforts have provided standardization sufficient to enable providers and insurers to consider mass customization opportunities. Examples of the latter include case management of catastrophic illness cases and the provision of deep Internet portals and customized feedback for insurance enrollees with chronic illnesses.

Mass customization does not imply an infinite variety of products and services, nor does it imply the end of invention and adaptation in medicine. It refers to a conscious effort to introduce ever-increasing levels of personalization and variety of outcomes. Configuring and delivering modules of service in response to patient needs and preferences accomplish it. For example, a child born with spina bifida may need a wide range of medical and social services, depending on the severity of the case, the stage of treatment, the resources of the family, the resources of the community, the policies of payers, and the child's rate of development. The professional individual or team assigned to configure that child's care would pick and choose among available providers and services to best meet the needs of that child and family. That would require access to and use of efficient and effective patient records, methods of communication, databases, and service contracts and relationships.

In the case of the insurance company, mass customization can involve concurrent review of claims data to update maintenance of a Web site for each enrollee, that provides information such as relevant patient education information, links to appropriate and reliable sources of information, and links to low-cost providers of supplies and drugs. For the doctor–patient relationship it might involve giving the asthma patient an air flow-measuring device that can be connected to the Internet so that the physician can monitor

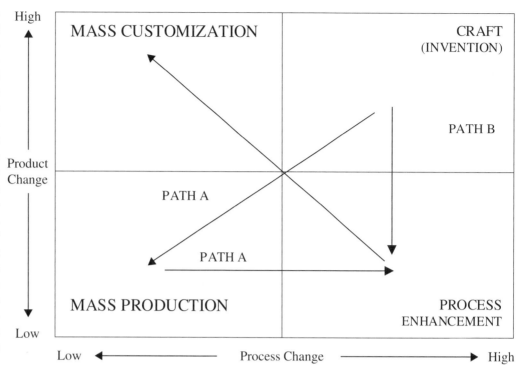

Figure 1 Stages of Industrialization

Source: Adapted from Victor & Boynton (1998).

patient status every few days and recommend modified inhaler dosage levels on an ongoing basis.

Trends that will enable and motivate mass customization include increased consumer demand for individualized care, reduced available physician face time per patient, exploding variety of disease classifications based on new genomic categories, and advancing and increasingly economical information technology. New requirements for electronic prescription ordering will rapidly speed up investment in the required underpinnings in real-time computer systems and interconnectivity among health care providers.

—Arnold Kaluzny and Curtis P. McLaughlin

See also Information Technology, Mass Customization, Quality Improvement Cycle

FURTHER READING

Davis, S. (1987). *Future perfect.* Cambridge, MA: Perseus.

McLaughlin, C. P., & Fitzgerald, C. Q. (2001). Converging genetics and information technologies and the emerging health care system. *International Journal of Health Care Technology and Management, 3*(5–6), 498–518.

McLaughlin, C. P., & Kaluzny, A. D. (1998, February). Managed care: The challenge ahead. *OR/MS Today, 25*(1), 24–27.

Victor, B., & Boynton, A. (1998). *Invented here.* Boston: Harvard Business School Press.

MATERNAL AND CHILD HEALTH (MCH)

Maternal and child health (MCH) is the professional and academic field that focuses on the determinants, mechanisms, and systems that promote and maintain the health, safety, well-being, and appropriate development of children and their families in communities and societies, in order to enhance the future health and welfare of society and subsequent generations. Maternal and child health is a collaborative, multidisciplinary specialty area within the field of public health. It uses the tools of other public health disciplines, such as health administration/policy, epidemiology, biostatistics, and health behavior, to address the health and developmental needs of the entire population of children. In keeping with public health in general, MCH is oriented toward health promotion and disease prevention. MCH employs public health's preventive philosophy in its efforts to ensure that the myriad health care and social systems, which are designed to promote and support the health, safety, and optimal growth and development of children, are available, accessible, coordinated, effective, and cost- efficient. Accordingly, MCH is distinct from pediatrics, obstetrics, maternal/fetal medicine, and other medical specialties that provide direct clinical services to women, infants, and children. Although MCH programs within public health agencies may provide direct clinical services, these gap-filling activities fall under MCH's overarching mission to assure the availability of and access to necessary, appropriate, and comprehensive systems of health care.

In the United States, maternal and child health evolved out of the child labor abolition and progressive reform movements of the late 1800s and early 1900s. The initial federal statutory agency focusing on MCH, the Children's Bureau, was established in 1912, based on a recommendation arising from the First White House Conference on Children in 1909. The Children's Bureau's mission was to "investigate and report upon matters pertaining to the welfare of children and child life among all classes of people." The course of MCH in the United States has since taken numerous directions and has been notably influenced by social events, including the Great Depression, world wars, and political movements. Nevertheless, the populationwide focus, coupled with an emphasis on needs assessment, assurance, and policy and advocacy functions, has remained a hallmark of MCH activities to this day.

Although there is variation across the country, state MCH programs within public health agencies typically encompass several distinct programs and services, including maternity, genetics, well baby, child health, children with special health care needs, adolescent health, family planning, EPSDT (Early and Periodic Screening, Diagnosis and Treatment), and WIC (Special Supplemental Nutrition Program for Women, Infants and Children). The scope of MCH efforts has extended beyond children to include mothers, women of reproductive age, fathers, and families, in recognition of the unique role parents and families play in child development and the importance of preconception health in improving the prospects of a healthy pregnancy and birth outcome.

—Greg R. Alexander

FURTHER READING

http://main.uab.edu/show.asp?durki=45534

Kotch, J. B. (Ed.). (1997). *Maternal and child health: Programs, problems, and policy in public health.* Gaithersburg, MD: Aspen.

Wallace, H. M., Nelson, R. P., & Sweeney, P. J. (1994). *Maternal and child health practices* (4th ed.). Oakland, CA: Third Part Publishing.

MATRIX STRUCTURE

See Structure

MATURE STAGE OF PRODUCT LIFE CYCLE

See Product Life Cycle (PLC) Analysis

MEASURING TRAINING OUTCOMES

Measuring training outcomes involves the systematic collection of information for the purpose of evaluating whether a planned learning event affects change in an individual, department, or organization. The outcomes of training help decision makers determine if a training program should be modified, continued, or terminated. Given the millions of dollars health care organizations spend annually on training programs, decision makers are concerned about the value and effectiveness of training, particularly in tight economic climates. For example, when a nurse specializing in patient care gets promoted to a management position and undergoes various management training programs, it is important to determine if those programs help him or her perform the new job better. In essence, by measuring training outcomes one is trying to answer the question "Does training work?"

Many professionals refer to Kirkpatrick's four levels of training outcomes when evaluating a training program. The first and most simple level is trainees' *reactions* to the training event. Reactions include trainees' perceptions that they learned something, will improve their performance, and felt the instructor and/or the program was effective. Questionnaires administered at the conclusion of a training event are used to gather reactions. The second outcome level is trainees' *learning* of the training content. Learning is often measured via trainees' memory or application of the training material. The importance of this outcome cannot be overstated—to change one's understanding, behavior, or performance, one has first to learn new knowledge, skills, or abilities.

The third outcome level is trainees' *behavior,* which reflects the extent training has created an actual change in trainees' behavior or on-the-job performance. Personal observation and behavioral rating forms are often used to assess behavioral change. There has been a great deal of research and practice in recent years aimed at improving the extent that skills and behaviors learned in training are transferred to the job such that performance is improved.

The final outcome is individual and organizational *results,* including such measures as revenue, absenteeism, accidents, patient complaints, and costs. Careful collection of this information can help decision makers examine the utility of a training program, such as whether benefits outweigh costs, and whether the training program adds value to other interventions, such as selection and on-the-job experience.

When attempting to measure training outcomes, practitioners should adhere to several guidelines:

- A careful training needs assessment should be conducted to determine the objectives of the training program.
- The training program's objectives should guide which outcome measures are used. For example, if the goal of a training program is greater awareness of other employee perspectives (such as sensitivity training), then reactions or learning may be more applicable than measuring organizational results.
- Standardized outcome measures that allow comparisons between different people, different training

programs, and training programs with other interventions, should be employed when possible.
- When measuring learning, behavior, or results, proper evaluation methodology should be used, such as control groups and pre- and posttraining measures. This will help determine whether improvements have been made and whether those improvements are attributable to the training program.

—Mark L. Poteet

See also Balanced Scorecard and Health Care, Management Development, Organizational Performance and Work Design

FURTHER READING

Bartram, S., & Gibson, B. (1999). *Evaluating training: A resource for measuring the results and impact of training on people, departments, and organizations.* Burlington, VT: Ashgate Publishing.

Goldstein, I. L., & Ford, K. (2001). *Training in organizations: Needs assessment, development, and evaluation* (4th ed.). Pacific Grove, CA: Thomson Learning.

Kirkpatrick, D. L. (1998). *Evaluating training programs: The four levels* (2nd ed.). San Francisco: Berrett-Koehler Publishers.

London, M. L. (1989). *Managing the training enterprise: High quality, cost-effective, employee training in organizations.* San Francisco: Jossey-Bass.

MEDICAID

Title XIX, "Grants to States for Medical Assistance Programs," also known as Medicaid, was created in Public Law 89-97, the Social Security Amendments of 1965. The Centers for Medicare and Medicaid Services (CMS), an agency in the U.S. Department of Health and Human Services (DHHS), has responsibility for the administration of the program. Medicaid, jointly funded by federal and state dollars, provides payments for medical services to over 40 million low-income individuals. In 2000, federal and state Medicaid expenditures amounted to $194.7 billion: $111.1 billion federal and $83.6 billion state funded. Federal expenditures have reached $85 billion during the first half of federal fiscal year (FFY) 2002. Medicaid is the largest single payer of long-term care services, providing over 44% of the funding, which in 2000 totaled $44.4 billion. Medicaid is the largest single payer of direct medical services to people living with AIDS, with expenditures estimated to total $7.7 billion in FFY 2002.

Medicaid evolved from two earlier federal grant programs. Federal matching funds were made available to states for payment of medical services provided to persons receiving public assistance in the Social Security

Amendments of 1950. The 1960 Kerr-Mills legislation provided federal matching grants to states providing medical assistance to the indigent aged. Medicaid became a joint entitlement program between federal and state governments that provides federal matching dollars to states that provide medical services to low-income persons receiving welfare assistance, pregnant women and single parents with dependent children, the needy aged, blind, and disabled, and supplemental coverage for low-income Medicare beneficiaries. Federal statutes and policies establish broad guidelines within which each state determines the eligibility standards, type, amount, duration, and scope of services, payment rate for services, and program administration.

Eligibility determination is based on both financial and categorical requirements. Medicaid, a means-tested program, requires the individual to have low income and to meet certain asset and resource standards established by each state within federal guidelines. In 1965, eligibility was linked to receipt of Aid to Families with Dependent Children (AFDC), and in 1972, Supplemental Security Income (SSI) was added as a qualifying program. Later legislation has allowed the coverage of certain Medicaid beneficiary groups based solely on income and resources and not on receipt of cash assistance. The Personal Responsibility and Work Opportunity Reconciliation Act (PRWORA) of 1996 replaced the AFDC cash assistance program with Temporary Assistance for Needy Families (TANF), a block grant program. PRWORA removed the automatic eligibility for Medicaid by TANF recipients but allowed families Medicaid coverage if they met AFDC requirements in effect before welfare reform, July 16, 1996.

Title XIX mandates the coverage of certain populations and allows the states the option of the inclusion of certain other groups. The groups that fall under the mandatory criteria known as the "categorically needy" include the following:

- AFDC-eligible individuals as of July 16, 1996
- Poverty-related groups: all pregnant women and children below the age of 6 years with incomes up to 133% of the federal poverty level (FPL)
- All children born after September 30, 1983, with incomes up to 100% of FPL
- Current and some former recipients of SSI
- Recipients of foster care and adoption assistance
- Certain Medicare beneficiaries

Low-income Medicare recipients that have limited resources may qualify for Medicaid benefits and are known as the "dually eligible." If qualified for full Medicaid coverage, Medicare benefits are supplemented by the state's Medicaid program. Other Medicare recipients may receive certain Medicaid supplemental assistance in the following categories:

1. *Qualified Medicare Beneficiaries (QMBs).* Medicare beneficiaries whose resources are at or below twice the allowable standard for SSI and whose incomes are at or below 100% of FPL for whom Medicaid (subject to state-determined payment rates) pays the Medicare Hospital Insurance (HI) and the Supplementary Medical Insurance (SMI) premiums, and the Medicare coinsurance and deductibles

2. *Specified Low-Income Medicare Beneficiaries (SLMBs).* Medicare beneficiaries whose resources are similar to QMBs but whose incomes are less than 120% of FPL for whom Medicaid pays only the SMI premium

3. *Qualified Disabled Working Individuals (QDWIs).* Medicare beneficiaries qualified by reason of disability who return to work though still disabled with incomes below 200% of FPL and ineligible for Medicaid by any other category for whom Medicaid can pay their HI premium

4. *Qualifying Individuals (QIs).* Medicare beneficiaries whose income is above 120% of FPL but below 175% of FPL and are otherwise ineligible for any other state medical assistance program may qualify for payment of some or all of their SMI premium 100% federally funded

States may choose to cover individuals from the following groups, known as "categorically related," which generally represent the same populations described in the mandatory categories but for whom more liberal income and resource tests are allowed:

- Poverty-related groups: pregnant women and infants with incomes up to 185% of FPL
- Medically needy: individuals that do not meet program financial limits but otherwise fit into one of the categorical groups
- Recipients of state supplementary income payments
- People in long-term care
- Working disabled
- "Optional targeted low-income children" included within the State Children's Health Insurance Program (SCHIP)

SCHIP, created by Congress in the Balanced Budget Act (BBA) of 1997 (Title XXI, State Children's Health Insurance Program) to meet the challenge of the growing number of uninsured children, provides states three options for program design: create a separate child health insurance program, expand coverage available under an existing Medicaid program, or use both strategies. SCHIP creates a new eligibility category, the "targeted low-income child."

The families of such children have an income below the greater of 200% of FPL or 50 percentage points above the state's Medicaid eligibility threshold. Congress authorized $40 billion in federal funding from 1998 to 2007 to offer states an enhanced match for children enrolled in this expansion program. Enrollment has grown from 1.96 million in FFY 1999 to 4.6 million in FFY 2001.

States also have the ability to expand eligibility through the research and demonstration project authority described in Section 1115 of the Social Security Act. The Health Insurance Flexibility and Accountability (HIFA) demonstration initiative is the most recent example of Section 1115 eligibility expansion options made available to the states.

Title XIX mandates certain covered services that must be provided by the states and defines certain optional services that may be provided by the states. Each state determines the amount, duration, and scope of the services. The mandatory covered services include the following:

- Inpatient and outpatient hospital services
- Rural health clinic and Federally Qualified Health Center (FQHC) services
- Laboratory and X-ray services
- Nurse practitioner and nurse midwife services
- Nursing facility services and home health services for individuals 21 years and older
- Early and Periodic Screening, Diagnosis and Treatment (EPSDT) for individuals under the age of 21 years
- Family planning services and supplies
- Physicians' services
- Dentists' medical and surgical services

EPSDT, established in 1967 and expanded in 1989, is a comprehensive and preventive child health program for Medicaid recipients under the age of 21 years. It provides periodic screening, vision, dental, and hearing services as well as any medically necessary health care service listed in Section 1905(r)(5) of the Social Security Act even if the service is not available under the state's Medicaid plan to the rest of the Medicaid population.

There are 33 optional services that the states may include in the Medicaid benefit package; the most commonly chosen include the following:

- Diagnostic services
- Clinic services
- Intermediate care facilities for the mentally retarded (ICFs/MR)
- Prescribed drugs and prosthetic devices
- Optometrist services and eyeglasses
- Nursing facility services for children under age 21
- Transportation services

- Rehabilitation and physical therapy services
- Home and community-based care to certain people with chronic impairments

States also have the option of providing an alternative to institutional care for people 55 years and older who require care at the nursing facility level, in PACE, Programs of All-inclusive Care for the Elderly, created by the BBA in 1997. States may also receive federal match funding if they provide medical services for certain women diagnosed with breast or cervical cancer or precancerous conditions authorized in the Breast and Cervical Cancer Prevention and Treatment Act of 2000.

Federal and state governments jointly provide funding for the Medicaid program. Disbursement of general revenue-derived federal funds to the states is based on the number of program participants and services provided in the state Medicaid program. States receive matching federal funds of 50% to 83% of the payments for services provided by the Medicaid program determined annually by a formula known as the Federal Medical Assistance Percentage (FMAP). The FMAP is determined by the average per capita income for each state relative to the national average whereby the lower the state average, the higher the federal match. Generally, 50% of administrative costs are eligible for FMAP.

States may pay for services provided under the Medicaid program on a fee-for-service basis or through various prepayment arrangements. Medicaid providers must accept state-determined Medicaid reimbursement amounts as payment in full. In FFY 2000, direct payments to providers totaled $146.4 billion. The Omnibus Budget Reconciliation Act of 1981 (OBRA 81) mandated states to make additional payments to certain hospitals providing a high proportion of inpatient care to Medicaid and other indigent patients known as Disproportionate Share Hospital (DSH) payments. DSH payments, $14.4 billion in FFY 2000, help ensure the "safety net" providers' participation in the Medicaid program. At the discretion of the states, cost sharing in the form of nominal deductibles, coinsurance, and copayments may be imposed on some Medicaid recipients for some medical services, but pregnant women, children under the age of 18 years, and hospitalized or nursing home patients who are expected to contribute most of their income toward institutional care must be excluded. In addition, emergency room and family planning services are exempt.

Because of mandated program expansion activity, the effects of the economic recession of the 1980s, and the rising costs associated with medical inflation, states sought budgetary relief from the rapidly escalating costs associated with the Medicaid program. A series of initiatives that all included managed care components were developed based on legislation first introduced in OBRA 81, known as

Section 19115(b) "Freedom of Choice Waiver," Section 1115 Waiver Research and Demonstration Projects, and in BBA–97 Section 1932(a). Section 1915(b) allows states to impose mandatory enrollment into Medicaid managed care programs. Section 1115 provides the secretary of DHHS the authority to approve experimental, pilot, or demonstration projects that test new methods of Medicaid program administration. This was further expanded in the Medicaid Voluntary Contribution and Provider-Specific Tax Amendments of 1991 where the waiver is allowed to cover nontraditional Medicaid populations and to expand managed care. Section 1932 provides a mechanism via the State Plan Amendment, by which a state can mandate managed care without prior receipt of a waiver.

Participation in Medicaid managed care has increased from 9.5% of all Medicaid enrollees in 1991 to 57% in 2001. As of June 2000, 31 states and the District of Columbia have implemented Section 1915(b) programs and 19 states have implemented Section 1115 programs. In August 2001 a new Section 1115 demonstration initiative, the Health Insurance Flexibility and Accountability (HIFA) program, was announced. This initiative is expected to expand coverage with limited benefits to uninsured individuals, primarily adults, with incomes below 200% of FPL.

—Barbara A. Nabrit-Stephens

See also Aid to Families with Dependent Children (AFDC), Centers for Medicare and Medicaid Services

FURTHER READING

http://cms.hhs.gov/about/history/pre35.asp

http://cms.hhs.gov/hiv/hivfs.asp

http://cms.hhs.gov/medicaid/2Tchartbk.pdf

http://cms.hhs.gov/medicaid/epsdt/default.asp

http://cms.hhs.gov/medicaid/managedcare/cover01.asp

http://cms.hhs.gov/medicaid/msis/mstats.asp

http://cms.hhs.gov/medicaid/waiver1.asp

http://cms.hhs.gov/statistics/nhe/historical/highlights.as

Rosenbaum, S. (2002). Medicaid. *New England Journal of Medicine, 346,* 635–640.

www.hcfa.gov/pubforms/actuary/ormedmed/default4.htm

www.ssa.gov/regs/ssasect.htm

MEDICAL APPROPRIATENESS OF CARE

Medical appropriateness of care has two meanings. The first is that the provider, the physician, is the only individual who can determine what is medically necessary or needed to bring the patient to an optimal level of health.

The other is that the federal government and managed care and other insurance companies a make the determination of what will be paid as a medical necessity. At times these two groups collide in determining what is medically needed. The term *medical necessity* is used interchangeably and should not be. Medical necessity for the physician can and frequently does have a different meaning than it does for the entities paying the bills. Generally, however, the services are covered if they are needed to prevent the onset of an illness or disability. (An example of this might be routine PAP tests, which, performed yearly on adult females, may determine in early stages cancer of the cervix; if treated at that time, extensive disease, high costs for treatments, and even death can be prevented.) The service will reduce the physical effects of an illness (an example of this may be immunization of children for childhood disease prevention). And, last, the service proposed will assist the patient in achieving maximum functional capacity (an example of this might include physical therapy, occupational therapy, or speech therapy).

Medical appropriateness is best defined as the care and services needed to bring the individual to the optimal level of well-being. The determination of appropriateness includes the extent that the service is needed and the efficacy of the expected outcome.

These services include ambulatory, outpatient clinic, or office care, acute inpatient hospital care, and finally, hospice or end-of-life care. With the high cost of health care, medical decision making is being challenged daily. Health care has changed enormously in the past three decades. What is considered routine medical intervention today was considered experimental only a few years ago. The need to spend the scarce health care dollar in a manner that will benefit most individuals is absolutely essential to the entire health care system's survival, to meet the needs of all individuals seeking health care.

Not so long ago an individual who was to undergo a simple procedure (elective cataract surgery) would be admitted to the hospital the day prior to scheduled surgery, have the necessary lab work completed, have the surgery the following day, and be cared for on an inpatient basis for several days. The length of stay might be five days for this procedure. Today, this procedure is done on an ambulatory basis, with all necessary lab work done before the day of surgery with the patient admitted to an ambulatory surgery area and discharged the same day. This is no longer an inpatient procedure.

One of the ways to determine medical necessity, for payment, in acute care is to use nationally recognized criteria that outline not only what is an acute care situation, but why it is. One such criteria set is InterQual. InterQual offers patient-specific criteria that encourage the reviewer to look at severity of illness (SI) and the intensity of services (IS) as part of the review process. This proprietary company,

McKesson, has a variety of other products to identify alternate level of care (ALC), length of stay (LOS), and pre-certification needs for procedures, durable medical equipment (DME) and imaging. This is a major source for substantiation for admission and continued stay and is used by many managed care companies as well as the peer review organizations (PROs) to address medical necessity for acute care. Physicians, nurses, and other health care practitioners usually generate criteria sets; these practitioners who look at past practices and draw on their experience to determine what care is needed, what the best setting (inpatient, outpatient, or ambulatory care), and when the care is needed.

The need to limit the scarce health care dollar has necessitated intervention in how and where it is spent. The managed care and other insurance companies defer to the physician in terms of what is necessary for optimal health but simply state that the care did not need to be rendered and decline to pay. They have determined that the decision to continue is between the physician and the patient to proceed without regard for their financial support. In many ways this is analogous to "free care" given to the patient for the insurance company. The patient receives the care needed, and the hospital and sometimes the physician are not paid. Medically appropriate care determination has been a shared responsibility of both the provider and the payer in the past decade and will continue in this fashion for some time to come.

—Edna Lee Kucera

FURTHER READING

www.cms.org
www.interqual.org
www.ipro.org
www.mccapny.org

MEDICAL CARE

The realm of medical care encompasses the continuum of services and products consumed by individuals to maintain health or to cure or ameliorate a clinical condition or disease. The scope of medical care is very broad and includes services provided in numerous settings from highly sophisticated medical centers and universities to neighborhood clinics in rural areas. Medical care can be divided into four separate categories:

- Primary care
- Secondary care
- Tertiary care
- Quaternary care

Primary Care: Primary care services involve health maintenance activities such as checkups, immunizations, treatment of common illnesses such as respiratory and digestive disorders, and caring for the psychosocial needs of individuals. Primary care providers in the United States come from a number of disciplines. Traditional concepts of primary care providers (PCPs) include specialties of family medicine, pediatrics, and internal medicine, and some authorities include obstetrics and gynecology in the mix of primary care specialties, because these physicians care for many of the primary care health needs of women. Physicians in these specialties can come from the ranks of either allopathic or osteopathic doctors. Allopathic physicians are trained in medical schools, undergo advanced training in a clinical specialty, and are licensed in their state of practice. The only difference in osteopathic training is that the educational curriculum occurs in schools of osteopathy, which include training in osteopathic manipulative treatment.

Over the past several decades, other health care providers have assumed the role of PCP. Advanced practice nurses, who undergo master's-level training and receive special certification, provide a number of primary care services, usually under the supervision of or in partnership with a physician. These health professionals are trained in performing histories and physical examinations, signs and symptoms of many common diseases, and use of diagnostic modalities such as lab and X-ray procedures. Many of these master's-trained nurses specialize in a particular medical discipline, such as pediatrics, and have distinguished careers in the health care delivery system. Other health professionals who may perform primary care services include home health nurses, parish nurses (affiliated with churches and religious organizations), and chiropractors.

Secondary Care: Primary care services are most often performed in outpatient settings, like medical offices or clinics, but many physicians who perform primary care also admit people to hospitals for secondary care. Secondary care has been most extensively defined in the National Health Service in the United Kingdom and includes more advanced outpatient services and procedures, such as outpatient surgery, as well as inpatient services that are less resource intensive. These services can include inpatient admissions for minimally invasive diagnostic procedures or therapies that require closer monitoring than can be performed in the outpatient environment. In the United States, economic pressures from payers have increased the number and types of services performed at free-standing outpatient centers, and hospital admissions for many procedures have declined substantially as a result.

Secondary care services may also be provided by a number of nonphysician practitioners. Advanced practice nurses and physicians' assistants frequently are involved in delivering secondary care services in both outpatient and hospital settings. These professionals usually specialize in a specific area, such as endocrinology or oncology, and become more knowledgeable about a specific illness or group of illnesses, unlike the advanced practice nurses who serve as PCPs. Other health practitioners who may work in secondary care settings include surgeons, medical specialists, podiatrists, behavioral health specialists, and radiologists.

Tertiary Care: Although secondary care services may be delivered in both outpatient and inpatient facilities, tertiary care services are nearly always performed in the hospital in the United States. This level of care often entails more complicated diagnostic or therapeutic procedures, such as complex surgical operations, invasive cardiac catheterization, advanced respiratory support using mechanical ventilation, or bone marrow transplantation. Because these procedures have greater potential for complications and harm to individual patients, they require closer supervision and are more resource intensive than primary or secondary care procedures. Thus, these procedures are best performed by health professionals who specialize in a specific clinical area that deals extensively with these disease entities and procedures. Examples of physicians who practice in the tertiary care environment include surgical specialists, such as cardiothoracic surgeons, orthopedists, and urologists as well as medical specialists such as pulmonologists, cardiologists, and intensivists. Although the scope of their services is usually very proscribed and supervised by physicians, nonphysician practitioners, such as advanced practice nurses, can also work in the tertiary care setting.

Quaternary Care: Usually reserved for highly specialized services for relatively uncommon clinical conditions, quaternary care in the United States is most often provided in university medical centers or very large hospital systems. Such care often requires the expertise of medical specialists who have training and experience in rare diseases, making treatment difficult because people lack understanding of the disease given its infrequency in the population. A medical or surgical specialist may become well known throughout the medical community for expertise in a particular rare condition, leading to referrals to the specialist's clinic or hospital, which enhances the treatment of the condition. Thus, the specialist must be located in an area with substantial medical resources, which in the United States entails either a university medical center or large hospital system. Because the clinical conditions are rare, diagnostic and treatment modalities are often not standardized, requiring continuing research into the disease—another characteristic of a quaternary care center.

The diversity of medical care in the United States is broadened substantially when viewed throughout the world. Although many of the developed countries have systems of care similar to that in the United States, developing countries may have significantly different health care delivery systems. For example, China has developed a three-tiered system of medical care, consisting of village stations, township health centers, and county hospitals in rural areas and street health stations, community health centers, and district hospitals in urban areas. Village stations are staffed by village doctors who are trained for three to six months after junior high school and receive an average of two to three weeks of continuing education each year. Township health centers usually have 10 to 20 beds overseen by a physician with three years of medical school education after high school, aided by assistant physicians and village doctors. County hospitals usually have 250 to 300 beds and are staffed by physicians with four to five years of medical training after high school, as well as by nurses and technicians.

In developed countries, some integration in the health care delivery system has been achieved. Primary care practitioners serve the vast majority of health needs for the population, and referrals for secondary through quaternary services are facilitated through a communications network that is fairly well developed. Payers in these systems often place barriers in the communications network to reduce unneeded referrals for more expensive services, or the availability of expensive resources is limited, creating queues. In contrast, in developing countries access even to primary care is frequently very limited by inadequate resources for medical care. In these countries, health care, even at the primary care level, is available only to wealthy individuals who can afford to purchase health resources.

Medical care involves all the services and products used for maintaining or improving the health of a population. The breadth of medical care throughout the world provides many models and scenarios, with varying degrees of effectiveness in delivering care. Because medical care is an essential component of human endeavor, most countries and the international community are working vigorously to improve the distribution of medical care services to individuals all over the globe.

—Donald E. Lighter

FURTHER READING

Bodenheimer, T., & Grumbach, K. (2001). *Understanding health policy.* Old Tappan, NJ: Appleton & Lange.

Institute of Medicine (Ed.). (2001). *Crossing the quality chasm: A new health system for the 21st century.* Washington, DC: National Academy Press.

Marmot, M., & Wilkinson, R. (Eds.). (1999). *Social determinants of health.* Oxford, UK: Oxford University Press.

Morrison, I. (2000). *Health care in the new millennium: Vision, values, and leadership.* San Francisco: Jossey-Bass.

Shortell, S., Gillies, R., & Anderson, D. (2000). *Remaking health care in America* (2nd ed.). San Francisco: Jossey-Bass.

www.aap.org

www.acog.org

www.acponline.org

www.ama-assn.org

www.aoa-net.org

www.who.org

MEDICAL ERRORS

In 1999 the Institute of Medicine (IOM) released a report entitled *To Err Is Human: Building a Safer Health System,* which defined medical error as the failure of a planned action to be completed as intended, or the use of a wrong action plan to achieve an aim.

The report, which suggested that as many as 98,000 people die annually from medical errors, generated a significant amount of media and congressional attention and triggered new scholarly research into this issue. If the estimates presented in the report are accurate, medical error is a leading cause of disability and death, responsible for more deaths annually than highway accidents, breast cancer, or AIDS.

Medical errors can occur in hospitals, physicians' offices, pharmacies, long-term care facilities, ambulatory care centers, and even in care delivered in the home. Examples of medical error include a nurse accidentally administering the wrong dose of a drug, a pharmacist misreading a physician's handwritten prescription and providing the patient with the wrong drug with a similar name, a hospital patient not being given a low-salt meal when one is clinically indicated, a diagnostic procedure being performed on the wrong patient, or a surgeon amputating the wrong leg.

Not all medical error results in actual harm to patients. For example, a provider may administer an incorrect medication without causing harm to a patient. However, many errors do result in harm, or adverse event, to the patient. An adverse event takes place when an injury occurs as a result of medical care prolonging hospitalization, producing temporary or permanent disability, or causing death. An error that does not lead to harm is called a "near miss" or "close call" event. One example of a near miss would be medical professionals realizing they are about to deliver the wrong drug to a patient and stopping themselves before actually doing so. Near misses are important to study because they may provide clues on why medical errors commonly occur and how people or health care systems could intervene to prevent error.

COST OF MEDICAL ERRORS

When error results in injury, it is a source of burden to patients, their families, caregivers, and health care organizations. These burdens can be both monetary and nonpecuniary losses. Monetary losses are typically expenditures from counteractive treatments and additional drug costs. Nonpecuniary losses can be opportunity costs and both social and emotional tolls taken on individuals and society as a result of error in health care delivery. The costs of repeated diagnostic tests, counteractive remedy drugs, and increases in insurance premiums (because of increased costs) are resources that become unavailable elsewhere. Other costs include loss of morale among providers, diminished patient satisfaction, increased discomfort, and loss of trust in the health care system. These factors may take their toll in the form of decreased worker productivity, reduced school attendance by children, and lower levels of overall population health status. The IOM report estimates the overall cost of medical error in the United States to be as much as $29 billion, with half of that attributable to medical care costs alone.

CAUSES AND PREVENTION OF MEDICAL ERRORS

Historically, there has been considerable reluctance among medical professionals to openly discuss their errors for fear of legal recourse or compromising their reputation. Deterrents to open discussion of errors may include the threat of malpractice suits, high expectations of the patients' family or society, possible disciplinary actions by licensing boards, and threats to job security. However, experts believe that individual providers are not the underlying cause of the medical errors problem. Instead they attribute the situation to the many suboptimal characteristics of the health care system. Among these conditions are the high levels of stress associated with delivering medical care, the similarity in the spelling and pronunciation of many drug names, the nationwide shortage of some key health care team members, and the lagging attention to safety in health care, especially when compared to other industries (such as aviation).

In preventing errors, interventions using a systemic approach seem most promising thus far. For example, enforcing a maximum consecutive duration for which resident physicians can work and assuring they receive adequate rest while working overnight shifts may help reduce errors associated with fatigue. In addition, the use of information technologies, such as computerized provider order entry systems (CPOE), can eliminate reliance on handwriting for medication ordering and other treatment needs. Such a system automates the medication order process and can force the indication of a precise dose, route, and frequency, thus eliminating the problem of illegible handwriting and incomplete or lost information, and it makes every prescription traceable to the provider. CPOEs, particularly when coupled with a decision support system, can also provide the latest information about a drug and can cross-reference allergies, interactions, and other patient-specific issues with the treatment being prescribed.

Other interventions being pursued to reduce error involve the standardization of treatment through the use of evidence-based clinical protocols to avoid reliance on memory, which is known to be fallible and the cause of many errors. Successful approaches to reducing medical error generally include making relevant information readily available, suggesting alternatives using decision support systems, pointing out redundancies, correlating links between pieces of information, doing boring or repetitive tasks, and making guidelines and new information accessible.

—Nir Menachemi

FURTHER READING

Bogner, M. S. (1994). *Human error in medicine.* Hillsdale, NJ: Erlbaum.
Institute of Medicine. (1999). *To err is human: Building a safer health system.* Washington, DC: National Academy Press.
www.ahrq.gov/qual/errback.htm
www.quic.gov/report

MEDICAL ETHICS

See Code of Ethics, Ethical Issues Faced by Managers, Ethics Officer

MEDICAL GENETICS

Medical genetics is the science or medical practice of identifying the human genetic code, in particular, those genes coding for faulty traits in the human organism, and then attempting to develop strategies for dealing with the deleterious effects of such traits. The use of exogenous factor VIII to compensate for its lack in hemophiliacs, even the use of insulin in diabetics, could be described as the early practice of medical genetics. In humans, the genetic code is contained in deoxyribonucleic acid (DNA), which codes for the production of ribonucleic acid (RNA), which in turn codes for the production of proteins. Each protein controls or influences an inherited trait, either directly, or indirectly by controlling or influencing the effect of other genes. Each human cell ordinarily contains 46 chromosomes, two copies of 23 different types, one copy contributed by each parent. Each chromosome is composed primarily of one DNA molecule, and each gene is located at a specific point on one of the chromosomes. The Human Genome Project is an international effort to delineate the entire human genome. The U.S. branch of the Human Genome Project is the National Human Genome Research Institute, a division of the National Institutes of Health (NIH). Celera Genomics, a privately funded research firm, has been in competition with the Human Genome Project, and during the past few years both organizations have claimed success. Despite differences in such basic concepts as the total number of genes (estimates range from 40,000 to greater than 60,000), it is clear that both groups have made notable contributions, and it can fairly be stated that most of the human genome has been determined. Some recent advances in medical genetics include the identification of genes that predispose to breast cancer, prostate cancer, ovarian cancer, and colon cancer, the differentiation of stem cells into specialized tissues, the ability to identify individuals by their "DNA fingerprint," and many more. As an organized branch of internal medicine, medical genetics has grown rapidly in the past few years. There now exist numerous scientific journals devoted to the specialty of medical genetics, an American College of Medical Genetics, an American Board of Medical Genetics, and numerous residency training programs in the field. In the United States, residency programs are accredited by the Accreditation Council for Graduate Medical Education, or ACGME, Residency Review Committee in Medical Genetics, and graduates of such programs may sit for the Clinical Genetics Board Examination, which is administered by the American Board of Medical Genetics. In general, a training program in medical genetics is a two-year residency for physicians who have already completed a minimum of two years residency training in a primary specialty in the United States. A specialist in medical genetics is expected to be able to diagnose a broad range of inherited diseases and congenital malformations, to be acquainted with the principles of genetic screening, to be able to provide counseling to patients and their families, and to be aware of the legal, social, and ethical implications of both genetic diseases and their potential treatments.

—Robert I. Katz

FURTHER READING

http://chid.nih.gov/subfile/contribs/mg.html
http://research.marshfieldclinic.org/genetics
www.genome.gov

MEDICAL SAVINGS ACCOUNTS (MSAS)

Medical savings accounts (MSAs) were enacted into law on a trial basis in the Healthcare Insurance Portability and Accountability Act of 1966, Public Law 104-191, also known as Kennedy/Kassebaum or H.R. 3103. The initial trial period ran through 2000, and there was an additional two-year extension through 2002. New legislation was being debated in the U.S. Congress as this encyclopedia was being edited in the summer of 2003. Federally tax-advantaged MSAs are governed by Section 220 of the Internal Revenue Code and are almost certainly going to continue for several more years as MSAs are included in the version passed by the House of Representatives (H.R. 2563) and are already included in the 2003 Bush administration budget.

Medical savings accounts are tax-deductible and tax-deferred savings accounts that may be used by persons covered by a high-deductible health insurance policy.

MSAs are aimed at the individual and small business owners with 50 employees or less. However, new legislation may expand the scope of MSAs and raise the dollar amount that may be invested tax free.

Presently, MSAs must meet several criteria:

- High-deductible insurance plan paired to the MSA. Individual deductibles of between $1000 and $2250 and family deductibles of $3000 to $4500 are required by law.
- The maximum legal "out of pocket" expenses are $3000 for individuals and $5500 for a family.
- Presently, tax-free contributions by employers or individuals to MSAs are limited to 65% of the deductible for an individual and 75% of the family deductible. Either the employee or the employer may make the contribution in any given year, but not both parties.

The key incentive for having a MSA is that any monies not used in the account at the end of the year may grow tax free. There is a 15% penalty tax plus regular income tax on early withdrawals before age 65 if this money is not used for medical purposes.

In addition, MSAs let the individual have some control over how his or her health dollars are spent. It gives the individual the choice of the health care provider, because an individual's MSA pays for the initial medical payments and expenses of the high deductible.

An individual may "save" money and be rewarded for not spending on health care. Any excess year-end MSA monies may accumulate in a savings account for the individual. Hopefully, this is also an incentive to stay healthy, spend medical dollars wisely, and live a longer, more prosperous life.

—Kenneth Steiner and Stuart Hochron

MEDICAL SPECIALTIES

There are 24 medical specialty boards in the United States that are recognized by (are members of) the American Board of Medical Specialties (www.abms.org). A medical doctor on graduation from medical school traditionally undertakes specialty training. Prior to this time a physician has gone through a minimum of four years of college and four years of medical school. The specialty training, also called *residency training*, consists of at least three years where the new physician works under supervision. At the completion of the residency period the physician will be able to apply for the certification examination of the specialty board in which he or she completed residency training. Successful completion of the residency and board examination(s) allows the physician to use the designation "board certified" in the medical specialty.

Many of the boards also have subspecialties. Certification in a subspecialty requires additional training. Subspecialty training may add a period of from one to three years of training, usually termed "fellowship" training. A subspecialist is one who has completed training in a general medical specialty and then takes additional training in a more specific area of that specialty.

In the following table (pp. 366–367), you will see the member boards of the American Board of Medical Specialties and the primary and subspecialty certifications offered, contact information, specialty information, and training requirements. It is also important to recognize that you may see physicians use other designations that are not part of this list. This is because not all medical specialty boards are part of the American Board of Medical Specialties. An example is the American Board of Oral and Maxillofacial Surgeons (www.aboms.org), which certifies dentists (D.D.S. degree) after completion of an approved residency. In addition, osteopathic physicians (D.O. degree) may be certified by similar osteopathic medical boards after successful completion of residency training. Further information about osteopathic medical boards can be obtained from the American Osteopathic Association (www.aoa.net).

—Stephen A. Vitkun

FURTHER READING

www.abms.org
www.abms.org/which.asp

Table 1   Member Boards of the Americans Board of Medical Specialties

Specialty Name	Description of Specialty	Training (After Completion of Medical School)
Allergy and Immunology	Treats immune system disorders. Examples include asthma, rhinitis, adverse reactions to foods/drugs, AIDS	Prior certification in medicine or pediatrics (3 years), plus 2 years in allergy/immunology
Anesthesiology	Provides pain relief and maintenance/restoration of stable condition during surgery, assesses surgical risk, optimizes condition Consults in critical care and pain management	4 years (subspecialty training additional)
Colon and Rectal Surgery	Diagnose and treat diseases of the intestinal tract, colon, rectum, and anal canal medically or surgically	6 years (including general surgery training)
Dermatology	Diagnose and treat disorders of the skin, mouth, genitalia, hair, and nails	4 years (subspecialty training additional)
Emergency Medicine	Diagnose and treat emergent conditions, also involved in prehospital care	3 years (subspecialty training additional)
Family Practice	Diagnose and treat a variety of conditions in patients of all ages. Focuses on total health care	3 years (subspecialty training additional)
Internal Medicine	Provides comprehensive long-term care of adolescents, adults, and the elderly	3 years (subspecialty training additional)
Medical Genetics	Diagnose and treat genetically linked diseases, coordinate genetic screening programs	2 to 4 years (depending on certification requested), subspecialty training additional
Neurological Surgery	Diagnose and treat (medically or surgically) diseases of the central, autonomic, and peripheral nervous systems	7 years (including general surgery training)
Neurology	Diagnosis and medical treatment of diseases of the brain, spinal cord, peripheral nerves, muscles, and autonomic nervous system	4 years (subspecialty training additional)
Nuclear Medicine	Specialist who uses radioactive atoms/molecules in the diagnosis/treatment of disease or for research	3 years
Obstetrics and Gynecology	Provides medical and surgical care of the female reproductive system. Can be a primary physician for women	4 years (subspecialty training additional)
Ophthalmology	Diagnose and treat (medically or surgically) conditions of the eye and visual system	4 years
Orthopedic Surgery	Diagnose and treat (medically or surgically) conditions of the extremities, spine, and associated structures (bones and joints)	5 years (including general surgery training), subspecialty training additional
Otolaryngology	Diagnose and treat (medically or surgically) conditions of the ears, nose, throat, and upper respiratory system and related structures of the head and neck	5 years (subspecialty training additional)
Pathology	Specialist who deals with the causes and nature of disease, provides diagnosis through laboratory applications	5 to 7 years (subspecialty training additional)
Pediatrics	Specialist concerned with the physical, emotional, and social health of children	3 years (subspecialty training additional)
Physical Medicine and Rehabilitation	Specialist concerned with diagnosis, evaluation, and treatment of physical disabilities (often called a *physiatrist*)	4 years (subspecialty training additional)
Plastic Surgery	A surgeon dealing with repair/reconstruction of physical defects. Often employs aesthetic surgical principles (grafts, flaps, etc.)	5 to 7 years (subspecialty training additional)

Table 1   (Continued)

Specialty Name	Description of Specialty	Training (After Completion of Medical School)
Preventive Medicine	Specialist who focuses on individual and community health to protect and promote well-being and prevent disease	3 years (subspecialty training additional)
Psychiatry	Concerned with prevention, diagnosis, and treatment of mental addictive and emotional disorders	4 years (subspecialty training additional)
Radiology	Specialist using radiological methods to diagnose and treat disease	4 years (subspecialty training additional)
Surgery	A general surgeon manages a broad spectrum of surgical conditions affecting almost any area of the body	5 years (subspecialty training additional)
Thoracic Surgery	A specialist who deals with surgical conditions of the chest	7 to 8 years (including general surgery training)
Urology	A specialist concerned with medical and surgical disorders of the genitourinary system and adrenal gland	5 years

MEDICARE

See Aging Society, Balanced Budget Act (BBA) of 1997, Centers for Medicare and Medicaid Services (CMS), Medicaid

MEDICARE RISK CONTRACT

Medicare beneficiaries can choose to enroll in the traditional Medicare program, a fee-for-service (FFS) program, or a managed care program under Medicare. The most common type of Medicare managed care health plan is risk-contracted HMOs. In the Medicare managed care risk contract program, each HMO has a defined geographic area for serving Medicare beneficiaries. They provide a full range of Medicare services and may offer benefits not covered by traditional Medicare, such as prescription drugs. After joining a risk contract HMO, a beneficiary selects a primary care physician affiliated with that HMO. All medical care is managed by the primary care physician, and referrals are made to specialists or other providers associated with the HMO, with the exception of emergency cases. The HMO is paid a flat fee per month for each enrolled Medicare patient, regardless of the medical services provided to that patient. Thus, the fewer or less expensive procedures authorized by the primary care provider, the more profitable the HMO risk contract becomes.

—Theresa DiMartino

MEDWATCH PROGRAM

The MedWatch program is the division of the Food and Drug Administration that is responsible for safety information and adverse event reporting. Products covered under MedWatch include prescription and over-the-counter medications, medical foods, infant formulas, dietary supplements, medical devices, and radiation-emitting devices (medical equipment, cell phones, and so forth). Products not covered by MedWatch include vaccines, cosmetics, blood products, and veterinary products. Serious adverse events that would be reportable to Medwatch could have patient outcomes of hospitalization, permanent disability, congenital anomaly, death, or event requiring intervention to prevent permanent injury or death. Consumer and independent health care provider reporting to this organization is entirely voluntary. Medwatch receives approximately 5000 voluntary reports per year. For these reports, the health care provider is not required to prove causality between event and product, a suspicion of association is sufficient. The FDA is also interested in problems with product contamination, therapeutic failures, or confusing or unclear labeling. In addition to MedWatch, the FDA has the Medical Device Reporting (MDR) Program, which receives approximately 100,000 reports per year. User facilities such as hospitals and nursing homes are required to report deaths suspected of being related to medical devices, to both the manufacturer and the FDA via the Medwatch 3500A reporting form. The determination of causality is made by personnel observing the event.

In 2001, 41% of MedWatch claims were filed by pharmaceutical companies, 11% by physicians, and the remainder by consumers. The apparent underuse of MedWatch by physicians is based primarily on lack of knowledge of its existence; it is estimated that 1% to 10% of severe adverse events are actually reported to MedWatch.

—Daryn H. Moller

FURTHER READING

www.fda.gov/medwatch

MENTORING

Mentoring reflects a relationship between two individuals, usually a senior and junior employee, whereby the senior employee takes the junior employee "under his or her wing" to teach the junior employee about the job, introduce the junior employee to contacts, orient the junior employee to the industry and organization, and address social and personal issues that may arise on the job. The mentoring relationship is distinguished from other organizational relationships (such as between supervisor and subordinate) in that the involved individuals may or may not formally work together, the relationship is typically not sanctioned by the organization, the relationship usually lasts longer than most organizational relationships, the issues addressed during the course of the relationship may include nonwork issues, and the bond between the mentor and protégé is usually closer and stronger than those of other organizational relationships.

MENTORING FUNCTIONS AND STAGES

Mentors fill two major functions for their protégés. Career-related functions focus on success and advancement within the organization and include sponsorship, coaching, exposure and visibility, protection, and challenging assignments. Psychosocial functions focus on enhancing sense of identity, competence, and effectiveness in the professional role and include role modeling, acceptance and confirmation, counseling, and friendship.

Mentoring relationships are described as occurring in four stages. Those stages are initiation of the relationship, cultivation of the relationship during which most lessons are learned and benefits attained, separation of the relationship when the protégé begins to assert independence, and redefinition of the relationship as one of peers or colleagues.

MENTORING BENEFITS

Mentoring relationships are reputed to provide substantial benefits to protégés, mentors, and organizations. Research shows that mentored individuals advance more rapidly in the organization, earn higher salaries, are less likely to leave the organization, and express more favorable work attitudes. This research includes studies that have been conducted within the health care industry. The benefits for mentors include the personal satisfaction that comes from passing knowledge and skills on to others, exhilaration from the fresh energy provided by protégés, improved job performance by receiving a new perspective on the organization from protégés, loyalty and support from protégés, and organizational recognition. In an effort to capitalize on the benefits of mentoring, a substantial number of organizations are implementing formal mentoring programs. Mentoring programs can help organizations in their efforts to develop and advance the careers of women and minorities who may not have access to informal social networks, can be used as a recruitment and retention tool, can be used to help groom employees for positions of greater responsibility and expose high potential junior employees to senior leadership, and can be used to foster cultural change within organizations.

WAYS TO ENCOURAGE MENTORING RELATIONSHIPS

Organizations can foster mentoring relationships among employees by encouraging an organizational learning and development climate. This can be done by recognizing and rewarding the efforts of those who mentor others, providing opportunities for junior and senior employees to interact, and helping employees develop the tools needed for coaching and counseling others.

—Tammy D. Allen

See also Culture and Culture Change, Employee Orientation Programs, Management Development, Organizational Change, Succession Planning

FURTHER READING

Allen, T. D., Poteet, M. L., & Burroughs, S. M. (1997). The mentor's perspective: A qualitative inquiry and future research agenda. *Journal of Vocational Behavior, 51,* 70-89.

Fagenson, E. A. (1989). The mentor advantage: Perceived career/job experiences of protégés versus non-protégés. *Journal of Organizational Behavior, 10,* 309–320.

Koberg, C. S., Boss, R. W., Chappell, D., & Ringer, R. C. (1994). Correlates and consequences of protégé mentoring in a large hospital. *Group and Organization Management, 19,* 219–239.

Kram, K. E. (1985). *Mentoring at work: Developmental relationships in organizational life.* Glenview, IL: Scott Foresman.

MERGER AND ACQUISITION

A highly controversial corporate strategy is merger and acquisition, referred to as *M&A.* The two terms are usually used together to refer to the legal and financial joining together of two separate organizational entities. However, the two terms, *merger* and *acquisition,* have different connotations.

Acquisition is an unfriendly or hostile takeover of one organization by another. In a sense, a larger fish swallows a smaller fish. The parent organization maintains control over the child organization, as measured by number of board seats in the new organization occupied by board members from the parent organization, or as measured by members of the top management team of the parent organization maintaining executive positions in the combined organization. The converse is true for the child organization in that former board members are in a minority in the combined board, and some executives are terminated or demoted. Frequently, after the acquisition the organizational name of the parent is used in place of the organizational name of the child organization.

A *merger* is the friendly joining together of two organizations as in a corporate marriage. In a merger, scrupulous attention is paid to power sharing between board members from the two old organizations, and between executives from the two old organizations. In a merger of equals, terminations and demotions are rare. Often a single new organizational name is assumed by both former organizations.

Whether a friendly merger or a hostile acquisition, M&A is controversial for at least three reasons. First, the resources involved are huge, sometimes reaching into several billion of dollars, and several thousand jobs. Second, the survival of the organization as currently known to management, employees, and customers is at stake. Third, the control, future direction, and ability of the organization to serve current customers are at stake.

In addition to short-term gain, there are other reasons why organizations are involved in M&A. It can be a way to implement other strategies. An organization might try to concentrate its market power by buying its competitors if government regulators will permit it. Alternatively, an organization might pursue diversification by acquiring an organization with different products and services from its own. M&A is an instant way to gain presence in an industry versus new product development or new market development. There may be a built-in bias toward M&A if executives are compensated in part on the basis of organizational growth or organizational size.

Good examples of M&A in the health care industry were found in the pharmaceutical industry in the mid 1990s. Per the *Wall Street Journal*, Eli Lilly acquired PCS Health Systems for $4 billion, Merck acquired Medco for $6.6 billion, and Glaxo acquired Wellcome Pharmaceuticals for $14.9 billion. Indeed, the amounts are substantial.

Unfortunately, M&A does not usually have a happy ending. Slightly more than 50% of acquisitions end in subsequent divestiture, just as slightly more than 50% of marriages end in subsequent divorce. Because the corporate divestiture and marital divorce rate are about the same, there may be unmet expectations and power issues in both situations.

—Michael J. Stahl

See also Concentric Diversification, Divestiture Strategies

FURTHER READING

Drug industry takeovers mean more cost-cutting, less research spending. (1995, February 1). *Wall Street Journal*, B1.

Ginter, P. M., Swayne, L. M., & Duncan, W. J. (1998). *Strategic management of health care organizations*. Malden, MA: Blackwell.

Porter, M. E. (1987, May–June). From competitive advantage to corporate strategy. *Harvard Business Review*, p. 43.

Stahl, M., & Grigsby, D. (1997). *Strategic management* (Chapter 5). Oxford, UK: Blackwell.

MERIT PAY SYSTEM

See Employee Compensation

MISSION

The *mission* defines the reason for an organization's existence and is generally reflected in a clear statement of the purpose of the organization or a subunit within the organization. It is a critical part of the strategic planning process. In its simplest form, a mission statement reveals what the organization does, how it does this (processes or technology), and to whom the organization's activities are targeted (customers, geography, and so on). Many mission statements also include the creed, ethics, and/or values the organization embraces. It is logical that companies and organizations in the health care industry will have different mission statements. The mission statement defines the industry sector in which the firm is operating and the method in which the organization chooses to differentiate itself within the sector.

The mission of an organization may be expressed in clear, precise, narrow terminology or in very broad general terms. However, a mission statement that defines the organization only by the products or services it provides is too narrow and incomplete. The service or product must meet a need in the marketplace and that need must be defined by where or to whom and how it will be met. It is important that the health care organization understands and recognizes the market it serves and the means by which it serves its market. Likewise, a health care organization that develops a mission that is broad and vague disseminates confusion or misinterpretation to its customers, management, employees, and stakeholders (such as suppliers, boards of directors, buyers, and investors) as to its real purpose. This may result in conflicting goals and objectives that inhibit organizational progress.

The mission statement provides management and shareholders with a definition of what the organization is and through its mission what it is not. Ideally the mission is known and understood by all employees, customers, and internal and external stakeholders. Some organizations post the mission statement throughout the organization, and include it on business cards, logos, and various forms of advertisement and promotion.

The health care industry, whether in the public or private sector, has gone through numerous industry changes. Mergers, alliances, and restructure are more common than exceptional in the health care industry. Redefinitions of customers, customer needs, regulation, methods of delivery, financial methods, and other factors critical to industry success provide a dynamic environment for management. To meet these challenges, a health care facility must know what "business it is in" before it can determine where it should be or what it should become. The mission statement provides this understanding. It is the foundation of a strategic plan.

WHO SHOULD DEVELOP THE MISSION STATEMENT?

Consultants, authors, and educators all purport different methods by which to develop the mission statement. Although different methods are advocated, a few truths prevail. (a) Contrary to popular belief, the mission statement should not be developed by the public relations arm of the organization. (b) It is important that key leadership "buy in" to the commonly understood definition of the mission. (c) Often, the process of developing the mission statement is as valuable as the definition itself. (d) Organizational input at all levels adds value to the process of developing the mission statement. And (e) the mission statement must be re-evaluated at regular intervals, especially in a dynamic industry environment.

The process of developing a mission statement is more than a process of writing a few key words that can be used for public proliferation. Rather the process should precipitate the feeling of an *esprit de corps* for the organization. An organizational knowledge of the mission statement can engender a sense of pride through a clear understanding of the organization's purpose. The mission can help individual organization contributors feel a sense of accomplishment by knowing what the organization values. The mission statement adds to the sense of organizational culture. Therefore, participation in the development and ongoing review of the organization's mission creates ownership of the organizational purpose.

Management must give careful consideration to the scope, level of participation, and time allocated in mission statement development. Too much participation can "bog down" the process; too little participation may be viewed as "top down" imposition. Adequate time must be given to the process. If the process is completed too quickly, insufficient reflective time will result in an inaccurate statement. If the process is perceived to take an inordinately long time, the organization may be viewed as unable to define its own purpose. The importance of the mission statement as viewed by managers, employees, and stakeholders is reflected by the attention given to its development by senior management. If senior management fails to know and communicate the mission, the organization will view it as superfluous.

THE MISSION OF DEPARTMENTS AND SUBUNITS

Often it is important for strategic business units, strategic service units, departments, or other organizational subunits to have a statement of functional mission. In contrast to the organizational mission statement, the functional mission must support the organizational mission. Such statements are usually more narrowly defined than the organizational mission.

Functional mission statements provide organizational role and clarity of responsibility. Organizations frequently experience suboptimization, which occurs when intraorganizational subunits focus more on internal competition among themselves than on external competition from the marketplace. Redundancy, inefficiencies, and ineffectiveness for the organization as a whole results from functional suboptimization. Functional mission statements provide direction for the organizational unit. The development of functional mission statements will help it identify conflicts, rivalries, and overlaps between departments.

The discussions and debates among subordinates and superiors during functional mission development focuses the organizational subunit on its purpose and direction, as well as, its contribution to the organizational mission. The organizational subunit will be able to better accomplish its responsibilities because it is clear on its purpose. Management can better direct employee efforts on the appropriate unit outcomes.

MISSION AS A PART OF STRATEGIC PLANNING

The mission on an organization provides a clear statement of the purpose of the organization. The mission statement focuses organizational attention on the reason for the organization's existence, not on what its existence should be or what it might be in the future. The mission is the foundation for strategic planning. It delineates the scope of operation. Based on the mission statement, the organization can begin to articulate its goals and objectives to meet the needs of its customers. In times of rapidly changing organizational environments, such as health care, it is important to clearly know the purpose of the organization.

—Rebecca I. Porterfield

See also Long-Range Planning, Organizational Vision, Strategic Planning

FURTHER READING

Carver, J. (1997). *Creating a mission that makes a difference.* San Francisco: Jossey-Bass.

Ginter, P. M., Swayne, L. E., & Duncan, W. J. (2002). *Strategic management of healthcare organizations* (4th ed.). Oxford, UK: Blackwell.

Graham, J. W., & Havlick, W. C. (1994). *Mission statements: A guide to the corporate and nonprofit sectors.* New York: Garland.

Jones, P., & Kahaner, L. (1995). *Say it & live it: 50 corporate mission statements that hit the mark.* New York: Doubleday.

MOBILE HEALTH UNITS (MHUs)

Mobile health units (MHUs) are portable, self-contained vehicles that can provide medical services to diverse populations in a number of different settings. Health care providers utilize these vehicles in order to provide goal-oriented medical care to a targeted patient population. Since the midcentury, various countries have been developing the concept of MHUs for use in both battlefield and humanitarian missions. In addition, MHUs have been evolved to permit provision of primary care to rural populations around the world.

Mobile health units have been shown to be beneficial in a number of different modalities. Most prominent is the MHU role in providing access to various aspects of primary care and preventive services to typically underserved rural populations. This has been very helpful in targeting the elderly population that is at higher risk for having suboptimal or no medical care. The best examples to date include immunization clinics, cervical and breast cancer screening, general diabetes care, and eye care. There are also MHUs that provide various types of radiological services, including plain X-ray, computed tomography (CT), and magnetic resonance imaging (MRI). These units have been shown to increase access to medical care providers by adding enrollment in health care plans supported by the mobile health unit. By managing primary care issues for these patients, MHUs have also been shown to decrease the number of emergency department visits patients typically have. Finally, MHUs have demonstrated their effectiveness in providing mental health services to the inner-city homeless population by decreasing the frequency of psychiatric admissions in these patients.

A cost–benefit analysis is always appropriate when evaluating a mobile health unit. The initial costs have historically been met through a combination of government grants, private funding, and corporate sponsorship. Although MHUs are expensive, the cost analysis must include long-term financial benefits such as decreased emergency department visits as well as hospital admissions. When analyzed in these terms, MHUs have proven to be fiscally responsible projects if targeted appropriately.

Utilizing these mobile health units has presented a number of problems beyond the actual functional costs of the operation. A targeted evaluation of the community is necessary to determine whether these units are feasible. Studies have shown that populations have unique characteristics that must be recognized when trying to ensure that people will use the mobile health unit. Funding the operation initially and then for continuation of the project must be addressed. How the project is going to be marketed is very important. Other factors that must be considered include community support and evaluation of an area's terrain and how this will affect a vehicle's ability to get to a population.

Overall, mobile health units have extended the ability of health care providers to get to patients who are in more remote locations. This ability has been extended in the form of either actual providers or services, such as radiography or ophthalmologic imaging. This model has proven cost-effective in certain circumstances and will probably play an expanded role in years to come.

—Bradley N. Younggren

FURTHER READING

Alexy, B. B., & Elnitsky, C. (1998). Rural mobile health unit: Outcomes. *Public Health Nursing, 15*(1), 3–11.

McEwan, S. R., Arthur, P., Scott, A., et al. (1999). A mobile screening unit, practicalities and problems. *Scottish Medical Journal, 44,* 106–110.

Moulavie, D., Bushy, A., Peterson, J., & Stullenbarger, E. (1999). Factors to consider when purchasing a mobile health unit to deliver services. *Journal of Nurse Administration, 29,* 34–41.

MONOPOLY

Monopoly is the condition under which a single *seller* sets prices in a market. This condition opposes that of perfect competition, where sellers have *no* pricing power.

Monopolistic sellers can exercise maximum *feasible* pricing power. However, this power is less than conventional wisdom frequently identifies. In short, a monopolist cannot just charge *any* price for its goods or services. Rather, it sets prices subject to consumers' willingness to pay.

Competitive firms are "atomistic" in the sense that their production decisions negligibly affect the aggregate level of output available to consumers. As a result, competitive firms are "price takers"; that is, they can sell *all* their output at a fixed market price.

Monopolistic firms, in contrast, are "price makers." Unlike their competitive counterparts, monopolists significantly affect aggregate output by altering their own output. Indeed, a monopolist's output not only contributes to aggregate output, it *is* aggregate output (at least for the market in which it operates). Consequently, rather than being able to sell all its output at a fixed price, the monopolist must lower its price to sell additional quantities.

To understand this necessity, suppose a monopolist sells soft drinks. A consumer might be willing to purchase a single drink for, say, $1.00. A second, less thirsty, consumer may only be willing to pay, say, $0.75. To the extent that the monopolist cannot price-discriminate (charge different prices to different consumers), it must choose in the present example between selling a single unit for $1.00 or two units for $1.50 ($0.75 each).

This example illustrates the more general phenomenon that, because consumers vary in their willingness to pay for goods and services (and because individual consumers often value additional units at lower marginal values), monopolists face "downward sloping demand curves." Should a monopolist want to supply more units to the market, it must do so at a lower price. To maximize profits, monopolists do not maximize price. Rather, they strategically trade off increased profit from increasing their output against decreased profit from lowering their price at higher output levels.

Although this tradeoff maximizes the monopolist's profit, it can constrain output to a less than socially optimal level. This adverse welfare consequence occurs because there exist consumers who are willing to pay more than the monopolist's marginal cost of production, but the monopolist is unwilling to sell to those customers because doing so would lower the price it charges to previous customers.

Monopolistic power can also create benefits, however. Consider the case of pharmaceutical innovations. Although monopolistic power has "natural" origins (such as that associated with first-mover advantages), it also has legal or regulatory origins. One such origin is patent law, which essentially confers monopoly power on those who create innovations in general and pharmaceutical companies in particular.

Absent this power, pharmaceutical companies would be reluctant to sink real resources into research and development efforts. Doing so would create significant costs while leaving consequent benefits for expropriation by other firms and consumers. *No* firm can invest for long in such an environment. Monopolistic power can thus offset, and perhaps overwhelm, associated welfare-decreasing effects (that is, constraining output) by, for example, encouraging potentially productive activity such as research and development.

—Dino Falaschetti

FURTHER READING

Bernanke, B., & Frank, R. (2001). *Principles of economics.* New York: McGraw-Hill.

Hirshleifer, J., & Glazer, A. (1992). *Price theory and applications* (5th ed.). Upper Saddle River, NJ: Prentice Hall.

Stigler, G. J. (1987). *The theory of price* (4th ed.). New York: Macmillan.

MONOPSONY

The term *monopsony* refers to the condition under which a single *buyer* sets prices in its market. This condition contrasts that of "monopoly" where a single *seller* sets prices.

In some cases, a monopsonist faces separate suppliers. For example, a remote town's sole employer may buy labor from a relatively large set of unorganized laborers. In other cases, a monopsonist faces a single supplier or a coordinated set of suppliers. Here, a large employer may buy labor from an organized set of labor (such as a union). The case where a single supplier faces a single buyer is sometimes referred to as a "bilateral monopoly."

Single-buyer health care programs offer a salient example of monopsonistic power. By aggregating the purchasing power of otherwise diffuse consumers, such organizations can pressure health care providers to lower their supply price. In this respect, the monopsonist can clearly check producers' potential market power.

The welfare consequences of this check, however, are less obvious. For example, to the extent that a monopsonist's activities encourage suppliers with market power to increase production, a monopsonist can increase welfare. However, these same efforts can decrease welfare if, for example, they reduce the cost of overturning patent protection.

Patent protection, in effect, confers monopoly power onto producers for a limited period of time. During this period, the monopolist can charge a price that exceeds society's "optimal" price. But this inflated price also encourages producers to engage in potentially welfare-enhancing research and development. Absent such price protection, or when this protection is ephemeral, a producer's claim to benefits that it creates are exposed to a relatively large expropriation risk. Consequently, producers will be reluctant to sink resources into producing future benefits.

Monopsonists, in principle, have an increased capacity to opportunistically overturn such protections, and thus increase this expropriation risk. In effect, a monopsonist is an organized interest whose constituency includes buyers. Buyers, in turn, prefer low prices (holding all else constant). The monopsonist's organizational capabilities thus increases buyers' ability to opportunistically retract patent protection or retard an innovator's ability to extract payment for the innovation. Although creating an immediate windfall for buyers, however, such an action can reduce net welfare in the long run. Indeed, to the extent that suppliers require price protection or pricing power to invest in knowledge production, a monopsonist's bargaining power can retard the rate at which an economy innovates.

Other channels also exist through which concentrating power in a single buyer can reduce welfare. For example, by aggregating the demands of its constituents, the single-payer precludes individuals from paying a price that exceeds that which the monopsonist sets. Individuals may value this opportunity if, say, the quantity available from a monopsonist does not satisfy their demand.

Like monopolistic power, monopsonistic power thus produces costs *and* benefits. If these market conditions were to produce *only* costs or only benefits, debates regarding their regulation would not be so contentious.

—Dino Falaschetti and Steve Parsons

FURTHER READING

Bernanke, B., & Frank, R. (2001). *Principles of economics.* New York: McGraw-Hill.
Hirshleifer, J., & Glazer, A. (1992). *Price theory and applications* (5th ed.). Upper Saddle River, NJ: Prentice Hall.
Stigler, G. J. (1987). *The theory of price* (4th ed.). New York: Macmillan.

MORAL HAZARD

See Code of Ethics, Ethical Issues Faced by Managers

MORBIDITY

To a physician, the word *morbidity* refers specifically to the presence of disease, though more colloquial interpretations have come to mean "gruesome" or sometimes "repelling." Morbid obesity is a condition where a patient's weight is so great that it is considered to carry a greatly increased risk of medical complications, possibly leading to death. Comorbidity is a cluster of conditions that seem related, for instance, the presence of heart disease is frequently accompanied by other medical conditions such as stroke, high blood pressure, obesity, and diabetes. Alcoholics and the morbidly obese are often clinically depressed, and substance abuse often accompanies other mental disorders. In such a case, one condition may or may not be caused by or be dependent on the other. In the United States, state and local governments, often acting in concert with the National Institutes of Health (NIH), collect statistics on morbidity and mortality. The NIH coordinates the collection and dissemination of such data, and changes in public policy often result. For instance, statistics on morbidity among pregnant women, the presence of HIV in segments of the general population, and the prevalence of West Nile virus have all led to the allocation or reallocation of health care resources. Recommendations regarding pediatric immunization, diet, and vaccination when traveling to foreign countries are a direct result of morbidity statistics. Federal law requiring the printing of health warnings on cigarette packages and those regulating the sale of tobacco and alcohol products are influenced by the known or suspected morbidity related to the use of such substances.

—Robert I. Katz

FURTHER READING

http://grants1.nih.gov/grants/guide/pa-files/PA-99-071.html
www.nih.gov

MORTALITY

The word *mortality* is derived from "mortal," in classical Greek mythology a human, as opposed to a god, who is "immortal" or immune to death. Mortals, unlike gods, are doomed to die. To a physician, *mortality* is generally used to refer to the rate of death in association with particular diseases or other factors, such as age, gender, income, and national origin. Statistics on mortality are kept by local, state, and federal governments, and the World Health Organization (WHO) maintains a database on cause-of-death records dating back to 1950. Data are supplied to WHO by those member states considered to have reliable and consistent information. For developed countries, data are supplied at frequent intervals, usually each year. For less developed countries, data reporting is intermittent and of lower reliability. WHO keeps data on the number of deaths according to cause, gender, age, year, nation, and geographic area. Data are coded according to the International Classification of Disease (ICD) code. As with morbidity statistics, mortality data are used by various governments to formulate health care policy and to allocate or reallocate health care resources. Statistics on infant mortality, maternal mortality, life expectancy, and cause of death may result in focused studies or in government-sponsored health care initiatives. In the United States, recommendations regarding pediatric immunization, diet, and vaccination when traveling to foreign countries are a direct result of morbidity and mortality statistics. Federal law requiring the printing of health warnings on cigarette packages and containers of alcoholic beverages, and those regulating the sale of tobacco and alcohol products are influenced by the known or suspected mortality related to the use of such substances.

—Robert I. Katz

FURTHER READING

www.ciesin.org/IC/who/MortalityDatabase.html
www.mortality.org/

MOST-FAVORED-NATION (MFN) CLAUSES

Most-favored-nation (MFN) clauses are used in global trade agreements. The term is now loosely used for favored or special treatment for one or more of the parties in business dealings.

In global trade, the General Agreement on Trade and Tariffs (GATT), which governs most international trade, specifies the general agreements on how different countries will deal with each other in trade—importing and exporting. Many countries have duties and tariffs designed to protect local businesses from imported products and to raise revenue for that country. These duties and tariffs can be quite large, effectively raising the prices of items so much that certain exporting countries are virtually prohibited from participating in that market.

For example, the United States is a large and lucrative market with relatively low or no duties and tariffs. A few industries still enjoy the protection of substantial barriers to imported products. One of the most recent examples was the imposition of large tariffs on foreign steel to protect the U.S. steel industry.

Under GATT, there is a classification by which a country can designate another country as most favored nation, thereby setting aside all duties and tariffs on products imported from the MFN. This is a great advantage for a developing country (such as China) in selling its products into a large developed market (such as the United States).

When MFN status is granted to a country, it becomes an important form of political currency, and one that the granting country can rescind if the grantee abuses it. In many cases, the threat of withholding MFN status can be used to extract other concessions between trading partners.

Thus MFN has become a shorthand phrase to signify favored treatment.

—John L. Mariotti

MOTIVATING EMPLOYEES

See Employee Absenteeism, Employee Turnover, Empowerment

MULTIHOSPITAL SYSTEMS

See Hospitals

MYSTERY SHOPPER

A mystery shopper is an individual who is normally employed by a market research firm, who visits client locations as a regular customer, evaluating the operation from the customer's perspective. Mystery shoppers rate the customer experience against predetermined criteria, and the information is processed into a usable format for the client company. Firms who use mystery shoppers are typically in pure service industries, where the quality of the service is measurable only at the point when the service is delivered. Common examples of industries that use mystery shoppers are retailers, restaurants, hotels, and repair facilities. Mystery shoppers are designed to give service providers a "report card" on the quality of the service being provided, and this report card is intended to be unbiased. The advantage of using mystery shoppers is that the employees providing the service are unaware that they are being evaluated, so the evaluation is indicative of their normal level of customer service.

Using mystery shoppers allows service providers to evaluate the level of customer service delivered by different employees, at different locations, and at different times of the day. Because the mystery shoppers fill out standardized evaluation reports, it allows the service provider to establish standards of customer service, and those standards can be evaluated across different service settings. Some areas of customer service that are often evaluated by mystery shoppers are salesmanship, facility appearance, timeliness, employee appearance, security procedures, hospitality, product quality, and use of promotions or marketing materials.

Some of the benefits that service companies realize from using mystery shoppers include the following:

- *Feedback.* Mystery shopper programs provide feedback for individual employees, giving client companies the ability to coach those individual employees to improve their performance to meet accepted standards.
- *Timeliness.* Because professional market research firms normally manage the mystery shopper program, reporting systems can be established to provide management with timely feedback.
- *Reliability.* Because professional market research companies are providing the mystery shopper evaluation, they can train and manage the mystery shoppers themselves and maintain quality control.
- *Consistency.* Each employee and location in a service company can be evaluated using the same standards.

- *Incentives and competition.* Ongoing analysis provides a basis for standardized bonus systems or discretionary incentives to reward service excellence.
- *Identification.* Provides information to reward areas that exceed quality standards and identify where improvement may be needed.

Health care providers, because of the purely service nature of their enterprises, can certainly benefit from mystery shopper programs. As health care becomes more and more competitive, and as consumers are presented with more choices, the quality of service provided to consumers becomes a critical point of differential advantage. Mystery shopper programs can provide health care companies with a tool to measure the quality of the service they are providing to their consumers.

—Mark A. Moon

NATIONAL ASSOCIATION OF COUNTY AND CITY HEALTH OFFICIALS (NACCHO)

The National Association of County and City Health Officials (NACCHO) is a membership organization representing local health officials. According to its mission statement, "NACCHO works to support efforts which protect and improve the health of all people and all communities by promoting national policy, developing resources and programs, and supporting effective local public health practice and systems." NACCHO is governed by a board and executive committee elected by the membership.

NACCHO provides many services to local health officials and serves as a forum for communication. NACCHO alerts member agencies to pressing public health issues and provides pertinent legislative updates. The staff of the agency works directly with the legislature and government officials at the national level to increase funding for public health and to advocate for issues to improve health. NACCHO staff working with local public health officials and other health agencies develops and provides tools to help local agencies assess the health of their communities and the level of services provided by the agencies. A survey of local health agencies by NACCHO in 1999 and 2000, published in *Local Public Health Agency Infrastructure: A Chartbook,* called attention to the diversity and needs of local agencies.

A similar agency, the Association of State and Territorial Health Officials (ASTHO), serves state-level public health officials.

—Carole W. Samuelson

See also Health Officer and Health Commissioner, Public Health

FURTHER READING

www.astho.org
www.naccho.org

NATIONAL COMMITTEE ON QUALITY ASSURANCE (NCQA)

The National Committee on Quality Assurance (NCQA) has changed dramatically since its inception in 1990. A private, not-for-profit organization, NCQA is governed by a board of directors that includes employers, consumer and labor representatives, health plans, quality experts, policymakers, and representatives from organized medicine. The organization was founded in 1990 with a grant from the Robert Wood Johnson Foundation and the support of large employers and health plans.

The organization's mission is to provide information that enables purchasers and consumers of managed health care to differentiate plans based on quality and to provide consumers and payers the information needed to make more informed decisions on health care purchasing. This approach anticipated that health plans would compete based on quality and value, rather than on price and provider network. NCQA's efforts are mounted in two areas: accreditation and performance measurement. These activities were integrated in 1999 under NCQA's Accreditation '99 program, which includes selected performance measures in such key areas as member satisfaction, quality of care, access, and service.

The organization introduced the concept of performance measurement for health plans in 1992, with the introduction of the Health Plan Data and Information Set (HEDIS®), a set of indicators for health plan performance. Since that time, HEDIS has become a standard in the health insurance industry to measure the performance of health maintenance organizations and as a means of benchmarking health plans against regional and national performance standards. In 1995, the development of HEDIS measures was assigned to the first Committee on Performance Measurement, a group of industry and health care professionals who provide oversight into development and management of the HEDIS performance measures.

From its early focus on commercial health plans, NCQA has branched out into other areas of health care accreditation. In 1995, the organization launched a program for accreditation of credentials verification organizations (CVOs). These organizations perform primary source verification of physician and health worker records, to ensure that the provider is qualified to perform services for a health care organization. The NCQA program on certification of CVOs is designed to ensure that these organizations perform the necessary functions to provide adequate information regarding a provider's qualifications and background. NCQA added other accreditation programs for managed behavioral health organizations (1997), physician organizations (1997), and preferred provider organizations (1999). In recent years, the organization has begun evaluating HMOs that are devoted to Medicare and Medicaid beneficiaries, as well.

Approaches to performance measurement have also changed over the life of the organization. In the early stages of HEDIS measures, the indicators were primarily concerned with process measures, such as health plan structure, committee functions, and lines of authority. Over the past 10 years, however, the focus has become more customer oriented and includes a customer survey as part of the indicator list. As the measures have become more codified, NCQA added an auditing process to the health plans' data submission process, to assure the validity of the data analyzed for HEDIS measures. The measures for 2001 included the following:

- Adolescent immunization rates
- Breast cancer screening (mammography) rates
- Cervical cancer screening (Pap smear) rates
- Childhood immunization rates
- Chlamydia screening rates
- Management of menopause
- Prenatal and postpartum care rates
- Advising smokers to quit rates
- Follow-up after mental illness
- Beta-blocker treatment after a heart attack
- Cholesterol management after a heart attack
- Comprehensive diabetes care
- Controlling high blood pressure
- Medication and management of asthma
- Communication by providers
- Overall ratings of doctors and specialists
- Claims processing

- Courtesy of office staff
- Customer service (by health plan)
- Access to care
- Access to needed care
- Overall rating of health plan

The organization now supports a number of Web-based health quality reporting initiatives through the NCQA HealthChoices Web site (www.healthchoices.org). The information on the site allows employers and individuals to rate health plans by their NCQA accreditation and some performance information, such as access to care, provider qualifications, preventive care, improvement in health status, and accreditation outcome. Individuals may search for specific health plans or create a listing of health plans in a particular area or zip code, as well as read detailed descriptions of the NCQA accreditation process and HEDIS measurement.

The accreditation process involves a site visit by a team of NCQA reviewers, who examine an organization's documents regarding five major areas, titled as follows:

- Staying Healthy (preventive care)
- Getting Better (health maintenance and avoiding illness)
- Living with Illness (management of chronic illnesses)
- Qualified Providers (credentialing of providers)
- Access and Service (access to care and effectiveness of services to plan members)

Health plans can be denied accreditation, or given provisional accreditation, if they do not meet NCQA standards. For those plans meeting standards, three levels of accreditation are bestowed: accreditation, commendable, and excellent. Each level connotes increasing adherence to NCQA standards. The accreditation process requires substantial management and organizational efforts by the health plan and also by providers, an issue that has led to criticism of the manner in which these reviews are performed (see Ohldin & Mims, 2002). Despite the criticism, many states consider NCQA accreditation satisfactory for licensing health plans.

NCQA's influence in the health insurance arena has grown substantially since the organization's inception in 1990. The annual report, *State of Managed Care Quality,* is used by the news media and governmental planners to evaluate health plans, as well as determine targets for health care policy changes. By focusing on health care quality, NCQA has broadened the evaluation of the health care industry from cost of care and price of services to a more value-based approach.

—Donald E. Lighter

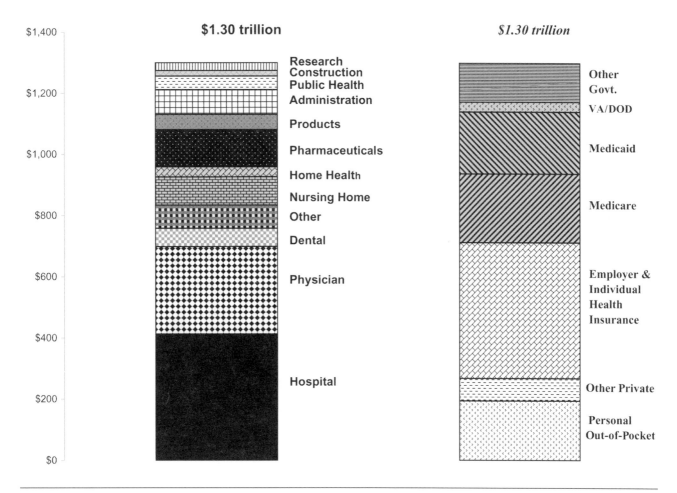

$1.30 trillion

$1.30 trillion

Figure 1   National Health Expenditures, 2001.

FURTHER READING

Ohldin, A., & Mims, A. (2002). The search for value in health care: A review of the national committee for quality assurance efforts. *Journal of the National Medical Association, 94*(5), 344–350.
www.healthchoices.org
www.ncqa.org

NATIONAL HEALTH EXPENDITURES (NHE)

National health expenditures (NHEs) are official measures of what is spent for health care—approximately $4637 per person or $1.3 trillion total in 2001 (Figure 1). As with the macroeconomic national income and product accounts, constructing national health accounts (NHAs) relies on an economic identity: All transactions have two sides, buyer and seller. "Expenditures" are *costs* to persons, firms that provide benefits to employees, government, and other payers, and are also *revenues* to hospitals, physicians, home health agencies, and other providers. A NHA is a matrix of the sources and uses of funds. Some informational elements are easier to obtain than others. For example, the American Hospital Association (AHA) reports total revenues for all U.S. hospitals every year. This number is taken as the measure of both the buy and the sell sides, because producer income is well measured, whereas spending (all the various payments, copayments, deductibles, discounts, and so forth paid by entities such as patients, insurance companies, government agencies) is not.

SOURCES OF FUNDS

Most health care funds come from third-party insurance payments. This break in the financial link means that most of time "prices" in health care are not relevant to patients, who care mostly about the 15% of costs that must be paid out-of-pocket; copayments, deductibles, uninsured drug bills, and so forth. Although the United States is often considered to have a mostly private market health care system, government is by far the largest source of funds. Medicare, Medicaid, other government agencies, and the tax breaks allowed for employer-paid health insurance premiums account for 55% of total expenditures.

USES OF FUNDS

Hospitals are the single largest category of health expenditures, and almost all (97%) of their revenues come from insurance. To some extent, these categories are overlapping. Also, note that the bulk of "research" for the rapidly advancing technology of medicine is not counted directly, but instead contained in the payments for pharmaceuticals, physicians, and so on.

The process of measurement forces consideration of central issues in health policy. Is unpaid care from a daughter uncounted, but home health agency visits are counted? Should a new allergy pill taken only once per week rather than twice per day really be valued 50 times as much? Are salary raises for nurse's aides to be interpreted as increases in health care quantity or quality? The first stage of health reform in many countries is creation of a NHA, because what is never measured consistently can rarely be improved efficiently. Studies in the United States and elsewhere indicate that aging, technology, number of hospital beds or visits, administrative organization, and mortality and morbidity are only secondary factors in NHE, whereas real per capita income (gross domestic product, or GDP) is the driving force that leads spending, and provider incomes, higher.

—Thomas E. Getzen

FURTHER READING

Levit, K., et al. (2002). Inflation spurs health spending in 2000. *Health Affairs, 21*(1), 172–181.
www.cms.gov/statistics
www.oecd.org/els/health
www.who.int/whr/2001

NATIONAL HEALTH SERVICE

See Health Care in China, Health Care in Eastern Europe

NATIONAL INSTITUTES OF HEALTH (NIH)

The National Institutes of Health (NIH, www.nih.gov) is one of the agencies of the Public Health Services, which is a part of the Department of Health and Human Services (DHHS, www.dhhs.gov) of the U.S. federal government. The NIH is responsible for medical and behavioral research for the United States. It has the mission of pursuing fundamental scientific knowledge about the nature and behavior of living systems and the application of that knowledge to treat illness and extend healthy life. The NIH has 27 separate components, mostly institutes and centers. The NIH has over 75 buildings on over 300 acres in Bethesda, Maryland. The NIH budget was just over $23 billion in 2002.

The goals of the NIH include (a) fostering fundamental creative discoveries and innovative research strategies as a basis for significantly advancing the nation's capacity to protect and improve health; (b) developing and maintaining and renewing scientific human and physical resources, to assure the capability to prevent disease; (c) expanding the medical science knowledge base, to enhance the nation's economic well-being and ensure a high return on the public investment in research; and (d) promote the highest level of integrity, accountability, and social responsibility in the conduct of medical science. These goals are accomplished by (a) conducting research in NIH laboratories, and supporting research of nonfederal scientists in universities, medical schools, hospitals, and research institutions throughout the country and abroad; (b) helping train medical research investigators; and (c) fostering communication of medical information.

The institutes and centers of the NIH include the following:

Office of the Director (OD): www.nih.gov/icd/od/

National Cancer Institute (NCI): www.nci.nih.gov

National Eye Institute (NEI): www.nei.nih.gov

National Heart, Lung, and Blood Institute (NHLBI): www.nhlbi.nih.gov

National Human Genome Research Institute (NHGRI): www.nhgri.nih.gov

National Institute on Aging (NIA): www.nia.nih.gov

National Institute on Alcohol Abuse and Alcoholism (NIAAA): www.niaaa.nih.gov

National Institute of Allergy and Infectious Diseases (NIAID): www.niaid.nih.gov

National Institute of Arthritis and Musculoskeletal and Skin Diseases (NIAMS): www.niams.nih.gov

National Institute of Biomedical Imaging and Bioengineering (NIBIB): www.nibib.nih.gov

National Institute of Child Health and Human Development (NICHD): www.nichd.nih.gov

National Institute on Deafness and Other Communication Disorders (NIDCD): www.nidcd.nih.gov

National Institute of Dental and Craniofacial Research (NIDCR): www.nidcr.nih.gov

National Institute on Diabetes and Digestive and Kidney Diseases (NIDDK): www.niddk.nih.gov

National Institute on Drug Abuse (NIDA): www.nida.nih.gov

National Institute of Environmental Health Sciences (NIEHS): www.niehs.nih.gov

National Institute of General Medical Sciences (NIGMS): www.nigms.nih.gov

National Institute of Mental Health (NIMH): www.nimh.nih.gov

National Institute of Neurological Disorders and Stroke (NINDS): www.ninds.nih.gov

National Institute of Nursing Research (NINR): www.nih.gov/ninr

National Library of Medicine (NLM): www.nlm.nih.gov

Center for Information Technology (CIT): www.cit.nih.gov

Center for Scientific Review (CSR): www.csr.nih.gov

John E. Fogarty International Center (FIC): www.fic.nih.gov

National Center for Complementary and Alternative Medicine (NCCAM): www.nccam.nih.gov

National Center on Minority Health and Health Disparities (NCMHD): www.ncmhd.nih.gov

National Center for Research Resources (NCRR): www.ncrr.nih.gov

Warren Grant Magnuson Clinical Center (CC): www.cc.nih.gov

To achieve its goals, the NIH funds medical and scientific research. The research is designed to acquire new knowledge to help prevent and detect disease, and to improve diagnosis and treatment. Nearly 84% of NIH money is used to support grants and contracts supporting research and training in over 2000 research institutions in the United States and overseas. About 10% of the budget funds the NIH's intramural research programs.

The NIH reviews over 43,000 research and training applications annually through a peer review system. It supports almost 47,000 grants in universities, medical schools, and other research and training institutions.

In the NIH 2001 report on investments, progress, and plans, the NIH director selected examples of achievement in the areas of genomics, advanced technologies, disease prevention, collaborative research, health disparities and health education/outreach. Public information from the NIH is available on a variety of diseases at http://health.nih.gov.

—Stephen A. Vitkun

FURTHER READING

Chow, S.-C., & Liu, J.-P. (1998). *Design and analysis of clinical trials: Concepts and methodologies.* New York: Wiley.

Office of the Director, National Institutes of Health. (2001, June). *The National Institutes of Health: Investments, progress and plans, selected examples from FY 1999–2003.* Bethesda, MD: National Institutes of Health.

www.nih.gov

NATIONAL LABOR RELATIONS BOARD (NLRB)

The National Labor Relations Act (also known as the "Wagner Act") created the National Labor Relations Board (NLRB) in 1935. The purposes of the NLRB are to conduct representation elections to see if workers at a particular employer are to be represented by a labor union, as well as to conduct hearings to determine if unfair labor practices have been committed.

Although the NLRB has jurisdiction over unionization issues "affecting interstate commerce," the NLRB has curtailed its jurisdiction to cover only larger employers. The exact extent of this coverage can be found by consulting the appropriate title of the Code of Federal Regulations (CFR).

—Bruce D. Fisher

FURTHER READING

Fisher, B. D., & Phillips, M. J. (2004). *The legal, ethical, and regulatory environment of business* (8th ed., Chapter 17). Mason, OH: Thomson-South-Western.

NEEDS/CAPACITY ASSESSMENT

See Capacity and Capacity Utilization

NEGATIVE DEMAND

See Demand

NEGLIGENCE

Negligence is probably the most important area of tort law. Here liability may be imposed for results that were not intended by the defendant, and originates from the defendant being at fault through failure to perform a required duty under a set of specific circumstances. There are two types of duties: the duty of due care, that is, the duty to act as any reasonable person would given the same or similar circumstances; and a special duty imposed by case law or statute. A prima facie case for negligence includes the following elements: act or actionable omission by defendant, duty of due care, breach of duty, actual cause, proximate cause, and damages. A negligent act per se consists of an act or omission, duty, and breach of that duty that exposes others to unreasonable risk of harm.

With regard to trades or professions, all individuals are held to certain minimum standards of care exercised by those in their professions, usually across a national standard. Physicians may be judged based on a same or similar community standard of care, although the modern trend is to accept standards set by nationally certified medical specialties as defining that "minimum standard of care." Here is an example of negligence: An obstetrician who discovers an inheritable disease in a pregnant patient is bound by duty to inform her of the possibility of genetic transmission to the fetus; he or she is also bound by duty to inform her of, although not necessarily personally offer, all available options under the duty of "informed consent." Failure to do so would constitute an actionable breach of duty.

—Benito A. Alvarez

FURTHER READING

American Medical Association. (1991). *The guide to medical liability insurance.* Chicago: Author.

NEGOTIATIONS

Negotiation (or bargaining) is "an interpersonal decision-making process by which two or more people agree how to allocate scarce resources" (Thompson, 2001). Health care managers must be able to negotiate effectively when dealing with boards, patient groups, employees, medical suppliers, insurance providers, labor organizations, and other stakeholders and constituents. In its simplest form, negotiations may involve two individuals who discuss and resolve an issue within a few minutes. A nursing supervisor, for example, may spend 10 minutes discussing and setting up a monthly work schedule with a pediatrics nurse. At the other extreme is a management team that negotiates a collective bargaining agreement with a union representing several hundred housekeeping employees at a large university medical center. Negotiations between union and management bargaining teams are known as *collective bargaining.* Other forms of high-level health care negotiations include merger talks between health care institutions, hammering out contractual terms with health insurance companies and medical suppliers, and dealing with patients' rights advocates, public officials, and financial backers.

TWO BASIC APPROACHES TO NEGOTIATIONS

The literature delineates two approaches to negotiation (Walton & McKersie, 1965). *Distributive bargaining* is characterized by a situation in which the gains achieved by one party result in an equal loss by the other party. For example, suppose a hospital administrator is negotiating salary with a staff physician. If the administrator concedes an additional $20,000 in pay, then the physician's monetary gain equals the hospital's monetary loss. Distributive bargaining is regarded as *zero-sum* (win–lose) because the size of the negotiating "pie" is fixed. *Integrative bargaining,* in contrast, is characterized by a situation in which both sides may gain. If the hospital administrator just mentioned negotiates a higher salary with a group of staff physicians, the financial "loss" to the hospital as a result of the higher salaries may be more than offset by lower physician turnover and a reduction in total labor costs. (*Note:* See the entry for *Employee Turnover* for an explanation regarding the costs associated with employee resignations.) The concept of integrative bargaining recognizes that some negotiation issues are variable-sum (win–win) issues. That is, the size of the bargaining pie is not fixed and can be expanded through intelligent and cooperative negotiations.

NEGOTIATION MYTHS

Thompson (2001) dispels four myths associated with the negotiations process. First, good negotiators are not born; they must develop and cultivate their negotiating skills. Second, experience is not necessarily the best teacher. Good negotiating skills are built by obtaining diagnostic feedback as to what worked and what failed in the negotiating process. Third, tough negotiators are not necessarily the most effective negotiators. Although tough negotiators are the stuff of legends, most negotiations can be conducted effectively without resorting to iron-fisted tactics. Fourth, good negotiators rely less on "gut" feelings and intuition; the keys to effective negotiation are thorough preparation and the effective use of bargaining tactics.

NEGOTIATION TACTICS

The negotiation process usually starts with one side making an offer (sometimes an extreme or preposterous offer); the opponent makes a counteroffer, and the two sides continue to talk and make counteroffers either until an agreement is reached or until the parties realize that further negotiations are not possible. During the process of negotiations, some parties want to get as much as they can from the other side (emphasizing a zero-sum approach). Other parties approach negotiations with the idea of broadening the size of the bargaining pie (emphasizing a cooperative, variable-sum approach).

Preparation

Knowing what you want to get out of negotiations is critical. Preparation involves gathering and organizing relevant information, identifying critical issues, anticipating what the other party is likely to offer, assessing the amount of risk one is willing to take during negotiations, and establishing sticking points beyond which you are willing to walk away from the negotiations.

Develop a Negotiation Style

Some negotiators adopt a "tough" and unyielding stance to negotiations, whereas others take a "soft" and conciliatory stance. Soft negotiators who are well prepared usually have an edge over tough negotiators who are poorly prepared. Table pounding, threats, name-calling, and other unreasonable behaviors are no substitute for extensive preparation. It is also important to use a negotiating style that is compatible with your personality and emotional style. Some negotiators function best when using an emotionless "poker face"; others are more comfortable using humor to break the tension of negotiations, and still others take a hostile and competitive approach to the negotiating table. One's style can have a profound effect on the outcome of negotiations. *Stabilizers* are individuals who strongly desire to reach an agreement, sometimes at any cost. These individuals may make concessions and negotiate agreements that are tilted strongly in favor of their opponent. A *destabilizer,* in contrast, may have little patience for the negotiation process, and view other negotiators with contempt. Destabilizers often regard those on the opposite side as pawns on a chessboard, to be manipulated as much as possible. Destabilizers may precipitate work stoppages and breakdowns in negotiations. In the middle are *quasi-mediators,* who want to reach a negotiating settlement that is fair and reasonable; they will neither sell out to nor will they attempt to ruin their opponent.

Effectively Using Negotiating Tactics

Here are some basic negotiating tactics to consider:

1. *Do not abuse power.* Negotiations are affected by power relationships that may be based on factors such as the number of alternatives available to them, their level of expertise and the information they possess, and their

financial resources. Even when one side has a temporary power advantage, it is not wise to unnecessarily exploit one's opponent, especially when the relationship is long term.

2. *Develop a reputation for being ethical.* You do not have to like your bargaining opponent, but you should keep your word when making agreements. If you agree to supply your opponent with salary survey information, then you should not later renege on your promise. Similarly, some negotiators try to take unfair advantage by asking for last-minute changes in agreements after negotiations are nearly complete. Such chiseling is the mark of an unethical negotiator.

3. *Keep your options open, and let the other party know that you have options.* One option or "out" is to convince the other side that you are prepared to walk away from the negotiations and take your business elsewhere (for example, a supply manager threatens to use another vendor).

4. *Manage the flow of information carefully.* Information is a form of power, and it can be used to your advantage. There are times when you may decide to withhold information, and there are times when you may want to reveal information to your opponent. The amount and quality of information you possess is based largely on what was done during the preparation stage. An ethical negotiator, however, does not falsify or distort information. Unfortunately, negotiators may walk a fine line between managing information to their advantage and engaging in unethical acts of deception.

5. *Be creative in offering solutions.* When making an offer, use a "selling" approach and stress how the offer is of benefit to you and your opponent. You may decide to package several options to make them more appealing, or you may provide cost estimates to your opponent to illustrate how it is to your opponent's advantage to accept a particular proposal.

6. *Control the rate at which you make concessions.* Conceding too quickly leaves the impression that you are anxious to settle, whereas conceding too slowly may mark you as an obstinate and unreasonable negotiator.

NEGOTIATION ERRORS

Negotiators often succumb to several negotiation errors. One error is to assume that your side has little in common with the other side. This mind-set is known as the *incompatibility error,* and it makes compromise solutions difficult to attain. The *fixed-pie perception* is the belief that the other party's interests are in direct conflict with your interests. In most cases, this assumption is not true, and effective negotiators look for common ground. Another error is *the transparency overestimation,* in which one party believes that its motives should be obvious to the opponent even when this is not the case. *Framing* is the tendency to avoid risk when confronting potential gains and to seek risk when confronting potential losses. When rejecting an offer, for example, a negotiator is viewing the offer as a potential loss and is willing to take the risk of holding out for a better offer. *Anchoring and adjustment* is the tendency to estimate values for unknown events or issues by starting from an initial value and adjusting from that point to reach a final solution. If the initial anchoring point is unrealistic (for example, a hospital administrator in the San Francisco area uses salary data from rural southern hospitals as a starting point in salary negotiations), it may make it difficult to negotiate a satisfactory settlement with the opposing side. *Availability* describes the situation in which information that is presented vividly is given greater weight in negotiations than information presented in a less vivid fashion (even though the latter information is just as important). This error has important implications for the way in which information is presented and evaluated during negotiations. *Overconfidence* occurs because negotiators overestimate their capabilities to judge and make decisions. In the context of negotiations, overconfidence leads the parties to assign an unrealistically high probability that their offer will be accepted. The *nonrational escalation of conflict error* occurs when negotiators refuse to budge from an initial offer even when it is in their best interest to do so. This error makes an agreement more difficult to reach. Finally, *ignoring the cognitions of others* is the tendency of negotiators to ignore the thought processes of their opponents (Kim, 1997).

THIRD-PARTY INTERVENTION IN NEGOTIATIONS

Mediators have long been used to help resolve deadlocks and avoid strikes in union-management negotiations, and their use is also feasible for other negotiation settings. The Federal Mediation and Conciliation Service, the American Arbitration Association, and other agencies provide mediators on an as-needed basis. Mediators help the parties by scheduling and monitoring negotiation sessions, keeping channels of communications open, defusing potential conflicts, allowing one side or the other to save face by suggesting alternative proposals, and helping the parties assess the cost if they fail to reach an agreement, among other possible activities. Unlike labor arbitrators, who have the power to dictate the settlement of contract interpretation disputes to the parties, mediators act in an advisory capacity that is not legally binding. The parties have the option of either listening to or ignoring the mediator's advice.

—Terry Leap

FURTHER READING

Kim, P. (1997). Negotiation biases. In L. Peters, C. Greer, & S. Youngblood (Eds.), *The Blackwell encyclopedic dictionary of human resource management* (p. 227). Malden, MA: Blackwell.

Leap, T. (1995). *Collective bargaining and labor relations* (2nd ed.). Upper Saddle River, NJ: Prentice Hall.

Thompson, L. (2001). *The mind and heart of the negotiator* (2nd ed.). Upper Saddle River, NJ: Prentice Hall.

Walton, R., & McKersie, R. (1965). *A behavioral theory of labor relations.* New York: McGraw-Hill.

NEONATAL CARE

Health care for newborns as a unique specialty began in the 1960s. Previously, technology had not existed to allow ventilation and surgical techniques for the premature or very ill newborn infant. Premature infants at that time were nurtured with oxygen and nutrition under the care of concerned pediatricians, and survival depended on their limited ability to mature rapidly outside the maternal environment. Specific physician training and environments for these patients began to develop during that decade and then began to explode in the 1970s. The March of Dimes Foundation formed the Committee on Perinatal Health, and in 1976 its publication *Toward Improving the Outcome of Pregnancy* defined a regional approach to delivery of neonatal care. The committee recommended defining three levels of care: Level I, newborn nurseries at birth hospitals providing routine care; Level II, larger nurseries at busy birth hospitals providing intermediate support for their moderately ill newborns; and Level III, regional centers that could supply tertiary and surgical care for newborns that would accept transports and support a regional network of lower-level nurseries. This system was the framework for the current situation that exists today, where much of the tertiary care technology and expertise has filtered down to the larger community nurseries.

There are approximately 3200 board-certified neonatologists in the United States. Currently the training requirement for this specialty involves a three-year pediatric residency after medical school, followed by three years of additional fellowship training at an approved program. These specialists staff a wide array of university- and community-based neonatal intensive care units (NICUs). Many are in teaching and administrative roles and have limited patient care exposure. There are approximately 830 NICUs, with a total of 19,000 beds for the delivery of specialized care.

In 2000, there were 4,058,814 births in the United States. Approximately 12% of these were preterm (less than 37 weeks completed gestation), and approximately 12% were born to teen mothers. These two groups account for the majority of the greater than 300,000 newborns per year who require specialized NICU admission. Health care costs of greater than $100,000 per discharge are typical for premature infants weighing less than 1500 grams at birth, accounting for approximately 60,000 births per year. One insurance review of health care claims demonstrated that 68% of all claims exceeding $25,000 per claim involved preterm births or congenital anomalies. This group also is a high-risk group for ongoing medical as well as medical-legal expenses after the initial discharges.

Neonatal care has been responsible for a dramatic reduction in the neonatal mortality rates that have occurred over the past few decades. This has prompted the CDC to credit this as one of the 10 most significant improvements in health care during the last decade. There is still room for improvement in the United States, as well as ample room for advancements to be demonstrated in developing countries, where the death rates for newborns are often 10-fold higher than in developed countries. Economic and cost–benefit analysis may have an inherent conflict with moral and ethical considerations as neonatal care continues to evolve driven by technological advances.

—Charles T. Hankins

See also March of Dimes

FURTHER READING

American Academy of Pediatrics. (2002). Understanding a practice venue. *Journal of Perinatology, 22*(Suppl.), 1–76.
American Academy of Pediatrics and The American College of Obstetricians and Gynecologists. (2002). *Guidelines for perinatal care* (5th ed.). Elk Grove Village, IL: Author.

NET INCOME

See Operating Cash Flow, Profit

NET OPERATING PROFIT AFTER TAXES

See Operating Cash Flow, Profit

NET PRESENT VALUE (NPV)

The net present value (NPV) of an investment is the present value of all the expected future cash flows less the initial investment. If the NPV is positive, then the investment recovers all of the initial investment and more, while taking into account the time value of the cash flows (see entry for *Time Value of Money*). If the NPV is negative, the investment does not recover all of the initial investment, taking time value of the cash flows into account. A common decision rule is to accept a project or investment only if its NPV is greater than or equal to zero.

Some examples will help illustrate the concept. Consider a new health care facility. It will cost $100 million to develop and launch a new facility, and the net cash flows are expected to be $30 million per year for 5 years. If the corporate cost of capital is 9%, is it a good investment? The cash flows are as follows:

Year	0	1	2	3	4	5
Cash Flow	100	30	30	30	30	30

The present values are

$$Year\ 0: -100.00$$
$$Year\ 1: 30/(1.09) = 27.52$$
$$Year\ 2: 30/(1.09)^2 = 25.25$$
$$Year\ 3: 30/(1.09)^3 = 23.17$$
$$Year\ 4: 30/(1.09)^4 = 21.25$$
$$Year\ 5: 30/(1.09)^5 = 19.50$$

The total of these is the net present value and is −$100 + $116.69 = $16.69.

This means the parent corporation would be $16.69 million better off by launching the new facility than not launching it.

A special case of the NPV decision rule is for zero NPV investments. An investment has a zero NPV if its cost exactly equals the present value of its benefits. In other words, a zero NPV investment is fairly priced. Should a company invest in zero NPV projects? The answer is "It depends." Just about all investments in marketable securities—from stocks, to bonds, to options, to futures contracts—are zero NPV investments. If the company has positive NPV projects, then certainly it should invest in those first. If it runs out of positive NPV projects, then its owners should be indifferent between the firm investing in a zero NPV project and just returning the money that would be spent to the owners—either through a dividend or perhaps a stock repurchase. However, the company should never invest in a negative NPV project. It is important to note that this applies only to for-profit concerns. A not-for-profit firm may legitimately invest in negative NPV projects if doing so furthers its mission—not-for-profits are not constrained to maximize NPV, as are for-profit concerns.

COMMON MISTAKES

Several mistakes are commonly made in calculating NPV. First, sunk costs are often included, when they should be ignored. For example, in the facilities launch described earlier, a total of $20 million was spent last year on planning and design. Should the $20 million have been included in the analysis? The answer is no. The planning expenditures were made before the current decision point—you can't get the money back by not undertaking the project, so you can't consider it as a cost of going forward.

The sunk cost issue is closely related to the second mistake, that of incorrectly identifying incremental costs. The only cash flows included in a NPV analysis should be ones that will occur as a result of the project. For example, the parent company has $30 million per year in overhead expenses that for accounting purposes it allocates among its various divisions. The new division for the new health care facility is going to be charged $5 million per year as its portion of the overhead. Should this charge be included in the cash flows? The answer is no. Even though the company is allocating part of its overhead to the new facility's division, the company would have to incur the $30 million in overhead expenses whether or not the new facility is built. So the overhead charge isn't relevant to the investment decision. In contrast, if the company must reclaim buildings for the new facility that it is currently leasing out to another company for $1 million per year, then this $1 million per year is an opportunity cost that must be charged to the project. This is because with the new facility the company will not earn $1 million in rental income.

A third mistake is to use the wrong discount rate. If the project is of the same riskiness as other projects or investments the firm makes, then the corporate cost of capital (see entry for *Cost of Capital*) should be used. However, if the project is more risky than the average project, then its discount rate should be adjusted upward. If the project is safer than average, then its discount rate should be adjusted downward.

—Phillip R. Daves

See also Cost of Capital, Discounted Cash Flows, Time Value of Money

FURTHER READING

Brigham, E. F., & Ehrhardt, M. C. (2001). *Financial management* (10th ed.). Mason, OH: South-Western.

NET WORKING CAPITAL

Net working capital is the difference between current (short-term) assets and current (short-term) liabilities.

Current assets typically include cash, marketable securities, accounts receivable, inventory, and other assets that can be converted to cash in one year or less. Current liabilities typically include accounts payable, the current portion of notes payable or other long-term debt, and accrued expenses payable. Working capital is the amount of money required by a company to manage differences between cash inflows and outflows. It covers the cash conversion cycle in a business from raw materials to collections on accounts receivable. Internal sources of funds for net working capital are retained earnings, savings from efficiencies, and generated cash.[1] Uses of net working capital include buying fixed assets, dividend payments, payment of long-term debt, and stock repurchases.[2]

The amount of optimal working capital varies by company, country, risk aversion, and industry. Net working capital can be beneficial to an extent, because a certain amount is usually required to cover expenses incurred in the firm's operating cycle. If a firm has high net working capital, that firm is less likely to fail in the short term, because it should be able to cover liabilities that it will incur in one year or less. Thus, the greater a corporation's net working capital, the better from a pure liquidity standpoint.[3] However, large amounts of short-term assets can indicate that the company is not managing funds well, because a greater return can generally be realized with longer-term investments. For example, increasing receivables are not always beneficial, because this may indicate that the company has inefficient collections policies. Likewise, increasing inventory may indicate obsolescence. Many companies that are either growing or experience a seasonal business often need to obtain cash from outside sources to finance working capital needs. This short-term funding can be obtained using commercial paper, lines of credit, short-term loans, and asset-based borrowing, including asset securitization.[4]

Fluctuations in net working capital can result from projects that affect current assets and current liabilities. Inventories typically comprise a small portion of project investment for health care providers, so the net working capital changes that result can often be overlooked without adversely or noticeably affecting the project analysis.[5] Whenever a capital project involves a significant positive change in net working capital (the increase in current assets exceeds the increase in current liabilities), the net investment in current assets and thus net working capital must be considered, to avoid overstating overall project profitability.[6]

Working capital management is significant to both lenders and investors. First, the amount of working capital required can have a strong effect on a company's cash flows and ability to repay debt. In addition, reducing working capital can increase a stock's price.[7] A lower required working capital policy allows a company to distribute more cash to investors.

—Edward Pershing

NOTES

1. Downes, J., & Goodman, J. E. (1998). *Dictionary of finance and investment terms* (5th ed., pp. 705–706). New York: Barron's.

2. www.amjoch-investors.com/fm01.html.

3. Gapenski, L. C. (2002). *Healthcare finance: An introduction to accounting and financial management* (2nd ed.). Chicago: Foundation of the American College of Healthcare.

4. Gamble, R. (1997, April). Fat-free working capital. *Controller Magazine*, p. 45.

5. Gapenski, *Healthcare finance*.

6. Gapenski, *Healthcare finance*.

7. Strischek, D. (2001, October). A banker's perspective on working capital and cash flow management. *Strategic Finance*, *83*(4), 38.

NETWORK-MODEL HMO

See Health Maintenance Organizations (HMOs)

NETWORKS

In the U.S. health care industry, the term *networks* can refer to groups of providers (such as physicians, hospitals, or cancer centers) that voluntarily coalesce in strategic alliances for some joint contracting purpose. These networks do not possess a common asset base, and there is no joint ownership.

To illustrate, managed care plans (such as health maintenance organizations and preferred provider organizations, or HMOs and PPOs) typically assemble networks of both doctors and hospitals for their enrollees to use. Here, each physician or hospital individually negotiates with the managed care plan for reimbursement in exchange for a defined set of services to be provided to enrollees. Physicians can themselves form their own networks to collectively negotiate with managed care plans—typically in the form of an independent practitioner association (IPA), the most popular form of HMO. Here, physicians voluntarily join the IPA, which then contracts with the HMO. Hospitals can likewise form networks of hospitals to share some services, cooperate on some endeavors, or to jointly contract with managed care plans. These hospital networks are much looser in organization and more nebulous in structure than are ownership-based hospital systems. Recent data collected by the American Hospital Association reveals that only 1% of hospital networks operated in a centralized fashion, whereas 61% were "moderately centralized," 4% were decentralized, and 34% acted autonomously.

Because networks are so loosely structured, there is little direct control over the members of a network. There is also a lot of variation in network arrangements, making it difficult for researchers to accurately describe them (other than just a snapshot in time). Because there is no common asset base to networks, networks are easy and relatively inexpensive to form. This explains much of their popularity in the HMO industry. Not surprisingly, they are also fairly easy and inexpensive to disband. This explains why there are a lot of market exits among these types of firms. Given these considerations, it is plausible to expect that networks may not perform as well as more organized systems. This hypothesis is true for hospitals: Networks exhibit lower levels of financial performance than ownership-based systems. The hypothesis also used to be true for IPA HMOs, in terms of their managing utilization (such as inpatient days per thousand enrollees). In recent years, however, IPAs have made considerable investments in information systems to improve their medical management and now exhibit utilization performance levels comparable to more organized HMOs such as group and staff models.

—Robert Lawton Burns

NEW DRUG APPLICATION (NDA)

A New Drug Application (NDA) tendered to the federal Food and Drug Administration is the method in which drug sponsors summarize all the preclinical, clinical, and manufacturing information in order to gain U.S. commercialization of the drug product. The data from the Investigational New Drug (IND) are part of the NDA.

The NDA application form is FDA 356h, which serves as a guide for the items needed for the NDA submission. These include 14 items, as follows:

1. Index
2. Summary
3. Chemistry, manufacturing, and control section
   a. Samples
   b. Methods validation package
   c. Labeling
      i. Draft labeling
      ii. Final printed labeling
4. Nonclinical pharmacology and toxicology section
5. Human pharmacokinetics and bioavailability section
6. Microbiology section
7. Clinical data section

8. Safety update section

9. Statistical section

10. Case report tabulations

11. Case report forms

12. Patient information on any patent that claims the drug

13. A patient certification with respect to any patent that claims the drug

14. Other (specify)

In addition, a pre-NDA submission conference should be held with the FDA, to provide a clear understanding to the agency of what is going to be submitted. It is also beneficial to the sponsor to get any preliminary FDA feedback on the application.

After it receives the NDA, the FDA has 60 days to determine if the application can be filed. Acceptance of the filing means that the FDA agrees all the required information is submitted in an acceptable format. The date of filing begins the 180-day clock wherein the FDA will either approve the application or determine that it is approvable or not approvable based on subsequent data.

—Anthony Sileno

See also Investigational New Drug Application (IND)

FURTHER READING

The FDA has many guidance documents to help prepare NDAs and the content of each section. For a list of all NDA guidances, see Section 21 Code of Federal Registration and www.fda.gov.

NICHE STRATEGIES

Niches are small markets that consist of people with similar characteristics or needs. Niche strategies are the methods that organizations use to meet the needs of those specific individuals. Organizations using niche strategies try to know the target market so well that they can serve it better than other, less focused, competitors. This requires an in-depth understanding of the customers' needs, as well as continual investment in internal capabilities.

Niche strategies involve identifying customers who have more than or different needs from those of the typical clients for a service. In the health care industry, for example, various people require specialized services in different areas ranging from alcohol and drug treatment to long-term care. Although large, multispecialty hospitals can provide care for these patients, they may not be able to offer the range and depth of specialty services that patients need. Smaller niche players, such as behavioral care providers or long-term care specialists, succeed because they recognize these needs and provide the appropriate mix of services, staffing, and care.

Effective niche strategies, therefore, arise from looking at the market creatively to find previously unmet needs. In the past 20 years, new possibilities have emerged in health care as well as many other industries due to rapid demographic and societal changes. Some of these changes include the increasing number of single-parent households, dual-income families and working women, an aging population, rapid technological advances, and increased demands on personal time. These changes influence patients' perceptions of services, their ability to utilize services, and their ability to pay for those services. Often clients are willing to pay more for extra services that save time or better meet their needs. In contrast, some niches consist of individuals with fewer needs and less ability to pay. Even these niches can be well served by organizations willing to streamline their processes and focus on the essentials.

The second critical element of a niche strategy is evaluating organizational resources and competencies and aligning them with the targeted customer needs. The ideal situation is when an organization's strengths are so well matched to the customer's needs that competitors are not able to match them. One way to work toward this fit is to involve clients in designing products or services. This involvement is also positive because it can help establish a close relationship with the client, building loyalty and making it more difficult for competitors to intervene.

Finally, health care organizations pursuing a niche strategy should clearly communicate the advantages and benefits of that strategy to current and potential clients. The objective is to clearly establish perceptions of the hospital's services in the minds of the targeted consumers.

—Barbara Spencer

See also Generic Strategies

FURTHER READING

Chalasani, S., & Shani, D. (1992). Exploiting niches using relationship marketing. *Journal of Consumer Marketing, 9*(3), 33–42.

McKenna, R. (1988, November–December). Marketing in an age of diversity. *Harvard Business Review, 66,* 88–95.

NOMINAL GROUP TECHNIQUE (NGT)

The nominal group technique (NGT) is a structured group meeting conducted by a facilitator. It has four steps:

generating ideas, sequential reporting of ideas, clarification of ideas, and ranking of ideas by importance. One of the advantages of the technique is the involvement of stakeholders in the outcome of the process. The NGT assures that each person has an equal opportunity to express his or her ideas. It stimulates the generation of ideas through silent writing in step 1 and the round-robin listing in step 2. Each member is asked to list 10 most important ideas for change in the organization. Then, in a round-robin fashion, one idea from each member is posted on a flipchart for all to see.

Then the second idea for each member is posted and so on. This continues until all the ideas are posted on a wall filled with flipchart paper. So far there is no questioning of any idea. This prevents closure of ideas before all the ideas are equally considered. All participants can reflect on all ideas and have their questions and concerns addressed in step 3. Thus, in step 3 one can argue against any of the points but all ideas still stay posted on the wall. Then, each member or participant is asked to decide which 10 ideas are most important to him or her. In step 3 all participants cast a selected number of votes on the ideas listed. Usually 20 or so ideas are listed. Each participant then has 10 votes. Voting usually consists of putting a sticky dot (dot sticker) alongside the ideas you vote for. The members can only use one vote per idea. The result is a clustering around the most important ideas that the collective agrees on. This is visually seen immediately, because the red or orange dots are seen clustered. The ideas that got little attention just go off the agenda without much objection. Silent ranking, step 4, gives equal weight to each opinion during decision making and reduces peer pressure to support only one idea. Also, the NGT is cost and time efficient, because it gathers a lot of data in a short period of time.

—Peter J. Dean

FURTHER READING

Dean, P. J. (1999). *Performance engineering at work* (2nd ed.). Washington, DC: IBSTPI [International Board of Standards for Training, Performance and Instruction] Publications, with the International Society for Performance Improvement.

NONCASH EXPENSE

Noncash expenses are operating costs that are recorded in the financial statements during a particular period but do not necessarily reflect cash disbursements by the organization in that period. Some noncash expenses are discussed in the following paragraphs.

Depreciation is the periodic expensing of an asset that was capitalized when purchased. When a piece of property or equipment is purchased that meets certain material thresholds for capitalization, the cost of that asset is recognized over its useful life as periodic depreciation. For example, when a hospital purchases a piece of equipment for $2 million and that equipment is expected to have a useful service life of 10 years, the hospital does not expense the entire $2 million in the year of the acquisition. Assuming no residual value at the end of the 10-year useful life period and assuming a straight-line method of depreciation, the hospital would annually recognize $200,000 in depreciation expense related to that piece of equipment over its useful life. In those years, the hospital recognizes a $200,000 expense while expending no additional cash.

Like depreciation, *amortization* is the periodic recognition of the cost of a capitalized asset. However, amortization generally relates to intangible assets such as goodwill, bond issue costs, or bond discounts and premiums. Goodwill results when an organization pays more than fair market value for an asset. Historically, the excess goodwill was amortized and expensed over the expected remaining life of the underlying asset. Recent changes in accounting principles related to amortization of goodwill call for the value of the asset that created the goodwill to be evaluated periodically and the goodwill adjusted for any changes. The periodic adjustments are recognized as a noncash expense in that period.

In the health care industry, especially in the not-for-profit sector, bond-related costs are very common. Bond issue costs include underwriter fees, legal fees, and other costs associated with the issuance of debt. These costs are generally included in the financed amount of a project or netted from the proceeds of a debt issuance. Because those costs relate to the financing of a project or asset with a long service life, the costs are established in an asset account and amortized over the term of the related debt issue. Bond premiums or discounts arise when bonds are sold for more or less, respectively, than their face or par value. For example, when a hospital issues bonds above their par value, they must recognize the excess amount as a premium paid. That premium is amortized over the life of the bonds.

There are numerous other forms of noncash expenses that are more infrequent in nature. When assets are sold for less than their book value, a loss on the disposal of that asset is recorded. However, that loss does not reflect a cash outlay; the loss only reflects the reconciliation of the sales price to the carrying value of the asset. Other forms of noncash expenses include extraordinary losses on the early extinguishment of debt. When debt is retired early, and that debt has related unamortized issue costs or discounts, the remaining unamortized issue costs and discount are expensed in the period of the extinguishment, resulting in a noncash expense.

In the statement of cash flows for an organization, noncash expenses that are included in the determination of net income must be added back to arrive at the true change in cash that has resulted from operations.

—Edward Pershing

FURTHER READING

Downes, J., & Goodman, J. E. (1998). *Dictionary of finance and investment terms* (5th ed.). New York: Barron's.

NONCOMPETE AGREEMENTS

Noncompete agreements are provisions in an employment contract that are intended to limit the employee's ability to compete with the employer either during the term of employment or after termination. The most common type of restrictive covenant in physician contracts is a noncompete agreement (or "noncompete"). Noncompetes are common in several types of physician contracts. In addition to physician employment contracts, noncompetes are also common in agreements involving physician practice purchases and establishment of group practices or partnerships. Any agreement that is designed to limit competition is considered a restraint of trade. Restraints of trade are not favored in a free-market society and are in fact illegal, absent proper justification. Therefore, only restraints considered *reasonable* are enforceable.

It is reasonable that physician contractors (whether employers, group members, partners, hospitals, or practice purchasers) would need to protect their business interests at the termination of the business arrangement. Valid business interests in physician contracts include investment in training, recruiting, marketing, and development of physicians, as well as protection of information concerning business practices and trade secrets. Client base retention is also a primary concern. It is also reasonable that physicians who have spent many years training to practice medicine would need to be free to practice their profession in the community of their choice and not be tethered to an unsatisfactory employment arrangement. Therefore, a restrictive covenant must strike a balance between these competing interests. Therefore, in most states noncompete agreements that are part of the employment contract and are designed to protect valid business interests are enforceable if the restraint is reasonable in scope, time, and place.

There are no established criteria as to how broad, how long, or how far a covenant can reach and still be considered reasonable. The reasonableness of each case is decided on its own facts and merits. Courts enforce only those restraints that are sufficient to protect the employer's interests, and no more. For instance, a family practice physician who leaves a group practice might be prohibited from opening a competing family practice office in close proximity to his or her former group but would not be restrained from joining the staff of emergency physicians in a nearby hospital. Thus, the scope of protection is limited only to the interest to be protected, that is, competition in a private family practice. The scope cannot reasonably inhibit the physician's ability to practice any kind of medicine within the same community. Reasonableness as to time and distance are treated similarly. The noncompete clause could prohibit the departing family practice physician from opening a competing practice within a few miles of the former group or perhaps within the same small community, but the protection would be too broad if it extended to the entire state, or perhaps even to other nearby communities. Again, the reasonableness would depend on the circumstances. Likewise, if a covenant restrained a physician from opening a practice for 10 years in the same community, it would probably not be enforceable. The same restraint for 1 or 2 years would likely be deemed sufficient but not excessive.

Because noncompetes are often considered burdensome, there is a growing trend by many courts toward favoring nonsolicitation clauses over noncompete clauses. Nonsolicitation clauses prohibit the departing physician from soliciting patients or employees of the previous employer. This is considered a less onerous method of protecting the employer's interest in patient and staff retention while allowing the departing employee the freedom to choose the community in which to practice.

Regardless of the type of restrictive covenant used in an employment contract, the promise not to compete must be bound by consideration. All contracts require valid consideration in order to be enforceable. Consideration is the exchange of something of value to bind the promise of the other party. Typically, consideration is provided by the exchange of promises by both parties to a contract. In an employment contract, the employee's promise not to compete is the consideration for the employer's promise to hire and vice versa. A noncompete agreement entered into *after* employment is often ruled unenforceable for "lack of consideration." It would be dangerous, however, for a physician to rely on this rationale in that some courts have determined that consideration was given by the employer's "retention" of the physician after the noncompete agreement was entered into.

Noncompete clauses are often deemed necessary to protect the value of the consideration paid in the purchase of the business. When a physician purchases a medical practice from another physician, it is common to include an agreement that limits the ability of the seller to compete with the purchaser for a period of time after the sale. Because it is likely that patients would follow their physician to his or her new location, the amount paid to purchase a physician's practice would be rendered virtually worthless if the selling physician were free to open a new practice and compete with the purchaser. Therefore, an agreement would be enforceable that limits the ability of the seller to directly compete and is reasonable as to scope, time, and distance.

Penalties for violating a noncompete clause range from injunctive relief to monetary damages to compensate for any financial losses incurred because of the violation. Some contracts specify liquidated damages—damages defined when entering the contract that will ensue if the noncompete provision is violated. In cases where the violation is deemed willful, malicious, or fraudulent, punitive damages may be awarded. Punitive damages are intended not only to compensate the wronged party for losses but also to punish the violator for particularly egregious behavior. Punitive damages are also intended to serve as a deterrent to others.

Although not favored in law, reasonable noncompetes in employment contracts are valid in most states if they meet certain criteria, that is, reasonableness, consideration, and valid purpose. But states vary considerably in their treatment of restrictive covenants. Some courts modify a restrictive covenant if it is deemed excessive, whereas other courts simply refuse to enforce them, and some states do not recognize noncompetes at all. All parties to physician employment contracts should be aware of the law and precedents in their state in order to understand the validity of restrictive covenants and the standards of reasonableness that are likely to be enforceable in that jurisdiction.

—Cheryl S. Massingale

FURTHER READING

Mann, R., & Roberts, B. (1970). *Smith and Roberson's business law* (10th ed.). Cincinnati, OH: South-Western.

NONPHYSICIAN PROVIDERS (NPPS)

See Physician Extenders

NONPRICE COMPETITION IN HOSPITALS

The term "nonprice competition in hospitals" describes a situation in which a particular institution has decided it can price its services without regard to the prevailing competitive market in which it operates. This might occur for a variety of reasons, ranging from unawareness of prevailing price competition to cost-driven reasons for noncompetitive pricing or a belief that a differentiated (and thus "noncompetitive") price is justified for a variety of reasons.

In a capitalist free-enterprise economy, price competition is an important factor in regulating growth, prosperity, the number of surviving entrants, and competitive behavior. Lower prices lead to higher demand and often to increased share of markets. Conversely, higher prices lead to lower demand, opening the market to new entrants or lower-priced competitors—all other things being equal.

However, when the same entity or parts of closely related entities can specify what is to be purchased, deliver the products or services, and establish the price, normal market factors no longer control competitive conditions. In the absence of competition, this might be called a *monopoly*. Occasionally normal competition is impaired by interference of outside agencies, a condition that effects the health care delivery systems in the United States. If competition is mitigated by a low availability or nonavailability of the particular product or service within a reasonable time or distance, a nearly monopolistic situation can exist and price competition is stifled, if not eliminated.

Where a prospective purchaser has a desperate need for a product or service, normal market controls also fail to operate normally. For people dying of thirst, water could be sold at almost any price, provided some purchasers had enough money to pay for it. Such is the case in medical care, especially at large medical institutions that dominate certain segments of the market, either by facilities, specialties, or geography.

When the entity that pays for the services is not the same as the one receiving them (a third-party payer), another of the normal price competition mechanisms is disrupted. This is the typical case in medical services and especially in hospital care. Only through the applied purchasing leverage of third-party payers (HMOs, PPOs, and so on) does the normal price competition mechanism come into play—and then only when viable competition exists in the facilities, specialties, or geography involved.

In conclusion, because most medical care is delivered with third-party payments, and the purchaser is in dire need of the services, the typical patient has little interest in price. The result is that most medical care is bought on decision criteria other than price. Thus, nonprice competition seems to be the norm, not only in hospitals but also in a wide range of health and medical care services.

—John L. Mariotti

FURTHER READING

www.strategicpricinggroup.com

NOT-FOR-PROFIT ORGANIZATION

Many health care organizations are not-for-profit. They do not have stockholders and no individuals may receive their residual assets, if any. They are also called *nonprofit organizations*. What distinguishes them from other private sector organizations is that profit is not their primary goal, although they are not constrained from being profitable. In fact, they must make some profits to maintain and upgrade their plant and equipment, repay debt, and adopt new technology.

TAX STATUS

Many in the general public associate tax exemption with not-for-profit status, but that is not a necessary condition. Most not-for-profit health care organizations qualify for federal, state, and local tax exemptions. They qualify as charitable organizations under Section 501(c)(3) of the Internal Revenue Code. If they qualify, profits are not taxable and gifts to them are deductible charitable donations for the donor. Most of the time their real property is also exempt from local property taxes. Not-for-profit organizations may choose to be tax exempt or may lose their exemption because they have devoted too many resources to influencing legislation and have too much business unrelated to their stated charitable purpose. Foundations are a separate type of not-for-profit organization and must also distribute most their annual income in accordance with their charitable purposes. Health insurers, even if not-for-profit, are not exempt from federal income taxes.

GOVERNANCE

Most not-for-profit organizations have a governance structure quite different from that of a stockholder corporation. The executive director or chief executive officer (CEO) is usually an ex-officio member of the board, and the voting members of the board are not employees. They are usually called directors, governors, or trustees. The board sets policies and instructs the executive director and staff to implement them. The board of a not-for-profit tends to be much more involved in financial and management decision making than the board of a for-profit. The executive director tends to be selected based on professional as well as managerial qualifications and usually reflects the professional ideology that dominates the organization. A professional orientation and value system is important to leadership, because high levels of performance incentives are not usually offered by not-for-profit organizations. High salaries and bonuses often are not acceptable to donors or to the general public. One place where the CEO often does not come up through the organization's dominant profession's ranks is the U.S. hospital. Here a separate profession of hospital administrator has established itself. This group has advanced management training useful to the organization, but the administrator often loses out to the physicians whenever there are professional differences.

There are three categories of not-for-profit organizations: donative, entrepreneurial, and membership. Each has a different form of governance. Most large nonprofits have activities that operate on each model in order to maximize income. In a membership organization, membership is voluntary and often carries a cost, so the members elect the board directly. An entrepreneurial organization generally has an independent self-perpetuating board, whereas the donative organization often selects its new and continuing members on the basis of their ability to generate gifts and other income. Most health care organizations are either entrepreneurial (hospital, hospice) or donative (cancer research center, medical school). Government funding for education and facilities would be donative, whereas medical research grants are highly entrepreneurial, moving with the investigator rather than being attached to the institution.

MANAGEMENT

Not-for-profit organizations are highly dependent on a clear definition of their mission and the needs of their primary constituencies. They cannot judge their performance solely against the bottom line, and there is so much demand for their services that they must work hard to stay focused on those two things. Measurement systems must be aimed at accountability and improved performance with the primary client group. In health care, most institutions involve a dominant professional group that must be respected and often includes the executive director, but an institution cannot limit itself to that one professional ideology or to any other single stakeholder. Many stakeholders—patients, professionals, donors, providers—must be considered in the decision-making process. Managing complex not-for-profit organizations requires very considerable managerial skills.

In many health care areas, for-profit and not-for-profit providers are in direct competition with each other. Examples include hospitals, nursing homes, home health agencies, insurers, and cemeteries. What are the pros and cons of each organizational form for health care organizations? For-profit organizations, especially those with publicly traded stock, are expected to produce steadily increasing earnings and maximize the wealth of the shareholders. Their stock requires a higher return on investment than borrowed money because of the risks to the stockholders from bankruptcy. Not-for-profit organizations are expected to meet their social objectives efficiently and effectively while staying solvent. Because of their access to the stock markets, for-profit organizations often have greater ability to raise capital for growth and modernization. Historically, the not-for-profits have relied more on retained earnings and borrowed money for growth. However, uncertainties in health care financing make it difficult to generate earnings or borrow the necessary capital. Hospitals used to be able to borrow 80% to 90% of their capital needs based on expected high occupancy rates. However, cost containment measures have lowered occupancies considerably and bond money is less available to them. Many states are trying to overcome that problem by setting up state bonding authorities that issue and stand behind tax-exempt bonds for local health care organizations.

—Curtis P. McLaughlin

FURTHER READING

Clement, J. P., White, K. R., & Valdmanis, V. (2002). Charity care: Do not-for-profits influence for-profits? *Medical Care Research Reviews, 59*(1), 59–78.

Drucker, P. F. (1990). *Managing the nonprofit organization: Principles and practices.* New York: HarperCollins.

McLaughlin, C. P. (1986). *The management of nonprofit organizations.* New York: Wiley.

Reinhardt, U. E. (2000). The economics of for-profit and not-for-profit hospitals. *Health Affairs, 19*(6), 178–186.

NURSING HOME

See Long-Term Care

OBJECTIVES

Objectives or goals are the results the organization seeks to achieve. As an integral part of the strategic or business plan, along with mission, vision, values, and strategies, objectives indicate what the organization plans to accomplish.

Objectives are meant to communicate desired outcomes for a number of organizationwide reasons. First, objectives communicate desired outcomes to organizational personnel so that they know how to allocate efforts in support of those desired results. Second, objectives communicate desired results to external stakeholders so they can understand the directions the organization is pursuing. Then, external stakeholders can decide if they wish to support the organization. Third, internal decision makers can allocate resources in the direction of the desired objectives and in appropriate amounts.

Objectives need to exhibit certain characteristics in order to communicate the preceding information to organizational personnel, external stakeholders, and internal decision makers. Objectives should be SMART: specific, measurable, attainable, result oriented, and time determinate.

Objectives should be *specific*. They should pertain to a certain task or program. Specific objectives help the organization decide the amount of resources to allocate.

Objectives should be *measurable*. Measurable objectives are quantifiable by date, outcomes, and responsibility. Thus, accomplishment can be verified.

Objectives should be *attainable*. Organizational personnel should be able to complete the objectives within the time indicated and with existing constraints. Goals that are totally unrealistic and not attainable lose their ability to motivate effort from personnel.

Objectives should be *result oriented*. Goals should be focused on outcomes so that personnel can see the results that affect stakeholders.

Objectives should be *time determinate*. The time frame should be established so that accomplishment can be verified.

An example of an objective that meets the preceding criteria is for a pharmaceutical company to establish a profitability objective of earnings per share of $1.40 in one year and $1.55 in two years. Or a hospital may establish an objective of reducing nursing staff turnover to 20% annually in one year and to 15% in two years.

—Michael J. Stahl

See also Business Plan, Long-Range Planning, Mission, Strategy, Values (Guiding Principles), Vision

FURTHER READING

Ginter, P. M., Swayne, L. M., & Duncan, W. J. (1998). *Strategic management of health care organizations.* Malden, MA: Blackwell.

Rich, S. R., & Gumpert, D. E. (1985). *Business plans that win $$$: Lessons from the MIT Enterprise Forum.* New York: Harper & Row.

Stahl, M., & Grigsby, D. (1997). *Strategic management* (Chapter 2). Oxford, UK: Blackwell.

OCCUPANCY RATE

See Capacity and Capacity Utilization

OCCUPATIONAL SAFETY AND HEALTH ACT (OSHA)

Passage of the Occupational Safety and Health Act (OSHA) of 1970 imposed a comprehensive scheme for regulating workplace safety. The Occupational Safety and Health Administration (also OSHA) is the federal agency responsible for promulgating and policing these workplace safety regulations. OSHA safety standards apply to health care facilities ranging from small physician offices to large multisite hospitals. These OSHA safety regulations relate to general safe working conditions such as methods to prevent employee slips, falls, and injury from machines, and emergency evacuation procedures as well as specific regulations pertaining to the health care work environment. These include the use of personal protective equipment (such as respirators, gowns, and eye guards), provision of first-aid equipment and training, and reducing exposure to bloodborne and airborne pathogens. In 1985, OSHA adopted a federal hazard communication standard requiring employers to notify their employees of the dangers associated with chemical hazards in the workplace. People manufacturing or importing hazardous chemicals are required to prepare a material safety data sheet (MSDS) that identifies the hazardous chemical and describes the physical and health hazards associated with exposure to it. Facilities that use the chemicals are required to inform their employees who may be exposed to such chemicals with information concerning risks associated with exposure and also protective and emergency response measures. In 1992, OSHA issued final regulations governing occupational exposure in the health care workplace to bloodborne pathogens including exposure to human immunodeficiency virus (HIV) and hepatitis virus B (HBV). The regulations provide for the identification and classification of "at risk" employees, training of employees, and the implementation of universal precautions and engineering controls and workplace controls to reduce the risk of exposure to such pathogens, as well as postexposure procedures.

—Theresa DiMartino

OCCURRENCE COVERAGE

There are two basic types of medical liability insurance coverage: occurrence and claims made. Occurrence policies cover all claims that arise from events that take place during a specific policy period, irrespective of when the claims are reported to the insurance company. Claims-made policies, in contrast, cover only those claims made, or reported, during the given policy's period and arising from incidents occurring during that policy's life. This latter type of policy was designed to limit the exposure of the insurers after the significant rise in medical liability claims in the 1970s. As such, most policies offered today are of the "claims made" type, with a few occurrence-style policies still being offered.

Thus, occurrence policies cover the claim if it occurred during the policy period. This obviates the need for additional coverage by the physician when changing insurance carriers (called "tail coverage"), but, where available, could result in higher premiums because the carrier is trying to minimize potentially large and unpredictable future payouts. Occurrence policies also might prove insufficient to cover awards if the limits were much higher than anticipated at some time in the future. An example of occurrence coverage would involve a physician who performs an emergency hysterectomy for a postpartum hemorrhage; the patient sues the physician for negligence five years after the doctor changes carriers. The insurance carrier at the time of the *occurrence* of the incident would assume responsibility for handling that claim, including its defense and payout if necessary.

—Benito A. Alvarez

FURTHER READING

American Medical Association. (1991). *The guide to medical professional liability insurance.* Chicago: Author.
www. coverageglossary.com
www. plusweb.org

OCCURRENCE SCREENING

As it relates to medical liability insurance, occurrence screening involves the evaluation of the physician seeking liability insurance coverage in the light of his or her risk to the insurer for possible claims-related losses. Some insurers use "experience rating," charging those doctors with "clean" claims records lower premiums (see entry for *Premium*); those with poor claims histories (numerous claims against them) are charged higher amounts (if at all covered). Other factors taken into consideration during the evaluation process are medical specialty, types of medical procedures performed, length of time in active practice, history of poor outcomes (so-called "potential negligence" cases against which a claim has not been formally launched), formal notifications by patient's attorney of intent to file a claim ("180-day letter"), geographic location of insured, and participation in risk management programs.

Participation in risk management programs has been increasing over the past few years, in an attempt by both physicians and insurers to limit their exposure. Some insurers offer a discounted premium with proof of attendance at these programs, whereas others make their policy renewal contingent on their completion. Some insurers have also begun considering discounts for those physicians and practices that employ an electronic medical record, recognizing the improved data capture these systems can achieve, resulting in improved documentation. An example of screening would be an insurer who assesses, based on a questionnaire describing actual claims history and potential claims, the risk of loss to come from insured; if coverage is granted (and it may be denied), the premium will reflect the level of such risk.

—Benito A. Alvarez

See also Premium

FURTHER READING

Alguire, P. (2002). *Malpractice insurance.* Philadelphia: American College of Physicians and American Society of Internal Medicine.
American Medical Association. (1991). *The guide to medical professional liability insurance.* Chicago: Author.

OFF LABEL

A drug product is approved for a certain indication, a method of administration according to controlled clinical studies. The FDA approves the product for that indication or label based on the contents of the New Drug Application. Health care workers may use the drug product "off label," which means not according to the approved indication or method of administration.

Physicians can use drug products off label without the requirement of submitting an Investigational New Drug Application or requiring institutional review board approval. However, the physician must follow good medical practice.

Examples of drug products used off label are pediatric and oncology medications. This can be a major issue, because there are no data available to learn how to administer the drug product safely.

A sponsor can publish in scientific journals, regarding the safety and effectiveness or benefits of "off label" uses for their marketed drug products. However, the FDA has policies for the use of promotional materials for off-label use. The FDA has proposed the provisions of the Food and Drug Administration Modernization Act (FDAMA) of 1997 allowing manufactures and sponsors of drug products greater flexibility to disseminate information on "off label" use.

—Anthony Sileno

See also Clinical Trials

FURTHER READING

Food and Drug Administration. (1998). *Institutional review boards and clinical investigators. FDA guidance for the industry.* Washington, DC: Author.

OFFICE FOR HUMAN RESEARCH PROTECTIONS (OHRP)

The Office for Human Research Protections (OHRP) is the federal office charged with the responsibility of promulgating policy, monitoring compliance, providing education and guidance, and assisting in quality improvement and assessment of programs pertaining to the protection of human subjects in research activities.

Formerly the Office for Protection from Research Risk (OPRR), this office was renamed OHRP and was moved up in June 2000 from under the jurisdiction of the National Institutes of Health to the Office of the Secretary, within the Department of Health and Human Services.

Institutions receiving federal funding must submit to the OHRP a Federal Wide Assurance (FWA) in which they certify their intent to comply with the federal regulations as 45 CFR 46 (Code of Federal Regulations at Title 45, Public Welfare, Part 46, Protection of Human Subjects) for federally funding human subject research. Most institutions extend this certification to cover all research, regardless of funding source or status. Registration of Institutional Review Boards (regardless of federal funding status) with the OHRP allows the office to efficiently disseminate new regulations and guidance.

For a period of approximately 3 years starting in the late 1990s, the Compliance Oversight branch of OHRP suspended human subject research at a number of institutions following audit findings of noncompliance with federal regulations and/or potential endangerment of human subjects. Subsequently, the Education and the Assurances and Quality Improvement branches of OHRP became particularly proactive in their efforts to work with institutions in assessing and preventing noncompliance, with the intended common goal of overall improvement in institutional human subject protection programs.

Compliance of institutions conducting research involving drugs, biologics, or devices is also monitored by the Food and Drug Administration (FDA). The federal regulations at 21 CFR 50 (Informed Consent), 56 (Institutional Review Boards), 312 (Investigational New Drug Application), and 812 (Investigational Device Exemptions) are all pertinent to investigators and institutions under FDA jurisdiction.

—Judy Matuk

See also Assurance of Compliance (Federal Wide Assurance, FWA), Institutional Review Board (IRB)

FURTHER READING

http://ohrp.osophs.dhhs.gov
www.access.gpo.gov/nara/cfr/waisidx_99/45cfr46_99.html
www.fda.gov/oc/ohrt/irbs/default.htm

ONE-TO-ONE MARKETING

One-to-one marketing is a philosophy based on the idea that an ideal size for a target market is one customer. Traditionally, one of the most important tasks for a marketer is the process of segmentation and targeting. Segmentation is the process of breaking a large heterogeneous group of potential customers into small, homogeneous groups of buyers with similar needs, characteristics, or behaviors who might respond to a unique marketing mix. Targeting, in contrast, is the process of choosing which of those segments is the most attractive, given the company's distinct competencies. When a company practices one-to-one-marketing, it takes the notion of segmentation to its logical extreme, and creates segments of individual consumers.

Implementing a one-to-one marketing philosophy requires that a company be able to understand what individual consumers want, be able to deliver value to consumers individually, and be able to communicate value with them individually. Historically, one-to-one marketing has been a common philosophy in business-to-business markets. Particularly for its largest customers, many companies will create custom marketing programs that respond to those important customers' individual needs. For example, DeRoyal is a supplier of acute care supplies to large hospitals, and its salesforce works directly with these large customers to provide custom solutions to their operating room needs. This has been relatively easy in business markets, because most companies have a relatively small number of large customers, and creating customized marketing programs for them has not been particularly difficult.

However, current trends are to provide such a program of one-to-one marketing in consumer markets as well. Such a program requires sophisticated database technology. A customer database allows the company to track individual buying behaviors, and make inferences about what customers value based on their past purchase and shopping behaviors. Analysis of these buying and shopping behaviors allows the company to create individualized bundles of products that are designed specifically for that segment of one customer. Finally, this database allows the company to keep in ongoing communication with individual customers, through direct mail, e-mail, and other direct marketing tools. Such communication should be a two-way dialog, where the company initiates a communication, the consumer responds, and the company remembers the response and then continues the dialog with further information or marketing offers. In other words, one-to-one marketing is an effort to engage individual consumers, in traditional mass-market settings, in the type of dialog that has always characterized business-to-business markets.

One company that has been extremely successful in implementing one-to-one marketing in both business and consumer markets is Dell Computer. For its large corporate customers, Dell employs a traditional salesforce that engages the customer in a one-to-one, face-to-face setting. Using advanced database technology, however, Dell is also able to engage in a meaningful dialog with individual consumers, and create customized product offerings that satisfy their individual needs. Although mass marketing has always been considered the most cost-effective way to go to market, thanks to information technology, "segments of one" are now becoming viable alternatives, even in consumer markets.

—Mark A. Moon

FURTHER READING

Lee, D. (2000). *The customer relationship management survival guide.* St. Paul, MN: HYM Press.

Newell, F. (2000). *Loyalty.com: Customer relationship management in the new era of Internet marketing.* New York: McGraw-Hill.

Peppers, D., & Rogers, M. (1993). *The one-to-one future: Building relationships one customer at a time.* New York: Currency Doubleday.

OPEN-ENDED STUDY

An open-ended study does not have a defined end point, such as a fixed dose quantity, but allows the ending to be determined based on the patient's response to therapy.

One type of open-ended study involves an escalating dose schedule, for example, according to a modified Fibonacci sequence. This type of study is very common in cancer clinical trials.

Here dose escalation is terminated when dose-limiting toxicity (DLT) is seen in over 50% of cases. The maximum tolerated dose (MTD) is defined as one level below the DLT. Further (phase 2) studies are usually planned at 80% of MTD. Phase 1 studies commonly have no benefit to the patient treated, and efficacy data (if any) should be used only to plan further studies.

—Steven C. Quay

OPEN-LABEL STUDY

An open-label study is a trial that is not "blinded" (meaning the patient is not told which arm of the trial he or she is on); both the doctors and patients know what treatment is being given. Note that an open-label study can be randomized or nonrandomized, as long as the patients and doctors know what treatment has been assigned.

—Steven C. Quay

OPERATING CASH FLOW

Operating cash flow is just the cash generated by operations. It is calculated as the sum of net operating profit after taxes (NOPAT) and any noncash adjustments to income, such as depreciation. The following accounting equation works for a simple company:

Sales

−   Operating expenses

=   Operating profit

−   Tax on operating profit

=   NOPAT

+   Depreciation (and any other noncash charges)[1]

=   Operating cash flow

[1] Only add back in depreciation and any other noncash charges that were deducted in the previous entries. See the discussion on depreciation.

The idea behind calculating operating cash flow rather than more common measures such as net income or earnings before interest and taxes (EBIT) is that it is important to know the actual cash generated by operations. A hospital can only pay its bills with cash, not with accounting earnings! Accounting rules require that many noncash and nonoperating items appear in the net income calculation, and these items obscure what is happening to operations and cash. Depreciation is charged off even though the company doesn't ever write a check to pay depreciation. Interest

income and interest expense are recognized even though they are the result of financing choices, not operating decisions. And all sorts of extraordinary and one-time items such as restructuring charges appear in net income. In short, if an analyst is interested in evaluating the core operations of a company, net income is often a poor measure to use. Operating cash flow is a better measure.

—Phillip R. Daves

FURTHER READING

Brigham, E. F., & Daves, P. R. (2002). *Intermediate financial management* (7th ed.). Mason, OH: South-Western.

OPERATING INCOME

See Operating Cash Flow, Profit

OPERATIONS MANAGEMENT

Operations management concerns the coordination of human resources, equipment, facilities, information, energy, and materials with the goal of providing a product, a service, or some combination of both. The value creation aspect of a business is often described as a *transformation process* and is defined by a set of inputs and outputs. For example, the inputs to an oil refinery consist of crude oil, equipment, and workforce, and the primary output is gasoline. The operation in this example would be considered a *physical transformation process* that creates value by converting crude oil into gasoline. Most manufacturing operations involve physical transformation processes through such activities as fabrication, assembly, blending, and chemical alteration. In contrast, *service operations* provide intangible outputs. Examples of service operations (and their associated transformation processes) include airlines (locational), hospitals (physiological), schools (informational), theme parks (entertainment), banks (financial), and department stores (exchange).

The management of operations involves decisions that are characterized as strategic, tactical, or operational. *Strategic decisions* represent long-term decisions focused on how a business will ultimately create value. Such decisions are often expensive and time-consuming to implement or change. They begin with such broad issues as defining product or service offerings, thereby effectively establishing what role a business shall play and how it will play it. Strategic decisions also include manufacturing process or service delivery system design, facility location and capacity, supply chain partnerships, outsourcing decisions, and large-scale technology decisions. *Tactical decisions* are considered medium-term decisions mostly concerned with planning. They include planned levels of workforce, capacity planning, materials acquisition planning, equipment maintenance and replacement, and inventory planning. *Operational decisions* (also referred to as *control decisions*) are short term in nature and include materials and inventory control, workforce scheduling, task assignment and scheduling, quality processes management, and order/customer flow management.

—Charles E. Noon

OPINION LEADERS

See Diffusion of Innovation

OPPORTUNITY

See Strength-Weakness-Opportunity-Threat (SWOT) Analysis

OPPORTUNITY COST

In making decisions, an agent (such as a person, organization, or firm) chooses actions from a set of competing alternatives. By choosing any particular action, an agent *must* forgo others. For example, spending an evening dining precludes one from simultaneously attending a movie. The value of such forgone alternatives is a decision's "opportunity cost." Continuing the present example, dining's opportunity cost is the utility (or value) one would have received from attending a movie.

Opportunity cost is, perhaps, economics' most fundamental notion. To see this, recognize that if resources are scarce (which they almost certainly are), then acting in a manner that "does no harm" is logically impossible. *Any* action causes resources to be employed in one way but not another. Consequently, even actions that produce tremendous benefits *must* simultaneously do so at some cost.

In using the term "opportunity cost," people frequently refer only to relatively obscure costs (such as the value of lost time). Strictly speaking, however, all economic costs are opportunity costs. Some are simply more obvious than others. For example, if one pays $1000 for medical supplies, then that $1000 can no longer be allocated to other

uses (such as meeting payroll). Such obvious costs are sometimes called "explicit" opportunity costs. These costs usually involve a market transaction with an explicit dollar payment. In contrast, "implicit" opportunity costs emerge from lost opportunities but do not necessitate a corresponding market transaction or payment. Often a single decision and consequent action create both explicit and implicit opportunity costs. Extending the present example, the value of time spent checking and stocking medical supplies adds an implicit opportunity cost to the $1000 explicit opportunity cost.

Identifying a prospective action's full opportunity cost (both explicit and implicit) is essential for making sound decisions. Consider how physicians allocate time. Time spent with a particular patient necessarily precludes that time from being allocated to an alternative endeavor. The opportunity cost of spending time with a patient is thus the value of, say, treating a different patient, contributing to a community outreach event, or even enjoying the company of family members. Even the best decision *must* produce an associated cost (lost opportunity) in this sense. Despite this necessity, however, a decision may still be "optimal" if the consequent action's opportunity cost is less than the ensuing benefit.

Identifying full opportunity costs is also essential for promulgating sound policy. Advocates sometimes extol a proposed policy's virtues by, in effect, arguing that the policy will be worthwhile if it "saves only one person." Although the magnitude of the policy's benefits may be difficult to measure, the advocate understands that even a poorly designed policy is likely to produce benefits for at least one person. By this standard, almost any policy's appearance can be made attractive.

What our hypothetical advocate ignores, however, is that allocating resources to his or her cause necessarily precludes those same resources from producing alternative benefits. If these forgone benefits (the policy's opportunity cost) exceed those produced by the policy, then the policy will *reduce* welfare. Notice that this net reduction occurs even if the policy truly saves at least one person! In this light, activities such as "fund raising" might be more accurately characterized as "fund transferring."

Indeed, when resources are scarce, society *must* forgo some policies (indeed, an infinite variety of possible policies), even those that "save at least one person." The problem for society, at least from a welfare perspective, is that institutions in which public decisions are made can encourage individuals to ignore, or at least discount, a policy's opportunity cost. To see how this problem might arise, consider two policies, say A and B. Suppose that implementing policy A would save more individuals than would implementing policy B. In addition, because resources are scarce, suppose that society can only implement one of the policies.

Clearly, from an opportunity cost perspective, society should implement policy A (its opportunity cost is less than that of policy B). However, suppose that individuals who would benefit from policy B are more easily identifiable than those who would benefit from policy A. Policy B might, for example, benefit 100 individuals who currently have a fatal disease, whereas policy A might benefit 1 million people, each of whom has a .001 chance of contracting a less prominent fatal disease. Although expected deaths amongst policy A's beneficiaries are 10 times those of policy B's beneficiaries, the cost of identifying policy B's beneficiaries is less than that of policy A's beneficiaries. Policy entrepreneurs may thus find B-beneficiaries a more attractive group with whom to curry political favor. This incentive exists despite the potential for alternative policies to create even greater benefits for more obscure individuals.

Although identifying full opportunity cost can, in principal, facilitate sound decisions, identifying these costs in practice can be difficult. This difficulty is sometimes sufficient for decision makers to ignore cost–benefit analysis altogether. Such ignorance almost certainly reduces the value of the decision maker's choice, however.

Instead of completely ignoring the cost–benefit calculus, one may simply want to hold back from a calculation the component that is particularly difficult to quantify. Consider, for example, an individual's decision of whether to return to school for a master's degree in health administration. Among the benefits of completing an advanced degree is the opportunity to engage in more interesting work. The value that one recognizes from such intellectual stimulation can be difficult to quantify, however.

A decision maker may thus want to treat this component of the opportunity cost calculus as "residual decision factors." Extending the present example, suppose that, after calculating the full opportunity costs of obtaining the degree, and comparing it to the likely increase in future earnings, our prospective student recognizes that returning to school would produce $20,000 of net costs (net of additional earnings). The optimal decision would then collapse to one of judging whether the value of increased interest in one's work exceeds $20,000. If it does, then the individual should pursue the degree.

—Dino Falaschetti and Steve Parsons

FURTHER READING

Bernanke, B., & Frank, R. (2001). *Principles of economics.* New York: McGraw-Hill.

Hirshleifer, J., & Glazer, A. (1992). *Price theory and applications* (5th ed.). Upper Saddle River, NJ: Prentice Hall.

Stigler, G. J. (1987). *The theory of price* (4th ed.). New York: Macmillan.

ORGANIZATIONAL BEHAVIOR MANAGEMENT (OBM)

Organizational behavior management (OBM) is a broad field devoted to the study of human capital in a work setting. Organizational behaviorists are primarily concerned with understanding the effects of human behavior on organizational effectiveness and advancing management theories. It is a field that draws on many domains, including anthropology, psychology, political science, ergonomics, and economics. Although most institutions do not have an OBM department, organizational behavior is a discipline that permeates all jobs and all functions of an organization. For this reason, a working knowledge of organizational behavior is advantageous for today's health care manager who spends most of his or her time working with and through people.

Unlike the hard sciences, OBM has advanced few universal laws about employee behavior, because of the complexity of human nature. Consequently, instead of advocating one best management practice applicable to all situations, organizational behaviorists embrace the contingency approach. That is, they believe that the best management practice depends on the circumstances. To be successful, the modern manager must be able to read situations and adapt accordingly. Although the contingency approach is a popular practice today, it took organizational behaviorists nearly a hundred years to conclude that there are no hard-and-fast rules to management.

THE HISTORY OF ORGANIZATIONAL BEHAVIOR

Before the 1900s, organizations were not concerned with understanding and improving management practices. It was not until the industrial revolution that employers became interested in finding new methods for managing workers. One of the most influential individuals of this time was Frederic Taylor, founder of scientific management. Taylor discovered that production workers were more effective when each task had been analyzed and broken down into its simplest components and each employee had been trained to do only those motions that were essential to the task. Advocates of the scientific management movement believed that employees were equivalent to machine parts. This led to growth in middle management and the development of new departments such as personnel and quality control.

Although scientific management resulted in increased productivity, many individuals opposed its dehumanization of work. Thus began the human relations movement, dedicated to the improvement of working conditions. Essential to this movement was Elton Mayo and his Hawthorne studies. Mayo found that employees were more productive when others observed them at work. From this finding, Mayo posited that employees have a psychological need to believe that their organization cares for them.

Another important contributor to the human relations movement was Douglas McGregor. He argued that traditional managers held the view that people are inherently lazy, dislike work, lack ambition, and must be coerced before they will work. He titled this assumption of human nature Theory X. In contrast, McGregor proposed Theory Y, suggesting that people are active, possess the potential to be responsible and committed to organizational goals, and are capable of self-direction. Furthermore, he maintained that managers would be more successful if they viewed humans from the Theory Y perspective.

Principles of the human relations movement remained popular until the 1980s, when North American companies began losing market share to Japanese companies. The need for better quality products brought about the need for new management practices. Out of this need grew total quality management (TQM). TQM is an organizational culture focused on continuous improvement, customer satisfaction, and employee development. Edward Deming, the founder of total quality management, proposed that when things go wrong there is an 85% chance that the system is at fault. Therefore, leaders should be helpful when mistakes are made, rather than punishing employees for something that is out of their control. Furthermore, he argued that organizations should be built on teamwork, trust, and mutual respect. TQM is a popular management practice embraced by today's leaders.

AN OVERVIEW OF MODERN ORGANIZATIONAL BEHAVIOR MANAGEMENT

Previously, we said there are very few universal truths in organizational behavior. Nevertheless, numerous management models, theories, and techniques are applicable to the health care industry. The following overview summarizes important aspects of OBM at the individual, group, and organizational levels.

At the individual level, organizational behaviorists are primarily concerned with individual differences, motivation, and leadership; essentially, research at the individual level focuses on the determinants of employee performance. Personality, attitudes, self-concept, abilities, and motivation are all related to an individual's performance on the job. To improve performance, managers can alter employees' attitudes, increase motivation, or influence action through various leadership techniques. For example, research on goal-setting theory (a motivation theory) has continually supported the proposition that setting specific, moderately difficult goals, followed by feedback, leads to higher performance. Furthermore, transformational leaders

(charismatic, inspiring leaders) are more effective at altering performance in changing environments than transactional leaders (leaders who influence others through rewards and punishment).

Organizational behaviorists devoted to studying the group level of analysis focus on group dynamics, teamwork, and conflict management in an effort to understand group effectiveness. For instance, research has shown that groupthink hinders the effectiveness of groups. Specifically, groupthink is the tendency of highly cohesive groups to ignore plausible solutions or alternatives to problems. Managers can prevent groupthink by assigning a group member to play the role of devil's advocate or call in outside experts to introduce new perspectives. Group research has also demonstrated that groups responsible for making decisions should be composed of five or fewer individuals.

Finally, at the organizational level of analysis, OB researchers are interested in organizational culture, structure, and change. In recent years, organizational behaviorists have argued that an organization's ability to learn is a determining factor of success. Leaders can enhance an organization's learning capabilities by promoting a climate of openness, committing to the continuous education of all employees, and scanning the external environment. Furthermore, findings of organizational-level research demonstrate that organizational change is less likely to be resisted when managers share information with employees, provide rationale for change, and conduct meetings to answer any questions about change.

—Katherine R. Helland

See also Conflict Management, Group Norms, Group Performance, Groupthink, Human Resource Management, Improving Employee Productivity, Job Satisfaction, Leadership, Learning Organizations, Management Development, Managing Organizational Change, Organizational Change, Organizational Communication: An Overview, Organizational Design and Discontinuous Change, Organizational Performance and Work Design, Organizational Structure, Quality Management, Team Building, Teamwork, Vision

FURTHER READING

Hersey, P., Blanchard, K. H., & Johnson, D. E. (2000). *Management of organizational behavior: Leading human resources* (8th ed.). Upper Saddle River, NJ: Prentice Hall.

Kreitner, R., & Kinicki, A. (2001). *Organizational behavior* (5th ed.). New York: McGraw-Hill.

Latham, G. P., & Lee, T. W. (1986). Goal setting. In E. A. Locke (Ed.), *Generalizing from laboratory to field settings* (pp. 101–117). Lexington, MA: Heath.

Robbins, S. P. (2002). *Essentials of organizational behavior* (7th ed.). Upper Saddle River, NJ: Prentice Hall.

Senge, P. (1990). *The fifth discipline: The art and practice of the learning organization.* New York: Doubleday.

Shortell, S. M., & Kaluzny, A. D. (2000). *Health care management: Organization design and behavior* (4th ed.). Clifton Park, NY: Delmar.

Walton, M., & Deming, W. E. (1988). *Deming management method.* New York: Perigee.

ORGANIZATIONAL CHANGE

Organizations are dynamic and complex social systems formed to accomplish goals. Organizational change is a field of study that focuses on viewing the organization as a system and on how the framework of that system interfaces and influences the performance of the individual. Factors considered in organizational change include the following:

- The people performing their jobs; the measurement of the performance
- The processes that make up the tasks the people perform
- The systems that compose the processes; the arrangements of the hierarchy and reporting relationships that make up the formal structure
- The informal structure professionals create for themselves
- How the strategy of the organization aligns itself to all the aforementioned factors (see Miles & Snow, 1978; Nadler & Gerstein, 1992)

These factors are underpinned by the following organizational behaviors of managers:

- Recognition of individual differences in workers
- Accurate perception of performance
- Correct assumptions about the motivation of workers
- Use of information technology in organizational communication
- Influence of conflict and collaboration on both group and team dynamics (Bowditch & Buono, 1997, pp. 37–39)

The principles that are important and relevant to the practice of organizational change today include the following:

1. *Understanding the interplay between the work environment and the individual worker is critical for change in organizations.* Any change in personal growth of individuals within a work group, caused by training, for example, should have a correlated attempt for social and cultural change within the entire organization. If there is no attempt to change both individuals and the environmental culture of an organization, no change is likely. That is why one training session is not likely to bring about significant organizational change. This principle is reflected in the formula $B = f(p,e)$, where behavior (B) change is the function (f) of the person (p) and the environment (e).

2. *To understand the system, you must first seek to change it.* Kurt Lewin (1948) called this *action research.* Accurate measurement of environmental and individual perceptions helps to clarify false perceptions and create correct knowledge about problems blocking performance of individuals. Gathering, measuring, and evaluating this evidence of perceptions must involve all who create the perceptions. For effective change of perceptions to occur, participants involved in change should feel a strong sense of belonging to the same group, which occurs as they participate in the corrective measures to clarify perceptions. Successful organizational changes are more likely to occur when workers affected by the change have an opportunity to participate in the process of change as early as possible and as long as is needed for the change to take place.

3. *Wed scientific thinking (action research) to democratic values for organizational change.* Democracy in the practice of change is critical, because every work system is a value system as well. It is not possible to have a value neutral work system. Whereas action research allows for the practice of accurate inquiry and measurement, democracy encourages participants to clarify their own feelings of ambivalence or frustration as well as their own perceptions of what would or would not work. The combination of action research and democracy creates new energy around accepting new values at work as well as the sense of belonging necessary for change in organizations, because the more cohesive the group, the greater the readiness for members to influence others and be influenced by others.

Lewin (1948) contended that it is very difficult to get productivity if you do things *to* people; it is better to do things *with* them. His re-educative approach was sometimes called an *action research approach,* which is only a partial use of the principles just stated. A re-educative approach was to involve those with a stake in the problem to help define accurately and solve it, because the less involved those affected by the change are, the less likely a solution will last long.

LEWIN'S RE-EDUCATIVE APPROACH TO ORGANIZATIONAL CHANGE

This re-educative approach is based on the idea of systems changing themselves through a communal effort by the people affected by the change: that is, whole systems engaging in the change of the whole system. The breakthrough vision of this approach, which involves the indispensability of groups as media of effective re-education, was captured by Lewin and Grabbe (1945) as follows:

> Acceptance of previously rejected facts can be achieved best through the discovery of these facts by the group members themselves. . . . Then, and frequently only then, do the facts become really *their* facts (as against other people's facts). An individual will believe facts he himself has discovered in the same way that he believes in himself or in his group. The importance of this fact-finding process for the group by the group itself has been recently emphasized with reference to re-education in several fields. . . . It can be surmised that the extent to which social research is translated into social action depends on the degree to which those who carry out this action are made a part of the fact-finding on which the action is to be based.

Re-education influences conduct only when the new system of values and beliefs dominated the individual's perception. The acceptance of the new system is linked with the acceptance of a specific group, a particular role, a definite source of authority as new point of reference. It is basic for re-education that this linkage between acceptance of new facts or values and acceptance of certain groups or roles is very intimate and that the second frequently is a prerequisite for the first. This explains the great difficulty of changing beliefs and values in a piecemeal fashion. This linkage is a main factor behind resistance to re-education, but can also be made a powerful means for successful re-education.

TRIST AND EMERY CONTINUED LEWIN'S WORK

Eric Trist, working with Fred Emery (1960), an Australian working from the accomplishments of Lewin, Wilfred R. Bion, and Douglas McGregor (1960), created a new group orientation to help people integrate the whole system. Bion, a psychoanalyst and much-decorated World War I tank commander, created a leaderless group method to deal with tension between cooperation and self-centeredness under stress. In 1957 the Tavistock Institute of Human Relations in London, England, pioneered a form of laboratory training based on Bion's ideas. Trist, an Army psychologist, joined Bion and used the work of McGregor. McGregor, author of the management classic *The Human Side of Enterprise*, also founded the Industrial Relations Section at the Massachusetts Institute of Technology and helped Kurt Lewin found the Research Center for Group Dynamics at MIT. McGregor emphasized that groups, if properly used, can improve decision making and problem solving, because effective groups require informality,

openness, frank criticism, self-examination of their own effectiveness, and shared responsibility for work and outcomes. In the 1950s in Great Britain, Trist and Emery worked together. This liaison brought systems thinking to the workplace. Trist, following the open systems thinking of biologist Ludwig von Bertalanffy (1950), created a way of thinking about management and change connecting the social and the technical systems to show that those who do the work get to have the power via information, control, and skills. The open systems idea was that all things, somehow, some way, link up and influence one another in all directions.

SOCIOTECHNICAL SYSTEMS

Trist coined the term sociotechnical system (STS) to represent the interaction of people (a social system) with tools and techniques (a technical system) that results from choosing to set up both as a catalyst for change and improvement. Lewin's core principle was that workers are likely to modify their own behavior when they participate in problem analysis and solution and are likely to carry out the decisions made during that process. Trist and Lewin's ideas are similar. In the article in *Human Relations* in 1951 entitled "Some Social and Psychological Consequences of the Longwall Method of Coal-getting," Trist and Bamforth give a definition of STS as an approach that connects mass-production engineering and a social structure consisting of the occupational roles that have been institutionalized. These interactive technological and sociological patterns are assumed to exist as forces having psychological effects in the life pace of the worker who must either take a role and perform a task in the system or abandon his attempt to work. Together, the forces and their effects constitute the psychosocial whole that is the object of the study. They concluded the study by stating that a qualitative change to the method would have to occur so that a social as well as a technological whole can come into existence. Only if this is achieved can the work be accomplished with a new social balance. The term "organizational choice" describing composite working, self-regulation, team organization, and maintaining production, along with workload stress and cycle regulation, are all included in STS.

Weisbord (1987) calls STS a revolution and uses a quote from Trist (1981, p. 59) to explain why: "Information technologies, especially those concerned with the microprocessor and telecommunication, give immense scope for solving many current problems—if the right value choices can be made." Ethics in change must be a constant. Weisbord (who was a newspaper reporter at one point in his life) goes on to report that Trist coined the term STS because he wanted to show that the interaction of people (social system) with tools and techniques (a technical system) results from choice, not chance. Those choices are influenced by the economic, technical, and human values present at the time. Trist emphasized the values of learning, caring, and collaboration as necessary for social change.

Weisbord (1987) sums up this work by stating that informed self-control, not close supervision, is the only way to operate new technologies without making mistakes. They can be mastered by the learner's direct involvement. Moreover, Weisbord continues, the future of democratic values, dignity and worth of each person, free choice and free expression, and social responsibility coupled to personal opportunity depends on what we do today. The recommendation is to integrate social, technical, and economic systems as soon as possible. The way to do that using the knowledge of Lewin and Trist and Emery is a way to have the whole system in one room.

—Peter J. Dean

FURTHER READING

Argyris, C., & Schon, D. A. (1980). *Organizational learning: A theory of action perspective.* Reading, MA: Addison-Wesley.

Dean, P. J., & Ripley, D. E. (1997). *Performance improvement pathfinders: Models for organizational learning systems.* Washington, DC: International Society for Performance Improvement Publications.

Dean, P. J., & Ripley, D. E. (Eds.). (1998). *Performance improvement interventions: Methods for organizational learning: Vol. 4. Culture and systems change.* Washington, DC: International Society of Performance Improvement.

Kochan, T. A., & Useem, M. (1992). *Transforming organizations.* New York: Oxford University Press.

Lewin, K. (1948). Resolving social conflicts: Selected papers on group dynamics. Gentude W. Lewin (Ed.). New York: Harper & Row.

Nadler, D. A., & Tushman, M. L. (1997). *Competing by design: The power of organizational architecture.* New York: Oxford University Press.

Weisbord, M. R., & Janoff, S. (1995). *Future search.* San Francisco: Berrett-Koehler.

ORGANIZATIONAL COMMUNICATION: AN OVERVIEW[1]

To borrow an axiom from logistics, effective organizational communication ensures that the "right" message is sent through the right channels and received by the right audience at the right time. How does this process occur? There is no shortage of research into the role, functions, and processes of communication in organizations, and approaches to these topics are virtually endless. The purpose of this article, however, is to examine organizational communication from a practical management perspective, by briefly discussing three basic issues: (a) the nature of communication in organizations, (b) the relationship between communication and organizational behavior, and (c) the link between an organization's communication processes and its orientation to management style.

WHAT IS THE NATURE OF ORGANIZATIONAL COMMUNICATION?

To answer the question "What is the nature of organizational communication?" one first needs to define communication in general. Although a virtual plethora of definitions exists, this entry defines communication as "a process that involves the sending and receiving of messages as a means of sharing ideas and experiences in order to create meaning." Note here the emphases on *process* and *meaning:* at its most basic level, communication is the process humans use to create meaning, to make sense out of their general environments and personal situations. Although some scholars still argue that communication is essentially a "sender" phenomenon, contemporary research suggests that it is better described as a "receiver" phenomenon, which implies that the "meanings" of messages reside in the receiver, regardless of what the sender intends—a notion of significant import for managers!

How does this process of "creating meaning" work? Again, countless charts and diagrams have attempted to describe the many variables found in communicative processes. However, in the context of "creating meaning," possibly the most significant concept to remember is that communication is symbolic—that is, communication is composed of verbal (words) and nonverbal[2] cues that not only "stand for" something else but also literally create the messages we attempt to send and receive. However, the *interpretations* or *meanings* of those messages tend to vary between individual message recipients (not to mention between senders and recipients). In short, messages consist of verbal and nonverbal "cues" or "symbols" that are encoded by senders and decoded by receivers, but the interpretation or "meaning" of these symbols is rarely, if ever, either absolute or universal. Thus, effective managers must both acknowledge and be sensitive to the potential problems (and even rewards) that can arise through these multiple interpretations.

Moreover, and perhaps even more significantly, communication is the process that essentially creates organizational realities, and thus serves as the foundation on which organizational behavior is shaped, maintained, and/or transformed. To paraphrase Hall, communication is behavior and behavior is communication. Thus, managers must be aware that this rather amorphous phenomenon called "communication"—messy as it can be and slippery as it is to grasp at times—is nonetheless key to efficient and effective organizational practices.

It is prudent to note here that communication processes do not occur in a vacuum. Any given communication is influenced (at the very least), by all interactors, by history, and by the environment in which the communication takes place. Thus, as they discern how interaction influences behavior, managers must remain aware of and account for the myriad influences on any given communication event or circumstance.

NETWORKS AND CHANNELS

Communication processes may be said to "flow" through organizational networks and channels, both of which profoundly influence the interpretation of messages.

Formal networks may be defined as "systems designed by management to dictate who should talk to whom to get a job done"[3]—also known as the organizational chart. Formal networks tend to be directional; that is, communication generally flows either *downward* (superior to subordinates); *upward* (subordinates to superiors); or *horizontally/laterally* (between peers or persons of relatively equal status). Managers should note that between one third and two thirds of their time is likely to be spent communicating downward; thus, organizations should take it on themselves to give and receive management training in supportive and motivational communication practices. Managers should also understand that message distortion occurs at all organizational levels and in all directions. For example, subordinates tend to distort messages traveling upward, whether consciously or not; most exhibit a tendency to tell superiors what they think the superiors want to hear. Naturally, distortion does not always pose a major stumbling block to interpreting messages; however, the effective manager must acknowledge that the process of creating meaning (communication) is by nature imperfect, often inaccurate, and always limited. Thus, effective communicators learn to deploy "distortion prevention" measures—such as channel management (see later discussion) and MBWA (management by walking around).

In addition to traveling through networks, organizational messages are delivered via many different channels—either oral, written, or both. Oral channels include face-to-face meetings, teleconferencing, telephone, and voice mail. Written channels include a variety of formats, ranging from memos, reports, and letters to email and computer conferencing (the latter of which may also contain oral elements). Modern technology not only increases the number of channels available but also enhances the complexity involved in making appropriate choices. As Adler suggests, "The question is not *which* communication channel to use, but *when* to use each one most effectively."[4] When making this decision, managers should consider, at the very least, the following:

- The degree of speed desired for establishing contact and receiving feedback

- Amount of information contained in the message
- Cultural expectations of the audience
- Nature of the intended message itself
- Relationship between communicators

In short, effective organizational communicators need to remember that channel choices have a momentous impact on how meaning is created in messages sent and received.

Finally, managers should recognize the fact that *informal* networks and channels affect communication at least as much, and often more, than do formal ones. Although formal protocols often receive the most attention—not to mention official sanctioning—mangers should never underestimate the power of the informal "grapevine"!

HOW DOES COMMUNICATION INFLUENCE ORGANIZATIONAL BEHAVIOR?

Scholars have identified several fundamental roles that communication plays in the execution of processes common to all organizations:

Process	Role of Communication
Socialization	Enables new entrants to become part of the organization and to understand appropriate "roles" and "ropes
Performance Control	Explains, coordinates, and evaluates goal-related behaviors
Decision Making	Influences the manners and modes in which decisions are made
Social Support	Influences the experience and creates the "meaning" of work
Conflict Management	Both creates and resolves conflicts
External	Connects the organization to its environment
Technical	Explains "mysteries" and enables effective deployment

Here it becomes obvious that a great deal of communication within organizations is task related. Thus in addition to its primary function of creating meaning in the organization, communication is also intimately related to accomplishing organizational and individual goals. Managers must not overlook the significant role that communication plays in executing organizational functions.

HOW IS COMMUNICATION INFLUENCED BY MANAGEMENT STYLE?

The manner in which communication is used and understood depends in large part on the organization's orientation to management. Despite overwhelming evidence suggesting that effective communication is key to organizational efficacy, not all organizations are managed in ways that foster effective communicative processes. In fact, research suggests that organizational communication practices tend to reflect, as well to be determined by, managerial philosophy.[5] Thus, organizational communication "works" only to the extent that its value is acknowledged and exploited by management.

THE CLASSICAL APPROACH TO MANAGEMENT

The classical approach to organization and communication, still evident in some organizations today, emerged during the industrial revolution's quest to create the perfect machine—hence, the organizational machine-as-metaphor model. Here, management is characterized (some would say plagued!) by a machinelike dependence on hierarchy and chain of command. This organizational model does not recognize the importance of communication other than as a downward "declamation and declaration" process. From this perspective, other communicative processes are unnecessary, costly, and are therefore discouraged, whereas a premium is placed on rules-based order and quantitative productivity. Clearly, in this atmosphere communication does not function to its fullest extent.

CONTEMPORARY APPROACHES TO MANAGEMENT

In contrast to the "classical" approach are more contemporary orientations, notably the "human resources" and "systems" orientations. Deriving from an emerging concern with the plight of workers during the Great Depression of the 1930s, the human resources approach is concerned with the total organizational climate and with how an organization can encourage participation, motivation, and ultimately enhance productivity through effective communication processes. Here, individuals are perceived as being "situated" in organizational circumstances that are discovered and even created through communication. Moreover, employees' motives for working productively are thought to be rooted in their needs and interests, which can be recognized not only with tangible rewards but also with information (feedback) they give and receive. Thus, management is concerned with "situating" the individual in whatever position maximizes his or her effectiveness and productivity. Clearly, communication's role in this management scheme is of utmost importance, as it requires open, honest, and thoughtful communication between managers and employees.

Likewise, the systems approach to management may be perceived as a subset of the human resources approach, by virtue of its emphasis on the importance of individuals as they relate to others throughout the system. This perspective works from the metaphorical concept that an organization is like a living organism where all elements are inextricably linked. Put simply, everything and everyone affect everything and everyone else. Thus, communication becomes not only the metaphorical glue that holds the system together, but also the means by which networks and relationships within the system may be analyzed.

CONCLUSION

Clearly, achieving effective organizational communication is a tall order by any standard. However, "creating meaning" through communication is likely the primal element underlying organizational behaviors of every stripe. So what's a manager to do? Although effective communication skills are honed throughout a lifetime (or a career), here are some positive steps managers can take at any time and in most any situation:

- First and foremost, understand that communication "creates meaning" and thereby influences (some would say "dictates") organizational behavior.
- Learn and practice supportive communication.[6]
- Maintain as "flat" an organizational structure as possible.
- Empower employees.
- Establish and use more than one channel through which to communicate.
- Be aware! Manage by walking around.

In sum, "effective managers strategically use communication"[7] to accomplish organizational goals. An awareness of what organizational communication entails is the first step in that strategy.

—Linda Lyle

NOTES

1. References used in preparing this document include K. Miller (1995); Daniels & Spiker (1994); Eisenberg & Goodall (1993); Adler & Elmhorst (2002); and Mohan (1993).

2. Nonverbal cues are most common to oral communication but are also present in written modes of delivery. Oral nonverbal cues include tone of voice, volume, emphasis, expression, and the like. Face-to-face delivery also includes visual cues, such as eye contact and facial expression. "Nonverbal" cues in written communication primarily involve spacing and formatting.

3. Adler & Elmhorst, p. 14.

4. Adler & Elmhorst, p. 29.

5. See generally Mohan.

6. An excellent resource for supportive communication practices and principles may be found in Whetten & Cameron (2002).

7. Timm & DeTienne (1995), p. xi.

FURTHER READING

Adler, R., & Elmhorst, J. (2002). *Communicating at work*. New York: McGraw-Hill.

Daniels, T., & Spiker, B. (1994). *Perspectives on organizational communication*. Madison, WI: Brown and Benchmark.

Eisenberg, E., & Goodall, H. L., Jr. (1993). *Organizational communication: Balancing creativity and constraint*. New York: St. Martin's Press.

Miller, K. (1995). *Organizational communication: Approaches and processes*. Belmont, CA: Wadsworth.

Mohan, M. (1993). *Organizational communication and cultural vision*. Albany: State University of New York Press.

Timm, P., & DeTienne, K. B. (1995). *Managerial communication: A finger on the pulse*. Upper Saddle River, NJ: Prentice Hall.

Whetten, D. A., & Cameron, K. F. (2002). *Developing management skills* (pp. 209–250). Upper Saddle River, NJ: Prentice Hall.

ORGANIZATIONAL DESIGN AND DISCONTINUOUS CHANGE

Continuous Change.   Learning that occurs in an incremental way, usually motivated by cost containment, efficiency, and evolutionary innovation.

Cooperative Learning.   Workers learning and helping each other learn for a specific outcome.

Discontinuous Change.   Learning that occurs in a radical way driven by performance or technological problems, competitive shifts in the market, or political conditions.

Learning in Organizations.   An organization where cooperative and reflective learning occurs in response to the needs of the organization thus helping the organization become self-designing.

Organization.   A system of formal arrangements in an organization encompassing the interaction of the strategy, structures, processes, and systems. These arrangements are designed in such a way to optimize the learning interface between people and their work environment.

Performance.   Both behavior, the actual observable activity, and its accomplishment, that which is left behind after the behavior occurs, define performance.

Processes.   Processes define and measure the sequence of steps, activities, and methods to produce a specific goal or outcome.

Strategic Vision.   The response of the organization to the needs of the marketplace.

Structures.   Structure addresses the division and coordination of tasks and the formal patterns of relationships between groups and individuals.

Systems.   Systems include all the procedures for budgeting, accounting, training, and so on that make the organization run. Systems use procedures, rules, policies, practices, and so on that help control processes.

The need for leadership of change in an organization emerges when the company is able to compete successfully by continuously aligning the strategy, structure, and processes, and learning to deal with the needs of incremental change while simultaneously preparing for radical change caused by the discontinuous pressure of the external market. This requires that the organization is to be designed in such a way to account for competition in a mature market where cost, efficiency, and incremental innovation is vital, while developing new products and services where speed, flexibility, and radical change is critically important (Lawrence & Lorsch, 1967, 1969; Tushman & O'Reilly, 1996). Both of these notions are easily understood, yet usurping one to make the other more sumptuous may create short-term success but will eventually lead the organization to long-term failure. Leading organizations proactively align their strategy, structure, processes, people, and culture through incremental evolutionary change. This change is punctuated by radical and discontinuous change that requires simultaneous shifting of the strategy, structure, processes, people, and culture to deal with sudden changes in technology, regulatory events, changes in the political environment, economic conditions, and competitive shifts in the market (Tushman & O'Reilly, 1996). It is the knowledge of many kinds of self-designing processes (Bunker & Alban, 1997) that is required by management to deal with this phenomenon.

All leaders' decisions to deal with organizational design depend on the performers in the organization and the process they are allowed to use, enabling them to deal with both incremental and discontinuous change. If leaders try to adapt to discontinuities through incremental adjustments they are *not* likely to succeed. If leaders try to do it alone, they are not likely to succeed. If you influence the design of the organizational system, you influence the system that has a direct influence over individual performers. People who use systems thinking for the entire organization and for dealing with performance improvement endeavors are called *organizational designers*. Organization design helps companies organize themselves and deal with the complexities of large organizational life. To lead the changing destiny of organizations in this country, the leader must have knowledge of organization design.

—Peter J. Dean

FURTHER READING

Argyris, C., & Schon, D. A. (1980). *Organizational learning: A theory of action perspective.* Reading, MA: Addison-Wesley.

Dean, P. J., & Ripley, D. E. (1997). *Performance improvement pathfinders: Models for organizational learning systems.* Washington, DC: International Society for Performance Improvement Publications.

Dean, P. J., & Ripley, D. E. (Eds.). (1998). *Performance improvement interventions: Methods for organizational learning culture and systems change* (Vol. 4). Washington, DC: International Society of Performance Improvement.

Kochan, T. A., & Useem, M. (1992). *Transforming organizations.* New York: Oxford University Press.

Nadler, D. A., & Tushman, M. L. (1997). *Competing by design: The power of organizational architecture.* New York: Oxford University Press.

Weisbord, M. R., & Janoff, S. (1995). *Future search.* San Francisco: Berrett-Koehler.

ORGANIZATIONAL DEVELOPMENT

See Organizational Change

ORGANIZATIONAL MISSION STATEMENT

See Mission

ORGANIZATIONAL PERFORMANCE AND WORK DESIGN

Galbraith and Lawler's book entitled *Organizing for the Future* captures the importance of organizational performance and work design and redesign: "organizations in the future will have to be able to innovate, to improve their processes, and to redesign themselves" (Galbraith & Lawler, 1993, p. 88).

Over the years, there has been an accumulation of tools and methods for innovation and improvement processes in organizations. In overview, these include the following:

1940s: Sensitivity training for the interaction of the person and the environment

1950s: Conflict resolution and team building

1960s: Intergroup development and open systems planning

1970s: Sociotechnical systems analysis and quality of work life

1980s: Organization transformation, total quality, large-scale change with future search

1990s: Re-engineering, large-group intervention, transcultural planning, and transnational community building

Organizational efforts to improve work design operate out of a set of core values:

- Integration of individual and organization needs
- Choice, freedom, and responsibility
- Dignity, integrity, self-worth, and fundamental rights
- Cooperation and collaboration
- Authenticity and openness
- Effectiveness, efficiency, interdependence, and alignment
- Holistic, systemic vantage point and stakeholder orientation
- Participation, confrontation, and adaptability

Organization change has traditionally relied on the interpersonal strategy of normative re-education without giving attention to the economic, political, technological, legal, and ethical issues that affect the organization. Organizational performance improvement and work design and redesign efforts have been added to the tools and methods of innovation. When dealing with the organization as a whole, one must ask questions that in their simplicity usually generate profound answers.

Where are we going? Develop goals for work, process, organization. (Goals)

How shall we get there? Develop design for attaining them. (Processes)

How will we know we've arrived? Develop management systems. (Feedback)

The primary question that encompasses the entire organization in its answer is, What intervention should we choose for organizational performance improvement and work design and redesign? There are three general categories of interventions that help improve organizational performance and work design and redesign, as follows.

TRAINING INTERVENTIONS

- Learner-controlled/self-paced instruction
- Instructor-led seminars, courses
- Experiential learning design
- Curriculum design
- Instructional design
- Evaluation design
- Computer-based training
- Health and wellness programs
- Employee assistance programs
- Networking systems
- Tuition reimbursement programs
- Scholarship programs
- Support for profession/civic activities
- Literacy programs
- Leadership and ethics development programs
- Team building
- Culture change programs
- Group dynamics
- Change management
- Value clarification
- Conflict management
- Organizational rites and rituals

ORGANIZATIONAL PERFORMANCE IMPROVEMENT INTERVENTIONS

Selection Systems Design

- Succession planning
- Personnel recruiting and hiring systems
- Leadership development programs

Information Systems Design

- Electronic performance support systems
- Expert systems
- Intranet delivery
- Internet delivery
- Interactive multimedia
- Online information/reference
- Prototyping
- Rapid application development
- On-the-job training
- Job aids

Career Development Design

- Internal recruitment systems
- Job rotation systems
- Work assignment rotation systems
- Cross-training
- Equal Employment Opportunity (EEO) programs

- Affirmative action programs
- Diversity programs
- Assessment centers
- Mentoring
- Coaching
- Loaned executive/job exchange
- Tuition reimbursement programs
- Scholarship programs
- Experiential learning
- Structured practices

WORK SYSTEMS DESIGN INTERVENTIONS

Management Science

- Strategic planning
- Goal setting
- Visioning
- Supervision and management
- Marketing systems
- Public relations
- Financial systems
- Problem-solving and decision-making systems
- Performance management systems

Job and Workflow Design

- Workflow analysis
- Job classification
- Work schedule/shift programs
- Business process re-engineering

Communication Systems Design

- Electronic mail
- Voice messaging systems
- Computer networking
- Memo distribution systems
- Meeting planning
- Corporate/organizational
- Newsletters and bulletins
- Memo design/format systems
- Negotiation systems

Feedback Systems Design

- Performance appraisal systems
- Identification of performance indicators
- Performance information systems
- Customer/client feedback mechanisms

Resource Allocations Involved in Work Design

- FTE allocation plans and ceilings
- Budgeting

- Reward/recognition systems design
- Compensation systems
- Merit award systems
- Bonus systems
- Motivation programs
- Incentive and recognition programs
- Benefits programs

Documentation and Standards

- Policies
- Procedures
- Guidelines
- Reference manuals
- Quality assurance documents
- Bylaws
- Articles of incorporation
- Partnership agreements
- Contracts, letters of intent, and so forth

Human Factors Involved in Work Design

- Facilities design
- Technological advances
- Tools and equipment acquisitions
- Equal Employment Opportunity (EEO) compliance (handicapped access)
- Safety planning

Continuous Improvement of Work Design

- Quality circles
- Quality assurance programs
- Quality of work life programs

Innovations, process improvements, and better work designs and redesigns in the preceding categories of interventions bring about the following results. First, they provide opportunities for employees to function as human beings rather than as resources in the productivity process. Second, they provide opportunities for each organization member and the organization itself to develop to their fullest potential. Third, they increase an organization's effectiveness by helping it achieve its strategic business goals and objectives. Fourth, they help create an environment in which employees find exciting and challenging work. Fifth, improved organizational performance provides opportunities for employees and managers to influence the way in which they relate to work, the organization, and the work environment. Sixth, they enable every employee to be treated as a human being with a complex set of needs and values, all of which are important in his or her work and life.

—Peter J. Dean

FURTHER READING

Dean, P. J. (1995). Examining the practice of human performance technology. *Performance Improvement Quarterly, 8*(2), 68–94.

Dean, P. J. (1999). *Performance engineering at work.* Washington, DC: International Board of Standards for Training, Performance and Instruction, IBSTPI Publications and International Society for Performance Improvement.

Dean, P. J., Blevins, S., & Snodgrass, P. J. (1997). *Performance analysis: An HRD tool that drives change in organizations.* In J. J. Phillips & E. F. Holton III (Eds.), *In action: Leading organizational change.* Alexandria, VA: American Society for Training and Development.

Dean, P. J., & Ripley, D. E. (1997). *Performance improvement pathfinders: Models for organizational learning systems.* Washington, DC: International Society for Performance Improvement Publications.

Dean, P. J., & Ripley, D. E. (Eds.). (1998a). *Performance improvement interventions: Methods for organizational learning: Vol. 2. Instructional design and training.* Washington, DC: International Society of Performance Improvement.

Dean, P. J., & Ripley, D. E. (Eds.). (1998b). *Performance improvement interventions: Methods for organizational learning: Vol. 3. Performance technologies in the workplace.* Washington, DC: International Society of Performance Improvement.

Dean, P. J., & Ripley, D. E. (Eds.). (1998c). *Performance improvement interventions: Methods for organizational learning: Vol. 4. Culture and systems change.* Washington, DC: International Society of Performance Improvement.

Galbraith, K., & Lawler, E. (1993). *Organizing for the Future.* San Francisco: Jossey-Bass.

ORGANIZATIONAL STRUCTURE

See Structure

ORGANIZATIONAL TRANSFORMATION

See Organizational Change

ORGANIZATIONAL VISION

See Vision

ORPHAN DRUG

Orphan drugs are products that treat rare diseases affecting fewer than 200,000 Americans. There are approximately 4000 orphan diseases in the United States. Because of the rarity of orphan diseases, there is limited commercial market for orphan drug products. The Orphan Drug Act of 1983 was intended to stimulate sponsors to conduct research on products to treat rare diseases. The act gives certain incentives, such as granting sponsors seven years of marketing exclusivity and tax incentives for clinical research; grant funding is also available.

The FDA also offers help through its Office of Products Development to help sponsors coordinate research and study design assistance for sponsors of drugs for rare diseases. The act has been successful in stimulating the industry to develop orphan drugs.

The problem with orphan drug research is that there are too few patients to demonstrate efficacy and safety. It can take great efforts to enroll enough patients. Study design issues, especially parallel double-blind placebo-controlled trials, may be impossible to conduct because of the availability of patients and the ethics of the study design.

—Anthony Sileno

See also New Drug Application (NDA)

FURTHER READING

www.fda.gov/orphan

OSHA

See Occupational Safety and Health Act (OSHA)

OUTCOMES RESEARCH

The term *outcomes research* is defined as determining the value of health care by evaluating clinical outcomes.

Health outcomes research combines features of clinical research, continuing medical education, and quality assurance. Patient outcomes can be characterized in terms of a number of dimensions, including clinical factors, death, disease, functional status, well-being, satisfaction, and cost.

Typically, outcomes research is distinguished from traditional clinical trials-based research by two factors:

(a) Outcomes research uses uncontrolled, observational data, which provide a "real-world" view of clinical practices and outcomes in representative patients; and (b) outcomes research frequently includes patients' self-reports that reflect quality of life, functional status, and satisfaction with care.

The outcomes movement was founded on the principle that patient care will improve if physicians are provided with timely and credible information linking local clinical practices and patient outcomes. Most physicians have little or no opportunity for ongoing, objective feedback about the relationship between their patterns of clinical practice and patient outcomes. Moreover, physicians may change practices in response to anecdotal information, such as a particularly good (or bad) outcome in an individual patient, which may not be representative of their overall clinical experience. Physicians need, but seldom have access to, benchmark data that allow comparison of individual practice patterns and outcomes with the experiences of their peers in caring for comparable patients.

From a pharmacoeconomic perspective, it is increasingly important for physicians and health care systems to demonstrate that they provide care that leads to superior outcomes, particularly in comparison with care rendered by other practitioners. Payers are shifting the increasing burden of health care costs to hospitals and providers. Hospital administrators are under intense pressure to reduce costs. Without objective data to substantiate the relationship between specific clinical care practices and clinical outcomes, payers and hospital administrators may limit care in ways that are harmful to patients. In contrast, objective data may demonstrate that certain types of care have no or very limited impact on health outcomes and thus can reasonably be discontinued.

Data from outcomes research empower clinicians to monitor and improve their practices and outcomes. These data can guide the development of educational programs to improve the care of patients and can provide a mechanism for physicians to evaluate the impact of their diagnostic and therapeutic decisions in a manner that is timely and objective.

—Frederick A. Anderson, Jr.

See also Quality Improvement Cycle, Quality Management

FURTHER READING

Blumenthal, D. (1997). The future of quality measurement and management in a transforming health care system. *JAMA, 278*(19), 1622–1625.

Ellwood, P. M. (1988). Shattuck lecture—Outcomes management: A technology of patient experience. *New England Journal of Medicine, 318*(23), 1549–1556.

Epstein, A. M. (1990). The outcomes movement: Will it get us where we want to go? *New England Journal of Medicine, 323*(4), 266–270.

OUT-OF-NETWORK SERVICES

In some managed care contracts there is a clause that addresses "out of network" service. Each insurance plan outlines what services will be paid, the amount of payment for the service, and what facilities and/or providers will be paid without additional cost. The contracts clearly outline these circumstances. When the insured signs up for the particular insurance carrier, a provider manual is generated that describes what services are considered "in network."

Each insurance company contracts with individual practitioners, hospitals, laboratories, and other health care providers in the areas of coverage. The rates are negotiated with these entities with the promise that there are a "guaranteed number of lives" that will be directed to them for care. The rates include office visits, radiology reimbursement, laboratory costs, and hospital rates. In some cases the hospital rates are paid for by specific DRG (diagnosis-related groups), per diem, or case rates.

In addition, there may be negotiated rates that outline home care services, long-stay facilities, and subacute care.

The decision to go to the hospital, practitioner, or laboratory that is included in the network assures either a small copayment or no payment from the insured. However, when the insured decides to use an out-of-network practitioner for care, there is either a large copayment or full payment.

According to the managed care companies, these networks keep costs and premiums down, provide a wide variety of services, and allow the insured to make personal choices of their health care providers.

—Edna Lee Kucera

OUTPATIENT CARE

See Ambulatory Care

OUTSOURCING

The term *outsourcing* is used to describe the practice of subcontracting certain services to an organization or company outside of the parent organization or company. It is important to understand that outsourcing is different from the act of contracting. With outsourcing, the parent organization (buyer) in essence transfers ownership of a business process to the supplier. It is the expertise that the supplier brings that is attractive to the parent organization. The buyer does not have the capabilities to dictate how they want the job done, just that the supplier needs to complete the task they are paid to perform. It is up to the supplier to develop the tools and processes necessary to achieve the end product. Buyers concerned about the specifics of how the task is performed should consider contracting for a service instead of outsourcing.

Health care practices today, whether hospitals or physicians' offices, have moved to outsourcing as a means of accomplishing many tasks. Determining the financial benefits of outsourcing is necessary to determine if an organization should opt for outsourcing or try to keep the task in-house. Expertise in a wide array of business practices is necessary to be an efficient profitable organization. Outsourcing is a way for even small companies to harness the efficiencies and expertise that only a large organization may achieve. Examples include companies (suppliers) that submit electronic claims, billing and collection agencies, dictation and transcription services, and companies that will handle and institute all issues related to human resources (payroll, benefits, and risk management). In the future there will be even greater proliferation of additional outsourced services that will contribute to running a profitable and successful health care business.

—Michael R. Marks

See also Billing, Electronic Claims, Human Resource Management

FURTHER READING

www.outsourcing.com
www.outsourcing-center.com

OVER-THE-COUNTER (OTC)

Over-the-counter (OTC) is a term used to describe products, especially medications, that can be purchased without a physician's prescription. Medications that are not over-the-counter must be obtained with a written prescription that must be submitted to a pharmacist for dispensing. Prescribed medications are restricted to the general public. They require special indications and usage as ordered by a health care provider with prescriptive privileges (such as a nurse practitioner). Not all medications are so restricted. These medications are readily available to the public for sale. They can be purchased in any store without a written prescription. The only barrier between a customer and the medication is the counter, hence the term *over-the-counter*.

Many different types of products are categorized as OTC. Cough syrups and nasal decongestants are typical examples of OTC medications. Other OTC medications include anti-inflammatory and analgesic products such as nonsteroid anti-inflammatory drugs.

When analgesic medications contain narcotics, these medications require a prescription and are not available OTC, because their use must be monitored by the prescribing licensed health care provider. This same type of supervision would apply to medications prescribed to control blood pressure, heart rate, and rhythm. Improper use of these medications could have morbid and fatal consequences for the individuals taking them. Hence, these substances are not available OTC.

In some situations, medications that were once only available with a prescription became available OTC. Classic examples are the gastric acid antagonist medications and some nonsteroid anti-inflammatory drugs. In this aspect, OTC may refer to those substances that have always been available without a prescription and those substances that were once only available with a prescription but have evolved (demonstrated safety and efficacy, and possibly also being made available in a smaller dose) to no longer requiring one. The category of OTC medications should be considered as a dynamic list, because a medication's status may change.

—Anthony J. Ippolito

FURTHER READING

Hardman, J. G., & Limbird, L. E. (2001). *Goodman and Gilman's The pharmacological basis of therapeutics* (10th ed.). New York: McGraw-Hill.

OWNERS' EQUITY

See Equity

P

PARETO CHART

The Pareto chart, or Pareto diagram, is one of the seven basic tools of quality improvement. It is named after the Italian economist Vilfredo Pareto (1848–1923), who observed that a small minority of Italian citizens held the majority of the wealth and means of production. His studies led him to conclude that 20% of the people in Italy owned 80% of the wealth. Quality expert Dr. Joseph M. Juran applied the "Pareto principle" to industry, and to specific processes within industry, noting that whenever a number of individual factors contribute to some overall effect, relatively few of those items account for the bulk of that effect.

Using the Pareto principle has proven an effective technique in the health services sector. The principle reinforces the practical reality that, given limited resources, efforts must be concentrated on issues that have the most potential impact. A Pareto analysis can assist a quality improvement team in setting priorities on its actions and also helps the team define and focus the problem.

The Pareto chart is graphically depicted as a bar chart, with each bar representing a separate problem cause. In the chart, the bars are ordered from left to right according to height, which signifies frequency. Thus the tallest bar, the most frequently occurring factor, is on the far left. Often included in the Pareto chart is a line graph that shows the cumulative percentage for all the categories of problem causes. Throughout the quality improvement process, the Pareto chart serves as a useful tool for identifying those factors that may produce the greatest effect in quality improvement.

A hypothetical example of the Pareto principle follows. Hospital A is focusing its quality improvement efforts on eliminating sources of outpatient dissatisfaction. An analysis of its most recent outpatient satisfaction survey reveals that all the sources of patient dissatisfaction fall into one of 10 survey questions. Each survey question represents a distinctive issue or category of dissatisfaction, such as long wait for an appointment, lack

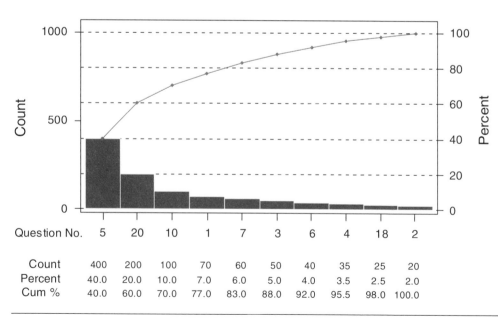

Question No.	5	20	10	1	7	3	6	4	18	2
Count	400	200	100	70	60	50	40	35	25	20
Percent	40.0	20.0	10.0	7.0	6.0	5.0	4.0	3.5	2.5	2.0
Cum %	40.0	60.0	70.0	77.0	83.0	88.0	92.0	95.5	98.0	100.0

Figure 1 Pareto Chart

of courtesy on the part of support personnel, and perceived lack of provider competence. The Pareto chart depicted in Figure 1 indicates that, from these 10 categories three (30%) account for 70% of the patient dissatisfaction. Thus from a purely practical perspective, the quality improvement team would initially focus its efforts on those three patient complaint categories. In a Pareto analysis, this is referred to as distinguishing "the vital few" from "the trivial many."

—Shonna L. Mulkey

FURTHER READING

Berwick, D. M. (1990). *Curing health care: New strategies for quality improvement.* San Francisco: Jossey-Bass.

Carey, R. G., & Lloyd, R. C. (1995). *Measuring quality improvement in healthcare: A guide to statistical process control applications.* New York: Quality Resources.

Shearer, C. (1994). *Practical continuous improvement for professional services.* Milwaukee, WI: ASQC [American Society for Quality Control] Quality Press.

PARTICIPATIVE DECISION MAKING

See Culture and Strategy, Leadership

PATIENT DUMPING

See Risk Adjustment, Risk Selection

PATIENT EXPECTATIONS

Patient expectations reflect the hopes, wishes, or desires of patients concerning health care needs and services. They include expectations about the structure, process, and outcomes of health care. Structural expectations focus on both the physical facilities (location, ambience, amenities, and equipment) and personnel (numbers, types, and appearance). Expectations centering on processes of care include technical (information gathering, physical examination, testing, prescriptions and referrals) and interpersonal (physician–patient communication including information exchange and active listening) aspects of care. Outcome expectations include aspects of somatic and psychosocial results of care, both in the short and the long term.

Expectations vary widely from person to person and from society to society. These differences are based on sociodemographic and biopsychosocial features and on prior experiences with the health care system. For example,

Americans have higher expectations for timeliness, involvement in health care decisions, and full recovery than do citizens of most other countries. Some of these expectations, especially those related to outcomes that are less under the control of health care providers, may be unrealistic.

The role of patient expectations in the health care system has increased dramatically in the past several years as patient autonomy and consumerism have supplanted paternalism as the main feature of the patient–provider interaction. Understanding patient expectations is important for several reasons. First, meeting patient expectations for care may be considered an intrinsic goal of medical care.

Expectations are also directly related to patient satisfaction; satisfaction may be viewed as the difference between what is expected and what is actually perceived. Patient satisfaction with care, in turn, is an important element in health care marketing as well as in assessing and determining quality of care. For example, high levels of satisfaction relate to greater levels of adherence with therapeutic plans, improved continuity of care, and fewer malpractice suits. Patient satisfaction also has a high correlation with quality of care as assessed by professionals, and studies have shown that patients can distinguish between the quality of the technical and interpersonal aspects of care.

Knowing an individual's personal expectations for care and for the outcome of care are critical in making clinical decisions in which personal preferences and values are important. This information can only come from the patients themselves. Including expectations and preferences in care planning is an intrinsic component of participatory decision making, a process in which the patient plays a major role, along with the clinician, in determining what course of treatment to pursue.

Patient expectations also provide guidance as to what health care services should be optimized to meet the patient's own desired outcomes. This includes decisions as to allocation of funds, designing delivery systems, and measuring quality of care.

Knowing and achieving patient expectations are also clearly important in a competitive health care market. Levels of satisfaction with providers, based on expectations, are a major determinant of staying or leaving providers and health care plans.

—David M. Mirvis

See also Customer Satisfaction Research, Customer Value, Empowerment (Delegation of Authority)

FURTHER READING

Davies, A. R., & Ware, J. E., Jr. (1988). Involving consumers in quality of care assessment. *Health Affairs, 7,* 33–48.

Kravitz, R. L. (1996). Patients' expectations for medical care: An expanded formulation and based upon a review of the literature. *Medical Care Research Review, 53,* 3–27.

PATIENT RIGHTS

See Customers' Consequences, Customer Value

PATIENT SATISFACTION

See Customer Satisfaction Research

PATIENT-CENTERED CARE

See Customer Desired Purpose or Goals

PATTERNS OF CARE

As health care analysts evaluate the quality of care provided to health care recipients, the continuum of care for a clinical condition can be described as a series of processes and subprocesses that correspond to specific events, such as a hospitalization or course of treatment for a respiratory infection in an ambulatory patient. Efforts to improve the quality of care examine the variation in these processes, then define changes in the process that improve quality and lower cost of care. As the processes of care are examined over large numbers of providers, similarities in the processes define models that can be analyzed for variation. These models are termed "patterns of care."

The approach to medical care that evaluates patterns of care has been applied in a number of situations. For example, the National Cancer Institute's Surveillance, Epidemiology, and End Results program, initiated in 1973, provides evaluations and data for cancer diagnosis, treatment, and survival in the United States. The SEER program has developed several registries around the United States that collect and publish cancer incidence and survival data from 11 population-based cancer registries and three supplemental registries covering approximately 26% of the population. The database contains information on more than 3 million in situ and invasive cancer cases, with the addition of nearly 170,000 new cases each year. The database includes information on patient demographics, primary tumor site, morphology, stage at diagnosis, first course of treatment, and follow-up for vital status, and the data are used for a number of reports on patterns of care, mortality, and distribution of cancer in the areas in which the SEER project operates. The longevity of the project has produced exceedingly useful information on patterns of care for cancer in the United States, and the database is used by clinicians and health planners alike.

Patterns of care often help in evaluating the cost of care, by codifying processes of care and then dividing them into subprocesses that can have costs assigned to each step. For example, in a study of the treatment of asthma, a group of researchers in Switzerland (Szucs, Anderhub, & Rutishauser, 2000) compared patterns of care and associated costs between general practitioners and specialists. The technique is used frequently in research studies, but it has also been increasingly applied by organizations that pay for health care services and insurance companies to perform cost effectiveness studies and quality assessments. Using appropriate statistical approaches, patterns of care can be discerned and stratified in a number of ways, such as by provider, by institution, by diagnosis-related group (DRG), by level of disease severity, and many other variables. This type of information can provide support for decisions on which patterns of care provide the greatest value. The development of data mining and statistical pattern recognition techniques over the past decade has increased the utility of large databases in identifying patterns of care.

Data sources for patterns of care analysis are diverse. Insurers usually use claims databases that are created from transactions submitted by practitioners for payment. Some of the more sophisticated payers create data warehouses that combine several sources of data into a very large database, adding content and value to the care patterns analysis. Although transaction data are readily available, they often lack sufficient clinical depth to perform the types of analysis necessary to determine optimum patterns of care. Thus these studies often provide suggestions for further analysis of care that requires abstraction of data from clinical records at the site of care. If an electronic medical record is not available, then paper chart reviews must be conducted by experienced chart abstractors.

Clinicians and researchers often use data directly from medical charts or from special data collection forms for analyzing patterns of care. These sources provide a much more robust clinical data resource, but they are generally less accessible and do not contain records of cost that are important in determining resource utilization. In most cases, the information from the transaction records must be combined with the clinical data to have a complete picture of the pattern of care for a clinical condition.

Patterns of care differences are of interest in a variety of settings. Practitioners find the information useful to determine the most effective methods of caring for a disease entity. Knowing the most effective modes of treatment can direct providers to the best processes for diagnosing and treating their patients. However, payers are interested in knowing which providers are practicing the highest quality, most effective medicine. Those providers can be rewarded with bonuses, or in some cases, with continuation of contractual relationships, whereas less effective providers can be targeted for educational or economic interventions. Health planners can also use the information to compare providers and payers in the health care delivery system. For example, the National Committee for Quality Assurance evaluates health plans based on its HEDIS measures, which examine outcome indicators as a reflection of patterns of care for health plans. Governmental institutions have taken a similar approach by publishing outcomes statistics for such procedures as cardiovascular surgery, as has been done in New York State, New Jersey, and Pennsylvania. The goal of these reports is to promote consumer choice of providers and to supply the information necessary to make informed decisions.

Evaluation of patterns of care has made the comparison of health care providers much more effective, because practitioners can be assessed on their ability to provide value to consumers. Better clinical and economic outcomes are reflected in comparisons, and the information can lead to better consumer choice. As more clinical data accumulate in electronic format, data mining and statistical pattern analysis can enhance the assessments of patterns of care, making them much more useful to clinicians, planners, and consumers.

—Donald E. Lighter

FURTHER READING

http://seer.cancer.gov

Lighter, D., & Fair, D. (2000). *Principles and methods of quality management in health care.* Gaithersburg, MD: Aspen.

Piland, N., & Lynam, K. (Eds.). (1999). *Physician profiling, source book for health care administrators.* San Francisco: Jossey-Bass.

Szucs, T. D., Anderhub, H. P., & Rutishauser, M. (2000). Determinants of health care costs and patterns of care of asthmatic patients in Switzerland. *Schweizerische Medizinische Wochenschrifft, 130,* 305–313.

www.health.state.ny.us/nysdoh/consumer/heart/homehear.htm
www.ncqa.org/communications/publications/hedispub.htm
www.phc4.org
www.state.nj.us/health

PEER REVIEW ORGANIZATIONS (PROs)

Peer review organizations (PROs) independently contract with the federal government to provide oversight for Medicare and Medicaid beneficiaries. These contracts are for a three-year duration and are called the "scope of service" (SOS). The details of the SOS are contained in the memorandum of agreement (MOA) and are sent to participating hospitals for acknowledgment and signature. The contracts outline, in detail, what activities are to be conducted during the ensuing three years for utilization of services and quality of care concerns. In addition to the oversight for the utilization and quality of services provided to the beneficiaries, the PROs have expanded their activities to national projects. These projects examine the care of the Medicare population using specific indicators and, over time, identify what outcomes of care result. These include studies for acute stroke, looking at the care of atrial fibrillation and transient ischemic attack (TIA); acute myocardial infarction (AMI); pneumonia and congestive heart failure (CHF). These studies are conducted on a large sample of cases with comparison data over time. Hospitals are strongly encouraged to participate in the study and be included in the outcome data. They receive a "report card" of how well they managed their cases, using the indicators as markers. These "report cards" measure how well they did compared with their own activities and how well they did compared with the national average.

There are additional activities the PROs are obliged to conduct. The DRG (diagnosis-related groups) validation; PEPP (Payment Error Protection Program); and cost outlier review are the major requirements for the SOS. Through these activities, the PROs have helped hospitals make changes and improve quality of care for the elderly and indigent populations.

—Edna Lee Kucera

FURTHER READING

www.cms.gov
www.ipro.org

PENETRATION STRATEGIES

See Market Entry Strategies

PERCEPTUAL GAPS IN SERVICES QUALITY

Health care quality is ultimately in the eye of the beholder. The concept of quality in health care has continued to advance and change as providers, consumers, regulatory agencies, and payer groups have maintained their interest in the topic, but it is the understanding of quality from the customer perspective that is currently emerging as a critical issue in health services delivery. And, for various reasons, consumers are not satisfied with the quality being offered.

In the 1980s, health care quality became a blend of clinical, profession, and consumer input, with the consumer perspective becoming the dominant perspective. Consequently, providers began trying to manage customer perceptions and used marketing strategies to accomplish that task. Since that time, providers have evaluated, reported, and marketed positive results such as patient satisfaction levels, managed care satisfaction, intentions to use a provider again in the future, Joint Commission for the Accreditation of Healthcare Organizations (JCAHO) survey results, compliance with advice and treatment regimens, turnover of staff, malpractice lawsuits' results, health care outcomes, and National Committee for Quality Assurance (NCQA) reports. All this work is directed toward demonstrating that the quality for a particular health care provider exceeds the competition and, in fact, does provide quality health care services. This effort seeks to eliminate the perception of gaps in one organization and to cast doubt regarding quality on another organization.

Another significant factor in perpetuating the concept of gaps in health care quality is the constant bombardment of the American public with negative reports and publicity issued by the media regarding clinical disasters and outcomes by health care providers. One need only listen to television or read the news occasionally to be made aware of poor outcomes of care provided. An investigative report by the *Chicago Tribune* stated that more than 100,000 deaths in the year 2000 were linked to infections that patients contracted in the nation's hospitals. The report indicated that most of the deaths were preventable and that nosocomial infections (those acquired in hospitals) represented the fourth leading cause of mortality among Americans, behind heart disease, cancer, and strokes. Another significant finding is that tens of thousands of those infections resulted from doctors and nurses failing to wash their hands.

The Institute of Medicine (IOM) issued a startling report in 1999, "The Urgent Need to Improve Health Care Quality." That investigation and report concluded that the quality of health care can be precisely defined and measured with a degree of scientific accuracy comparable with that of most measures used in clinical medicine and that serious and widespread problems exist throughout U.S. medicine. The problems could be classified as underuse, overuse, or misuse and occur in small and large communities alike. The report also proposed that the problems occur with equal frequency between managed care and fee-for-service systems of care, with the effect that very large numbers of Americans are harmed in the process. In fact, the report indicated that

U.S. hospitals were responsible for between 45,000 and 98,000 deaths each year. This is equivalent to one 747 airliner crashing every other day. The report called for massive reforms and improved reporting systems.

These data reflect poorly on the U.S. health care system. But to what extent is this a fair standard, by which judgment should be made? When an error in health care is defined as the failure of a planned action to be completed as intended, or the use of a wrong plan to achieve an aim, one must consider the level of control the provider wields in the entire process. Efforts to assess the importance of various types of errors are currently hampered by the lack of standardized taxonomy for reporting adverse events, errors, and risk factors. Attempts to classify adverse events according to root causes are complicated by the fact that several interlocking factors contribute to an error or series of errors that in turn result in an adverse event. Simply put, errors and adverse events are quite complicated when it comes to eliminating sources of error.

One cannot assess perception of quality just by focusing on the societal impact of counting and reporting errors but must also consider a perception of quality from an economic view as well. When Americans think about quality, they may be thinking about outcomes—or lack thereof—and outcomes may be a function of access and affordability. For example, a perception of quality, especially poor quality, may arise because the service is either not available or not affordable. Many Americans do not have access to health care because of their geographic location, whereas others have geographic access but not financial access. That brings into question whether or not perception of quality would increase if media reports reflected more positive outcomes. One study revealed that some health care services save more lives for fewer dollars; the Centers for Disease Control (CDC) sponsored a study that ranked by priority those preventive health services recommended for average-risk patients based on the services' health benefits and cost effectiveness. Among those services ranking high on the list of opportunities for prevention were tobacco cessation counseling, screening older adults for undetected vision impairments, screening adults over 50 years for colorectal cancer, screening young women for chlamydia infections, screening and counseling adults for problem drinking, and vaccinating older adults against pneumococcal disease. Although these rank high on positive results and outcomes, they are often not covered or delivered, because of lack of funding. This outcome is not usually widely reported, because it is not "newsworthy." Therefore, the public has a negative perception of the quality of health care services in this country.

Coile (2000) suggests improving customer satisfaction using 10 strategies that require gaps to be closed or narrowed and notes that organizations that do not focus on customer service today will no longer exist tomorrow.

Several strategies are recommended such as starting with visible board and management support for high quality and ending with a rule that puts patients first. Perhaps with that approach health care quality could be "as good as it gets."

—Patti Elaine Griffin

FURTHER READING

Chassin, M., & Galvin, R. (1998). *Statement on quality of care, Institute of Medicine, national roundtable of health care quality.* Chicago: Institute of Medicine.

Coile, R. C., Jr. (2000). *New century healthcare.* Chicago: Health Administration Press.

Editor. (2002, July 24). Dirty hospitals: Are hospitals spreading germs to patients? *Good Morning America.* ABCNews.

Editor. (2001, June 22). New study reveals which healthcare services save more lives for fewer dollars. Washington, DC: Partnership for Prevention.

Kohn, L., Corrigan, J., & Donaldson, M. (Eds.). (1999). *To err is human: Building a safer health system.* Institute of Medicine. Washington, DC: National Academy Press.

Uribe, C. L., et al. (2002, July–August). Perceived barriers to medical-error reporting: An exploratory investigation. *Journal of Healthcare Management, 47*(4), 263–280.

PER DIEM PAYMENTS

Per diem payments are payments for all services provided during a single day of care. A fixed payment level is set regardless of the actual services provided. This may apply to all patients or to patients that have been subgrouped by diagnosis, age, or other risk-related characteristics.

The goal of per diem billing is to reduce the risk to the payer for the large number of individual services provided to a patient. With traditional fee-for-service payments, a provider is paid more for performing more tests, procedures, and so on. With per diem payments, the provider receives the same payment regardless of which and how many services are provided on a single day of care. The risk is thus partially transferred from the payer to the provider. The provider loses rather than gains from providing more health care services on a single day. However, the payer remains at risk for the number of days of care.

This shifting of risk established different incentives for the payer and the provider. The provider is rewarded for providing fewer services or for spreading the same care over a longer period of service, that is, increasing *length of stay.* The incentive for the payer is to use strict utilization review methods to limit length of stay and to reduce the time required for treatments and tests.

Per diem billing also simplifies billing procedures. It is not necessary to track the individual services that are provided. All that is needed is the length of stay in the hospital or the number of days during which services were provided.

—David M. Mirvis

See also Billing, Length of Stay (LOS)

PERFORMANCE APPRAISAL

Performance appraisal is the process of evaluating the effectiveness of an employee's performance. Performance appraisal is a critical human resources practice that helps ensure employees' efforts support and link to group, department, and organizational objectives. Performance appraisal has been a standard practice in organizations for the past 50 to 60 years. Today, the company that does not use some form of performance appraisal is the exception rather than the rule. Early use of performance appraisal tended to focus on evaluating people on the basis of general qualities or personality traits, such as friendliness, attitude, and work ethic. These criteria are still used frequently. Over time, performance appraisals have focused more on measuring actual employee behaviors and results. This change has occurred partly because of legal rulings and concern for greater accuracy in measurement.

REASONS FOR CONDUCTING PERFORMANCE APPRAISALS

Performance appraisal serves a number of purposes for organizations and human resource professionals. First, results of performance appraisals are used to make administrative decisions, such as salary raises, promotions, and termination. Management also uses appraisal results to provide employees with feedback as to how well they are doing and what they can do to improve. Third, performance appraisal information is used for human resources and succession planning purposes. Finally, organizations use performance appraisal for research purposes, such as validating selection tests and evaluating the effectiveness of training programs.

MEASUREMENT OF PERFORMANCE

Job performance can be appraised with several types of measures. Objective performance measures include behaviors, such as absenteeism, accidents, and number of claims processed, and outcomes, such as patient volume, number of products made, and service costs. A main advantage of objective measures is that they reduce subjectivity in the appraisal process. However, such measures are not applicable to many jobs, particularly given the shift from a manufacturing to a service-oriented industry base, such as in the health care industry. In addition, objective counts of behaviors or outcomes are not always complete portrayals of the full range of performance. Finally, objective measures are often influenced by external factors beyond the employee's control, such as illness, equipment breakdowns, inadequate supplies, and cooperation of management and coworkers.

Consequently, subjective judgments are used frequently for appraising employee performance. Typically, supervisors rate an employee's performance along a variety of criteria, including personal traits or characteristics (such as dependability, work ethic), work-related dimensions (such as quality of work, work output), and specific behaviors. Using subjective judgments of work dimensions and behaviors makes the performance appraisal process applicable to a wider variety of jobs, gives the rater the ability to factor in external influences of performance, and can result in a more comprehensive performance assessment.

However, this approach requires a significant amount of time for the rater to observe, review, and evaluate performance. Further, there can be several biases and errors in the subjective appraisal process. For example, a rater may give the same rating to an employee across all work dimensions, regardless of how much the person's performance varies on each dimension. Known as "halo error," this happens when a rater allows a general impression about the employee to influence ratings on all dimensions. Other biases occur when a rater rates everyone unjustifiably low on the rating scale ("severity error"), unjustifiably high on the rating scale ("leniency error"), or unjustifiably in the middle of the rating scale ("central tendency"). Some raters allow their first impressions of an employee's performance or behaviors to overly influence their ratings ("primacy effect"), whereas other raters overly weight the most recent behaviors ("recency effect"). Finally, performance appraisal ratings can be influenced by the fundamental attribution error. Specifically, this error suggests that a rater will tend to attribute an employee's success to external or situational factors beyond the employee's control, whereas employee failure will be attributed to factors *within* the employee's control. Failures, then, tend to receive more attention when a rater makes his or her ratings.

To deal with biases and errors, practitioners and researchers have devoted considerable time and effort toward improving the accuracy of performance ratings. Practitioners have used multiple types of appraisal formats and methods, implemented rater training programs, and increased the number and types of raters.

METHODS AND FORMATS FOR MAKING PERFORMANCE APPRAISAL RATINGS

Multiple formats exist for the rater to make subjective performance appraisal ratings. One of most frequently used formats is the *graphic rating scale* (GRS), in which a set of performance criteria are evaluated along a rating continuum with general descriptors at each rating point, such as 1 ("Unacceptable Performance") to 5 ("Superior Performance"). With this method, the rater is required to observe an employee's performance and judge the effectiveness of the performance. An example of the GRS is the *behaviorally anchored rating scale* (BARS). A BARS expands on the GRS concept by specifically defining each rating scale point with actual job behaviors. With BARS, the rater is required to match the employee's on-the-job behaviors with behaviors listed for a point on the rating scale. For example, if the employee's on-the-job behaviors are most similar to the example behaviors for the "Successful" rating scale point, then the employee receives a rating of "Successful." The *behavioral observation scale* (BOS) is similar to the BARS in that it defines performance in terms of job behaviors. With this approach, however, each important job behavior is listed on the appraisal form, and the rater is required to rate the frequency at which the behavior occurs. The *mixed standard scale* (MSS) is similar to the BARS and BOS in its focus on observable behaviors. However, for each performance dimension, three different behaviors are presented, representing high, medium, and low levels of performance, respectively. These behaviors are then combined with behaviors from other performance dimensions, all of which are randomly ordered on the appraisal form. For each behavior, the rater is required to indicate whether the employee's performance is better than, the same as, or lower than the behavior. According to proponents of this approach, because the performance dimensions and the "favorableness" of the behaviors are not immediately known, some rater biases and errors are less likely to occur. Further, inconsistent raters (such as those who rate an employee as "lower than" the low-level behavior, yet "higher than" the high-level behavior, for the same performance dimension) can be identified and given further training on avoiding such errors.

Each of the rating formats just described falls under the "absolute" method of evaluation. Specifically, these approaches require the rater to rate an employee's performance against a predefined and absolute standard. This standard of performance is usually the same or very similar for all employees. However, some rating formats require that the rater actually compare an employee's performance with others in the department and work group. Hence, evaluations are made based on "relative" comparisons. Examples include *rank-ordering,* where a rater is simply required to order his or her employees from highest to lowest performing on a performance dimension. Another type of relative method is the *forced-distribution rating system,* where a rater is required to assign a percentage of people to a different level of performance—for example, 25% of employees rated as "Superior," 50% rated as "Average," and 25% rated as "Below Average."

RATER TRAINING

One training method for increasing rater accuracy is to teach raters how to observe and document performance objectively, consistently, and nonjudgmentally. Typically such training will advise raters on the differences between behaviors and inferences or judgments, and give them techniques for maintaining accurate records. Another type of training is *frame-of-reference training*, which teaches raters how to make accurate judgments and ratings based on behaviors they have documented. Typically this type of training communicates the company or department's performance standards and then has raters make practice ratings of fictional employees. The raters' ratings are then compared with "true" ratings (usually an expert panel's ratings), and discrepancies are discussed. A third type of training is *rater error training*, which focuses on teaching raters about various errors and biases, and methods for avoiding them.

SOURCES OF PERFORMANCE APPRAISAL INFORMATION

An employee's immediate supervisor is often the person who rates his or her performance. In many organizations, supervisors are held responsible for an employee's performance and behaviors. Because they are usually given the authority to control employee assignments, make salary decisions, and determine disciplinary or punitive actions, it makes sense that supervisors should be given responsibility for rating performance.

However, several trends have brought into question the assumption that supervisors are the best raters. First, organizations have become more decentralized, thus increasing supervisors' span of control considerably. Second, employees today are using special work arrangements, such as flextime and telecommuting, that reduce their face time at the company. Third, many employees work in team settings, some of which are self-managed with minimal direct supervision.

As a result, other stakeholders are sometimes used to appraise employees' performance. These sources include immediate peers, immediate subordinates, customers, suppliers, colleagues from other departments, and even oneself. The inclusion of multiple evaluation sources has most often been done within 360-degree feedback systems. Including these sources may provide a more comprehensive perspective because they see a greater number of performance behaviors compared with a supervisor. Further, because multiple ratings are used, the reliability of ratings is often increased. However, there are some concerns with using these sources as raters. For example,

self-evaluations tend to be overinflated. Subordinates may hesitate to give their bosses unfavorable ratings due to fear of reprisal. Consequently, 360-degree appraisal has been used mostly for providing employees with *developmental* feedback. However, in recent years more organizations have begun to use multisource appraisal for administrative purposes. The practical and legal impact of this practice is still unresolved.

LEGAL ISSUES IN PERFORMANCE APPRAISAL

Several countries have antidiscrimination laws that protect certain groups, such as women and minorities. In the United States, when performance appraisal results are used to make administrative decisions such as hiring, terminating, promoting, and transferring people, the practice of performance appraisal is viewed as a "measurement device" and, as such, becomes subject to various employment discrimination laws. If a performance appraisal system is being used to intentionally discriminate unfairly between people from protected groups, or if, on average, people in protected groups receive substantially lower ratings compared with the majority group, then the system runs the risk of being ruled unlawful. This is particularly relevant for subjective performance appraisals.

If an employee challenges an employment decision that was wholly or partly based on his or her performance appraisal, a judge or arbitrator essentially tries to answer the question "Does the performance appraisal process discriminate unfairly against a protected group?" To answer the question, the judge or arbitrator reviews information about how the performance appraisal system was designed and how it is being used. In this scenario, the entire appraisal system (not just the specific person's appraisal results) may come under legal scrutiny. Readers are encouraged to pursue other authors for a complete review of performance appraisal case and rulings history, such as Malos (see Further Reading).

GUIDELINES AND TECHNIQUES FOR PERFORMANCE APPRAISAL DESIGN

Historically, performance appraisal has not been done very successfully within organizations. Appraisal systems designed to improve employee motivation and performance often fail to achieve those objectives. The following practices have often been recommended as ways to increase the accuracy of performance ratings, legal defensibility, employee buy-in, and the value of the performance appraisal process.

- Conduct job analysis to determine key requirements and performance dimensions. Performance dimensions should be defined in terms of specific behaviors, and examples of good and bad performance should be used to define rating scale anchors. These dimensions can then be used as performance criteria on the appraisal form.

- Ensure that performance measures are job related, valid, free from contamination, and meaningful. Performance measures can dictate the behaviors that employees emphasize on the job. For instance, performance measures that focus solely on work quantity may lead employees to produce a high number of units but of potentially dubious quality.
- Seek employee input into the design of the appraisal form and process. This helps ensure that performance criteria are accurate and job related, and potentially increase employee buy-in.
- Provide training to raters on how the performance appraisal process will operate, how to avoid and overcome errors, how to observe and document performance, and how to make accurate ratings.
- Raters should keep documentation and records of their employees' performance.
- Allow ratees an opportunity to appeal their ratings to a third party for review.
- Monitor the system periodically to determine whether average ratings or decisions based on appraisal ratings (such as promotion rates) differ between protected groups.

—Mark L. Poteet

See also Balanced Scorecard and Health Care, Critical Success Factors, Employment Discrimination, Job Analysis, Performance Management

FURTHER READING

Bernardin, H. J., & Beatty, R. W. (1984). *Performance appraisal: Assessing human behavior at work.* Boston: Kent.

Landy, F. J., & Farr, J. L. (1983). *The measurement of work performance: Methods, theory, and applications.* New York: Academic Press.

Malos, S. B. (1998). Current legal issues in performance appraisal. In J. W. Smither (Ed.), *Performance appraisal: State of the art in practice* (pp. 3–48). San Francisco: Jossey-Bass.

Mohrman, A. M., Jr., Resnick-West, S. M., & Lawler, E. E., III (1989). *Designing performance appraisal systems: Aligning appraisals and organizational realities.* San Francisco: Jossey-Bass.

Murphy, K. R., & Cleveland, J. N. (1995). *Understanding performance appraisal: Social, organizational, and goal-based perspectives.* Boston: Allyn and Bacon.

Smither, J. W. (1998). *Performance appraisal: State of the art in practice.* San Francisco: Jossey-Bass.

Toropov, B. (1999). *Manager's portfolio of model performance evaluations: Ready-to-use performance appraisals covering all employee functions.* Paramus, NJ: Prentice Hall.

PERFORMANCE FEEDBACK

See Performance Appraisal

PERFORMANCE MANAGEMENT

Performance management is an integrated human resource process and system designed to enable employees to perform their work in a high-quality and efficient manner, to improve their skills and abilities, and work in direct support of the company's strategic goals and values. It is a continuous process that starts with performance planning and progresses through employee performance appraisal and development.

Performance management can best be described as a series of steps or activities that occur at different points in a performance management cycle (typically defined as a yearly interval during which the employee's performance goals are set and the employee is evaluated and given feedback). Steps to the performance management process include (a) performance planning, (b) observation and monitoring, (c) rating and appraisal, (d) feedback and communication, (e) reward and recognition, and (f) individual development. It is important to note that the ordering of the steps just listed does not imply a purely sequential process. In fact, one of the key features to performance management is that it is not a once-a-year, orderly process. Rather, managers may simultaneously be at multiple steps with different people. For example, rather than waiting until after an appraisal is made before giving feedback, proponents of performance management advocate managers provide regular and ongoing feedback throughout the process in order to manage and improve performance.

Many human resources professionals use the terms "performance appraisal" and "performance management" interchangeably. Indeed, the two are related. However, performance management takes performance appraisal to the next logical step. Performance management is a larger, more comprehensive practice that includes performance appraisal as one of its major steps or functions. Unlike performance appraisal's large focus on accuracy in evaluating an employee's performance, performance management is viewed as a vehicle for

- Increasing employee understanding of company and department goals and strategy
- Linking employee performance and objectives to company goals and values
- Increasing communications between managers and employees
- Helping employees broaden their strengths, expand their career opportunities, and develop their weaknesses through training and development

- Reinforcing positive, value-added work efforts and motivating employees to progress in their careers
- Providing frequent and regular performance feedback to employees
- Translating capabilities and factors crucial for business success into individual goals and competencies
- Helping employees realize their full potential to contribute to the company's success

Managing employee performance has received growing attention in recent years due to several factors. There is greater domestic and international competition that has required companies to sharpen their strategic focus and to infiltrate their strategy, goals, values, and mission into employee everyday behavior. Companies recognize the critical role that employees play in helping them achieve strategic goals and, consequently, employees are being relied on to do more with less, reduce costs, and continuously improve operations. Further, growing recognition of the problems with performance appraisal in motivating employees and helping them develop their skills has resulted in a more integrated approach to performance management.

PERFORMANCE PLANNING

When beginning to manage performance, is it imperative that the supervisor and employee meet to discuss goals, outcomes, plans, and performance expectations for the coming year. Ideally this is a collaborative effort between the supervisor and employee. Goals, outcomes, and plans help establish the road map for employee efforts. The supervisor and employee should review the company's strategic goals, the goals for their department, and the employee's job description, roles, and responsibilities. From this information, the supervisor and employee select a reasonable number (such as three to five) of objectives that the employee should accomplish. These job objectives should support both department and company goals. Then the supervisor and employee should discuss and agree to a plan for achieving the objectives, complete with action steps, expected outcomes, measures of those outcomes, performance tracking tools, progress check dates, support mechanisms, and deadlines. The supervisor should also communicate his or her expectations and standards for the factors and work dimensions that the employee will be rated on during the performance appraisal step.

OBSERVATION AND MONITORING

Many companies build formal progress reviews into their performance management systems. These reviews typically occur bimonthly, quarterly, or semiannually. They serve as an opportunity for the supervisor and employee to monitor progress and make midcourse adjustments to action plans and goals, as needed. Further, they encourage regular communication and feedback between the supervisor and employee.

Throughout the performance management cycle, it is the job of the rater to observe and document the employee's performance. Raters should keep track of the employee's accomplishments, colleagues' and customers' comments, subordinate feedback, observations of critical incidents of performance, letters of recognition, mistakes, and so on. Using a "journal" or keeping a separate file for each employee often suffices for documenting performance. It is important that the rater attend to and record behaviors that the employee shows, rather than make inferences about the behavior. The rater should document the situation, the employee's behaviors, and the outcome of the situation. This ensures that developmental feedback and performance ratings are actionable (that job-relevant behaviors will be undertaken) and useful. When receiving feedback, employees are typically less defensive when they are told precisely what they did and the outcome of those actions, rather than how the evaluator feels or thinks about those actions.

RATING AND APPRAISAL

The performance management process requires that the supervisor evaluate the quality and effectiveness of the employee's performance. Informally, managers do this frequently; for example, whenever an employee's project is completed, a task is done, an employee's interaction with a customer is observed, or a report is turned in. These informal evaluations establish the basis for ongoing feedback and communications.

Many performance management systems include a formal appraisal process whereby raters rate the employee's performance on an appraisal form. Often this is done annually. After making ratings, the supervisor will meet with the employee to review the appraisal, discuss reasons for performance, give and receive feedback, and discuss developmental actions. Several companies give the employee an opportunity to evaluate him- or herself and sometimes the rater includes the employee's self-appraisal in his or her own ratings.

Companies have the option of evaluating an employee against an absolute, consistent performance standard, or of evaluating employees strictly against one another, as in rank-order systems. There are a variety of rating forms and formats available to raters, ranging from graphic rating scales to written essays to mixed standard scales. Each form differs in its behavioral specificity, standardization, and purpose. Companies also vary to the extent they evaluate employees on trait-based factors, such as work ethic, attitude, and friendliness, or on specific behaviors and performance dimensions that are demonstrated on the job.

Table 1	Example Competency

PATIENT SERVICE ORIENTATION

Skill and proficiency in showing the highest levels of care, compassion, empathy, and sincerity in all interactions with patients, in order to positively affect their understanding and comfort.

Behavior Examples:

- Responds promptly to patient calls and inquiries.
- Answers patients' questions openly, honestly, and compassionately, within their expertise and job responsibility.
- Seeks patients' questions and input, and ensures that patients have the information and care that they need.
- Administers all medical treatment to patients correctly and on time.
- Provides medication information to patients.
- Documents any reaction to medication treatment.
- Demonstrates respect for the patient's feelings, concerns, fears, and questions.
- Assists patients and their families with their questions, concerns, grief, and suffering.

In recent years, companies have begun measuring employees' performance on general *competencies* (sometimes called *critical success factors*). Competencies are broader than performance dimensions, specific behaviors, and abilities, although they often contain elements of each in their definition. For example, Table 1 lists a competency defined in both behavioral and ability terms.

Further, competencies are linked to business strategy and company values. For example, the competency just described could have been derived from a hospital's strategic objective to "Be the recognized leader in total patient care for our region." In designing performance competencies, human resource professionals conduct a job analysis on affected positions, as well as an organizational analysis of the company's goals, values, strategic goals, challenges, and competitive strategies. A company's values or strategic objectives are defined in behavioral terms that serve to set performance expectations for all employees. Competencies can be tailored to individual jobs (such as shift supervisor level I, or administrator) or general job families (such as management or administration).

FEEDBACK AND COMMUNICATION

The majority of companies require at least one feedback meeting between a rater and an employee that usually coincides with the annual performance appraisal. However, the key to successful feedback is that it be informal, consistent, and regular (that is, not just once or twice per year). Most employees want to have at least some idea as to how they are doing on the job, where they are excelling, and what they need to do to get better. Feedback also helps to validate employees' efforts and provide them with a sense

of recognition. Not all employees respond to feedback the same way, so a manager has to adapt his or her communication somewhat to the needs, style, and temperament of the employee. Some people prefer a direct, "Tell it to me like it is" approach, whereas others may respond better to messages that are more empathic.

Regardless of the style chosen, managers should follow several guidelines to give effective feedback:

- Describe the specific behavior that occurred in a clear and direct manner, as close in time to when it occurred as possible.
- Gather information from the employee about the behavior; for example, what led up to the behavior, what caused it, and so on.
- Describe the consequences, good or bad, of the behavior.
- Provide actionable tips for the employee to improve performance. Above all, the supervisor should demonstrate he or she is trying to help the employee and wants the employee to succeed.

REWARD AND RECOGNITION

Providing recognition is key to reinforcing an employee's successes, accomplishments, and efforts to improve. In some organizations monetary rewards are tied directly to the performance management system. For example, an annual "Successful" rating may provide a 4% pay increase, whereas an "Outstanding" rating may provide a 7% raise. Practice and research indicate that monetary awards only go so far in motivating employees, so some companies have expanded their formal rewards to include extra days off, stock options for management, dinner vouchers, or gift certificates to company or retail stores. Organizations with limited budgets or greater restrictions on their ability to use monetary rewards have used plaques and company trinkets, increased responsibility, opportunities for training and development, challenging and high-profile assignments, and letters of recognition to recognize employee efforts.

Rewards and recognition should be given as close as possible to the performance so that the employee sees the link between performance and consequence. Further, rewards must be distributed fairly and consistently. Each employee must have equal opportunity to work for the reward; otherwise, perceptions of favoritism and bias may arise.

INDIVIDUAL DEVELOPMENT

A key component to an organization's ability to adapt and respond to changing business, societal, and economic demands is having a highly competent and qualified workforce. This is why performance management systems provide training and development opportunities for employees to improve their current job performance and become better prepared for future opportunities. The feedback given to employees is instrumental in directing them to the knowledge, skills, abilities, or competencies that need further development. To supplement performance feedback, employees may also participate in formal assessment processes that target specific skills and abilities that need development in order for the person to become more ready to advance. From there, the supervisor will work with the employee to create a specialized individual development plan. Developmental activities may include, but are not limited to, projects and assignments, formal classroom training, informal reading, mentoring and coaching, and on-the-job activities. Career development activities, such as career planning and career mapping, are sometimes integrated with performance management systems.

EFFECTIVE PERFORMANCE MANAGEMENT

Performance management systems become more effective when the following practices are implemented:

- Seek employee input into the design of the process.
- Communicate the purposes of the performance management system, its steps, its desired outcomes, and so on.
- Make employees more responsible for managing their performance and improving their skills; couching the system as something that is done for or to them lessens employees' accountability for performing.

- Give training to supervisors and employees who will participate in the system.
- Continually monitor and evaluate the process to ensure it is meeting objectives.

—Mark L. Poteet

See also Balanced Scorecard and Health Care, Critical Success Factors, Management Development, Organizational Performance and Work Design, Performance Appraisal

FURTHER READING

Bacal, R. (1998). *Performance management.* New York: McGraw-Hill.

Banks, C. G., & May, K. E. (1999). Performance management: The real glue in organizations. In A. I. Kraut & A. K. Korman (Eds.), *Evolving practices in human resource management: Responses to a changing world of work* (pp. 118–145). San Francisco: Jossey-Bass.

Bernardin, H. J., & Beatty, R. W. (1984). *Performance appraisal: Assessing human behavior at work.* Boston: Kent.

Cook, M. J. (1999). *Effective coaching.* New York: McGraw-Hill.

Nelson, B. (1993). *1001 ways to reward employees.* New York: Workman Publishing.

PERFORMANCE MEASUREMENT

See Performance Appraisal

PERFORMANCE PREDICTION

See Employee Selection and Hiring

PERFORMANCE RATING ERRORS

Performance rating errors are systematic or consistent misevaluations of an individual's or several individuals' performance. Employers who rely on assessment systems requiring individuals to make subjective judgments about the performance of others should be concerned with rating errors because they can reduce the accuracy of the performance appraisal system. Biases in ratings may be due to either intentional or unintentional processes. Intentional errors are commonly attributed to political issues. For instance, a head nurse may want his or her unit to look good, so he or she rates all of his or her employees favorably. Supervisors may also inflate ratings to avoid giving negative feedback to their subordinates. Finally, raters may distort ratings as a way of discrimination.

Unintentional errors typically stem from inaccuracies in the way humans process information. In general, raters can only store and recall a limited amount of performance information for each employee. Consequently, people commonly organize and store information according to cognitive categories (that is, schemas) such as "good worker" and "poor worker." Therefore, when a rater is asked to recall information about the performance of a coworker who he or she has processed as a "good worker," he or she will typically rate the individual according to his or her prototype of a good worker and not on the ratee's actual behaviors. Furthermore, unintentional errors may be attributed to ambiguous dimensions on the performance appraisal form or the rater's failure to observe behavior.

TYPES OF RATING ERRORS

Common rating errors include leniency errors, severity errors, central tendency errors, restriction of range, halo errors, and recency errors. Leniency errors occur when a rater gives employees higher ratings than their actual performance warrants. For example, supervisors who rate all their average performing subordinates as "above average" on all the performance dimensions could be accused of a leniency bias. For most organizations, leniency is a very common type of rating bias; according to performance appraisal researchers Murphy and Cleveland, it is not unusual to discover that approximately 80% to 90% of all employees are rated as "above average."

In contrast to leniency errors, severity errors transpire when a rater evaluates employees more unfavorably than their true performance justifies. Using the preceding example, a supervisor with a severity bias would rate his or her average performing coworkers as "below average." Both severe and lenient ratings are thought to be present when the mean of all ratings given by a particular rater differs substantially from the true mean level of performance. Thus, a rater with a low mean rating is believed to be overly severe and a rater with a high mean rating is believed to be overly lenient.

Similarly, if ratings cluster around the midpoint of a performance scale, central tendency errors are assumed present. That is, a rater with a central tendency bias gives few if any employees very high or very low ratings. Central tendency, severity, and leniency errors are constant misjudgments across individuals. Thus, a rater does not have a severity bias if he or she rates only one person lower than his or her performance warrants.

All the errors just discussed are examples of restriction of range (that is, little variance in a rater's ratings). A relatively small standard deviation regarding the extent to which the ratings are spread is usually a strong indicator that a rater has engaged in restriction of range. Restriction of range can occur at any point on a scale.

Halo errors involve the tendency of raters to evaluate a single individual similarly across several performance dimensions based on a general assessment of that individual. For example, a physician is asked to evaluate a resident on leadership skills, communication skills, patient satisfaction, and initiative. The resident is a strong leader and a strong communicator, but is average in regard to patient satisfaction and initiative. Nevertheless, the physician gives the resident nearly identical performance ratings on all the performance dimensions resulting in a very high correlation among the ratings stemming from a general evaluation of the resident.

Finally, raters make recency errors when they give greater weight to a coworker's recent behaviors than his or her performance over the entire appraisal period. Recency errors are common when a critical situation has affected the ratee's recent performance. For example, a conscientious nurse who is rarely tardy or absent from work has been late three times and absent twice in the last two weeks because his children were sick with chickenpox. When his supervisor conducted the annual performance appraisal at the end of the week, she based many of her ratings on the nurse's performance in the last two weeks instead of the entire year. Thus, the supervisor's ratings were strongly influenced by her recency bias.

HOW TO REDUCE RATING ERRORS

A performance appraisal system plagued by rating errors cannot accomplish its purpose of evaluating the true performance of employees or differentiating between strong and weak workers. Thus, it is important that any organization relying on individuals to make subjective evaluations of others, take precautions to reduce rating errors. Diary keeping, rater error training, and frame-of-reference training are three ways to improve raters' abilities to make accurate assessments. More specifically, with diary keeping raters document critical incidents regarding their coworkers' performance throughout the assessment period. The diary serves as a tool to aid in the rater's recall process as they complete the appraisal form. In rater error training (RET), raters view examples of common rating errors and receive suggestions on how to avoid making these errors. Last, in frame-of-reference training (FOR), raters observe examples of good and poor performance. Raters are trained to use these examples as standards against which to judge performance. Both training methods are more effective when raters are allowed to practice evaluating performance and are provided with feedback on their ratings.

—Katherine R. Helland

See also Judgment, Performance Appraisal

FURTHER READING

Balzer, W. K., & Sulsky, L. M. (1990). Performance appraisal effectiveness and productivity. In K. Murphy & F. Saal (Eds.), *Psychology in organizations: Integrating science and practice.* Hillsdale, NJ: Erlbaum.

Bernardin, H. J., & Buckley, M. R. (1981). Strategies in rater training. *Academy of Management Review, 6,* 205–212.

Cardy, R. L., & Dobbins, G. H. (1994). *Performance appraisal: Alternative perspectives.* Cincinnati, OH: South-Western.

DeNisi, A. S., & Williams, K. J. (1988). Cognitive approaches to performance appraisal. In G. R. Ferris & K. M. Rowland (Eds.), *Research in personnel and human resources* (Vol. 6). Greenwich, CT: JAI Press.

Funder, D. C. (1987). Errors and mistakes: Evaluating the accuracy of social judgment. *Psychological Bulletin, 101,* 75–90.

Murphy, K. R., & Cleveland, J. N. (1995). *Understanding performance appraisal: Social, organizational, and goal-based perspectives.* Thousand Oaks, CA: Sage.

PERISHABILITY OF HEALTH CARE SERVICES

See Health Care Services

PER MEMBER PER MONTH (PMPM)

Per member per month (PMPM) is the ratio commonly used to designate the critically important average insurance cost and average insurance revenue of health plans. Because insurance premium payments are collected from employers monthly, this is reported as revenue per member per month that can be matched against the corresponding period's cost information.

Capitation reimbursement rates are almost always expressed in terms of a fixed payment per member per month. Enrollments are continually changing both within a practice and with the insurers. More frequent changes in the denominator would be too cumbersome, whereas less frequent changes could lead to serious payment inequities.

PMPM data are a useful basis for comparison among plans and among service alternatives. They enable comparisons when enrollments are changing or differ significantly across plans. At any point in time a comparison can be made by dividing the total cost of an alternative by the number of currently active enrollees involved in a plan. This gives the same information as an appropriate marginal

cost analysis. Any changes in costs on a PMPM basis can be transformed directly into a corresponding change in the monthly premium per enrollee using the organization's standard markup over cost. In the literature, premium revenue, other income, variable costs, fixed costs, and profits are all found reported on a PMPM basis. Utilization data such as hospital days and emergency room visits are generally reported annually on a basis of per 1000 members.

PMPM data are easily understood by decision makers, yet are not always the appropriate basis of comparison. PMPM data are an average of all enrollees and do not take into account case mix differences in the populations being compared. Where decisions are to be made based on a comparison made using data from two or more patient populations, a case mix adjustment should be made. PMPM data comparisons may also ignore the longer-run market strengths and weaknesses of any proposal as well as its qualitative performance implications.

If enrollees do not have the same coverages, be careful to adjust the denominator to the relevant population. Suppose only 50% of the enrollees have a drug benefit. In that case the PMPM cost or revenues apply only to those members having that benefit.

—Curtis P. McLaughlin

See also Capitation/Capitated Health Plans, Case Mix, Premium

FURTHER READING

Cleverey, W. O., & Cameron, A. E. (2002). *Essentials of health care finance* (5th ed.). Gaithersburg, MD: Aspen.

Kongstvedt, P. R. (2001). *Essentials of managed health care* (4th ed.). Gaithersburg, MD: Aspen.

PHARMACY BENEFIT MANAGEMENT

See Formulary

PHASE 1 STUDY (PHASE 1 CLINICAL TRIAL)

A clinical trial is a prospective, rather than retrospective study. It employs one or more interventional techniques and contains a control group. A carefully designed clinical study is a powerful experimental instrument for assessing the effectiveness of an intervention. Clinical trials are generally grouped into four phases. The term *phase 1 study,* or *phase 1 clinical trial,* refers to the testing of an investigational new drug in humans. It is the first type of study performed in humans after animal testing, in vitro (laboratory cell culture) testing, and toxicology studies have been performed. This first step uses a small number of volunteers (usually about 20 to 80 people). Depending on the type of drug, the individuals may be patients who have already tried and failed to improve on existing standard interventions.

A phase 1 study generally is used to define the bioavailability, pharmacokinetics, pharmacodynamics, and metabolism of the drug, as well as the side effects (possible toxicity) as the dose range of the drug is established. Participant safety is most important. Regulatory agencies such as the Food and Drug Administration (FDA) require an assessment of safety. Extensive safety information such as laboratory evaluations is necessary at frequent intervals. The study generally involves about 20 to 80 volunteers. Although healthy volunteers are usually involved, some studies, such as those involving cancer or AIDS drugs, may involve severely ill patients who have not responded to standard treatments. A drug company, a contract research organization (CRO), a health care facility, or a university medical center may have a specialized phase 1 unit to conduct trials.

A well-designed phase 1 study provides information about the experimental drug's absorption, metabolism, pharmacokinetics, pharmacodynamics, side effects, and safety information. This provides the basis on which the phase 2 studies are based. For example, a phase 1 study might be titled "Pharmacokinetics Studies of a Single Dose of Experimental Drug X in Normal Volunteers."

—Stephen A. Vitkun

See also Clinical Trials, Phase 2 Study, Phase 3 Study, Phase 4 Study

FURTHER READING

Chow, S.-C., & Liu, J.-P. (1998). *Design and analysis of clinical trials: Concepts and methodologies.* New York: Wiley.
Friedman, L. M., Furberg, C. D., & DeMets, D. L. (1998). *Fundamentals of clinical trials* (3rd ed.). New York: Springer.

PHASE 2 STUDY

A phase 2 study is generally the first trial in patients. The primary purpose of a phase 2 study is to provide the first indications on the safety and efficacy of the drug or device being tested. This is the study phase where optimized interventions and clinical end points are established. A control group meeting strict inclusion/exclusion criteria is used. Other important information obtained by phase 2 study is

the determination of doses, dosing ranges, and research conditions for phase 3 study as well as common short-term side effects and associated risks. A phase 2 study is populated by 100 to 300 patients who have a condition the study item is designed to treat, diagnose, or prevent. This study phase is often conducted in hospitalized patients under close monitoring. Several thousand patients may be enrolled in an expanded phase 2 study. Information obtained from this study phase helps refine subject inclusion/exclusion criteria by age, comorbidity, and illness symptomatology. The pharmacokinetic differences between healthy volunteers and patients are also assessed. Additional information obtained from phase 2 study includes dose response, best patient type, and frequency of dosing. These data provide the basis for refining the protocol and evaluating its theoretical framework and constructs. The outcome of a phase 2 study may be different from what is ultimately used in phase 3.

Some pharmaceutical companies subdivide this study phase into either phase 2A or phase 2B. Phase 2A studies are designed to evaluate dosing, whereas phase 2B studies are designed to determine the effectiveness of the drug. This phase of study represents the most rigorous demonstration of a medicine's effectiveness. For example, a phase 2 study might be titled "A Double-Blind Study Evaluating the Safety and Efficacy of 1 mg/kg of Test Drug X vs. Placebo in Disease State Patients."

—Linda M. Cimino

See also Clinical Trials, Phase 1 Study (Phase 1 Clinical Trial), Phase 3 Study, Phase 4 Study

FURTHER READING

Association of Clinical Research Professionals. (2002). *Certification examination review for clinical research coordinators* (pp. 21–24). Alexandria, VA: Author.
Chow, S.-C., & Liu, J.-P. (1998). *Design and analysis of clinical trials: Concepts and methodologies.* New York: Wiley.
Glossary: Clinical research terminology. (2001, December). *Applied Clinical Trials,* pp. 36–48.
Kolman, J., Meng, P., & Scott, G. (1998). *Good clinical practice* (pp. 2–3). Chichester, UK: Wiley.
Wittemore, R., & Grey, M. (2002, Second Quarter). The systematic development of nursing interventions. *Journal of Nursing Scholarship,* pp. 115–120.

PHASE 3 STUDY

A phase 3 study or phase 3 trial is the last set of preapproval trials to evaluate a new drug before obtaining final approval. Phase 3 studies are generally designed to assess the effectiveness and safety of a new drug or intervention and start to establish its role in clinical practice. They are generally controlled, randomized, comparative studies. Phase 3 studies may have a short follow-up period for evaluation. The main focus of a phase 3 study is effectiveness, but a knowledge of safety is also necessary to fully evaluate the proper role of a new drug or intervention. The more long-term evaluations are part of the phase 4 studies.

Phase 3 studies are usually multicentered, run at more than one site, because they usually involve 1000 to 3000 patients (or more) in the sample for whom the investigational drug or treatment is eventually intended. The larger number of patients allows additional safety data to be obtained. These data often provide much of the information needed for the package insert and product labeling.

In addition to the types of studies just described, which are sometimes referred to as *phase 3A studies,* there are also phase 3B studies. These are conducted after submission of the New Drug Application (NDA) but before the product's approval and marketing. A drug company may also look to expand indications during the phase 3B period between submission for approval and receipt of marketing authorization. The results of phase 3 trails are usually those that are pivotal in obtaining approval of authorities for the marketing of a drug.

A series of well-designed phase 3 studies are used by the pharmaceutical manufacturer to demonstrate safety and efficacy in a larger population. The results of these studies are considered pivotal to obtaining the approval of authorities for marketing of the drug. Postmarketing phase 4 studies are then undertaken. For example, a phase 3 trial might be titled "A Study of the Safety and Efficacy of Experimental Drug X Compared With Marketed Drug Y in Patients With Disease Z."

—Stephen A. Vitkun

See also Clinical Trials, Phase 1 Study (Phase 1 Clinical Trial), Phase 2 Study, Phase 4 Study

FURTHER READING

Chow, S.-C., & Liu, J.-P. (1998). *Design and analysis of clinical trials: Concepts and methodologies.* New York: Wiley.
Glossary: Clinical research terminology. (2001, December). *Applied Clinical Trials,* pp. 36–48.
Kolman, J., Meng, P., & Scott, G. (1998). *Good Clinical Practice* (pp. 2–3). Chichester, UK: Wiley.

PHASE 4 STUDY

Phase 4 studies are conducted after the test item has been marketed. These studies cannot be conducted until after the

FDA has approved the product. The purpose of this phase of clinical research is to provide additional information about the product's safety and efficacy with widespread usage in actual practice. This is the study phase where patients from diverse demographic groups are observed, as the product is available to the general public and there is no need for a control group. Formulations, dosages, treatment durations, and other factors are evaluated. The findings generated by the outcomes of phase 4 study are significant. The detection and identification of previously unknown or inadequately quantified related risk factors and adverse reactions takes place in this study phase. Any side effects associated with long-term use are also determined in this step of the research process. Because these results are concerned with the future, phase 4 study is considered to be prospective.

FDA approved drugs that have been "fast tracked" (approval granted before all conclusive premarketing data has been collected) are mandated to undergo phase 4 testing. The study sponsor must return to earlier phase testing if a new therapeutic indication or different labeling is being sought based on new evidence obtained from findings in this study phase. An example of a phase 4 study might be titled "The Pharmacoeconomics of Short-Term Treatment With Approved Drug X vs. Approved Drug Y in Disease State Patients."

—Linda M. Cimino

See also Clinical Trials, Phase 1 Study (Phase 1 Clinical Trial), Phase 2 Study, Phase 3 Study

FURTHER READING

Association of Clinical Research Professionals. (2002). *Certification examination review for clinical research coordinators* (pp. 21–24). Alexandria, VA: Author.
Chow, S.-C., & Liu, J.-P. (1998). *Design and analysis of clinical trials: Concepts and methodologies.* New York: Wiley.
Glossary: Clinical research terminology. (2001, December). *Applied Clinical Trials,* pp. 36–48.
Kolman, J., Meng, P., & Scott, G. (1998). *Good clinical practice* (pp. 2–3). Chichester, UK: Wiley.

PHILANTHROPIC GOVERNING BOARDS

See Boards of Directors

PHILANTHROPY IN HEALTH CARE

To generate financial resources sufficient to make a significant impact on an institution's ability to meet its mission, the institution, through its fundraising arm (hereafter referred to as "foundation"), must provide prospective donors with a variety of giving opportunities designed to meet the needs of both the donor and the institution.

The components of a successful fundraising program include the following:

- *Institutional strategic plan.* An effective institution must have a comprehensive strategic plan from which high-priority programs, services, and equipment can be identified. Applications for funding from the foundation should be evaluated in light of the institution's strategic plan.
- *Annual giving.* The backbone of any effective fundraising operation is its annual giving program. Although the annual giving program may not generate large amounts of money, it does provide large numbers of donors with the opportunity to support the institution's work while at the same time enabling the foundation to expand its donor base and identify major gift prospects for the future.
- *Special events.* Special events, though expensive and time-consuming, present opportunities for the foundation to generate income while at the same time drawing attention to itself through the publicity associated with each event.
- *Major gifts.* The success of any foundation's major gift fundraising effort rests on the ability of staff and volunteers to develop relationships with prospective donors who have both the ability to make large gifts and the proper motivation to do so. For a foundation to be successful in developing its major gift program, staff and volunteers need to develop a list of prospects with whom the foundation can develop relationships and for whom specific cultivation strategies can be developed.
- *Planned giving.* Much of any foundation's long-term success depends on its ability to take advantage of the transfer of wealth from one generation to the next. Foundations must develop significant bequest programs while at the same time making use of charitable remainder trusts, gift annuities, and insurance products as vehicles for charitable giving.

CAPITAL CAMPAIGNS

From time to time foundations may be called on to organize capital campaigns for specific major projects. In each case, specific appropriate projects should be identified and realistic goals set. It is important that foundations be selective in identifying campaign prospects, making certain that requests match donor interests and that campaign solicitations do not interfere with "asks" that might be planned for other institutional priorities. Among the important issues confronting any foundation board and staff is whether or not to engage professional counsel to assist with feasibility studies and campaign management.

WEB SITE

Although the amount of money generated through Web sites remains a small percentage of that raised by most foundations, it is nevertheless true that increasing numbers of donors make their contributions via the Internet each year. Foundations should develop mechanisms through their Web sites for online contributions.

PUBLICATIONS

Although publications do not raise money, they are an important part of any foundation's ability to communicate with its various constituencies. At a minimum, foundations should develop a generic foundation publication as well as a series of brochures on various forms of planned giving and the use of specific types of assets to meet particular charitable goals.

RECOGNITION

Although most donors give without regard to the potential for personal recognition, it is nevertheless important that we recognize their generosity. A formal recognition system that appropriately recognizes every level of contribution must be developed.

—Jerry W. Askew

FURTHER READING

Dove, K. E. (2001). *Conducting a successful fundraising program: A comprehensive guide and resource.* New York: Wiley.

Fitzpatrick, J., & Dellar, S. (2000). *Fundraising skills for healthcare executives.* New York: Springer.

Flanagan, J. (1999). *Successful fundraising: A complete handbook for volunteers and professionals.* New York: Contemporary Books.

Marwick, M., & Hitchcock, S. (2001). *Ten steps to fundraising success: Choosing the right strategy for your organization.* San Francisco: Jossey-Bass.

Sharpe, R. F. (1999). *Planned giving simplified: The gift, the giver and the gift planner.* New York: Wiley.

Sturtevant, W. T. (1997). *The artful journey: Cultivating and soliciting the major gift.* New York: Bonus Books.

PHILLIPS CURVE

The term *Phillips curve* refers to a negative relationship between inflation and unemployment. The Figure 1 illustrates such a relationship.

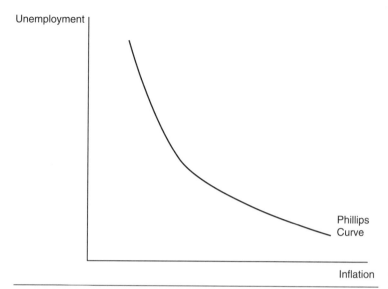

Figure 1   Phillips Curve

Through (roughly) the 1960s, economists tended to think of this relationship as being causal. As a consequence, they argued that pursuing a policy of increased inflation would reduce unemployment.

Channels through which monetary policy would exert this influence included the asymmetric adjustment of input and output prices. To understand such an asymmetry's potential, consider how quickly the price for labor (that is, wages) might respond to inflation relative to how quickly the price for outputs (such as automobiles) might respond. To the extent that laborers sign fixed-wage contracts, as they might in a unionized setting, their wages cannot respond quickly to changes in inflation. However, a manufacturer may not have entered any such contracts with buyers of its output; that is, prices it charges for transforming labor into goods and services can respond rapidly to changes in inflation. In such a setting, an employer's nominal cost of production is relatively constant, whereas the price at which it sells associated output increases. The real cost of labor (inflation-adjusted cost) thus decreases.

This decrease in real labor costs, in turn, induces employers to increase the quantity of labor that they demand—as with other goods, labor's quantity demanded increases when its real price decreases. In this setting, inflation thus reduces unemployment. Given the political appeal of such arguments, central bankers fell under increasing pressure to manage real economic activity by strategically adjusting the money supply to control inflation *and* (they believed) unemployment.

Subsequently, economists such as Milton Friedman began to question whether the inflation–unemployment relationship was indeed causal. Their criticism developed as follows. For inflation to reduce unemployment, it must asymmetrically affect prices, that is, it must produce a smaller increase in

labor prices than in output prices. Under this condition, labor *appears* more productive, because its nominal cost remains relatively constant while the price for associated output increases. As a consequence, firms can increase profits by expanding their labor forces. In aggregate, this behavior thus reduces unemployment.

Why, though, would this process *systematically* fool laborers? In other words, in the face of repeated inflations, why wouldn't laborers demand higher wages (or wages that automatically adjust to inflation)? Such a demand could indeed offset any benefit that the firm might recognize from the increased input–output price gap. Economists following Milton Friedman argued that, once one accounts for such expectations, monetary policy is impotent as a tool for manipulating real economic activity in general and unemployment in particular.

Indeed, data from the 1970s forward tend to lack the inflation–unemployment tradeoff that data from the 1960s exhibited so markedly. Nevertheless, talk of the Phillips curve persists in both academic and political circles. In academic settings, researchers are interested in alternative channels through which inflation might exert an asymmetric force on prices and thus influence real economic activity. Politicians, in contrast, frequently exploit arguments based on the Phillips curve to blame economic fluctuations on "unaccountable" central bankers.

—Dino Falaschetti

FURTHER READING

Hubbard, R. G. (1996). *Money, the financial system, and the economy* (2nd ed.). Reading, MA: Addison-Wesley.

Mishkin, F. S. 1997. *The economics of money, banking, and financial markets* (5th ed.). Reading, MA: Addison-Wesley.

PHYSICAL THERAPY

See Rehabilitation

PHYSICIAN EXTENDERS

Physician extenders are individuals that aid physicians in the practice of health care. They primarily include physician assistants and nurse practitioners. Most states require that they practice under the supervision of a physician who is on the property; however, they do generally have the right to gather history, complete physical examinations, order appropriate tests, diagnose and design an appropriate treatment plan, and prescribe medications.

Physician extenders can typically generate charges and payments at the same level as a physician, but salaries are much less than a physician. Training is generally extended beyond a bachelor's program but less than medical school training. Physician assistants and nurse practitioners often are trained and eventually work in a field that is more specific than general medicine. They often serve in rural areas to increase the accessibility of patients to care, allowing physicians such as primary care providers to hire additional physician extenders at a lower cost and as an easier-to-find alternative to another physician. All areas of health care are becoming accessible to physician extenders. They often serve as primary care providers as well as assistants in specialized areas of medicine.

Physician extenders are gaining in popularity as a profession because of their increasing utility, decreased training time compared with physicians, role in increasing accessibility of medical care, and financial advantage to the health care industry. Increasing acceptance of physician extenders by the public and by health care providers has led to a greater role in health care today. The physician assistant profession is generally thought to have begun in 1965 at Duke University, where the first training program began with four military corpsmen. It is a vibrant and growing profession today. Nurse practitioners are generally registered or bachelor's nurses with a master's degree in nursing. Both professions require a sponsoring physician. Specific state requirements dictate the amount of supervision needed by the sponsoring physician. Both professions find their greatest demand in underserved areas of health care, especially rural areas.

Physician extenders increase efficiency for practices by freeing up physicians to concentrate on more difficult cases. They can decrease the patient load of a physician allowing the physician to care for more patients in less time. They often serve a vital role in patient education, which leads to better compliance with treatment plans. Patients seem to be generally pleased with the care they receive from a physician extender with improved access and decreased waiting times, and seem to trust that their physician is aware of the care offered by the physician extender.

Many practices have found particular usefulness for physician extenders in performing time-consuming tasks that improve patient care but do not traditionally generate great amounts of revenue such as patient education and preventive health care. The key to the success of physician extender usefulness is a trusting, coordinated relationship with the physician team leader. Applying concepts of team management to patient care with physician extenders will help create a new paradigm in medical care. Physician extenders are now shaping that paradigm by their various strengths and weaknesses.

—Kenneth R. Robertson

PHYSICIAN–HOSPITAL ORGANIZATIONS

Physician–hospital organizations (PHOs) can mean two things. Most specifically, they refer to a joint venture between one or more hospitals and a group of physicians. Physicians contract individually with a larger physician corporation in which they also invest capital and have an ownership interest. This physician corporation then contracts with the PHO, and invests in and owns it together with the hospital(s).

More generally, the term *PHO* refers to the panoply of joint venture arrangements between physicians and the hospitals in which they practice. These arrangements include the PHO joint ventures just noted, independent practitioner associations (IPAs) organized by medical staff, management services organizations (MSOs), foundation models, and salaried physician arrangements. Definitions and detailed descriptions for each of these models are commonplace.

Here, we restrict attention to the more specific definition of a joint venture. The PHO is typically established as a defensive measure to counteract rising penetration of managed care and the increased number of HMOs contracting in the local market. The PHO attempts to sell itself as a unified entity that can go at risk for capitated contracts and manage utilization effectively. Unfortunately, most research suggests that PHOs rarely solicited capitated contracts from managed care or developed the capability to manage lives at risk. Data from the American Hospital Association's annual survey reveal that the percentage of community hospitals with PHOs peaked in 1996 and has been declining ever since.

—Lawton Robert Burns

FURTHER READING

Burns, L. R., & Thorpe, D. P. (1993). Trends and models in physician–hospital organization. *Health Care Management Review, 18*(4), 7–20.

Burns, L. R., & Thorpe, D. P. (1997). Physician–hospital organizations: Strategy, structure, and conduct. In R. B. Conners (Ed.), *Integrating the practice of medicine* (Chapter 17, pp. 351–371). Chicago: American Hospital Publishing.

PHYSICIAN–PATIENT RELATIONSHIP

The physician–patient relationship is a trusting relationship between the caregiver and the patient necessary to ensure the best possible outcome for patient and caregiver. There is more emphasis today than in the past on ensuring that physicians and patients learn to listen and trust each other. Medical science is realizing the vital role patients play in their own recovery. A relationship where physicians and patients trust one another improves the role patients play in their own recovery.

Physicians have always known that compliance of the patient with the care plan was an essential element in the success of any care plan. Modern patients are often more educated about their diseases than people were in the past. Today, more time is spent explaining the reason for the care plan. Patients are taught by caregivers to understand the treatment offered and are often given choices for care. As the physician–patient relationship is expanding in scope, more physicians are encouraging patients to take control of their own treatment.

Many things in recent years have proven to decrease the strength of the physician–patient relationship. One includes less loyalty among patients to their physicians. Patients no longer depend on one physician for all their medical care. This is due to many factors, including such things as specialization and third-party payers of medical care. Primary care physicians are often unaware of care provided by specialists. In addition, patients are forced to be loyal to their insurer instead of to their provider, because of the ever increasing cost of health care. The litigious nature of society also tends to undermine the physician–patient relationship. A focus on litigious issues in medical care by physician and patient can lead to mistrust between physician and patient.

Another important element of the physician–patient relationship is the accessibility of the physician to the patient. Improving access to the physician increases the trust the patient has in the physician. Key features of newer models of patient care include options that increase the patients' access to care and to their caregivers. Improved use of technology can help increase accessibility to physicians for patients. The use of e-mail and online scheduling are good examples. Patients also need to be able to trust that physicians caring for them have access to all information needed to design the most appropriate medical care plan. Integrated care has an increasing need of proper use of available technology to become a viable reality (see entry for *Electronic Medical Record*). Integrated care includes linking all caregivers to each other, increasing accessibility on behalf of the patient between primary care and other caregivers.

Decreasing medical errors and improved quality control of medical care also improve the physician–patient relationship. National initiatives to improve standardization of medical care are being enacted with hope that the physician–patient relationship will improve. Patients have a right to trust they are receiving the most appropriate care. Physicians have a responsibility to design efficient, effective, and safe treatment plans with patient input.

—Kenneth R. Robertson

See also Electronic Medical Record

PIVOTAL STUDIES

Pivotal studies are trials conducted after the early clinical development program establishes the overall efficacy and safety of the drug. These trials are an expansion of the clinical trials program.

These trials are designed to satisfy the requirements of the regulatory agencies. Primary and secondary end points are chosen based on FDA recommendations or previous clinical data. There are guidances for identifying primary end points for certain disease states, such as female sexual dysfunction, for example. Please refer to the FDA guidance for clinical studies (see Further Reading).

Pivotal trials are the sponsor's phase 3 trials. These studies are expanded controlled and uncontrolled trials after preliminary evidence of effectiveness and safety has been established in the previous phases. This phase establishes the clinical requirements of regulatory agencies and provides the company's marketing department with information on which to base marketing themes.

Phase 3 studies are usually designed as double-blind, placebo-controlled trials that include an increase in patient number, exposure, and length of drug administration. It is important during phase 3 studies to arrange several meetings with the regulatory agencies to discuss the format of the registration application, any new indications, and the core of the clinical submission.

—Anthony Sileno

See also Clinical Trials

FURTHER READING

Guarino, R. A. (Ed.). (1987). *New drug approval process.* New York: Marcel Dekker.

Food and Drug Administration. (2001). FDA Guidance for the Industry. *Choice of control group and related issues clinical trials.* Washington, DC: Food and Drug Administration.

PLACEBO

A placebo is a nonactive control of a clinical trial. The placebo has the components of the drug product minus the active ingredient. FDA guidelines suggest that placebo groups should be used very early in clinical trials to interpret efficacy and safety data. In all phases of clinical investigations, the main objective in using a placebo is to control the study adequately. However, for ethical reasons, in pain studies, pediatric cases, or life-threatening disease states, the use of an active control drug rather than a placebo is desirable.

In placebo-controlled trials the subjects are randomly assigned to a test treatment or an identical appearing treatment that does not include the active test drug. These trials are usually double-blind studies, to control for placebo effect, wherein the subject improves as a result of their impression that they are actually taking the drug. Allowing blinding and randomization in the placebo-controlled studies facilitates control for all potential influences, such as subject's or investigator's expectations, effect of being in the trial, and subjective elements. Placebo control trials help the investigator distinguish the causality of the adverse effects caused by the drug from adverse effects caused by the concomitant disease state.

—Anthony Sileno

See also Clinical Trials, Pivotal Studies

FURTHER READING

Food and Drug Administration. (2001). FDA Guidance for the Industry. *Choice of control group and related issues clinical trials.* Washington, DC: Food and Drug Administration.

PLAN-DO-STUDY-ACT CYCLE

The plan-do-study-act (PDSA) cycle consists of a circle or a wheel as depicted in Figure 1. The wheel is divided into four quadrants, each representing a significant step in the quality improvement process. The continuous, circular motion of the PDSA cycle symbolizes the central component of the quality improvement philosophy—that improvement is a never-ending cycle, a continuous movement, as opposed to a linear project with a discrete beginning and ending. The PDSA cycle is often referred to as "the Shewhart cycle" or "the Deming cycle" after the two men who were instrumental in its conception and dissemination.

Statistician Walter Shewhart (1891–1967), employed by Bell Laboratories in the 1920s and 1930s, pioneered the use of new statistical methods to improve the quality of manufactured goods. At the time, quality inspection in the manufacturing industry consisted of using classical statistical techniques to detect products that were outside of the specification limits. Shewhart introduced the use of statistical process control tools that could be used to forecast

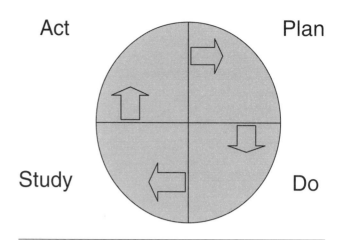

Figure 1   The Plan-Do-Study-Act (PDSA) Cycle

or predict. This contradicted the linear manufacturing model, which was to specify, produce, and inspect. In proposing a circular, closed-loop model, Shewhart emphasized that each area of production requires statistical knowledge from each of the other areas. Shewhart's work promoted a fundamental change of focus from detection to prevention. Integral to this change was his emphasis on work processes rather than the manufactured goods themselves. Shewhart asserted that proper control of the processes of production was far more efficient than end point inspection of the product.

Quality expert W. Edwards Deming (1900–1993) studied Shewhart's work, expanded upon it, and is credited with disseminating it throughout the world. In 1950, Deming presented an influential series of lectures to Japanese engineers and top executives. In the lectures he explained the meaning and use of the PDSA cycle. The four stages of the PDSA cycle are as follows:

Plan: The quality team plans a change or tests a pilot program by first observing and analyzing the current process. This establishes a baseline from which to later evaluate the effectiveness of the team's actions. Throughout this step, team members ask, "What is the purpose of this change or test?"

Do: Next, the plan is implemented, preferably on a small scale. All relevant changes that occur during the implementation are documented, and all data are collected systematically for later evaluation.

Study or Check: The effects of the change or test are then measured and evaluated. The team asks itself, "Has the purpose been achieved?"

Act: Depending on the outcome of the evaluation, the change is acted on or tested. If the test result is positive, the change is standardized to remove variation in the process, and the cycle begins again.

In teaching the PDSA cycle, Deming emphasized the central role of the customer in the learning cycle. He asserted that there are many stages of work and these stages all form a process. If you look at a single process, every stage of that process has a customer—the next stage. In the final stage, there is an ultimate customer, the one who buys the product or the services. Thus the customer plays a significant role in planning for the future by helping clarify what needs to be done for improvement. Thus the PDSA cycle represents a never-ending cycle of learning in which the results of a change must be studied, analyzed, and acted on in a scientific manner.

—Shonna L. Mulkey

See also Continuous Quality Improvement (CQI), Quality Management

FURTHER READING

Berwick, D. M., Godfrey, A. B., & Roessner, J. (1990). *Curing health care: New strategies for quality improvement.* San Francisco: Jossey-Bass.

Deming, W. E. (1986). *Out of the crisis.* Cambridge, MA: Massachusetts Institute of Technology.

Latke, W. J., & Saunders, D. M. (1995). *Four days with Dr. Deming.* Reading, MA: Addison-Wesley.

PLANNING LEVELS

See Long-Range Planning, Strategic Management

POINT-OF-SERVICE (POS) ARRANGEMENTS

An alarming rate of growth in health care expenditures observed over the past 20 years has led to a number of strategies to control cost and utilization. Restrictive delivery systems, utilization management, and the gatekeeper responsibility that places a primary care physician between an insured member and access to services were hallmarks of the HMO boom of the 1990s. There is some evidence that other models can accomplish the same controls that resulted in savings for HMOs when the member who seeks services has substantial financial responsibility for which service is chosen.[1]

The point-of-service (POS) arrangement allows a member to seek discounted care from a network of contracted providers at a lower out-of-pocket expense. To the degree that a member uses the network like an HMO, the member's costs mimic HMO costs, which are usually lower and provide richer benefits. There is typically a primary care practitioner assigned to each member, but it is up to the member whether to seek care and referrals from the PCP or to access specialty care directly. The costs to the member take the form of copayments for visits that increase substantially for care from out-of-network (OON) providers. Even more aggressive cost sharing occurs in the form of coinsurance that is a fixed percentage of the charges incurred. Both copayments and coinsurance rates are significantly lower for in-network than for OON care. There is usually a ceiling on these out-of-pocket expenses, which can be twice as high for OON care.

From the purchaser's standpoint, the POS arrangement is a hybrid that allows more fiscal control than the extensive delivery networks and limited medical management of the preferred provider organization (PPO). Insured individuals do not have to choose a restrictive network to reduce their financial responsibility. POS members may choose to buy up or down at any time, depending on their personal needs. As long as the member seeks routine care inside the network and obtains OON care for special needs, the cost remains considerably lower than if an HMO member decided to purchase care directly from a provider who did not participate in the member's insurance plan.

In the battle over choice, physicians may be unhappier with managed care than their patients, particularly regarding the adequacy of specialty networks.[2] The POS arrangement may not make life easier for primary care physicians for some aspects of care such as restrictive drug formularies. However, it does allow them to keep their patients when the member is forced to change to a plan in which the physician does not participate, as long as the patient is willing to pay the difference. POS also allows the physician and patient to discuss the value of services for which the member may experience increased financial responsibility.

The POS appears to be gaining popularity as open-access HMOs, as restrictive PPOs, and as a possible compromise between managed care and the proposal for a patient's bill of rights. It is reasonable to think that these flexible arrangements will attract even more membership over the next few years.

—Gregory Preston

REFERENCES

1. Escarce, J. J., Kapur, K., Joyce, G., et al. (2001, January 12). Medical expenditures under gatekeeper and point-of-service arrangements. *Health Services Research, 36*(6), 1037.

2. Flocke, S. A., Orzano, A. J., Selinger, H. A., et al. (1999, October). Does managed care restrictiveness affect the perceived quality of primary care? A report from ASPN. *Journal of Family Practice, 48*(10), 762.

POSITIONING STRATEGIES

See Advertising

POSITRON EMISSION TOMOGRAPHY (PET)

Positron emission tomography (PET) is a method principally used for imaging brain activity, particularly during cognitive tasks. PET uses a radioactive tracer to measure the amount of blood flow to different regions of the brain. Blood constantly flows through the brain, carrying glucose and oxygen, which are necessary for cellular metabolism. The more active an area of the brain is, the more nourishment it needs, and the more blood that flows to it. A radioactive tracer, usually ^{15}O in the form of H_2O (although ^{11}C, ^{18}F, and ^{13}N are also used), is injected at the time of mental activity and is carried throughout the circulatory system. All parts of the body receive the isotope, but during cognition only areas of the brain whose activity is increased show increased flow. Under this theory, the PET scanner measures relative, rather than absolute, metabolic activity. The results are usually reported as a change in regional cerebral blood flow (rCBF) between the more active and the resting conditions. ^{15}O, an unstable isotope with a half-life of 123 seconds, emits positrons as it decays. The PET scanner works by picking up the photons (or gamma rays) given off in opposite directions by the collision of these positrons with electrons, and then calculating their source. In addition to cognitive studies, PET scans have been used to localize seizure foci in patients with normal MRI scans and also to image fetal dopaminergic cells that were surgically implanted in Parkinson's disease patients.

—Robert I. Katz and Erica L. Katz

FURTHER READING

Gazzaniga, M. S., Ivry, R. B., & Mangun, G. R. (2002). *Cognitive neuroscience: The biology of the mind* (2nd ed., pp. 136–137). New York: Norton.

Kandel, E. R., Schwartz, J. H., & Jessell, T. M. (Eds.). (2000). *Principles of neural science* (4th ed., pp. 378, 927). New York: McGraw-Hill.

POWER

In general, power is the capability of one party (a social unit such as an individual, a group, or an organization) to influence another party. More specifically, power is typically viewed as an important aspect of leadership, referring to a leader's ability to influence followers. Leadership power is derived from the opportunities inherent in a person's position and personal attributes of the leader. French and Raven, researchers of leadership power, developed a taxonomy to further classify sources of power. Their taxonomy includes three types of position power (legitimate, reward, and coercive) and two types of personal power (expert and referent).

Legitimate power is influence that stems from the formal authority over work that is associated with an organizational position. However, a person who holds a title such as "chief of staff" does not necessarily have legitimate power. For a person of authority to have influence over others, individuals must be willing to comply with requests. The way in which legitimate power is exercised, either positively or negatively, can affect a follower's willingness to comply. For example, a polite request that is followed by an explanation is likely to be more effective than a curt demand. Legitimate power is more likely to be prevalent in health care institutions with very clear chains of command.

Reward power is influence that is derived from followers' perception that a leader has the ability to deliver valued rewards. Leaders may have control over rewards such as pay increases, bonuses, promotions, a more flexible work schedule, and a better office. The authority to grant rewards varies greatly within and between organizations. For instance, a physician who is the sole owner of a private practice likely has greater control over rewards than the chair of a pediatrics department at a teaching hospital.

Similarly, coercive power is based on the leader's capacity to deliver punishments to employees. Both threats of punishment and actual punishment give a leader coercive power; however, if a punishment does not follow a threat when the wrong behavior occurs, the usefulness of coercive power is lost. Coercive power should be used with caution, because it is likely to result in undesirable side effects such as resentment, decreased job satisfaction, and turnover.

Leaders have expert power when they possess superior task-relevant knowledge. For example, specialized physicians have potential influence over generalized practitioners because they have unique information about the best way to approach a particular medical issue. Furthermore, when an individual has extensive expert power and is perceived to be a reliable source, a follower may be willing to comply with the leader's request without an explanation. This is frequently the case when interns take orders from supervising physicians.

Finally, referent power originates from employees' desire to please a leader toward whom they have strong feelings of loyalty and admiration. Charismatic leaders are often described as possessing referent power. Leaders can increase their referent power by acting supportive, making self-sacrifices, defending their followers, and keeping promises.

THE IMPORTANCE OF POWER

Power is a dominant force in any organization because an individual is incapable of leading if they do not have influence over another party. A leader's ability to influence others is commonly derived from more than one source of power and is constantly changing. The most effective leaders typically influence others through expert and referent power. Unfortunately, it is not clear how much power a leader needs to be effective. Too much power can be detrimental to an organization's goals. Thus rules and regulations such as grievance procedures should be enforced to ensure that leaders remain responsive to their followers' needs.

—Katherine Helland

See also Authority, Compliance, Leadership

FURTHER READING

French, J., & Raven, B. H. (1959). The bases of social power. In D. Cartwright (Ed.), *Studies of social power* (pp. 150–167). Ann Arbor, MI: Institute for Social Research.

Hinkin, T. R., & Schriesheim, C. A. (1990). Relationships between subordinate perceptions of supervisor influence tactics and attributed bases of supervisory power. *Human Relations, 43,* 221–237.

Podsakoff, P. M., & Schriesheim, C. A. (1985). Field studies of French and Raven's bases of power: Critique, reanalysis, and suggestions for future research. *Psychological Bulletin, 97,* 387–411.

Yukl, G. (2002). *Leadership in organizations* (5th ed.). Englewood Cliffs, NJ: Prentice Hall.

PRECLINICAL TESTING

Preclinical testing is conducted to determine safety and efficacy in nonhuman animal studies as well as studies to characterize the chemical properties of the drug, its formulation, and the conditions of storage. Preformulation studies covering the physical and chemical characterization of the new drug substance are also conducted.

Preclinical testing involves the following:

- *Safety pharmacology.* The purpose of the safety pharmacology is to investigate the effects of the test substance on vital functions. In this regard, the cardiovascular, respiratory, and central nervous systems are usually considered the vital organ systems that should be studied in the core battery.
  - *Central nervous system.* Effects of the test substance on the central nervous system should be assessed. Motor activity, behavioral changes, coordination, sensory/motor reflex responses, and body temperature should be evaluated.
  - *Cardiovascular system.* Effects of the test substance on the cardiovascular system should be assessed. Blood pressure, heart rate, and the electrocardiogram should be evaluated. In vivo, in vitro, and ex vivo evaluations, including methods for repolarization and conductance abnormalities, should also be considered.
  - *Respiratory system.* Effects of the test substance on the respiratory system should be assessed, including respiratory rate, and other measures of respiratory function (such as tidal volume or hemoglobin oxygen saturation) should be evaluated.

Effects of the test substance on organ systems not investigated elsewhere should be assessed when there is a reason for concern. For example, dependency potential or skeletal muscle, immune, and endocrine functions can be investigated.

- *Toxicology.* Toxicology studies in the preclinical stage are conducted to
  - Select or reject lead candidate
  - General indication of suitability
  - Dose selection and guidance to clinician

The basic studies conducted are
  - Mutagenicity: in vitro Ames test
  - One-week or two-week range finders: mouse or rat, dog or primate
  - Maximum tolerated dose
  - Gross effects, clinical chemistries: What are the toxicities?
  - Gross pathology to indicate target organs

- *Pharmacokinetics.* The primary objective of pharmacokinetics is to quantify drug absorption, distribution, biotransformation, and excretion of the drug. Based on pharmacokinetics,
  - The performance of dosage forms can be evaluated in terms of rate and amount of drug delivered to the blood
  - The dosage regimen of a drug can be adjusted to produce and maintain therapeutically effective blood concentrations with little or no toxicity

—Steven C. Quay

PREFERRED PROVIDER ORGANIZATION (PPO)

Simply defined, a preferred provider organization (PPO) consists of at least one network of providers of health care that is organized to contract for the delivery of its services on a discounted fee basis to a purchaser or purchasers. The network can be small, single specialty, and local. The network can be broad based and nationwide, and can include nontraditional providers. A PPO may own several such networks. Unlike a health maintenance organization (HMO), PPOs emphasize self-directed access to providers and do not require a relationship with a primary care practitioner often known as a *gatekeeper*. The number of PPOs in the United States grew 36% between 1994 and 1999,[1] but demonstrated a 9% decline in 2000.[2]

More than two thirds of PPOs are owned by health plans and third-party administrators (TPAs). Hospitals and physician groups own approximately 10% of existing PPOs. Employer groups showed interest in owning PPOs in the past, but that number has declined to insignificance. The remaining 20% to 25% are distributed among multiple types of owners, including states, investors, and even members.[1,2]

While HMOs move toward elimination of the need for referrals (open access) or away from restriction to the HMO network (point of service), PPOs are adding HMO-like services, including utilization management, pharmacy benefits management, case management, and disease management to their operations. Originally, managed care was perceived as a continuum where the starting point was a discounted fee-for-service, uncredentialed PPO and the goal was to evolve to a highly integrated HMO. The current strategy appears to have become a race for the middle ground of care management.[3]

As the popularity of HMOs declined between 1995 and 2001, PPO enrollment increased from 34%[4] to 44%[5] of all employees in employer-sponsored health plans. This growth came from employees walking away from traditional indemnity plans and HMOs. There are a number of reasons why PPOs are the most popular type of employer-sponsored health plans. Restrictive networks, heavily managed limits on access to care not provided by a primary care practitioner in the office setting, and provider backlash all led to movement of members from HMOs to PPOs. Poor coverage and high out-of-pocket expenses make indemnity plans unappealing to employees. During the boom years of the last decade low rates of unemployment made attracting new people difficult. The relative cost containment offered by PPOs encouraged employers to offer these plans in place of traditional indemnity group insurance and HMOs. Finally, PPOs were attractive to self-insured groups because they were exempt from ERISA regulations and allowed more flexibility in designing benefits.

In comparing the benefits provided by one large health plan for its HMO and PPO members, there were 55 distinct categories that ranged from allergy testing to hospice care. Behavioral benefits were also included. Thirty-two (58%) of the benefits descriptions were identical. In the cases

where there was a discrepancy, the covered services were similar or identical. However, in-network and out-of-network payment rules created distinct differences between the two types of plans. Copayments were fixed and limited in the HMO for covered benefits, and except for emergencies or approved exceptions, claims for out-of-network services would not be paid. The same services in the PPO would be covered in a fashion similar to the HMO in-network; however, out-of-network services carried as high as a 50% coinsurance that did not apply to the out-of-pocket maximum contribution by the member if the services were not authorized by the health plan.

Both types of plans carried medical management services that included requirements for prior authorization and concurrent review of hospital care, hospice care, home health care, and certain surgeries. Case management was offered for high-risk members and for members receiving long-term outpatient therapies. The HMO required prior authorization for a more extensive list of services including referrals for specialty care, all outpatient therapy, rehabilitation programs, and durable medical equipment. In addition, more extensive medical management services were provided to HMO members including disease management and pharmacy management.

The differences in the insurance coverage lie in the flexibility of the PPO model. Employers who offer an HMO are usually required to accept a fairly extensive benefit package that has become progressively more costly over the past 15 years. The PPO offers choice based on size of network (access), types of providers and services covered (availability), and the ability for members to "buy up" for expanded networks or coverage in the form of deductibles, coinsurance, and copayments. And even though PPO premiums are higher than HMO premiums, the gap is closing.[2]

The cost savings associated with PPOs appear to arise from two sources. Network savings (7% to 14%) are realized from medical management programs such as case and utilization management (18% of savings), cost sharing (57% of savings), and contract leverage (25% of savings).[6] The second source of savings is related to the fact that overall utilization rates by PPO members are substantially lower than for HMO members. Inpatient utilization rates have declined every year since 1994 and continued their favorable trend through 2000.[2] If there is a selection bias where healthier members choose PPOs because they anticipate less care and lower out-of-pocket expenses, it may well disappear as HMOs lose ground.

The PPO at one time was considered a transition plan to take health care from traditional indemnity to the HMO world. The new and popular PPO may well continue to carry the managed care banner as the principal form of managed care in the future. As health care inflation escalates, PPOs will have to adopt more aggressive management strategies to contain costs. It is unclear if they will become the HMOs of the future or will leverage the development of communication and integration strategies to become a truly new managed care model.

—Gregory Preston

REFERENCES

1. Schroeder, S. (2000). Section 11. Who runs a PPO? In K. Greenrose, G. Carneal, & K. Makwana (Eds.), *Rise to prominence: The PPO story* (pp. 93–98). Jeffersonville, IN: AAPPO [American Association of Preferred Provider Organizations]/URAC.
2. Aventis Pharmaceuticals. (2002). *Managed Care Digest Series 2001*. Bridgewater, NJ: Author.
3. Cassidy, T., & Fairman, H. (2000). Section 16. Employer coverage trends. In K. Greenrose, G. Carneal, & K. Makwana (Eds.), *Rise to prominence: The PPO story* (pp. 129–132). Jeffersonville, IN: AAPPO [American Association of Preferred Provider Organizations]/URAC.
4. Section 2. AAPPO Market Report Summary. (2000). In K. Greenrose, G. Carneal, & K. Makwana (Eds.), *Rise to prominence: The PPO story* (pp. 29–32). Jeffersonville, IN: AAPPO [American Association of Preferred Provider Organizations]/URAC.
5. www.aappo.org.
6. Smith, D. G., & Betley, C. L. (2000, June 1). Cost management activities of PPOs. *Journal of Risk and Insurance, 67*(2), 219.

PREMEDICATE (PREMEDICATION)

The term *premedicate* has come to mean something very specific in the practice of medicine. Namely, it refers to the administration of medication prior to a procedure or test. This is interesting, because if the word were analyzed by its components the reader might get confused. *Pre-* means "before," and *medicate* means "to administer medicine." If anything, the term should be *pre-procedure medication*. Nevertheless, the word *premedicate* has its place and is universally understood in modern medicine.

For the variety of procedures performed, from a colonoscopy to open heart surgery, premedication has its purpose. First and foremost, the goal of premedication is anxiolysis (reduce anxiety). This state can be achieved by a number of medications and administered through a number of routes. The most commonly used drugs are benzodiazepines, which are used to treat anxiety. However, medications that contain narcotics or antihistamines can be used for premedication because of their calming effect on patients. There are several options for the route of administration. The intravenous route is preferred because of the reliability of medication uptake. Other routes such as intramuscular (into the muscle) or subcutaneous (under the skin) can be used. These routes are not as reliable in uptake because factors such as soft tissue and fat affect medication absorption. Other administration routes are oral and rectal. The oral route is especially advantageous when administering medication to children as they are more amenable to drinking a liquid than having a needlestick injection. The second purpose of premedication is analgesia (relief of pain) prior to the offending procedure. The analgesic is given to treat a future painful stimulus. Thus, premedication can consist of more than one medication.

—Anthony J. Ippolito

FURTHER READING

Miller, R. D. (2000). *Anesthesia* (5th ed.). Philadelphia: Livingstone.

PREMIUM

A premium is a monetary payment made by an insured individual to a liability insurance carrier (insurer). This is a contractually established fee between the insured and insurer, which provides the insured (e.g., a physician) coverage for the defense and payment of medical liability claims that may arise during a set policy period according to type of policy. Policy payout limits (liability limits) are defined on initiation of the agreement by both parties, and premiums vary depending on the ceiling of such limits; that is, the higher the coverage amount, the higher the premium. Premiums are calculated based on various factors taken into consideration during the insured's initial evaluation (or re-evaluation if a policy renewal situation) process (see *Occurrence Screening*). In the event of a settlement or loss of a negligence (malpractice) case, the liability insurance company provides payment (an "award") to a third party (e.g., an injured patient). This payment is also called an *indemnity*. Most policies also provide payment on behalf of physicians for the legal costs associated with the defense of a claim.

Premiums provide a mechanism for insurers to spread the risk of insurance among policyholders. They are, for all practical purposes, set at rates that would be sufficient to pay present and future losses, cover the insurers' administrative and operating expenses, generate investment income, and allow the company to continue as an ongoing business. Reinsurance describes the situation where an insurance company buys insurance from another company to cover part of any potential losses it might incur in the usual course of its business.

—Benito A. Alvarez

See also Occurrence Screening

FURTHER READING

The guide to medical professional liability insurance. (1991). Chicago: American Medical Association.

www.coverageglossary.com

www.plusweb.org

PREPAID HEALTH PLAN

See Health Insurance

PRESCRIPTION

A prescription is an order for medication issued by a physician, dentist, veterinarian, or other duly licensed medical practitioner. The purpose is to specify a particular medication to be administered to a patient at a designated time. It is then dispensed by a licensed pharmacist. The prescription is a type of "conversation" between the prescriber, patient, and pharmacist. Medications dispensed legally by prescription only are often referred to as "legend drugs" and are intended for use exclusively by the patient indicated and cannot be transferred for use to another individual.

Prescription drugs play a critical role in contemporary medicine. This is illustrated by U.S. spending of $116.9 billion in 2000, almost triple that of 1990, with expected spending reaching $243 billion by 2008. Prescription drug spending is only 9% of personal health care spending, but is one of the fastest growing components. National prescription spending increased 15% from 1997 to 1998 compared with a 5% increase for physician services and a 3% increase for hospital care. The number of prescriptions purchased, 2.6 billion, increased 37% from 1992 to 1998, compared with a U.S. population growth of 6%. The average number of prescriptions per person increased from 7.3 to 9.6, with Tennessee leading the nation in prescription drug use in 1998 with a per capita consumption 40% above the national average. The average retail prescription price in 2000 was $19.33 for generic drugs and $65.29 for brand drugs. Generics accounted for 42% of total prescriptions dispensed whereas brands accounted for most of the top-selling prescriptions.

—Donna Sym

FURTHER READING

U.S. Department of Health and Human Services. (2000, April). *Report to the president: Prescription drug coverage, spending, utilization, and prices.* Washington, DC: U.S. Government Printing Office.

www.kff.org

PRESS RELEASE

A press release is the formal communication of information to media personnel for distribution by targeted media to identified audiences. It is an important tool in a comprehensive public relations strategy. The intention of a press release is to attract the attention of editors and reporters for subsequent inclusion of key information in published or broadcast announcements, articles, stories, and editorials. Media personnel receive large numbers of press releases daily. They *shortlist* (as a reduction strategy) those releases that are targeted to the audiences they desire to reach. Thus the writer of a press release needs to capture the main promotional points in a clear, concise, and enthusiastic manner, keeping a focus on the specific target of the message (for example, a pharmaceutical company introducing a new breakthrough drug to a target audience of physicians).

Over time, press releases have expanded in scope. Today, press releases may range from a simple release of a single statement to something more elaborate, such as a pack of supporting materials (often referred to as a media pack). The latter might include information sheets, photographs, artwork, video and audio tapes, CDs, and DVDs. Video and audio news releases (VNRs and ANRs) may contain significant material that will preclude the editor needing further related material. Press releases can be found in all forms of media, including print, broadcast, and interactive electronic (such as Internet and e-mail).

Many areas of the health care industry take advantage of press releases. Examples would include a hospital introducing a new staff physician or director, a new service, research discoveries, and so on. Likewise, health care insurance companies use press releases to announce policy or procedural changes. Finally, medical suppliers and pharmaceutical companies use press releases to announce new discoveries or inventions.

—David W. Schumann

FURTHER READING

Aronson, M., & Spetner, D. (1998). *The public relations writer's handbook.* San Francisco: Jossey-Bass.

McIntyre, C. V. (1992). *Writing effective news releases . . . : How to get free publicity for yourself, your business, or your organization.* Colorado Springs, CO: Piccadilly Books.

Pickton, D., & Broderick, A. (2001). *Integrated marketing communication.* Upper Saddle River, NJ: Prentice Hall.

PREVENTIVE MEDICINE

See Wellness

PRICE CONTROL IN THE PHARMACEUTICAL INDUSTRY

Pharmaceutical companies are accused of having excessive profit rates compared with those of other industries. Economists would argue that large profits invite others to enter into the business, causing competition that would correct excessive profits (such as in the computer industry). However, in the pharmaceutical industry recent history has shown that there are usually no new entrants, only mergers. Medicaid, HMOs, pharmacy benefit managers (PBMs), hospitals, retail pharmacies, federal law, and individual states have all explored various strategies to control the costs of prescription drugs.

The Omnibus Budget Reconciliation Act of 1990 (OBRA 90) governs the provision of pharmaceutical benefits under Medicaid. Under this law, pharmaceutical manufacturers are required to enter into rebate agreements with the U.S. Department of Health and Human Services (DHHS) in order to sell their products to the state Medicaid programs.

In 2001, forty state lawmakers have introduced proposals aimed at curtailing drug spending, and various bills have been passed. Certain bills aimed at consumer savings include New Jersey's implementation of a senior discount program allowing lower-income individuals to pay 50% of the reasonable cost of the drug. West Virginia approved a plan to form a multistate purchasing pool open to consumers. Maryland has requested permission from the federal government allowing Medicare patients to buy drugs at lower Medicaid program prices. The strongest impact has come from the state of Maine. It has received federal approval to let residents with incomes up to 300% of the federal poverty level buy drugs at a discount. Another bill, the Maine Rx Program, passed in 2000, allows price controls by permitting the state to negotiate with drug manufacturers to lower prices. If the state is not satisfied with these prices, Maine's commissioner of human services will be able to establish maximum retail prices effective in 2003. Companies refusing to negotiate could face their products, restriction in the state's Medicaid program. Lawmakers in 27 other states are including parts of Maine's law in their own proposals. The pharmaceutical industry has filed lawsuits against such programs.

Congress has also commented that the cost of prescriptions for Americans continues to rise, which has resulted in millions of people on fixed incomes having to choose between purchasing prescriptions, housing, or food. They noted that drugs manufactured by U.S. pharmaceutical companies are available at lower prices in other countries and Americans should be able to purchase these medications at comparable prices. Hence, the Medicine Equity and Drug Safety Act (MEDS) of 2000 was enacted by Congress with the intention of providing the U.S. consumer with lower-priced pharmaceuticals. It would have permitted pharmacists and licensed wholesalers to re-import U.S.-manufactured, FDA-approved prescription drugs from countries in which the drugs were sold at lower prices. Prior to the MEDS Act only manufacturers could re-import drugs back to the United States. This act would legalize parallel trade. Signed by Clinton and passed by Congress in October 2000, it was terminated in December 2000 by Donna Shalala, then Secretary of the DHHS. Shalala argued she could not certify that the MEDS Act would meet its objectives: to pose no additional risk to the public's health and safety and result in a significant reduction in the cost of pharmaceuticals to the American consumer. The pharmaceutical industry argued that the MEDS Act would reduce aggregate economic welfare, reduce the ability of the manufacturer to recover costs of research and development (R&D), and damage long-term economic efficiency in the industry.

There are approximately 40 PBMs in the United States, with the top five accounting for 75% of the market. They act as intermediaries among employers, pharmacists, patients, managed care organizations, and third-party payers. An important way they control costs is through the use of closed formularies. The term *open formulary* refers to the reimbursement of all drugs, whereas a closed formulary means the reimbursement of specific drugs only. For example, multiple brand name drugs, called "me-too" drugs, may be available to treat a condition or disease. The PBM may choose one drug in this category to be included in its formulary. This drug is often chosen by having manufacturers compete with their rebate and discount packages; those with the best offers would be included in the formulary, whereas the higher-priced drugs would be excluded. Rebates and discounts are often granted to compete with generic drugs, although PBMs often encourage the use of cheaper generics. Rebates are paid directly to the PBM, often based on the number of prescriptions filled for a given drug or based on the PBM's ability to move the market share of that drug, that is, to cause a significant increase in the number of prescriptions filled for that given drug. Several pharmaceutical manufacturers own PBMs, raising concern as to whether this gives rise to unfair competition. Such PBMs may include their own drugs to the unfair exclusion of other manufacturers' products. PBMs also control prescription costs by encouraging or requiring enrollees to use mail-order pharmacies for maintenance drugs for chronic conditions. Patients are often given incentives to use mail-order by discounting or eliminating copayments. Mail-order pharmacies can offer prescription drugs at lower prices because of the volume of drug purchases and economies of scale and because of lower overhead than retail pharmacies.

Pharmaceutical manufacturers also have preferred pricing for hospitals, either individually or through buying groups, and HMOs. It often entails rebates similar to that offered to PBMs. Prices paid by federal agencies are determined by the Federal Supply Schedule (FSS). The Veterans Health Care Act of 1992 states that pharmaceutical manufacturers must make drugs available to those covered by the FSS as a condition of Medicaid reimbursement eligibility.

To control costs, retail pharmacies join buying groups, enabling them to concentrate market power and buy drugs at volume discounts. They have warehouses of prescription drugs and distribute them to members in order to reduce costs. Retail pharmacies also participate in a network to provide services to members of contracted health plans that allow them to be included in third-party reimbursement programs. Pharmacies included in the network sign contracts agreeing to comply with the health plan's rules and regulations and accept the reimbursement level.

—Donna Sym

FURTHER READING

U.S. Department of Health and Human Services. (2000, April). *Report to the president: Prescription drug coverage, spending, utilization, and prices.* Washington, DC: U.S. Government Printing Office.
Wire Reports. (2000, December 27). U.S. kills program to import cheap drugs. *Arizona Daily Star*, p. A1.
www.kff.org
www.phrma.org

PRICE DISCRIMINATION

Patients may think the charges posted to their bill represent what is paid to the provider. Charges tend to be the highest price anyone might reasonably be expected to pay. All prominent group buyers in health care demand and receive negotiated discounts, often 40% to 60%. These negotiated prices represent *price discrimination* against those payers (individual or group) who exert less bargaining power. Discounting occurs widely, including physician office visits, specialists' procedural fees, hospital days, and prescription and generic drugs.

Under the Robinson-Patman Act of 1934, price discrimination among competing customers is illegal per se, except on the basis of differences in costs of servicing those competing customers. However, individuals receiving personal services are not considered to be in competition with each other. Airlines and hotels offer differing rates to customers using the same flight or identical rooms, based on the willingness of customers to pay. Health care providers rarely adopt such pricing policies, called *yield management,* based on the timing

of demand and the perishable capacity available, because it also requires prior reservations, something that is not appropriate for the acute care portion of health care. Furthermore, it is unlikely to be socially acceptable. Provider–payer price negotiations tend to take place annually based on historical and projected annual patient volumes and utilization.

When health insurance became widespread during and after World War II, some providers agreed to bill on the basis of costs rather than list prices. As price competition intensified, providers, especially hospitals, raised their charges to cover the amount that costs exceeded revenues. Other customers, especially indemnity insurers, made up the difference, a practice that became known as *cost shifting.* Gradually, all third-party purchasers have demanded the opportunity to negotiate or dictate rates, reducing the discrimination against large corporate buyers, but increasing discrimination against others, especial individual payers. The only way to avoid price discrimination would be to have a single payer with community rating for underwriting and rate-setting purposes. So long as health plans compete against one another to service individual employers, it is likely that one group or another will experience some form of price discrimination. What vendors lose on the apples, they have to make up on the oranges.

—Curtis P. McLaughlin

See also Cost Shifting

PRICE SENSITIVITY IN HEALTH INSURANCE

Price sensitivity is the degree to which consumers of health insurance buy less insurance when faced with higher premiums. (See the entry for *Elasticity of Demand.*) Most research has focused on the effects of out-of-pocket premium contributions on a worker's choice of health plans offered by their employer. Price sensitivity depends on the number of plans offered and the nature of those plans. For a given increase in out-of-pocket premium, workers with more plan offerings are more likely to switch plans.

The key finding is that workers are enormously sensitive to out-of-pocket premiums. Dowd and Feldman (1994) found that a 1% increase in the out-of-pocket premium of one managed care plan relative to the others offered by the employer, led to a 7.9% reduction in that plan's share of single-worker coverage at the firm. Other research yields similarly large estimates of price sensitivity. A limitation of this work is that it has not explicitly explored the role of the overlap of provider networks across plan offerings. Presumably the price sensitivity is much greater when individuals can switch plans without switching providers.

In principle, employer demand for health insurance is derived from worker demand. As such, firm demand for coverage should reflect a degree of price sensitivity similar to worker demand. Few studies have explored this. Feldman et al. (1997) examined the demand for coverage by 2000 small Minnesota firms. They found that a 1% increase in premiums reduced by 3.9% the probability that a small firm would offer single coverage and reduced by 5.8% the probability that such a firm would offer family coverage.

This substantial price sensitivity was a driving force behind the changes observed in health insurance markets over the 1990s. Because workers were willing to change plans for modest reductions in out-of-pocket premiums, insurers were under considerable pressure to contain costs. As a result, insurers selectively contracted with hospitals and physicians, and promised case volume in exchange for lower prices. Over the 1989 to 1996 period, annual increases in premiums for employer-sponsored health insurance dropped from 18% to less than 2% (Morrisey, 1998).

Worker sensitivity to out-of-pocket premiums has also led to employer initiatives to implement "level dollar premium contribution" models. Under these approaches, employers set their premium contribution at the cost of the least costly plan. Workers wanting more extensive coverage must pay the extra costs in the form of higher out-of-pocket premiums. The effect has been to shift workers into less costly plan options (Buchmueller & Feldstein, 1996).

—Michael A. Morrisey

FURTHER READING

Buckmueller, T. C., & Feldstein, P. J. (1996). Consumers' sensitivity to health plan premiums: Evidence from a natural experiment in California. *Health Affairs, 15*(1), 143–150.

Dowd, B., & Feldman, R. (1996). Premium elasticities of health plan choice. *Inquiry, 31,*438–444.

Feldman, R., Dowd, B., Leitz, S., & Blewett, L. A. (1997). The effect of premiums on the small firm's decision to offer health insurance. *Journal of Human Resources, 32*(4), 635–658.

Morrisey, M. A. (1998). *Managed care and changing health care markets.* Washington, DC: AEI Press.

PRICE SENSITIVITY OF HEALTH CARE SERVICES

The term *price sensitivity* refers to the degree to which consumers of health services use fewer services when faced with higher out-of-pocket prices. (See the entry for *Elasticity of Demand.*) Differences in out-of-pocket prices typically arise because of the presence of health insurance. With health insurance an individual may be required to pay only 20% of the price of a diagnostic test or she may be required to pay only $10 or $20 out-of-pocket for a physician visit. The insurance company pays the balance.

There have been numerous efforts to estimate the degree of price sensitivity of health services. Many of the studies are confounded because people who are more likely to use health services also tend to choose health plans that require lower out-of-pocket payments for hospital, physician, and other health services (Morrisey, 1992). (See entry for *Adverse Selection.*)

The best evidence on health services price sensitivity comes from the Rand Health Insurance Experiment (Newhouse et al., 1993). It randomly assigned people to one of 14 health plans with differing levels of out-of-pocket payments and monitored their use of health services for four to five years. The study was conducted between 1974 and 1977. The findings continue to be used in health policy analysis today.

Price sensitivity tends to be similar within broad categories of care, but different across categories. Free care relative to paying the full price of physician visits resulted in approximately 67% more visits. Prescription drugs were about as price sensitive as physician visits. Hospital admissions were much less price sensitive; free care increased admissions by approximately 29%. Free care for emergency department visits increased visits by approximately 54%. The vast majority of these additional visits were nonurgent. Mental health services tended to be very price sensitive. Free care for outpatient mental health services increased visits by 300%. Mental health service use also increased over time in response to lower prices. In contrast, medical service use was equally price responsive throughout the life of the Rand study. Dental services were about half as price sensitive as physician services, but had a much greater sensitivity to price in the first year.

The differences in price sensitivity across categories of health services explain differences in health insurance coverage. Utilization review in the form of preadmission certification and concurrent review are commonly used for hospital care, arguably because out-of-pocket prices have only a small impact on use. In contrast, managed care plans and other insurers increasingly rely on copayments to limit the use of physician visits and prescription drugs. Mental health services are so price sensitive that insurers often impose limits on the number of visits or days of care that are covered or exclude coverage entirely.

—Michael A. Morrisey

FURTHER READING

Morrisey, M. A. (1992). *Price sensitivity in health care: Implications for health care policy.* Washington, DC: NFIB [National Federation of Independent Businesses] Foundation.

Newhouse, J. P., & Insurance Experiment Group. (1993). *Free for all? Lessons from the RAND health insurance experiment.* Cambridge, MA: Harvard University Press.

PRIMARY ADVERTISING

See Advertising

PRIMARY CARE

The term *primary care* has some conflicting interpretations. For the purposes of this book it is defined as the care provided to patients by the caregiver they consider to be the individual they are most likely to present to when they develop an illness or concern regarding their health care status.

The term *primary care* first appeared in the literature in the early 1960s and appears to have been most often used within the context of the "primary care practitioner." In more technical literature, however, it was often used to refer to the initial contact with the health care system, whether that actually was a physician or another service provider such as the emergency room in a hospital.

Part of the difficulty of defining the term and its use results from two divergent definitions of the word *primary*. This word may be interpreted as meaning the first in time or order, and in that context narrows the definition of primary care to the initial contact with the system. The other use of *primary* is to imply main or principal, which allows a much broader description of primary care. Within that second frame of reference, *primary care* may refer to the initial contact with the system, or as is more commonly perceived today, it may refer to the care provided by the individual patients consider their principal caregiver or by the people principally responsible for managing and coordinating care during their current episode of illness.

According to WHO, *primary care* is defined as the first point of entry into the health care system for all patients of all ages with all diseases. Primary care providers traditionally were physicians, such as family practitioners, pediatricians, internists, or obstetricians, but today they frequently are nurse practitioners or physician's assistants.

It is important to understand that primary care practitioners typically see a patient population that is broad based in many ways, such as age, sex, ethnicity, and degree of illness. Patients presenting to a primary care practitioner may have a specific complaint related to a particular diagnosis. They are, however, much more likely to present nonspecific complaints influenced by multiple factors in their life such as ethnicity, religion, prior experience, allergies, current medications, and even other current, concomitant illness. These practitioners must therefore be multidisciplinary in their approach, widely educated in a variety of types of illnesses, and open to a large variety of inputs to be used in their approach to diagnosis and disease management. They must be prepared to coordinate the use of specialists and subspecialists, to interpret the results of various forms of diagnostic studies, and to facilitate the patient's progress through the diagnostic and management process.

Primary care should be differentiated from secondary and tertiary care. Secondary care typically involves the use of consultants who help resolve a diagnostic dilemma and then return the patient to the primary care practitioner. Tertiary care is care provided at highly technical, subspecialized levels most often related to complex illnesses (e.g., organ transplants). In its best form tertiary care also incorporates primary care physicians utilizing their broad knowledge of the patient.

—C. Bevan Stuart

See also Ambulatory Care, Health Care Utilization, Hospitals, Tertiary Care

FURTHER READING

http://archinte.ama-assn.org/info/auinst_term.html

Institute of Medicine. (1996). *Primary care: America's health in a new era.* Washington, DC: National Academy Press.

www.umanitoba.ca/centres/mchp/concept/thesaurus/thesaurus_P.html

PRIVACY ISSUES

Protection of the security and confidentiality of information is an essential responsibility of health care managers. Health information systems contain sensitive information. Clinical systems process medical information about individual patients. Human resources information systems contain personal information about employees. Financial and decision support systems include proprietary data used for planning, marketing, and management of the enterprise.

Clinical information systems require comprehensive programs to protect the privacy of patient medical records. Three categories of clinical systems must be considered: patient care systems, public health information systems, and medical research information systems.

- *Patient care systems* contain information about a patient's medical history, diagnoses, and treatment plans. Organizations that provide care are required by law and by ethical considerations to ensure that patient-specific information is available only to authorized users.

- *Public health information systems* support disease prevention and surveillance programs. Protecting public health requires the acquisition and storage of health-related information about individuals. Public health benefits sometimes conflict with threats to individual privacy. Individuals concerned about privacy who avoid clinical tests and treatments may endanger the health of others in the community.

- *Medical research information systems* use large repositories of individual patient records to study patterns of health and disease in populations. Data mining techniques are used to search for potential relationships among patient characteristics and other factors. Research data often are accessible to a number of investigators and their staff, and information security measures are essential to protect patient privacy rights.

Enterprise-wide standards must be established to protect information privacy and confidentiality in health care organizations. A comprehensive information security policy should include three elements: (a) physical security, (b) technical controls over access, and (c) management policies that are well known and enforced in all organizational units.

Physical security includes such elements as using keys or badges to unlock computer terminals and using dial-back procedures to determine that a request to access data has come from a specific terminal and modem.

A number of technical controls to data access can be built into operational information systems. Passwords are the most common. Each user is assigned a password that is known only by that individual and the data security manager. Users should be warned never to share their passwords with anyone else, and passwords should be changed periodically. Passwords should allow access only to those portions of the organization's database appropriate to the individual user and his or her departmental affiliation.

Encryption is a method of coding or altering information such that it is unintelligible if obtained by unauthorized users. Encryption is used with very sensitive information such as lists of passwords or diagnostic information on mental health or sexually transmitted diseases. It is not a practical method for providing general data protection. The data security manager should be the only one able to decode encrypted information.

The most important technical safeguard may be the maintenance of audit logs that track every transaction associated with use of critical data files. The logs identify the user and/or terminal, the date and time of access, and the type of transaction carried out (simple access, addition, changes, or deletions to the record). If employees are aware that all transactions are being monitored for violations, they will be deterred from seeking unauthorized use of sensitive information.

Management policies support the physical safeguards and technical controls that protect data confidentiality. Training of all users is essential to be sure they understand the importance of data confidentiality and the procedures in place to protect privacy of records. Every employee should be required to read the organization's privacy protection policy, and sign a statement indicating that he or she will not violate provisions of the policy. Strict disciplinary measures, including termination, should be followed when employee violations occur.

The Health Insurance Portability and Accountability Act (HIPAA) was passed by the U.S. Congress in 1996. HIPAA is designed to allow individuals who change jobs to retain health insurance coverage by eliminating the use of exclusions for "pre-existing" conditions, refusal to cover health problems that exist at the time of a job change.

Privacy protection components of this law limit the nonconsensual use and release of private health information and give patients new rights to access their medical records and to know who else has accessed them.

HIPAA compliance and modification of information systems to meet HIPAA standards have become major issues for health care organizations. Many organizations have established HIPAA task forces. Some have appointed compliance and/or privacy offices to lead the efforts. Others are using existing organizational units including the office of the chief information officer, medical records, and risk management.

Software vendors will play a critical role in HIPAA compliance, because most organizations use vendor-supplied software in their information systems.

—Charles J. Austin

FURTHER READING

Austin, C. J., & Boxerman, S. B. (2002). *Information systems for healthcare management* (Chapter 13). Chicago: AUPHA [Association of University Programs in Health Administration] Press/Health Administration Press.

PRIVATE NETWORK

See Virtual Private Network (VPN)

PRIVATIZATION OF HEALTH CARE

Health care privatization is the process of enabling market forces to perfect health care delivery to a specified community. In that regard an efficient market (a state in health care that does not exist today!) is a status where we cannot make anyone better, without making someone else worse. A balance between government regulation and efficient market forces would enable many countries to start this process and continue the tug and pull at their own pace to reach an acceptable bargain to the enterprise, competitors, suppliers, customers, other stakeholders, and the state.

The World Trade Organization (WTO) is squeezing many of the nonmarket anticompetitive strategies (such as public services) out of governmental practices by charging higher margin to those who value the services or increasing market shares in face of greater competition. Unfortunately, this will lead to abandoning those who cannot pay the marginal cost. The loss of financial aid as a right for the poor in the United States, under the 1996 welfare reforms, helped reduce social services caseloads but also left 60% of working single mothers with incomes at or near the poverty level, and 700,000 people who left welfare remained without health insurance.

As the market gets saturated, the profit begins to fall. Private health care providers, to increase their profits, then develop strategies to raise their productivity, diversify services, and create new markets. Privatization programs emphasize cutting cost, substitution of high-intensity for low-intensity services, cost shifting, or outright cost avoidance. Some have entered the public services and dismantled their programs having made extensive short-term profits. This rapid entry into and exit from public markets has resulted in disasters.

The implementation of the WTO action plan has spelled trouble in some countries, such as Mexico, Indonesia, and Thailand, where other regulations are not necessarily operational (such as antitrust, fraud, and *qui tam* laws). Partly because of regulations, there have been highly successful public service programs in some European countries such as France, the Netherlands, the United Kingdom, and Sweden. One advantage of the European system is that the standard and range of cover is a judgment call by the people, as they see on their pay slips how much they are paying for health care and judge whether the cost is justified. This practice is one way of making the market serve everyone.

The World Health Organization has acknowledged Malaysia's public health care system as second only to Cuba's in terms of geographic distribution and access to primary health care. Malaysia's infant mortality rate is approaching that of the United States, a remarkable achievement considering the country spends only about 2.5% of its gross national product (GNP) on publicly funded health care (whereas the United States spends 16% of its GNP on publicly funded health care).

There is a lesson to be learned from the stock market and its recent scandals, such as Enron, WorldCom, Martha Stewart, and ImClone. Vigilant oversight is of paramount significance to keep up the confidence of all stakeholders (patients, care providers, suppliers, public, institutes, and the state) in the process of health care privatization.

—Fareed A. Khouqeer

FURTHER READING

Feldstein, P. J. (1998). *Health care economics* (5th ed.). Cincinnati, OH: Delmar.

Musgrave, G. L. (2000). *The evolving bargain: Strategic implications of deregulation and privatization.* Boston: Harvard Business School Press.

Waitzkin, H., & Iriart, C. (2001). How the United States exports managed care to developing countries. *International Journal of Health Services, 31*(3), 495–505.

www.efpia.org/default.htm

www.igc.org/lpa/lpv25/lp05.htm

www.medscape.com/viewarticle/421474

PRIVILEGE

Privilege is defined in legal terms as a right or immunity granted as a benefit or favor. In health care, *privilege* refers to the right to treat patients or use specific facilities granted to a health care practitioner based on his or her training or status. These rights extend to hospital admission, the ability to perform skills, and specified tests or procedures.

In general, any health care provider seeing patients in an institutional setting has defined treatment and assessment capabilities. Admitting privileges may be temporary, conditional, or full. Procedural privileges are granted for each specific skill, generally after specialty training (for example, a cardiothoracic surgeon is granted admitting and operative privileges). Privileges are granted by the medical staff of the facility and are based on established intrainstitutional policies. The process of obtaining privileges, called credentialing, involves review of education, experience, and peer reference, and most institutions have specific committees devoted solely to this purpose.

—Brian J. Daley

PRIVILEGE SYSTEM

See Privilege

PRODUCT

Product is everything that a marketing organization offers to potential customers as viewed from the perspective of the organization. Product is often viewed as the first or most important of the 4 P's (controllable variables of the marketing mix) ahead of price, place, and promotion in the decision-making hierarchy. Product includes tangible things (goods) and intangible things (services), as well as ideas, opinions, or suggested actions about activities, causes, people, places, and even the organization itself. Some organizations prefer to think of their product as their offering to potential consumers and, therefore, use the word *offering* instead of *product* in their conceptual models and in-house communications. Success in an organization's product strategy and product design seems to occur when the organization is focused on the benefits customers receive when they acquire, use, or consume the product, not when the organization is focused on the features of the product.

A product has some value for what it inherently contains (an automobile is an assemblage of steel, rubber, plastic, and so on), but more important, the value comes from the function it performs (an automobile provides transportation) and the expectations created about its nonfunctional aspects (an automobile can secure the admiration of others). Charles Revson of Revlon Cosmetics is reputed to have said, "In the factory we manufacture lipstick; in the store we sell hope," clearly suggesting that the value lay in the benefits expected by the purchaser/user, not in the physical components.

Professor Philip Kotler has made distinctions about various components of product that he calls the levels of the product—the core product, the actual product, and the augmented product. The *core product* level consists of the problem-solving aspects or the benefits the product provides (what it does). The *actual product* level includes elements of the product such as its design, brand, packaging, features, and quality level (how it does what it does). The *augmented product* level contains things that enhance the product's benefits and value to the user such as easy-to-understand instructions, warranty, delivery, installation, and after-sale service (that makes it more valuable).

Most organizations produce a number of products (see the entry for *Product Classes*) that may or may not be related to each other (see *Product Mix*) and pursue long-run success through a number of strategies involving the nature and direction of the growth of their collection of products (see *Product Line Extension*).

—David W. Glascoff

PRODUCT CLASSES

Product classes are groupings of products into meaningfully different categories based on aspects of their marketing characteristics and/or characteristics of their purchasers. Products are normally classified as either consumer products (purchased by final household consumers for their own personal use and satisfaction) or organizational products (purchased by organizations for the production of other products and services). This distinction, for example, can make health insurance an organizational product (when it is purchased by the employer) and can make health care a consumer product (when it is purchased by the consumer). The marketing of the product "health insurance" is thus focused on benefits and features that are significant to the organizational purchaser, and the marketing of the product "health care" is focused on benefits and features that are significant to the final household consumer.

Consumer products are classified by how they are purchased (the amount and type of shopping effort), whereas organizational products are classified by how they are used in the production process. Consumer products are generally agreed to have four major categories. *Convenience products* are purchased with minimal shopping effort and include subcategories of staple, impulse, and emergency products. *Shopping products* are purchased with considerable shopping effort and include subcategories of homogeneous shopping products where the basis for shopping is price alone and heterogeneous shopping products where the basis for shopping is suitability (meaning that the purchaser endeavors to see, feel, try, or in some manner examine the product prior to purchase). *Specialty products* are purchased with the shopping effort having been expended in advance of purchase, because of brand insistence and inelastic demand for the particular item. *Unsought products* are divided into subcategories of regularly unsought products, purchased with reluctant shopping effort, because the purchaser does not wish to buy the product, and new unsought products, not purchased because the potential customer does not know about the product.

Organizational products are normally classified as being of six types, but they may be collapsed into three categories based on whether the product is used to make the product, to become the product, or to facilitate the production process. *Installations and major equipment* and items that are *accessories and minor equipment* are long-lived, depreciable assets used to manufacture the product. *Raw materials* along with *finished and semifinished component parts and materials* actually become the product. *Business services* such as accounting, legal, and personnel activities and *supplies* such as maintenance, repair, and operating supplies are necessary to facilitate the production process or the organization's purpose.

Some individuals believe that *services* generally (banking, travel, medical advice) should be classified and treated separately because some of their characteristics (intangibility, lack of being able to be stored in inventory, and inseparability from the service provider) make them differ in a material manner from tangible products. Other individuals acknowledge that although services have characteristics that make them different from tangible products, the difference is one without distinction in a marketing sense.

—David W. Glascoff

PRODUCT CONCEPT

See Marketing Concept

PRODUCT LIFE CYCLE (PLC) ANALYSIS

To say that a product has a life cycle is to assert four things:

1. Products have a limited life.

2. Product sales pass through distinct stages, each posing different challenges, opportunities, and problems to the seller.

3. Profits rise and fall at different stages of the product life cycle.

4. Products require different marketing, financial, manufacturing, purchasing, and human resource strategies in each stage of their life cycle.

Most product life cycle (PLC) curves are portrayed as bell-shaped (Figure 1). Such curves are typically divided into four stages: introduction, growth, maturity, and decline.

1. *Introduction*: A period of slow sales growth as the product is introduced in the market. Profits are nonexistent in this stage because of the heavy expenses incurred with product introduction.

2. *Growth*: A period of rapid market acceptance and substantial profit improvement.

3. *Maturity*: A period of a slowdown in sales growth because the product has achieved acceptance by most potential buyers. Profits stabilize or decline because of increased competition.

4. *Decline*: The period when sales show a downward drift and profits erode.

The PLC concept can be used to analyze a product category (medical devices), a product form (signal managers), a product (pacemaker), or a brand (Medtronics).

- *Product categories* have the longest life cycles. Many product categories stay in the mature stage indefinitely and grow only at the population growth rate. Some major product categories, such as typewriters, seem to have entered the decline stage of the PLC. Some others, such as cellular telephones, are clearly in the growth stage.

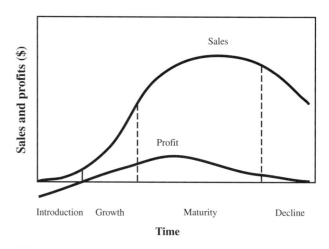

Figure 1   Bell-Shaped Product Life Cycle Curve

- *Product forms* follow the standard PLC more faithfully. Manual typewriters passed through the stages of introduction, growth, maturity, and decline; their successors, electric typewriters and electronic typewriters, passed through these same stages.
- *Products* follow either the standard PLC or one of several variant shapes.
- *Branded products* can have a short or long PLC. Although many new brands die an early death, some brand names, such as Bayer Aspirin, have a very long PLC.

Not all products exhibit a bell-shaped PLC. Researchers have identified over a dozen PLC patterns.[1] Three common patterns are shown in Figure 2. Figure 2(a) shows a *growth-slump-maturity pattern*, often characteristic of some newly launched drugs. The drug, if successful, exhibits early sales growth that later slumps, and then its sales remain at a "petrified" level.

The *cycle–recycle pattern* in Figure 2(b) describes the sales of other launched drugs. The pharmaceutical company aggressively promotes its new drug, and this produces the first cycle. Later, sales start declining and the company undertakes another promotion push, which produces a second cycle (usually of smaller magnitude and duration).[2]

Another common pattern is the *scalloped PLC* in Figure 2(c). Here sales pass through a succession of life cycles based on the discovery of new product uses or users. It is illustrated by a pharmaceutical company that discovers new applications of its drug or moves its drug into new countries.

MARKETING STRATEGIES: INTRODUCTION STAGE

Because it takes time to roll out a new product and fill distribution pipelines, sales growth tends to be slow at the

(a) Growth-slump-maturity pattern

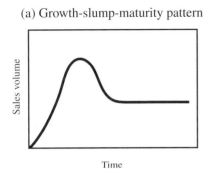

(b) Cycle–recycle pattern

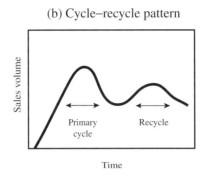

(c) Scalloped pattern

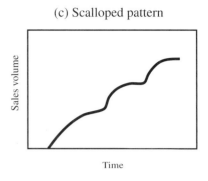

Figure 2   Common Product Life Cycle Curves

introduction stage. Buzzell identified several causes for the slow growth: delays in the expansion of production capacity, technical problems ("working out the bugs"), delays in obtaining adequate distribution through retail outlets, and customer reluctance to change established behaviors.[3] Sales of expensive new products such as CAT scanners are delayed by additional factors such as product complexity and fewer buyers.

Profits are negative or low in the introduction stage because of low sales and heavy distribution and promotion expenses. Promotional expenditures are at their highest ratio to sales because of the need to (a) inform potential consumers, (b) induce product trial, and (c) secure distribution in retail outlets. Firms focus their selling on those buyers who are the readiest to buy, usually higher-income groups. Prices tend to be high because costs are high, given relatively low output rates, technological problems in production, and high required margins to support the heavy promotional expenditures.

In launching a new product, marketing management chooses among four strategies:

1. *Rapid skimming*: Launching the new product at a high price and a high promotion level

2. *Slow skimming*: Launching the new product at a high price and low promotion

3. *Rapid penetration*: Launching the product at a low price and spending heavily on promotion

4. *Slow penetration*: Launching the new product at a low price and low level of promotion

MARKETING STRATEGIES: GROWTH STAGE

The growth stage is marked by a rapid climb in sales. Early adopters like the product, and additional consumers start buying it. New competitors enter, attracted by the opportunities. They introduce new product features and expand distribution.

Prices remain where they are or fall slightly, depending on how fast demand increases. Companies maintain their promotional expenditures at the same or at a slightly increased level to meet competition and to continue to educate the market. Sales rise much faster than promotional expenditures, causing a welcome decline in the promotion–sales ratio.

Profits increase during this stage as promotion costs are spread over a larger volume and unit manufacturing costs fall faster than price declines owing to the producer learning effect. To prepare new strategies, firms have to watch for a change from an accelerating to a decelerating rate of growth.

During this stage, the firm uses several strategies to sustain rapid market growth as long as possible:

- It improves product quality and adds new product features and improved styling.
- It adds new models and flanker products (that is, products of different sizes, flavors, and so forth that protect the main product).
- It enters new market segments.
- It increases its distribution coverage and enters new distribution channels.
- It shifts from product awareness advertising to product preference advertising.
- It lowers prices to attract the next layer of price-sensitive buyers.

MARKETING STRATEGIES: MATURITY STAGE

At some point, the rate of sales growth slows, and the product enters a stage of relative maturity. This stage normally lasts longer than the previous stages and poses formidable challenges to marketing management. *Most products are in the maturity stage of the life cycle, and most marketing managers cope with the problem of marketing the mature product.*

The sales slowdown creates overcapacity in the industry, which leads to intensified competition. Competitors scramble to find niches. They engage in frequent markdowns. They increase advertising and trade and consumer promotion. They increase R&D budgets to develop product improvements and line extensions. They make deals to supply private brands. A shakeout begins, and weaker competitors withdraw. The industry eventually consists of well-entrenched competitors whose basic drive is to gain or maintain market share.

Dominating the industry are a few giant firms—perhaps a quality leader, a service leader, and a cost leader—that serve the whole market and make their profits mainly through high volume and lower costs. Surrounding these dominant firms are a multitude of enterprises exploiting market niches, including market specialists, product specialists, and customizing firms. The issue facing a firm in a mature market is whether to struggle to become one of the "big three" and achieve profits through high volume and low cost or to pursue a niche strategy and achieve profits through low volume and a high margin.

In the maturity stage, a company can consider three strategies:

1. *Market modification.* The company can try to expand the number of brand users by attracting nonusers, or entering new market segments, or winning over competitors' customers. The company can also try to convince current brand users to increase its brand usage by using the product in new ways, or using more of the product, or using the product on more occasions.

2. *Product modification.* Managers also try to stimulate sales by modifying the product's characteristics through quality improvement, feature improvement, or style improvement.

3. *Marketing mix modification.* Product managers may also try to stimulate sales by modifying other marketing mix elements such as price, distribution, advertising, sales promotion, salesforce size, or service.

MARKETING STRATEGIES: DECLINE STAGE

The sales of most product forms and brands eventually decline. The decline may be slow, as in the case of oatmeal; or rapid, as in the case of the Edsel automobile. Sales may plunge to zero, or they may petrify at a low level.

Sales decline for a number of reasons, including technological advances, shifts in consumer tastes, and increased domestic and foreign competition. All lead to overcapacity, increased price cutting, and profit erosion.

Unless strong reasons for retention exist, carrying a weak product is very costly to the firm. The cost is not just the amount of uncovered overhead and profit: There are many hidden costs. Weak products often consume a disproportionate amount of management's time, require frequent price and inventory adjustments, generally involve short production runs despite expensive setup times, and require both advertising and sales force attention that might be better used to make the healthy products more profitable, and they can cause customer misgivings and cast a shadow on the company's image. The biggest cost might well lie in the future. Failing to eliminate weak products delays the aggressive search for replacement products. The weak products create a lopsided product mix, long on yesterday's breadwinners and short on tomorrow's.

In a study of company strategies in declining industries, Harrigan identified five decline strategies available to the firm:

1. Increasing the firm's investment (to dominate the market or strengthen its competitive position)

2. Maintaining the firm's investment level until the uncertainties about the industry are resolved

3. Decreasing the firm's investment level selectively, by dropping unprofitable customer groups, while simultaneously strengthening the firm's investment in lucrative niches

4. Harvesting ("milking") the firm's investment to recover cash quickly

5. Divesting the business quickly by disposing of its assets as advantageously as possible[4]

When a company decides to drop a product, it faces further decisions. If the product has strong distribution and residual goodwill, the company can probably sell it to another firm. If the company can't find any buyers, it must decide whether to liquidate the brand quickly or slowly. It must also decide on how much inventory and service to maintain for past customers.

The PLC concept is best used to interpret product and market dynamics. As a planning tool, the PLC concept helps managers characterize the main marketing challenges in each stage of a product's life and develop major alternative marketing strategies. As a control tool, the PLC concept helps the company measure product performance against similar products launched in the past. The PLC concept is less useful as a forecasting tool, because sales histories exhibit diverse patterns, and the stages vary in duration.

—Philip Kotler

NOTES

1. J. E. Swan & D R. Rink (1982, January–February), Fitting market strategy to varying product life cycles, *Business Horizons,* pp. 72–76; and G. J. Tellis & C. M. Crawford (1981, Fall), An evolutionary approach to product growth theory, *Journal of Marketing,* pp. 125–134.

2. See W. E. Cox Jr. (1967, October), Product life cycles as marketing models, *Journal of Business,* 375–384.

3. R. D. Buzzell (1956), Competitive behavior and product life cycles, in J. S. Wright & J. Goldstucker (Eds.), *New ideas for successful marketing* (Chicago: American Marketing Association), p. 51.

4. K. R. Harrigan (1980, Fall), Strategies for declining industries, *Journal of Business Strategy,* p. 27.

PRODUCT LINE EXTENSION

A *product line extension* is an addition to the current collection (line) of goods and services offered by a marketer. A product line normally consists of all the related products offered by an organization and the usual dimensions of the product line are its width, depth, and length. The *product line width* is the number of different types of items that the manufacturer offers (for example, the product line width of a furniture manufacturer may be chairs, sofas, and tables). The *product line depth* is the number of different categories of items within each type (the depth of the furniture manufacturer's product lines are easy chairs, dining chairs, and desk chairs; two-cushion sofas, three-cushion sofas, and sleeper sofas; and Early American tables, Danish modern tables, and contemporary tables). The *product line length* is the number of different choices within the various categories that make up the product line depth (within the easy chair category, the length could characterize such items as traditional, overstuffed, recliner, and rocker; within the dining chair category, the length could include captain's, Windsor, cane seat, and dinette; and within the desk chair category, such items as executive, secretary, swivel, and upholstered).

The other common use of product line extension, sometimes simply called *line extension,* is to describe one of four growth strategies pursued by a marketer who offers branded items to potential customers. Sales growth for the marketer can come from using existing or new brand names on existing or new product categories. Using the existing brand name on similar products that are essentially little more than changes in flavor, ingredients, or product forms in order to capitalize on the favorable image of the existing brand is called a *line extension,* in contrast to a brand extension. Among the best examples of successful *line extension* strategy are the product variations introduced by Coca-Cola, such as its caffeine-free Coke, diet Coke, caffeine-free diet Coke, cherry Coke, lemon Coke, and so on. In contrast, a *brand extension* strategy is using an existing brand in a different product category. Honda, for example, in addition to automobiles and motorcycles, has extended its brand to somewhat unrelated categories including lawn mowers and snowmobiles. Because the success of *brand*

extensions is difficult to predict (Colgate mouthwash and Listerine toothpaste seem to have succeeded, but Clorox laundry detergent and Life Saver gum have not been as successful), most marketers are reluctant to use their valued brand names on a product too far away from the product class that brought the original success. The other two line-related strategies are *multibranding* (using a new brand name for a product in an existing product category, such as Coca-Cola's Tab—its initial entry in the diet drink market) and *new branding* (using a new brand name for a product in a new product category, such as Procter and Gamble's introduction of Pringles).

—David W. Glascoff

PRODUCT MIX

The product mix encompasses all the products and services offered by a marketer. The aspects of the organization's product mix include diverse topics such as assortment creation, profitability, research and development, growth, and branding strategies. Product mix is often, however, thought to have four dimensions: width, depth, length, and consistency, with the first three also being characteristics of the organization's product line. (See the entry for *Product Line Extension* for a discussion of width, depth, and length.) Consistency, as a dimension of the product mix, is a measure of the appropriateness, in both the customer's mind and the producer's mind, of the quality level and relatedness of the offering. It would be inconsistent, for example, for Cadillac's product mix to include inexpensive in-line roller blades or, some would suggest, for a physician's office to sell cosmetics.

The idea of assortment creation, credited to W. Alderson, suggests that a successful marketer puts together a heterogeneous group of goods into a collection that makes sense to customers. This collection becomes that organization's product mix and can be most readily seen in the assortment available in many retail stores. Facial tissues, soft drinks, motor oil, and ballpoint pens have little in common except that most consumers expect to find them at a nearby gas station or convenience store. These unrelated items, along with magazines, cigarettes, and small boxes of laundry soap, make up the store's offering or product mix.

The profitability of the individual items that make up the product mix has a tremendous impact on the nature of the mix. Most marketers seek a balanced approach to profitability, based on the idea that some items will contribute more to the organization's overall profitability than will others, either because of the per unit profit contribution or the percentage of total profit with which they are associated. A fast-food chain makes a larger per unit percentage contribution (profit) on its beverages than on its hamburgers or french fries, but the overall product mix is priced to achieve a target contribution (profit) based on the expected sales of the component items. (See also entries for *Complementary Product* and *Substitute Product*.)

Research and development activities are related to the product mix as an organization seeks growth. H. Igor Ansoff is generally given credit for developing the product–market matrix approach to classifying various growth strategies a marketer might pursue in terms of a product mix. Ansoff identified and labeled each of four possibilities in terms of sources of growth: existing or new products in existing or new markets. Pursuing growth through existing products in existing markets is called *market penetration.* Growth from bringing existing products to new markets is called a *market development* strategy. Growth by creating new products for existing markets is known as a *product development* strategy, and developing new products for new markets is called growth by *diversification.* Successful marketers probably have a product mix in which sales growth has been based on research and development activities leading to ventures of all four strategies.

Branding strategies are also a part of an organization's product mix and include a number of possibilities for both manufacturers and distributors. A brand's value, sometimes called *brand equity,* is created by customer loyalty to the brand. A *manufacturer's brand,* often called a national brand, is owned by a manufacturer or producer, and extreme loyalty (brand insistence) is seen when a customer goes to a different store or supplier because the desired brand is not available. For example, a customer may want only Lenox china and will not accept a substitute. A *dealer's brand,* sometimes called a private label or store brand, is owned by a retailer or wholesaler and thus the loyalty is to the outlet where the item is available. For example, Road Handler shock absorbers or Craftsman tools are only available at Sears Roebuck stores. Most general-line retailers have a product mix that consists of a combination of brands (their own and those owned by manufacturers) to provide products at different quality levels or at different prices for a broad range of customers.

—David W. Glascoff

PRODUCTION POSSIBILITIES CURVE

Available technology defines the maximum feasible level of output that a given quantity of inputs can produce. For example, equipped with *any* particular technology, a surgeon can produce only so many surgeries. The "production possibilities curve" summarizes this relationship over a range of input levels. Continuing the present example, and treating surgeons as inputs, the production possibilities curve identifies how many surgeries different numbers of surgeons are capable of producing, holding all other inputs constant.

As an empirical regularity, production possibilities curves appear concave; that is, past some level of input the rate at which additional inputs increase production decreases. Put more precisely, inputs eventually exhibit "diminishing marginal products." To see this phenomenon, consider the surgeries example again. Given a surgeon, that is, an input to the production of surgeries, a quantity of surgeries exists beyond which medical technology does not permit one to exceed without additional factor inputs. The production possibilities curve identifies this limiting quantity for each level of input.

Note, however, that two surgeons may be capable of producing more surgeries than is one. Nevertheless, the second surgeon's marginal product may be less than that of the first, perhaps because the two must share equipment or operating room space. Likewise, because adding a third surgeon further increases competition for other factor inputs (which we have assumed are held constant), the marginal increase of surgeries is likely to be smaller still. In short, adding surgeons increases the number of surgeries that can be produced, but (eventually) does so at a diminishing rate.

Eventually, significant output expansions are likely to be available only if the practice expands its use of related inputs or adopts a more productive surgical technology. In the present example, the surgeons might expand their production possibilities by renting more operating room space or employing more support staff. Alternatively, they might employ a more productive operating technology, such as one that increases the rate at which they can perform certain procedures.

Figure 1 (p. 454) illustrates this phenomenon, as well as the "decreasing returns" feature that regularly characterizes production possibilities.

For a *given* technology or level of related inputs, Production Possibilities A in the figure represents the quantity of output (such as surgeries) that is feasible for different levels of a *particular* input (such as surgeons). Because a particular input's marginal productivity regularly decreases past some level (that is, shows decreasing marginal returns), increased output levels might only be feasible from increased employment of related inputs (such as operating rooms) or the adoption of a superior transformation technology (such as one that decreases the amount of effort that a surgeon must exert to produce an operation). Production Possibilities B represents the quantity of output that can be produced from a particular input when the quantity of related inputs increases or the technology for transforming that particular input to output improves.

—Dino Falaschetti and Steve Parsons

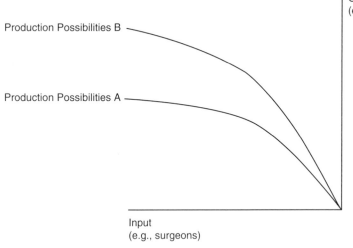

Production Possibilities B

Production Possibilities A

Output
(e.g., surgeries)

Input
(e.g., surgeons)

Figure 1   Production Possibilities Curve

FURTHER READING

Bernanke, B., & Frank, R. (2001). *Principles of economics.* New York: McGraw-Hill.

Hirshleifer, J., & Glazer, A. (1992). *Price theory and applications* (5th ed.). Upper Saddle River, NJ: Prentice Hall.

Stigler, G. J. (1987). *The theory of price* (4th ed.). New York: Macmillan.

PRODUCTIVITY

Productivity is the rate at which inputs can be transformed into outputs. An input's productivity is not constant. Rather, it depends on the level at which it is already employed, the level at which related inputs are employed, and the nature of available technology.

The production of physician office visits is illustrative. Suppose that a physician's production capacity is 10 visits per day. By employing an office assistant, our hypothesized physician might increase this capacity to, say, 15 visits. In this case, the office assistant's marginal productivity is 5 office visits.

Introducing a second assistant is likely to further expand the physician's production capacity. This assistant's "productivity" can be higher or lower than that of the first. A higher marginal product, say 6 additional office visits, could emerge from economies associated with specialization (for example, the first assistant specializes in maintaining the group's financial records and the second specializes in filing insurance claims). Nevertheless, the law of diminishing marginal returns says that the office assistants' marginal product (and that of every other input) must eventually fall. If this were not the case, a firm would have no boundaries.

Understanding the term "productivity" facilitates optimal decision making. For example, to maximize profits one needs to choose a combination of factor inputs so that each factor's productivity-to-cost ratio is identical. When this condition does not hold, a "free lunch" is available from hiring additional inputs whose ratio is high (for example, 20 units/$5) and firing those whose ratio is low (for example, 10 units/$5).

—Dino Falaschetti and Steve Parsons

FURTHER READING

Bernanke, B., & Frank, R. (2001). *Principles of economics.* New York: McGraw-Hill.

Hirshleifer, J., & Glazer, A. (1992). *Price theory and applications* (5th ed.). Upper Saddle River, NJ: Prentice Hall.

Stigler, G. J. (1987). *The theory of price* (4th ed.). New York: Macmillan.

PROFESSIONAL CORPORATION

A professional corporation (PC) is a corporation formed under state law that restricts its ownership interests to only members of a particular profession. Thus a PC formed to practice medicine has only physicians as shareholders. By choosing corporate status, the PC shareholders have all the liability protections afforded to any other kind of corporation. PCs are formed by filing a certificate of incorporation with the appropriate state agency (usually the secretary of state), and in many states, one must obtain approval from the governing licensing authority (that is, department of education) before filing the certificate of incorporation. PCs use corporate bylaws and shareholder agreements to delineate the rights, duties, and obligations of their shareholders, officers, and directors. To avoid paying corporate income taxes, many PC owners elect Subchapter S status with the Internal Revenue Service.

—Theresa DiMartino

PROFESSIONAL STANDARDS REVIEW ORGANIZATIONS

For the health care industry, several organizations and federal agencies are responsible for the promulgation and review of professional standards. These include the Joint Commission on Accreditation of Healthcare Organizations (JCAHO), the National Committee for Quality Assurance (NCQA), and the U.S. Department of Health and Human Services (DHHS) Centers for Medicare and Medicaid Services (CMS), among others. The JCAHO is an independent not-for-profit organization that has standards manuals for, and conducts physical surveys of, hospitals, home care agencies, long-term care organizations, and ambulatory health care organizations, among others. Accreditation by the JCAHO is mandatory for these various organizations to participate in federal and state health care reimbursement programs, including Medicare and Medicaid. The JCAHO publishes annually its Accreditation Manuals, which contain required standards of performance for these health care organizations. The NCQA is the main accreditation agency providing standards and guidance to the managed care industry. The NCQA reviews quality assurance, utilization management, credentialing, preventive health services, members' rights and responsibilities, and medical records and has developed standards for accreditation in each of these areas. The CMS promulgates regulations (Conditions of Participation) that govern the quality of health care services. Hospitals that are successfully accredited by the JCAHO are deemed to be in compliance with the CMS Conditions of Participation.

—Theresa DiMartino

PROFIT

Profit is easy to define; it is equal to income less expenses. The difficulty comes when you need to define income and expenses, and do so in a way that provides useful information about a firm's performance. The financial statements that most people see are prepared under a set of rules called *generally accepted accounting principles,* or GAAPs. These rules are designed to provide investors with financial statements that are consistent from company to company. Of course, if managers falsify their financial statements or do not follow GAAPs, as has happened recently in several high-profile cases, the financial statements are not consistent with other companies' statements, and the conclusions that investors may draw will be based on incorrect information. However, even when GAAP accounting is used and financial statements are consistent from firm to firm, the standard summary measures, such as revenue or net income, may not be the most useful measures for evaluating a company's performance. Therefore, most analysts modify published financial statements to come up with their own measures. Figure 1 shows the items that would make up a typical income statement and how the items are calculated.

Sales

– Cost of goods sold

= Gross profit

– Selling, general, and administrative expenses

– Depreciation

= Earnings before deducting interest and taxes (EBIT)

– Net interest expense

= Earnings before deducting taxes

– Taxes

= Net income before deducting extraordinary items

– After-tax extraordinary items

= Net income after deducting extraordinary items

– Preferred stock dividends

= Net income available to common stockholders

– Common stock dividends

= Additions to retained earnings

Figure 1   A Typical Income Statement

INCOME

Income consists of sales receipts, interest income, and a variety of other items that are often lumped together into a category called *nonoperating income.* Because most firms use accrual accounting, the sales line item on an income statement usually includes both cash received from sales, and also the selling price of goods that have been sold, but for which money has not been collected. Other items that would be included in income are dividends on shares of stock the firm owns, and license or royalty payments.

EXPENSES

Expenses are more complicated. Expenses include many of the obvious items that a firm writes checks to pay for: costs of raw materials, labor wages, electricity, maintenance, advertising, interest payments, and taxes. It also includes some items that a firm does not actually pay for, called *noncash expenses,* such as depreciation. Under GAAPs accounting, a firm is not allowed to deduct the entire amount it spends on capital equipment in the year the equipment is purchased. Instead, the firm must "depreciate" the equipment over its expected life, which means charging a portion of the initial cost of the machine each year of its life. So, for example, if a firm were to purchase a $100,000 piece of equipment, it typically would not be allowed to include as an expense in the purchase year the $100,000 it paid for the equipment. Instead, the $100,000 must be expensed over the expected life of the equipment. If the expected life is 10 years, then the firm records $10,000 per year as an expense. In the first year the firm pays out $100,000 for the equipment, but only claims an expense of $10,000. In years 2 through 10, the firm records a $10,000 expense when, in fact, it pays out nothing for the equipment. This means the expenses a firm records do not correspond to the cash the firm pays out! In years 2 to 10 the firm records noncash expenses of $10,000 each year.

NET INCOME, OR PROFIT

Net income is the figure most accountants and investors call the "bottom line." It is just income less expenses. It is also known as *profit* or *net profit after tax.*

ALTERNATIVE MEASURES OF PROFIT

Although net income is a common and widely recognized measure, other measures of profitability are frequently calculated. Managers need performance measures for parts of the business that are under their direct control. Investors need performance measures that reflect the cash flows that belong to them. For example, it is often important to distinguish between a firm's performance in its core, or ongoing, day-to-day business, and its performance because of one-time events (called *extraordinary items*) or its investments in securities. This is important because firms have relatively more control over their operations, and knowing how profitable these operations are gives management feedback it can use to improve operations. Several of these alternative measures of profit are discussed next.

GROSS PROFIT

Gross profit is sales less cost of goods sold. This measures the contribution that sales themselves make to the firm's bottom line. Cost of goods sold includes materials cost and labor, and is the variable cost associated with sales; thus gross profit measures the contribution that sales make to covering all the overhead, administrative, and financing expenses that the company incurs.

OPERATING PROFIT, OR NET OPERATING PROFIT AFTER TAXES (NOPAT)

It is often convenient to differentiate between a firm's operations and its other activities. For a manufacturing firm,

operations consists of selling activities, manufacturing, investing in plant and equipment, and the like. A large manufacturing firm may also have other activities in which it engages that are ancillary to its line of business. For example, the firm may own marketable securities from which it receives interest or dividends, or it may have a partially owned subsidiary that engages in some completely different line of business. Finally, the firm may own real estate that it is holding for speculative purposes rather than for use in future expansions. These assets are called *nonoperating assets* and any income that they generate is called *nonoperating income.* Along the same lines, a firm's interest payments depend not on how it operates, but on how it is financed, so interest expense is a nonoperating expense. Operating profit, then, is the profit derived from these core operations, and omits such things as interest income, interest expense, and any other nonoperating income. Based on the sample income statement in Figure 1, operating profit is calculated as earnings before interest and taxes (EBIT) minus taxes on EBIT. Of course, there is no separate entry on the income statement for taxes on EBIT; the reported taxes figure is the taxes on all the pretax income, including nonoperating sources of income, so the analyst or investor has to figure out how much taxes the firm would owe only on EBIT. As a rough cut, the taxes on EBIT can be approximated as EBIT multiplied by the tax rate, T. So as a rough cut, operating profit can be approximated by $EBIT \times (1 - T)$.

EARNINGS BEFORE INTEREST, TAXES, DEPRECIATION, AND AMORTIZATION (EBITDA)

EBITDA (earnings before interest, taxes, depreciation, and amortization) is another commonly reported measure of pretax profitability. It is calculated by adding back depreciation and amortization charges to EBIT. Because depreciation and amortization are noncash expenses (the company doesn't really have to write a check for these charges), adding them back gives a measure of the cash that the company generates from operations, before paying taxes. This is important because even a company that reports zero EBIT, or even negative EBIT, may still be generating plenty of cash if it depreciating many assets. And this cash, less any taxes to be paid, is available for reinvestment in the firm or distribution to shareholders.

NET CASH FLOW

Net cash flow is calculated as net income plus depreciation, amortization, and any other noncash expenses, and minus any noncash revenues that were included in net income. Net cash flow, like EBITDA, measures cash the firm generates but also subtracts the taxes it pays.

FREE CASH FLOW

Free cash flow is probably the most useful of all of the measures of profitability. The measures of profitability just discussed do not take into account the fact that firm must invest in operating assets if it is to continue to grow. Although investment in assets isn't an expense, it does require cash, and the cash that is used for investment within the company cannot be used for other purposes, such as paying interest or dividends. Free cash flow takes this required reinvestment into account. Free cash flow is calculated as net operating profit after taxes (NOPAT) less any required net reinvestment in operating assets. As in the calculation of NOPAT, there is no line item on the income statement or balance sheet that reports "required net reinvestment in operating assets." The analyst must calculate this as the increase in net operating assets during the year. Rapidly growing firms often have negative free cash flows during the early years, even if net income is positive, because of the huge investment in assets that growing firms often require. However, once growth slows and the required investment in assets subsides, then the firm can generate positive free cash flows.

A picture is worth a thousand words, and an accounting equation is worth two thousand words. Here is an accounting equation that shows the hierarchy of expenses when constructing various profitability measures.

Equation 1: Operating Profit (NOPAT) Calculation

EBIT
− Taxes on EBIT

= NOPAT

Equation 2: EBITDA Calculation

Earnings before deducting interest and taxes (EBIT)
+ Depreciation and Amortization

= EBITDA

Equation 3: Net Cash Flow Calculation

Net income after deducting extraordinary items
− Noncash revenue
+ Depreciation and amortization

= Net cash flow

Equation 4: Free Cash Flow Calculation

NOPAT
− Net required reinvestment in operating assets

= Free cash flow

—Phillip Daves

FURTHER READING

Brigham, E. F., & Daves, P. R. (2002). *Intermediate financial management* (7th ed.). Mason, OH: South-Western.

PROFIT SHARING

Profit sharing is a performance incentive plan that distributes a fixed percentage of an organization's pretax profits to qualified employees. According to a 2001 survey by *Medical Economics,* 30% of physicians in the United States participate in a profit-sharing plan. The goal of profit sharing is to focus workers on a company's profitability and to link their performance to the company's goals. The amount an employee receives is based on salary (for example, 6% of annual pay), position in the company (such as partner or staff member), or on a combination of these and other variables. Payouts can take the form of cash given directly to employees or of deferred compensation via a retirement account. In general, companies use standard accounting metrics (such as net income, return on equity, earnings per share) to measure profitability. However, other longer-term strategic metrics are gaining in popularity, most notably the "balanced scorecard" approach, which tracks data from financial, customer, growth, and internal process goals to assess success of an organization.

Profit-sharing plans work best when a company is stable and profitable, when employees perceive their efforts have an impact on organizational goals, and when incentives based on individual merit are also included in the overall compensation package. In addition, payouts should not become an expectation of employees; expectation not only reduces the motivating force of profit sharing but also may cause significant backlash if a company reduces or stops sharing profits because of economic hardships. Implemented thoughtfully, profit-sharing plans can be a powerful tool for retaining not only doctors but also nurses, billing staff, and other vital employees.

Profit-sharing plans must comply with complex federal tax codes and labor laws. An accountant or other individual with expertise in this area should review all components of any profit-sharing plan.

—E. Kate Atchley

See also Balanced Scorecard and Health Care, Employee Compensation, Incentive Pay

FURTHER READING

Allen, E. T., Jr., Melone, J. J., & Rosenbloom, J. S. (1997). *Pension planning: Pensions, profit-sharing, and other deferred compensation plans.* New York: McGraw-Hill.

Berger, L. A., & Berger, D. R. (1999). *The compensation handbook* (4th ed.). New York: McGraw-Hill.

Burg, B. Young doctors face a steep climb. *Medical Economics, 78*(16), 82–84, 89–90, 93.

Kaplan, R. S., & Norton, D. P. (1996). *The balanced scorecard: Translating strategy into action.* Boston: Harvard Business School Press.

PROGRAM EVALUATION

See Balanced Scorecard and Health Care

PROGRAM EVALUATION AND REVIEW TECHNIQUE (PERT) AND PROJECT MANAGEMENT

Program Evaluation and Review Technique (PERT) is a project management tool that was introduced and developed by the Navy in the 1950s to analyze and control the large number of activities involved in complex projects. It is a powerful tool that lays out all tasks involved in the project in a graphic form. It helps the project manager identify the critical activities that need to be closely monitored if the project is to be completed on time. PERT also identifies what activities are noncritical, namely activities that could be delayed without affecting the completion time of the entire project. Software tools available for project management include Microsoft Project and PERT Chart Expert.

At the heart of a PERT analysis is the PERT chart, which visually depicts the tasks in the project, their task times, and the order in which the tasks should be completed. The chart starts with an initiation node from which the first task (or set of tasks) originates and ends with a completion node, which signifies the completion of all tasks in the project. The nodes in PERT depict events in the project. More specifically, they represent the start or the completion of one or more tasks. A task is represented by a directed arrow that starts from one node and ends on another. The description of the task, and the task time, is typically placed above the arrow representing the task. Each task is connected to its succeeding task in this manner, resulting in a network of nodes and arrows, clearly establishing the precedence structure among the tasks and their task dependencies. Determining task times can pose challenges, especially because PERT charts are used for unique projects that typically have not been undertaken before. Typically, for each task the analyst estimates the *best* time, the *worst* time, and the *most likely* time, and computes a weighted average task time in which the best and worst times have a weight of 1 and the most likely time has a weight of 4.

Once the PERT chart is complete, the analysis determines the *critical path,* which is the sequence of tasks that determine when project completion is expected (the critical tasks). Any delay in completion time of a critical task delays project completion time, so there is no "slack" for any of these tasks. Therefore, the project manager has to monitor these tasks very carefully. All tasks *not* on the critical path, by definition, have some degree of slack. For each

task in the network, PERT provides four values—an earliest start time, an earliest finish time, a latest start time, and a latest finish time. These times, which have the obvious meanings, define how much slack time is present in any of the noncritical activities. For the critical activities, the earliest and latest start times are the same, and the earliest and latest finish times are the same. All these times are deterministic estimates. To model randomness, more sophisticated techniques often consider the standard deviation of task times in the analysis.

—M.M. Srinavasan

PROGRESSIVE DISCIPLINE SYSTEM

A progressive discipline system is the set of successive consequences administered to redirect employee behavior after a violation of work policy or procedure. Organizations using such systems often respond to misconduct initially with some minimal warning, followed by more severe punishments up to and including termination or discharge. An example of a progressive disciplinary program is outlined as follows:

- Verbal warning
- Written warning copied to supervisor's file
- Written warning copied to human resources (HR) department file
- Suspension or demotion
- Termination

Using a progressive approach has two main purposes. First, progressive discipline is a logical and structured way to document infractions. Over time, undesired worker behavior may necessitate weighty human resource decisions such as total compensation decreases, demotions, and termination. Having appropriate documentation in place increases the fairness of these types of actions while protecting the organization from wrongful termination lawsuits. Second, when executed correctly, progressive discipline is effective in extinguishing unwanted behavior through the set of processes implicated in reinforcement theories of motivation. To avoid the negative outcome of the discipline procedures, employees will likely refrain from behavior that they know leads to disciplinary action.

PROGRESSIVE DISCIPLINE SYSTEM POLICY

After putting a general progression of disciplinary actions in place, organizational leaders must then determine the appropriate starting point along the continuum given the severity of each specific violation of policy. To do this, categories of infractions are often created. Each category is associated with a different progression along the discipline continuum. Minor, correctable infractions, such as lateness and absenteeism, lend themselves readily to a multiple-step, progressive discipline approach. A verbal warning is an acceptable consequence for the first incident of lateness. In contrast, severe infractions, such as stealing large amounts of money from operating funds or divulging confidential patient information, can lead to more serious consequences such as immediate termination, and even the pressing of criminal charges. Clearly, severe misconduct should not be handled merely with a verbal warning. A third category of significant but not severe infractions, such as inadvertently misfiling insurance claims, may be disciplined with a written warning as a first step. Progressive discipline steps for each category of infraction should be outlined in an employee handbook.

Any discipline policy should also allow for exemption from progressive discipline if there are mitigating circumstances. Disciplining employees despite such circumstances undoubtedly creates feelings of unfairness and resentment. For instance, accidents and emergencies may be the cause of lateness, absenteeism, or personal use of the company telephone. Alternatively, employees may disclose a medical reason for the infraction. If a medical disclosure is made, a lawyer or HR specialist should be consulted to determine the Americans with Disabilities Act or Family Medical Leave Act implications of the matter.

USING A PROGRESSIVE DISCIPLINE SYSTEM

Before any discipline takes place, an investigation should be launched to find the causes for the employee's errant behavior, to be sure the employee is to blame. In courts of law, organizations are held responsible for having made a thorough investigation. Employees terminated for behavior that either never occurred or was uncontrollable have won large settlements against former employers.

When the employee is clearly to blame, a causal analysis should be conducted to determine the best tactics for preventing the misconduct in the future. Briefly, one should determine if the problem resulted from misunderstanding, lack of knowledge, or motivation. If an employee does not *understand* why his or her behavior was inappropriate, the best course of action is to communicate with the employee in addition to or instead of discipline. If the employee does not *know how* to perform properly, training may be necessary in addition to or instead of discipline. Finally, if the employee is not *motivated* to perform correctly, systems or cultural issues may be partially to blame. Motivation issues may be the hardest to address through disciplinary procedures, but cases of misconduct are a good opportunity to examine motivational factors in the workplace.

Provided the investigation conclusively indicates that discipline is warranted, enforcement is imperative. Ignoring

employee misconduct allows problem employees to perform at a level of decreased productivity and efficiency. Moreover, failing to use progressive discipline may also have undesirable, yet indirect effects. Managers can easily lose credibility in the eyes of other employees if they do not carry out established policies and procedures. Furthermore, the morale of the entire team may suffer when one employee does not carry his or her own weight. Employees are often more sensitive to these issues than most managers think; many employees become disgruntled and leave organizations because they don't see problems being appropriately handled by their managers.

Research provides several other suggestions for successful execution of a progressive discipline system. Discipline should focus on one specific behavior, not on a pattern of behavior. If a pattern of behavior develops, managers have not been using the progressive discipline system appropriately. Discipline should also be administered by someone the employee trusts and respects. Likewise, the manager administering the punishment should maintain his or her credibility by enforcing the rules and by refraining from rewarding the employee to overcome any guilt for having to administer discipline. Finally, progressive discipline should also be provided consistently across time, people, and situations. If the progressive discipline system changes in any way, policy and procedure manuals and other materials should be updated to reflect the modifications.

PROPER USES OF PROGRESSIVE DISCIPLINE

Discipline discourages unwanted behavior and should be used only to extinguish unacceptable behaviors such as insubordination, lackluster productivity, or policy violation. Although the use of discipline is an effective motivational technique for helping employees reach an acceptable level of behavior, exceptional performance cannot be attained using discipline. Rather, rewarding employees is the means by which a manager can encourage performance above an acceptable level. Therefore, it is important that managers use discipline when it is warranted, but capitalize on other motivational techniques when encouraging merely acceptable performers to become outstanding ones.

—Jennifer R. D. Burgess

See also Americans with Disabilities Act (ADA) of 1990, Family and Medical Leave Act (FMLA), Motivating Employees, Organizational Behavior Management (OBM)

FURTHER READING

Bernardin, H. J., & Russell, J. E. A. (2002). *Human resource management* (3rd ed.). Boston: Irwin McGraw Hill.

Fisher, C. D., Schoenfeldt, L. F., & Shaw, J. B. (1999). *Human resource management* (4th ed.). Boston: Houghton Mifflin.

Latack, J. C., & Kaufman, H. G. (1988). Termination and outplacement strategies. In M. London & E. M. Mone (Eds.), *Career growth and human resource strategies.* New York: Quorum Books.

Mitchell, T., & O'Reilly, C. (1983). Managing poor performance and productivity in organizations. *Research in Organizational Behavior, 1,* 201–234.

Raines, C. (1997). *Beyond Generation X: A practical guide for managers.* Menlo Park, CA: Crisp Publications.

Whetton, D. A., & Cameron, K. S. (2001). *Developing management skills.* New York: HarperCollins.

PROSPECTIVE PAYMENT SYSTEM

In 1983, the U.S. federal government initiated a new method of payment for Medicare hospital services. The prospective payment system (PPS) created a reimbursement mechanism in which scientifically clustered diagnoses known as diagnosis-related groups (DRGs) would have predetermined compensation amounts, regardless of the hospitals' actual costs. The concept of DRGs was created by a group at Yale University in the 1970s and adopted by Medicare for the prospective payment system for hospital inpatient services. Medicare pays physicians using a modified fee-for-service system based on a resource-based relative value scale (RBRVS).

Each year the Center for Medicare and Medicaid Services (CMS, formerly the Health Care Financing Administration, or HCFA) determines hospital Medicare reimbursement based on DRGs. Since 1983, CMS has instituted a PPS for home health care, skilled nursing facilities, and outpatient care.

The PPS for hospital inpatient services has served as a model for all the other types of services that CMS currently pays through the PPS. The payment cycle can be described as follows:

1. Hospitals submit a bill for each Medicare patient they treat to their Medicare fiscal intermediary (a private insurance company that contracts with Medicare to carry out the operational functions of the Medicare program). Based on the information provided on the bill, the case is categorized into a diagnosis-related group (DRG), which determines how much payment the hospital receives. Most hospitals have software in their billing systems that optimize DRG classifications for maximum reimbursement.

2. The base payment rate is composed of a standardized amount, which is divided into amounts that are labor related and those that are not. The labor-related amount is adjusted by the hospital's local wage index. Hospitals in Alaska and Hawaii also receive an adjustment for cost of living. The base payment rate is then multiplied by the DRG relative weight to arrive at a DRG-adjusted base payment rate.

3. If the hospital cares for a disproportionate share (DPS) of low-income patients, it receives an additional amount for each case paid through the PPS, depending on the percentage of low-income patients served. The DPS factor is then applied to the DRG-adjusted base payment rate and any outlier payments received for services not meeting DRG criteria, such as catastrophic cases that generated costs outside the limits of the DRG.

4. Teaching hospitals receive a percentage add-on payment for each PPS case, depending on the ratio of residents to beds.

5. The hospital's costs for the case are evaluated to determine whether the case qualifies as an outlier. In the event that the case does meet the criteria as an outlier, an additional payment may be provided to protect the hospital from serious financial losses from unusually expensive cases. The outlier payment is added on to the DRG-adjusted base payment rate generated in the second step of the payment calculation.

6. The costs for each case are then summed to calculate the total payment due the hospital.

Several costs are excluded from PPS reimbursement. For example, direct costs of medical education for interns and residents are reimbursed to teaching hospitals based on a fixed amount per resident. In addition, bad debts from failure of patients to pay Medicare deductible and coinsurance amounts are reimbursed, but only at a rate that reasonably compensates the hospital for its costs. Finally, organ procurement costs at transplant facilities are also reimbursed separately.

Elements of a PPS payment thus include the following:

- Base payment amounts, fixed for each DRG and determined each year
- A wage index to account for local labor costs
- DRG relative weights, designed to adjust for case mix
- DPS payment
- Medical education payment
- Payment for outliers

The base payment amounts have been adjusted each year using an update factor since 1981 to account for differences in case mix, wage rate inflation, disproportionate share, and payments received for medical education. Update factors are set by Congress to account for annual inflation while maintaining incentives for hospitals to be efficient. There are currently two separate standardized amounts: hospitals in large urban areas (population over 1 million) and all other hospitals. These base payment amounts serve as the basis of payment for every fee for service Medicare discharge from an acute care hospital.

Ambulatory hospital services have also been converted to a PPS through the Balanced Budget Refinement Act of 1999 (BBRA). All services paid under the new PPS are classified into groups called ambulatory payment classifications, or APCs. Using methodology similar to that for creating DRGs, services assigned to each APC are similar clinically and in terms of resource requirements. A payment rate is established for each APC, as are coinsurance amounts, and the payments are adjusted for geographic wage differences using the hospital wage index. Similarly, home health services, hospice, rehabilitation services, and long-term care facilities have been converted to a Medicare PPS.

The effectiveness of the PPS in limiting Medicare cost escalation prompted many commercial insurers to adopt similar payment strategies. These payment methods either mimicked that of Medicare or provided a fixed amount per day (per diem amount), with only minor adjustments for severity or complexity of a case. Per diem reimbursement can vary by type of service, such as medical, surgical, or intensive care, and frequently vary with type of hospital (urban versus rural, teaching versus community). The effect of limited reimbursement in both the commercial and government sectors has created difficult financial circumstances for many hospitals in the United States. Faced with rising costs for labor and pharmaceuticals, many hospitals have been forced to delay additions of capital equipment to remain current with medical technology.

The 1983 revolution in Medicare reimbursement known as PPS has changed the health care delivery system in the United States. As commercial payers adopt the same methods of reimbursement, funds available to hospitals for expansion and updating capital equipment have nearly disappeared, but the health care delivery system has become much leaner and more efficient.

—Donald E. Lighter

FURTHER READING

Carter, G. (Ed.). (2002). *Analyses for the initial implementation of the inpatient rehabilitation facility prospective payment system.* Santa Monica, CA: Rand.

Congressional Office of Technology Assessment. (1986). *Medicare's prospective payment system.* New York: Springer.

Garg, M., & Barzansky, B. (Eds.). (1986). *The Medicare system of prospective payment: Implications for medical education and practice.* New York: Praeger.

Goldfield, N., & Kelly, W. (Eds.). (1999). *Ambulatory care services and the prospective payment system.* Gaithersburg, MD: Aspen. http://cms.hhs.gov/hcprofessionals/payment.asp

Stewart, M. (2001). *Coding and reimbursement under the outpatient prospective payment system.* Chicago: American Health Information Management Association.

PROTOCOL (INVOLVING HUMAN SUBJECTS)

For a research activity involving human subjects to be conducted at an institution, a submission must be made to its institutional review board (IRB) for review and approval. The documents reviewed include the local application, the investigator's brochure (for experimental drug or device research), applicable consent documents, any recruitment tools (such as advertisements) proposed for use, and a detailed research protocol.

General scientific protocols include the background, aims, and actual procedures to be employed to answer the scientific hypothesis in question. However, when humans are proposed as subjects to be enrolled in the research, specific federally mandated criteria must be met for a study to be granted approval. To meet most of these criteria, a protocol involving human subjects must *additionally* contain information about foreseeable risks and (therapeutic) benefits to the subject, inclusion and exclusion criteria, provisions for protecting privacy of subjects and confidentiality of the subject's data, plans for safety monitoring, and additional protections for subjects who may be considered vulnerable to coercion or undue influence.

The protocol's description of foreseeable risk and benefit is critical in the assessment of whether or not a study may be approved by an IRB. The IRB is federally mandated to ensure that a protocol's risks are reasonable in relation to anticipated benefits. The review of inclusion and exclusion criteria helps an IRB meet its ethical and legal obligation to ensure that the selection of subjects is fair, given the purpose of the research.

The protocol details concerning purpose, research procedures, risks, benefit, and so on must be accurately presented in the research consent form that is used to enroll subjects into the study. The consent form, unlike the protocol, must be written in lay terminology to ensure readability by subjects; it also includes details concerning the subjects' rights as a participant, including the right to refuse participation and the right to withdraw from the research without affecting the subject's status at the institution.

—Judy Matuk

See also Institutional Review Board (IRB)

FURTHER READING

www.access.gpo.gov/nara/cfr/waisidx_99/45cfr46_99.html

PROVIDER

In the health care context, a provider is a health care professional who acts at the interface between a patient (customer) and the health care delivery system. Providers can have many different faces, from the physician who serves to direct the overall care of a patient to nurses who make sure that specific elements of care are delivered, to professionals, such as physical therapists, who treat a specific portion of a patient's clinical condition. Thus *health care provider* is a generic term for any health care professional in the system who interacts with patients to improve their health.

Health care providers are usually divided into primary care providers (PCPs) and specialty care providers (SCPs). Primary care services involve a number of health maintenance and preventive activities:

- Routine health maintenance checkups
- Immunizations
- Treatment of common illnesses, such as respiratory and digestive disorders
- Caring for psychosocial needs
- Counseling on good health practices
- Nutritional counseling

As with any health care professional, PCPs must be especially attuned to the psychosocial situation of each individual to better customize medical care. Physician specialties devoted to primary care include pediatrics, internal medicine, and family practice. Some experts also include obstetrics and gynecology as a primary care specialty, because these practitioners frequently assume responsibility for the primary care of women. Other health professionals may also provide primary care services, including advanced practice nurses, home health nurses, school nurses, and parish nurses (affiliated with religious institutions). The degree to which these professionals may engage in providing independent services varies according to licensing requirements and community practices.

Specialty care providers include practitioners who focus on one aspect of patient care. SCPs are generally divided into medical specialists and surgical specialists. Most medical SCPs in the U.S. health care system tend to focus on one organ system, such as neurology, which concentrates on diseases of the brain and nervous system, or pulmonology, which focuses on disorders of the lungs. Surgical SCPs specialize in types of procedures. For example, cardiothoracic surgeons perform surgical procedures on the chest, heart, and lungs; or neurosurgeons perform operations on the brain and spinal cord. Although most surgical specialty providers are physicians, some do not have traditional medical training, such as podiatrists, who operate on feet.

Nontraditional providers include those who practice complementary and alternative medicine. These approaches to health care vary considerably in efficacy and include such modalities as acupuncture, acupressure, chiropractic, biofeedback, energy healing, herbal medicine, massage therapy, homeopathy, reflexology, and a host of others.

—Donald E. Lighter

FURTHER READING

www.aap.org
www.aaos.org
www.abms.org
www.acog.org
www.acponline.org
www.ama-assn.org
www.aoa-net.org
www.facs.org
www.fda.gov/oashi/aids/fdaguide.html
www.thoracic.org

PROVIDER-SPONSORED ORGANIZATION (PSO)

A provider-sponsored organization (as defined by the Balanced Budget Act of 1997) is a public or private managed care contracting and health care delivery organization that is owned and governed by health care providers, and accepts full risk for beneficiary lives. The PSO receives a fixed monthly payment to provide care for Medicare beneficiaries.

A PSO must supply all medical services required by Medicare law and must do so primarily through its network. A PSO's providers must deliver at least 70% of the full range of services; the remainder may come from contracts with other providers. PSOs contract with the Centers for Medicare and Medicaid Services (CMS) to deliver the scope of services normally provided under Medicare Part A and Part B in return for a fixed payment. PSOs may be for profit or not-for-profit; however, 51% must be owned and governed by health care providers (physicians, hospitals, allied health professionals).

The concept of PSOs emerged in the 1980s, as a response to the need to cut health care costs. In 1989, the National Health Policy Council recommended the development of "provider-owned accountable healthcare plans," that could directly contract with employers. The language "provider-sponsored network" was first used in policy language in 1995 and included in the "Medicare + Choice" provision of the BBA of 1997.

Two rule changes were enacted to help reduce the entry barriers faced by providers who wanted to contract directly for Medicare-risk lives. These include the elimination of the 50/50 rule requiring Medicare risk plans to maintain at least 50% commercial membership, and a potential waiver of the requirement that PSOs obtain a state license.

PSOs have been criticized as creating conflicts of interest, as providers desire to maximize the earnings from the plan and the PSOs need to be competitive in the marketplace, achieve cost control, and maintain the PSO operations.

—Donald Levick

FURTHER READING

HCFA releases regulations on PSO definitions. (1998, June 1). *MGM Update, 37*(11).

Hull, B. (1998, September 15). PSOs—Big opportunities, big risks. *MGM Update, 37*(18).

McDaniel, R. D., Jr. (1999, May–June). Is a PSO right for you? *MGM Journal, 46*(3).

www.aasha.org

PSYCHIATRIC CENTERS

Psychiatric centers fill the sensitivity, support, and security needs of the mentally ill population and their families and caregivers, optimally in a well-designed and up-to-date psychiatric facility. In meeting the determinable needs of the patients (clients), their specific type must be identified (for example, adults, children, or adolescents). The types of conditions the facility is able to treat or renowned for treating is also identified or identifiable (for example, psychosis, substance abuse, personality disorders, "locked unit" patients). The types of patients with their different treatment modalities have a clear delineation of separation in their treatment regimens. All the preceding defines the design and type of psychiatric center. There are many additional facets of psychiatric centers. Some psychiatric centers are so-called centers of excellence and are usually associated with universities affiliated with a medical school. These are also known as *tertiary* or *consultative facilities*. These facilities are often centrally located and regional. Large metropolitan areas can more easily support these types of facilities with the volumes of patients and the appropriate funding needed. Several types of psychiatric centers are inpatient units (open or voluntary, closed or involuntary), outpatient facilities, community mental health centers, private clinics, hospital clinics, intensive outpatient (more intensive outpatient care), partial hospital programs, and incarceration (prison) facilities. Crisis intervention or screening centers often are the "stepping stones" before admission or treatment at psychiatric centers.

There are multiple funding sources for mental health care at psychiatric centers in the United States. The federal government, through its Veterans Administration systems, Medicare, and various disability programs, along with the sovereign state where the facility is located, is a large provider for the cost of care and treatment at psychiatric centers in the United States. Other funding sources for psychiatric centers are private insurance plans such as Blue Cross/Blue Shield, Aetna Insurance, Prudential Insurance, and so on. Managed care has had a tremendous impact on the funding for the care and treatment at psychiatric centers. Counties and states have continued to look for ways to minimize the costs necessary to provide mental health services at psychiatric centers. They have been turning to managed care organizations (MCOs) to replace the relatively more expensive fee-for-service arrangements at psychiatric centers. A recent survey conducted by the National Alliance for the Mentally Ill (NAMI) stated that the managed care industry has not been successful in providing adequate treatment to the seriously mentally ill at psychiatric enters.

Psychiatric centers provide treatment and care that is provided in accordance with the current standards of professional care outlined by the appropriate accreditation and licensing authority whose jurisdiction it is under (depending on the state, county, country, or territory). Another consideration is based on whether the standards are governed by the Joint Commission on Accreditation of Healthcare Organizations or not. Other governing bodies or licensing bodies can sometimes have jurisdiction over psychiatric centers (for example, medical school or health care organizations). The patient (consumer and client) must not be lost in the maze.

—Richard A. Robin

FURTHER READING

www.NMHA.org

PSYCHIATRY

See Psychiatric Centers

PSYCHOGRAPHIC SEGMENTATION

See Market Segmentation

PSYCHOLOGICAL CONTRACT

The term *psychological contract* is the term used to describe each employee's understanding of what he or she is to provide the organization (such as hard work, effort, loyalty) and what the organization is to provide in return (such as pay, benefits, job security). Unlike a written or explicit contract, psychological contracts are perceptions or understandings on the part of the individual; each individual has his or her own psychological contract, and the contract may vary greatly from person to person.

Functionally, psychological contracts accomplish three things. First, they reduce uncertainty. Believing one has an agreement with one's employer (whether accurate or not) increases one's feelings of security and assurance. Second, psychological contracts guide behavior at work; the worker will accomplish those things for which he or she feels obligated without having to be constantly monitored by a superior. Last, a psychological contract provides a sense of control in that the individual believes that he or she has "agreed" on its terms.

Despite the idiosyncratic nature of the psychological contract, it is assumed that people form one of two general types of contracts: relational or transactional. Relational psychological contracts are long-term, often very subjective agreements that entail such exchanges as company loyalty on the part of the employee in return for job security provided by the organization. Because of the long-time horizon of the relational psychological contract, the exchanges between organization and employee may not be immediate. For instance, an employee may stay late to accomplish an important company objective, not expecting to be "repaid" for his or her work immediately. By extension, the relational psychological contract is very flexible; employees feel comfortable accomplishing any number of tasks without the expectation of immediate reward or recognition. Because of this flexibility, relational contracts are typically desired by organizations.

Transactional contracts, in contrast, are very short term in nature, observable or objective, and typically based on very extrinsic exchanges. The worker may wish to exchange only the work outlined in his or her job description for a paycheck and benefits. In the transactional contract, then, exchanges are immediate. For instance, one expects to be paid in a reasonable time frame after the work is completed; in most organizations, paychecks are distributed roughly every two weeks. Likewise, workers with transactional contracts often do not put forth effort that is not likely to be immediately or tangibly rewarded. In sum, immediate reciprocity is desired by those holding transactional psychological contracts.

Although they are purely perceptual, it is important that psychological contracts are at least somewhat accurate when compared with the objective contributions expected from the employee and the objective inducements provided by the organization. Psychological contracts operate in similar ways to promises or obligations. If they are fulfilled in the individual's eyes, positive outcomes result. Job satisfaction and "going that extra mile" are associated with contract fulfillment. Likewise, unfulfilled or violated contracts may have negative results. Employees who feel as if the contract has been violated may exhibit negative attitude changes, a reduction in performance, turnover, and other withdrawal behaviors. It becomes important, then, for employers to be aware of, and to some extent manage, the psychological contracts that employees may hold. Helping employees create realistic psychological contracts lessens the likelihood that the individual will perceive the contract to be broken.

Psychological contracts are partially formulated and then reinforced based on messages received from the organization. The organization's mission and vision, policies and procedures, and the variety of messages sent by supervisors and peers may contribute to an individual's psychological contract. For instance, organizational practices such as the presence of internal career ladders may include implicit promises about the promotional rewards to be received if the employee completes training or a certain set of assignments. Policy and procedure manuals may outline the conditions for probationary employment, performance standards, and the infractions for which employees can be disciplined. Finally, managers or peers may make promises and communicate expectations to employees that help in the formulation of a new contract or the reinforcement of an existing one.

The other major force in creating a psychological contract consists of the individual's own personality, goals, and work experiences. These personal characteristics are the lenses through which individuals see the objective information in the environment. In other words, what a person expects may be due in large part to what he or she has experienced. Thus, if someone has aspirations of creating a long-term relationship in an organization, he or she may frame information received in such a way as to form a relational psychological contract. Likewise, if someone believes strongly in a fair day's pay for a fair day's work, he or she may form a more transactional contract.

Collectively, individuals' psychological contracts are changing such that they may be harder to manage and control. In the past, companies were readily able to provide job security in return for loyalty, initiating the more desirable relational contract, but because of downsizing and pressures for short-term results few promises for long-term employment still stand. Moreover, owing to the flattening of organizational charts, or the removal of many layers of management, organizations can no longer promise promotions and career paths for workers. In response to these organizational trends, workers have come to expect different things from organizations. Individuals now demand challenging work, developmental experiences, and training that can be transferred to other organizations. These desires are often termed "employability," because they allow the worker to maintain his or her skills such that when a downsizing occurs, the worker is marketable. In return, these workers provide hard work and creativity to the organization, but not loyalty. In other words, they will leave the organization if better opportunities exist elsewhere. This presents challenges for organizations in that the best way to attract this type of worker is by offering training, but the training that is offered makes them marketable for any number of positions they may wish to pursue.

—Jennifer R. D. Burgess

See also Organizational Behavior Management, Structure

FURTHER READING

Cavanaugh, M. A., & Noe, R. A. (1999). Antecedents and consequences of relational components of the new psychological contract. *Journal of Organizational Behavior, 20,* 323–340.

Ehrlich, C. J. (1994). Creating an employer–employee relationship for the future. *Human Resource Management, 33,* 491–501.

Rousseau, D. M. (1995). *Psychological Contracts in Organizations.* Thousand Oaks, CA: Sage.

Rousseau, D. M. (2001). The idiosyncratic deal: Flexibility versus fairness? *Organizational Dynamics, 29*(4), 260–273.

Rousseau, D. M., & Greller, M. M. (1994). Human resource practices: Administrative contract makers. *Human Resource Management, 33,* 385–401.

Shore, L. M., & Tetrick, L. E. (1994). The psychological contract as an explanatory framework in the employment relationship. *Trends in Organizational Behavior, 1,* 91–109.

Spindler, G. S. (1994). Psychological contracts in the workplace— A lawyer's view. *Human Resource Management, 33,* 325–333.

PUBLIC ASSISTANCE AND HEALTH INSURANCE

See Access

PUBLIC GOODS

A distinguishing feature of public goods is "nonexclusivity," that is, the marginal cost of accessing public goods is negligible. National defense illustrates this concept. If one offers national defense to an individual, then excluding, say, that individual's next-door neighbor from recognizing

associated benefits would indeed be difficult. Because the marginal cost of accessing goods such as national defense is so small, excluding individuals from recognizing the consequent benefits (or costs) can be prohibitively difficult. Such goods are thus referred to as being "public."

Nonexclusivity makes producing public goods problematic. Continuing the present example, notice that each neighbor has little incentive to contribute to the production of defense. The first neighbor realizes that, because defense is nonexclusive, he or she can consume all of the neighbor's defense and avoid any of the production costs. Recognizing this opportunity to "free ride" off of the neighbor's efforts, the first neighbor will tend to exert less effort toward producing defense than he or she would have if defense was a "private good" (that is, if defense benefits accrued solely to those who contributed to their production).

Nothing is special about the example's first neighbor, however: A symmetric opportunity to free-ride also confronts the second neighbor. As a consequence, each neighbor simultaneously has an incentive to free-ride off the other. Given such incentives, the neighbors may produce *no* defense jointly, even if each would have produced defense if the associated benefits were exclusive.

Both individuals would be better off contributing to the public good's production, but each is unwilling to do so without a mechanism that precludes the choice of opportunistic actions (that is, actions that increase individual welfare but decrease social welfare). This type of argument is frequently cited to rationalize private and public governance structures. Absent such authorities, individuals are reluctant to expose themselves to the type of opportunism that the defense production example illustrates. As such, they may forgo transactions that, in the presence of an appropriate enforcement mechanism, would be mutually beneficial.

Rules such as patent laws can be understood in this context. Consider, for example, the case of knowledge production. Just as excluding individuals from consuming defense benefits is difficult, so is excluding individuals from consuming benefits that emerge from producing knowledge. Recognizing that knowledge exhibits this property of public goods, individuals have an incentive to free-ride off others' knowledge production. The consequence here, however, parallels that from the defense example; that is, unconstrained individuals produce inferior levels of knowledge.

Institutions such as patent laws can check this difficulty. In effect, patents increase the cost of consuming others' production of knowledge. By "excluding" others from such consumption, patents thus transform what would otherwise be a public good into one that produces sufficient private benefits. To the extent that they make the product of knowledge investments costly to expropriate, patent laws thus facilitate endeavors such as pharmaceutical research and development.

—Dino Falaschetti

FURTHER READING

Bernanke, B., & Frank, R. (2001). *Principles of economics.* New York: McGraw-Hill.

Hirshleifer, J., & Glazer, A. (1992). *Price theory and applications* (5th ed.). Upper Saddle River, NJ: Prentice Hall.

Stigler, G. J. (1987). *The theory of price* (4th ed.). New York: Macmillan.

PUBLIC HEALTH

THE U.S. PUBLIC HEALTH SYSTEM

In 1988 the Institute of Medicine, as part of a landmark study *The Future of Public Health,* defined the mission of public health as "fulfilling society's interest in assuring conditions in which people can be healthy."[1] Within this mission, the primary business of the U.S. Public Health Service is prevention. Prevention can be defined as activities that reduce the incidence, prevalence, and burden of disease and injury and enhance (or preserve) health by improving physical, social, and mental well-being. Basic prevention activities can be classified as health promotion—activities involving personal health behaviors that maintain good health, such as smoking cessation programs; health protection—activities to change the social or physical environment in order to restrict personal exposures to known risk factors, such as highway safety programs; and clinical health services—such as vaccinations, delivered in a clinical setting to prevent the onset or progression of specific diseases. This entry describes the complex system of federal, state, and local agencies that form the basis for governmental involvement in organized community efforts for prevention.

Governmental involvement in organized community effort is the essence of what differentiates preventive activities in the context of public health from prevention in the context of medical care. This is important because it limits this discussion to public health activity within the purview of government. Many voluntary and nongovernmental organizations participate in activities related to public health. However, this entry deals only with governmental public health.

A BRIEF HISTORY OF GOVERNMENTAL PUBLIC HEALTH

Given that our focus is public health as government effort, it is appropriate to begin by pointing out that the origins of public health activity coincide with the evolution of human communities. George Rosen, in his well-known *History of Public Health,* originally published in 1958, begins by stating, "Throughout human history, the major problems of health that men faced have been concerned with community life. . . . Evidence of activity connected with community health has been found in the very earliest civilizations."[2] Clearly, the Old Testament book of Leviticus, deals with defilement, uncleanness, and isolation from the community to prevent the spread of contamination. Many scholars consider such contamination to be contamination for ritualistic purposes and not for medical or health promotion reasons. However, it is clear that these biblical writings, no matter their original purpose, did become the basis for some very early forms of community health promotion and health education.

An example of the biblical origins of some public health promotion activities can be found in the emergence of quarantine for Hansen's disease. A skin condition designated as *tzara'at* in Leviticus is a reason prescribed for isolation. *Tzara'at* is rendered in Greek translations of the Old Testament as "lepra" meaning, "a scaly condition." In an attempt to combat leprosy in 583, the Christian church adopted the precepts delineated in Leviticus and restricted association with lepers.

As we move closer to the modern era, one of the more significant factors in the growth of communities in size and public health complexity was the industrial revolution. The 18th and 19th centuries saw profound economic changes that radically altered the nature, structure, and size of cities and increased the need for organized community effort to protect health.

In England, the creation of factories and rail transportation encouraged large-scale population movement from towns and rural communities into the cities. Factories required concentrations of inexpensive labor, and rail transportation provided a means for people to move to the new work opportunities provided by industrialization. In a brief span of 40 years, from 1801 to 1841, the population of London increased from 958,000 to nearly 2 million. Congestion and lack of organized sanitation, as well as poor nutrition, created highly effective vectors for communicable disease.

Cholera, typhoid, tuberculosis, and other diseases rapidly increased in the filthy and crowded conditions of English cities in the early 1800s. For example, between 1831 and 1844 the mortality rate in Birmingham rose from 14.6 to 27.2 per 1000. The economic consequences of this morbidity and mortality soon became apparent. Not only were lives shortened and living conditions deteriorating, but the ability of the workforce to endure long hours in the factories was decreasing.

One of the most famous and influential governmental reports of this era, written by Edwin Chadwick, was entitled "Report on an Inquiry Into Sanitary Conditions of the Labouring Population of Great Britain." Chadwick's report is considered one of the defining documents of modern public health. It articulates not only the basis for the environmental causation of disease, but also the relationships among disease prevention, governmental action, and financial well-being.

There are many individual instances of American colonies and later states establishing governmental acts with the purpose of preventing disease. Some of these ordinances were passed as early as the mid 17th century.[3] The causes of disease were not well understood, and prevention activities during this period focused on quarantine and hygiene. Efforts at quarantine revolved around the periodic outbreaks of epidemic infectious diseases but were hampered by a lack of knowledge about causation.[4] The following briefly describes some of the more significant events in the United States that established the foundations for public health practice:

1794   *Act of June 9, 1794.* Authorized the appointment of a health officer for the Port of Baltimore, Maryland. Because of the maritime nature of commerce and national defense, port cities were magnets for industrial growth and epidemic contagion.

1796   *Act Relative to Quarantine.* Directed revenue officers to execute health and quarantine regulations at U.S. ports of entry.

1798   *Act for the Relief of Sick and Disabled Seaman.* Imposed a 20-cent tax per month on the seaman's wages to provide for mariners' health care. This act, which led to the creation of the Marine Hospital Service, is considered by many to be the genesis of the U.S. Public Health Service. An Act of Congress in 1902 changed the name of the Marine Hospital Service to the Public Health and Marine Hospital Service and created the Hygienic Laboratory, which, in 1930, became the National Institutes of Health.

1845   *Publication of a "Census of Boston," by Lemuel Shattuck.* This document laid the foundation for the accurate reporting of vital statistics in the United States. The census revealed the high general mortality, especially among infants and new mothers. Five years later, Shattuck followed this document with one of the most famous documents in U.S. public health history, the Massachusetts Sanitary Commission Report known simply as "The Shattuck Report." This report, which recommended most of the public health policies that were put into effect in later years, had little impact at the time it was published.[5]

1860–   *The U.S. Civil War* fostered a new consciousness
1865   of infectious disease. Between two thirds and three fourths of all casualties in this war were due to disease and not to battle-related injury.

1869   *Functioning state boards of health* began to form. By 1875 boards of health existed in Massachusetts, California, the District of Columbia, Virginia, Minnesota, Maryland, and Alabama.

1879   *Act to Establish a National Board of Health.* A serious yellow fever epidemic in 1879 encouraged the Congress to create a board to cooperate with state and local boards of health on "all matters affecting the public health." This body was responsible for trying to formulate quarantine regulations that involved commerce and travel between the states. The board was soon involved in bitter states' rights battles, and it was disbanded in 1883.

1880s   *The new science of bacteriology* identified the organisms responsible for tuberculosis, cholera, typhoid, and diphtheria. By the mid 1890s, laboratory tests had been developed to detect these diseases and others.[6] These developments led to a dominance of the disease-oriented approach to public health. However, public health has always been characterized by a diversity of views, and nutrition, environment, and education also had strong advocates for their importance in public health practice.

1908   *Establishment of the first unit within a health department to deal specifically with infant health.* The Division of Child Hygiene in the New York City Health Department demonstrated the importance of prevention in reducing infant deaths.

1912   *An Act to Establish a Children's Bureau.* This federal agency was charged with investigating and reporting on "all matters pertaining to the welfare of children and child life among all classes of people."

1921   *Sheppard-Towner Act.* The first federal measure to appropriate funds for a health and social welfare purpose. Provided matching funds to states for prenatal and child health clinics. After seven years, well-organized opponents of this type of government action were able to persuade Congress to discontinue the program.[7]

1935   *Social Security Act.* Added grant-in-aid functions to the Children's Bureau for maternal and child health activities and created federal government assistance in the areas of rehabilitation of crippled children, general public health activities, and aid for dependent children under age 16.

1940s   Introduction of antibiotics, penicillin, and sulfonamides gave physicians their first effective therapies for treating infectious diseases. These drugs accelerated the shift from infectious diseases to chronic diseases as the chief source of mortality in the United States.

1948   *Water Pollution Control Act.* Authorized the U.S. Public Health Service to help states develop water pollution control programs and to aid in the planning of sewage treatment plants.

1955   *Air Pollution Control Act.* Provided aid to states, regions, and localities for research and control programs to protect air quality.

1960s   *Extension of the adult life span.* An increase of about two years per decade during each decade subsequent to the 1950s. This represents a significant change as life expectancy had been increasing because of decreases in infant deaths. Now life expectancy is increasing because of years added at the end of life.

1964   Surgeon General's *Report on Smoking and Health.* Identified cigarette smoking as one of the primary preventable causes of morbidity and premature death.

1965   *Social Security Amendments.* Passage of Medicare and Medicaid marked the first large-scale federal initiative to provide health insurance for major segments of the population.

1970   *Public Health Cigarette Smoking Act.* Banned cigarette advertising from radio and television.

1970   *Occupational Safety and Health Act.* Provided federal program of standard setting and enforcement to assure safe and healthful conditions in the workplace.

1972   *National School Lunch and Child Nutrition Amendments.* Added funds to support nutritious diets for pregnant and lactating women and for infants and children (the WIC program).

1977   *World's final case of smallpox* is identified in Merka, Somalia. Marked the ultimate success of the world's first disease eradication program begun by the World Health Organization in 1967.

1980s   *New era in human disease begins with the recognition of the global AIDS epidemic.*

A DESCRIPTION OF THE CURRENT U.S. PUBLIC HEALTH SYSTEM

Activities designed to protect the health of the population in the United States are carried out by government agencies, by the health care sector, by voluntary health agencies, and increasingly by various other segments of society such as school systems, faith communities, law enforcement, business, and others. However, there are certain functions that only government can perform. These functions were defined by the Institute of Medicine in *The Future of Public Health* as assessment, policy development, and assurance.[8]

Federal-Level Public Health Activity

The size and diversity of federal organizations, and the numerous constituencies directly affected by public health regulation, have led to an often confusing allocation of public health responsibility within several different agencies of the executive branch of government. Significant public health responsibility exists within the U.S. Department of Agriculture and the Environmental Protection Agency, among others. However, most activity takes place under the auspices of the Department of Health and Human Services (DHHS). Within DHHS there are agencies clearly focused toward public health and prevention activity. Key DHHS public health agencies include the following:[9]

* *Centers for Disease Control and Prevention (CDC).* Conducts epidemiologic surveillance and research of communicable and chronic diseases, injuries, and occupational illness throughout the world.
* *Health Resources and Services Administration (HRSA).* Provides health services for special populations such as maternal and child health, rural health care, care for underserved through the National Health Services Corps and Community Health Center support, care for persons with HIV/AIDS. In addition, HRSA monitors the training, supply, and distribution of health professionals in the United States.
* *Food and Drug Administration (FDA).* Regulates over one fourth of all goods and services bought and sold in the United States.[10] FDA researchers and regulators evaluate new products in development before they are brought to market, including experimental drugs, cosmetics, food additives, radiation-emitting devices, and new medical devices.
* *Substance Abuse and Mental Health Services Administration (SAMHSA).* Organizes and supports a wide range of services for the prevention and treatment of substance abuse and mental impairments. Programs are focused on both prevention and treatment of conditions.
* *Agency for Toxic Substances and Disease Registry (ATSDR).* Administered by the CDC director, investigates the human effects of toxic materials.
* *Indian Health Service (IHS).* Operates health care facilities for Native American populations. Facilities may be administered by the IHS or by the tribes.
* *National Institutes of Health (NIH).* Funds basic biomedical research done through major medical teaching centers. The agency also has a large in-house research program.

- *Agency for Health Quality and Research (AHQR).* Improves the quality and effectiveness of health care services including research into health services delivery, medical effectiveness, and health outcomes.

State-Level Public Health Activity

Every state and eight U.S. territories have a state health agency (SHA) that is responsible for the administration of public health services within its geographic boundaries. These agencies tend to be independent cabinet-level organizations reporting directly to the governor (64%) or subunits of a state "superagency" for health and welfare. In 80% of the states, some type of board of health or health council is used for citizen input into the administration of the public health programs of the state.

The activities of state health agencies are quite varied. Although 100% of these organizations are the designated state public health authority, their responsibilities beyond this role are heterogeneous. The activities may include licensure of health facilities or personnel and/or management of state-owned health facilities.

Local-Level Public Health Activity

Variability characterizes the organization and functions of local health departments and is more extensive than that found among SHAs. Depending on which definition one uses, there are between 2850 and 2950 local public health agencies (LPHAs) in the United States. The results of a 1989 survey of LPHAs by the National Association of County Health Officials (NACHO) indicate that approximately 42% of LPHAs serve populations of less that 25,000 and nearly 66% of the LPHAs serve populations of less than 50,000.[11]

Over 80% of all LPHAs, regardless of size of population served, reported providing immunizations, collecting and analyzing reportable disease data, providing some type of child health services, and tuberculosis control activities. Less than 25% of all LPHAs provided primary care, obstetric care, radiation control, or occupational safety and health services.[12] The availability of services from local public health agencies is highly variable even within individual states.

NOTES

1. Committee for the Study of the Future of Public Health (1988), *The future of public health* (Washington, DC: Institute of Medicine), p. 7.

2. G. Rosen (1958), *A history of public health* (New York: MD Publications), p. 1.

3. J. J. Hanlon & G. E. Pickett (1984), *Public health administration and practice* (8th ed.), (St. Louis: Times Mirror/Mosby), p. 30.

4. F. Mullan (1989), *Plagues and politics, a history of the United States Public Health Service* (New York: Basic Books), p. 14.

5. Rosen, pp. 217–218.

6. P. Starr (1982), *The social transformation of American medicine* (New York: Basic Books), pp. 137–138.

7. Starr, p. 261.

8. Institute of Medicine, p. 31.

9. B. Turnock (2001), *Public Health: What is it and how it works* (2nd ed.), (Gaithersburg, MD: Aspen), p. 140.

10. Turnock, p. 141.

11. National Association of County Health Officials [NACHO] (1990), *National profile of local health departments: An overview of the nation's local public health system* (Washington, DC: Author).

12. NACHO.

—Stuart A. Capper

See also Evidence-Based Medicine (EBM), Public Health Core Disciplines, Strategic Management

PUBLIC HEALTH CORE DISCIPLINES

Public health practitioners employ a multidisciplinary approach to fulfill their core functions of health assessment, assurance, and policy development. The five disciplines at the core of public health practice are epidemiology, biostatistics, environmental health, health behavior and education, and health services administration.

Epidemiology. The oldest of all public health disciplines, epidemiology is the study of disease patterns through the systematic examination of the distribution, frequency, and causes of illnesses. Epidemiologists develop and test hypotheses about the sources, transmission modes, and possible interventions that might reduce the incidence of a disease. Interestingly, a complete clinical understanding of an illness is not always necessary to create an effective intervention. For example, Charles Snow's discovery of how cholera was transmitted preceded the identification of the causative agent by 30 years (Tulchinsky & Varavikova, 2000).

Biostatistics. Taken together with epidemiology, biostatistics provides the basis for the assessment function of public health. Biostatistics uses mathematical and statistical theories to develop tools for the analysis of health-related issues. In addition to complementing epidemiology in public health management, biostatics has numerous other applications, including biomedical research, clinical trial design, and assessing environmental issues.

Environmental Health. Improvements in environmental health, primarily through sanitation, have been a mainstay of public health efforts throughout the world (Jackson,

2002). Environmental health professionals have a significant role in the assurance of safe food sources, sanitary water supplies, and clean air. The success of environmental health practitioners has led to dramatic changes in the leading causes of death in the more developed countries. One effect of this success has been an increased emphasis on educating populations about the relationship between health behavior and chronic disease.

Health Behavior and Education. Health behavior and education seeks to understand and influence the attitudes and habits that affect a population's health status. The major goals of health behavior and education are to help individuals, families, and communities adopt healthier lifestyles. Engaging a community in participatory needs assessment, health behavior practitioners help design, implement, manage, and evaluate health-related programs and interventions. In this capacity, health behavior addresses the assurance function of public health. Because health promotion is related to many other social factors, such as economic status and health insurance availability, it also plays a significant role in health policy development.

Health Services Administration. Health services administration is a multidisciplinary field that engages in both health service research and health care organization management. The research function is intended to provide scientific evidence that contributes to the core function of policy development. In addition to informing policy, health service administrators have a leadership role in creating strategies that guide and coordinate the financing, structure, and goal setting of health care organizations.

In addition to the five core disciplines, public health is also interested in occupational safety, maternal and child health, nutrition, public health dentistry, biomedical and laboratory practices, and international health. Also, the field of preparedness against bioterrorism has taken on new importance after the attacks in New York.

—Eric W. Ford

FURTHER READING

Jackson, R. J. (2002). *A strategy to revitalize environmental health services in the United States.* Atlanta, GA: Centers for Disease Control and Prevention.

Tulchinsky, T. H., & Varavikova, E. A. (2000). *The new public health.* San Diego, CA: Academic Press.

PUBLIC HEALTH DEPARTMENTS

See Public Health, Public Health Core Disciplines

PUBLIC HEALTH SERVICES

See Public Health, Public Health Core Disciplines

PUBLIC HEALTH TEN ESSENTIAL SERVICES

See Public Health, Public Health Core Disciplines

PUBLIC HOSPITAL

The public hospital is rooted in the traditions of the 18th-century almshouses that cared for the sick and poor and emerged as the backbone of our hospital system with the advances in treatments and nursing care during the Civil War. Today, of the almost 5000 community hospitals in the United States, approximately 1200 are public hospitals owned or operated by state and local governments. There are less than 100 large urban public hospitals, such as Cook County Hospital in Chicago or Charity Hospital in New Orleans.

Urban public hospitals provide more than ¼ of uncompensated care costs in the nation although they represent less than 2% of all hospitals; 80 hospitals provide 25 million outpatient visits. These institutions are heavily dependent on Medicaid, disproportionate share hospital payments, and local government subsidies. The large urban public hospitals typically provide services not found elsewhere in a community, including burn units, neonatal intensive care units, Level One trauma units, and AIDS treatment programs. Many of these hospitals are major academic medical centers that train 16% of all residents in the country. Hospital governance is by an appointed board, a health authority, or elected officials.

The legacy of public hospitals such as Boston City Hospital, Charity Hospital in New Orleans, or Cook County Hospital in Chicago, for example, extends to every nook and cranny of our health care system from the care of unusual and expensive disorders to the training of our health care workforce to the discovery of new treatments for disease.

—Max Michael

See also Disproportionate Share Hospital (DSH), Medicaid, Aid to Families with Dependent Children (AFDC)

FURTHER READING

Dowling, H. F. (1982). *City hospitals: The undercare of the underprivileged.* Cambridge, MA: Harvard University Press.

Rosenberg, C. E. (1987). *The care of strangers.* New York: Basic Books.

Stevens, R. (1989). *In sickness and in wealth: American hospitals in the twentieth century.* New York: Basic Books.

PUBLIC RELATIONS

The term *public relations* (also commonly referred to as *PR*) refers to a set of communication activities used to manage perceptions and reputation. Normally these activities are initiated by a PR agency or a PR department within a company or institution, and have a specific objective of communicating targeted information to relevant stakeholders. These stakeholders may include employees, consumers and customers, government agencies, stockholders, financial managers, public interest groups, or society as a whole. PR usually reflects an effort to promote a desired message and reinforce a relationship between an organization and a targeted audience(s) (such as a hospital and the population it serves). However, it may also seek to promote the position of a single individual with a specific public (such as the U.S. surgeon general and the U.S. school-age population).

PR and marketing are often confused in terms of their respective purposes. This suggests significant overlap between the two and considerable debate. Is PR part of marketing? Is marketing included within PR? Are they both independent of each other or are they interdependent? Regardless of one's position within this debate, one important differentiating aspect of PR is its consistent focus on goodwill and public understanding. As such, PR may be viewed as an important subset of activities under the larger umbrella of an *integrated marketing communication* strategy.

PR messages may either reflect a one-way communication or be interactive. PR employed in health care management may be one-way government health warnings, for example, or may be two-way, as in the case of asking for the public's attitudes and intentions on key health issues.

The specific activities of PR include press releases, exposure of expertise, lobbying, event management and sponsorship, presentation of research findings, the promotion of public affairs and community relations, corporate communications, and crisis management. Over 70% of PR is corporate-based messages to various publics. This type of PR (sometimes referred to as *marketing public relations*) is used to reinforce such marketing activities as product or service introduction (such as new pharmaceutical advancement approved by the FDA, introduction of a new hospital service), price changes (such as raising of health insurance premiums), or a change in procedures or structure (such as change in hospital procedures, corporate restructuring or re-engineering).

In sum, public relations provides a valuable set of tools. In attempting to use the media to reach specific audiences, it focuses on goodwill and public understanding, and is typically part of a larger comprehensive marketing communications strategy.

—David W. Schumann

See also Advertising

FURTHER READING

Caywood, C. L. (1997). *The handbook of strategic public relations and integrated communications.* New York: McGraw-Hill.

Cutlip, S. M., Center, A. H., & Broom, G. M. (1999). *Effective public relations* (8th ed.). Upper Saddle River, NJ: Prentice Hall.

Harris, T. L., & Kotler, P. (1999). *Value-added public relations.* New York: Contemporary Books.

Pickton, D., & Broderick, A. (2001). *Integrated marketing communication.* Upper Saddle River, NJ: Prentice Hall.

Shimp, T. A. (1997). *Advertising, promotion, and supplemental aspects of integrated marketing communications* (4th ed.). Cincinnati, OH: Dryden Press.

PUBLIC SECTOR

The public sector distinguishes itself from the private by allocating resources via collective choices. Consider, for example, goods and services such as public transportation, infrastructure, and police protection. Unlike goods and services such as foodstuffs or lawn care, those directed via the public sector often do not have an *explicit* price attached to them (or user prices do not match associated costs). Instead, whether a community receives a light rail line, new bridge, or increased police patrols depends in significant part on the capacity for that community's members to produce political support. Others, such as organized interests, may also attempt to sway such allocation processes but do so in a manner that avoids a system of explicit prices. Even in "market" economies such as the United States, the public sector directs over 40% of national resources in this manner.

What's more, even private goods and services such as foodstuffs and lawn care rely (at least indirectly) on the public sector for their direction. Indeed, without institutions that define and enforce the "rules of the game," explicit prices that appear to direct private allocations would be impotent. Why, for example, would individuals pay the asking price for groceries if prospective retribution for stealing was negligible? In this light, the public sector appears to allocate *all* of an economy's resources, whether it does so directly or indirectly.

One's standing in the market sector can be very different from that in the public sector. As a consequence, determining which goods and services are allocated via the public and market sectors has anything but trivial consequences. Consider, for example, health care's allocation. Although developed countries tend to regulate their health care sectors rather heavily (that is, compared with their regulation of other sectors), significant cross-country differences exist. In the United States, for example, the health care sector receives relatively light regulation (at least from a comparative perspective). As a result, the capacity for individuals to pay for health care services in pecuniary terms (dollars) appears to exert a magnified influence on the quantity and quality of health care that individuals receive. The capacity for individuals to pay for services in nonpecuniary terms (for example, waiting time), in contrast, appears to exert a relatively small influence.

Although calls for public sector control frequently abound when market sector allocations produce unpalatable disparities (that is, unpalatable to at least a vocal minority), public sector allocation mechanisms *need not* induce superior results. Indeed, to the extent that organized interests exert "undue influence" on public decisions, it would be difficult to rationalize how moving a transaction from the market to the public sector would "improve" matters. This possibility certainly does not imply that moving allocations from the private to the public sector *cannot*

improve welfare—it can. Rather, it simply implies that the manner in which the private and public sectors interact is complex and can thus produce inferior outcomes from even well-intentioned policy interventions. Although the public sector is, in some sense, more fundamental than is the private sector, understanding how interested adversaries stand in the private as opposed to the public sector is nevertheless important.

—Dino Falaschetti

FURTHER READING

Bernanke, B., & Frank, R. (2001). *Principles of economics.* New York: McGraw-Hill.

Hirshleifer, J., & Glazer, A. (1992). *Price theory and applications* (5th ed.). Upper Saddle River, NJ: Prentice Hall.

Stigler, George J. (1987). *The theory of price* (5th ed.). New York: Macmillan.

PURCHASING GROUP

See Coalitions (Business)

QUALITY ASSURANCE

Quality assurance in health care is a broad topic that may also be referred to in a general way as *continuous quality improvement, total quality management,* or *quality control,* or by other terms. The name applied may suggest the specific type of quality model used by the institution or program. In general, quality assurance programs ensure that there are criteria for assessment and quality improvement activities that evaluate, maintain, and improve the quality of health care provided to patients.

The concept of total quality management (TQM) was developed by W. Edwards Deming, after World War II, for improving the production quality of goods and services. The concept was not taken seriously until the Japanese, who adopted it in 1950 to resurrect their postwar business and industry, used it to dominate world markets by 1980. By then most U.S. manufacturers had finally accepted that the 19th-century assembly-line factory model was not effective if they were to remain competitive in the new global economic markets.

There are many approaches to quality assurance. These approaches generally employ the principles of measurement, customer focus, and statistically based decision making. A quality assurance, or performance assessment, and continuous quality improvement includes structural criteria, process criteria, and outcome criteria as well as peer review and appropriateness evaluation.

Structural measures include board certification of physicians, licensure of facilities, compliance with safety regulations, and so on. Many of these criteria are delineated in state and local laws and regulations. Accreditation and regulatory agencies may focus on structural criteria, because such criteria may be clearly documented.

Process criteria measure the way care is provided. Process measures can include screening rates, follow-up rates, and so on, which may be evaluated against national criteria or benchmarks. Process measures may also include service measures such as appointment waiting times.

Outcome criteria evaluate the outcome of the care or service. Standard outcome measures include infection rates, morbidity, and mortality. Poor outcomes generally mandate a careful review. Although structural criteria and process criteria should be linked to outcomes, unfortunately a poor outcome often offers little insight into the causes of poor performance.

Peer review involves a comparison of individual practices either by peers or by comparison to an acceptable standard of care. These standards may be developed within a local community (practice guidelines) or by national professional associations. Cases may be identified through noting when specific quality indicators are not met or through review of medical records. Managed care companies may also consider appropriateness evaluation (such as appropriateness of admission or procedure) in their quality review process.

Methods of building on the traditional quality assurance programs may be described as *quality management programs.* In addition to the quality assurance criteria, they include a clear aim or purpose that is not a part of a traditional quality assurance program. Organizational goals may be achieved by identifying customer (patient) needs, thereby unifying the purpose within the organization. Having this vision, customer focus becomes a cornerstone of a modern quality management program. Key customers, customer needs, and improvement processes to meet those needs are then integrated into the program. Issues identified for change and the implementation of changes are often evaluated through the "plan-do-study-act" cycle that is used as the framework for a trial-and-learning model.

Many organizations evaluate health care quality in different ways. These independent review organizations have promulgated standards and regulations that mandate quality improvement activities as part of the requirements to achieve accreditation. They include the Joint Commission on Accreditation of Healthcare Organizations (JCAHO, www.jcaho.org) and the National Committee on Quality Assurance (NCQA, www.ncqa.org), among others. The Joint Commission's ORYX initiative's core measures are designed to permit more rigorous comparisons using standardized evidence-based measures. The NCQA has promulgated the HEDIS measures (Health Employer Data Information Set), which drive the quality improvement activities in institutions that the NCQA reviews. Nearly all health organizations are regulated in some way or participate in accreditation by an independent agency.

Many large commercial enterprises, including Fortune 500 companies and other large public and private sector employers, have joined together in the Leapfrog Group (www.leapfroggroup.org). The group represents about 33 million health care consumers and works with medical experts and hospitals to improve the quality of health care. Other concepts being applied to health care quality now include "six sigma" quality control (www.isixsigma.com) which in essence means quality control to 6 standard deviations (about 3 quality issues per million occurrences or outcomes). The International Organization for Standardization (www.iso.org) also publishes quality standards (ISO-9000, ISO-14000, and others) for many industries that are recognized in 130 countries. ISO also has an accreditation program.

Health care organizations are mandated by regulatory and accrediting agencies to have an effective program for quality assurance, quality improvement, and quality management. It is incumbent on the institution to develop the proper infrastructure and resources to maintain an effective quality program. For many institutions, this may involve integrating the quality program into the institutional mission, as well as an institutional culture change among physicians, nurses, administrators, and other health care workers to have an effective quality program. In addition to regulatory and accreditation agencies, the public is becoming more informed about health care and will not only expect, but will also have a role in defining, quality health care.

—Linda M. Cimino and Stephen A. Vitkun

See also Health Plan Employer Data and Information Set (HEDIS), Joint Commission on Accreditation of Healthcare Organizations (JCAHO), National Committee on Quality Assurance (NCQA), Quality Improvement Cycle, Quality Management

FURTHER READING

Kongstvedt, P. R. (1996). *The managed health care handbook* (3rd ed.). Gaithersburg, MD: Aspen.

Lighter, D. E., & Fair, D. C. (2000). *Principles and methods of quality management in health care*. Gaithersburg, MD: Aspen.

QUALITY IMPROVEMENT CYCLE

The term *quality improvement cycle* has been used throughout the literature in a variety of ways. It is sometimes used in a general sense, for example, to represent a never-ending cycle of experimentation and continuous improvement. The term has also been used in a specific sense, to translate the well-known plan-do-study (or check)-act cycle (PDSA) into operations. Similarly, the term has been used to describe the circular and continuous flow of the PDSA cycle, a model frequently used in the health services arena to help quality improvement teams move through a step-by-step quality improvement process.

In its broadest sense, the quality improvement cycle symbolizes the continuous movement of the quality process and the belief that quality cannot be achieved merely by implementing a series of projects with a discrete beginning and ending. The concept of continuous quality improvement has been introduced and shaped by a succession of thinkers including Walter Shewart, W. Edwards Deming, Joseph Juran, Philip Crosby, and Armand Feigenbaum. It has been applied to the field of health care by several scholars, most notably Donald Berwick.

The significance of the continuous improvement cycle, and the importance of planning to the total process, is illustrated by Juran when he discusses a manager who is up to his waist in alligators. The manager's attempts to slay the alligators one by one are analogous to a project-by-project quality improvement approach. This approach, although common, is not satisfactory, because more and more alligators will simply emerge from the swamp. Juran instead suggests it is best to begin by establishing the vision and then the policies and goals of the organization. To convert the goals into results ("making quality happen"), he promotes the use of three basic managerial processes: quality planning, quality control, and quality improvement. In the planning stage, planners identify their customers and the needs of their customers. They then develop product and process designs to respond to those needs and, finally, turn the plans over to the operating forces. During the quality control stage, actual performance is evaluated and compared with quality goals. Managers then act on the difference. In the quality improvement stage, improvement projects are identified, controls are established to hold the gains, and a permanent infrastructure is established to hold the gains.

—Shonna L. Mulkey

See also Continuous Quality Improvement (CQI), Plan-Do-Study-Act Cycle

FURTHER READING

Berwick, D. M., Godfrey, A. B., & Roessner, J. (1990). *Curing health care: New strategies for quality improvement.* San Francisco: Jossey-Bass.

Juran, J. M., & Godfrey, A. B. (Eds.). (1999). *Juran's quality handbook.* New York: McGraw-Hill.

McLaughlin, C. P., & Kaluzny, A. D. (1999). *Continuous quality improvement in health care* (2nd ed.). Gaithersburg, MD: Aspen.

QUALITY MANAGEMENT

Quality management in health services delivery has two components: quality assurance and quality improvement. Quality assurance is an approach to quality management typically composed of a formal retrospective process of identifying medical delivery problems, finding means for overcoming them, and taking corrective actions to address them. Quality improvement is a management philosophy to improve health system performance by identifying medical care process failures through ongoing monitoring, empowering workers to make changes, and using the scientific method to continuously reduce process variation by removing wasted action and rework in process activities. Both types of quality management measure quality with regard to the structure, process, and outcomes of medical care delivery. These measurements may occur with regard to specific clinical situations or a population of individuals in a community, state, or the nation.

THE ASPECTS OF QUALITY MANAGEMENT

Donald M. Berwick identifies quality management as having three primary aspects: (a) knowing what works, (b) using what works, and (c) doing well what works. To this list, a fourth element should be added: knowing the resources needed for what works. Quality assurance and quality improvement emphasize the second and third aspects of quality management.

The resources needed to create quality are reflected in the operational structures of health care organizations, especially physical facilities and personnel requirements. The earliest quality assurance procedures employed professional or organizational measures of structure in developing licensure, certification, and accreditation for individuals, health care institutions, and educational programs. Contemporary evidence indicates, however, that structure is not highly related to process or outcomes measures of quality, providing a necessary but not a sufficient condition for quality care.

Knowing what works requires information on the efficacy of specific technologies, pharmaceuticals, and clinical interventions under controlled conditions and on the effectiveness of medical treatments and surgical procedures as well as diagnostic, preventive, and rehabilitative care in the course of practice (outcomes research). Both approaches provide evidenced-based knowledge of the impact of technical interventions or processes on the health outcomes of a segment of the population. Because of its greater use of experimental controls, efficacy studies produce results that have clearer causal implications but are less generalizable to a cohort of patients who have or might contract a disease. Effectiveness studies have become an important source of knowledge regarding the effects of medical interventions on patient mortality, morbidity, perceived health status (health-related quality of life), and satisfaction with care. For example, a study of the medical outcomes for patients experiencing low back pain when treated, respectively, by surgeons, chiropractors, or physical therapists demonstrated little difference in overall results. The study did, however, produce a storm of controversy among the professional groups.

Specific outcome indicators and benchmarked standards for them are used by accreditation groups such as the National Committee for Quality Assurance or the Joint Commission on the Accreditation of Healthcare Organizations as well as federal agencies such as the Center for Medicare and Medicaid Services and private entities such as Oregon's Foundation for Accountability.

Using what works requires health care managers to consider the appropriateness of care provided, that is, its underuse, overuse, or misuse. The term *underuse* refers to the omission of services that could benefit the patient, overuse to the implementation of a service that has no or a harmful result, and misuse to the improper or incorrect use of a beneficial service. Appropriateness is generally identified in two ways. First, one may assess whether the risks of doing a clinical or preventive process outweigh the benefits for a specific class of patients. Second, a process of care may be compared with a standard of care established through efficacy or effectiveness research or through a consensus among experts in the field. The results of such investigations are practice guidelines or protocols that organize knowledge for providers. The acceptance of these guidelines by providers, however, depends on a variety of factors, including provider education, feedback on their practice, incentives, peer and leader opinions, patient education, and the involvement of providers in the guideline development process.

Once established, individual institutions or governmental agencies regulate the behavior of providers using standards for diagnosis, treatment, and prevention. Concurrent and post hoc assessment by committees in hospitals or other health services organizations is the routine means through which physicians and other health professionals perform peer review. State boards and professional review organizations also use standards of care as the basis for quality assurance in response to individual behavior failures.

Doing well what works results from a process of continuous quality improvement (CQI) that focuses on misuse of services that results in medical errors and on the wide variation in medical care, geographically, that is often provided for the same condition. The concepts and principles of CQI result from the early work of W. Edwards Deming and have been most fully used by Berwick's Institute for Healthcare Improvement in Boston, Massachusetts. In CQI, organizations emphasize the management of processes and systems of care rather than behavior of individual providers or other workers. In other words, the vast majority of quality problems are said to result from failures in the design or operation of a process or the suppliers or inputs to it, whereas only a small minority occur from idiosyncratic events, including the behavior of individuals.

Managers must view their organization and its processes as a system, identify the causes of variations in the processes, and empower their workers to make ongoing changes in these processes. The change process requires substantial effort in problem identification and then the systematic implementation of an improvement, using the scientific method to assess its effect on a specific outcome. For example, New England cardiac surgeons performing coronary artery bypass surgery reduced their mortality rate by 24% through training in CQI, increased communication among surgical team members, feedback of data, benchmarking against excellent hospitals, and establishment of clinical protocols.

Quality management is a complex process that is only beginning to be implemented in health care institutions and by state and federal organizations.

—Richard S. Kurz

See also Continuous Quality Improvement (CQI), Quality Assurance

FURTHER READING

Berwick, D. M. (1989). Health services research and quality of care: Assignments for the 1990s. *Medical Care, 27,* 763–771.

Bodenheimer, T. (1999). The movement for improved quality in health care. *New England Journal of Medicine, 340,* 488–492.

Institute of Medicine. (2001). *Crossing the quality chasm: A new health system for the 21st century.* Washington, DC: National Academy Press.

Weingarten, S. (2002). Assessing and improving quality of care. In S. J. Williams & P. R. Torrens (Eds.), *Introduction to health services* (6th ed., pp. 373–391). Albany, NY: Delmar.

QUEUING

The word *queue* is the common English term for "waiting line." The study of queuing, or *queuing theory,* concerns how and why people or objects incur waiting. Waiting occurs in situations where servers are unable to provide immediate service for all requests. A classic queuing system is a ticket window at a movie theater. A waiting line forms when the rate of customers arriving to purchase tickets exceeds the cashier's rate of selling tickets. Not all queuing situations have an obvious line of waiting customers. Situations where people or objects are waiting for a server to arrive and provide service are also considered a queuing system. For example, during inclement weather a call for police to respond to a nonserious automobile accident represents a request for service that takes its place in a virtual waiting line.

Queuing is an integral part of most service operations. Because services cannot be "inventoried" ahead of time, some degree of waiting for an occupied server is likely to occur. In health care, queuing systems are commonplace. Some examples include (a) patients waiting for treatment in an emergency room, (b) hospital rooms waiting to be cleaned by housekeeping, (c) blood samples waiting to be processed through a lab, and (d) patient backlogs for surgical resources.

The term *queuing system* refers to a system in which waiting may occur. A queuing system is characterized by (a) a calling population, (b) an arrival process, (c) a queue configuration, (d) a queue discipline, and (e) a service process.

The term *calling population* refers to the group of customers or objects that may generate requests for service. For example, the calling population to an emergency room is the collection of all individuals in reasonable geographic proximity to the facility. In such a case, the calling population is very large and is modeled differently from a queuing system with relatively fewer people or objects potentially requesting service. For example, in a nursing unit the calling population consists only of those patients currently in the unit.

The term *arrival process* refers to the manner in which requests for service are generated from a calling population. Requests usually emerge in a random rather than predictable fashion. Characteristics of arrival processes include the rate and timing of requests, whether requests occur individually or in batches, and whether the calling population is homogeneous or contains subgroups. For example, the average rate of arrivals to an emergency department depends greatly on the day of week and time of day. Arrivals may occur individually or in batches (larger accidents) and may be subgrouped as requiring either critical or noncritical care.

The term *queue configuration* refers to the arrangement of queues and servers within a queuing system. The most common queue arrangements are either single line or multiline. Most grocery stores allow a separate queue to develop for each checkout, thus requiring a customer to choose which queue to join. Airline check-in counters, in contrast, often use a single waiting line in which customers are directed to the "next available agent." Grocery stores often differentiate servers by offering an "express checkout" for customers with few items.

The term *queue discipline* refers to the manner in which the next customer is selected for service. The most common and "socially just" queue discipline is first-come-first-served. Hospital emergency departments, in contrast, must use a triage system to select and treat waiting patients according to severity of condition.

The term *service process* describes the server arrangements, assignments, and processing time characteristics. Servers may be assigned specific tasks and arranged in series (cafeteria servers). Alternatively, servers may be able to perform a variety of tasks and be arranged in parallel (cosmetics counter clerks).

Customer perceptions of queuing experiences depend on objective measures such as waiting time before service and the time required performing the service. Customer perceptions can also be positively or negatively affected according to how customer expectations are managed, how queue status is communicated, and the queuing environment itself.

—Charles E. Noon

See also Health Care Service Operations, Service Operations, Waiting Time

FURTHER READING

Fitzsimmons, J., & Fitzsimmons, M. (2001). *Service management.* New York: Irwin McGraw Hill.

QUI TAM ACTIONS

The words *qui tam* are the short form of a Latin phrase that, loosely translated, means "one who sues for the king as well as for himself." *Qui tam* provisions derive from a 150-year-old law known as the False Claims Act (FCA). The FCA was passed to address military procurement fraud during the Civil War. To aid in controlling fraud against the government, the FCA encouraged private citizens with knowledge of false or inflated claims against the government to sue on behalf of the government. This type of lawsuit is known as a *qui tam* action, and the person bringing the suit is known as a *relator.* Under the FCA the incentive

for the private citizen's *qui tam* action is that the relator is allowed to keep a portion of the money awarded in the lawsuit or settlement.

During the last 100-plus years, the FCA has fallen in and out of favor as a prosecutorial tool and has undergone several revisions. But since the last major revision in 1986, it has become the weapon of choice in the battle to stem health care fraud and false claims against government health care programs. The cost of health care in the United States has been a matter of growing concern for decades. It is estimated that billions of dollars are lost annually to health care fraud and abuse, and enormous efforts have gone into making and enforcing laws to address the problems. The False Claims Act remains the kingpin of fraud and abuse laws and has been responsible for significant recoveries from *qui tam* actions.

The FCA is a civil statute that provides for treble damages (three times the amount of loss suffered by the government) and civil penalties of $5,500 to $11,000 per claim. The statute targets anyone who knowingly makes a false or fraudulent claim against the government. The penalties are assessed on each claim submitted and can add up to astronomical awards in the health care context. *Qui tam* relators are responsible for a significant number of health care false claims actions and billions of dollars returned to the health care program. Once a *qui tam* action is filed, it remains under seal for at least 60 days while the government performs a preliminary investigation and assessment of the claim. If the government believes that the claim is meritorious, it may elect to join the *qui tam* action and assume responsibility for investigating and prosecuting the case. If the government joins the action the *qui tam* plaintiff will be entitled to 15% to 25% of the recovery or settlement. If the government declines to join the case, the *qui tam* relator has the right to pursue the case and bears the costs of discovery and expenses of trial. If the case is successful, the defendant is required to pay the relator's attorney fees and costs as well as the damage award and penalties. When the government does not intervene, the relator's share of the award is 25% to 30%. If the government believes the *qui tam* case lacks merit, the government has the right to dismiss the case. Relators can be anyone with knowledge of facts that lead to a false claim. Typically relators are current or past employees, competitors, suppliers, consultants, or others with knowledge about the activities within the company. Their motives for bringing a suit range from genuine concern for correcting wrongdoing to vengeance by a disgruntled employee or simply personal greed. Health care enforcement authorities are vigilant in attempting to determine when a *qui tam* suit is based less on facts than on the relator's personal agenda. Relators are allowed a portion of the recovery only when they are the "original source" of the information leading to the *qui tam* case. An original source is one who has direct and independent knowledge of the information and voluntarily provides the information to the government before filing the complaint. The 1986 amendments to the FCA protect relators who bring *qui tam* actions against their employers. Employers are barred from retaliating in any terms or conditions of the relator's employment. Thus the employer cannot fire, demote, alter benefits for, deny promotions to, or use any other means to retaliate against any employee who participates in a *qui tam* case.

The FCA imposes penalties only on those who act "knowingly." This term is broadly construed, however, and includes actual knowledge of the falsity of the information, deliberate ignorance of the truth or falsity of the information, or reckless disregard of the truth or falsity of information. The provisions of the FCA are not intended to punish innocent mistakes, but someone seeking reimbursement under government health care programs has an affirmative duty to determine that the claim is legitimate and accurate. "Mistakes" that occur from the provider's failure to employ proper filing procedures or correct system errors are at risk of being classified as deliberate ignorance or reckless disregard, even where the provider lacks specific knowledge of the problems.

The number of *qui tam* suits has risen dramatically in recent years. Recoveries in some high-profile cases have amounted to hundreds of millions of dollars, and collectively, billions of dollars have been returned to the Medicare trust fund and state Medicare programs from *qui tam* actions. Insiders with specific knowledge about practices within their companies have access to information that outside sources might never uncover. *Qui tam* actions have proven valuable in ferreting out abuses of government health care programs. False claims actions now incorporate widely varying facts that go far beyond billing errors. Filing a claim for services that were never rendered, claims for services deemed medically unnecessary or of substandard quality, claims involving up coding and unbundling, or claims by providers who routinely waive copayments may be deemed false claims. Although some of these actions are blatant abuses, others involve professional judgment or mistakes. As new uses of the FCA proliferate, so too do the risks of abuse by overzealous relators seeking financial gain, and we must take great care to ensure that we do not trade one form of abuse for another.

—Cheryl S. Massingale

FURTHER READING

Becker, S. (1998). *Health care law: A practical guide* (Section 5.05). New York: Matthew Bender.

False Claims Act, 31 U.S.C. § 3729 *et seq.*

http://oig.hhs.gov

R

RANDOMIZATION

Randomization is a process that assigns research participants by chance, rather than by choice, to either the investigational group or the control group of a clinical trial. Each study participant has a fair and equal chance of receiving either the new intervention being studied (by being placed in the investigational group) or the existing or "control" intervention (by being placed in the control group). The goal of randomization is to produce comparable groups in terms of general participant characteristics, such as age or gender, and other key factors that affect the probable course the disease would take. In this way, the two groups are as similar as possible at the start of the study. At the end of the study, if one group has a better outcome than the other, the investigators will be able to conclude with some confidence that one intervention is better than the other. A randomized, controlled trial is considered the most reliable and impartial method of determining what medical interventions work the best.

HOW DOES RANDOMIZATION PREVENT BIAS?

Research participants are randomized in clinical trials so that bias does not weaken the study results. Bias consists of human choices, beliefs, or any other factors besides those being studied that can affect a clinical trial's results. If physicians or participants themselves choose the group, assignments might be personally influenced and therefore unevenly slanted toward one side or the other.

For instance, if a study is not randomized physicians may unconsciously assign participants with a more hopeful prognosis to the experimental group, thus making the new therapy seem more effective than it really is. Conversely, participants with a less hopeful prognosis might pick the experimental treatment, making it look less effective than

it really is. Randomization prevents such bias. In a randomized trial, investigators use a computer program or a table of random numbers to assign each study participant to a group. Randomization introduces a deliberate element of chance into the assignment of treatments to patients in a clinical trial. During subsequent analysis of the trial data, it provides a sound statistical basis for the quantitative evaluation of the evidence relating to treatment effects. It also tends to produce treatment groups in which the distributions of prognostic factors (known and unknown) are similar. In combination with blinding, randomization helps to avoid possible bias in the selection and allocation of patients arising from the predictability of treatment assignments. The randomization schedule of a clinical trial documents the random allocation of treatments to patients. In the simplest situation it is a sequential list of treatments (or treatment sequences in a cross-over study) or corresponding codes by patient number. The logistics of some studies, such as those with a screening phase, may make matters more complicated, but the unique preplanned assignment of treatment, or treatment sequence, to patient should be clear. Different designs of study require different procedures for generating randomization schedules. This procedure should be capable of being reproduced (if the need arises) through the use of the same random number table, or the same computer routine and seed for its random number generator. Although unrestricted randomization is an acceptable approach, some advantages can generally be gained by randomizing patients in blocks. This helps to increase the comparability of the treatment groups, particularly when patient characteristics may change over time, as a result, for example, of changes in recruitment policy. It also provides a better guarantee that the treatment groups will be of nearly equal size. In cross-over trials it provides the means of obtaining balanced designs with their greater efficiency and easier interpretation. Care must be taken to choose block lengths that are sufficiently short to limit possible imbalance but that are long enough to avoid predictability toward the end of the sequence in a block. Investigators should generally be blind to the block length. The use of two or more block lengths, randomly selected for each block, can achieve the same purpose, the prevention of bias. (Strictly, predictability does not matter in a double-blind trial, but the pharmacological effects of medicinal products often provide the opportunity for intelligent guesswork.)

—Steven C. Quay

RANKING OF HOSPITALS

See Coalitions (Business), Hospitals, Outcomes Research

RATE OF RETURN

Rate of return is expressed as a percentage of the total amount of an investment over a period of time (typically expressed on an annual basis). Unfortunately, different people may use this representation in different ways. You may hear rate of return expressed as the interest returned on an investment or the profit margin received over a defined period of time.

If an investment of $100,000 over one year of time yielded a balance of $110,000, then the rate of return would be $10,000. The rate of return would be expressed as 10% ($10,000 divided by $100,000 (initial investment) = 0.10 or 10%).

There are multiple types of calculations for "rate of return," such as internal rate of return, tie-weighted rate of return, and so on—not to be confused with the basic rate of return just described. Many calculations take into consideration other factors such as time value of money, inflation, deflation, taxes, and other criteria that may be applicable for analysis. These should all be understood to the degree of how and why it affects the analysis being done. For example, if the 10% rate of return were adjusted for an annual 2% inflation, then the adjusted rate of return would be 8% (10% – 2% = 8%).

Uses of the rate-of-return calculation vary as well. Most often rate of return is used in evaluating investment criteria for future decisions and for measuring performance of current or past investments. For instance, a hospital is considering expansion to another location. The hospital has $20 million for the expansion in liquid assets. The decision has been made to go through with the project, because it is projected to pay for itself in five years and double the revenues of the hospital. Now the stakeholders are discussing how to pay

for it. Should they use the $20 million, which is currently earning 9% (rate of return on the $20 million), or should they borrow the money at a 7% rate of interest (their cost of capital). If they used the current $20 million they would give up 2% (9% – 7% = 2%) on their potential earning power on the $20 million. So, they would be better off borrowing the money, and if the earning potential of the $20 million ever goes below the cost of capital (7%), then they would have the opportunity to pay the loan off.

The rate of return is a powerful tool in projecting and setting priorities on investments. Even if the preceding investment example had not met the exact criteria for the financial model, the hospital might have gone through with it anyway because it met the strategic goals and the opportunity costs for not doing now would have been greater later. Other investment decisions that have a negative rate of return may need to be accomplished as a necessity, such as a leaky roof. This tool can help in looking at the financial or resource investment aspects but should never be the sole criterion for a "wise" investment strategy.

—Terry Moore

See also Investment, Return on Assets (ROA), Return on Owner's Equity

FURTHER READING

Freidman, J. P. (2000). *Dictionary of business terms.* Hauppauge, NY: Barron's.

Gepenski, L. C. (2001). *Healthcare finance: An introduction to accounting and financial management.* Chicago: Health Administration Press.

Zelman, W., McCue, M. J., & Millikan, A. R. (1998). *Financial management of healthcare organizations: An introduction to fundamental tools, concepts and applications.* Malden, MA: Blackwell.

RATIO ANALYSIS

Basic analytic procedures include horizontal and vertical analysis of the balance sheets and income statements, solvency analysis, and profitability analysis. Comparisons can be made over time for a particular practice, between competing practices, and with industry averages.

BASIC ANALYTIC PROCEDURES

Horizontal analysis of the balance sheets and income statements is accomplished by computing the dollar amount, direction, and percentage of the change in each balance sheet or income statement account from one period to another or by comparing the changes of one or more periods to a selected base period. The data derived can be reviewed to determine if particularly favorable or unfavorable trends are indicated.

Vertical analysis of the balance sheet requires that the dollar amount of each asset account is expressed as a percentage of the total assets, and that the dollar amount of each liability and equity account is expressed as a percentage of the total of the liabilities and equity. After vertical analysis percentages are determined, a horizontal analysis of the data can be prepared for comparison with one or more preceding periods or with industry-wide trends.

Common-size statements reflect the horizontal analysis data or the vertical analysis data as percentages. Similar percentages are computed and then compared with those of competing businesses or industry averages in order to determine trends.

SOLVENCY ANALYSIS

The ability of a business to meet current and long-term financial obligations to creditors is of great interest to business owners, creditors, and investors. Some of the techniques, which can be useful to a medical practice, include the following:

Working capital is computed as the difference between total current (short-term) assets and total current (short-term) liabilities on the balance sheet. The dollar amount should be positive; however, if the working capital seems too large in comparison with industry averages, further examination of the individual current accounts is indicated.

The *current ratio* is determined by dividing the total current assets by the total current liabilities. If the current ratio is less than 1, current liabilities exceed current assets; a short-term solvency problem could exist with respect to meeting creditor claims. How large the current ratio should be is determined by many factors. As with working capital, if the current ratio is very large in comparison to industry averages, the business may need to reassess its capital structure.

The *quick (or acid test) ratio* is a more conservative variation of the current ratio. The quick ratio is computed as (cash + marketable securities + receivables), all divided by total current liabilities. A quick ratio of 1 or slightly higher generally indicates good short-term solvency or instant debt-paying ability.

The *ratio of operating cash flows to current liabilities* is computed by dividing cash flows from operations by the average current liabilities (the average current liabilities may be computed by adding the beginning and ending current liabilities and dividing the total by 2). As current liabilities are generally satisfied by paying out cash, the operating cash flows to current liabilities is a more conservative measure of solvency than the current and quick ratios, which include noncash current assets.

The *accounts receivable turnover ratio* is computed by dividing the net sales on account (the net credit sales) by the average accounts receivable (the average accounts receivable can be approximated by adding the beginning and ending accounts receivable and dividing the total by 2). The accounts receivable turnover is an indicator of the efficiency in collecting receivables and the effectiveness of credit policies.

The *supplies inventory turnover* is the total cost of supplies used during the year divided by the average supplies inventory (the average supplies inventory can be approximated by adding the beginning and ending supplies inventory amounts and dividing by 2). If the turnover is low in comparison to industry averages, too much may be invested in supplies, with resulting risks of obsolescence or spoilage. If the turnover seems too high, time spent in reordering supplies may be excessive and quantity discounts available with larger orders may not be available.

The *number of days supplies in inventory* can be determined by dividing the year end supplies inventory by the average daily cost of supplies (the average daily cost of supplies can be determined by dividing the annual cost of supplies used by 365 days). As with the supplies inventory turnover, the reasonableness of the number of days supplies in inventory would have to be determined through examining trends within the business and comparing them with competitors and industry averages.

Fixed assets to long-term debt is a solvency measure, which indicates some degree of security to long-term creditors and may have an impact on the borrowing ability of the business. Fixed assets such as land, buildings, furniture, and equipment tend to be financed through mortgages or other long-term debt. The ratio of the net fixed assets (the total amount of the fixed assets less any accumulated depreciation) is divided by the total long-term debt. The larger the resulting ratio, the greater the perceived margin of safety for the long-term creditors.

Debt-to-equity ratio (or *ratio of total liabilities to total owner's equity*) is another measure of solvency that is of interest to creditors. The total liabilities are divided by the total owner's equity to yield a ratio that indicates the relationship between debt (creditor financing) and equity (owner financing). As creditors have a higher priority in claims against firm's assets than owners do, a low ratio of debt to equity is perceived as an extra margin of security for creditors.

Debt to total assets is similar to the debt-to-equity ratio with respect to the margin of safety offered to creditors. The total assets are divided by the total liabilities to indicate the relationship between the debt versus the equity financing of the total assets. The lower the ratio of the debt to total assets, the lower the level of risk as perceived by the creditors.

Times interest earned is computed by dividing (interest expense plus income before income taxes) by interest expense. The higher the ratio, the greater the margin of safety as perceived by the debt holders with respect to the debtor's ability to pay interest.

PROFITABILITY ANALYSIS

The *profit margin ratio* is calculated by dividing net income by net sales. The ratio can be compared with earlier data for the firm, competitors, and industry averages.

The *asset turnover (or net sales to assets ratio)* is computed by dividing net sales by average total assets (beginning total assets plus ending total assets all divided by 2). The higher the ratio, the more effectively the assets are being used to generate sales.

The *rate earned on total assets (or return on assets)* is calculated by adding interest expense (net of tax effect) and net income, all divided by average total assets (as computed earlier). The resulting ratio is an indicator of the overall profitability of the assets of the firm.

Return on equity is an assessment of the profitability of the investment in the firm by the owners. The ratio is computed by dividing the net income by the average owners' equity (beginning owners' equity plus ending owners' equity, all divided by 2). A high return on equity indicates high profitability of the investment of the owners.

As financial statements are derived from the accounting equation, which essentially involves assets = liabilities (debt) + owners' equity + revenues − expenses, ratios derived from the financial statements may be influenced by changes to any of the components of the overall equation. Therefore, care must be exercised in drawing conclusions from any single ratio, because a favorable trend indicated by one ratio may be offset by an unfavorable trend indicated by another ratio.

—Harry N. Hughes

FURTHER READING

Fraser, L. M., & Ormiston, A. (2001). *Understanding financial statements* (6th ed.). Upper Saddle River, NJ: Prentice Hall.

Harrison, W. T., Jr., & Horngren, C. T. (2001). *Financial accounting* (4th ed.). Upper Saddle River, NJ: Prentice Hall.

Penwell, T. L. (1994). *The credit process: A guide for small business owners*. The Federal Reserve Bank of New York, Public Information Department, 33 Liberty St., New York, NY 10045.

Risk Management Association. (2001). *Annual statement studies*. Risk Management Association, One Liberty Place, Philadelphia, PA 19103.

Warren, C. S., Reeve, J. M., & Fess, P. E. (2002). *Financial and managerial accounting* (7th ed.). Mason, OH: South-Western.

RATIONING

Most governments control health spending by using price controls in the form of price ceilings. When prices are not free to change in response to the interplay of supply-and-demand forces, some other mechanism must replace the role of prices in allocating goods and services among competing uses. Price ceilings result in shortages. Rationing carries out the allocation function normally associated with price changes. Health care is typically rationed through longer waiting times, a decrease in the overall quality of health care, and reduced access to certain health care services.

The interaction of supply and demand is key to resource allocation in a private enterprise system. Prices are determined by the interplay of supply and demand forces. Given quantity supplied, an increase in demand for a health care service not only increases the price but also leads producers to supply greater qualities of the service. Price changes allocate scarce resources among competing uses on the basis of priorities. Higher prices stimulate production to meet the needs of consumers who are willing to pay more for a health service.

Government-sponsored health care programs control spending by setting a price ceiling for each service that is less than the market-clearing equilibrium price. Excess demand exists at the administered price. This excess demand, in part, represents consumers who are queued and are willing and able to pay more to avoid long waits. Because the market price cannot rise above the ceiling, rising demand does not expand output despite the needs of consumers and their willingness to pay more. One effect of efforts to hold prices down is to limit production and make the product less available. Because prices are not left to the free interplay of supply and demand, some form of rationing must be used to allocate health care services among competing uses.

Health care is rationed through longer waiting times, a reduction in the quality of health care, and reduced access to certain services. Patients will wait longer in emergency wards, months for referral to a specialist, or a year for a long-term bed. Only patients willing to wait will have access to certain health services. Some patients will seek health care in other countries. Physicians will be encouraged to devote less time to each patient. Lower prices and profits may reduce capacity and limit the use of new technologies. Hospitals will raise the threshold for admission and for performing expensive diagnostic and therapeutic procedures. Attention will be focused on providing primary and emergency care, and less specialty care services. A government's refusal to approve a new drug because it is not deemed a significant improvement over an existing drug is a form of health care rationing. The effect of a system that depends on rationing access to health care is often to delay, or simply not provide, certain health care services.

—Don P. Clark

See also Access, Queuing

FURTHER READING

Folland, S., Goodman, A. C., & Santo, M. (2001). *The economics of health and health care* (3rd ed.). Upper Saddle River, NJ: Prentice Hall.

Martin, S., & Smith, P. (1999). Rationing by waiting lists: An empirical investigation. *Journal of Public Economics, 71,* 141–164.

REAL GROSS DOMESTIC PRODUCT

See Gross Domestic Product (GDP)

RECEIVABLES MANAGEMENT

See Average Collection Period, Factoring of Accounts Receivable

RECRUITMENT

PATIENT RECRUITMENT

Recruitment of clinical trial study participants involves careful consideration that the subjects meet the inclusion/exclusion criteria set forth in the protocol. In addition, the recruitment of certain patient populations may bias your study. For example, you may identify patients who have a favorable outcome to your product or may have less likelihood to have a favorable response or adverse effect. For example, African Americans respond poorly to the blood pressure effects of beta-blockers, so a comparison of a new antihypertensive with these drugs in such patients would show favorable efficacy outcomes.

The choice of a patient population for your clinical studies covers a wide range of possibilities, such as etiology, disease state, age, gender, concomitant diseases, and medications. Therefore, the measures of efficacy and safety are directly related to the restrictions placed on patient eligibility.

Certain restrictions in the protocol or the disease state being studied may cause study enrollment issues, such as a delay in patient recruitment and completion of the study.

Other issues that can affect patient recruitment are the amount of compensation for the study, length of the study, the amount of in-clinic visits, patient privacy issues, and the chances of getting a placebo.

It is important to recruit patients who are able to read and understand the informed consent and their requirements in the study. They must understand how to fill out all the trial-related documentation, such as questionnaires.

—Anthony Sileno

See also Clinical Trials

FURTHER READING

Anderson, L. D. (2001). *A guide to patient recruitment, today's best practices and proven strategies.* Boston: CenterWatch.

International Conference on Harmonization of Technical Requirements for Registration of Pharmaceuticals for Human Use. (1996, April). *Good clinical practice: Consolidated guidance.* Rockville, MD: Center for Biologics Evaluation and Research, Food and Drug Administration, Center for Drug Evaluation and Research, U.S. Department of Health and Human Services.

REFERRAL

Making a referral means Physician A is recommending a patient to Physician B or to another health care entity for services essential to the patient's overall care. When Physician B sees a patient at the request of the referring physician, Physician B bills the patient for a consultation. However, Medicare and other carriers do not consider referral to be a consultation. From the Medicare point of view, a referral means Physician A has transferred the care of the patient to Physician B, which for billing purposes is not the same as a consultation.

For Physician B to bill for a consultation, the patient must be referred by Physician A (or another physician) for opinion, advice, or management of a specific problem. A physician consultant (Physician B) can initiate diagnostic or therapeutic services at the same or a subsequent visit. Physician B should send a consultation letter to the referring physician (Physician A) documenting the request for consultation, the patient's history, the physical examination, an impression, recommendation, and any specific tests that were ordered for rendering the opinion. The consultation letter should clearly state that the patient was sent for consultation. The usual billing mistake made by consultants is that they use the term *referral* and *consultation* interchangeably and commonly state, in such a letter, "Thank you for referring this patient." However, from the Medicare point of view this is incorrect. Physician B should state, "Thank you for sending this patient for consultation." In addition, during a consultation the patient should see his or her own doctor (Physician A) after the services have been completed.

A referral initiated by a patient or family and not requested by Physician A cannot be billed as consultation. Physician B must bill such a visit either as "new patient" or as "established patient visit." A new patient is defined as one who has not been seen by the physician or any other physician in the same group for at least 3 years.

—Ramesh K. Gandhi

FURTHER READING

Current procedural terminology. (2003). (Professional ed., p. 14). Chicago: American Medical Association.

REGULATORY AFFAIRS

See Institutional Review Board (IRB), Office for Human Research Protections (OHRP)

REHABILITATION

REHABILITATION MANAGEMENT

As in any business venture, providing customer value in rehabilitation medicine is paramount for success. The following discussion highlights the strategic concepts important for the success of a rehab program in providing customer value.

Successful management of a rehabilitation program begins with four main principles: (a) Determine the market segment in which to focus, (b) understand the competitive forces impacting the market segment(s), (c) establish a method of measuring outcomes and staff performance, and (d) create functional teams that meet the demands of the chosen market segment(s) and competitive forces.

Market Segment

The scope of rehabilitation medicine is diverse, ranging from sport injuries to long-standing neurological conditions. As a result, wide ranges of market opportunities exist. This necessitates understanding market segmentation as it relates to providing customer value. Managers must understand that missing a targeted segment could result in an inability to provide a needed rehabilitation service. Determining the market segment involves deciding between a niche focus and a broader scope. In this determination, one should ask if there are relevant and distinguishable market groups and if so, to what groups value services could be provided effectively. For example, a large referral rehabilitation hospital that targets patients with catastrophic illnesses and injury would find it operationally difficult to see a high volume of new sports injuries. Determining the market segment has significant implications on how the service is provided and how much it will cost. Often expansive efforts cost more to maintain. Managers should not overlook that critical step in establishing or maintaining a rehabilitation program.

Competitive Forces

The competitive landscape often shapes the strategy of a rehabilitation program and influences the likelihood of success. Competitive forces include new entrants into a market, leverage from consumers and suppliers, as well as threats from substitute services. For example, managed care has dominated the competitive landscape and therefore influenced the decisions of managers. If this dominance were to lessen, managers would have to adapt and perhaps focus on valued services provided directly to patients. Another example might be the influence of alternative medicine as a substitute for rehabilitation services. Increased competition from alternative medicine providers would influence the management decisions of a rehabilitation program.

Outcome Measurement and Staff Performance Measurement

Understanding the relationship between rehabilitation staff performance and patient outcome is critical to success in a changing environment. For example, prospective payment (lump sum prepayment) for inpatient rehabilitation for Medicare beneficiaries has forced rehabilitation hospitals to allocate resources more efficiently. Managers who understand what staff activities lead to the best outcomes under this prepayment model could realize cost savings without compromising quality. The rehabilitation literature is replete with outcome measurement tools that can aid in this process. Establishing continuous quality improvement teams allows for implementing measures that improve efficiencies.

Functional Teams

Rehabilitation services are primarily provided via teams. Management should create a culture that ensures synergy among team members. Well-functioning teams behave more reliably and with little variation. This in turn stabilizes the processes of care and lays the groundwork for a program of process improvement.

In summary, understanding market segmentation and competitive forces will help formulate an overall strategy for the rehabilitation program. Measuring patient outcome and staff performance is critical to success in changing environments. Finally, well-functioning teams promote performance improvement in rehabilitation programs.

—Christopher J. Garrison

FURTHER READING

Baker, J. (1998). *Activity-based costing and activity-based management for health care.* Gaithersburg, MD: Aspen.

Lighter, D., & Fair, D. (2000). *Principles and methods of quality management in health care.* Gaithersburg, MD: Aspen.

Porter, M. E. (1980). *Competitive strategy: Techniques for analyzing industries and competitors.* New York: Free Press.

Schultz, D., Tannenbaum, S., & Lauterborn, R. (1993). *Integrated marketing communications: Pulling it together & making it work.* New York: NTC Business Books.

Ware, J. E., Jr., with Snow, K. K., Kosinski, M., & Gandek, B. (2000). *SF-36® health survey manual & interpretation guide.* Lincoln, RI: QualityMetric Incorporated.

REHABILITATION ACT OF 1973

The Rehabilitation Act of 1973[1] was the first federal statute creating substantial federal rights for individuals with disabilities. Before then, government programs mainly sought to increase public awareness and to provide assistance in gaining employment, vocational training, and insurance programs for people with work-related disability. Generally, the Rehabilitation Act applies to federal agencies, as well as to programs that receive federal funding, and bars discrimination and other barriers against employees because of their disability. Numerous states have adopted its language in the creation of their own statutes, and the act also provided the conceptual framework for the Americans with Disabilities Act of 1990.[2]

Section 501 of the act requires nondiscrimination and reasonable accommodations for the "hiring, placement, and advancement" of disabled persons by federal agencies, departments, and "executive instrumentalities." The federal employer need not provide accommodation, however, if to do so would result in "undue financial and administrative burdens" or require "fundamental alteration . . . of [the] program." For example, in a case where an employee was aggressive toward other employees because of his mental impairment, it was found not to be a reasonable accommodation to require the employer extensively to change duties of other employees in order to isolate the disabled employee.[3] Poor job performance or employee misconduct

also may remove the employee from the protection of Section 501. For example, an employee who failed to report to work and who had exaggerated her physical limitations was found not to be otherwise qualified.[4] Poor job performance or misconduct need not be excused even where the disability had not been reasonably accommodated.[5]

Section 501 also is noted for the affirmative action obligations that are imposed on federal government employers. In addition to the requirement to "seek out" disabled prospective employees, mentally retarded and severely physically disabled people may be afforded "excepted service" employment. Under that program, a person occupying an excepted service position may acquire competitive seniority rights, if job performance has been satisfactory for two years, without being required to take a competitive examination.

Section 502 of the act directs removal of physical barriers to access by the disabled in federal buildings financed with federal funds, in accordance with the Architectural Barriers Act.[6]

Section 503 imposes affirmative action duties on federal contractors (as well as on their subcontractors) for contracts of more than $10,000. Contracts with any federal agency or department are required to include "a provision requiring that the party contracting with the United States shall take affirmative action to employ and to advance in employment qualified individuals with disabilities." The implementing regulations also require that contractors not otherwise discriminate against disabled individuals.

Section 504 has accounted by far for most of the litigation activity involving the Rehabilitation Act, and most understanding of the act has come through published cases from the courts. Section 504 prohibits discrimination against an "otherwise qualified individual with a disability . . . solely by reason of her or his disability . . . under *any program or activity receiving federal financial assistance*" (emphasis added). No minimum amount of financial assistance is stated for an entity to be covered under Section 504.[7] What constitutes "federal financial assistance" is not defined in the act. It has been held, however, that a hospital, by accepting Medicare and Medicaid payments, has received federal assistance.[8]

The section as written applies to both governmental and private recipients. The Civil Rights Restoration Act of 1987 significantly extended the reach of Section 504. Whereas before only specific programs or activities that received funds were covered, Section 504 now reaches much further. "Program or activity" of a state or local government includes "all of the operations of . . . a department, agency, special purpose district, or other instrumentality of a State or of a local government; or . . . the entity of such State or local government that distributes such assistance, and each such department or agency . . . to which the assistance is extended."

Operations of educational programs include "a college, university, or other postsecondary institution, of public system of higher education; . . . or a local educational agency . . . , system of vocational education, other school system."

Private entities are included as "an entire corporation, partnership, or other private organization . . . if assistance is extended to such corporation . . . as a whole; or . . . which is principally engaged in the business of providing education, health care, housing, social services or parks and recreation; or . . . the entire plant or other comparable, geographically separate facility to which federal financial assistance is extended."

The full extent of the reach of Section 504 continues to be a matter of considerable debate. The U.S. Supreme Court had held that only direct recipients of financial assistance were subject to Section 50, and that only the specific program receiving assistance was covered, not the whole entity. The Civil Rights Act of 1987 overruled those holdings, however, so that an entire organization apparently is subject to the requirements of nondiscrimination.

Lower courts have not interpreted this principle so broadly. For example, an employee diagnosed as legally blind alleged that he had been discriminated against because the City of Chicago did not accommodate his disability by adequately modifying his job duties. The court held that although Chicago received federal assistance, the employee still needed to show that the department in question had benefited from that assistance.[9]

At the time of this writing, it is unsettled whether states, as compared to local governments, are subject to Section 504. The Civil Rights Act of 1964 was amended in 1986 to provide that a "State shall not be immune under the Eleventh Amendment of the Constitution . . . from suit in Federal court for a violation of [Section 504]." However, the Supreme Court restated the authority needed by Congress to abrogate state immunity, and subsequently concluded that Congress had exceeded its authority when it passed the Americans with Disabilities Act.[10] The Rehabilitation Act is silent as to the constitutional authority intended by Congress. Lower courts have disagreed whether states' Eleventh Amendment immunity was properly abrogated when the act was passed.

—Donald Zink

NOTES

1. Pub. L. No. 93-112, Title V, § 501 *et seq.*, 87 Stat. 394 (1973). (Codified as amended in 29 U.S.C. § 791 *et seq.*)

2. In some respects the ADA provides more extensive substantive provisions and coverage. The ADA, however, does not apply to federal sector employers. In addition, the Rehabilitation Act imposes affirmative action requirements on federal employers and contractors, which are not found in the ADA. A 1992 amendment of the ADA "harmonized" the ADA and the Rehabilitation Act. As a result, rulings under either statute since then are governed according to ADA rules.

3. *Mazzarella v. United States Postal Service* (1994), 849 F.Supp. 89 (D. Mass.).

4. *Francis v. Runyon* (1996), 928 F.Supp. 195 (E.D. N.Y. 1996). *See also Husowitz v. Runyon*, 942 F.Supp. 822 (E.D. N.Y.). (Employee was not qualified for his position, where he was threatening to others, insubordinate, and uncooperative.)

5. *Butler v. Department of the Navy* (1984), 595 F.Supp. 1063 (D. Md.).

6. See also Section 508 and Titles II and III of the ADA.

7. No minimum number of employees is stated, as well. It is possible, therefore, for an employer to be covered under Section 504, but not under the ADA.

8. *United States v. Baylor University Medical Center* (1984), 736 F.2d 1039 (5th Cir.).

9. *Winfrey v. Chicago* (1997), 957 F.Supp. 1014 (N.D. Ill.).

10. *Board of Trustees of the University of Alabama v. Garrett* (2001), 531 U.S. 356.

REIMBURSEMENT

See Health Insurance

REIMBURSEMENTS IN INSURANCE

See Health Insurance

RELATED DIVERSIFICATION

See Diversification Strategies

RELEASE

A release is the relief from obligation, liability, or responsibility; in legal terms, the giving up of specific rights or claims to the benefit of another. Releases in health care deal with the granting of specific rights to another, with the presumption of a benefit accruing to the patient. Releases are granted for transfer of information, care for a minor or incapacitated individual, and liability. Most release forms are available commercially.

Releases for the care of minors when parents are not immediately available have been used in the health care setting for some time. Releases for photographs or specimens for studies or teaching are commonly included in admission and operative consents. As individuals spell out their health care choices in premorbid documents, surrogate decision makers are assigned (the autonomy of decision making is *released* to the health care proxy). With the passage of the Health Insurance Portability and Accountability Act of 1996 ensuring privacy of health information (Section 264), the transfer of personal health information between providers, third-party payers, and any other appropriate and legal interested party must be granted by a release.

Releases must specifically spell out what rights are transferred and be executed by the individual surrendering those rights. In distinction, a contract is an agreement between parties that creates a duty to do or not to do something and a right to performance of that duty. Consent is the voluntary and uncoerced agreement or acquiescence by an individual with capacity and understanding.

—Brian J. Daley

FURTHER READING

Merriam-Webster's dictionary of law. (1996). Springfield, MA: Merriam-Webster.

REMINDER ADVERTISING

See Advertising

RESIDENCY PROGRAM

The term *residency* as a descriptor of medical education first appeared in the American Medical Association (AMA) Council on Medical Education's publication "Essentials" in 1928. Early residency programs were designed to provide physicians with at least one year of practical experience under faculty supervision after internship. The residency program allowed graduate physicians to assume increasing responsibility in the care of patients.

Prior to the 1880s, graduate physicians in the United States often went directly into the private practice of medicine. Some graduate physicians apprenticed with a practicing clinician, frequently in Europe, and an elite minority served a one-year internship at a university hospital under attending physicians. Physicians entered the internship through personal connection or from affiliation agreements with medical schools. The value of internships in providing practical clinical experience became increasingly evident in the early 1900s. By 1914 about 80% of medical graduates entered internships and by the late 1920s nearly all graduates did. In 1914 the AMA developed a list of approved internships and produced "Essentials" for internship approval.

The concept of a physician specializing in an area of medicine led to residency program development. By 1915, 80% of graduate physicians sought specialized training either through on-the-job training, formal specialist education, or university degrees. Beginning in the late 1880s, a few university graduate medical schools offered specialized instruction in branches of medicine. The development of specialty boards formalized the course of study leading to certification in a discipline of medicine. Prior to 1917 when the American Board of Ophthalmology defined the type of training and content of the certifying examination there were no standardized requirements to practice a discipline of medicine.

The American Board of Medical Specialties was formed in 1937 by those medical disciplines having certifying boards and the Association of American Medical Colleges, the Federation of State Medical Boards, the Council on Medical Education and Hospitals of the AMA, and the National Board of Medical Examiners. This board sought to advise graduate medical education (GME) programs on the coordination of medical education and certification by medical specialties. Following World War II, residency review committees (RRCs) were formed to oversee the training programs of individual specialties. Concern about the control and quality of GME raised from special reports of organized medicine in the mid 1960s resulted in the Liaison Committee on Graduate Medical Education (present Accreditation Council on Graduate Medical Education, ACGME) being given authority for residency programs. The ACGME, whose membership is taken from its five parent organizations, established general requirements for GME and develops procedures for the accreditation process. The RRCs develop the special requirements for residency education in their specialty areas and accredit residency programs. Currently, there are 26 RRCs.

Functionally, residency programs provide the clinical infrastructure for faculty to teach graduate physicians the skills incumbent in their specialties and facilitate research performance. Each residency program is administered by a program director. Residency education is funded through a combination of federal Medicare dollars, research grants, endowments, and clinical practice revenues. With the exception of some community primary care residency programs, almost all programs are university based.

—Gregory H. Blake

See also Residency Review Committee (RRC)

FURTHER READING

Graduate medical education directory. (2002). Edited by F. Donini-Lehhoff, Medical Education Products, American Medical Association, Chicago, IL 60610.

Stevens, R. A. (1978). Graduate medical education: A continuing history. *Journal of Medical Education, 53,* 1–18.

Morris, T. Q. (1992). Taking charge of graduate medical education: To meet the nation's needs in the 21st century. *Transactions of the American Clinical and Climatological Association, 104,* 130–136.

RESIDENCY REVIEW COMMITTEE (RRC)

The Accreditation Council for Graduate Medical Education (ACGME) is a regulatory agency whose purpose is to establish and maintain national standards for graduate medical (resident) education in all specialties. Subcommittees of the ACGME include the Institutional Review Committee (IRC) and the Residency Review Committee (RRC). The IRC periodically reviews hospitals, medical schools, and clinics at which residents train. The RRC maintains residency requirements in each specialty and periodically inspects each residency program to ensure compliance with RRC requirements. A separate RRC exists for each specialty, which contains representatives appointed by the American Medical Association, by the appropriate specialty board, and sometimes by a professional specialty organization (for example, the American Society of Anesthesiologists). Rules and requirements established by an RRC often include the qualifications and responsibilities of program directors, faculty, and chairpeople, specific topics to be taught, and clinical as well as supervisory requirements. Quality-of-life issues are also addressed, which can establish the maximum amount of call and hours worked per week. Inspections of residency programs are carried out at set intervals, varying by both the specialty and the status of individual programs, most usually every three to five years. Physicians within a given specialty perform site visits and survey each program. Such visits include interviewing faculty and residents, inspecting the individual program curriculum, and inspecting facilities. The ACGME maintains a Web site (www.acgme.org) that lists the current registration status of all residency programs in the United States. An established residency program may be given full accreditation or may be placed on probation, and if such a program fails to achieve compliance with RRC requirements, its accreditation can be revoked. New programs may be granted provisional status prior to the granting of full accreditation.

—Robert I. Katz

FURTHER READING

www.acgme.org

www.asahq.org/Newsletters/1999/05_99/Resident_0599.html

www.cordem.org/mono/acgme.htm

RESTRUCTURING

See Contraction Strategy

RETRENCHMENT STRATEGIES

See Contraction Strategy

RETURN ON ASSETS (ROA)

Return on assets (ROA) is an indicator, expressed as a percentage, of an organization's profitability. ROA is calculated as follows:

$$\frac{\text{Net income}}{\text{Total assets}}$$

Net income is the total annual or annualized revenue less expenses and nonoperating gains or losses. For example, assume the following related to ABC Medical Center:

Income Statement	*For the 12 months ending 12/31/0X*
Net patient service revenue	$1,000,000
Other revenue	100,000
Total revenue	1,100,000
Operating expenses	
Salaries and benefits	400,000
Supplies and other	150,000
Depreciation and amortization	150,000
Interest	100,000
Total operating expenses	800,000
Income from operations	300,000
Nonoperating gains	50,000
Net income	$350,000
Balance Sheet	*As of 12/31/0X*
Assets	
Current assets	$3,000,000
Property plant and equipment	6,000,000
Other long-term assets	1,000,000
Total assets	$10,000,000

Liabilities and fund balance

Current liabilities	$2,000,000
Long-term debt	3,000,000
Other liabilities	1,000,000
Total liabilities	6,000,000
Fund balance (retained earnings)	4,000,000
Total liabilities and fund balance	$10,000,000

Using the this information, the return on assets calculation for ABC Medical Center for the year 200X would be net income of $350,000 divided by total assets of $10,000,000, or 3.5%.

Return on assets is an indicator of how well an organization's invested capital is generating earnings. The higher the ROA value, the better an organization is leveraging its assets in the generation of earnings, and presumably the generation of cash.

Return on assets is an important ratio for a number of reasons. First, the ratio tells creditors and shareholders of public companies how well the organization's assets are being deployed in the generation of income. Investors look at return on assets as a key evaluation criterion for companies. However, it is important to note that return on assets varies greatly from industry to industry. For example, health care is an asset-intensive industry, relying on large amounts of buildings, major medical equipment, and other assets to generate its profits. In contrast, many service industries utilize few capitalized assets in the generation of its earnings. Even within the health care industry, return on assets can vary significantly between different types of organizations. For example, an acute care medical center generally utilizes more assets in the generation of earnings than a home health agency, which has relatively few capitalized assets.

Return on assets is also important in evaluating investment in new projects. Along with return on investment (ROI), this measure is important for companies deciding whether or not to initiate a new project. The basis of this ratio is such that if a company is going to start a project and expects to earn a return on that project, ROA is the return it would receive. Generally speaking, if the expected ROA is above the rate at which the company borrows funds or above some other predetermined hurdle rate for new investments, then the project should be undertaken; if not, then the project is rejected.

—Edward Pershing

FURTHER READING

Downes, J., & Goodman, J. E. (2002). *Dictionary of finance and investment terms* (pp. 705–706). New York: Barron's.

Gapenski, L. C. (2002). *Healthcare finance: An introduction to accounting and financial management* (2nd ed.). Chicago: Foundation of the American College of Health Care Executives.

RETURN ON OWNER'S EQUITY

Return on owner's equity is one of the most important measures of an organization's profitability. It allows observers to measure the rate of return of an owner's investment. Observers use the information to discover trends through comparison of current and prior periods and to determine competitiveness through comparison with industry peers. The standard calculation for return on owner's equity (ROE) is expressed as a percentage and is computed using the following formula:

$$ROE = \text{net earnings/stockholder's equity}[1]$$

Net earnings, also known as the *net income of the organization,* is the profit or loss after consideration of all revenues and expenses recognized during an accounting period. The term *net earnings* is also used to refer to the accrued profit available for distribution to the stockholders or owners. Stockholder's equity is equal to all assets minus all liabilities. Often referred to as *common equity,* stockholder's equity is composed of common stock and retained earnings. For not-for-profit organizations, including many hospitals, stockholder's equity is referred to as *fund balance* or *net assets.*

ROE is often used with return on assets (ROA), defined as net income to total assets, to measure the overall efficiency of an organization's management. ROE is significantly different from ROA, however, in that ROE addresses the organization's debt leveraging. Thus ROE—unlike ROA—can provide an observer with information on how the organization's management team uses the tools of profitability, asset management, and financial leverage to influence an organization.[2] The DuPont analysis provides an alternative method for calculating ROE that allows observers to determine the impact of the decisions and the activities of the organization's management by examining the trend of the measurements found in the DuPont analysis.

The DuPont analysis calculates ROE using the following method:[3]

Profit Margin[4]		*Total Asset Turnover*		*Financial Leverage*		*Return on Equity*
$\dfrac{\text{Net income}}{\text{Revenues}}$	×	$\dfrac{\text{Revenues}}{\text{Total assets}}$	×	$\dfrac{\text{Total assets}}{\text{Total equity}}$	=	$\dfrac{\text{Net income}}{\text{Total equity}}$

The profit margin measurement shows the impact of raising and lowering charges. Charging for a procedure to remain profitable while also sustaining patient volume is challenging and vital to creating profits. The impact of new service lines or markets and contracts with managed care organizations are seen in the measure of profit margin.

Total asset turnover measures an organization's ability to manage its assets. By generating more revenue with fewer assets, an organization can decrease expenses required to maintain capital equipment and can return the increased gains from operations to its owners. Finally, financial leverage measures the organization's use of debt to support operations. Debt can be used to add capacity to an operation that ultimately increases earnings by greatly increasing volumes at a slightly lower profit margin, which leads to an increase in ROE. The danger is that too much debt eventually erodes profit margins through increased interest costs and decreases asset turnover, thus decreasing ROE. Therefore, ROE allows an observer to determine if the organization's management is properly managing profits, assets, and debt to the benefit of the organization's owners.

—Edward Pershing

NOTES

1. L. M. Fraser & A. Ormiston (2001), *Understanding financial statements* (6th ed.), (Upper Saddle River, NJ: Prentice Hall), p. 253.

2. www.fool.com.

3. L. C. Gapenski (1996), *Understanding health care financial management* (2nd ed.) (Chicago: Foundation of the American College of Healthcare Executives), pp. 511–512.

4. Operating margin (operating income/revenues) should replace profit margin in the DuPont analysis for not-for-profit organizations to account for variations in nonoperating gains common to not-for-profit organizations.

FURTHER READING

Brigham, E. F., Gapenski, L. C., & Ehrhardt, M. C. (1999). *Financial management theory and practice* (9th ed.). Cincinnati, OH: Dryden Press.

Downes, J., & Goodman, J. E. (1998). *Dictionary of finance and investment terms* (5th ed.). Barron's Educational Series. Hauppauge, NY: Barron's.

Needles, B. E., Jr. (1989). *Financial accounting*. Boston: Houghton Mifflin.

REVENUES

See Income Statement (IS), Profit

RISK ADJUSTMENT

Risk adjustment is any mechanism for reflecting differences in health status across individuals or groups of individuals. When risk adjustment is used in studies of costs or other outcomes of hospitalizations, episodes, or specific procedures, it is often called *case mix adjustment*. The diagnosis-related groups (DRGs) classification system is used to make risk-adjusted payments for hospital admissions. DRGs are also used to identify groups of hospitalizations that are sufficiently similar that it makes sense to try to identify systematic factors associated with variations in their content, costs, or health care outcomes. A fairly comprehensive discussion of risk adjustment for measuring cost and other health care outcomes is given by Iezzoni (1997). Risk adjustment is also used to describe a process for measuring or predicting health care expenditures (or other outcomes) of individuals or groups of individuals during a specified period of time, such as a year. A distinction is sometimes made between the process of measuring differences in medical risk (risk assessment) and the methods used to modify payments to providers, based on these assessed differences (risk adjustment). Risk adjustment is being used by public insurers, employers, health plans, hospital and provider networks, and even by individual providers. Glazer and McGuire (2001) define "formal risk adjustment" as the use of formulas that incorporate demographic, diagnostic, or other health information to calculate individual-level health premiums. They document that formal risk adjustment is widely used by public payers such as Medicare, Medicaid, and state governments, but used less often by private employers, who may have other strategies for offsetting risk selection incentives. Risk adjustment is also increasingly used within health plans to evaluate provider efficiency, and to identify, manage, and evaluate the management of individual high-cost cases.

Many kinds of information may be used for risk adjustment. The most widely used risk adjusters are age and gender, which explain 10-fold differences in expected health care costs across individuals. Employment status and whether or not a person is in a nursing home are examples of other demographic variables that have been used. The use of such demographic information alone leaves considerable opportunity for risk selection by health plans, because people with similar demographics may differ widely in their health care needs. In recent years health plans and payers have explored other types of information for risk adjustment, including survey-based measures, particularly self-reported health status data, and prior utilization measures. Some groups are beginning to use pharmacy information for risk adjustment; however, concerns about incentives (that derive from paying more for patients when they receive additional drugs) may limit the use of such data for adjusting payments. A clear preference has emerged for using diagnostic information for risk adjustment, with many employers and public programs currently basing payment to health plans on diagnostic information, age, and sex.

The U.S. Medicare program is a leading proponent of using risk adjustment to correct problems of risk selection. Prior to January 2000, capitation payments to health plans with Medicare risk contracts were risk adjusted using only demographics, and risk selection (that was not offset by risk-adjusted payments) was convincingly shown to be a serious problem (Brown et al., 1993). Since 2000, Medicare has been calculating part of its risk-adjusted premium payments to plans using inpatient diagnoses based on a payment formula called the Principal Inpatient Diagnostic Cost Group (PIP-DCG) model. The program has announced that from 2004 onward, it is expanding its risk adjustment formula to recognize multiple diagnoses from both inpatient and outpatient encounters.

—Randall P. Ellis

See also Case Mix, Risk Selection

FURTHER READING

Brown, R. S., et al. (1993, December). *Does managed care work for Medicare? An evaluation of the Medicare Risk Program for HMOs.* Washington, DC: Mathematica Policy Research Inc.

Glazer, J., & McGuire, T. G. (2001, Fall). Why don't private employers use formal risk adjustment? Conference overview. *Inquiry, 38*(3), 242–244.

Iezzoni, L. I. (Ed.). (1997). *Risk adjustment for measuring health care outcomes* (2nd ed.). Ann Arbor, MI: Health Administration Press.

Pope, G. C., Ellis, R. P., Ash, A. S., et al. (2000, Spring). Principal inpatient diagnostic cost group models for Medicare risk adjustment. *Health Care Financing Review, 21*(3), 93–118.

Van de Ven, W. P. M. M., & Ellis, R. P. (2000). Risk adjustment in competitive health plan market. In A. J. Culyer & J. P. Newhouse (Eds.), *Handbook in health economics* (Chapter 14, pp. 755–845). Amsterdam: North Holland.

RISK SELECTION

Risk selection occurs when health plans differ systematically in the expected costs or utilization of their enrollees. Economists use the term somewhat differently from the way actuaries use it. Economists emphasize the broad concept that if competing health plans differ in any observable dimension from each other, then plans will tend to attract enrollees that attach greater importance to this dimension. If people who value these plan features differ from average in their health care utilization and costs, then risk selection causes plans to differ systematically in their expected costs and health care utilization. For example, a health plan that offers a prescription drug benefit (or access to a specific teaching hospital, or expanded mental health treatment) tends to attract people for whom this benefit is relatively important. Because people for whom these benefits are important tend to be more expensive than average in using that feature, if any plan offers greater coverage in these dimensions then risk selection will occur: High-cost enrollees end up in high-coverage health plans, and low-cost enrollees end up in low-coverage health plans. Plans receiving the high-cost enrollees experience "adverse selection," whereas plans enrolling low-cost enrollees experience "favorable selection," which collectively are called "biased selection." Biased selection is a particular problem when health plan premium payments are capitated rather than experience rated. Biased selection is perceived to be a serious problem in the U.S. Medicare program (Greenwald, Levy, & Ingber, 2000).

Actuaries use the term *risk selection* to describe what happens when underwriters introduce eligibility criteria to restrict the kinds of people who enroll in an insurance plan. For example, in the individual health insurance market a health plan may deny coverage to individuals with certain pre-existing conditions (such as cancer, AIDS, or diabetes) or require a medical examination as a precondition for offering insurance. Another form of explicit risk selection is selective disenrollment, whereby unprofitable enrollees are dropped or encouraged to leave a health plan. These forms of explicit risk selection are often illegal or prohibited by employers and the government. The U.S. Medicare program, for example, prohibits explicit risk selection. Implicit risk selection mechanisms, through benefit design, for example, may also cause biased selection. Health plans with lower deductibles and copayments or higher coverage limits tend to attract higher-cost enrollees. Rothschild and Stiglitz (1976) provide the classic description of this process. Recent literature has highlighted that individual choice of health insurance may be influenced in subtle ways by such factors as level of coverage for high-cost chronic conditions, numbers of specialists, degree of access to specialty hospitals or primary care physicians, or even waiting times. Health plans that offer only certain types of providers or that utilize observable forms of care management may also lead to risk selection. Risk adjustment (that is, making payments that vary with assessed health risk) is the most commonly recommended strategy for addressing risk selection among capitated providers.

—Randall P. Ellis

See also Adverse Selection, Medicare Risk Contract, Risk Adjustment

FURTHER READING

Greenwald, L. M., Levy, M., & Ingber, M. J. (2000). Favorable selection in the Medicare + Choice program: New evidence. *Health Care Financing Review, 21*(2), 127–134.

Rothschild, M., & Stiglitz, J. (1976). Equilibrium in competitive insurance markets: An essay on the economics of imperfect information. *Quarterly Journal of Economics, 90,* 629–649.

ROOT CAUSE ANALYSIS (RCA)

Root cause analysis (RCA) is an approach for post hoc analysis of an undesirable situation to determine what happened and, more importantly, why it happened. This makes it possible to identify strategies for preventing the situation from recurring. Thus RCA is a tool for identifying prevention strategies and continuous process improvement.

At the heart of RCA is the distinction between proximal and root causes. The proximal cause is the obvious cause. For example, suppose that a physician ordered medication that had a subsequent adverse effect on the patient. The proximal cause is human error by the physician. Knowing that the cause is human error, however, is not very useful in determining strategies for preventing this situation from recurring. More important to the development of prevention strategies is determination of the root cause or the cause that underlies the proximal cause. For example, the root cause of this situation could be that the physician had been working long hours and was not thinking clearly, that the physician had a cognitive impairment that should have been identified by credentialing activity, or that once the error had been made, the nurse didn't feel sufficient authority to question the medication order. Note that there are obvious strategies for dealing with each of these situations and preventing such a situation in the future, compared with trying to deal with the proximal cause of "human error." This is typical of root causes; once the root cause is known, the solution is usually obvious.

RCA is typically conducted by an interdisciplinary team that includes knowledgeable individuals from all involved levels. Data analysis tools such as flowcharts, cause-and-effect diagrams, failure modes, and effects analysis and fault trees are used to analyze the evidence to separate proximal causes from the root cause. At the heart of these tools is asking "why" at each level of cause and effect to remove noncontributing causes. There are a number of commercially available software packages and consultants specializing in RCA training for health care organizations.

RCA is particularly important for health care organizations because of the September 1998 directive of the Joint Commission on Accreditation of Healthcare Organizations, the accrediting body used by the U.S. Department of Defense to validate military treatment facilities. This directive mandates that DOD facilities must comply with the sentinel event reporting process for identifying certain patient care events as potential markers of quality problems.

However, effective process improvement would move beyond mandated RCA of sentinel events to use it for a variety of adverse effects, from excessive waiting times for appointments and parking lot problems to surgical errors and increased suicide rates.

Once the root cause has been determined, it is critical to develop a set of recommendations for corrective action, including designating a person responsible for implementation of the corrective action and a reporting date. The plan should include a means for measuring the effectiveness of the changes. The corrective actions do not necessarily need to be designed to prevent the root cause from occurring. Rather, by understanding the entire logical chain of cause and effect, breaking the chain of events at any point will prevent the final failure from occurring.

—Barbara Flynn

FURTHER READING

www.downtimecentral.com/Root_Cause_Analysis.htm

www.jcaho.org/accredited+organizations/ambulatory+care/sentinel+ events/form+ and+tools/root+cause+analysis+matrix.htm

www.patientsafety.gov/tools.htm

www.rootcauseanalyst.com

RUN CHART

A run chart is a visual tool used to display the variations in a process over time. Run charts can be used to plot any type of data. Examples of process data include the quantity of a specific drug administered in a hospital by shift, the number of patient complaints per month, and the number of walk-in patients in a clinic per week. The major benefit of a run chart is its simplicity. It requires minimal statistical knowledge and can easily be understood by all members of a quality improvement team. The sample run chart in Figure 1 illustrates the number of patient complaints per month over a period of 20 consecutive months.

A run chart helps one determine whether the variation in a specific process has a common or a special cause. Common cause variation is inherent in every process and is a part of the regular rhythm of a process. Processes that demonstrate common cause variation are stable, predictable, and "in control." Special cause variation, in contrast, is due to irregular or unnatural causes that often occur unpredictably. When special cause variation exists, the process is "out of control," or unstable. To improve a process, the special causes must first be identified and eliminated. Only after this has occurred should one consider changing or improving the process. Attempting to change processes that contain special causes is futile and a waste of resources.

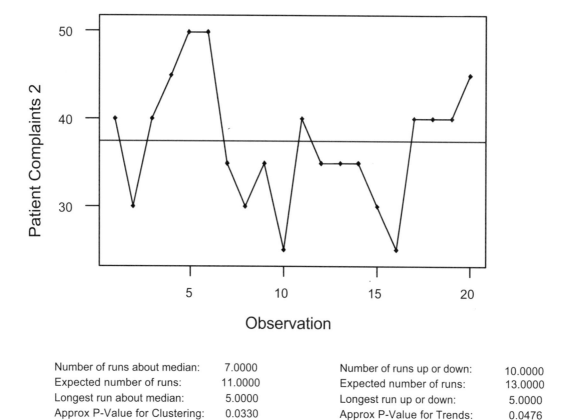

Number of runs about median:	7.0000	Number of runs up or down:	10.0000
Expected number of runs:	11.0000	Expected number of runs:	13.0000
Longest run about median:	5.0000	Longest run up or down:	5.0000
Approx P-Value for Clustering:	0.0330	Approx P-Value for Trends:	0.0476
Approx P-Value for Mixtures:	0.9670	Approx P-Value for Oscillation:	0. 9524

Figure 1   Sample Run Chart for Patient Complaints by Month

To construct a run chart, the following actions must occur: (a) Collect the appropriate amount of data. (b) Draw a horizontal axis and label it with the unit of time, such as hours, days, weeks, or the sequence of occurrence. (c) Draw a vertical axis and label it with the characteristic, or variable, that is to be plotted. (d) Plot each data point in the order that it occurred. (e) Connect the points on the graph with a solid line. (f) Determine the median for the data, plot it for each data point, and connect the points with a straight line. (g) Count the number of runs on the chart. A "run" is one or more consecutive data points on the same side of the median not counting the data points on the median. (h) Compare the number of runs to a pre-established statistical computation. The statistical computation indicates the lower and upper run limit according to a specified number of data points.

If there are too few or too many runs in the data, a special cause variation exists. There are several other types of runs to include "shifts," "trends," and "zigzags," but each shares the common element of exhibiting a distinctive pattern. Again, if the pattern exceeds the established statistical limit for the number of data points, special cause variation exists. One must attempt to mitigate or eliminate the special cause(s) so that process stability can be achieved. Once stable, the goal is to continuously improve the process by reducing variation.

—Shonna L. Mulkey

FURTHER READING

Carey, R. G., & Lloyd, R. C. (1995). *Measuring quality improvement in healthcare.* New York: Quality Resources.

Shearer, C. (1994). *Practical continuous improvement for professional services.* Milwaukee, WI: ASQC Quality Press.

S

SAFETY NET PROVIDERS

In recent years the term *safety net* has been applied to the programs taking care of people who do not have employment-related benefits of various types. It implies that a safety net of programs is in place, such as unemployment insurance, welfare programs, and Medicaid. Services for Medicaid enrollees may or may not be available in a community. In health care the term *safety net providers* refers primarily to those who care for the uninsured and the underinsured. In some communities this is a local health department that provides primary care services. In other cases it may be the outpatient department of a city or county hospital, a rural health center, or a school nurse. If these public health providers are not available in a community, there is either no safety net or there is a second tier of charity providers such as a clinic run by church groups or by medical students or uncompensated care given by existing providers, such as hospitals or community physicians. As budgetary restraints have led to reductions in the payments made by Medicare and Medicaid, more and more providers have withdrawn their services from the medically needy populations, forcing more and more of such people onto safety net providers.

The biggest group in need of a medical safety net is the working poor, who work for relatively low wages and whose employers usually do not provide much in the way of health care insurance. The wealthy can purchase their own insurance and typically work in organizations with good health benefits, whereas the unemployed and disabled are eligible for government-financed health programs such as Medicaid. However, the working poor, even when employed or on Social Security, have trouble meeting the ever-increasing deductible and copayment requirements of their health insurance programs.

There is no national plan to provide the so-called safety net for health care. There is still an unresolved debate over whether health care is a right or a privilege in the United States. Available services for uninsured and the working poor are sparse and quixotic. Full funding is available for individuals needing kidney dialysis, but not for transplants. Mental health treatment costs are covered under Medicare, if one is ruled disabled, but not under most employer-financed health plans. A separate mental health delivery system functions in most states. Although receiving some federal support, it is inadequately funded. Many centers have tended to wander away from their original objective of focusing on the chronically and severely mentally ill. Coordination between community mental health clinics and state hospitals is poor, and many mentally ill fall through the cracks, adding to the burden of homeless shelters and prisons. The one group experiencing increasing access to medical care is children. Each year another cohort of children is added to those receiving Medicaid coverage at incomes up to almost twice the local poverty level.

What must precede the design of a health care safety net system is consensus about what level of care the working poor are to be afforded and where payment is to come from. Then expert opinion can be called on to design a more reliable and comprehensive safety net system.

—Curtis P. McLaughlin

SALES FORECASTING

Sales forecasting is defined as *a projection into the future of expected demand, given a stated set of environmental conditions.* This is distinguished from the sales plan, which we here define as a set of specified managerial actions to be undertaken to meet or exceed the sales forecast. Notice that our definition of a sales forecast does not specify the technique (quantitative or qualitative), does not specify who develops the forecast within the company, nor does it include managerial plans. Managerial plans for the level of sales to be achieved should be based on the forecast of demand, but the two management functions should be kept separate. For this reason, our definition of the sales plan (or any other managerial plans, for that matter) does not include the activities of making projections of demand levels.

Notice that these definitions imply different performance measures for sales forecasts than for sales plans. Because the goal of sales forecasting is to make the projections within a defined environment, a key measure of performance is accuracy of the forecast, and a key method to explain variances in accuracy is how the environment varied from the one defined. This explanation is not intended to excuse forecast inaccuracy but rather to help us understand the business environment and forecast more accurately in the future.

In contrast, the goal of the sales plan is not to achieve accuracy, but rather to meet, and in some cases to exceed, the plan. The purpose of the sales plan is not to accurately project future demand levels. It is to provide sales goals for marketing and sales based on this projected future demand, and the motivation to meet or exceed these goals.

If we can simply set a sales goal and expect marketing and sales to exceed it, why do we even need a sales forecast in the first place? This is a question many managers ask and often answer incorrectly (saying, "We do not need a forecast"), to their eventual sorrow.

The correct answer is that every time we develop a plan of any kind, we first make a forecast. This is as true of individuals as it is of profit and not-for-profit companies, government organizations, and in fact any entity that makes a plan. It can be as simple as planning what we will wear tomorrow. When we decide to wear wool slacks and a sweater, we are forecasting it will be cool. If we add an umbrella to our ensemble, we are forecasting rain. The plan was predicated on the forecast, whether we consciously thought about it or not.

This is not much different from a company making financial plans based on expected demand and the costs of meeting that demand. The trick is not to get caught in the trap of making "inadvertent sales forecasts." Inadvertent sales forecasts are made when we are so intent on developing the plan that we simply assume what demand will be, rather than giving any concentrated thought and analysis to the market conditions that will be necessary to create this level of sales.

One great example of such an inadvertent forecast came from a manufacturer in the health care products industry. The owner of the company explained to us that the sales plan called for an increase in sales of 5% for the next year. However, we had also been told that this industry in this country was not growing and that any attempt to grab market share from the competition was only met by countermoves that caused greater promotional expenditures but no shift in market share. "Wait a minute," we said to the owner. "How

can industry size not change, market share not change, but sales grow? It doesn't take a math major to figure out this is not going to work." The answer was that management would simply have to motivate everyone to work harder to achieve the (mathematically impossible) plan. Of course, it is obvious what happened—no amount of motivation is going to overcome an impossible situation, and the sales plan was not achieved. It was not achieved because it was based on an inadvertent and uninformed forecast.

Let's look at one more example. A large regional distributor of medical products to hospitals develops an elaborate annual profit plan. Hundreds of person-days go into the development of this plan, but it always starts with such comments as "We need profits to increase next year by 6%. Let's figure out how much sales have to be to achieve that goal." Notice that the term "goal" sneaked into that quote. Where these executives should have started was to ask about market and environmental conditions facing the company during the planning horizon and what levels of sales could be expected based on these conditions. The plan then becomes one of determining what marketing and sales efforts will be necessary to meet and exceed these projections to a level necessary to achieve the profit plan. The plan cannot drive the forecast; it has to be the other way around.

—John T. Mentzer

FURTHER READING

Mentzer, J. T. (1999, Fall). The impact of forecasting improvement on return on shareholder value. *Journal of Business Forecasting*, pp. 8–12.

Mentzer, J. T., & Bienstock, C. C. (1998, Fall). The seven principles of sales forecasting systems. *Supply Chain Management Review*, 76–83.

Mentzer, J. T., Bienstock, C. C., & Kahn, K. B. (1999, May–June). Benchmarking sales forecasting management. *Business Horizons, 42*, 48–56.

Moon, M. A., Mentzer, J. T., Smith, C. D., & Garver, M. S. (1998, September–October). Seven keys to better forecasting. *Business Horizons, 41*, 44–52.

SALES IN HEALTH CARE

See Revenues

SALES PROMOTION

See Advertising

SATISFACTION

See Customer Satisfaction Research, Job Satisfaction

SCOPE OF PRACTICE

Scope of practice is defined as all the accepted services provided by a particular profession. It provides the parameters within which a profession provides services. A scope of practice may be determined in a number of ways. A recognized professional organization may develop and define the scope of practice for a particular profession. Health care examples would include the various medical specialties with their specialty boards, such as the American Association of Nurse Anesthetists for Nurse Anesthesia. The hospital credentialing process defines the scope of practice for any single individual health care provider within the hospital setting. State statute or law may more rigidly define the scope of medical practice. It is done to specifically separate and define the services provided by nonphysician health care providers (that is, physician assistants and nurse practitioners) from the practice of medicine, which only physicians can perform. This is usually performed through the state licensure boards, which license health care providers to provide services within their scope of practice.

CONFLICTS ARISING OVER THE SCOPE OF PRACTICE

Conflicts between health care providers or provider organizations can arise when scopes of practice overlap. These can be as minor as conflicts over hospital credentialing when two medical specialties provide similar services or procedures. Conflicts can become more serious when health care providers, other than physicians, are providing services traditionally provided by physicians. Most of these conflicts have been resolved by state statutes that clearly define the scope of practice for these nonphysician health care providers. Conflicts may also arise in the development of these "legal" scopes of practice, because they more often focus on boundary setting between the professions and what discrete activities belong to a specific specialty than on the overlapping competencies of the professions.

—George V. Jirak

FURTHER READING

Furrow, B. R., Greaney, T. L., Johnson, S. H., Jost, T. S., & Schwartz, R. L. (2001). *Health Law: Cases, Materials, and Problems* (4th ed., pp. 117-125). St. Paul, MN: West.
www.aana.com

SECONDARY DATA

See Marketing Research

SEGMENTATION

See Market Segmentation

SELECTION BIAS

See Risk Adjustment, Risk Selection

SELECTIVE ADVERTISING

See Advertising

SELECTIVE DISTRIBUTION

Selective distribution is one of three levels of distribution intensity that companies may choose from as they develop their marketing channels; intensive and exclusive are the others. Each manufacturer must determine the extent of market coverage it considers adequate for providing consumers access to its products. This decision is affected by a number of factors, including the type of product being distributed and the target markets (consumer segments) being pursued.

For example, a candy manufacturer such as M&M/Mars wants to have its markets thoroughly covered because consumers buy candy frequently, so its products are available in grocery stores, convenience stores, and many other retail outlets. This is intensive distribution. In contrast, other products are bought less frequently, involve more risks, and require that consumers spend more time in the decision-making process.

Selective distribution is used by manufacturers of automobiles and furniture, among others. Consumers like to compare prices, so retailers tend to locate relatively close to each other. This is why one sees automobile dealers clustered together along a major highway, or furniture stores located within several blocks of each other in a city's downtown area.

A pharmacy chain store such as Walgreen's follows this selective strategy in locating its pharmacies in smaller cities. If the city is big enough, Walgreen's will open more than one pharmacy location, much like one finds several Ford dealerships in a major metropolitan city.

—Jeffrey W. Totten

See also Exclusive Distribution, Intensive Distribution

FURTHER READING

Lamb, C. W., Jr., Hair, J. F., Jr., & McDaniel, C. (2002). *Marketing* (6th ed., Chapter 12). Cincinnati, OH: South-Western/ Thompson Learning.

SELF-CARE

See Wellness

SELF-INSURANCE

When health insurance companies create the products they sell, they manage risks of the cost of health care against the premium they expect to receive from purchasers. The costs include administrative expenses, and the medical expenses for hospital and physician services, pharmacy, and multiple other, ancillary categories of services, such as durable medical equipment and home health care. Insurance companies offer and charge for additional services that include provider network development and management, managed care activities such as case management, and the cluster of administrative services that lead to the accurate payment of claims based on thousands of combinations of benefits selected by purchasers of individual and group health insurance. The entire package, extent and availability of benefits, cost and payments, and communications to and about recipients, all need to be managed within a regulatory environment that becomes more complex each year. An entire industry of third-party administrators (TPAs) has evolved to deliver different combinations of the services required to provide health insurance.

Group health insurance linked to employment has been institutionalized in this country for decades. Employers have tried to manage the cost against the tide of inflation, with brief periods of success followed by periods of rising cost. Managing the cost by undertaking the risk themselves, employers have become self-insured or have managed so-called captive companies that provide health insurance to employees. Another option that is gaining recognition and may offer employers respite from health care inflation is defined contribution plans (DC plans).

GROUP HEALTH INSURANCE

Employers of large groups with 1000 or more beneficiaries down to companies with as few as 50 employees purchase almost all nongovernmental group health insurance. Like other large employers, government agencies purchase services for their employees and also for recipients of entitlement programs. They have all been through the insurance wars of the past 20 years. Employers also have to purchase benefits for retirees, a growing class of recipients.

To control the ever-rising cost of health care and the costs associated with administering these benefits, most purchasers have taken on the risk of some of the activities listed earlier. Each service is available from health plans or specialty vendors individually or as a complete package, for which the purchaser designates a fiduciary, and the risk is born totally by the purchaser. Most self-insured people mitigate the risk by buying reinsurance that covers catastrophic costs above a predefined level. Like other aspects of the health insurance market, reinsurance is becoming more costly too. In general, midsize groups of 100 to 500 recipients move in and out of the self-insurance market as prices fluctuate, whereas larger companies find that assuming the risk themselves is more attractive and tend to continue in the market once they enter.

Two areas of risk appear to be the reasons why employers are attracted to self-insurance. The cost of health care services continues to increase and the trend that slowed during the early to mid 1990s has accelerated to double digits in most of the drivers of health care delivery. The most visible cost component is the trend toward pharmacy benefits, which now generates more health costs in most plans than inpatient hospital care. As the costs of services and the demand for services continue to rise, the margins and taxes passed on to purchasers as part of the cost of health insurance represent potential savings.

The second category of risk is especially important to large groups. When an employer group enters a fully insured risk pool, the insurer may base the risk on community rating. If an employer maintains a relatively young or otherwise more healthy employee group, then the employer's health insurance costs support more unfavorable groups in the same risk pool. For example, that may mean being included in a fully insured pool with smaller or midsize groups where there are one or two catastrophic cases and the insurer is also the reinsurer. Purchasing insurance can be unfavorable compared with the group's own experience with the cost of health services, but can be favorable, if expensive, to some older, more stable employee groups.

Some self-insureds may purchase services directly from large medical groups or hospitals. Most, however, rent a contracted network from a health plan or other TPA along with a number of support services. Sometimes medical management and customer services (such as member handbooks) are included with the network. Many of these services, such as case management, utilization management, and disease state management, can be purchased individually from specialized vendors or selected from a menu provided by the TPA. Pharmacy benefits managers (PBMs) can provide a network, a formulary, drug-purchasing strategies, customer service, and claims payment for one carved-out benefit. Likewise, behavioral health, specialty services such as radiology, and laboratory services can be purchased individually. The organizations that provide carved-out or "boutique" services often assume risk through capitation or through pricing based on guaranteed savings.

Claims payment and customer service can be purchased from TPAs that specialize in efficient transaction management and nothing else. As the Internet becomes more secure, many administrative services, especially traditional customer services, could be delivered directly to members in their homes and could represent savings in the future. E-commerce between providers and payers may enable self-insureds to obtain better pricing based on more rapid reimbursement that includes direct deposit to providers' accounts.

Renting or purchasing services directly carries the additional risk of managing the delivery system. Self-insureds can be protected to some extent by requiring accreditation from recognized agencies that also require some proof of regulatory compliance for accreditation. HIPAA, ERISA, and the Patients' Bill of Rights (PBR) all contribute to the cost of managing health benefits. These regulations, particularly HIPAA, require that a firewall between the company and the health benefit be maintained to protect the confidentiality of an individual benefit recipient's medical information. COBRA administration is an added function mandated by HIPAA, ERISA, and the PBR that requires eligibility and the benefits determination process to be managed in a way that protects the self-insured from legal liability.

Benefit packages are designed by the employer or by a TPA and should be based on more than cost. The benefits need to be supported by medical evidence and should be delivered effectively and at a fair price for groups to realize the benefit of self-insurance. Claims payment, contracting with providers, and member contracts all need to be based on the standard of care and medical evidence. This standard changes, often during the course of a contract. The pipeline for new technology continually introduces new and innovative care that was not considered during the original benefit design. Self-insureds need to maintain a relationship with a resource that can filter and provide reliable recommendations for changes in benefit based on compelling evidence of increased value or savings.

DEFINED CONTRIBUTION

Limiting choice by carefully limiting benefits made employer-sponsored health insurance a useful bargaining chip for employee negotiations. This relatively inexpensive, visible benefit offered security from catastrophic expense to employees, and tax savings to employers for nearly 40 years following World War II. The HMO revolution spun off the physician organization (PO) and physician hospital organization (PHO) and the vertically integrated delivery system. Demands for more health care freedom led to the open-access HMO, the point-of-service plans, and to tremendous growth in preferred provider organizations (PPOs) to balance cost and demand.

This 20-year round of restricted networks, restricted access within networks (for example, to specialists), and juggling risk between payers and providers has run out of steam. Mandated coverage, recipient demand, provider backlash, and new technology all have re-created the inflationary health care trends of the period before managed care, between 1980 and 1990. During the managed care storm of design and reinvention, recipients have remained isolated from the true cost of health care. Even though out-of-pocket expenses appear higher than ever with copayments, coinsurance, deductibles, and out-of-network penalties, recipients' share of the actual cost of care is still nearly 25% lower now than it was in 1990 (Coddington et al., 2002).

Initial efforts to educate beneficiaries about quality and cost have not compelled people to become good consumers of health care. Most insureds think only in terms of the cost directly to them for health insurance, which in many cases is unrelated to their own health care expenses. The next proposal to shift risk is from employers directly to employees in the form of consumer-driven health care. This form of risk sharing is also known as a *defined contribution (DC) plan,* in which the employer creates a fixed dollar subsidy to the employee based on the lowest contribution that might be made in the current list of plan choices available to the employee. The expectation exists that employer costs will be lower and more predictable. Because the employee will be stretching those dollars to cover all routine health care costs, another expectation is that the employee will want to be a better consumer.

The concept is tentative at the present time. Some employers and insurance companies have offered DC plans, but the experience is limited. The two DC plans currently available are medical savings accounts (MSAs) or a voucher toward the purchase of health insurance (Ford, 2002). DC plans need to be administered. These plans require most if not all of the infrastructure necessary to provide self-insurance to groups. The funds need to be used for their intended purpose, catastrophic or reinsurance need to be available to the employee, and some form of contract between providers and employee groups will make pricing to beneficiaries more reliable. Companies that manage DC plans are emerging in anticipation of the need for administrators.

E-platforms for both information, and self- or physician-directed health care are being developed but do not attract a lot of consumers yet. This may be one product where the Internet becomes a valuable source of information for consumers, and cost savings to employers.

—Gregory Preston

FURTHER READING

Coddington, C., Fischer, E. A., Moore, K. D., & Clarke R. L. (2000). *Beyond managed care* (Chapter 3, pp. 59–72). San Francisco: Jossey-Bass.

Ford, E. W. (2002). Economic implications of defined contribution health plans: Their impact on employers, insurers, employees, and healthcare providers. *Business Economics, 37*(1), 38.

SELF-REFERRAL

A self-referral occurs when a physician refers a patient for services to another health care entity in which the physician or an immediate family member owns financial interest. The referral itself must be for one or more designated health service (DHS), and furthermore must not be an exception to the Stark law (a safe harbor; see entry for *Stark Law*). The financial interest can be direct, such as an investment or stock ownership, or indirect, such as a salary for being the medical director or a rental arrangement with a hospital-owned building.

The self-referral laws were developed to prevent physicians or their immediate family members from benefiting financially from a higher volume of services than would otherwise be recommended if they did not own interest in the health care entity. The laws assume that doctors who own ancillary services would be induced to refer patients there in order to increase their own return on the investment.

Another set of laws, antikickback rules, also apply to self-referral. Under the antikickback rules, it is a crime to knowingly and willfully offer, pay, solicit, or receive any remuneration to induce a person to refer an individual for a service covered under a federal health care program. Its violation can result in civil monetary penalties equal to three times the amount of illegal remuneration, plus $50,000 per violation, plus possible exclusion from the Medicare system. If the violation is proven beyond a reasonable doubt, criminal penalties may also apply.

DHS AND SAFE HARBORS

When a physician wants to enter any financial relationship with another health care entity, such as investing in imaging or ambulatory surgical centers, it is very important for the physician to understand the DHS and the exceptions to the law (safe harbors). The exceptions were developed in order to clarify ambiguities in the self-referral law, which then made it

easier to decide if an investment was safe under the law. The exceptions are also called *safe harbors,* and the complete set of exceptions that were approved as of January 2001 are known as *the final rule.* The first self-referral law, also called the *Stark law,* was passed in 1989. The first final rule was passed in July 1991, in which 10 original safe harbors were described to clarify safe investments. These rules still left open ambiguities for investors, and further clarifications were added in 1992, 1993, 1994, 1996, and 1999, until the final rule was issued in January 2001. The final rule has made it relatively easier for physicians to invest in other health care entities.

The following is a list of the DHSs: clinical lab services; physical therapy, occupational therapy, and speech/ language pathology services; radiology and other imaging services; durable medical equipment and supplies; prosthetics, orthotics, and prosthetic supplies; home health services; outpatient prescription drugs; inpatient hospital services; outpatient hospital services; and parental and enteral nutrients and related supplies and equipment.

The initial 10 safe harbors that were issued in July 1991 concerned the following 10 areas:

1. Investment interests

2. Space rentals

3. Equipment rentals

4. Personal services and management contracts

5. Sale of practice

6. Referral services

7. Warranties

8. Discounts

9. Employees

10. Group purchasing organization

To clarify ambiguities about "investment interests," three additional safe harbors were approved in the final rule on July 29, 1991:

- *Investment in rural area:* The original "60–40" rule was made more flexible.
- *Surgeons who refer patients to ambulatory surgical centers (ASCs) and perform surgery themselves on these patients are protected.* Profits from these entities should not be based on the volume of referral, but rather on the investment interests. ASCs located on the premises of the hospital are not covered.
- *Investment interests in group practices composed exclusively of active investors.* More clarification was given.

These new exceptions were very helpful, and ASCs sprang up all across the country. However, significant ambiguities were still preventing group practices from making certain investments that could be useful to patients. On January 4, 2001, Centers for Medicare and Medicaid Services (CMS) issued phase 1 of the final rule, which provides more flexibility to physicians in investments and compensation arrangements. These new exceptions included the following:

- *Physician service exception:* This exception allows physicians to refer patients to other physicians of the group, or the independent contractors in the group practice or under the supervision of a physician member or contractor in the group practice. This exception is important because it considers an independent contractor physician as a part of the group practice as long as he or she is in contractual agreement for at least one year. This allows referral to independent contractors to fall within the exception.

- *Office ancillary service exception:* This allows physicians to refer patients within their own practice for certain ancillary DHSs such as imaging services and lab and pathology services. Certain conditions regarding the location, billing, and group must be satisfied. The service should be provided in the same building where all the other activities of the group take place. It can be provided in the satellite office where a broad range of services are provided that are the same as those provided in the main office. However, the relationship between the referring physician and the patient should not be grounded solely on the basis of the service. For example, the physician may send a nursing home patient whom he (or she) treats on a regular basis to his office for imaging studies, but not other patients whom he does not treat on a regular basis. Simply sending these other patients for imaging studies does not make him their main treating physician. In addition, the billing should be performed under the group billing number. To get the exception, the definition of the group practice must be satisfied. The group consists of at least two or more physicians who are recognized by state law. It should operate as a unified business with one governing body and proper financial management practices. Each physician of the group should provide at least 75% of his or her work in the confines of this group's joint space, using joint equipment and employees. Finally, the compensation of the physicians should not be based on the volume of DHS referrals

- *Exceptions for compensation arrangements:* They protect the medical staff's incidental benefits provided by a hospital. These include free parking provisions and free compliance training to physicians on the hospital staff. However, the most important member of this category is the fair market value compensation exception. Under this exemption, the physician can enter into a compensation arrangement with an entity for performing DHSs. To get this exemption, the antikickback provision has to be satisfied. The contract should be in writing regarding the services to be provided, and the duration of the contract should be for at least one year. The compensation is set in advance and is consistent with the fair market value.

- *Radiological services have been redefined.* Nuclear medicine, preventive screening procedures such as mammograms, and certain invasive procedures such as cardiac catheterization and endoscopies are included in the exemptions. Radiation therapy and supplies also qualify for the exemption.

In conclusion, several aspects of the self-referral and anti-kickback statute should be kept in mind whenever a business relationship is being planned to provide DHSs. Some of the safe harbors are clear-cut, such as building an ASC that is owned and operated by the group. The new final rule allows the groups to provide ancillary services to their patients provided all conditions just described are met. Legal advice should be obtained to construct proper contracts and compensation arrangements. Despite this new clarity of the law, challenges remain to clarify further ambiguities in the future. If your legal counsel has any doubt about the financial arrangement being proposed, advisory opinion can be obtained from the U.S. Inspector General regarding it. However, even if advisory opinion allows the exemption, it does not guarantee that the office of Inspector General will not challenge the financial arrangement in the future because the opinion was based solely on the facts provided at the time.

—Ramesh K. Gandhi

FURTHER READING

www.cms.hhs.gov
www.oig.hhs.gov/fraud.html

SENIOR CARE

See Long-Term Care

SENTINEL EVENT

The term *sentinel event* was created by the Joint Commission on Accreditation of Healthcare Organizations

(JCAHO). It is an unexpected occurrence involving death or serious physical or psychological injury or risk thereof. Serious injury specifically includes loss of limb or function. The phrase "risk thereof" includes any process variation for which a recurrence would carry a significant chance of serious adverse outcome. Said differently, a sentinel event is an event that has resulted in an unanticipated death or major, permanent loss of function not related to the natural course of a patient's illness or underlying condition. The phrase "major permanent loss of function" means sensory, motor, physiologic, or intellectual impairment not present on admission and requiring continued treatment or lifestyle change. When major, permanent loss of function cannot be immediately determined, reporting is not expected until either the patient is discharged with continued major loss of function or two weeks have elapsed with persistent major loss of function, whichever occurs first. A distinction is made between an adverse outcome that is related to the natural course of the patient's illness or underlying condition and a death or major permanent loss of function that is associated with the treatment or lack of treatment of that condition. JCAHO considers the following to be mandatory sentinel events (even if the outcome is not death or permanent loss of function):

- *Patient suicide or attempted suicide with serious injury in a setting where the patient is housed around the clock, or death, or serious injury following elopement from a hospital setting.* An "elopement" is an unauthorized and unexpected patient departure from a facility.
- *An infant abduction or discharge to the wrong family.* An abduction is when a child has been taken from the facility without the knowledge and approval of the patient's physician and parent or legal guardian. Discharge to the wrong family occurs when a child and/or parents are misidentified. This most often occurs with newborns, when proper identification processes have not been initiated or maintained. An example is misplacement of identification bands, resulting in patient misidentification.
- *Rape of a patient.* This is a legal definition and differs according to state. Consult legal counsel to determine the strict legal interpretation of the term (for example, New York State Penal Law, Sections 130.35, 130.00, and 130.25, specifies definitions of first-, second-, and third-degree rape).
- *Hemolytic transfusion reaction involving administration of blood or blood products having major blood group incompatibility.*
- *Surgery on the wrong patient or wrong body part.*

—Kathleen Ferrara

FURTHER READING

www.jcaho.org

SERVICE AREA COMPETITOR ANALYSIS

Business organizations have long engaged in competitor analysis, viewing it as an essential part of environmental analysis. However, health care organizations were not concerned with service area competitor moves and countermoves, because most organizations cooperated rather than competed. Hospitals, long-term care facilities, and physicians focused on trying to meet the demand for their services rather than on competing. This history of noncompetition changed when legislation led to an increased number of hospital beds, an increased number of physicians (particularly within certain specialties), and a prospective- (rather than cost-) based system. Every segment of the health care industry has become more competitive because of the oversupply of beds and physicians as well as fundamental changes within the industry brought about by the influences of managed care, efforts to reduce costs, emphasis on increasing efficiency, and the increasing presence of for-profit health care organizations.

In the past, a regional area contained few competitors. More recently, alliances have brought in additional competitors. As competition escalated, some formerly friendly competitors have become far more aggressive in their efforts to attract and keep consumers, sensing that survival is at stake. In some markets, mergers among previously independent hospitals to form competing systems intensified competition. Academic medical centers, with their focus on research, have traditionally viewed only other academic medical centers as competitors. However, with the impact of managed care and lowered reimbursements, new competitors exist.

"Managed care" was supposed to control costs by restricting consumer choice. Economies of scale were to be achieved by limiting patients' choices for hospitals and physicians. Primary care physicians became "gatekeepers" directing patients to only one hospital to obtain the best possible rates. Strong competition emerged among health care providers for the managed care organization's insured group.

Despite the lack of experience in performing competitor analysis and the difficulty in identifying specific competitors for the many services offered, health care organizations need to understand their immediate competitive environment to develop successful strategies. A significant contribution of competitor analysis is the development of a clear definition of the service category (industry or industry segment).

DEFINING SERVICE CATEGORIES

To have a clear idea of what is to be accomplished by service area competitor analysis, it is important to first understand and define the service category, starting narrowly with direct competitors, and then expanding the category to include more indirect competitors. To avoid a too narrow focus, the service category must be defined in the broadest terms that are useful. Competition may come from very nontraditional competitors. For example, using its success in hotels the Marriott Corporation drew on its expertise in accommodations management to create Senior Living Services. Previously, multihospital systems and nursing home chains dominated this category.

Market entry by competitors from outside the metropolitan area, the region, or the state is quite common. Expansion by multihospital for-profit systems (such as HCA, the Healthcare Company) represent competitive challenges in many markets. Nationally recognized clinics, such as the Mayo Clinic and the Cleveland Clinic, have expanded to locations in Florida and Arizona.

Many health care organizations have several service categories, each of which may have different geographic service areas. For a multihospital chain deciding to enter a new market, the service category may be defined as acute care, but for a rehabilitation hospital, service categories may include physical therapy and orthopedic surgery. Further, because many health care services can be broken down into subservices, the level of service category specificity should be identified. For example, pediatric care may be categorized as well-baby care, infectious diseases, developmental pediatrics, pediatric hematology-oncology, and so forth. Certainly pediatric hematology-oncology as a service category would have a far larger service area than well-baby care. A parent with a child who has cancer would travel farther to see a specialist than a parent who was seeking well-baby care.

Plastic surgery is a medical specialty that can be defined as a service category; however, there are additional subservice categories. For instance, reconstructive plastic surgeons often specialize on the face, dealing with congenital deformities and injuries from trauma. Ear, nose, and throat physicians as well as oral surgeons are performing similar procedures. Cosmetic plastic surgeons may offer a full range of services, including reconstructive surgery, or they may specialize on the face, breast, or other body parts. Plastic surgeons may specialize on the basis of procedures used, such as laser or liposuction. To understand how customers perceive the organization's service category is an important determination.

DEFINING SERVICE AREA

Service area is the geographic location surrounding the health care provider. A health care organization must analyze in detail all relevant and important aspects of the service area including economic, demographic, psychographic (lifestyle), and disease pattern characteristics that will help position the service category and tailor the service to the needs of the service area. Usually limited by fairly well-defined geographic boundaries, services may be difficult to render beyond these borders because of distance, cost, time, and so on. Managed care contracts define service areas as well.

Understanding the geographic boundaries is important to define the service area but is often difficult because of the variety of services offered. In an acute care hospital, the service area for cardiac services may be the entire state or region, whereas the service area for the emergency room may be only a few square miles. Thus, for a health care organization that offers several service categories, it may be necessary to conduct several service area analyses. At the same time, defining only one service category may suffice (as in the case of a long-term care facility).

Although service area is determined by customers, it is based on the health care providers that are available. For example, some rural areas have no doctors. Rural residents have to travel to the nearest town that has a doctor. The service area for that doctor may be very large in terms of geography (but have few residents).

In more densely populated areas, consumers drive past some providers to seek health care from the doctor they prefer. The distance consumers are willing to travel depends on a variety of factors, including the kind of care, reputation, perceived treatment from doctor and staff, and proximity to home or work. Consumers are "shopping" for health care today because of the higher costs of care, including insurance premiums, out-of-pocket costs (copayments and percentages), and wait time costs.

Determining the geographic boundaries of the service area may be highly subjective and usually depends on patient histories, the reputation of the organization, available technology, physician recognition, and so on. In addition, geographic impediments such as a river, mountains, and limited-access highways can limit the service area. In general, health services are provided and received within a well-defined service area, where the competition is clearly identified and critical forces for the survival of the organization originate.

SERVICE AREA PROFILE

Once the service category and service area have been defined, a profile should be developed. The service area profile includes key competitively relevant economic, demographic, psychographic (lifestyle), and community health status indicators as these facts relate to service category delivery by the organization and its competitors. Relevant economic information may include income distribution, major industries and employers, types of businesses and institutions, economic growth rate, seasonality of businesses, unemployment statistics, and so forth. Demographic variables commonly used in describing the service area include age, sex, race, marital status, education level, mobility, religious affiliation, and occupation. Psychographic (lifestyle) variables, which are often better predictors of consumer behavior than demographic variables, include values, attitudes, lifestyle, social class, or personality.

Health status of the service area is important in considering its viability, because disease may be related to age, occupation, environment, or economics. Health status includes any data normally considered to represent the physical and mental well-being of a population. Demographic, psychographic, and health status information should be included in the analysis only if relevant to competitiveness.

SERVICE AREA STRUCTURE

Harvard's Michael E. Porter suggested that the level of competitive intensity within an industry is the most critical factor in an organization's environment. In Porter's model, competitive intensity is a function of the threat of new entrants to the market, the level of rivalry among existing organizations, the threat of substitute products and services, the bargaining power of buyers (customers), and the bargaining power of suppliers. The strength and impact of these five forces must be carefully monitored and assessed to determine the viability of the service category today and in the future.

STRATEGIC GROUPS

The next step in the service area competitor analysis process is to evaluate the strengths and weaknesses of competitors, characterize their strategies, group competitors by the types of strategies they have exhibited, and predict competitive responses to strategic initiatives by other organizations. Evaluation of competitors' strengths and weaknesses provide clues as to their future strategies and to areas where competitive advantage might be achieved. Such information may be obtained through local newspapers, trade journals, Web sites, focus groups with customers and stakeholders, consultants who specialize in the industry, securities analysts, outside health care professionals, and so on.

Organizations within a strategic group are each other's primary (direct) competitors. As management writer Bruce Henderson noted, "Organizations most like yours are the most dangerous." Members of a strategic group primarily compete with each other and do not compete with organizations outside their strategic group, even though other competitors outside the group may offer similar products or services.

Organizations within a strategic group use similar resources to serve similar markets; however, management in an individual organization must find ways (sometimes subtle) to differentiate its organization and achieve competitive advantage. Strategic group analysis may indicate important market dimensions (niches) that competitors are

not capitalizing on. Lack of attention to critical success factors by other competitive organizations offering the same or a similar service may provide an opportunity for management to differentiate its services.

Within a service category or service area, there may be only one strategic group (if all the organizations follow the same strategy), or there may be several different groups. Strategic group analysis differentiates between "within-group" rivalry and "between-group" rivalry.

SERVICE CATEGORY CRITICAL SUCCESS FACTORS

Sometimes organizations have inflexible commitments to historical critical success factors (traditional inpatient services) and do not attempt to forecast future success factors (outpatient approaches). Typically a limited number of activities within a service category in a service area must be achieved at a high level if an organization is to be successful. It is possible to identify critical success factors through careful analysis of the environment and the competitors in that environment.

Generally, once the service category critical success factors have been identified, several goals may be developed for each success factor. At that point, a strategy may be developed around the goals. Establishing linkages among the environment, the critical success factors, the goals, and the strategy is important. In addition, it is important to evaluate competitors on these critical success factors, because excellence in any of these factors may be the basis for competitive advantage. Further, these factors form the fundamental dimensions of strategy. Possible differences among an organization's strategic options in a given service area may include specialization, reputation, service or product quality, technological leadership, vertical integration, cost position, and service.

LIKELY COMPETITOR ACTIONS OR RESPONSES

Strategy formulation is future oriented, requiring that management anticipate the moves of competitors. These moves may be projected by evaluating competitor strengths and weaknesses, membership in strategic groups, and the characterization of past strategies. A thorough analysis of the key strategic decisions of competitors may reveal their strategic intent.

SYNTHESIZING THE ANALYSES

To be useful for strategy formulation, general external environmental analysis and service area competitor analysis must be synthesized and then conclusions drawn. It is easy for strategic decision makers to be overwhelmed by information. To avoid paralysis by analysis, external environmental analysis should be summarized into key issues and trends (including their likely impact). Then service area competitor analysis should identify the strategic group for a service category and competitors' likely future actions.

—Linda E. Swayne

See also Competitive Advantage, Critical Success Factors, Environmental Analysis, Industry Analysis, Strategic Groups

FURTHER READING

Baum, J. A. C., & Korn, H. J. (1996). Competitive dynamics of interfirm rivalry. *Academy of Management Journal, 39*(2), 256.

Ginter, P. M., Swayne, L. E., & Duncan, W. J. (2002). Service area competitor analysis. In P. M. Ginter, L. E. Swayne, & W. J. Duncan, *Strategic management of health care organizations* (4th ed.). Oxford, UK: Blackwell.

Henderson, B. D. (1989, November–December). The origin of strategy. *Harvard Business Review, 67,* 139–143.

Porter, M. E. (1980). *Competitive strategy: Techniques for analyzing industries and competitors.* New York: Free Press.

Reger, R. K., & Huff, A. S. (1993). Strategic groups: A cognitive perspective. *Strategic Management Journal, 14*(2), 103–123.

Zahra, S. A., & Chaples, S. S. (1993). Blind spots in competitive analysis. *Academy of Management Executive, 7*(2), 7–28.

SERVICE OPERATIONS

Value creation systems can be divided into two broad categories; goods-producing operations and service operations. Goods-producing operations are characterized by tangible outputs and are the result of physical transformations such as fabrication, assembly, blending, and chemical alteration. Service operations are characterized by intangible outputs and are relatively more labor intensive. Examples of service operations (and their transformation processes) include airlines (locational), hospitals (physiological), schools (informational), theme parks (entertainment), banks (financial), and department stores (exchange).

Service operations are distinct from goods-producing operations in several ways. First, services are created and consumed simultaneously. As a consequence, service operations lack the option of using inventory as a buffer between demand and capacity. For example, a toy manufacturer may spend the summer months building up inventory for the heavy demand of Christmas season. In contrast, a tax preparation service cannot "inventory" services but instead must temporarily ramp up capacity to satisfy heavy demands during tax season. This characteristic of services creates heightened challenges in the areas of demand forecasting, workforce planning, job scheduling, and customer wait-time management.

A second distinction is the degree of customer participation in the service creation process. Most goods are produced in a factory far away from the eventual consumer. Most services, in contrast, involve considerable customer participation and often directly involve the customer. Hence, a retail store must be laid out to make it easy for a customer to self-navigate, and great attention must be paid to cleanliness, lighting, and customer service training. Customer participation also implies considerable visibility into the design and operation of the service delivery process. Inefficiencies or inadequate staffing may be readily apparent and could negatively affect customer perception.

A third distinction is that most manufacturing operations strive to produce products that correspond to a particular definition of quality. Because services are often delivered on an individual basis, the definition of "quality service" can differ from person to person depending on each customer's needs. In health care, for example, some patients greatly value spending time with physicians and discussing a wide range of health or personal issues. Other patients may wish to spend the minimum time possible and perceive any other chat time as wasteful and not as adding value.

A fourth distinction stems from the intangible nature of a service itself. Service concepts, as opposed to product concepts, cannot easily be protected by patents and may be readily imitated. Also, the intangible nature prevents a customer from thoroughly evaluating a service before deciding to buy it. Hence, reputation plays a greater role in customer decisions.

The management of service operations requires the careful coordination of workforce, facility, equipment, information, and facilitating materials. For example, a health care clinic requires a proper mix of workforce skill sets, a physical facility, equipment for performing on-site tests, information in the form of patient records, and adequate inventories of supporting materials such as medications.

—Charles E. Noon

See also Health Care Service Operations, Operations Management

FURTHER READING

Fitzsimmons, J., & Fitzsimmons, M. (2001). *Service management.* New York: Irwin McGraw Hill.

SERVICE QUALITY

Quality is a most ambiguous word. It means different things to different people. It means different things to the same person at different times and in different circumstances. So quality is difficult to define and understand, and difficult to examine and evaluate. It is typically in the eye of the recipient. When it comes to service quality in the health care sector, the examination of quality would explore such areas as the effectiveness of an intervention, the appropriateness of a particular intervention and under what circumstances, and determining whether its benefits exceed its costs. Even this explanation is limited in scope. To consider an additional definition and broaden the understanding about quality, it might be described as that kind of care that is expected to maximize an inclusive measure of patient welfare, after one has taken account of the balance of expected gains and losses that attend the process of care in all its parts.

In 1984, the American Medical Association (AMA) defined high quality of care as care that consistently contributes to the improvement or maintenance of quality and/or duration of life. And in 1990, the Institute of Medicine (IOM) proposed that quality consists of the degree to which health services for individuals and populations increase the likelihood of desired health outcomes and are consistent with current knowledge.

Service quality encompasses three areas: quality assessment, quality improvement, and quality assurance, where quality assessment measures the essential elements of quality of care. Quality improvement consists of a set of techniques for continuous study and improvement in the process of delivering health services and products to meet the needs and expectations of customers of those services and products. To complete this circle, quality assurance embraces the full cycle of activities and systems for maintaining the quality of patient care.

Service quality as a systemwide approach is relatively new. Only in the 1970s did it receive a publicly concerted effort by providers. Most practitioners provided care independently of how others may have accomplished that same procedure. This was particularly true of surgical interventions, and a study in Vermont demonstrated that of 10 surgical procedures performed in 13 hospitals, there was wide variation in resource input, utilization of services, and expenditures. There was also variation and uncertainty about the effectiveness of different levels and specific kinds of aggregate health services.

As the focus on quality became more intense, it was suggested that quality of care and shaping the ways in which it is measured should include concepts of structural, process, and outcome measures of quality. Structural measures considered the characteristics of the system, and included such things as the number, type, size, and location of hospitals, the number and qualifications of providers, and other system amenities. These measures are the most tangible and most easily identified, and often reveal more about access to care than about quality of care received.

Process measures considered the components of the interactions between providers and the patient and focused on the technical quality of care and interpersonal interactions that occurred between the participants. Finally, outcome measures concentrated on the patient's subsequent health status following an intervention. As one might expect from the definition, outcomes are the least tangible and often most difficult to measure. Recall again, quality is most often in the eye of the recipient of care.

Because outcome is the final step in the process, one must know how to measure the outcome of care and services to determine the level of quality experienced by the customer/patient. To that end, organizations throughout the country have weighed in on this aspect of service quality and mandated compliance with processes to measure outcomes. For example, the Joint Commission for the Accreditation of Healthcare Organizations (JCAHO) carries much weight in this area.

The focus by JCAHO is on standards that require procedures for identifying, reviewing, and evaluating all key patient care processes as part of the performance improvement standards. Health care organizations must demonstrate that they have identified these processes, have collected data to validate the efficacy of these processes, and have in place a plan for an ongoing course of improvement based on the collected data and the analysis of those data. In addition, since JCAHO introduced the Sentinel Event Policy, organizations must also demonstrate that as they set priorities on their performance improvement efforts, they have also taken into consideration any high-risk issues identified in their organizations by sentinel events or near misses. These organizations must also consider the data generated from the monitoring of sentinel events and other resources in the literature.

Another organization, the National Committee for Quality Assurance (NCQA), accredits health maintenance organizations (HMOs), as proof to providers, consumers, and payers of their ability to provide high-quality services. The NCQA developed the Health Plan Employer Data and Information Set (HEDIS) in 1991 so that employers could compare health plans among all those companies. Several versions have been issued, but the concepts still remain: HEDIS measures six dimensions of prepaid managed care plans: quality management, physicians' credentials, members' rights and responsibilities, preventive health services, utilization management, and medical records. The organization incorporates more than 60 performance indicators to assist in the measurement of quality of care, access to and satisfaction with care, use of services, plan finances, and plan management. Of the nine indicators for quality of care, one focuses on outcomes: low birth weight. A second one, hospitalization rates for patients with asthma, focuses on a proxy for an outcome. The others focus on access to preventive services.

A discussion of service quality would not be complete without information regarding quality-of-care policy issues. Those issues include use of a carrot or a stick as most effective in making improvements, provider attitudes toward quality assessment, and the frequent blurring of lines between the issues of cost and quality. The debate rages on about the best approach between the carrot and the stick. It has more recently piqued interest in achieving a better understanding of processes as the cause of problems rather than blaming an individual.

—Patti Elaine Griffin

FURTHER READING

Barton, P. L. (1998). *Understanding the U.S. health services system*. Washington, DC: AUPHA [Association of University Programs in Health Administration] Press/Health Administration.

Coile, R. C., Jr. (1997). *The five stages of managed care*. Chicago: Health Administration Press.

Coile, R. C., Jr. (1998). *Millennium management*. Chicago: Health Administration Press.

Coile, R. C., Jr. (2000). *New century healthcare*. Chicago: Health Administration Press.

Cudney, A. E., & Reinbold, O. (2002). JCAHO: Responding to quality and safety imperatives. *Journal of Healthcare Management, 47*(4), 216–219.

Griffith, J. R. (1998). *Designing 21st century healthcare*. Chicago: Health Administration Press.

Griffith, J. R. (1999). *The well-managed healthcare organization*. Chicago: AUPHA Press/Health Administration Press.

SERVICES

Health care services can be expressed as a combination of resources, organizations, financing, and management that society uses to maintain a state of health, prevent disease, or manage the disease once it has begun. The health care services system in the United States is a market-based system in an affluent, industrialized, information-based, biotech-savvy economy.

To facilitate understanding the scope of health care services, the following topics are included as appropriate in each service presented: services available, providers of services, financing and payers for services provided, and the delivery system.

HEALTH CARE SERVICES AVAILABLE

Health care services in the United States can be divided into at least two discreet provider groups: public health and private health. A third group, special populations and special disorders, are discussed.

Public Health Care Services

The public health services sector is an organized function of the federal government and is supported by tax dollars from its citizens. It is organized and managed by a cabinet-level executive with an emphasis toward the prevention of disease, promotion of health, reporting and control of communicable diseases, responsibility for environmental factors such as air and water quality that affect the public's health, and collection and analysis of vital event data to provide indicators of the public's health.

The public health service has undergone numerous revisions as it has matured, but as of 1995 the essential public health services included monitoring health status to identify and solve community problems; diagnosing and investigating health problems and health hazards in the community; informing, educating, and empowering people about health issues; mobilizing community partnerships and actions to identify and solve health problems; developing policies and plans that support individual and community health efforts; enforcing laws and regulations that promote health and ensure safety; linking people to needed personal health services and assuring the provision of health services when otherwise unavailable; assuring a competent public health and personal health services workforce; evaluating effectiveness, accessibility, and quality of personal and population-based health services; and researching for new insights and innovative solutions to public health problems.

These activities and services are provided within the public health agencies as follows: Centers for Disease Control (CDC), Food and Drug Administration (FDA), Health Resources and Services Administration (HRSA), National Institutes for Health (NIH), the Substance Abuse and Mental Health Services Administration (SAMHSA), the Indian Health Service (IHS), and the Agency for Health Care Policy and Research (AHCPR). Although the public health service may directly deliver some primary care services, the focus is not on service delivery, but on shaping the nation's public health system to promote health and to prevent disease.

Although these organizations are under the umbrella of the U.S. Department of Health and Human Services (DHHS), other ministry-level health functions in the system provide health care services. For example, the U.S. Department of Defense (DOD) administers health services for active duty military personnel and their dependents and for military retirees. As well, the Department of Veterans Affairs (DVA) provides services to military veterans in a nationwide system of hospitals, clinics, and nursing homes. The U.S. Department of Justice (DOJ) manages the correctional health services in the country's prisons; the Drug Enforcement Agency (DEA) within the Department of Justice governs the use of narcotic prescription drugs; the

U.S. Department of Agriculture (USDA) administers the Women, Infants, and Children (WIC) nutritional program. WIC does not provide direct health services but is closely linked to programs that assist low-income recipients.

The Department of Labor (DOL) has oversight of the Occupational Safety and Health Administration (OSHA), which enforces healthy and hazard-free workplaces, and is generally categorized as a provider of health-related services. Finally, the Environmental Protection Agency (EPA) has responsibility for the protection of the environment, including water and air quality, and for removing contaminants such as toxins and pollutants from sites contaminated by those agents.

The public arena of health service providers includes two more groups, quasi-governmental organizations and voluntary agencies. Included in the quasi-governmental agencies are peer review organizations (PROs). These organizations perform statutorily mandated services under contract to the government. The agencies are generally organized as private, not-for-profit corporations, but their sole or primary function is to carry out a legislatively specified scope of work.

The last groups to be discussed in the public arena of health services providers are voluntary agencies. They are typically disease-specific agencies that focus their energies on subsets of the population. For example, the Children's Defense Fund lobbies for programs to improve the health and well-being of children and provides data on the health status of children. Another voluntary agency is the American Association of Retired Persons (AARP). This agency concentrates on health, social services, and other needs of the older population. The Red Cross assists in disaster relief and procures health services, food, shelter, and other services for victims of natural disasters.

Several voluntary professional associations indirectly provide or assist with the provision of health services; perhaps the two most recognized ones are the American Hospital Association and the American Medical Association. The American Hospital Association promotes the interests of health care organizations such as hospitals, and the American Medical Association represents physician interests across the nation.

Private Health Care Services

Private health care services are delivered by professionals in almost every community in the country. It is unlikely that most American citizens go without some level of care for any length of time. Personal care may be further explained and understood by reviewing the levels of care. For example, primary care, secondary care, tertiary care, long-term care, and palliative care are delivered in a variety of general clinics, specialty clinics, acute care hospitals, specialty hospitals, rehabilitation centers, long-term care

centers, assisted living facilities, hospice centers, people's homes, and numerous other venues. The private division also includes medical equipment and devices designed to assist people in mobility, activities of daily living, and maintenance of life. In addition, pharmaceuticals and other medical supplies constitute an important component in the private U.S. health care system.

To better understand the levels of health care services available to the public, one needs to discriminate among the various levels, starting with primary care. Primary care is usually the patient's first contact with the treatment system or provider, and can be defined as a service that includes a diagnosis of illness or disease, and provision of initial treatment. It is generally for episodic care for common, nonchronic illnesses or injuries. Primary care providers are physicians, physician assistants, nurse practitioners, nurse midwives, nurses, and other categories of providers considered to be clinicians. Primary care providers also include physical and speech therapists, mental health providers, diagnostic and therapeutic laboratory staff, podiatrists, optometrists, home health aides, respiratory therapists, and social workers.

Secondary care includes special ambulatory medical services and commonplace inpatient hospital acute care. Contrasted with ambulatory primary care, which is centered on episodic, often one-time common illnesses or injuries, secondary care is generally continuing care for sustained or chronic conditions. Providers of secondary care are predominantly physicians. Secondary care is provided in sites such as ambulatory surgery centers, radiology centers, urgent care centers, childbirth centers, and end-stage renal disease centers established by groups of physicians, hospitals, and other sponsors. Secondary care is expensive because it addresses persistent and recurrent health problems and conditions, and a significant and growing proportion of the U.S. population needs this level of care for their sustained or chronic health problems.

Tertiary care is the next level in the discussion of health care services. Tertiary care can be defined as care that centers on highly specialized, procedurally intensive inpatient care that may require a prolonged length of stay in a hospital. Because of the extended length of stay and intensity of the illness, the cost is significant. Some examples of tertiary care include surgical procedures as well as specialized diagnostic testing. Coronary artery bypass grafts (CABGs) are probably the most widely recognized surgeries in this category. Specialized diagnostic technologies such as magnetic resonance imaging (MRI) and positron emission tomography (PET) are used in tertiary care centers. Providers of tertiary care are commonly those that have an academic health center affiliation. Because of the intensity of the illness and subsequent diagnosis, it is imperative that clinicians gain experience through caring for large numbers of patients. This helps ensure provider proficiency and achievement of optimal outcomes in treating special conditions. This then suggests centralization or regionalization of tertiary care centers.

Long-term care (LTC) is the next stage in the health care services continuum. This stage is an array of services provided in a range of settings to individuals who have lost some capacity for independence, usually because of a chronic illness, significant injury, or long-term physical condition. The length of service usually extends beyond 90 days and assists individuals with basic activities and routines of daily living. It may also include skilled and therapeutic care for treatment and management of those conditions. The need for long-term care is usually determined by measuring an individual's functional abilities, activities of daily living (ADLs). More than 12 million people now need long-term care services, and almost 50% of those are severely disabled. Many analysts believe this need for services will increase significantly in the next three decades because of an aging population, medical advances that save and sustain more lives, and medical advances that lengthen lives in general.

Formal providers of long-term care include those who are trained to provide such care and are reimbursed accordingly. Although many of the services include medical and nursing care, many do not and are nonclinical in nature. Those formal specialists are homemakers, home health aides, visiting nurses, social workers, mental health providers, meal deliverers, therapists (speech, physical, occupational, and recreational), and adult day-care providers. These specialists may be associated with a nursing home, community center, adult day care center, retirement center, board and care or shelter homes, or the client's home.

The next level of health care services is palliative care. This care is offered during a person's terminal illness when no further therapeutic interventions hold promise for improvement. It is generally a result of a decision made by the person, the person's family, and the physician in charge of the care. The care may be provided by informal caregivers such as family members in a home setting. In more recent years, a new yet old concept and location called *hospice* was developed, whereby the person may be cared for and live out the remainder of life. Further defined, hospice care is provided to ease the pain and stress of a terminal condition when no other medical or surgical interventions are available to ameliorate the condition. Specific services may include physician care, pain management with prescription drugs, nursing care, psychological counseling, short-term hospitalization based on a specific need, homemaker and home health aide services, social services, and some therapy support. Physician certification is usually required in order to gain access to hospice care, especially if reimbursement is sought through Medicare or Medicaid.

It is generally accepted that the person has a life expectancy of six months or less.

Hospice care can be delivered in the person's home, in a designated unit of a hospital or long-term care facility, or a freestanding hospice center. People of any age with a terminal condition may be cared for by a hospice center. Diagnoses such as cancer, diabetes, and heart disease lead the conditions of people seeking hospice care.

Special Populations and Special Disorders

Special populations and special disorders occur outside the unified delivery system of health care services. These conditions are usually in the physical or mental disorders category defined as a heterogeneous collection of unrelated disorders that affect a sizable proportion of any population and affect an individual's ability to function in society. The diagnoses most commonly linked to chronic mental illness include schizophrenia, schizophrenia disorder, and bipolar disorder. Providers of care include psychiatrists, psychologists, counselors, therapists, social workers, and advanced practice nurses.

—Patti Elaine Griffin

FURTHER READING

Barton, P. L. (1998). *Understanding the U.S. health services system.* Chicago: AUPHA Press/Health Administration Press.

Coile, R. C., Jr. (1997). *The five stages of managed care.* Chicago: Health Administration Press.

Coile, R. C., Jr. (1998). *Millennium management.* Chicago: Health Administration Press.

Coile, R. C., Jr. (2000). *New century healthcare.* Chicago: Health Administration Press.

Griffith, J. R. (1998). *Designing 21st century healthcare.* Chicago: Health Administration Press.

Griffith, J. R. (1999). *The well-managed healthcare organization.* Chicago: AUPHA Press/Health Administration Press.

Long, M. J. (1998). *Health and healthcare in the United States.* Chicago: AUPHA Press/Health Administration Press.

www.healthcare-informatics.com/issues/2001/05_01/cover.htm

SETTLEMENT

A settlement is an agreement between the parties of a lawsuit or claim that resolves the legal dispute. It usually involves the payment of a specified amount to the plaintiff to resolve the claim without a decision on the merits of the case. A legal release from the plaintiff regarding any future defendant liability from the incident is obtained in exchange for the payment. The release usually includes a statement that the settlement is not an admission of any fault.

Settlement may be more desirable than proceeding with litigation for a number of reasons. It can limit defense costs, avoid uncertainty by establishing a fixed amount, reduce the stress of litigation, and avoid unfavorable publicity. The plaintiff avoids delay in obtaining compensation for damages.

The settlement process initially begins with the plaintiff's attorney demanding a monetary figure for damages and the defendant's attorney responding with a denial, acceptance, or counteroffer. The judge may order formal mediation, which involves an impartial third party such as another judge who helps the parties come to an agreement. The third party helps both sides see each other's view and realistically addresses the merits of the case.

MEDICAL LIABILITY SETTLEMENT AND THE PHYSICIAN

A physician involved in a medical liability case needs to be directly involved with the settlement process. A liability insurance plan must spell out the physician's right to consent to settlement, otherwise it can settle the case without the physician's consent. Some liability insurance plans have a "hammer clause" that spells out the monetary consequences of not agreeing with the insurer's recommendations for settlement in the event the trial results in a larger award. In the case of resident physicians, consent to settlement need not be obtained.

Because all settlements must be reported to the National Practitioner's Databank, the implications of a medical liability settlement on a physician may be significant in obtaining hospital privileges, insurance plan credentialing, and future liability insurance coverage.

—George V. Jirak

FURTHER READING

Melendez v. Hospital for Joint Diseases. (1991). 575 N.Y.S.2d 636 (N.Y. Sup. Ct.)

Showalter, J. S. (1999). *Southwick's The law of healthcare administration*. Chicago: Health Administration Press.

SHORT-TERM DEBT

See Liabilities

SHORT-TERM INVESTMENT

See Capital Investment, Capital Structure

SINGLE-SPECIALTY CARVE-OUT MODEL

See Carve-Out

SINGLE-SPECIALTY GROUP PRACTICE

A single-specialty group practice consists of three or more physicians who practice the same medical specialty as a single legal entity. They share clinical and administrative facilities, patient records, and employees. Income and expenses are distributed among the physicians according to a prearranged plan. The AMA publication *Medical Group Practices in the U.S. 1999 Edition* reveals that the number of medical groups continues to increase. About 70% of all groups are single-specialty. The average size of a single-specialty group is 6.4 physicians, although 6.1% of primary care and 1.6% of nonprimary care single-specialty groups have more than 100 physicians.

One of the main challenges of a single-specialty practice is to create a group system of control in governance, personnel, financial, and other practice decisions. Single-specialty group practices create advantages over solo practices including revenue enhancement opportunities such as improved receivables management, improved managed care contracting, and opportunities to generate new revenue through the addition of ancillaries. Economies of scale associated with group practices create multiple expense-reduction opportunities, greater efficiencies, and additional cash flow through reduction of overhead percentages. Group practices also have more access to capital to invest in technology and information system upgrades.

Single-specialty group practices give the opportunity for physicians to have more palatable practices and personal lifestyles. The positive attributes include improved call coverage, easy access to consultation from other members of the group, and decreased personal responsibility for the daily administration of the practice. Groups are more likely to utilize midlevel providers who can leverage and optimize physician time.

—James H. Leigh, Jr.

FURTHER READING

Havlicek, P. L. (1999). *Medical group practices in the U.S. 1999 edition*. Chicago: American Medical Association.

Wassenaar, J. D., & Thran, S. L. (Eds.). (2001). *Physician socioeconomic statistics 2000–2002 edition*. Chicago: American Medical Association.

SIX-SIGMA PROGRAM

The six-sigma program is a business improvement program that focuses on processes, variation reduction, and delivery of quantitative financial results. Six-sigma operates project by project with rigorous documentation of financial results. Other goals of the six-sigma program are to increase customer satisfaction and overall quality.

Six-sigma uses a measurement scale of process variation based on the normal distribution called the *sigma scale*. The higher the sigma, the fewer defects produced by the process. A process operates at a six-sigma level if it produces no more than 3.4 defects per million opportunities for defects. A three-sigma process produces 66,810 defects per million opportunities, a four-sigma process 6,210, and a five-sigma process produces 233.

Six-sigma programs require quality leaders or champions. These are high-level managers who develop the implementation plan, set objectives, allocate resources, and monitor progress. The other important members of six-sigma programs are the black belts. These are individuals with high leadership potential who have received training in statistics and other process improvement tools. This training typically takes six weeks. The black belts work full-time leading teams that work on the six-sigma projects. These projects typically take three months to complete and have definite financial targets. At General Electric (GE) the typical target has been $175,000. At GE most project teams have a member from the finance department who documents the financial impact of the project. The black belt position is intended to be temporary—typically two years. At GE a typical black belt completes 8 to 12 projects for a net savings of about $1 million. Being a black belt is intended to be a step to promotions. One of the goals of six-sigma is to develop managers with a continuous improvement mind-set.

Other positions in six-sigma programs are the green belts. These people have received more limited training and do not work full-time on six-sigma projects. There are also the master black belts. These are black belts who have advanced training in statistics and other quality improvement tools. They are responsible for all six-sigma work done in a particular area or function. Theirs is a more managerial function than that of the black belts. They select, train, and mentor the black belts. They help on project selection or approval, training, and review of projects completed. It is common for them to have weekly hourlong meetings with the black belts whom they are mentoring. Their position is full-time.

Six-sigma projects use the DMAIC methodology. DMAIC stands for five project stages: define, measure, analyze, improve, and control. In the define stage, the right problem is selected. In the measure stage, the cost of the problem is quantified. In the analyze stage, the causes of the problem are found. In the improve stage, the problem is

fixed. And in the control stage, measures are put in place so that the problem does not recur.

It is claimed by some that the great impact of six-sigma programs is due to the creation of full-time positions for improving critical business processes.

—Ramón V. León

SKILL-BASED COMPENSATION

See Employee Compensation

SKILLED NURSING FACILITY (SNF)

See Long-Term Care

SOCIAL MARKETING

WHAT IS SOCIAL MARKETING?

Kotler and associates (2002, p. 5) offer the following definition: "Social marketing is the use of marketing principles and techniques to influence a target audience to voluntarily accept, reject, modify, or abandon a *behavior* for the benefit of individuals, groups, or society as a whole."

WHAT ISSUES CAN BENEFIT FROM SOCIAL MARKETING?

Social marketing is used to influence specific behaviors that improve health, prevent injuries, protect the environment, and contribute to communities. Major issues that social marketing can benefit include

- *Health:* tobacco use, binge drinking, obesity, physical activity, immunizations, nutrition, sexually transmitted diseases, blood pressure, oral health, high cholesterol, and skin, breast, prostate, and colon cancer
- *Injury prevention:* traffic safety, drowning, safe gun storage, falls, household fires, suicide, sexual assault, domestic violence, disaster preparedness, and usage of safety belts, car seats, and booster seats
- *Environmental protection:* waste reduction, water conservation, water quality, energy conservation, air pollution, litter, wildlife habitat protection, forest preservation, disposal of hazardous waste
- *Community involvement:* organ donation, blood donation, volunteering, voting, crime prevention, animal rights

WHO DOES SOCIAL MARKETING?

Social marketing practitioners most often include professionals working in governmental agencies responsible for public health, safety, and environmental protection. In addition, not-for-profit organizations, associations, and foundations develop and implement social marketing campaigns, and for-profit corporations frequently support and participate in social marketing campaigns, as do marketing professionals providing services in areas such as marketing research, advertising, and public relations.

WHAT ARE THE STEPS IN THE PLANNING PROCESS?

Kotler, Roberto, and Lee (2002) outline the following steps in developing a social marketing campaign:

1. Analyze the social marketing environment.

2. Select target audiences.

3. Set objectives (desired behaviors) and goals (quantifiable measures).

4. Deepen understanding of target audiences and the competition, relative to desired behaviors.

5. Develop marketing strategies using the 4 *P*'s (product, price, place, promotion).

6. Develop an evaluation plan.

7. Establish budgets and funding sources.

8. Complete an implementation plan.

WHAT ARE THE KEY PRINCIPLES FOR SUCCESS?

Kotler, Roberto, and Lee (2002) suggest 12 important campaign tactics:

1. Take advantage of existing and prior research and campaigns.

2. Start with target markets that are (most) ready for behavior change.

3. Promote a single, doable behavior, explained in simple, clear terms.

4. When possible, incorporate and promote tangible objects and services that support the desired behavior.

5. Understand and address perceived barriers to adopting the desired behavior.

6. Make access easy.

7. Develop attention-getting and motivational messages.

8. Use appropriate media for target audiences.

9. Provide response mechanisms that make it easy and convenient for inspired audiences to act on recommended behaviors.

10. Allocate appropriate resources for media and outreach.

11. Allocate adequate resources for research.

12. Track results and make adjustments.

McKenzie-Mohr and Smith (1999) suggest increased success from

- Using prompts as reminders
- Using commitments to increase participation
- Using social norms to your advantage

WHAT ISSUES AND CHALLENGES DO SOCIAL MARKETERS FACE?

Common challenges for social marketers include balancing the desire to serve markets of greatest need with the resource efficiencies gained by targeting those most ready for change, utilizing strategies beyond communications to effectively impact behaviors, finding sufficient campaign funding, and measuring and reporting campaign impact.

—Nancy R. Lee

FURTHER READING

Andreasen, A. (1995). *Marketing social change: Changing behavior to promote health, social development, and the environment.* San Francisco: Jossey-Bass.

Kotler, P., Roberto, N., & Lee, N. (2002). *Social marketing: Improving the quality of life.* Thousand Oaks, CA: Sage.

McKenzie-Mohr, D., & Smith, W. (1999). *Fostering sustainable behavior: An introduction to community-based social marketing.* Gabriola Island, Canada: New Society.

Prochaska, J., Norcross, J., & DiClemente, C. (1994). *Changing for good.* New York: Avon Books.

Siegel, M., & Doner, L. (1998). *Marketing public health: Strategies to promote social change.* Gaithersburg, MD: Aspen.

SOLO PRACTICE

As the name implies, a solo practice has only one physician who maintains responsibility for all aspects of the practice. These responsibilities are in addition to the physician's primary duty of providing medical care. All the income and liabilities attributable to the practice are retained and controlled by the practitioner. Data from the American Medical Association's Socioeconomic Monitoring System surveys indicate that the percentage of solo practitioners decreased from more than 40% in 1983 to less than 25% in 1997. Solo practitioners generally earn less than their counterparts in group practice.

Probably the most desirable feature of a solo practice is that the physician has total control over all practice decisions. When compared with small group practices with several physicians who produce income and share expenses, the overhead of the solo physician is higher and there is more financial risk. Because the practice income is totally dependent on the solo practitioner's work, any disruption caused by factors such as illness, travel, unfortunate business decisions, or bad economic conditions could cause large variances in funds available to pay expenses or distribute as income.

The lifestyle of a solo practitioner basically depends on the type of practice and predetermined goals with regard to income and free time, but in most cases the solo practitioner must spend more time working than do counterparts in group practice. The workload can be decreased by sharing night call and vacation coverage with other physicians in the area. In many cases administrative assistance can be obtained from local management service organizations or professional consultants.

—James H. Leigh, Jr.

FURTHER READING

Wassenaar, J. D., & Thran, S. L. (Eds.). (2001). *Physician socioeconomic statistics 2000–2002 edition*. Chicago: American Medical Association.

SPECIAL CAUSE VARIATION

Special cause variation is variation in a process that is caused by specific factors, and occurs over and above normal process variation (also known as *common cause variation*). If measurements from a process are charted in a control chart, special cause variation manifests itself in one of several ways: one or more points above the upper control limit or below the lower control limit; runs of seven or more points all on the same side of the center line, indicating a process shift; or other patterns indicative of a nonrandom pattern (such as trends). Processes that display special cause variation are regarded as being unstable and unpredictable.

The successful management of a process involves the identification of special cause variation and the reason(s) for its presence. However, uncovering special causes is the responsibility of the local workforce, because those who have ongoing exposure to the process are in the best position to correctly identify it. This knowledge then allows for the special cause to be potentially eliminated, leading to greater process stability and predictability. Thus management must provide workers with the ability to act on special cause variation.

The random variation in processes that show no special cause variation is called *common cause variation*. Process improvement usually involves first the identification and elimination of special cause sources of variation, then the reduction of common cause variation.

As an example of special cause variation, suppose that hospital rooms are subject to an inspection according to some schedule. Based on the inspection criteria, consider the proportion of rooms that pass inspection each day. If we examined these data over a period of, say, a month, we might observe that the average proportion is, say, 95%, with some small variation about this average if we look at the day-to-day value. This would represent common cause variation. If we found a day on which only 60% of the rooms pass inspection, this would be very surprising, and in fact we would seek to identify a special reason, or cause, why this occurred on this specific day. A possible explanation would be that a new room inspector was being used who didn't understand the application of the inspection criteria.

—James L. Schmidhammer

SPECIALTY

See Medical Specialties

SPENDING ON HEALTH CARE

Both the level and growth rate of U.S. health care spending are reaching new highs, not only with respect to historical domestic spending patterns but also to other countries' contemporary patterns. This spending pattern, however, does not exhibit a positive association (at least not a strong one) with U.S. population health.

To understand why U.S. health care spending is increasing so rapidly (and thus why contemporary spending levels are so high), one must first understand why individuals demand health care. Notice that individuals do not demand health care, at least not directly. Rather, they demand health care to the extent that it produces health.

Health, in turn, is a "normal" good; that is, empirically, its demand increases with wealth. Consequently, to the extent that health care produces health, growing wealth increases health care spending. The United States's rapid growth in wealth thus appears to be one contributor to its steep increase in health care spending.

In addition to health care, however, other goods, services, and behaviors influence health. For example, health maintenance activities such as exercise contribute to health's production. Why, then, might individuals increasingly allocate resources to health care, as opposed to these other items, to produce health?

Notice that individuals recognize health care costs in a different form from the way they recognize these substitutes' cost. Engaging in health maintenance activities, for example, tends to consume more time than does visiting a physician. Although this time may not appear costly in a direct pecuniary sense, it does when one recognizes that time allocated to one activity cannot be allocated to alternative productive endeavors (such as employment). In short, time has an "opportunity cost." Moreover, medical insurance's favorable tax treatment may implicitly subsidize health care whereas no such treatment may exist for, say, health maintenance activities. Given this distortion, and the increasing price at which individuals can sell their time on the market (that is, the increasing productivity of time spent working), rational individuals migrate toward less time-intensive health production factors (for example, physician visits as opposed to regular exercise). This incentive to "buy" health, rather than "make" health oneself, not only has the capacity to increase the rate at which individuals allocate resources to health care, but can do so without improving health!

Other explanations for the U.S. health care spending experience are also available. For example, price inflation for health care services appears to be growing rapidly and independently of the behavioral forces just identified. This price increase may reflect an expanding capacity for interested players to sway relevant regulations. For example, pharmaceutical manufacturers may be improving their ability to prolong patent protections (for example, by accumulating knowledge about relevant regulatory processes) and thus extend the period over which they can exercise pricing power.

Each of these forces, and many more not listed here, potentially increases the rate at which health care spending grows and in a manner that need not improve health. Because the list of candidate explanations is so large, and the potential for interaction among the explanations is so complex, however, significant disagreement remains about what, if any, type of policy should be promulgated as a response.

—Dino Falaschetti

FURTHER READING

Feldstein, P. J. (1999). *Health care economics* (5th ed.). Albany, NY: Delmar.

Phelps, C. E. (1997). *Health economics* (2nd ed.). Reading, MA: Addison-Wesley.

STAFF MODEL HEALTH MAINTENANCE ORGANIZATION (HMO)

See Health Maintenance Organizations (HMOs)

STANDARD OF CARE

In a legal proceeding, *standard of care* is the standard against which the defendant's conduct is measured. The defendant is expected to act as an ordinary, prudent person with similar training and skill would have acted in a similar situation. If the defendant's conduct falls below this standard, the defendant may be determined to have acted in a negligent manner. Professional malpractice liability involves an act or omission that causes injury, representing a departure from accepted standards of medical care. This comparative standard weighs a particular medical decision against specific medical standards.

The criteria for meeting the standard of care has shifted over time with the demise of the locality rule. The locality rule virtually limited testimony to the standard of care in the defendant's practice area. Now plaintiffs have access to a wider array of previously unavailable testimony from experts outside the local area. The change in the standard has been affected by changes in technology. It is likely that the introduction of new technology has raised what is considered to be customary care to a higher level. The practice of defensive medicine has also influenced the standard of care. To the extent that physicians order additional tests as protection against subsequent liability, the added tests become part of the changing standard of care.

In medical malpractice, the applicable standard of care is established by the medical profession itself, through expert medical review and testimony. In addition to expert testimony, professional standards may be evidenced by regulations promulgated by outside organizations such as the Joint Commission on Accreditation of Healthcare Organizations, conditions of medicare participation, statutes, state health and hospital codes, as well as internal policies and bylaws.

The *res ipsa loquitur* doctrine ("the thing speaks for itself") is applicable when the negligence of the defendant is so obvious that it is unnecessary to present expert testimony to prove that there was a breach in the standard of care. Some jurisdictions retain the requirement of expert testimony despite application of *res ipsa loquitur*. Others require the plaintiff to choose between *res ipsa loquitur* and the use of expert testimony. An application of the *res ipsa loquitur* rule involves cases in which foreign objects have been left in the patient's body during surgery.

—Kathleen Ferrara

FURTHER READING

Smith, J. W. (1995). *Hospital liability* (Chapter 4). New York: Law Journal Seminars Press.

STANDARD OPERATING PROCEDURES (SOPs)

As defined by the International Conference on Harmonization of Technical Requirements for the Registration of Pharmaceuticals for Human Use (ICH), standard operating procedures (SOPs) are "detailed, written instructions to achieve uniformity of the performance of a specific function." SOPs document what the clinical research site does in its daily practice and are uniformly formatted to contain the purpose, policy, scope, and definitions associated with this practice. The goal of SOPs is to provide a method of clinical trials performance and documentation that embodies the high standards of good clinical practice. SOPs clarify and simplify the organization and documentation of clinical trials. In addition to the medical/clinical components of a trial, sponsors, monitors, and investigators (study team) must be well versed in their respective responsibilities as well as in those of the others. Everyone involved in clinical trials research must maintain up-to-date knowledge regarding the protection of trial subjects and informed consent as detailed in the Declaration of Helsinki. These individuals are obligated to conduct the research in the most ethical manner.

SOPs delineate the responsibilities of sponsors, monitors, and investigators. For example, a SOP defining the responsibilities of the study team would include the following: Sponsors choose the investigator and provide the study medication and all pertinent information for documentation of adverse event reporting; monitors provide the communication link between sponsors and investigators, conduct site visits with the investigator to determine if the trial is being performed correctly, and determine that information on source documents and case report forms (CRFs) are compatible; and investigators provide a subject pool and maintain familiarity with properties of the study medication, drug accountability, and procedures a study coordinator will follow.

—Linda M. Cimino

See also Clinical Trials, Investigational New Drug Application (IND)

FURTHER READING

Kolman, J., Meng, P., & Scott, G. (1998). *Good clinical practice: Standard operating procedures for clinical researchers.* Chichester, UK: Wiley.

STANDARDS, ETHICAL ISSUES

See Ethical Issues Faced by Managers

STANDARDS OF PERFORMANCE

See Balanced Scorecard and Health Care

STANDARD TREATMENT

In the introduction of a new drug or treatment modality, a researcher must show that it is at least as efficacious, or perhaps better than the existing or standard treatment. Standard treatments are what is considered common clinical practice in medicine and has been approved by the Food and Drug Administration for treatment of a specific disease or medical condition.

If a new drug is being introduced, it will already have gone through phase 1 and phase 2 trials to show that it is capable of providing its therapeutic endpoint. However, whether it is able to do so better and with fewer side effects is the purpose of a phase 3 trial, in which the standard treatment is compared with the experimental. In a nonresearch setting, the term *standard treatment* may be used synonymously with *standard of care*. This is a series of practices developed in the clinical setting for the treatment of a specific medical condition. It is assumed that given the same diagnosis, most reasonable practitioners would adhere to these standards.

—Daryn Moller

See also Clinical Research, Clinical Trials, Phase 1 Study (Phase 1 Clinical Trial), Phase 2 Study, Phase 3 Study

FURTHER READING

Day, S. (1999). *Dictionary for clinical trials.* Chichester, UK: Wiley.

STARK LAW

The Federal Physician Self-Referral Act is commonly referred to as "Stark." The Stark law, so named for its congressional proponent, Congressman Pete Stark, is a prohibition against "self-referrals" in the health care system. Specifically, Stark prohibits a physician from making referrals to an entity for certain designated health services if that physician or a member of the physician's immediate family has a direct or indirect financial relationship with that entity and payment for those services will be made by Medicare or Medicaid.

The Stark law was actually passed in two phases. Phase 1 pertained to only one designated health service—clinical laboratories. The law was passed following a study that found that where physicians had a financial interest in a clinical lab, there was a tendency to order more tests than in situations where there was no financial relationship. Because extra tests represent extra costs to the health care system, Stark 1 was passed in an effort to contain health care costs by prohibiting referrals to clinical labs in which the referring physician had a financial interest. In 1993, the Stark law was amended to include 10 additional designated health services. The new designated health services include

- Physical therapy services
- Occupational therapy services
- Radiology services (MRIs, CT scans, PET scans, ultrasound, and so on)
- Radiation therapy services and supplies
- Durable medical equipment and supplies
- Parenteral and enteral nutrients, equipment, and supplies
- Prosthetics, orthotics, and prosthetic devices and supplies
- Home health services
- Outpatient prescription drugs
- Inpatient and outpatient hospital services

The Stark law applies only to physician referrals, only to the eleven specific health services named in the statute, and only when payment is to be made by Medicare or Medicaid. Violation of the statute occurs when such a referral is made to an entity with which there is a personal or familial financial relationship. A financial relationship includes both ownership or investment interests and a compensation arrangement. A compensation arrangement involves an arrangement between a physician and an entity whereby the entity pays remuneration to the physician.

No specific intent is required to violate the law, but the sanctions for violating Stark can be quite severe. For instance, if a physician refers Medicare patients to a laboratory for blood tests and that physician is an investor in that lab, this may constitute illegal referrals under Stark if no exception applies. The lab is not entitled to collect payment from Medicare for the tests, because of the prohibited referrals. Therefore, on discovery of the improper payments the lab would be required to report improper payments and return the payments to Medicare. In addition, the lab may be subject to civil monetary penalties of up to $15,000 per claim and possible exclusion from the Medicare program. Failure to report the improper payment in a timely manner following

discovery could result in additional penalties of up to $10,000 per day and possible liability under the False Claims Act.

There are numerous exceptions to the general prohibitions under Stark. For instance, one such exception exists where there is a *bona fide* employment arrangement. In this example, if the physician's financial relationship was based on the fact that the physician was an employee of the lab rather than an investor in the lab, the referrals would be allowed provided that the remuneration to the physician was fair market value and not based on the volume or value of referrals.

Other exceptions pertain to in-office ancillary services, personal services arrangements, rental of equipment or space, academic medical centers, medical staff incidental benefits, fair market value, and nonmonetary compensation up to $300 per year. These exceptions are complicated and often difficult to apply given the myriad fact situations and financial arrangements common in the health care field. To avoid a Stark violation, the physician's financial arrangement must adhere fully to all the provisions of the relevant exception. In addition, it is clear that even if certain financial arrangements fail to violate the Stark law, they may still violate other fraud and abuse laws including the antikickback statute.

The Centers for Medicare and Medicaid Services (CMS), formally HCFA, has attempted to offer guidance through regulations interpreting the Stark law. The process has taken years, but as final regulations emerge, they have provided gradual clarification of the Stark provisions. Despite the additional guidance offered by the final regulations, health care providers must continue to take great care in structuring any business arrangements that involve physician referrals.

—Cheryl S. Massingale

FURTHER READING

Becker, S. (1998). *Health care law: A practical guide.* (§ 5.04[1]). New York: Matthew Bender.

False Claims Act. (1863). 31 U.S.C. § 3729.

Social Security Act. (1992). Prohibition on certain referrals. 42 U.S.C. § 1395nn.

STATEMENT OF CASH FLOWS

See Discounted Cash Flows, Operating Cash Flow

STATEMENT OF CHANGES IN NET ASSETS

The statement of changes in net assets was created through the adoption and implementation of Statement of

Financial Accounting Standards No. 117, *Financial Statements of Not-for-Profit Organizations* (FAS 117). The statement was created to provide financial reporting consistency among the various types of not-for-profit organizations. FAS 117 requires that not-for-profit organizations, including many hospitals and health care entities, prepare a statement of financial position (which is analogous to the balance sheet of for-profit entities), a statement of activities (income statement), and a statement of cash flows. The statement of changes in net assets is an integral part of the statement of activities. In fact, the "statement of activities" is typically named the "statement of activities and changes in net assets," if the two statements are combined for reporting purposes. (See presentation examples A, B, and C.)

The primary purpose of the statement of activities and changes in net assets is to provide information about the events and circumstances that change net asset amounts. This statement and the related disclosures in the notes to the financial statements provide information to creditors, donors, and others to evaluate an organization's performance during a period; namely, to assess current service efforts, ability to continue services, and management's allocation of resources. The change in net assets measures whether an organization maintained its net assets, drew on resources provided in past periods, or added resources that can be used for future periods.

A review of the types of net assets is necessary to understand what events and circumstances may occur to change the dollar amount and nature of net assets. Net assets, which may also be referred to as *net equity* or *fund balance,* are classified as unrestricted, temporarily restricted, or permanently restricted for not-for-profit entities under Statement of Financial Accounting Standards No. 116, *Accounting for Contributions Received and Contributions Made.* Unrestricted net assets consist of those assets that have not been externally restricted by a donor. Temporarily restricted net assets are donor-restricted net assets that may be used by an organization once a certain event has occurred; that is, a restriction has been met or a certain amount of time has passed. Permanently restricted net assets (such as an endowment) are those assets with donor-imposed restrictions that do not expire with the passage of time. Such net assets are to be held in perpetuity by the entity, because the related restrictions cannot be removed.

The statement of activities and changes in net assets must report the amount of the change in net assets (unrestricted, temporarily restricted and permanently restricted) during a period. This change is highlighted on the statement of activities through a descriptive caption such as *change in net assets* or *change in equity.* The ending net assets should agree to the face of the statement of position (balance sheet) for each class of net assets. Generally, revenues and gains increase net assets, and expenses and losses decrease net assets. Revenues and

NOT-FOR-PROFIT HOSPITAL *Format A*

Statement of Activities
Year Ended June 30, 20XX (in thousands)

Changes in unrestricted net asset	
Revenues and gains:	
Net patient service revenue	$22,468
Other revenue	5,400
Other investment income	1,000
Total unrestricted revenues and gains	28,868
Net assets released from restrictions:	
Satisfaction of program restrictions	10,000
Satisfaction of equipment acquisition restrictions	1,500
Expiration of time restrictions	1,000
Total net assets released from restrictions	12,500
Total unrestricted revenues, gains, and other support	41,368
Expenses and losses:	
Operating expenses	19,526
Management and general expenses	8,540
Provision for bad debts	674
Interest	1,500
Depreciation and amortization	1,730
Total expenses	31,970
Loss on sale of equipment	80
Total expenses and losses	32,050
Increase in unrestricted net assets	9,318
Changes in temporarily restricted net assets:	8,110
Income on long-term investments	2,580
Actuarial loss on annuity obligations	(30)
Net assets released from restrictions	(12,500)
Decrease in temporarily restricted net assets	(1,840)
Changes in permanently restricted net assets:	
Contributions	280
Income on long-term investments	120
Increase in permanently restricted net assets	400
Increase in net assets	7,878
NET ASSETS, BEGINNING OF YEAR	266,140
NET ASSETS, END OF YEAR	$274,018

gains are considered increases in unrestricted net assets unless the use of the assets received is limited by donor-imposed restrictions (purpose and/or time). In the absence of a donor's restriction, the asset is reported as an unrestricted revenue or gain. Assets with donor-imposed restrictions shall be reported as either increases to temporarily restricted net assets or permanently restricted net assets, depending on the type of restriction. Once the

NOT-FOR-PROFIT HOSPITAL   Format B

Statement of Activities
Year Ended June 30, 20XX (in thousands)

	Unrestricted	Temporarily Restricted	Permanently Restricted	Total
Revenues, gains, and other support:				
Net patient service revenue	$22,468			$22,468
Other revenue	5,400			5,400
Contributions		$8,110	$280	8,390
Other investment income	1,000			1,000
Income on long-term investments		2,580	120	2,700
Net assets released from restrictions:				
Satisfaction of program restrictions		10,000	(10,000)	
Satisfaction of equipment acquisition				
Restrictions	1,500	(1,500)		
Expiration of time restrictions	1,000	(1,000)		
Total revenues, gains, and other support	41,368	(1,810)	400	39,958
Expenses and losses:				
Operating expenses	19,526			19,526
Management and general expenses	8,540			8,540
Provision for bad debts	674			674
Interest	1,500			1,500
Depreciation and amortization	1,730			1,730
Total expenses	31,970			31,970
Loss on sale of equipment	80			80
Actuarial loss on annuity obligations		30		30
Total expenses and losses	32,050	30		32,080
Change in net assets	9,318	(1,840)	400	7,878
NET ASSETS AT BEGINNING OF YEAR	103,670	25,470	137,000	266,140
NET ASSETS AT END OF YEAR	$112,988	$23,630	$37,400	$274,018

restrictions related to temporarily restricted net assets have been met, the assets are transferred from temporarily restricted net assets to unrestricted net assets, and are classified as *net assets released from restrictions* in an entity's statement of activities and changes in net assets. If donor-imposed temporary restrictions are met in the same reporting period in which the asset is recognized, the increase may be shown as unrestricted in that period, provided the organization reports consistently from period to period and discloses its accounting policy.

The statement may be formatted in a variety of ways. Each format may have a different advantage, depending on the needs and type of the organization. Three common formatting schemes are provided (A, B, and C).

—Edward Pershing

STATEMENT OF OPERATIONS

The operations function in an enterprise involves activities required to convert inputs to desired outputs. Operations management is based on a systems approach in which a process is viewed as follows:

Inputs → transformation process → outputs

A health care enterprise consists of a number of operations processes that must be managed. These processes may include not only delivery of medical services but also procurement of materials and supplies, maintenance of patient records, hiring/training/deployment of human resources,

NOT-FOR-PROFIT HOSPITAL   Format C, Part 1 of 2

Statement of Unrestricted Revenues, Expenses and Other
  Changes in Unrestricted Net Assets
Year Ended June 30, 20XX (in thousands)

Unrestricted revenues and gains:	
Net patient service revenue	$22,468
Other revenue	5,400
Other investment income	1,000
Total unrestricted revenues and gains	28,868
Net assets released from restrictions:	
Satisfaction of program restrictions	10,000
Satisfaction of equipment acquisition restrictions	1,500
Expiration of time restrictions	1,000
Total net assets released from restrictions	12,500
Total unrestricted revenues, gains, and other support	41,368
Expenses and losses:	
Operating expenses	19,526
Management and general expenses	8,540
Provision for bad debts	674
Interest	1,500
Depreciation and amortization	1,730
Total expenses	31,970
Loss on sale of equipment	80
Total unrestricted expenses and losses	32,050
Increase in unrestricted net assets	$9,318

NOT-FOR-PROFIT HOSPITAL   Format C, Part 2 of 2

Statement of Unrestricted Revenues, Expenses and Other
  Changes in Unrestricted Net Assets
Year Ended June 30, 20XX (in thousands)

Unrestricted net assets:	
Total unrestricted revenues and gains	$28,868
Net assets released from restrictions	12,500
Total unrestricted expenses and losses	(32,050)
Increase in unrestricted net assets	9,318
Temporarily restricted net assets:	
Contributions	8,110
Income on long-term investments	2,580
Actuarial loss on annuity obligations	(30)
Net assets released from restrictions	(12,500)
Decrease in temporarily restricted net assets	(1,840)
Permanently restricted net assets:	
Contributions	280
Income on long-term investments	120
Increase in permanently restricted net assets	400
Increase in net assets	7,878
NET ASSETS AT BEGINNING OF YEAR	266,140
NET ASSETS AT END OF YEAR	$274,018

processing of accounts payable and receivable and, in some cases, preparation and delivery of food services and housekeeping services.

In a health care setting, the inputs to a process may be patients needing services, blood or tissue samples requiring testing, or data that must be posted into appropriate patient and billing records. The transformation process typically consists of physical activities involving treatment of patients, analysis of laboratory specimens, processing of records, and so on. The outputs reflect completed activity that adds value to the enterprise such as improved patient health or updated information.

Operations management is critical because the operations function is the part of the organization where most assets and people should be employed. Effective operations management involves a number of activities related to the inputs, transformation process, and outputs.

With regard to inputs, forecasting and capacity planning are necessary to estimate and accommodate the anticipated levels of demand. A hospital or clinic must have some idea of the volume of patients that will require services. This information is necessary to plan for the resources that will provide those services. A laboratory must anticipate workloads in order to have sufficient staff and equipment for the testing and analysis that must be done. Similarly, the anticipated volume of transactions must be known or estimated to provide necessary computer facilities and personnel to maintain information systems supporting admissions, discharges, billing records, and so forth. In general, the more that is known about the inputs to a process, the better. Manufacturing companies have recognized this concept for many years, and some manufacturers have established supply chain relationships with customers and suppliers to reduce uncertainty regarding the quantity and quality of inputs to their production systems.

Management of the transformation process in an operations system requires good design principles and effective day-to-day planning and scheduling. The design principles address location and physical layout issues. Health care facilities specializing in certain types of treatments will find it advantageous to organize equipment and facilities around the basic workflow involved in providing the specialized service. This may involve an "assembly line" approach to the facility layout. In contrast, clinics or other facilities providing general treatment of a wide variety of health care issues will find it necessary to have a physical layout that provides maximum flexibility by having multiple pieces of equipment in examination or treatment areas. This would resemble a "job shop" in a manufacturing environment. The design of the operations system is relatively stable and is influenced by the strategic goals of the enterprise.

Effective scheduling is usually necessary to manage the transformation process. Scheduling involves the detailed, day-to-day assignment of "jobs" to resources in specific time periods. In a doctor's office the physician's time is the limiting resource, and an appointment schedule is used to match the availability of the doctor with the arriving patient load. In a hospital operating room, the availability of both the facility and the surgeon is critical, and the operating room schedule becomes an important tool to coordinate these resources. Scheduling activities of this type often require the use of priority rules to resolve conflicts created by multiple requests for the resource in a given time period. Once established, the hospital operating room schedule drives the assignment of surgical nurses and other support personnel, and is the basis for material planning to provide needed items to support the scheduled surgical procedures. In general, scheduling activities affect the direct deployment of resources on a day-to-day basis.

The outputs of any operations system must meet quality standards. Both the inputs and the transformation process affect quality of the outputs, and issues in quality control are important throughout the system. Quality reflects how the various operations processes are managed.

Quality in a health care environment may be measured in a number of ways. Patient satisfaction surveys in a hospital provide overall data that may reflect how the various processes—such as admissions, medical services, food service, and housekeeping—are working from the perspective of the customer (patient). More specific measures of individual processes, such as the time required to admit a patient, provide data to monitor performance and possibly identify areas for improvement. An important element of the systems approach to managing an operations process is to identify clearly the output of the process so that meaningful measures can be established to monitor quality.

Feedback is an important part of any operations management system. Information about the time required to process admissions in a hospital may lead to an examination of the system that results in improvements in the inputs or transformation process. For example, it may be determined that delays in the hospital admission process are often caused by incomplete information provided by the admitting physician. In this case, simplifying or standardizing the forms to be completed by the admitting physician might lead to improvements in the inputs to the hospital admission process.

In summary, complex organizations such as health care facilities consist of a number of operations processes. Each operations process consists of inputs, a transformation process, and outputs. Effective operations management involves identifying these process components and their relationships.

—R. Lawrence LaForge

FURTHER READING

Haksever, C., Render, B., Russell, R. S., & Murdick, R. G. (2000). *Service management and operations* (2nd ed.). Upper Saddle River, NJ: Prentice Hall.

Render, B., & Heizer, J. (2001). *Principles of operations management* (4th ed.). Upper Saddle River, NJ: Prentice Hall.

STATISTICAL PROCESS CONTROL (SPC)

Statistical process control (SPC) is the application of various statistical tools and techniques to data acquired from a process, with the intention of process improvement. The term is related to *statistical quality control* (SQC), an older term that includes techniques such as acceptance sampling, which are no longer in widespread use. At the heart of statistical process control is the control chart, and its use for process understanding and improvement. All processes manifest variation in characteristics (measurements) of its output, and understanding and reducing this variation results in process improvement. Variation that is observed in a process can either be random variation inherent to the process (called *common cause variation*) or sporadic variation that is not part of the normal process (called *special cause variation*). Control charts provide the ability to distinguish between these two types of variation. More generally, control charts can be used to identify and characterize different sources of variation that act on a process. This comes about by the application of rational sampling and rational subgrouping. For example, control charts can be used to separate variation arising from the measurement process itself from inherent process variation.

Various kinds of control charts have been developed to handle different types of data and different methods of data collection. Charts designed to display data involving counts of attributes include p charts, np charts, c charts, and u charts. A p chart could be used to chart the percentage of medication orders that had one or more errors. A c chart could be used to chart the number of errors per 100 medication orders. A u chart would be used to chart the number of errors per week (where each week would have a potential different total number of orders). Charts designed to display data involving measurements of process variables include X-bar and R charts, X-bar and s charts, and individuals' charts. Various financial ratios like net operating margin would be an example of a measure from a financial process. Laboratory turn-around time would be an example of a measure from a medical production process. Statistical process control also includes the assessment of the ability of a process to meet requirements, often expressed as the ratio Cp or Cpk. Cp is the ratio of the allowable range of values to the range of values that the process actually yields (determined statistically). Cpk is a modified version of Cp that also measures how well the process is on target.

Another chart used for statistical process control is the cusum chart, which is used for maintaining the status quo, and is designed to detect small shifts of known magnitude. Also, the exponentially weighted moving average chart serves a similar purpose. However, these charts are more complex and harder to use, and usually fare not much better than the classic control charts when they are used with additional tests for runs.

—James Schmidhammer

STATISTICAL THINKING

The term statistical thinking is used to describe the application of statistical techniques and concepts, and other structured techniques, to a wide variety of situations, including process management and problem solving. As such, it involves the use of data in a process of learning and action.

Statistical thinking is necessary for process improvement, in the sense that the key to process improvement involves the understanding and reduction of variation in the process, and this variation manifests itself in data collected from the process. Process variation can typically be classified as either common cause variation or special cause variation, with each type of variation requiring a different strategy for action. Control charts are used to distinguish special cause variation from common cause variation. More generally, control charts can be used to identify and characterize different sources of variation that act on a process. This involves the understanding and effective use of sampling and subgrouping strategies, which are essentially intelligent ways of gathering data from the process that support process understanding and can thus lead to process improvement.

Statistical thinking is necessary to understand the capability of processes to meet requirements. More advanced statistical techniques for process understanding and improvement include the use of experimental designs, regression analysis, and survival analysis. A graphical tool useful for understanding relationships among variables is a scatterplot. Other tools that support statistical thinking include process flow diagrams, Pareto diagrams, and cause-and-effect diagrams.

The acquisition of the ability to do statistical thinking typically involves training in statistical methods and other methods of process improvement, as well as ongoing practice in the application of these techniques.

—James Schmidhammer

STATUTE OF LIMITATIONS

The statute of limitations is defined as the period of time in which a lawsuit may be filed. This is determined by state statute and most commonly is two years for medical malpractice lawsuits. This is shorter than for other types of tort litigation. The statute of limitations may be longer if other causes of action are claimed such as breach of contract, negligence from a negligent act (not malpractice), and intentional tort such as battery (intentional nonconsensual touching).

The issue is when does the statute of limitations begin? The statute of limitations usually begins (accrues) when the incident occurred. This is usually true of intentional torts such as battery, because it is easy to determine when the battery occurred. In medical malpractice cases it may be difficult to determine when the negligent incident occurred. Some states determine that the statute of limitations begins at the time the treatment was provided. Others use the "discovery rule" where the statute of limitations begins at the time the patient discovers or should have discovered the malpractice. The statute of limitations may be extended in the case of birth injuries and minors to the age of majority in some states. One needs to inquire about the specific requirements within a particular state's jurisdiction.

—George V. Jirak

FURTHER READING

Dobbs, D. B., & Hayden, P. T. (1997). *Torts and compensation: Statutes of limitations* (pp. 278–297). St. Paul, MN: West.

STEP-DOWN FACILITY

The term *step-down facility* or *step-down unit* is a generic term that can have various meanings in different settings. It is used to designate movement to a less intense level of care where the patient-to-nurse ratio is greater. A step-down unit can be used after a hospitalization for patients who are not strong enough to return home. These facilities are also called subacute or transitional units and are usually located in a hospital or nursing home.

A step-down unit can also be a transition between intensive care and a medical or surgical floor in a hospital. Examples include (a) a postcoronary unit for a patient who suffered a heart attack several days previously or (b) a step-down surgical unit for a surgical patient who no longer needs intensive care.

In recent years, lengths of hospital stays are decreasing, and hospital step-down units are less common. Moving patients from room to room incurs additional costs and disrupts bonds between patients and nurses. Nurses on the general medical floors are now trained to care for patients who are coming directly from intensive care. Patient-focused care encourages bringing the necessary care to the patient, rather than moving the patient to various sites as needs change. Step-down units within hospitals can disrupt patient-centered care.

—Jean Stretton

See also Subacute Care

FURTHER READING

Calkins, E., Bould, C., Watner, E. H., & Pacala, J. T. (1999). *New ways to care for older people: Building systems based on evidence.* New York: Springer.

STRATEGIC ALLIANCES

See Alliances

STRATEGIC ALTERNATIVES

Alternatives are the set of choices available to an organization in any decision-making situation. Alternatives are present in all decision-making activities at all (corporate, business, and functional) levels of the organization. Typically, "*strategic*" alternatives refer to the set of strategies under consideration at the corporate and business levels of an organization as a result of a formal planning process. These strategic decisions often involve increasing or decreasing the scope of the organization's activities. Basic types of strategic alternatives include expansion, contraction, and maintenance strategies.

In planning models, the generation and evaluation of strategic alternatives is the process step that follows analysis of the organization's internal and external environments.

Armed with this analysis and the mission and objectives of the organization, the strategist can formulate strategic alternatives for where the organization wants to be, can be, and should be in the future. After evaluating the strategic alternatives based on each one's ability to achieve the objectives (financial as well as nonfinancial), the alternative would be implemented (the next step in the planning process).

The word "strategic" implies a greater degree of uncertainty distinct from functional decisions. Fundamentally, strategic alternatives are direction setting in nature and involve the entire organization as opposed to a single operating unit or department. No hard and fast criteria exist to delineate strategic from operational alternatives. However, Russell L. Ackoff proposed that the more enduring the effect and the greater difficulty in reversing it, the more strategic a decision is. Important operational alternatives exist in all organizations. Decisions to lease or buy equipment or outsource services may have far-reaching influence on the organization, but they are subordinate to strategic alternatives just as the strategic alternatives under consideration at any time are subordinate to the organization's chosen mission. Although the choice of the organization's mission is the ultimate strategic decision, the term *strategic alternative* usually assumes that the mission has already been established or reaffirmed. Evaluating the consequences of pursuing one alternative versus another, regardless of the level of the decision, consumes much managerial activity in most organizations. The set of strategic alternatives under consideration at any given time is context specific. In addition to organization level, strategic alternatives are often discussed as they relate to emergent, growth, mature, and declining industries. Regardless of the context, there are a finite number of strategic alternatives although the possibilities for their implementation may be infinite.

CORPORATE-LEVEL STRATEGIC ALTERNATIVES

Corporate-level alternatives deal with possible alterations to the organization portfolio of activities. The question "What business(es) are we in?" is a key one at this level, and the answer may require altering the organization mission statement. Alternatives at the corporate level may be grouped into growth and contraction as they relate to the basic goals available to any organization. Strategies to achieve those goals are typically thought to constitute strategic alternatives. Growth alternatives include related and unrelated diversification, and forward and backward vertical integration.

At different times, most organizations grapple with diversification as a growth mechanism. The addition of new services may be related or unrelated to the organization's current markets, services, or dominant technology. Obviously, these three areas represent a continuum of relatedness. The more unrelated the activity, the less chance management will be able to transfer past experiences to the new endeavor. Related diversification involves entry into service areas different from current services but related in terms of either the markets served, services offered, or technology employed. The movement of acute care hospitals into skilled nursing facilities is an example of related diversification. An unrelated diversification strategy, adding services considered unlike your current markets, customers, or technology, is also a strategic growth alternative. Acute care hospitals' entry into parking facilities and into catering services are examples of unrelated diversification. Vertical integration involves adding services along a channel of distribution. Addition of services along a continuum of care can be considered vertical integration. Backward vertical integration includes adding services aimed at wellness, whereas forward vertical integration might add activities such as a home health unit.

Contraction alternatives at the corporate level include divestiture and liquidation. Selling a business to another organization that plans to continue the business is known as *divestiture*. Selling all assets of the business for what the assets may bring to one or more organizations or individuals is known as *liquidation*.

BUSINESS-LEVEL STRATEGIC ALTERNATIVES

Business-level strategic alternatives are more focused on "how to compete in a given business" (than at the corporate level). Expansion, contraction, and stability or maintenance may be goals at this level of the organization. Strategic alternatives such as market development (entering new geographic markets with existing services), product development (addition of new services for existing customers), and market penetration (increasing utilization of existing services in markets currently served) are examples of business-level alternatives focused on growth.

Contraction alternatives include harvesting and retrenchment. Attempting to reap short-term benefits from business units in markets that are experiencing long-term decline is known as *harvesting*. Regional hospitals used this strategy in managing the decline in facilities with smaller numbers of beds, in rural health networks. *Retrenchment* is the scaling back of services in terms of markets served, personnel employed, or assets utilized. The service remains viable, but increasing costs reduces profitability, prompting the retrenchment.

Maintenance or stability alternatives include enhancement and status quo strategies. When management believes the organization is making progress toward its goals but needs "to do things better," the organization embarks on an enhancement strategy. Continuous quality improvement (CQI) and total quality management (TQM) are enhancement strategies. Status quo (the current position, without changes) is maintained in stable or mature markets where an organization attempts to defend its current position without adding additional services. Typically, organizations seek to preserve their status quo in one service area while pursuing market or product development in another.

Each of these corporate- and business-level strategic alternatives has its own benefits and constraints related to cash flow, return on investment, time to implement and see results, and expertise needed. Selection of one of these strategic alternatives requires supporting decisions at the next level, thereby exposing a fresh set of alternatives.

—Woodrow D. Richardson

See also Contraction Strategy, Expansion Strategies, Strategy, Strategic Management

FURTHER READING

Ackoff, R. L. (1970). *A concept of corporate planning.* New York: Wiley-Interscience.

Fox, W. L. (1989). Vertical integration strategies: More promising than diversification. *Health Care Management Review, 14*(1), 49–56.

Ginter, P. M., Swayne, L. E., & Duncan, W. J. (2002). *Strategic management of health care organizations* (4th ed.). Oxford, UK: Blackwell.

Pearce, J. A., II. (1982). Selecting among alternative grand strategies. *California Management Review, 24*(3), 23–31.

STRATEGIC ASSUMPTIONS

In strategic planning, managers analyze the company's external and internal environments, as well as its goals, and then select appropriate strategies. However, selections of appropriate strategies stem from assumptions, or unquestioned beliefs, that the managers make about their environments, rates of change, and relevant stakeholders. Strategic assumptions affect the processes of generating ideas, arriving at consensus, making decisions, formulating plans, influencing colleagues, and charting progress. Conflicting strategic assumptions may also disrupt teamwork and effectual organization. Consequently, strategic assumptions can perpetuate decision-making biases and lead to poor decisions.

To enhance the quality of strategic decisions, some companies have instituted processes such as strategic assumption analysis. Strategic assumption analysis allows the decision makers to step back, to question assumptions, and to rethink hypotheses.

For example if a company's brainstorming session leads to two opposing strategies or positions, the analysis begins when each side states its position. Lynn Oppenheim and Barbara Langham have discussed how a pharmaceutical company's research and development (R&D) team could debate a strategy for allocating its research budget. One side wants to pursue promising leads in antifungals, whereas the other side feels that, given the budgetary constraints, antibacterials would provide more profits.

Next, each side lists all assumptions underlying its position. Then members step back to examine their beliefs—the ideas and information that led to their present positions. For example, the antifungal side might explain that the company has the world's best scientists in the field and that consumers find current antifungals on the market hard to administer. The other side might argue that the company's antibacterial research group consistently makes better use of investment dollars, and given the huge market for antibacterials, the company stands to make a substantial profit.

Once the sides make their assumptions explicit, the leader breaks the team into groups of three to five, making sure each group has representatives of both sides of the dispute. This action separates alliances, and members feel less compelled to represent their departments or interests. Each subgroup then analyzes the assumptions according to truth and importance. They should ask, for each assumption, How certain are we that this is true? and, How important is this assumption to the outcome?

The ensuing dialog usually gives team members insights into their colleagues' thoughts: Hearing the underpinnings of the other side's assumptions allows one to rethink problems. Suppose the antifungal side realizes that market size indeed should play a dominant role in the decision, and the market for an antibacterial would dwarf that of even a very good antifungal. At the same time, the antibacterial side might realize that an innovation in antifungals could lead to breakthroughs in ancillary applications and have great impact.

When each group feels it has sufficiently analyzed all relevant strategic assumptions, the team reconvenes to review findings. By focusing on the assumptions the team targets the problem. By analyzing the truth and relevance of assumptions, members can identify the precise areas of disagreement and resolution becomes possible.

—Usha C. V. Haley

See also Strategic Decisions, Strategic Planning, Strategy

FURTHER READING

Emshoff, J. R., & Finnel, A. (1979). Defining corporate strategy: Using strategic assumption analysis. *Sloan Management Review, 20*(3), 41.

Haley, U. C. V. (1997). The MBTI personality inventory and decision-making styles: Identifying and managing cognitive trails in strategic decision-making. In C. Fitzgerald & L. K. Kirby (Eds.), *Developing leaders: Research and applications in psychological type and leadership development* (pp. 187–223). Palo Alto, CA: Consulting Psychologists Press.

Openheim, L., & Langham, B. A. (1994). Resolving team conflicts. *R&D Innovator, 3*(4), 19–23.

STRATEGIC BUSINESS UNIT (SBU)

A strategic business unit (SBU) is a form of organizational structure that clusters individual businesses together under a single manager or management group, for purposes of synergy. Synergy may take the form of similar or common customers, like distribution networks, common resource needs, and similarities where economies of scale or economies of scope can be realized. The strategic business unit allows management to focus attention on common customers, geography, or product groups with the expectation of cost efficiencies. Strategic business units are commonly found in very large organizations or conglomerates where a single corporation owns multiple businesses. SBUs provide a structure for the management of the entire business portfolio by organizing individual business into units that build on similar relationships while maximizing resource capability.

In large health care organizations, businesses may be clustered into strategic business units based on the product or service needs of the end user or to realize supply chain advantages. As an example, consider a large health care corporation that owns assisted living facilities, emergency delivery companies, and financial services companies, including insurance and lending institutions. Clustering these businesses into business strategic units capitalizes on human resource knowledge, supplier efficiencies, and marketing efforts that are uniquely different to each strategic business unit. Managing each company separately would diffuse management attention in multiple directions without realizing individual efficiencies.

Strategic business units allow strategic decisions to be directed toward the unique aspects of the businesses clustered. SBUs maximize customer responsiveness while minimizing shared or common costs.

—Rebecca I. Porterfield

See also Organizational Structure, Value Chain for Health Care

FURTHER READING

Markides, C. C., & Williamson, P. J. (1996, April). Corporate diversification and organizational structure: A resource-based view. *Academy of Management Journal, 39*(2), 340–367.

STRATEGIC CHANGE

Strategic change is the means by which a significant and new organizational order is created over time so that the organization is better aligned with its current and/or future environment. When an organization is better aligned with its environment, organizational survival is preserved and organizational performance is enhanced. Because health care environments are changing quickly and often in unpredictable ways, the ability to prepare for or bring about strategic change is increasingly important to successful health care organizations.

In the preceding definition, strategic change is conceptualized as both an outcome (that is, significant new organizational order) and a process (that is, means by which a new order is created). When we speak of strategic change outcomes, experts often refer to "first-order" and "second-order" strategic change. First-order strategic change deals with such things as adding new service lines or entering new geographic markets. It is strategic in nature because the organization's alignment is altered, but it does not challenge the cultural values or identity of the organization. In contrast, second-order strategic change deals with first-order changes, but it also challenges the cultural values and identity of the organization. Clearly, second-order changes are more complicated, uncertain, and challenging than first-order strategic changes.

When we speak of strategic change as a process, experts usually refer to three types of processes. The oldest and most widely acknowledged form of strategic change is the formal planning process. However, it isn't always possible to know where an organization needs to go or to designate in advance how to get there in a predetermined fashion, because of the complexity and uncertainty of most health care environments.

Consequently, some organizations have focused on developing their capabilities in anticipation of upcoming strategic changes. Rather than a discrete annual planning ritual, some organizations focus on continuous improvement in areas such as improving the new product development process or developing leaders within the organization. Once again, however, it isn't always possible for strategic leaders to know what capabilities will be needed in the future. Therefore, a select few progressive organizations are investing in becoming learning organizations. This approach requires all of the organization's associates to experiment, learn, and adjust individually and collectively so that the organization's alignment with its environment can be enhanced.

Strategic change is complex and messy. There is no one technique for thinking about or bringing about strategic change as each organization's situation determines what will and will not work. Usually, strategic change efforts focus on one or more of the following aspects of an organization: (a) the way people do their jobs, (b) the way an organization structures or controls itself, (c) the way that strategy is developed and/or the strategic goals pursued, and (d) the way that cultural norms and values operate within the organization. Clearly, the scope and complexity of the strategic change expands with each successive level of focus.

—William Q. Judge

See also Discontinuous Change, Downsizing, Emergent Strategy, Hypercompetition, Learning Organizations, Managing Organizational Change, Organizational Change, Organizational Communication: An Overview, Organizational Culture, Organizational Structure, Power, Strategic Leadership, Strategic Management Process

FURTHER READING

Anderson, D., & Anderson, L. (2001). *Beyond change management: Advanced strategies for today's transformational leaders.* San Francisco: Jossey-Bass.

Argyris, C. (1985). *Strategy, change, and defensive routines.* Marshfield, MA: Pitman.

Nadler, D., Shaw, R., & Walton, E. (1994). Discontinuous change: Leading organizational transformation. San Francisco: Jossey-Bass.

Rowden, R. (2001). The learning organization and strategic change,. *Advanced Management Journal, 66*(3), 11–16.

STRATEGIC COMPENSATION ISSUES

See Employee Compensation

STRATEGIC CONTROL

Strategic control is a process through which an organization measures its performance, and then through a feedback loop, makes appropriate changes to its strategies going forward. Feedback from the system signals the appropriateness of the organization's strategies, given the conditions in the external environment and the organization's own competitive advantages.

Strategic control evolved as a component of a structured system of planning. As large balance sheets and corporate wealth were amassed during the industrial revolution, hierarchical reporting structures developed. Large, efficient organizations were built that dominated markets through sheer size, by means of market share and financial clout.

Corporate America borrowed heavily from the military system's top-down chain of command and from its formal structure for gathering and analyzing information.

The traditional hierarchical planning process is carried out in a serial fashion. Strategies are formulated and then implemented in the organization. Strategic control is essentially a feedback system that compares performance to a predetermined set of goals. The process becomes a never-ending loop, with *potential* for feedback at any point in the process. Yet in reality, most assessment occurs at strict intervals, such as quarterly or yearly financial reporting periods. Lengthy time lags are prevalent, in that feedback and change are often tied to an annual planning cycle. This type of control system is appropriate when the environment is relatively stable and when simple quantitative goals, such as physical output or sales quotas, can be measured with a high degree of certainty. The performance measures and the underlying strategies produced by the strategic planning process become codified, allowing all levels of the organization to develop detailed operating plans.

21ST-CENTURY STRATEGIC PLANNING

The sophistication of the planning now required by health care organizations is a reflection of several decades of fast-paced growth and consolidation in the industry. In such a rapidly changing environment, the effectiveness of strategic control depends on both the quality and the timeliness of the performance measures, which translate to an organization's ability to communicate throughout all levels of hierarchy. Even organizations that have been extremely successful in the past can become complacent and miss important shifts when they rely too heavily on a lengthy planning cycle. The demands on the organization change too quickly to rely on a static, detailed strategic plan, particularly at the business unit level. As a result, effective strategic control involves constant monitoring of the internal and external environment. Change proceeds incrementally as information is fed back to the system, with managers serving as resources to the system. Their job is to judge the feedback in the context of the bigger picture and make judgments concerning the appropriateness and timing of changes to the strategic plan.

STRATEGIC CONTROL AT THE CORPORATE LEVEL

As strategic planning has evolved, a clear distinction has been drawn between corporate-level strategic control and business-level strategic control. Control at the corporate level assesses the top-level strategies of the organization, and is typically subjective in nature, relative to more quantifiable financial controls common at the business level. Corporate-level strategic control focuses on establishing an information system that shares strategic factors such as

knowledge, markets, and technologies across business units. This in turn requires that top management have a thorough understanding of the business-level strategy for each unit. As a consequence, as organizations grow, either internally or through acquisitions of existing businesses, a strong case can be made for a strategy of related diversification. Strategic controls are sometimes difficult to apply in situations where an organization has grown through a strategy of unrelated diversification. Managers simply cannot synthesize the needs for disparate controls into one meaningful set of strategic, subjective performance objectives. In these situations, managers must rely on more quantitative financial measures in judging each business unit's contribution and long-term strategic fit.

For example, a health care system in a large metropolitan area may compete in several areas of providing health care, such as a hospital, an emergency care facility, and home health care. Sharing information across these business units is accomplished through corporate-level strategic control. Information such as demographics, health care competitors, health plans of area employers, and government policies constitute vital input for each of these businesses, and it is important that new information is handled in an integrated, cooperative fashion. If Medicare changes a policy on hospital stays, both the hospital and the home health care business will be affected. Budget items for both businesses will be affected, from food costs to payroll expenses. Managers must coordinate the resulting reallocation of resources among the business units with an eye to the effects on the overall organization.

STRATEGIC CONTROL AT THE BUSINESS LEVEL

In a large, diversified health organization, the real business of health care takes place at the business unit level. Control at the business level, involving operating and financial feedback, is essential as organizations face better-informed patients and shareholders, as well as increasing government oversight. Controls are in place to verify that critical business-level strategies and tactics are being properly emphasized and executed in the pursuit of operational goals.

Strategic control at the business level assesses the fit between what a firm might do, based on opportunities in the external environment, and on what its competitive advantages will allow. Specific operating and financial measures are compared with forecasts to determine if the strategies in place are achieving intended goals; these measures then form the basis for suggested improvements to the business-level strategy. For example, the manager of the fitness center at a community hospital might discover plans for a competing fitness center, threatening the virtual monopoly enjoyed by the hospital. Management, regardless of the financial goals and strategies in place, must reassess the effectiveness of the strategy going forward. A pre-emptive action may be appropriate, such as buying new fitness machines or dropping the monthly fees, yet it may be prudent just to wait and see if the competitor materializes. The key for effective strategic control lies in asking timely questions that challenge the current strategy.

—Kipling M. Pirkle

See also Capital Asset Pricing Model, Diversification Strategies, Strategic Fit, Strategic Plan, Subsidiary Corporations

FURTHER READING

Cleverley, W. O., & Cameron, A. E. (2002). *Essentials of health care finance.* Gaithersburg, MD: Aspen.

Dess, G. G., & Lumpkin, G. T. (2003). *Strategic management: Creating competitive advantages.* New York: McGraw-Hill.

Hitt, M. A., Ireland, R. D., & Hoskisson, R. E. (2003). *Strategic management: Competitiveness and globalization.* Mason, OH: South-Western.

STRATEGIC DECISIONS

Schwenk (1988) defines three elements of a strategic decision. He theorizes that strategic decisions are

- Ill-structured and nonroutine
- Especially important to an organization
- Very complex

Strategies are different from tactics. Although good companies can develop bad tactical and even strategic decisions, few firms obtain sustained competitive advantages without good decisions (Schwenk, 1988).

We can view decisions through two theoretical lenses in the strategy field: the resource-based view and strategic choice.

- **The resource-based view of the firm: Internal resources are key.** The resource-based view (Barney, 1991, 2002; Priem & Butler, 2001; Wernerfelt, 1984) holds that firms obtain sustained competitive advantages through developing resources that are rare, valuable, inimitable, and nonsubstitutable. Effective strategic decisions in the health care industry could be a valuable, rare, nonsubstitutable, and inimitable resource and thus produce sustained competitive advantage. Many health care leaders see strategic decisions as a potential source of sustained competitive advantage. They would argue that decisions that include Schwenk's (1988) three elements are rare, valuable, inimitable, and nonsubstitutable.

- **Strategic choice: Strategy defines financial performance.** The Holy Grail of strategy research is the correct relationship between strategy and performance. Many argue that the only reason for strategy is to improve performance. The strategic choice theory (Child, 1972, 1997) holds that a firm's strategies drive performance (Powell, 1990). Traditionally, performance focused on financial performance. Firms chose a particular strategy if the financial benefits outweighed the costs. Thus, strategies determined financial performance. Those strategies where costs outweighed the benefits produced poor financial performance. Strategies that produced benefits that outweigh costs, produced better financial performance. An eclectic group of stakeholders drive the health care industry. Thus, health care firms need to consider multifaceted forms of performance. Financial performance may not be the fundamental type of performance in the health care industry. Indeed, financial performance can be less important than the relationships among the firm, the insurance industry, and the regulatory agency. Strategic choice theory could be especially relevant in the health care field. The health care industry is inherently complicated, because of the number, complexity, and jurisdictional issues of regulations as well as the number, complexity, diversity, and importance of stakeholders. As such, strategic choice theory could explain managers' attempts to apply a rational framework in such a disorganized environment. Again, strategic choice theory predicts that strategies are related to performance and as such, firms that implement effective strategic decisions as defined by Schwenk (1988) will consistently perform better financially over the long term.

To be successful, managers in the health care industry should develop a specific yet flexible process for strategic decision making. Two popular texts provide examples of the strategic decision process:

- Williams (2000) recommends "rational decision making." His steps include defining the problem, identifying decision criteria, weighting the criteria, generating alternative courses of action, evaluating each alternative, and computing the optimal decision.
- Wheelen and Hunger (2002) propose a more detailed process, including evaluating current performance results; reviewing corporate governance; scanning and assessing the external environment; scanning and assessing the internal corporate environment; analyzing strategic (SWOT) factors; generating, evaluating, and selecting the best alternative strategy; implementing selected strategies; and evaluating implemented strategies.

In summary, effective strategic decisions are an important element to the successful health care firm.

—Bruce Clemens

FURTHER READING

Barney, J. B. (1991). Firm resources and sustained competitive advantage. *Journal of Management, 17*(1), 99–120.

Barney, J. B. (2001). Resource based theories of competitive advantage: A ten-year retrospective on the resource-based view. *Journal of Management, 27,* 643–650.

Child, J. (1972). Organizational structure, environment and performance: The role of strategic choice. *Sociology, 16,* 1–22.

Child, J. (1997). Strategic choice in the analysis of action, structure, organizations and environment: Retrospect and prospect. *Organization Studies, 18*(1), 43–76.

Powell, W. W. (1990). Neither market nor hierarchy: Network forms of organizations. *Research in Organizational Behavior, 12,* 295–336.

Priem, R. L., & Butler, J. E. (2001). Is the resource-based view a useful perspective for strategic management research? *Academy of Management Review, 26*(1), 22–40.

Schwenk, C. R. (1988). *The essence of strategic decision making.* New York: Lexington Books.

Wheelan, T. L., & Hunger, J. D. (2002). Strategic management and business policy. Upper Saddle River, NJ: Prentice Hall.

Williams, C. (2000). *Management.* Cincinnati, OH: South-Western.

STRATEGIC FIT

Strategic fit is a management concept used as organizations expand and contract their offerings in the marketplace. Related diversification is the basic tenet in an ongoing examination of a firm's various operating divisions. As strategic alternatives are considered as a part of corporate-level strategy, only those options that align with the organization's distinctive competencies are pursued. Also known as *concentric diversification,* the premise is to maintain a common business thread throughout all business activities. An organization builds on the activities that it is already competent at doing, always asking whether new opportunities "fit" with its a core competencies.

The result of strategic fit is synergy in some fashion. Synergy exists when the whole of the organization is greater than the sum of its parts, for example, 2 + 2 = 5. Related diversification creates value not only in the operating divisions but across the entire organization as well. By putting together operating divisions that are related in areas such as technology, resources, or skills, these divisions can draw on one another and on corporate-level strengths to become more effective and profitable. The key to achieving strategic fit is to identify and leverage the firm's distinctive competencies across closely fitting businesses to create new sources of value.

Strategic fit is typically cast in three areas. Product–market fit can be achieved when distribution channels, sales force, and promotion techniques, or customers can be handled at the same time for more than one product or service. Operating fit involves economies being realized in areas such as purchasing, warehousing, production and operations, research and development, or personnel. Management fit occurs when managers are given responsibility over areas in which they have experience.

For example, Orthopedic Associates (OA) has been in business for 10 years. The owners are a group of orthopedic surgeons from the metropolitan area. OA started as a two-person partnership, and as the practice grew, more physicians and specialty services were added, including a radiology group and three physical rehabilitation facilities. Each of the new subsidiaries was funded through a separate legal entity; shares are 100% owned by the parent company, OA. The partners have learned the hard way over the years not to stray too far afield from what they know best—orthopedics. Early on, the partnership started a medical supply business and a fitness center. The competition was fierce and margins were thin; both businesses were eventually shut down. OA has since declined the opportunity to invest in several potentially lucrative health care deals that were not related to its core competencies.

—Kipling M. Pirkle

See also Diversification Strategies, Strategic Service Unit (SSU), Subsidiary Corporations, Synergy

FURTHER READING

Gaughan, P. A. (1996). *Mergers, acquisitions, and corporate restructurings.* New York: Wiley.

Hitt, M. A., Ireland, R. D., & Hoskisson, R. E. (2003). *Strategic management: Competitiveness and globalization.* Mason, OH: South-Western.

Pitts, R. A., & Lei, D. (2003). *Strategic management: Building and sustaining competitive advantage.* Mason, OH: South-Western.

Stahl, M. J. (1989). *Strategic executive decisions: An Analysis of the difference between theory and practice.* Westport, CT: Greenwood Press.

STRATEGIC GOALS

See Objectives, Vision

STRATEGIC GROUPS

A strategic group is a collection of health care organizations that use similar strategies. All the members of a specific strategic group must be direct competitors (that is, all members must compete head-to-head in identifiable markets). For example, two acute care hospitals would be considered direct competitors, whereas an acute care hospital and a behavioral health hospital would likely not be considered direct competitors.

The competing firms that make up a strategic group are clustered together based on similar patterns of various strategic factors. The clustering process seeks to find the common ground among competing firms, as opposed to identifying outlier organizations. Categorizing competitors into strategic groups is an intermediate level of analysis. In other words, the concept of strategic groups lies somewhere between the firm level of analysis and the industry level of analysis. Classifying competitors into strategic groups facilitates the overall understanding of how all the firms in a given market position themselves.

Strategic groups are created based on strategic (that is, competitive) factors that each organization internally controls. The clustering technique used to create strategic groups must measure the strategic decision-making processes within each organization. The different types of strategic decision-making factors can include specific competitive strategies, the way stakeholder relationships are managed, specific facility structures, types of products and services offered, specific target markets, top management personnel decisions, physician credentialing processes, resource allocation algorithms, short-range versus long-range perspective, profitability objectives, quickness and flexibility in the product development process, technology investment goals, and even the range of organizational collaborative activities.

Although strategic group creation is based on similarities of strategic decision making among direct competitors, the operations within each organization can actually vary quite a bit between members of the same strategic group. What this means is that, even though firms may utilize similar macro-level strategic decision making, these firms may have created radically different operational processes to carry out similar strategic goals.

One purpose of classifying firms into strategic groups is to determine, for all the competitors in an identified market, which specific pattern of strategic factors leads to the highest performance. For example, a metropolitan area may have 10 primary care (PC) medical practices. If a strategic group analysis results in three identifiable strategic groups, we may find that group 1 contains four PC practices, group 2 includes four other PC practices, and group 3 counts the remaining two PC practices as members. Once this clustering of the ten PC practices into the different strategic groups is accomplished, the performance outcomes of the medical practices are compared to ascertain if any of the three strategic groups exhibits a significantly higher level of performance. For example, if group 2 had the best-performing PC practices, then the pattern of strategic decision-making processes that characterize group 2 would be deemed to produce higher performance, given the specifics of the market.

—Dawn M. Oetjen and Timothy Rotarius

See also Strategic Decisions, Strategic Planning

FURTHER READING

Daems, H., & Thomas, H. (Eds.). (1994). *Strategic groups, strategic moves, and performance.* New York: Pergamon.

Marlin, D., Huonker, J. W., & Sun, M. (2002). An examination of the relationship between strategic group membership and hospital performance. *Health Care Management Review, 27*(4), 18–29.

McGee, J., & Thomas, H. (1996). Strategic groups: Theory, research and taxonomy. *Strategic Management Journal, 7,* 141–160.

Reger, R. K., & Huff, A. S. (1993). Strategic groups: A cognitive perspective. *Strategic Management Journal, 14*(2), 103–124.

STRATEGIC ISSUE DIAGNOSIS (SID)

A *strategic issue* is a change factor in the external environment that has the potential to affect an organization's ability to fulfill its strategic goals. Typical criteria used to classify an issue as "strategic" include probable impact on the organization as a whole, significant financial implications due to resources required to respond or resulting from failure to respond, and the probability that the effects of the issue will be felt over several years. Strategic issues might result from legislative or regulatory actions, changes in market dynamics, or other environmental jolts.

The concept of strategic issue diagnosis (SID) entered the management literature in 1983 to describe the process by which decision makers interpret environmental data and determine if the probable organization impacts of trends, events, or specific circumstances have strategic implications. Emerging strategic issues typically are identified during environmental scanning activities. Initially, issues may be poorly defined, requiring the organization's leaders to monitor developments over time to evaluate the magnitude and extent of probable impact on the organization.

The SID process is pivotal to initiating adaptive changes in the organization's existing strategy. As organization leaders gain understanding of the various facets of a strategic issue and anticipate the type and extent of its organizational effects, incentive for change increases. Therefore, strategic responses may be incremental in nature, depending on the perceived urgency of the need to respond as the issue becomes more clearly understood.

Strategic issue diagnosis has two distinct phases. First, decision makers identify environmental issues that are perceived as worthy of further investigation. Dutton and Duncan refer to this as the *issue recognition stage.* Second, decision makers evaluate the *urgency* of the issue—perceived importance, time pressures, visibility, and responsibility—and *feasibility*, the organization's ability to pose a solution to the problem(s) arising from the issue.

Additional factors affecting decision makers' choice of possible actions include confidence in their ability to understand the issue, and belief that the organization has the resources and capabilities required for successful solutions. These factors may be visualized as two dimensions producing a four-cell (or four-outcome) matrix. When both understanding and capability are judged low, decision makers feel incapable of resolving the issue. When understanding is low and capability is high, uncertainty delays or prohibits decision-making activity. When understanding is high and capability is low, action may be considered but not implemented. Only when both understanding and capability are high is successful intervention likely to occur.

The Health Insurance Portability and Accountability Act of 1996 (HIPAA), P.L. 104–191, provides an excellent example of a strategic issue for most health care organizations. Potentially the most comprehensive piece of health legislation passed to date, HIPAA's implementation guidelines were released in 2003. Hospitals and other health care organizations were forced to plan for making significant modifications to the infrastructure of existing information systems and information management policies and procedures, a time- and resource-intensive undertaking under the best circumstances, without adequate knowledge of what the actual requirements would be.

—Donna J. Slovensky

FURTHER READING

Dutton, J. E. (1993). Interpretations on automatic: A different view of strategic issue diagnosis. *Journal of Management Studies, 30*(3), 339–358.

Dutton, J. E., & Duncan, R. B. (1987). The creation of momentum for change through the process of strategic issue diagnosis. *Strategic Management Journal, 8,* 279–296.

Dutton, J. E., Fahey, L., & Narayanan, V. K. (1983). Toward understanding strategic issue diagnosis. *Strategic Management Journal, 4,* 307–323.

Dutton, J. E., & Jackson, S. E. (1987). Categorizing strategic issues: Links to organizational action. *Academy of Management Review, 12*(1), 75–91.

STRATEGIC ISSUES

See Environmental Analysis, Strategic Issue Diagnosis (SID)

STRATEGIC LEADERSHIP

Strategic leadership is the process of showing others the way in order to protect and/or enhance the organization's alignment with its external environment. Because health care organizations are confronted with enormous changes in their environments through such things as changing customer demands, shifting government regulations, and new competitive threats, effective strategic leadership is essential to organizational survival and performance. In short, strategic leadership enables the organization to move to a new state that is better aligned with its environment.

Strategic leadership is the responsibility of the person or persons in charge of the overall organization. Usually, this is the chief executive officer or president, and the rest of the top management team. However, this does not mean that all strategic leadership must emanate from the top of the organizational hierarchy. In progressive health care organizations, strategic leadership is exercised throughout the organization, particularly at the middle management level and at the board of director/trustee level.

Many health care organizations are confronted with conflicting pressures—improve quality while reducing cost, reorient care toward the patient and community while not alienating physicians, collaborate or integrate with other providers of care while preserving the institution's core values and competencies. Effective strategic leadership creates a shared and inspiring vision for how these conflicts can be addressed and enables the organization to move toward that vision. To do this, strategic leaders must command not only leadership skills, but also character and integrity.

The strategic leadership process is fundamentally a transformational process. To be an effective strategic leader, one must be willing to have faith in the vision and be willing to be personally transformed along the way. Because this process requires organizational leaders to publicly and/or privately admit and confront their shortcomings while becoming dependent on their followers, effective strategic leadership is rare within organizations.

Because of the enormous impact that strategic leaders have on the overall organization, these individuals must be developed and selected very carefully. Too often, strategic leaders come to their roles because of their excellent technical knowledge and transactional interpersonal skills, without understanding or being groomed for their strategic leadership role and responsibilities. When this happens, the organization loses focus, responds to crises reactively, and its very survival becomes threatened. In progressive organizations, significant and ongoing investments in leadership and strategic leadership training are made.

An excellent illustration of strategic leadership is provided by Phil Newbold, president and CEO of Memorial Hospital and Health System, located in South Bend, Indiana. Newbold has transformed the system's associates from exclusive focus on acute care to a wider focus on the overall clinical and economic health of its service area. Using a broad array of leadership skills and considerable personal character, Newbold has been recognized as a transformational strategic leader on numerous occasions within the health care industry. Rather than reacting to crises, Newbold has led the enterprise into the future. Unfortunately, strategic leaders like Newbold are the exception rather than the rule.

—William Q. Judge

See also Chief Medical Officer/Medical Director, Culture and Strategy, Leadership, Strategic Change, Strategic Management Process, Succession Planning, Vision

FURTHER READING

Blair, J., & Fotler, M. (1998). *Strategic leadership for medical groups.* San Francisco: Jossey-Bass.

Coile, R. (1996, May–June). Steering toward the end game. *Healthcare Forum Journal, 39*(3), 72–75.

Gabel, S. (2001). *Leaders and healthcare organizational change: Art, politics, and process.* New York: Kluwer Press.

Gilkey, R. (1999). *The 21st century health care leader.* San Francisco: Jossey-Bass.

Judge, W. (1999). *The leader's shadow: Exploring and developing executive character.* Thousand Oaks, CA: Sage.

STRATEGIC MANAGEMENT

Strategic management is an externally oriented philosophy of managing an organization that links strategic thinking and analysis to organizational action. As a continuous, explicit philosophy of managing an organization, strategic management

- Provides a framework for thinking about the "business"
- Creates a fit between the organization and its external environment
- Provides a process of coping with change and organizational renewal
- Fosters anticipation, innovation, and excellence

- Facilitates consistent decision making
- Creates organizational focus
- Represents the process of organizational leadership

Strategic management provides an ongoing philosophy for developing and managing the plans and actions of the organization. It seeks to orchestrate a fit between the organization's external environment (political, regulatory, economic, technological, social, and competitive forces) and its internal situation (culture, organization structure, resources, products and services, and so on). In some cases orchestrating the fit may mean responding to external forces, whereas in other cases the organization may attempt to actually shape its environment (change the rules for success). Change in health care has been quite dramatic and often disruptive. When change occurs, new opportunities and threats emerge. Strategic management is an organization's mechanism for understanding and constructively managing change. It is the leadership process for reinventing or renewing the organization.

Strategic management focuses on anticipating external change, fostering innovation in the services and processes of the organization, and promoting excellence. At the same time, strategic management sets direction for the organization and—through a common understanding of the vision and broad goals—provides everyone in the organization a template for making consistent decisions. Such management defines where the organization is going and, sometimes more important, where it is *not* going. Strategic management creates organizational definition and focus.

Strategic management is no longer viewed as a separate discipline; rather, it has become integral in leading and managing organizations. Strategic managers constantly relate the organization to its external environment, not merely to ensure compatibility and survival, but also to understand or alter the environmental trends so as to "create the future." Thus, strategic management represents an evolving process of analysis and evaluation to continuously monitor the environment and adapt the organization to create momentum. Strategic management is the process of organizational leadership.

STRATEGIC THINKING, STRATEGIC PLANNING, AND STRATEGIC MANAGEMENT

Strategic thinking is the intellectual orientation or mindset underlying the strategic management philosophy. *Strategic planning,* a term sometimes used interchangeably with *strategic management,* is the periodic process of creating strategy using strategic thinking. Therefore, strategic planning is the set of organizational processes for identifying the desired future of the organization and developing decision guidelines. The result of the strategic planning process is a plan or *strategy.* Strategic management is continuous and is the philosophy of managing an organization using strategic thinking and periodic strategic planning.

WHAT STRATEGIC MANAGEMENT IS NOT

Strategic management should not be regarded as a technique that will provide a "quick fix" for an organization that has fundamental problems. Successful strategic management often takes years to become a part of the values and culture of an organization. If strategic management is regarded as a technique or gimmick, it is doomed to failure. Similarly, strategic management is not an annual retreat where the management of an organization meets to talk about key issues only to return to the office and continue "business as usual." Although retreats can be effective in refocusing management and for generating new thinking, strategic management must be adopted as the philosophy of managing the organization.

If strategic management has reached a point where it has become simply a process of filling in endless forms, meeting deadlines, drawing milestone charts, or changing the dates of last year's goals and plans, the process is not strategic management. Strategic management is not a process of completing paperwork; effective strategic management actually requires very little paperwork. It is an approach to managing supported by strategic thinking, not by a series of documents. Similarly, strategic management is not initiated merely to satisfy a regulatory body's requirement for a "plan."

Strategic management is not a process of simply extending the organization's current activities into the future. It is not based solely on a forecast of present trends. Strategic management attempts to identify the issues that will be important in the future. Health care leaders should not simply ask the question "How will we provide this service in the future?" Rather, they should be asking questions such as "Should we provide this service in the future?" "What new services will be needed?" and "What services are we providing now that are no longer needed?"

STRATEGIC MANAGEMENT IN THE HEALTH CARE INDUSTRY

Historically, individual health care organizations had few incentives to employ strategic management because most health care organizations were independent, freestanding, not-for-profit institutions, and health services reimbursement was on a cost-plus basis. Efforts at health planning were initiated by federal, state, or local governments and implemented through legislation or private or nongovernmental agencies. For the most part, these planning efforts were disease oriented; that is, they were categorical approaches directed toward specific health problems.

Strategic management concepts have been employed within health care organizations since the early 1980s.

Many of the management methods adopted by health care organizations, both public and private, were developed in the business sector. In many respects health care has become a complex business using many of the same processes and much of the same language as the most sophisticated business corporations.

Strategic management has become the essential process for coping with external change and is the major philosophy guiding the management of all types of contemporary organizations. For example, business organizations have almost universally embraced strategic management as a way to anticipate and cope with a variety of external forces beyond their control. Government agencies and nonprofit organizations have increasingly adopted strategic management to set direction and create organizational focus amid a chaotic environment. Similarly, health care organizations have embraced strategic management as a mechanism for coping with the increasing amount and pace of environmental change.

—Peter M. Ginter

See also Hypercompetition, Long-Range Planning, Strategic Planning, Strategic Thinking, Strategy

FURTHER READING

Duncan, W. J., Ginter, P. M., & Swayne, L. E. (1998). *Handbook of health care management.* Malden, MA: Blackwell.

Ginter, P. M., Swayne, L. E., & Duncan, W. J. (2002). *Strategic management of health care organizations* (4th ed.). Oxford, UK: Blackwell.

Horak, B. J. (1997). *Strategic planning in healthcare: Building a quality-based plan step by step.* New York: Quality Resources.

Prince, T. R. (1998). *Strategic management of health care entities.* Chicago: AHA Press.

Zuckerman, A. M. (1998). *Healthcare strategic planning: Approaches for the 21st century.* Chicago: Health Administration Press.

STRATEGIC MANAGEMENT PROCESS

The term *strategic management process* refers to the means by which critical human, technical, financial, and informational resources are obtained, combined, and discarded so that an organization can survive and prosper. Typically, upper-echelon managers take responsibility for this process, but progressive managers involve the entire organization as much as possible in this process. Because there are many misconceptions about this process, it is helpful to examine what it is not before further exploring what it is.

First, the strategic management process is not the same as the strategic planning process. This process subsumes strategic planning, particularly in dynamic and uncertain environments. Increasingly, the aim of the strategic management process is to promote effective resource allocation decisions and activities, whereas the strategic planning process is an important communication tool that promotes coordination within the organization.

Second, this process is not the same as strategic leadership. Management deals with the effective use of organizational resources within an existing order; leadership deals with showing others the way so that a new organizational order can be created. Both sets of activities are important and sometimes overlap, but each activity has a different aim and usually requires different skills sets.

Finally, this process is not the same as strategic thinking or decision making or control. Although strategic managers often think carefully and make important decisions, they also act on those decisions and oversee the execution of those decisions. As such, the strategic management is a holistic process that subsumes these three activities.

Top managers in the health care industry have not historically used the strategic management process because tactical excellence was emphasized in a cost-plus-reimbursement framework. Today, this has all changed. Tactical excellence is still important, but attention to "big picture" strategic issues within the strategic management process is essential as well.

The strategic management process, if done well, should ensure the long-run health and viability of the organization. Organizational health is best judged from a balanced and holistic perspective that considers financial and nonfinancial considerations as well as a broad range of organizational stakeholders. The balanced scorecard is a useful framework to create a strategy-focused organization from a holistic perspective.

In our information-based global economy, innovation is increasingly the only option that strategic managers and leaders can pursue to be successful. Because information is increasing in comprehensiveness and velocity, cost efficiencies are quickly apparent and eventually copied by competitors. Although continuous attention to cost efficiencies will always be important to "remain in the game," the only viable option for long-term growth is for the strategic management process to focus on creative ways to produce new and valuable products and services or to literally "change the game." As such, strategic managers must work with strategic leaders to deal with the increasingly paradoxical strategic situations that demand maintaining stability while trying to change, balancing short-term goals with long-term ones, and acting to reconcile the multiple, and sometimes conflicting, interests of organizational stakeholders.

—William Q. Judge

See also Balanced Scorecard and Health Care, Business Plan, Critical Success Factors, Culture and Strategy, Long-Range Planning, Strategic Alternatives, Strategic Assumptions, Strategic Control, Strategic Issues Diagnosis (SID), Strategic Thinking, Strategy

FURTHER READING

Ginter, T., Swayne, L., & Duncan, W. (2002). *Strategic management of health care organizations* (4th ed.). Oxford, UK: Blackwell.

Kaplan, R., & Norton, D. (2001, May–June). The strategy-focused organization. *Strategy & Leadership, 29*(3), 41–42.

Muller, C. (2002). Strategic management: A tool for growth in the biotechnology sector. *Journal of Commercial Biotechnology, 8*(3), 226–234.

STRATEGIC MAPPING

See Strategic Management

STRATEGIC MOMENTUM

See Strategic Issue Diagnosis (SID)

STRATEGIC PLAN

See Long-Range Planning, Strategic Management

STRATEGIC PLANNING

See Strategic Management

STRATEGIC SERVICE UNIT (SSU)

A strategic service unit (SSU) is a form of organizational structure that groups all functions needed to provide a product or service to a set of customers in a self-contained unit. The purpose of the unit is precise and clear, and all goals for the unit are priority-ranked around service outcomes. Service units are found in large complex organizations where skill sets and resources can be identified specifically to the product or service provided.

Strategic service units have the advantage of coordinating all efforts around the needs of the service recipient. Because of the clearly defined resource needs for the service, strategic service units can respond rapidly to changing situations and bring the best and appropriate service to the situation. Specific yet appropriate, service-oriented responsiveness leads to a high level of customer satisfaction. Strategic service units are capable of crossing functional boundaries. Individuals representing different functional backgrounds will collaborate to meet service goals with minimal conflict.

The mission of many health care organizations is excellent customer service. The strategic service unit structure is consistent with organizational mission. Although customer satisfaction may be high, the cost of the strategic service unit may also be high. SSUs result in duplication of service resources from unit to unit and lack of coordination between and among other strategic service units, because of the decentralized autonomous operation of the service unit.

Strategic service units provide a mechanism for health care organizations to provide excellent customer service, in rapidly changing situational needs. Although high in costs, service goals can be realized.

—Rebecca I. Porterfield

See also Organizational Structure, Service Area Competitor Analysis

FURTHER READING

Sullivan, E. J., & Decker, P. J. (2001). *Effective leadership and management in nursing.* Upper Saddle River, NJ: Prentice Hall.

STRATEGIC THINKING

Strategic thinking is an intellectual process, a mind-set, or a way of thinking that asks people to think as leaders. Vision and a sense of the future are an inherent part of strategic thinking. Strategic thinkers are constantly reinventing the future, creating windows on the world of tomorrow. As the writers on leadership James Kouzes and Barry Posner have indicated, all enterprises or projects, big or small, begin in the mind's eye. They begin with imagination and with the belief that what is merely an image can one day be made real. Strategic thinkers draw on the past, understand the present, and can envision a better future.

Strategic thinkers are always asking, "What are we doing now that we should stop doing?" "What are we not doing now, but should start doing?" and "What are we doing now that we should continue to do but in a fundamentally different way?" For the strategic thinker, these questions are applicable to everything the organization does—its products and services, internal processes, policies and procedures, strategies, and so on. Strategic thinkers examine assumptions, understand systems and their interrelationships, and develop alternative scenarios. Strategic thinkers forecast external technological, social, and demographic changes, as well as critical changes in the political and regulatory arenas.

Therefore, strategic thinking is directed toward the "big picture" and concerns effectiveness more than efficiency. The assumption underlying strategic thinking is that organizations should first focus on being effective (doing the "right" thing) and then concentrate on doing it well (doing things "right").

WHY ENGAGE IN STRATEGIC THINKING?

The fundamental reason to engage in strategic thinking is that the world is undergoing dramatic change. This change is often referred to as *whitewater change* or *hypercompetition.* Organizations need some type of intellectual process to identify and cope with this change if they are to remain relevant, some way to consider how to renew or reinvent themselves.

Managers who operate in an environment where there is little change probably do not need strategic thinking. However, today few industries do not face massive change—technological, economic, social, political, regulatory, and competitive—that can devastate a successful organization. Health care is certainly one of the most dynamic industries and thus requires strategic thinking. Moreover, to assume that what a health care organization is currently doing will always be valuable and relevant is the type of arrogance that has destroyed many organizations in other industries. As the world changes, the "rules for success" change as well. New technologies, social values, demographics, political environments, regulations, economic conditions, and competitive changes call for new approaches, new products and services, and new ways to deliver them.

Strategic thinking is an important foundation of strategic management. However, strategic thinking is not confined to just the CEO or the top level of the organization. For strategic management to be successful, everyone should be encouraged to think strategically. Strategic thinking is supported by the continuous process of strategic management and documented through the periodic process of strategic planning.

—Peter M. Ginter

See also Hypercompetition, Long-Range Planning, Strategic Management, Strategic Planning, Strategy

FURTHER READING

D'Aveni, R. A. (1995). Coping with hypercompetition: Utilizing the new 7S's framework. *Academy of Management Executive, 9*(3), 45–60.

Dixit, A. K., & Nalebuff, B. J. (1991). *Thinking strategically.* New York: Norton.

Ginter, P. M., Swayne, L. E., & Duncan, W. J. (2002). *Strategic management of health care organizations* (4th ed.). Oxford, UK: Blackwell.

Kouzes, J. M., & Posner, B. Z. (1995). *The leadership challenge: How to keep getting extraordinary things done in organizations.* San Francisco: Jossey-Bass.

STRATEGY

A *strategy* is a plan to accomplish a desired end result. Strategy links management's understanding of the organization today with where it wants, can, and should be at some point in the future (for example, three to five years in the future). Strategy is the road map to the future.

A strategy may be viewed as a behavioral pattern that emerges from a stream of decisions concerning the positioning of the organization within its environment. In other words, when a sequence of decisions relating the organization to its environment exhibits a logical consistency over time, a strategy will have been formed. Decision consistency is central to strategy; when an organization exhibits a consistent behavior, it has a strategy.

The requirements of decision consistency suggest that a strategy is the means an organization chooses to move from where it is today to a desired state some time in the future. Thus strategy may be viewed as a set of guidelines or a plan that helps assure consistency. Strategy provides parameters that indicate what types of decisions are appropriate or inappropriate for an organization.

Without some type of organizing framework or theory, the process of creating strategy becomes overwhelming. However, there are many ways to think about strategy in organizations. Analytical or rational approaches to strategy creation rely on the development of a logical sequence of steps or processes (linear thinking). Emergent models, in contrast, rely on intuitive thinking, leadership, and learning. Both approaches are valid and useful in explaining strategy.

THE EMERGENCE OF STRATEGY

During the past several decades, practitioners have been interested in examining and understanding the strategies of health care organizations. Few industries have experienced more "whitewater change" and "turbulent times" than health care. How health care organizations strategically respond to such change has been, and will continue to be, an important topic.

An interest in strategy for organizations emerged as a response to the difficulties of managing efficiency *and* effectiveness. The first half-century of management and management research was preoccupied with efficiency and focused almost exclusively on internal controllable factors. However, by the 1950s this internal focus was clearly inadequate.

Managers increasingly recognized the limitations of a management theory that did not account for and deal with the external and uncontrollable factors. Events in the 1960s intensified the need for a revision of management theory. This era was characterized by radical new technologies, a dramatic increase in competition, the cold war, shifts in regulatory policy, racial unrest, and a demand for social justice, as well as many other changes.

STRATEGY TOPICS

A variety of topics have been incorporated under the general rubric of *strategy.* Elements of strategy include process, content, contextual issues (the external environment), competitive advantage, strategic groups, the role of the strategist, performance, structure, strategic competencies, decision making, and complexity and chaos as well as a number of related subcategories. However, central to the understanding of strategy is the distinction between strategy as *process* and strategy as *content.*

STRATEGY AS PROCESS VERSUS STRATEGY AS CONTENT

The strategy *process* has been described as primarily focused on the actions that lead to and support strategy including planning methods and decision making (*how* strategy is formulated and implemented). In contrast, strategy *content* is characterized as the strategic decision itself, including such decisions as merger, acquisition, divestment, market entry and exit, mobility barriers, product or market differentiation, turnaround, and vertical integration as well as the content of decisions regarding scope and competitive strategies.

Strategy as Process

Strategic planning is the periodic process of creating *strategy.* It is the set of organizational processes for identifying the desired future of the organization and developing decision guidelines. The result of the strategic planning process is a plan or *strategy.* However, the development of the strategy is more specific than strategic planning and is usually referred to as *strategy formulation.* Strategy formulation is one part of the strategic planning process and does

Figure 1   Normative Model of Strategy Formulation

are developed. Implementation strategies are the means to accomplish competitive strategies.

Strategy as Content

As illustrated in Figure 1, the content of strategy is typically viewed as those strategies that determine scope, market entry, and competitive posture or positioning. Directional strategies (mission and vision) are most often treated separately and, because of their lack of specificity, are not generally viewed as content strategies. Similarly, implementation strategies are viewed as tactical and cover a broad range of organizational activities including finance, marketing, operations, human resources, structure, culture, and so on.

A discussion of strategy content may be organized using the normative strategy formulation model. Table 1 presents a schema or map of strategy content using normative strategy formulation decision logic focusing on scope, marketing entry, and competitive strategies. This map not only identifies the alternative strategies (content) but also illustrates a hierarchical relationship among the strategies.

Expansion strategies—at both the corporate and business levels—have been quite prevalent in health care. Corporate-level strategies are directed toward creating the best mix of semiautonomous businesses operating in separate markets with distinct products or services. Corporate-level strategies address the question "What business(es) should we be in?" Corporate expansion strategies increase the scope of the organization and include diversification and vertical integration.

In contrast to corporate strategies, business-level strategies are concerned with a single well-defined market and with a product or service line that serves a specific market or service area. Business-level strategies deal with the question "How should an organization compete in a given market?" Business-level strategic alternatives are concerned with competing within a service area. Prevalent health care business-level strategies are market-based strategies and include market development, product development, and penetration.

Strategies for decreasing scope occur at both the corporate level and business level, as well. As shown in Table 1, corporate-level contraction strategies include divestiture and liquidation and business-level strategies include harvesting and retrenchment.

not include situational analysis (the external environment and internal environment), implementation, or control.

From a normative viewpoint, strategy formulation may be viewed as a series of increasingly specific decisions. Generally, the acquisition of one health care organization by another one is part of a series of decisions rather than a single decision or an end in itself. In other words, a broader strategy precipitated the acquisition decision and subsequent decisions must be made to support the acquisition and make it successful. Therefore, a normative model of strategy formulation may be constructed consisting of increasingly more specific decisions. These strategies, beginning with the most general and moving to the more specific, include directional strategies, scope strategies, market entry strategies, competitive strategies, and implementation strategies. These strategy decisions should be made sequentially with each subsequent decision more specifically defining the strategy of the organization. This approach is illustrated in Figure 1.

Theoretically, the cascading of strategy types from directional to implementation strategies forms an "ends-to-means chain." Directional strategies develop consensus on the organization's mission, vision, values, and broad goals, and from a normative perspective must be made first. Next, organizational scope strategies become the means to accomplish the directional strategies (the desired end result for the organization) and are concerned with contraction, or maintenance of operations. Market entry strategies are the means to accomplish the organizational scope strategies and indicate how expansion or maintenance strategies will be carried out. Next, the organization's strategic posture and positioning vis-à-vis other organizations must be determined (competitive strategies); and finally, specific functional and organizationwide implementation plans

Table 1   Map of Strategy Content

Scope Strategies	Market Entry Strategies	Competitive Strategies
Expanding Scope	**Purchase**	**Strategy Types**
• Diversification	• Acquisition	• Generic strategies
• Vertical integration	• Licensing	• Strategic postures
• Market-based strategies	• Venture capital	• Strategy archetypes
• Market development	**Cooperation**	• Strategic groups
• Product development	• Merger	
• Penetration	• Alliance	
Decreasing Scope	• Joint Venture	
• Divestiture and liquidation	**Internal Development**	
• Harvesting and retrenchment		
Maintaining Scope		
• Enhancement		
• Status quo		

Often organizations pursue maintenance strategies when management believes past decisions have been appropriate and few changes are required in the target markets or the organization's products or services. Maintenance does not necessarily mean that the organization will do nothing, but rather that management believes the organization is progressing appropriately. There are two maintenance strategies: enhancement and status quo.

Typically, enhancement strategies take the form of quality programs (CQI, TQM) directed toward improving organizational processes, cost reduction programs designed to render the organization more efficient, innovative management processes, speeding up the delivery of the products or services to the customer, and adding flexibility to the design of the products or services (marketwide customization). A status quo strategy is based on the assumption that the market has matured and periods of high growth are over. Often the organization has secured an acceptable market share and managers believe the position can be defended against competitors. Typically, organizations attempt a status quo strategy in some areas while engaging in market development, product development, or penetration in others to better utilize limited resources. For instance, a hospital may seek to hold its market share (status quo) in slow-growth markets such as cardiac and pediatric services and pursue market development in higher-growth services such as intense, short-term rehabilitation care (renal dialysis, ophthalmology, or intravenous therapy, for example).

Selecting the expansion or maintenance-of-scope strategies dictates that the next decision to be made concerns market entry. (If a decreasing scope strategy is selected, there is no reason for market entry.) The expanding scope strategies specify entering or gaining access to a new market, and the maintenance strategies often call for obtaining new resources.

As shown in Table 1, an organization can use its financial resources and purchase into the market, join with other organizations and use cooperation to enter a market, or use its own resources and develop its own products and services. It is important to understand that market entry strategies are not ends in themselves but serve a broader aim—the scope strategies. Any of the scope strategies may be carried out using any of the market entry strategies, but each one places different demands on the organization.

Purchase strategies may be divided into acquisition, licensing, and venture capital investments. Cooperation strategies may be grouped into merger, alliance, and joint venture strategies. Internal development uses the existing organizational structure, personnel, and capital to generate new products, services, or distribution strategies.

Competitive strategies are business-level strategies and are primarily concerned with market positioning and direct competition. Using the decision logic in the normative strategy formulation model, after having selected the scope strategies and market entry strategies, managers then decide their competitive posture and positioning. Competitive strategies are presented as taxonomies of strategy types and strategic groups and specify common strategic behaviors or patterns resulting in strategy classifications such as cost leadership, differentiation, analyzers, prospectors, market leaders, and so on. These taxonomies have frequently been referred to as *gestalts, strategic archetypes, generic strategies,* or *strategic groups.* Thus competitive strategies identify strategy behavior types. Strategic groups are particularly important in health care because of the complexity of the industry. There are often many organizations that offer similar services, have similar strategies, or serve a common market and yet are not direct competitors and therefore not a member of the strategic group.

There are a limited number of strategy types, but an infinite number of ways they may be implemented. In addition, organizations typically engage in more than one type at a time. Combination strategies are used, especially in larger complex organizations, because no single strategy alone may be sufficient. In addition to an organization using several different strategies at once, a strategy may have several phases. It may be necessary to "string together" several strategic alternatives as phases or elements to implement a broader strategic shift.

—Peter M. Ginter

See also Competitive Advantage, Contraction Strategy, Expansion Strategies, Long-Range Planning, Strategic Management, Strategic Planning

FURTHER READING

Blair, J. D., & Boal, K. B. (1991). Strategy formation process in health care organizations: A context-specific examination of context-free strategy issues. *Journal of Management, 17*(2), 305–344.

Fahey, L., & Christensen, H. K. (1986). Evaluating the research on strategy content. *Journal of Management, 12*(2), 167–183.

Ginter, P. M., Swayne, L. E., & Duncan, W. J. (2002). *Strategic management of health care organizations* (4th ed.). Oxford, UK: Blackwell.

Huff, A. S., & Reger, R. K. (1987). A review of strategic process research. *Journal of Management, 13*(2), 211–236.

STRATEGY FORMULATION

See Strategy

STRATEGY IMPLEMENTATION

See Strategy

STRENGTH

See SWOT (Strength-Weakness-Opportunity-Threat) Analysis

STRUCTURE

Studies on formal structure in organizations have encompassed vertical and horizontal differentiation, hierarchies, formalization, delegation, specialization, and divisionalization. Some researchers have argued that structure results from functional imperatives such as size or technology. Managerial decisions on structure then reflect the inevitable logic of survival. Joan Woodward, however, noted that the scale she developed could only predict structure at its extremes; in the middle, managers had discretion in deciding on structure.

Almost all the studies on organizational structure have concentrated on the formal aspects of structure as in procedural manuals. Almost none of the researchers asked how the formal offices worked in practice and whether people lived up to their formal roles as the manuals defined them. Also, almost all the studies dealt with cross-sectional variables or snapshots in time, and so one cannot draw conclusions on causality.

Researchers have found some relationships between structure and technology at the organizational level, but not particularly strong ones. As technology becomes more explicit in manufacturing, the number of staff specialties increase, overall formalization increases, chief executives' spans of control increase, and the subordinate ratios first increase, then decrease. Specialization and certain aspects of formalization may stimulate innovation, but when researchers control for size this pattern becomes adversely affected. Chris Argyris has convincingly argued that rather than technology, leadership style may have a strong influence on structure.

Alfred Dupont Chandler, John Child, and others represented this open-system view in which managers could create and choose among alternative structures, many of which could facilitate organizational viability and effectiveness. Several questions then arose: Which structure provided the best choices? How did managers choose the best structure? What did "best" mean for the managers? Among other measures, studies have analyzed the relationships among formal structure, innovation, technology, and profits.

Peter Drucker labeled the process of developing a corporate structure as divisionalization or federal decentralization. According to management theory, decentralization comes from sheer necessity. Except in very small business groups, top managers cannot make all decisions and decentralize for efficacy. In large domestic U.S. corporations, divisionalization has moved from functional divisions (marketing, finance, and so on) to product divisions, to matrix structures that combine both functional and product divisions, and finally back to functional divisions for some corporations!

Several studies have explored the relationships between formal structure and organizational strategy. In his groundbreaking book, *Strategy and Structure,* and employing case analysis, Chandler illustrated the unique ways in which Dupont, General Motors, Sears Roebuck, and Standard Oil adopted decentralized, multidivisional structures after World War I. These corporations' changes in formal structure resulted from their managers' varying outlooks and approaches. Chandler argued that structure followed strategy for these large American corporations.

A number of historical studies have indicated that diversification by business corporations preceded their moves from functional to divisional structures, thereby supporting Chandler's dictum on strategy and structure. However, the time lags between strategic and structural changes have extended over very long periods, which again raises some questions about causal connections.

Other studies have displayed no relationship between structure and strategy. For example, Jerald Hage and Robert Dewar, analyzing data from 16 health and welfare agencies, discovered that program innovations correlated more closely with values of the organizational elites than with organizational structure.

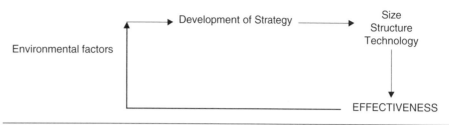

Figure 1 The Relation Between Strategy and Structure, According to John Child

Richard Rumelt's research pointed to fashionable managerial practice, rather than strategy, as another viable influence on structure. For example, managers in some corporations come to believe that a product division structure would lead to better performance than a functional structure. As Rumelt explained, rather than strategy, "Structure also follows fashion."

John Stopford and Louis Wells reported how 187 U.S. multinational corporations evolved as they diversified their products for foreign markets. They concluded that they evolved from (a) functional structures to (b) divisional structures to (c) product division structures plus international divisions to (d) global structures often based on worldwide product divisions. Another path included adding international divisions to functional structures before stage c. Stopford and Wells also presented data to show that corporations that matched their structures to balance between foreign product diversity and relative importance of foreign sales, on the whole achieved higher levels of profitability and growth. However, the role of imitation and fashion in these developments remains an open question.

If one accepts Chandler's dictum that strategy leads to structure, then design processes should include steps from formulation of strategy to implementation. Central in these design principles should loom measures of effectiveness by which managers gauge whether they should alter strategies or continue with more of the same. In this vein, Child argued that environmental factors affect the development of strategy that in turn affects size, structure, and technology (see Figure 1). Managers should evaluate both structure and strategy against measures of effectiveness, should and successful organizations modify both in response to performance fluctuations—that is, measures of effectiveness should guide both strategy and structure.

—Usha C. V. Haley

See also Organizational Design and Discontinuous Change, Organizational Performance and Work Design, Strategy

FURTHER READING

Argyris, C. (1972). *The applicability of organizational sociology.* Cambridge, UK: Cambridge University Press.

Chandler, A. D. (1962). *Strategy and structure.* Cambridge, MA: MIT Press.

Child, J. (1973). Predicting and understanding organization structure. *Administrative Science Quarterly, 18,* 168–185.

Drucker, P. (1954). The practice of management. New York: Harper.

Hage, J., & Dewar, R. (1973). Elite values versus organizational structure in predicting innovation. *Administrative Science Quarterly, 18,* 279–290.

Rumelt, R. P. (1974). *Strategy, structure and economic performance in large American industrial corporations.* Boston: Graduate School of Business Administration, Harvard University.

Stopford, J., & Wells, L. T. (1972). *Managing the multinational enterprise.* London: Longman.

Woodward, J. (1965). *Industrial organization: Theory and practice.* London: Oxford University Press.

STRUCTURED SETTLEMENT

A structured settlement is an agreement between the defendant and plaintiff to provide periodic payments of damages over a specified period of time. The settlement is usually financed by purchase of an annuity. The annuity is usually purchased from an annuity insurance company.

A structured settlement is usually considered when there are long-term medical or income needs because of significant disability or where the plaintiff would have difficulty managing large sum awards. It may involve up-front cash to cover costs before the settlement and then periodic payments for medical expenses, income, and educational costs. A properly designed structured settlement flows tax free to the plaintiff. It provides lifelong financial security, taking advantage of the increasing investment value of the money deposited for the settlement over time.

—George V. Jirak

FURTHER READING

www.nssta.com

STUDY ARMS

A study arm of a clinical trial includes the active arm, which is the test product, a possible reference arm, which could be another active approved product, and a placebo arm. Additional arms of the study can include other approved reference products or additional doses of the drug product.

Study arms can be implemented in a parallel design, whereas two or more drugs are randomly assigned to different patients or a crossover design where the patient takes each treatment in a random fashion.

It is important to determine the appropriate number of study arms in your clinical trial because the outcome of your clinical trial may depend on this. In order to present reliable data to the agency, well-designed studies are important. Statistical plans depend on the number of study arms employed in your study.

In addition, the number of subjects in each arm is important. It is feasible to make the active groups larger than the placebo groups to improve the precision of the active drug comparison.

Combination or factorial design studies can be employed to add several dosing arms in combination with several doses of approved agents in combination. This is common in antihypertensive therapies where combination therapy is a standard of care.

In addition, study arms could also have a placebo group for each drug, a double-dummy placebo-controlled trial design. When comparing the efficacy and safety of two products that have different routes of administration, a double-blind double-dummy study design can be used. A placebo can be given for each route, along with its corresponding active treatment to maintain the integrity of the blinding.

—Anthony Sileno

See also Clinical Trials, Placebo

FURTHER READING

FDA guidance for the industry. (2001). *Choice of control group and related issues in clinical trials.* Washington, DC: Food and Drug Administration.

SUBACUTE CARE

Subacute care units are also called *transitional care units.* In the 1990s, subacute units were developed to fill the gap for those patients who no longer needed acute hospital care, but were not strong enough to return home. This gap was widened by the Medicare prospective payment system that began for hospitals in the United States in the mid 1980s. This payment system is based on diagnosis-related groups (DRGs). Hospitals are paid a predetermined amount for each admission based on the DRG, regardless of the length of the hospitalization or the costs incurred. Under the DRG payment system, hospitals have an incentive to shorten lengths of stay. In contrast, since the inception of Medicare and for most of the 1990s, long-term care facilities were reimbursed on a "cost plus" basis. Individuals who had an established treatment plan but continued to have complex medical needs were ideal for the subacute unit. These units were directly reimbursed for the specialized equipment, medications, or personnel required.

Subacute units must follow state and federal regulations for long-term care, which in most cases are more stringent than hospital regulations. These units are almost exclusively located in hospitals or nursing homes. A unit must include a minimum of 15 beds and be located in a designated area. Subacute patients cannot be scattered among other patients in the facility. Affiliations with hospitals and nursing homes provide savings from economies of scale and a built-in referral base.

Subacute units provide complex medical care and rehabilitation. The ratio of nurses to patients is higher than in a nursing home. The cost of care in a subacute unit is intermediate between hospital and nursing home care. Physical, occupational, and speech therapists must be available as employees or on a contracted basis. The unit must have a certified nursing home administrator, a social worker, and a medical director. Because the care is more complex, attending physicians typically visit the subacute unit once or twice a week, in contrast to nursing home visits, which are often monthly.

Team meetings that include all participants in the patient's care occur on a regular basis to share information and develop an individualized treatment plan. Patient and family participation in these meetings is encouraged. The patient's goals are integral to the treatment plan. Most admissions are for two weeks or less, and most residents return to their homes.

Current Medicare regulations require a three-day hospital stay before admission to a subacute unit. Managed care organizations pay for subacute care without a recent hospitalization if there is a sudden change in the patient's condition and subacute care can meet the needs. Examples of situations where a person could be directly admitted to a subacute unit include (a) a fracture that requires pain control and nursing care and (b) pneumonia that requires intravenous antibiotics. Examples of subacute care after a hospitalization include (a) rehabilitation after joint replacement and (b) treatment of an infected surgical wound that is too complex for home care. Some subacute units can also manage ventilator dependent patients.

At the end of the 20th century, Medicare reimbursement for subacute units and nursing home changed to payment based on resource utilization groups (RUGs). RUGs are analogous to the DRGs used to reimburse hospitals. This limited reimbursement has increased the challenges of providing care for these transitional and fragile patients.

—Jean Stretton

See also Home Health Care, Step-Down Facility

FURTHER READING

Hyatt, L. (1995). *Subacute care: Redefining health care.* New York: McGraw-Hill.

Von Sternberg, T., Connors, K., & Calkins, E. (1999). Subacute care. In E. Calkins, C. Bould, E. H. Watner, & J. T. Pacala, *New ways to care for older people: Building systems based on evidence* (Chapter 8). New York: Springer.

SUBINVESTIGATOR

A subinvestigator is any member of the clinical trial team that has been so designated by the trial's investigator. This individual is under the direct supervision of the main investigator. Performance of procedures related to the critical trial, as well as the authority to make important trial-related decisions, are tasks of a subinvestigator at the study site. In essence, the investigator and subinvestigator have a collaborative agreement regarding the conduct of the trial. This agreement is the result of their discussions on the manner in which the trial will be conducted so that good clinical practices are strictly adhered to. These discussions occur before the first patient is screened, whenever questions arise, and continue throughout the trial.

In certain institutions the role of subinvestigator is assigned to individuals who meet certain criteria. For example, nurse practitioners can be designated as subinvestigators. Their advanced practice privileges allow them to perform physical examinations, diagnose disease states, and write prescriptions.

—Linda M. Cimino

See also Investigator (Principal Investigator)

FURTHER READING

Chow, S.-C., & Liu, J.-P. (1998). *Design and analysis of clinical trials: Concepts and methodologies.* New York: Wiley.

Glossary: Clinical research terminology. (2001, December). *Applied Clinical Trials,* 36–48.

Kolman, J., Meng, P., & Scott, G. (1998). *Good clinical practice* (pp. 2–3). Chichester, UK: Wiley.

Whittemore, R., & Grey, M. (2002, Second Quarter). Systematic development of nursing interventions. *Journal of Nursing Scholarship, 34*(2), 115–120.

SUBJECT, HUMAN RESEARCH

The federal regulations define two ways in which an individual becomes a human research subject. The first involves having a researcher obtain data about the individual via actual intervention or interaction with the individual. Once the person agrees to participate in the research study, he or she becomes a human research subject. The second circumstance does not require the individual to be present in the research setting in order to be considered a human subject. Once an individual's identifiable private information (for example, from a medical record, or obtained from investigation of biological specimens, and so on) is proposed for research use, that individual becomes a human research subject as well.

Human research subjects are afforded important rights that must be protected. One of the most important rights a subject has is the ability to choose whether or not to participate in the research; that is, participation must be voluntary. Further, even if a subject agrees to participate, the subject must retain the right to withdraw from the research at any time, without any effect on his or her status with the investigator (this is particularly important when the investigator is also the treating physician).

The protection of human subjects occurs at many levels. The Office for Human Research Protections (OHRP) and the Food and Drug Administration (FDA; for research involving drugs, biologics, and devices) at the federal level, and the institutional review boards (IRBs) and research investigators at the local level, must all maintain levels of communication, education, and monitoring to ensure that the rights and welfare of human subjects are protected.

—Judy Matuk

See also Belmont Report, Institutional Review Board (IRB), Office for Human Research Protections (OHRP), Vulnerable Research Subject Populations

FURTHER READING

http://ohrp.osophs.dhhs.gov
http://ohrp.osophs.dhhs.gov/humansubjects/guidance/belmont.htm
www.access.gpo.gov/nara/cfr/waisidx_99/45cfr46_99.html
www.fda.gov/oc/ohrt/irbs/default.htm

SUBSIDIARY CORPORATIONS

A subsidiary corporation is a company that is at least 50% owned by a parent company, or holding company. A subsidiary typically has a distinct stable of products or services, and functions as a separate profit center. If a subsidiary corporation has its own board of directors, that board is controlled or at least heavily influenced by the holding company. The parent company acts as an internal banker, allocating resources among its various subsidiaries. The subsidiary's financial statements are consolidated into the holding company's statements, along with those of other subsidiaries. Tax returns are filed by the holding company, based on the combined operations of its subsidiaries.

For example, Metro Health Care (MHC) is a holding company that owns 100% of the stock in three subsidiary corporations: Metro Hospital, Metro Emergency Care, and Metro Physical Therapy. Each of these units is a stand-alone business, with its own president and staff. Each unit is a profit center, and each unit has a distinct mission in the metropolitan area. MHC, the holding company, generates no patient revenues of its own, but consolidates the financial statements of its three subsidiaries. Investors own shares in the parent company, MHC.

—Kipling M. Pirkle

See also Strategic Business Unit (SBU)

FURTHER READING

Cleverley, W. O., & Cameron, A. E. (2002). *Essentials of health care finance.* Gaithersburg, MD: Aspen.
Collin, P. H. (2001). *Dictionary of business.* London: Peter Collin.
www.toolkit.cch.com

SUBSTITUTE PRODUCT

A substitute product is a product for which another product can provide a similar level, or an acceptable level, of satisfaction to the customer on the particular purchase or usage occasion. Coca-Cola and Pepsi-Cola are obvious examples of substitute products for each other. However, both are members of the beverage category; and other cold beverages, such as water, iced tea, or beer could prove satisfactory substitutes on a hot day. But if the purpose for which the Coke or Pepsi were being sought was as an item to be used during a break from work, then a cup of coffee, a donut, or an energy bar might be an acceptable substitute in the mind of the potential customer.

In addition to the usage occasion and the customer's perspective, the actions of competitors help to establish the range of substitute products. The Polaroid camera initially was not a particular threat as a substitute for Kodak's Brownie camera (because its price was too high), nor was it viewed as a substitute for the existing top-end 35mm SLR cameras (because the resolution of the picture was not comparable). As Polaroid improved the technology and was also able to reduce the price because of an increase in volume, it became a viable substitute product for many other cameras.

It is generally agreed that Toyota Corollas do not compete with luxury sport utility vehicles and also that the Lincoln Navigator and Cadillac Escalade do compete with each other. However, expensive jewelry, an extended vacation, or original artwork could all be substitute products for the Lincoln and Cadillac for someone who is seeking the benefit of admiration from others or possession of a status symbol, not the benefit of transportation from point A to point B.

—David W. Glascoff

SUCCESSION PLANNING

Succession planning is a human resources process that typically includes an evaluation of individual potential to help determine which employees are likely to be able to fill critical leadership roles at some point in the future within a single organization. The purpose of succession planning is to help management build the human resource capability necessary to achieve business results and enable the organization to be successful in the future. There are a variety of reasons why succession planning makes sense for organizations of all sizes. Some of the most popular reasons include the following: It aids the organization in developing its people, helps ensure continuity of leadership, and helps the organization assess its talent within the employee pool. In sum, succession planning is necessary to ensure that leadership and employee skill growth keeps pace with organizational growth.

Structured properly, systematic succession planning can result in many benefits for the organization. For example, succession planning engages senior management in a disciplined review of leadership talent and provides specific guidance for what the key development opportunities are within the organization so that there can be a continual pipeline of employees ready to assume key leadership positions. A practice of regular succession planning should help alleviate transition problems with critical senior leadership roles within the organization. Finally, a robust succession planning process can help to retain key employees by showing employees available career paths and job opportunities.

CHARACTERISTICS OF A SUCCESSION PLANNING PROCESS

A succession planning process is often very unique to an organization; however, most succession processes include a few similar components. These characteristics are identified and discussed below:

- *Cascading reviews.* The term *cascading reviews* refers to the fact that in most organizations, the employee succession reviews start lower in the organization and work up (cascade) to the top level of management. As the succession information is cascaded upward, the names of high-potential employees from all levels of the organization are forwarded, and ultimately a selection of those candidates is reviewed at the highest level of the organization.
- *Skill/ability assessment of employees.* There is normally an evaluation of the employees that often includes an assessment of employees' skills on the leadership competencies that are relevant to the particular organization. Frequently used leadership competencies include coaching skills, business acumen, communication, flexibility, decision-making ability, strategic thinking, initiative, and risk-taking ability.
- *Evaluation of readiness for a potential future position.* Using a job description as a reference point, employees being considered as successors are frequently evaluated based on work experiences and other key factors to determine how prepared they are for a future position. Evaluations typically designate the employee as being "ready now" for the position or designate a time frame (normally between one and five years) when it is anticipated that the employee will be ready to assume the future position.
- *Creation of a development plan.* Depending on the employee's readiness for a future position, a development plan is usually created to clearly map out the actions that the individual needs to take to be ready to assume a promotion in the future. Development plans may include a summary of additional work experience needed, educational requirements, or leadership competencies that need further refinement.
- *Information is systematically gathered from employees.* During the succession planning process, it is critical to solicit uniform information from all participating employees. This often includes information about the employees' desired future position, career expectations, willingness and desire to pursue a given specific career path, and willingness and ability to possibly relocate.
- *Process occurs regularly.* Succession reviews should occur approximately every 12 to 18 months, and it is advisable to have a process that is separate and distinct from the annual performance appraisal process.

- *Creation of a candidate slate.* Most succession planning processes culminate with a draft of a candidate slate that summarizes the key organization positions and lists potential internal candidates for those positions. Each internal candidate's readiness for future positions should be noted on the slate. In other words, people who are ready now to assume a greater role should be identified, as well as those who may be anywhere from one to five years away from assuming a leadership role. This final candidate slate is a document that should only be seen and accessed by the very highest organization officials (such as the CEO) and the human resources support personnel. As positions become available, this candidate slate serves as a good starting point to determine the availability of internal talent versus the need to initiate an external candidate search.

WHAT HAPPENS AFTER SUCCESSION PLANNING?

Identifying viable backup candidates for key leadership positions within the organization is only the first step to ensuring that the organization will have the human resource capability to succeed in the long term. Through systematic and vigorous evaluation of internal employee talent, an organization should have a more solid idea of what positions, if vacated, will require an external job search, versus those for which internal talent can be accessed to succeed the predecessor.

The ultimate success of a succession planning process lies in the creation of development plans for key employees within the organization to ensure their readiness for their next organizational role. These development plans require both employee and organization commitment to ensure that the developmental actions or activities are realized. Moreover, progress on these plans should be reviewed periodically by both the employee and his or her manager.

OBSTACLES TO SUCCESSFUL SUCCESSION PLANNING

Succession planning, when done with rigor and frequency, has the potential to be a very strong HR planning tool. However, many potential pitfalls could minimize the effectiveness of succession planning. Some of the key challenges and potential obstacles are reviewed next.

Because the ultimate success of the succession plan lies in the accuracy and validity of the review of internal talent, it is critical that managers and leaders be honest and discuss only relevant information during the succession review process. Succession planning will be hampered if organizational politics are allowed to interfere with the free and accurate exchange of information.

Since it is likely that only a few individuals will be seen as "ready now" for their next career move, the succession planning process needs to include a development planning component. As discussed, it is useful to identify a manageable number of development needs and to create actions plans to address those needs over an agreed-on amount of time.

A process that starts with an open dialogue between the organization's management team and the human resource function about business goals, priorities, and human resource needs to realize those goals, is a critical first step in the succession planning process. Throughout the process, the management team needs to work in constant coordination with the human resource function to ensure that the organizational needs can be met by taking the appropriate steps to develop internal talent and prepare current employees to lead the company in the future.

—Laura Gniatczyk

See also Human Resource Planning, Performance Appraisal

FURTHER READING

Atchley, K. P., Gniatczyk, L. G., Ladd, R. T., & Little, T. W. (1999). Transitioning leadership styles: Physicians preparing for health care leadership. In M. J. Stahl & P. J. Dean (Eds.), *The physician's essential MBA: What every physician leader needs to know.* Gaithersburg, MD: Aspen.

Beeson, J. (1998). Succession planning: Building the management corps. *Business Horizons, 41,* 61–66.

Byham, W. C., Smith, A. B., & Paese, M. J. (2002). *Grow your own leader: How to identify, develop, and retain leadership talent.* Upper Saddle River, NJ: Prentice Hall.

Greengard, S. (2001). Why succession planning can't wait. *Workforce, 80,* 34–38.

SUMMONS

A summons is, simply put, a notice that a lawsuit has been filed against someone or some entity. As would be expected of any notice, the following applies:

- Every reasonable effort must be made to deliver the notification. This requires the person doing the notifying (referred to as the summoner, most often a county court sheriff) to deliver the notice in person. This is known as *personal service.* If personal service is impossible, then court rules may allow for delivery by certified or even regular U.S. mail.
- The summons must contain the name(s) of the party pursuing the lawsuit.

- Where and when the person being summoned must go in order to answer the lawsuit that has been filed against them.
- The time within which a response is required (or the recipient will lose the lawsuit).

In the event that all the preceding items are not included in the summons, then the summons is deemed to be "improper" and cannot be relied on as adequate "proper notice" by the person suing. A lawsuit cannot proceed without the person suing first proving that the other party has received proper notice. Proper notice in nearly every state includes receipt by the defendant of both the summons and complaint.

A summons is generally accompanied by a complaint. A complaint is a relatively detailed outline of the case written by the attorney for the complaining party. The summons is separate and apart from the complaint.

Summonses should not be confused with subpoenas, which are formal requests for documents and/or records in a legal case. Subpoenas may be delivered by hand or by other court-approved methods. Subpoenas may be delivered to nonparties and simply seek the information outlined in the subpoena along with a time frame for response. Subpoenas are issued directly by attorneys after a lawsuit has been filed, and, unless service is improper, must be answered as directed or attempts made to "quash" the subpoena in court.

Medical entities and medical professionals should be directed by their advisers to respond immediately to both subpoenas and a summons. This response, in every case, should be to contact their legal adviser. In the case of a medical malpractice (medical negligence) case, the summons should be referred to the malpractice insurance carrier and/or in-house counsel. In the case of another type of matter, the summons should be referred to an attorney who has agreed to represent the defendant. In some cases when lawsuits are expected, an attorney will often ask his or her client if the attorney may "accept service" in lieu of the defendant. If permission is forthcoming, then the defendant's attorney will receive the summons and complaint and the attorney will then contact his or her client with further legal advice.

—Kenneth Steiner and Stuart Hochron

SUPPLEMENTAL MEDICAL INSURANCE

See Health Insurance

SUPPLY CHAIN MANAGEMENT (SCM)

A supply chain is defined as a set of three or more companies directly linked by one or more of the upstream and downstream flows of products, services, finances, and information from a source to a customer.

It is important to realize that implicit within this definition is the fact that supply chains exist whether they are managed or not. Thus we draw a distinction between supply chains as phenomena that exist in business and the management of those supply chains. The former is simply something that exists, whereas the latter takes overt management efforts by the organizations within the supply chain.

The idea of viewing the coordination of a supply chain from an overall system perspective, with each of the tactical activities of distribution flows viewed within a broader strategic context, is called a *supply chain orientation*. The actual implementation of this orientation, across various companies in the supply chain, is supply chain management. This leads us to the definition that a supply chain orientation is the recognition by a company of the systemic, strategic implications of the activities and processes involved in managing the various flows in a supply chain.

Thus, a company possesses a supply chain orientation (SCO) if its management sees the implications of managing the upstream and downstream flows of products, services, finances, and information across their suppliers and their customers. A company does not have a supply chain orientation if it only sees the systemic, strategic implications in one direction. Further, this does not mean the firm with the SCO can implement it—such implementation requires a SCO *across* several companies directly connected in the supply chain. The firm with the SCO may implement individual, disjointed supply chain tactics, but this is *not* supply chain management (SCM) unless they are coordinated (a strategic orientation) over the supply chain (a systemic orientation).

In other words, supply chain management is the implementation of a supply chain orientation across suppliers and customers. Companies implementing SCM must first have a supply chain orientation. Stated differently, a supply chain orientation is a management philosophy, and supply chain management is the sum total of all the overt management actions undertaken to realize that philosophy.

Pulling together these disparate aspects of supply chain management, supply chain management is defined as the systemic, strategic coordination of the traditional business functions within a particular company and across businesses within the supply chain, for the purposes of improving the long-term performance of the individual companies and the supply chain as a whole.

An example of supply chain management applied to medical practice involves scheduled surgery. In an unmanaged supply chain, on the day of the surgery the head surgical nurse must gather all the surgical supplies from around the hospital for each operation—a time-consuming wasteful use of the head surgical nurse's time that often also results in the discovery that the required supplies are not available. In one managed supply chain, however, the surgeon communicates his or her surgical schedule to the hospital, which in turn communicates the schedule to a surgical supply provider. The provider then puts together a packet of all the surgical supplies for each operation (keeping in mind the brand preferences of the surgeon), and packs them (already sterilized) in a container in the order of the operations for that particular surgeon for a particular day. The night before the surgical schedule, the packet is delivered to the hospital. On the morning of the operating schedule, all the head surgical nurse has to do is wheel the container into the surgical theater and the team is ready (at least from the perspective of surgical supplies) to perform all the operations of the day. After each operation, the used surgical supplies are repacked in the container for pickup that night by the provider. The provider then recycles the appropriate supplies and properly disposes of the rest. The result of the management of this supply chain from surgical supplies provider to hospital to surgical team and, ultimately, to patient, is the reduction of inbound delivery costs, reduction in hospital storage costs, reduction in surgical team time spent finding supplies, the elimination of the incidence of supplies out of stock, and reduction in the cost of recycling or disposing of used surgical supplies. Clearly, supply chain management can have a considerable impact on medical supply chains.

—John T. Mentzer

FURTHER READING

Mentzer, J. T., DeWitt, W., Keebler, J. S., Min, S., Nix, N. W., Smith, C. D., & Zacharia, Z. G. (2001). Defining supply chain management. *Journal of Business Logistics, 22*(2), 1–26.

Mentzer, J. T., Foggin, J. H., & Golicic, S. L. (2000, September–October). Collaboration: The enablers, impediments, and benefits. *Supply Chain Management Review, 4*, 52–58.

Mentzer, J. T., & Williams, L. R. (2000). The role of logistics leverage in marketing strategy. *Journal of Marketing Channels, 8*(3–4), 29–48.

SWOT (STRENGTH-WEAKNESS-OPPORTUNITY-THREAT) ANALYSIS

A SWOT analysis involves analyzing both the external and internal environments of an organization to determine the threats and opportunities presented by the external forces as well as the strengths and weaknesses within the organization. *Threats* are trends or changes in the external environment that challenge traditional ways of doing business, threaten growth prospects, or create profit pressures. *Opportunities,* in contrast, are trends or changes in the external environment that create new growth prospects, allow performance improvements, or improve existing competitive conditions. *Strengths* are characteristics of an organization that can help it pursue its mission and achieve performance goals, whereas *weaknesses* are characteristics of the organization that create vulnerabilities and inhibit the ability of the organization to perform.

The information from the SWOT analysis is an essential input into an overall strategic planning process, providing a focus for the planning efforts. The analysis process helps administration and stakeholders come to a common understanding about the context within which a strategic plan will be developed. The idea is to develop strategies that buffer threats, seize opportunities, capitalize on strengths, and correct weaknesses.

In preparing a SWOT analysis, a manager or administrator usually starts with an analysis of the organization's external environment. The external environment is often classified into two parts: the remote environment and the operating environment. The remote environment consists of forces and trends that affect the organization but are not subject to influence or change *by* the organization. The remote environment includes demographic, economic, sociocultural, political/legal, and technological forces and trends. The operating environment is composed of constituents, forces, and trends that affect the organization but that the organization can influence through its strategies and actions. The operating environment includes suppliers, customers, competitors, and communities. The steps in analyzing the external environment are (a) define the relevant external constituents and forces, (b) gather information about trends and expected changes, (c) determine the implications of each identified trend or change for the organization, and (d) determine whether the implications create a threat, an opportunity, or both for the organization.

For example, in analyzing the external environment of a regional hospital, the administration may conclude that demographic changes in the region will result in a lower-income, more elderly patient load than experienced in previous years—a change that will influence services offered, the types of physicians recruited, accounts receivables and cash flow, and facility and equipment investments. In assessing the operating environment, administrators may identify regional nursing shortages (a form of labor supply) and the expansion plans of another hospital in the region (a competitor) as threats, while noting that there may be an opportunity to extend the services of the hospital into satellite urgent care facilities and services for the homebound in response to some

competitors leaving the area. They may also conclude that the sociocultural trend toward use of herbal medicines provides an opportunity to create a new educational program through the hospital's outreach efforts and that cost reductions and quality improvements in wireless communications and computer technology will present opportunities to improve patient care while reducing time and cost of delivery, if the appropriate investments are made soon.

After identifying the sources of threats and opportunities in the external environment, administrators will then turn to the internal environment. In framing an analysis of strengths and weaknesses inside the organization, it is useful to think in terms of both resources and activities. In general, resources may be grouped into five categories: *human* (such as physicians, nursing staff, laboratory staff, administrative staff), *physical* (such as facilities, equipment), *information* (databases, experience), *financial* (cash and borrowing capacity), and *reputation* (perceptions of doctors, of patients). Resources create value for the organization when they are applied effectively to the organization's work or activities. Some of the key activities in a hospital, for example, include the many, varied medical procedures, nursing care, and the administrative processes of record-keeping, supplier management, and billing and insurance processing, among many others.

In making an assessment of strengths and weaknesses, it is important to collect information from many sources—to get an objective, independent evaluation of resources and activities. After a thorough assessment of all resources and activities, hospital administrators may find weaknesses in some areas (such as personnel shortages in critical nursing areas, and administrative processes that are burdensome, redundant, or inaccurate) and strengths in others (such as high levels of patient satisfaction with medical care, strong reputation that helps recruitment of doctors, and improving supply chain management practices leading to essential cost reductions).

It is important to consider strengths and weaknesses in light of what was learned in the external analysis of threats and opportunities. For example, a fully staffed, highly respected neonatal group may be a strength for a hospital when there is sufficient demand for neonatal services. If the demographics of the area change and demand for neonatal services falls to low levels, the specialized skills and facilities may no longer serve as a strength for the hospital and may even be a source of underutilized capacity and high fixed costs.

The SWOT analysis should conclude with an interpretation of how the information will be incorporated into the strategic plan. That interpretation should address the severity of the threats and weaknesses, and the plans for blocking or correcting them. It should also address the ways in which the identified opportunities and strengths should direct the strategic plan. Continuing the example given, the challenge for the hospital with the neonatal unit will be to determine what to do to correct this weakness, for example, either scale down the unit to a more appropriate size, market the expertise to other hospitals in the region to increase referrals, or close the unit altogether.

The final interpretation may be framed from the following questions: Do any of the external threats have the power to challenge the survival of the hospital? What changes must be made to buffer or block the hospital from the threats that were identified? Should any of the new opportunities be incorporated into the hospital's strategic plan? If so, does the hospital have the resources and capabilities needed to capitalize on those opportunities? Are any of the identified internal weaknesses so serious that they threaten the survival of the hospital? What changes must be made to correct the weaknesses? Do the hospital's strengths set it apart from competition? Are there ways to take advantage of these existing strengths through new strategic initiatives?

—Caron St. John

FURTHER READING

Harrison, J., & St. John, C. (1998). *Strategic management of organizations and stakeholders: Theory and cases* (2nd ed.). Cincinnati, OH: South-Western.

SYNERGY

An effort by managers and leaders in organizations to bring about continued and systemic forms of change practiced by teams is essential for organizational learning. Yet change is not comfortable for many organizations, and it does not occur automatically.

Organizations display enormous structural and cultural inertia in response to change. However, the costs of failing to overcome this inertia can be damaging to the organization itself.

Kochan and Useem (1992) and Dean (1999) suggest that continuous systemic organizational change must be integrated and consistent among an organization's major components and designed for the long term to provide a more suitable foundation for cooperation, learning, and innovation. They call these organizations *transforming organizations.*

The systemic change can take place only when the technological, organizational, and human resources are altered and aligned together. One part of the system can be fully realized only when developed with all other parts. Moreover, systemic change involves more than changes within each of these parts. It challenges the underlying assumptions, tacit knowledge, and standard relationships that link these different organizational parts.

To engage in systemic, continuous change and go beyond the isolated shifts and periodic lurching observed in so many organizations, it is essential to have all organizational parts learning together. This integration results in faster innovation and flexibility to reduce the stress of hierarchic authority, centralized control, and fixed boundaries. Then the organizational designs rely on work teams, decentralized decision making, and informal networks crosscutting formal boundaries. Also there is more reciprocal information sharing, shared commitment to sustained cooperation, and a common set of values. Next, the learning organization must have a learning culture that stresses learning above the bottom line. Finally, the learning organization learns from diversity, and does not simply manage it or value it. This approach lays the groundwork for practice of synergy in an organization.

SYNERGY AND ORGANIZATIONAL CHANGE

Weisbord and Janoff (1995) suggest that over the last century a learning curve has been traversed with respect to organizational change. In 1900 any change efforts came about by an expert solving problems. This was a "great person" approach to change: Whether for good or bad or for acceptance or resistance, change occurred and revolved around one person. In the 1950s, the learning was that everybody solves problems, just not all together. In 1965, the attention was around experts improving whole systems, where the system endured, not the expert. And in 2003, the philosophy is that "everybody improves whole systems." This latest philosophy evolved from the initial attempt of Taylor, the focused work of Lewin, and the workable application of Trist and Emery. Others were involved, but these were the key pathfinders along the journey.

From this philosophy, Weisbord and Janoff (1995, p. 69) recalibrated the principles of Lewin and tips of Trist and Emery into the seven learning practices for organizational change that they use in their action for change in organizations:

1. Each person has a unique learning style. Some learn best by reading, others by doing, still others by discussing or listening.

2. Each person learns at a different rate. Hence some may be confused or lost in early stages. It is okay not to get it the first time you hear it. Try to be patient with yourself and others.

3. Each person learns different things from a common experience. Hence we encourage trading of perceptions and acceptance of different feelings and views.

4. Each person learns best from his or her own experience. Hence we urge testing ideas against your own situation and support a healthy skepticism toward a one best-way-approach to process change in organizations.

5. Each person learns more than the world will permit us to apply. Hence we focus on local action within a global context.

6. Each person has the ability to help and teach others. Hence we encourage participation and drawing on each other's expertise as well as ours.

7. Each person benefits from trial, error, and feedback, if given support and a chance for success. Hence we provide opportunities for this to happen in relatively low-risk situations. No one is required to invest in these opportunities.

—Peter J. Dean

FURTHER READING

Kochan, T. A., & Useem, M. (1992). *Transforming organizations.* New York: Oxford University Press.

Weisbord, M. R. (1987). *Productive workplaces: Organizing and managing for dignity, meaning, and community.* San Francisco: Jossey-Bass.

Weisbord, M. R. (1992). *Discovering common ground.* San Francisco: Berrett-Koehler.

Weisbord, M. R., & Janoff, S. (1995). *Future search.* San Francisco: Berrett-Koehler.

T

TAIL COVERAGE

Medical malpractice insurance generally falls into four categories:

- Claims made
- Occurrence
- Claims paid
- Tail coverage

The most common type of policy is the claims-made type. This policy covers acts of malpractice that occur and are reported to the insurance carrier during the policy time period. A practitioner may continue this policy for many years; however, at some point he or she may want to switch insurance carriers or may have a change in career including retirement. Then the practitioner must purchase "tail" coverage for liability protection. Regardless of the reason, when a practitioner terminates a claims-made policy, he or she must purchase tail coverage for the period during which the former policy was in place.

A tail coverage policy extends insurance coverage for acts of malpractice that may be reported beyond the policy coverage date of the claims-made policy. The practitioner is then covered by his tail policy if he faces a malpractice claim years after the claims-made policy was in effect. When purchasing a claims-made policy, the insured should look for a guaranteed right to purchase tail coverage. The price of tail coverage varies with specialty, location, and length of practice. Obviously, the further back in time the tail policy must cover, the more expensive it will be to purchase. Recent market conditions surrounding the costs of malpractice insurance have made tail coverage difficult to obtain for some high-risk specialties and costs for such coverage have skyrocketed.

Occurrence coverage policies insure for malpractice incidents that occur while the policy is in effect, *regardless of when an actual claim may be made*. Therefore, tail coverage is not needed when this type of insurance coverage is terminated.

Claims-paid coverage is often used by trusts. Premiums are based on claims settled during previous years and projected for the future.

The coverage is similar to claims made, with different considerations for what is considered a claim or a formal complaint. Regardless of their differences in legal nuances, a claims-paid policy requires the insured to have tail coverage to protect against future litigation that would arise out of acts during the years the claims-paid policy was in effect.

Obviously, if an individual practitioner is not prudent enough to be protected by an occurrence policy, under any other scenario he or she must at some point purchase tail coverage to protect oneself.

—Kenneth Steiner and Stuart Hochron

TASK FORCES

The organization is a sum-total system of formal arrangements that houses the interaction of the forces of strategy, structure, processes, systems, competence, and culture of the enterprise. These forces influence the tasks of individual workers. Leaders and managers need to understand the influence these task forces have on work if they want to better improve the interface between humans and the work the enterprise sets out to accomplish.

The task forces can either enhance or hinder accomplishment of the purposes of the enterprise. The manager crafts these arrangements to bring about congruence and alignment among these task forces to better lead change in the organization.

- *Strategic vision* presents the mental picture of what the organization has to do to survive in business.
- *Structure* describes how the tasks are divided and coordinated using specialization and integration, decentralization and centralization, and formal patterns of relationships between groups and individuals (for example, which department reports to a division).
- *Processes* define and measure sequences of steps, activities, and methods that produce a specified goal, result, consequence, or an output for a particular internal or external customer or market.
- *Systems* entail the procedures for budgeting, accounting, and training that make the organization run, and a particular set of procedures or rules, policies, devices, guides, and practices, designed to control process(s) in a predictable way.
- *Competence* looks at the way managers manage, the way employees are selected, placed, oriented, developed, and rewarded, and the skills of both managers and employees. In a high-performance organization, management and employees work together for an integration of goals, policies, procedures, standards, information and feedback systems, incentive systems, training, and budget.
- *Culture* presents the patterns of basic shared assumptions, beliefs, attitudes, expectations, and values (Nadler & Tushman, 1997) as revealed in everyday work performance and practices. The formal aspects of culture such as policies, processes, and procedures influence those patterns and the balance between suppliers of resources such as labor, materials, tools, equipment, facilities, and so on and the efficiency and effectiveness of organizational performance.

The challenges of change in business today are often global in scale. Business, sociopolitical, and economic forces also drive the need for organizational change in strategies, policies, structures, processes, systems, and tactics. Managerial expertise in the design, development, and deployment of the task forces listed as well as the externalities of political, economic, social, and technological forces just mentioned has become even more critical than in the past. Learning, learning how to learn, participative informational exchanges with two-way communications, decentralized decision making, informal networks, and a common values set are the essential capacities to deal with the task forces. Leaders should avoid trying to "fix" the individuals in the workplace, rather than influencing task forces that influence the performance of the individuals.

AREAS OF EXPERTISE FOR DEALING WITH THE TASK FORCES

Health care professionals need to develop several areas of expertise for leading change and dealing with the task forces regardless of their professional practice preference. These include the following:

- *Establishing and managing client relationships.* Establishing and managing client relationships is one of the most critical elements in improving organizational performance. This area of expertise is necessary for fostering trust and cooperation between consultants and their clients.
- *Conducting analyses.* Rossett (personal communication) believes that conducting analysis requires interacting with clients to determine the business need, performance problem, and expected outcomes.
- *Identifying root causes.* Health care professionals need to be able to determine whether the root cause is a gap caused by the organization, its people, their behavior, consequences for performance, feedback, or other environmental factors.
- *Recommending and implementing solutions.* Rossett (personal communication) believes that performance consultants need to be able to recommend solutions eliminating the barriers to performance. This is done by addressing root causes of performance deficiencies, which requires a proficient knowledge of organizational performance and work system design and redesign.
- *Evaluating results.* Task force professionals must be able to measure the overall success of the project by determining whether initial performance improvement goals have been achieved and the business issue resolved.
- *Facilitating learning.* Change professionals are responsible for helping employees acquire new skills, knowledge, insights, awareness, and attitudes needed to implement change. These may include problem-solving skills, giving and receiving performance feedback, listening skills, leadership development, goal setting, resolving conflicts, and diagnosing group interactions.
- *Building partnerships.* Becoming a task force professional requires you to develop an expertise in building partnerships. Such partnerships help professionals decide which change initiatives provide the highest value and have the greatest impact on the organization. They also promote establishment of working relationships based on shared values, aligned purpose and vision, and mutual support.
- *Facilitating change.* The task force professional's final area of expertise is to become proficient in

change facilitation. A facilitator is an individual who guides a group toward a destination or goal. The goal for a change professional is to bring about a change within an organization. To achieve this objective, change professionals need to develop the change facilitation area of expertise in future search conferences and nominal group technique.

—Peter J. Dean

REFERENCE

Nadler, D., & Tushman, M. (1977). *Competing by design: The power of organizational architecture* (2nd ed.). Oxford, UK: Oxford University Press.

TAX CREDITS FOR THE UNINSURED

See Access

TEAM-BASED COMPENSATION

Team compensation consists of pay, benefits, and other rewards delivered to members of work teams in return for their contributions to the performance and capabilities of their teams. In contrast to individual compensation for individual work, *team* compensation refers to rewards for cooperative products or services of teams, for which members share both the responsibility and accountability, and which they accomplish together through coordinated, interdependent efforts. Compensation systems in team-based organizations ideally reward team performance while motivating individual performance and fostering cooperation among teams.

Team compensation represents part of an employee's total compensation, in addition to components linked to individual capabilities or performance. Individual pay components, such as base salary, usually reflect education, work experience, training, and the labor market. An additional pay-for-skill component may compensate an individual's demonstrated, special skills, such as proficiency with specific medical procedures or software. A typical component of an individual compensation package is the organization's benefits package for all employees: medical and life insurance, retirement contributions, education assistance, stock options, and others. Compensation packages differ greatly in the combinations of components they include and the designs of the components.

Many organizations use team compensation to motivate and reward team performance. Team compensation usually consists of variable pay based on performance against a measurable target or objective on one or more performance indicators. Compensation can involve incentive pay for team performance, pay bonuses for exceptional performance by teams, or individual bonuses for contributions by team members to their teams' accomplishments. Examples include a 20% annual salary bonus to members of a project team for completing their project within budget and within specifications, a one-time $100,000 bonus split among members of a medical research team on approval of their patent for a new drug, and a monthly salary bonus to members of hospital patient care teams whose customer satisfaction ratings exceed a certain minimum.

Organizations may use team compensation when individual compensation fails to motivate the cooperation required by the business. For example, individual members of patient care units at a hospital might deliver excellent care but collectively exceed cost targets. Their managers might organize them into teams and offer team compensation focused partly on cost efficiency, perhaps a monthly bonus to teams who meet targets for both quality of care and cost efficiency.

Team compensation can help in recruiting, hiring, and retaining capable individuals, motivating them to cooperate, and providing incentives for continuous improvement and learning. Team compensation, as part of the organization's compensation system, helps express and reinforce the culture. Ideally, all components of a compensation system, including the team component, link performance incentives with the organization's mission, values, and success.

Dilemmas in designing and administering team compensation include (a) how to appropriately measure team performance; (b) how to link measures of team performance to the organization's success; (c) how to create a clear *line of sight* for team members—a psychological link between efforts toward improving their team's performance and the rewards for those efforts; and (d) how to minimize competition among teams eligible for team-based rewards.

MEASURING TEAM PERFORMANCE

Key to the success of team compensation is a measurement system that team members accept as accurately reflecting their cooperative performance of team duties. For example, a patient care team might have the responsibility of delivering high-quality care—as perceived by patients—while keeping controllable costs within budget. To the extent that all members understand and accept the measurement procedures used to evaluate their performance, they experience the measurements as fair. For example, a patient care team might accept a measure of quality of care based on ratings by patients, and a cost-tracking system keyed to the team's orders for medical supplies and services as well as controllable cleaning, maintenance, and equipment costs they incur. They might not as readily accept a measure of costs that included vaguely defined "overhead" beyond their control.

Critical to members' acceptance of performance measures, or "buy-in," is participation in their development. For example, a patient care team might help identify controllable costs. Besides helping buy-in, participation draws on the knowledge and experience of team members and can lead to better measures than managers might develop alone.

LINKING MEASURES OF TEAM PERFORMANCE TO THE ORGANIZATION'S SUCCESS

Managers must assure that measures of team performance appropriately reflect each team's relevant contributions. This means linking team performance measures to corresponding department- and organization-level indicators. For example, a hospital's performance scorecard might include quality-of-care indicators. For departments and teams that deal directly with patients, measures of performance might incorporate a standard method of tracking patient satisfaction used throughout the organization. (Managers would have some difficulty, of course, in combining the results of measures that differed from one unit to another; for instance, if one unit used a five-point satisfaction rating and another used a yes/no question.) In effect, part of the manager's job is to assure that measures of team performance can be aggregated to form accurate measures of performance for larger units and ultimately of the whole organization's success.

Besides creating standardized measures of team performance that align with the organization's higher-level indicators, team managers also have responsibility for fostering development of measures that reflect teams' unique contributions worthy of compensation. For example, a marketing team might have a special performance measure that reflects monthly sales of health care services to new clients, consistent with an organizationwide objective of increasing market share. One test of whether a team performance measure belongs in a compensation system is a demonstrable connection with the organization's success.

Ideally, team managers facilitate timely, accurate recording and reporting of data on team performance into the database used in calculating team compensation. Part of the task of developing performance measures is creating procedures for recordkeeping—standard across teams, if possible—and available for audit. The same database can serve the organizationwide reporting on its key performance indicators.

Line of Sight to Team Rewards

The term "line of sight" refers to the individual's perception of a connection between effort toward team objectives and reward commensurate with that effort. This connection constitutes the psychological key to the motivating effect of team rewards. To feel motivated by team rewards, a team member must perceive that successful effort by the team will be rewarded in a timely way and that the reward is worth the effort. If members believe a cooperative effort will probably fail, or if they see the reward as not worth the effort, it becomes a weak source of motivation.

Perception that effort leads to reward depends on confidence in being able to influence the outcomes reflected in performance measures. For example, the measures for a surgical team might include counting surgical tools and accounting for 100% of the tools. Team members may have little trouble seeing that they can influence such a measure.

Members' perceptions of whether their team rewards are equitable, or worth the effort, depend on two factors: (a) levels of performance required for payout, and (b) sizes of contingent rewards. For example, a patient care team at a hospital might have as one of its performance measures the promptness of patient billing, indicated by average number of business days from discharge to mailing of a hospital statement. If their average is 12 business days, and the proposed payout occurs when the average reaches 5 business days, team members may calculate that they can, with effort, reach that threshold.

Team members' psychological evaluations of equity also take account of size of team rewards. Experts have varying opinions on the magnitude of rewards needed for a significant boost in motivation. Some say 10%, others say 20% or more. Participation by team members is critical to the effectiveness of team rewards. Managers also need to take account of financial variables such as revenue generated by teams in meeting performance targets.

Teams typically must satisfy certain minimum standards to become eligible for team rewards. For example, many team-based organizations delegate responsibility for scheduling people for certain jobs that can easily be rotated, such as occupying a nursing station, for certain time periods. To be eligible for team rewards, a team may have to achieve 100% coverage by at least one person during all its shifts in a given month. Such standards might exist for attendance, safety, security, waste disposal, and other factors.

Maintaining a clear line of sight between individual effort and team rewards calls for the rewards to arrive promptly after requisite performance. Ideally the schedule of team bonuses matches that of paychecks. If recordkeeping requires delays, quarterly or even annual bonuses may prove motivating.

Potentially controversial decisions in managing team rewards concern individual shares of the team reward within teams. One decision concerns the responsibility for establishing a policy for sharing team rewards among individual members. Team managers can make the decision, or involve team members in a joint decision, or delegate the decision entirely to the teams. (Greater involvement by the teams may yield better results.) A second decision concerns the actual sharing formula within teams. Simplest is equal sharing by all members. Unfortunately, if members contribute differentially to their team's success, equal shares may be inequitable, and may cloud the line of sight to team rewards. Unequal sharing, sometimes called "equity-based" sharing, may lead to what individuals see as fairer rewards for individual members. However, weighted distributions of rewards depend on having an adequate procedure for assessing individual team members' performance of team responsibilities, for example, through peer ratings. Even with individual assessments of team contributions, arriving at a sharing formula within a team without divisive conflict requires skilled teamwork or external facilitation. Research on team-based rewards suggests that successful procedures for differential distribution of rewards within teams can produce favorable results.

PROMOTING COOPERATION AMONG TEAMS

One possible problem with team-based rewards is that teams may compete for scarce or shared resources in order to assure that their team receives its reward, even at the expense of other teams. At sites where teams share such facilities as laboratories, videoconference centers, and software libraries, interteam competition can cause problems. Motorola had to redesign a team compensation program for just this reason. Its solution, now common, was to implement a site-based gain-sharing program in which all employees shared in payouts from a bonus pool based on performance by the whole organization at the site. Linking the bonus pool to performance at the local site retains the needed line of sight and gives teams an incentive to cooperate with one another to promote performance of the whole site.

Implementing Team-Based Compensation

Because of the many factors that can affect the effectiveness of team rewards, the task of designing and implementing them is both complex and inherently dynamic. Organizations that make successful use of team rewards treat them as work in progress and as opportunities for learning and continuous improvement. For managers considering team rewards, benchmarking visits to other organizations can help.

—Eric D. Sundstrom and Elaine Seat

See also Employee Compensation, Group Norms, Group Performance, Team-Based Organization

FURTHER READING

Deckop, J. R., Mangel, R., & Cirka, C. C. (1999). Getting more than you pay for: Organizational citizenship behavior and pay-for-performance plans. *Academy of Management Journal, 42*(4), 420–428.

DeMatteo, J. S., Eby, L. T., & Sundstrom, E. (1998). Team-based rewards: Current empirical evidence and directions for future research. *Research in Organizational Behavior, 20,* 141–183.

Jones, S. D., & Schilling, D. J. (2000). *Measuring team performance.* San Francisco: Jossey-Bass.

Lawler, E. E. (1999). Creating effective pay systems for teams. In E. Sundstrom & Associates, *Supporting work team effectiveness* (pp. 188–212). San Francisco: Jossey-Bass.

Welborne, T. M., & Gomez-Mejia, L. R. (1991). Team incentive in the workplace. In M. Rock & L. Berger (Eds.), *The compensation handbook: A state of the art guide to compensation strategy and design* (3rd ed., pp. 236–247). New York: McGraw-Hill.

Zenger, T. R., & Marshall, C. R. (2000). Determinants of incentive intensity in group-based rewards. *Academy of Management Journal, 43*(2), 149–163.

TEAM-BASED ORGANIZATION

In a team-based organization the primary units consist of *work teams,* or interdependent collections of individual employees who share responsibility for specified outcomes in the organization. An example of a team-based organization is Florida's Cape Coral Hospital, which organized all of its employees into teams and held them accountable for defined results. Among several kinds of teams at Cape Coral, patient care teams delivered medical services to the hospital's patients, ordered supplies, maintained budgets, and handled patient logistics.

Today many enterprises incorporate team-based organizations, including private sector businesses such as automobile manufacturing, public sector institutions such as schools, and various health care organizations. Team-based organizations proliferated in the 1990s after widely publicized stories of dramatic improvements in performance, cost efficiency, and customer satisfaction.

Team-based organizations have their roots in the 1950s, when new technology in coal mining and textile mills clashed with traditional forms of organization. Advocates of the "sociotechnical systems" approach called for joint optimization of automated equipment and social relationships. They experimented with "semiautonomous work groups" with responsibility for scheduling their work, sharing tasks, assigning individual members to specific tasks, rotating jobs, and other duties formerly delegated only to supervisors. Early trials showed such success that many organizations were experimenting with work groups in the 1960s and 1970s. With the advent of total quality management in the 1980s, team-based organizations had gained widespread acceptance.

The hallmark of a team-based organization is a relatively flat structure, with few hierarchical levels and delegation of authority to employees who compose teams at the front line. Teams have responsibility for tasks once considered the exclusive province of supervisors, especially scheduling work, budgeting, cross-training, individual work assignments, conducting maintenance, quality checks, and evaluating members' performance. The key feature of work teams is interdependence among individual members for a coordinated output.

SUPPORT SYSTEMS FOR WORK TEAMS

Effective, team-based organizations provide nine kinds of support for work teams:

1. *Team roles.* Each team in a team-based organization ideally has a well-defined role in relation to the organization's mission and the other teams. Definition of teams' roles include specification of primary counterparts (such as suppliers and customers), responsibilities, outputs, workflows, performance measures, and reporting relationships.

2. *Leaders' roles.* Managers have the responsibility of defining leadership roles for teams, including an internal role such as supervisor, and an external leadership role such as team manager or coordinator of several teams. Many team-based organizations elect team leaders who hold the same rank as other team members.

3. *Staffing.* Well-managed systems for selecting and placing employees assure that teams have members with necessary knowledge, skills, abilities, and other attributes. As more organizations incorporate work teams, more employees acquire the needed teamwork skills.

4. *Training.* Systems for employee education and development in team-based organizations often focus on both teamwork skills and coordination of technical skills. Most successful team-based organizations incorporate needs assessments and ongoing training of team members and managers.

5. *Measurement.* Team measurement systems can objectively gauge team performance, including customer satisfaction, efficiency, and other key outcomes.

6. *Rewards.* Team-based reward systems can provide extrinsic incentives and reinforcement for sustained, cooperative performance by teams.

7. *Information systems.* Teams require up-to-date information systems to maintain data on work processes, supplies, customers, and their performance. The same computer-based systems provide information to managers and customers. As information systems become more central to teamwork, computer skills become more essential for team members.

8. *Communication technology.* Many teams need specialized equipment beyond telephones, e-mail, and computers to communicate effectively. New technology promotes group interaction via teleconferencing, videoconferencing, and computer-supported collaboration.

9. *Facilities.* The physical working environment may be as important as any other factor in supporting work teams. Layout of workstations promotes or inhibits face-to-face interaction, access to equipment, and the capacity to isolate or display work in progress, hold meetings, and move among work areas.

TYPES OF WORK TEAMS

Work teams take many forms. They can be self-managing, virtual, permanent, or temporary. Six common types of work teams appear in team-based organizations, distinguished mainly by the kinds of work they do:

1. *Production teams* repeatedly produce a tangible output. They usually consist of front-line employees, and have elected leaders or appointed supervisors who report to management. Many production teams schedule their members' work and assignments, maintain their own equipment, and do housekeeping for their work areas. Examples include pharmaceutical production teams and electronic equipment assembly teams.

2. *Service teams* cooperate to provide repeated transactions toward meeting customers' needs. Examples include patient care teams, facility maintenance teams, and insurance claims units. A hospital maintenance team might have an electrician, plumber, carpenter, and environmental control technician who cooperate to serve internal or external customers.

3. *Management teams* consist of an executive or senior manager and those managers who report directly to him or her. Management teams coordinate work units and conduct joint planning, policymaking, budgeting, staffing, and logistics. They determine their own team structures.

4. *Project teams* (also called task forces) perform specialized, time-limited assignments and disband after finishing. Generally cross-functional, they bring together special expertise needed for a new effort

such as medical research, construction, and facility design.

5. *Action and performing teams* engage in time-limited, complex performance events involving audiences or adversaries. Members consist of expert specialists who have complementary, interdependent roles. Examples include emergency rescue teams, specialty surgical teams, and environmental accident response teams.

6. *Advisory groups* often are not work teams, and instead operate parallel to the work stream. Examples, such as ad hoc committees, problem identification groups, and selection committees, produce recommendations and disband; they generally lack authority to implement their suggestions. Members are not chosen as much for their specialized skill as for their work area or title, and are interchangeable.

—Elaine Seat and Eric D. Sundstrom

See also Group Performance, Team-Based Compensation

FURTHER READING

Sundstrom, E. (1999). The challenges of supporting work team effectiveness. In E. Sundstrom & Associates, *Supporting work team effectiveness* (pp. 3–23). San Francisco: Jossey-Bass.

Sundstrom, E., De Meuse, K. P., & Futrell, D. (1990). Work teams: Applications and effectiveness. *American Psychologist, 45*(2), 120–133.

Sundstrom, E., McIntyre, M., Halfhill, T., & Richards, H. (2000). *Group Dynamics, 4*(1), 44–67.

Wellins, R. S., Byham, W. C., & Dixon, G. R. (1994). *Inside teams: How 20 world-class organizations are winning through teamwork.* San Francisco: Jossey-Bass.

TEAM BUILDING

The term *team building* refers to activities by work groups intended to improve their cohesion or effectiveness. Traditionally led by external facilitators, team building usually focuses on improving interpersonal communication, cooperation, and relationships among team members.

One common type of team building, "ropes" courses, calls for members to cooperate in supervised, outdoor activities such as climbing over high walls together with ropes, or crossing rivers on rope suspension bridges. The trainer debriefs the team afterward and leads discussion on opportunities for improving communication and teamwork.

Other team-building activities focus on solidarity and cohesion through mutual, personal acquaintance. Icebreaker exercises, for example, ask individuals to tell about their lives away from work. Exercises based on personality differences, such as those revealed by the Myers Briggs Type Indicator (MBTI), help team members understand different ways of gathering information, making decisions, and communicating.

Some exercises focus on group processes, such as consensus decision making. Practice exercises like NASA's "Lost on the Moon" call for groups to consider a list of items rescued from a wrecked spaceship and, using consensus, rank them in order of their importance to survival. Trainers help groups learn from their successes and failures in capitalizing on members' knowledge.

Research evaluating the effectiveness of team building has failed to demonstrate a consistent link with group performance. Some studies found the link, whereas others found no relationship or even a drop in performance. Research on team building has, however, generally found increases in group cohesion and members' satisfaction.

Because team building focuses on interpersonal skills, managers routinely combine team building with training on task-related or technical skills, such as coordination of specialized roles or role clarification.

Team building exercises are most helpful for new teams and individuals new to teamwork. The exercises can help build skills in group decision-making, conflict resolution, managing individual differences, and basic communication.

—Elaine Seat and Eric D. Sundstrom

See also Team-Based Organization, Teamwork

FURTHER READING

Biech, E. (2001). *The Pfeiffer book of successful team building tools.* San Francisco: Jossey-Bass/Pfeiffer.

Powell, K. (2001). *Communicating with your team: Skills for increasing cohesion and teamwork.* Chicago: American Medical Association, AMA Press.

Quick, T. L. (1992). *Successful team building.* New York: AMA-COM–American Management Association.

TEAMWORK

Teamwork is effective cooperation among the members of a work team. Teamwork depends on a team's success in coordinating individual members' specialized roles and expertise, which in turn depends on key interpersonal and self-management skills needed for teamwork.

INTERPERSONAL TEAMWORK SKILLS

Interpersonal skills that enhance teamwork help members with conflict resolution, collaborative problem solving, and communication. Conflict resolution skills allow the team to understand conflict as a part of developing new ideas and strategies. Conflict resolution strategies call for fostering useful conflict in the form of divergent approaches to the group's work, while avoiding personal conflicts. Team members who have mastered this skill can distinguish the types of conflict and use tactics that help the group move toward win–win solutions.

Skills for collaborative problem solving include inviting and encouraging others' ideas and suggestions, especially about ways of improving the team's work processes. Collaboration can require individuals to serve the interests of the whole group over their own ideas or interests. Unfortunately, collaboration takes more time and energy than more directive approaches. Team members can obtain training in methods of collaborative problem solving, such as consensus decision making.

Communication skills for teamwork focus on active listening, reinforcing others' suggestions and ideas, and participating by offering constructive input to the group. Specific skills include paraphrasing others' contributions, acknowledging teammates' views, articulating ideas, identifying positive features of others' ideas, probing for additional information and reasoning, observing and understanding nonverbal messages, and engaging team members in personal conversation about everyday matters.

SELF-MANAGEMENT TEAMWORK SKILLS

Self-management skills conducive to teamwork concern many of the responsibilities traditionally assigned to supervisors before the spread of team-based organizations and self-managing teams. Self-management skills related to work evaluation include goal setting to meet team responsibilities and capabilities of receiving, interpreting, and acting on team performance feedback. Requisite skills include developing measures of performance, data collection, recordkeeping, charting, trend spotting, problem identification, problem solving, and action planning.

A second set of self-management skills concerns planning and coordination. Ideally, team members can take full responsibility for scheduling all members' activities, including vacations, coverage of absences, overtime, assistance to other teams, and related logistics. Teamwork also depends on the members' skills at balancing members' workloads and managing internal cross-training, job coaching, job rotation, and asking for training or other outside help.

Self-management also requires meeting management skills. Ideally a team can conduct effective meetings that maximize the use of members' time.

MANAGER'S ROLE IN FOSTERING TEAMWORK

Development and sustenance of teamwork calls for team managers to maintain an appropriate balance between directive and nondirective styles. If a manager takes a highly directive approach, as seen in some traditional hierarchies, team members may react by becoming passive and dependent. If, in contrast, a manager takes a completely nondirective or hands-off approach, team members may experience ambiguity about their responsibilities and might respond with unwelcome initiatives or with confusion and indecision. A manager can promote teamwork by providing a moderate amount of structure and support for self-management, including clearly defining roles and responsibilities, helping define team performance measures, providing assistance in obtaining training and resources, helping with conflict and diversity, and encouraging independent handling of the details of the work.

—Elaine Seat and Eric D. Sundstrom

See also Group Performance, Team Building

FURTHER READING

LaFasto, F. M. J. (2001). *When teams work best: 6,000 team members and leaders tell what it takes to succeed.* Thousand Oaks, CA: Sage.

Stevens, M. J., & Campion, M. A. (1994). The knowledge, skill, and ability requirements for teamwork: Implications for human resource management. *Journal of Management, 20*(2), 503–530.

Stevens, M. J., & Yarish, M. E. (1999). Training for team effectiveness. In E. Sundstrom (Ed.), *Supporting work team effectiveness* (pp. 126–156). San Francisco: Jossey-Bass.

TECHNOLOGY ASSESSMENT

Many technologies are germane to health care. These technologies include information processing technologies, drug research, treatment methods, medical devices, and so on. A key decision that must be made is the selection of the optimum technology for a given situation. This selection must be based on key decision criteria that adequately consider the following:

- Estimated benefit of the technology
- Risk associated with utilizing the technology

The first decision criterion, estimated benefit of the technology, must be assessed giving consideration to several key factors. The first factor that must be considered is the estimated size of the population of people that could conceivably benefit from successful development of the technology. This size might be considered as a potential market size. This is the number of people who might use the technology. Also considered in evaluating this criterion is the relative benefit to the patient, the ultimate end beneficiary of the technology. For example, the potential to lower the cost of a treatment would not be given the same importance as the potential to develop a vaccine for a communicable disease, and a technology with the potential to relieve low levels of pain would not be given equal weight with a technology that has potential for greatly increasing the mobility of paraplegics.

The second decision criterion that should be used in the assessment of health care technologies is that of risk. This risk criterion should not be considered as a simple one-dimensional value. Rather, the risk spoken of here involves such considerations as

- Patient risk
- Risk to the caregiver
- Financial risk
- Risk of becoming obsolete
- And so on

The first of these is simply the risk of an adverse impact on the patient. Assessing this should include consideration of the probability of adverse health reactions versus the patient's current condition. For example, more possible risk to the patient may be acceptable if the patient is severely distressed and their chances of recovery are low. The risk to the caregiver should also be considered. A technology should not be used if there is an inherent danger to the person using the technology for the patient's benefit. The financial risk is the most pure economic assessment. However, when assessing health care technologies consideration should be given to the cost of the technology, the expected allowable costs to be paid by insurance companies, and the possibility of obtaining government-sponsored grants.

Assessing health care technologies must include consideration of many factors, some of which are objective and some, subjective.

—Terry L. Payne

See also Technology Change

FURTHER READING

Maidique, M. A., & Patch, P. (1988). Corporate strategy and technological policy. In M. L. Tushman & W. L. Moore (Eds.), *Readings in the management of innovation* (2nd ed., pp. 236–248). Cambridge, MA: Ballinger.

Stahl, M. J. (1984). *Strategic executive decisions: An analysis of the difference between theory and practice.* New York: Quorum Books.

TECHNOLOGY CHANGE

One of the strongest motivating forces known is the will to survive. Abraham Maslow recognized its importance in his famous motivational theories by acknowledging that, if one does not satisfy the need to extend life, the effectiveness of all other motivating forces is limited. The strength of the motivational force driven by this desire to extend and improve the quality of life is apparent in the health care industry. Specifically, the health care industry is constantly extending the boundaries of technology in its attempts to satisfy the unquenchable thirst for immortality. This thirst, accompanied by an abundance of funding from sources ranging from governments to pharmaceutical companies to private foundations, results in many technologies germane to the health care industry being highly turbulent, that is, frequently changing.

By definition, turbulent technologies experience frequent improvements and changes. In the health care industry, this turbulence is most evident in

- Development of new drugs
- Development and application of new treatment methods, procedures, and approaches
- Development of new diagnostic devices

Accompanying each of these changes in technology are necessary changes in administration and human resources.

In anticipation of and to facilitate the frequent implementation of technology changes, the health care industry should foster an environment that embraces technological change. In the determination of the most supportive environment for implementation of technology changes, two important stakeholders must be considered, namely, the patients and the health care providers. The technology change must be implemented in a manner that assures that the health care provider is comfortable in utilizing the technology change. This may require continuing education for the provider community. Likewise, the patient will need to be informed of the advantages the technology change affords them. The patient will largely be interested in advantages associated with the new technology that indicate an improvement(s) in the effectiveness of the new technology in the treatment process.

What is anticipated with regard to the turbulence of technologies related to health care? Spawned by an increase in our basic understanding of the human body, most forecasts project an increase in the turbulence of technology change within the health care industry.

Consider the following as a few possible areas where technological changes may soon be evident:

- New drugs that slow the aging process
- New robotic limb prostheses
- Artificial eyes

The development of each of these health care-related technologies, and many others, will result in modifications to the way in which illnesses are detected and treated. In addition, the discovery of new illnesses and diseases will require the development of new treatment methods involving technology. Thus, technologies in the health care industry are expected to frequently change for all of the anticipated future and therefore all aspects of the health care industry, including key business decisions, should anticipate and plan for changes in technology.

—Terry L. Payne

See also Technology Change

FURTHER READING

Ansoff, H. I. (1984). *Implanting strategic management.* Upper Saddle River, NJ: Prentice Hall.

Maslow, A. H. (1966). *The psychology of science.* New York: Harper & Row.

TELECOMMUTING

Telecommuting, also known as *telework,* refers to a work arrangement where employees perform all or some of their work from an alternate work location. In most cases, a telecommuter works from a home office. However, recent trends suggest that organizations in large cities are setting up smaller, remote offices to accommodate individuals with lengthy commutes. Telecommuting often occurs at the request of an employee, but increasingly organizations are asking some employees to telecommute, to reduce overhead costs.

Telecommuting has become a very viable work alternative with the increased availability of personal office equipment, including fax machines, personal photocopiers, and virtually limitless access to the Internet. However, because this increased dependence on technology is essential for a telecommuter's success, people pursuing such a work alternative need to feel comfortable with technology.

Although telecommuting may be a preferred method of work for some employees, the needs for strong technology skills, self-discipline, and lack of social contact, suggests this work style is not appropriate for all employees.

When allowing an employee to telecommute, it is necessary to establish clear work goals and objectives, because the employee's output will be the primary method for evaluating job performance. In addition, all new telecommuting work arrangements should be frequently evaluated to help avoid work performance problems and ensure a smooth transition to this new work style.

Telecommuting is one of several work scheduling alternatives an employer may want to consider offering. Other options include compressed workweeks and flextime.

—Laura Gniatczyk

See also Compressed Workweeks, Flextime

FURTHER READING

Adgar, M. (1998). The alternative workplace: Changing where and how people work. *Harvard Business Review, 76,* 121–137.

Froggatt, C. C. (2001). *Work naked: Eight essential principles for peak performance in the virtual workplace.* San Francisco: Jossey-Bass.

Mariani, M. (2000). Telecommuters. *Occupational Outlook Quarterly, 44,* 10–17.

TELEMEDICINE

Telemedicine (TM) can be defined as the practice of medicine at a distance, using the definition of the Greek word *tele-* for "far" with "medicine." This literal definition does not represent the full use of the word in this growing method to deliver health care using communication technologies. Another word, *telehealth* (TH), is increasingly being used to define the broader application of distant communications to health care and information.

Although projects using TM existed earlier, the present growth of TM began in the early and mid 1990s. This growth has been facilitated by improved, lower-cost technology and communications infrastructure making new applications of TM feasible. Because the field of TM is relatively new, the definitions of terminology are changing as the participants in the field advance the applications. One of the new descriptions of TM is the use of telecommunications and information technologies to provide or support clinical care at a distance (Puskin, 2002), which includes the growing field of information technologies.

TM can be considered to be care exclusively provided by a physician to a patient. This concept does not include the care given by physician assistants, nurse practitioners, nurses, and other providers. A broader definition includes any health care from any provider. Including all providers is more consistent with the present methods of delivering health care. Thus, the definition of TM should be consistent with present practice.

TH can be defined as the delivery of health care services at a distance (Darkins & Cary, 2000). The term can represent a broader set of applications in which information and telecommunications technologies support long-distance clinical care, consumer and professional health-related education, public health, health administration, research, and use of informatics/electronic medical records (Puskin, 2002). Because TH can include care for patients, education for patients, education for students in health care, continuing education for providers, administrative conferences, and the communication of medical records, TM can be considered as a subset of TH (Darkins & Cary, 2000; Puskin, 2002). Sometimes the two terms are used interchangeably.

The application of TM for patient care can be accomplished using several methods. Interactive videoconferencing led the development of TM in the 1990s because new technology made it possible and video emulated an in-person visit between the patient and a provider. It is possible to use this technology in patients' homes, clinics, and hospitals. Compressed videoconferencing technology provides this service using standard home telephone lines (POTS—Plain Old Telephone System); ISDN (Integrated Services Digital Network) telephone lines for typically 128, 256, and 384 kbps (kilobytes per second) rates; T-1 lines for up to 1.54 mbps; and the Internet for typically 384 and 768 kbps. In addition to videoconferencing, the standard telephone can be used for interactive audio communication between a patient and provider to provide TM services. The use of technology that permits interactive, real-time communications between a patient and a provider is synchronous TM.

Other technologies provide asynchronous communications for the delivery of TM services. These include the rapidly growing use of remote monitoring. For example, vital signs including blood pressure, pulse, oxygen saturation, and blood glucose can be measured in the home by a patient using electronic instruments and can be transmitted by telephone lines to a central monitoring station. Asynchronous communication such as remote monitoring can also be referred to as "store-and-forward" TM. The transmission of radiological films and digital images is an example of store-and-forward TM that has been used for several years.

Another example of asynchronous communications is a question-and-answer session between a computer program and a patient. The purpose of this communication is to determine the present health status (usually on a daily basis) of the patient by asking questions similar to an interaction between a provider and the patient, and by obtaining data provided by the patient from an instrument such as a glucometer. One method of providing this communication is an electronic box that displays the questions and is connected to the patient's home telephone line. The patient responds by pressing buttons to communicate to the central computer presenting the questions. Another method uses the standard telephone in the home. The questions are presented in audio by a computer and the patient uses the telephone keypad for responses and entry of data from instruments. A third method uses an Internet Web site to interact with the patient.

—Samuel G. Burgiss

FURTHER READING

Darkins, A. W., & Cary, M. A. (2000). *Telemedicine and tele-health: Principles, policies, performance and pitfalls.* New York: Springer.

Maheu, M. M., Whitten, P., & Allen, A. (2001). *E-health, tele-health, and telemedicine: A guide to start-up and success.* San Francisco: Jossey-Bass.

Puskin, D. S. (2002). An overview of telemedicine: Through the looking glass. In M. L. Armstrong & S. Frueh (Eds.), *Telecommunications for nurses* (2nd ed., pp. 135–165). New York: Springer.

TERTIARY CARE

Tertiary care is highly specialized care, requiring the skills of individuals with advanced educational and practical experience in the management of complex illness. It also typically is provided in facilities that have high-technology equipment capabilities and are accustomed to providing subspecialty services not available in general acute care hospitals.

Such care should be differentiated from primary care and secondary care. Although dependent somewhat on the definition used, *primary care* usually refers to care provided by family practice, internal medicine, obstetric, and pediatric physicians. *Secondary care* typically refers to short-term care provided by specialists or subspecialists in their offices or in the general acute care hospital, often helping the primary care physician solve a diagnostic dilemma.

Physicians involved in providing tertiary care typically are subspecialists with special training either in diagnostic procedures such as cardiac catheterization or surgical procedures such as neurosurgery. Because tertiary care often requires high-technology equipment, other individuals involved may be highly skilled technicians or nurses.

Hospitals providing tertiary care often are large, regional referral centers or university- and medical school-affiliated facilities. They may, however, be community hospitals that have developed certain specialized service lines such as cardiovascular surgery or cancer care.

Both the physicians and the hospital facilities involved in providing tertiary care are also often involved in providing primary and secondary levels of care. It is therefore the level of care being provided rather than the provider that determines the appropriate application of the term tertiary.

—C. Bevan Stuart

See also Ambulatory Care, Health Care Utilization, Hospitals, Primary Care

FURTHER READING

http://cpmcnet.columbia.edu/texts/guide/hmg01_0002.html

www.umanitoba.ca/centres/mchp/concept/thesaurus/thesaurus_T.html

THEORY OF CONSTRAINTS

The theory of constraint (TOC), developed by Dr. Eliyahu Goldratt, is a method of operations management and organizational problem solving. The premise underlying TOC is that all systems have at least one constraint that is preventing the system from reaching its goal. Primacy is given to systemic goals rather than local efficiencies. TOC is applicable to the management of entities that produce products or services, including health care operations.

The TOC was initially popularized in Dr. Goldratt's business novel, *The Goal*, in which the protagonist, Alex Rogo, the manager of a factory, has been told, by the senior management of his company, to make his factory profitable, or the factory will be closed. Rogo enlists the help of a consultant, Jonah, who guides Rogo, using the Socratic method to help Rogo discover the principles of TOC, until Rogo is ultimately able to save the factory.

Because the initial description of TOC presented in *The Goal* was in a manufacturing setting, readers may have the misconception that the applicability of TOC is limited to the identification and elimination of production bottlenecks in a manufacturing, job-shop environment. In reality, the TOC provides managers with a methodology that allows them to clearly state their organization's global goals, for example (for most businesses), to make money, identify and remove the constraints that are preventing the organization from reaching its goal, and to enable the manager to logically approach the organizational conflicts that occur when mutually exclusive a priori assumptions are proposed as the basis for making key decisions.

An algorithm is provided whereby managers can identify and eliminate the impediments to achievement of these goals, that is, the constraints, or, in a manufacturing environment, the production bottlenecks. This algorithm is as follows:

1. Identify the system's constraints.

2. Figure out how to best exploit those constraints.

3. Subordinate everything else to these efforts.

4. Remove the constraints.

5. Once the constraints have been removed, go back to step 1 and start again.

The system's constraint is typically the resource in the chain of production or service, with the least capacity. This is referred to as the *capacity constraint resource* (CCR). However, Goldratt stresses that constraints often appear that are the result of the organization's policies. Although identifying policy constraints can be very difficult, removing them does not typically cost money.

By "exploiting" the system's constraints, Goldratt means to make sure that the CCR is fully utilized; that is, don't waste the CCR. For instance, in a physician's office practice, if the CCR is the physician's time availability for seeing patients, exploiting the constraint in this instance means making sure the physician's time is spent doing billable activities related to patient care. An example of "subordinating everything else" is to enlist the aid of nurses or physician extenders to increase the amount of time the physician has available to see patients, and to make sure that patient flow is optimized by making sure that all lab data and other information needed by the physician at the time of the visit are tracked down by the office staff prior to the visit, rather than by the physician at the time of the visit. Ultimately, it may become necessary to "remove the system's constraints." In the example given, this may involve hiring additional physicians once the current physician's patient panel reaches a given level.

As noted, the TOC gives primacy to achieving systemic, organizational goals rather than local efficiencies. For example, the goal of a multispecialty, outpatient practice is, ultimately, to make money, albeit in the context of providing high-quality care. The TOC, therefore, focuses on measuring "throughput," which, in this case, is the amount of revenue generated by seeing patients, rather than, for example, the cost per visit. The cost per visit is a local optimum. A practice may be able to reduce cost per visit by decreasing staff salaries or by downsizing the staff. However, this may result in decreased net profits because of diminished service capacity; that is, focusing on cost reduction, per se, may create operating constraints. This puts TOC directly at odds with traditional cost accounting and has led to the development of "throughput accounting," a technique of managerial accounting used to measure the real-time financial performance of organizations employing TOC (see the entry for *Throughput Accounting*), and to assist such organizations with regard to financial decision making.

Aside from the techniques employed by TOC aimed at eliminating operating constraints, a major component of TOC methodology involves the TOC "thinking process." This thinking process is aimed at alleviating the policy constraints mentioned earlier. Many managers have found that as they eliminate constraints from the actual production or service operation they manage, additional constraints originate outside of the actual production process. The principle behind the TOC thinking process is that what are referred to in TOC terminology as the organization's "undesirable effects" (aptly described in some TOC literature as akin to the symptoms of a disease) have a root cause. The TOC thinking process provides managers with the ability to identify this root cause. The process is similar to the one used by physicians as they narrow down the list of potential diagnoses that may be causing symptoms in a patient. For instance, a patient's shortness of breath may be due to chronic lung disease or congestive heart failure. The findings on a physical exam and the results of diagnostic testing allow the physician to make a diagnosis of congestive heart failure. The physician then seeks to change the patient's heart function by prescribing agents to improve the patient's cardiac function, such as angiotensin-converting enzyme inhibitors and diuretics. By identifying the root cause of the problem, appropriate and logical changes in the system can be made. TOC uses the following algorithm when approaching such problems:

1. What should be changed?

2. What should it be changed to?

3. How should the change be implemented?

The TOC literature describes, in detail, the techniques needed to employ this algorithm, such as the construction of a "present reality tree," the use of the "evaporating cloud" technique, and so on. Detailed description of these methods is beyond the scope of the current treatment of this topic, and the reader is referred to the suggestions for further reading.

—Darren S. Kaufman

FURTHER READING

Gaither, N., & Frazier, G. (1999). *Production and operations management.* Cincinnati, OH: South-Western.

Goldratt, E. (1984). *The goal.* Great Barrington, MA: North River Press.

Goldratt, E. (1990). *The theory of constraints.* Great Barrington, MA: North River Press.

Goldratt, E. (1990). *The haystack syndrome.* Great Barrington, MA: North River Press.

Swain, M., & Bell, J. (1999). *The theory of constraints and throughput accounting.* New York: McGraw-Hill.

THIRD-PARTY ADMINISTRATOR (TPA)

A third-party administrator (TPA) is an individual or company that provides health insurance administrative functions through contracts with employers who self-insure the health of their employees. It is estimated that about 60% of all U.S. workers are currently covered by self-funded health plans, most of which are managed by TPAs. The typical TPA develops and coordinates self-insurance programs, usually with significant input from the employer, who may mandate certain benefits and reimbursements. (For example, if the workforce is dominated by women of child-bearing age, the plan may need to include high levels of maternity coverage.) The TPA also works to market the program to the employees and provide customer support. The TPA processes and pays the claims on behalf of the employer and may help locate stop-loss insurance for the employer. The TPA can also analyze the effectiveness of the program and trace the patterns of those using the benefits. Many TPAs can function as an independent health insurance company for those companies that do not wish to self-insure or cannot afford to bear the risk of self-insurance.

Each employer forges a custom arrangement with its TPA, which can perform as many or as few tasks as the client delegates. A TPA can help design insurance plans, administer claims, ensure compliance with government regulations, review how employees use the health plan, arrange participation in preferred provider organizations (PPOs), maintain plan records, and prepare materials to explain health care changes to employees.

—Donald Levick

FURTHER READING

Sosnin, B. (2000, February). 10 tips for picking a TPA. *HR Magazine, 45*(2), 83.

THIRD-PARTY PAYERS

See Health Insurance

THREAT

See SWOT (Strength-Weakness-Opportunity-Threat) Analysis

THREAT-OPPORTUNITY-WEAKNESS-STRENGTH (TOWS)

See SWOT (Strength-Weakness-Opportunity-Threat) Analysis

THROUGHPUT ACCOUNTING (TA)

Throughput accounting (TA) is a managerial accounting methodology that gives primacy to the identification and elimination of a system's operating constraints. As opposed to cost accounting, throughput accounting methods do not allocate costs to products or activities. TA is based on the theory of constraints, developed by Eliyahu Goldratt. The concepts of the theory of constraints were introduced in Goldratt's seminal work, *The Goal.*

THROUGHPUT ACCOUNTING: BASIC ASSUMPTIONS AND DEFINITIONS

As a managerial accounting methodology, the purpose of TA is to provide management with information that allows accurate decisions to be made, such as optimal allocation of resources, product-service mix, and so on. In addition, a managerial accounting system must provide management with an accurate picture of where the firm is, and where it should be going forward.

In TA, priority is given to the generation of revenues by the firm. Three basic metrics are used in the TA system: throughput, operating expense, and investment. Throughput (*T*) is defined as the rate at which the firm generates money. In most cases, throughput can be equated with sales revenue. The strict definition of throughput is given by the following equation:

$$Tu = Ru - TVC$$

where *Tu* = throughput per unit produced

Ru = revenue per unit produced

TVC = totally variable costs

The term *"totally" variable costs* serves to distinguish TA from the other extant managerial accounting methodologies, such as cost accounting and activity-based costing. TVC is restricted to the cost of selling one additional unit of product or service. In a manufacturing setting, TVC would be equated with raw material cost, whereas the TVC of a patient visit to a doctor's office would be the cost of the materials used during the visit such as gowns, gloves, printed forms, and so on. Throughput is similar to contribution margin, which is defined as revenue minus variable cost. This is equal to the dollar amount of revenue available to cover fixed costs. However, in TA, only totally variable costs are subtracted from revenues, as just shown. All other costs, other than totally variable costs, are included in operating expense (OE).

The second metric used in TA is "investment." Goldratt uses the term "inventory," and other managerial accountants utilizing TA sometimes use the term "assets." In any event, whichever terminology is adopted, the parameter measured is the amount of money that the entity uses to purchase the items it plans to sell, or, if a service operation, the amount of money used to purchase the items needed to produce the service. For example, in a TA system the funds used to purchase dialysis machines and equipment by a dialysis provider are recorded under the category of investments. This somewhat restricted definition of assets used in TA differs from that recognized in the more standard accrual accounting treatment. For instance, in a manufacturing firm the expenses attendant to producing work in process and finished goods inventory are not recognized until the product is sold, via the matching principle of basic accounting. TA asserts that, although this GAAP-mandated methodology of recognizing expenses is appropriate (and required) when reporting financial data to outside agencies and shareholders, it does not provide an accurate managerial accounting picture of the firm's true profitability and cost structure. In TA, the only value attributed to inventory is the totally variable cost of producing the inventory. Importantly, the cost of producing a product or service, using TA, is recognized at the time the product or service is produced or rendered, rather than when the product is sold or payment is received for the service.

Operating expense, as used in the TA system, is defined as the amount of money used by the entity to convert investment into throughput. Hence, operating expense represents the entire cost attendant to producing a good or service, other than totally variable costs. TA does not seek to allocate costs to a particular product or service. Therefore, all wages and salaries, such as those paid to executives and line workers alike, as well as rent, energy expenses, and so forth, are included under operating expense, and no attempt is made to further classify costs as being fixed, variable, semifixed, and so on.

DECISION MAKING USING THROUGHPUT ACCOUNTING

Two additional, key metrics are used in TA: net profit (NP) and return on investment (ROI). The utility of any managerial accounting system is its ability to allow managers to make both short-term and longer-term operational and strategic decisions using readily available data that result in an improvement in the entity's bottom line. Net profit (NP) and return on investment (ROI) are linked to the aforementioned terms *throughput* (in this case the firm's total throughput), *operating expense* and *investment*, as follows:

$$NP = T - OE$$
$$ROI = (T - OE)/I$$

Clearly it will be attractive to elect to produce a good or service that increases throughput while decreasing operating expense or investment. When making such decisions, management will seek to produce goods and services that create an increase in NP and ROI. Projects that are predicted to have positive incremental net profits, or that have a return on investment that meets or exceeds a requisite value, will be accepted. In TA, primacy is given to ROI when making such decisions.

THE USE OF THROUGHPUT ACCOUNTING IN OPERATIONS MANAGEMENT

One additional metric that is key to the application of TA to actual day-to-day operations management and planning is throughput per unit time used by the capacity constraint resource (CCR). The capacity constraint resource is the actual limiting resource in the chain of production. The CCR can be envisioned as the weak link in the chain, as discussed in theory of constraints literature. For example, in a physician's outpatient practice, the actual time availability of the physician for seeing patients represents the CCR. Hence, continuing with this example, a key managerial accounting metric should be the throughput generated per patient visit, per unit of time spent by the physician with the patient. In fact, it may be more accurate to include the time spent by the physician before, during, and after the visit dealing with the issue addressed during the office visit, because the physician may have had to call the patient after the visit to discuss abnormal laboratory values, to arrange follow-up testing and additional treatment; this treatment of time on the CCR is an important issue in health care management because delegating certain pre- and postvisit administrative tasks to a nonphysician results in less time used by the CCR, and greater operational effectiveness. Hence, when making operating decisions, such as whether or not to hire a nurse practitioner for the practice or deciding whether to administer IV medication infusions in the office, the effect on throughput per unit time on the capacity constraint resource should be analyzed. Ultimately,

however, the effect of any decision on ROI needs to be examined.

—Darren S. Kaufman

FURTHER READING

Corbett, T. (1998). *Throughput accounting.* Great Barrington, MA: North River Press.

Goldratt, E. (1984). *The goal.* Great Barrington, MA: North River Press.

Goldratt, E. (1990). *The haystack syndrome.* Great Barrington, MA: North River Press.

Goldratt, E. (1990). *The theory of constraints.* Great Barrington, MA: North River Press.

Noreen, E., Smith, D., & Mackey, J. (1995). *The theory of constraints and its implications for management accounting.* Great Barrington, MA: North River Press.

Swain, M., & Bell, J. (1999). *The theory of constraints and throughput accounting.* New York: McGraw-Hill.

TIME VALUE OF MONEY

The term *time value of money* refers to the concepts and calculations behind the simple observation that a dollar to be received in one year, or at some arbitrary time in the future, is worth less than a dollar to be received today. Mortgage payments for physician offices, interest expense on equipment loans, and investment annuities are all examples of time value of money calculations. In what follows, the variable P represents an amount today, also called a *present value*. The variable F represents an amount to be received sometime in the future, also called a *future value*. The letter n represents the number of periods from now that a payment will be received or paid. Usually the periods will be years, but sometimes they will be months. The letter r represents the periodic interest rate. This rate is also called the *discount rate*. Usually this will be an annual rate, but sometimes it will be a monthly rate. See the entries *Compound Growth Rate* and *Annual Percentage Rate* for more information on interest payments that occur more frequently than once a year.

PRESENT VALUES

The present value, P, of an amount, F, to be received in n years when the interest rate is r is

$$P = F/(1 + r)^n$$

For example, if you will receive $10,000 in three years and the interest rate is 6% then you will be indifferent to the choice between receiving the $10,000 three years from now and receiving $10,000/(1.06)^3 = $8,396.19 right now. We say, "The present value of $10,000 to be received in three years is $8,396.19." Another way of putting it is that $10,000 to be received in three years is worth $8,396.19 today if the interest rate is 6%.

Note that to use the formula, n doesn't have to be measured in years, and r doesn't have to be an annual interest rate. It is common to calculate monthly payments for mortgages and auto loans, so n might be in months and r might be a monthly interest rate. Frequently, there will be a series of equal payments, such as with a mortgage, or the interest payments on a bond. This is called an *annuity.* In these cases the present value of an annuity is just the sum of the present values of the individual payments. If there are more than a few such payments, then the calculations become tedious and it is more convenient to use a formula. The *present value interest factor of an annuity* when the interest rate is r% and there are n equal payments is denoted $PVIFA(r\%, n)$ and is the present value of $1 to be received at the end of each of n periods when the interest rate is r% per period:

$$PVIFA(r\%, n) = \frac{\$1}{1 + r} + \frac{\$1}{(1 + r)^2} + \frac{\$1}{(1 + r)^3} + \cdots \frac{\$1}{(1 + r)^n}$$

$$= \frac{1 - \dfrac{1}{(1 + r)^n}}{r}$$

Financial calculators and spreadsheet programs such as Microsoft Excel can perform this calculation automatically. To simplify the exposition we will use the expression $PVIFA(r\%, n)$ instead of the preceding formula when discussing how to perform the various calculations. Using this expression, the present value of an annuity of $100 per year for 20 years at an annual interest rate of 12% is $100 $PVIFA(12\%, 20)$ = $100 × 7.4694 = $746.94.

The annuity formula can be used to find the payment on an auto loan or mortgage. Suppose an automobile costing $30,000 will be financed for 60 months at a monthly rate of ½% per month. The bank would call this a five-year loan at 6% (that is, 0.5% per month × 12 months = 6%) with monthly payments. If *pmt* is the payment, then the present value of the stream of 60 payments of *pmt* must be equal to the loan amount of $30,000:

$$30,000 = pmt × PVIFA(0.5\%, 60)$$
$$30,000 = pmt × 51.7256$$
$$pmt = 30,000/51.7256$$
$$= \$579.98$$

So the monthly payment would be $579.98.

Sometimes a financial instrument is a combination of an annuity and a fixed payment, like a corporate bond. A 15-year 8% corporate bond is a bond that makes interest payments of $40 every six months for 15 years (for a total of $80 per year), and then an additional final payment of $1,000, called the *principal payment.* The bond is called an "8%" bond because $80, or 8% of the $1,000 principal amount, is paid out each year. If the going 6-month interest rate is 3.5%, then the price of this bond should be

Price = present value of $40 annuity for 30 six-month periods
   + value of final principal payment in 15 years (in 30 six-month periods)
   = 40 × $PVIFA(3.5\%, 30)$ + 1000/(1 + 0.35)^{30}
   = 40 × 18.3920 + 356.28 = $1,091.96

FUTURE VALUES

The future value of an amount today is how much that amount would grow to at a given interest rate. For example, $100 invested today at 6% will grow to $100 + $6 = $106 at the end of one year. At the end of two years you will have the initial $100, the $6 in interest from the first year, another $6 in interest on the $100 from the second year, and finally $6 × (0.06) = $0.36 from the interest in the second year earned on interest from the first year. This totals $112.36. This accumulation of interest on interest is called *compounding* and plays a big role in the mathematics of saving and investing.

The formula for the future value, F, of an amount invested today, P, at an interest rate of r% for n periods is

$$F = (1 + r)^n$$

So $100 invested at an annual rate of 15% for 20 years will grow to $100 × (1.15)^{20} = $1,636.65, an increase in value of $1,536.65. Notice that only $15 × 20 = $300 of the extra $1,536.65 is actually interest on the initial $100. The rest, $1,236.65, is actually interest on interest. So compounding is very important.

Just as with present values, many financial problems or investments involve a series of equal payments, or an annuity. The future value of a series of payments is just the sum of the future values of the individual payments. But because the calculations can quickly grow tedious, if there are more than a couple of them we will refer to the *future value interest factor of an annuity,* or $FVIFA(r\%, n)$, as the amount that a series of $1 payments at the end of each period for n periods will grow to if the periodic interest rate is $r\%$:

$$FVIFA(r\%, n) = \$1(1 + r) + \$1(1 + r)^2 + \cdots + \$1(1 + r)^n$$

$$= \frac{(1 + r)^n - 1}{r}$$

Consider a savings plan for college education. If you invest $100 per month in an account earning 0.5% a month for 18 years ($18 \times 12 = 216$ payments) you will have $100 $FVIFA(0.5\%, 216) = \$100 \times 387.353 = \$38,735$ at the end of the 18 years. Of this total, you actually only contributed $18 \times 12 \times 100 = \$21,600$. The rest, $17,135, is interest and interest on interest. If you pick riskier investments that are expected to earn, on average, twice as much, or 1% a month, then the total grows to $75,786.

AMORTIZATION

Time value of money calculations are used to figure out how much of a mortgage payment is interest and how much of it is principal. The list by month of how much of the mortgage payment is interest and how much is principal repayment is called an *amortization schedule.* This matters because the mortgage company needs to keep a running total of how much is owed on the loan so if the borrower refinances or pays off the loan early everyone knows how much the balance is. This also matters because home mortgage interest is tax deductible so homeowners need to know how much interest they have paid during the year so they can file their taxes.

Take, for example, a 30-year mortgage for $200,000 with monthly payments and a monthly interest rate of 0.75%. This corresponds to a stated annual interest rate of $0.75 \times 12 = 9\%$. Using the present value of an annuity formula, we can figure out the monthly payment for 360 months:

$$
\begin{aligned}
P &= pmt \times PVIFA(0.75\%, 360) \\
200,000 &= pmt \times 124.2819 \\
pmt &= 200,000/124.2819 \\
&= \$1,609.25
\end{aligned}
$$

Note that in most cases this would not be the total amount you would write a check for, because most mortgages also require monthly payments to the mortgage company to cover homeowner's insurance and property taxes. Depending on the value of the home, the mortgage amount,

the area's tax structure, and the mortgage interest rate, the total payments to the mortgage company may be from 25% to 100% higher.

In the first month of the loan, a total of $200,000 \times 0.75\% = \$1,500$ in interest is owed on the loan. That leaves the balance, $1,609.25 - \$1,500 = \$109.25$, for principal repayment. So after the first payment the homeowner now owes $200,000 - \$109.25 = \$199,890.75$.

In the second month of the loan, a total of $199,890.75 \times .75\% = \$1,499.18$ in interest is owed. This leaves $1,609.25 - \$1,499.18 = \$110.07$ for principal repayment. So after the second payment the homeowner now owes $199,890.75 - \$110.07 = \$199,780.68$. This calculation is made in each of the 360 months of the loan. In the first years of the loan most of the mortgage payment is interest because the outstanding balance is so high, so the homeowner gets a large tax deduction. In the later years of the mortgage most of the payment is principal because the outstanding balance is small, so the homeowner gets only a small tax deduction.

RETIREMENT PLANNING

Time value of money calculations can help you establish savings goals for retirement. It takes several steps to do the appropriate calculations, and we will lay them out here. Note importantly that each step requires assumptions about rates of return and life span. The assumptions here are just for illustrative purposes.

Assumptions

Suppose you are starting early on your retirement planning. You are 25 years old and expect to work for 40 years and then retire at age 65. You anticipate drawing retirement funds for 20 years and do not plan on leaving anything in your retirement account to pass on to your estate. You can tolerate risk fairly well and so plan to invest your savings in a mutual fund that earns on average 10% a year. Although no one knows what will happen to inflation, the inflation rate is low now, and you anticipate that inflation will hover around 3% over your working career.

Step 1: Lifestyle

How much will you need to live on when you retire? If you think that $50,000 per year in today's dollars would be enough to live on, then in 40 years at a 3% inflation rate you will need $50,000 \times (1.03)^{40} = \$163,102$ per year to maintain the same lifestyle that $50,000 buys you now. For simplicity, let's assume you are planning on funding your retirement so you can draw $200,000 per year for 20 years, starting in 40 years. Of course the spending power of the

$200,000 per year will erode with inflation during your retirement, which is why we started with a higher retirement benefit.

Step 2: How much must you accumulate?

Starting in 40 years, you plan on spending $200,000 per year for 20 years when the investment rate is 10%. This is an annuity and the present value of this, as of the day you retire, is $200,000 *PVIFA*(10%, 20) = $200,000 × 8.51356 = $1,702,713. So in order to retire as planned, you need to accumulate $1.7 million in your retirement account. If you have this amount earning 10% you can spend $200,000 per year for 20 years and have a zero balance at the end of 20 years.

Step 3: How much must you save?

Let's assume that you will make monthly contributions to your retirement account, which earns on average 10/12 = 0.833% a month. You will contribute for 40 × 12 = 480 months. If *pmt* is your contribution, then the future value of an annuity formula shows how much this will grow to:

$$F = pmt \times FVIFA(0.833\%, 480)$$
$$1,702,713 = pmt \times 6,316.4$$
$$pmt = 1,702,713/6,316.4$$
$$= \$269.57$$

So in order to retire as you have planned, you need to save $269.57 per month if your investments earn, on average, 10% per year.

—Phillip R. Daves

See also Annual Percentage Rate (APR), Compound Growth Rate

FURTHER READING

Brigham, E. F., & Ehrhardt, M. C. (2001). *Financial management* (10th ed.). Mason, OH: South-Western.

TITLE VII OF THE CIVIL RIGHTS ACT OF 1964

Title VII of the Civil Rights Act of 1964 (42 U.S.C. 2000e) was enacted to provide equal employment opportunities in the workplace for all individuals. The act is a federal law that prohibits discrimination by employers who engage in any business or industry affecting commerce. Title VII makes it unlawful for employers to hire, fire, or otherwise take adverse employment action against an individual or a class of people because of the individual's or group's race, color, religion, sex, or national origin. Adverse employment action can include hiring, firing, promotions, compensation, terms and conditions of employment, or privileges of employment. The law has been interpreted to cover harassment in the workplace when the harassment occurs because of race, color, religion, sex, or national origin. The act also encompasses both pregnancy discrimination and sexual harassment in the workplace under the provision prohibiting gender discrimination. Title VII applies to all employers who have 15 or more employees for each working day in each of 20 or more calendar weeks in the current or preceding calendar year.

Sexual harassment is a unique and important component of the protections of Title VII as the law developing around this topic has continued to grow and provide employers more guidance. Sexual harassment includes harassment between members of the opposite sex as well as harassment between members of the same sex. Harassment can occur between supervisor and employer, or between coworkers. As issues of harassment continue to be pursued by employees, the courts are using sexual harassment case law to interpret other forms of harassment such as harassment based on race, color, and other protected classifications. Employers may be protected from some sexual harassment claims if the employer can show the existence of a strong sexual harassment policy and application of that policy.

Title VII includes an antiretaliation provision that prohibits an employer from retaliating against an individual who opposes any discriminatory act by filing a complaint, testifying, or assisting, or who is involved in any manner in an investigation, proceeding, or hearing under Title VII. An individual participating in an internal investigation conducted by an employer as a result of an allegation of discrimination is included in the protection from retaliation afforded under Title VII.

Title VII requires that a complainant exhaust available administrative remedies before filing in court. The administrative remedies available under Title VII include filing a complaint with the Equal Employment Opportunity Commission (EEOC) or the appropriate state human rights organization. The EEOC will investigate the charge and make a determination or will issue a "right to sue" letter allowing the person complaining to file a case in court.

Remedies for violations of Title VII may include all forms of relief such as back pay, front pay, hiring, promotion, reinstatement, wages, salary, fringe benefits, reasonable accommodations, attorney's fees, expert witness fees, court costs, and injunctive relief. Compensatory damages may be awarded for future losses, emotional distress, pain, suffering, and mental anguish. In the case of willful or malicious discrimination, punitive damages may also be available.

Employers should keep in mind that all states also have legislation prohibiting discrimination under states' human rights acts. It may be important to consult these state acts, as individual states may have more expansive nondiscrimination protections (such as laws that may prohibit discrimination based on sexual orientation) than those provided through federal legislation.

—Jennifer L. Richter

See also Civil Rights Acts of 1964 and 1991, Employee Rights, Equal Employment Opportunity Commission (EEOC)

FURTHER READING

www.eeoc.gov

TOTAL QUALITY MANAGEMENT (TQM)

See Quality Management

TRANSFORMATIONAL LEADERSHIP

See Leadership

TRANSFORMATION PROCESS

See Organizational Change

TRAUMA

The word *trauma* originated from the Greek word τραεμα, which means wound. There are references to trauma in the ancient Greek, Egyptian, and Indian literature. Injuries result from acute exposure to physical agents. The physical agents could be varied, such as heat, mechanical force, chemicals, electricity, and radiation. When the magnitude of force of the physical agent exceeds the normal human tolerance, injury results.

Injuries are classified by various methods. They are categorized based on mechanism of injury, for example: a motor vehicle crashes, pedestrian struck. The type of injury caused by blunt forces are called *blunt trauma* and the injuries caused by sharp objects that penetrate the skin before causing internal damage are called *penetrating trauma.* Examples of blunt trauma are motor vehicle crashes, falls, and so on; examples penetrating trauma are stab wounds and gunshot wounds. Another way to classify traumatic wounds is as "intentional" and "unintentional" depending on the intent of the perpetuator. The intentional injuries are further classified as homicide and suicide.

The impact of trauma on American society is devastating. It is the leading cause of death in the first four decades of life. Trauma causes devastation to the young and potentially more productive members of society. With the advancing age of the American population, geriatric trauma is becoming an increasing social issue. No subset of the population is immune from trauma. Trauma ranks third, behind cancer and arteriosclerosis, as a leading cause of death in all decades of life.

Two people are killed, approximately 350 sustain a disabling injury, and $7.8 million is spent every 10 minutes in this country as a result of trauma. Approximately 60 million injuries occur in this country every year. Of these injuries, 50% require medical treatment. Every year 3.6 million trauma hospital admissions occur. Approximately 9 million of these injuries are disabling, 300,000 permanently and 8.7 million temporarily. The trauma-related costs exceed $400 billion annually. It is ironic that despite such an amount of financial loss to the economy of this country, only four cents of every federal research dollar are spent in trauma research.

Death from trauma follows what is known in trauma circles as the *trimodal death distribution.* The first peak of deaths occurs in the field and occurs within the first few seconds or minutes of injury. This peak of deaths is beyond control of the medical profession. Only legislation and law enforcement can make a significant impact on this peak of death. Enforcement of laws against drunken driving, helmet laws, and safety belt laws would significantly reduce this peak of trauma death. Public education about trauma prevention would significantly help to reduce trauma death. The American Trauma Society and National Safe Kids Coalition have spearheaded trauma prevention education. Public awareness of battered spouse syndrome, battered child syndrome, and elder abuse would help prevent trauma in those vulnerable subsets of society. The second peak of deaths occurs within a few minutes to several hours of the injury. Dr. Adam Cowley therefore popularized the Golden Hour concept. The concept is that if the trauma patient is taken to a specialized trauma care center within an hour of injury, then the trauma victim has a better chance to survive the injury. Based on that concept, specialized centers to treat trauma were created all around the country. These are called *trauma centers.* There are various levels of trauma centers depending on the resources of the trauma centers. They are classified as level I, II, or III trauma centers. To use the Golden Hour concept effectively, the prehospital trauma care (the care provided by emergency medical service at the scene) has been streamlined and integrated into trauma care.

The prehospital care is to stabilize and rapidly transport the trauma victim to the nearest trauma center for the definitive care. Standardization of trauma care across the board has a major impact in improving the morbidity and mortality of the trauma victims in this country. Multiple studies in the past decade have confirmed the notion that trauma victims do have a better chance of survival if they are brought to a trauma center. The third peak of deaths occurs in several days to several weeks after the initial injury. The mode of death is sepsis and multiple organ failure, and such mortality can be decreased by better ICU care.

The only way to reduce the economic, social, and personal perils of trauma is to educate the public about effective trauma prevention.

—Ramanathan Raju

FURTHER READING

Fiemu, N., & Thal, E. (1999). *Parkland trauma handbook* (2nd ed.). Philadelphia: Mosby.

Greaves, I., Ryan, J. M., & Porter, K. M. (1998). *Trauma.* Oxford, UK: Arnold & Oxford University Press.

Mattox, K., Feliciano, D., & Moore, E. (2000). *Trauma* (4th ed.). New York: McGraw-Hill.

TRUST FUND BALANCE

See Fund Balance

UNANTICIPATED OUTCOME DISCLOSURE

An unanticipated outcome is a result that differs significantly from what was anticipated to be the result from a treatment or procedure. Every treatment and procedure carries with it anticipated and unanticipated consequences. Legal and ethical standards now require all hospitals and physicians to inform patients of both of these types of results. In order to make decisions about their care, patients have a need and right to know what is happening to them at all times (so long as this information does not pose a danger to the patient). A recent policy adopted by the JCAHO (Patient Safety Standards, R1.1.2.2) states, in part, "Patients and, when appropriate, their families, are informed about outcomes of care, including unanticipated outcomes." Compliance with this and other similar standards requires a balance between strict compliance and risk to the patient. Generally, if there is no risk to the patient, information regarding both types of outcomes are required to be transmitted to the patient.

Positive unanticipated outcomes are simple, such as healthy triplets when twins were expected. Issues arise, however, when an outcome is *negative and unanticipated*, as in the case of a rare surgical complication which causes serious postoperative problems. It is important to note that no legal, ethical, or JCAHO standard requires a professional, faced with telling a patient of an unanticipated outcome, to admit liability. Rather, facts, education, and support remain the cornerstones of these communications.

Managing the risks of communicating unanticipated outcomes requires candor, empathy, and documentation. Informed consent is critical to a patient's right to determine his or her own care. Informed consent standards are of two types in the United States, namely the reasonable patient standard and the reasonable physician standard. Each requires that the physician inform the patient of

- The disease state to be treated
- The proposed treatment or procedure
- Alternatives to the proposed treatment or procedure
- Anticipated outcomes of the procedure or its alternatives (unanticipated outcomes are also often included)

The reasonable physician standard requires communication of all information that a reasonable physician would give to a patient for him or her to make an informed decision. The reasonable patient standard (the standard in the majority of states) requires the communication of all information that a reasonable patient would need to make an informed decision. Such information and consent lays the groundwork for any future communications regarding outcomes. If the physician has been open, empathetic, and honest, then the risk of liability is reduced. The opposite also applies.

Posttreatment, the disclosure of unanticipated outcome information does not require admission of liability but does require an explanation of outcome or results, recommended next steps, and the offering of assistance appropriate to benefit the patient. This may include a bioethical, religious, social service, or other consultation.

All policies regarding unanticipated outcomes should include the following:

- Training for professionals and support staff to include the issues of liability, informed consent, and ethical standards
- Limitations on personnel entitled to inform patients of outcomes, and ways to contact those who can
- Patient grievance policies, family contact policies, and corrective action policies

- A statement that obtaining a detailed informed consent is the best means of avoiding risk after the disclosure of an unanticipated outcome

—Kenneth Steiner and Stuart Hochron

UNCOMPENSATED CARE

See Indigent Health Care

UNDERSERVED POPULATIONS

Underserved populations are residents of catchment areas for whom the availability of health care limits the amount of care consumed to something less than what experts believe they should be using. Note some of the qualifications of that statement. The appropriate service level is not determined by market demand but by experts' estimates of need. People who decide not to go to the doctor because they choose to ignore their symptoms are not poorly served, but someone who lacks access is. That lack of access may be due to the inability to pay or to a lack of providers in the area.

The U.S. Department of Health and Human Service administers a number of programs aimed at protecting and improving the health of underserved populations. Therefore, it has developed guidelines for designating Medically Underserved Areas (MUAs) and Medically Underserved Populations (MUPs). Areas and populations that meet these guidelines are eligible to receive grant funding for Community Health Centers and, if rural, as Rural Health Centers and have personnel assigned by the U.S. Public Health Service. Eligible health centers that meet the guidelines but do not receive grants may be certified as Federally Qualified Health Centers and become eligible for cost-based Medicaid reimbursement.

The population of individuals whose attributes are used to determine whether an area is underserved is the whole population of a set of counties, minor civil divisions, or census tracts that represent a homogeneous socioeconomic or demographic neighborhood. The population for the MUP is a subset of the individuals in an area who experience economic, linguistic, and/or cultural barriers to private medical care.

The four basic criteria for MUA or MUP designation are the percentage of the area population at or below 100% of the federal poverty level, the percentage over 65, the infant mortality rate over the last five years, and the ratio of full-time–equivalent physicians per thousand population. The values for each of these variables are assigned a score and these four scores are added to form an Index of Medical Underservice. A cutoff score is then applied to determine eligibility. Populations that do not meet the cutoff score may also apply based on the existence of "barriers to access to or the availability of personal health services" if they have the support of the state's governor and local health officials. Note that these determinations are not based directly on measures of health needs or utilization, but on available secondary data often associated with poor access to services.

The uninsured are a major group of the underserved, making up roughly a sixth of the under-65 population. For the most part they are working members of minorities, Hispanic and black, and young. Although their age makes them a generally healthy population, they also are closed out of preventive medical services. Most states have special Medicaid programs for children with less stringent eligibility requirements that the program for adults, although they often have waiting lists due to lack of funding.

—Curtis P. McLaughlin

See also Access, Medicaid

FURTHER READING

www.bphc.hrsa.dhhs.gov/dsd/muaguidelines
www.cms.gov/medicaid/
www.ebri.org

UNIFORM GUIDELINES ON EMPLOYEE SELECTION PROCEDURES

See Employee Selection and Hiring

UNINSURED PATIENTS

A patient is said to be medically insured when a third party assumes financial responsibility for medical costs associated with the management of the patient. An uninsured patient is one who for various reasons does not have the arrangement of a third party assuming responsibility for medical costs.

In the United States, having health insurance has traditionally been used as a proxy for determining access to health and medical services. Lack of health insurance is therefore considered a significant barrier to medical care. Estimates indicate that about 14% or about 38 million Americans lack health insurance at all times. The major reasons why these individuals lack insurance coverage include excessive cost of the insurance, nonavailability through employment, ineligibility for public assistance, and in some cases making too much money for public assistance and not enough to purchase insurance directly.

Lack of health insurance is more prevalent among low-income persons and those described as poor and near poor. Many uninsured persons are also employed, but earn low wages, are unskilled laborers, service workers, and small business employees. Because of the strong association between availability of health insurance and use of medical services, research shows that uninsured children and adults are less likely to receive preventive care, and to be hospitalized for ambulatory care sensitive conditions—medical conditions that can be managed as outpatient care. People who lack medical insurance also tend to delay entry into care, thereby not benefiting from early intervention for debilitating diseases such as cancer and other metabolic disorders.

Lack of health insurance tends to increase during periods of economic downturn because the majority of Americans, for example, receive their medical insurance through their employers. Even among those who are employed and insured through their employers, companies saddled with higher premium costs are passing the higher costs to employees as higher deductibles and copayments, leading to some employees deciding to withdraw participation in the employer-sponsored programs.

In the United States, social and economic factors influence whether individuals would be uninsured. In a majority of states in the United States, poor adults may be uninsured because such adult individuals have no children. Family status therefore is an important factor in determining whether an adult who would otherwise qualify for insurance assistance would be uninsured. Additionally, the rising health care cost is forcing many people to forgo medical care and medical insurance, even as society in general continues to exhibit an insatiable appetite for new treatments, expensive drugs, and new technology.

Many studies have demonstrated the adverse health consequences of patients who lack health insurance. Among women, diagnostic procedures for various forms of cancer are delayed, leading to higher cancer mortality rates due to diagnosis at later stages of the disease. Among men and women, screening tests for heart diseases, which are important for early diagnosis and treatment, are delayed in the uninsured, leading to higher mortality rates, and when care is available to these patients, the uninsured are less likely to receive aggressive interventions.

In summary, lack of health insurance is a major indicator of poor health outcome among patients. Until the availability of health insurance ceases to be a primary indicator of access to health care services, society will continue to pay a high price for the care of uninsured patients.

—Ken Oranefo Okolo

FURTHER READING

Haas, J. S., & Adler, E. N. (2001). *The causes of vulnerability: Disentangling the effects of race, socioeconomic status and insurance coverage on health.* Washington, DC: Institute of Medicine.

Hadley, J. (2002). *Sicker and poorer: The consequences of being uninsured.* Menlo Park, CA: Kaiser Commission on Medicaid and the Uninsured.

Hoffman, C., & Pohl, M. (2000). *Health insurance coverage in America: 2000 data update.* Menlo Park, CA: Kaiser Commission on Medicaid and the Uninsured.

Sales, J. (2000). *Tennessee: Profile on the uninsured.* Washington, DC: Alliance for Health Reform.

UNION

See Labor Unions

UNRELATED DIVERSIFICATION

See Diversification Strategies

U.S. AGENCY FOR INTERNATIONAL DEVELOPMENT

U.S. Agency for International Development (USAID) is an independent federal government agency established in 1961. The creation of an agency to administer international economic assistance programs was mandated when the Congress passed the Foreign Assistance Act. USAID provides economic and humanitarian assistance to developing countries around the world. The agency's aim is to support U.S. foreign policy interests while improving the lives of the citizens of the developing world.

USAID is headquartered in Washington, D.C., and has field offices in Africa, Asia, Latin America, and eastern Europe. The agency is organized around three functional bureaus that conduct worldwide programs: (a) global health; (b) economic growth, agriculture, and trade; and (c) democracy, conflict resolution, and humanitarian assistance.

USAID PROGRAMS IN GLOBAL HEALTH

USAID's strategy for global health is to stabilize world population and protect human health through programs in maternal and child health, reproductive health, infectious diseases, environmental health, and nutrition. USAID's

Table 1   Summary of USAID Global Health Program Focus, Goals, and Strategies

Focus	Goal	Strategy
Environmental Health	To reduce childhood mortality and morbidity	Improve environmental conditions and reduce exposure to infectious diseases
Population and Reproductive Health	To allow couples to determine the number and spacing of their children	Expand reproductive health care choices
Health Policy and Systems Strengthening	To provide quality health care services at the national and local levels	Improve the capacity of health care systems
HIV/AIDS and Other Infectious Diseases	To reduce the threat of HIV/AIDS, tuberculosis, and malaria	Provide prevention, care, and support for individuals, communities, and nations
Maternal and Child Health	To improve the future for mothers and children	Support prevention and treatment for primary causes of maternal and childhood mortality
Nutrition	To prevent malnutrition in women and children	Support programs in breastfeeding, micronutrients, and food and nutrition policies

Global Health Bureau aims to address these global health challenges by improving the quality, availability, and use of health care services. From 1985 to 2000, USAID provided approximately $13.8 billion in global health assistance to developing countries, making it the largest international donor in this sector in the world. In fiscal year (FY) 2001, estimated funding for the health sector totaled $1,422 million.

USAID supports health programs in more than 60 countries around the world, focusing in countries with the highest potential for worldwide health impact. These countries include Bangladesh, Cambodia, Egypt, India, Indonesia, Jordan, Morocco, Nepal, Pakistan, Philippines, Vietnam, West Bank/Gaza, and Yemen. The agency also supports programs in other countries, which have important health sector activities or because of policy considerations and crisis conditions.

USAID programs focus on improving the quality, availability, and use of health care services in the technical areas listed in Table 1.

USAID collaborates and works in partnership with the governments and indigenous organizations of assisted countries, other U.S. government agencies, private voluntary organizations, universities, and private business to tackle global health challenges. The agency also has relationships with other bilateral donors and private foundations.

—Pinar Senlet

See also Public Health

FURTHER READING

www.usaid.gov

U.S. DEPARTMENT OF HEALTH AND HUMAN SERVICES (DHHS)

The U.S. Department of Health and Human Services (DHHS) is a Cabinet-level department of the federal government. It is the leading agency involved in protecting the health of every American and providing essential human services. A prime focus is on the underserved.

DHHS encompasses more than 300 programs, such as the National Institutes of Health (NIH), Food and Drug Administration (FDA), the Centers for Disease Control and Prevention (CDC) and the Centers for Medicare and Medicaid Services (CMS), formerly the Health Care Financing Administration (HCFA).

DHHS focuses on comprehensive health services for Native Americans, services for older Americans, medical and social research, food and drug safety, services for low-income families, preventing outbreaks of infectious diseases, preventing domestic violence, substance abuse, services for the disabled, and maternal/infant health. It is the largest grant-making agency in the federal government (about 60,000 grants per year). The DHHS annual budget for 2002 was $460 billion, and it employs 65,100 people. DHHS works closely with state, local, and tribal governments and many funded services are provided by area agencies or private sector grantees. The DHHS Medicare program is the nation's largest health insurer (over 900 million claims per year). Programs are administered by 11 operating divisions; eight agencies are in the U.S. Public Health Service and three are human services agencies. DHHS programs also provide for impartial treatment of recipients nationwide and allow for the collection of national health data.

The Social Security Administration (SSA) was once a part of the DHHS. It became an independent federal agency in 1995. The two agencies continue to work closely together.

—Doreen T. Day

FURTHER READING

U.S. Department of Health and Human Services Web site: www.hhs.gov

U.S. DEPARTMENT OF LABOR (DOL)

The U.S. Department of Labor (DOL) is the federal government agency that oversees all issues arising in the workplace and protects the interests of all job seekers, current employees, and retirees. The department seeks to improve working conditions, assists employers in finding potential employees, protects retirement and health care benefits, and tracks changes in employment, wages, and other economic indicators via the Bureau of Labor Statistics. Furthermore, this branch of government also administers and enforces more than 180 federal labor laws. The most well known of these laws include the Fair Labor Standards Act (FLSA), which regulates employees' rights to a minimum hourly wage and overtime pay; the Occupational Safety and Health Act (OSHA), which ensures workers' rights to safe working conditions; the Employee Retirement Income Security Act (ERISA), detailing employees' rights regarding pension and welfare benefit plans; and the Family and Medical Leave Act (FMLA), which requires organizations of over 50 employees to allow employees leave for the birth or adoption of a child or for serious illness to the employee or spouse, child, or parent. Last, the department offers several forms of compliance assistance to organizations to ensure that their policies and practices are in accordance with federal laws. This assistance ranges from training seminars and written brochures to detailed information on the internet available via the department's home page.

—Elizabeth M. Smith

See also Bureau of Labor Statistics; Employee Retirement Income Security Act (ERISA); Employment Law; Family and Medical Leave Act (FMLA); Occupational Safety and Health Act (OSHA)

FURTHER READING

www.dol.gov

U.S. HEALTH CARE SYSTEM

The U.S. health care system is a complex network composed of the thousands of organizations and millions of individuals that deliver health care services to the population of the United States and work with other governments and multinational organizations to protect the public's health domestically and globally. The system provides services across the continuum of care: from health promotion and prevention, to disease or injury diagnosis and treatment, through rehabilitation and maintenance for those suffering from lingering illness or chronic disease. Several characteristics distinguish the U.S. health care system from other segments of the domestic economy and from its counterparts in other industrialized nations.

SIZE

An immediately observable characteristic of the U.S. health care system is its sheer size. The $1.3-trillion industry is a major feature in the U.S. economy, representing 13.2% of the nation's gross domestic product (GDP) in 2000. Current projections call for continuing growth, with the sector reaching 17% of GDP, or $2.8 trillion, by 2011.

COORDINATION

Health care systems of most industrialized nations are governed by a central authority that specifies how the components will link to each other. The health care system in the United States, however, is highly fragmented, having evolved as a result of government policies and economic, technological, and social forces into a loosely linked network of public and private providers, payers, financing arrangements, and payment mechanisms.

SPECIALIZATION AND TECHNOLOGY

The U.S. health care system leads the world in sophisticated medical technology, research, and education as a result of significant investments in scientific and medical research made by the federal government begun following World War II and continuing today. In 2000, funding for the National Institutes of Health (NIH) reached $18.8 billion, up from $770 million in 1967. In addition to the federal government, medical technology firms, such as pharmaceutical, medical device, and biotechnology companies, also invest in research and development. Corporate domestic research and development channeled into health and medicine was an estimated $10.4 billion in 1997.

The explosion in medical knowledge and technology multiplied the amount of information that clinicians had to master in order to be proficient in their field. U.S. medical schools began training physicians with increasing levels of in-depth knowledge in increasingly narrow fields of practice. In 1999, approximately two thirds of all M.D.s in the United States were specialists, with the remaining one third in primary care. This specialist–generalist ratio differs from most other nations, where primary care physicians predominate.

PAYMENT METHODS

Another distinctive feature of the U.S. health care system is the way services are paid for. Most industrialized countries have some variation on a single-payer system, where providers are paid by an agency of the government or insurance pool. In contrast, the United States has a multiple-payer, third-party reimbursement system financed from both private and public sources. Introduction of the insurance or payment entity as a third party to the health service transaction separates the delivery of services from the payment for services, thus interrupting normal market dynamics. Insulated from the full cost of treatment, patients may demand more services than they would if they paid out-of-pocket for their care.

In 2000, 55% of total U.S. national health expenditures (NHE), or $712 billion, came from private sources, principally from employment-based health insurance. Employment-based health insurance is unique to the United States and can be traced to wage and price controls during World War II. Most nonelderly Americans receive their health insurance coverage through their employment. The percentage of the nonelderly population covered this way has held steady over the past decade, increasing only from 65.5% to 66.7% from 1990 to 2000.

In 2000, 45%, or $587 billion, of NHE came from public sources. Of that amount, $412 billion or 70% came from the federal government in the form of payments from Medicare, the federal program providing insurance coverage for the elderly and certain disabled individuals, and from the federal portion of Medicaid, the joint federal–state program to provide coverage for the economically indigent population. State and local governments were responsible for the remaining 30% or $176 billion.

COMPONENTS

The U.S. health care system is characterized by an enormous diversity, complexity, and dynamism of its elements.

Besides differing by types of care delivered across the continuum, system components vary from relatively simple individual physician practices to large, complex organizations such as academic medical centers. Relationships among system components are constantly evolving in response to shifting market dynamics.

Hospital and Inpatient Services

Hospitals and inpatient care have long been a central feature of the U.S. health care services industry. With the development of antibiotics and improved surgical techniques and anesthesia in the mid-20th century, the hospital became the hub for the practice of medicine, earning its designation as "the physician's workshop." Hospital care accounted for $412.1 billion, or 32% of NHE, in 2000, representing the largest category of health care spending.

Although for-profit, investor-owned hospital organizations have generated much attention since their rise in the 1970s, ownership status of community hospitals has remained fairly constant. About 70% are not-for-profit, 13% are investor owned, with the remainder owned by state and local governments.

A wave of hospital closures, mergers, and consolidations swept the industry in the 1990s, reducing the number of acute care facilities from a peak of around 7200 in the 1970s to 5160 in 2000. Even more dramatic has been the reduction in bed capacity, falling from a 1975 high of 6.79 beds per 1000 people to 3.49 beds per 1000 people in 2000, a decline of nearly 50%.

Several factors have driven the contraction of inpatient capacity. First, because inpatient services are among the most expensive care to provide, inpatient care has been the target of much cost containment activity. The introduction of the Medicare prospective payment system and managed care techniques, such as preauthorization and utilization review, has reduced hospitalizations and lengths of stays dramatically. Second, clinical factors are also driving health care delivery away from the inpatient setting. Less invasive surgery techniques, faster-resolving anesthesia, and improved pharmaceuticals permit procedures and treatments once requiring overnight hospital stays now to be done on an outpatient basis. Hospital organizations have responded to the decline of inpatient care by adding outpatient departments or redefining themselves as hubs of integrated delivery systems, which provide services across the continuum of care.

Ambulatory and Outpatient Services

Concurrent with the contraction in inpatient services has been the explosion of growth in the outpatient sector, as financial incentives and clinical advances drive treatment into ambulatory settings. Outpatient services encompass care not requiring an overnight stay in a hospital, including visits to physician offices, urgent care centers, hospital outpatient and emergency departments, and ambulatory surgery centers. Between 1995 and 1998 alone, visits to physician offices and hospital outpatient and emergency departments increased 17% from 861 million to just over 1 billion visits. Private physician office visits are the core of outpatient care in the United States, accounting for an estimated 756.7 million visits compared to an estimated 84.6 million visits to hospital outpatient and emergency departments.

Postacute and Long-Term Care

With the aging of the U.S. population, the growing predominance of chronic illness, and the search for less costly delivery settings, postacute and long-term health care services are increasingly important. Expenditures for nursing homes and home health care have grown as a percentage of NHE from 8% or $48.9 billion in 1988, to 13.2% or $171.5 billion in 2000.

Nursing homes are the principal institutions for long-term care delivery. In 2000, there were 17 thousand federally qualified nursing homes in the United States. Medicaid is the primary payer for nursing home services, accounting for 68% of nursing home patients in 1999. Although most long-term care users are over 65 year of age, Medicare covers only a small percentage of nursing home services, accounting for 9% of patients in 1999. In contrast to hospitals, two thirds of all of nursing homes are under private, for-profit ownership.

Expenditures for home health care have risen from $2.4 billion of NHE in 1980, to $32.4 billion in 2000, a 13-fold increase. The growth in the number of home health care agencies was primarily among hospital-based and freestanding proprietary agencies, which account for 30% and 40% respectively of total Medicare-certified agencies. Consumer out-of-pocket payments account for the largest category of home health payments, representing 28% of home health care expenditures in 2000. Medicare is the largest single payer, accounting for 26%.

As the number of Americans requiring long-term care services has grown, the industry has responded with innovative approaches to long-term care. Adult day care programs offer community-based day care as an alternative to institutionalization. Assisted living facilities provide residents support for activities of daily living while allowing them to maintain independence. Continuing care retirement communities enable residents to transition from independent to assisted living, and then to skilled nursing facilities as their health needs change.

PHYSICIANS AND THE HEALTH CARE WORKFORCE

Physicians and clinical services are second only to hospitals in terms of total national health expenditures. In 2000, spending for physicians and clinical services accounted for 22% or $286 billion of NHE. The organization of medical practice in America is changing as physicians respond to forces in the health care marketplace, primarily the need for increased leverage in negotiations with managed care plans. The change is evidenced by the dramatic growth in the number of medical group practices, which approximately doubled during the period between 1980 and 1995. Prior to the 1950s, most physicians were in solo practice. By 1999, one third of physicians practiced in medical groups with just a quarter remaining in solo practice. Another facet of changing practice patterns is the growth in the number physicians who are salaried employees, rising from 25% in 1983 to 41% in 1999.

Delivering health services is a labor-intensive activity, and health care is among the most significant employment sectors in the nation. In 2001, about 1 in 10 Americans was employed in the health care industry in jobs ranging from unskilled support personnel to highly trained physician specialists. Although cost containment efforts have slowed growth in the health care workforce somewhat over the past several years, the growth rate is predicted to increase as the American baby boom generation retires, with nursing and home health aides leading the expansion.

MANAGED CARE

In the face of out-of-control health care benefit costs that threatened their global competitiveness, large American employers turned to managed care as a remedy for the ills of the indemnity health insurance. By linking the delivery and financing of health care services, managed care seeks to reverse the incentives of fee-for-service indemnity insurance that favor higher utilization.

From its modern beginnings with the 1973 federal HMO act, managed care has grown to become the dominant form of coverage for employment-based health insurance. By 2001, 93% of workers were enrolled in some form of managed care health plan, compared to 17% in 1988.

Many of managed care's cost-saving practices, such as limited provider networks, controlled access to specialists, and preauthorization requirements are antithetical to American values of individualism and choice, resulting in what has been termed the "managed care backlash." As a result of the backlash, much of the growth in managed care has been among the less tightly managed forms such as preferred provider organization (PPO) and point-of-service (POS) plans rather than the more tightly managed health maintenance organization (HMO) plans.

PUBLIC HEALTH

In the United States, personal health care services are delivered predominantly in the private sector, whereas public health activities are conducted primarily by the federal, state, and local governments. Despite the potential population-wide benefits from public health promotion and prevention activities, funding priorities in the United States have favored curative care. In 2000, only $44.2 billion, or 3.4% of the $1.3 trillion NHE, flowed into government public health activities. Times of crisis in the United States historically have brought additional resources to the public health sector. For example, the September 11, 2001, terrorist attacks brought substantial new resources into public health programs. Whether this response signals a permanent reallocation of resources into public health activities remains to be seen.

ISSUES OF COST, QUALITY, AND ACCESS

Despite its leadership in high-tech medicine, the U.S. health care system has suffered problems of cost, quality, and access. Along with the benefits of highly sophisticated specialized medicine have come spiraling costs, complexity, and fragmentation. Although the United States leads the world in the amount spent per capita on health care, it ranks 15th among member nations in the 1997 World Health Organization index of overall health system attainment, a composite index based on levels and distribution of health and health system responsiveness, and on fairness of financial contribution.

In contrast to other industrial nations whose health systems aspire to make health care universally available to all citizens, in the United States access to care is primarily predicated on insurance coverage. Although the absolute number of uninsured Americans declined during the economic boom of the 1990s, the percentage of Americans without health insurance remained steady at about 17% from 1994 through 2000. In 2001, 41 million Americans reported not getting or delaying needed medical care, with cost being the most commonly reported barrier to care. The combination of a slowing economy and rising provider costs passed along as double-digit increases in health insurance premiums will likely exacerbate access problems.

—Julia A. Hughes

See also Ambulatory Care, Health Insurance, Hospitals, Long-Term Care, Managed Care Organization, Managed Care Plans, Medicaid, National Health Expenditures (NHEs), National Institutes of Health (NIH)

FURTHER READING

Anderson, G., & Hussey, P. S. (2001). Comparing Health System Performance in OECD Countries. *Health Affairs, 20*(3), 219–232.

Heffler, S., Smith, S., Won, G., Clemens, M. K., Keehan, S., & Zezza, M. (2002, March–April). Health Spending Projections for 2001–2011: The Latest Outlook. *Health Affairs, 21*(2), 207–218.

Kaiser Family Foundation. (2002, May). *Trends and Indicators in the Changing Health Care Marketplace, 2002.* Menlo Park, CA: Chartbook.

Levit, K., Smith, C., Cowan, C., Lazenby, H., & Martin, A. (2002, January–February). Inflation spurs health spending in 2000. *Health Affairs, 21*(1), 172–181.

National Center for Health Statistics. (2001, August). *Health, United States, 2001.* Bethesda, MD: Centers for Disease Control and Prevention, Department of Health and Human Services.

Sultz, H. A., & Young, K. M. (2001). *Health care USA: Understanding its organization and delivery.* Gaithersburg, MD: Aspen.

World Health Organization. (2000). *World Health Report 2000–Health systems: Improving performance.* Geneva: Author.

www.aha.org/resource/newpage.asp

Zinner, D. (2001, September–October). Medical R & D at the turn of the millennium. *Health Affairs, 20*(5), 202–209.

UTILIZATION REVIEW

Utilization review represents a quality assurance function with the primary purpose to promote and assure the most efficient utilization of hospital services and facilities. In addition, identification of problems in health care practices, trending information, and working toward improvements are major utilization functions. Utilization review must be performed with discretion, fairness, and respect. Any and all reviews are done regardless of payment source to assure that the same standard is applied throughout the process. Often criteria are used to guide appropriate practice and to assure application is uniform. Reviews are conducted on a concurrent and, at times, on a retrospective basis. The most effective process is concurrent review for the admission and continued stay. During these activities, the underutilization and, in some cases, overutilization of services can be identified and corrected.

Criteria that are used need to be tested and validated for adequate utilization review. InterQual is a commonly used criteria set for the inpatient setting and outpatient setting. InterQual offers patient-specific criteria that encourages the reviewer to look at the severity of illness (SI) and the intensity of services (IS) as part of the review process. This proprietary company, McKesson, has a variety of other products to identify alternate level of care (ALC), length of stay (LOS), and precertification needs for procedures, durable medical equipment (DME), and imaging. This is a major source for substantiation for admission and continued stay and is used by many managed care companies as well as the peer review organizations (PROs).

Typically, the utilization review nurse is a registered nurse with three to five years clinical experience. This experience assists the nurse to review the medical record and speak to the attending physician with some knowledge of disease states and comorbid states. Certification for the utilization review nurse is an important credential. To be considered to take the exam, the nurse must have three years direct utilization review experience. Certification assures the expertise of the reviewer.

The medical record is the primary source for utilization review activities; however, conversations with the medical team may assist in completing the entire picture of what is happening with the patient on a given day. The physician and nurse are asked to document the care rendered, the plan of care anticipated, and the outcome(s) of the care given to support the need for both the admission and the continued stay. The old adage of "If it is not written, it is not done" is aptly applied in utilization review activities.

The utilization review activities assist the practitioner in making essential decisions not only about the need for the care but also in what setting the care should take place.

Data are usually collected about practices and are provided to the practitioner for consideration and action.

—Edna Lee Kucera

FURTHER READING

www.cms.org
www.ipro.org

VALUE CHAIN FOR HEALTH CARE

The value chain concept was developed by Michael Porter of the Harvard Business School in his *Competitive Advantage: Creating and Sustaining Superior Performance,* published in 1985. The value chain is a way of viewing a business firm, hospital, or any other type of organization in terms of value-adding opportunities.

The value chain is composed of two major components, primary activities and support activities. Primary activities are those activities that are involved in getting resources and customers into the organization, transforming the resources into products or providing services, marketing, and distribution. Porter called the collection of activities devoted to getting resources and customers into the system *inbound logistics* and included things such as production scheduling and the receipt of inputs into the manufacturing process. The manufacturing and service delivery processes were labeled *operations,* and *sales and marketing activities* are designed to promote products and services; *outbound logistics* include those activities that distribute the products to the wholesalers, retailers, and so on.

Support activities are designed to aid the primary activities in transforming resources or providing services. Support activities include such things as the organization's infrastructure (accounting and purchasing systems, organization structure, and so on), information technology, and human resource system.

VALUE CHAIN AND HEALTH CARE

The conventional value chain is applicable, in principle, to almost any type of organization. However, it best describes the stereotypical business and manufacturing firm. For this reason, some find it difficult to apply the value chain concept to service-oriented and, specifically, to health care organizations. For this reason, some modifications have been suggested that make the value chain concept more directly applicable to health care organizations.

One of the most important changes that has been proposed in the value chain to make it more applicable to health care organizations has to do with the primary activities. Analysts generally agree that the primary places where value can be added in health care organizations is before service delivery, at the point of service delivery, and after the health care service has been delivered. In this case, the primary activities are reduced to three: preservice, point-of-service, and postservice.

In health care organizations, value can be added prior to service delivery by efficient appointment systems, convenient parking facilities, appropriate signage, and similar measures. At the point of service, patient-friendly providers, clean and well-designed medical facilities, and so on can add value to the patient–provider encounter. After service, value-adding activities include follow-up telephone calls, understandable and self-explanatory invoices for services, and related activities. Support activities in health care organizations include infrastructure items such as modern medical technologies, appropriate organization structures, information support systems, and an organizational culture that promotes and encourages a patient orientation.

USING THE VALUE CHAIN

Health care organizations can use the value chain in a variety of ways. For example, the value chain can be a useful tool in helping managers and employees understand the importance of value and value-adding behaviors. In an industry such as health care, value is a critically important concept. Because of third-party payers and the importance of a person's health, many consumers of health care services are not extremely price sensitive. However, most consumers are value sensitive. People want and need to feel they are receiving high value for their health care expenditures. The value chain is a useful way of demonstrating where and how value can be added in health care organizations.

The value chain can also be used as an aid in internal environmental analysis. Rather than thinking of the hospital or health clinic in terms of its subsystems such as clinical operations, finance and administration, information systems, human resources, and so on, the value system can be used as a way to focus the search for organizational strengths and weaknesses. For example, in assessing the internal environment, strengths and weaknesses can be developed relative to preservice, point-of-service, and post-service as well as with regard to the various support activities. These value-adding strengths and weaknesses can then be evaluated in terms of their potential for obtaining a competitive advantage of experiencing a competitive disadvantage.

A final important implication of the value chain has to do with the linkages between and among various value adding activities. By using systems thinking and breaking the total system of the value chain into its component parts, we can focus more on each area where value can be added. However, care should be taken not to think only of discrete activities. Some of the greatest opportunities for adding value are obtained from linking activities. For example, linking operations and marketing, information technology and point-of-service, or organizational culture and postservice follow-up can provide important synergies that can provide unique competitive advantages.

—W. Jack Duncan

See also Competitive Advantage, Internal Environmental Analysis, SWOT (Strength-Weakness-Opportunity-Threat) Analysis

FURTHER READING

Duncan, W. J., Ginter, P. M., & Swayne, L. E. (1998). Competitive advantage and internal organizational assessment. *Academy of Management Executive, 12*(3), 6–16.

Porter, M. E. (1985). *Competitive advantage: Creating and sustaining superior performance.* New York: Free Press.

VALUES (GUIDING PRINCIPLES)

Values or guiding principles are those beliefs or attitudes held by an organization that shape its internal operating culture (employees) and its response to its customers, suppliers, buyers, and other external constituencies. Organizational values or guiding principles often are manifested in written documents such as codes of behavior or codes of ethics. Patterns of behavior by individuals or groups within the organization also exemplify values that are understood to exist with or without documented statements.

In health care organizations, values and ethical statements are often prescribed through the professional licensure required for health care providers such as physicians and nurses. An example is found in the American Nursing Association's code. This document forms a code of ethics, which describes beliefs that guide individual behaviors and decision making in the nursing profession. Although individual commitment to professionally explicit values form the basis for individual participation in organizational values, the concept of organizational values or guiding principles is the broad-based expectation of the behaviors, decisions, actions, and expected performance of all employees that in total reflect the organization as a whole.

Other terms for values or guiding principles in an organization are creed, philosophy, core values, commitment to quality, and so forth. Values in an organization concern the philosophy of work that accomplishes the organization's mission and the nature, rights, and expected behaviors of those providing the product or service and the customers, clients, or patients being served. Value statements or statements of shared values may be found as part of the mission and vision statements in many organizations.

UNDERSTANDING AND COMMUNICATING ORGANIZATIONAL VALUES

Organizational values are transmitted through formal and informal channels of communication. Formal channels include, in written form, booklets, banners, quotes, logos, business cards, slogans, posters, press releases, and articles. Executives in the organization use organizational value statements in speeches, employee "pep talks," employee town meetings, and performance evaluations. Employees state organizational values through actions, comments, conversations, stories, decisions, memos, and letters. Whether formally documented or informally understood, all organizations have a set of working values that guide individual activities within the organization and that shape organizational reputation.

USING ORGANIZATIONAL VALUES EFFECTIVELY

Excellent organizations make use of statements of shared values in numerous ways:

- To set expectations for customers or clients that the organization values quality in its service and products or that it places value on its service to its customers or clients

- As a clear message of the value the organization places on the importance of its employees
- As a means to better define key components of its mission statement
- As a framework for individual decision making within the organization
- To delineate boundaries of behaviors of executives and employees
- To form the basis for the corporate culture
- To articulate the level of social responsibility or organizational citizenship the organization embraces, such as commitment to healthy children
- To articulate its priorities as related to social issues, such as a clean environment

DEVELOPING AND MAINTAINING ORGANIZATIONAL VALUES (GUIDING PRINCIPLES)

In the past decade health care organizations have sought to create a new vision for the performance and delivery of the services provided to health care recipients. Coupled with a new vision is the need for a new set of core values or guiding principles. However, the adoption of cultural values in an organization is a slow process frequently taking years. This is in part due to the changing mores of society in which organizational personnel live and operate. Capturing the sagas, stories, and myths about the perception of existing values provides the first step. Organizational values may not be blatantly obvious but rather are imbedded in the informal communications and actions of the organization's employees. Building on existing values that are consistent with the new vision, the organization can restate old values under the new paradigm. This method can help hasten the acceptance of new values.

Developing new guiding principles for organizational behaviors demands that the principles be related to the mission and vision of the organization. The new values or guiding principles can be developed by a senior management team or a team comprised of cross-functional representatives. The imperative is not who develops the principles but rather the pace at which they will be accepted. The pace can only be accelerated by the continuous reinforcement of top leaders who not only adopt the principles but also enact them in tangible, personal ways that reinforce the importance and executive commitment to the newly shared values.

Although the focus here has been on creating new sustainable values that reinforce organizational mission, organizations often develop value systems that work against the overall good of the organization. These attitudes and beliefs perpetuate negative work ethics and ultimately undermine organizational reputation. If a health care facility develops a bad reputation based on its perceived value structure, management must find the means to create immediate change and can ill afford the usual slow-paced adaptation of a new organizational culture. Swift, decisive action must exaggerate the new value system so that managers, employees, customers, clients, suppliers, buyers, and others recognize that the organization has changed. The new value code must be exemplified frequently and dramatically to gain attention. Proliferation of communication methods enhances this process.

Values, value statements, guiding principles, statements of creed and philosophy, and codes of ethics all help to define and shape the organizational culture. The reinforcement of the written word must come through the actions, behaviors, and decisions of all employees. If an organizational value system is truly engrained in the organization's culture, individual contributors will not have to reflect on the appropriate action based on what the organization's value system would dictate. They can act with knowledge that their decision will be received in the organization system of values. The actions of senior executives will magnify both the positive and negative values identified throughout the organization. Therefore, organizational values are only as strong as the senior executive group exemplifies them through actions and words.

—Rebecca I. Porterfield

See also Culture, Ethical Issues, Mission, Organizational Change, Strategic Planning

FURTHER READING

Edge, R. S., & Groves, J. R. (1994). *The ethics of healthcare: A guide for clinical practice*. Albany, NY: Delmar.

Keeney, R. L. (1992). *Value-focused thinking: A path to creative decision-making*. Cambridge, MA: Harvard University Press.

Kozier, B., Erb, G., & Blais, K. (1997). *Professional nursing practice: Concepts and perspectives*. Menlo Park, CA: Addison-Wesley.

Rokeach, M. (1972). *Beliefs, attitudes and values: A theory of organization and change*. San Francisco: Jossey-Bass.

Shi, L., & Singh, D. A. (2001). *Delivering health care in America: A systems approach*. Gaithersburg, MD: Aspen.

VARIABILITY OF SERVICES

See Services

VENTURE CAPITAL INVESTMENT

Venture capital investment typically means the process and activity by which private equity is provided by a venture capital firm to an organization or venture that is not publicly traded (not registered with the Securities and Exchange Commission and not openly traded via the New York Stock Exchange, American Stock Exchange, NASDAQ, and so on). Private equity can take several forms, including preferred stock or loans. A venture capital firm is generally regarded as a private independent organization that is professionally managed. The ventures that seek venture capital investment are in various stages of development from entities that have not been incorporated to older, private firms that need additional funding to support growth initiatives.

Many of these ventures are limited in their ability to gain access to capital; thus venture capital most often comes at a substantial premium. Despite this high cost, many ventures have flourished. Within health care, venture capital investment has assisted in the development of new and established firms in the sectors of medical devices, biotechnology, pharmaceuticals, nursing homes, hospitals, physician practice management companies, and pharmacy benefit management companies, among others. Venture capital investment has played a crucial role in the development of the health care industry.

VENTURE CAPITAL FIRM ACTIVITY

Venture capital firm activity can be segmented into five stages: origination, screening, evaluation, structuring, and postinvestment activity. Origination is the process by which venture capital firms become aware of different ventures. Scanning for new opportunities characterizes this stage. Screening involves the initial sorting of identified opportunities for investment. The venture capital firm relies heavily on its network of contacts to effectively pursue origination and scanning activities.

As many of the potential opportunities represent ventures without prior histories, the evaluation of potential investments relies heavily on the venture capital firm's ability to assess both the market for the venture's products or services, and the venture's management ability. Assessment is critical to the venture capital firm's future success. To lessen the risk, venture capital firms will often seek other venture capital firms as investors and coassessors.

If the venture is assessed positively, the next activity is structuring the business arrangement. Within this stage the arrangement between the venture and venture capital firm is memorialized (the parties enter into a contractual arrangement), and unlike other providers (such as commercial banks offering loans) of capital, venture capital investment is active investment. Typical attributes of this arrangement include specification of the equity stake in the venture by the venture capital firm, designation of board seats, covenants to limit the venture's expenditures (including management's salaries), circumstances under which the

venture capital firm may take control of the venture, and restrictions on the acquisition of additional capital. This sets forth the conditions under which both parties can act during the fifth stage.

The fifth stage is postinvestment. Many venture capital firms participate as board members and offer advice with respect to strategy, management, and business development. The venture capital firms are generally organized under a general partnership model. Under this model, the venture capital firm creates a subsidiary, usually in the form of a limited liability partnership (LLP) or limited liability corporation. The venture capital firm acts as the general partner (or manager) of this subsidiary. It is into this subsidiary that individual or institutional investors provide venture capital.

Individual or institutional investors are the limited partners of the subsidiary and have limited roles, rights, and liabilities. It is the limited partners that provide the vast majority of the funds available for venture capital investment, with the venture capital firms themselves providing little of the capital that is to be invested. In addition, the venture capital firm or general partners are responsible for investing and managing the funds of the LLP and receive a management fee for this activity. The funds from the LLP may be invested in one or more ventures. In this respect, venture capital investment is similar to mutual fund investment in which individuals or institutional investors invest in a pooled fund that invests in multiple entities.

There are several differences between venture capital investment and mutual fund investment. Venture capital investment is generally viewed as being a riskier investment, as these investments are in entities that are in various stages of organization and operation. Venture capital involves investing in firms that typically do not have common stock; thus, its investment may be in the form of a loan or preferred stock. The LLP has a limited, preset life span. Liquidation of its funds is often set at 10 years.

VENTURE CAPITAL FOCUS

To help with the difficulties surrounding the five venture capital firm activities, many venture capitalists also specialize. They choose an area of expertise, such as health care, and focus their activities in this area. In addition, venture capital investment is often staged. Thus, the venture receiving financing from a venture capitalist know that they only have a certain amount of capital available to meet predefined goals. This limiting of funds acts to focus the activities of those receiving venture capital, as venture capitalists typically reserve the right to abandon the investment, thus denying the venture needed future capital.

Because the LLPs have limited life spans, the goal for many LLPs is to convert the ventures from privately financed entities to publicly traded firms via initial public offerings. At this point, many LLPs receive common stock or cash in exchange for their investment. These receipts are then disbursed to the limited partners with the LLP ending its operation with the dispersal of all funds. Through the process of venture capital investment, many health care firms have access to not only capital but also management expertise. Thus venture capital investment provides resources for ventures in various stages of development that are otherwise unavailable to these ventures.

David R. Williams

See also Initial Public Offerings

FURTHER READING

Barry, C. B., Muscarella, C. J., Peavy, J. W., & Vetsuypens, M. R. (1990). The role of venture capital in the creation of public companies. *Journal of Financial Economics, 27,* 447–471.

Ginter, P. M., Swayne, L. E., & Duncan, W. J. (2002). *Strategic management of health care organizations.* Oxford, UK: Blackwell Business.

Sahlman, W. A. (1990). The structure and governance of venture-capital organizations. *Journal of Financial Economics, 27,* 473–521.

Tyebjee, T. T., & Bruno, A. V. (1984). A model of venture capitalist investment activity. *Management Science, 30*(3), 105–106.

VERTICAL INTEGRATION

Complete vertical integration is the operation of the organization across an entire spectrum of activities ranging from the source of raw materials at one end of the spectrum, through operations, to retailing to the end-use consumer at the other end of the spectrum. Thus, there are two opposite ends of the vertical integration spectrum. The term *backward vertical* or *upstream integration* refers to operation near the stage of raw materials in the industry. The term *forward vertical* or *downstream integration* refers to operation near to retailing the product or service.

Some organizations seek upstream activities to protect a source of supply or to insulate the parent firm from price fluctuations in the raw material. A good example of backward or upstream vertical integration to protect a source of supply was the practice of many hospitals in the mid 1990s of buying the practices of physicians. By buying those practices, the hospitals were acquiring a necessary input in the health care process, namely physicians, and protecting the referral of patients.

Other organizations seek forward vertical integration so that the consumer will identify with the parent organization and demand its product by name. A good example of forward or downstream vertical integration was the practice of many pharmaceutical companies to advertise prescription drugs by name directly to consumers (patients) in the media with the identity of the pharmaceutical companies. The objective was to cause patients to demand prescriptions from their physicians for the drugs.

Increasing vertical integration is a form of diversification. Becoming more integrated in addition to one's current position spreads risk and leads to areas wherein management has limited competence. Highly vertically integrated organizations report lower profitability than others. Apparently, the diversification activities required of increased vertical integration detract attention and resources from the firm's core of distinctive competence. This yields lower profitability, just as unrelated horizontal diversification does.

—Michael J. Stahl

See also Acquisition, Diversification, Divestiture, Merger

FURTHER READING

Ginter, P. M., Swayne, L. M., & Duncan, W. J. (1998). *Strategic management of health care organizations.* Malden, MA: Blackwell.

Harrison, J., Hall, E., & Caldwell, L. (1990, Spring). Assessing strategy relatedness in highly diversified firms. *Journal of Business Strategies, 7,* 34–46.

Porter, M. E. (1987, May–June). From competitive advantage to corporate strategy. *Harvard Business Review, 65,* 43.

Stahl, M., & Grigsby, D. (1997). *Strategic management* (Chapter 5). Oxford, UK: Blackwell.

VICARIOUS LIABILITY

You didn't do it, but your employee did. Sorry, you are liable. Such is vicarious liability. Strictly defined, vicarious liability is the imposition of responsibility on one party for the negligence or intentional tort (an action that injures) of another.

It is easiest to appreciate the vicarious liability standard in the case of an employee who is authorized by the employer to perform an act and who, in the course of his or her employment, negligently injures another person. The injury would not have occurred but for the negligence of the employee, which would not have occurred but for his or her employment. Vicarious liability ties the employer to the actions of the employee relative to the following:

- The degree of control the employer has over the actions of the employee
- The benefit to the employer of the actions of the employee

- The degree of power deferred to the employee by the employer and the vulnerability of the victim
- The degree of notice which the employer had or should have had relative to the negligent or intentional actions of the employee
- The degree of oversight reasonably required of an employer in the circumstances of the employer–employee relationship

Efforts to prevent vicarious liability in the health field should be concentrated in the areas of sexual harassment, billing and collections, and compliance with government regulations. The classic scenario is the hospital or physician using a billing service. Progress notes are forwarded to the service, which "appropriately" codes for the level of care of each visit. If overcharging occurs, regulators will look to the provider and not to the billing agent for reimbursement of overcharges, and any penalties that result from improper billing will be directed to the provider. The provider must maintain close review of all agents representing its financial interests and follow a strict compliance policy with periodic reviews to assure compliance with governmental regulations.

Automotive accidents and injuries are common cases where vicarious liability attaches to employers. If an employee is driving during working hours or on behalf of an employer, then the employer will be held liable for accidents caused by the employee. Hospitals and physician employers are often subject to the vicarious liability of sexual harassment cases. As such, every employer should have and actively maintain a sexual harassment policy. An incident in which an employee sexually harasses another employee or a patient must be addressed immediately. For employees who feel they are subject to sexual harassment, a means to seek redress should be in place. Any complaint should be taken seriously and immediately investigated. If it is determined that the potential for repeated harassment exists, then the offending employee should be educated, monitored, reprimanded, and possibly terminated.

Suffice it to say, all actions of employees should be known to and authorized by the employer. An employer cannot claim ignorance as a defense when it is reasonable and possible to create and adhere to compliance policies.

—Kenneth Steiner and Stuart Hochron

VIRTUAL PRIVATE NETWORK (VPN)

A virtual private network uses secure paths, often called *tunnels,* to create a private network environment inside of public networks such as the Internet. Until the creation of VPNs, companies had to either lease dedicated lines or build and maintain their own lines to confidentially communicate information with business partners and associates. VPNs accomplish the same goal as private networks, but at a fraction of the cost.

Simply put, tunneling is the process of preparing a message to be sent, encapsulating the message, and then sending it over the common carrier network. The preparation process uses a special method called a *passenger protocol,* the encapsulation process uses an *encapsulation protocol,* and the sending process uses a *carrier protocol* common to that network. For example, TCP/IP is a common carrier protocol for the Internet.

VPNs are commonly used in businesses today to support confidential sharing of information through extranets and intranets and trusted mobile users and business affiliates. Consequently, the three most common types of VPNs are called remote access, or access, intranet based, and extranet based.

There are two common methods for configuring access VPNs. The first, the *client-initiated* method, requires the remote user to establish an encrypted tunnel from its machine, through the network and into the corporate network. This type of VPN provides a high level of data security from the client computer to the corporate network, but users need to take measures to ensure that remote equipment is protected. For example, notebook computers equipped with tunneling software should at the very least be password protected and should never be left on and unattended.

The second type of access VPN, called a *network access server VPN,* requires remote users to dial into a third party service provider, which in turn initiates a secure connection to the corporate network. The main advantage of this method is that the service provider can authenticate a user before giving it access to the corporate network. The disadvantage is that the data are only encrypted from the service provider to the corporate gateway.

Companies with two or more locations or branches often need to share information. Intranet-based VPNs are used to create secure connections among different corporate locations. Similarly, extranet-based VPNs are used to create secure communications channels between two or more business partners.

Benefits of VPNs include

- Improved security
- Assurance of data reliability
- Improved productivity via secure remote connectivity
- Relatively inexpensive mechanism for global networking
- Cost effectiveness over traditional wide area network configurations
- Scalability—it is much easier to add more users to a VPN than to a leased line

Additional investments that may be required to ensure proper functionality of a VPN include firewalls, dedicated VPN servers, network access servers, and client software for each remote user. Some companies, such as Cisco, offer complete turnkey solutions as an option for companies interested in VPNs.

VPNs can play a vital role in protecting confidential information including data, voice, and video that is commonly exchanged among hospitals, physician offices, insurance companies, pharmaceutical companies, and other health care-related organizations.

—Amy W. Ray

See also Electronic Commerce, Encryption, HIPAA

FURTHER READING

Busby, M. (2000). *Demystifying virtual private networks.* Wordware.

Yuan, R., & Strayer, W. T. (2001). *Virtual private networks: Technologies and solutions.* Reading, MA: Addison-Wesley.

VISION

The *vision* for an organization is generally reflected in a statement of direction and future for the organization. The vision statement reflects organizational aspiration, whereas the organization's mission statement reflects the organization's purpose. The gap between the mission statement (what we are) and the vision statement (what do we aspire to be) provides the basis for the setting of goals and objectives to move the organization from the mission to its vision.

The vision statement, in its best form, provides an energizing force around which the organization's executives, employees, stakeholders, and financial analysts rally.

The statement typically is brief, consisting of one or two sentences. A well-conceived, effective vision statement will

- Convey a broad sense of direction that unifies organizational direction
- Aid in changing organizational direction and the rationale for redirection when internal resistance exists
- Provide all levels within the organization a clear understanding of where the organization's future lies
- Provide executives with an opportunity for a clear, consistent compass for resource justification and allocation
- Rally and energize employees and stakeholders
- Set an expectation of energy and action
- Provide confidence in the organizational leaders to set direction

When the organizational leader communicates the organization's vision, it sends a signal throughout the organization that change is happening. The vision may serve as a catalyst for new thinking and at the same time may ferret out internal resistance to change. The vision for the organization's future, by definition, will necessitate the rethinking of resource alignment to accomplish the vision.

The vision statement is frequently considered the "drumbeat" of the organization. It is clear, consistent, resonant, and often repeated. The vision statement frequently is written as a logo or catchy phrase that captures the internal and external public. It is the "march" of the organization providing a cadence and direction for the organization's future purpose. The vision often sets a tone for organizational pride, thus stimulating ideas and a new work ethic. The drumbeat must be repeated often and reinforced at every opportunity to ensure organizational acceptance and commitment.

DEVELOPING AND COMMUNICATING THE VISION STATEMENT

A vision statement is not just plucked from the air. Rather, it is the result of thoughtful analysis and assessment of the environment in which the organization exists. Technology, regulation, economics, competition, politics, demographics, and the social environment are just a few of the factors that mold and change the dynamics in which an organization operates (the external environment). Some of these factors will provide opportunities for the organization; others pose threats to the organization's viability. The tone and direction of the vision statement is developed by the analysis of the industry's driving forces and the possible directions available to the organization as a result of this analysis.

A vision statement must be perceived as achievable. It is not essential that all strategies be known when the vision statement is developed; however, the vision must be viewed as possible. Slogans and platitudes without substance will not engender the outcomes sought through an appropriate vision statement. Over time the articulated vision would be viewed as a dream rather than a potential reality. The organization will become disenfranchised to future change. Thus it is important to frequently communicate successful progression toward accomplishing the vision.

Finding the most effective means of communicating the vision statement is as critical as its development. The statement should create a visual image that evokes excitement and pride. Ideally it should be simple enough to be remembered yet complex enough to establish commitment. The vision should be transmitted through media that gets the attention of the organization. Most important, the highest-ranking executive must consistently and clearly articulate the vision in every forum in which he or she participates.

The vision must always be recognized as coming from the top of the organization.

VISION STATEMENTS AND STRATEGIC PLANNING

Unlike mission statements, which are frequently developed down to the department level, vision statements are generally developed for the organization as a whole. The exception to this is for those very large multinational conglomerates that have unrelated business units. The multinationals may have a strategic vision for the corporation as a whole and one for each of the strategic business units, depending on the level of diversity among the units.

As the vision directionally sets the purpose for change and the mission statement focuses on the existing purpose, the gap between these two statements necessitates goals, objectives, and strategies to move the organization from its mission to its vision. The external environmental analysis used to develop the vision and the internal assessment of the organization's strengths and weaknesses supporting its mission must converge. This convergence effectively links internal resources with external factors essential to accomplish the vision and is reflected through the strategic plan at the corporate level.

The vision statement, broadly defined, sets the direction, whereas the strategic plan charts the course. As an example, if a local hospital sets a vision to become a regional hub, the strategic plan will articulate the steps (both short term and long term) to accomplish the vision.

VISION STATEMENTS IN HEALTH CARE

The health care industry has, over the past decade and into the foreseeable future, been highly affected by government regulation, population demographics, and political legislation. These factors have required health care providers to reassess who they are and the services they will deliver. Some organizations have narrowed their scope of operations in favor of specialized services, while others have expanded their scope of operations through acquisition and other strategies to large and specialized population segments. Each strategy, whether product based or customer based, requires changes in operations. It is critical, especially in times of dynamic environmental shifts, to develop and articulate a new strategic vision. By communicating the vision, confidence is gained that senior management is willing and ready to meet new challenges, that employees do not have to be worried about changes ahead, and that stakeholders (the community, the customers, the stockholders) are assured that the organization understands its industry and can provide and deliver the services or product to meet these challenges.

—Rebecca I. Porterfield

See also Leadership, Mission, Organizational Change, Strategic Planning

FURTHER READING

Brill, P. L., & Worth, R. (1997). *The four levers of corporate change.* New York: AMACOM.

Collins, J., & Porras, J. I. (1996, September–October). Building your company's vision. *Harvard Business Review, 74*(5), 70–82.

Horak, B. J. (1997). *Strategic planning in healthcare: Building a quality-based plan step by step.* New York: Quality Resources.

Lipton, M. (1996, Summer). Demystifying the development of an organizational vision. *Sloan Management Review, 36,* 83–92.

VISITING NURSES ASSOCIATION

In 1983, the Visiting Nurse Associations of America (VNAA) was established as the official national association of the Visiting Nurse Agencies (VNAs). The Visiting Nurse Agencies are nonprofit health agencies that provide nursing services in the home, using nurses and other personnel as home health aides trained to give bedside personal care. VNA services include skilled nursing, mental health care, hospice services, social work, and physical therapy. High-tech services such as ventilator care, blood transfusions, pain management, and chemotherapy can also be done at home by VNAs.

More than a century ago, there were limited hospital resources in some communities. The Visiting Nurse Agencies created home health care as a means of dealing with those patients that either had no access to hospital care or were deemed not seriously ill enough to require it. Families were caring for the ill at home. VNAs began making house calls to care for patients as well as to offer support to their families.

With the advent of managed care and the need to decrease the costs of medical care, patients are being discharged from hospitals earlier. As the length of hospital stays decrease there is again a need for visiting nurses as patients are cared for at home. VNAs care for almost 10 million people annually and account for a quarter of all not-for-profit, freestanding home health care services in the United States. A voluntary community board of local leaders, assuring that community health care concerns are addressed, governs each VNA.

—Doreen T. Day

FURTHER READING

www.vnaa.org

VITAL SIGNS

Vital signs are a rapid, objective method of assessing a patient's clinical status and well-being. There are five vital signs: blood pressure, heart (pulse) rate, respiratory (breathing) rate, temperature, and as of 2001, pain score. Hospitalized patients have their vital signs taken at regular intervals, most commonly every eight hours by hospital assistants or nurses. When the patient is under closer monitoring such as on intensive care or intermediate care, or when receiving certain medications or blood products, vitals signs are taken more frequently. This allows for rapid identification of problems as well as close following of trends. In operating rooms and critically ill intensive care unit patients, vital sign monitoring is frequently done on a continuous basis. The usage of pain as a "vital sign" was first initiated by the Veterans Administration Hospital, and was adapted by the Joint Commission on Accreditation of Health Care Organizations (JCAHO) in January 2001. Pain can be assessed by several scales such as the Verbal Analog Score (VAS), which rates pain on a scale of 1 to 10. For children under 3 years of age or nonverbal individuals, various pain assessment scales such as the "Wong Pain FACES" can be used. This consists of a series of faces with expressions ranging from frowning/crying to smiling/happy; the child is asked to point to the appropriately descriptive face.

—Daryn H. Moller

FURTHER READING

www.jcaho.org

VITAL STATISTICS

See Vital Signs

VOLUNTARY ALLIANCES

See Alliances

VOLUNTARY HOSPITAL

See Hospital

VULNERABLE RESEARCH SUBJECT POPULATIONS

Federal law mandates that individuals who participate as volunteers in research must not be coerced, or subject to undue influence during recruitment, the consent process, or during the conduct of the research. Vulnerable research subject populations are those considered to be particularly susceptible to coercion or undue influence.

The determining factors for a subject population to be considered vulnerable are varied. Minors are considered vulnerable by virtue of their age and, therefore, their immature decision-making capability. Patients who have had a stroke, or who are experiencing the later stages of Alzheimer's disease are vulnerable because of their probable inability to determine for themselves whether or not to participate in research. The same can be said for certain psychiatric disorders. The economically disadvantaged are considered vulnerable to coercion where there may be payments made for participation. Prisoners are considered vulnerable by virtue of their confinement, with their decisions potentially influenced accordingly. Other vulnerable populations include, but are not limited to, pregnant women, women of child-bearing potential, minorities, and the educationally disadvantaged.

An institutional review board (IRB), which reviews and monitors research involving human subjects, must carefully review a protocol's inclusion and exclusion criteria to assess the proposed use of a vulnerable population. It must determine whether or not such inclusion is justified, given the aims of the research. If justified, the IRB must identify additional protections that are needed, above and beyond those normally afforded research subjects. For example, if an IRB reviews a study involving a drug with unknown adverse effects on developing fetuses, and determines that the inclusion of women of child-bearing potential is justified, then the committee will confirm that appropriate scheduling of pregnancy tests, and requirements for abstinence or birth control, are in place in the protocol, and clearly explained in the consent document.

—Judy Matuk

See also Belmont Report

FURTHER READING

http://ohrp.osophs.dhhs.gov/humansubjects/guidance/belmont.htm
http://ohrp.osophs.dhhs.gov/irb/irb_chapter6.htm

WAITING TIME

Waiting time is the time between an expectation for service and the beginning of the service delivery. It occurs when a request for service cannot be satisfied immediately due to a server being occupied with other requests or due to a server being temporarily out of service. Waiting (or *queuing*) occurs in most service operations and is primarily due to the variation in customer arrivals and service times. Customers arriving for service can be either scheduled appointments or unscheduled walk-ins. Arrivals for scheduled appointments may exhibit variation around their appointment times; however, such variation can often be reduced by reminder calls, communication, or late penalties. Walk-in customers generally arrive according to a *Poisson process* and are characterized by extremely high levels of variation in interarrival times.

As an example of the effects of random (Poisson) arrivals, suppose the time between patients arriving to a one-physician walk-in clinic averages 15 minutes. If the time to treat each patient were exactly 12 minutes, it would seem there would be no waiting, because the rate of arrivals is less than the rate of service. With the arrival process being random, however, the result is that the average patient wait before being treated will be 24 minutes.

If there also exists variation in the time it takes to provide a service, the waiting time can increase substantially. Continuing with the example, suppose the treatment time averages 12 minutes but exhibits considerable variation (such variation is sometimes modeled using an exponential distribution). In this example, the combined effects of the random arrivals and the random treatment times would increase the average waiting time to 48 minutes.

Within health care, waiting time is often cited as the most common reason for patient dissatisfaction. Even with considerable efforts in variation reduction, some degree of waiting is inevitable in health care systems. As such, careful attention should be given to the waiting environment and to managing the customer's perceptions of the wait. Several practices have been shown to be effective in combating negative perceptions of wait.

The waiting environment should be designed to keep a waiting customer comfortable and occupied. Standard techniques for keeping a waiting customer occupied include magazines, television, and informational brochures. More recently, such techniques include free phone and Internet access, as well as computer-based games and information services. Staff should be in constant communication with customers regarding a waiting situation, beginning with a simple acknowledgment that the customer is in the system ("We'll let the doctor know you're here"). In cases where a wait may be long, customers should be advised and updated of the likely or worst-case wait and the reasons for the wait ("Dr. Smith had an emergency delivery this morning, and so we are running about an hour late"). It is also important to maintain fairness in waiting situations or to explain situations that could be perceived as unfair. For example, many emergency departments make it clear that life-threatening cases will be taken ahead of minor injuries. It's important to recognize that many waiting situations in health care are anxiety filled and warrant special attention. For example, a patient awaiting test results may wrongly interpret a growing wait as an increasing probability of "bad news." In such situations, it may be important to communicate a "no news" status in the event of delayed results.

—Charles E. Noon

See also Health Care Service Operations, Queuing

FURTHER READING

Maister, D. (1985). The psychology of waiting lines. In J. A. Czepiel, M. R. Solomon, & C. F. Surprenant (Eds.), *The service encounter.* Lexington, MA: Lexington Press.

WEAKNESS

See SWOT (Strength-Weakness-Opportunity-Threat) Analysis

WELLNESS

The terms *wellness* or *health and wellness* or *wellness and prevention* represent the absence of sickness and the prevention of many illnesses that result from unhealthy lifestyle choices. In the *Encarta World English Dictionary, wellness* is defined as physical well-being, especially when maintained or achieved through good diet and regular exercise. Today a growing industry in health care is looking at the "upstream" of illness or how many serious health care issues could be averted if providers of health care understood and practiced "wellness medicine" rather than "sickness medicine."

As those born between 1947 and 1960, the baby boomers, age, health care and technology must advance to take care of a growing number of chronic illnesses. However, this generation of people is also the most informed and proactive in dealing with health care issues. Through advancements in the dissemination of information through the Internet, people are better empowered to keep and maintain good health. These people are also more informed of the cost of health care than ever before, and with the influence of managed care and medical savings accounts, the logical approach is to stay healthy both for physical and financial reasons.

The next generation of health care is evolving to deal with the demands of this population of consumers. The new paradigm in health care delivery systems should include as its very core a philosophy and a facility centered on prevention and wellness. These "centers of wellness" as stated in *Wellness Centers* by Gallup define where the emphasis of all health care providers should start. With the aging of the population and people living longer, if the model does not change to one of prevention and wellness, our acute care institutions will not be sufficient to handle the number of sick patients.

Innovative health care delivery systems have begun to include outpatient wellness centers in the continuum of care. A very successful example of such a center is the Akron General Health and Wellness Center in Akron, Ohio. Akron General Medical Center is a 511-bed tertiary care teaching hospital whose administration, with the help of physician leadership, changed its mission from acute sick care to true "health" care in 1996. The center is located 12 miles from the main facility, covers 190,000 square feet, and has been rated the number one health and wellness

center in the United States for design and programmatic development. The mission of the facility is based on community education, health maintenance, prevention, rehabilitation back to health, and wellness. The hub of the center is "Lifestyles," a medically supervised exercise facility integrated with rehabilitative services. Since the center opened in 1996, Akron General has been recognized as the leader of wellness services in the area.

There are now over 400 medical fitness centers in the United States, and the number is growing. The 21st-century hospital system must include a wellness component to be viable. The cost of sick care is out of control and in spite of all efforts to curb expenditures and control costs on the delivery side, real savings will not be realized until the emphasis changes from sick care to wellness and prevention.

Over 80% of the daily expenditures on "sick care" are the result of a lifestyle decision by the patient. Obesity, lack of exercise, smoking, poor nutrition, and not wearing safety belts are just a few "choices" that are made every day that result in significant sick care. Programmatic efforts within the wellness centers addressing these lifestyle choices are having a significant influence on the prevention of the downstream results.

In her book *The Last Sick Generation*, Polenz reviews many such facilities and programs throughout the country. She also outlines how the education of physicians needs to be altered at the medical school level to include teachings about wellness and preventive medicine. The discipline of preventive medicine should not be left only to those physicians who choose public health as their specialty. All providers should have a broad knowledge base of illness prevention and wellness initiatives. The new centers are providing these services to the public; providers need to embrace and encourage their usage.

Managed care companies or the payers of health care in this country are slow to understand wellness and prevention. Their payment systems are based on codes of "illness" or procedures. The leadership of these companies sould see that the only true way to control the "cost" of health care is to help their members stay well.

Only when providers, patients, and those who pay the largest portion of the expenditures are aligned with prevention and wellness initiatives as their priority, will the escalating costs come under control.

—Thomas L. Stover

FURTHER READING

Gallup, J. W. (1999). *Wellness centers: A guide for the design professional.* New York: Wiley.

Polenz, J. M. (2000). *The last sick generation: A proposal for healthcare reform.* Tampa, FL: American College of Physician Executive Press.

Shortell, S., Gilles, R. R., Anderson, D. A., Erickson, K. M., & Mitchell, J. B. (2000). *Remaking healthcare in America.* San Francisco: Jossey-Bass.

WOMEN AS MAJOR HEALTH CARE CONSUMERS

Women are the major consumers of health care services and are responsible for 70% to 90% of health care decisions for their families. As such, it is imperative for the long-term viability of health care organizations to address the needs of this consumer group.

The National Ambulatory Medical Care Survey of 2000 indicates that 823.5 million visits were made to physician offices, with women accounting for 59.3% of all visits. Inpatient hospital procedures totaled 41.3 million in 1999. Sixty percent of these procedures were accomplished in women; only 25% of this total were obstetrical in nature. Sixty percent of discharges from the hospital (reflecting admissions) were for women. Outpatient department visits in 2000 totaled 83.3 million, with women constituting 59.6% of those visits. Women also use preventive services to a greater extent than men.

Women represent 51% of the population of our country, have a longer life expectancy than men (79 years for women versus 74 years for men), and represent 43% of the labor force with 60% of those eligible, employed. Women have achieved higher educational levels than men with 89% of women completing high school (87% men) and 30% with bachelor degrees or higher (28% men). Despite entering the employment ranks in increasing numbers, women also continue in their traditional roles as homemakers, providing primary responsibility for child care and caring for the elderly. As a consequence, 80% of women feel they have too much to accomplish during the day and their personal health care issues are their last priority. Already time challenged, this consumer group receives health care in a fragmented fashion, which requires that women utilize multiple providers and separate encounters for each organ system.

Traditionally, women's health care has centered on obstetrical and reproductive services with federal funding ensuring access to prenatal care, family planning, and the detection of breast and cervical cancer. A survey conducted by Johns Hopkins University in 1993 identified 3600 women's health centers in the United States. The majority of these facilities (71%) focused on reproductive health with only 12% offering primary care services. With the median age of the U.S. population at 35.3 years and baby boomers ranging in age from 36 to 64 in the year 2000, the focus of women's health care needs to shift to reflect this new demographic.

Current interest in women's health care issues can be traced to the women's movement of the 1970s and 1980s as well as to the general acceptance of women as the determinant consumer group in directing health care expenditures. Women represent a significant, well-educated economic force that is demanding access to health information and collaboration with providers, and they have increased expectations as a result of customer service in the retail sector. Disparities in funding of health care initiatives, exclusion of women from clinical trials and allocation of resources that impact a only fraction of a woman's life, has resulted in a paucity of information on women's health that is often conflicting.

In 1983, Assistant Secretary of Health Dr. Edward N. Brandt, Jr., developed the Public Health Task Force on Women's Issues, to determine the role of the Department of Health and Human Services in women's health care. In 1985 this task force made recommendations on a broad array of health care issues spanning the lifetime of girls and women. As a result, the National Institutes of Health (NIH) in 1985 established a policy of including women in clinical trials. This policy was communicated in the 1987 *NIH Guide to Grants and Contracts* and amended later that year to include minorities. In 1990, the Congressional Caucus for Women's Issues requested that the U.S. General Accounting Office (GAO) study the NIH's implementation of the guidelines for inclusion of women. The resulting GAO report stated that the implementation of this policy was slow, it was not well communicated, gender analysis was not incorporated, and the impact could not be determined. Exclusion of women from clinical trials has left many unanswered questions on the most effective ways to treat women. Three months after the release of the GAO study, the resulting media coverage and public reaction resulted in the formation of the Office of Research on Women's Health (ORWH). ORWH is charged with assuring that research conducted and supported by the NIH appropriately addresses issues regarding women's health and that there is appropriate participation of women in clinical trials. In 1991 the the NIH launched the Women's Health Initiative (WHI), the largest clinical trial ever undertaken in the United States. The WHI has enrolled 160,000 women (recruitment completed December 1998) and is designed to impact the most common causes of death, disability, and impaired quality of life in postmenopausal women. It is expected that the WHI will provide many answers concerning possible risks and benefits associated with use of hormone replacement therapy, dietary supplements, and other interventions in preventing cardiovascular disease, breast and colorectal cancer, and osteoporosis in postmenopausal women.

The Office on Women's Health (OWH) within the Department of Health and Human Services (DHHS) was established in 1991 to improve the health of American women by developing a comprehensive health agenda. The

OWH has established National and Community Centers of Excellence in Women's Healthcare to provide models of health care delivery for women in a comprehensive, integrated, and multidisciplinary fashion. The centers are responsible for developing professional and public education, outreach, and collaboration with stakeholders in the community.

The vertical integration of women's health services in collaboration with multiple disciplines will provide accessibility, convenience, and a holistic approach to women's health care. By viewing a woman not as the sum of her parts, but as a complete being with socioeconomic and cultural influences impacting her health, and acknowledging that women are physiologically different from men, health care improvements throughout the lifetime of a woman may be achieved.

—Melissa Trekell

FURTHER READING

MHS Staff. (2000, Fall). Women's health: Marketing challenges for the 21st century. *Marketing Health Services*, pp. 5–10.

Noonan, M. D. (2000, Fall). Beyond mauve walls. *Notes from the field*, pp. 32–36.

Towery, M. (1998). *Powerchicks*. Marietta, GA: Longstreet.

Weisman, C. S. (2000). The trends in health care delivery for women: Challenges for medical education. *Academic Medicine, 11*, 1107–1113.

www.cdc.gov/nchs

www.census.gov

WOMEN, INFANTS, AND CHILDREN (WIC) PROGRAM

Established in 1974, the Women, Infants, and Children (WIC) Program is a federal grant program administered by the Food and Nutrition Service (FNS) of the U.S. Department of Agriculture. The goal of the program is to provide nutritious foods to supplement diets, education on healthy diets, and referral to health and social services to low-income women, infants, and children who are at nutritional risk. Currently serving 47% of infants born in the United States, the program has expanded substantially from 3.4 million enrollees in 1988 to over 8 million in 1998 at an annual cost of $4 billion. The program undergoes biennial review, as required by the FNS, to determine policy changes and funding requirements.

Fifty state health departments, 32 tribal organizations, American Samoa, the District of Columbia, Guam, Puerto Rico, and the Virgin Islands accomplish administration of the program. The 10,000 clinic sites determine eligibility and provide the required nutritional assessment, nutrition education, and referral to other needed services. Food vouchers for products high in specific nutrients, which are typically lacking in the targeted low-income family, are provided to the participants and can be redeemed at 46,000 locations nationwide.

Eligibility for the Women, Infants, and Children Program is based on income, residence, and nutritional risk assessment.

- *Women*
- Pregnant (during pregnancy and up to six weeks postpartum
- Postpartum (up to six months after birth or end of pregnancy)
- Breastfeeding (up to the infant's first birthday)
- *Infants* (up to first birthday)
- *Children* (up to child's fifth birthday)
- *Income:* 185% of poverty level or less. Automatic eligibility occurs if individual qualifies for Food Stamps, Medicaid, or Temporary Assistance for Needy Families
- *Residence:* State where administered or tribal organization residency requirements
- *Nutritional Risk:* Must be assessed by health care professional such as physician, nurse, or nutritionist to determine nutritional risk

Most participants are certified for six months. States may certify infants up to one year and pregnant women for the duration of their pregnancy.

Based on findings of the National Survey of WIC Participants and their local agencies (NSWP, 1998), participant surveys indicate a high level of satisfaction with the program. Most WIC enrollees learn of the program through friends, family members, and physicians, not through advertisement of the program. Caucasians represent the majority of participants (39.2%), followed by Hispanics (32.3%), African Americans (22.9%), Asians (3.2%), and Native Americans or Alaskans (1.5%). In 1998, 10% of women were less than 18 and only 7% older than 35. Only 44% of women enrolled in WIC were married, whereas 51% of mothers of enrolled infants and children were married. The majority of women enrolled in the WIC program had completed 12 years of education. Three fourths of WIC participants reside in households with wage earners.

The average size of the WIC family is 4.0 persons. Most participants reside in single-family residences with 15% residing in multifamily households. Two thirds of WIC participants reside in households below the poverty level. An additional 23% of participants have income between 100% and 150% of poverty level and qualify for WIC based on eligibility for other programs, such as Medicaid.

Women who participated in WIC had lower Medicaid costs for themselves and their infants. The program has demonstrated reduced infant mortality, increased birth weight, and improved growth and intellectual development of nutritionally at-risk infants and children. Infants and children who participate in the program are more likely to have access to medical care and maintain current immunization status. Women participants achieve earlier access to prenatal care, improved nutritional intake before and after pregnancy, as well as improved weight gain during pregnancy, resulting in longer gestation and improved fetal outcomes.

—Melissa Trekell

FURTHER READING

Kowaleski-Jones, L., & Duncan, G. J. (2002). Effects of participation in the WIC program on birth weight: Evidence from the national longitudinal survey of youth. *American Journal of Public Health, 92*(5), 799–803.

Shefer, A. M., Fritchley, J., Stevenson, J., Lyons, B., Friedman, R., Hopfensperger, D., Mize, J., & Rodewald, L. (2002). Linking WIC and immunization services to improve preventive health care among low-income children in WIC. *Journal Public Health Management Practice, 8*(2), 56–65.

www.fns.usda.gov/wic

WORK DESIGN

See Organizational Performance and Work Design

WORKERS' COMPENSATION INSURANCE

Workers' compensation insurance laws were enacted at the state level in the early 1900s and are designed to provide income and medical expenses to employees who are injured in work-related accidents. All states have laws that provide no-fault insurance with the cost of insurance borne by the employer. The purpose of the insurance is to provide reasonable and prompt benefits to employees who are injured or killed on the job regardless of fault. Therefore, if an employee is injured at work, performing the normal duties of his or her job, then workers' compensation will pay for medical expenses and compensation for lost wages. The regulations concerning reimbursement vary from state to state, so managers must be fully aware of the policies and procedures of their organization. Every state has a Web site that contains information about its workers' compensation laws and procedures.

Workers' compensation has become an important concern to corporate America, as well as state governments and employee groups. Corporations have witnessed escalating costs in their workers' compensation programs and have been forced to pay increased administrative costs to reduce medical and lost time claims costs. States (such as Texas) have been pressured into overhauling their workers' compensation laws in order to do a better job protecting employees and attracting new businesses to their states. Employees have become increasingly frustrated by the red tape and by the loss of income that occurs because workers' compensation reimbursement for lost time is generally only a fraction of the wages lost by an employee.

Workers' compensation costs can be well managed by programs that include medical case management, return to work in temporary modified duty, and experience-rated assessment of fees within an organization. Medical case management includes developing preferred provider lists, active management of medical treatment after injury, and medical follow-up when necessary. Modified duty programs arrange for the gradual return to full functioning in a job. Companies that return injured employees to work as they continue to heal demonstrate lower workers' compensation costs and happier employees. Employers can encourage units to reduce workers' compensation costs by providing economic incentives to reduce costs. These incentives come in the use of experience ratings to determine future costs. For example, a hospital may set a charge back for workers' compensation insurance for the physical plant department by averaging workers' compensation claims over a three-year period. Thus, the physical plant could save money by more effective workers' compensation insurance management.

Front-line supervisors bear great responsibility in managing workers' compensation cases. They are responsible for filing the necessary paperwork when the injury occurs, assuring that the employee gets appropriate medical attention, maintaining contact with the employee during rehabilitation, developing a temporary modified service program to bring the employee back to work, and removing any safety problems that were identified as a result of the accident. The supervisor must accomplish these tasks in accord with the Americans with Disabilities Act, Environmental Health and Safety laws, and company policies and procedures.

Alan P. Chesney

FURTHER READING

Bialk, B. (1987). Cutting workers compensation costs. *Personnel Journal, 66*(7), 95–97.

Dressler, G. (1999). *Human resource management.* Upper Saddle River, NJ: Prentice Hall.

Fisher, C., Schoenfeldt, L., & Shaw, J. (1999). *Human resource management (*4th ed.). Boston: Houghton Mifflin.

Swauke, J. (1992, February). Ways to tame workers comp premiums. *HR Magazine, 42,* 39–41.

WORKING CAPITAL

See Net Working Capital

WORLD HEALTH ORGANIZATION

The World Health Organization (WHO) was founded in 1948 as a special agency of the United Nations. With 191 member states, WHO endorses technical cooperation for health among nations and implements programs to control and eradicate diseases. WHO aims to improve the quality of human life by providing worldwide guidance and setting global standards in the field of health. The organization also cooperates with member governments to strengthen national health programs and to develop and transfer appropriate health technology and information. WHO describes its goal as "the attainment by all peoples of the highest possible level of health." Health, as defined by the WHO constitution, is "a physical, mental and social well-being and not merely the absence of disease or infirmity."

WHO is governed by the World Health Assembly, which is the supreme decision-making body. The assembly meets annually and is attended by delegations from all member states. Its main function is to determine the policies of the organization. The budget of WHO is made up of assessed contributions from the member states. The organization also receives voluntary contributions from member states and from other sources. Altogether, WHO's annual budget approximates $900 million.

WHO PROGRAMS

Infectious Diseases

The fight against infectious diseases is a top priority for WHO. The organization is a key player in control and elimination of infectious diseases worldwide. A major accomplishment was the global eradication of smallpox in 1977, owing to global immunization programs supported by WHO. Other diseases such as polio and guinea worm and leprosy are also on the threshold of eradication. Along with these old diseases known to humankind for a long time, WHO also has programs to control new diseases, which are constantly emerging, such as HIV/AIDS and viral hemorrhagic fevers. Re-emerging diseases, which have returned with new vigor after they seemed to decline, such as tuberculosis, malaria, and cholera, are also diseases to which WHO remains alert.

Noncommunicable Diseases

WHO supports worldwide programs to address cardiovascular diseases, cancers, and respiratory diseases. These programs target to prevent, treat, and rehabilitate major chronic diseases. The organization's approach involves the integration of disease-specific interventions into a disease control package. Application of existing cost-effective methods of detection, and management of global campaigns to encourage healthy lifestyles and healthy public policies are promoted within such packages.

Health Promotion and Environment

The impact of environment on human health is a priority concern for WHO. WHO supports health promotion projects such as Healthy Cities and Villages, Health Promoting Schools and Workplaces. Major environmental projects are concerned with improved access to safe drinking water, prevention and control of ionizing radiation, and issues related to increasing depletion of the ozone layer.

Health Research

WHO gathers, analyses, and disseminates data on health conditions and needs on a very large range of public health topics. Such research ranges from evaluation of school health programs to epidemiological research and to monitoring the progress of genetic engineering.

—Pinar Senlet

See also Public Health

FURTHER READINGS

World Health Organization. (2001). *Global Health Issues: 107th Session of the WHO's Executive Board.* Geneva: Author.

World Health Organization. (2002). *Report of the Director General, 2001.* Geneva: Author.

YEAR 2010 OBJECTIVE

See Healthy People 2010

Z

ZERO DEFECTS

The term *zero defects* refers to the goal of achieving output from a process with no defects. It was introduced by the quality guru Philip Crosby, but is now used both by practitioners of total quality management, or process improvement, such as the Six-Sigma approach, and by practitioners of Lean Manufacturing. The Six-Sigma approach involves the aggressive reduction of process variation to the point where as little as 3.4 parts per million are defective. The Lean Manufacturing approach has evolved out of the Toyota Production System, and uses techniques like mistake-proofing (Poka-Yoke) to reduce the occurrence of defects to near-zero levels. This often involves 100% inspection of the process material that occurs early in the process. Reconfiguring the process to achieve just-in-time product flow is central to this approach as well.

Zero defects management is based on the premise that it is better to detect problems before they cause accidents or product defects. Airlines must use a zero defects approach to maintaining and flying their planes. Hospitals would like to achieve zero defects for medication errors, or for infections. Administrators would certainly want zero accounting errors, since their presence could adversely affect the financial condition of the company.

—James L. Schmidhammer

Index

92408

CONSTANTS AND CONVERSION FACTORS

Constants

Avogadro's number, N_A	0.6023×10^{24} mol^{-1}
Atomic mass unit, amu	1.661×10^{-24} g
Electric permittivity of a vacuum, ϵ_0	8.854×10^{-12} C/(V $\cdot$ m)
Electron mass	0.9110×10^{-27} g
Elementary charge, e	0.1602×10^{-18} C
Gas constant, R	8.314 J/(mol $\cdot$ K)
	1.987 cal/(mol $\cdot$ K)
Boltzmann's constant, k	13.81×10^{-24} J/K
	86.20×10^{-6} eV/K
Planck's constant, h	0.6626×10^{-33} J $\cdot$ s
Speed of light (in vacuum), c	0.2998×10^{9} m/s
Bohr magneton, μ_B	9.274×10^{-24} A $\cdot$ m^2

SI Prefixes

giga, G	10^9
mega, M	10^6
kilo, k	10^3
milli, m	10^{-3}
micro, μ	10^{-6}
nano, n	10^{-9}
pico, p	10^{-12}

Conversion Factors

Length	1 meter $= 10^{10}$ Å $= 10^9$ nm
	$= 3.281$ ft
	$= 39.37$ in.
Mass	1 kilogram $= 2.205$ lb$_m$
Force	1 newton $= 0.2248$ lb$_f$
Pressure	1 pascal $= 1$ N/m^2
	$= 0.1019 \times 10^{-6}$ kg$_f$/mm^2
	$= 9.869 \times 10^{-6}$ atm
	$= 0.1450 \times 10^{-3}$ lb$_f$/in.^{2}
Viscosity	1 Pa $\cdot$ s $= 10$ poise
Energy	1 joule $= 1$ W $\cdot$ s
	$= 1$ N $\cdot$ m
	$= 1$ V $\cdot$ C
	$= 0.2389$ cal
	$= 6.242 \times 10^{18}$ eV
	$= 0.7377$ ft lb$_f$
Temperature	$^\circ$C $= $ K $- 273$
	$= (^\circ$F $- 32)/1.8$
Current	1 ampere $= 1$ C/s
	$= 1$ V/Ω

PERIOD TABLE OF THE ELEMENTS

I A																		0
1 H 1.008	II A												III A	IV A	V A	VI A	VII A	2 He 4.003
3 Li 6.941	4 Be 9.012												5 B 10.81	6 C 12.01	7 N 14.01	8 O 16.00	9 F 19.00	10 Ne 20.18
11 Na 22.99	12 Mg 24.31	III B	IV B	V B	VI B	VII B	VIII			I B	II B		13 Al 26.98	14 Si 28.09	15 P 30.97	16 S 32.06	17 Cl 35.45	18 Ar 39.95
19 K 39.10	20 Ca 40.08	21 Sc 44.96	22 Ti 47.90	23 V 50.94	24 Cr 52.00	25 Mn 54.94	26 Fe 55.85	27 Co 58.93	28 Ni 58.71	29 Cu 63.55	30 Zn 65.38	31 Ga 69.72	32 Ge 72.59	33 As 74.92	34 Se 78.96	35 Br 79.90	36 Kr 83.80
37 Rb 85.47	38 Sr 87.62	39 Y 88.91	40 Zr 91.22	41 Nb 92.91	42 Mo 95.94	43 Tc 98.91	44 Ru 101.07	45 Rh 102.91	46 Pd 106.4	47 Ag 107.87	48 Cd 112.4	49 In 114.82	50 Sn 118.69	51 Sb 121.75	52 Te 127.60	53 I 126.90	54 Xe 131.30
55 Cs 132.91	56 Ba 137.33	57 La 138.91	72 Hf 178.49	73 Ta 180.95	74 W 183.85	75 Re 186.2	76 Os 190.2	77 Ir 192.22	78 Pt 195.09	79 Au 196.97	80 Hg 200.59	81 Tl 204.37	82 Pb 207.2	83 Bi 208.98	84 Po (210)	85 At (210)	86 Rn (222)
87 Fr (223)	88 Ra 226.03	89 Ac (227)	104 Rf (261)	105 Db (262)	106 Sg (266)												

58 Ce 140.12	59 Pr 140.91	60 Nd 144.24	61 Pm (145)	62 Sm 150.4	63 Eu 151.96	64 Gd 157.25	65 Tb 158.93	66 Dy 162.50	67 Ho 164.93	68 Er 167.26	69 Tm 168.93	70 Yb 173.04	71 Lu 174.97
90 Th 232.04	91 Pa 231.04	92 U 238.03	93 Np 237.05	94 Pu (244)	95 Am (243)	96 Cm (247)	97 Bk (247)	98 Cf (251)	99 Es (254)	100 Fm (257)	101 Md (258)	102 No (259)	103 Lw (260)